What's New in the Third

This third edition of *Windows NT 3.51 Unleashed* offers you significant changes from the first two editions.

Part IV is now devoted to the issues involved in utilizing NT as a server on the WWW. This section covers everything from selecting proper hardware for your Windows NT web site to creating web pages on your new web server using proper HTML standards. The section also includes the following:

- How to publicize your new web site on the web by registering it with various search engines and databases.
- References to various web sites for more information regarding HTML.
- Reviews of various Windows NT tools that can be used to make web site development easier. These tools range from utilities that analyze your web server's log file to image-map editors and various HTML editors.
- How to make your web site interactive by using CGI (Common Gateway Interface) to design feedback forms and provide customized content based on the web browser being used to access your web site.
- Various Internet services such as e-mail and FTP that are related to hosting a web site.

The book's text has been expanded considerably, with a new chapter (Chapter 7) covering a host of new features that NT 3.51 has to offer over and above those in 3.5. This includes such new areas as disk compression, unattended installation, new command-line utilities, and configurable command prompt sessions.

We've also added Windows 95 information with such topics as how Windows 95 should figure into your overall operating system strategy, how to incorporate Windows 95 clients into NT networks, and how Windows 95's design and operation differs from NT.

Windows NT 3.51

UNLEASHED

Third Edition

Robert Cowart

SAMS
PUBLISHING

201 West 103rd Street
Indianapolis, IN 46290

THIRD EDITION

International Standard Book Number: 0-672-30902-5

Library of Congress Catalog Card Number: 95-72342

99 98 97 96 4 3 2 1

Interpretation of the printing code: the rightmost double-digit number is the year of the book's printing; the rightmost single-digit, the number of the book's printing. For example, a printing code of 96-1 shows that the first printing of the book occurred in 1996.

Composed in AGaramond and MCPdigital by Macmillan Computer Publishing

Printed in the United States of America

Trademarks

Publisher and President *Richard K. Swadley*

Acquisitions Manager *Greg Wiegand*

Development Manager *Dean Miller*

Managing Editor *Cindy Morrow*

Marketing Manager *Gregg Bushyeager*

Acquisitions Editor
Kim Spilker

Development Editor
Kelly Murdock

Software Development Specialist
Steve Straiger

Copy Editors
Cheri Clark
Lisa Lord
Ryan Rader
Bart Reed

Technical Reviewer
Vincent Mayfield

Editorial Coordinator
Bill Whitmer

Technical Edit Coordinator
Lynette Quinn

Formatter
Frank Sinclair

Editorial Assistants
Sharon Cox
Andi Richter
Rhonda Tinch-Mize

Cover Designer
Tim Amrhein

Book Designers
Gary Adair
Alyssa Yesh

Copy Writer
Peter Fuller

Production Team Supervisor
Brad Chinn

Production
Georgiana Briggs, Sonja Hart, Kevin Laseau, Erika Millen, Casey Price, Nancy Price, Beth Rago, Erich Richter, Craig Small, Christine Tyner, Todd Wente, Colleen Williams

Overview

Part IV Setting Up a World-Wide Web Site Using NT Workstation

Part V Appendixes

Contents

Part III Networking Windows NT

About the Authors

Robert Cowart has been writing for computer magazines and book publishers for more than 14 years. Specializing in instructional books about computer software, he has a strong background in PC operating systems. He cut his teeth writing 8080 assembler code for CP/M systems in the early 1980s when he built his first personal computer from scratch. After earning a BS degree in digital electronics, he performed technical support and training services for North Star Computers in the early 1980s. Subsequently, he started his own dBASE consulting company, programming for small businesses. He has written approximately 100 feature articles for magazines such as *PC Week, PC Tech Journal, A+, Keyboard, PC World, MacWorld,* and *MacWeek.* He also has written a variety of computer-related books and user manuals, including *Mastering Windows 3.xx, Mastering Windows 95, ABCs of dBASE, Mastering Microsoft Works, ABCs of Microsoft Access,* and *Windows Quick and Easy.*

Howard Marks has been a LAN enthusiast and educator since 1984. He is Founder/Wizard of Networks Are Our Lives, Inc., a network consulting and teaching firm that specializes in NetWare/Windows integration. He is a co-author of *Networking Windows, NetWare Edition* (Sams Publishing, 1992).

Sanjaya Hettihewa is a consultant specializing in integrating Windows NT-based information systems on the World Wide Web. He is also an accomplished webmaster and an HTTP addict who has been spending more than five hours a day on the Internet and the WWW since high school. He is also a Computer Science and Information Systems major attending the University of Maryland. Sanjaya can be reached at `http://wonderland.dial.umd.edu/` or, if you prefer the old-fashioned way, `sanjaya@wam.umd.edu`.

Acknowledgments

A book of this size and technical substance takes considerable effort. A number of people have helped over the almost nine months involved in completing this Herculean task. Developing a book that isn't just another user's guide took a great deal of thought and interaction among people scattered across the country. In its first edition, Robert Cowart thought a book on NT could be pretty much a simple adaptation of his existing books on Windows 3.xx and Windows 95. As talks progressed, it seemed that this would be less and less the case. NT was an entirely new animal requiring special treatment, with an emphasis on network administration, installation, maintenance, and troubleshooting. More people were brought to the table, and, thanks to CompuServe and the Internet, the physical proximity of the writers was not an issue. Daily e-mail and file transmission over the wires sufficed. Perhaps one day the writers and editors will meet in real, not virtual, space.

Robert wishes to thank the powers that be at Sams Publishing for offering the opportunity to work on such a timely project as this. I believe NT to be a pivotal product in a field that has captivated my attention and that has been the focus of my professional activity for more than a decade. I'm pleased to have been given the chance to head up the project. Thanks certainly go to my agent, Bill Gladstone, for putting me in touch with Sams. Thanks to Gregg Bushyeager for initially refining this book's proposed contents. To Mark Taber, who originally developed this book, great thanks on a number of counts, not the least of which is patience. Several glitches along the way were unnerving to us all, and Mark held steady in the storm, keeping me on track and applying just the right amount and right kind of pressure—the kind but firm whip-cracking that every writer knows he or she needs! For this third edition, thanks to Kim Spilker for her patience, and for her help in locating a writer knowledgeable in Internet Web setups utilizing NT. And last, but not least, thanks to my friends and family who regularly have to put up with my seemingly eternal disappearance.

Howard would like to acknowledge his wife Kristin's eternal patience with having a grumpy writer around the house, especially during the holidays. Honey, you're the greatest.

Sanjaya would like to thank his parents Walter and Lakshmi for their support and a special note of appreciation to Gerry and Monique Feffer and Irving Stern. And of course, thanks to Kim Spilker, my acquisitions editor, for letting me be part of an exciting project.

All three of us want to thank the technical reviewer, Vincent Mayfield, for his thoughtful commentary that ensured the timeliness and accuracy of the material.

And, of course, considerable thanks goes to the entire Sams team, from editorial and production to sales and marketing—the often invisible and underappreciated people who make the book business happen.

Introduction

Windows NT is an incredibly pivotal software product. In an industry where few can even be sure what type of computer they'll be using tomorrow, much less what software will be running on it, Windows NT (which stands for *New Technology*) brings to the table a whole new set of questions—and capabilities.

The first real "industrial strength" operating system intended for the enormous installed base of IBM-compatible computers, Windows NT offers what PC tinkerers of a decade ago could only have classified as a mainframe operating system. Not merely an upgrade of Windows 3.xx (although it looks much like it), NT is a serious operating system intended to meet the computing needs of power users, government agencies, and large industry. And rather than being a bandage approach to meeting a need, Windows NT was ported "down" to PCs from its mainframe UNIX predecessors rather than ported "up" from a single-user system, with some spit and bailing wire to hold it together.

Fearing NT's strengths, computer monoliths such as IBM, Sun, and Novell have mounted major marketing campaigns and product development efforts to derail a potential industry-wide shift to the Microsoft NT camp. After all, these competitors (most notably Novell) have for years enjoyed the lion's share of success in PC-based local network networking. NT disinformation—or at least obfuscation—abounds, especially in the press, which is constantly at odds with itself over NT's rewards versus its shortcomings.

Debates about hefty hardware requirements, questionable DOS and Windows 3.xx performance, and where Windows 95 fits into the 32-bit landscape keep us all entertained. But make no mistake about it. The chemistry is very, very good. A 32-bit multitasking, multithreading, fault-tolerant, networkable, and highly secure operating system, combined with the many thousands of Windows applications available today, along with the visionary software company Microsoft, makes Windows NT the hands-down winner in the battle for a mission-critical operating system in the corporate enterprise setting.

Although these paragraphs might have the ring of press hype, this wasn't necessarily the attitude of this book's authors prior to their approximately one year of experimentation with NT while researching and writing the first edition of *Windows NT Unleashed.* Based solely on our collective experience with computer operating systems, with corporate clients dependent on real-world applications and networking, and with market trend analysis, we forged our opinions.

This book attempts to explain what makes NT such a strong product, why the industry is leaning in its direction, and how to get the most out of it.

What You Should Know Before Reading This Book

Windows NT Unleashed explains both basic and advanced material on the topic of Windows NT. It doesn't assume that you know anything about Windows NT. However, it does assume that you have knowledge about Microsoft Windows 3.xx and possibly about Windows 95, and that you've used them somewhat. This book also assumes that you have been around IBM PCs and are familiar with their operation, such as how MS-DOS works, how printers and modems work, and to some degree how local area networks (LANs) operate. Furthermore, this book assumes that you're probably using NT because you're either in a work environment where Windows NT is running on your workstation or that you're managing such a network or workgroup in one way or another. Beyond that, this book doesn't make assumptions. Technobabble computer terms often are explained the first time they appear. Complex concepts also are explained when they first appear. In addition, a glossary is included. So, whether you're an NT novice or a hard-core computer junkie, you're likely to learn quite a bit. You're neither "snowed" by geek-speak nor condescended to.

Audience

Writing a book about a software product as ambitious as Windows NT hasn't been easy. Finding writers who know enough about such a new and feature-rich product was difficult enough. But divining just who will be using NT and what they will want to know posed another serious challenge.

Clearly, just doing a port of an existing Windows 3.xx book was not in order. Windows NT is a much richer product aimed at a more sophisticated audience with different needs. In developing a strategy for determining this book's coverage, we had to carefully consider just who will be using NT, and to what ends. "Will single users really want it?" "What about developers?" "Will it be installed primarily in corporate settings?" "Will NT servers be used primarily for application servers, or as workstations?" "How much coverage of NT Advanced Server should we include?" "Should integration of existing systems such as LAN Manager and Novell with Windows NT be a key topic?" "Should we discuss NT multimedia, software development on the NT platform, Remote Access Services?" You get the idea. The strategy time and again came down to including as much as possible for all users.

Single NT Users

There are cases when a person would want to use Windows NT on a single, nonnetworked workstation. Typically, this would be in instances where system stability, the ability to have separate user accounts on a single workstation, multioperating system capability, or development of NT applications would be high-priority needs.

If you're such a user, *Windows NT 3.5 Unleashed,* Third Edition, provides all you need to know in the way of installing NT, converting from Windows 3.xx, partitioning your hard disk, booting alternative operating systems such as DOS and OS/2, and even running with hard disks formatted with other file systems, such as FAT and HPFS.

Of course, all the basics of NT are covered, and these apply to single users too: Program Manager, File Manager, Control Panel (which is extensive in NT), Schedule+ (for organizing your daily appointments), Disk Administrator, and User Manager. You'll also find more-than-ample coverage of multimedia hardware and driver installation, installing on RISC machines such as the DEC Alpha and MIPS 4000, and system maintenance guidelines pertaining to topics such as adding and removing hard drives, upgrading your hardware (memory, video, processor), running automated backups, recovering lost data from stripe sets, and so forth.

NT Users on a Network

Should you already be on, or if you upgrade to, a networking installation of Windows NT, you're in for a treat. All the basics are covered here—in English. Networking is a complex world in and of itself. Hundreds of buzzwords, not to mention numerous types of network cards, cabling, interrupt settings, topologies, and protocols, make networking one of computing's black arts. The author of Part III, "Networking Windows NT," has (figuratively speaking) a black belt in networking with Windows, Novell, and UNIX. Both WAN and LAN operations are covered, as is remote access into NT systems via modem. If you haven't yet installed the physical network, this book provides ample help in the decision-making process. Text and illustrations explain clearly the issues that pertain to networking theory, topologies, cabling types, optimum workstation organization, NT's "domain-based" architecture, and many other advanced topics. The chapters were written by people who design, install, maintain, teach, and write about PC-based networks.

Systems Administrators

If you're a systems administrator or an MIS professional, managing PCs can be a nightmare. Windows NT can make your job much easier if you know what you're doing. *Windows NT 3.5 Unleashed,* Third Edition, takes the attitude that most readers will be administrators—either of their own system or of an extended network of NT or non-NT workstations. This book emphasizes not just what a particular command or utility does to the NT system, Registry, network, or domain, but when and why an administrator would want to use it.

Under one cover are not only all the basic instructions for running NT's supplied systems-administrator applications—User Manager, Disk Administrator, Event Viewer, and Performance Monitor—but also detailed instructions on topics such as

- Installing NT to new workstations over the network
- Maintaining security and passwords for users and workstations you supervise
- Running network OLE so that your users can share their Clipbook data
- Setting up, using, and managing printer servers
- Preparing for power outages using NT's UPS service
- Maximizing mass storage and guarding against data loss using volume sets, stripe sets, and stripe sets with parity
- Managing and automating local and remote tape backups
- Remote systems administration
- Setting up the Replicator service to synchronize directories across the network
- Understanding and using trusted domains
- Optimizing the NT system, with coverage ranging from Control Panel to CONFIG.NT and AUTOEXEC.NT, SCSI drives, CD-ROMs, RAM upgrade tips, and NT Setup migration of Windows 3.xx .INI settings
- Using and optimizing alternative operating environments—DOS, Windows 3.xx, POSIX, and OS/2
- A wide variety of troubleshooting tips and tricks

Web Developers

Because NT is well on its way to becoming the most popular PC-based operating system for Internet Web servers, budding webmasters will benefit from reading this book. Part IV of the book discusses all the ins and outs of piecing together a complete NT-based Web server. Sanjaya Hettihewa, well-established as a Web expert, covers such topics as copyright legalities, secure transactions on the Web, and how to design your own Web pages.

How to Use This Book

This book was written by three authors. Robert Cowart wrote Parts I and II, Howard Marks wrote Part III, and Sanjaya Hettihewa wrote Part IV. Each part deals with a different angle of NT's use. Depending on your particular interest in NT, you might decide to focus on one part more heavily than another.

We've written this book so that the parts—and even the chapters—can stand pretty much on their own. When a discussion assumes prior knowledge, there is often a cross-reference.

Although the early chapters have some basic NT orientation material, you should have little difficulty understanding the discussions, even if you read them out of order. Don't hesitate to scan the table of contents and jump directly to the topics you're interested in. Many readers just starting with NT, for example, will want to read Chapter 8, "Installing Windows NT," before reading Chapters 3 and 4, which cover the basics of running NT.

How This Book Is Organized

The lay of the land is as follows. Most readers will want to read the first two chapters to get a little academic background on what NT is, where it comes from, how it fits into the world of operating systems, and what it can do. After that, I suggest that you at least skim the rest of Part I, because it covers File Manager and the basics of running applications of various kinds from Program Manager. If you're already quite familiar with Windows, the basics of these sections will be old news. However, because Part I also covers some new features in the NT versions of these programs, you probably shouldn't skip the rest of this part entirely. Common program groups in Program Manager and security features such as auditing in File Manager are just a couple of examples of new and interesting features.

After covering Program Manager and File Manager, Part I goes on in Chapter 4 to provide detailed discussions of the Print Manager program for setting up local and shared printers.

Chapter 5 discusses data-sharing methods, ranging from the tried-and-true Windows Clipboard to more advanced procedures such as applying network OLE to compound document creation.

We decided to skip coverage of the supplied accessory programs because most NT users probably are already quite familiar with the likes of Notepad, Paintbrush, Calendar, and so forth. However, Chapter 6 covers the two feature-rich, network-based applications, Mail and Schedule+, that are bundled with Windows NT, as well as the Chat program.

Chapter 7 discusses all the new features of NT version 3.51. We've put that information in a separate chapter because many people may still be using version 3.5.

Beginning with Chapter 8, *Windows NT 3.5 Unleashed,* Third Edition, moves on to administrative and system maintenance issues. If you haven't already installed NT on your system or if, as an administrator, you must install NT on a number of workstations, read Chapter 7. It covers many aspects of setting up NT, ranging from hardware requirements and IRQ conflicts to the most advantageous means of installing over top existing operating systems.

Chapter 9 examines many aspects of NT system configuration, ranging from all the Control Panel settings to the use of NT Setup for maintaining system drivers and files. Configuration of alternative environment subsystems (DOS and OS/2) also is discussed.

If you're an administrator, Chapter 10 is essential reading. It details the supplied systems administration tools, User Manager and Disk Administrator, as well as security options in Print Manager and File Manager. All the details of setting up user accounts; managing directory, file, and printer shares over the network; and organizing your applications effectively for multiuser workstations are explained.

If you're into trying to get the most output per megahertz from your system, check out Chapters 11 and 12. Chapter 11 discusses NT optimization, from system software tricks to installing new hardware, choosing hardware, and watching out for traps.

Chapter 12 is a general maintenance and troubleshooting chapter that covers such topics as using Event Viewer, recovering crashed disks, recovering a crashed NT installation, running Windows 3.xx applications, understanding how NT boots, and using the Registry Editor.

Part III begins our in-depth coverage of NT and networks. Chapter 13 provides an overview of networking, and Chapter 14 dives into network installation. This is essential reading for anyone running NT on either new or existing networks.

If relatively modest networking is what you have in mind for NT, Chapter 15 covers the bulk of salient issues for you. Howard covers the ins and outs of simple networking arrangements utilizing NT's built-in peer-to-peer networking. He also discusses interfacing with existing peer-to-peer systems such as Windows for Workgroups.

For more advanced networking arrangements using Windows NT Advanced Server, turn to Chapter 16. The details of NT Advanced Server (NTAS) are covered, including creating domains and workgroups, using Remote Access Server, remote managing of NT clients, and connecting to Macintosh computers.

Chapter 17 moves on to even more esoteric networking considerations. If you're internetworking NT with other brands of networks, such as Banyan VINES, Novell, or LAN Manager, you'll find this interesting and vital reading.

As its popularity grows, NT likely will be utilized in large corporate settings that are not necessarily restricted to single geographical settings. Chapter 18 discusses wider-area networking on "the enterprise," with coverage of such topics as setting up domains and managing intradomain trust relationships. Chapter 19 moves further into WAN concepts, covering leased and switched services, Remote Access Services, and the Internet, among others.

Chapter 20 covers network-specific optimization, with topics such as improving server performance, using Performance Monitor to avoid network bottlenecks, and other tricks of the trade for maximizing your overall network throughput. The last chapter in the networking portion of the book, Chapter 21, dives into the many means for troubleshooting your network to iron out elusive bugs and hardware misconduct.

Part IV, "Setting Up a World-Wide Web Site Using NT Workstation," begins a very interesting, timely discussion of a recently popular use of NT: setting up Web sites.

You start in Chapter 22 with an introduction to the World Wide Web, web sites, and home pages. By providing you with a brief introduction to the World Wide Web, how it evolved and where it is headed, you'll be in a better position to visualize how the contents of this part will aid you in creating an outstanding web site. This chapter also provides a glimpse of how web servers work and how web browsers communicate with web servers to retrieve information.

Before setting up your web server, you need to evaluate various hardware options for your web site. Chapter 23 covers these options. By analyzing the pros and cons of various hardware platforms and price/performance issues, you will be able to determine the right hardware platform for your web server.

Choosing the right software for your web server is just as important as choosing the right hardware, and Chapter 24 provides information to help you make the right software decisions. First, this chapter covers various web server software options and different features you should look for when selecting a web server. Then you learn about various tools that enable you to create and enhance your web site. By using these tools, you can save time while adding a professional touch to your web site. The chapter shows you how to use these tools and where they can be found on the Internet.

Chapter 25 helps you with the next step: determining what kind of bandwidth you will need for your web site. Depending on the magnitude of your project, you might want to choose between POTS (Plain Old Telephone Service), ISDN (Integrated Services Digital Network) or a T1 (digiTal, 1st Carrier System) link.

Chapter 26 deals with putting your pages together and creating a user-friendly web site. The audience you will be serving generally has a short attention span—similar to that of someone flipping through channels on a television set. Consequently, you need to create a captivating, easy-to-navigate web site. This chapter includes tips to help you effectively plan the architecture of your web server. The chapter also covers various HTML standards, tools to verify whether your HTML is correct, and various graphic file formats and their suitability for various tasks.

Chapter 27 helps you get your web site up and running. The chapter shows you how to be innovative in designing your web site, how to keep your information up-to-date, how to register (for free) your web site with various search engines/databases.

Chapter 28 explains how to make your web site interactive. You will learn how to use CGI (Common Gateway Interface) to extend the capabilities of your web site, how to set up an e-mail feedback form so that users browsing your web site can e-mail feedback to you, and how to write CGI programs to performs tasks such as displaying a customized web paged depending on the browser being used to access your web site. Because PERL is a popular CGI programming language, this chapter also has an introduction to PERL and how PERL for Windows NT can be utilized to write CGI scripts.

Chapter 29 explains how to further extend the capabilities of your web site by setting up an Internet mail server as well as an FTP server to make files available to users browsing your web site. This chapter also covers how to set up the Windows NT FTP service and customize it so that it can be accessed with web browsers to download various files.

Finally, Chapter 30 tells you where to go for help on the web if you have a question about Windows NT or have problems getting an application to work with NT. This chapter will also cover other Windows NT resources on the Internet such as mailing lists, FTP sites, and user groups and how to best use them.

Finally, we've supplied some useful appendixes for your convenience. You'll find a listing of the command-prompt commands, functions, and other settings in Appendix A. Appendix B has a discussion of NT's error and information messages, how to look up error messages, and where to find additional explanations for them using the NT-supplied Messages database. Appendix C is a compilation of NT terms and definitions—a very useful and essential inclusion in a highly technical area fraught with nascent terminology.

This Book's Conventions

In this book, the term *NT* often replaces the term *Windows NT*. Likewise, *DOS* often is used interchangeably with MS-DOS.

Windows commands often are double-barreled because you often have to open a menu and then choose a command. In this book, such an action is written with the menu name and command name separated by a vertical bar. For example, the command "Choose File | Save" means "Open the File menu and choose Save."

Code lines, error messages, and things you type appear in `monospace`. Placeholders appear in *`italic monospace`*.

Problem avoidance is 90 percent of success in network and systems management, so helpful notes, tips, cautions, and warnings are presented along the way in hopes of avoiding calamity. Dialog-box options are often included in a table, with discussions and notes about complex choices. In addition, many numbered lists are included that guide you through a process step-by-step.

I

PART

An Introduction to Windows NT

IN THIS PART

What Is Windows NT?

1

IN THIS CHAPTER

Windows NT is Microsoft's top-of-the-line, corporate-oriented operating system. Targeting the needs and demands of corporate MIS departments and hoping to woo corporate buyers sniffing out OS/2 or UNIX alternatives to DOS, Windows 3.x, and Windows 95, Microsoft spent at least four years developing a robust and feature-rich operating system intended to meet the rigorous demands of enterprise-wide corporate settings.

If you've kept up with press reviews and articles about Windows NT, you might already know a bit, if not a lot, about NT.

NOTE

Most NT users (or those considering a switch to NT) are highly computer-literate, so I will dispense with detailed explanations of fundamental computer terminology. Appendix C contains definitions of some of those terms.

Windows NT is a multithreaded, preemptive multitasking operating system with full 32-bit memory addressing. It supports DOS, Windows, Win32 GUI and character-based applications, POSIX-compliant and character-based OS/2 1.x applications, and it includes integrated networking, security, and administration tools. It can run on single or multiple CPUs without modification, and it supports Intel processors as well as DEC Alpha, MIPS, and PowerPC, chips. Bundled electronic mail (MS-Mail) and group scheduling (Schedule+) programs round out the NT package.

A key feature of Windows NT is that it was designed as *the* future operating system from Microsoft. Newer Microsoft operating system products such as Windows 95 will borrow heavily from NT, but will be short-term bridges to the more reliable and robust NT platform. Of significant importance are NT's internal *client/server* model, in which the internals of the operating system are divided into these two categories (client and server), and dynamic disk-caching, which utilizes disk space across multiple drives as available, significantly enhancing performance.

Half of these adjectives probably sound like marketing hype, so the next sections contain the initial breakdown of this terminology. Further discussion is found later in this chapter.

Preemptive Multitasking

In systems that can run multiple programs at once (not just switchers such as Software Carousel, which suspends one application while resuming another), some means of keeping all the tasks running is needed.

A good analogy is a major intersection with a traffic cop standing in the middle and blowing a whistle. Suppose you have a spreadsheet recalculation going, a COM port is receiving a fax, and you're typing a letter at the keyboard. As you know, all these activities can occur simultaneously in a typical Windows 3.1 or a Windows 95 session (although not always smoothly).

NOTE

When I use the term *Windows 3.1,* this is also inclusive of Windows 3.11 and Windows for Workgroups 3.11.

In Windows 3.1, simultaneous application execution might not behave as you expect. This is due to the way Windows 3.1's traffic cop works. Windows 3.x doesn't really have an intelligent scheduler. Applications are supposed to be written in such a way that they relinquish CPU time at regular (very short) intervals so that other tasks can be serviced. Not all applications do this religiously, however, and Windows itself can't enforce adherence to the standard. A poorly written Windows 3.1 application can actually hog the CPU for enough time to effectively kill some time-dependent applications, such as data-acquisition programs. Try formatting a disk using File Manager (not in a DOS window) while trying to run a communications session (or anything else) and you'll see what I mean.

Windows 3.1's method of multitasking was called *cooperative multitasking.* By contrast, Windows NT's preemptive multitasking scheduler actually empowers the traffic cop to direct traffic as it sees fit. That is, NT can preempt one program in favor of another, democratically allotting CPU cycles or even stealing them when necessary.

Windows 95 provides a bit of each of these worlds. Under Windows 95, 16-bit applications do not and cannot run any "smarter" than they did under Windows 3.1. Instead, they can still tie up the operating system. Even 32-bit programs must wait for 16-bit applications to yield before they can continue. On the other hand, if you are running 32-bit apps under Windows 95, you can expect smoother performance because preemptive multitasking will be in effect. By contrast, NT runs 16-bit applications in a separate "virtual machine" that is treated as a separate 32-bit program and smoothly multitasked. The result is that 16-bit applications cannot tie up an NT system.

One result of preemptive multitasking is that the user no longer needs to consider the resources that a certain task will consume; nor does he have to allow the processing of one task to finish before starting another. Process mixes that previously might have caused problems in Windows 3.1 shouldn't cause even a hiccup in NT. Background communications sessions, for example, shouldn't drop data while other CPU-intensive tasks are running.

Here's another example. Any veteran Windows user almost instinctively allows one program to launch before trying to launch another from, for example, Program Manager. This is because you see the hourglass cursor, the symbol Windows puts on the screen to say "Hey, I'm busy." With NT, waiting isn't necessary. The icon does change, but to an hourglass with a pointer on it (called the StartGlass in NT). The pointer is still functional, and as long as you keep double-clicking on icons, programs keep loading. NT keeps track of the workload and doesn't balk.

NOTE

Actually, the number of programs that can load and execute in an NT system is limited by the amount of virtual memory available, as set by the paging file size (similar to the swap file in Windows 3.1). When this amount is exceeded, NT will lag, just as Windows 3.1 does. Setting the paging file size is accomplished from the Control Panel's System applet. This is covered in Chapter 9, under "Setting the Virtual Memory File Size."

In NT, a single task is much less likely to hold up the system for more than a blink of an eye. What's more, pressing tasks can be given a higher priority than others. For example, keyboard input, mouse movement, or data coming in through a port could be given special attention by NT's scheduler.

Multithreading

There has been enough talk about NT's (and Windows 95's) capability to run *threads* and about its *multithreading* capabilities to make you wonder whether you're in a sewing class. Before I continue, here's a quick rundown—in common language—of the significance of threading, in case you don't know. (I cover this topic more in Chapter 2.)

All tasks performed by NT can be classified as *processes*. During any given period of time, NT is executing a wide variety of processes. These might include checking a user's password, keeping track of the system's clock, accessing data from a disk, doing a memory fetch from RAM, or doing a mathematical calculation.

In NT, processes can be broken down even further into *threads*. In fact, the scheduling of events in NT is actually based on the thread unit, not the process. Most processes contain only a single thread, but they can consist of multiple threads if the programmer chooses.

The important point is that programs devised to take advantage of NT's capability to service threads can be run very smoothly—more smoothly than under Windows 3.1. For example, one complaint about multimedia programs in Windows 3.1 is that live video sometimes doesn't execute smoothly if a sound file is being played simultaneously. Although this can be due to a slow processor, it's more likely that the CPU's cycles aren't being evenly distributed between processes—even with a lightning-fast CPU. Under NT, this is much less likely to happen. In addition, as explained later in this chapter and in Chapter 2, the architecture of NT allows threads in a single application (as well as in separate applications or NT services) to be offloaded to secondary CPUs in the case of multiprocessor systems, further smoothing thread execution.

Is NT Really New Technology?

Although NT stands for *new technology,* what it affords the user isn't really all that new. Most of NT's features existed before its release and were available in other forms. NT looks and feels just like Windows 3.1, it has networking not unlike the best Novell has to offer, and internally it's much like UNIX.

Windows NT and the Windows family of operating systems provide a common interface—encapsulation of many common tasks into one package. Slowly dying are the days of the cryptic character-based operating systems. Further, Windows NT is cheaper at $389 (for the WorkStation version) than many competitors. NT allows us to leave the arenas of expensive proprietary operating systems and equipment such as the WANG, with the freedom of greater connectivity.

NT wraps it all up nice and neat in one package—a package that works right out of the box. With just a little work, you can have NT up and running on a single station or on hundreds of machines. Installation from a CD-ROM is almost automatic, and installation across a network is even easier.

Your networked mix can incorporate any collection of DOS, Windows, Windows for Workgroups, Windows 95, OS/2, UNIX, Novell NetWare, and NT machines. Support for IPX/SPX, TCP/IP, and remote access services via modem also extend the interoperability of NT outside of normal PC domain into the mainframe and WAN territories.

OS Features Aren't Everything

If the demand was only for a serious operating system with most or even all of these features, NT might not have been worth waiting for. Corporations heavily invested in PC-based information systems could have adopted UNIX or OS/2 *en masse* by now. Both of these offer much of what NT has. But the success of an operating system, particularly in business settings, has more to do with application availability than with any other variable.

Apple was aware of this basic OS truth when it dispersed its Apple evangelists to entice application developers into writing programs for their new brainchild, the Macintosh. Without application availability, the Mac never would have taken off. Its predecessor, the Lisa, went over like a lead balloon for just that reason. The demise of the NeXT "cube" is another good case in point. It was a terrific machine, but due to a scarcity of applications, loyal users of PCs and Macs just couldn't be wooed away. (Of course, its lofty price didn't help any, either.)

The operating system market isn't only application-driven, however. It's also driven by cost practicalities. As the PC market has matured, users have become less prone to overnight conversions from one type of machine—or even application—to another. The learning curve and data commitments involved in today's systems and applications are much greater than they were back in the days of the Apple II or the CP/M. It behooves MIS professionals to seriously consider the long-term investment cost of conversions to new applications, hardware, and training when they're shopping for operating systems. Over the last 10 years, compatibility and interoperability have become more and more of an issue when people are making critical hardware and software choices.

Perspective

As of this writing, the personal computer world can be divided into three primary operating system camps: Mac, DOS, and Windows. A fourth, UNIX, is also manifesting in greater numbers and various forms on the desktop. Interoperability of PCs has become an issue only since MIS departments and corporations in general have finally come to terms with the irrefutable fact that PCs are here to stay, and that the bulk of applications these days—even games—are being designed for the Windows environment. This happened in the late 1980s after a significant installed base of IBM PCs came into existence, many of them networked.

Since the advent of the Apple II and VisiCalc, MIS directors have slowly lost a desperate battle to hold onto and wield absolute control over corporate data processing via their mainframes. Independent single users in the corporate setting experienced a new freedom over their computing chores as soon as they learned to perform many simple tasks by themselves, such as running a spreadsheet for data analysis. Suddenly the days of waiting for a batch job to be done or a letter to be typed became a thing of the past.

Aside from interdepartmental power struggles that resulted from this democratization of CPU time in the workplace, some very real issues concerning data integrity were born. In a sense, personal computing was great, because it took a portion of the workload away from the MIS departments. But concerns over data validity and security—problems that MIS people thought had been addressed by their software years ago—now lurked around the corner again. In so-called *mission-critical* or *line-of-business* applications, large and often valuable corporate databases can't realistically be put in the hands of everyday users without jeopardizing the health of a company's data processing backbone.

Numerous advances over the past 10 years have attempted to address this problem and serve the needs of MIS professionals, power users, and others with high-end computing requirements. Novell (among others) has made great strides in providing networking extensions to MS-DOS. With products such as Novell's "fault-tolerant" system, DOS has became a fairly reliable networking platform, offering at least a fair amount of security for sensitive, valuable data. Likewise, the downward price spiral of minicomputer workstations running UNIX or UNIX-like operating systems has brought multitasking, mainframe-like power to many smaller corporations.

Where Do NT Workstation and NT Server Fit In?

Windows NT addresses many of these issues, and then some. Due to the impact NT will have on the huge installed base of Windows users, it's likely to usher in a new era of high-end computing on the desktop for the following reasons:

- It runs on 386 and higher PCs (albeit with some probable hardware upgrades). Thus, the millions of IBM machines and their clones in places of business can actually run NT.
- It runs most existing DOS and Windows applications. Therefore, programs were instantly available for NT the moment it was released. This is a central NT feature.
- It offers security and robust kernel solidity—features that many corporations and governmental institutions require for their mission-critical applications.

Consider these additional key features that make Windows NT an attractive operating system for the power user or corporate computing MIS professional:

- NT is written from the ground up as an operating system. It's not just a GUI laid on top of DOS.
- NT has the look and feel of Windows. Windows users don't have to be retrained to use NT. Soon, for those becoming accustomed to the Windows 95 interface, there will be an NT with that new appearance.
- Scalable architecture. This means that NT can run on different types of computers—from single CPUs (both Intel x86 and RISC chips) to multiple processor-based systems (sometimes called *symmetric* multiprocessor systems).
- High reliability. Unlike DOS and DOS/Windows, NT incorporates a robust *microkernel* design that prevents a single misbehaving application from pulling down the whole system. The microkernel is based on both the well-accepted and time-tested UNIX derivative called the Mach microkernel and the VMS operating system.

NOTE

Dave Cutler, the designer of the VMS operating system, was hired by Microsoft to create Windows NT. He and his team combined aspects of the Mach microkernel design and VMS to produce a composite design that led to the final Windows NT.

- Application compatibility. NT can run a mix of any of these classes of applications: DOS, Windows 3.x, POSIX-compliant, MS OS/2 1.x character-based programs, and new 32-bit NT applications. A command prompt similar to the DOS prompt in Windows 3.1 supports execution of DOS, 16-bit Windows, POSIX, OS/2, or 32-bit NT applications from the command line. (POSIX is a UNIX implementation that ensures source-code compatibility of UNIX applications that comply with the standard. NT complies with character-based POSIX application requirements.)

NOTE

OS/2 1.x Presentation Manager applications are also supported via the OS/2 PM Subsystem Add-On for NT package available from Microsoft.

- Complete support for Windows Object Linking and Embedding (OLE) version 2.0 is supported for data sharing between applications—even over the network.
- File system compatibility. Windows NT can work with four types of file systems: FAT, HPFS, NTFS, and Windows 95's VFAT. FAT (DOS's file scheme) is widely used. HPFS is used by OS/2. NTFS is the proprietary Windows NT file system. Because NT supports an installable file system, future file systems are easy to add and support. Because one of the key selling features of Windows 95 is support for long filenames via its VFAT system, NT's compatibility with it is key. You can actually dual-boot a single system either in NT or Windows 95 and have access to VFAT drives complete with long filenames.
- File system enhancements. Aside from being able to convert FAT and HPFS partitions to NTFS, NT's file system offers advanced security features, supports long filenames (up to 256 characters), and provides automatic error correction if a bad sector is detected. Advanced features allow creation of *stripe sets* in which multiple disks are used simultaneously to speed disk I/O, and *mirrored disks* are used to increase data safety through storage redundancy.

NOTE

Although Windows NT supports long filenames on FAT partitions, only NTFS partitions support the advanced security features.

- A built-in networking solution. The basics of LAN Manager and Windows for Workgroups are built into NT for simple peer-to-peer or client/server networking, with no need for add-on software modules. NT supports industry-standard network protocols, with built-in drivers for NetBEUI, IPX/SPX, TCP/IP, and other transports. NT is compatible with popular existing networks such as Novell NetWare, Banyan VINES, and Microsoft LAN Manager. For larger networks and remote access capabilities, the NT Server product (available at additional expense) provides additional features such as Macintosh and mainframe connectivity.

- Security. NT provides U.S. government C2-rated security features. For most intents and purposes, NT has essentially bulletproof security that can prevent an unauthorized user from entering the system or in other ways gaining access to files on the hard disk. NTFS partitions can't be reached without a proper password, so files are protected. Tools for assigning permission levels for various tasks are supplied, providing great flexibility in security arrangements.
- Multiple users can have accounts on the same NT machine. A user account on a machine includes a username and password and a series of user privileges assigned by the administrator. Users can hide directories or files from other users and set custom File Manager, Program Manager, and Control Panel settings. Logging on to the system automatically activates all saved settings from the user's previous sessions. If users have been assigned high enough privileges, they can share or stop sharing system resources on the Net (such as printers and files), or they can alter the rights other net users have when accessing them.
- NT is part of the Microsoft product line. Microsoft has been fairly good (although not perfect by any means) at designing products that mesh. As of NT's release, this is still fairly true. NT was designed to fit smoothly into the existing product line of operating systems and GUIs. As a result, if you're using MS-DOS, Windows 3.x, Windows for Workgroups, or Windows 95, migration to NT is relatively easy. Most of your existing applications will work fine. Although there have been reports that some 16-bit applications run slower under NT, many will actually run faster due to NT's incorporation of 32-bit disk, screen, and printer drivers. Just as when upgrading from Windows 3.x to Windows 95, an upgrade to NT can be done such that your Windows 95 or Windows 3.x settings are imported into NT. After installation, your NT Program Manager and Control Panel settings will be automatically preconfigured to previously existing settings.

NOTE

In all fairness, although this isn't typically mentioned in magazine reviews of NT, some 16-bit Windows applications run significantly faster under NT than in Windows 3.x or Windows 95—especially disk-intensive applications. This is due to NT's dynamic disk cache, mentioned earlier. However, to gain this benefit, you must add additional RAM, typically well above the 12MB or 16MB minimum suggested for NT systems. For example, a 32MB NT Server platform runs such disk-intensive applications very efficiently.

NT Versus DOS and Windows 3.x

Although some NT users will be making a lateral (some would say downward) move from UNIX or OS/2, most newcomers to NT will be migrating upward from the DOS/Windows 3.x platform or the Windows 95 platform. Because these are the most likely scenarios, they beg comparison for most readers.

Because you've read the press announcements and reviews, or possibly because you've read other books on the subject, you might have already decided to switch to Windows NT for specific reasons.

NOTE

One book devoted to an in-depth look at the advantages and disadvantages of NT from many points of view is *Windows NT: The Next Generation* by Len Feldman (Sams Publishing, 1993).

Because the DOS/Windows 3.x marriage has been with us for so long and is still highly prevalent despite the explosion of Windows 95 in the market, let's look at how NT compares to that operating environment. Subsequently, I'll compare NT to Windows 95 and other operating systems such as OS/2 and UNIX.

The Role of DOS

Despite the enormous popularity of Windows 3.0 and 3.1 (some estimates put the user base as high as 60 million), these GUIs are really only shells placed on top of DOS. This is also true of other PC-based GUIs, such as Digital Research's GEM, the now-defunct TopView from IBM, and VisiCorp's VisiOn.

The real culprit in this scenario is DOS—not that DOS is any slouch, of course. After all, it's been estimated that more than 100 million copies of DOS are in existence and that more than 10,000 applications are available for it. As a result, no responsible MIS professional or computer user would want to discount the importance of DOS compatibility when making an operating system choice. All too often, programs—whether major applications or minor utilities—are available only in a DOS version.

But as strong a workhorse as it is, DOS never was designed to be a multitasking operating system, much less to have a graphical user interface tacked on top of it. In other words, Windows has been a "kludge job"—something held together with spit and baling wire. As any veteran Windows user knows, strange and frustrating anomalies often crop up in Windows as a result of this unlikely marriage.

For example, when one Windows program (or DOS program running under Windows) crashes, it might very well bring the whole system and any other running applications to their knees. This is particularly a problem with Windows 3.0. Windows 3.1 is more forgiving about runaway programs, but limitations in the architecture of DOS still prevented the building of a crashproof shell.

On the up side, many DOS lovers converted to Windows simply because it provided a pretty good means of task switching and multitasking. They could run multiple DOS applications and switch between them—much as Software Carousel, Multiple Choice, and DesqView allow—but with the added convenience of also running Windows applications and of windowing DOS applications into small boxes that could be jumped to simply by clicking on them.

NT's DOS

How does NT's DOS work, and how does NT do DOS without the limitations of DOS? For starters, when NT boots, DOS does not. You can opt to install NT so that you have an option of booting DOS *or* NT, but never do you load both. NT does have a kernel operating system, one responsible for much of what DOS does under Windows 3.x—for example, keyboard and screen I/O, managing loadable device drivers, and handling disk I/O requests. Then, on top of that, NT contains modules called *environment subsystems* that emulate the DOS environment. (There are also modules for POSIX, OS/2, 16-bit Windows, and 32-bit Windows environments.) The DOS environment subsystem provides all the system services that DOS normally does. However, these functions are integrated seamlessly into NT; they don't sit below it.

DOS lovers need not feel abandoned while in NT, however. Many DOS diehards can achieve a greater throughput of work using nothing but the keyboard than they can with menus, dialog boxes, and the mouse. Microsoft is aware of this and, in keeping with its strategy of supplying backward compatibility between its operating systems, has provided a *DOS box* similar to the one in Windows 3.x.

The DOS box is not a DOS session *per se,* as it is in Windows 3.1. There, Windows actually spawns a session of DOS, running COMMAND.COM. In NT, the system architects decided to offer DOS's functionality while avoiding the limitations of DOS and utilizing the benefits of NT CPU scheduling, system security, and crash protection. This is achieved through DOS emulation via a 32-bit application called CMD.EXE, which is a superset of MS-DOS that not only provides MS-DOS compatibility but also lets you run Windows, OS/2, and POSIX applications from the command line.

NOTE

The DOS session that is created when you run a DOS application from the command window (CMD.EXE) is quite flexible in that it is configurable. Just as DOS that boots on a PC can be configured from AUTOEXEC.BAT and CONFIG.SYS, the DOS session that gets created within NT can be configured with loadable device drivers, TSRs, and so forth. Chapter 9, "Configuring Windows NT," covers this in detail.

The NT DOS emulator supports all the usual DOS commands, and then some. When you launch a DOS program under NT, NT creates a *VDM* (*virtual DOS machine*) that tricks the DOS program into thinking it's running on its own PC. NT sets up one VDM for each DOS application you run. Each VDM has all the hooks needed to handle both 16-bit and 32-bit DOS calls, in compliance with DOS 6. A full 16MB of standard DOS (segmented) application and data memory space is supplied to the VDM. In addition, the documentation states that the popular memory managers are supported. Figure 1.1 illustrates how virtual DOS machines run independently of one another on top of NT.

FIGURE 1.1.
Several DOS sessions running on top of NT in virtual DOS machines (VDMs).

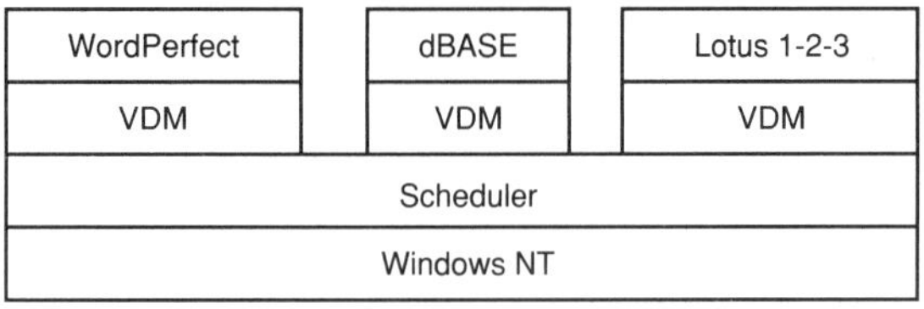

There are certain limitations to the DOS support, which you might expect. In order for NT to ensure data security and system stability, its DOS emulator intercepts all I/O processes, routing data to their destinations. This is handled by I/O interceptors, which in turn hand data to the *NT executive* for dispatching.

Any traditionally designed DOS programs that perform their I/O using standard DOS system calls will run under NT as expected. Those that write directly to hardware for which device drivers prevent direct access—for example, the hard-disk drivers—will be thwarted by NT, leading to an error message and termination of the program. Typical programs that do this are disk caching and communications applications. Overall, this approach provides a high level of system security. The result should be fewer virus problems with DOS programs under NT, because most viral programs attempt to write directly to the hard disk boot tracks or directories, and NT won't allow this.

Another limitation of NT's DOS emulator concerns device drivers. If your DOS application requires a loadable device driver to operate, you might have trouble running it in NT because the driver won't be loaded. If NT allowed loading of device drivers, it would probably mean circumventing the security features of the NT Executive because many device drivers attempt to access hardware directly. In time, modified versions of DOS applications will become available for NT, but in the meantime you might have to run the application under real DOS running outside of NT.

Windows on Win32 (WOW)

As with DOS applications, 16-bit Windows programs run in an emulation VDM created on the fly by NT—but there's a catch. Here's how it works. You launch a 16-bit Windows application in NT just as you do from Windows 3.x. That is, you can double-click on icons in the NT Program Manager, or you can use the File | Run command from Program Manager or File Manager.

NOTE

You also can type the program's .EXE filename at the DOS prompt (called the *command prompt* in NT) or enter the program's name in the Task List box.

From information in the header of the file, NT then recognizes the 16-bit Windows program and launches a VDM, just as when you run a DOS program. The VDM includes DOS and an emulation of Windows called *Windows on Win32* (*WOW*). As with DOS emulation, the Windows emulation fakes all the standard system calls (called *APIs* in Windows, for *application programming interfaces*). When a program makes a call to a standard Windows 3.x API, WOW intercepts the call and routes it to the appropriate source—usually the NT Executive or a Win32 API call. Some APIs are mapped to internal code integrated into the WOW environment. The Windows NT 32-bit *graphical display interface* (*GDI*) manages the display of the application on-screen for such things as image and text display, window locations, and so forth.

The interesting thing about 16-bit Windows applications is that, unlike DOS sessions, after the first application is run, launching additional Win 3.1 apps doesn't create an additional VDM and WOW session. It's no more necessary than running multiple copies of normal Windows 3.1 when you want to run Terminal and Notepad at the same time. This arrangement is necessary to allow maximum Windows 3.1 compatibility, as well as DDE and OLE communication between applications.

NOTE

To offer additional robustness, NT provides the capability to execute 16-bit Windows in separate VDMs. Although this requires more system resources, such as paging file space, it offers the advantage that if the application crashes, the WOW won't come down with it.

After a WOW VDM environment is launched the first time, additional Win 3.1 applications are just dumped into it as separate program threads, as shown in Figure 1.2.

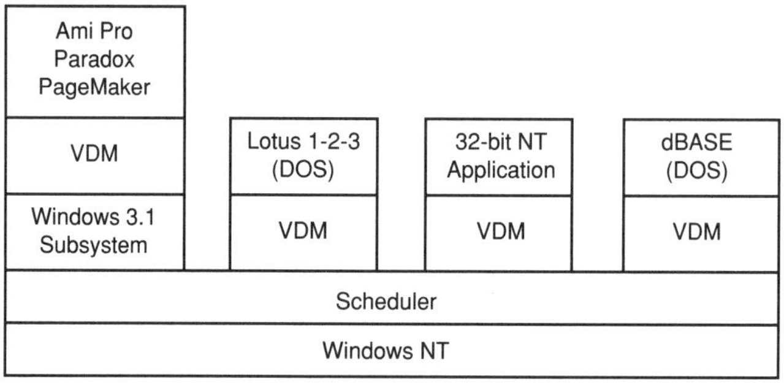

FIGURE 1.2.
Multiple 16-bit Windows applications run in the same VDM.

The good news is that this way there is less software overhead to NT and, because the NT thread manager is preemptive, no unruly application is allowed to hog the CPU's attention and slow down your other applications. The bad news is that because all 16-bit Windows applications are running in the same VDM, an errant application can pull down the whole VDM like a house of cards, as shown in Figure 1.3. This won't crash NT, but conceivably it could crash any running 16-bit Windows applications.

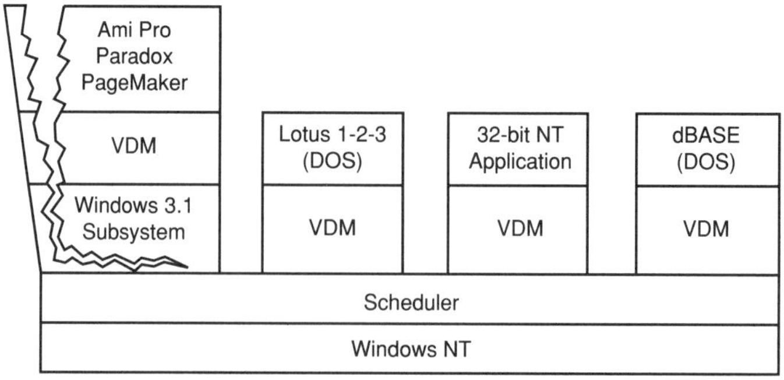

FIGURE 1.3.
One crashed 16-bit Windows program can pull down the WOW VDM, but not the whole system.

TIP

Although the WOW VDM might crash due to a misbehaving Windows application, you don't have to restart NT to launch the WOW environment again. Simply running another 16-bit Windows application will suffice.

This leads to the last point. As with DOS applications, only well-behaved Windows applications are likely to run successfully under NT. So beware: Some Windows 3.x programs write directly to the Windows GDI (usually to speed up display performance) instead of making calls to the API. Under NT, the GDI isn't going to be where the application expects it, so these unruly programs may not execute properly. (See Chapter 12, "Maintenance and Troubleshooting," under the topic "Running DOS and Windows 3.x Applications.")

Speed Issues: DOS and Windows 3.x Applications in NT

As I mentioned earlier, the big plus to running DOS and Windows 3.x apps on NT is the additional security that the system offers. The applications will still run (in fact, Microsoft believes that more than 90 percent of them will run without a hitch), and you can rest peacefully in the knowledge that your hard disk *FATs* (*file allocation tables*), files, or boot tracks aren't going to be creamed by runaway programs, and that no unauthorized personnel will have access to your files. And because all I/O calls are intercepted and mapped by NT, you can have multiple applications vying for I/O ports (for example, serial and parallel ports), and NT will run interference to prevent data collisions.

That's the good news. The bad news is that emulation, particularly with the kind of security that's built into NT, takes big-time computing power. The end result is that your DOS and 16-bit Windows applications run slower under NT than in their native environments. On average, 16-bit Windows applications run between 10 and 50 percent slower under NT, depending on the type of computation process being performed. As mentioned earlier, some disk-intensive applications on hardware with enough RAM installed might improve in performance.

As a rule, graphically intensive applications such as CorelDRAW! and full-blown graphical word processors such as WordPerfect for Windows take the greatest hit. Programs primarily doing calculations (for example, spreadsheets) exhibit less degradation because the CPU is just doing calculations as it normally does, as opposed to moving lots of graphics around on-screen and internally converting lots of 16-bit API calls to 32-bit calls. Speed degradation on DOS applications isn't as clearly delineated between graphical and nongraphics-oriented programs, but you can assume that programs running in character-mode DOS perform faster than those running in graphics mode.

Windows NT Versus Windows 95

Because virtually all popular applications have been or are now being converted for Windows 95, 16-bit Windows programs are soon to be a thing of the past. In fact, to garner the Windows 95-compatible logo from Microsoft, Windows 95-compatible applications must be written to the Win32 API and be capable of running on NT. There is a strong incentive for software makers to convert their apps to such a state that they will perform nicely on NT. The upshot is that NT is a natural next step for Windows 95 users, without any performance penalty or application incompatibility whatsoever. With that perspective in mind, let's take a closer look at how Windows 95 compares with NT.

Although many PC users are itchy for a 32-bit operating system, the vast majority of them will upgrade first to Windows 95, not to NT. Early numbers prove this point. Despite its admirable capabilities, in the first year of release, for example, only 400,000 copies of NT were sold, versus 2.4 million copies of OS/2 (International Data Corp, Framingham, MA.) Of course OS/2 is bundled with IBM PCs, so this figure may not represent an actual user demand. Resistance to NT is probably due to its hardware requirements, particularly in the RAM area. NT is overkill for most PC users, at least at this point. Still, Microsoft has its grand plan, and NT plays a big part in that scheme. So does Windows 95.

As mentioned earlier, well aware of the kludge of the DOS/Windows 3.x marriage, Microsoft set out to create a real operating system. Six million lines of code and $150 million later, NT was born. Ideally, Microsoft wants to support only a single operating system, but because many PCs still can't run NT (there are a lot of 386s out there, as well as machines with less than 12MB of RAM), this isn't possible now. Eventually though, if Microsoft has its way (and it probably will if history is any measure), everyone will be running NT in one form or another.

For the time being, Microsoft has provided a bridge from Windows 3.x to NT. That bridge—with a relatively short life of about three to five years—is Windows 95. Windows 95 will run most 32-bit NT programs as well as DOS and Windows 3.x programs. This is because Windows 95 utilizes essentially (with slight modifications) the same API as NT. It will also run on "legacy" 386-based machines having as little as 4MB of RAM.

To get developers to port their applications to 32-bits, Microsoft has made the public hungry for features built into the Win32 API and Windows 95 operating system, such as long filenames, preemptive multitasking, and memory protection. Another plus is that 32-bit versions of popular programs run faster than their 16-bit counterparts do when compared on the same Windows 95 system. The industry at large has recognized the importance of Win32 API, so that now even competitors are adopting it. For example, both DEC and IBM now offer developer's extension APIs for VMS and OS/2 that allow easy porting of applications to the Win32 API.

Despite the hoopla and technical advances such as Plug and Play, an attractive interface, additional memory protection, and a 32-bit file system, much of Windows 95 borrows from Windows 3.x's architectural anachronisms. Why did Microsoft cut corners when it already had an impressive blueprint for a true 32-bit operating system from which it could borrow? Because scaling down NT into something like "NT-Lite" wasn't possible, much less desirable, from Microsoft's point of view. Here's why.

NT's design fits a different category altogether. It is oriented toward client/server at its core level, and turning it into a small-workstation operating system would be like trying to get an elephant through your front door. Instead, a few NT architectural concepts were cut and pasted into Windows 95, a few completely new ones such as Plug and Play were added, and a flashy interface was pasted on. As a result, vestiges of the DOS/Windows kludge job are still evident in Windows 95. The result is an operating system that still acts unstable, runs multiple programs jerkily at times, and crashes for unknown reasons.

To commend it, Windows 95 does sport an impressive interface, well-integrated communications, and the capability to run more programs simultaneously than does Windows 3.x. Implementation of Plug and Play is impressive indeed. Plug in a new card (especially in a notebook), plug in a Plug and Play printer, or insert your portable into its docking station, and Windows 95 reconfigures itself accordingly. Network support is strong as well, with all the popular protocols included. Windows 95 is highly compatible with a plethora of existing hardware (moreso than is NT), runs almost every existing 16-bit and DOS application, is great for playing games, and earns high marks in the appearance category. The new interface is much easier to master than the Windows 3.x interface, so productivity for users will likely be higher.

Does it have serious problems for use in the Enterprise? Yes. For example, one errant 16- or 32-bit application can pull down the whole operating system, not just the 16-bit VDM as in NT. This is because critical portions of the operating system core code are left bare as unprotected 16-bit code. (This was done intentionally for backward compatibility reasons.) House-cleaning after a crashed application is better than it was in Windows 3.x, but it's still not perfect; so even if an application crashes and the system continues to run, it might become "unstable" and crash later. To increase support for 16-bit and DOS applications, Windows 95 allows programs to access central operating system code and directly manipulate system interrupts. Either of these can potentially crash the system.

Another serious problem is the so-called improved interface. If you're an IS manager or trainer responsible for hundreds or thousands of employees, all of whom have become conversant in use of the Windows 3.x interface, moving to Windows 95 might pose a problem. Yes, you can opt to use the Windows 3.x interface on Windows 95, but many people seem to want to migrate upward due to ease of use. Still, additional training and commensurate budgetary impact will be incurred.

Should you need to compare features of the members of the Microsoft Windows family, Table 1.1 should prove helpful. There you'll find the most salient operating system features compared.

Map of Windows Products to Come

As you might have heard or expected, numerous future releases of Windows are in the making. I couldn't include them in Table 1.1 because design specs for products such as

Table 1.1. A comparison of Windows NT and the rest of the Windows family.

Feature	*16-bit Windows 3.1*	*Windows 3.1 with Win32s*
Virtual memory	Yes	Yes
Multitasking	Cooperative	Cooperative
Preemptive Multitasking for 16-bit apps	No	No
Preemptive Multitasking for 32-bit apps	No	No
Multithreading	No	No
Symmetric multiprocessing	No	No
Portability	No	No
Access security	No	No
Runs 16-bit Real-mode Windows applications	Yes	Yes
Runs 16-bit Standard-mode Windows applications	Yes	Yes
Runs 16-bit Enhanced-mode Windows applications	Yes	Yes
Runs 32-bit Windows applications	No	Yes
Runs OS/2 applications character mode only	No	No
Supports POSIX	No	No
Supports DOS FAT	Yes	Yes

NT with the Windows 95 interface and refinements to Windows 95 are in flux. Table 1.2 illustrates Microsoft's game plan as of this writing.

Notice, firstly, that NT is the destination for both classes of users. This will be the ideal, but it must wait until the hardware is in place. Both Memphis and Nashville will be minor upgrades to Windows 95. Exact inclusions are not known at this time. Table 1.3 details some of the NT developments along the way.

Windows for Workgroups	*Windows 95*	*Windows NT*
Yes	Yes	Yes
Cooperative	Preemptive	Preemptive
No	No	Yes
No	Yes	Yes
No	Yes	Yes
No	Yes	Yes
No	No	Yes
No	No	Yes
Yes	Yes	No
Yes	Yes	Most
Yes	Yes	Yes
No	Yes	Yes
No	No	1.x
No	No	Yes
Yes	Yes	Yes

continues

Table 1.1. continued

Feature	16-bit Windows 3.1	Windows 3.1 with Win32s
Supports OS/2 HPFS	No	No
Supports NTFS	No	No
Built-in networking	No	No
Built-in e-mail	No	No
386 or higher CPU required	No	Yes
Supports RISC chips	No	No
Supports multiprocessors	No	No
Fault tolerance	No	No

Table 1.2. A time line of Microsoft's Windows offerings.

Year	*Home users or under-endowed business machines*	*Business users or well-endowed home machines*
1994	Windows 3.1	Windows 3.1 or Windows for Workgroups 3.11
1995	Windows 95	Windows NT 3.51
1996	Update of Windows 95 code-named *Nashville*	Windows NT 3.52
1997-1998	Update of Windows 95 code-named *Memphis*	Windows NT 4.0 code-named *Cairo*
1999-?	Windows NT	Windows NT

Table 1.3. A few of the past and expected upgrades to Windows NT.

NT 3.51	Dialog boxes and controls compatible with Windows 95, including networking and VFAT interoperability.
NT 3.52	Same interface as Windows 95; integration of Microsoft Network.
NT 4.0 (Cairo)	OFS support (see sidebar), object-oriented architecture, Network OLE ("distributed OLE"), ATM (asynchronous transfer mode) networking, enhanced authentication and security, directory services.

Windows for Workgroups	*Windows 95*	*Windows NT*
No	No	Yes
No	Yes	Yes
Yes	Yes	Yes
Yes	Yes	Yes
Yes	Yes	Yes
No	No	Yes
No	No	Yes
No	No	Yes

MICROSOFT'S EVENTUAL FILE SYSTEM SOLUTION: OFS

The FAT (File Allocation Table) method, which is the file system that all DOS PCs and Windows 3.x machines use, is inefficient. A little-known fact is that, due to FAT's limitations, much of the space on your disks isn't used. This is because FAT specifies a fixed number of sectors on the disk, and breaks up data across those sectors in predetermined chunks. Although a file might be only 2 bytes long, for example, it can often consume as much as 1K (1,000 bytes) of disk space because that is the size of the smallest block or sector the disk operating system can allocate.

The problem gets worse. As hard disk sizes increase, so do the sizes of sectors that are only partially consumed by data. Increasingly large amounts of precious data potential will be thrown away.

There are several solutions to this problem. NT's next incarnation, Cairo, will provide a much improved file system that will address this and other disk issues. Cairo will support disks up to the incredible size of 427 trillion MB. That should be enough for most users!

Then again, this poses additional problems related to data retrieval. Another real challenge is how to effectively locate desired data and documents when you need to. Simply using the hierarchical approach of folders within folders or subdirectories within directories will eventually fall short. As applications and documents become more complex and more integrated and linked to one another, a new paradigm of data organization and mass storage will be mandatory.

An upcoming addition to NT will be what Microsoft calls OFS (Object File System), which is an elaboration of NTFS. OFS, in collaboration with *OLE structured storage,* allows (among other things) for a file system to have extensible fields. Instead of just the filename, date, and a few flags such as read/write, each directory entry could include other important information such as fields for the creator of the file or object, which other files or documents are linked to it, and so on. Some of today's applications support one or two of these features, but only indirectly—not officially via the file system. OFS will represent the first real advance since long filenames, and will be as pivotal to efficient data storage and retrieval as the introduction of subdirectories was in DOS version 2.0.

NT Versus OS/2

Windows NT and IBM's OS/2 have similar roots. Both were born at Microsoft. OS/2 came first, originally a joint development effort of Microsoft and IBM. When a falling-out between the two companies occurred in 1990, IBM took over OS/2 and Microsoft began work on NT. Subsequently, the companies have developed these two 32-bit operating systems independently. Due to their common ancestry and similar design philosophies, however, OS/2 and NT have many similar features.

In general, OS/2 offers slightly speedier performance than NT, has less demanding system requirements, and is more compatible with DOS applications, while NT offers somewhat better crash protection and security, and decidedly superior device support.

OS/2 (I include Warp and Warp Connect when using this generic term) are multithreaded, preemptive multitasking operating systems with a graphical user interface similar to Windows. The difference between Warp and Warp Connect is that Connect includes additional network protocols. Otherwise the packages are much the same. This is unlike the distinction between NT Workstation and NT Server, which are significantly different packages; Server sports an impressive set of advanced functionality above that of Workstation.

As opposed to NT, OS/2 runs only on Intel-based processors. OS/2 can run 16- and 32-bit OS/2 applications, as well as 16-bit DOS and Windows applications (the latter via Windows 3.1, which is included with or accessed by Warp). On the other hand, OS/2 Warp doesn't run Win32 or NT 32-bit applications or programs written exclusively for Windows for Workgroups.

Multitasking performance is comparable between NT and OS/2. However, OS/2's multitasking works somewhat differently than NT's in the way it queues I/O requests from applications. OS/2's design can result in I/O bottlenecks that can slow system responsiveness as perceived by the user, whereas NT isn't likely to suffer in this way.

The graphical interface in OS/2 is called the Workplace Shell. Compared to Program Manager and File Manager, Workplace Shell is more object-oriented. OS/2 applications actually can modify the Workplace Shell, creating new operating system objects that can take advantage of OS/2's built-in functionality. These features then can be used by the application.

Both NT and OS/2 support large amounts of memory, the addressable memory area for both is 4GB. OS/2 applications are allotted 4GB (NT apps only 2GB) but OS/2 limits space for the application code to 512 MB, allowing the applications private access to the remaining portion of its own 4GB address space for data. Not that this is really a big deal—at least not yet. Even with the explosive growth of application size (so-called *bloatware*), the biggest programs I've seen are in the range of 2MB or 4MB. Besides, your applications can really see no more memory than is free (including virtual hard disk memory set aside by a paging file).

OS/2 doesn't use TrueType fonts, except when you're running Windows applications. Otherwise, it uses Adobe's ATM. Although ATM is available for Windows 3.1 and Windows for Workgroups, most Windows users prefer TrueType because it's built into Windows and because TrueType fonts are cheap and readily available. Some even come packaged with all versions of Windows.

HPFS Versus NTFS

OS/2 Warp supports an advanced file system called High Performance Files System (HPFS), similar to NT's NTFS. HPFS supports filenames up to 254 characters long, as well as "extended attributes" above and beyond the normal DOS (FAT) attribute settings (date, time, system, hidden, archive, and read/write). Extended attributes allow programs to store notes about a file, such as key phrases, the editing history of the file, the author of the file, and so on, as part of the directory entry. NT offers similar features in NTFS but also includes support for access control security, enabling an administrator to assign individual and group permission rights to every file and directory. Also, NT's disk fault-tolerance such as RAID 5 and mirror disk sets exceed those of OS/2.

OS/2 Networking

The networking version of OS/2, called OS/2 Warp Connect, provides built-in peer networking services, a NetWare requester, along with the TCP/IP support and the full set of Internet software tools that come with the standard version of Warp. Connect includes support for the following clients and protocols: IBM Peer for OS/2, IBM OS/2 LAN Requester 4.0, Novell NetWare Client Version 2.11 for OS/2, LAN Distance Remote 1.11, Gopher, FTP, telnet, and TCP/IP for OS/2 version 3.0.

Due to its IBM background, SNA (systems network architecture) is well supported. This is an important feature in the many settings that historically have been connected to IBM mainframes. In addition, many other popular protocols such as TCP/IP, APPC, NetBIOS, and LU 6.2 are supported, so OS/2 machines can be connected as workstations (clients) on most popular LANs. One particularly strong point is that an OS/2 machine can perform as a Novell NetWare server, whereas an NT machine as of this writing can't because Novell seems uninterested in sharing its server code with Microsoft. No doubt this is an issue that Microsoft will address quickly in hopes of capturing more of the Netware server market.

Stability and Crash Protection

At the time of NT's initial release, OS/2 was more successful at running DOS and Windows 3.x applications without error—partly because OS/2 has been around longer and bugs have been resolved, but mostly because NT's security prevents programs not in strict compliance with API rules from wreaking havoc on the system. It's a trade-off between compatibility and robustness at this point, with robustness taking the upper hand. For those concerned with security, the trade-off is an acceptable one.

Final Analysis

In the final analysis, NT has a leg up on OS/2 Warp and OS/2 Connect in a number of ways:

- NTFS is more capable than HPFS due to security and fault-tolerance features.
- NT's internal security is more advanced and pervasive than OS/2's, extending not only to disk operations but to all system events (application threads, system calls, memory accesses, and so on).
- NT is portable to RISC and multiprocessor systems.
- NT is directly compatible with Windows for Workgroups, Windows 95, and LAN Manager. Simply install the necessary network cards, cable the machines together, boot up, and you have a functioning LAN.

- NT has built-in networking, and extensive, secure networking is available with NT Server.
- NT is fully 32-bit, whereas parts of OS/2 are written in 16-bit left over from earlier versions. In addition, NT can easily be modified to support other operating systems with the simple addition of operating system emulator modules (environment subsystems, discussed in Chapter 2). This probably will ensure a longer life span and faster upgrading for NT than for OS/2.

Refer to Table 1.4 for a comparative listing of Windows NT and OS/2 features. Notice particularly the C2-level security, 32-bit application support, and NTFS differences.

Table 1.4. Feature comparisons of Windows NT and OS/2.

Feature	*OS/2 Warp*	*Windows NT*
Portability	Planned	Yes
Symmetric multiprocessing	No	Yes
Virtual memory	Yes	Yes
Object-oriented user interface	Yes	No
Internationalization	Codepage	Unipage
C2-level security	No	Yes
DOS FAT file system	Yes	Yes
High-performance file system (HPFS)	Yes	Yes
NT file system (NTFS)	No	Yes
Runs DOS applications	Yes	Yes
Runs 16-bit Windows applications	Yes	Yes
Runs OS/2 16-bit applications	Yes	Text-only†
Runs OS/2 32-bit applications	Yes	No
Runs 32-bit Windows applications	No	Yes
Application protection	Yes	Yes
Multitasking	Yes	Yes
Multithreading	Yes	Yes
Multiple message queues to prevent data bottlenecks	No	Yes

†With the addition of the OS/2 PM Subsystem Add-On for NT package available from Microsoft, NT can also support OS/2 1.x Presentation Manager applications.

NT Versus UNIX

Contrary to popular opinion, UNIX is no longer the inscrutable operating system usable only by engineers and computer geeks. Its popularity among nonacademics is on the rise as a graphical operating system. In fact, much of Windows NT has its origins in a variant of UNIX called Mach, developed at Carnegie-Mellon University. In the last several years, standardization of UNIX among its many vendors has resulted in its gaining an even stronger foothold in the marketplace. With its recent acquisition of the portion of AT&T that invented UNIX (AT&T's UNIX Systems Laboratory), Novell might indeed give Microsoft a run for its money with its own UnixWare product. Other major players in the UNIX market are SCO, IBM, DEC, SunSoft, and NeXT, with their products SCO UNIX, AIX, ULTRIX, Solaris, and NeXTSTEP, respectively.

NT and UNIX have much in common, which is good news. The multiprocessing, multitasking, and networking capabilities of NT's Object Manager and Process Manager owe much to UNIX's own time-tested architecture (as well as to VMS design concepts, as mentioned earlier).

In addition to the multitasking mentioned earlier, UNIX and NT have another important commonality. According to some analysts, in fact, this is the *most* important feature of NT. It's called *RPC* (remote procedure call) support. This feature allows NT to offload computing tasks to another networked CPU (that is, a workstation) detected as sitting idle. Such a chore typically is a subtask or thread of a currently executing program or procedure. In this arrangement, there are RPC *clients* and RPC *servers.* Clients are processes that look for CPU power across the distributed computing network. A server is such a CPU, available for use by the client. Windows NT Server provides RPC support services that let programs written to take advantage of them do so. In the future, this might result in very efficient execution of complex programs, in effect turning a network into a huge multiprocessor computer that can be dynamically assigned to any number of tasks that network users are running.

> **NOTE**
>
> See Chapter 2 for more details on the internal architecture of NT and for descriptions of the Object and Process Managers.

Devices

A major similarity between NT and UNIX is in how they interact with devices attached to the computer. In order to design an operating system that's as flexible as possible, UNIX and NT both connect to the world through device drivers that appear as files. When either

UNIX or NT wants to send data to or fetch data from a screen, keyboard, I/O port, memory, or disk file, the same internal approach is used: They simply route the process to a device that appears to the operating system as a sequential file. Regardless of the physical nature of the device (such as a pressed key, a memory location, or a COM port), all of these objects are treated in the same manner.

Memory Allocation

Another major similarity is the way NT and UNIX use memory. Both can access a large, "flat" memory space of many megabytes. NT and UNIX programmers don't have to deal with any of the problems inherent in a 16-bit PC application's need for segmented addressing schemes. NT typically offers a memory space of 4GB per application. (This is virtual memory, of course, because you'll probably have only 16MB of real RAM.) Actually, only 2GB of that space is available for the application; the rest is for NT's use. Many UNIX systems offer about the same amount. Both systems prevent applications from stepping on each other's toes, because memory blocks allotted to one process or application can be protected from access by another process. A key difference between UNIX systems on PCs and NT is that, however annoying it is that NT requires 12MB to 16MB of RAM, UNIX systems tend to require more.

GUI Treatment

Over the years, a number of graphical interfaces for UNIX have appeared, and due to the open design philosophy of UNIX, little standardization has ensued. One of the key advantages of NT over UNIX is simply that it adopted the Windows GUI, an interface that through mass popularity has more or less been set in stone. In the UNIX world, contending GUIs such as OPEN LOOK and Motif present problems for users and applications developers alike. Users can be confused when jumping between systems with different GUIs, and developers have to decide which GUI or GUIs they'll tune their application for.

Software Compatibility: Market Considerations

Reiterating the point about software applications driving the operating system market is certainly applicable here. Although UNIX and its variants such as Solaris and NeXTSTEP offer advantages (NeXTSTEP is a great development environment for programmers due to its true object-oriented metaphor), few of them offer significant support for DOS or Windows applications. For establishments that are moving upward in processing power and that are already well ensconced in a DOS/Windows applications mix, UNIX won't cut the mustard. However, for those who have previously invested in UNIX applications, systems, terminals, networking, and so forth, one of the PC-based UNIX contenders could make good sense as an affordable alternative when you consider the addition of fully loaded workstations.

It's true that UNIX has some advanced features, such as distributed file services and parallel processing, that NT does not. And almost like a religion, its followers are loyal and ubiquitous. A huge pool of UNIX experts worldwide has been developing utilities, applications, and extensions to the operating system for many years. Microsoft is only in the infant stages of developing support for NT. On the downside, however, UNIX is a behemoth, and it's not fully standardized. A full-blown version V of UNIX takes up a huge amount of disk space (almost 100MB) and comes on close to 100 disks. It also requires significant upkeep.

In the long run, the phenomenal popularity of DOS and Windows applications in the horizontal market (nonspecific applications such as spreadsheets, databases, and word processors) will ensure NT's success (or that of other Windows derivatives), and it makes NT the better choice for most power-user business needs—whether on the network or on the stand-alone desktop. Although NT is much like UNIX in terms of features, it's more elegant and more efficient. UNIX incorporates advances inspired by Dave Cutler and his VMS development team as well. It offers much of UNIX's functionality without the ever-growing plethora of nonstandard functions and add-ons that UNIX has accumulated over the years.

Based on the Carnegie-Mellon Mach microkernel and VMS model, NT was designed to be the real Windows that PC people were waiting for, or the manageable operating system that UNIX hackers dreamed of taking home with them. As future versions of 32-bit–compatible Windows programs become readily available (Win32s and NT apps from many vendors are available now, and more are on the way), UNIX's hope of widespread popularity on the desktop is likely to be dashed.

NT's Advanced Features

So much for a brief look at NT's basic features and the main contenders against NT. Before I move on to discuss the detailed architecture of NT, this section takes a quick tour of the NT services and features that distinguish it from Windows 3.x and Windows 95:

- Networking
- NTFS file services
- Multiprocessor support
- Hardware support
- Fault tolerance
- System administration tools

Networking

Windows NT comes in two versions, in which the significant differences pertain to networking. These versions are called simply Windows NT Workstation and Windows NT Server. With the standard NT desktop operating system, you get peer-to-peer networking, server networking, remote access services, and all the administration tools typically needed to maintain a network server. (See the section titled "Other Advantages of NT Server," later in this chapter.)

For a little more than twice the price (about $699 versus $319), you can purchase an introductory package of NT Server and get a serious enterprise-wide server solution. Windows NT Server has no arbitrary limit on the number of users who can be connected, aside from the client licensing issue. However, a Windows NT Workstation has a maximum of 10 *inbound connections* (connections from an external client) and an unlimited number of *outbound connections* (connections to an external server or other workstation).

NOTE

The base product doesn't include the client licenses. These must be purchased separately. At the time of this writing, a special upgrade had been announced for Windows NT Advanced Server 3.1 users. You can upgrade to Windows NT Server 3.5 with a 250-client user license for $699, and you can upgrade from Windows NT 3.1 to Windows NT Server 3.5 with a 20-client license pack for $149.

Both systems are built around the same basic core NT kernel and interface, and both have C2-level government security features. NT Workstation is meant to connect smaller workgroups, typically within a single site on a departmental level. However, with the Server package, you get a greater degree of fault tolerance and larger network capabilities and connectivity options. You also get remote access administration capabilities, meaning that you can perform administrative duties from a remote station (even over the phone) instead of having to perform them at the server station. You even get additional support for AppleTalk, enabling Apple Macintosh users to coexist happily on your NT network.

Both systems are built around the Network Device Interface Specification (NDIS) version 3.0 specification. This means that you can connect to other Microsoft products (and other brands) such as LAN Manager for OS/2. TCP/IP support in both NT and NT Server means connectivity to UNIX systems. Other support packages can provide IBM and VAX connectivity, which might be even more important, especially in the corporate environment.

Windows for Workgroups Support and Windows 95 Support

In the forthcoming battle of the high-end operating systems, the likely focal point will be the LAN. Thus, Windows NT was made compatible with as many existing network types as possible. The good news is that, unlike many networking solutions (including the many capable but complex UNIX PC systems), networking with NT is simple and fairly painless right out of the box. This fact alone might win the hearts of many MIS managers.

Both NT and NT Server allow connection of hardware systems running NetWare, Banyan VINES, and Microsoft LAN Manager networks, as well as Windows for Workgroups (WFW) and Windows 95. The first three are far more likely to be found in the field than Windows for Workgroups (despite Microsoft's efforts to push that product). However, if you're running WFW or Windows 95, getting up and running is a no-brainer. NT really is plug-and-play compatible with WFW and Windows 95 as well as with Microsoft's DOS networking analogue, Workgroup Connection. Just hook up an existing WFW or Windows 95 network to a standard NT Server, share some directories and printers from the server, and you're in business. What you've got is a peer-to-peer network with the NT station also acting as a server.

NOTE

Due to the similarities of network interaction and presence between WFW and Windows 95 peer-to-peer networks or stand-alone stations, WFW will often be used to represent both types of systems. When you see *WFW* in reference to connections, shares, or other management issues, Windows 95 workstations are also implied.

The advantage over what you had on a standard WFW peer-to-peer network is that your server can be locked up tight as a drum with serious password protection, assignable user privileges, and fault-tolerant hard disk functions. Not only can WFW stations access FAT partitions on the server, they also can take advantage of the advanced features of the NTFS file system (such as security and media fault-detection and repair).

NOTE

Long filenames are not available to DOS or DOS/Windows 3.x users attached to NTFS partitions over the network. NT truncates filenames for use by non-NT workstations, as explained later in this chapter in the section titled "NTFS File Services." However, Windows 95 users will see long filenames.

NOTE

Windows for Workgroups version 3.11 is an extension of WFW containing a few features that allow it to interface more neatly with NT. For example, 3.11 adds domain support for NT Server networks, which provides for user authentication, much as the NT client machines do. Windows 95 has similar features.

Network administrators also have sophisticated control over file and directory accessibility and user rights on a network, even with WFW clients. For example, rights to a host of activities such as read/write privileges, programmer privileges, forcing obligatory password changes or uniqueness, backing up files, forcing a system shutdown, and changing the system time can be individually assigned on a user-by-user basis. Administrators also can opt to build an audit trail using an automatic event logger, recording who logs on and off the system, which files and directories were accessed, and other details.

The sharing of network resources in NT uses the same metaphor as Windows for Workgroups. This makes it probably one of the simplest to manage. To share a directory, simply highlight the directory's file folder in File Manager and click on the Share icon in the toolbar. Fill in a few details in a dialog box, and the task is complete. To share a printer, open Print Manager, highlight a printer, and click on the Share button.

NOTE

An important distinction between NT and WFW/Windows 95's sharing models needs to be highlighted. When you share a resource such as a directory or a printer in WFW, security is set at the share level. That is, you have the option of declaring some properties about the share, such as whether the directory is read-only or read/write. Specific network users who will have access to the resource aren't declared. You can declare a password in some cases, but this restricts access only for people who don't know the password. With NT, shares can easily be restricted to use by individual users or to preset groups of users. When a user tries to access a resource, the resource server (that is, the workstation containing the shared resource) checks the identity of the potential client and either grants or refuses access to the resource based on the user's identity (username and password).

Installing NT automatically results in the installation of 32-bit versions of Microsoft Mail and Schedule+. Although Mail works seamlesslywith the 16-bit Windows for Workgroups version of this program, the 32-bit Schedule+ has a much different feature set from its 16-bit counterpart, causing some compatibility problems.

Other Network Support

The majority of networked PCs run Novell products such as NetWare or NetWare Lite. Novell has cooperated with Microsoft over the years by offering to share its client-side software. Assuming that hardware requirements aren't a big issue, one of the key advantages of NT is the ease with which getting Windows onto a Novell network can be achieved. Connection to a NetWare network with Windows 3.1 requires three levels (four modules) of software. Connection with NT requires just one, with the inherent security and connectivity advantages of NT.

Novell and Microsoft have, through their collaborations, seen to it that clients running Windows 3.1, Windows for Workgroups, Windows NT, and Windows NT Server can connect to Novell servers just as easily as they can to other servers such as LAN Manager.

For obvious reasons, Novell is not interested in sharing its code for the server side of the equation. After all, NT Server is an arrow aimed directly at Novell's heart in hopes of capturing some of the networking market share Microsoft has failed to gain with LAN Manager and Windows for Workgroups. Microsoft has been forced to write its own server code, and by most accounts it looks as though NT Server is a fairly successful challenge to Novell's servers. It matches much of the functionality of Novell, such as file and print serving, and it contains significant additional functionality such as RPC support, extensive fault tolerance and security, Remote Access Services, environment subsystems, disk striping and volume sets, and very good user administration tools.

Some analysts suggest that Microsoft intends NT Server servers to perform as 32-bit NT application servers on established Novell networks. Therefore, instead of converting your Novell servers to NT, just add some NT Server units to your network mix and allow users to run high-performance 32-bit NT applications from them.

Fault Tolerance Extensions

NT Server affords a couple of fault-tolerant options worth noting. These are well known by Novell aficionados. They are generically known as *disk mirroring* and *disk striping*. Specifically, they're known as RAID 1 and RAID 5. (*RAID* stands for *redundant array of independent drives.*)

RAID 1 enables you to set up each hard disk in the server with a mirror disk that contains a carbon copy of the disk's data. Whenever a write occurs on the primary drive, an identical change is made to the mirror disk. Although this procedure requires two hard disks for every one you want in action, the advantages can be well worth it. If the operating system detects an error such as a lost file or sector, the second drive is accessed in order to retrieve it. In a worst-case scenario, when the primary drive crashes or fails, the backup takes over without a hiccup.

NOTE

To fully implement hard-disk fault tolerance, you should install multiple disk controllers as well as disks. Windows NT lets you do this. The mirror disk will then be on a second controller, so that if the first controller card fails, the second one will take over instantaneously.

RAID 5 is a different story. It wasn't designed for avoiding down-time and data loss *per se.* Instead, RAID 5 enables you to create *volume sets,* or *arrays.* A volume set combines between two and 32 disk drives to speed up the reading and writing of data. An array looks like a single volume (for example, drive E:) to the system. When the system attempts to write a file to disk, the information is spread (striped) across several disks instead of written on a single one, resulting in a significant throughput increase. What's odd is that the data is broken up among drives, so it doesn't exist on any single drive. However, if striping is used with the parity option, enough data is stored on the set to allow operation of the system (and access to the files) even if one disk in the array becomes crippled.

Finally, a third fault-tolerant option enables uninterruptible power supply (UPS) operation of NT clients and servers. Through a serial port connection between the UPS and NT machines, NT is warned of a power outage or a brownout. All users connected to the server are notified of the problem, and after a specified period of time (dependent on the capacity of the UPS), NT begins to shut down.

Remote Access Services (RAS)

Remote access services enable the user to dial into the network from a remote computer (such as a laptop) over phone lines. Operationally, interaction is just as if the user is in the office. As soon as users are logged on and recognized as valid, they have access to any service for which they are authorized, even if that service attaches them to another domain, a mainframe, or another type of LAN. Therefore, you could call from home, log in, send a print job to a laser printer, use some data on a mainframe, run applications, leave e-mail for other users, interact with company scheduling programs such as Schedule+, and so on.

Remote access is included in the standard NT product too, but only one user can call it at a time. On the NT Server version, multiple callers can log in simultaneously. (The maximum is 256, but this number is limited by the number of COM ports you have available.)

NT's built-in RAS is not the same as commonly used products such as PC-Anywhere, Close-Up, and Carbon Copy. These DOS products let you log in and run Windows or DOS programs from afar, but they actually control the host machine, which is different than logging into a network or a workstation as a user and being validated with a password. With those DOS products, applications still run on the host machine while the remote access software simply shunts keyboard and screen I/O to the remote machine. With NT's

RAS, you tie into the network just as any workstation does. Additional security is provided by an optional "dial-back" setting that forces the workstation to dial up the remote computer at a predetermined location (phone number) to further prevent unauthorized users from gaining access. All this is built into NT. In addition, an administrator can easily enable or disable dial-up authority for each user.

Other Advantages of NT Server

Windows NT is designed to be the local workgroup solution when you need more control than is offered by a peer-to-peer network (such as Windows for Workgroups, LANtastic, or Novell Lite). But what about really large corporations or agencies with many departments, and possibly even different physical sites around the country?

For the complex requirements of sophisticated interdepartmental networking communications or for interplatform networking, you might want to consider the more sophisticated NT Server. NT Server shares the core design and desktop appearance of the standard $300 NT. The price is higher, however, and extensions to NT are added, supplying support for the following:

- The "domain" model for establishing very large networks, meaning enterprise-wide connectivity and interconnectivity with other networking platforms and the necessary tools for administering such domains
- Wide area networking capabilities
- Remote access software
- Connectivity services for mainframes and minicomputers
- Macintosh connectivity

Although it's not truly complete in its first release, NT Server is a long-range project for Microsoft. It clearly is the direction Microsoft intends to take for serious corporate users. In the works for NT Server, Microsoft has promised the following:

- SNA support for IBM and compatible mainframes. AS/400 environments via 5250 emulation will be supported.
- An enterprise-wide messaging system called EMS (Enterprise Message System).
- An enterprise-wide network management system called SMS (System Management Server).
- SQL Server for NT Server.

In the domain model, each NT Server typically services a departmental workgroup; then you network the Server machines to create a domain. Any collection of network servers and clients that shares the same security access database is considered to constitute the domain; therefore, the design is flexible. However, the topography is normally laid out as shown in Figure 1.4.

FIGURE 1.4.
Two domains of five workstations each are attached to create a single, larger network. Each domain has at least one NT server.

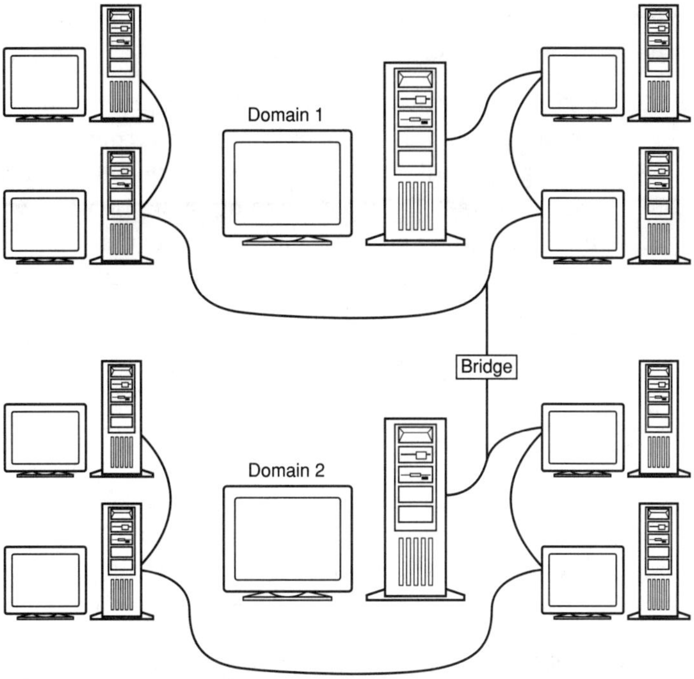

Windows NT Server comes with administrative tools beyond those supplied with standard NT: management tools for administering domains, a Server Manager for both local and remote management of a particular server, and a Profile Editor to tweak the specifics of each user's rights and account details.

NT Server domain cooperation is based on an interserver relationship called *trust*. Trust is employed as a hedge against the inevitable network slowdown that comes with the level of security that NT incorporates. Without trust, each time a user attempted to use a file or other service from a server on the network, a complex series of authentication procedures would have to ensue, just to ensure that the user was legitimate. To prevent this security-checking replication, servers have *trust relationships* with one another. In essence, if one server has validated a user, other servers with whom that server has a trust relationship will honor the user. On a properly configured network with full trust between servers, a user has to log on to the system only once. Passwords are not required each time the user requests another service.

Multiple CPU Support

Both versions of NT support multiple processors running in the same machine. Although the standard NT version supports only one or two CPUs, Server allows up to four. For systems with more than four CPUs, you must rely on the hardware developers to supply proprietary NT drivers.

Adding CPUs is the perfect solution to sluggish performance as networks get larger, the application mix grows heavier, high throughput becomes a must, or custom applications grow exceedingly extensive. Of course, the traditional fix of adding RAM helps too, and throwing CPUs at an NT machine running applications not written with multiprocessor execution in mind won't give you a leg up, to say the least. Although the NT Executive automatically dispatches threads to detected CPUs, effectively divvying up the workload across them, the application must be written to take advantage of NT's multithreading to do so. (NT itself handles the dispatching of threads to the detected CPUs.) Microsoft's SQL Server supports NT multiple threads on SMP systems. Other developers are following suit.

NT's CPU detection and performance upgrading is automatic. For example, a multi-CPU machine called the AcerFrame 3000 MP50 enables you to add additional 486 DX-50s at will. To get NT to recognize and utilize additional CPUs, simply plug in the new CPU cards and reboot NT. The NT kernel detects the additional computing power, and the thread dispatcher begins dishing it tasks as soon as you run multithreaded applications.

NOTE

The multi-CPU arrangements that NT supports are *SMP* (*symmetric multiprocessing*) only. *Asymmetric multiprocessing* (*AMP*) with a number of dissimilar CPUs, or with CPUs running at varying speeds, isn't yet supported. Windows NT can support an AMP type of architecture in a limited fashion by dedicating a CPU to a particular service. For example, SQL Server for Windows NT can increase SQL Server performance by dedicating a CPU for its own use.

NOTE

Notice that there is an interesting distinction between SMP and AMP. In AMP, a single CPU typically is used for executing the operating system, while additional CPUs are used for executing different tasks, such as SQL Server (as in the LAN Manager model). The CPU assigned to running the operating system can't share its CPU cycles with other tasks and hence limits its overall effectiveness. In SMP, CPU cycles are shared more democratically, increasing overall operating system and application efficiency.

NTFS File Services

Chief among NT's strong points is the NT File System (NTFS). Based largely on Microsoft's experience with OS/2, NTFS ups the ante over OS/2's High Performance File System (HPFS) by adding a few additional features.

As I mentioned earlier, NT can read and work with both DOS (FAT) and HPFS disks in their native formats. It also can convert them to the file system optimized for use with NT. Windows NT can also recognize and work with VFAT partitions created under Windows 95. Hard disk volumes also can be partitioned into a mix of all three. NT recognizes and works with directories and files from any host partition, meaning that you can share NTFS, FAT, and HPFS on a network. Other NT clients (actually running NT on their machines) will have access to any of the three file formats. Windows for Workgroups or other DOS-based systems can have access to shared FAT and NTFS partitions. However, NTFS long filenames will be truncated.

TIP

If you intend to share NTFS directories with non-NT workstations, you might want files in those directories to comply with standard "8.3" DOS-style filenames so that those workstations won't have to deal with truncated names.

Long Filenames

As Mac, OS/2, and now Windows 95 users (among others) will certainly agree, DOS's 8.3 filename restriction (eight characters, a period, and a three-letter extension) is a perennial frustration. Most PC people have grown used to it, but Microsoft seems to have finally gotten the message. NT allows names up to 256 characters, including spaces and periods, and it differentiates between uppercase and lowercase letters.

NOTE

The uppercase/lowercase distinction applies only to the on-screen display of filenames, not to NT's recognition of filenames for access or execution. It's merely a visual convenience.

In File Manager, a typical file listing might look like this:

```
History of Asian Music
```

However, you can't create files with long names with any DOS or Windows 3.1 application; you get an error message stating that such a filename isn't valid. Only programs designed for NT allow the actual use of long filenames, so relief from DOS's naming limitation isn't going to be instantaneous. (Of course, you can rename files in NT's File Manager if you must.)

The key question is, "What does NT do with filenames to make them usable by DOS and Windows 3.1 applications running under NT?" When running under NT, these programs can access the NTFS directory, but normally they couldn't read the longer filenames.

Here's the trick. When you save a file using an NT application, it automatically generates a shorter, 11-character name that DOS and Windows 3.1 can read. That name is also stored on disk, along with the long filename. Windows 95 users, when networked to the NTFS directory on the NT machine, will see the whole name. Figure 1.5 shows what happens to filenames when they're saved and reloaded with various operating systems and file formats.

FIGURE 1.5.
How NTFS serves long filenames to other operating systems.

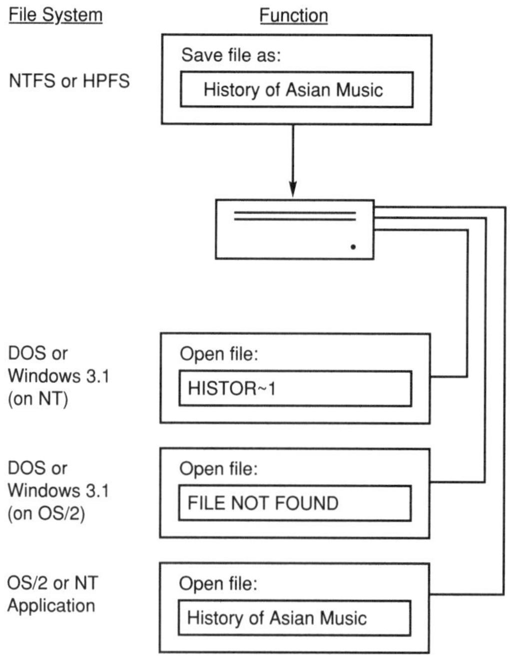

Summary

This chapter discussed the specific features that clearly make Windows NT one of the most powerful operating systems available for PCs. It compared NT to competing PC- and mainframe-based operating systems on a number of counts. Clearly, NT is much more powerful, flexible, and configurable than its predecessor, Windows 3.1, though in appearance they are almost identical. Although Windows 95 represents an important waystation toward a full 32-bit model, it too has limitations that are vestiges of DOS and Windows 3.x. More like UNIX or VMS in internal design, NT is much more portable, extensible, and practical due to the number of compatible applications it can run. In a nutshell, Windows NT provides:

- mature multitasking
- fault tolerance
- extensive networkability
- RPC support
- extensibility
- plug-and-play connectivity with Windows for Workgroups, Windows 95, LAN Manager, TCP/IP, and RAS
- backward compatibility with DOS, 16-bit Windows applications, some OS/2 packages, and character-based POSIX applications

Add to this its government C2-level security compliance, and the package is very complete. Despite the additional hardware requirements NT demands (particularly in the RAM and CPU departments), NT clearly is an operating system with a bright future. Forthcoming Microsoft operating system products will most definitely be based on the NT model, ensuring NT's success even moreso. Windows NT should figure strongly in any far-sighted corporate or government projections for operating system and networking system allocations for this reason alone. It will eventually be in every laptop and desktop computer if Bill Gates and Microsoft get their way. And there's little to suggest they won't.

The Architectural and Operational Design of Windows NT

2

IN THIS CHAPTER

As you probably surmised from Chapter 1, Windows NT is a complex and capable operating system—certainly a far cry from its DOS/Windows 3.1-combination predecessor. Windows NT is a full-blown multiuser operating system that borrows from sophisticated mainframe operating system design principles such as preemptive multitasking and multithreading. You've also seen how NT compares to other PC and mainframe-based operating system alternatives such as OS/2 and UNIX.

This chapter goes a bit more into the inner workings of NT, discussing its architectural design and some specific differences between 16-bit Windows and NT. First, though, let's look at how NT fits into a larger overall Microsoft Windows strategy.

NT's Market Position

NT's appearance is deceiving. The first time I saw NT running, it was at a Microsoft-sponsored expo in San Francisco about a year before NT's release. Having written several books about Windows, I was quite interested in how NT's changes in user interface and overall functionality would impact rewrites of my existing books. I was surprised to find that, for the most part, it looked and acted just like Windows 3.1, with a few added applications (primarily administrative management tools for networks) thrown in.

Clearly, Microsoft has achieved what it set out to do: make potential NT users feel at home with something that looks just like the Windows they know but, under the skin, is actually a very different animal with additional functionality. In fact, this is the design philosophy behind all Microsoft Windows products, from Modular Windows to Pen Windows, Mobile Windows, Windows 3.1, Windows for Workgroups, Windows 95, and finally, Windows NT. Other new Windows categories probably will be coming down the pike, such as Windows for interactive television. (The functionality details for this medium are being hotly debated at this time, but Microsoft currently is a big player in the discussions.)

Microsoft's bet is that once people are familiar with the Windows metaphor, any permutation of it will be easily learnable. Table 2.1 illustrates Microsoft's multiplatform market attack for its Windows products.

Table 2.1. Microsoft's multilevel Windows products.

Product	*Platform*	*Audience*
Windows NT	High-end CISC and RISC machines, including those with up to 16 multiprocessors	Power users and corporations needing enterprise-wide network services and mainframe connectivity. Good platform for developing mainframe applications.

Product	*Platform*	*Audience*
Windows for Workgroups and Windows 95	IBM PCs and compatibles with Intel-compatible CPUs 386 and higher	Small businesses needing peer-to-peer networking or interconnectivity with NT. Many users say that even on a stand-alone system such as a laptop, these are the versions of Windows to consider if you're not running Windows NT. The feature set of both is rich, and NT compatibility is high.
Windows 3.1/DOS or Windows 95	IBM PCs and compatibles with Intel-compatible CPUs	Most desktop PC application users who have no need for networking.
Mobile Windows/ Pen Windows	Notebook and subnotebook computers with Intel-compatible CPUs	Typical PC users who need computing power on the road.
Modular Windows	Home interactive multimedia systems/pocket PDAs (personal data assistants) with various CPU types	Games and other services on home appliances; users who want small electronic organizers for various functions.

Windows NT sits at the top of the current heap, at least for the time being. Other higher-end products are sure to appear, both to augment NT and to update other existing products (for example, Windows 95, BackOffice, and various Internet server software packages). In any case, emphasis is on the painless transition as you move up the Windows ladder, with Microsoft's hope of cornering the market on graphical user interfaces. The essentials of the Microsoft Windows design are likely to endure for some time.

Some analysts feel that one of NT's main strengths is that it provides an excellent downsizing platform for corporate developers and, eventually, the perfect upsizing target for workstation users. For example, corporate folks can utilize the Microsoft C/C++, COBOL, and FORTRAN compilers on NT machines to develop applications for the mainframe. These applications often can even be tested on the NT platform as well. Then, after the application passes its testing and development stages, it can be uploaded and recompiled for the mainframe. This has the potential to save the corporation considerable money, because mainframe CPU time is quite costly. In fact, it could save the company enough money to pay for the NT machines and software required for the development.

An Overview of NT's Design

Now that we've looked at NT in relation to other Microsoft operating systems, let's look at the inner workings of NT. Having taken 150 million dollars and comprising several million lines of code, a project of such magnitude can't be undertaken lightly or without extensive forethought. Coding began only after a thorough architectural design and line of attack were agreed upon by the main programmers and system architects involved. Much of the design, coding, and thinking behind NT were the work of Dave Cutler, who also developed an operating system for the DEC PDP-11 (called RSX-11M) and the VMS operating system that runs on the DEC VAX system.

NOTE

Although it began with about 10 members, the NT programming team is reported to have eventually grown to about 50, with as many as 200 working on ancillary items such as applets and drivers.

The NT design model included a number of primary higher-order goals separate from applications, tools, or utilities—that is, inner functionality mostly invisible to the user. The apparent achievement of these goals is primarily what renders Windows NT superior to its predecessor. Although other design issues exist in addition to these, the main architectural premises were to make NT

- compatible with existing code
- easily extensible
- scaleable
- portable
- networkable, with distributed processing
- secure

The next sections briefly examine what each of these design goals means and how NT implements them. Then we'll look at the architectural model and the components of NT.

The NT System Model

Any further discussion of NT's design requires an understanding of the basic model that NT draws upon. An operating system's functioning is very complex, requiring code built in many layers. Without a basic theoretical model to build upon, an operating system's writers could easily become mired in detail, lost in their own code as if it were a huge pile of spaghetti. Decisions at critical junctures are more difficult to make without the guidance of the model. Over the years, operating systems engineers have developed a number of basic theories (and resulting models) that are employed when they design a new operating system. The three most common models are

- monolithic
- layered
- client/server

User and Kernel Modes

All three models have one thing in common: They each divide operating system tasks into at least two categories—*user mode* and *kernel mode*. The kernel, as you might recall, is the innermost (core) part of the operating system. Code that runs in kernel mode has access to system hardware and system data. To protect the operating system and stored data (such as files), only certain code is allowed to run in kernel mode. All other code, such as that for applications, runs in user mode.

For example, in most operating systems, applications typically run in user mode and thus don't have direct access to system resources such as the hard disk. The user-mode application must ask the kernel to access the hard disk. The application isn't permitted to write directly to the disk, because a mistake in the writing process could scramble other unrelated data files—including the operating system itself.

NOTE

Some mainframe operating systems actually divide into more than two modes (sometimes called *rings*) of the CPU to provide additional protection layers. The VAX, for instance, might utilize ring 0 for the kernel but also utilize ring 1 for other kernel services (such as a database engine), and utilize ring 2 for additional services while utilizing ring 3 for the user portion of the operating system. Instead of just the user/kernel distinction then, an operating system can provide such additional extensions to provide more security and robustness. Microsoft could have implemented additional rings in NT but decided not to because of the software overhead involved in ring transitions. The result is faster performance and a more robust system model.

NOTE

Virus programs are an example of a breach of this "containment field" approach. A virus program that writes to the boot tracks of a hard disk circumnavigates the user/kernel privilege agreement by using its own code to write on the hard disk, rather than asking the operating system (which normally would prevent the system-track modifications).

This distinction between the nonprivileged user mode and privileged kernel mode is important in understanding how NT is designed.

System Model Descriptions

Now, getting back to the three types of models, I'll explain each one and where NT fits in.

Monolithic Model

In typical monolithic operating systems, many functions (or procedures) are built into the system. Each procedure can call another procedure, with messages passing between them. In other words, there is no central traffic cop ensuring the integrity of the messages or controlling the flow in a specific direction. (See Figure 2.1.) Errant programs can cause failures of the system. Another problem with monolithic systems is that it's difficult to extend the system's functionality. Monolithic systems are usually not modularized enough to allow updating of one procedure without causing problems with other procedures.

FIGURE 2.1.
A flow diagram of a monolithic operating system.

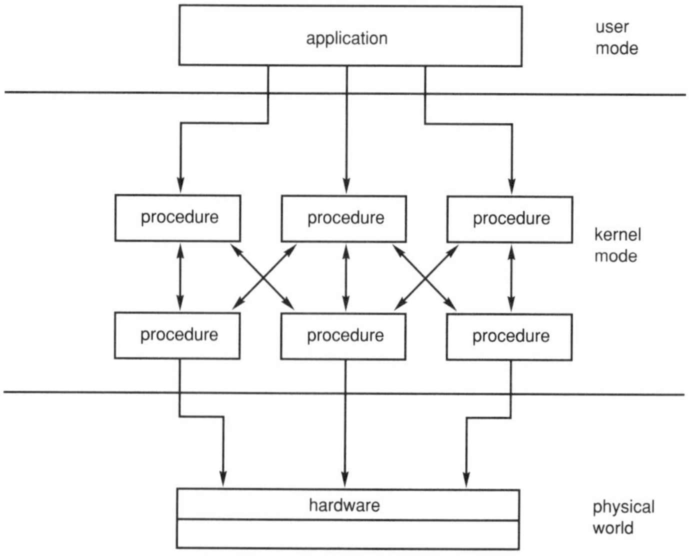

Layered Model

Layered systems are somewhat better at directing traffic flow because data can't be passed between procedures in an ad hoc manner. Instead, data must be sent through a hierarchy of layers, much like communication down a chain of military command. As in the military model, commands are passed only down to lower layers, not upward. (See Figure 2.2.) This adds more structure to the way operations are performed and at least prevents lower layers from wreaking havoc on the whole system. It also aids in debugging. Due to a more modular design, replacing subsystems is easier; thus, updating the operating system is simpler. In general, layered operating systems provide a much more resilient and stable backbone for computing systems than nonlayered models do.

FIGURE 2.2.
A flow diagram of a layered operating system.

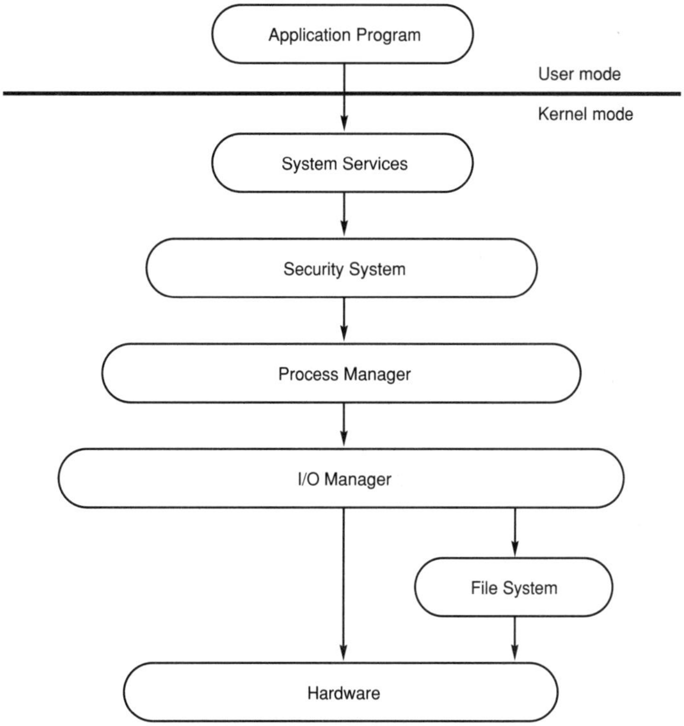

Client/Server Model

NT's design draws heavily from the client/server model.

NOTE

There's a distinction to be made between client/server as it applies to networking models and as it applies to the inner workings of an operating system discussed here. Typically, when people talk about client/server in network discussions, they're talking about client workstations and server workstations and the sharing of resources such as printers and directories. In operating system models, the terms refer to the sharing of internal services. The same term is used in both cases because each involves both a client and a server entity, and both involve the sharing of resources of one type or another. In the case of NT, these models have more in common with one another than with some other operating system. For example, with NT, a programmer can simply replace any RPC call in a program with an LPC call, and NT will request the service of the local computer (or vice versa). As a result, distributing even the operating system itself among multiple machines is a possibility.

In this model, applications are clients because they ask for various services, from having the operating system put a window on the screen to having data sent to the printer or written to a disk. These requests are made through the *NT Executive,* which manages the requests, queuing them up and passing them on to the appropriate servers. Servers supply canned functions built into the operating system. Because servers can supply their services to any number of clients (applications), this keeps down the size of the operating system.

The NT Executive isn't limited to calling local servers only. NT's client/server model is extensive enough to support servers located on other machines or other processors. NT can do this seamlessly, without the application knowing that it's happening. (See Figure 2.3.)

FIGURE 2.3.
A flow diagram of a client/server operating system.

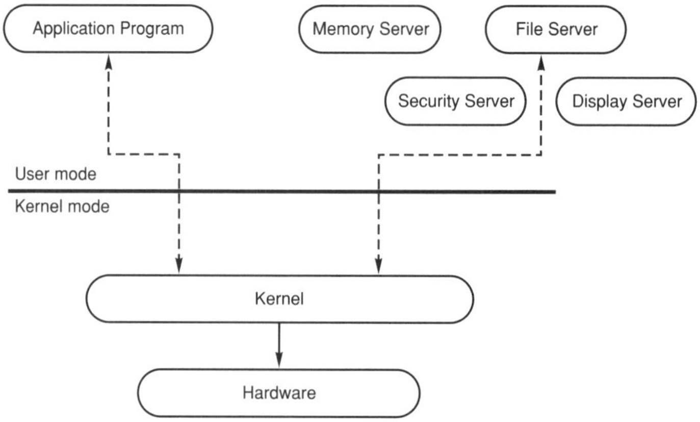

Now that you have a general understanding of NT's OS model, the next section considers compatibility issues and how the client/server works to meet the compatibility design requirements of NT.

Compatibility

Any new operating system hoping to compete in an existing market must offer high compatibility with existing software. In order for NT to stand a chance of survival, it not only had to offer users new features but it also had to support existing features that users had become accustomed to. This meant that, at the least, NT had to be compatible with Microsoft products, but ideally with others as well.

It was finally decided by the design team that NT should be compatible with popular existing file systems, applications, and networks.

As discussed in Chapter 1, the final outcome amounted to a unique compatibility mix not offered by other operating system products available today (although OS/2 comes the closest). Through the use of various tricks, such as software emulation and modularization of key software components, NT compatibility with other products ended up as follows:

- Existing file system compatibility: FAT, HPFS, and most recently Windows 95's VFAT.
- Existing application compatibility: DOS, Windows, Windows 95, OS/2 version 1.x character-based (except on MIPS and DEC Alpha, where OS/2 compatibility is not available at all), LAN Manager, and POSIX-compliant applications.
- Existing networks: NetWare, Banyan VINES, LAN Manager, Windows for Workgroups; connectivity for TCP/IP, SNMP, SNA, NetBEUI, and data link control (DLC); remote access services to support Point to Point (PPP), Serial Line Internet Protocol (SLIP), and X.25 protocols.

Types of Compatibility

Compatibility is a difficult goal, requiring significant amounts of patience and lots of testing with existing applications. Sometimes even *reverse engineering* (analyzing an operating system by close dissection of its components) is required when operating system specifications aren't available.

NOTE

NT has fallen prey to software compatibility complaints in some magazine reviews. This is common problem in early releases of an operating system. However, it usually improves over time as the operating system's compatibility modules are debugged and as application developers modify their programs to work around an operating system's peculiarities. This certainly has been the case as newer versions of NT have hit the streets. Typically, programs that don't coexist with NT peaceably are those that skirt the standard rules, such as avoiding direct hardware addressing. One of the good things about Microsoft is that the company is pushing industry-wide standards that force hardware and software developers to comply or face the wrath of users. These standards benefit all as long as they are open and available.

Compatibility is further complicated by variations in the CPUs of target computers. Because it was decided that NT would run on a variety of CPUs, existing applications run on NT might not be *binary-compatible* with the target CPUs and therefore might not run.

Here's an example. Suppose a user wants to run WordPerfect for Windows under NT running on a MIPS R4000 or a DEC Alpha-based machine. WordPerfect for Windows was written to run under DOS/Windows 3.1, and therefore on Intel CPUs. However, the CPUs of MIP and DEC machines have different internal instruction sets than the Intel x86 chips; therefore, they can't directly execute the binary code (for example, .EXE files) of programs written for Intel CPUs.

NOTE

Due to the virtually exclusive use of Intel processors in PCs over the years, PC users have been protected from most binary compatibility issues. Intel's design philosophy (partly in coordination with Microsoft) has been to build in backward compatibility, allowing later chips such as the 486 and the Pentium to directly execute programs written even 10 years ago for 8086 and 8088 16-bit processors.

One way around this problem is to build *source-code compatibility* into the operating system instead of *binary compatibility,* requiring that each application be recompiled into new binary code for each CPU. In this scenario, users would have to purchase all-new versions of each application they wanted to run on a different CPU, just as Macintosh and PC programs aren't interchangeable. For this reason, source-code compatibility was deemed an unacceptable solution.

Environment Subsystems Provide Compatibility

To solve this binary compatibility problem, NT uses *environment subsystems.* An environment subsystem's job is to intercept each binary code request of a CPU or operating system and translate it into appropriate instructions that NT can successfully execute.

An environment subsystem is really just a program, called a *virtual machine,* that makes an application feel or act as if it's running on its own machine (or at least is in the environment it was written for). When a DOS program runs in the DOS subsystem, for example, it behaves just as if it were the only program running on a PC. When it asks DOS to print to the printer, write to the screen, read the keyboard, or read a sector from the hard disk, it thinks it's really interacting with DOS, even though it isn't. The DOS environment subsystem is simply programmed to respond to the application in such a way that its system calls are appropriately responded to.

When you try to run any type of program in NT, here's what happens:

1. NT attempts to determine what type of environment the program is designed for. If the program type isn't recognized, an error message is generated, and nothing happens.
2. If recognition is successful, NT calls up the requisite environment subsystem.
3. NT loads the program into the environment and executes it.

As the program is running, the environment subsystem is busy doing translations of various types, which can include translating actual CPU instructions. However, because many applications that will run on NT are actually written for and will execute on Intel-compatible processors, most of the translations that actually happen are API translations.

NOTE

APIs, or *application programming interfaces,* are tools built into operating systems that programmers use to help perform a job in a program. For example, an API might put a window or a dialog box on-screen at a certain location or store a file on the hard disk.

If an environment subsystem is to successfully run programs written for the environment it's emulating, it has to recognize calls to the source operating system's API and translate (map) them to NT APIs that effectively perform the same functions.

Here's an example. Suppose an OS/2 application running under NT asks to write a file to the disk because the user has chosen to save some work. The OS/2 application calls the appropriate OS/2 API for writing to disk. The application isn't aware that it's running in a simulated OS/2 environment under NT, but this doesn't matter. NT's OS/2 environment subsystem intercepts the disk call and maps it to an NT (Win32) call. This call is in turn passed to the NT Executive, which effectively performs the same function—writing the data to the disk.

One advantage of doing all this under NT is the additional security and functionality (such as multiprocessor support and disk fault-tolerance) that are supplied to the program. For example, NT prevents programs of various types from "stepping on each other," which can cause system crashes. This is achieved by giving each subsystem its own memory space that can't be touched by other subsystems or programs. For this reason, the environment subsystems are called *protected subsystems.* Working through NT's executive and I/O functions also allows the writing of data on disk in a number of formats, as discussed earlier. It can allow applications to run faster, using more advanced CPU arrangements such as multiple processors or superfast processors such as the DEC Alpha 150.

Because NT's environment subsystems are written as stand-alone server modules (remember the client/server operating system design idea), they can easily be replaced or upgraded. Thus, as bugs are uncovered or extensions to NT are desired, modified environments can easily be added.

Environment Subsystem Details

In the current version of NT, several environment subsystems each provide a specific environment and API to programs. They are

- Win32
- DOS
- Windows 3.x
- OS/2
- POSIX

As I mentioned earlier, NT treats the environment subsystems as servers. Thus, they can have many clients, meaning that they each can service a number of applications at once. Suppose you're running two Windows 3.1 applications. Both applications are managed by the same copy of the Windows 3.1 environment subsystem. The Windows 3.1 subsystem's API server can be called by both applications to perform the same functions, and the subsystem decides which one to service first. Because only one copy of the code provides the service, the system impact of maintaining duplicate resources is minimized.

Also note that each subsystem operates in user mode rather than in kernel mode. This helps to protect the kernel of the operating system from a subsystem or application that goes awry.

Win32 Subsystem

Of the four environment subsystems, the Win32 subsystem is the most central to NT's functioning. This is the subsystem that controls the NT interface—the screen, keyboard, input, and mouse activities for whatever you're doing in NT, even if you're running an OS/2 program or another type of program. The other subsystems—OS/2, DOS/Windows, and POSIX—all send their translated API calls to the Win32 subsystem for execution. Because it's also used to run 32-bit programs written for NT or Windows 95, this subsystem performs double duty. Figure 2.4 depicts the relationship between the other subsystems and the Win32 subsystem.

FIGURE 2.4.
The relationship of the environment subsystems.

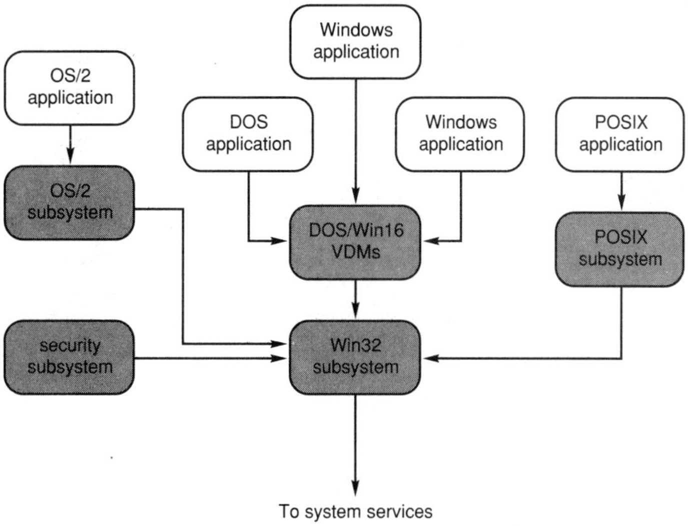

DOS Subsystem

The DOS environment subsystem is interesting and worth understanding. Because DOS is not a multitasking operating system, its subsystem differs from the others. When you try to run a DOS program, NT launches the DOS protected subsystem, which creates a *Virtual DOS Machine* (*VDM*). A VDM is an emulator that creates a simulated or virtual PC with its own 16MB of segmented memory space, required device drivers, support for most memory managers, and I/O system call support. In the case of DOS applications, each new DOS application you launch gets its own VDM and separate "DOS window," just as in Windows 3.x.

The DOS VDM window under NT is compatible with all the specifications of DOS 5.0, and it will operate properly as long as the DOS application behaves itself—that is, as long as the application uses the DOS system calls for all input and output and doesn't try to access hardware directly. When an I/O request is trapped (detected) by the subsystem, it's passed on to the NT Executive (or, in some cases, the Win32 API) and processed accordingly. An application that attempts to write directly to hardware is terminated, and a message to that effect appears on-screen.

There are two particularly interesting additions to the NT DOS window over the Windows 3.1 version. First, you can launch Windows NT applications from it by entering the .EXE filename at the command prompt. Second, you can alter the foreground and background colors of the box—something that should have been included in Windows 3.1!

16-Bit Windows Subsystem

The 16-bit Windows protected environment subsystem is an interesting beast. Actually, it's built upon the DOS VDM. When you launch the first 16-bit Windows application, NT creates a new VDM. As I explained earlier, this VDM is a simulated PC with DOS running in it and with a significant amount (16MB) of virtual memory assigned.

After the VDM is created, the Windows emulator (WOW, discussed in Chapter 1) is loaded, providing a multitasking simulation (cooperative rather than preemptive, however) of Windows 3.1. Although it provides all the APIs of 16-bit Windows, its internal structure is significantly different. System calls made by an application are mapped to Win32 calls and executed by the Win32 subsystem or the NT Executive.

As with DOS programs, any Windows application that attempts direct hardware access will fail; the call is trapped by NT and the application is terminated. However, unlike when multiple DOS applications are running, multiple Windows applications don't need additional VDMs. Each new 16-bit Windows application launched after the first one is set up as a separate thread within the same instance of WOW in the VDM.

OS/2 Subsystem

The OS/2 subsystem is less complicated, at least in theory. For starters, because the base NT configuration supports only character-based OS/2 programs, no GUI support is required. Second, because OS/2 applications are designed with 32-bit multiuser capabilities, the protected-mode subsystem has a little less mapping to do. A VDM isn't necessary—only a subsystem that properly maps the OS/2 calls to the relevant NT services.

NOTE

It should be emphasized that NT won't run OS/2 2.x or OS/2 Warp applications, but only character-mode applications that will run under OS/2 version 1.x.

NOTE

NT does support OS/2 1.x Presentation Manager applications with the OS/2 PM Subsystem Add-On for NT extensions, available from Microsoft.

POSIX Subsystem

Before I discuss the POSIX subsystem, a little background is in order. As covered in Chapter 1, a number of different interface standards exist for UNIX applications and systems. UNIX is so ubiquitous, and in use by so many institutions that have taken it upon themselves to modify it, that little exists in the way of standards—especially when it comes to interface with the user.

POSIX, a response to this problem, is an attempt to standardize UNIX application code so that it can be more easily ported to other systems. At this point, NT's POSIX subsystem supports only character-based applications, so once again, the subsystem is not as complex as it would be if a GUI such as Motif were being emulated. No VDM is created—just a protected space to run the application and a call interceptor that remaps calls to the Win32 environment subsystem and NT Executive. As with the other systems, illegal hardware calls are trapped by the NT Executive.

Extensibility

One of the highest priorities for NT designers was to make NT flexible and extensible. Extensibility refers to a feature of applications and operating system software that enables a programmer to quickly and in a cost-efficient manner upgrade or extend the functionality of the software. Considering the rapidly changing face of computer hardware and application hardware requirements, extensibility of an operating system is key to its continued success. For this reason, NT was written in such a way that modifying it for future upgrades and porting it to other computer classes are possible with relatively little hassle.

As you've seen from previous discussion and illustrations in this chapter, NT is modular in its design, making extensibility easy. For example, the protected environment subsystems, although intimately woven into NT's fiber while running, are actually stand-alone modules that, if needed, can be rewritten independently and plugged into NT. They aren't even loaded into memory unless they're needed.

Likewise, all the other major portions of NT are written and function as modules: the security subsystem, the hardware abstraction layer (HAL), and the NT Executive (kernel, I/O manager, object manager, security reference monitor, process monitor, local procedure call (LPC) facility, and virtual memory manager).

How does extensibility work? If you've experimented with the Windows 3.1 Control Panel or File Manager, you might know that these are both modular and extensible (though they're much simpler programs, of course, than NT). They can easily be upgraded to supply new services to the user, thus requiring no changes to the core application. Simply altering the initialization file listing for File Manager (WINFILE.INI) or adding .CPL files to the system directory (for Control Panel) is all you need to do.

As the needs of NT users grow, NT can grow too. Simply replace an old module with a new one. Modularity is such a strong feature in NT that many system services can be started via Control Panel's Services applet, after NT is booted and running. Future upgrades of NT (unlike DOS) likely will consist of a disk with a few add-on modules that can support a new class of applications, fix a bug, or offer new services such as additional security or network protocol support.

If Microsoft proves responsive to user requests for such extensibility, availability might not be a problem. At the worst, Microsoft might at least share enough code with other software vendors so that extensions to NT become available through other channels. Time will tell how generous Microsoft intends to be in sharing the innermost secrets of its operating system code. No doubt deals with vendors will be limited to those that pose no threat to Microsoft's future marketing of their own NT extensions.

Symmetric Multiprocessing

As I mentioned in Chapter 1, NT uses symmetric multiprocessing (as opposed to asymmetric multiprocessing) as its model for scaleability. Figures 2.5 and 2.6 help explain the differences.

FIGURE 2.5.

In symmetric multiprocessing, all processing (including the operating system and applications) is spread among available CPUs.

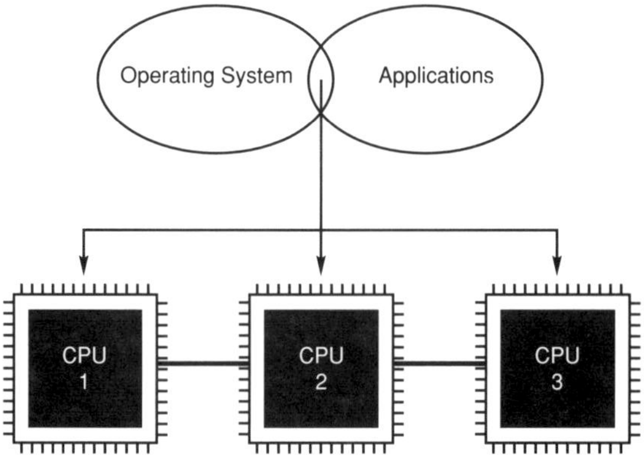

FIGURE 2.6.
In asymmetric multiprocessing, the operating system code is run by one CPU, and other CPUs run applications.

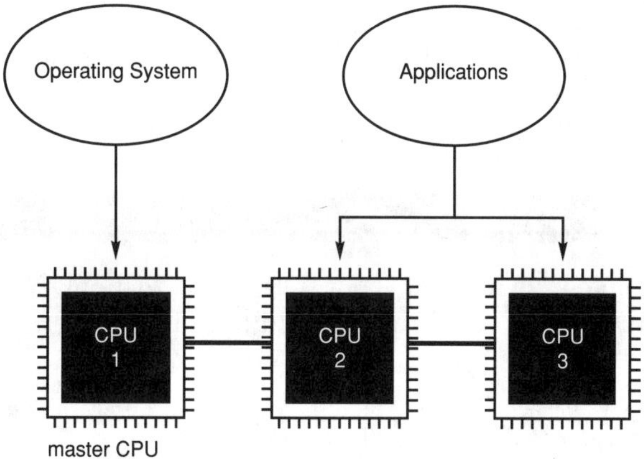

The end result of employing symmetric methodology is that the operating system is less likely to come to a standstill if the master CPUs cease functioning for some reason. Also, because operating system tasks can be shuffled off to other processors, the system runs more smoothly and (possibly) with greater throughput.

Asymmetric operating systems are easier to design and build, and they can even be monolithic in nature. An efficient use of symmetric processing, on the other hand, is more difficult and requires that the operating system itself be threaded, or broken down into separate processes. The benefits, however, are great. For example, operating system subtasks can be routed to different processors, increasing system efficiency and making it less likely that CPUs are underutilized. I/O processing could be handled by one CPU while, for example, the security subsystem is handled by another.

Scalability

Scalability refers to an operating system's capability to take advantage of additional resources—particularly additional CPU resources that might be added to a computer's hardware arsenal. When installed on a uniprocessor machine, NT's thread manager sends all processes to the only CPU in the system. When there is only one processor, however, system performance can be slowed by bottlenecks in the single-thread queue.

Due to its internal design, NT is not necessarily bound by the limitations of single-CPU constraints. This is because NT's built-in CPU detection enables it to automatically redirect threads and processes to available CPUs (from 1 to 16), increasing system operational throughput. Various RISC and CISC systems support easy installation of extra CPU cards. In most cases, simply installing the CPU and rebooting NT are all that's required to prod the thread dispatcher into divvying up the workload between processors. Not all multi-processor stations use fancy RISC chips. We'll be seeing more PCs based on multi-Intel chips like the 486DX. A case in point is the Wyse Series 70001, which has five 486DX2/66s in it, or the AcerFrame 3000MP50.

NOTE

Something to keep in mind about scalability is that only Windows NT programs designed to take advantage of the multithreading will benefit from it. Even if a developer writes a program using the Win32 API, this doesn't mean that the program can use multiprocessors. The program has to specifically utilize the multithreading hooks in the API.

Also note that the Win32s subset of the Win32 API doesn't support multithreading. Therefore, although it offers the advantage of creating programs that will run under both Windows 3.x and Windows NT, such programs won't profit from multiple processors. This doesn't mean that overall system throughput won't improve with multiple processors, just that an application might not work as quickly or smoothly as it could. For example, you might have to wait for a word processor to quit printing (or at least spooling to the Print Manager) before you can get back to writing on it, or for a spreadsheet to recalculate before punching in some new numbers. Note also that Win32 programs won't benefit from NT's application-level security features.

The one exception to this scenario is when there are enough CPUs to provide one CPU per application. Even if the application weren't written to take advantage of symmetric multiprocessing, NT could route the application to an otherwise idle CPU, which might execute the application more quickly than if its threads were split between multiple CPUs tied up with other tasks as well.

Portability

NT's nemesis, UNIX, is well-endowed when it comes to portability. One of UNIX's great virtues is that it has been ported (made runnable) on myriad platforms. UNIX or UNIX work-alikes have been seen running on CPUs ranging from 8-bit Zilog Z-80s running in tandem (using a UNIX spin-off called Micronix, written by Gary Fitts—the same software pioneer who wrote TOPS, the first peer-to-peer networking system to connect Macs and PCs—and marketed by Morrow Designs in the early '80s) to 32-bit and larger CPUs from Texas Instruments, AMD, and Motorola. UNIX is available for numerous workstations, ranging from DEC to Sun, IBM, Silicon Graphics, and Hewlett-Packard, to name but a few. Obviously, UNIX's calling card is flexibility. The result? Users can upgrade their hardware without having to throw away their operating system and applications.

Of course, DOS users have enjoyed flexibility in this department to some degree. Upward mobility from 8088s all the way to Pentiums has been a great boon both to Microsoft (which has promoted DOS phenomenally) and to DOS users. With little effort except the expense, most of us have brought our favorite DOS and Windows applications up through the ranks of CPUs to super-fast 32-bit processors we couldn't have imagined being able to afford only a few years ago. Due merely to the vast numbers of PC clones in the workplace today, hardware prices have been forced down to rock-bottom levels, making powerful systems available even to students on shoestring budgets.

Still, DOS and Windows have required Intel or (now, due to legal judgments that enable other chip manufacturers to compete with Intel) Intel-compatible CPUs in order to run. UNIX, on the other hand, has enjoyed much more platform independence.

With NT, Microsoft wants to make dependence on Intel a thing of the past. With modularity of design and code portability in mind, NT is already runnable on CISC and RISC chips in various formations. The Intel 80x86, MIPS R4000, and DEC Alpha currently are supported. With a recompilation of NT's modules (using software compilers), other future CPUs can be accommodated.

NOTE

At the time I was writing this, Windows NT was being ported to the PowerPC CPU, which is being developed jointly by IBM, Apple, and Motorola. Other CPUs will no doubt follow, based on user demand.

Note, however, that although Microsoft claims that 32-bit NT applications are fully portable, requiring only a "simple recompile," this doesn't represent the whole picture. Applications still have to be troubleshot, and software developers need to decide whether they have the requisite support resources before jumping onto a new hardware platform. We're likely to see many 32-bit applications on Intel-based NT before seeing much for MIPS or Alpha. Software manufacturers are already cautious enough about jumping on the NT bandwagon without having to decide whether they should fine-tune their programs for other CPUs.

Another down-side reality regarding portability is the fact that DOS and Windows 3.1 applications are written for Intel chips. What's the problem with this? Well, if you're intending to soup up your NT arrangement with a MIPS or Alpha and you want to run DOS and Windows programs, you might be disappointed in performance. Sure, you're going to get great performance on these chips (especially the 150 MHz Alpha) with 32-bit programs written for the host machine. But DOS and Windows 3.x programs will be run through emulators that might slow down performance of the applications. Depending on how the application is written (the ratio of native CPU code to the number of API calls), it's conceivable that applications will run faster, but this probably can be determined only by testing. Before you jump to another NT platform, you should ask some probing questions or perform some real-life experiments.

On the bright side, NT's portability is likely to spark a lively competition between CPU makers. The beneficiaries will be the users, who will begin to see a CPU speed and price war worth staying tuned for. We can expect to see serious NT-compatible workstations go through an evolution similar to what we've seen with DOS workstations. A super-loaded NT workstation today can cost as much as $37,000. In a couple of years, the same system likely will cost a tenth of that. Not only will the battle be pitched over Intel, Alpha, and MIPS-based machines, but we'll also see NT on new CPUs such as Intergraph's Clipper chip.

Networkable, with Distributed Processing

As you already know, Windows NT comes with networking built in. Both the base version of NT and NT Server support peer-to-peer and client/server networking topologies. An NT network can be constructed "out of the box" without anything other than network cards and cables to connect it, or it can be added to an existing network, such as a preexisting Novell or LAN Manager client/server system. This type of plug-and-play functionality has been well implemented in NT. Whether you're interested in giving up your existing investment in another network operating system is another question. There probably will be some bugs to iron out if you switch immediately to NT or NT Server, and (as mentioned in Chapter 1) NT Server isn't exceedingly cheap. So, for large enterprise-wide networks, you'll have to consider the fiscal impact of the per-server price tag.

NOTE

When you're pricing network server software (and even application software), licensing fees are an issue to factor in. Although the up-front cost of NT Server might be higher, the overall cost might be lower. Licensing fees aren't issued based on the number of client connections per server, but rather on a per-service basis. Server and client licenses have been separated. A single server license is required for each physical server on the network, while a single client license can connect to an unlimited number of servers.

One feature that might tip the scales is another network-related feature—distributed processing. NT implements something called *remote procedure calls,* or *RPCs.* Similar to the *local procedure calls* that operating systems such as NT sometimes use to send messages between applications, RPCs are calls that a computer running an application can send to another computer for CPU assistance. NT's multithreading is designed to support RPCs to distant computers spread across a network. In an ideal arrangement, if an NT server finds itself bogged down in a large queue of threads, it can dispatch or offload some threads to other processors on the network, thus lightening its own burden. This spreads the CPU's chores out to any idle networked CPUs in much the same way that multiple processors coexisting on the local machine cooperate.

Security

In addition to the environment subsystem, another type of subsystem exists, called an *integral subsystem.* NT has a number of integral subsystems, but chief among them is the *security subsystem.* This subsystem is a user-mode client, just like the environment subsystems. However, its purpose is exclusively to provide security for the NT system.

For example, a user who hasn't been granted rights might try to access the system. The security subsystem prevents this by requiring a password for each user. If the password is entered incorrectly, the user is denied access to the system. In addition, each user can have a certain set of specific privileges controlling the level of access to the system resources—files, directories, drives, networks, modems, ports, and so on. These are assigned to the user by the system administrator.

Virtually all aspects (inner and outer) of NT are overseen by security management services that make NT quite secure. Windows NT meets U.S. government requirements for what is called C2-level security. This isn't the highest level of security an operating system can achieve, but it's respectably high and good enough for the bulk of work run on computers.

NOTE

NT will be upgradable to B2-level security in future custom versions.

The NT Executive

During the course of this discussion, I've referred several times to the NT Executive. The Executive is the heart of NT's architecture, and it includes everything except the protected-mode subsystems and the actual hardware.

Recall that the operating system code can run in two modes: user (unprivileged) mode and kernel (privileged) mode. Recall also that all the subsystems (such as the DOS, POSIX, and OS/2 environment subsystems) run in user mode. By contrast, the NT Executive runs in kernel mode. This means that the NT Executive has access to all the critical internal data structures and procedures of NT. Figure 2.7 shows where the Executive fits into the picture.

FIGURE 2.7.
The NT Executive forms the heart of Windows NT.

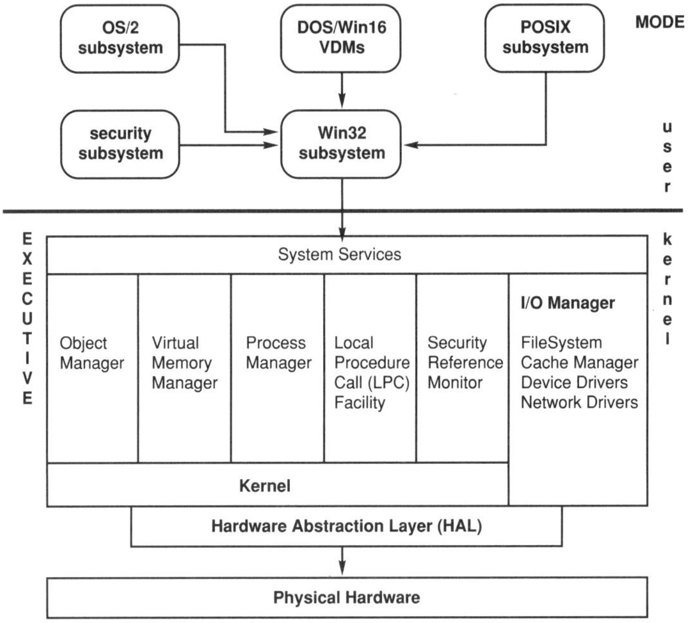

Note in Figure 2.7 that the Executive is comprised of all the components below the dark line, except for the hardware itself. Thus, the Executive provides all the *native services* that the client environment subsystems can't—virtual memory management, I/O, thread scheduling, and so forth. When a subsystem needs a service performed, it sends the call to the appropriate NT Executive manager. NT then runs in the restricted kernel mode momentarily, protecting itself from foreign intervention, and performs the action. When the task is completed, control returns to the calling party (typically a subsystem).

A necessary element of the Executive is made up of the *primitives*. The NT Executive primitives represent an important design concept, because they allow for multiple subsystem compatibility. Without them, applications running in the different subsystems might clobber one another. For example, applications running in the Win16 and OS/2 modules ask for resources differently. Conceivably, two subsystems could request the same service simultaneously. The primitives negotiate such contentions between the environment subsystems.

About the System Services

Actually, when a subsystem asks to have a service performed (such as getting some memory allocated for a program you just launched), it must ask the System Services module to handle it. The System Services module then sends the message to the Virtual Memory Manager (VMM). The same would be true of any other service. As an example, when a program is launched, NT must supply at least one thread for it. The subsystem would request a thread from System Services, which in turn asks the appropriate manager for the thread. Only after the thread is created is control returned to the subsystem.

When System Services is used as the buffer between the subsystems and the executive services and managers, critical components of NT can be more easily updated. As an example, imagine your local telephone system. If a central switching office didn't connect your phone to other phone lines, making changes to numbers or services could mean major rewiring. The phone company might have to run new wires across town or even across the country. By using central offices, the phone company can easily change and update equipment, change phone numbers, and change services without you even knowing about it. The System Services portion of the Executive provides similar conveniences.

The Other Modules

Now let's consider the remaining eight sections of the Executive:

- Object Manager
- Virtual Memory Manager
- Process Manager
- Local Procedure Call Facility
- Security Reference Monitor
- I/O Manager
- Kernel
- Hardware Abstraction Layer

Each of these modules performs a specific class of task necessary for internal operation of NT. Because this book isn't intended for programmers or computer scientists, but for professionals managing NT-based systems, I won't go into intimate detail about each of them. Instead, I'll offer just a few sentences about each one. If you need more details, refer to another book, such as *Windows NT: The Next Generation* (Sams Publishing, 1993).

Object Manager

Although it's not truly an object-oriented operating system, NT does use so-called "objects" as the basic operating element for interaction between user mode and kernel mode—for example, when a subsystem needs access to shared resources.

An object is a data structure that represents a service that can be shared by more than a single process. For example, a physical device such as a port could be shared by a number of applications. When port access is requested, the source subsystem calls the service manager and asks for it. The service manager in turn calls the object manager, which creates a new object that represents the request. But even invisible processes such as threads can be objects, so it's a little hard to visualize.

By creating objects, NT (and human programmers) can more easily keep track of system resources such as shared memory, ports, processes, and files. In a sense, it democratizes important events and resources within an NT session by giving them what's called a *handle*. After being given a handle, all these types of objects—whether a physical resource, a process, or an event—can be dealt with uniformly by the object manager and other modules of NT. For example, the security reference monitor can examine an object for validation, or prevent unauthorized use of it.

The object manager makes sure that objects don't gobble up too much memory and that there aren't too many objects of a specific type (which might overrun system resources). It also gets rid of objects that seem to have been abandoned by their source ("garbage collection").

Virtual Memory Manager

As you probably know, virtual memory is simulated RAM memory created by sleight of hand. When RAM memory is low, NT uses hard-disk space to simulate what looks like RAM space to applications, but what is actually the result of temporarily "swapping" data in RAM to the hard disk to free up some RAM for the requested activity. The result looks and acts like a computer system with more RAM memory than is physically present. Later, the data is read back into RAM without the application being aware of it. The advantage of virtual memory is cost: Hard-disk space is significantly cheaper than physical RAM. The disadvantage is speed: Hard-disk reading and writing is much slower than RAM-based data transfer.

The Virtual Memory Manager manages the virtual memory for each process that might request it. This primarily means preventing processes from overwriting other virtual memory "pages" on disk and managing other options, such as preventing swapping to disk in cases when an application requests faster performance.

Process Manager

The process manager's job is to create and terminate processes and threads when calling applications need them. For example, suppose an application wants to create a new file. This file request is sent through the active server environment subsystem to the system services. It's then sent to the process manager, which creates a formal process request and sends that to the object manager, which in turn creates an identity for it. The process is then started.

When the process is finished (for example, the file is fully written to disk), the process manager terminates the thread.

The importance of the process manager is hard to underestimate. Hundreds of processes can seem to be executing simultaneously. This is because the process manager quietly plays traffic cop to the threads waiting to execute. The process manager can cause any application's threads to be executed, suspended, restarted, or terminated.

Local Procedure Call Facility

This module's job is simply to supply a communication link between two threads that belong to separate processes. Recall that processes are composed of threads (at least one thread per process). For example, the printing and editing functions of a word processor could be coded into the application as two separate threads.

Sometimes separate threads need to exchange data. For example, a spell checker written as a separate thread might want to pass a correctly spelled word to the editor for placement in a document. Normally, no easy avenue exists for this data passage, because threads are executed by the CPU as separate entities. In such a case, when one thread needs to send data to another thread belonging to a separate process, the LPC facility steps in. Such message passing is achieved via requisition of a temporary memory pool from which the data is handed off to the second thread. After the handoff, the memory is freed up for other use.

Security Reference Monitor

As I mentioned earlier, the object manager often works in tandem with this monitor to ensure that objects aren't accessed (accidentally or intentionally) by unauthorized users. A user can be an actual person (in the case of someone trying to access a file or a port, for instance), or it can be a process, thread, or some kind of event. In any case, preventing illegal attempts to access objects is called *object access control.* This is what the security reference monitor does.

All processes in NT are given an *access token,* which contains a list of the permissions (rights) that have been granted to the user who started the process. Typically, these rights are assigned by the system administrator to a specific user. For sake of illustration, let's say the user is Joe. When Joe starts a process (a word processor, for example), his process might try to access an object, such as a file. Each object (recall that objects are maintained by the object manager) also has a list of access rights (called an *access control list,* or *ACL*). When Joe's process tries to access the file, the file's ACL and Joe's access token are compared by the security manager. In other words, it looks to see whether Joe has permission to use the file. If the two compare favorably, the object is made available to Joe's process. The file opens, and Joe can start editing the document. Otherwise, access is not allowed and a dialog box appears on-screen, alerting the user to an illegal attempt. In some cases, NT just doesn't display certain objects—directories, printers, menu items, and so forth—that are out-of-bounds for a certain class of user.

It's worth noting that NT's security reference monitor is intelligent in the way it does its security checks. Rather than checking the lists against each other every time Joe wants access to the file (such as each time the file is saved during a working session), NT checks only the first time. This prevents the system from slowing to a crawl when many processes and users log on to the system and begin working.

I/O Manager

Input/output systems are one of the gnarliest black holes of computer science and operating systems design. Actually, interfacing with the outside world often takes a little spit and baling wire. As a result, getting printers, modems, data-acquisition devices, video displays, SCSI devices, keyboards, mice, and other such real-world objects to work correctly and efficiently is often a nightmare. It's a well-known fact that programmers often have to work *around* an operating system (DOS or the combination of DOS and Windows, for example) just to get an application or peripheral to work efficiently enough to keep users happy.

NT's I/O manager attempts to make life easier both for users and for programmers. For starters, most I/O software drivers can be loaded on-the-fly, without restarting Windows NT. This is a nice feature. It means that while NT is running, you can power up a tape drive unit, a network card, a new printer, an external CD-ROM drive, or whatever; load the driver in NT; and you're up and running. This is of particular importance on large networks, where taking down the server just to load a new driver would be a nuisance. Secondly, NT's I/O system is designed so that removing and installing new drivers of any sort (including file system drivers such as those for FAT, HPFS, and NTFS) can be done as a module replacement.

NOTE

Unfortunately, not all NT drivers can be loaded and unloaded without a reboot. For example, loading a new video or tape backup driver requires a reboot.

The I/O manager's job, as you might expect, is simply to process the I/O requests of applications. The following describes how the I/O manager handles an I/O request: When an application asks for an I/O service, such as sending data to a printer, the message first goes through the environment subsystem running the application. It's then passed through System Services to the I/O manager. The I/O manager determines which driver should be used and sends the data to the proper driver in the form of an I/O request packet, or IRP. The driver then processes the data accordingly for the physical device. This often entails some sort of translation—for example, into PostScript code for that type of printer, or into HPCL code for an HP printer. After the data is successfully sent to the device (through the hardware abstraction layer explained later in this chapter), the driver returns the IRP to the I/O manager, which then deletes the packet. Figure 2.8 details this process.

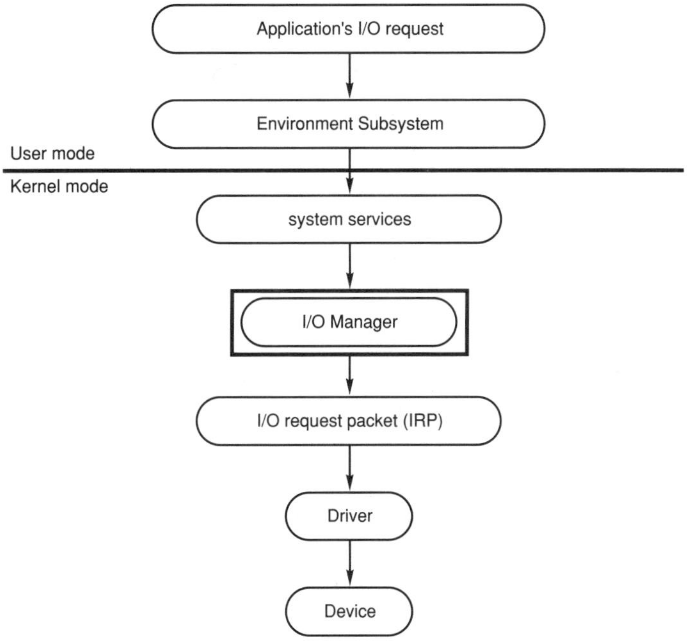

FIGURE 2.8.
A flow diagram of the I/O process.

System Kernel

The kernel is the Grand Central Station of NT. Almost everything that happens in NT passes through the kernel in one way or another. As I mentioned earlier, NT's kernel is of the "microkernel" variety. In other words, it's a scaled-down version of larger kernels used in big systems such as UNIX and Digital Equipment Corporation's VMS operating system. Some of this down-scaling was achieved by offloading traditional kernel chores to the executive modules discussed earlier.

Still, the kernel plays a key role in the operation of NT. Its main job is to schedule and dispatch threads and processes. Therefore, it continually queues up data, sends it to the CPU(s), and routes it after processing. The kernel also handles interrupts from various sources (the keyboard or other physical devices) and is responsible for managing *exceptions*—error conditions resulting from system violations such as divide-by-zero errors or attempts to write over protected memory areas.

Two other jobs of the kernel are to synchronize multiple CPUs (by carefully managing how data threads are divided up between them) and to prepare and restart the system in case of a power failure.

Hardware Abstraction Layer

Ideally, NT's design is so modular that running it on different computers requires only replacing the hardware abstraction layer and some of the I/O drivers. This might actually turn out to be true someday. Based on its experience with installable device drivers in DOS, and then with even greater system independence with Windows, Microsoft apparently has realized that keeping hardware as far out of the operating system as possible is the way to ensure success in the operating system market.

One of Windows strongest selling points, for example, has been that software drivers for a zillion different types of screens, printers, mice, SCSI devices, sound cards, video cards, and a plethora of sundry hardware items can easily be written for it. To a great degree, this isolates Windows and DOS from their supporting hardware on any given system. As a result, application developers know that if their programs run on one Windows machine, they're pretty likely to run on another—regardless of whether the screen on that system has VGA, SVGA, or other resolution, and regardless of what printer, network, keyboard, or mouse is attached.

NT takes this approach of hardware isolation a step further by using not only device drivers, but a whole replaceable layer of the operating system responsible for interacting with the hardware. The hardware abstraction layer, or HAL, is this layer. It's the final barrier between the system hardware (including the CPU, memory, I/O ports, keyboard, video, and so forth) and the rest of NT. The only parts of NT that communicate directly with

kernel and the I/O drivers. Applications, the other executive modules, ıent subsystems don't know anything about what type of computer they're at type or number of processors are involved, or whether the system is on

a replaceable HAL module will allow NT to be ported to any number of with minimal recoding of the executive modules (various managers) and sys- This is probably overly hopeful, because differences exist in the way dissimilar upport hardware (such as caches and hardware memory managers) schedule data, and such management is a part of the HAL; some rewriting seems inevi- ever, by abstracting the hardware layer of a system as much as possible, rewrite be minimized.

Summary

This chapter discussed the architecture and operational design of Windows NT. It covered the functionality of the various modules and subsystems that comprise NT, and it showed the significance of these elements as they relate to a modern, extensible operating system. You also learned about the overall design philosophy that the Microsoft and NT design team applied while developing the system.

You should now have a pretty good handle on what NT is, how it compares to competitive operating systems and graphical user interfaces, and where it fits into the Microsoft marketing landscape. You also should have a healthy grasp of NT's modular structure and overall operational design.

In the next chapter I discuss, from the user's point of view, how the basics of the NT interface—Program Manager, File Manager, Control Panel, and Print Manager—differ from their counterparts in Windows 3.1.

NOTE

Administrative tools such as the User Manager, Registry Editor, and Event Viewer are covered in Part II of this book.

Working with Windows NT

3

IN THIS CHAPTER

This chapter covers the basics of working with Windows NT. The primary focus is on running and using Program Manager and File Manager, running applications under NT, and working with user-oriented Control Panel settings (as opposed to administrator-related settings). The discussions assume that you are familiar with Windows 3.1's usage of these programs, so the emphasis is on differences between Windows 3.1 and Windows NT. However, there is some review material in case you're a little rusty on your Windows techniques, or if you're a user on an NT network or workstation who isn't a Windows "jock."

Logging On

One of the first differences any user notices with NT is that you're asked to log on to the system before you gain access to anything. The logon information (username, domain, and password) lies at the heart of the NT security system. After the username and password are correctly entered, all resource privileges assigned to that user by the administrator, such as access to drives, directories, applications, printers, and backup devices, go into effect.

Each time you boot NT, you see the dialog box shown in Figure 3.1.

FIGURE 3.1.
Welcome dialog box.

Although pressing Ctrl-Alt-Delete causes a DOS machine to reboot, it doesn't have the same effect on NT. This key combination is used to thwart potential "Trojan horse" viruses or programs that attempt to bypass NT's security system by luring users into typing their passwords into phony dialog boxes. When you press Ctrl-Alt-Delete, NT attempts to flush out any such insidious programs, and it brings up the NT Logon dialog box, shown in Figure 3.2.

NOTE

Figure 3.2 shows a logon dialog for NT Server. If you're using Windows NT Workstation, this dialog will have a Shutdown button as well.

The username is assigned by the system administrator when a new account is made for a user, and it must be unique.

FIGURE 3.2.
Logon dialog box.

> **NOTE**
>
> Accounts are set up with the User Manager program, explained in Chapter 10.

On a single-person system, only one user account and one administrator account are likely. In fact, if during installation you opt to skip setting up a user account, only the administrator account is set up. (The administrator always has at least one account.)

The password is always selected by the user. Regularly changing it can be enforced by the system administrator. The password can be changed when the user presses Ctrl-Alt-Delete *after* logging onto NT. (Changing the password is covered in Chapters 10 and 12.)

In the From box, enter either the name of the local computer (if you want access to what's stored on it) or the name of the NT Server domain you want to connect to (assuming one exists). Of course, you can't connect to an NT Server domain until your local computer has been made a member of the domain.

When you click on OK in the password dialog box, NT checks the password database. If the fields in the database don't match, you'll see an error message. Press Enter and try typing it again. If the account policy for this user account has the Account lockout option enabled, the account will be locked after the maximum number of attempts have been made within the selected time frame. This prevents would-be intruders from breaking in by trying a series of incremental entries. The account can be enabled by clearing the Account Locked check box for the user account in User Manager.

Restoring Connections at Boot Time

If the last time you ran NT you were using files on another workstation's drives, NT attempts to restore those *connections,* as they're called, when you log in.

> **NOTE**
>
> Connections are explained in detail later in this chapter, in the section titled "Connecting to Network Directories."

If the remote computer to which your NT system is trying to reconnect isn't online, or its directories aren't shared for network use, you'll see an error message like the ones in Figure 3.3 and Figure 3.4.

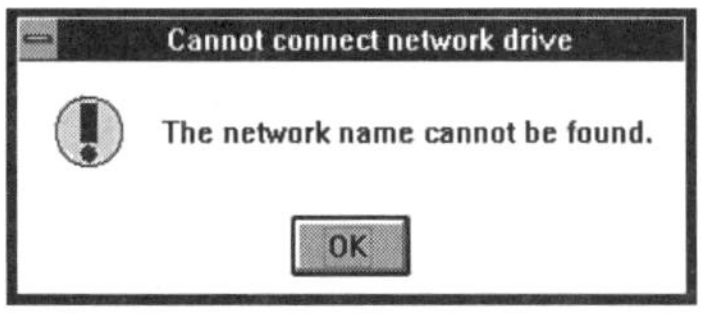

FIGURE 3.3.
A typical error message seen when a network connection can't be restored for some reason.

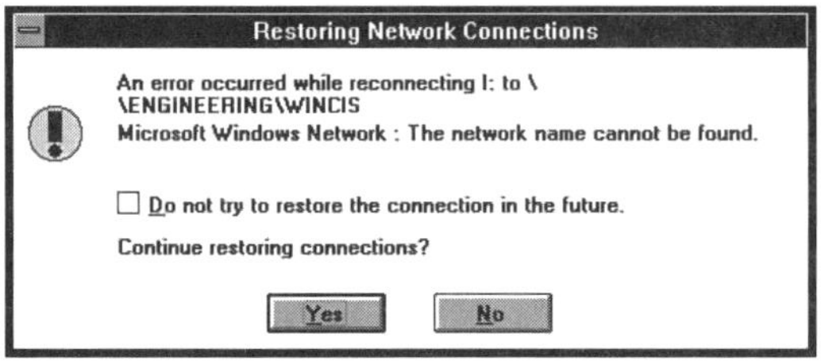

FIGURE 3.4.
Another typical error message.

Clicking on Yes isn't like a "Retry" in DOS; rather, it causes NT to abandon the attempt to make the current connection (the one listed in the dialog box) and move to the next one. Clicking on No abandons the process for any and all connections that were made and saved from the previous session.

Typically, failure to connect is the result of other workstations not being online or having failed to republish (share) the directories to which you were previously connected. This is often the case at the start of a new workday, because not everyone powers up at the same time. In this case, NT or Windows for Workgroups adds the appropriate drive icons to File Manager, just as if the connection had been made, but they don't actually make the connection. Clicking on the drive icon in File Manager, or performing some other action that calls on the remote drive, initiates an attempt to reconnect. If the workstation is then online, things will work as expected. Typically, all you have to do is click on Yes for each dialog box that comes up.

Using Program Manager

As you probably know, Program Manager helps you organize documents and applications so that they're easier to access. It is, however, a little clunky, particularly to anyone familiar with more object-oriented metaphors such as the Mac, OS/2's Workplace Shell, or WinTools for Windows 3.1.

An obvious shortcoming of Microsoft's Program Manager is that it's not hierarchical. You can't create classes and subclasses of documents and applications the way you can set up directories and subdirectories on a hard disk, or the way the Mac lets you put folders within folders. If you want to create a program group for correspondence, for example, then further subdivide it into personal and business letters, you're out of luck. You just have to mix them all together in one Program Manager group, or set up two separate groups—one for personal and one for business.

Until NT shell replacements start hitting the streets, you'll have to live with it. Why not use shells designed for Windows 3.1? Although Windows 3.1 shell alternatives abound, at this point I don't recommend using them in NT, particularly in a networking corporate environment. Microsoft specifically warns against using shells not designed for NT. This is because NT's Program Manager has integral multiuser security and settings for each user account on the workstation. Non-NT add-on shells don't know about such settings.

TIP

Unless the same shell replacement is mandated for all the users in your corporate setting, I don't even recommend changing shells for Windows 3.1 users. Replacing Program Manager with Norton Desktop, PC Tools for Windows, NewWave, or some other shell defeats one of the primary advantages of Windows in the first place—a standard user interface that everyone can easily recognize when they sit down at a workstation. Customized shells might be attractive to users, and many users feel that customization is the big attraction of Windows. However, in the wrong setting, it might lead to additional user training or support that isn't worth the hassle.

Using alternative shells in NT gets extra hairy due to security features and other options, such as common group icons (explained later in this chapter). Technically, you can run shells such as Norton Desktop for Windows 3.1 in NT, but because they're run on the 16-bit Windows emulator (WOW), not 32-bit Windows, they'll work slowly and with limitations.

Organizing Applications

The NT Program Manager, shown in Figure 3.5, is almost identical to its Windows 3.1 counterpart, with a couple of twists.

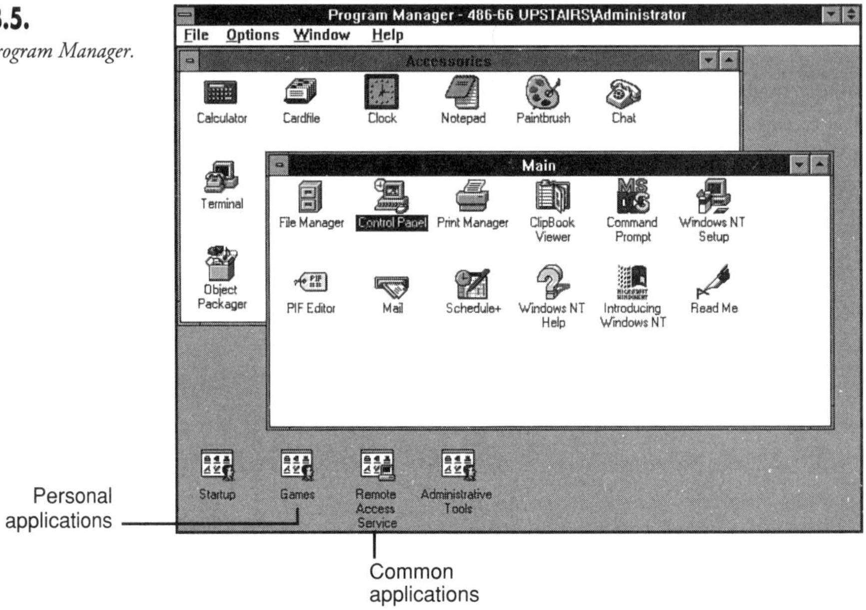

FIGURE 3.5.
The NT Program Manager.

Notice the familiar groups Main, Accessories, Applications, and Games. If you chose to migrate settings from an existing Windows 3.1 installation when you ran NT Setup, you probably will have those additional groups, meaning all your Windows 3.1 groups.

NOTE

Migration of Windows 3.1 settings is an option only if you install NT over an existing installation of NT. (Installation is covered in Chapter 8.) Also, note that migration of Windows 3.1 settings will not occur for the Administrator account—only for the new user accounts as you create them.

Notice also in Figure 3.5 that, unlike the single group icon type in Windows 3.1, NT has two types: *personal* and *common.*

When you create a new program group (as explained later in this chapter), you can declare which type it is. Personal icons appear only during a session in which the user who created them has logged onto the system. Common icons appear to all users, regardless of who has logged on.

The common icon makes it easier for administrators to give all the users on a machine access to a suite of applications or documents. For example, if the computer is in the Finance department, you might want all users to have access to Quicken, Excel, and 1-2-3.

Just create a common group with these icons in it, and all users will see that group in their Program Manager window.

NOTE

The downside to this arrangement is that common groups can be altered by any user on the workstation. If one user modifies the group by adding or deleting icons, rearranging them, or altering their properties, this affects all workstation users.

Supplied Groups

A new NT setup comes up initially with six groups:

- Main: Basic tools for running NT
- Applications: Programs NT Setup found on your system

NOTE

Several accessory groups might be created if NT Setup finds more than 40 applications during installation. Each Applications group will hold 40, after which another will be created.

- Accessories: Helpful day-to-day tools bundled with NT
- Games: Distractions such as Solitaire
- Startup: Empty group to which you add auto-startup programs
- Administrative Tools: System administration tools for NT managers

The administrators' program group appears only when the administrator (or a user given administrative privileges) logs on. That group, shown in Figure 3.6, contains administrative tools such as the User Manager, Event Viewer, Backup, and Disk Administrator, all of which are used for managing the server or local NT machine.

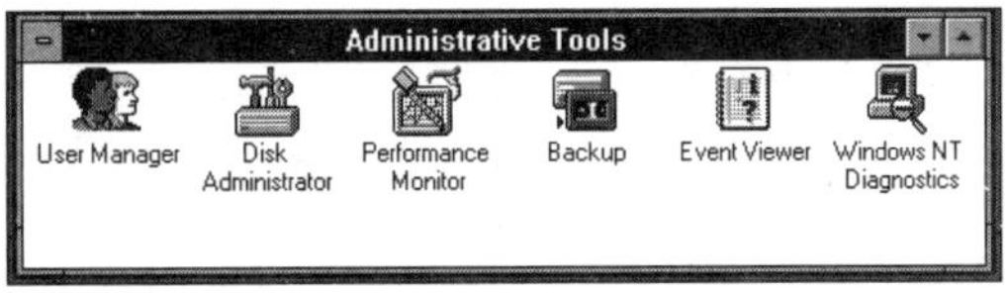

FIGURE 3.6.
The Administrative Tools group.

Startup Group

The Startup group has the same function in NT as in Windows 3.1. The only difference is that each user can have his or her own Startup group. This feature offers a bit of flexibility for system administrators because it allows for fine-tuning the NT environment for each user.

TIP

You might want to create several NT setups for yourself, with specific applications groups, applications, documents, startup applications, and desktop arrangements. To achieve this, you have to create multiple user identities for yourself via User Manager (explained in Chapter 10), then set up Program Manager to your liking and save the configuration.

Adding New Group and Program Icons

As with 3.1, you can create, move, copy, and delete icons. Here's a quick reminder in case your skills are rusty.

Adding Icons

To add a new item, follow these steps:

1. Choose File | New, which gives you the dialog box shown in Figure 3.7.

FIGURE 3.7.
Creating a new group or application icon.

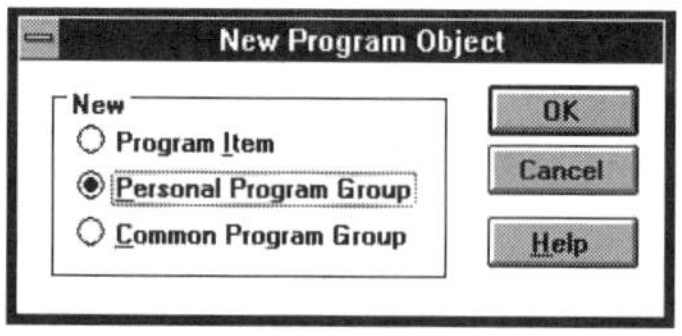

NOTE

You have a choice of two types of groups—personal and common. Personal groups appear only for the user currently logged in. Common groups appear for all users who have accounts on the workstation.

2. Choose the type of item you want to create and click on OK.
3. If it's a group, fill in the description. See Figure 3.8.

FIGURE 3.8.

New group dialog box.

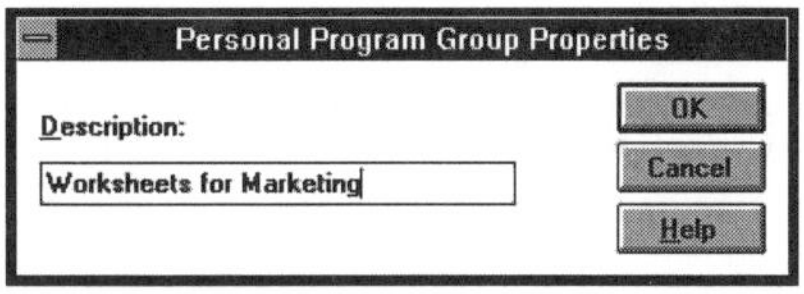

As shown in Figure 3.9, if you're setting up an application dialog box, you have to fill in a little more information.

FIGURE 3.9.

New application dialog box.

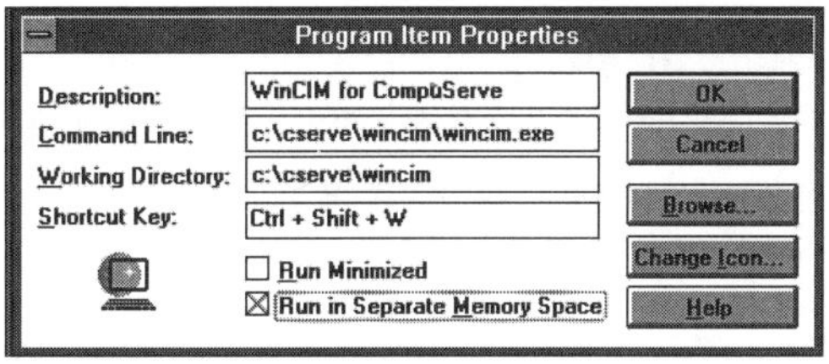

Use the Browse button to look for the application or document, unless you already know its path. Don't forget that any document with an association can be added as an icon. Clicking on that icon runs the associated program and loads the document.

TIP

If you're working on the same document every time you log on, just drop its icon in the Startup group. The application will run as soon as you log on.

Because an NT machine is likely to be networked, a user can add application and document icons pointing to files stored on remote machines. Clicking on the icon loads the application or file across the network. However, setting up icons that point to a remote machine will result in error messages if the NT machine attempts to launch a program from a remote drive that's not connected to the network at the time. (See Figures 3.10 and 3.11.)

FIGURE 3.10.

An error message.

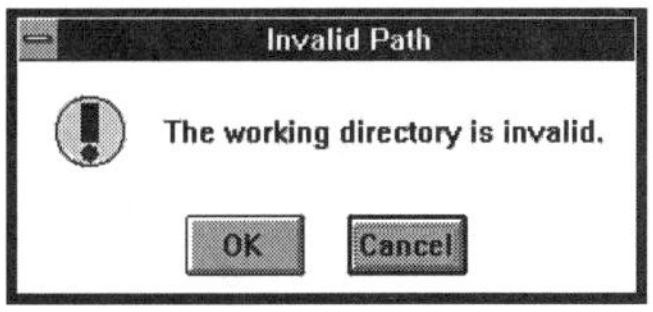

FIGURE 3.11.
Another error message.

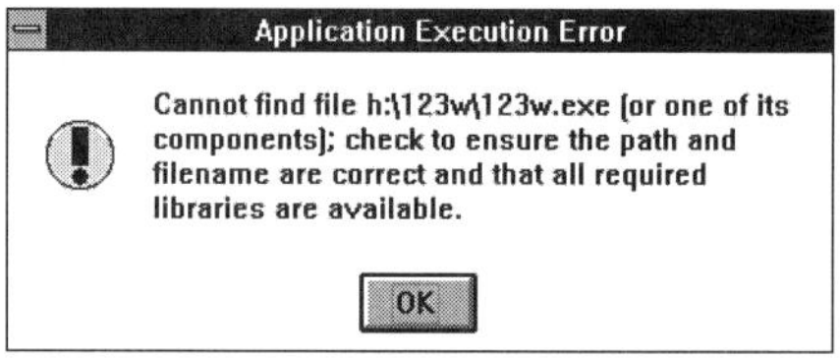

You also can add program and document icons to groups from File Manager.

1. Arrange the screen so that File Manager and Program Manager are both visible.
2. Fine-tune the arrangement so that the application or document file in File Manager is visible and the destination group window in Program is visible.
3. Drag the file from File Manager into Program Manager, dropping it into the destination group window. Its icon will appear in the group automatically.

NOTE

If you're dragging in a document rather than an executable file, the icon of the associated program (the Word for Windows icon, for example, in the case of *.DOC files) is given to the item. If the file has no association, you are warned of this. You can still add it, but it is given a generic icon design and will not execute when you double-click on it in Program Manager.

Copying, Moving, and Deleting Icons

You can easily copy, move, and delete program and application icons, just as in Windows 3.1. To move a program icon into a new group, follow these steps:

1. Select the icon.
2. Choose File | Move and stipulate the destination, or drag the icon into the destination window and release it.

Pressing Ctrl while dragging an icon copies it instead of moving it.

To delete a program or document icon, follow these steps:

1. Highlight it.
2. Press Delete and answer Yes in the confirmation dialog box.

To delete a group, follow these steps:

1. Iconize its window.
2. Highlight the icon.
3. Press Delete and answer Yes.

Arranging Icons and Windows

Program Manager isn't very good at keeping things neat and tidy, as Windows 3.1 users know. A little intervention and housekeeping are required from time to time. First, arrange and size the group windows as desired. Some groups typically will be open; others will be closed. Most users like a few choice groups open in a window so that often-used programs and documents are showing.

To neatly line up all the icons in a group window, choose Window | Align Icons. To line up group icons, first select any iconized group icon by clicking on it, then choose Window | Arrange Icons.

If you want icons in a group window to automatically rearrange themselves to fit the window when you change its dimensions, choose Options | Auto Arrange.

TIP

To save the settings of windows and icons, including the "restored" size of each group window, choose Options | Save Settings Now. This is analogous to pressing Shift and double-clicking on the Program Manager control box in Windows 3.1. I recommend this method over the Options | Save Settings on Exit command, which saves settings when you log off from NT, because with that option you might accidentally save a window arrangement you didn't intend to. I suggest you make sure that this option is turned off (in other words, that there is no check mark next to it).

Ways to Run Programs in NT

Programs can be run several ways in Windows NT. These include a couple of choices not available in Windows 3.1:

- Icons
- File | Run command
- File Manager

- Command line
- Batch files
- Task Manager

Executing Programs from Icons

The easiest way for typical users to run programs is via Program Manager icons. All the user has to do is double-click on a program icon. NT generates an appropriate window for the application type and launches the application in the window. If the program is of the DOS variety, for example, a DOS VDM is spawned and the DOS application runs in it, using the color and font settings last saved. (Details of those settings are described in Chapter 5.)

As I mentioned earlier, NT offers a Startup group too, just like Windows 3.1 uses for automating program execution. Simply adding some icons to the Startup group causes those applications (or documents) to run when you log onto NT.

TIP

Applications in the Startup group aren't necessarily executed in the order in which the icons appear in the Startup group window. They're executed in the order they were added to the group. If you want to change the order of execution, you must move the icons to another group, save the settings, and add them to the Startup group in the desired order.

NOTE

Windows applications will execute before non-Windows applications, regardless of the order in which applications are added to the Startup group.

After an icon is created and added to a group, its *properties* are stored with it. You can change properties by highlighting the icon and pressing Alt-Enter, by pressing Alt and double-clicking on the icon, or by highlighting the icon and choosing File | Properties. With any of these methods, the properties are displayed and can be edited via a dialog box, as shown in Figure 3.12.

FIGURE 3.12.
The Properties dialog box.

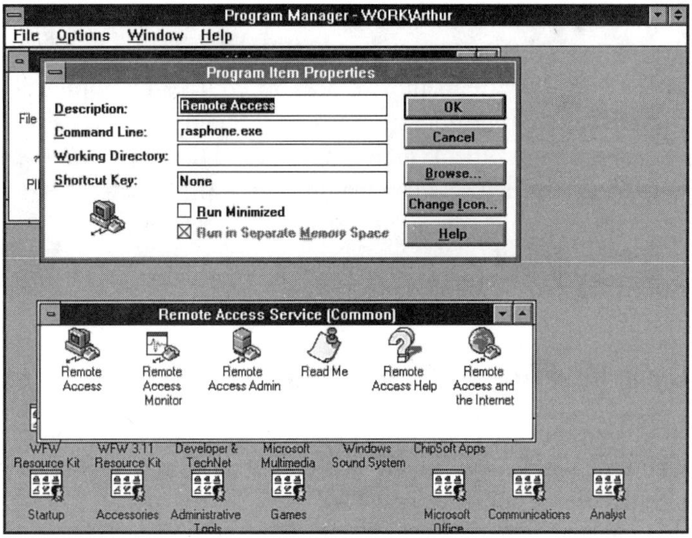

This dialog box has the following options:

- Description: The words that appear under the icon
- Command Line: Filename and path (network path, drive, and directory) of the file
- Working Directory: The directory the application uses as a default (typically for temporary or support files)
- Shortcut Key: The key combination that, when pressed while Program Manager is the active window, runs the application, or, after the program is already running, immediately switches to the application regardless of where you are

TIP

The icon can be changed by clicking on the Change Icon button and searching for an icon you prefer. You can borrow an icon from any program file or icon collection. For example, the Windows 3.1 file called MORICONS.DLL contains numerous icons to choose from, as does PROGMAN.EXE. Both are stored in your Windows 3.1 directory, typically C:\WINDOWS. Windows NT offers a similar icon collection stored in the file MORICONS.DLL in the \SYSTEM32 directory.

- Run Minimized: Starts the application in an iconized state
- Run in Separate Memory Space: Creates a separate VDM in which the application executes

TIP

Utilizing separate memory spaces for your 16-bit applications will completely isolate the application from other 16-bit applications, aside from the supported datasharing protocols such as OLE and DDE. This can be particularly useful for applications that perform lengthy processing (such as a graphics conversion program), which normally prevent other 16-bit applications from receiving their fair share of CPU time.

Using the File | Run Command

Both Program Manager and File Manager have Run commands on their File menus. Choosing the Run command brings up the dialog box shown in Figure 3.13. Just enter a program name and click on OK.

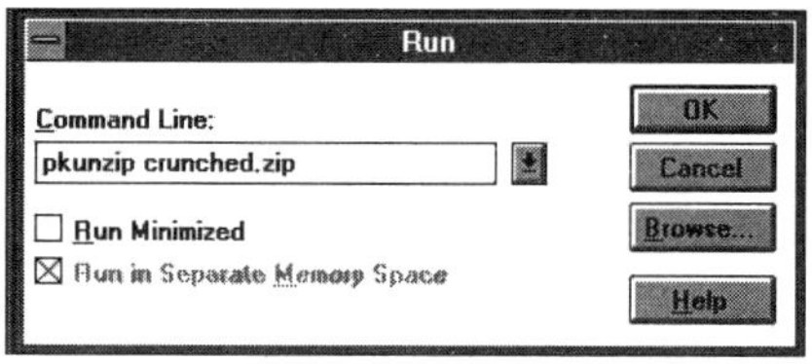

FIGURE 3.13.
The File | Run dialog box available from Program Manager and File Manager.

TIP

The Windows 3.1 environment can be fine-tuned based on your Windows 3.1 WIN.INI and SYSTEM.INI settings. Windows NT has a feature that synchronizes settings changes made by Windows 3.1 and Windows NT. See Chapter 5 for details. Note that this feature applies only if you installed NT over an existing 16-bit Windows setup.

Executing Programs from File Manager

For experienced users, File Manager is a good alternative to Program Manager for running programs. To launch a program, double-click on any executable file or any file that has an application associated with it. NT does the rest.

Six types of file icons display in File Manager:

Directories
Directories shared for network use

Executable program files (.EXE, .COM, .BAT, .PIF, .CMD)
Documents with associations
Documents without associations
System or hidden files

Obviously, you can launch only two types of files using this technique: executables and documents with associations. If you double-click on other types of files, such as DLLs, you get the error message shown in Figure 3.14 because they aren't programs.

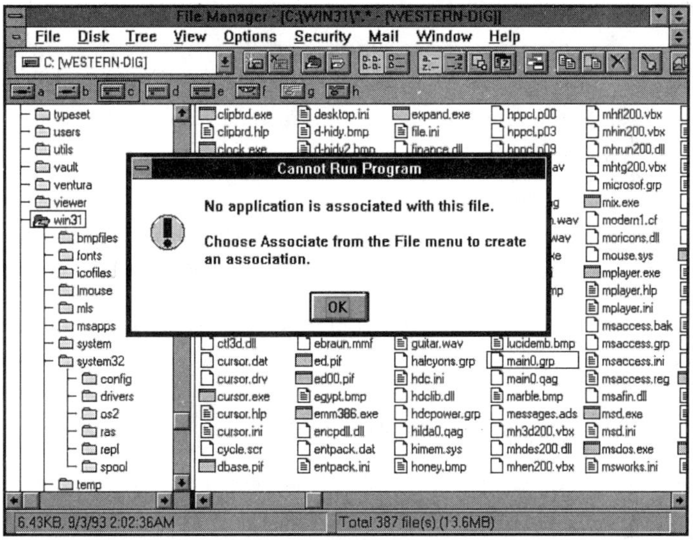

FIGURE 3.14.
This dialog box appears when you double-click on a file other than an application program or a document with a program association.

NOTE

In case you don't know, an *association* is a declared link between files with a specific three-letter extension and an application that can work with that file. Clicking on a .WRI file, for example, runs Write and loads the .WRI file because there is an association between the two. You create an association using File Manager's File | Associate command.

Running Programs from the Command Line

The NT command-line interpreter (DOS prompt equivalent) is more versatile than its DOS counterpart. Although the NT command line appears to be functionally equivalent to DOS 5 (and much of DOS 6), recall from Chapters 1 and 2 that it really is a DOS emulator, not a true DOS session as in Windows 3.1. Some DOS applications run more slowly under the emulator than under real DOS. This isn't necessarily the case, however. The speed penalty depends on the application design. A program that is disk-intensive or that makes many API calls typically runs *faster* under NT than in its native DOS due to the emulator's use of NT's disk caching and 32-bit API mapping. By contrast, applications running significant amounts of native 16-bit DOS code will be slowed down by the translation from 16- to 32-bit machine language (a process called *thunking*).

The NT command prompt isn't called the DOS prompt because it isn't DOS, and also because it's not restricted to running DOS programs. In Windows 3.1, typing a Windows program name at the DOS prompt (for example, `pbrush`) and pressing Enter only results in the error message `This program requires Microsoft Windows.`

With NT, no such error message exists. The program runs, regardless of whether it's a DOS, OS/2, 16-bit Windows, Win32s, or Windows NT application. NT simply spawns the appropriate application window, loads the application into it, and gets you up and running.

So, if you're a command-prompt keyboard type, bring up a command-prompt box and start running your programs from it if you like. Commonly used commands such as `DIR`, `FORMAT`, and `CHKDSK` are supported, too. See Appendix A for a complete listing of the DOS prompt commands and syntax, and see the following section for more information.

NOTE

> Windows NT lets you configure the MS-DOS environment based on settings in your AUTOEXEC.BAT files as well as using two other files, AUTOEXEC.NT and CONFIG.NT. Using these files, you can load TSRs and device drivers, or set up memory managers prior to running a DOS application. In addition to these files, you also can create PIFs similar to the ones in Windows 3.1 for declaring specifics about how NT services the DOS session. See Chapter 5 for information about configuring the DOS environment.

When you start an application by simply entering its name at the command prompt, the current window is taken over by the new application. If you want to retain use of the window and start a new application in its own window, use the `start` command. For example:

```
start wp5
```

Running Programs from Batch Files

In addition to having a more intelligent command prompt, NT supports batch files for programs other than DOS programs. This was a major drawback of Windows 3.1, and a number of third-party programs attempted to address it. The problem specifically was that no facility existed for running Windows programs from batch files. Because the NT command prompt is intelligent enough to identify program types, batch files are possible even with a mixture of program types. For example, you can run this file at the command prompt:

```
cls
echo Here comes Microsoft Word for 16-bit Windows
pause
c:\winword\winword
cls
echo Here comes a DOS DIR command
pause
dir c:\winword\*.doc
echo Here comes an OS/2 application
word
echo All Done!
```

NOTE

Just as with DOS batch files, you can write the files using any nonformatting ASCII/ANSI text editor, such as Notepad, or you can use the command

```
copy con: filename.bat
```

and then enter the lines for the batch file. On the last line (that is, a new blank line), end the file by pressing Ctrl-Z and pressing Enter.

You can assign the batch file to an icon in Program Manager or execute it from the command prompt. When the batch file executes, each program is run in order from the top down, just as in a normal batch file. For instance, in the previous example, WinWord runs first, in a new window; the batch file moves to the background but stays open. When you quit WinWord, its window closes and the command-prompt window comes to the foreground, doing a `DIR` listing. After that, the OS/2 program runs.

As you might imagine, this can be a boon for anyone wishing to automate procedures in Windows. Perhaps you regularly perform a series of tasks in the same order. For example, you might go about acquiring some data through a communications program or data acquisition board, then run a spreadsheet or statistical analysis package to work with the data, then catalog the data somewhere or send it across the network or to another user via modem. Batch files that can mix and match programs running on a variety of platforms could be great.

TIP

In addition to standard DOS batch file commands, you also could use Windows 3.1 Recorder to automate tasks while a 16-bit Windows program is running. Note, however, that no 32-bit version of Recorder is supplied with NT. This is probably because the Recorder program is finicky, requiring a good deal of care to prevent it from bombing—particularly when you attempt to record and replay mouse movements. My experience using Windows 3.1 Recorder macros with 32-bit NT applications was that they didn't work, causing error messages from NT when macros were executed. Using Recorder macros with 3.1 applications running under NT tends to work better, probably by virtue of the fact that all Windows 3.1 apps are running in the same WOW session and thus can share resources such as those provided by Recorder. Keep your eyes peeled for third-party NT macro programs capable of sophisticated multiapplication program automation and scheduling. As of this writing, none are available. If all you're interested in doing is scheduling program or batch file execution for a specific time, check out NT's `at` command (see Appendix A).

Running Applications from Task Manager

The final means of running an application is from Task Manager. This is a very convenient method, replacing the popular method many Windows veterans use of switching to Program or File Manager, executing the File | Run command, and typing in a DOS command. Instead, just press Ctrl-Esc to bring up Task Manager. There's a text area in the dialog box where you can enter a program name.

Windowing DOS Applications

Command-prompt sessions can be displayed either in a window or full-screen. As a default, double-clicking on the command-prompt icon in the Main group of Program Manager runs the command prompt in a full-screen session. However, you might want to see other windows on-screen at the same time or copy, cut, and paste between windows using the mouse. You can do this just as in Windows 3.1:

1. Press Alt-Enter. Whatever is on the screen is minimized to a window.
2. Press Alt-Enter again. The window jumps to full-screen size.

While in full-screen mode, you can press Alt-Tab (just as in graphical Windows mode) to task switch. The little box doesn't appear in the middle of the screen, however. Instead, the names of running applications appear at the top of the screen. Release the Alt key when you see the name of the application you want to switch to.

NOTE

Data sharing between the various environments is discussed in Chapter 5.

Terminating the Command-Prompt Window

Command-line windows you execute by clicking on the Command Line icon in Program Manager don't terminate until you intentionally kill them. To remove the window and thus the memory it consumes, just type `exit` and press Enter at the command prompt.

This isn't necessary when a DOS program has been run from an icon in Program Manager or if another application such as File Manager has spawned the DOS window. For example, say you choose File | Run from File Manager, type `c:\ws\ws`, and press Enter to run WordStar. When you quit WordStar, the DOS window disappears.

Terminating Crashed Applications

Of course, applications sometimes crash. For the first iteration of NT, this actually happens more than it should. The good news is that a crashed app doesn't a crashed OS make. Even a crashed application is likely to leave your NT system intact—except, as explained in Chapters 1 and 2, when a single errant Windows 3.1 or DOS application can take down a VDM and all other DOS or Windows 3.1 apps.

When an application dies in NT, an error message usually is generated. NT kills the application itself, brushing it aside and freeing up the memory it was utilizing. If this doesn't occur automatically, you have to take the following steps:

1. Bring up the Task List by pressing Ctrl-Esc.
2. Select the dead program and click on End.
3. A dialog box advises you to use this practice only as a last resort. Confirm your choice.

Another approach, if you can't seem to get to the Task List, is to press Ctrl-Alt-Delete. This brings up a box with a button on it that you can click to get to the Task List.

If the program is running in an NT command-prompt window, you have another option. You can terminate the application by opening the Control menu and choosing Close or Terminate.

Running Multiple Programs Simultaneously

It probably isn't necessary to mention this, but you can run many applications simultaneously under NT. Windows NT's thread dispatcher takes care of slicing up CPU time between the applications, at least making it appear that they are all running at the same time.

To run multiple programs at once, simply continue launching them using any of the techniques explained earlier. The actual number of applications you can run is determined by the combined amount of RAM and virtual memory available. If you have 16M of memory or more, you will be able to run a good number of applications at once without NT issuing messages about low memory. If you begin seeing error messages about low memory, it's time to increase your virtual memory allocation or add more physical memory.

No More System Resource Shortages

In Windows 3.1, an enigmatic feature called *system resources* often is responsible for error messages about low memory, even when plenty of physical and virtual memory is left. System resources is a small amount of memory (64K) set aside for applications to use for certain internal functions, such as tracking small graphics like those in application toolbars.

NOTE

The seemingly arbitrary size of 64K is a limitation of the 16-bit architecture of the Intel 8086 and 80286 CPUs and the associated code required for compatibility. Even Enhanced-mode Windows 3.1 on 386 and higher processors utilizes 16-bit code and therefore suffers the same problem.

WARNING

Because Windows NT has no noticeable resource limit, a problem might occur if you commonly migrate data files from Windows NT to Windows 3.1. For instance, I have used the Microsoft Office products (Word for Windows, Excel, Access, and Powerpoint) as front-end and analysis tools utilizing custom macros. This can cause a problem if you do it under Windows 3.1, because Windows 3.1 normally doesn't have sufficient system resources to execute all of these applications simultaneously and display the applications' associated data. A large Powerpoint slide show might also demonstrate this portability issue.

After you run only a few programs in Windows 3.1, system resources often can run low, triggering low-memory messages. Checking the available memory using the Help | About command in Program Manager or File Manager, or using other programs that list this data, often sends users off scratching their heads because, typically, plenty of memory is left. What users often don't understand is that their system resources are low, not their system memory. The computer can have much physical and virtual memory available but still be unable to run more programs. This is particularly bad news if you just dropped big bucks to purchase extra RAM, thinking it would solve the problem.

The good news is that NT doesn't allocate system resources the same way Windows 3.1 does. It's much more intelligent. Because NT doesn't run on top of DOS, the 64K limit doesn't arise; for all intents and purposes, NT's WOW environment subsystem simply never runs low on system resources. If, in fact, you run Windows 3.1 utilities that measure system resources when in NT, they'll report that you have used none whatsoever, regardless of the number of Windows 3.1 applications running.

Running Multiple Instances of the Same Program

When you're running multiple applications, remember that each one does use up some memory. Eventually you will run out of application space if you keep launching programs and/or opening documents. You'll want to limit the number of open applications, or at least experiment with the program mix if you're running out of space. Some POSIX applications, for example, might be quite large and might precipitate memory shortage messages when you run them. You might have to close an application or two to load a new large one.

TIP

Many applications enable you to run multiple instances of them. For example, you can run Microsoft Word as many times as you like. Others, such as Clock (CLOCK.EXE), can be run only once. Typically, you'll run multiple instances of an application to open several files and to enable easy cutting and pasting between them or to edit several documents at once. There are some advantages, but the down side is that each instance consumes more system memory because it amounts to loading a separate copy of the program each time. If you make a habit of opening files from File Manager by double-clicking on them (for example, clicking on .DOC files to open them in Word), you can end up with more than a few instances of a large program in memory, and thus have little room for others. The memory-efficient solution is to run the program once, then use the application's File | Open command to load additional files. Of course, this works only for applications that enable you to open multiple documents at one time.

Switching Between Applications

Switching between running applications is as simple as it is in Windows 3.1. You have several choices:

- Click on the window you want
- Alt-Tab to the application
- Press Ctrl-Esc to bring up the Task List
- Press Ctrl-Alt-Delete and choose the Task Manager option from the resulting dialog box

The most intuitive approach is simply to click on the window containing the application you want to activate. This technique assumes that you have a mouse and that all your applications aren't maximized (that is, with the window taking up the whole screen).

Personally, I usually have my applications maximized, so my preferred switching technique is to press Alt-Tab. Each press of the Tab key (while you hold down the Alt key) advances you to the next application. A little box in the middle of the screen reports the name and displays the application's icon, as shown in Figure 3.15.

FIGURE 3.15.
Pressing Alt-Tab brings up this box.

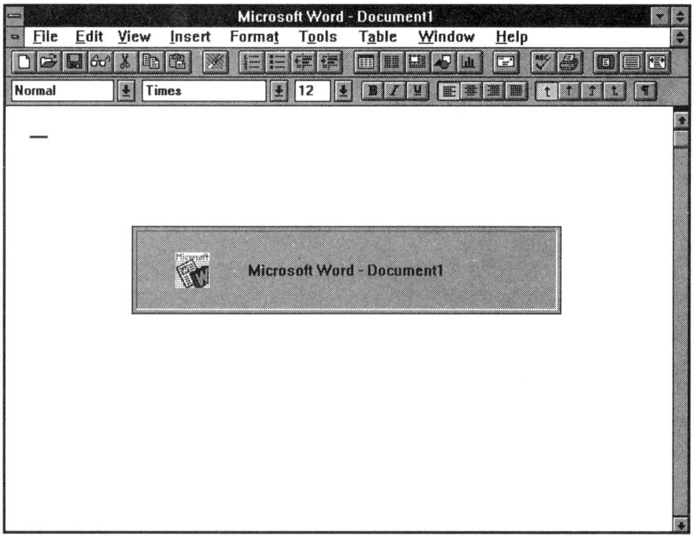

Release the Alt key when you see the name of the application you want to switch to. When you do, that application's window jumps to the foreground. This is called *fast application switching*.

NOTE

The Fast Application Switching feature can be defeated. You can turn it off or on from Control Panel's Desktop applet. When it's turned off, Alt-Tab simply jumps you between application windows. This arrangement is a little less intuitive, however, and you have to scan the screen to see which window will be activated next.

TIP

Often with Alt-Tab, you pass the application you're looking for because the tendency is to do it quickly. Rather than tab your way around the applications circle again, hoping to stop at the right one, press Shift-Alt-Tab. Each press moves you backward through the same list of applications. It's like putting a car in reverse to back into a parking space.

Another alternative is the Task List. Pressing Ctrl-Esc while you're anywhere in NT causes a program call TASKMAN.EXE to execute. TASKMAN.EXE presents the Task List, shown in Figure 3.16, which lists all the currently running applications—well, usually. Actually, many NT services and certain applications designed to "hide" in the background don't show up in the list. You have to use a craftier program if you really want to see a complete list of what's running. A program called PVIEWER.EXE, included in the NT Resource Kit and in the Win32 Software Developer's Kit (SDK), displays a complete list.

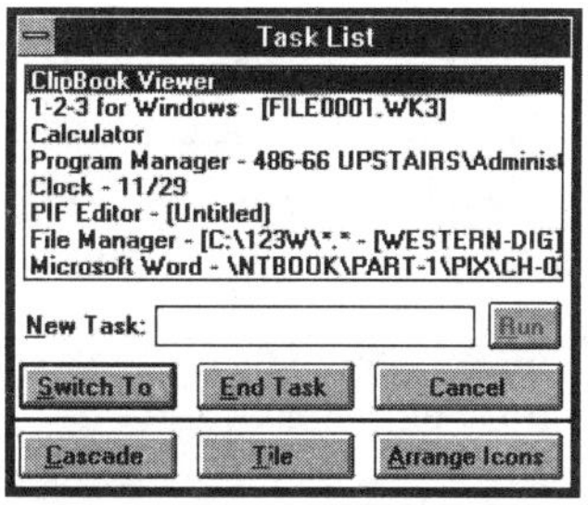

FIGURE 3.16.
The NT Task List.

Just double-click on the program you want to jump to, or select it and click on Switch To. Note that you also can use the Task List for other purposes, such as cascading or tiling the running applications to neatly organize them, or to end the task (quit the application).

TIP

As I mentioned earlier, the Task List also has a RUN line in it. This line is functionally equivalent to the command-line interpreter explained earlier. Therefore, another quick way to run a program whose name you know is to press Ctrl-Esc, type in the name, and click on the Run button.

Sharing Network Applications and Documents

Because NT is a networking multiuser system, some additional considerations not affecting single-user systems can crop up when you're running applications. In general, issues arise around shared resources. At any time on a network, two or more people might be sharing the same applications, files, or physical devices (such as a printer). Although NT is quite capable of precluding networked device and application conflicts, it's useful for users as well as administrators to understand the process of data, application, and device sharing.

For anyone accustomed to local area networking on PCs, this discussion is elementary and therefore may be skipped. However, if you're new to networking or you're upgrading from a more casual system (for example, a pure peer-to-peer system such as Windows for Workgroups or LANtastic), these issues will be more germane.

Network Software, File Locking, and Record Locking

Networking a number of PCs does not, by itself, magically transform your current software—for instance, database managers such as dBASE, Access, or Paradox—into multiuser software. Single-user programs usually enable more than one person to run them at the same time (for example, two people can run the same copy of Excel stored somewhere on an NT server), but when it comes to opening and sharing the same data file simultaneously, look out. If NT let you do that, you could have what I call a "data collision."

If NT were to allow two people to, for example, open and modify the same letter at the same time, what would happen? Figure 3.17 gives the answer.

Whoever saves the letter last will wipe out the earlier version. Losing a letter is enough of an inconvenience, but the effect can be far worse when single-user databases are used simultaneously from a number of network stations. Invaluable data records can be lost if the last saved version of the file doesn't include changes made by another user.

With correct network management (implementing a data protection scheme called *file locking,* which prevents more than one person from using a file at one time), this type of data collision scenario can be prevented. Windows NT (as well as Windows 3.1 and Windows for Workgroups) applications typically implement file locking, so when you try to access a file that has been opened by another user (whether on your computer or on a remote one), you receive a message like the one shown in Figure 3.18.

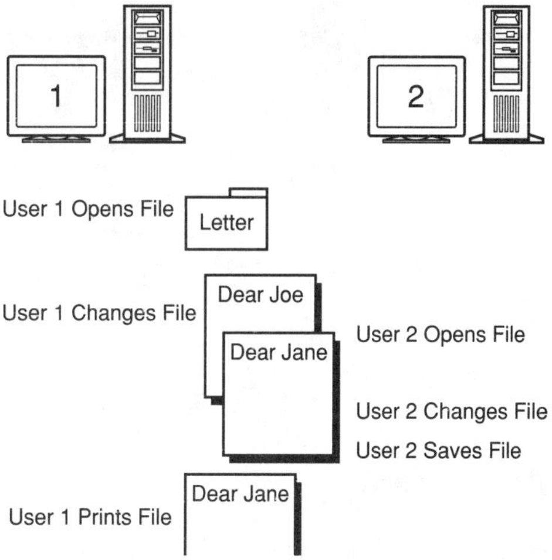

FIGURE 3.17.
Flow diagram of a data conflict if two users have write privileges and the operating system doesn't support file locking.

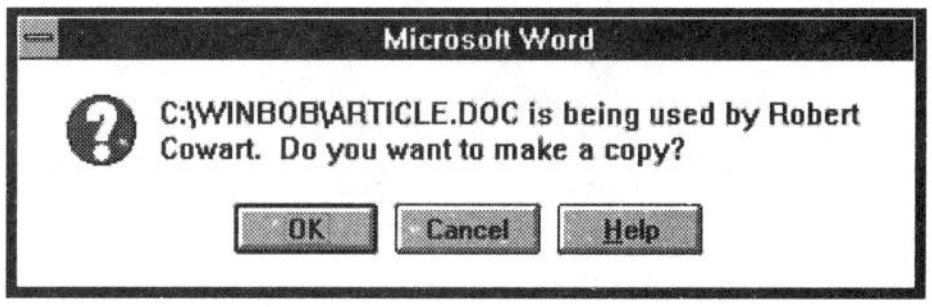

FIGURE 3.18.
This message means that the file is in use by another network user.

The actual message you receive may vary from program to program. In Figure 3.18 you see a conflict message generated by Microsoft Word. Making a copy of the file is Word's solution to the access problem. First it makes a copy, then it lets you edit the copy instead of the original. As a result, you actually can save your work.

When you're attempting to open files with other programs, you might instead see a dialog box that asks about opening the file as read-only. Figure 3.19 shows such a message generated by Lotus 1-2-3 for Windows.

Opening the file as read-only means that you can display the file on-screen (or possibly print it), but you can't make changes to it. Not until the other user has closed the file does NT make it available to you for changes. So, if you answer Yes to such an interrogative, don't expect to be able to save any changes you've made to the file. One way around losing changes you've made is to use the File | Save As command and give the file a new name.

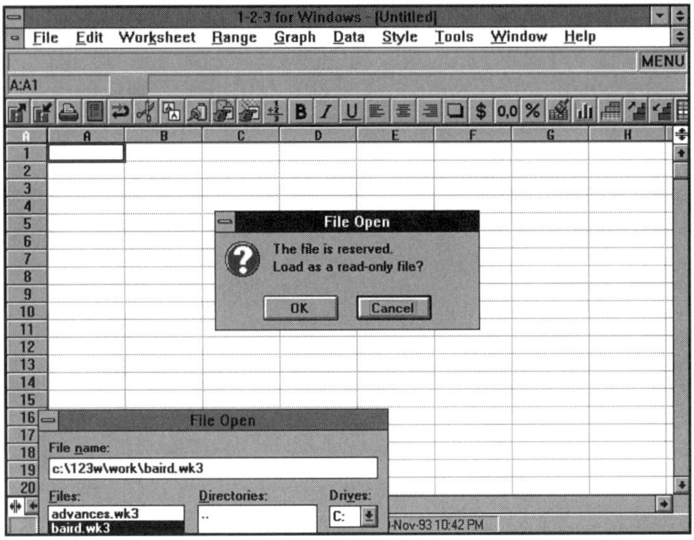

FIGURE 3.19.
A file-in-use message by Lotus 1-2-3. Lotus' solution is to load the file in read-only mode.

Sharing Applications

Sharing application programs is much simpler than sharing data files. Most programs can be used by any number of people simultaneously because they are simply read into your computer. Merely using a program doesn't alter its program file. Occasionally, the changes you make to a program's settings or performances are written to disk, but they usually go into an initialization (.INI) file stored in the Windows directory or elsewhere.

As a rule, most non–network-aware programs can be used on networks by multiple users. Some exceptions at the time of this writing are PageMaker 4.0 and CorelDRAW!, apparently because they use support or temporary files that can be opened by only one user at a time. If multiple users are having trouble running a program simultaneously, contact the manufacturer of the program to determine a possible fix. When purchasing new programs for use on your network, look for Windows for Workgroups or NT compatibility statements in the advertising or on the product box. Also, buy networking products when possible, or ones that give you a discount on upgrades as they become available.

NOTE

System administrators have the option of denying read-write privileges and assigning read-only privileges to any user on an NT system. Attempting to change a file for which you have read-only rights results in a dialog box announcing that what you are attempting to do isn't possible. It doesn't necessarily mean that the file has been opened by another user.

Groupware to the Rescue

Some applications are written specifically for network use and are intended for multiuser platforms such as NT, Novell NetWare, or UNIX. Two simple cases are MS-Mail and Schedule+, both of which are bundled with NT and Windows for Workgroups.

NOTE

MS-Mail and Schedule+ are discussed in Chapter 6.

Such programs implement more advanced data-sharing schemes devised for networks—schemes enabling many users to have access to the same data file, rather than limiting it to a first-come, first-served basis.

The software protocol that manages multiuser data access is often referred to as *record locking*. Instead of locking a user out of a file altogether, record locking allows any number of users into the file but limits their access to one record (a discrete portion of the file) at a time. Record locking's most obvious application is in databases, where files are actually broken into discrete records. As long as users are editing different records, no conflict occurs. If simultaneous access to the same record is attempted, an error message is generated, typically advising the user to wait a few seconds until the record is unlocked.

Until recently, few attempts had been made to write multiuser word processors or spreadsheets. However, a rash of multiuser *groupware* programs, ranging from games to messaging software such as MS-Mail and Lotus Notes, have gained attention in the network software market. These products are setting the stage for a new class of network software that enables network users to interactively modify documents while sitting in different offices.

Pointers for Sharing Files Across the NT Network

The main points to keep in mind when sharing applications and document files across the network are as follows:

- If you intend to run applications stored on a remote machine, consider whether the remote machine is always going to be turned on and connected to the network when you need the application. If not, copy the application onto your local workstation's hard disk and run it locally.
- Are the data files you'll be using stored on a mainframe that you'll be connecting to via NT's TCP/IP capabilities or other connectivity add-on modules? If so, do you need to use NT's remote access services, or is the mainframe local? How many

users can connect at once, and which NT machine or domain provides the gateway to the mainframe? Talk with the network administrator about scheduling such complex activities.

- Will you need access to the same data files that other workers are using? If so, are those files accessible via multiuser software? If not, you need to arrange a schedule with coworkers for file access and coordinate management of the files. You might want to create and maintain an audit trail listing times, dates, and the nature of changes made.

TIP

The NT Administrator's utility program is called Event Viewer. It keeps track of a wide variety of system events, including the date and time any file on an NT machine is opened, read, or modified, and by whom. The Event Viewer log can be used as a means of tracking file access. Although it's not an elegant solution to the problem of tracking a workgroup's access to files, it works.

- As a rule, if an evolving document is going to be worked on by more than one person, keep only *one* copy of the file and store it in a central location. Duplication of files leads ultimately to confusion among people in a workgroup. If necessary, keep another file, such as a simple text file that contains a log of changes made. Better yet, add a section for such a log at the beginning of the file in question (for example, in a large text cell in a spreadsheet, or on the first page of a report) so that users on the network will know what's going on with the file. This way, whenever the file is opened, the user will see the notes.
- Consider buying a groupware version of the programs you use for group activities. Some of the newer programs are very intelligent in design and might even improve a workgroup's efficiency by facilitating communication between workers.
- Remember that even though DOS-based workstations can access files stored on shared NTFS or HPFS partitions, filenames will be truncated to the "8.3" format for those users. Check and possibly modify filenames for the DOS-based workstations.
- Make use of your network's e-mail program to send notes to other users about modifications you've made to files. A simple note such as "Sharon, I added the latest sales figures to the monthly balance sheet on the NT server" is often all that's needed to prevent mishaps.
- Make backups of vital shared files on a regular basis.
- Don't shut down your computer if you know that others have files open on your system. (Later I discuss how to handle shutdowns when files are in use.)

Using File Manager

Like Windows for Workgroups, the NT File Manager is much improved over its Windows 3.1 predecessor. For example, the NT File Manager has a user-configurable toolbar to speed up common tasks, and it also sports new icons that indicate shared directories and networked drives. Additional menus and menu options also have been added to supply needed networking functions—for instance, connecting to and disconnecting from network resources, determining who is using files on your system, declaring security levels for directories and files, copying a file to the Windows Clipboard, and viewing proprietary information about programs that manufacturers store in the file's NTFS file header (such as an application's version number).

General Operation

In general, the operation of File Manager is identical to that in Windows 3.1 and Windows for Workgroups. Running the program from Program Manager's Main group results in the screen shown in Figure 3.20 (or a reasonable facsimile).

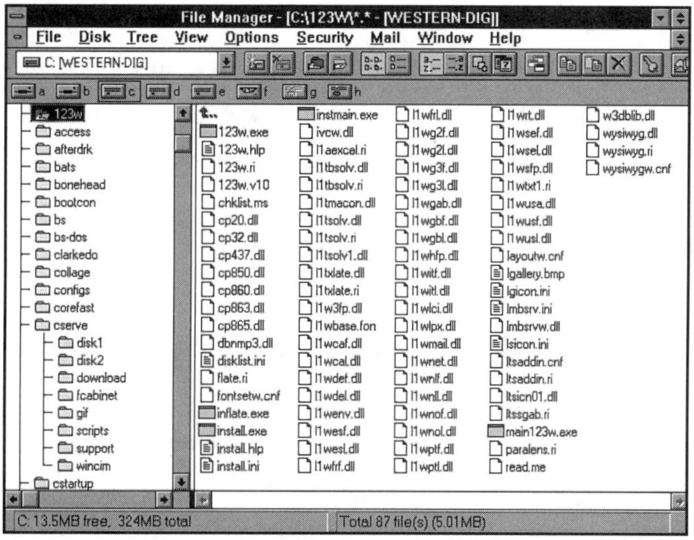

FIGURE 3.20.
The basic File Manager screen.

Notice that the layout of the window (the directory and file panes, the tree, and the file icons) are almost identical to Windows 3.1. The NT File Manager, however, has a slightly new look that includes a configurable toolbar, some new icons, and some new commands. Note that the drive bar contains a special icon for networked hard disks. Also note the new icon for shared directories (the little hand under the file folder). This shows up after you share one of your directories, meaning that other users have access to it. All drives now are case-sensitive and support longer filenames. Case-sensitivity is for display purposes only. You can access a file or directory with any combination of upper- and lowercase letters.

Functionally, however, many features are not new. As with Windows 3.1, you can

- drag-and-drop files into new destination directories, or drag-and-drop from the file windows to a drive icon
- drag entire directory branches to new destinations, effectively grafting entire sections of a hard disk
- drop a document icon on top of an executable file for the purpose of opening the file
- display the contents of multiple drives at once in separate windows, which can be sized, cascaded, or tiled as you please
- print from File Manager, using either the File | Print command or drag-and-drop to pull a file onto an iconized Print Manager (you have to run Print Manager first, then iconize it where you can see it)
- format and label disk volumes
- save your window setup for future File Manager sessions

Because most of these features are identical to NT's Windows 3.1 cousins, I'll spare you the details. (If you've never used File Manager and you have questions about basic File Manager operation, check the System Guide supplied with NT.) Instead, I'll focus on the new features of File Manager that pertain only to NT. These include the following:

- Using and customizing the toolbar
- Connecting and disconnecting network drives
- Sharing your directories and drives with others
- Setting permissions for your shared drives and directories
- Sending mail with attached files that you select in File Manager
- Working with long filenames

NOTE

Advanced File Manager options such as NTFS security options prevent copying or moving of files, enable changing ownership of files, and let you keep an audit list of who uses your shared drives and directories. These and other security features are covered in Chapter 8.

Using and Customizing the Toolbar

As with toolbars in other programs, File Manager's toolbar, shown in Figure 3.21, is just a shortcut for common procedures. Just click on a button and something happens.

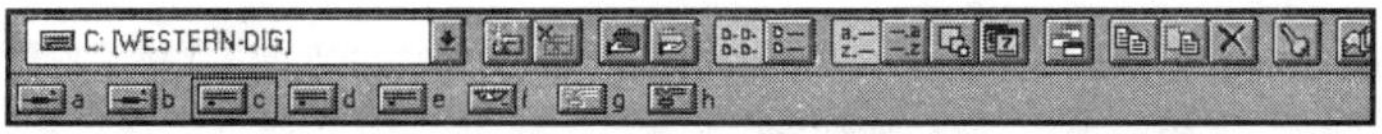

FIGURE 3.21.
The File Manager toolbar.

At first you won't remember what the buttons do because the pictures on them are so small. The easiest way to figure it out is to choose Options | Customize Toolbar. From here you can see the description of each button, as shown in Figure 3.22. You also can add buttons from the left side and remove buttons from the right side. Any buttons that appear in the right side of the box when you click on OK subsequently appear on the toolbar.

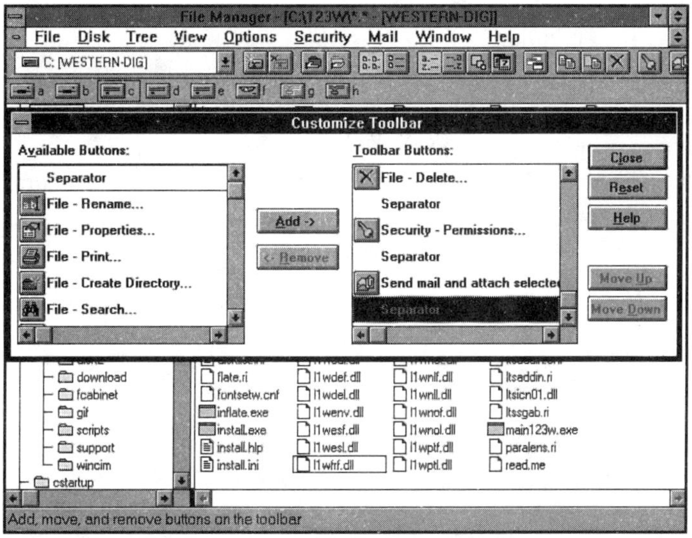

FIGURE 3.22.
Configuring the toolbar.

TIP

If you click and hold a button on the toolbar, a description will be displayed in the status bar in the lower-left corner. If you decide not to perform the action, just move the mouse cursor away from the icon while still pressing the mouse button, then release the mouse button.

Connecting to a Network Directory

Before you can use someone else's directory, that person has to intentionally *share* it, and you have to *connect* to it. Sharing and connecting are both achieved via File Manager commands. In general, this is referred to as *making connections.*

NOTE

Actually, a user with Administrator status can connect to any machine's hard disk, even if it's not shared. This is because all machines create a hidden share for each root directory in the machine. For example, in a two-drive machine called SRV, an administrator can connect to the hidden shares `\\SRV\C$` and `\\SRV\D$`. NT automatically creates these hidden shares.

After connections are established between workstations on the net, they are by default remembered (although this can be defeated), both by NT and by some other network types such as Windows for Workgroups. The next time you boot up, the operating systems will attempt to reestablish the connections. With NT and WFW, this is true even if your system powered down unexpectedly (that is, due to a power outage or inadvertent flip of the switch) or if a system crash occurred. The reconnection is simply part of the boot-up sequence.

Before you can use files stored on other network workstations, you have to connect to the drive and directory where they are stored. This operation is done through File Manager.

NOTE

Some applications, such as Notepad, are UNC file-aware and can be accessed without mapping a drive to a remote drive. You can specify the UNC name \\ROADTRIP\C\AUTOEXEC.BAT in the File Open dialog to open a remote computer's AUTOEXEC.BAT file.

1. From File Manager, choose Disk | Connect Network Drive, or click on the Connect Network Drive button in the toolbar. A large dialog box appears, as shown in Figure 3.23.
2. Double-click on the workgroup, then choose the user station. The shared directories appear in the lower pane.
3. Double-click on the directory you want to gain access to. After a few seconds, during which NT polls the network for shared directories, you see a listing of workgroups and stations in the bottom window.

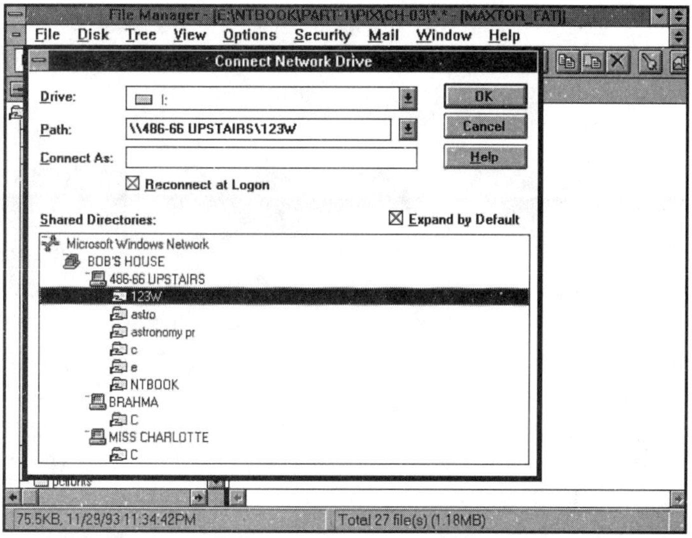

FIGURE 3.23.
Connecting to a network drive is achieved from the Disk menu.

NOTE

The volumes available to you, as well as the exact layout of dialog boxes, might look different if you're using Novell NetWare or another network in addition to Windows for Workgroups.

4. File Manager assigns the next available drive letter to any new connection, and thus the top line is filled in. You don't have to change this unless you want to. You can change this from the drop-down Drive list if you desire, but normally, leaving it alone suffices.
5. In the bottom pane, double-click on the workgroup containing the station you want access to (unless workstations on the group are already showing). All the workstation users in the group appear under it in a list. This is like double-clicking on a directory to see a list of its subdirectories.

TIP

If the Expand by Default box is enabled, workgroups and workstations on the network are automatically listed in the dialog box, so you don't have to double-click your way down the list. On smaller networks, you'll want to keep this setting enabled. On larger networks with lots of stations and shared directories, however, this can slow down the opening of this box, because polling all the workstations takes time. It also takes a bit of a toll on the network's overall throughput, because the polling ties up the net at least momentarily.

6. Double-click on the workstation you think contains the directory you want to use. Its shared directories now appear below it, along with their *sharenames* (the name the directory was published with—something the person sharing the file decided to name it).

NOTE

Your station also appears in the listing of workstations on the network when you select your workgroup in the list. Any directories you might have shared also appear. At first blush it doesn't make sense to connect to your own directories over the network, although NT allows it. However, being able to connect to one of your own shares can be quite useful. You can use it like the MS-DOS `ASSIGN` command, or you can use it to copy or back up data from your CD-ROM drive. Normally, you can't back up a CD-ROM to tape, for instance, but if you share it, then connect to it, it becomes a regular network drive and can be accessed as such. You never know when this feature might come in handy.

7. Double-click on the directory you want to connect to. If the drive is password-protected, you're asked to enter the password; if not, no dialog box appears. A new drive icon appears on the drive bar near the top of your File Manager window; you can use it like you use any other disk icon. Select it to see the files it contains, run programs, and so forth.
8. Normally, when a connection is made to another machine, the network uses your current username to identify who is making the connection. (This information is stored in the workgroup or domain's user database, and it determines the level of accessibility to remote directories you have.) The *current* username is the name you logged in with and is the default unless you fill in the Connect As text area. If you want to connect to a remote NT system's directory and have higher privileges than those assigned to the current username, enter a different username in the Connect As portion of the dialog box. (Of course, you must already have an account under this alternative name for this to work.)

NOTE

That last point might be academic, but remember that what appears in your File Manager as a network drive is in reality the directory on a remote drive. This typically is a subdirectory, not the root directory, so you're not really seeing everything on the drive—just selected portions that the owner decided to share. Also remember that drive letters on your workstation are assigned in the order that you connected to remote directories. If you set up some Program Manager icons that point to files on a network drive, you want to make sure that the drives are reconnected in the same order, or at least that you give the connections the right drive letter assignments when you reconnect.

TIP

The Path line in the dialog box lists the last 10 network paths you have connected to. If you regularly connect to the same paths, you might want to use that list rather than work your way down the tree in the lower box.

TIP

If you know the name of the computer you want to connect to but don't know the directory names, you can enter just the computer's name in the Path box and click on OK. This lists the shared directories, which you can then choose by clicking on them.

A special type of shared directory called an *administrative root share* is restricted to those logged on as administrators or backup users (two types of user groups that have a high level of permissions). Administrative root shares aren't displayed in the big dialog box that lists available directories on the network. To connect to such a root share, you have to manually type in the pathname, such as \\SERVER1\C$.

In Microsoft-based networks, the path for a network drive is preceded by a double backslash (\\), followed by the workstation name and the sharename. To connect to a share called PROJECTS on a server named SALES, for instance, the path would be written \\SALES\PROJECTS.

Disconnecting from a Network Directory

When you finish using a network directory, you might want to disconnect from it. To disconnect from a network directory, do the following:

1. Finish any work you're doing with that drive, such as editing files and running programs.

2. Choose Disk | Disconnect Network Drive, or click on the Disconnect Network Drive icon.
3. Choose the drive from the resulting list, shown in Figure 3.24.

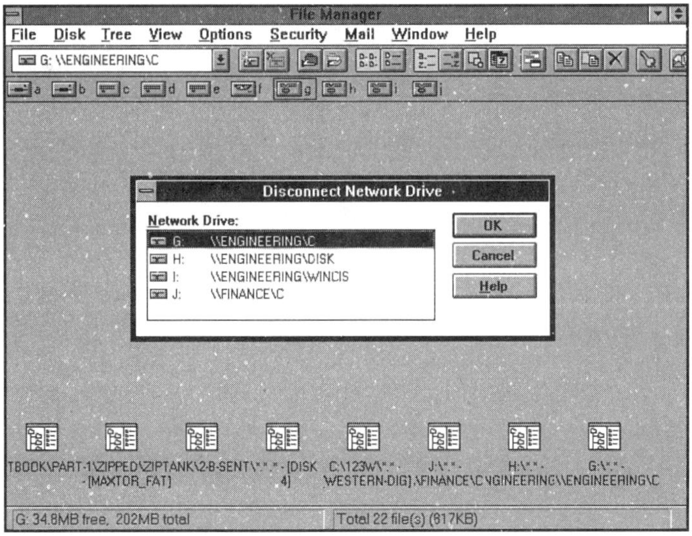

FIGURE 3.24.
The Disconnect Network Drive dialog box.

4. Click on OK. The drive is eliminated from the drive bar in File Manager, and your access to that drive ends.

Sharing Directories with Others on the Network

Before other workgroup or domain members can use *your* files, you have to *share* the directory containing them. Shared directories can have passwords, and they also can have specific privileges (read-only or read/write). If you have a bunch of files that you want people to be able to see but not alter, just put them into a new directory and share it as read-only. If you want only specific people to be able to alter the files, share them protected by a password by following these steps:

TIP

You can also use NTFS enhanced security features to restrict directory and file access to individual groups and users. For instance, you could set up a share called SALES that contains monthly reports. By using the Security menu option, you could specify read-only access for management while providing read-write access for accounting. Permissions are discussed in greater detail in Chapter 10.

1. Click on the directory.
2. Chose Disk | Share As. If you don't have the privilege to share a directory, a dialog box appears, stating `The network request is not supported`. Assuming you do have sharing privileges, a dialog box like the one shown in Figure 3.25 appears.

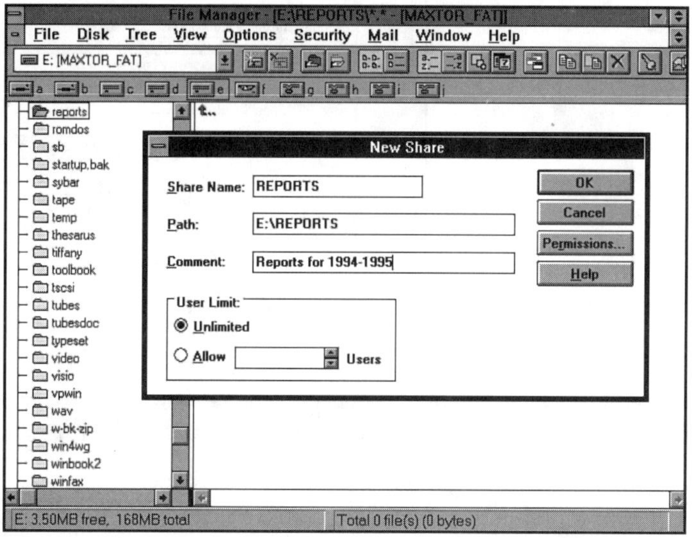

FIGURE 3.25.
The New Share dialog box.

3. Notice that I've filled in some information. I wanted to share the E:\REPORTS directory. Other users see it listed with the directory name REPORTS and a description of `Reports for 1994-1995` (if the networking operating system attaching to it supports this feature). Fill in these areas according to your needs. The comment area is optional.

   The Share Name is, by default, the same name as the directory itself. If the directory has a long filename, a dialog box alerts you that DOS (and therefore Windows 3.1) workstations cannot see the entire name and asks whether you want to shorten it. See Figure 3.26.

   Note that other NT stations can see the long name.

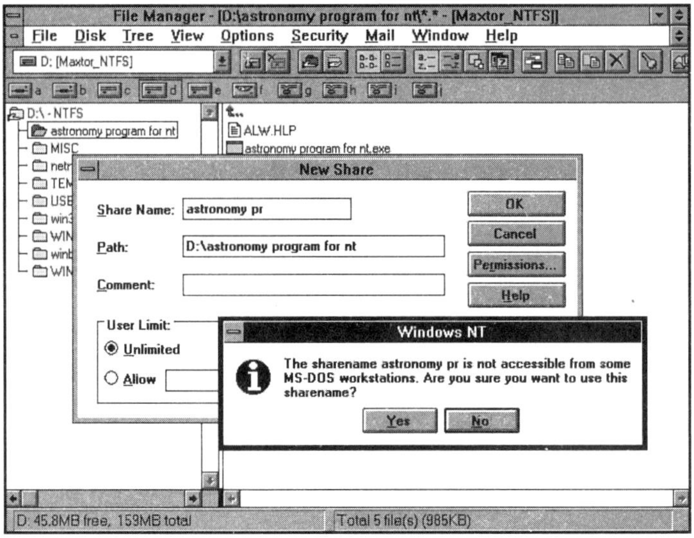

FIGURE 3.26.
The Alert box for long filename directory sharing.

CAUTION

Because publishing the root of a disk allows network users into all directories on the disk, doing so can be dangerous. Be cautious when doing this. As I mentioned, NT automatically creates root shares, but only administrators can access them, as indicated by the $ after the drive letter.

TIP

Because MS-DOS applications are limited by the DOS eight-letter file-naming convention, you might want to elaborate on a FAT directory name that you're sharing. Still, you have only 12 spaces to work with here, and the name must conform to DOS file-naming conventions (spaces and some characters are illegal). You might, for example, lengthen REPORTS to REPORTS.94.

4. You might want to limit the number of users who can simultaneously access the directory. Why? Because your system's local performance, or even its ability to service remote users, might bog down if too many users connect to the directory at once. If you share a popular directory and notice significant system sluggishness, or if you find that other workers complain of slow service from your server, try decreasing the user limit.

5. Next, you have the option of setting specific permissions in order to restrict the use of the directory by others.

NOTE

The protection to set from this dialog box is available regardless of whether the volume is of the FAT, HPFS, or NTFS type. However, these permissions apply only to directories and files accessed over the network. Recall that NTFS partitions also can have special permissions already set on them by the particular NT system's administrator. If they do, these permissions will operate in addition to those set here. The NTFS permissions are discussed in Chapter 8.

CAUTION

If you don't set the permissions, anyone can access the directory, and everyone will have full access (meaning read/write access and even the ability to delete files in the directory, if they wish).

Set the share permissions (called *permissions through a shared directory,* incidentally) by clicking on the Permissions button in the New Share dialog box. The dialog box shown in Figure 3.27 appears.

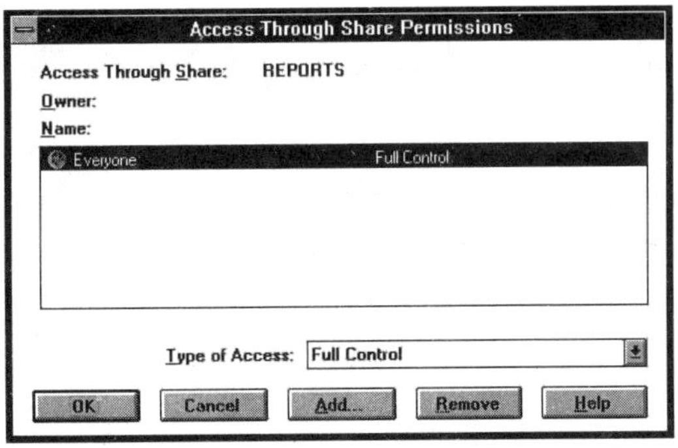

FIGURE 3.27.
Set permissions for access from this dialog box.

Change the general permission level by opening the drop-down list box in the Type of Access area. You have four choices:

Type	*Result*
No Access	Nobody can get into the directory. You might use this setting to temporarily block access for some reason.
Read	Enables viewing filenames, changing the shared directory's subdirectories, running applications in the directory, and opening document files.
Change	All permissions listed previously, plus adding files and subdirectories, altering data in files, and deleting subdirectories and files.
Full Control	All permissions listed previously, plus changing permissions and taking "ownership."

NOTE

These last two permissions apply only to NTFS partitions.

NOTE

A more in-depth discussion of permissions and security as it pertains to directory and file sharing can be found in Chapter 10.

CAUTION

Note that a user has the same rights to all the subdirectories of a shared parent directory. Be careful not to share directories that have subdirectories unless you want those to become accessible with the same level of restriction. However, you can manually set the access rights for each subdirectory from File Manager on NTFS partitions only.

6. The permission level you choose applies to all groups of users shown in the list at the top of the dialog box. Normally this is "Everybody," encompassing all classes of users (from administrators to guests). If you want to fine-tune which groups have access to the directory or directories you're sharing, click on Remove (to remove everyone), then click on Add (to add select groups of users).

NOTE

NT comes with a standard set of 10 groups. However, the system administrator can create new groups. By creating a group that includes only certain employees, such as "Finance Group," the system administrator provides an easy way to enable a user to limit directory access to just a few individuals.

7. Click on OK. The directory becomes available to any other users who are attached to your workgroup. It appears in the File Manager window with a little hand under it—a reminder that you're making an offering to the public.

Changing a Share's Properties

You can change permissions or other settings pertaining to the share after the fact, if necessary. For example, you might decide to limit the number of connections to the share.

1. Highlight the directory in File Manager, and choose Disk | Share As or click on the Share Directory button in the toolbar.
2. The Share dialog box that appears, letting you make changes, is the same one that appeared when you originally shared the directory.

TIP

You can't make changes to the sharename from this box. You can choose other names that the same directory is currently shared under (a directory *can* be shared more than once under different names), but you can't add a new name. To change the name of a share, click on New Share, then share it with the new name. If you want, you can delete the original sharename, as I explain in the following section.

Unsharing a Directory You've Shared

When you want to remove a workstation's directories from the network, follow these steps:

NOTE

You can stop the sharing of files or directories only if you're a member of the Administrator or Power Users groups.

1. Choose Disk | Stop Sharing, or click on the Stop Sharing button in the toolbar. The dialog box shown in Figure 3.28 displays a list of your shared directories.

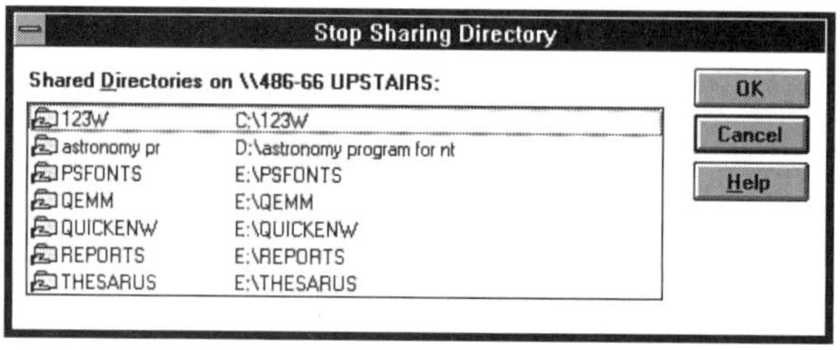

FIGURE 3.28.
The Stop Sharing dialog box lists currently shared directories on the workstation.

2. Double-click on the directory you want to stop sharing. (You can select more than one by pressing the Ctrl key and clicking on each directory, then clicking on OK.) If workgroup users are currently connected to the directory, you see a message indicating this and warning you against terminating the share. See Figure 3.29.

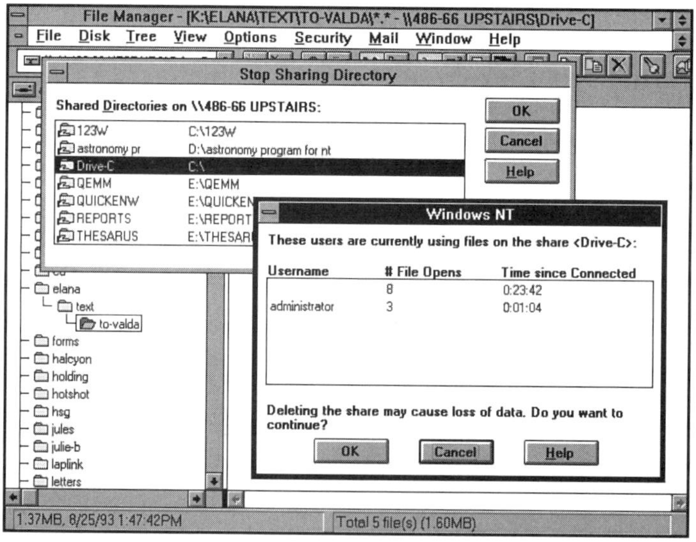

FIGURE 3.29.
NT warns you if others are using your shared directory and asks for confirmation.

> **NOTE**
>
> In Windows NT 3.1, this box has a bug and therefore doesn't function properly. (This problem has been fixed in version 3.5.) Names of users might not appear, but the number of files they have open will. Notice in Figure 3.29 that someone has eight files open, but it isn't reported who. If you must know (for example, to warn that person to close the files before you quit sharing), follow the steps listed next.

If you really want to terminate, click on Yes, but be aware that other users might lose their data—particularly if the dialog box indicates that files are open. Closing a shared directory like this is a great way to lose friends, so normally you would click on No, get the other user to sign off from your directory, and then try again later.

TIP

You might want to use the Chat program (covered at the end of Chapter 6) or make a quick phone call to users of the directory to alert them of your intention to remove the drive from the network.

If you want to know what's really going on with a directory (that is, who's using it and whether files are open), do the following:

1. Run Control Panel and choose Server.
2. Click on the In Use button. A dialog box like the one shown in Figure 3.30 appears, displaying information about each file, its location, and its user.

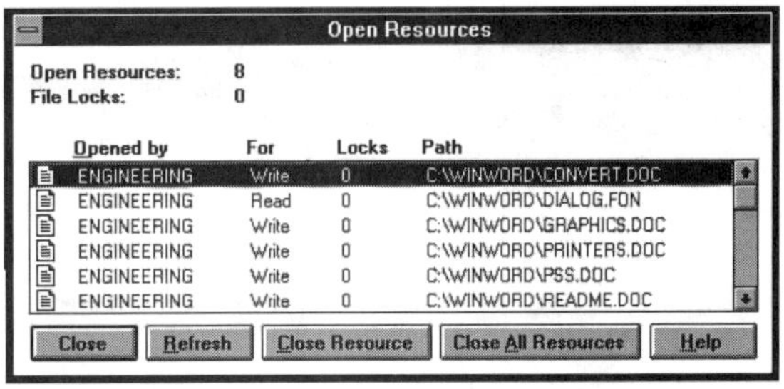

FIGURE 3.30.
Examining who is using files on your NT machine.

3. Click on Close, then click on Cancel.

CAUTION

Be careful not to click on Close Resource or Close All Resources unless you mean to immediately cut users off. The list is just to help you make a decision about terminating the connection using this procedure.

Seeing Who's Using a Particular File

Even without using Control Panel, perhaps, you might want to determine which files on your machine are likely to be in use. If you do, you can list current users of the file right from File Manager.

1. Select the file in the file pane of File Manager.
2. Choose File | Properties or press Alt-Enter. This brings up the Properties box.
3. Click on Open By. This will list the current users, as shown in Figure 3.31.

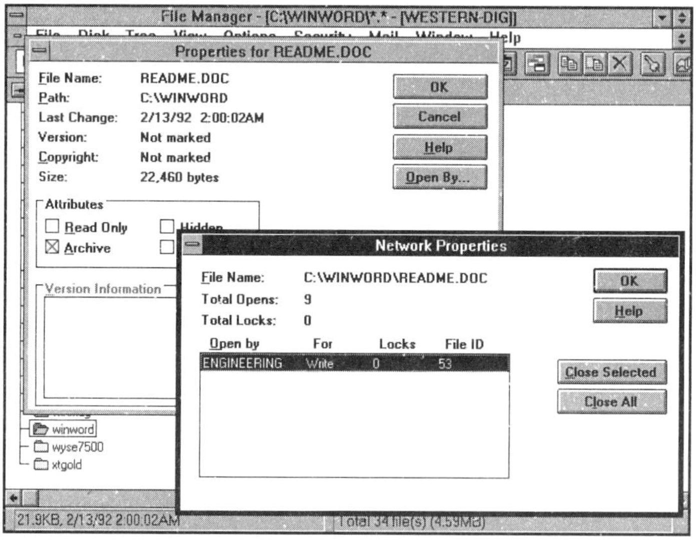

FIGURE 3.31.
The list of current users of a file can be displayed from File Manager, using the Open By button in the Properties box.

Sending Mail with Attached Files Selected in File Manager

The Mail | Send Mail option on the menu bar has a simple purpose. It lets you easily send a file to another person on the network, embedding the file in a letter. If the file is a sound or a picture, this is a neat way of including it in a communiqué to a colleague. Because it's embedded using Windows OLE (object linking and embedding), all the recipient has to do is double-click on the icon that represents the file, and it will run or open. Embedding a file in a missive also can be achieved through the MS-Mail program without the aid of File Manager. This feature is explained in Chapter 6.

Working with Long Filenames

This section discusses naming files with long filenames. Chapter 2 explained briefly what happens to long filenames when they're saved under the various disk file systems that NT supports. The following are the NTFS and DOS file-naming rules and some hints for using them.

The following rules apply to long filenames:

- NTFS and FAT enable you to give files and directories names of up to 256 characters in length.
- You can include an extension, separated from the rest of the name by a period, such as `1994 Sales Reports.WK3`.
- Spaces can be included.
- Special characters not allowed are `?`, `"`, `\`, `/`, `<`, `>`, `*`, `¦`, and `:`.
- Uppercase and lowercase are both allowed, and they display in listings. However, they won't be interpreted by NT or NT applications as being different from one another.

NT automatically generates shorter DOS-compatible filenames for every long name you create. It does this by

- removing illegal characters and replacing them with an underscore (_)
- removing any spaces in the name
- using only the last period that has three consecutive letters after it as the extension
- truncating the first name to six letters and adding a tilde (~) and a single-digit number as the last two characters of the first name

  For example:

Long Filename	*DOS Name*
Quarterly Sales Reports.WK3	QUARTE~1.WK3
Quarterly Sales Reports.Atlanta.Georgia.WK3	QUARTE~1.WK3
Qrtr[Sales]Reports from Atlanta,Georgia.WK3	QRTR_S~1.WK3

TIP

Recall that DOS programs with files that have long filenames can be used in two ways: in a DOS window under NT, or by sharing the directory they're on. (If you boot up with DOS on the NT machine, NTFS partitions are invisible.) After a directory is shared for the network, NT does its magic on the filenames. Even

DOS-based workstations, seeing their shortened names, can connect to the directories and use the files. Of course, 32-bit programs won't be able to run, but document files and 16-bit executables work fine. In any case, you might want to adopt a naming convention that makes sense to you when the longer names are converted to shorter DOS names. Try to use only one period and use the extension that the application expects. Because the first six letters are the ones that are retained, pack as much description into those as possible. For instance, SALES for Frambo Computers 1994.WK3 would convert to something like SALES~1.WK3.

Just in case you're a bit rusty on DOS file-naming conventions, here are the rules that govern them:

- Eight letters maximum in the first part of the name
- After the first name, a period and up to three letters as the extension
- No spaces
- Any characters except <, >, +, *, ?, ,, =, ¦, ;, :, [,], /, \, ", or .
- Illegal names include PRN, COM1, COM2, COM, COM3, CON, LPT1, LPT2, LPT3, LPT4, NUL, and AUX

Displaying Short Filenames

Finally, if you're working with long filenames and you'd like to see the MS-DOS filenames, follow these steps:

1. Switch to the relevant drive window in File Manager.
2. Choose View | Partial Details. The dialog box shown in Figure 3.32 appears.

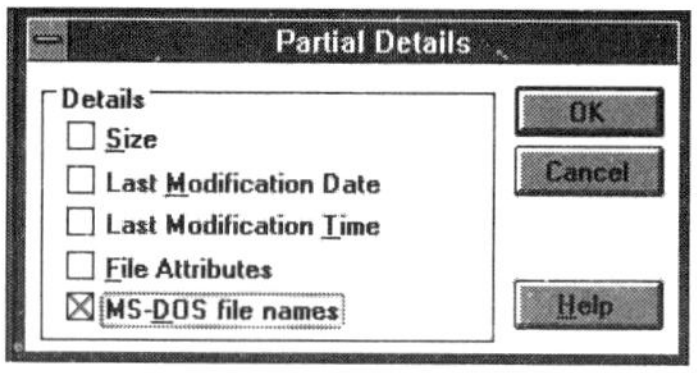

FIGURE 3.32.
Changing the viewing details to display short filenames.

3. Enable the check box to select MS-DOS filenames.

Using Control Panel

Like File Manager, Control Panel is in large measure identical to its Windows 3.1 relative.

TIP

All Control Panel settings are stored in the Windows NT Registry. The Registry is NT's analogue of Windows 3.1's WIN.INI, SYSTEM.INI, and several other .INI files, along with settings specific to NT (for example, usernames, passwords, auditing options, and other security features). Each user on a system has a separate batch of Registry settings. Most Control Panel settings a user makes won't carry over to all other users of a system. This rule has some exceptions, notably Fonts, which, when modified, affect all user sessions on that workstation.

Table 3.1 is a complete list of the Control Panel subprograms (applets) and their respective functions.

Table 3.1. Control Panel subprograms.

Applet	*Description*
Color	Customizes the colors Windows uses on-screen
Fonts	Adds or removes type styles from Windows and Windows applications
Ports	Initializes serial communications ports
Mouse	Fine-tunes mouse speed and button assignments
Desktop	Sets desktop background, icon spacing, screen saver, fast Alt-Tabbing, full drag, and cursor blink rate
Keyboard	Sets key repeat rate and delay before repeat
Printers	Runs Print Manager to install/remove printers, assign printer ports, select network printers, and manage print queue
International	Makes settings that vary between countries, such as formats for currency, date, and keyboard special characters
System	Sets virtual memory paging size, DOS Window environment variables, default bootup operating system, and tasking priorities
Date/Time	Sets the computer's internal date and time
Network	Joins a workgroup/domain, adding, removing, and configuring network drivers for various types of network cards

continues

Table 3.1. continued

Applet	*Description*
Cursors	Fine-tunes the various system cursors
Display	Selects the video driver, resolution, refresh frequency, font size, and color palette
Sound	Assigns sounds to system events and disables/enables sounds
MIDI Mapper	Adjusts MIDI key and patch assignments for non-Microsoft standard synths attached to your computer
Drivers	Adds, removes, and configures software drivers for add-in cards such as sound and video cards
Server	For network administrators: Allows observing who is connected to the local system's directories and what local resources are shared and/or open; manages directory replication and system alert routing (such as impending power-down)
Services	Manages the various system software services by individually starting and stopping them and by configuring which ones automatically start at bootup
Devices	Controls when hardware device services (drivers) start and stop
UPS	Sets how an optional uninterruptible power supply (UPS) alerts the NT machine of a power failure, and how NT powers down and warns users without loss of data

You might notice several interesting (and possibly confusing) additions here, particularly those pertaining to system services and devices. If you've experimented with these at all, or at least opened their dialog boxes, you know what I mean. The distinction between such things as devices and services, what you can start and stop, and so forth, can be confusing to anyone familiar with DOS's way of loading device drivers at bootup. After a device driver is loaded in DOS, it's in memory and running, period; there's no control after that. Those familiar with UNIX will be more at home with the notion of being able to load, start, or stop devices while the operating system is running.

Details of all the Control Panel settings can be found in Chapters 9 and 10.

NOTE

Print Manager is a substantial topic warranting a separate chapter. Refer to Chapter 4 for information on printer installation, configuration, use of network printers, and the NT print spooler.

Aside from the self-explanatory Cursors, which lets you change some of the cursor shapes a bit, the other new Control Panel choices primarily concern NT system administration. These options are not available to all users, but only to those with higher-level privileges. Therefore, coverage of them has been relegated to Chapter 10.

Locking Your Workstation

All the computer security in the world is of no value unless you take advantage of it. It doesn't take a "back-door man" or a hacker to get into your computer files if you just walk away from your desk with File Manager sitting right there on the screen. When you get up to go to the lavatory or out to lunch, think about the value of your files and take precautions. It's probably not necessary to be paranoid about computer crime, but it can't hurt to be safe.

NT has a built-in, easy-to-use trick for locking your computer without logging off and having to restart again. It's also good protection from prying eyes.

1. Press Ctrl-Alt-Delete. A dialog box with a Lock button in it appears.

NOTE

Your network or system administrator might ask you to change your password from time to time. You do so using this box.

2. Click on Lock. A dialog box reports the time you locked (so people can see when you were last physically present at the station) and reminds you how to get back in.
3. To unlock the station, press Ctrl-Alt-Delete as instructed. You see a box similar to the original login dialog box you see when you start an NT session.
4. Enter your password, and you're back up, happy in the knowledge that nobody accidentally (or intentionally) messed with your system.

Logging Off and Shutting Down

It's important to remember to tell users (and to remember yourself) that correct NT session termination is imperative. It's also achieved differently than in Windows 3.1. Correct termination of a session is more important for NT machines than for Windows 3.1 machines, partly due to the possibility that other users are connected to resources on your system. You certainly don't want to just hit the power switch while other users are in the middle of a print job or editing files when your NT machine is acting as a server.

But that's only part of the story. The other pivotal point is that a typical NT multiuser machine supports a number of separate users from one single machine. Recall that a complex file called the Registry stores numerous settings pertaining to each user's work habits (such as Program Manager, File Manager, and Control Panel settings) and a host of other preferences and administrator-declared permissions. Shutting down an NT session improperly can cause damage or loss in the Registry. This can be a real bummer, particularly because there's only one Registry, and it contains information about all the users on the system. Loss of or damage to the Registry can render the system completely unusable, which sometimes requires a complete reinstallation. In some cases, even the NT Emergency Repair disk won't help you recover your configuration unless you update the repair information periodically.

WARNING

The primary problem in just shutting down the system with the on/off switch is that data is cached in NT's dynamic disk cache. This cache includes the Registry files. Just turning off your machine instead of performing an orderly shutdown can make NT completely unusable. Many NT installations have had to be reinstalled because the user forgot this single point. Always use the Shutdown command before powering down.

TIP

You can use the RDISK utility to update your repair information and create a new repair disk to aid in preventing catastrophic loss due to a power failure or accidental shutdown.

Logoff Versus Shutdown

Before getting into the actual procedure of logging off and shutting down, a little theory is in order—particularly for anyone raised on DOS and Windows.

As you might have gathered along the way, NT's executive kernel offers certain services—resource sharing, screen and keyboard I/O, and so forth. These functions are internal to NT, and they run as long as NT is up—and NT is running as long as the NT logon screen is up. This means that even if nobody has logged onto an NT machine, its services still are running over the network and are available to network users. All the shares that were last made (typically by an administrator) become available as soon as the machine boots.

Therefore, when a user logs off, this isn't really analogous to terminating a Windows or Windows for Workgroups session. You won't be cutting off users who might be connected to your workstation, and you don't really have to think about other users unless you're considering a shutdown of the system.

A true shutdown, on the other hand, closes all open files and terminates all service on the NT machine, so you should consider who's using what before running one. If, however, you want to take the lazy approach, NT will cover you. If network users are connected to the station's resources, an alert box notifies you of this and asks you to confirm the shutdown.

TIP

Incidentally, a shutdown can take a little time. Be prepared to wait a minute or so for it to complete.

CAUTION

If nobody is logged onto the system and the Ctrl-Alt-Delete message is displayed, this doesn't mean that you can power down. If you're working on a Windows NT Server system, someone must log onto the system and either choose Shutdown from Program Manager's File menu or press Ctrl-Alt-Delete again and choose Shutdown. On a Windows NT Workstation, the logon dialog includes a Shutdown button that can be used to shut down the system. You can enable this same dialog option for NT Servers by setting the registry key `HKEY_LOCAL_MACHINE\SOFTWARE\Microsoft\WindowsNT\CurrentVersion\Winlogon\ShutdownWithoutLogon` to 1.

Logging Off

Here are the steps for logging off:

1. Close any open applications, especially if you haven't saved files you've been working with.

NOTE

Most applications are good at warning you if you've forgotten to save edited files, but don't count on it.

2. Switch to Program Manager.
3. Choose File | Logoff or File | Shutdown. The dialog box shown in Figure 3.33 appears.

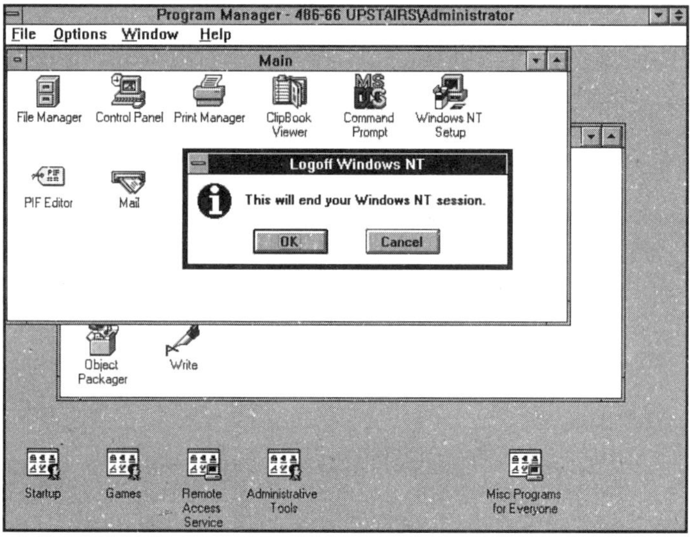

FIGURE 3.33.
Logging off.

4. Click on OK to end your user session.

An alternative method precludes having to get to Program Manager. Just press Ctrl-Alt-Delete from anywhere in NT. A multipurpose dialog box appears. Just click on Log Off.

Shutting Down

Take care when shutting down, because network users might be affected by a shutdown.

1. Check who is on the system and make sure they won't lose data. (Refer to the section titled "Using File Manager" earlier in this chapter and to the section titled "Server" in Chapter 10 for the techniques to use.)
2. Close any open applications, especially if you haven't saved files you've been working with.
3. Switch to Program Manager.
4. Choose File | Shutdown. The dialog box shown in Figure 3.34 appears.
5. Click on OK to end your NT session.

An alternative is to press Ctrl-Alt-Delete from anywhere in NT. A multipurpose dialog box appears. Just click on Shutdown.

With either method, wait until a dialog box appears that says it's OK to turn off the computer before you actually do so.

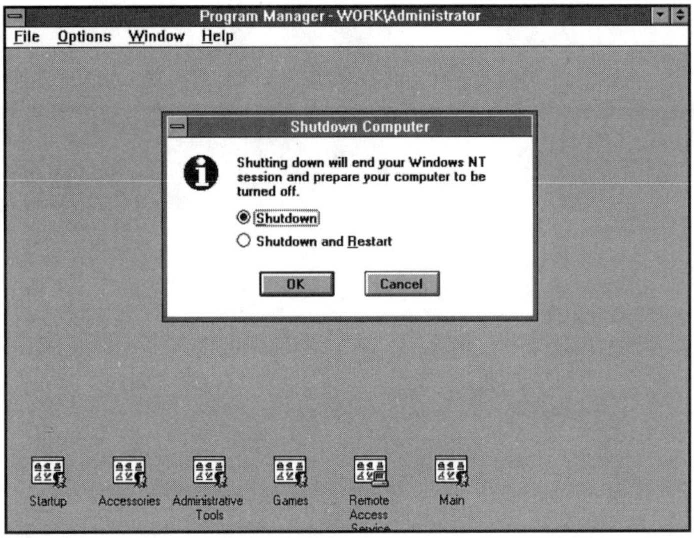

FIGURE 3.34.
Shutting down.

Summary

This chapter covered NT's basic operational procedures. Typical NT workstation users reading this chapter will have gained enough knowledge to organize their documents and applications, run applications in a variety of ways, manage files and directories over the network, and make some changes to their Windows environment.

The next chapter covers the use of the Print Manager for setting up, sharing, and managing printers, both locally and over the network.

Print Manager

4

IN THIS CHAPTER

Chapter 8, "Installing Windows NT," discusses the installation of printer driver software during the Setup process. If you stipulate a local printer type at that time, the NT system will have a default printer driver already installed. If not, you have to use Print Manager to install one.

As with Windows 3.1, unless Print Manager is disabled, Windows applications running under NT hand off data to NT, which in turn invokes Print Manager to spool the data to a specified printer. This is true with both 32-bit and 16-bit Windows applications.

Unlike Windows 3.1, however, NT prevents any application from writing *directly* to the printer port. (In Windows 3.1, DOS applications don't pass through Windows; they must handle printer interfacing independently, and they *are* allowed direct port access.) In NT, any such attempt by applications to directly write to hardware is trapped by the security manager and either is rerouted to the NT printer driver or simply fails.

NOTE

Unlike Windows 3.1, incidentally, Windows for Workgroups *does* provide printer port access contention.

In this way, Print Manager automatically takes control of all printing jobs, whether from OS/2, POSIX, Win32, Win16, or DOS applications. Print Manager receives the data, queues up the jobs, routes them to the correct printer, and, when necessary, issues error or other appropriate messages to print job originators. As in Windows 3.1, a Print Manager user interface provides a facility for users or administrators to manage jobs (that is, reorder the queue, delete jobs, and reroute jobs).

In Windows 3.1, printer driver installation and configuration (making connections) are done through the Printers applet in Control Panel, while print job management is done through the Print Manager application program. Windows NT combines both functions into Print Manager. (Control Panel still has a Printers icon, but it simply calls up Print Manager.) Menus in Print Manager enable you to install, configure, connect, disconnect, and remove printers and drivers.

This chapter explains these features, as well as procedures for local and network print queue management. Some basics of print management also are discussed, providing a primer for the uninitiated or for those whose skills are a little rusty.

Print Manager Basics

As you may know, when you print from non-Windows programs in DOS, your computer and printer cease to be available for other tasks. You're reduced to taking a coffee break, going for a jog around the block (probably not a bad idea), or pulling out a pencil and paper to continue your work. Programs or hardware add-ons called *print spoolers* get around this problem, effectively fooling the computer into thinking the print job is done, and letting you get back to work while the program prints your files in the background.

A spooler program (PRINT.COM or PRINT.EXE, depending on your version of DOS) is supplied with every copy of DOS. UNIX systems have similar utilities, as does OS/2. They let you specify a list of files to be printed (such a list is called the *print queue*), and they print it while you return to your work. However, using them is often awkward at best.

Although the Windows 3.1 Print Manager came under fire for being a bit sluggish (especially with graphics) and for lacking features, at least it was a system-wide spooler with the graphical interface and convenience typical of Windows applications. The NT Print Manager might not be perfect, but it's far superior to its predecessor, and it certainly is much stronger in its networking support. For example, after a printer is set up, the user never needs to know which physical port a printer is connected to. Therefore, there are no more "Is it LPT1 or LPT2?" hassles. As of release 3.1, NT's Print Manager feature mix was quite rich. Here are the highlights:

- You can install, configure, and remove printer drivers right from Print Manager. There's no need to run Control Panel.
- A toolbar makes execution of frequently used commands convenient.
- NT's Print Manager has security management for printer sharing. Groups of users (administrators, guests, power users, and so forth) can be assigned rights for ownership, sharing, unsharing, and queue management.
- If you're on a network, you can manage network printer connections by displaying available printers, sharing your local printer, and connecting to and disconnecting from network printers.
- Due to NT's multithreading and preemptive multitasking, simultaneous printing and application functioning are smoother than under Windows 3.1. You can start printing and immediately go back to work, not having to wait until spooling for Print Manager to finish.
- While one document is being printed, other applications can run and print. Print Manager simply adds subsequent documents to the queue.
- Default settings for such options as number of copies, paper tray, page orientation, and so forth are automatically used during print jobs so you don't have to manually set them each time.
- A window displays jobs currently being printed or in the queue waiting to be printed, along with an indication of the current print job's progress.
- Easily rearranges the order of the print queue and deletes (cancels) print jobs.

- Adjusts CPU priority for Print Manager to balance printing and application/ network throughput.
- Temporarily pauses or resumes printing without causing printer time-out problems.
- Sets printer properties, such as times of day when a network printer is available for use.
- Chooses among 48 different *forms* drivers—canned forms sizes such as stationery, business letter, legal, and envelope sizes—to include as part of the printer driver.
- Creates a *pool* of printers, all of which are specified as the default printer. When you print a document, the first available printer is used.
- Administers and audits the use of network print servers locally or remotely.

Installing and Configuring a Printer

As I mentioned, the Setup program prompts you to install a printer. If you elected to do so, or if you've installed printers in Windows 3.1, you'll be somewhat familiar with the procedure. If your printer is already installed and seems to be working fine, you probably can skip this section. However, if you need to install a new printer, modify or customize your current installation, or add additional printers to your setup, read on.

This section covers the following topics:

- How to install (or, in NT terms, *create*) a new printer
- How to select the printer port and make other connection settings
- How to set preferences for a printer
- How to install a printer driver that's not listed
- How to set the default printer
- How to select a printer when more than one is installed
- How to set up a printer pool
- How to remove a printer from your setup

About Printer Installation

First, a reminder. As I mention in Chapter 8, "Installing Windows NT," before installing hardware, including printers, you should read the README.WRI file that comes with NT for possible pertinent information about your brand of printer. You should read this file because it's full of helpful hints not included in the manuals. It includes a section on printers so recent that I can't include it reliably in this book—it changes too often, particularly as Microsoft adds new printers to their list.

TIP

Another file, PRINTER.WRI (*not* PRINTERS.WRI—that's the Windows 3.1 printer file), contains a list of printers and the DIP-switch settings necessary to work with NT.

With that said, here is the overall game plan for installing a printer:

- Install the printer driver file onto your hard disk from the NT master floppy or CD, or from a disk supplied with your printer.
- Select the printer's port and relevant port settings.
- Check and possibly alter the default printer settings, such as the DPI (dots per inch) setting and memory settings.

After these steps are complete, your printer should work, and you probably won't need to do anything more. However, you can make several more customizations to your setup along the way. The options vary from printer to printer, but those of note include the following:

- Specifying the amount of time you want Windows to keep trying to print a document before alerting you to a printer problem
- Specifying the sharename for the printer, for other network users to see when they search the network for printers
- Setting job defaults pertaining to paper tray, two-sided printing, and paper orientation
- Stipulating a *separator file*—a file, usually one page long, that prints between each print job
- Selecting the default printer if you have more than one printer installed
- Choosing whether your printer should substitute its own fonts for certain Windows TrueType fonts
- Selecting printer settings relevant to page orientation, scaling, type of paper feed, halftone imaging, and when file header information (such as a PostScript "preamble") is sent to the printer
- Arranging security for the printer by setting permissions

If you want to modify only one of the settings for your currently installed printer, look for the section in this chapter that explains that topic and skip to it. You might, however, have to work your way toward the dialog box that contains the pertinent setting. Also note that Print Manager has context-sensitive Help built in. Point to an element on the screen and press F1. A relevant Help topic will likely appear.

NOTE

Printer security issues such as setting permission, conducting printer access auditing, and setting ownership are covered in Chapter 10.

Creating a Printer

As I mentioned earlier, printer setup in NT is called *creating a printer*. This is a another one of those weird Microsoft terms. This means installing a printer driver, setting some preferences, and, if it's networked, giving the printer a network name. You create a new printer under the following circumstances:

- You're connecting a new physical printer directly to your computer
- You're connecting a new physical printer to the network
- You want to print to formatted disk files that can later be sent to a particular type of printer
- You want to set up multiple printer configurations (preferences) for a single physical printer so you can switch between them without having to change your printer setup before each print job

Notice that a great deal of flexibility exists here, especially in the case of the last item. Recall that NT interfaces with the physical world through a hardware abstraction layer, and that internally NT is object-oriented. So, although printers are physical hardware, most of NT (up to the point where the hardware abstraction layer interfaces with printers) deals with printers as virtual devices. As a result, you can create any number of printer definitions for a given physical printer.

TIP

These definitions are actually called *printers,* but you can think of them as printer names, aliases, or named virtual devices.

For example, for a local printer (one connected directly to your computer) you could create a printer that prints in landscape orientation on long paper. Then you could create another printer for network users, one that prints in portrait orientation with standard paper and gives access only to specified users. You could even specify a lower priority for network print jobs so that your local print jobs would always be processed first.

NOTE

It's important to remember that the word *printer* (in NT documentation, online help, and this book) usually doesn't mean a physical printer. It usually means a virtual printer that you've set up in advance with Print Manager and that you choose to print to. It's a collection of settings that typically *points* to a physical printer, but it could just as well create a print file instead of paper output. Also remember that a single physical printer can have a number of printer setups with different configurations.

About Printer Drivers

A *printer driver* is a file whose job is to translate the data you want to print so that your printer knows how to print it. NT needs a specialized printer driver for each type of printer. Because many printers are actually functionally equivalent, a driver for a popular brand and model of printer (for example, an Epson or a Hewlett-Packard) often masquerades under different names for other printers. Although many popular printer drivers were supported by NT in its initial release, some offbeat printers aren't included. In cases where a driver for your printer isn't included with Windows, the printer's manufacturer might be able to supply one. The procedure for installing manufacturer-supplied drivers is covered later in this chapter.

A good printer driver takes advantage of all your printer's capabilities, such as its built-in fonts and graphics features. A poor printer driver might succeed in printing only draft-quality text, even from a sophisticated printer.

NOTE

If your printer isn't included in the list, consult the section in this chapter titled "What to Do if Your Printer Isn't Listed."

Creating a New Printer

You begin creating a printer by installing the printer driver.

NOTE

Only administrators and power users can create new printers. If you're logged on under another standard NT group, your permissions won't let you create a printer.

1. Open Control Panel and double-click on Printers (or run Print Manager from the Main group). Print Manager's main screen appears, as shown in Figure 4.1.

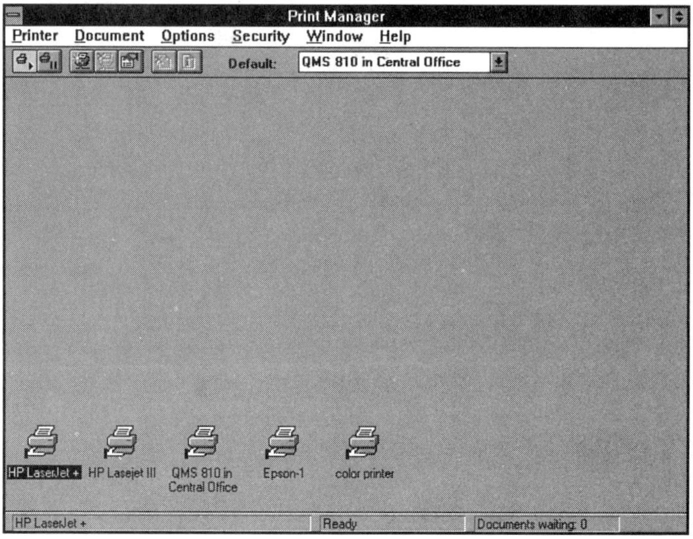

FIGURE 4.1.
Print Manager's main screen.

2. Choose Printer | Create Printer. A dialog box like that in Figure 4.2 appears.

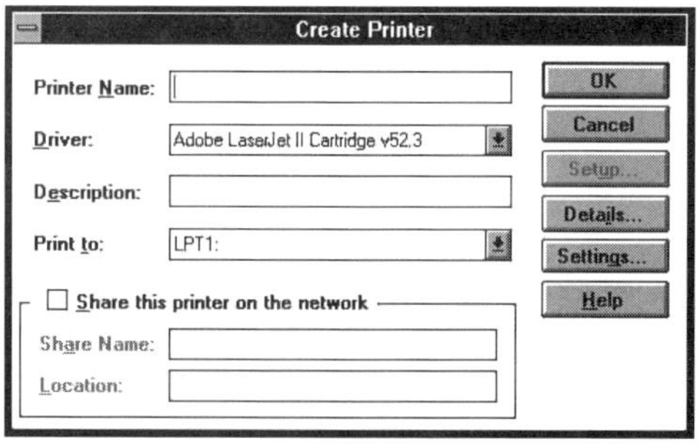

FIGURE 4.2.
The Create Printer dialog box. From here you can install a printer or modify a printer setup.

3. Type in a name for the printer. The maximum length is 32 characters. Try to make it meaningful. Typically, the name of the department—Sales, Marketing, and so forth—suffices. Network users see this name on their screens when they cruise the network for printers.

NOTE

If the printer will be shared with DOS and 16-bit Windows users, you might want to limit this name to 12 characters, because that's the maximum length those users will see.

4. Select your printer from the drop-down Driver list. Be sure to select the exact printer model, not just the correct brand name. Consult your printer's manual if you're in doubt about the model. What you enter here determines which printer driver file is used for this printer's definition.
5. Fill in the optional Description field with some information about the location, or other pertinent information. Something like `Joe's Laser Printer in Room 23` would be useful. Network users also see this description.
6. The Print To box contains a list of physical destinations for the printer data. In other words, where is the printer actually connected to your computer?

Port	*Notes*
LPT1:, LPT2:, LPT3:	The most common setting is LPT1, because most PC-type printers hook up to the LPT1 parallel port.
COM1:, COM2:, COM3:, COM4:	If you know your printer is of the *serial* variety, it's probably connected to the COM1 port. If COM1 is tied up for use with some other device, such as a modem, use COM2. If you choose a COM port, click on Settings to check the communications settings in the resulting dialog box. Set the baud rate, data bits, parity, start and stop bits, and flow control to match those of the printer being attached. Refer to the printer's manual to determine what the settings should be.
File	This is for printing to a disk file instead of to the printer. Later, the file can be sent directly to the printer, or sent to someone on floppy disk or over a modem. When you print to this printer name, you are prompted to enter a filename. (See the section in this chapter titled "Printing to a Disk File.")

Port	*Notes*
Other	Use this when you don't see the name of a local port you want to add to the standard list. Also use this when the printer is network-capable, such as an HP that has a network port, or a shared UNIX printer. For a networked HP printer, you'll have to stipulate the HP port address by choosing HP Network Port in the Print Destinations box. Another box comes up, asking for the port address and asking you to name the port. For a shared UNIX printer, stipulate Other in the Print Destination box, then specify LPR Port. Another box appears, asking for the IP address and the name of the shared printer.

NOTE

You won't see either the HP Network Port option or the LPR Port option unless the Data Link Control Protocol or the TCP/IP Protocol services have been added to the workstation's NT setup by way of Control Panel. Run Control Panel, choose Network, and choose Data Link Control or TCP/IP Protocol. For more information about network protocol installation, see Chapter 9, "Configuring Windows NT," which covers Control Panel.

7. If you want to make the printer available for network users, check the Share box and fill in the Location. The sharename is filled in for you, based on the Printer Name box above it. The Printer Name is the name that network users with NT-based workstations see when they're browsing for printers, so the Share Name is irrelevant. But DOS-based workstations need a name that conforms to DOS naming standards; this is what the Share Name supplies. The name you enter here (if you decide to change it) has to conform with DOS 12-letter naming rules.

NOTE

Filling in the location is optional, but it lets users know where to pick up their documents.

TIP

To allow UNIX clients to print to shared network printers, enable the TCP/IP Print Server service in Control Panel's Services applet. Select Startup, and configure the Startup Type as Automatic. Then start the service.

UNIX clients will need the IP address or DNS name of the print server (which is specified in the HOSTS file of the UNIX client) and the sharename of the printer in order to connect.

8. Click on OK. You likely will be instructed to insert one of the Windows NT disks into a floppy drive so that Windows can copy the appropriate printer driver from it onto your hard disk. If necessary, insert the disk, make sure the pathname of the drive is correct, and click on OK.

NOTE

If the printer driver with the correct name is already on the hard disk, you won't be instructed to insert a disk; the existing driver will be used. Also, NT remembers the location you installed NT from originally. If you installed from a CD-ROM, it's likely that the default location for files is always going to be the CD-ROM drive's logical name (typically some higher letter, such as E: or F:).

9. You are alerted to insert additional disks if they are needed for the font files. Just follow the instructions on-screen. After the printer is created, a Setup dialog box appears from which you can choose options (properties) that pertain to the type of printer. (See Figure 4.3.)

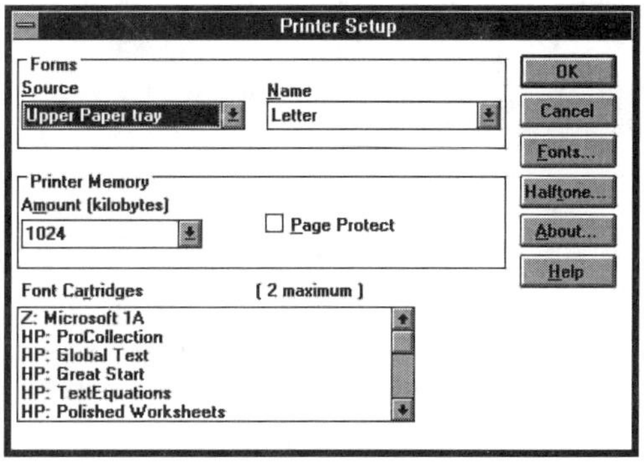

FIGURE 4.3.
The Printer Features dialog box appears after the driver is loaded.

You can change properties at this time if you wish, or you can just cancel the box and do it later. Chances are you won't have to make any changes if all you want to do is ensure that the printer works.

10. Click on OK. The printer is then given its own window, as shown in Figure 4.4.

FIGURE 4.4.
Each installed printer gets its own window.

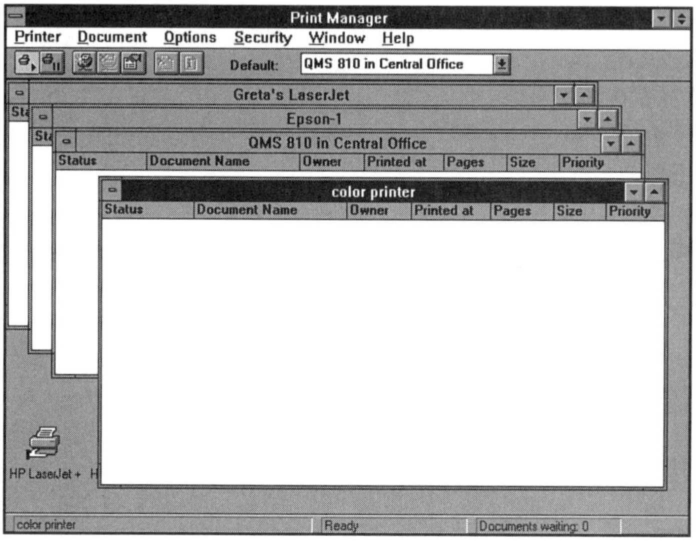

TIP

The fact that each printer is represented by a window or an icon is a little confusing at first. But think of a printer like you'd think of a document in a word processor or a spreadsheet program. In Print Manager, each printer is essentially a document, so it gets its own window within Print Manager's window. The name of the printer appears in the title bar of the window. The printer's window lists print jobs sent to the printer, as discussed in the section titled "Viewing the Queue." The printer's window can be iconized at the bottom of the Print Manager window.

11. Notice the Default Printer drop-down list near the top of the Print Manager window. The name that displays here before the list is opened is the *default printer.* The default printer is the printer that an application will use unless another is specifically chosen. Also, it's the printer that programs which don't provide an option for selecting a printer will use. (Notepad is an example of a program that doesn't allow you to choose a printer.) Normally, the first printer you install is the default. Change this if you want.

Supporting RISC and x86 Machines on the Same Printer Server

In three instances, you need to manually install a new driver for a printer that's already been created or that you are creating:

- When NT doesn't come with a driver for your printer
- When you've received an updated driver and you want to replace the old one with the update
- When your printer server is connected to both RISC and x86-based machines and thus needs two drivers per printer

The first two of these circumstances can be handled using the instructions in the next section. The third situation is discussed here.

Recall from Chapter 2 that recompilation is needed for applications to run on RISC stations. This is because RISC and x86 machines have dissimilar CPUs, each with its own instruction set. Because printer drivers are a type of program, they too must be rewritten or at least recompiled to run on RISC workstations.

When an application prints a document, it's passed to the operating system, which then directs it to the chosen virtual printer. The virtual printer contains all the preference settings, including the location (local or network path) of the driver. The driver is read in from disk and launched, and the data is processed by the driver and then passed to the printer (or to the printer server, which in turn passes it to the printer). Figure 4.5 shows this in block diagram form.

If a network contains a mix of RISC and x86 workstations, and these stations want to share a printer server, drivers for both systems must be available. Figure 4.6 illustrates this.

Typically, the drivers are stored in their respective workstations, but they can be placed on the server. In fact, driver files can be stored anywhere on the network, as long as the workstation doing the printing can access the driver at print time. The advantage of putting both drivers on the server is that any RISC workstation on the network can then use the printer.

If you want to store both drivers on an x86-based printer server, perform these steps at the server:

1. Create the x86 version of the printer using the steps explained earlier for creating a new printer. This printer is the one that other x86 workstations connect to. You can name it something like `x86 version of Joe's printer`.
2. Create another printer now for the RISC station. In the Create printer dialog box, open the drop-down Driver list box, scroll to the bottom of the list, and choose Other. Then click on OK.

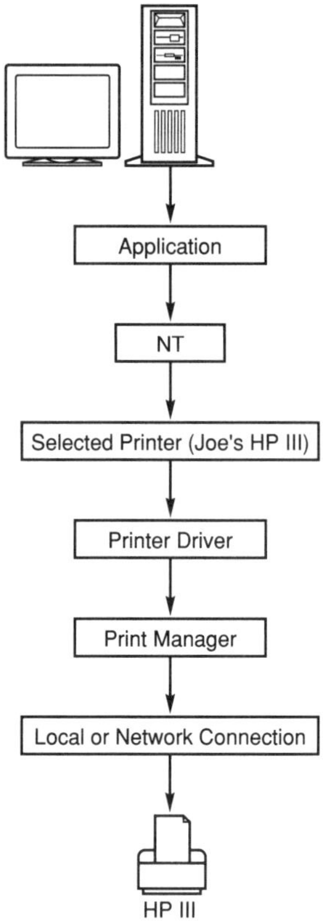

FIGURE 4.5.
The data path when an application prints.

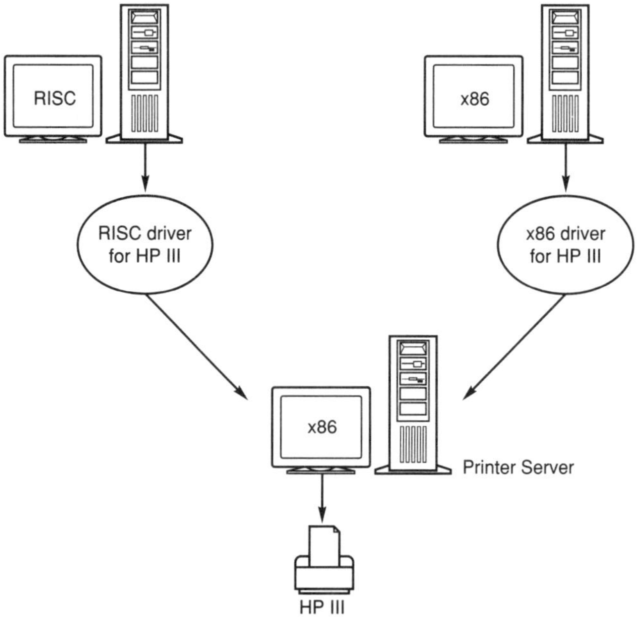

FIGURE 4.6.
RISC and x86 machines need separate printer drivers for the same printer.

3. You're prompted to enter the path where the PRINTERS.INF file and the RISC printer drivers files are located. See Figure 4.7.

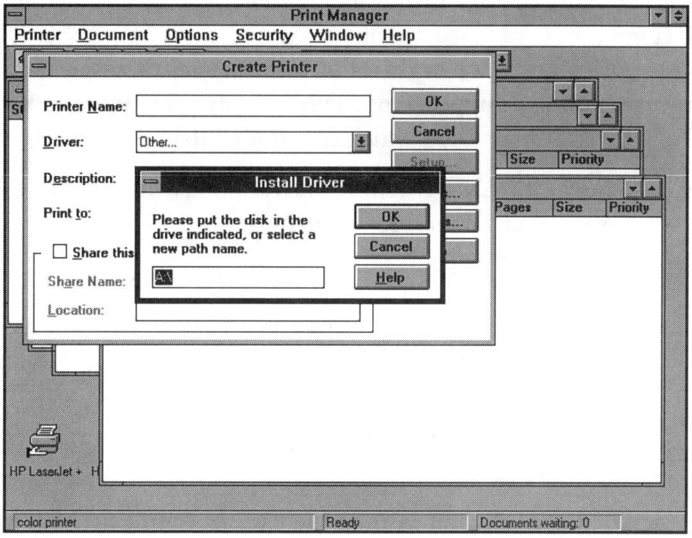

FIGURE 4.7.
Enter the path for the printer driver files.

4. Enter the path name in the dialog box. This could be a floppy drive, a CD-ROM containing RISC printer drivers, or a path on the network.

> **NOTE**
>
> You must acquire the RISC drivers and either copy them onto a hard disk whose path is accessible or insert a floppy or a CD-ROM containing them.

5. A new dialog box, Select Driver, comes up. The Printer Driver box lists the available RISC drivers. Choose the correct one and click on OK.

What to Do if Your Printer Isn't Listed

If your printer isn't listed among those supplied with Windows NT, there is still hope. As I mentioned earlier, many off-brand printers are designed to be compatible with one of the popular printer types, such as the Apple LaserWriters, Hewlett-Packard LaserJets, or the Epson MX series.

Check the hardware compatibility listing to see whether the printer in question is listed. If it is, you can use the driver designed for the printer your printer is compatible with. Even if the printer isn't listed there, it might still be compatible. Check the printer's manual for indications of compatibility. You also might have to set the printer in a compatibility mode using DIP switches or software. Again, check the printer's manual for instructions.

Finally, if it looks like there's no mention of compatibility anywhere, contact the manufacturer for their NT-compatible driver. If you're lucky, they'll have one. It's also possible that Microsoft has a new driver for your printer that wasn't available when your copy of the program was shipped. Contact Microsoft at (206) 882-8080 and ask for the Windows NT Driver Library Disk, which contains all the latest drivers.

CompuServe also has a Microsoft driver library online. Try `GO`ing `WINNT`, `WINADV`, or `WDL` (Windows Driver Library) for more info.

Assuming that you do obtain a printer driver, follow these instructions to install it:

1. Follow the instructions in the section titled "Creating a New Printer" for naming and describing the printer, setting the port, and specifying its share-name.
2. Instead of selecting one of the printers in the Driver list (it isn't in the list, of course), scroll to the bottom of the list and choose Other.
3. Click on OK.
4. Windows asks you to enter the path where the driver is located (typically a floppy disk). Insert the disk (or make sure the files are available somewhere), enter the path, and click on OK.
5. You might have to choose a driver from a resulting list if multiple options exist.
6. Configure options if you want, or just click on Cancel and do it later.

Changing a Printer's Properties

Each printer driver has an associated box or two from which you can fine-tune certain details of the driver as it's applied to that printer. Many variations exist, due to the number of printers supported. The following sections describe the gist of these options without necessarily going into detail about each printer type.

The settings pertaining to a printer are called *properties.* When you create a printer, you can declare its properties or accept the default properties. In any case, you can change them later, but only if you're logged on with Administrator or Power User privileges, *or* if the administrator has given you those privileges.

1. Run Print Manager.
2. Select the printer's icon or window.
3. Click on the Properties button in the toolbar, or choose Printers | Properties. The Printer | Properties dialog box, shown in Figure 4.8, appears.

FIGURE 4.8.
Alter a printer's properties from this box.

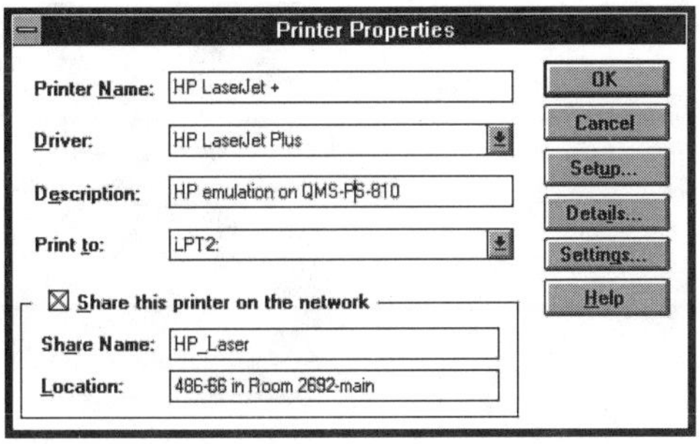

4. Change any of the text boxes as you see fit. (Their significance was explained earlier in this chapter.)
5. Click on the Setup, Details, or Settings buttons to alter a variety of settings. These buttons are confusing in name, and there's no easy way to remember what's what. Here's the general breakdown:

Button	What It Changes
Setup	Paper tray, form, printer memory, soft fonts, font substitution, halftone settings
Details	Time availability, separator file, additional ports, printer priority, print directly to ports, job prints while spooling, print spooled jobs first, landscape/portrait, number of copies
Settings	Time-outs for LPT ports, baud rate, data bits, parity, stop bits, and flow control for serial ports; add additional serial ports

Figures 4.9 through 4.12 show the dialog boxes you would see for an HP LaserJet III when you press the buttons. Other printers' Setup boxes will differ.

FIGURE 4.9.
The dialog box that appears when you press the Setup button.

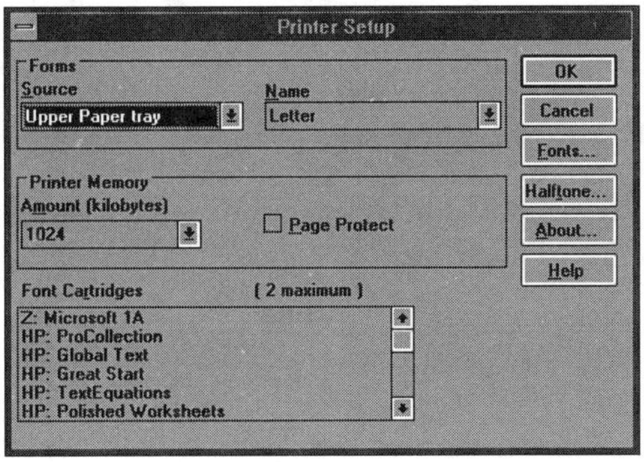

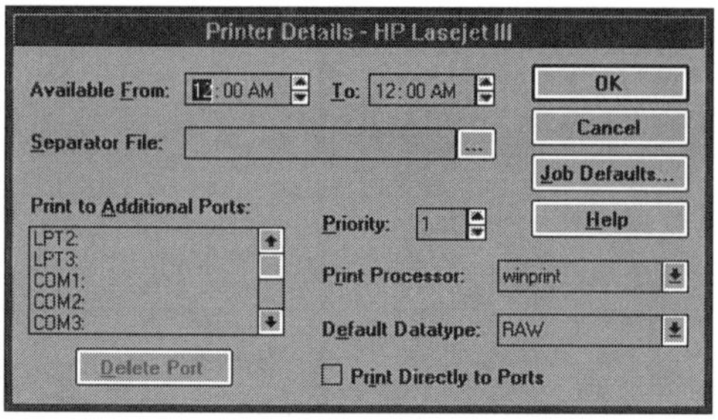

FIGURE 4.10.
The dialog box that appears when you press the Details button.

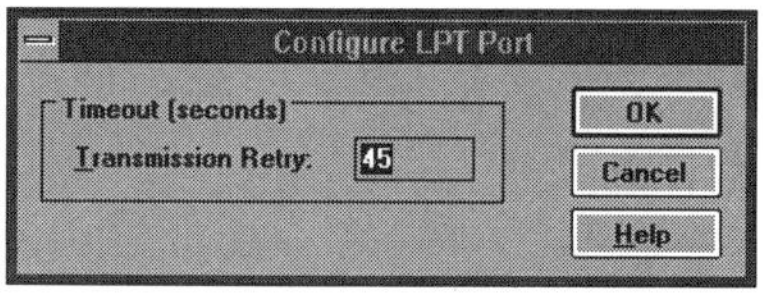

FIGURE 4.11.
The dialog box that appears for a parallel port when you press the Settings button.

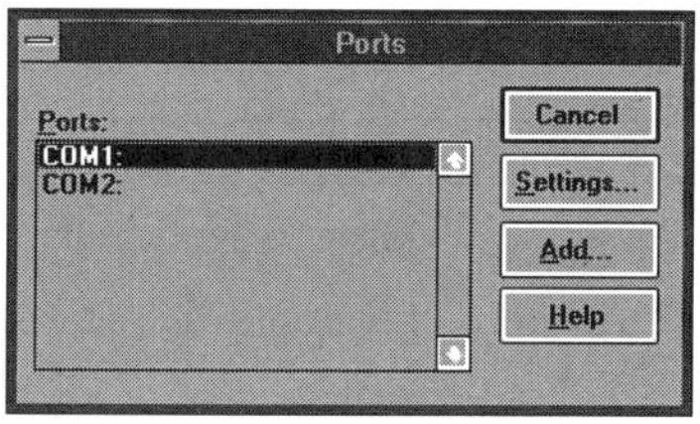

FIGURE 4.12.
The dialog box that appears for a serial port when you press the Settings button.

The next three sections explain the options in these dialog boxes in more detail.

Setup

The Printer Setup dialog box varies widely between types of printers. Some printers, such as older Epson dot-matrix types, have only a single option; others, such as HP lasers, have many. You might have to consult the online help if you're in doubt about a specific one not described here. The following section gives a breakdown of the basic dialog box and of the dialog boxes that appear when you click on Fonts or Halftone.

The Basic Setup Dialog Box

Table 4.1 describes the most common settings from this dialog box for both PostScript and HP-compatible printers.

Table 4.1. The options in the Basic Setup dialog box.

Setting	*Description*
Forms Source/Name (HP) or Paper Tray/Form (PostScript)	Choose a source, such as a lower tray. Then choose a form name to match with the source. When the user chooses a form name (such as A4 small) at print time, the printer driver tells the printer which tray to switch to. The user doesn't have to think about it. Repeat the process for each form name you want to set up.
Printer Memory	How much memory does the printer have installed?
Page Protect	If turned on, this option prevents the printer from printing until an entire page is imaged inside the printer. It's available only on printers with enough memory to store an entire graphics page in internal RAM.
Font Cartridges	Choose the names of the cartridges that are physically installed in the printer. You can select only two.
Use Printer Halftoning	Normally, NT processes the halftoning of graphics printouts. Activate this check box if you want the printer to process halftoning. (Only printers that can do halftoning offer this option.) However, you have more halftoning flexibility if you let NT do it. (See the section titled "Halftone.")

Fonts

If you click on the Fonts button, the dialog box you see is determined by the type of printer. Three types of dialog boxes pertain to fonts:

- PostScript Soft Font Installer: Used for downloading Adobe type 1 soft fonts to PostScript printers
- Raster Printer Font Installer: Used for downloading bitmapped fonts to HP printers
- TrueType Font Substitution Table: Used for PostScript printers to declare when internal fonts should be used in place of downloading TrueType fonts, in order to speed up printing

Figures 4.13, 4.14, and 4.15 show the three font dialog boxes in sequence. Tables 4.2, 4.3, and 4.4 describe the options in these dialog boxes.

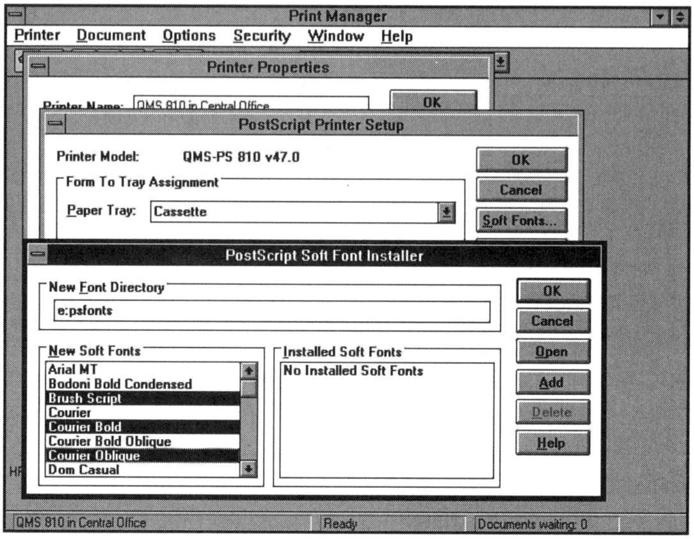

FIGURE 4.13.
The PostScript Soft Font Installer dialog box.

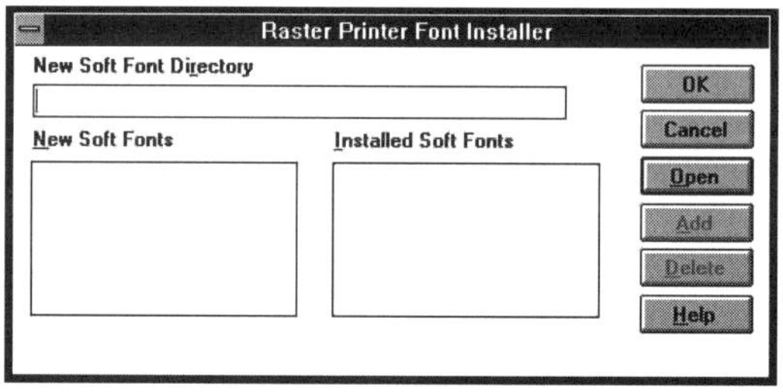

FIGURE 4.14.
The Raster Printer Font Installer dialog box.

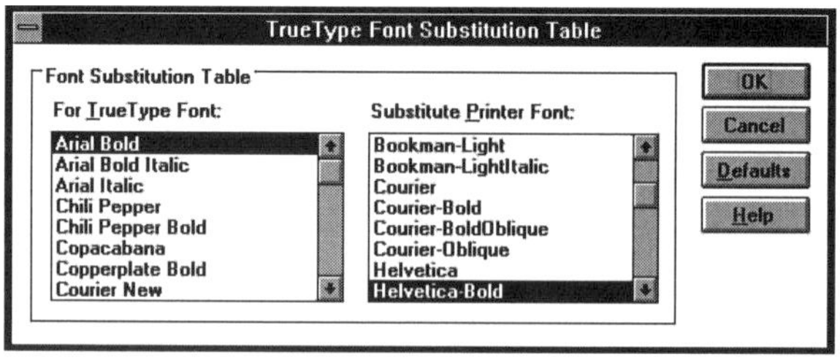

FIGURE 4.15.
The TrueType Font Substitution Table dialog box.

Table 4.2. The options in the PostScript Soft Font Installer dialog box.

Setting	*Description*
New Font Directory	Indicates where the new soft font files are located. Enter the path and click on the Open button.
New Soft Fonts	Displays a list of soft fonts available from the path you enter. To install fonts, select them in this box and click on the Add button.
Installed Soft Fonts	Displays a list of the soft fonts already installed in the printer. To remove fonts, select them in this box and click on the Remove button.

Table 4.3. The options in the Raster Printer Font Installer dialog box.

Setting	*Description*
New Soft Font Directory	Indicates where the new soft font files are located. Enter the path and click on the Open button.
New Soft Fonts	Displays a list of soft fonts available from the path you enter. To install fonts, select them in this box and click on the Add button.
Installed Soft Fonts	Displays a list of the soft fonts already installed in the printer. To remove fonts, select them in this box and click on the Remove button.

Table 4.4. The options in the TrueType Font Substitution Table dialog box.

Setting	*Description*
For True Type Font	This box contains the list of TrueType fonts that are installed in the NT system. Click on a font that you want to set up a substitution for. Click on only one at a time.

continues

Table 4.4. continued

Setting	*Description*
Substitute Printer Font	This box contains the list of outline fonts internal to the PostScript printer. After a TrueType font is selected in the left box, choose the font you want substituted for it in this box. If you want no substitution (if you want to print the TrueType font), scroll to the top of the list and choose Download as Soft Font. This takes longer at print time, initially, because the TrueType font has to be downloaded, but your printout more closely resembles the screen image.
Defaults	This button returns the substitution assignments to the factory settings. For example, Arial equals Helvetica, Courier New equals Courier, and Times New Roman equals Times-Roman.

NOTE

See Chapter 9 for a discussion of system-wide font management.

Halftone

A good number of printer drivers offer a Halftone button for configuring the manner in which color and grayscaling are converted to printer-generated patterns. Halftoning is a process that converts shades of gray or colors to a pattern of black and white dots. A newspaper photo is an example of halftoning. When the arrangement of dots (pixels) on the page is varied, a photographic image can be simulated with only black and white dots. Because virtually no black and white printers and typesetters can print shades of gray, halftoning is the closest you get to realistic photographic effects.

Default halftone settings typically are set up fine and don't need any futzing. You might have a preference that requires adjustment, however. Click on the Halftone button in a printer's Setup dialog box. This brings up the Halftone dialog box, shown in Figure 4.16. The options in this dialog box are listed in Table 4.5.

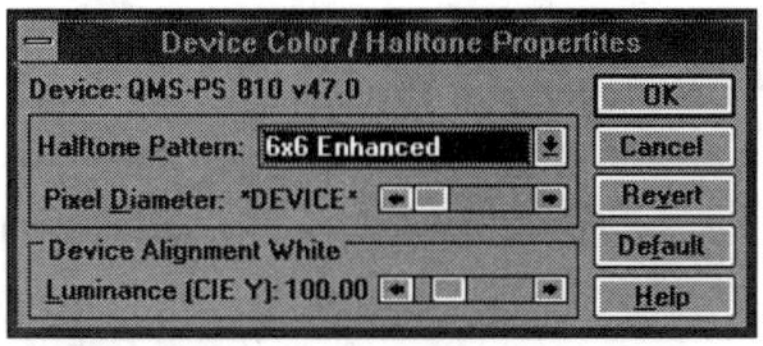

FIGURE 4.16.
The Black-only Printer Halftone dialog box.

Table 4.5. The options in the Black-only Printer Halftone dialog box.

Setting	*Description*
Halftone Pattern	Sets the cell (rectangle) size of the grid pattern used for halftoning. Cells are measured in pixels.
Pixel Diameter	Determines how fat the pixels in the grid are, and thus the density (darkness) of the halftone image. When set to the far left (*DEVICE*), this is automatically calculated by the driver. Some settings are not actually reproducible by most printers—for example, 1/12,000", which would require a typesetter capable of 12,000 DPI.
Luminence (CIE Y)	Uses International Commission on Illuminations standards for brightness of output. Basically, this sets to the ratio between white and black in your final output. Normally, this should be set to 100.
Default button	Returns all variables to factory settings.

If you have a color printer, this box is more complex, enabling you to adjust not only brightness (luminence) but also *chromaticity,* which is like changing the color settings on a television. (See Figure 4.17.) You might have to do this to achieve a match between printed colors and what you see on-screen. Table 4.6 lists this dialog box's options.

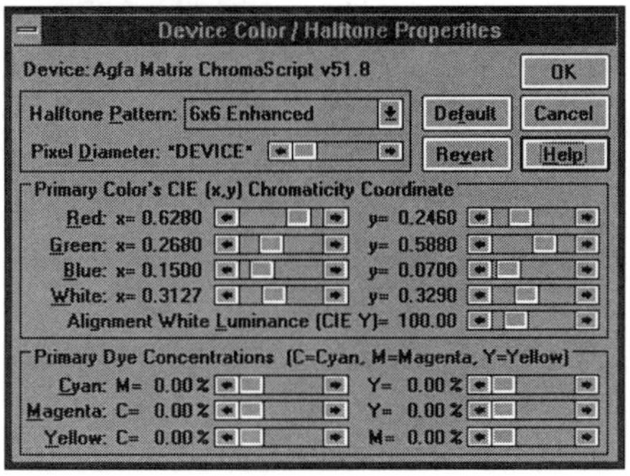

FIGURE 4.17.
The Halftone dialog box for color printers.

Table 4.6. The options in the Halftone dialog box for color printers.

Setting	*Description*
Primary Colors (CIE)	Enables you to adjust the color of your printouts using figures congruent with the International Commission on Illuminations standard. Each printer color (R, G, B) has an *x* and a *y* slider. White has only one slider.
Primary Dye Concentrations (CMY)	This setting enables you to adjust the actual shade or tone of each of the primary colors, as opposed to adjusting the ratio of the primary colors in a printout to one another.
Revert	Returns to the last saved values.
Default	Returns values to factory settings.

Details

The Printer Details dialog box, shown in Figure 4.18, doesn't vary between types of printers; the same options show up for each one. (See Table 4.7.)

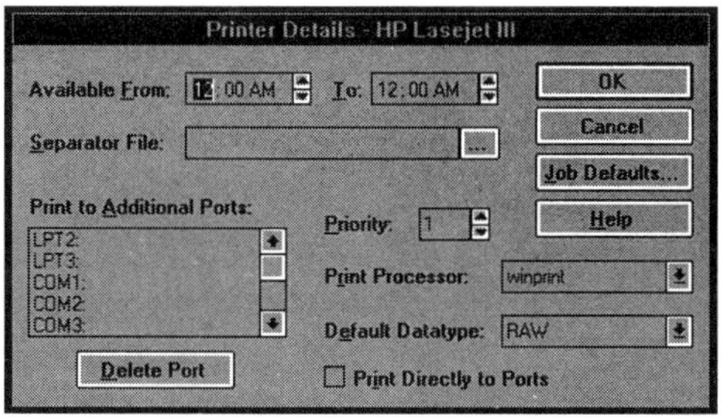

FIGURE 4.18.
The Printer Details dialog box.

Table 4.7. The options in the Printer Details dialog box.

Setting	*Description*
Available From/To	Times when the printer is available for use. At other times, the printer can still be printed to, but physical printing is attempted only during available hours. As a way of managing printing priorities when the number of physical printers is limited, you can create multiple printer setups based on the same physical printer. Set one of the printers to off-hour availability (for example, during the night or over lunch hour). Then instruct users to send their low-priority print jobs to that printer.
Separator File	A preassigned file can be printed between jobs, usually just to place an identification page listing the user, job ID, date, time, number of pages, and so forth. Files also may be used to switch a printer between PostScript and PCL (HP) mode for printers that can run in both modes. Type in the name DEFAULT.SEP for a basic page before each PCL print job. Choose other separator files by clicking on the ... button and switching to the SYSTEM32 directory. PSLANMAN.SEP prints a basic ID page on a PostScript printer, PCL.SEP switches the printer to PCL mode, and PSCRIPT.SEP switches to PostScript mode.
Print to Additional Ports	Use this option to set up a printer pool. This means that several printers are connected to the same server, but to a number of different ports on that server. Everyone on the network can send print jobs to the same virtual printer, but the server doles out the jobs to the first available printer. (See Figure 4.19.) If the port you want to print to isn't listed, go back to the Printer Properties dialog box. In the Ports listing, scroll down to Network Printer and select it. In the resulting dialog box, choose Local Port and click on OK. Enter the name of the port you want to add.
Priority	Printers can have a priority setting from 1 to 99. The default setting is 1. Print jobs sent to a printer that has a priority level of 2 always print before a job sent to a printer with a level 1 setting if both setups use the same physical printer.

continues

Table 4.7. continued

Setting	*Description*
Print Processor	Usually doesn't need changing. Default is WinPrint. A very specialized application might ask you to create a printer with another print processor for use when printing its documents.
Default Datatype	Usually doesn't need changing. Default is RAW. A very specialized application might ask you to create a printer with another data type setting for use when printing its documents.
Print Directly to Ports	This option prevents documents sent to the printer from being spooled. Thus, printing doesn't happen in the background; instead, the computer is tied up until the print job is completed. There's virtually no practical reason for doing this, unless your printer and Print Manager are having difficulty communicating or you find that printing performance (page per minute throughput) increases significantly when this option is enabled. When a printer is shared over the network, this option isn't available.

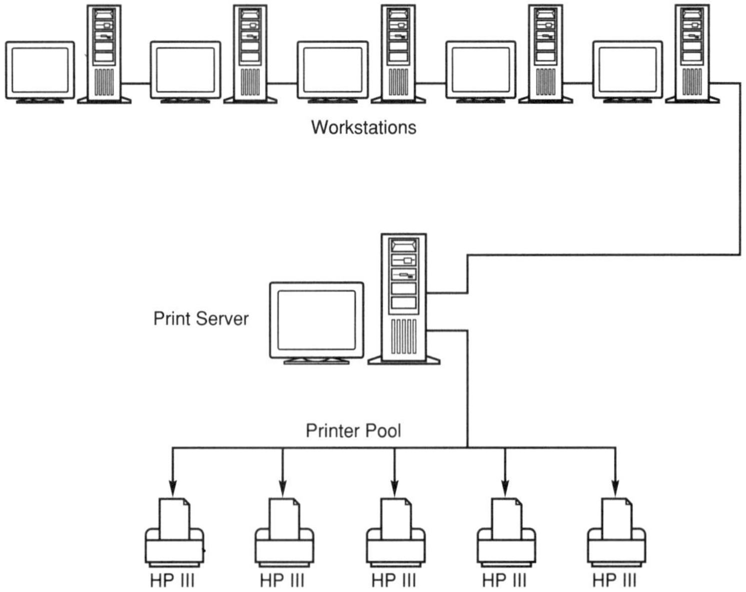

FIGURE 4.19.
A printer pool lets one printer configuration connect to several physical printers. Documents sent to the server are automatically routed to the first available printer.

NOTE

When connected and being used locally (on your computer), the following printers can't use separator pages: Canon LBP-4, LBP-8 II, and LBP-8 III, IBM Laser Printer 4019, Olivetti DM 109, and Olivetti DM 309.

Setting Job Defaults

One button I haven't yet discussed is the Job Defaults button. When you print from an application, you usually see a box that lets you choose the number of copies, page orientation, and so on. The Job Defaults box from Print Manager lets you set up defaults that you normally would use so that you don't have to enter them each time. Unlike with Windows 3.1, these are not system-wide settings. They pertain only to the printer you've created. Thus, you can create several printers, each with different defaults (such as portrait or landscape orientation), print to the desired printer, and not have to worry about making changes in the Print Setup dialog box from an application's File menu. When you do make changes from an application at print time, they override the job defaults.

When you click on the Job Defaults button in the Details dialog box, you see the dialog box shown in Figure 4.20.

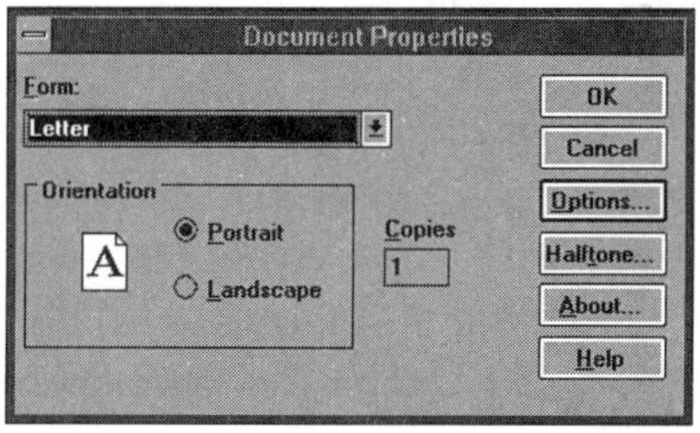

FIGURE 4.20.
The Job Defaults dialog box.

The options that you see depend on the type of printer driver you installed. Some options might be unavailable for your printer. In any case, Table 4.8 gives all possible options and an explanation of each.

Table 4.8. The options in the Job Defaults dialog box.

Option	*Description*
Resolution	Some printers can render graphics in more than one resolution. The higher the resolution, the longer printing takes, so you can save time by choosing a lower resolution. For finished, high-quality work, choose the highest resolution.
Form	Normally, it's assumed that you're using 8 1/2- by 11-inch paper. Change this if you're using a different paper size. Seven sizes are available.
Orientation	Page orientation. Normal orientation is Portrait, which, like a portrait of the Mona Lisa, for example, is taller than it is wide. Landscape, like a landscape painting, is the opposite.
Copies	Controls the number of copies of each page printed. Normally you want just 1, but if you typically need an extra copy or two, change it.
2 Sides	Enables or disables double-sided printing for printers that support this feature.
Fonts	Chooses whether to download TrueType fonts for all fonts you want to print or whether to use the substitution table (discussed earlier), substituting the printer's internal fonts for some of the more commonly used TrueType fonts.
Color	Alternates between color mode and black-and-white printing on color printers to print all colors except white as black, or to print a reverse image (a negative).
Options	Some printers have additional options available, as determined by the brand and model of printer. For example, PostScript printers have an option for printing to an encapsulated PostScript file and for scaling a page. To change these options, click on Options, and then make the adjustments from the resulting dialog boxes. For information about each of the settings, click on the Help button in the dialog box. The Help screens have "hot spots" (spots where the pointer changes to a pointing finger that will bring up more information when you click) that explain each setting more fully.

Job Default boxes for a number of high-resolution printers, such as lasers, have a Halftone button. This brings up a complex box that's even more detailed than the Halftone settings box you reach from the Setup dialog box. For example, Figure 4.21 shows the Halftone Color Adjustment box for a PostScript printer.

FIGURE 4.21.
The Halftone Color Adjustment box, available from the Job Defaults box.

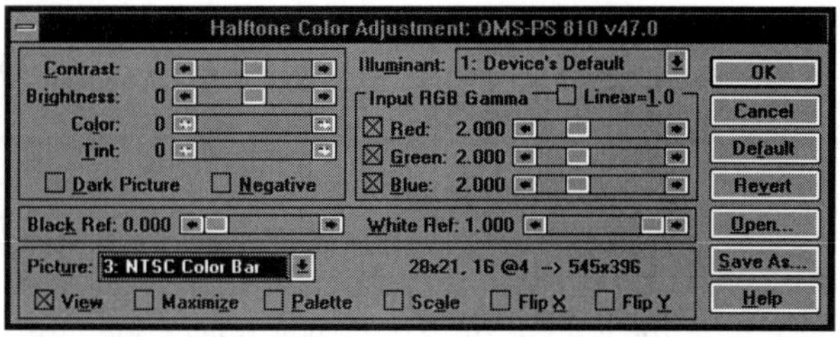

This dialog box even lets you load graphics files, modify them, and save the modified file on disk, much as a graphics drawing program or file-conversion program does. For an explanation of options, click on the Help button.

Settings

This set of options, which pertains to port settings, is the simplest. There are two resulting dialog boxes, depending on whether the printer is connected to a parallel or serial port.

Setting the Time-Outs for LPT Ports

When you're adjusting a printer connected to a parallel port, only one setting can be made—time-outs. When there's a problem with your printer—running out of paper, for example—printers often aren't very gracious. The result can be a printing job that gets unceremoniously terminated. At times you're left sitting and waiting while your laser printer's data light flashes and you assume that your print job is going along fine. Eventually, you realize that nothing is happening.

Printers and operating systems don't always agree on how long to wait in case of an error before giving up. You could be busy adding paper to the tray or changing a ribbon with the printer top open, making NT think the printer is dead. Or perhaps you forgot to put the printer online to start with and are just getting to it.

The time-out settings determine how long Windows NT (actually Print Manager) should try before sending you an error message. Of course, the error message dialog box (like the one in Windows 3.1 or the DOS `Abort, Retry, Fail` message) lets you retry the transmission from the point where it left off. As long as you're around to monitor the printing process, it's no big deal if your time-out setting isn't perfect.

If your printer needs a little more time, however, or you're likely to have to change the paper often and NT is regularly timing out, you'll want to increase the number of seconds

Print Manager waits before throwing in the towel. You can alter the default time-out settings. Assuming that the printer is connected to a parallel port, click on Settings. The Configure LPT Port dialog box, shown in Figure 4.22, appears.

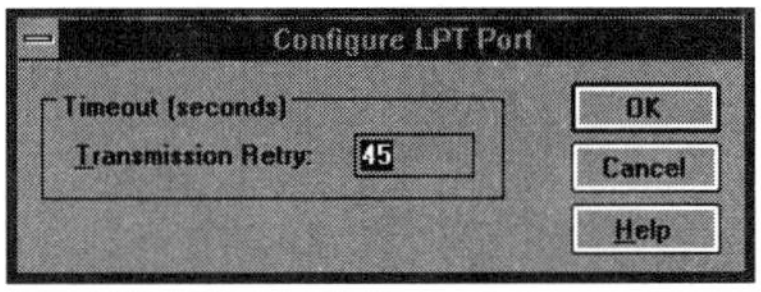

FIGURE 4.22.
Setting the time-outs.

The default setting is 45 seconds, which is long enough for most purposes. If printing from your application regularly results in an error message about transmission problems and retrying seems to work, increase the setting. The maximum is 999 seconds.

NOTE

Windows 3.1 contains a number of specific time-out parameters. NT has only one.

Making COM Port Settings

When you're adjusting a printer connected to a serial port, you can make a few settings. They pertain to the serial port's communications settings, such as baud rate and parity. In fact, clicking on the Settings button runs the Control Panel Ports applet. I won't repeat that information here. See the section titled "Ports" in Chapter 9, "Configuring Windows NT." Suffice it to say that the serial port's baud rate, data bits, parity, stop bits, and flow control must match that of the printer's, or you're in for some garbage printouts. If you have trouble, check the printer's DIP switch or software settings and the printer manual to ensure that the settings agree.

NOTE

Also see the section titled "Maintenance and Troubleshooting" in Chapter 12.

Sharing a Printer

You must share a printer before it becomes available to other network users. Sharing was mentioned earlier in this chapter, in the section titled "Creating a New Printer." Here, briefly, is the method for sharing a printer:

1. Create the printer by choosing the driver, port, and name.
2. Set up the desired properties for the printer, as shown in Figure 4.23.

FIGURE 4.23.
Sharing a printer.

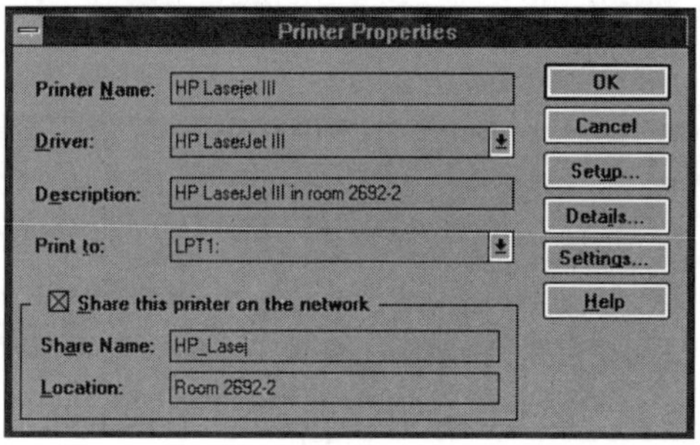

3. In the printer's Properties dialog box, activate the Share This Printer option in the Network check box.
4. A sharename based on the Printer Name is automatically generated. You can leave the sharename as is or give it another name. DOS-based network users see this name, which must conform to DOS file-naming rules.
5. Fill in the location of the printer so that users know where to pick up their printouts.

Connecting to a Network Printer

Assuming that your Windows NT network system is successfully cabled and running, network printing should be possible. Before a network user can access a network printer, the following must be true:

- The printer must be cabled to the sharing computer
- The printer must be created and working properly for local use
- The printer must be shared
- The printer's security settings and network users wishing access must match

TIP

By default, new printer shares are given a security setting that gives all users ("Everyone") access for printing. Only the creator, power users, and administrator can *manage* the printer, however. Managing the printer means rearranging the print job queue: starting, stopping, and deleting print jobs.

Connecting to the Desired Printer

Assuming that the network user has decided which printer she wants access to, she simply connects to the printer via Print Manager by following these steps:

1. Run Print Manager.
2. Choose Printer | Connect to Printer, or click on the Connect button in the toolbar.
3. The Connect to Printer dialog box appears. Shared printers are listed under their respective domains, NT servers, and workgroups in a tree fashion similar to the format of File Manager. Double-click on the network, domain, workgroup, server name, or workstation to eventually arrive at the printer level. Eventually, shared printers appear, as shown in Figure 4.24.

FIGURE 4.24.
Listing shared printers across the network.

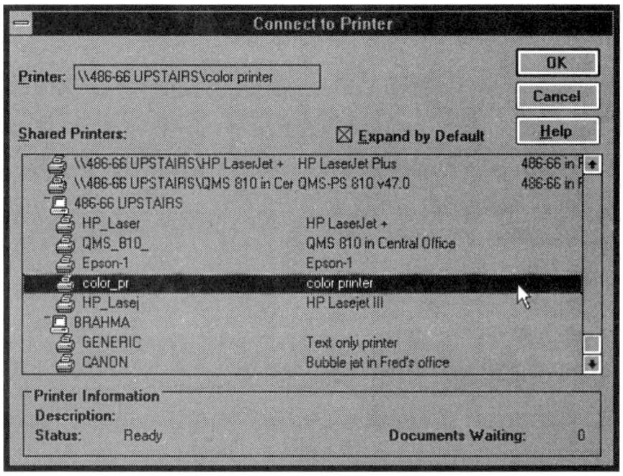

> **TIP**
>
> Disable the Expand check box if your network is slow (or huge) and you don't want to wait for all the workstations and printers to list out.

4. Highlight the desired printer and click on OK. The printer is connected. You should see a new printer icon in the Print Manager window. It's identified by the share path and printer name, as shown in Figure 4.25.

   Only if both workstations (sharing and connecting) are NT-based and of the same NT type (x86 to x86 or RISC to RISC) will the connection engage without an additional step. Otherwise, NT issues an error message like the one shown in Figure 4.26.

FIGURE 4.25.
The new printer icon.

FIGURE 4.26.
What you see if the printer driver on the sharing computer doesn't jibe with the computer that's attempting to connect to the printer.

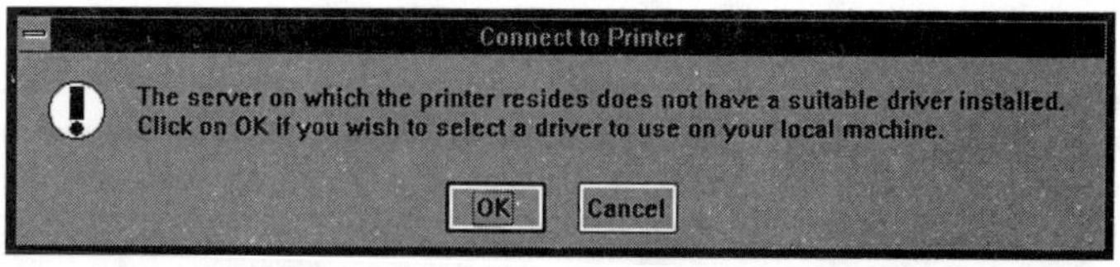

NOTE

The connecting NT computer must have access to the appropriate 32-bit NT-compatible driver to send data to the connected printer. If the printer driver on the sharing workstation is determined by NT to be either the wrong processor type (RISC versus x86) or 16-bit rather than 32-bit (for example, a Windows for Workgroups share), you see a message that prompts you for a new driver.

5. After you click on OK to the prompt for the new driver, you see the box shown in Figure 4.27.

FIGURE 4.27.
When NT determines that you need to install a new driver on your system in order to use a remote shared printer, you see this box.

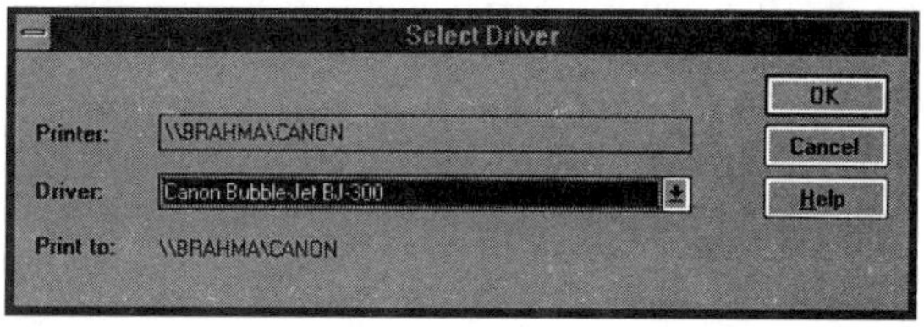

6. Choose the correct printer driver from the list (it *isn't* preselected!). You might have to contact the sharer of the printer to determine the exact model of printer.
7. Click on OK. You're asked where NT can find the printer driver files, as shown in Figure 4.28.

FIGURE 4.28.
Indicate the location of the printer driver files.

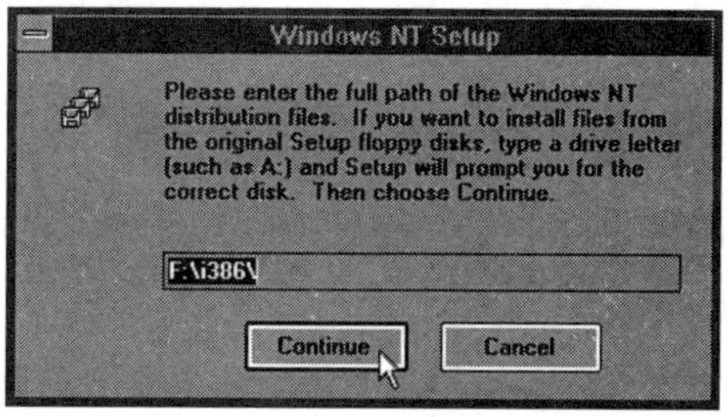

8. Enter the path for the files and click on Continue. Now the printer is connected.

When you want to disconnect a network printer from Windows, highlight the printer in the Current Printer Connections area and click on the Disconnect button.

Removing a Printer

You might want to decommission a printer you've created if

- you want to disconnect from a network printer you're through using
- you've connected a new type of printer to your computer and you want to delete the old setup and create a new one with the correct driver for the new printer
- you've created several slightly different setups for the same physical printer and you want to delete the ones you don't use

In any of these cases, the trick is the same:

1. Run Print Manager.
2. Select either the icon or the window for the printer setup you want to delete.
3. Choose Printer | Remove Printer.

Depending on whether the printer is local or remote, you see two different dialog boxes. One asks whether you want to delete the printer; the other asks whether you want to delete the connection to the printer. In either case, click on Yes. The printer icon or window disappears from the Print Manager dialog box.

NOTE

The removal process removes only the virtual printer setup from NT's registry for the currently logged-in user. The related driver file and font files are not deleted from the disk, however. Therefore, if you want to re-create the printer, you don't have to insert disks or be prompted for the location of driver files. This is convenient, but be aware that if you're tight on disk space, the printer fonts and drivers could take up considerable room. To remove fonts, use the Fonts applet from Control Panel, as described in Chapter 9, "Configuring Windows NT."

Printing from Applications

As I explained earlier, Windows applications *and* all applications—OS/2, POSIX, DOS, Win32, and Win16—are shunted to Print Manager. If no particular printer has been chosen (perhaps because the application—a DOS app, for example—doesn't give you a choice), the default printer is used.

NOTE

The default printer is set from Print Manager's toolbar.

All the printer settings you made in Print Manager with the Create and Properties commands go into effect, controlling the print job.

The exact appearance of your printed documents might vary from program to program, depending on the degree to which your Windows application can take advantage of the printer-driver setup. Some programs, such as Write, enable you to change fonts, for example, while others, such as Notepad, don't. DOS, OS/2, and POSIX applications aren't likely to utilize any of NT's advanced font support.

TIP

In fact, if you choose as a default a printer that your non-NT application can't support, your printouts might be garbled. For example, if you're running WordPerfect 5.1 for DOS and have it installed for an Apple LaserWriter, but the default printer as set in Print Manager is an Epson dot matrix, your printouts will be nothing but a listing of PostScript commands. Make sure your non-NT applications and your default printer are in accord before you try to print.

When you print from any program, the file actually is printed to a disk file instead of directly to the printer. Print Manager then spools the file to the assigned printer(s), coordinating the flow of data and keeping you informed of the progress. Jobs are queued up and listed in the Print Manager window, from which their status can be observed; they can be rearranged, deleted, and so forth.

Before You Print

To print from any application, including Windows and Windows NT applications, follow these steps (which are exact for Windows applications but only approximate for other environments):

1. Check to see that the printer and page settings are correct. Some applications provide a Printer Setup or other option on their File menu for this. Recall that settings you make from such a box override the Job Default settings made with the Printer | Properties command.
2. Select the Print command on the application's File menu and fill in whatever information is asked of you.

3. Click on OK (or otherwise confirm printing). NT intercepts the print data and writes it in a file, then begins printing it. If an error occurs—a port conflict, the printer is out of paper, or what have you—you see a message such as the one shown in Figure 4.29.

FIGURE 4.29.
A typical printer problem error message.

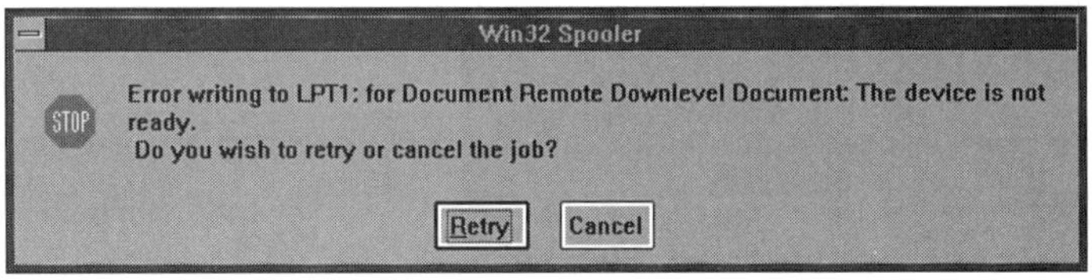

Attempt to fix the problem by checking the paper supply and so forth.

Printing by Dragging Files into Print Manager

You can quickly print Windows application document files by dragging them from a File Manager window into the running Print Manager. This is an easy way to add files to the print queue.

1. Run File Manager.
2. Run Print Manager.
3. Arrange the two windows so that you can see the file(s) you want to print as well as either the Print Manager window or the iconized Print Manager.
4. Drag your document files into the Print Manager icon or window. The file is loaded into the source application, the Print command is automatically executed, and the file is spooled to Print Manager.

NOTE

Note that printing is directed only to the default printer—you can't control the destination printer when you're dragging files into Print Manager. This also is true when you're using the File | Print command in File Manager to print files.

NOTE

Documents must have associations; otherwise, printing by dragging them to Print Manager won't work.

TIP

If your jobs seem to be going to the wrong printer, run Print Manager and verify that the default printer is set correctly.

Viewing the Queue

After you have a number of documents printing in the queue, you might want to know more about the status of your print jobs. The thing you probably want to do most often from the Print Manager window is check the status of the queue.

For each printer, the window displays

- which job is currently printing
- document names, sizes, and page count of other print jobs in the queue
- who the owner of each print job is
- when each print job was sent to the print queue
- the priority level of each job

Figure 4.30 shows a sample printer with a print queue and related information.

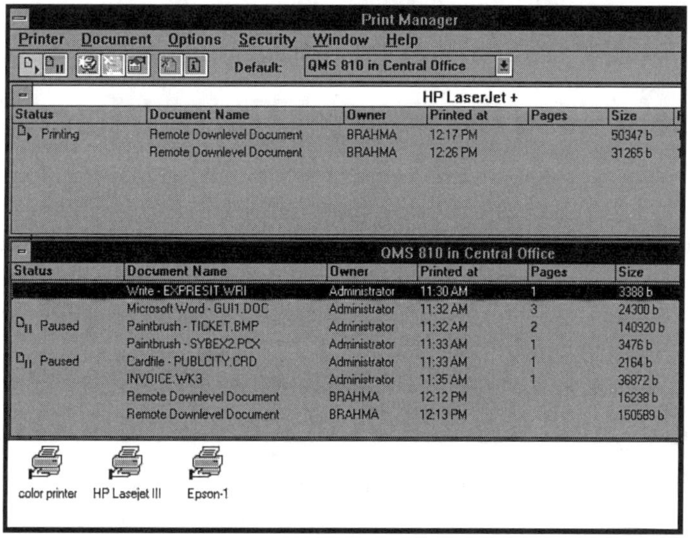

FIGURE 4.30.
The Print Manager screen with several print jobs pending.

Notice the following pieces of information in the Print Manager dialog box:

- Each printer existing on the NT machine gets its own icon and window. Print jobs sent by network users are placed in the appropriate window based on the network printer they chose to print to.
- The printer windows can be iconized or windowed. Windows can be cascaded, tiled, or arranged by hand. Use the Window menu to cascade, tile, or switch to a particular window. You also can arrange printer icons with the Arrange Icons command.
- Below that, each print job queued up for that printer occupies one line, called a *file information line*. The currently printing file shows the word Printing to its left.
- If the print job originated from a non-NT machine, the Document Name is not known. It's listed as Remote Downlevel Document, meaning that it came from a lesser (downlevel) workstation. For example, the source could be a DOS/Windows station. Note that downlevel sources typically don't use a printing format embedded with enough data to tell the NT printer the page count.

TIP

You can resize the columns in the display to see more data in a small window. Move the pointer to the dividing line in the header display (for example, to the immediate left of "Document Name") and drag the line left or right.

Refreshing the Network Queue Information

The network cabling connecting workstations and servers often is quite busy, so NT usually doesn't bother to add even more traffic to the net by polling each workstation for printer queue information. Occasionally this is done when necessary, such as when a document is deleted from a queue. However, if you want to refresh the window for a printer to get the absolute latest information, just choose Windows | Refresh or press F5. This immediately updates the queue information.

Checking the Details of the Network Queues

If you have a choice of network printers to print from, or you're managing a network, you might want to check the queue status of various shared printers.

1. Run Print Manager.
2. Choose Printer | Server Viewer.

3. A box appears, listing domains, servers, workgroups, and workstations in a tree fashion. Work your way down the tree by double-clicking on domains and workgroups until you reach the workstation you're interested in. Double-clicking on it shows the printers connected to it with a listing of pending print jobs, as shown in Figure 4.31.

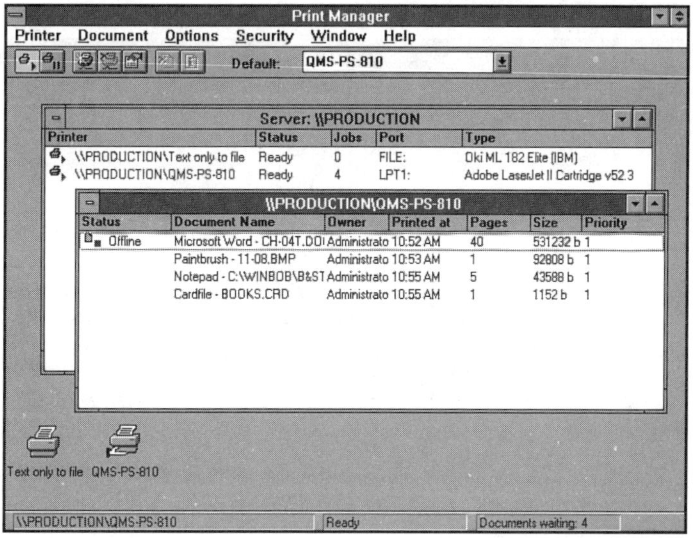

FIGURE 4.31.
Listing print jobs queued up for a given network printer.

4. To examine details of each pending print job, double-click anywhere on a specific printer's line. A new dialog box appears, listing details about the queue.
5. When you're finished examining the information, close the window by double-clicking on the window's Control box in the upper-left corner of the window.

Deleting a File from the Queue

After sending a file to the queue, you might reconsider printing it, or you might want to re-edit the file and print it later. If so, you can simply remove the file from the queue.

1. Select the file by clicking on it in the queue.

> **NOTE**
>
> Sometimes, especially with laser-type printers, deleting a file while it's printing in graphics mode necessitates resetting the printer to clear its buffer. To reset, either turn the printer off then on, or use the Reset option (if it's available).

2. Click on the Delete Document button, choose Document | Delete, or press Delete. The document item is removed from the printer's window. If you're trying to delete the job that's printing, you might have some trouble. At the very least, the system might take some time to respond. Sometimes you have to pause the printing document before you can delete it. (This appears to be a bug in Print Manager 3.1.)

NOTE

Print jobs will survive an NT server power-down. Any documents in the queue when the system goes down, whether due to an intentional shutdown or a power outage, reappear in the queue when you power up.

TIP

When an error occurs during a print job, NT tries to determine the cause. If the printer is out of paper, you might see a `Paper Out` message in the status area. At other times the message is ambiguous, and the word `Error` might appear in the status area. Add paper; make sure that the printer is turned on, online, and correctly connected; and make sure that the settings (particularly the driver) are correct for that printer.

Canceling All Pending Print Jobs on a Given Printer

You can't easily cancel all print jobs for all servers, but if you have the right privileges, you can cancel all print jobs one printer at a time.

1. Select the printer's icon or window.
2. Choose Printer | Purge Printer. A confirmation dialog box like the one shown in Figure 4.32 appears.

FIGURE 4.32.
Purging all pending jobs for a particular printer.

All queued jobs for the printer are canceled.

Pausing the Printing Process

You can temporarily halt the printing process for a particular job or all jobs on a particular printer at any time. This might be useful in cases where you want to adjust the printer for some reason, or to quiet the printer (if it's a dot-matrix or an impact type) so you can take a phone call, have a conversation, and so forth.

Pausing or Resuming Printing

When you feel the need to pause or resume the printing process, follow these steps:

1. Select the document's information line.
2. Click on the Pause button (the second button from the left) or choose Document | Pause. The current print job is temporarily suspended, and the word `Paused` appears in the status area. (The printing might not stop immediately, because your printer might have a buffer that holds data in preparation for printing. The printing stops when the buffer is empty.)

TIP

You can pause documents anywhere in the queue. Paused documents are skipped and subsequent documents in the list print ahead of them, essentially moving ahead in line. You can achieve the same effect by rearranging the queue, as explained in the section titled "Rearranging the Queue Order."

3. To resume printing the document, click on the Resume button (the furthest button to the left) or choose Document | Resume.

Pausing or Resuming All Jobs on a Printer

You can temporarily pause all jobs on a given printer. You might want to do this for a number of reasons:

- To repaper or adjust the physical printer
- To alter printer settings from the Printer | Properties dialog boxes
- To allow jobs sent to other printers based on the same physical printer to print first

Follow these steps to pause or resume all jobs for a printer:

1. Deselect any documents in the printer's window; press the Spacebar if a document is selected.

2. Click on the Pause button or choose Printer | Pause. The printer window's title bar changes to say `Paused`.
3. To resume all jobs on the printer, click on the Resume button in the toolbar or choose Printer | Resume. The `Paused` indicator disappears, and printing should resume where the queue left off.

TIP

You can restart a printing document from the beginning if you need to—for example, if the printer jams, the wrong paper was loaded, or some other error warrants it. Select the document and choose Document | Restart.

Rearranging the Queue Order

When you have several items on the queue, you might want to rearrange the order in which they're slated for printing. Perhaps a print job's priority has increased because it's needed for an urgent meeting, or you have to get a letter to the post office. Whatever the reason, it's easy to rearrange the print queue.

1. Click on the file you want to move and keep the mouse button depressed. The cursor changes to include a little document page.
2. Drag the file to its new location. A solid line moves to indicate where the document will be inserted when you release the mouse button.
3. When you release the mouse button, your file is inserted in the queue, pushing the other files down a notch.

Viewing and Changing Document Details

For a more detailed view of information pertaining to each document, you can open a Details dialog box. A few settings, such as priority and the time of day the document will be printed, also can be made from this box.

1. Click on the information line for the print job in question.
2. Click on the information button (the "i" button) or choose Document | Details.

TIP

As a shortcut, you can just double-click on the job's information line.

The dialog box shown in Figure 4.33 appears. Table 4.9 lists the options found in this dialog box.

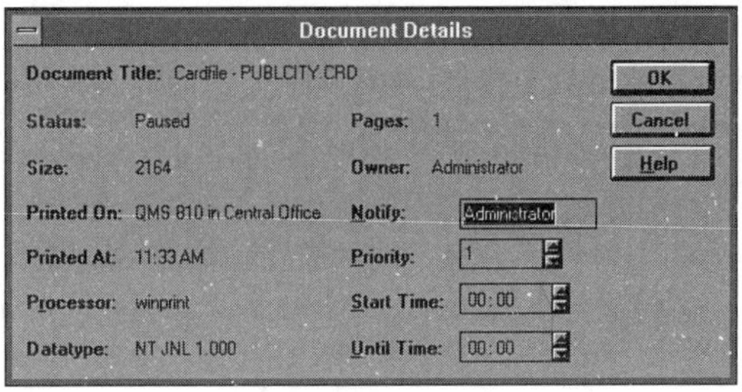

FIGURE 4.33.
The Document Details dialog box.

Table 4.9. The options in the Document Details dialog box.

Item	*Description*
Document Title	The name of the disk file queued for printing. From a non-NT source, the name might be generic—for example, Remote Downlevel Document.
Status	Current status of the print job—for example, Printing, Error, or Paused.
Size	Size of the print file in bytes.
Printed On	Which printer the job was sent to.
Printed At	Time the file was sent to the queue.
Processor	The print processor software (internal to NT; normally Winprint) that is used to process the document.
Datatype	NT's category type for the data. Could be NT JNL 1,000, TEXT, or RAW. Normally it's RAW.
Pages	Number of total pages in the final printout. Non-NT documents won't list this figure.
Owner	Who sent the document.
Notify	The person to notify when the document is finished printing.

continues

Table 4.9. continued

Item	*Description*
Priority	All documents normally have the same priority, 1. You can increase this to as high as 99 to push the print job through. The job with the highest priority is printed before all other jobs on that printer. Remember, however, that when you create a printer, it can have a priority setting too. That setting overrides the document setting you make here. Therefore, even if you increase the priority of a print job to 99, it won't print before a job with a priority of 1 that's been sent to the same physical printer via a setup with a higher priority.
Start Time/Until Time	You can specify that a job be printed only between certain hours, such as night (when the network printing load is low) or during lunch hour. Make sure the hours are compatible with the hours the printer is set for, as described earlier in this chapter.

Using Forms

Most printers have feeders, trays, or some other kind of accommodation for a variety of form sizes. Common examples are legal, letter, and envelope. Every printer you create is given a default form, usually 8 1/2- by 11-inch—the common letter size. More than 30 canned form sizes are supplied with NT.

A form is really nothing complicated. It's just a few numbers that plug into the printer driver, stipulating the paper size and margin settings. Although they're simple, forms are an essential option in everyday business computing. Spreadsheets, legal briefs, envelopes, mailing labels, and company stationery with a logo at the top are all examples of forms that require special handling by the printer so that text is printed in the correct location on the form and the paper is advanced properly.

You can create a printer for each task that you or users might need. For example, one printer could be for envelopes, and another for stationery. When network users want to print a particular form, they just choose the correct printer based on the description or the sharename, which should indicate something about the form size the printer is set up with.

NOTE

If the physical printer has multiple paper trays, each one can be assigned a form size.

Assigning a form was explained in the section titled "Setup." However, assigning a form when you're creating a printer only draws upon the preexisting forms stored in the computer. Because form needs are widely varied, NT enables you to create your own and add them to the list. This list must be stored in the server for the physical printer. After forms are stored, they can be assigned to any printer—either a preexisting one or a new one you create.

Creating a New Form

Setting up a new form is easy. Simply specify the paper size and margins, then give the form a name.

NOTE

Do this at the computer connected to the physical printer in question.

1. Choose Printer | Forms. The dialog box shown in Figure 4.34 appears.

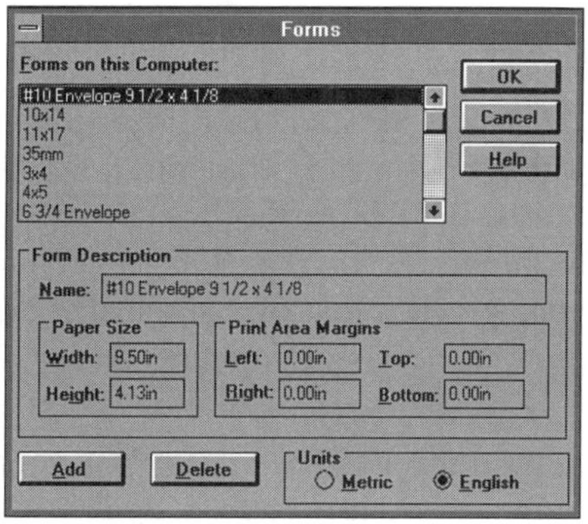

FIGURE 4.34.
The Forms dialog box. Create a new form here, or redefine settings for a preexisting form size.

2. If you want to modify an existing form, choose it from the list. Even if you don't want to modify an existing form, you might want to choose the form that's closest in layout to what you want to create.

3. Enter the paper size and margin dimensions for your form.
4. If you're creating a new form rather than modifying an existing one, type in a name.
5. Click on Add, then click on OK.

CAUTION

Don't modify an existing form name (such as Letter) without due consideration. Unless you change the form's name, changing its settings affects all printers on the server that use the form.

You can remove a form from the computer by highlighting it and clicking on the Remove button.

Printing to a Disk File

Sometimes you might want to print to a disk file rather than to the printer. When you print to a disk file, the output from the application program that normally would be sent to the printer is shunted to a disk file, either locally or on the network. The file usually isn't just a copy of the file you were printing; it contains all the special formatting codes that control your printer. Codes that change fonts, print graphics, set margins, break pages, and add attributes such as underline, bold, and so on are all included in this type of file. Print files destined for PostScript printers typically include their PostScript preamble, too.

Printing to a file gives you several options not available when you print directly to the printer:

- You can send the file to another person, either on floppy disk or over the phone lines, with a modem and a communications program such as Terminal. That person can then print the file directly to a printer (if it's compatible) with Windows or a utility such as the DOS `COPY` command. The person doesn't need the application program that created the file, and he doesn't have to worry about any of the printing details—formatting, setting up margins, and so forth. It's all in the file.
- You can print the file later. Maybe your printer isn't hooked up, or there's so much stuff on the queue that you don't want to wait, or you don't want to slow down your computer or the network by printing now. Print to a file, which is significantly faster than printing on paper. Later, you can use the DOS `COPY` command or a batch file with a command such as `COPY *.PRN LPT1 /B` to copy all files to the desired port. This way you can queue up as many files as you want, prepare the printer, and then print them without having to be around. Be sure to

use the `/B` switch. Because the print files are binary files, the first control-Z code the computer encounters will terminate the print job.

- Sometimes print files are used by applications for specific purposes. For example, you might want to print part of a database to a file that will later be pulled into a company report. Or you might want to print an encapsulated PostScript graphics file to be imported into a desktop publishing document.

In some applications, this choice is available in the Print dialog box. If it isn't, you should modify the printer's configuration to print to a file rather than to a port. Then, whenever you use that printer, it uses all the usual settings for the driver but sends the data to a file of your choice instead of to the printer port.

1. In Print Manager, select the printer's icon or window.
2. Choose Printer | Properties.
3. In the Print to: section, choose FILE:.
4. When the file is at the top of queue, you're prompted for a filename. Note that you're not asked for the filename when you initially print the file from the application.

TIP

If you want to print the file as ASCII text only, with no special control codes, you should install the Generic/Text Only printer driver. Then select that as the destination printer.

TIP

If you want to print to an encapsulated PostScript file (.EPS), print to a printer that uses a PostScript driver (the Apple LaserWriter or the QMS PS-810, for instance) or set up a phony printer that uses such a driver. No physical printer is needed. Then, modify the properties of the printer via the Properties | Details | Job Defaults | Options dialog box to set an Encapsulated PostScript filename.

Summary

This chapter covered all important aspects of printing from Windows NT. This includes creating and setting up new printers, sharing printers, connecting to printers over the network, managing printer queues, and setting some printer security features. Some additional printer security features, such as audits of printer use, are covered in Chapter 12. Also, be sure to see Chapter 10 for lots of information about system administration, including the setting of user privileges, some of which relate to the use and control of network printers.

5

Sharing Data Between Applications Using Clipboard, Clipbook, DDE, and OLE

IN THIS CHAPTER

In a perfect world, operating systems would provide a seamless meshing of applications. Although this is only an ideal that has yet to be completely realized by any operating system, Windows has bridged a few significant gaps. The capability to run several programs at once, switching between them at will, is a strong move in this direction. This chapter considers a common issue that results from this new freedom—that of sharing data between these applications.

Due to developers' conformity with the Windows API and Microsoft's vision of a world where dissimilar applications can communicate, there are now thousands of applications that can easily share data through cutting, copying, and pasting—that is, the Windows Clipboard. This was a major advancement in PC programs that previously couldn't even come close to doing these things.

Still, today's applications often continue to use proprietary file and data formats, a move that often seems promoted by developers' marketing departments in hopes of establishing their own industry standards. Whatever their motives, the end result seems to be that actually sharing data files (as opposed to copying portions of data between programs) is seldom easy. For example, just try to open and publish a dBASE data file in Microsoft Word. Things become even more complicated as multimedia applications gain popularity. We are now seeing competing formats for live-motion video, audio recording, and MIDI files.

As time passes, we see more conversion programs and input filters built into programs as solutions to application intercompatibility. As an example, Word for Windows can read and write numerous text and graphics file formats. Likewise, database management programs such as Paradox and desktop publishing programs such as Ventura Publisher both offer a plethora of conversion options. Standards such as Rich Text Format (RTF) are now emerging to facilitate data transfers between programs, and with time, more elegant solutions will appear.

Aside from actual file swapping, which I don't discuss here, Windows NT offers three internal vehicles for exchanging data between programs: the Windows Clipboard (and Clipbook, an extension of Clipboard), *dynamic data exchange* (*DDE*), and *object linking and embedding* (*OLE*). If you're a veteran Windows user, you're certainly familiar with at least the Clipboard, and you know that both DDE and OLE are built into "vanilla" Windows as well. So why discuss them here, in a technical book about NT, you might wonder? After observing Windows users over the years and writing books on the topic, I've found that, aside from the very basics, people are confused about Windows data sharing. As a result, its many possibilities are widely underutilized. Second, Windows NT itself introduces some new wrinkles due to the inclusion of network DDE and OLE capabilities, the capability to share Clipboard material via the Clipbook, and NT's security system that can affect how and when data can be shared. Therefore, this chapter presents a review of some Windows Clipboard, OLE, and DDE concepts and procedures, as well as a thorough discussion of how Windows NT's treatment of them differs from Windows 3.1's treatment. Included are some special considerations for data sharing across the NT network.

The Clipboard

Although it's not capable of significant data conversions between file formats (such as .TIF to .PCX or .RTF to WordPerfect) or of any radical sleight-of-hand to miraculously render all programs compatible, the trusty Windows Clipboard comes in handy for many everyday tasks. As a result, virtually all Windows programs that allow editing of data utilize the built-in functionality of the Clipboard.

Using the Clipboard, you can move text, graphics, data cells, portions of multimedia files, and OLE objects from one location to another. The Clipboard works with a number of data formats, on both 16-bit and 32-bit Windows programs, as well as with non-Windows programs. However, certain limitations pertain to non-Windows applications. These are explained later.

The Clipboard uses system memory (RAM and virtual memory) to temporarily hold information that is in transition. The data waits in suspension until the user is ready to copy or move it to its new location—typically a document that is open in a window. The data remains on the Clipboard until you delete it, replace it, or exit Windows. This enables you to paste the information any number of times. You can paste into several documents or into the same document several times if you wish.

The Clipboard's contents can be viewed, stored to disk, and later retrieved via the Clipboard Viewer utility. Clipboard data is stored in .CLP files.

Selecting, Copying, and Cutting in Windows Applications

In Windows NT, the Windows 3.1 standards and procedures for copying, cutting, and pasting apply because NT's WOW supports all the Windows 3.1 calls for these services. Also, because the WOW subsystem shares a common clipboard with the Win32 subsystem, data can be passed between 32-bit and 16-bit applications.

In a nutshell, when running NT, you'll use an application's Edit menu and the Edit menu's shortcut keys for these tasks just as you've done before, minus a few limitations that were imposed by Standard mode operations in Windows 3.1.

Concerning the selection of portions of documents for copying or moving to another document, the following steps still hold true:

1. For text, the usual techniques of dragging across the text, using the Shift key in conjunction with the arrow keys, and other techniques such as double-clicking in

the left margin to select complete lines, still apply in NT. These techniques vary from application to application.

For graphics, again, the techniques for selection vary, even more greatly than for text-based programs such as word processors. Typically, users have to consult the application's instructions or Help files for clarification of selection procedures.

2. After selecting, choose Edit | Copy or Edit | Cut, depending on whether you want to copy the material or delete the original with the intention of pasting it later.
3. Reposition the cursor, either in the same document or in another document, and choose Edit | Paste. The material will appear in the new location.

TIP

Some programs might have shortcuts for copying, cutting, and pasting, so you should read the manual or the Help screens supplied with the program.

Copying Selected Text or Graphics from Non-Windows Applications

You can copy a selected area of graphics or text from non-Windows programs such as DOS applications. You might want to do this to paste text data or graphics into a Windows document. However, you can do this only when the non-Windows program is running windowed (not full-screen). If the program won't run in a window, you're out of luck. This usually works if you have a standard 640×480 screen driver.

POSIX and OS/2 applications by necessity run in character-based screens because NT can't run graphics programs in those environments. Thus, the information you copy from these windows will be character-based. When you're running DOS applications, the story is different. NT knows whether the application is running in character mode or graphics mode and processes the grabbed (copied) data accordingly. If the data is detected as text, it's copied as a character stream. If the data is detected as graphics, it's pasted into the destination application as a bitmapped graphic. The data can then be pasted into any Windows program that will accept text or graphics from the Clipboard (for example, Notepad, Write, Cardfile, Paintbrush, Terminal, Word, and so on).

TIP

Note that some DOS programs might appear to be in text mode (because they are displaying text) but in fact are not. In this case, copying text might not work as expected. Sophisticated DOS-based word processing programs such as WordPerfect or Microsoft Word for DOS can run in graphics mode to better represent the final printed page on-screen. If you copy text from the DOS window when a program is running in this mode, you might be surprised to find that what's been copied to the Clipboard is a graphic, not text. Thus, you won't be able to paste it into another text file. Switch the DOS program back into text mode before copying and then try again.

Here are the steps for copying text and graphics out of a DOS-based program window (the command-prompt window):

1. Window the DOS application. If it's currently full-screen, press Alt-Enter to make it a window. (Some applications can't run in a window. See the coverage of the PIF Editor in Chapter 9, "Configuring Windows NT," for DOS application quirks.)
2. In the DOS application, open the document to be copied from. Scroll it so that you can see the item to be copied. (You can copy only what's actually on-screen.)
3. From the window's control box, choose Edit | Mark. This puts the window into selection mode. Select the text or graphics area to be copied by dragging the mouse pointer as explained earlier in this chapter. Start in the upper-left corner of the target area and move down to the lower right.
4. Release the mouse button. The selected area will be highlighted. An example is shown in Figure 5.1, in which some text from a WordStar document has been selected.

NOTE

The moment you first click in the window to begin selecting, its menu bar changes. The word Select precedes the window name, indicating that you're in select mode. You can't use your application again until you finish the selection process or press the Esc key.

5. Open the DOS application's Control menu and choose Edit | Copy, as shown in Figure 5.2. (Note that there's no Cut command.) This places the text on the Clipboard.

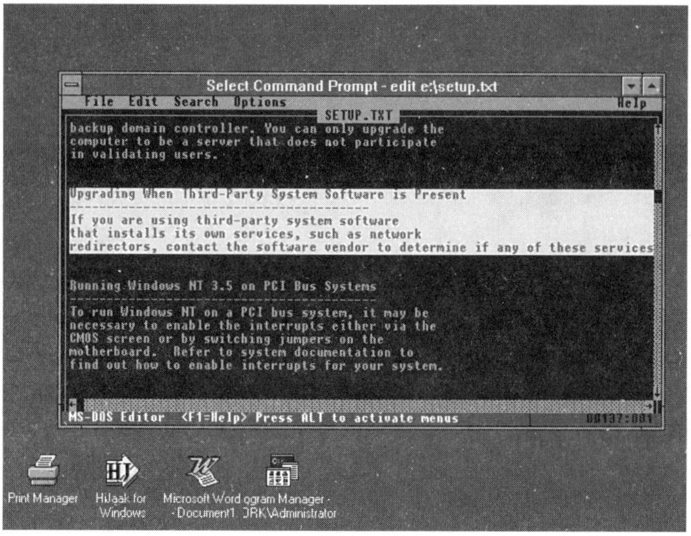

FIGURE 5.1.

To select text or graphics from a DOS application, first window the document, then select the desired text with the mouse.

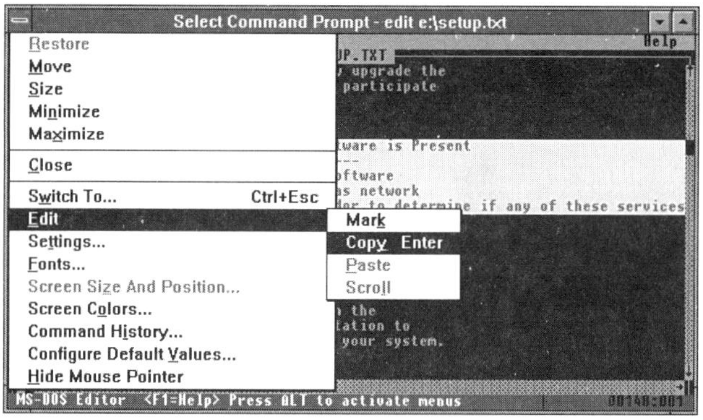

FIGURE 5.2.

The Edit | Copy command.

6. The text or graphic is now on the Windows NT Clipboard. Switch to the destination Windows application, position the cursor, and choose Edit | Paste to paste the Clipboard's contents at the cursor position.

> **NOTE**
>
> Windows figures out the format of the copied material based on the screen mode the DOS application uses when it runs. If the application is running in a recognizable graphics mode such as one of the VGA graphics modes, Windows copies a graphic bitmap to the Clipboard. Otherwise, it copies the selection as text.

Copying a Bitmapped Image of the Active Window

In order to create documentation or marketing information about software, you can capture the screen or portions of it, such as the active window, using the Clipboard. The screen or window you capture may contain either a Windows or non-Windows application. The Clipboard translates the selection into a bitmap format that some graphics programs, such as Windows Paintbrush, can read, print, or convert into another file format such as .PCX or .TIF for use with desktop publishing programs.

TIP

If you don't want to work with the window's image right away, you can save it on disk as a .CLP file or put it in the Clipbook for later use. See the sections in this chapter titled "Saving the Clipboard's Contents to a File" and "Using Clipbook."

TIP

If you write lots of documentation, remember that some 16-bit Windows screen-capture techniques that work in NT are superior to using the Clipboard. Collage was used to capture the screen shots in this book. Other programs of note are Tiffany, PixelPop, Hotshot, and Hijaak. These tend to be very flexible in their capture modes and file formats, including gray-scaling capabilities.

To copy the active window's image to the Clipboard, follow these steps:

1. Open the application in a window.
2. Adjust and size the window as needed. Note that if a dialog box is open, this window usually is considered the "active" window.
3. Press Alt-Print Screen. The image of the active window is copied to the Clipboard.

NOTE

If Alt-Print Screen doesn't seem to copy the image, try Shift-Print Screen. Some older keyboards use this key combination instead.

4. Follow the steps in the section in this chapter titled "Pasting Information from the Clipboard" to paste the copied information.

Copying a Bitmapped Image of the Entire Screen

If you want to capture an image of the entire screen, follow these steps:

1. Set up the screen appropriately. For DOS applications, the screen can be either windowed or full-screen.
2. Press the Print Screen key. (On some keyboards, this key is called Prt Scr or something similar.)

NOTE

If pressing Print Screen doesn't work, try Shift-Print Screen or Alt-Print Screen. Some older keyboards use this combination.

The image will be copied to the Clipboard. See the section titled "Pasting Information from the Clipboard" and the sections that follow it for information on pasting the Clipboard's contents.

Copying a File to the Clipboard from File Manager

You can use File Manager to embed or link files into other files using the Clipboard as an intermediary. Follow these steps:

NOTE

The details of object linking and embedding (OLE) are covered later in this chapter.

1. Select the source file from the File Manager window.
2. Choose File | Copy.
3. In the Copy dialog box, choose the Copy to Clipboard option. The entire file is copied to the Clipboard as an object.
4. Return to your destination document, position the cursor if necessary, and choose Edit | Paste Special | Paste Link. The document is embedded.

Pasting Information from the Clipboard

As soon as you've copied or cut a graphic, some data, or another type of object (such as a portion of sound or video) to the Clipboard, you have three choices:

- Paste it into a document you're working with (or that you open later)
- Save it to a Clipboard file
- Save it on a Clipbook page

Saving data in a Clipboard file or on a Clipbook page are described later in this chapter. For now, I'll discuss just the options pertaining to pasting:

- Pasting information into Windows applications
- Pasting information into full-screen non-Windows applications

Pasting Information into Windows Applications

The vast majority of Windows applications have a Paste command on their Edit menus. However, if nothing is on the Clipboard, this option will be grayed out, meaning that you can't choose it. Also, some applications have their own internal clipboard, so even though you've copied something, it might not be on the system-wide Windows Clipboard. Such setups are for use only between separate documents created in the same application. Word for Windows "large clipboard" is an example of this.

> **NOTE**
>
> Some Windows applications can provide more than a single data format when material is cut or copied to the Clipboard. This allows more flexibility when you're pasting into the destination document. This can provide live "data conversions" (instead of actual data being stored in the Clipbook) for particular formats. When you paste, the destination document and the Clipboard together figure out which stored format to use. See the section titled "Changing the View Format" for more discussion of this.

In any case, to successfully paste information, all you have to do is set up the right conditions and issue the Paste command.

1. Copy or cut the desired text or graphics onto the Clipboard.
2. Switch to the application and document to receive the information and position the cursor or insertion point. The exact technique for positioning differs from application to application.
3. Choose Edit | Paste or press Ctrl-V. (Pressing Ctrl-V won't work with all applications, however.) The Clipboard's contents will appear in the destination window.

The Clipboard's contents remain static until you copy or cut something new, so you can paste the same material repeatedly.

Pasting Information into Non-Windows Applications

Pasting into non-Windows applications is a little trickier, and the results might not be what you expect because not all non-Windows applications accept data in the same way.

NOTE

Keep in mind that any formatting contained in text will be lost when you paste data into non-Windows documents.

You can paste only text (not graphics) into non-Windows applications. To paste graphics, you have to cut or copy the graphic into a program such as Paintbrush or CorelDRAW! and save the graphic in a file that can be read by the DOS graphics program. Because so many graphics programs are Windows-based these days, you're probably not using DOS-based graphics programs anyway, so this shouldn't be a common problem.

The easiest way to paste into a non-Windows application is to follow these steps:

1. Make sure the application is windowed. Press Alt-Enter if it isn't.
2. Using whatever method applies to the destination application, position the cursor at the location where you want to insert the Clipboard's material.
3. Open the destination application's Control menu. Choose Edit | Paste. (Make sure you're not in Select or Mark mode, or Paste will be grayed. Press Esc if you are.) The text will be copied into your document.

The internals of the process are interesting. The Clipboard's contents are sent to the portion of the environment subsystem responsible for buffering keyboard data entry. Thus, the data is dumped into the keyboard buffer for the non-Windows application. The result is that the application thinks you've typed the text from the keyboard. For the procedure to work correctly, however, the recipient program has to be written in such a way that it doesn't balk at receiving information faster than a normal human could type it. Figure 5.3 shows an example in which I inserted Clipboard text copied from a Help screen into a WordStar file running in a window.

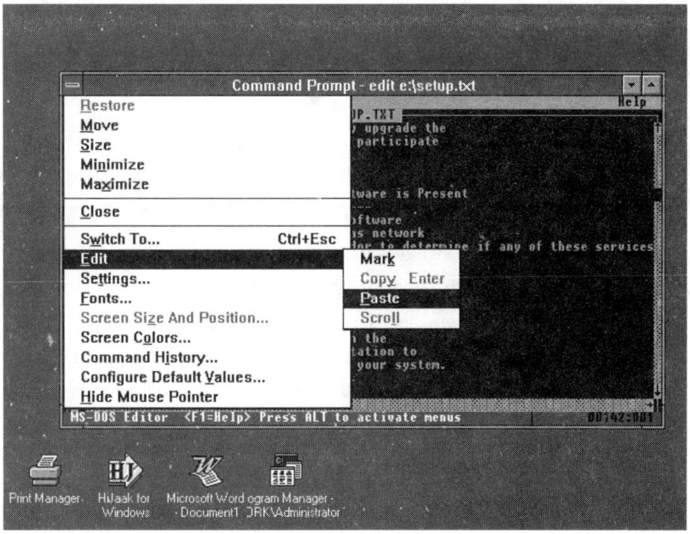

FIGURE 5.3.
To paste text into a non-Windows application running in a window, position the cursor and select Edit | Paste from the Control menu.

Working with Clipboard Viewer

After you put data on the Clipboard, you might not want to paste it immediately. The Clipbook Viewer program in Program Manager's Main group facilitates other Clipboard-related activities you might need. With it, you can

- view the Clipboard's contents
- save the Clipboard's contents to and retrieve the Clipboard's contents from a file
- clear the Clipboard's contents

Viewing the Clipboard's Contents

Sometimes you'll forget what information is on the Clipboard. Every time you cut or copy, the Clipboard's contents are replaced with the new material, so you might forget what's there. Pasting the wrong thing can be a hassle, so viewing the contents in advance can be useful. Another time when viewing is useful is when you're trying to get a particular item into the Clipboard, but you can't quite see how well you're doing. If you bring up the Viewer and position it in the corner, you get instant feedback when you cut or copy.

In any case, here's how to view the Clipboard's contents:

1. Run the Clipbook Viewer program by double-clicking on its icon in Program Manager's Main group.

2. The Clipbook Viewer window comes up. Double-click on the Clipboard icon in the bottom-left corner of the window. The iconized Clipbook icon turns into a window that displays the Clipboard's current contents.

Changing the View Format

The contents of the Clipboard might look different in the viewer window than in the source application. Text line breaks might be in new positions, or graphics might be mottled or distorted. Graphics and text both can have a considerable amount of formatting material associated with them, such as font type and size, and graphics settings for resolution, color, aspect ratio, gray-scaling, and so on. The application you cut or copy from is supposed to inform Windows NT, and thus Clipboard, of the nature of the material. The NT Clipboard does its best to capture all the relevant information, but it doesn't necessarily display all of it in the viewer window.

Based on this information from the source application, Clipboard knows in which formats the data can be viewed and accepted. As an example, a Paintbrush picture can be passed on to another application as what Windows NT calls a bitmap-enhanced metafile, picture-enhanced metafile, or Windows-enhanced metafile. Other information that relates to object linking and embedding also can be included in an item placed on the Clipboard, but these aspects don't appear in the viewer window.

In any case, check the View menu for display options. The options won't affect the Clipboard contents, only its display. The Default setting returns the view to the original display format the material was first shown in.

NOTE

When you paste into another Windows application, the destination program does its best to determine the optimal format for accepting the information. This isn't determined by the Display menu's setting or the current Clipboard window display. If the destination's Paste option is grayed, the contents are not acceptable.

Saving the Clipboard's Contents to a File

When you log off, shut down, or place new material onto the Clipboard, its current contents are lost. Also, because the Clipboard isn't network-aware, its contents can't be shared with other users. However, you can save Clipboard contents to disk in .CLP files and reload them later. If you do lots of cutting and pasting of specific items, you might want to use this technique. Additionally, if network users have access to the drive and directory containing the .CLP file, they can in effect use your Clipboard.

NOTE

.CLP files use a proprietary file format that is readable by virtually no other popular programs. Clipbook Viewer provides what you might consider a more elegant technique for achieving the same results, however.

1. In the Clipboard Viewer utility, choose File | Save as. The Save As dialog box appears.
2. Type in a name. As usual, you can change the pathname and extension. You should leave the extension as CLP, however, because Clipboard uses this as the default when you reload the file.
3. Click on OK. The file is saved. It can be loaded again as described in the next section.

Retrieving the Contents of a Stored Clipboard File

You can reload a .CLP file into the Clipboard. too. Note that when you do so, anything currently on the Clipboard will be lost.

1. Run Clipbook Viewer.
2. Click on the Clipboard icon.
3. Choose File | Open in Clipboard Viewer's window. The Open dialog box appears.
4. Select the file you want to pull onto the Clipboard. (Only legitimate .CLP files can be opened.)
5. If something's already on the Clipboard, you're asked whether you want to erase it. Click on OK.
6. Change the display format via the View menu if you want to (assuming that options are available on the menu).
7. Paste the contents to the desired destination.

Clearing the Clipboard

Although NT machines tend to have a lot of RAM and sizable hard disks, system requirements are likely to consume significant amounts of these resources. Thus, memory and application management can be important. Keep in mind that information stored on the Clipboard can affect the amount of memory available for use by the system and other applications. If you're cutting and pasting small bits of things, as most people do during the course of a workday, you have nothing to be concerned about. However, some items, such as graphics, video, sound samples, or large amounts of formatted text, take up considerable space on the Clipboard. This is especially true of items stored on the Clipboard in multiple formats.

If you're running into memory shortages, you might occasionally want to clear the Clipboard's contents.

NOTE

In Windows 3.1 you can get an idea of how much system memory an item on the Clipboard is occupying by referring to Program Manager or File Manager's Help | About... boxes before and after copying (if you cleared the Clipboard first). NT's dialog boxes don't report free memory, so it's harder to know what's going on. You'll need to use the NT Performance Monitor to determine the amount of free memory. Performance Monitor is covered in Chapter 20, "Optimizing Your Network."

To clear the Clipboard, follow these steps:

1. From Clipbook Viewer, select the Clipboard view by double-clicking on the Clipboard icon or by clicking on its window.
2. Choose Delete from the Edit menu. Click on the X button in the toolbar or press the Delete key.
3. Click on OK. The Clipboard's contents will be deleted.

Using Clipbook

The Clipboard suffers from a variety of shortcomings. The three most glaring ones are the following:

- You can't store more than one item at a time. Copying a new item erases the previous one.
- You can't share Clipboard data with network users.
- It's a hassle to store and retrieve Clipboard files. Saving a number of small clip-art bitmaps, for example, means naming multiple files and remembering their names when you reload them.

A Clipboard enhancement called Clipbook first appeared in Windows for Workgroups. It's been updated to a 32-bit version for NT. Clipbook offers a number of key features:

- It allows up to 127 pages of Clipboard storage. Each page is like a separate Clipboard.

- Each page can be given a description of up to 47 characters in length.
- Pages can be displayed as "thumbnails" for easy reference.
- Individual pages can be shared for use by network workstations.
- It contains enhancements for network OLE that make linking to objects on another computer easier.

Running Clipbook

To run Clipbook, double-click its icon in the Main program group. Its window appears, as shown in Figure 5.4.

FIGURE 5.4.
Clipbook Viewer.

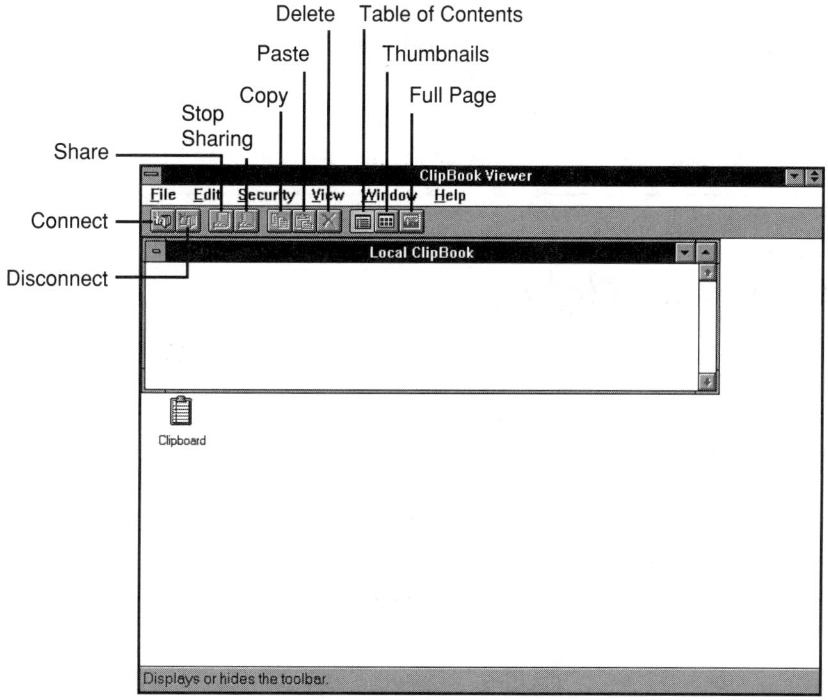

The toolbar offers a number of useful options. Table 5.1 lists the toolbar's buttons and their meanings.

Table 5.1. Clipbook Viewer toolbar buttons.

Button	*Effect*
Paste	Pastes the contents of the Clipboard to the Clipbook
Copy	Pastes a selected Clipbook page to the Clipboard
Table of Contents	Lists the named pages in the Clipbook
Thumbnails	Displays thumbnails of the Clipbook's pages
Full Page	Full display of a selected Clipbook page
Delete	Deletes the contents of a selected page (or the contents of the Clipboard if they're showing)
Connect	Connects to a Clipbook on a remote (networked) computer
Disconnect	Disconnects from a Clipbook on a remote (networked) computer
Share	Shares a page of your Clipbook for network users to access
Stop Sharing	Stops sharing a page

Pasting into Clipbook

Clipbook doesn't replace Clipboard. Instead, like many of the Clipboard enhancements from third-party software developers, it works with it. Cutting, copying, and pasting into applications is still done via the Clipboard. Clipbook is simply a convenient storage tank for Clipboard items. Figure 5.5 illustrates the relationship of Clipboard to Clipbook.

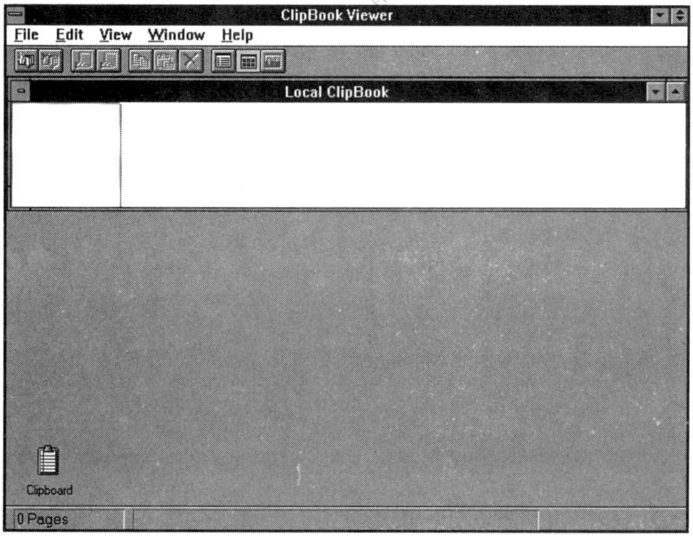

FIGURE 5.5.
Items are added to the Clipbook when you paste them from the Clipboard.

When you want to add an item to the Clipbook, follow these steps:

1. Put the information on the Clipboard using the source application's Edit menu.
2. Switch to Clipbook Viewer.
3. Choose Edit | Paste. A Paste dialog box appears, asking for a name for the new page (see Figure 5.6). Each time you paste into Clipbook, you have to name the page.

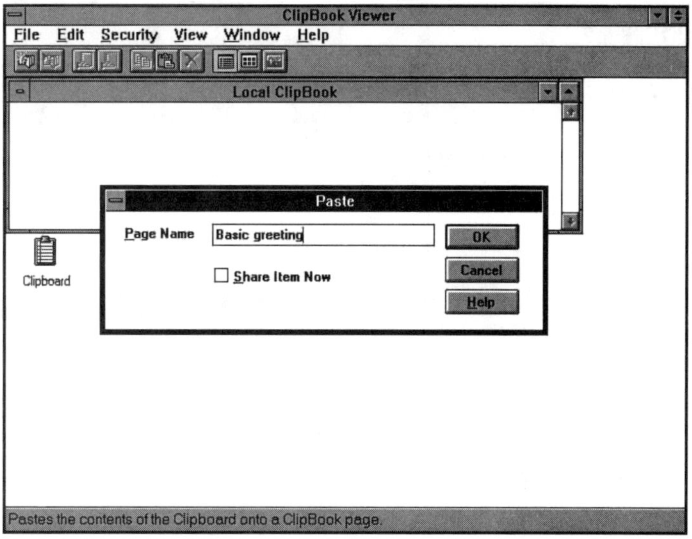

FIGURE 5.6.
Naming a Clipbook page.

4. Enable the Share Item Now box if you want to make the item immediately available to network users.

Pasting from Clipbook

As soon as items have been copied to the Clipbook, you can paste them into documents on the NT workstation or share them with networked workstations. Follow these steps to paste an item from the Clipbook to the Clipboard for use in other applications:

1. Open Clipbook Viewer.
2. Select the page containing the information you want.
3. Click on the toolbar icon for pasting to the Clipboard, or choose Copy from Clipbook Viewer's Edit menu. This places the material on the Clipboard.
4. Switch to the application you want to paste into. Place the cursor where you want to paste the information and choose Edit | Paste.

Sharing Clipbook Pages for Network Use

When you want to share a Clipbook page so that others on the network can link to it or copy it into their documents, do the following:

1. Select the page in Clipbook Viewer.
2. Click on the Share button or choose File | Share. You see the dialog box shown in Figure 5.7.

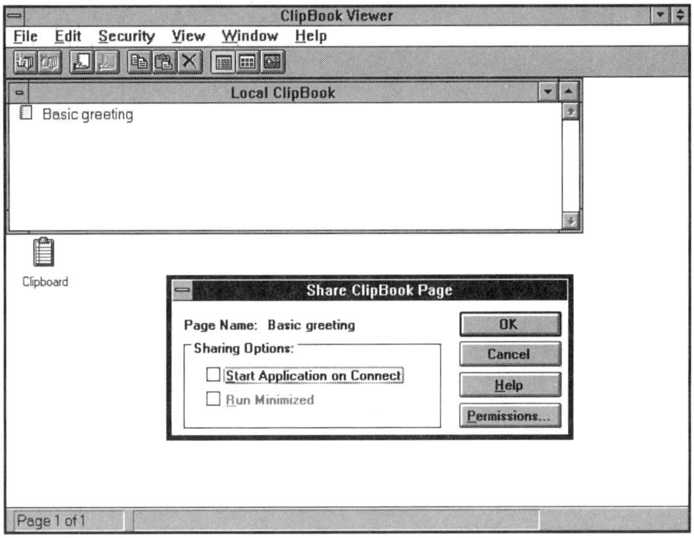

FIGURE 5.7.
The Clipbook Page dialog box for sharing.

3. Notice the Start Application on Connect check box. You have to enable this check box if the data on the Clipbook page is more complex than a bitmap or unformatted text. If you don't, network users won't be able to access the data.

TIP

When the Start Application on Connect check box is enabled, the source application will run when a remote user accesses the specific page. If you don't want the running of the application to interrupt your work by opening a window on the serving workstation, enable the Run Minimized check box.

4. Unless specified otherwise, pages are shared with a permission level that enables others to only link to it or read it. Only the creator has permission to change, erase, or share the data.

Setting Permissions for Shared Clipbook Data

Each page of the Clipbook can have separate permission levels assigned to it. If you created the Clipbook page or if you've been assigned a high enough permission level on the system, you can adjust the permissions assigned to the page. This means that you can control who has access to the page. Normally, all users have read and link access to pages, but you might want to limit access to power users or administrators, or to another group of users set up by an administrator, such as "art personnel," "finance personnel," and so forth. Alternatively, you might want to extend the access to allow some users to alter the Clipbook data by giving them write access.

Suppose, for example, that a group of artists is working on a corporate logo that exists on one system's Clipbook but that has been linked into a number of documents in the network, such as the company letterhead, envelopes, and memos. You might want to allow any of the artists to alter the logo to update it as it evolves. This would require altering the default rights.

Follow these steps to alter the permissions for a page:

1. Select the Clipbook page in question.
2. Choose Security | Permissions. The dialog box shown in Figure 5.8 appears.

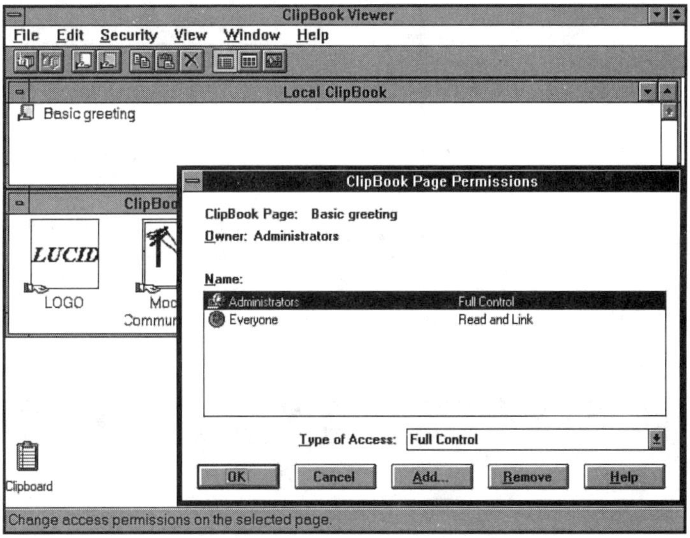

FIGURE 5.8.
Changing permissions for a Clipbook page.

3. Choose the individual (or group) whose permission level you want to alter.
4. In the Type of Access area, choose the permission level you want to assign.

TIP

If you want to prevent any access to the page by a group or individual, select the group or person and click on Remove.

Rather than changing permissions for an existing user, you might want to add a new user to the list. You also do this from the Permissions box.

1. Choose Security | Permissions.
2. Click on the Add button. The Add Users and Groups dialog box, shown in Figure 5.9, appears.

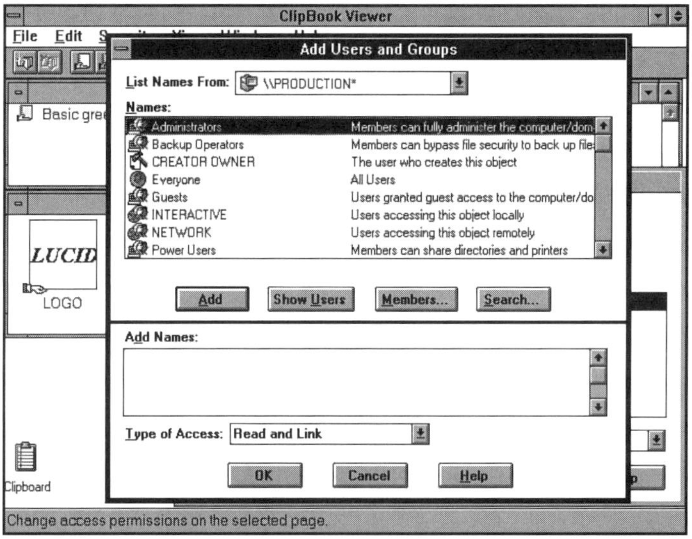

FIGURE 5.9.
Adding a new user to the list of people allowed access to your Clipbook page.

3. If the person's name isn't showing, choose a new domain or computer in the List Names From section.

TIP

You can use the other options in the dialog box to find users and groups on the network, including which domain they're in. Most often you'll use the Show Users button after you select a computer or a domain from the List Names From section. If you've selected a domain or a group and you want to see who's in it, click on the Members button.

4. When you see the user or group name you want, click on it to select it, then click on the Add button.
5. In the Type of Access box, choose the permission level you want to assign to the groups or users.
6. Click on OK.

> **TIP**
>
> The NT Clipbook server can be set to create an audit trail, recording the use or attempted use of your Clipbook pages. Your audit report can list a variety of variables, such as day and date of access, users' names, and so on. Auditing is covered in Chapters 10 and 12.

Object Linking and Embedding Under NT

One of the big draws to Windows was that it enabled users to run multiple programs in concert, almost as if they were designed as a single piece of software. Even die-hard DOS users have been caught using Windows 3.x simply as a task switcher, running multiple DOS sessions so that they didn't have to quit one to start another. The additional advantages of a consistent user interface across applications and Clipboard's data transferral capabilities have converted some hard-core DOS users to the GUI world of Windows despite the issues of speed and stability.

As I discussed earlier, the Clipboard enables you to freely pass information—text, numeric data, sounds, drawings, charts, and so on—from one program to another. But post-Windows 3.0 products (Windows 3.1, Windows for Workgroups, Windows NT Workstation, and Windows NT Server) have gone a step further with an information sharing system called object linking and embedding (OLE), which allows the information passed to other programs to remain "linked" to its source program.

As a power user or a systems administrator, undoubtedly you are aware of the existence of OLE. You might even use it regularly. Maybe you've set up complex arrangements on your network based on OLE protocol. On the other hand, many veteran Windows users have only a cursory knowledge of OLE and don't understand its nuances, so they stick with the tried-and-true Clipboard for interapplication data passing. Because not all applications are "OLE-aware" or implement it in the same way, it sometimes seems to some users like opening a can of worms. Add to this some confusion over the differences between dynamic data exchange (DDE) and OLE, and additional confusion over rules governing the use of OLE over a network, and you've got a rich topic that could use some elucidation! Therefore, this section offers a short OLE primer. This is followed by a discussion pertaining to the use of OLE under Windows NT.

Advantages of OLE

Let's look at a classic business application of OLE. Say you're starting a business and you want to construct a convincing, professional-looking business plan using a Windows word processor such as WordPerfect, Word, or AmiPro. You want to include financial projections for the new company, substantiating them with financial data taken from a spreadsheet. You could cut and paste numbers from your spreadsheet into the document, but the projections change daily as you update your spreadsheet input. Instead, you link the relevant cells from the "live" spreadsheet directly to the document. When you change the numbers in the spreadsheet, they automatically change in your business plan. Figure 5.10 shows a Lotus 1-2-3 spreadsheet linked to a Word for Windows document, illustrating this effect.

FIGURE 5.10.
Data linked between a 1-2-3 spreadsheet and a Word for Windows document.

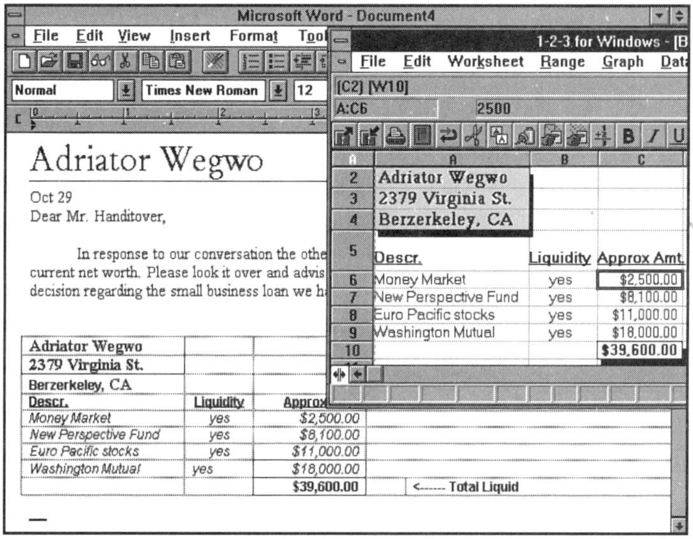

Even simpler, when you need to enter new figures in the spreadsheet, you don't need to manually locate and open it. Windows knows which document and program the numbers came from, so you can bring up the spreadsheet and edit it just by double-clicking on it in the word processing document. This causes the source application (such as 1-2-3) to run and to automatically load the spreadsheet, ready for your changes. As soon as your changes are entered, you close 1-2-3. The changes appear in the Word document and in any other document linked to the spreadsheet.

Using this same technique, you can link charts, graphics, sounds, and even video to documents. For example, you might want to add a chart from that same spreadsheet program to your business plan to communicate the numeric information graphically, or a sound clip that explains a concept when you click on it. In the case of a chart, you would want the chart to be redrawn automatically to reflect any changes in the underlying data.

OLE Versus DDE

Although OLE is the more powerful of Windows' data-sharing devices, the older and less-nimble DDE is still included in Windows NT, so you should become familiar with it. With earlier versions of Windows, you could achieve some of the same results you get with OLE using DDE. (NT and Windows for Workgroups have included an updated network version of DDE called NetDDE.)

The drawback of DDE is that it leaves much of the work of sharing information to each individual application. As a result, the steps you have to go through to ensure that data is updated in linked documents varies greatly from program to program. You have to consult the manual for each application when you want to link data to another document. Because OLE came out with Windows 3.1, and because it's been updated even since then (with OLE version 2), most major Windows applications support OLE rather than DDE for user-related data sharing. Internally, though, programs can use DDE for behind-the-scenes communications between documents or applications. One application that uses DDE in this way is Microsoft Excel, which uses some DDE functions in macros that control some linking and embedding actions.

Understanding OLE Concepts

It's important to have a thorough understanding of the basic OLE terms and concepts before you try to create documents using OLE. Otherwise, you might end up creating a mess, especially over the network.

Let's start with the differences between the terms *linking* and *embedding*. With OLE, you have the option of using either one. They're different in functionality and in how you work with objects that are linked as opposed to embedded. Study Figures 5.11 and 5.12 for a moment.

Notice that in the case of linking, two separate files exist. The spreadsheet data can be edited either from within the word processing document or separately from its source file in the spreadsheet application. In the second figure, the graphic file is more intimately connected to the word processing document. The embedded picture can be edited only from within the document and doesn't need to have a separate source document.

With both linking and embedding, both documents are categorized as *compound* documents. A compound document is any document composed of two or more dissimilar document types joined via OLE.

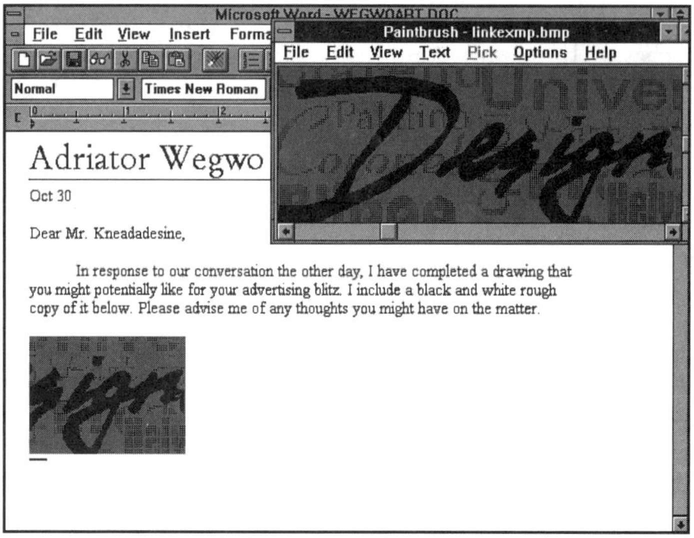

FIGURE 5.11.
A section of one document linked to another.

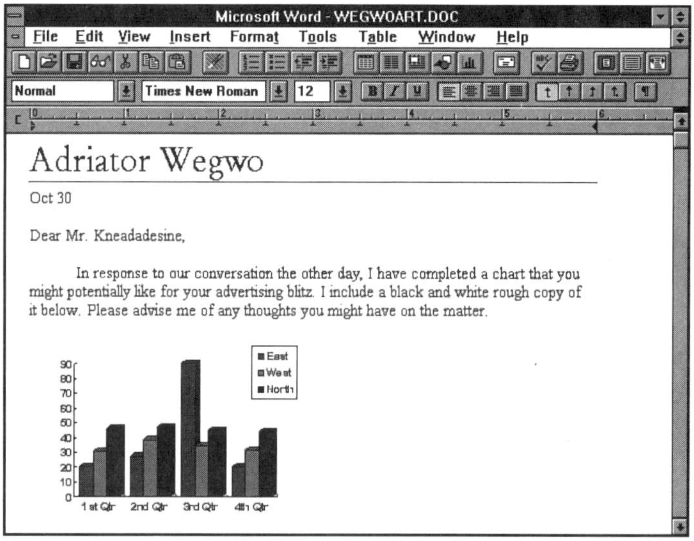

FIGURE 5.12.
One document embedded in another.

Servers and Clients

To refine this discussion a bit, let's consider a few other concepts. Programs play two distinct roles in the process of sharing information via OLE:

- One program originates the object that is to be embedded or linked. This is called the OLE *server.*
- The other program accepts the object. This is called the OLE *client.*

NOTE

An *object* is any chunk of information passed as a bundle from one program to another. An object can consist of as little as a single spreadsheet cell, database field, or graphic element, or as much as an entire spreadsheet, database, or complete picture.

For example, in Figure 5.10, Lotus 1-2-3 is the originating (server) program and the word processor is the accepting (client) program.

High-end applications often work as both OLE servers and clients. For example, a spreadsheet program might supply charts and worksheet objects to a word processor or a desktop publishing program, but it might also be able to accept embedded database objects from a DBMS (database program). However, client/server capability in a single application isn't always the case. Some programs, such as Sound Recorder and Paintbrush, can act only as servers. Others, such as Write and Cardfile, can function only as clients.

Two other OLE terms that are fairly self-explanatory refer to the documents with which an object is associated. The *source document* is the one in which an object is originally created. The *destination document* is the one into which you place the object.

In-Place Editing

A new OLE 2.0 feature is *in-place activation.* The examples I've been discussing demonstrate OLE 1.0-compliant applications, where each application utilizes a separate window (as shown in Figure 5.10). An OLE 2.0-compliant application, however, will seamlessly change the application's behavior.

Look back at Figure 5.10, which shows a Word for Windows document and a 1-2-3 spreadsheet, and compare it to the Word for Windows document and Excel spreadsheet shown in Figure 5.13. They look pretty similar, don't they?

However, double-clicking on the displayed chart doesn't invoke an instance of Excel to display the chart for editing. Rather, it modifies the menu and toolbars to those contained in Excel, as Figure 5.14 demonstrates. This is known as *visual editing,* or in-place activation.

Packages

Aside from the two basic OLE options of linking and embedding, there is a third variant of OLE—*packaging.* You can use packaging to essentially wrap up a server document in a bundle represented by an icon. As soon as the package is embedded, the icon (rather than the document itself) appears in the destination document. Figure 5.15 shows an example of a Cardfile card with a sound file package embedded in it.

FIGURE 5.13.
An example of an OLE 2.0 embedded object.

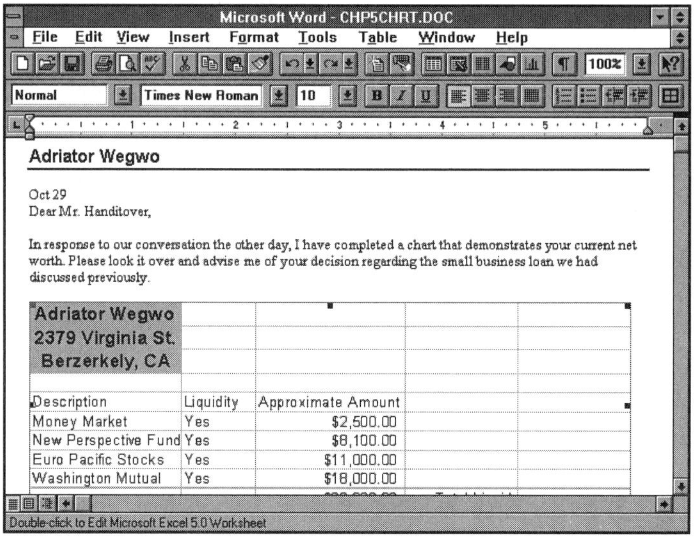

FIGURE 5.14.
An example of in-place editing of an OLE 2.0 embedded object.

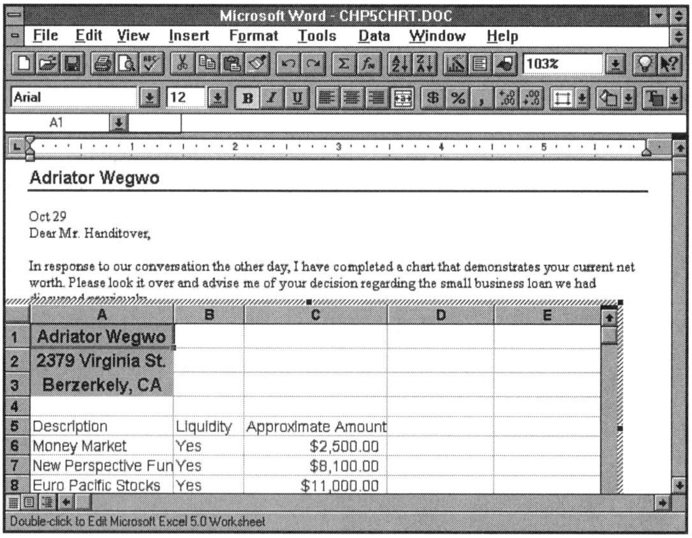

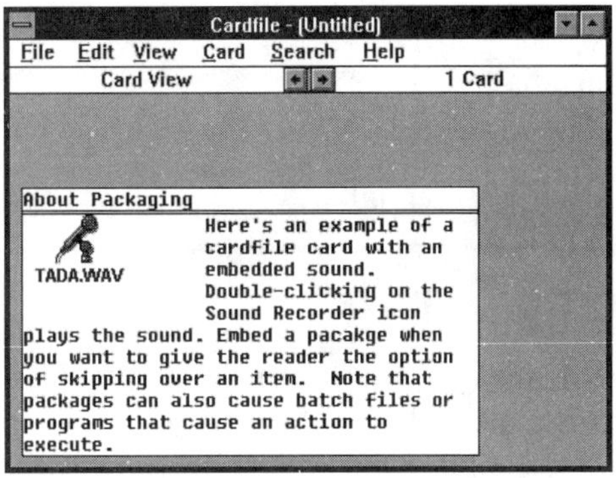

FIGURE 5.15.
Packaging a document iconizes it for later replay, but the document doesn't display automatically.

Packaging is achieved either from File Manager or by using the Packager program.

NOTE

It's worth mentioning that DDE and OLE functionality requires that there be enough memory to load both involved applications (server and client) simultaneously. I've known several users who have forgotten this fact and have been seriously discouraged when utilizing DDE and OLE, particularly in very complex compound documents. Also, note that very complex documents created under NT might not function properly if the same document is loaded under Windows 3.x, due to differences in system resources.

OLE Methodology Variations

Despite a greater consistency among OLE-aware programs relative to DDE, there are still idiosyncrasies and slight variations in the way you work with OLE in different applications. You might have to snoop through an application's menus or consult its manual to determine how to edit OLE items. In Cardfile, for example, you don't have to place the cursor over a linked picture before you edit it, because Cardfile knows that the picture is in the upper-left corner. Similarly, because you play a linked or embedded sound object in a destination document by double-clicking on the Sound Recorder icon, you can't use the double-click method to edit the object. Instead, you choose Edit | Sound Object and then choose Edit from the cascading menu.

With that general understanding about the nature of OLE out of the way, I'll now review the procedures for using embedding, linking, and packaging objects in Windows NT. I'll also discuss some networking and security issues that pertain to linked objects. The discussion breaks into the following topics:

- Embedding objects
- Linking objects
- Packaging objects
- Maintaining object links

Embedding Objects

Embedding an object is almost identical to pasting a static copy of it from the Clipboard into an old-style non-OLE application. These two processes—embedding and plain old pasting—are very similar, because neither involves a link to any external files. The only difference between standard Clipboard cutting and pasting and OLE embedding is that when you embed an object you can easily edit it by clicking on it or by choosing an Edit menu option. This is possible simply because the embedded object contains a pointer to its source application.

Here are the basic steps for embedding an object into a document:

1. Open the source application and document. Make sure that the application can perform as an OLE server.
2. Select the portion of the document you want to embed in the other document.
3. Switch to the destination application and document. Position the insertion point and choose Edit | Paste. If the application is OLE 2.0-compliant, position the insertion point and choose Edit | Paste Special.

Assuming that both applications are OLE-aware, you might get what looks like a static copy of the material (such as a bitmap), but the destination application will know from whence it has received and thus can be easily edited.

TIP

With some OLE applications, you can embed an object using a command choice such as Insert | Object. This leads to a dialog box from which you choose the type of object. (All the OLE-aware programs on your system are listed.) After you choose, the source application runs. You can then create the object and exit, returning to the calling application. When you exit, the object is placed in the destination document.

Editing an Embedded Object

When you want to edit an item you embedded, follow these steps:

1. Double-click on the item. The source application will run, and the object will be loaded into it.

NOTE

With some applications, double-clicking on an embedded file won't have any effect until you change modes. In Cardfile, for example, you have to choose Edit | Picture first.

2. Choose File | Update and then File | Exit and answer Yes to any resulting dialog boxes about updating. (Alternatively, you can just choose File | Exit.)

TIP

As an alternative to this technique, an application might have an Edit menu option for editing the object. Select the object and check the Edit menu.

Linking Objects

As I mentioned earlier, linking an object is similar to embedding it. However, there is an important difference. When you link, the connection between the source and the destination document is maintained. So, instead of copying the object's data to the destination document, the link tells the destination application where to find the original source file.

The user can open the source document in the original program without leaving the destination document. Any changes made to the object will be stored in the source file and reflected in the destination document. Likewise, editing the source document the ordinary way also works—the changes will be reflected in the destination document the next time it's opened.

Remember that you can drop the same object into multiple destination documents. Changes to the source object will be reflected in all destination documents. As a result, linking is the technique to use when you want to use data that must always be identical in two or more documents.

To link two files, follow these steps:

1. Create or find the server document you want to link (the source document). For example, you could open Paintbrush and draw something.

NOTE

Before you can link a file, it must be saved on disk. You can't link a file that's still called Untitled. Also, if you make changes to the document, be sure to save it before linking.

2. Select the portion of the document, drawing, and so on that you want to link.
3. Choose Edit | Copy to put it onto the Clipboard.
4. Switch to the destination document, such as a word processing document.
5. Move the insertion point to the place where you want to insert the linked item.
6. Choose Edit | Paste Link (not Edit | Paste).

NOTE

You also can choose Edit | Paste Special, choose a specific data format, and then click on Paste Link. (See the section in this chapter titled "Changing the View Format" for a discussion of choosing data formats.)

7. If you want to establish a second link, repeat steps 4 through 6, selecting a different destination document in step 4.

The linked item should appear in the correct position in the destination document. If all goes well, the object will appear in its original form. That is, a graphic will look like a graphic, not like the server application's icon. In some cases, though, you'll see the source application's icon instead. For example, if you're trying to link some Word for Windows text into Write, you'll see a Word icon instead of the text. If you really just want the text, you should use the Paste command. Otherwise, you get essentially a packaged object. (See the section titled "Linking and Embedding with Packages" and the sections that follow it.)

Editing a Linked Object

As soon as you've linked an object to one or more destination documents, you can edit the object starting from any of the places it appears. The technique for doing the editing is the same as editing an embedded object. The result, however, is different, because changes you make to a linked object appear in all the documents you've linked it to.

Here's the basic game plan for editing a typical linked object:

1. In any of the documents the object has been linked to, double-click on the object. The source application will open with the object loaded.

TIP

As an alternative, check the Edit menu. If you click on the object once and open the Edit menu, it might have an option such as Edit Object on it. Choosing this also works.

2. Make your edits.
3. Choose File | Save, then File | Exit. Changes you made should appear in any destination documents containing the link.

Linking and Embedding with Packages

So far, we've discussed embedding and linking objects by placing the objects themselves into destination documents. As an alternative, however, you can embed or link an object in the form of an icon that represents the object. This type of icon is called a *package.* When the user double-clicks on such a package, the object contained in the package opens in the application that created it (or, in the case of sound or animation objects, the object plays).

Why use packages instead of the ordinary embedding and linking method? Packages provide a simple yet powerful means of allowing access to supplemental information in documents that are designed primarily to be used on-screen rather than printed.

So, instead of presenting users with a confusing document displaying many pictures, charts, or tables, you can give them the option of clicking on icons that will open to reveal only what they choose. Each package can be labeled with a helpful description such as "For more about ostrich eggs, double-click here." Packages are a good way to include support documents in e-mail sent over the network.

Remember to use packages when you want to give the user the option of skipping over or ignoring the object, or of opening or running a program, batch file, or multimedia event with a double-click.

You can create a package in several ways:

- From File Manager
- From the Object Packager application
- From File Manager and Object Packager together

TIP

Because you can embed .EXE, .PIF, .BAT, and .CMD files, you can easily construct what amounts to a graphical menu of options in a document, with instructions next to each one. Write your comments and instructions to the user in an OLE-aware text processor such as Write. Then embed the appropriate file after each description, such as "Double-click here to back up the data files." Non-Windows applications' packages should be created using the Object Packager program detailed in the next section.

Packaging an Entire Document

A program called Object Packager is included with Windows NT (as well as with Windows 3.1, Windows for Workgroups, and Windows 95). It's used specifically for creating packages. You'll find it in the Accessories group.

NOTE

Packages can contain either an embedded or a linked object. Object Packager can package only embedded objects. To package a linked object, you must use File Manager as explained in the next section.

1. Open Object Packager. As shown in Figure 5.16, Object Packager has two windows, Content and Appearance.

FIGURE 5.16.
Object Packager.

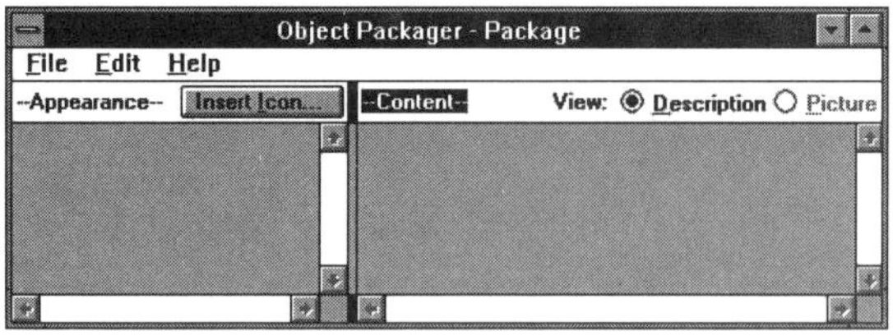

2. Select the Content window by clicking on it.
3. Choose File | Import to display the Import dialog box.
4. Use the Browse button to select the document you want to package.
5. Click on OK. At this point, you'll see the filename of the document you chose in the Content window and the icon for it in the Appearance window.

6. Choose Edit | Copy Package. This puts the document on the Clipboard.
7. Run the destination application and open a document.
8. Place the insertion point where you want to place the package.
9. Choose Edit | Paste. The package appears in the document in the form of an icon labeled with the document's filename.

You can now bring up the document, run the program, and so on by double-clicking on the package. Some Edit menus have other options such as Edit | Package.

Using File Manager to Package Document Objects

For packaging complete documents, File Manager is actually easier to use than Packager, and it's also more flexible. If you make a habit of keeping File Manager open, you might as well rely on it for packaging documents. Recall that in fact you must use File Manager to prepare packages containing linked objects.

File Manager packaging is very flexible. You have three ways to package documents (although all three aren't available with all programs):

- Drag the document to the destination document.
- Use the Clipboard to copy the document from File Manager, pasting it into the destination document as a package.
- Use the Clipboard to copy the document from File Manager to Object Packager, from which you the copy it to the destination document and paste it as a package.

Packaging an Entire Document from File Manager by Dragging

You can easily create packages by dragging documents to their destinations with the mouse.

1. In File Manager, open the directory that contains the source document, batch file, and so on.
2. Open the destination document and position the cursor.
3. Arrange the File Manager and destination document windows so that you can see the source file and its intended destination.
4. Drag the file into the destination document window. This creates an embedded object. To create a linked object, hold down Ctrl-Shift while dragging the source document icon to the destination window.
5. Release the mouse button to place the package at the insertion point. Figure 5.17 illustrates this process.

FIGURE 5.17.
Embedding a document with File Manager.

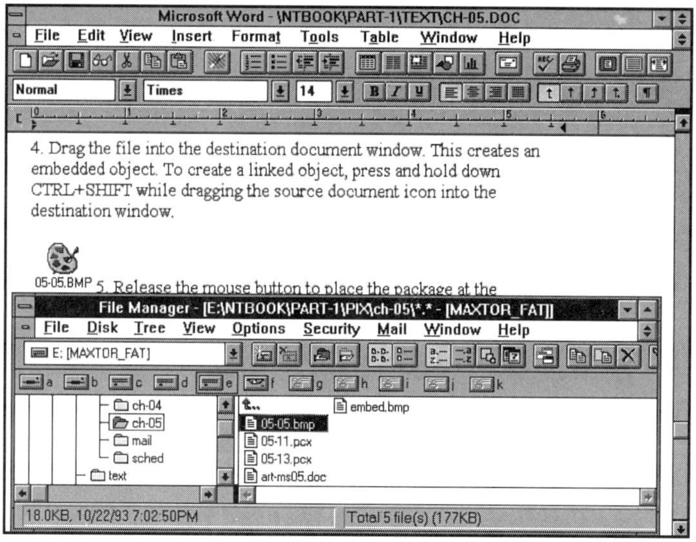

TIP

A plus sign should appear in the document pointer when the cursor is over the destination document. If instead you see the international "no" symbol cursor (as in No Smoking, No Turkeys, and so on), the destination application isn't OLE-capable.

Packaging an Entire Document Using File Manager and the Clipboard

Here's how to use File Manager in concert with the Clipboard to package an entire document:

1. In File Manager, select the file you want to package.
2. Choose File | Copy. The Copy dialog box appears.
3. Choose Copy To Clipboard and click on OK.
4. Open the destination document.
5. If necessary, position the cursor or insertion point where you want to place the package.
6. Choose Edit | Paste Link to place the document package as a linked object. Choose Edit | Paste to place the package as an embedded object.

Creating a Package Using File Manager with Object Packager

You can use transfer a document from File Manager to Packager using the Clipboard as an intermediary. This method involves an extra step, but it offers some advantages. With this approach you can change the icon or label used to represent an embedded package, and you also can create linked packages.

1. In File Manager, select the source document.
2. Choose File | Copy.
3. In the Copy dialog box, choose Copy To Clipboard and click on OK.
4. Run or switch to Object Packager. Select the Content window.
5. Choose Edit | Paste Link to create a linked document package; choose Edit | Paste to create an embedded document package. The filename of the source document shows up in the Content window. The Appearance window displays the icon of the source application.
6. Choose Edit | Copy Package to put the package on the Clipboard.
7. Open the destination document, move the cursor to the location where you want to insert the package, and choose Edit | Paste. The package appears in the document.

Packaging Part of a Document

The primary advantage of Object Packager over File Manager when you're creating packages is that you can limit the package to just a specific portion of the source document. You might want to limit the package to a few cells of a spreadsheet or a paragraph of text, for example.

Here's how to package just a portion of a document and place it in a document either as an embedded or linked object:

1. Create or open the source document. In this case, the object must have been created by an OLE server—that is, an application designed to originate linked or embedded objects. As always, if you want to link the object rather than embed it, you must first save the source document on disk.
2. Select the document section you want to package.
3. Choose Edit | Copy.
4. Open Object Packager and select the Content window.
5. In Packager, choose Edit | Paste if you want to embed the object or Edit | Paste Link if you want to link it. The Content window shows the path and filename for

the source document, and the Appearance window shows the source application's icon.

6. In Packager, choose Edit | Copy Package.
7. Open the destination document. Position the insertion point or cursor where you want to insert the package, then choose Edit | Paste. The package's icon appears at the spot.

Packaging .EXEs, .PIFs, .BATs, and Command Lines

As I mentioned earlier, you package an application just as easily as you package a document. For example, you might place the Calendar program at the top of your "to do" list for easy reference. You also can package a DOS or other command line (POSIX or OS/2, for example) in a package.

Just use any of the techniques outlined earlier to package the documents. Simply select the filename or icon of the application or batch file during the process. The application's icon will appear in the destination document, labeled with the program's full filename. Double-clicking on the package runs the application just as if you typed it at the command prompt or from File Manager or Program Manager. When you quit the application or batch task, Windows returns you to the original document.

Packaging an MS-DOS Command-Line Command with Packager

Object Packager has a little feature that facilitates creating a command-prompt package. Such a packaged command line might execute a single program or a number of commands from a batch file you've created. You can use it for packaging series of NT-compatible command-prompt commands.

TIP

Remember that because NT can execute any mix of programs from its command-prompt window, this can be a rich feature. You can mix Windows, POSIX, OS/2, and DOS commands in a batch file.

1. In Object Packager, choose Edit | Command Line.
2. Enter a command acceptable to the command prompt in the dialog box that appears. If you're typing the name of a batch file or a program file, enter the full pathname of the batch file.
3. Click on OK. The command you entered will appear in the Content window.

4. Before you can package the command, you must assign an icon to it. Click on the Insert Icon button in the Appearance window. The Insert Icon dialog box appears.
5. Select the icon of your choice from the scrolling display. Choose Browse if you want to change the icon. Find a file containing icons and choose one. Click on OK.
6. Choose Edit | Copy Package.
7. Insert the new package into your destination document in the standard way.

Managing OLE Links

Windows NT normally takes care of managing, linking, and updating all linked files and packages when alterations are made to OLE server documents. However, there are times when you might want to make manual changes or set some features of a link. The next several sections explain why and how to do this.

Manually Updating a Linked Object

Normally, any changes you make to the original version of a linked object immediately appear in all the linked copies of that object in other documents. When circumstances dictate, however, you can set up a link so that the changes appear only in destination documents when you manually execute an update command. You might want to do this when a source document is in flux and the destination document would read inaccurately or appear unfinished if the source were being updated before your work was done.

Here's how to set a link for manual updating:

1. Open the destination document.
2. Click on the object to select it.
3. Choose Edit | Links. You'll see the Links dialog box, shown in Figure 5.18.

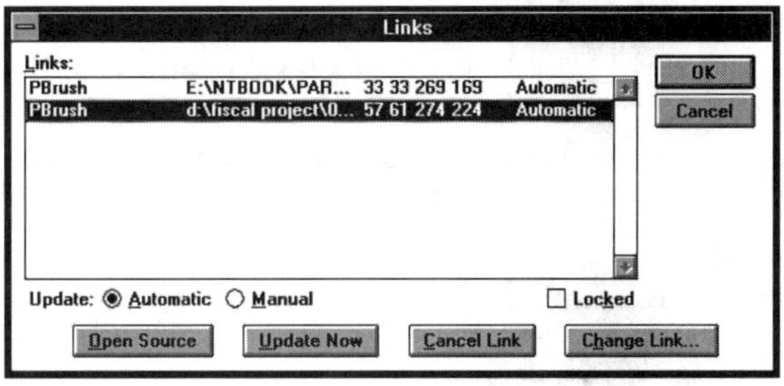

FIGURE 5.18.
Changing details of a link.

NOTE

If the Links dialog box lists two or more links, you can select multiple consecutive links by holding down the Shift key while you click with the mouse. You also can select multiple links that don't appear consecutively by pressing Ctrl while you click.

4. The Links dialog box lists all the links in your document, identifying each link by the source document's filename.
5. Click on the Manual button at the bottom of the Links box, then click on OK.

You can return to automatic updating for any link whenever you like. Repeat the process just described, clicking on the Automatic button in the Links dialog.

TIP

As soon as a manual link is declared, no changes will occur in the destination document until you manually update it. Just open the Links dialog box again and choose Update Now.

Using the Links Dialog Box to Manage Links

The Links dialog box also can be used to break or delete links, fix broken links, and alter existing links to refer to different source documents. Repairing broken links, especially on a network, is not an uncommon need. Source files can be lost or moved to other directories if they're scattered across the network or if they're under the supervision of many different users, and source machines can be offline.

Canceling and Deleting Links

Sometimes you'll want to break or cancel a link, destroying the connection between the source and destination documents. In this case, the object continues to appear in the destination document, but it can't be edited from within that document. A static copy of the material exists in the destination document, as though it were simply pasted in. That is, two separate copies of the material now exist: one in the source document and one in the destination, assuming that the destination document can actually display that type of material in the source file.

TIP

You probably can still edit the object if you need to by copying it to the Clipboard and pasting it back into the originating program.

When would you want to break a link? Only when you're fairly certain that you'll never be revising the object as it appears in the destination document.

In contrast to breaking a link, deleting a link goes a step further by actually removing the object from the destination document. The source document is left intact, of course.

You use the Links dialog box to break or delete links.

1. Start from the program containing the object with the link you want to break or delete.
2. Select the object and choose Edit | Links to display the Links dialog box.
3. Highlight the object in the list of links.
4. To cancel the link, click on the Cancel Link button. To delete the link, press the Delete key.
5. Click on OK.

Fixing Broken Links

As I mentioned, links can be broken accidentally. Common causes of broken links are moving or renaming files. Because Windows NT relies on the document's filename and pathname to locate the original object, OLE applications get confused when they can't find an OLE resource, so they break the link. Here's how to reestablish a link:

1. Open the document containing the object with the broken link.
2. Select the object and choose Edit | Links. The Links dialog box appears with the object already highlighted in the list of links.

TIP

You also can use Edit | Change Link to replace one link with a completely different one. Just select a different filename for the source document.

3. Click on the Change Link button. A new Change Link dialog box appears.
4. In the File Name list, select the filename of the source document that contains the original object. Click on OK. The Links dialog box reappears, showing the new name of the source document as the selected link.

5. Click on OK. When the dialog box closes—and assuming that the link is set for automatic updating—the current version of the linked object appears in the destination document.

Objects Located on Other Computers

Although you can use File Manager, the Link dialog box, or possibly commands in some programs to create links based on source objects stored on drives in other people's workstations across the network, the Clipbook application can make linking objects easier.

As I mentioned earlier, other network users can make information available to you by placing it on pages of their Clipbooks and then publishing the pages containing that information.

Likewise, when you want to link to a source document stored on their computers, they can put the file or a portion of it on a Clipbook page and share it. You can then copy that information to your Clipboard and paste the link into your document.

1. Run Clipbook and choose File | Connect.
2. Choose the computer and Clipbook page containing the information you want to link.
3. Choose Edit | Copy in Clipbook Viewer. This puts the information on your local Clipboard.
4. Switch to your destination document, position the cursor, and choose Edit | Paste Link (or Edit | Paste Special if you need a specific data format and the command is available).

Coping with Server Error Messages

As I mentioned earlier, if a destination document contains links to source documents on a remote workstation, errors can occur if that computer is unavailable for some reason. Maybe the computer is busy, dead, or offline. Or maybe the directory containing the document hasn't been shared, the file has been moved, the server application is busy printing, or a dialog box is open.

In such instances, you might see an error message saying `Server Unavailable` when you try to open a link or a package in hopes of playing, editing, or updating it. Here are your options:

- Just wait. The server might get it together after some process is completed. Your computer will keep calling for the information as long as the dialog box is onscreen.

- Use the Cancel button in the dialog box to cancel the box and alert the other computer's user that there's a problem. Make sure that the server application and document are shared and available and that your permissions allow you access to the directory.

OLE Security and Permissions

Keep in mind that every user on an NT network has certain rights and privileges applicable to all files, directories, and disks to which they're connected. Complex documents present a particular challenge to NT's security system because they can combine elements supplied from various sources. The text in a document could come from a file the user has read/write (full) access to, while an embedded portion of a spreadsheet is supplied by a workstation or a directory to which the user has only read privileges.

As far as security goes, there's an important distinction between embedded and linked documents. Recall that in the case of embedded documents, there really is only one document. Therefore, the access restrictions assigned to that file apply to all portions of the complex document. In other words, when you embed an item, it takes on the security level of the destination document.

By contrast, when you link a document, there are still two documents, each with its own access restrictions. These restrictions might be identical, or they might be different. If the user tries to edit a portion of a complex document to which he or she doesn't have access privilege, NT won't allow it, and a dialog box will issue an appropriate message.

Summary

This chapter discussed the various methods available for sharing data between applications and workstations. Note that many of the procedures explained here can apply equally well to Windows for Workgroups, because that platform supports network OLE and Clipbook page sharing using the same techniques I've described. The information in this chapter should make it clear that data sharing need not be limited by the simple cut, copy, and paste commands that virtually all Windows (and even Mac) users are familiar with.

Remember that with OLE, complex and rich documents that combine the talents of seemingly disparate programs can be pulled together, calling upon elements spread across even huge NT-based networks. It's not inconceivable that a company report could contain live spreadsheet data from the Houston office, a newly updated logo from the San Francisco art department, and freshly edited text from the New York office, all pulled together and updated when you open the document first thing in the morning. Changes that the remote offices made during the previous day would immediately appear in the document as NT reached across the network to load the document's objects.

Also remember that you can use the Windows Clipboard to create screen captures to illustrate user documentation, and that Clipbook pages make sharing bits of clip art, spreadsheet sections, pages of text, bits of sound, or even whole files a simple task. You rarely have to copy material onto a floppy disk and walk it around the office to another workstation just to share a little data with a coworker.

6

Network User Applications: MS-Mail, Schedule+, and Chat

IN THIS CHAPTER

Like Windows for Workgroups, Windows NT comes bundled with several very useful productivity-enhancing programs for use on networks—MS-Mail, Schedule+, and Chat. MS-Mail and Schedule+ are known as "MAPI-aware" programs in the industry. That is, they utilize the Microsoft Mail API (application programming interface) to allow network users to interact in some way through the medium of a mail post office that resides on a mail server within the network. These two programs are full-blown workgroup applications (nowadays colloquially dubbed *groupware*) that can help keep open the lines of communication between workers and help manage corporate and agency employee scheduling. The third program is really just a utility that makes on-the-fly communication between workstation users easier. I cover all three programs in this chapter. Whether you're simply using these programs as a network client or you're a network administrator or the postmaster for a workgroup, you'll want to read this chapter.

Sending and Receiving Mail with MS-Mail

Bundled with the Windows NT package is a 32-bit version of Microsoft's e-mail application called Microsoft Mail. This application enables you to communicate easily with other users over a network using a common post office set up on a server. You can send memos to other people on the system and attach documents such as word processing, spreadsheet, or database files, as well as OLE objects such as sound, graphics, charts, and video clips.

E-mail is a step in the direction of the "green office" because it cuts down on paper usage (assuming that you don't give in to the temptation to print your mail on paper!). It eliminates the need to print, copy, and physically distribute interoffice memos. It's also satisfying to know instantly that your message was sent (and optionally, that it was read) without having to pick up the phone and make a call. Options also enable you to

- organize your sent and received mail into bins called *folders*
- print selected mail
- search through messages to find specific ones

An Overview of MS-Mail

Here's a brief overview of an MS-Mail system for Windows NT. First, a person must be assigned the task of being the post office administrator. This person creates a *workgroup post office* (*WGPO*) on his or her machine or on a server somewhere. This WGPO consists of a directory with some files in it. The machine must be on and the directory shared for messages to be sent and received. The computer can be turned off after the business day is over if no one expects to process mail and if no one will be calling in using remote access services.

The administrator creates an account for herself, and she can optionally create accounts for other users. The other users can create their accounts themselves, though, if they want to.

NOTE

Users on the network can create a new account for themselves only the first time they run Mail. Once an account is set up for a user, that user can't create a new account on the Mail server.

Creating an account consists of entering a name, mailbox ID, password, and some optional data such as phone numbers, department, and so on. As soon as an account is open for a user, he or she can send and receive mail.

When a letter is sent to a user, it's stored in the post office machine. A file in your NT hard disk directory called MSMAIL.MMF is updated by the WGPO to indicate that the user has a message. (This file is called the local MMF file.) The user can then read the message, keep it for future use, or dispose of it.

You don't have to be on the network to use Mail. A feature enables you to download messages from the post office server to your machine, then read your mail offline and compose responses. Later you attach to the network again and send your mail.

So much for the basics. Now for the specifics of using Mail. There are two parts:

- Using Mail
- Setting up and administering the WGPO

Establishing Accounts

Each user has to establish a post office account. The following are the steps for a typical user. (Note again that this can be done only the first time the user runs Mail after NT is installed on his or her workstation.)

1. Run Mail from your workstation.
2. You will see a dialog box about creating a new account, as shown in Figure 6.1. Choose Connect to Remote Post Office.
3. You'll be asked the location of the post office. Use the resulting dialog box, shown in Figure 6.2, to browse the network and find the WGPO directory on the post office workstation. Choose this directory and click on OK. The directory you stipulate must be shared for network use and grant full read/write access to all users.

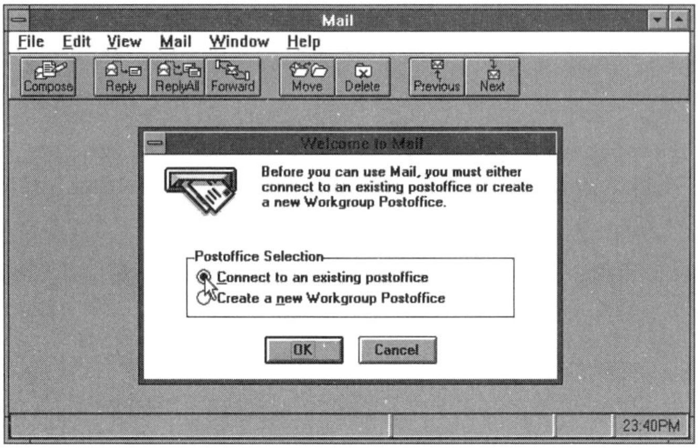

FIGURE 6.1.
Connecting to a WGPO.

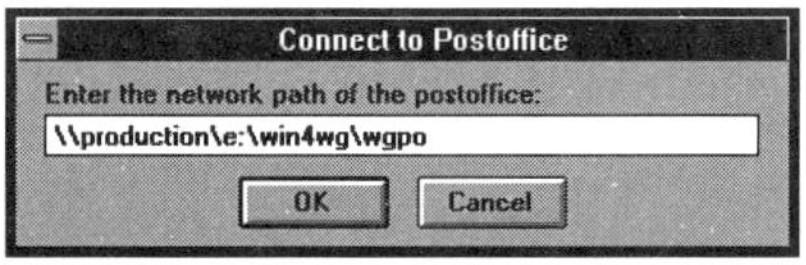

FIGURE 6.2.
Enter the path of the WGPO.

NOTE

Unfortunately, there is no Browse button, so you can't easily scan the network. If you don't know the path of the network post office, you'll have to ask someone who does. Remember that workstation paths start with a double backslash, such as \\bigserver\wgpo.

TIP

If you already have a Windows for Workgroups WGPO set up, NT machines can use it without modification. Simply log on as usual if you already have an account, or create a new account using the Windows for Workgroups WGPO path.

4. You'll be asked if you have an account on the post office, as shown in Figure 6.3. If you don't, answer no. If you do have an account, simply log on as usual and skip the rest of this section.
5. You'll see the Enter Your Account Details dialog box, shown in Figure 6.4. Fill in the information about yourself. Only the first three fields are required. The second field is already filled in.

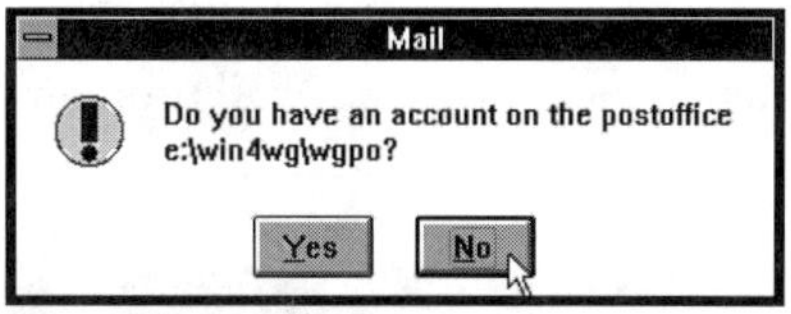

FIGURE 6.3.
Click on No, assuming that your administrator hasn't set up an account for you already.

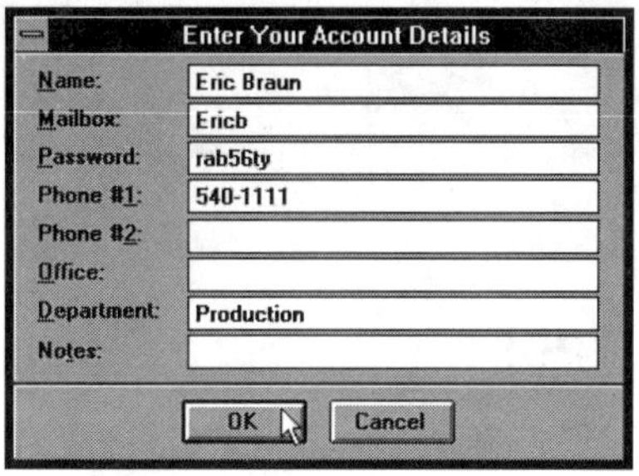

FIGURE 6.4.
Enter your account information.

The following are some notes on each of the items:

Item	*Maximum Length*	*Description*
Name	30	If not blank, this defaults to the name you used when you installed NT, although you can change it for the Mail system if you like. Typically, you'll use a full name such as John Doe.
Mailbox	10	This is a unique and personal mailbox name. It defaults to the username for your NT account. Try not to use anything you'll have trouble remembering. Typically, a username or a mailbox name is a first name and a last initial, such as JOHND.
Password	8	If you don't change this, it defaults to PASSWORD, which is very easy to remember.
Phone #1	32	Your primary phone number.
Phone #2	32	Your secondary phone number, such as a fax.
Office	32	The location of your office.
Department	32	Your department in your company.
Notes	128	Any special comments you might have about this particular mail account.

As soon as you fill in these items and click on OK, an account is now established in the post office. When you next run the Mail program, you'll be prompted to enter your mailbox and password before you can exchange mail.

NOTE

If later you want to change your password or mailbox, ask the postmaster. These items have to be changed from the post office workstation, using the Mail | Postoffice Manager command.

Checking Your Mail

When you first log on to Mail, you see the two panes shown in Figure 6.5. This is the basic Mail setup.

FIGURE 6.5.
The Mail screen.

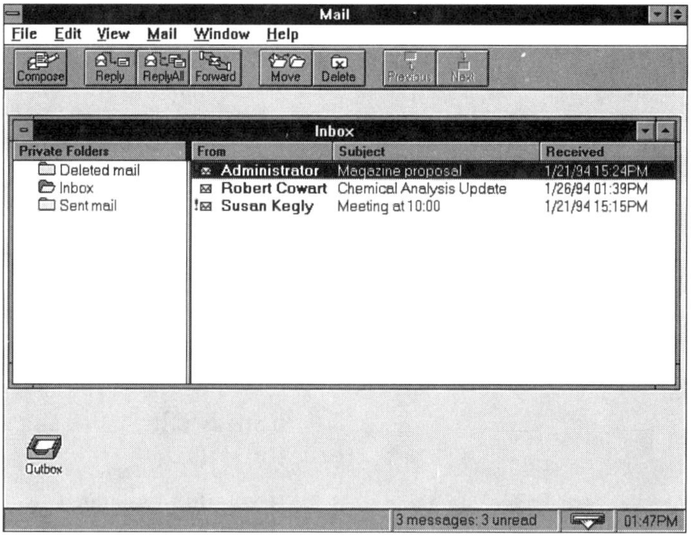

In the left pane is a list of folders, much like directories in File Manager. You create and use folders to store mail you've already received and want to file. The number of folders you can create isn't limited, so you can set up as many as you find necessary to keep your mail organized and accessible.

In the right pane are short descriptions (*headers*) of the mail you've received. When a piece of mail hasn't been read, the envelope icon to the left of the sender is still sealed. As soon as you read an e-mail missive, the envelope icon opens. A red exclamation mark (!) next to the item means that the sender tagged this message as high priority. A paper clip means that the communiqué has a file of some kind attached to it.

The following are the actual steps for checking and reading your mail.

1. Open the View menu and choose New Messages. This causes your workstation to check for new messages that might have come in after you ran Mail.
2. Click on the Inbox folder on the left side of the screen (see Figure 6.5). If the Inbox is iconized at the bottom of the screen, double-click on it. It might be down there if you iconized it at some point.
3. In the right pane, click on From, Subject, or Received to sort the items if you have lots of new mail and want to see the messages in a particular order. Each button sorts the messages in a different order (sender, subject, or date).
4. Double-click on the message you want to read. It pops up in a message window like the one shown in Figure 6.6.

FIGURE 6.6.
Reading a message by double-clicking on it.

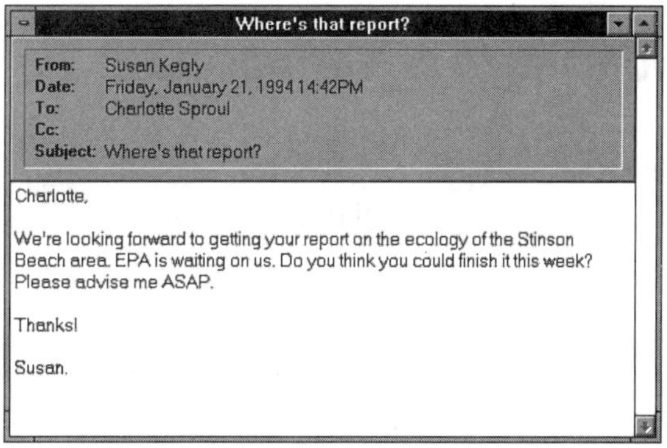

The message heading at the top of the window tells you who sent the message, who else it went out to, and the subject matter. If a file or files are attached to the message, it appears as an embedded icon with the file's name below it. You can double-click on the icon to open the file or run the application.

NOTE

You can open a file only if the following are true:

- There's an association for it set up in your system.
- The necessary application is available either on your system or on one you're connected to.
- The association points to the correct network path.

You can have several documents open at once. You can continue to read messages while other messages are waiting. Each opens in a window. You close a message window just as you close any window—by double-clicking on its control box. You also can iconize it to get it out of the way temporarily.

After reading a message, you can do several things with it:

- Respond to the sender
- File it in a folder
- Delete it

TIP

You can save any message you're reading or composing as a text file on disk. With the message's window open, choose File | Save and fill in a filename.

Responding to a Message

E-mail often is a continuing conversation between office workers that you'll often want to respond to. Mail makes it easy by giving you a Reply button and by automatically addressing the e-mail to the sender. Here's how to use the Reply button:

1. Click on the Reply button in the toolbar.

TIP

If you want to send mail to everyone who was sent the message, click on Reply All instead.

2. A new type of window called a Send Note form appears. (See Figure 6.7.) The sender's name and the subject (carried over from the original missive) are already typed in. The message you're responding to is included in the note, with pipe characters (|) down the right margin. You might want to remove this text or reference it in your response.

TIP

A simple way to reference individual sections or paragraphs is to enter your responses within the body of this copy. Your newly entered material won't have pipe characters next to it.

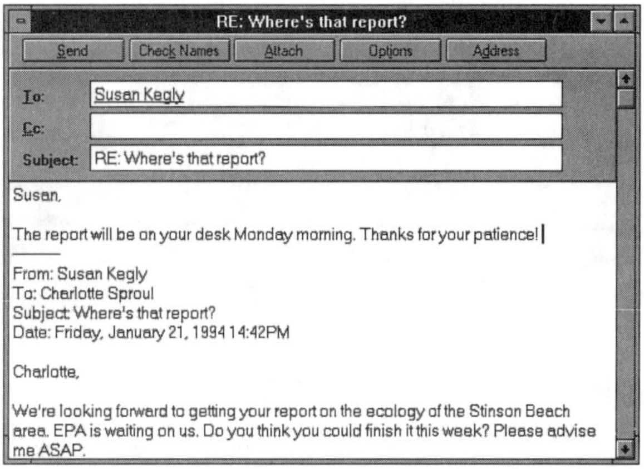

FIGURE 6.7.
Entering your response to mail. The message you're replying to is entered automatically, below the horizontal line.

> **NOTE**
>
> See the section titled "Sending a New Message" to learn how to attach files and objects to a message.

3. When you're finished editing, click on Send. The message is sent down the line and stored in the WGPO directory on the post office machine. The recipient mail boxes are updated to indicate that mail has been received.

Deleting a Message

If you want to delete a message, the easiest way is to follow these steps:

1. If the Inbox is closed, open it by double-clicking on it.
2. Click on the Delete button in the toolbar, or choose File | Delete.

> **TIP**
>
> Alternatively, you can drag the file into the Deleted folder.

Actually, the message doesn't get deleted. Instead, it gets put into the Deleted folder. You can undelete the message at any time up until you quit Mail.

CAUTION

Normally, the Deleted folder's contents are erased when you quit Mail. If you delete a message and then change your mind and want to reclaim something you deleted during the current session, open the Deleted folder and pull the message back out before you quit Mail. See the section titled "Moving and Copying Messages Between Folders" for more information about moving messages around.

Sending a New Message

Creating a new message and sending it are easy when you know a few basic steps.

1. Click on the Compose button in the toolbar, or choose Mail | Compose Note. A Send Note window, shown in Figure 6.8, appears.

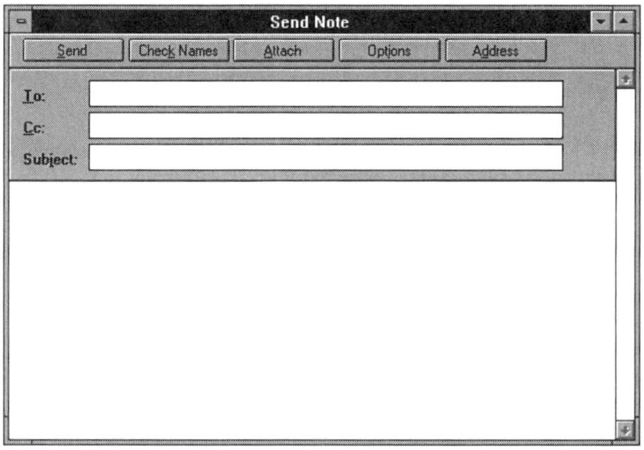

FIGURE 6.8.
Creating a new message.

TIP

If you're composing multiple notes and you want to see one as you're writing another, click on the Compose button again. A new window will open with each click.

2. Click in the To: field, then click on the Address button. A list of people who have accounts in your post office appears. Choose the recipient(s) to whom you want to send the missive. You can choose multiple people by Shift-clicking or Ctrl-clicking, just as when you select files in File Manager. Typing a letter takes you to the first entry that starts with that letter. (See Figure 6.9.)

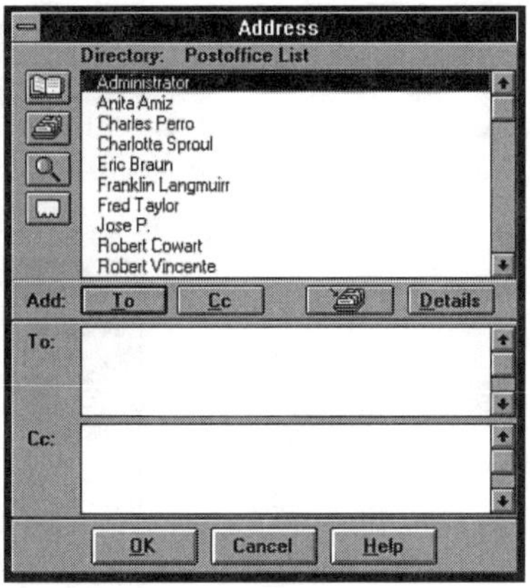

FIGURE 6.9.
The Address dialog box.

TIP

Entering just the first letter of a person's name in the To: or Cc: lines and then clicking on Check Names displays a list of only names starting with that letter.

3. Click on the To: button, and the selected name or names are added to the list in the lower half of the Address list. Multiple names are separated by a semicolon.

TIP

If you want to know more about a possible recipient, select the name and click on Details. A dialog box appears that lists specifics such as the location of the post office, the phone number, and the network name of the user.

4. The major recipients have now been specified. Next you need to choose the people you want to send copies to. You do this the same way you choose the primary addressees. Choose the names, then click on the Cc: button. (If you leave the Cc: area blank, no one will get copies.) Again, recipients' names are separated by semicolons, as shown in Figure 6.10.
5. Click on OK to accept the addressees. They'll show up in the To: and Cc: areas in the Send Note window.
6. Fill in some information in the Subject area. What you enter here will be seen in the recipient's in-box listing.
7. Enter the message in the message window.

TIP

Text wraps automatically. It will rewrap to fit the window if you resize it.

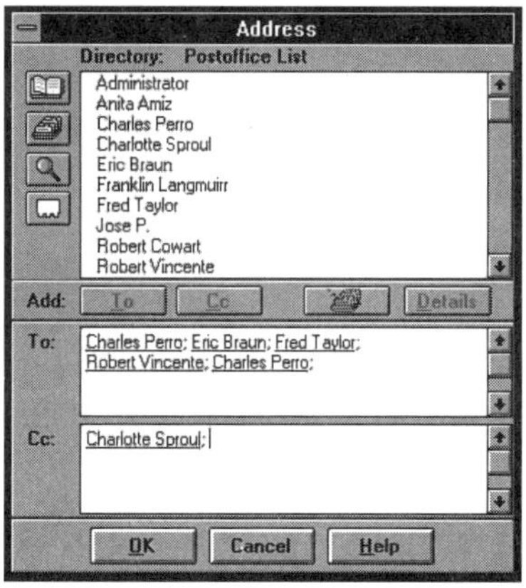

FIGURE 6.10.
Addressees filled in.

8. Click on Options if you want a return receipt when the recipient reads the message, or if you want to tag the message as high priority or low priority. (See Figure 6.11.) (A low-priority message displays a little down-arrow to the left of the message on the recipient's screen.)

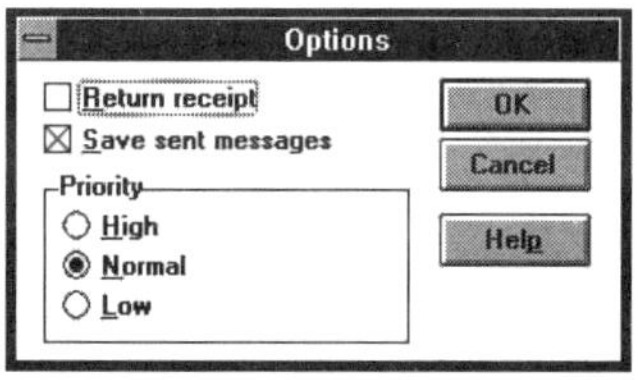

FIGURE 6.11.
Optional settings for the message.

9. Use the Attach button to attach an external file to the message. As I mentioned earlier, typically this would be a formatted word processing file, database, spreadsheet, graphics file, or executable program. If it's a document file, the receiver will need access to a program that can read the file. When you click on Attach, a standard File dialog box appears. Choose the file and click on the Attach button in the dialog box. A file icon is placed in the text area of your message.

TIP

If you prefer to write and edit text in your favorite word processor, attaching a file lets you accomplish this. Just address the note and attach the file you've written.

Note that you also can attach other types of OLE objects to a message via Mail's Edit | Paste Special command. (See Chapter 5 for more about the use of OLE.)

10. If you want to spell-check the message before you send it, choose Edit | Spelling or press F7. You'll see a typical spell-check dialog box. Figure 6.12 shows the spelling dialog box, which is similar to the one in Word for Windows.

FIGURE 6.12.
Spell-checking can be performed on a selection of text or on the whole message.

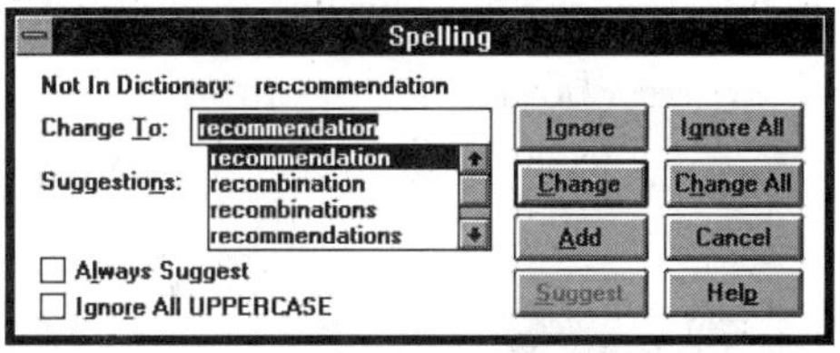

TIP

To spell-check a word after you've typed it, double-click on it to select it and press F7. To always have Mail check your spelling before you send a letter, choose Mail | Options and enable the Check Spelling... check box.

11. Click on Send to send the message.

NOTE

If you want to bail out and not send the message, just double-click on the message window's control box.

Filing Messages in Folders

Though the most commonly needed categories for message organizing are supplied (everybody has Inbox, Deleted, and Sent Mail), you can create as many as you like using the File | New Folder command. Some can be private and others public. Dragging a message into a public folder enables any user in your Workgroup to read the file.

Working with folders is much like working with directories in File Manager. You can create new folders, delete folders, and copy or move messages between folders. Folders can have subfolders, just as directories can have subdirectories.

NOTE

The metaphor of File Manager is, in fact, being implemented more and more by Microsoft. The Windows NT Tape Backup program uses the same layout.

Moving and Copying Messages Between Folders

To move or copy your files among folders, follow these steps:

1. Open the correct box (inbox or outbox).
2. In the left pane, double-click on the folder containing the message to be moved or copied.

NOTE

You must double-click on a folder in the left pane to open it, not single-click as you do in File Manager to see files in a directory. Unless the folder's icon looks "open," you're not looking at its contents in the right pane.

3. In the right pane, select the message and drag it to the destination. Alternatively, click on the message name, click on the Move button in the toolbar, choose the destination folder, and click on the OK box. To copy the message rather than move it, press Ctrl while dragging. A plus sign in the cursor indicates that you're making a copy. You also can use the File | Copy command if you prefer menus and dialog boxes or if you don't have a mouse.

Creating a New Folder

If you want to create a new folder to better organize your letters, follow these steps:

1. Choose File | New Folder. The dialog box shown in Figure 6.13 appears.

FIGURE 6.13.
Creating a new folder using the File | New Folder command.

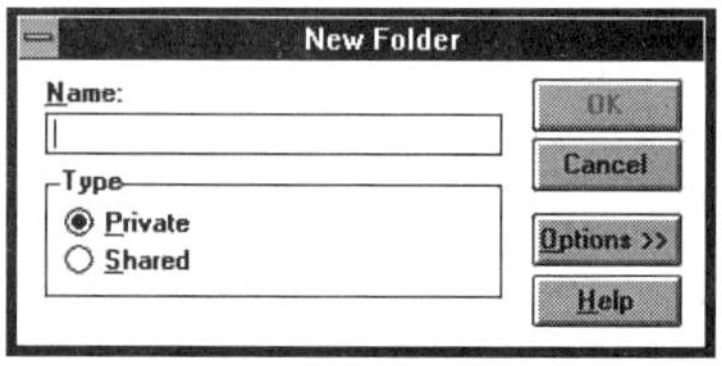

2. Choose whether you want the folder to be available only to you or to anyone with an account in your post office. Shared folders are useful for posting items for public access, such as general company announcements or documents for distribution. When you create a shared folder, it appears in the list of shared folders on everyone's computer.

TIP

You switch between viewing shared and private folders by clicking on the words Private Folders or Shared Folders at the top of the left pane of the Inbox window.

NOTE

You also can share documents in other ways, such as by sharing a directory with File Manager, or by embedding or linking a document to a Clipbook page and sharing that page. However, it might be easier to simply send the document to the post office. That way, your machine doesn't have to be on when other people need access to the information.

3. Just as when you create a new directory, a new folder will be created as a subfolder below the currently selected folder. However, there's no "root" folder, so you can't select the root first if you want a top-level folder (on the same level as Inbox, Deleted Mail, and Sent Mail). You have to use the Options button for that. In the New Folder dialog box, click on the Options button. The dialog box expands to the size shown in Figure 6.14.

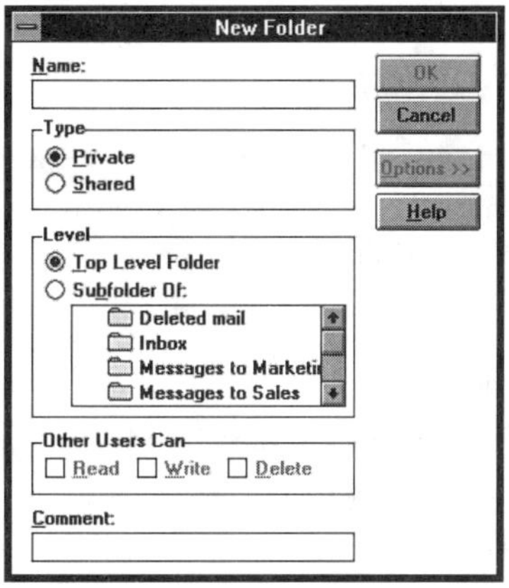

FIGURE 6.14.
Set folder options from this box, including whether a folder is a top-level folder.

Click on Top Level Folder if that's what you want, or choose the folder that you want the new folder to be a subfolder of. If you share the folder, you can set whether other users have Read, Write, or Delete permissions on the folder. They will need Write privileges in order to add new messages to the folder.

4. Click on OK for any open boxes. The newly created folder appears in the left pane.

TIP

If you want to adjust the folder properties after the fact, highlight the folder in the left pane and press Alt-Enter or choose File | Folder Properties. The Folder Properties dialog box appears.

Changing Passwords

Your post office password is separate and distinct from the system password you use to log on to NT. Occasionally you might want to change your mail password to protect your mail from others. Regularly changing your password is a good idea if mail security is of importance in your setting. The postmaster (administrator) can change your password, or you can do it yourself. Here's how to change the password on your own:

1. Choose Main | Password.
2. Type your old password and press Tab or click in the next section.
3. Enter the new password in the New Password box.
4. Confirm the new password by entering it in the Confirm box, then press Enter. The new password will become effective the next time you sign in to Mail.

Locating Messages

It's not uncommon to find yourself poring over scads of stored messages, attempting to unearth a memo that contains an important phone number, date, or whatever. The Find command searches through your messages based on text, subject, recipient, or sender criteria you specify.

1. Choose File | Message Finder. The Message Finder dialog box, shown in Figure 6.15, appears. Enter any pertinent information and leave the other fields blank.
2. Click on the Where to Look button to refine the search.
3. Click on the Start button to begin the search. If it looks like it's going to take forever, or the message has been found, click on Stop.

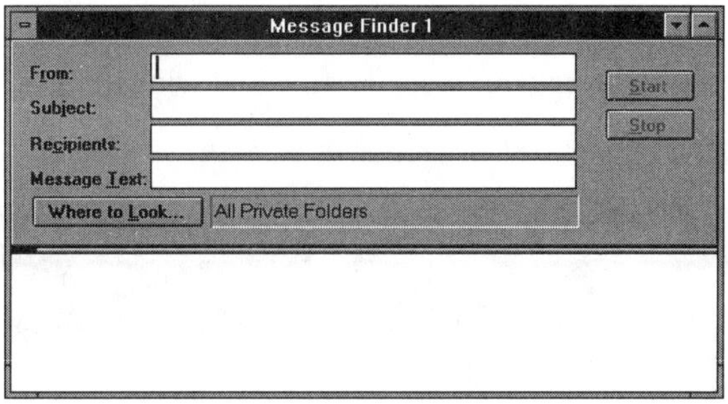

FIGURE 6.15.
Use this dialog box to search for a message.

Using Message Templates

Message templates are similar to document templates you might have used in, for example, Word for Windows. Templates typically are some type of form (such as a time sheet) or a regularly scheduled announcement sent to a specific group. To create a template, you set up a document (note) just as though you were going to send it. When you save it as a template, it's stored complete with attachments, a message, and a list of recipients (if you specify these). The next time you need to send the message, it's ready to go.

1. Use the Compose button to set up the note and address it.
2. Don't send the message. Just close its window by double-clicking on its control box. You'll be asked whether you want to save the message. Choose Yes. This puts the message in your Inbox.

TIP

You might want to create a Templates folder and move your templates to it.

3. The next time you need to send a message using the template, open the appropriate folder, select the message, and click on Forward.
4. Fill in the message and check that the list of recipients is correct.
5. Click on the Send button.

Working Offline

There are several occasions when you might want to work offline with the Mail program. Why? When you work offline, you can still read and compose mail, rearrange your mailbox, and so forth. By contrast, when you're connected to the mail server and there's an active session between you and the server, you're working *online*. Working offline makes sense when

- the mail server is down or your connection to it is impaired
- you're taking your work on the road with a laptop computer
- you want to work at home

NOTE

In order for you to work offline, the Mail program has to be on your computer.

When you want to work offline, Mail stores your saved messages in your outbox. The next time your computer is connected to the network (or your message file is imported from your laptop to your desktop machine that's connected to the network), messages in your outbox are sent automatically.

It's easy to work offline on your networked machine when the server is down. When you run Mail, you're asked whether you want to work offline. Just say yes and start composing messages. You can't receive mail because you're not connected to the post office server.

To work out of the office, you have the choice of taking your message files and address book with you. If you don't want them, there's nothing to do. Just compose messages offline. Make sure you have Mail on your system at home or on your laptop. If you do want them with you, use the File | Export command to put all (or selected) folders of messages on a floppy disk and put the disk in your laptop or home machine. When you get back to the office, use the File | Import command to put the message file back into your networked system.

Here's the setup to work on a laptop or at home:

1. Choose File | Export. A dialog box, shown in Figure 6.16, asks where you want to copy your message file (.MMF extension).

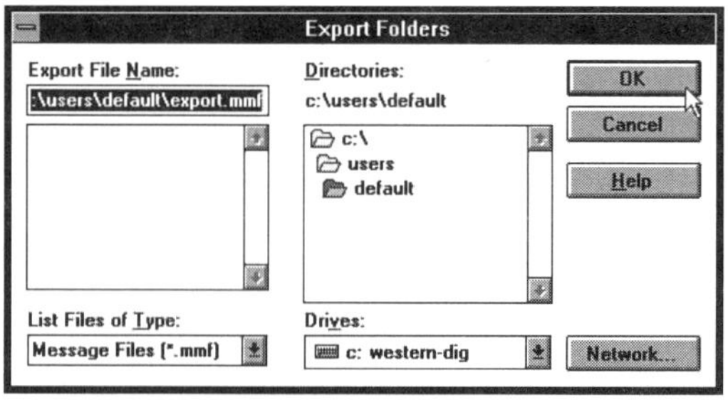

FIGURE 6.16.
Exporting your message file for use on another computer.

2. Fill in or choose the appropriate disk, filename, and so on. EXPORT.MMF is the default filename, and it's okay to use. If you're asked whether you want to create the file, choose Yes. After some thrashing, the file is saved on disk. Of course, if your laptop is networked, you can send the file over the network, which is faster than writing to a floppy. Make sure there's enough room on the disk to store your messages.
3. You're presented with a list of folders to export, as shown in Figure 6.17. Click on All Folders to export them all, or make your selections. Ctrl-click to select or deselect folders.

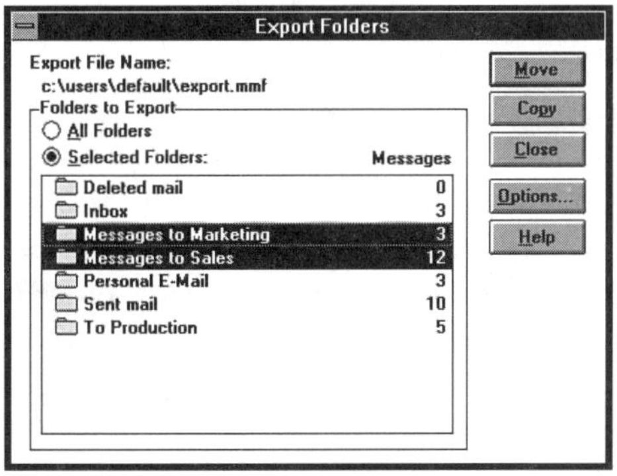

FIGURE 6.17.
Choosing which folders to export.

4. To choose only messages in the selected folders that fall within certain dates, click on Options.
5. Click on Copy. The selected folders, messages, and your personal address are copied to the floppy in the form of a single file with an .MMF extension, typically EXPORT.MMF. Close the dialog box.

TIP

You must have MS-Mail and Windows on your laptop. Ideally, the easiest way to do this is to install Windows for Workgroups. Unless you're running NT on your laptop or home machine, the 32-bit version of Mail that comes with NT won't run under Windows 3.1. Sixteen-bit MS-Mail is included with Windows for Workgroups. If you're running Windows 95, you should be okay because it has Mail. However, to be perfectly legal, you should either buy MS-Mail or Windows for Workgroups.

6. Run Mail on your laptop or home machine. Insert the floppy. Use the File | Import command to bring in the file. When you do, you see the warning box shown in Figure 6.18. Make your choices. Typically you'll want the top option, which is the default.

FIGURE 6.18.
Importing folders from a laptop or a floppy when duplicate folders exist.

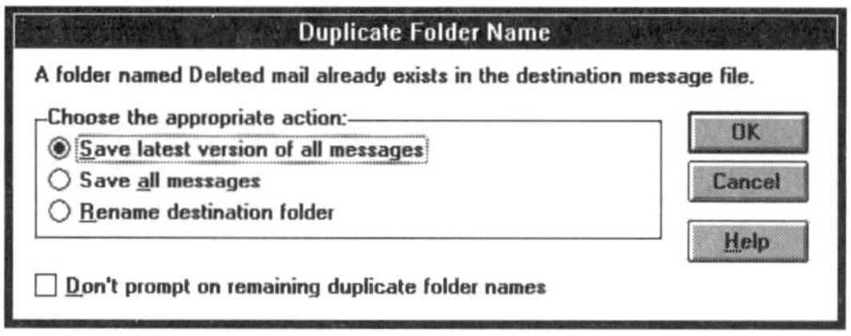

Using the Address Book

An address book is built into Mail. The earlier instructions for sending a new piece of mail illustrated this feature briefly. The address book feature enables you to choose whom to send a letter to. You can see a list of all post office members, or you can set up a custom personal list of people you contact regularly so that you don't have to wade through the whole list each time. The list also can include special groups of people that you can open separately.

1. Choose Mail | Address Book. The resulting dialog box is shown in Figure 6.19.

FIGURE 6.19.
The Address Book dialog box.

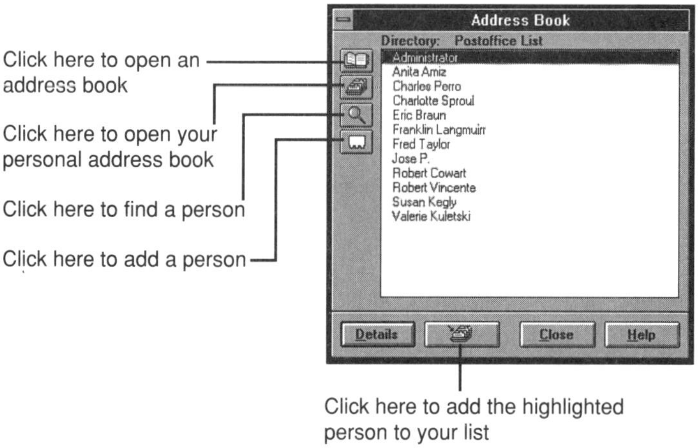

2. Notice the buttons on the left. When you want to add someone to your personal address list, first make sure that the full post office list is showing. Click on the top button and choose Postoffice List.

3. Click on a person, then click on the card file/arrow icon at the bottom of the dialog box. The person is added to your personal list. Click on the Personal list icon (second from the top) to see.
4. To delete a person from your list, open the personal directory using the top button. Highlight the person's name and click on Delete.

Creating Groups

Custom groups are like subdirectories in your address book. They show up in bold letters. Double-clicking on them opens a sublist from which you choose message recipients. To create a group, follow these steps:

1. Choose Mail | Groups. A box like the one shown in Figure 6.20 appears.

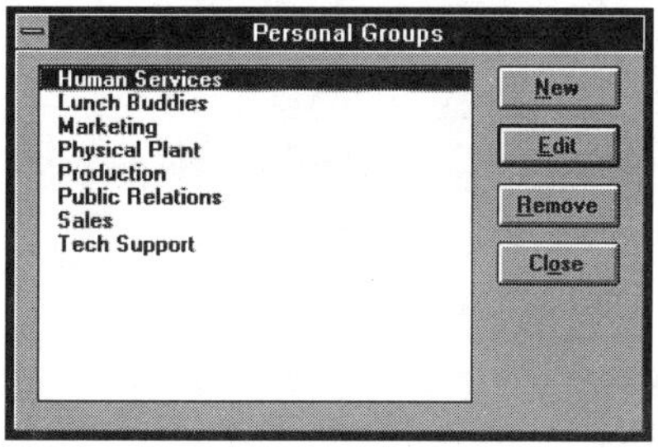

FIGURE 6.20.
Creating new groups. Here you see a few examples of typical group names.

2. Click on New to create a new group or click on Edit to change an existing one. If you click on New, enter the group name and click on Create. The dialog box shown in Figure 6.21 appears.

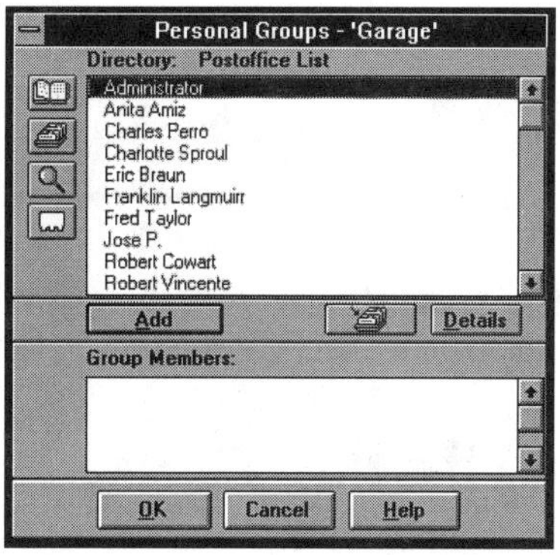

FIGURE 6.21.
Adding or editing group members.

3. Add names by selecting them and clicking on Add. Click on OK.

The next time you send a message, click on Address in the Create Note window. When you open your personal directory, you'll see the group name in bold letters. Double-click on a group to include it in the recipient or Cc: list. All the members in the group will receive the message, even though as entered only the group name will display ("sales," for example) rather than the names of the group members.

Backing Up Your Data

If your messages are important to you, you'll probably want to back up your message files once in a while. You can do so easily with the backup command. The backup option finds your personal message file (.MMF extension) and copies it to the network or local drive of your choice.

TIP

If regular backups are being performed on the post office server by the administrator, you might not want to bother doing individual backups on your own.

1. Choose Mail | Backup.
2. In the resulting dialog box, shown in Figure 6.22, enter the name you want to give the file and the destination drive.

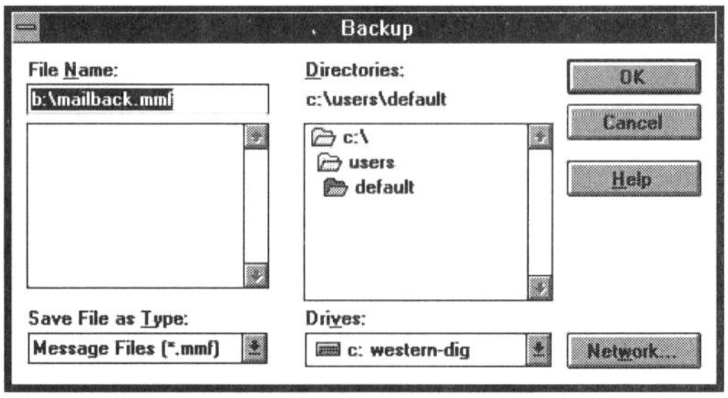

FIGURE 6.22.
Backing up a Mail file.

If you ever need to restore the backup, the easiest way is to use the File | Import command. Mail will see to it that the Microsoft Mail file (MMF) is copied to the correct directory.

Establishing the Post Office

This section explains how to create a new WGPO. Unless you stipulate otherwise with Custom setup, Mail is installed automatically, and a Mail icon appears in each user's Program Manager Main group. Thus, everyone on the network probably already has the program at their disposal. Note that the program constitutes not only MSMAIL32.EXE, but numerous support DLLs. You can't move the Mail program around just by copying the .EXE file.

When you create the post office, you also create one user account automatically—the "admin" account (the administrator's account). You can't remove this account, but you can modify its password.

NOTE

Only users with accounts on the same WGPO can share mail. You'll probably want to set up only one post office per network if there will be a need to communicate between workgroups. Also note that because only the user of the machine that hosts the post office can maintain and manage post office accounts, you should make sure that that person is willing to do so before deciding where the post office will be located.

1. Decide (by consensus, volunteer, or decree) who's going to be the postmaster. The postmaster has to maintain and administer the post office, deal with people who forget their passwords, and so on. Administration doesn't take a significant amount of time, but it does take some commitment.
2. Check for disk space. The Mail system is stored on a single computer, and it requires
   - 360K for a post office with no accounts
   - 16K per each user account added
   - In addition, each user's machine needs space for mail. Mail is stored in the server in encrypted form until it's downloaded by the user. It's then shipped to the user's machine and decrypted. Typically, a user's machine needs 100-200K of free space. But if file attachments and OLE objects are added to Mail, this can easily increase to a megabyte or more.
3. Run Mail. A dialog box that says "Welcome to Mail" appears. If there isn't already a post office, you'll have the choice of creating a new one. Choose that option.
4. You're asked to choose the directory for the post office. Choose a directory on your local computer or on a network machine. Mail will create a subdirectory to that directory and call it WGPO. All mail and associated files will go in WGPO and in a number of subdirectories that Mail creates below WGPO. (See Figure 6.23.)

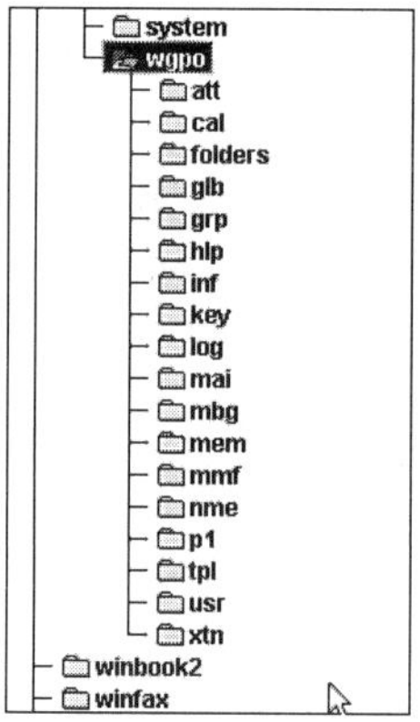

FIGURE 6.23.
The WGPO directory structure.

The post office is really nothing more than a series of directories, each with its own purpose:

Directory	*Purpose*
ATT	Encrypted file attachments
CAL	Calendar files for Schedule+
FOLDERS	Private and public folders
GLB	Global system files
GRP	Pointer files for NT multipostoffice system extensions available from Microsoft. Directories marked with an asterisk (*) are also used for this purpose.
HLP	Help files
INF	Information files
KEY	Index files pointing to the header files in .MBG files
LOG	Output logs*
MAI	Mail files stored in encrypted format until they're read
MBG	Mail headers used with the .MAI files
MEM	Information on post office members is stored here
MMF	Actual message files for each user
NME	Alias files used to map usernames to post office aliases
P1	Temporary storage
TPL	Stored templates
USR	User and group names and addresses
XTN	Extra directory to store files added by multipostoffice upgrading*

5. You're presented with a new user "account form" to fill in as a user of the new post office. As explained earlier in this chapter, you only have to fill in the first three fields in the box. Other boxes are optional and for the benefit of other users on the network. The Mailbox name is a unique ID that can be up to 10 characters long. Typically, it's the user's first name, but it can be a nickname. It can't have spaces, punctuation, or special symbols in it. The password can be up to 10 characters, and it can't have spaces, punctuation, or special symbols.

   You're reminded that you have to share the WGPO directory with full access rights with all users.

NOTE

Mail will give you an error message if it can't create the directories. This could happen if the disk is too full or if you don't have write access to the disk or directory you've chosen for the post office. Therefore, make sure you have access to the directory.

6. As soon as all the directories are set up, you have to share the parent WGPO and subdirectories, or users will be unable to send or receive mail. Make sure you do the following:
   - Share the WGPO directory with full access
   - (Optional) Declare a password for the directory
   - Enable the Re-share at Startup option

Refer to Chapter 3 if you have questions about sharing directories.

NOTE

You might have realized that because the WGPO directory has to be shared with full access, anyone on the network can connect to the directory and trash the Mail system. The only safeguard you have against such nefarious (or accidental) activity is to declare a password when you set up the directory share. Mail users will be prompted for the password before Mail activity can begin. All users on the network probably already have to enter passwords to get on to the network anyway, so there's some accountability built into the NT system. However, if you want to restrict the post office to a limited subset of system users, use the additional password.

Managing the Post Office

The postmaster might have to perform a few basic activities:

- Adding and removing users
- Editing a user's account information, including the password
- Checking and optionally compressing messages stored in shared folders

All three of these functions can be performed only by the postmaster using the Postoffice Manager dialog box. Choose Mail | Postoffice Manager to display this dialog box, shown in Figure 6.24.

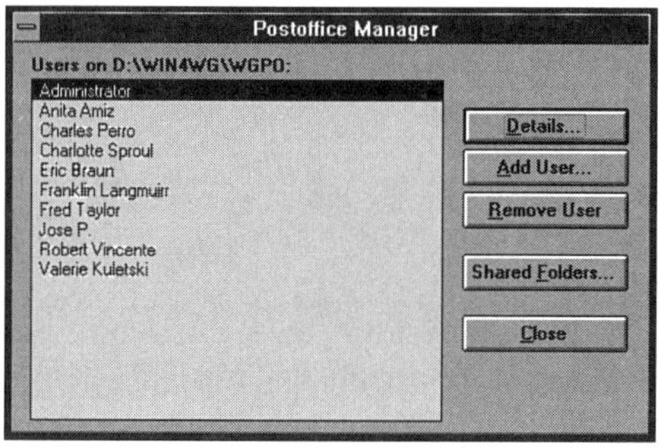

FIGURE 6.24.
Use this dialog box to manage the post office.

Adding and Removing Users

New users can add themselves, as explained earlier in this chapter. However, the postmaster can do it too.

1. Click on Add User.
2. Fill in the dialog box as explained in the section titled "Establishing Accounts."

To remove a user, just highlight the user's name and click on Remove User. Note that you can't remove the administrator from the list.

Editing a User's Account Information

Occasionally you'll have to edit a user's details. The user might get a new phone number, or you might need to change his password because he forgot it.

NOTE

You can't change the administrator's password, so don't forget it. Write it down somewhere. If the postmaster forgot her password, she would have to create a whole new WGPO.

Follow these steps to edit a user's details:

1. Click on the user's name.
2. Choose Details.
3. Make the changes and click on OK.

Checking and Compressing Shared Folders

Private folders and the messages in them are stored on individuals' computers. However, Mail puts shared folders on the post office system (in the WGPO directories on the Mail server). The messages in these folders can take up considerable disk space, leading to Mail malfunctions. It's a good idea to regularly check how many shared directories Mail users have set up, and possibly compress them to free up space on the hard disk.

1. In the dialog box that you see after choosing Mail | Postoffice Manager, click on Shared Folders. You see the dialog box shown in Figure 6.25.

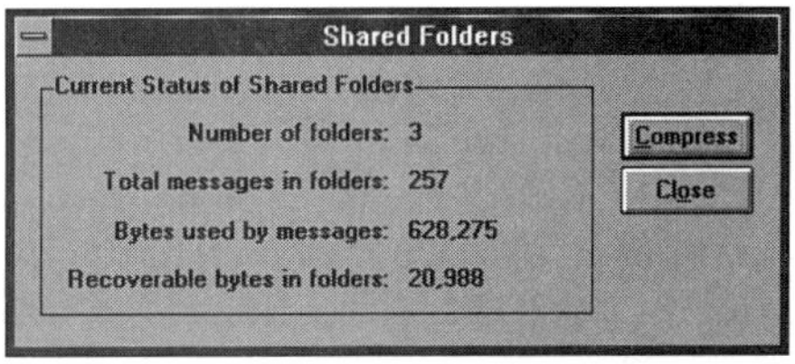

FIGURE 6.25.
Check and possibly compress your shared message folders using this dialog box.

2. The Compress button will be grayed out if there's not enough stuff to compress. If the Recoverable bytes figure looks significantly large, go ahead and compress the folder, but make sure nobody's using the folder when you do this. Nobody should be reading or composing messages stored in the folder. A little horizontal gauge appears on-screen, keeping you apprised of the compression progress. It could take a while if there are lots of messages, or it could be a very quick process.

Quitting Mail

When you've finished reading and sending mail, you can quit it just as you would quit any other application. When you rerun Mail, the post office is checked for mail. If you don't quit Mail, that's OK too.

If you receive mail while Mail is running, what happens is determined by your Options settings. (Choose Mail | Options to view and change the settings.) As a default, your computer will beep and your mouse cursor will change to the shape of an envelope. The iconized Mail program on your desktop will change to look like a piece of mail coming through a mail slot.

You've probably noticed that Mail has many menu options, with more commands than this book has room to cover. The Help system for Mail is very good, so you shouldn't have trouble finding on-screen assistance to explain some of the more advanced features.

Scheduling Workgroup Activities with Schedule+

Managing time is a chore that most of us perform poorly. Managing our own time is difficult enough. Add to this the chore of managing office time—scheduling meetings, lunches, and so forth—and you've got a real job on your hands.

Schedule+ is an application bundled with Windows NT that can aid in the process. Schedule+ is a time and task organizer that not only runs on NT but also interfaces with your NT Mail post office. If other post office users keep their schedules with Schedule+, you can easily coordinate a workgroup for meetings and appointments. When a meeting of coworkers is required, you simply enter a few parameters and the program figures out the rest—and alerts everyone via the e-mail system.

A personal daily scheduler enables you to keep track of your daily appointments. Schedule+ graphically displays how the appointments dovetail—or conflict—with others' schedules or with group meetings. Alarms can be set as reminders of your appointments. They also can be sent to your secretary, receptionist, social director, valet, or whatever at another workstation.

A Task List option enables you to track, categorize, and prioritize chores you need to tackle. Tasks can be organized alphabetically, by due date, or by their description. Related tasks also can be grouped as projects, and the program will help you block out time to work on the tasks.

Running Schedule+

Follow these steps to start the Schedule+ program:

1. Double-click on the Schedule+ icon in the Main group.
2. You'll be prompted to enter your mailbox name and password if you aren't already logged onto Mail. The Schedule+ main window appears, as shown in Figure 6.26.

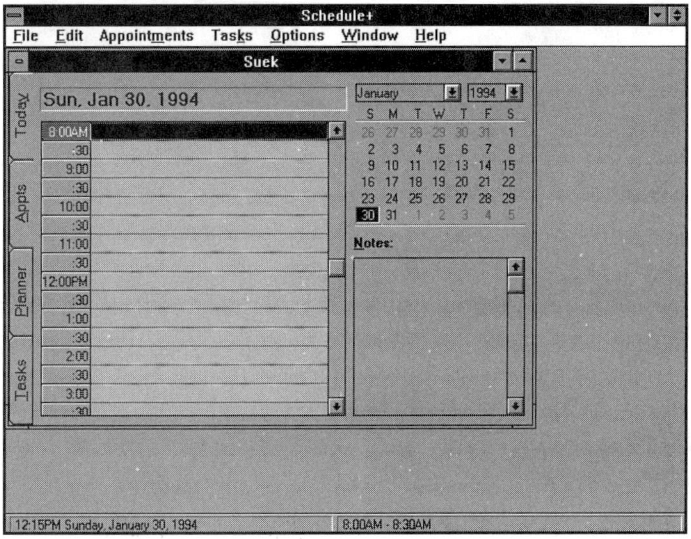

FIGURE 6.26.
The Schedule+ workspace. Clicking on the tabs on the left of the screen changes views.

Creating New Appointments

Before you get into any advanced options with Schedule+, you have to set up a personal appointment list. This not only helps you keep track of your own schedule, but it also is the basis upon which Schedule+ arranges meetings with other users. If you intend to do group scheduling, each user should keep his or her personal appointments in Schedule+.

1. Make sure your schedule is being displayed. It's possible to show others' schedules, which can be confusing. To ensure that you're observing your own, access the Window menu and choose your name from the list. (Other users' names might be on the list, too.) Your schedule will appear, and it will look something like Figure 6.26.

TIP

You might have to click on the Appts. tab on the left side of the window if one of the other screens is showing.

2. In the upper-right part of the window, choose the month and year of the appointment. Click on the exact day in the little calendar.
3. In the left side of the window, in the lined area, double-click on the start time for the appointment. For example, click on 12:00 PM to schedule a lunch appointment. A dialog box appears, asking for some details (see Figure 6.27).

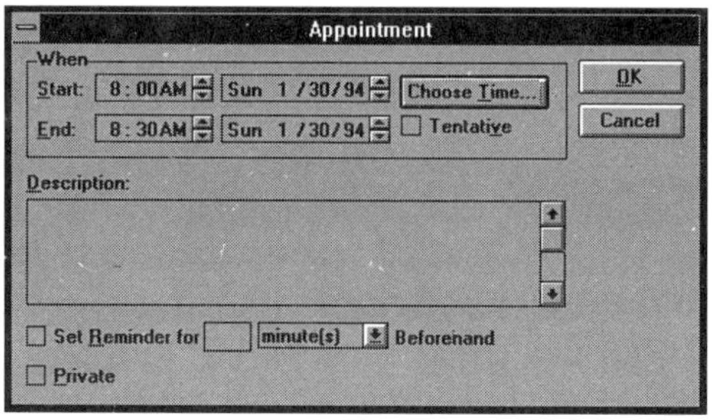

FIGURE 6.27.
Creating a new appointment.

4. In the When area, adjust the End time to reflect the duration of the appointment. If you prefer to choose the time graphically from a time grid, as shown in Figure 6.28, click on the Choose Time button.

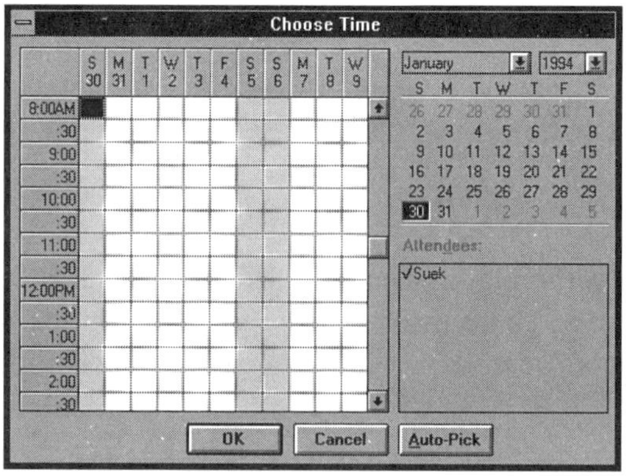

FIGURE 6.28.
You can choose a time graphically by using this box.

To set the time using the grid, drag the mouse pointer across the appropriate blocks in the grid. A dark square appears at the correct start time to help you get oriented to the grid. Click on OK when you're happy with the grid.

NOTE

Ignore the stuff in the box that pertains to attendees. This is for calling meetings.

5. Want to "pencil someone in"? Turn on the Tentative check box. When you make a tentative appointment, it will still appear in your appointment schedule, but in a lighter gray. The appointment won't appear in your Planner, however. (The Planner is a graphical display of appointments marked with vertical colored bars that others on the network can see.) If other users look at your schedule, your tentative appointments won't show up. Thus, it will appear that you're available at those times. Therefore, it behooves you to solidify your tentative plans as soon as possible to avoid confusion.

NOTE

Although you could use the Tentative option to schedule "secret" appointments that you don't want others to see, the *private* option described later is designed for that purpose.

6. You can enter a description of the appointment in the large text area if you want to. This area can hold a significant amount of information, such as directions to a meeting, dress code for the event, who's going to attend, and so forth.
7. Schedule+ can alert you before the meeting. Turn on the Set Reminder for check box and set the amount of advance warning you want. (This box normally is turned on, but it can be turned off using the Options | General Options command.) An alert can happen even months ahead of the actual appointment if you wish. Just choose from the Beforehand drop-down list.
8. Enabling the Private box hides your appointment from other network users. They'll still know you're busy, but they won't know whether you're actually closing that important deal with B.F. Goodrich or whether you hopped on the Concorde for a quick cappuccino in Paris.
9. Click on OK. The appointment is added to your schedule for that day.

Setting up Recurring Appointments

Many important dates are of the recurring type. For example, perhaps you have a faculty, staff, or sales meeting every Monday morning at 9:00. You can set up such dates easily, and the program will block them in and even remind you of them if you like.

1. In the upper-right corner of the window, select the day of the first appointment.
2. In the appointment area on the left, click on the correct starting time for the appointment.
3. Choose Appointments | New Recurring Appointment. The dialog box shown in Figure 6.29 appears.

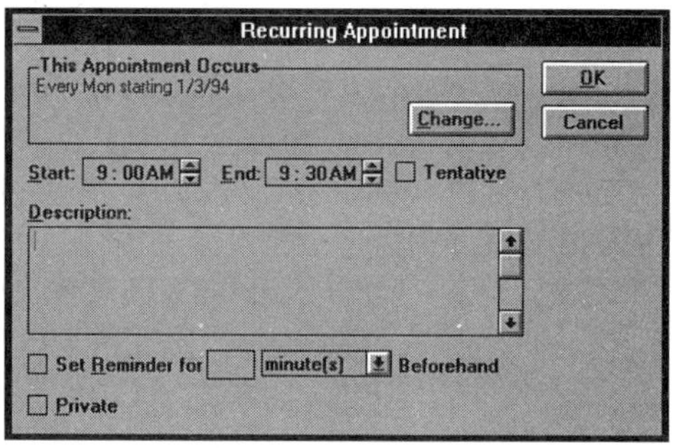

FIGURE 6.29.
Setting up a recurring appointment.

4. Complete the dialog box. Pay attention to the start and end times and the description.
5. To declare how often the appointment recurs, click on the Change... button. The dialog box shown in Figure 6.30 appears.

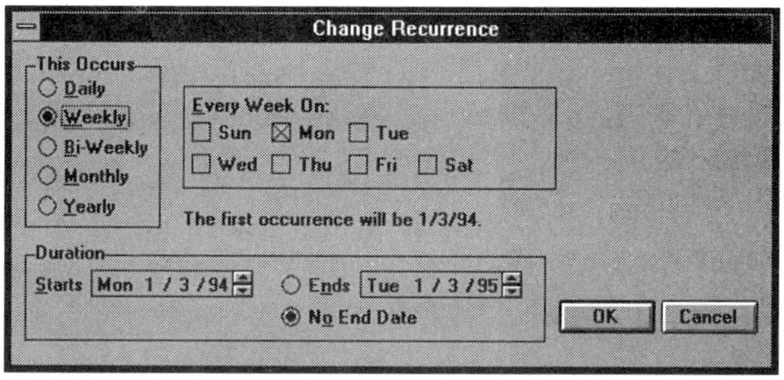

FIGURE 6.30.
Setting up the details of a recurring appointment.

6. Make the appropriate settings in the box. Note that as a default there is no end date to the appointments, which means you'll be scheduled until the year 2019 unless you stipulate otherwise.
7. Click on OK in the Change Recurrence box and you're returned to the Recurring Appointment box. Click on OK in that one, and you're done. The appointment line now has a new icon in it, indicating that it's a recurring appointment. (See Figure 6.31.)

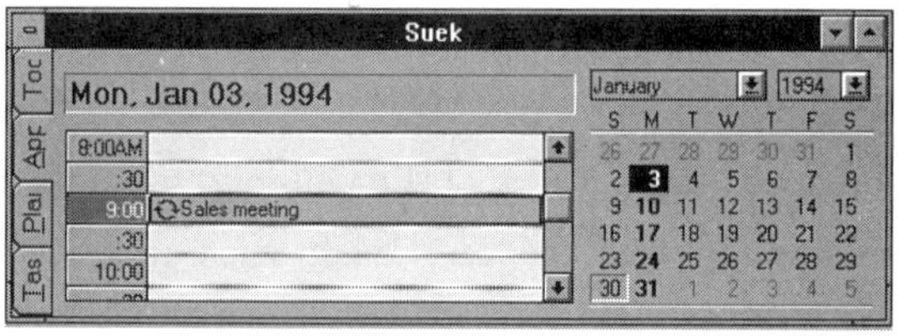

FIGURE 6.31.
An appointment line with a circular arrow indicates a recurring appointment.

NOTE

A recurring appointment is displayed in the Planner as a narrow vertical bar.

TIP

You can easily move an appointment to an earlier or later time by dragging the upper (dark blue) edge of the appointment in the Appointment list view. You can decrease or increase the length of time of an appointment by dragging the bottom line of the appointment's perimeter (the gray bar) up or down.

Organizing Your Tasks

The next major section of Schedule+ is the Task List. It helps you track your projects and assign time to get that old "to do" list done. This section explains how to add new tasks to your list, prioritize them, schedule time for them, and mark them as completed when they're done.

1. Switch to the Task List by clicking on its tab (on the left side of the window).
2. Type an unfinished task description in the New Task box and press Enter or click on Add to add it to your Task List. (See Figure 6.32.) Repeat for each task.

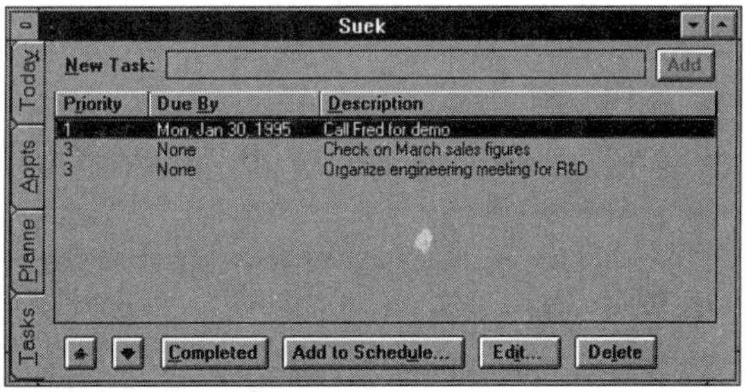

FIGURE 6.32.
The Task List with a few tasks entered.

3. Double-click on any task (or highlight it and click on Edit) to open a details dialog box (see Figure 6.33) that enables you to declare a few things about the task. Here you can assign the task to a project and set the due date and priority.

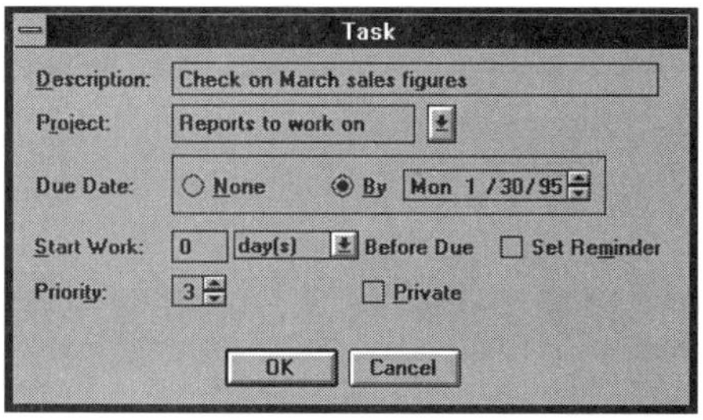

FIGURE 6.33.
Task dialog box for setting details of a task.

4. Until you name some projects, the Project drop-down list will read <none>, which means that all tasks are lumped together in the list. You can group tasks under project categories, though. To create a project, type one in the Project box. For example, in Figure 6.33, I've entered `Reports to work on`.
5. If the task has a due date, enable the By button and set the due date. You can type it in or click on the tiny arrow buttons. The Start Work option lets you estimate the amount of time you'll need to finish the project. You can enable this option and then enable the Set Reminder check box to have the program remind you to get started on the project well in advance—a little tickler.
6. Each task can have a priority setting. This number or letter is used to sort your tasks in order of importance. This makes it easier to see what's slipping through the cracks. You set the priority by typing a number from 1 to 9 or a letter from A to Z or by choosing with the little arrows.

NOTE

When organized by priority, tasks with numbers will come before those with letters.

7. When you click on OK, the item's changes are reflected in the Task List, as shown in Figure 6.34.

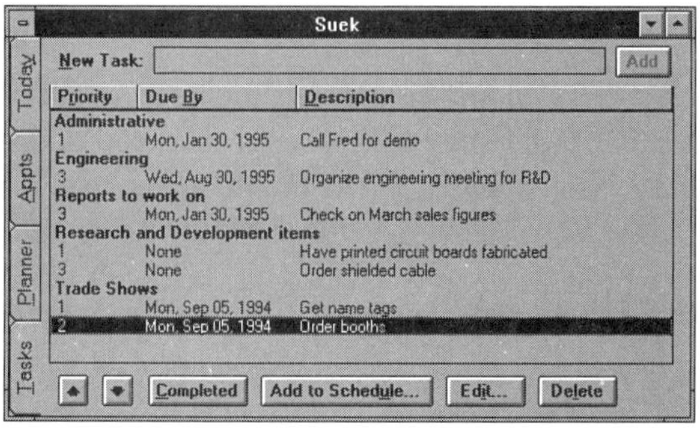

FIGURE 6.34.
You can set up project categories and add tasks under each, as well as sort the tasks and prioritize them.

As soon as you have items in the list, you can

- drag tasks up and down in the window, moving them to other project categories
- add new tasks under any project
- create as many projects as you like, using either a task's detail box or the Tasks | New Projects command
- double-click on a task to bring up the details box to edit the task description
- double-click on a project line to change its name
- highlight a task and click on the up- and down-arrow buttons to change its priority
- highlight a task and click on Delete to kill the task
- click on the Priority, Due By, or Description buttons to sort the tasks in corresponding order
- set events as private so that nobody using Schedule+ can see them

When you're finished with a task, just highlight it and click on the Completed button at the bottom of the screen. The task will be added to the Notes box on your Appointment screen—a little pat on the back for having completed a task, I suppose.

Deleting a Task from the List

You can eliminate a task from the list if you decide not to continue with it. Thus, the task is not completed; it's just canned.

1. Access the Tasks screen.
2. Click on the task in question.
3. Press the Delete key or choose Edit | Delete Task.

Scheduling Time for a Task in Your Appointment Book

You can have the Task List schedule time in your appointment book to ensure that you keep a time slot open for working on the task. Here's how:

1. From the Tasks screen, select the task.
2. Click on the Add to Schedule button. The Choose Time box, shown in Figure 6.35, appears. The current date and time are highlighted.
3. Choose the time slot by selecting the date and then dragging the mouse pointer across the grid.
4. Click on OK. The task is now on the Task List and your appointment schedule.

FIGURE 6.35.
Scheduling a time for working on a task.

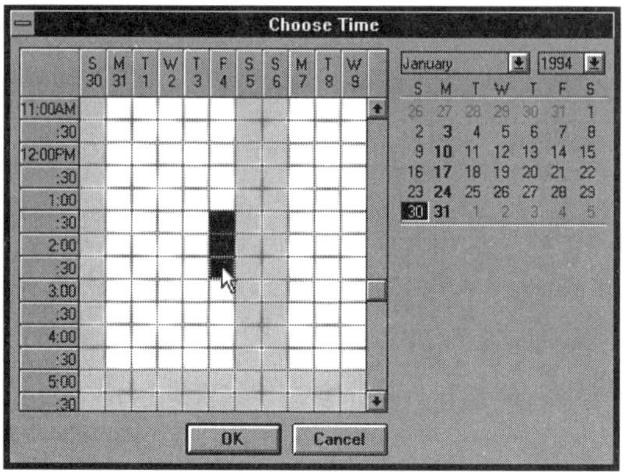

Scheduling a Meeting

When you want to schedule a meeting with users in your workgroup, do the following:

1. Make sure you're logged onto the post office. If you aren't, Schedule+ can't send out the requisite meeting announcements to each person you'd like to attend.
2. Switch to the Planner screen by clicking on its tab.
3. Check out the part of the window under Attendees. Because you're calling the meeting, your name is already in the list. Click on Change to add or remove people from the list. You see the dialog box shown in Figure 6.36.

FIGURE 6.36.
Selecting attendees for a meeting.

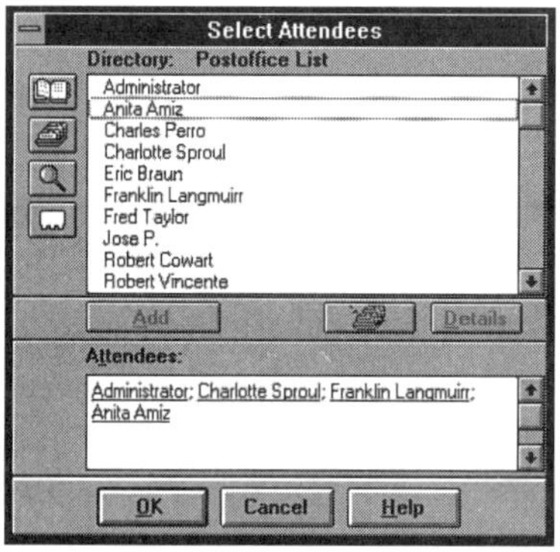

4. Construct your list of desired meeting attendees by clicking on their names in the list, then clicking on Add. Just as in Mail, you can select several nonadjacent names by Ctrl-clicking and select a range of contiguous names by Shift-clicking. You also can select one at a time by double-clicking on each desired name. Click on OK when the list is complete. The attendees' names will appear in the Attendance list on the Planner screen.

5. Now you have to set the meeting time. In the upper-right corner of the window, set the month, year, and day of the meeting. Any personal appointments you have will show up on the Planner as vertical bars. Other people's appointments also will show, collectively overlaid on your Planner. Your appointments will be in one color and everyone else's will be in another. To schedule a meeting, you need to find a free time long enough to accommodate it. Look for an area that has no bars. Choose an acceptable meeting day and time by dragging the mouse pointer vertically over the grid.

NOTE

When your appointments and others' appointments coincide, the colors are combined.

TIP

Alternatively, you can display or remove an attendee from the grid to see whose schedule might conflict with the desired meeting time. The Planner will show everyone's schedule simultaneously only if all the check marks to the left of the names are turned on.

CAUTION

Don't drag the mouse pointer horizontally unless you want to schedule a very long meeting that spans complete days!

TIP

If you want Schedule+ to help choose the time, choose Appointments | Auto Pick. It only searches forward in time from the location of the cursor on the Planner grid.

6. Click on the Request Meeting button to prepare your meeting announcement. Figure 6.37 shows an example.

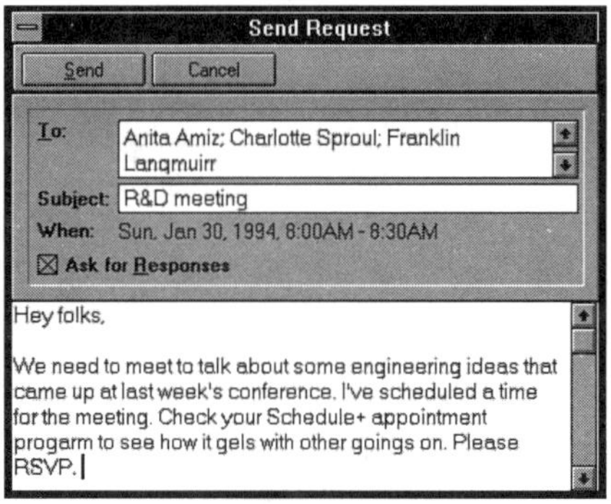

FIGURE 6.37.
Filling in the announcement for a meeting.

7. Click on Send. Schedule+ sends out the announcements with the time of the meeting automatically entered into the memos. If there are no conflicts with other people's schedules, you're informed that the meeting was successfully booked. Schedule+ also sends all attendees a meeting announcement.

Other Options

Schedule+ has many more options, but the ones discussed in this chapter should get you started. The File and Options menus contain most of the options. Of particular note are settings that allow the following:

- Responses to requests for meetings. Attendees then have to let you know if they plan to attend a meeting.
- Printing schedules
- Privileges can be altered to allow the Planner to directly enter meeting times into everyone's schedule without waiting for responses (sort of fascist meeting planning).
- You can create archives of schedule data for later reference. Archives save disk space because the calendar information (which can get cumbersome) is compressed.
- You can import and export schedule files for working offline, just as with Mail, as explained earlier in this chapter. The next sections contain more information about working offline.

About Schedule+ Calendar Files

Schedule+ relies on Mail for much of its functionality, and it uses the Mail Application Program Interface (MAPI) standard for communicating with other workstations. Therefore, Schedule+ uses the Mail program as its basis for interworkstation communications when you're working over a network (online), and it relies on its own resources when you're working offline.

Schedule+ data resources consist primarily of individual calendar files that contain scheduling information. Every user has a calendar file on the local machine and another on the mail server (in the WGPO\CAL directory). The online calendar file has the mail user's name as the filename and .CAL as the extension (for example, JDOE.CAL). The offline calendar file uses a random filename and a .CAL extension.

You can work either online or offline, using either calendar, with no problem. You don't have the advantage of seeing others' appointments when you're working offline, however. When you connect to the network again and run Schedule+, the program actually synchronizes the two files so that your latest appointments are reflected. This is done fairly intelligently. Even if you have an assistant making changes to your schedule online while you're making changes offline, there probably won't be any problems when the files are synchronized. This is because the files are merged, not just overwritten.

NOTE

Some specific restrictions pertain to which file will take precedence. In general, if there is a conflict between the two, the offline file will win when you go back online. Rules governing file merging can be found in the Windows NT Resource Guide.

Taking Your Calendar on the Road

Working offline is a little different from going remote—that is, out of the office. If your main computer at work is a desktop machine, the offline .CAL file is stored there. If you want to take your scheduler on the road, you have to get your .CAL file off the desktop and put it into the laptop or onto a floppy in order to take it to a remote computer, such as at home. Here are the steps to follow to ensure that you don't lose important scheduling data:

1. Run Schedule+ on the office machine.
2. In Schedule+, choose File | Move Local File and copy the file to a floppy.
3. Make sure that Schedule+ is on the remote computer. Run it there and use the File | Move command again to pull the schedule in from the floppy. Store it in a directory on the remote computer's hard disk. It doesn't really matter where.
4. Do your scheduling. When you're finished, do the reverse—that is, move the file to the floppy, take it back to the office, and move it back into the source directory.

NOTE

You can move your .CAL file to any directory and Schedule+ will keep track of its location if you use the File | Move Local File command. The .INI file for Schedule+ (called SCHDPL32.INI) is updated each time to reflect the location.

Chatting with Other People on the Network

The Chat program is a convenient little item that comes with Windows NT (and Windows for Workgroups). I like this program. Though modest, it's quite useful for communicating with coworkers, especially if you want to stay off the phone. It's particularly effective for contacting workgroup members who are always on the phone, because you can call them on the network instead. Here's how:

1. Run Chat from the Accessories group.
2. Click on the Dial icon or choose Conversation | Dial.
3. A dialog box appears. In it, choose the workstation you want to call and click on OK. The user will be called.

NOTE

If either the caller or callee's machine is sound-equipped, that person will hear the sound of a phone ringing. A little phone icon on the recipient's desktop appears, bouncing around as if the phone is ringing really loudly. The caller's name appears under the icon.

4. The called party must click on the pick-up icon or choose Conversation | Answer.
5. Both the caller and the callee type in the upper halves of their Chat windows, respectively. The responses are seen in the lower half. (See Figure 6.38.)

TIP

You can change the font you type in and the font the other person sees. The font you choose should be available on that person's machine, but if it isn't, something else will be substituted. To make a loud statement, choose a large font.

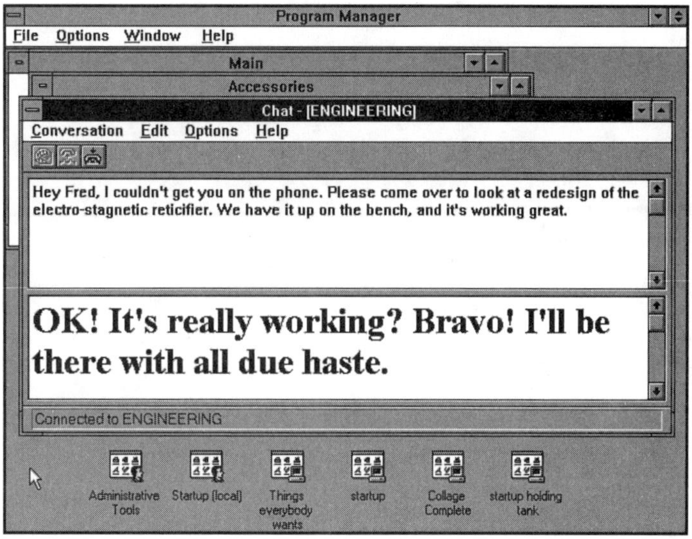

FIGURE 6.38.
Having a chat. Just type away.

6. When you're finished talking, just click on the hang-up icon or choose Conversation | Hang Up.
7. Quit Chat when you're through.

Summary

This chapter discussed the three user-oriented, productivity-enhancing tools included in NT—MS-Mail, Schedule+, and Chat. By following the instructions in this chapter, you should be able to set up these programs and begin electronic communication and scheduling with your coworkers. If used and managed wisely, these tools can improve the tracking of office communications, reduce paper waste, and increase overall efficiency in the workplace. Mail and Schedule+ are feature-rich products that might take some time to master. The most important aspects of these programs were covered in this chapter. However, for more information, don't overlook the online Help system.

Improvements, Enhancements, and Additions in NT Work-station Version 3.51

7

IN THIS CHAPTER

A number of changes and enhancements were made since the release of NT 3.5, and although a hundredth place increment in the version number of software products typically represents only a bug fix version, Windows NT Workstation 3.51 is an exception. Significant items and functionality were added to the feature list of this product, some of which will be transparent to the typical user, and some of which will be more noticeable. This chapter discusses the most important differences and how they might affect the way you work with Windows NT.

NOTE

For additional coverage (particularly of more arcane or highly technical details of the 3.51 update), refer to the NT Workstation manuals, or use the Books Online command covered later in this chapter. This chapter only covers NT Workstation/Server upgrades, not those pertaining solely to NT Server.

In some cases, the new enhancements affect the procedures used to perform specific tasks that are explained elsewhere in this book. Because many users still work with version 3.5 of NT rather than version 3.51, those procedures were not changed for this edition of *Windows NT Unleashed.* So, make a point of referring here for 3.51-specific information as the need arises. Also, some topics discussed here (such as using the Registry Editor) imply knowledge of topics covered in other chapters, so you might want to refer to the table of contents to locate associated materials.

Here is the quick list of the new features added to Windows NT 3.51 after NT 3.5:

- Setup changes: 5.25-inch setup floppy disks cannot be used. The setup (`winnt` and `winnt32`) programs can run in unattended mode. The floating-point division error exhibited by some Intel Pentium processors is detected and can be corrected during setup.
- Windows 95 common controls: Windows 95 common controls and Help are supported in this release of Windows NT Workstation.
- PCMCIA cards: Windows NT Workstation now includes increased support for certain Personal Computer Memory Card International Association (PCMCIA) cards.
- Online documentation: Books Online allows you to point to the location of the online Windows NT Workstation or Windows NT Server manuals.
- Console: This is a new Control Panel option that enables you to change the appearance and position of character-based and command prompt windows.
- Command-line utilities: Windows NT Workstation 3.51 includes three new command-line utilities: `pentnt`, Books Online (the `ntbooks` command), and `compact`.
- Miscellaneous changes: These affect existing programs such as File Manager.

The following sections discuss each of the preceding topics in order.

Setup Changes

As indicated earlier, support for installing from 5.25-inch floppy disks is a thing of the past. Microsoft determined that there just aren't enough high-end machines with this disk format to warrant distribution in this format, not to mention the reduced capacity of the disks relative to the new compressed 3.5-inch distribution format, which gets close to 2MB on a smaller disk. So, if you're going to install from floppies (which is not recommended, incidentally, due to the hassle factor), make sure your machine has the correct type of drive. Not much more needs to be explained here.

One of the boring hassles of installation of many programs—especially monolithic operating systems such as NT—is having to sit around and answer questions as the installation proceeds. Now, finally, the NT setup program can run in unattended mode, which lets you install or upgrade Windows NT Workstation without being present. Unattended setup is particularly useful when you upgrade or install on a number of computers. It also eliminates the need for feeding in the floppy disks at predetermined times, because the necessary files are temporarily copied to your computer in advance. The down side to this is that you must make sure you have a lot of space available on the hard disk before beginning—enough to hold the contents of all the floppies, *plus* the space that is normally needed for an NT installation of the type you desire. Of course, if you're installing from a CD-ROM, this additional disk space isn't an issue.

Here's how unattended setup works. The answers that you would normally supply by interacting with the setup program are instead fed to it from a text file that you create before running the setup program. The format of this control file is explained in a text file called UNATTEND.TXT—a file on the Windows NT Workstation CD-ROM. You'll find a copy of it in any of the \I386, \ALPHA, \MIPS, or \PPC directories. It's quite a lengthy bit of instructions, but with a little study, you'll be up and running unattended installations, saving yourself the headache of jumping around between cubicles at your corporation or business to insert disks or click on options or the OK button.

NOTE

The floating-point division error found in some Pentium chips isn't performed during an unattended setup. Determining whether your system exhibits the floating-point division error is no big deal, though. You just run the pentnt utility at a DOS prompt after setup completes. The file is found in the system32 directory. For more information about the pentnt utility, see the section "Detecting and Correcting the Floating-Point Division Error," later in this chapter.

Performing Unattended Upgrades

After you have the text file constructed, you begin the unattended installation via the `winnt32` command, using the `/u` parameter (U for *unattended*). If you named your control file UNATTEND.TXT, you won't have to specify the name of the control file because UNATTEND.TXT is assumed. If you want to create a variety of control files for different types of computers, either rename one of them to UNATTEND.TXT before beginning, or specify the one you want to use when executing the command.

> **NOTE**
>
> The unattended setup command syntax is as follows. Remember to use the `winnt32` command only when upgrading from an earlier version of NT. Otherwise, when upgrading from DOS/Windows 3.x, use the `winnt` command. See Chapter 8, "Configuring Windows NT," for more about installation.

Syntax for executing the unattended setup command (from a DOS prompt):

Syntax:

```
winnt/u:<answer_filename>/s:<source>
winnt32/u:<answer_filename>/s:<source>
```

Parameters:

`/u` indicates unattended setup mode.

`answer_filename` includes the location of the answer file.

`/s` indicates the source of the distribution files if they are located on a different drive.

For more information about using the `winnt32` command, see Chapter 8.

The Floating-Point Division Problem in Pentium CPUs

As you probably know, some early Intel Pentium processors exhibited a floating-point calculation error under rare circumstances. Some experts argued that the possibility of this affecting the work of the average user was about as likely as being hit by lightning. Still, it was shown to be possible, and it did affect computations in some banking spreadsheets and the work of academic mathematicians who use many decimal places. Intel located and fixed the problem, so later Pentium chips' floating-point units (a section within the Pentium) no longer calculate erroneously.

Unlike unattended setup (explained earlier), the manual setup program has been updated to automatically detect whether your Pentium processor's floating-point hardware has the much-dreaded division error. If, during setup, the malfunction is detected in the computer's CPU, the setup program will alert you. You'll then have the option of disabling the floating-point unit (FPU) on the processor. When this is disabled, calculations that would normally be performed by the FPU are handed off to the CPU where they are done "long-hand." Such calculations might take a bit longer to complete, but at least you can be assured that they will be correct to over 100 decimal places. You don't have to decide during setup to disable the FPU. You can do it later, using the command-line utility called pentnt. For more information about using the pentnt utility, see the section "Command-Line Utilities" later in this chapter, or type the pentnt /? command at the command prompt.

Common Controls

Version 3.51 Workstation incorporates Windows 95's *common controls*. Common controls are a set of dialog boxes and windows provided by a common control library. This means that programs can have a consistent user-interface and look much like Windows 95's control boxes and windows if those programs make use of the library. The dialog boxes and toolbars in the following programs have changed in Windows NT Workstation 3.51 to incorporate common controls: File Manager, Print Manager, Clipboard Viewer, Command Prompt, Chat, CD Player, Media Player, and Sound Recorder.

The most notable additions are such things as tabbed dialog boxes instead of menus, or a question mark (?) displayed in the upper right corner of a dialog box window. The question mark is the "what's this?" icon. Clicking on it changes the pointer to a question mark. Then, clicking on a section of the dialog box should cause a pop-up description to appear. If the program's toolbar has changed, tool tips are displayed about the program's toolbar options if you rest the pointer on a toolbar button for a couple of seconds. Figure 7.1 shows a new-style common dialog box.

The Windows NT Help engine has been changed as well, emulating Windows 95's fancier Help system. The Windows 95 Help format has tabs for Index and Find, and it lets you do full-text search of everything on all the help screens for a given program or the operating system's Help files. These two tabs enable you to view the index or search within a single Help file or a group of Help files. The facility works with all Windows 3.1 and Windows NT Workstation Help files, regardless of whether they were specifically compiled for full-text searching.

The first time you perform a full-text search in a Windows NT Workstation 3.51 Help file, you are prompted to build a full-text word list (*.FTS) file if one was not built when the system was shipped. The new Help system doesn't support the previous full-text search indexes (files ending with the .IND extension) that were created for Windows 3.1, Windows for Workgroups 3.11, or Windows NT Workstation 3.5 Help files. Figure 7.2 shows an example, using the NT Help file available in the Program Manager's Main group.

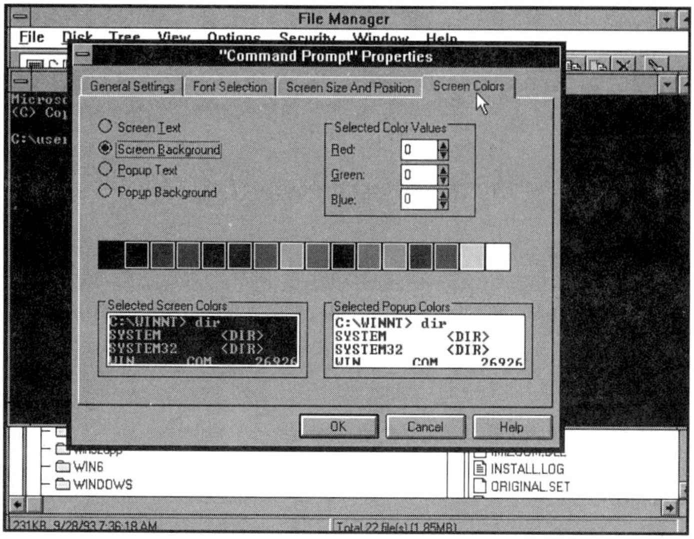

FIGURE 7.1.

Common controls allow programs to present the new tabbed dialog boxes.

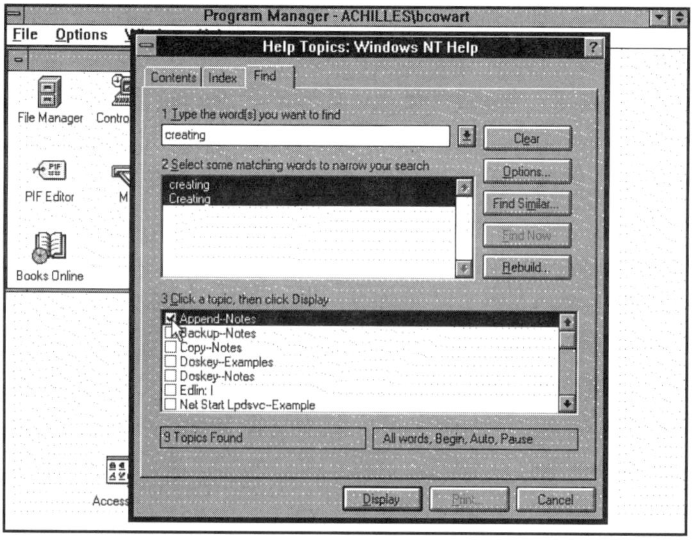

FIGURE 7.2.

A typical new Help screen's Find tab.

Performing a full-text search means that you can search for specific words and phrases in Help topics as opposed to searching for Help by category. In some instances, you can search across multiple Help files. Before you perform a full-text search, you must first build the full-text search index. The new Windows NT Workstation Help includes a Find Setup Wizard that aids you in setting up a full-text search file. You only need to build a full-text search word list (*.FTS) file the first time you perform a full-text search in a Help file. After that, the full-text search word list is available each time you open the Help file for which you built the word list.

The first time you try to do a full-text search (Find) in an application that supports this new type of Find box (not all apps will be supported under 3.51), you're prompted to create a word index based on the application's Help information. Here's what happens.

1. First, open a Help file, and then choose the Find button. The Find Setup Wizard then comes up, asking how thorough an index you want created based on the Help file associated with the application. Choose the option that makes the most sense to you.

Option	*Description*
Minimize database size	This option is recommended. It saves room on your disk. It lets you do full-text searches of all words, but it doesn't search for phrases.
Maximize search capabilities	This option lets you do full-text searches of all words in the Help file, including phrases and matching phrases, untitled topics, and annotated or bookmarked topics.
Customize search capabilities	This option lets you decide the extent to which you'll be able to search the Help file.

2. You'll see several dialog boxes with instructions in them. Just follow the instructions.

The new Help engine is capable of grouping files for cross-file full-text searches. In some cases, you'll see a search word list from a number of files. The index for the groups of files has already been created in this case, so you won't be prompted to use the Find Setup Wizard for each of them before you can search.

To perform a full-text search, even on an older Windows 3.x or NT program, do this:

1. Open the Help file in the usual way (F1 or Help menu), and click the Find button. Either the Wizard runs (if the index doesn't exist) or the Help dialog box is displayed with the Find tab selected.
2. Type the text for which you want Help.
3. Optionally, choose one of the buttons in the dialog box to specify more options about the search.
4. Click the Display button to see Help about a topic you have selected, or double-click the topic.

You can also search the index for keywords rather than doing a full-text search. Then only preassigned keywords are listed. Here's how you do that:

1. Open a Help file, and then choose the Search button. The Help Topics dialog box is displayed with the Index tab selected. (See Figure 7.3.) Some applications will have a Search for Help on... choice from the Help menu that will take you directly to this box.

FIGURE 7.3.
Searching for keywords is done by choosing the Index tab.

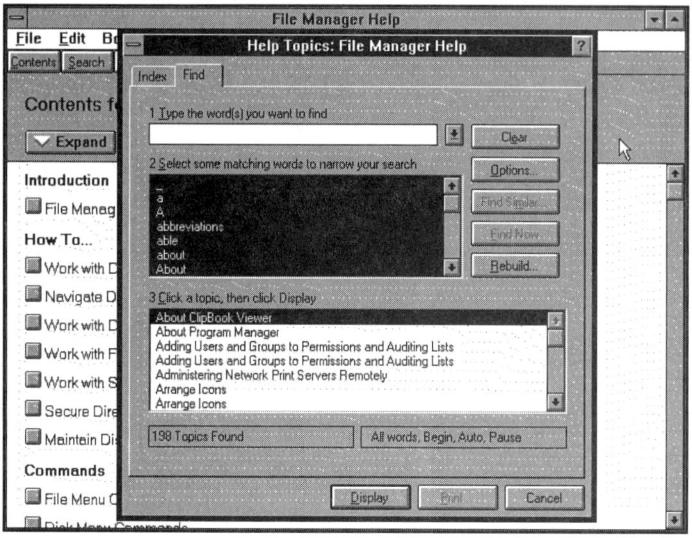

2. Type in the keyword or phrase that you are looking for, or select a keyword or phrase from the index list.

NOTE

Index files that the Wizard creates are stored in the same directory as the Help (HLP) files they pertain to. However, if the Help files are stored on a server in a directory that has read-only access, the full-text search files (*.FTS) can't be written into this location, obviously, because NT won't allow writing to the directory. In that case, they are stored on the local computer rather than in the server. In the interest of saving disk space on the local computer, an administrator can create the required *.FTS file in the server's directory so that the files can be accessed by the users on the network. This could be done by anyone who has read/write access to the directory. Simply open Help for the application in question, click on Search or Find, and let the Wizard create the index.

PCMCIA Card Support

PCMCIA cards (the little ones that plug into the side of laptop computers) have become very popular. If you've wanted to add a modem, SCSI controller, proprietary CD-ROM controller, Ethernet, or sound card to a laptop, you've most likely used a PCMICA (or simply PC) card. Contrary to popular belief, PCMCIA doesn't stand for People Can't Memorize Computer Industry Acronyms (but maybe it should). It stands for Personal Computer Memory Card International Association, a group created in 1989 as a standards body and trade association consisting of manufacturers of semiconductors, connectors, peripherals, and systems, and device and software developers.

Windows 95 was the first operating system to have Plug and Play support for PC cards. Just inserting a card resulted in the card being detected. Powering down wasn't necessary, nor was rebooting. Once the card is inserted, Windows 95 loads the proper device driver and configures itself accordingly so that the device can be used.

Now, with Windows NT 3.51, support for certain modem cards, small computer system interface (SCSI) controller cards, network adapter cards, and hard disk PCMCIA cards has been included, too. However, unlike Windows 95's complete one-stop shopping, PCMCIA card and socket support has not been included. (Card and socket services are the low-level drivers needed to make your PCMCIA cards work under an operating system.) This will come in time, of course, but not with this revision. Microsoft says to be sure to check the Hardware Compatibility List to determine which cards and computers are supported.

When you know that your card and computer are among those supported, using them is a little less elegant than under Windows 95. For one thing, you can't do "hot" inserting and removal.

1. First, you shut down the computer.
2. Insert the card.
3. When the computer is restarted, Windows NT Workstation should detect the card in the socket.
4. To remove the card, you must also shut down Windows NT Workstation.

Here are a few additional notes about PCMCIA cards.

- Integrated Device Electronics (IDE) PCMCIA hard disks should be inserted before you install Windows NT Workstation, so that it can recognize the drive and write a signature on it, which NT uses to keep track of the mass storage devices in each system.
- For Windows NT Workstation to detect a supported SCSI or network adapter PCMCIA card, you first have to load the appropriate NT-compatible SCSI device driver, or configure the network adapter card before shutting down to insert the card. Then shut down, insert the card, and reboot. For example, to install a SCSI device driver, double-click the Windows NT Setup icon in the Main program group, and then choose Add/Remove SCSI Adapters.
- Before you insert a PCMCIA card, you might want to check certain applications or system settings, or look for a related key in the Registry, so that after the card is

inserted you can verify whether NT detected the card. For more information about viewing and searching the Registry, see Chapter 12, "Maintenance and Troubleshooting." Here's an example. Suppose you are inserting a modem card and want to know whether it's been detected:

1. Prior to shutting down the computer, double-click the Ports icon in Control Panel to display the number of communication ports you have.
2. Exit NT and shut down the computer.
3. Insert the modem PCMCIA card.
4. Restart Windows NT Workstation.
5. When the computer is restarted, repeat step 1. If the PCMCIA card has been detected, an additional communication port is listed in the Ports dialog box.

Or, suppose you want to know whether a SCSI card was detected:

1. After you have enabled and configured your SCSI PCMCIA card, but before you shut down Windows NT Workstation to insert the SCSI card, check the Registry for the following key:

   ```
   HKEY_LOCAL_MACHINE\HARDWARE\DEVICEMAP\SCSI
   ```
2. Reboot and check the value again.

NOTE

For additional information about using the Registry Editor, also see "Editing Registry Values" in the README.WRI file. Using the Registry Editor can be dangerous to your system if you don't know what you are doing.

Online Documentation: Books Online

This is a terrific new feature. You might notice a new icon called Books Online in the Program Manager's Main group. Books Online gives you searchable access to the hard-copy manuals for NT Workstation or Server. (See Figure 7.4.) Although you might have to do a little digging, you'll at least be able to do text-based searches of the entire manual.

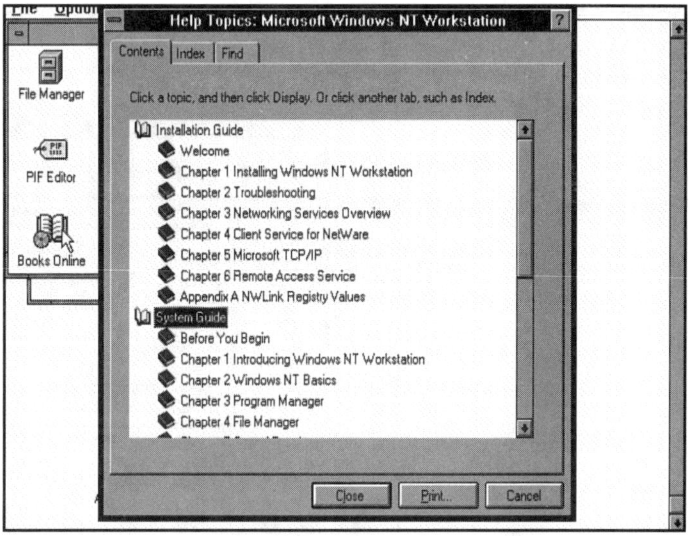

FIGURE 7.4.
The Books icon in the Main group of Program Manager provides on-screen access to the NT manuals.

NOTE

You need to have purchased both products or NT Server in order to have access to both manuals.

If you performed a new installation of Windows NT Workstation or Windows NT Server, the Books Online icon is automatically created for you and put into the Main program group. Perhaps in an oversight by Microsoft, an upgrade from Windows NT 3.x to Windows NT Workstation 3.51 or Windows NT Server 3.51 *doesn't* put the Books Online icon into your Main program. However, you can still run the program because the Books Online utility was actually installed.

In that case, you can run the Books Online utility from the command line by typing the `ntbooks` command. You could also use Program Manager to create a program item for the utility. (For more information about creating program items, see Chapter 3, "Working with Windows NT," in the section entitled "Using Program Manager." For more information about the `ntbooks` command, see the section "Command-Line Utilities," later in this chapter.)

When you first run the Books Online icon, you set the location of the online books. Thereafter, whenever you select the icon, you automatically open the online books if they remain at the location specified. If they aren't at the previous location, you'll be prompted to type in a new source, as shown in Figure 7.5. If the location is correct but the CD-ROM just isn't in the drive, replace it and click on OK.

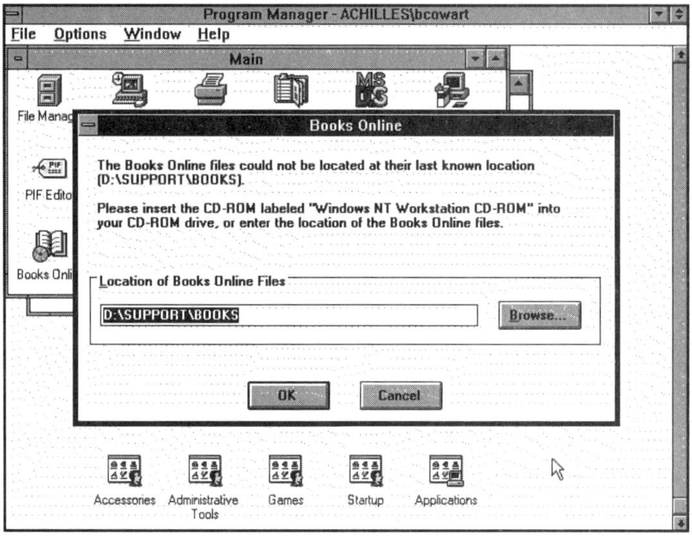

FIGURE 7.5.
If the online books files have been moved or you've removed the CD-ROM from the drive, you'll see this box asking for the new location.

Console

Console is a new Control Panel option that enables you to change the appearance and position of character-based and command prompt windows. If you've used Windows 95's DOS boxes much, you'll know about the features provided by Console. They are roughly identical in functionality.

Most of the options affect character-based programs only (not graphics programs such as games), letting you alter the default white-on-black appearance of typical character-based windows. With Consoles you can

- Change the cursor size, screen buffer size, and position of the window.
- Enable QuickEdit mode and insert mode.
- Select the colors of the text and background for character-based windows and pop-ups.
- Alter the font and font size displayed in the window.

As you might already know, the Properties command of a Microsoft-DOS window (reached by clicking on the Control Box and choosing Properties while in a window) lets you determine the window settings for a specific DOS program. The console window properties that you can set using Console are identical to the properties you can set using this Properties command. The difference with the Console command is that it will affect the properties of any character-based Microsoft-DOS window. The settings specified using the Properties command pertain only to the currently open console window or to windows with any windows that sports the same title.

Here's how to use Console:

1. Open the Control Panel.
2. Double-click the Console icon as shown in Figure 7.6.

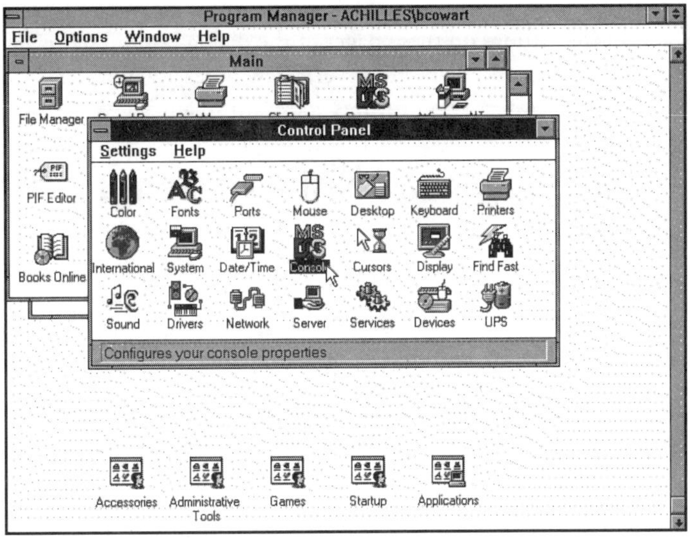

FIGURE 7.6.
The new Console applet in Control Panel lets you configure all DOS boxes.

3. The Console Windows Properties dialog box is displayed, as in Figure 7.7.

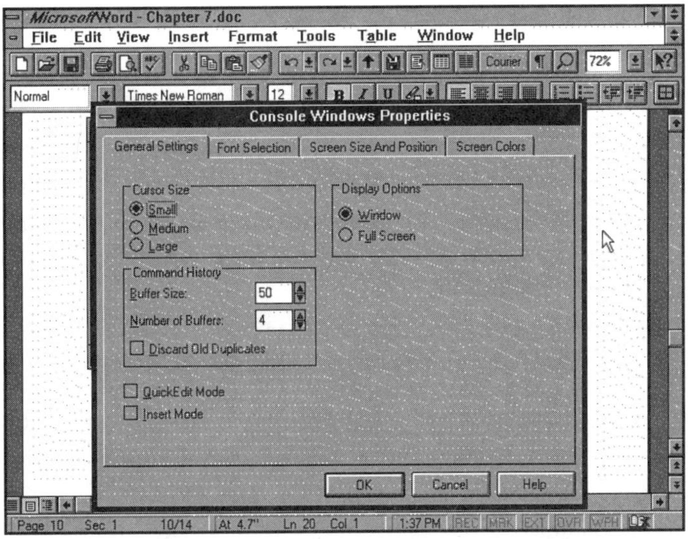

FIGURE 7.7.
The Console dialog box.

4. Make your settings, and click on OK to save them.

NOTE

The first time you open Console, the General Settings tab is selected. Thereafter, the Console Windows Properties dialog box is displayed with the last selected tab showing.

Most of the settings on these pages of the dialog box are self-explanatory, so I won't bore you with a discussion of them. However, a few notes are in order. Obviously, you click on the tab indicating the category of features you want to alter.

Making Command History Settings and Using Command History

The Command History settings are like the DOSKEY command. NT can store recently executed commands in an internal buffer. If you use the same commands often, this can save you time because you don't have to retype the commands each time you use them. You just access them using the procedure explained next.

By default, the buffer size is set to store 50 commands, but you can reconfigure it to store more commands. On the down side, storing the command history uses up some memory, so you might not want to increase it too far.

Incidentally, the command history can also retain commands used within character-based programs that accept buffered input, such as software program debuggers. One history buffer is set up for each running program that accepts buffered input. Use the Number of Buffers option in the General Settings tab to specify the number of buffers to be created for command history.

How do you use the command history list while working with a DOS window? You can use one of three different ways:

- Use the up and down arrow keys to recall stored commands in sequence.
- Press F7 to display a pop-up box with a list of stored commands. You use the arrow keys to scroll through the list until the command you want is selected. Press Enter to issue the command.
- Type part of a command, and then press F8 as many times as necessary to retrieve the correct command. You can then edit the command. Press Enter to issue it.

TIP

If you have issued the same command numerous times, command history contains each instance of the command. To maximize the number of different commands that can be retrieved, select the Discard Old Duplicates check box.

Changing Window Mode Settings

The QuickEdit mode enables you to use a pointing device (mouse) to cut and paste text in a DOS window quickly, without having to open the Control menu; simply click in the upper-left corner of the window and choose Edit commands from a right-click menu as described below. But remember, QuickEdit mode copies data only when the command prompt is running as a window, although you can paste in QuickEdit mode when the command prompt is either a window or a full screen. Copied data is always treated as text, so you can't do this with graphics. Also, some DOS programs such as fancy word processors might look like they are displaying only text, but they might be in a graphics mode to allow display of fancy fonts and text attributes. You'll have to switch back to character mode before cutting and pasting in this manner.

NOTE

When QuickEdit mode is on, the mouse is disabled in all programs started at that command prompt. You have to use the Start command to retain use of the mouse when starting a program from a command prompt window with QuickEdit mode enabled.

To cut and paste text at the command prompt using QuickEdit mode, perform the following steps:

1. If necessary, use the Settings command from the Control menu to turn QuickEdit mode on. If you've turned it on from the Console command, it will be on for all DOS windows unless specifically turned off from a particular window.
2. Position the arrow cursor at the beginning of the text you want to copy. Press the left mouse button. Keeping the left mouse button depressed, drag the cursor to the last character of the section you want to copy and release the left mouse button. The portion of the screen you want to copy is highlighted.
3. Press the right mouse button to copy the highlighted area to the Clipboard. The highlight will disappear.
4. Press the right mouse button to copy the contents of the Clipboard to the command prompt cursor. If the area copied was more than one line, a carriage return (Enter) is added at the end of each line.

NOTE

You must still use the Paste command from the Edit menu to paste the contents of the Clipboard into Windows applications.

The Insert mode check box determines whether text is inserted at the cursor or overwrites existing text. If Insert mode is not selected, text typed at the cursor replaces or overtypes any existing text.

Changing Fonts for Window Mode

You can easily choose from a variety of different fonts and font sizes for a Microsoft-DOS window display. When you change fonts, the window size changes to accommodate the new font size so that you still have the standard 24 lines by 80 characters that the traditional DOS screen allows.

To change fonts for a console window or command prompt window, just choose a font and then choose a size. The Window Preview box shows how the size of the window changes based on the font and font size you selected. To use bold fonts, select the Bold Fonts check box and the window will slightly increase in size.

Changing Screen Size and Position

The settings on this tab of the dialog box determine the size of the virtual DOS screen when windowed. Actually, it's pretty nifty because you can create DOS boxes that have more than the standard 25 lines, which is great for things such as long DIRectory listings.

The screen buffer size is memory that's reserved for a DOS-box's display. The buffer size is determined by the number of characters of width multiplied by the number of lines of height. The Window size controls the number of characters in a line and the number of lines. The default settings are 80 and 25 for both the Window Size and Buffer Size. You can use the little arrows or type in new numbers to affect any changes you want. Remember, unless other Microsoft-DOS programs have been customized with their own settings (from the Control Box | Properties command), the settings you make here will affect all DOS boxes you open.

The position setting determines where on the screen a DOS box will open. Use the arrows to adjust the coordinates. The preview window moves around on the little screen to give you a graphical idea of what the effect will be. You don't have to know the coordinates; just fiddle with the little arrows.

Suppose you set the DOS box to a size that is larger than your display allows. No problem. Scroll bars are displayed if the current size of the window is smaller than the screen buffer size settings or larger than your screen. You can't resize a console window to be larger than the area set by the screen buffer settings.

NOTE

When you switch to full-screen mode by pressing Alt+Enter, NT displays the number of lines (25, 43, or 50) that most closely matches your window mode. (Only on x86-based computers.)

Command-Line Utilities

Windows NT Workstation 3.51 includes three new command-line utilities: Books Online (the `ntbooks` command), pentnt, and compact.

- The `ntbooks` command opens the NT manuals for searching and viewing.
- The `pentnt` command checks your Pentium chip for the floating point error that some chips exhibit.
- Compact compresses your hard disk or specific directories on your hard disk.

Books Online

You learned earlier about the means for accessing Books Online via Program Manager. However, the Books Online command is also available from a DOS box. The Books Online utility enables you to point to the online manuals for Windows NT Workstation 3.51 or Windows NT Server 3.51. You can use the `ntbooks` command to access both Windows NT Workstation and Windows NT Server manuals (if you have both products or have Server). If you only have Workstation, you only get the Workstation books.

As with the Program Manager-based approach for running Books Online, the `ntbooks` command remembers the last path you specified as the source for the manuals. Typically, this is your CD-ROM drive, although it could be across the network. If the CD-ROM is not in the drive or the other source isn't present, you are prompted to insert the CD-ROM.

The following table lists the parameters you can use with the `ntbooks` command from the DOS prompt:

Parameter	*Description*

`ntbooks /s`
or
`ntbooks /server`
	Forces the utility to access the Windows NT Server books even though you installed Windows NT Workstation.

`ntbooks /n`	Indicates that you are providing a new location for the online books. If this parameter is used, the last connection made is replaced by the new location.

`ntbooks /w`
or
`ntbooks /workstation`
	Forces the utility to access the Windows NT Workstation online books even though you installed Windows NT Server.

pentnt

As mentioned earlier in this chapter, if your system is Pentium-based and you're concerned about the floating-point division error, you can use the pentnt utility to detect and correct the floating-point division error by disabling the floating-point hardware in the CPU. This fix actually emulates the floating-point hardware, using what's called *floating-point emulation.*

There are two approaches to disabling floating-point hardware and turning on floating-point emulation: conditional and forced. Conditional emulation is used to disable the hardware and turn on floating-point emulation if the floating-point division error is detected on your system. Conditional emulation is implemented by specifying a `-c` parameter with the `pentnt` command. For example, at the command prompt, type

```
pentnt -c
```

Forced emulation is used to disable the hardware and turn on floating-point emulation, even if the floating-point division error isn't detected on your system. Forced emulation is implemented by specifying a `-f` parameter with the `pentnt` command. For example, at the command prompt, type

```
pentnt -f
```

NOTE

For more information about the pentnt utility and its parameters, type the `pentnt /?` command at the command prompt.

Compact Command for File Compression

The compact utility is the command-line version of a new compression functionality in File Manager. The compact command—either from File Manager or command line—only works on NTFS partitions, not on FAT partitions, as does DiskSpace for Windows 95, Stacker, or other programs. Compact also displays the compression state of directories and lets you compress individual directories—a great way to selectively reclaim space without erasing entire contents of directories.

NOTE

The use of the File Manager's file compression command is covered in the next section, "Miscellaneous Changes to Existing Programs."

Here's the gist of NT's compression. A new flag or bit settable on each file's Property sheet indicates to NT whether the file should be compressed or not compressed. NT will decompress it when you want to use it and recompress it when you save it.

As another attraction, you can set the attribute for an entire directory. Then, whenever you move files into that directory, they will be compressed. Note that this doesn't affect files that are already in the directory. You must move files out of the directory and back into it to compress them.

To check out the existence of the Compressed attribute setting, you can run File Manager, click on a file, and press Alt+Enter. There you'll see the Compressed option box for the file. The same holds true for directories.

Personally, I find that using the File Manager for compression is easiest. Still some folks need to write batch files, or they just like using the Command prompt for operations like this. The following table lists some of the parameters you can use with the compact command.

TIP

For more information about compact and its parameters, type the `compact /?` command at the command prompt.

Example	*Effect*
`compact /c /s`	Compresses the files in the current directory and all subdirectories. Additionally, the compressed attribute is set on the current directory and all its subdirectories, which causes files that are moved to these directories at a later time to be compressed automatically. Files that are already compressed are unmodified.
`compact /c /s C:\TMP\*.BMP`	Compresses all files that end with the filename extension .BMP in the `\TMP` directory and all subdirectories of `\TMP`. The compressed attribute of these directories is not modified unless one of the directories ends with the filename extension .BMP.
`compact /c /f C:\filename`	If the system crashes during a compression operation, the file that was being compressed might be left in a partially compressed state. Such a file already has the compressed attribute set, so the `/f` parameter is required to force the file data to be recompressed in its entirety.

continues

`compact /u C:\TMP`	Removes the compressed attribute from the directory C:\TMP. Files subsequently created in this directory are not compressed unless the user takes explicit action to compress them. Files currently in the C:\TMP directory are unaffected; if any are compressed before the operation, they are still afterward.

Miscellaneous Changes to Existing Programs

Here is a quick list of additions and enhancements that have been made to existing utilities and programs in NT:

- Command Prompt. The property settings for command prompt windows can be configured using the new Properties command, which has been added to the command prompt window's control menu. This is discussed somewhat in the previous section on the Console command.
- File Manager. Windows NT file system (NTFS) file compression functionality has been added to Windows NT Workstation and Windows NT Server.
- Command-Line Utilities. The functionality of the format and route command-line utilities has changed.
- Print Manager. A new dialog box has been added to change the tray/form assignment of a PostScript printer.
- Registry Size. The maximum Registry size can be changed using the System option in Control Panel.
- Schedule Service. The `cmd` command does not load by default.
- Sound Recorder. A new Properties command has been added to Sound Recorder's File menu.
- Telnet. New functionality has been added that enables Telnet to output command operations to a log file.
- Uninterruptible power supply (UPS). Administrators cannot specify command files that require user input.

- User Manager For Domains. User profile paths can be assigned to the user accounts in the security database of a Windows NT Workstation.
- User Profile Editor. Logon scripts can complete execution before Program Manager appears on screen.

Unless you are a network or system manager, the most important changes here are the first two. Because I've already covered the Properties box for DOS windows (it works the same way as the Console settings from Control Panel, explained earlier), I'll focus only on the File Manager's new compression capability.

File Manager Compression and Toolbar Customization

The basics of the new NTFS file compression were explained earlier, in the section "Compact Command for File Compression." The console command for performing compression provides great flexibility in applying compression to groups of files. (Suppose you want to compress all Microsoft Access MDB files anywhere on your disk, for example.) However, the File Manager makes visual sense out of what you're doing and gives a graphical leg up for most users simply because it's easier to use.

With File Manager, you can now select a file or group of files to compress, click on the Compress button (assuming you've added it to your toolbar) or choose the File/Compress command, and the job is done. The files or directories you've chosen will be compressed. Or, they will be decompressed if you use the Decompress command or button. It's pretty straightforward. Modification of the toolbar is another new feature of NT 3.51, incidentally. Let's look at compression first.

Suppose you want to compress a series of files on an NTFS partition. Choose one of these methods:

- Select the files, and then select Compress or Uncompress from the File menu as shown in Figure 7.8.
- Alternatively, you can select the files and then open the File menu in File Manager. Choose Properties (or press Alt+Enter) to display the Properties dialog box, and then select the Compressed check box and click on OK as shown in Figure 7.9.

FIGURE 7.8.
Compressing selected files via the File menu.

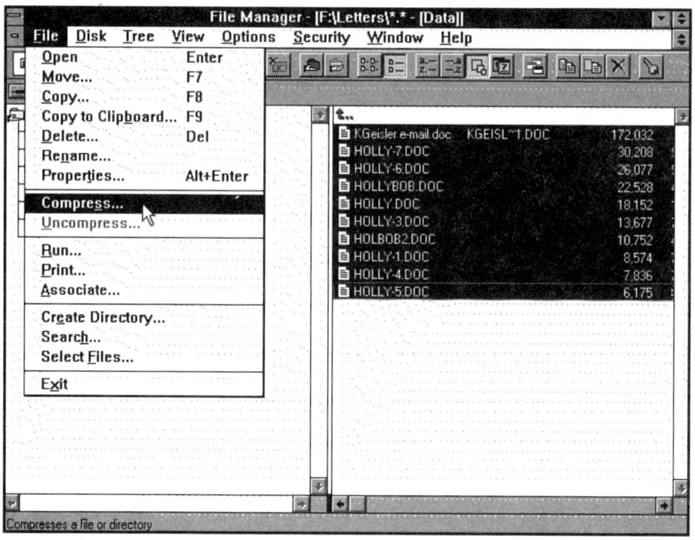

FIGURE 7.9.
Compressing selected files via the Properties box.

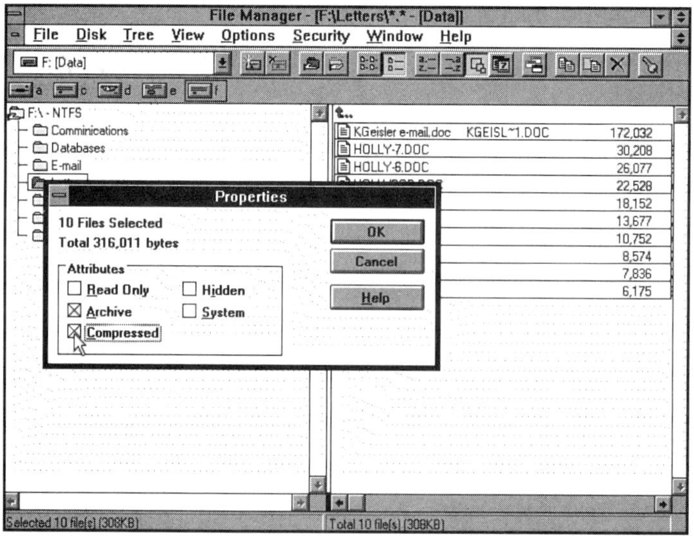

After compressing, the files turn a different color (typically, blue) to indicate that they are compressed. If you want to compress/decompress directories, you just select the directory folder icon and either bring up the Properties box and set the compression, or use the File menu or toolbar to make the setting.

TIP

A little tip is in order here. Files can be compressed in a directory that isn't itself set to be compressed. If you want to quickly decompress all the files in such a directory, you first set the directory's compression to on and click OK. Then you turn it off and click OK. You are asked whether you want to decompress all the files in the directory.

The Properties dialog box can also be used to view the compressed size and compression ratio of a selected file. Figure 7.10 shows an example. An important note here is that the standard File Manager panes will only display the full, uncompressed size of the files—not the compressed size. You have to open the Properties box for a report on the compression ratio and compressed file size.

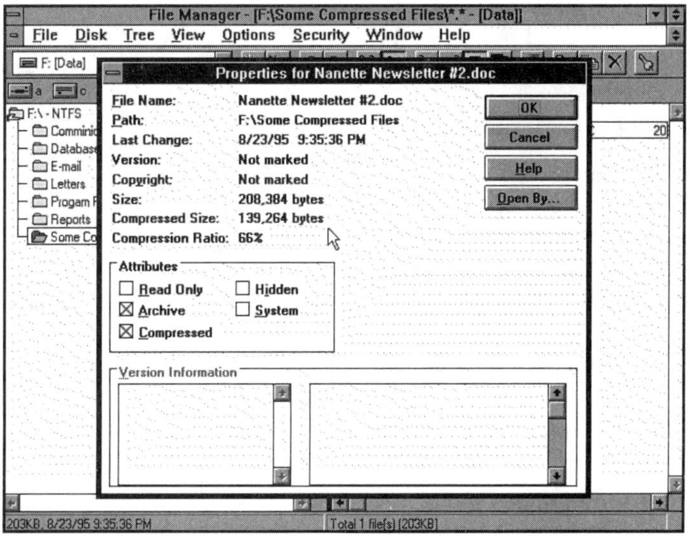

FIGURE 7.10.
Viewing the compression ratio and file size is done via the Properties box after compression.

To set up buttons on the toolbar for compression or decompression (or other options as well), follow these steps:

1. Run File Manager.
2. Choose Options | Customize Toolbar. The box shown in Figure 7.11 appears. Scroll down to the bottom of the list in the left pane and choose Compress.

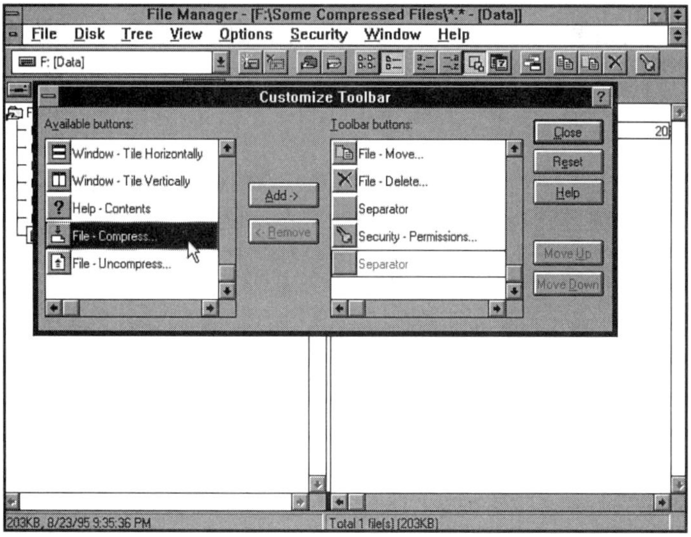

FIGURE 7.11.
Customizing the File Manager toolbar.

3. Click on Add.
4. Repeat for Decompress.
5. Click on OK.

Summary

This chapter discusses the enhancements and additions to Windows NT Workstation in version 3.51. It includes information about unattended setup routines, additional programs for reading online manuals, checking Pentium errors, compacting files, support for PCMCIA cards, and additional controls for DOS windows. The next chapter goes more thoroughly into installation and configuration of Windows NT.

PART

II

IN THIS PART

Windows NT System Administration

Installing Windows NT

8

IN THIS CHAPTER

In general, the actual software installation of Windows NT is a self-explanatory and automated process. In some ways, it's significantly simpler than installing other major operating systems, GUIs (such as Windows 3.1), or even some Windows applications. This is especially true if NT is installed from a CD-ROM or over a network.

However, you'll still want to read this chapter before installing NT on the target system. You have a number of choices to ponder (some of them new to PC users) before you start the installation process. An incorrect choice could lead to lots of extra work later.

NOTE

For the time being, most NT installations will be on Intel x86 systems because RISC-based MIPS ARC/R4000 or DEC Alpha systems are rather expensive and lower in availability. Therefore, this chapter (in fact, most of this book) assumes that you have an x86-based system. If you're installing on a RISC-based computer, see the section titled "Installing NT on a RISC Computer."

NT Hardware Compatibility

Before attempting an NT installation, you should check your hardware for compatibility with NT.

- You need a speedy processor. If you can afford a multiprocessor such as a DEC or a MIPS machine, great. If you're planning to install on a uniprocessor x86 machine, make sure that the CPU and bus design are pretty fast. Microsoft says you can run NT on a 33Mhz 386, but I suggest that it be at least that speed in the 486DX class. Even with a DX2/66, NT can sometimes seem slow, especially when you're running Windows 3.1 applications on top of NT. When choosing a bus design, remember that any 32-bit I/O bus is superior to any 16-bit bus. EISA, MCA, PCI, and VLB are all 32-bit buses. If you already have an ISA machine and it has VLB (VESA local bus) slots, consider using them for your video and hard-disk controllers. SCSI controllers typically are faster than IDE, but make sure that the one you want to use is supported by NT.

NOTE

More specific advice on system upgrades can be found in Chapter 11, "Optimizing Windows NT: Performance Determinants."

NOTE

Hardware caching controllers are great in theory, but NT does software caching and in some cases requires hardware caches to be disabled. NT supports caching controllers, but only if the controller has an NT driver that supports caching, if write caching is disabled, or if caching by the controller is completely disabled.

NOTE

Testing has shown that Windows 3.1 applications will run slower on NT than under Windows 3.1. For this reason alone, if you intend to run Windows 3.1 applications you might want to upgrade your processor. With the street price of a 66Mhz 486DX/2 motherboard with CPU being about $600, the expense of a speedup isn't prohibitive.

- You need to ensure that you have enough disk space. You must have about 90M of free space on the target disk for an express setup. This allows space for the NT files and a 20M paging file (virtual memory). You can get away with less if you use the custom setup, but don't bother unless you're really pressed. If you choose the custom setup option, the required disk space will be reported. This amount will vary, depending on which NT components you choose to install.
- Next, note or look up how your network card is installed. What are the IRQ and base port addresses? If possible, check that your system is working correctly under less-demanding operating systems such as DOS, Windows 3.1, or Windows for Workgroups. If your network, sound, video, and mouse cards are working correctly in Windows for Workgroups (WFW), NT probably will install smoothly. (See the next section for help with add-in card configuration.)
- If you're using an x86-based system and you don't have at least 12M of RAM, get ready for painfully slow loading, lots of hard-disk thrashing, and lots of waiting for each dialog box to appear. Contrary to what Microsoft says, NT will load and run with only 8M of RAM. But do yourself a favor and get some more RAM first—it's less frustrating. RISC machines need 16M. There is no more important factor than physical memory in determining NT's performance.

NOTE

NT supports up to 4G of RAM. In 16-bit ISA-based machines, the speed limitations of the 24-bit DMA hardware of these machines is overcome by NT's use of double-buffering. Microsoft claims this works almost as fast as 32-bit DMA. They warn, however, that on some ISA systems, adding memory above 16M actually degrades performance instead of improving it. You might want to borrow some memory and try it both ways if you're considering upgrading beyond 16M for your workstation or server, especially with memory prices going through the roof these days.

- You need a minimum of a VGA resolution video display adapter. A generic VGA screen driver is used for the setup process. At the end of the installation, you will be given an opportunity to either select a video driver based on the detection process or manually select and install a video driver. You can change this selection later using the Windows NT Display icon in Control Panel.

Check Your Hardware Settings Before Starting

Often, configuration and installation problems are due only to incorrect settings on network, I/O, sound, and other cards. The result is cards that conflict with one another for the same *IRQ* (interrupt request line), *base I/O port address, DMA,* or *base memory address.*

Usually, these settings are made by changing jumpers or DIP switches on the board. Cards that typically require settings are

- network cards
- bus mouse cards
- sound cards
- tape backup controller cards
- SCSI cards
- fax/modem cards

NOTE

There is a move afoot by VESA for manufacturers to design software-configurable cards when possible. Some cards (for example, Novell's NE2000 PLUS) use software programs to set the IRQ and port addresses. You might have to run a DOS program to make the settings before running NT Setup.

In case your understanding of board configuration settings is somewhat foggy, the next few sections provide a quick review.

IRQs

When an add-in card (or program) needs to grab the attention of the CPU, it issues a message called an *interrupt* directly to the CPU. The CPU then services the request accordingly. A common example is when data targeted for a specific workstation arrives at its destination network card. The card "pulls" the predetermined interrupt line, and the CPU then jumps to the appropriate code related to that interrupt in order to service it. This is achieved by using what's called the *interrupt handler*.

As a rule, no two boards should share the same interrupt request line or IRQ. When two devices attempt to use the same interrupt at the same time, a data collision can happen and the system can hang, or nothing happens at all.

TIP

With some operating systems, such as DOS/Windows, there is an exception to this case, wherein some IRQs can be shared. You might be familiar with this. For example, under DOS it's often possible to share the LPT1 (IRQ 7) with other devices, as long as you're not printing through that port at the time the second device tries to use it. NT handles IRQ sharing differently. It does *not* share IRQs on ISA machines. (It does support sharing on EISA, MCA, or PCI machines, but only if no ISA card is sharing the same IRQ as another card.) Instead of IRQ sharing, if two devices are detected as sharing the same IRQ, NT will switch to a "polling" mode, wherein the CPU regularly checks for and services I/O requests rather than waiting for IRQ lines to be activated. This can slow down overall NT performance, because it creates another software "loop" that the operating system has to service. The bottom line is that NT will either hang, fail to load a service or driver, or, at best, will slow down a bit if boards have IRQ conflicts. Therefore, do your homework on IRQ assignments.

The bad news is that there are not a lot of IRQ lines to go around. You might have to decide to leave something out of the system if you have boards that aren't very flexible in their IRQ options. For example, older Novell NE2000 boards give you only a few IRQ options, and the Logitech Bus Mouse board lets you choose from only IRQs 1 through 5.

If you're configuring a network card, most likely you can use IRQ 3 or 5. Table 8.1 might be of help in setting IRQ and port addresses for your cards. Refer to the manuals with the cards to determine how to make the settings and to determine which IRQs are already in use.

Table 8.1. Typical IRQ assignments in 80286-based or later x86 systems.

IRQ	*Typical Assignment*	*Availability*
2	EGA/VGA video	Almost never available because it's redirected to IRQ 9.
3	COM2:, COM4:	Available sometimes.
4	COM1:, COM3:	Usually not available.
5	LPT2:	If a second parallel port is installed, probably available. Not available if a Trantor or Future Domain 8-bit SCSI card is used, unless polling is used for one of the devices.
6	Floppy disk controller	Almost never available.
7	LPT1: (printer port)	Almost never available, but if it is, it will be sharable only on EISA, MCA, and PCI devices. If an ISA peripheral is detected on the same IRQ, this prevents sharing.
8	System clock	Never available.
9	EGA/VGA	Seldom available, because devices using IRQ 2 will be redirected here as well.
10		Available.
11		Available if no 16-bit SCSI card is in use and set to this default IRQ.
12	PS/2 mouse	Available only on systems that don't have a PS/2-style mouse connector. Compaq and NEC, for example, have this connector, and thus this IRQ is not available on these systems.
13	Math coprocessor (if installed)	Never available.

IRQ	Typical Assignment	Availability
14	Hard-disk controller	Never available if an ST-506-compatible hard-disk controller (that is, MFM, RLL, ESDI, or IDE) is used. But possibly available if a SCSI hard-disk controller is used.
15		Available.

TIP

Microsoft recommends disabling COM2/COM4 in your ISA system's CMOS settings if you decide to use IRQ 3 for your network board. This prevents an interrupt conflict in case the two are being used simultaneously. Even if your system works properly under DOS/Windows 3.x, it probably won't work properly under NT due to the manner in which NT services interrupt requests.

DMA Channels

Your PC has eight DMA channels that can be used for rapidly transferring data between memory and peripherals such as a hard disk, sound cards, and so on. Some cards even use several of these at once. (For example, the ProAudio Spectrum 16 uses two DMA channels for high-speed transfer of digitized audio sound data.) The DMA numbers are 0, 2, 3, 5, 6, and 7. Typical users of DMA channels are

- tape backup controllers
- network cards
- proprietary printer cards such as PostScript cards
- scanner cards
- SCSI controllers

In general, you shouldn't share DMA channels. If you're really pressed, you can share certain ones. However, you should never share DMAs that are in use by network cards or hard-disk controllers. Important data might be lost. As a rule, just try to make sure that no two devices use the same DMA channel at the same time.

Table 8.2 lists the typical DMA controller assignments in x86 (286 and higher) machines.

Table 8.2. Typical DMA controller assignments in x86 machines.

Channel	*Typical Assignment*
0	Generally used for DMA refresh
1	Available
2	Floppy disk controller
3	Available
4	NT's cascade channel (not available)
5	Available
6	Available
7	Available

Base I/O Port

Some devices send and receive data through input/output ports (I/O ports) rather than DMA numbers. In PC architecture, I/O ports are mapped into system memory and therefore are accessed using memory addresses. Again, each device that uses an I/O port must have a different port address.

Table 8.3 shows commonly used and unused port addresses in hexadecimal.

Table 8.3. Commonly used and unused port addresses.

Port	*Device*	*Port*	*Device*
200 to 20F	Game port	300 to 30F	
210 to 21F		310 to 31F	
220 to 22F		320 to 32F	PS/2 model 30 hard-disk controller
230 to 23F	Bus mouse	330 to 33F	
240 to 24F		340 to 34F	
250 to 25F		350 to 35F	
260 to 26F		360 to 36F	
270 to 27F	LPT3	370 to 37F	LPT2
280 to 28F		380 to 38F	
290 to 29F		390 to 39F	
2A0 to 2AF		3A0 to 3AF	

Port	Device	Port	Device
2B0 to 2BF		3B0 to 3BF	LPT1
2C0 to 2CF		3C0 to 3CF	EGA/VGA
2D0 to 2DF		3D0 to 3DF	CGA/MCGA; also EGA/VGA when operating in color
2E0 to 2EF		3E0 to 3EF	
2F0 to 2FF	COM2	3F0 to 3FF	Floppy-disk controller; also COM1

TIP

A common source of I/O contention is between video cards, SCSI devices, and network cards. As soon as NT is up and running, a program in the Administrative Tools group reports such conflicts in a pretty understandable manner (quasi-English).

Base Memory Addresses

Similar to the I/O port address, the *base memory address* is the beginning memory address that some cards use to communicate with the CPU. Sometimes this setting is called the *RAM starting address* (or *start address*).

Some cards (particularly network cards) must have their base memory address set by a jumper or software. Then a corresponding software setting in the NT driver must be set to match. A typical base memory address reads like this: D3000. Sometimes the last zero is dropped, so the address reads D300.

Another consideration with cards using base memory addresses is the amount of RAM space they will occupy. Some cards will use 16K of space, and others will use 32K or more. Check the card's manual for options. Using more memory might improve the operation of the card, but it will decrease your system's memory availability because that space will be occupied.

Note that most ISA cards utilize an upper memory address that falls somewhere between A000 and FFFF. However, many EISA, MCA, VL-Bus, PCI, and some ISA cards can utilize address space above 1M, or even above 16M in the case of 32-bit cards. If your card can utilize such an address, it's better to do so because it will minimize the chances of bumping into the operating system.

TIP

If you have an ISA computer, check the BIOS and video card shadow RAM addresses being used. They've been known to conflict with memory-mapped add-in cards. This kind of data collision can definitely cause a system crash or at least major erratic behavior.

NOTE

Some cards don't specify a base memory address because they don't use RAM address space for data transfer.

NT Device Driver Availability

With the second release, NT's driver support was pretty impressive. Among the usual host of mouse, video, and printer drivers, there was support for

- 94 SCSI host adapters
- 72 CD-ROM drives
- 87 SCSI tape drives
- 24 SCSI removable media systems and scanners

All the basics were there. However, it's still possible that some of the devices in your system won't be supported by NT out of the box.

For example, fax/modem, fancy monitor, sound card, video card, SCSI adapter, or network adapter board might not be recognized by NT and might not work. As of the initial release, no fax/modem drivers were available, so I couldn't use WinFax to send or receive documents while running Win 3.1 apps under NT. Nor could I use a 1280x1024 resolution grayscale monitor/card combo that works fine with Windows 3.1 and Windows for Workgroups.

Note that third-party fax/modem pooling solutions do exist. For instance, FACSys from Optus Software is an enterprise-wide faxing solution with built-in e-mail integration. Net2Com 2.0 from ESDL offers modem pooling to MS-DOS, Windows, and Windows NT clients.

Just as it took device manufacturers some time to come out with drivers for OS/2 and Windows 3.1, you might have to wait a bit or do some digging. On the up side, though, what Microsoft has supplied will at least get NT booted on most systems.

NOTE

Look for the NT Hardware Compatibility List if you're in doubt about whether your computer or hardware will work with NT. This booklet comes in the box with NT. Be aware that even if your products aren't listed, NT might still work with them. For example, a call to Colorado Memory Systems informed me that another of the supplied tape backup drivers would work with my unit. The same was true of a video card not named, but because it used the Tseng Labs ET4000 chip set, the generic ET4000 screen driver worked fine.

Check README.WRI and SETUP.TXT

After you've installed NT, be sure to read the last-minute additions to your release of NT. These additions are listed in the Write files called README.WRI and SETUP.TXT. README.WRI is dumped into the Main Program Manager groups. It's well worth scanning. The table of contents, shown a little later, helps you to quickly determine whether there's anything pertinent to your system. SETUP.TXT can be found on the CD-ROM.

TIP

You can't easily read this file until NT is installed. This is sort of a Catch-22 if you're having trouble installing! If you think you might have a problem that's listed in the release notes, find a friend with NT installed and view or print the document. If you have a CD-ROM player, just look for README.WRI in the MIPS directory. (This assumes that your CD-ROM drive is functional under another operating system—preferably Windows 3.1 because the file is in Write format.) If you don't have a CD-ROM drive, shuffle through your NT floppy disks, look for the file called README.WR_ on disk 17, and use the Expand program (probably in your DOS directory) to load the file onto your hard disk. Use the syntax

```
expand a:readme.wr_ c:\ readme.wri
```

where `a:` is the source disk and `c:` is the destination disk. Then look through the file for possible mentions of your hardware. First read the table of contents, then use the Find command in Write.

As it pertains to Setup, the readme file as shipped with version 3.5 of NT contains discussions of the following topics. These exact topics might change somewhat as newer versions of NT are shipped. However, scanning this topic list will give you an idea of the general categories of topics and some specifics that might still apply to your setup:

Additional installation information
Installing over the network without floppy disks
Booting floppy disks
Creating backup disks
Upgrading Windows NT 3.1 to Windows NT Server 3.5
Upgrading when third-party system software is present
Running Windows NT 3.5 on PCI bus systems
Update required when retaining Windows NT 3.1
Installation directory
Installing to mirrored partitions
Selecting keyboard layout
NextStep changes to partition tables
Disk fragmentation can prevent installation
MS-DOS undelete sentry blocks
Using MS-DOS-based disk utilities
Interrupt conflicts
ROM shadowing on multiprocessor systems
CD-ROM installations require a local CD-ROM drive
SCSI devices must be on for setup
Disconnect UPS serial connections
ACER AcerFrame 3000 MP
Digital Alpha AXP Firmware must be upgraded
Gateway Nomad and TI Travelmate notebooks
IBM Personal System/2
IBM ThinkPad

Intel EtherExpress 16 LAN adapter

Toshiba T4400SX monochrome

Caching disk controllers and drives

Installing Windows NT on an ESDI disk drive with more than 1,024 cylinders

File Sources for Setup

There are a number of ways to install NT, depending on the source file location:

- From a CD-ROM
- From a network location (called a *sharepoint*)
- From floppies

Installing from a CD-ROM or across a network definitely are the preferred techniques. They don't require feeding in many floppies. If you don't mind inserting 20 floppies and waiting for dialog boxes, there's nothing inherently wrong with floppy installation. However, using a CD or the network as a source is significantly simpler and quicker. Considering all the other tweaking an administrator has to do later—not to mention the learning curve for getting up to speed on the advanced aspects of NT—you don't need the additional aggravation.

Where to Put NT Disk Partitioning Schemes

As soon as you've decided on the setup source, but before you install, one of the biggest issues to consider is the type of partition into which you want to install NT. Windows NT supports three file systems:

- DOS's FAT (File Allocation Table) format
- Windows NT's NTFS (NT File System) format
- OS/2's HPFS and HPFS386 (High Performance File System)

The advantages and disadvantages of each are listed in Table 8.4.

Table 8.4. Types of partitions.

File System	*Advantages*	*Disadvantages*
FAT	Usable by DOS and Windows 3.1 without running NT, so you can boot either NT or DOS from a FAT partition with the *boot loader* option that NT automatically installs on a drive containing an existing operating system.	Provides little security. No file or disk recovery features without add-on programs.
NTFS	Extensive file protection (security) and file/drive recoverability. Long filenames—up to 256 characters instead of eight characters or less plus extension. Usable by DOS apps running in a DOS VDM under NT. (Long filenames are truncated to supply DOS with 8.3 filenames.)	DOS and Windows 3.1 can't see or work with NTFS partitions. However, DOS and Win 3.1 apps running under NT can.
HPFS	Lets you boot and run OS/2 and NT on the same drive, using the boot loader. Because NT can recognize HPFS and OS/2 can't recognize NTFS, this is the only choice for NT-OS/2 coexistence.	Not a Microsoft product anymore. Could be argued that there is less file security than under NT. DOS and Windows 3.1 apps can't use HPFS long filenames when you're running DOS and Windows 3.1 emulation (Windows on Windows, or WOW) under NT.

CAUTION

FAT partitions can also support long filenames, but without the enhanced security and file recovery options. Also, extreme care should be used when utilizing MS-DOS utility applications that are not aware of long filename support. At worst, these applications can potentially destroy the data on a FAT drive with long filenames. At best, they will convert the long filenames to truncated 8.3 filenames.

If you intend to make a major commitment to NT and you need the safety and security features of NT, you should lean in the direction of NTFS. Remember, though, that once a partition is reformatted as NTFS, DOS won't recognize it. Also, although you can convert a FAT partition to NTFS nondestructively, the reverse is not true. To do so without losing data, you have to do a backup, reformat the disk, and do a restore. In other words, it's a hassle.

The bottom line is this: The DOS-to-NT migration path that makes the most sense for DOS and Windows 3.1 users is to install NT on the existing DOS or DOS/Windows 3.1 FAT partition and preferably *on top of* the existing Windows 3.1 or Windows for Workgroups installation. Installing on top of the existing 16-bit Windows makes switching to NT easier, because this gives you the option of "migrating" various Windows 3.1 settings (such as application-specific WIN.INI settings, font setting, desktop settings, and Program Manager settings) to NT automatically. Just be sure to clear off 80M of free space before you run the NT Setup program.

You'll probably want higher security for some files or disks, so create an NTFS partition elsewhere to experiment with NT's security or use it for sensitive files or applications that require a higher degree of safety and protection. A common solution among beta testers of NT was to purchase another drive and format at least part of it as NTFS.

Another solution, short of purchasing an additional drive, is to divvy up your existing drive into a couple of partitions (assuming that you have enough disk space). Leave the current system drive in its current format (typically FAT) and create an NTFS partition for use with directories that need security.

NOTE

You have the option of migrating Windows 3.1 settings into NT only if you opt to *upgrade* Windows—that is, if you install NT on top of the existing Windows directory. When you do so, Setup adds numerous files to your Windows directory and adds a \WINDOWS\SYSTEM32 directory to hold additional support files, similar to the \WINDOWS\SYSTEM directory used by Windows 3.1.

NOTE

Another option you have is to install the basic boot files (about 2M worth) on the normal boot disk (drive 0), but locate the NT support files elsewhere, such as in another partition or on another physical drive. If you can't figure out how to reclaim 90M of disk space on drive 0, you can instruct NT to install the support files on another drive while still doing the initial boot-up from drive 0. The boot drive must have the NT boot sector, NTLDR, NTDETECT.COM, NTBOOTDD.SYS (if SCSI), and BOOTSECT.DOS in the C:\ directory. The rest of the files can go wherever you indicate.

NOTE

If you plan to use the multiboot option to alternately boot OS/2 2.x and NT, the preceding scenario is not recommended. This is because OS/2 and NT order primary partitions differently. This can lead to confused pathnames, various icons pointing to the wrong drive, and so on, and it can be a general annoyance. Because of this, if you plan to use the multiboot option with OS/2 and NT, using separate boot disks isn't recommended.

Coping with DoubleSpace and Stacker

NT does *not* support any current disk compression schemes, which can be a real inconvenience. NTFS compression is in the works. Perhaps this is an admission that such schemes are not safe enough for mission-critical applications. One authority suggests that incorporation of disk compression into NT would have delayed the release just that much more, so Microsoft went ahead and released the product without support for compression. In any case, Microsoft reports that compression might be supported in the future, but for now, you're up a creek if you're using DoubleSpace or Stacker. For many corporations, considering the low cost of hard disk storage, this is not an important factor.

Simply put, NT doesn't recognize virtual drives created by compressing software. Therefore, before you can even begin, you must remove the disk compression scheme, restoring all your files to a decompressed format on volumes you want NT to recognize. This can be a hassle, particularly if your hard disk is packed (and whose isn't?). Look in the manual that came with your disk compression software for help with this.

Here's the approach I took before installing NT. I had a 205M drive that, when compressed with DoubleSpace, gave me about 350M of files. It was gridlock city, because I had only a 40M decompressed portion on the drive, not enough to unsquish much data into. Short of doing a total backup and restore, you might try the following steps, using a new drive.

1. Install a second physical drive or locate a decompressed partition to copy to. (In my case it was a new 340M physical drive.)
2. Start copying directories to it. (Dragging from File Manager is the easiest way.) Because the target drive isn't compressed, this in effect decompresses the files.
3. Occasionally exit Windows, and from DOS run DoubleSpace using its menu interface. Choose to resize the compressed volume, decreasing its size as much as possible. (You might have to defragment the compressed drive a couple of times using the defragment option before DoubleSpace will let you decrease the compressed volume's size.)

NOTE

Be aware that even with defragmentation, it can appear that there are arbitrary limitations on the amount by which you can decrease the compressed volume's size. These limitations don't always make sense and can prove frustrating. Often the culprit is a file (or files) marked *hidden, system,* or *read-only.* These files can't be moved; thus, they limit the minimum size of the compressed drive. Try using File Manager or another file-management tool that displays file attributes to look for such files and change these attributes. Then try decreasing the compressed partition size again.

4. Repeat steps 2 and 3 as many times as you need to, depending on how much data you have to decompress.
5. If you're still out of space, zip or otherwise archive some directories. I use PKZIP (DOS) or QUINZIP (Windows). You can unzip the archives later when you get your compressed volume back in usable form. Eventually, get everything copied out of or backed up from the compressed volume.
6. Delete the compressed volume. With DoubleSpace this can be done by erasing the hidden system volume file. The name of this file takes the form DBLSPACE.*XXX,* where *XXX* is a number—for example, DBLSPACE.000.

TIP

Another way to delete a DoubleSpace drive is to use the DOS command line `dblspace /delete x:`, where `x` is the logical drive letter of the compressed drive. Note that you can't delete drive C: in this way.

7. Unzip directories, move directories back to their original drive, and, in general, try to reestablish the same drive/directory tree structure you had before. (Many applications, particularly Windows 3.x programs, expect support DLLs, fonts, and other related files to be where they were when you installed them.) Try to arrange for about 90M of free space if you want to set up NT on the same disk.

TIP

An alternative to the preceding steps for the gradual juggling of files is to use a tape backup system and do a complete backup and restore. Or, if you're on a network, find a hard disk with enough temporary space to hold your directories. A third alternative is to make sure your second hard disk is large enough to take everything on your compressed drive in one fell swoop. Remember, though, that files will bloom to approximately twice their compressed size when copied out of their volume.

Basic Installation

The following steps describe the basic installation procedure, regardless of whether the source is CD-ROM or floppies. (Upgrading an existing installation is covered in the section titled "Upgrading an Existing Installation," and installation across a network is covered in the section titled "Installing Over a Network with WINNT.")

NOTE

If you intend to load NT from a SCSI-controlled CD-ROM, make sure that the drive isn't set to device 0 or 1. If it is, Setup might report the CD as an active hard-disk partition rather than as removable media.

Running Setup

Before you start, you'll have to know the type of display, mouse, printer, printer port, keyboard, network adapter address and IRQ, and finally the computer name and domain name if you're going to connect the NT machine to a Windows NT Advanced Server *domain.*

1. Insert the NT Setup Boot Disk in drive A. Find the correct size of disk. (NT typically comes with a boot disk of each size.) If your drive A is a 5 1/4-inch drive, use that disk. If you have only one size of disk, you might have to switch your floppy drive cables so that drive A: is the drive that matches the size of the setup disk.

> **TIP**
>
> Most Intel-based PC systems use a floppy data cable with two connectors, one for drive A and one for drive B. The drive A connector is the one that has a few of its wires twisted just before the connector.

2. Reboot your machine and optionally reset the CMOS BIOS settings to cause your system to read the floppy drive for startup if you've changed that in the past.
3. The boot disk takes over your system and loads enough of the operating system to bootstrap the Setup program and identify your SCSI disk controller. During this process, you will need to insert the additional setup disks as prompted.
4. You will be asked several things about your system and your preferences for installation. First, Setup prompts you for your installation media choice (3 1/2-inch or 5 1/4-inch disks or CD-ROM), and then it identifies your hardware. Next, it asks you to make choices regarding the file system you want to use and the directory for storing NT files.
5. Get out a blank high-density disk of the same size as your A drive. NT uses the disk during installation to create a backup Emergency Repair Disk that you'll use in case NT ever has trouble booting. (Typically this happens when you've made system modifications such as adding drivers that just won't work with your system.)
6. You'll be asked whether you want to do a custom or an express setup, just as with standard Windows. Express setup is a better choice in most circumstances, simply because it requires less intervention. Although custom setup lets you opt out of installing certain modules of NT such as Help, Accessories, and so forth, and to declare system hardware settings manually, express setup does its best to work around disk space shortages, bagging trivial components not necessary for NT to work. It then searches for applications, adding icons to the relevant NT Program Manager groups.

TIP

Custom setup lists your detected hardware and lets you modify the list. It also lets you change the target directory, configure network adapters, and join a workgroup. In addition, it gives you more control of setting up applications by letting you choose the path and drives you want it to look for apps on. Again, express setup is easier. But if for some reason the auto-detection capabilities of express setup hang the Setup program (this can happen particularly if network cards or video cards are incorrectly detected), run custom setup and manually scrutinize and/or modify the detected hardware settings as they are presented in dialog boxes. This might get you through the installation successfully.

NOTE

Custom setup presents a screen asking you to declare virtual memory (paging or swap file) settings. Express setup does this automatically. Virtual memory (paging file) considerations are covered in Chapter 9, "Configuring Windows NT." In the meantime, you can choose the default settings suggested by Setup.

7. Proceed with the installation. The program scans for SCSI adapters and examines the hard disk partition scheme on your system. If your NT CD-ROM is in the drive connected to the SCSI adapter that Setup finds, it assumes this to be the file source for the installation.

TIP

If you've tried to install NT from your CD-ROM before, and you know that the driver for your CD-ROM drive isn't included on the startup disk, there's a solution. If you have an NT-compatible SCSI device driver for your CD-ROM, use the custom setup option. When you're prompted for SCSI detection, select Other. Supply your OEM driver disk when prompted.

8. Setup then looks for an existing Windows NT installation or a 16-bit Windows installation if no prior NT installation is found. If one is found, Setup suggests installing NT in the same directory (C:\WINDOWS, for example). If you want NT installed on a FAT partition, this is the thing to do. NT system files will land in a new directory—C:\WINDOWS\ SYSTEM32—not in your Windows or \WINDOWS\SYSTEM directory, so don't worry about file collisions or more confusion in those already overloaded directories.

TIP

There's an advantage to installing in the existing Windows directory: Many of your existing Windows settings (notably Program Manager groups, application .INI files, and so on) will be maintained and still work with the existing path names. If you choose to put NT elsewhere, Win 3.1 apps are more likely to issue error messages because they're less likely to find their related support files.

9. Next NT Setup does a `CHKDSK` of your entire disk to ensure that there aren't any errors, and then it copies a zillion files to the hard disk. Using the CD-ROM, this is painless and takes just a couple of minutes.
10. You'll see a message about doing a three-key reset. Do it, and note that the boot-up sequence is very different now. You'll see a message about the "NT OS loader" booting, and a message about NT checking the hard-disk media. It's looking for broken chains, much like `CHKDSK`. Not until the volume is considered "clean" (free of errors) will NT boot. If errors are detected, NT attempts to correct them.

NOTE

On most VGA screens, these messages are in a smaller-than-normal font. Instead of 25-line print, they're in 48-line print.

11. During the first boot-up, you'll be prompted to enter your name and your company's name and to verify them. As with other Microsoft products, this information shows up in NT-related dialog boxes such as About boxes. It's Microsoft's way of recording who is supposedly the registered owner.
12. Next you'll be prompted to give the computer a name. If you've been using the computer using another networking scheme such as Windows for Workgroups, use the same name. This way, other stations on the network will be able to connect to the new NT station, not even knowing it's changed status from a WFW peer to an NT peer.
13. You'll be prompted to choose the language locale. Usually English (American) is fine. This affects primarily date, currency, and time displays, just as in 16-bit Windows.
14. When you're prompted about printers, in the Model area choose the type of printer that's attached to your system, set the correct port, and give the printer a name. This name is the name users on the network will see when they're browsing around to attach to a printer. Use a name that makes sense, such as "HP Laser Printer in Room 302." A name like this tells users where to pick up their print-outs.

15. Next you'll be asked about the network card(s) in the machine. Set the IRQ, port address, DMA channel, or other relevant information. Defaults for the detected card are displayed (assuming that your card is installed and was detected properly). Change them if necessary. (See Chapter 11 and this chapter for more details on network installation.) Setup now copies a significant number of files.

NOTE

If the network card isn't detected, you still can set up the driver for the card. Just stipulate the IRQ and base address, or whatever else you're asked about. Later you can adjust the card's jumpers (or run a DOS-based software configuration program). Then try rebooting NT until the card is properly detected.

16. After lots of little advertisements about how great NT is, and after the installation of other files, the network modules are started, and you're asked to declare the name of the workgroup or domain you want to join and/or to declare a password. If you want to connect to an already existing Windows for Workgroups workgroup, just enter the name of the group and click on OK.

NOTE

If at this point your connection to the network doesn't commence, it's probably either because the network isn't running (check the other workstations/servers) or, more likely, because Setup didn't recognize your network card. You should try reinstalling NT using the Custom setup, because it lets you declare the network card and settings. Alternatively, as soon as NT gets up and running fully, you can run the Network applet in Control Panel and adjust the card and driver settings there.

17. Next you'll see the Administrator Account Setup. Each NT machine can have multiple accounts or sets of passwords, privileges, and so on for each user. But each NT machine you set up must have at least one "administrator account." This is the account that the system administrator will use to log onto the system and perform certain maintenance tasks such as setting up and altering passwords, creating a post office for use with the Mail program, and controlling the sharing of directories and other resources. Setup assumes that the person doing the installation is an administrator and grants Administrator status by allowing him or her to enter the password. Enter a password and write it down somewhere so that you'll remember it.

NOTE

Incidentally, the default password is *Administrator*. If you don't enter a password and you're later prompted for the administrator's password, try it. It might work.

18. Next you'll have the option of creating a local account for the "user" (as opposed to the administrator). Initially the user will have the same privileges as the administrator, but this can be changed later via the User Manager program. No two accounts can have the same password, so even if the same person is both the local user and the administrator, the accounts must have different assigned passwords.

NOTE

You can set up multiple user accounts on the same NT machine via the User Manager applet (available only to those with Administrator status), but at this point you're just given the option of creating one. Chapter 10, "Windows NT Administration," covers establishing new accounts with User Manager.

19. Check the date and time dialog box for accuracy. Normally, you just have to change the time zone.
20. When you're prompted, insert a high-density floppy disk in the boot drive for NT to make an Emergency Repair Disk. It gets formatted and then written to with backup information.

NOTE

The Emergency Repair Disk contains the directory structure, the NT Registry information, and the computer name. (The Registry is NT's version of Windows 3.1's .INI files, among other things.) The disk can be used only with the computer it was made on. It can't be transferred to another machine unless the other machine is *identical* (physically and logically) to the one on which the disk was created. This isn't likely, but it's possible.

21. Remove the floppy and restart your computer. If you already had DOS on the system disk, your system tracks are modified so that the multiboot OS Loader runs at boot time. You'll see an option for starting MS-DOS or NT.
22. Make sure that Windows NT is highlighted and press Enter. Alternatively, just wait 30 seconds and NT will boot by itself.

23. The first time you log on as a user, if NT was installed into a directory containing a preexisting Windows 3.1 install, you'll be prompted to
    - migrate Windows 3.x WIN.INI and CONTROL.INI files into NT
    - migrate Windows 3.x Program Manager group files into NT

    As a rule, I suggest doing this if you want the smoothest migration path from 16- to 32-bit Windows. When you opt for this, some major disk thrashing will ensue. You'll suddenly have lots of groups, and your color settings, desktop setup, and so forth will be the same as they were under Windows 3.1. You will still have to adjust the Program Manager windows, however (choose Arrange Icons). Also note that your WINFILE.INI won't have migrated, so File Manager will need arranging too.

NOTE

If you install NT in an existing Windows for Workgroups installation with the Microsoft At Work fax support or other mail extension DLLs, MS-Mail might report several error messages about invalid images. These error messages occur because the NT version of MS-Mail doesn't support 16-bit DLLs. The easiest method of correcting the problem is to use the registry editor and delete the undesired keys. Having experienced several problems attempting to correct these situations, I suggest deleting all but the following key in HKEY_CURRENT_USER\Software\Microsoft\Mail\Microsoft Mail. The tree should be completely empty except for this single key. This will restore the application to its initial state, ready for you to configure the application as desired. See Chapter 6 for a more in-depth discussion of MS-Mail.

Installing on an Unformatted Hard Disk

This section describes installation on a new hard disk or one that hasn't been formatted. Normally, NT assumes that you want to keep the existing partition type (FAT, NTFS, HPFS) intact. On an unformatted disk, however, Setup gives you the option of formatting the disk as a FAT or NTFS volume.

1. At the beginning of Setup, you'll see this message:

```
Setup has determined that your computer's startup hard disk contains a
nonstandard OS or has never been used. If a nonstandard operating system
is installed, continuing Setup may interfere with or destroy the
operating system's ability to start.
```

If the hard disk has never been used, or you wish to discard its current contents, choose to continue Setup.

Then you see the following:

```
Please select the partition where you like to install Windows NT.

The list below shows the existing partitions that Setup has found, as
well as space available for new partitions. Use the Up and Down arrow
keys to highlight your choice in the list.
```

At this point you can create a partition by pressing P. On a new disk, the default is to partition the whole disk. You can decrease the size of the partition if you want. Press Enter to continue. This just creates a partition; it doesn't format it.

NOTE

Sometimes 1M or so of space is left unpartitioned. Older drives in particular list this unused 1M or so. This unused space is actually one cylinder on the hard disk that is reserved as a *test track*. Some newer drives, such as late-model SCSI drives, don't set aside a test track, so you won't see the unused space after you partition these drives. Some older SCSI drives (for example, Adaptec 154x drives) used to have a test track, but with the newer NT drivers, they can be repartitioned to regain this extra 1M.

2. Now you will have a choice to format the partition as FAT or NTFS.

NOTE

To take advantage of the security features of NT (such as recovery from media glitches and prevention of unauthorized access), you must use NTFS. As discussed earlier, be aware that you don't have access to NTFS partitions when you boot MS-DOS.

3. Setup warns you that formatting will erase data on the partition. When you choose to continue, a "gas gauge" appears, keeping you apprised of the formatting progress.
4. After the format, you're asked which directory you want to put NT in. The default is \WINNT. This option is the best overall choice. If you later install another Windows version (such as 3.1 or Windows for Workgroups), its Setup program will detect NT and suggest that you install into the \WINNT directory to allow a symbiotic relationship between the two and to allow migration of settings.

```
\winnt    {--- NT files
system32   {--- NT system files
```

If you later perform an installation of a 16-bit Windows 3.1, or Windows for Workgroups, you'll end up with the following:

```
\windows   {--- NT and 16-bit Windows files
   ¦
system32 {--- NT system files
   ¦
system {--- 16-bit Windows system files
```

NOTE

To force a Windows 3.1 to NT migration after installation is over, you have to create a new User account.

5. After installation is over, reboot. If there was another operating system on your computer before you installed NT, you'll see a Windows NT Boot Loader message asking which operating system you want to load—NT or MS-DOS (and optionally OS/2 if that was the previous system). Select NT, and NT starts. It checks the system first, and then it asks you to press Ctrl-Alt-Delete to sign in.

NOTE

You might wonder why NT makes you press the traditional "three-key reset" command keys to log on. In DOS, these keys are the "abandon ship" keys. Microsoft claims that using these keys prevents Trojan Horse viruses or "back doors" from being available after logon.

Upon the first boot, the volume check will report that your volume is a FAT volume. Don't worry. If you chose to create an NTFS partition, it will be converted after the partition is determined to be "clean" by the OS loader. The OS loader will then self-run the convert program, converting the FAT to NTFS, and finally reboot.

Installing Over a Network with WINNT

Network administrators might want to set up a number of NT machines along a network. This can be done easily by creating a shared directory on the network. This directory will hold the NT files. After the files are copied there by Setup, you use a supplied command-prompt program, WINNT.EXE, to install the NT files on the target machine. Setting up such a shared directory for NT installation is called (by Microsoft) creating a sharepoint. As soon as the sharepoint is created, an administrator can install NT for a user with the WINNT command. These steps are covered in the next section.

Setting Up the Network Sharepoint for Subsequent Network NT Installations

Here are the steps for creating the sharepoint:

1. Run NT on the machine that the sharepoint will reside on.
2. Make sure that the network is alive and functioning. Any kind of network will do, as long as all the workstations you want to set up NT on can access the network via MS-DOS.
3. Check your directory permissions. The drive you're going to install the sharepoint on must have read/write permission by you because you're going to write files there.
4. From NT File Manager, switch to (or connect to) the target drive.
5. Create a fresh directory to receive the files—for example, `md netnt`.
6. Open a DOS session (command prompt) from Program Manager or choose File | Run from File Manager and type `COMMAND`.
7. Enter the following command:

   ```
   xcopy SourceDirectory\Platform DestinationDirectory
   ```

   For example, to copy the files for the Intel platform, the command would appear as `XCOPY E:\I386 \\SRV\SETUP\I386` where `E:` is the local CD-ROM (source files), and the destination directory `\SETUP\I386` resides on the server `SRV`.

NOTE

If you are installing to a shared directory on another network, just specify the drive letter you used to connect instead of an UNC filename for the destination directory.

8. After all of the files have been copied to the sharepoint, you're ready to proceed with the client installations.

Follow the instructions in the next section to install NT on one of the workstations connected to the network.

Installing NT from a Network Sharepoint

As soon as the sharepoint is set up, you're ready to install NT on any workstation that can access the sharepoint. Microsoft says it doesn't matter which NOS (network operating system) connects the stations, as long as each can access the sharepoint via MS-DOS or some operating system that can run an MS-DOS program from the DOS command line, such as Windows for Workgroups, OS/2, or Windows 3.1 with a compatible network link such as Banyan VINES or NetWare. The only catch is that the DOS command-line interpreter must be running in an environment that allows only a single instance of MS-DOS. That is, you can't be running Windows in Enhanced mode—it must be running in Standard mode. Nor can you be running OS/2 2.x—it must be 1.x. Obviously, just quitting OS/2 or Windows and running a plain old DOS session might be the easiest way to do such an installation.

NOTE

Even though you can install NT across a non-NT network, that doesn't mean NT will recognize it after it's installed. NT recognizes only specific networks.

TIP

Instead of installing across a network, you could pass around a CD-ROM drive. But network speed often is higher than that of a CD-ROM, so installation is faster, with less hassle. Also, because all WINNT does is copy files, multiple workstations can be installing NT at the same time with no network conflicts.

1. Make sure that the sharepoint (NT file source directory) is shared for network access.
2. At the target workstation, log onto the network and connect to or otherwise access the sharepoint directory.

NOTE

If your target station is a Windows for Workgroups 3.1 machine, you have to follow a few more steps. As mentioned earlier, you must not run WINNT in Enhanced 386 mode—only in Standard mode. To start Windows for Workgroups in Standard mode, you first have to start the network manually. Follow these steps:

1. Boot the machine into DOS and type `net start workgroup`.
2. Enter your computer name and password. Then type `win /s`.

NOTE

Windows for Workgroups 3.11 doesn't support standard mode. However, `win/t` provides the same basic functionality—with one exception. If your network driver is an NDIS 3.0 (that is, a protected-mode driver), your network won't start. To solve this problem, either use the Network Setup applet in the Network Group to install an NDIS 2.0 driver for your network adapter, or configure your current driver to support real mode and enhanced mode.

3. Use File Manager to connect to and log onto the sharepoint. Then continue with the following steps.
4. There should be an .EXE file in the sharepoint directory called WINNT. Run this program.
5. NT installs pretty much as explained in the section titled "Basic Installation," but with a few twists:
   - First, WINNT prompts you to insert a disk in drive A. It then creates three floppies, which are essentially the same NT installation floppies you use on a normal install.
   - Next, it copies the NT source files from the sharepoint into the target directory on the local machine, dropping them in a temporary directory called WIN_NT.~LS.
   - It then prompts the installer to reboot the machine so that the boot floppy is read.
   - A standard installation occurs, except that Setup *moves* files from the temporary directory into the target directory (instead of copying them from a CD-ROM or floppy).
   - If less than 8M of RAM is detected in the target machine, Setup terminates.

NOTE

Because files are moved rather than copied between directories on the target partition, you don't need to ensure double the normal amount of hard-disk space. Approximately 90M is still adequate.

TIP

Your company might have NT customization requirements or preferences. If you alter the source NT files at the sharepoint before network installation, all subsequent network installs will reflect those changes immediately upon installation without the need to fine-tune each workstation's setup. This can save significant workstation configuration time. See Chapters 9 through 12 for customization information.

Upgrading an Existing Installation

There are several ways to upgrade an existing installation of NT. You can use either of the setup methods just discussed, or you can use WINNT32. WINNT32 is a native NT application that can be configured to use a network sharepoint to upgrade an existing NT installation with or without any boot disks. My favorite method utilizes the "no floppy boot" option, because it's essentially a hands-off upgrade requiring minimal user interaction.

NOTE

You can't use WINNT to upgrade a RISC-based computer. Either follow the standard method of installation as described in the next section, "Installing NT on a RISC Computer," or use WINNT32.

To perform an upgrade and create the three boot floppies, follow these steps:

1. Make sure that the sharepoint (NT file source directory) is shared for network access.
2. At the target workstation, log onto the network and connect to or otherwise access the sharepoint directory.
3. There should be an .EXE file in the sharepoint directory called WINNT32. Run this program.
4. NT installs as explained in the section titled "Installing NT from a Network Sharepoint."

To perform an upgrade without creating the three boot floppies, follow these steps:

1. Make sure that the sharepoint (NT file source directory) is shared for network access.

2. At the target workstation, log onto the network and connect to or otherwise access the sharepoint directory.
3. There should be an .EXE file in the sharepoint directory called WINNT32. Run this program with the `/s:\\ServerName\SharePoint /b /x` command-line parameters. This specifies the source path and floppyless operation and tells NT not to create the boot floppies, respectively.
4. NT installs pretty much as explained in the section titled "Installing NT from a Network Sharepoint," but with a few exceptions:
   - First, it copies the NT source files from the sharepoint into the target directory on the local machine, dropping them in a temporary directory called WIN_NT.~LS. Another temporary directory called WIN_NT.~BT contains the boot files required for setup (basically the same files contained in the three boot floppies).
   - Next, an entry is added to BOOT.INI for the NT upgrade, and you're prompted to either restart the computer or exit to Windows NT. After the computer is restarted, the upgrade process continues.
   - A standard installation occurs, except that Setup moves files from the temporary directory into the target directory (instead of copying them from a CD-ROM or floppy). Also, as an upgrade to an existing installation, even if a custom setup is specified, there are no options to customize the exiting network settings, user account, domain, or other settings. In fact, the only configurable options are remote access (if the TCP/IP protocol has been previously installed) and the display settings.

Installing NT on a RISC Computer

There is some variation in the way you run Setup on RISC-based computers. First, you have to check that your hard disk has been initialized. It doesn't all have to be partitioned, but at least some of it has to be. Unlike x86 systems, RISC systems can split the boot track and the NT system files between two partitions. Your primary partition (called the *system partition*) must be FAT, and it must have at least 2M of space in order to handle the NT hardware-specific NT boot files. If you're not sure where the system partition is or whether you have one, study the manuals or call the manufacturer.

NOTE

After you install NT, the system partition will have a directory called \OS\NT, which will include two boot files called OSLOADER.EXE and HAL.DLL.

Next, you should check the manual to determine how to run a program located on a CD-ROM. As soon as you have that under control, the following instructions are typical of what you'll have to do.

NOTE

Due to differences between machines, these steps are approximate. However, the general principles are the same.

1. With the NT CD-ROM in the disk, restart the computer.
2. Choose to run a program. For example, on an ARC machine, choose Run A Program from the menu.
3. You should see a command prompt. Enter the following line (or something similar):

   ```
   CD:\mips\setupldr
   ```

   The gist is that you're trying to run the SETUPLDR program.
4. Now go through the basic installation as described earlier in this chapter, responding to the on-screen dialog boxes.

Configuring Windows NT

9

IN THIS CHAPTER

Configuring Windows NT was explained somewhat in Chapter 8, "Installing Windows NT." For many typical NT systems, the Setup program oversees configuration quite well. As a result, in many cases, any adjustments need only be minor.

Because NT is based on an entirely different model than Windows running on DOS, configuration (although achieved in some cases via similar paths such as Control Panel) actually works quite differently in NT. For example, 32-bit applications written for NT no longer use traditional 16-bit Windows .INI files for saving their settings, nor does Windows NT. (16-bit Windows applications running under NT still do, of course.) No longer does Windows configuration entail laborious scrutiny of the WIN.INI, SYSTEM.INI, AUTOEXEC.BAT, and CONFIG.SYS files. In place of these files, NT relies on a totally new hardware and software configuration concept that helps MIS personnel locally or remotely configure and maintain hundreds or even thousands of computers and applications.

This is achieved through the *Configuration Registry*—a centralized database that stores information about hardware, applications, and operating system settings for each computer on the network.

Due to the introduction of the Registry, there's no longer a SYSEDIT program for modifying your system files, nor are new applications allowed to run amok among your configuration files, potentially wreaking havoc on a finely tuned system. Instead, when absolutely necessary (which isn't often), you can use the Registry Editor to dig into things.

NOTE

Use of the Registry Editor is covered in Chapter 12.

Under most conditions, actual direct manipulation of the Registry isn't necessary or recommended. The supplied administration tools such as Control Panel offer an easier interface and ensure that Registry alterations are properly maintained.

This chapter covers the most likely avenues through which you can tailor Windows NT settings on the workstation or server. Topics covered in this chapter include

- Control Panel
- System Setup
- Configuring other application environments

NOTE

Settings specific to NT Server aren't covered here. Look for these in Part III of this book.

Control Panel

The NT Control Panel has extensions above and beyond those in Windows 3.1. Aside from actual system administration involving passwords, user profiles, and disk management, the majority of NT configuration can be achieved via Control Panel. Any Control Panel changes you make are stored in the Registry in the active account's section (tree). This means that each user on any given system can have unique Control Panel settings such as screen savers, mouse sensitivity, screen colors, and so on.

NOTE

Some settings, such as Fonts, are system-wide. Adding or removing fonts on a given workstation affects all users.

As with Windows 3.1, Control Panel is in the Main Group. Each user has a Main group and a Control Panel. When you run Control Panel, the box shown in Figure 9.1 appears.

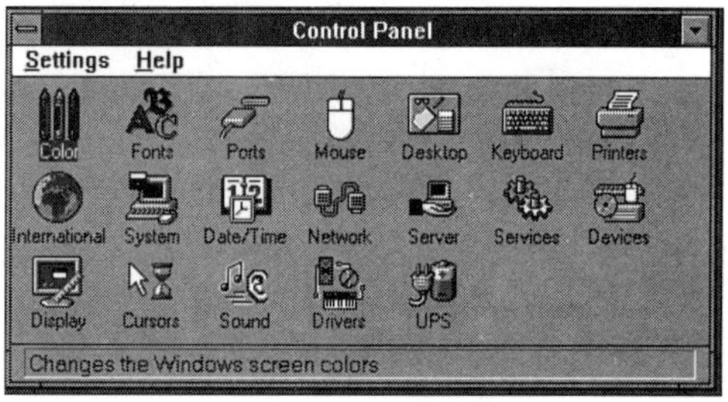

FIGURE 9.1.
The NT Control Panel.

Table 9.1 lists Control Panel options (applets) and their uses. Some you'll be familiar with, and others are new with NT. An asterisk indicates that the function is identical (or nearly identical) to Windows 3.1. "Local" means that settings may be individually set for a specific user on a workstation. "Global" means that changes affect the accounts of all users on the workstation.

Table 9.1. Control Panel options and their uses.

Applet	*Local or Global*	*Description*
Colors*	Local	Sets the colors of Windows elements such as workspace background, scroll bars, title bars, and so on.
Fonts*	Global	Installs, removes, and views installed TrueType fonts.
Ports	Global	Configures serial async ports with settings such as baud, parity, data bits, flow control, base port address, and IRQ.
Mouse*	Local	Sets sensitivity, double-click speed, and left/right buttons.
Desktop*	Local	Sets cursor blink rate, desktop pattern or wallpaper, desktop alignment grid, icon spacing, fast tabbing, full drag, and screen saver.
Keyboard*	Local	Sets key repeat rate and delay before repeat.
Printers	Global	Runs Print Manager.
International*	Global for language, local for everything else	Sets currency formats, special characters, and the date/time display format.
System	Global	Sets virtual memory page size, system and application environment variables, system recovery options (logging STOP events, administrator alerts, system reboots), and the startup operating system (OS/2, MS-DOS, or NT).
Date/Time	Global	Sets the system's clock.
Network	Global	Sets the network interface card. Sets card parameters such as IRQ, DMA, and port address. Installs network drivers and software components. Joins workgroups or domains.

Applet	*Local or Global*	*Description*
Server	Global	Lets you see who's connected to your local computer, which devices you share, and who's using them. You also can disconnect others from these resources, as well as declare which users will receive alert messages in case of a system emergency such as an impending power-down. Also allows managing directory "replication," described in Chapter 10.
Services	Global for administrators, local for other users. Specific services can be installed either way.	Many of NT's inner workings are divided into modules called *services*. For example, the capability to act as an OLE server to others on the network and the capability to browse the network for other machines are both services. This applet lets you start or stop such modules without quitting and restarting NT. You also can declare when each service becomes active.
Devices	Global	Devices are like services, but they pertain specifically to devices such as a CD-ROM drive. In fact, they are loadable device drivers such as those you're used to loading via CONFIG.SYS in DOS. This applet lets you interactively start, stop, and declare when each device driver is loaded (such as at boot time).
Display	Global	Installs and removes video drivers, video resolution, color palette, font size, and refresh rate.
Cursors	Local	Configures cursor shapes such as the pointer, the "waiting hourglass," and others. Some animated cursors are supplied too, which can be fun.
Sound*	Local	Assigns system sounds if you have a sound card, or turns off the annoying beep if you don't want the computer talking back to you.

continues

Table 9.1. continued

Applet	Local or Global	Description
MIDI Mapper*		Lets you remap MIDI key or patch commands to work with MIDI synthesizers that don't comply with the "general MIDI" spec that Microsoft uses.
Drivers*	Global	Lets you install, configure, and remove software drivers for add-on multimedia sound boards, video boards, TV boards, and so forth.
UPS	Global	If you have an uninterruptible power supply, you'll want to set it up with certain options here, such as how long to wait before saving files and shutting down the system, which serial port its communication line is connected to, and so on.

Colors

This applet alters the colors assigned to the various Windows screen elements. Because colors on gray-scale screens (such as many laptops) are mapped to shades of gray, changing the color settings will have some effect on those too. The default setting (called Windows Default) is fine for most screens. However, users can make modifications. Each user's settings are stored in the Registry and reactivated when he or she logs on.

You can modify the color setting of just about any part of a Windows screen, either manually or by choosing one of the predefined color schemes. Manual color choices are picked from a palette of premade color choices. If none satisfies you, custom colors can be mixed, just like in a paint store. After you create custom colors and color schemes, you can save them for later use.

It's possible that the screen driver you chose when you installed NT will have some effect on the color rendering on the workstation's screen. Experimentation is the key. For example, choosing the standard color-VGA driver, even when you're using a noncolor VGA screen, can give you a more agreeable display, particularly if the screen is capable of gray-scaling. Therefore, if you chose a monochrome VGA driver when you installed NT, you might want to switch to a color one.

NOTE

Configuring the video display is covered a little later in this chapter in the section titled "Display Usage."

In any case, as soon as the driver is installed and operational, you can fine-tune the display from Control Panel. When you run the applet, you see the dialog box shown in Figure 9.2. Each Windows NT screen element is displayed in a sample area. When you select different color schemes, the sample area changes to display the effect.

FIGURE 9.2.
The dialog box for setting screen and window colors.

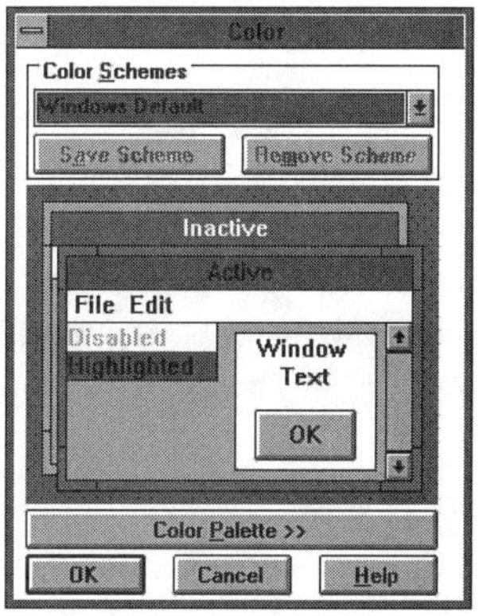

Loading a Color Scheme

To try an existing color scheme, follow these steps:

1. Open the drop-down Color Schemes list.
2. Make a selection using the arrow keys or by typing the first letter of the selection you want to move to. The colors in the dialog box change, showing the scheme.

TIP

You can quickly cycle through the color schemes. Highlight the Color Schemes space and press the up and down arrow keys. The sample screen elements change to reflect each color scheme as its name appears in the Color Schemes space.

3. Click on OK. The new colors go into effect.

The following are some tips on color schemes for laptops:

- If you have a gas plasma screen, you might want to use the Plasma Power Saver color scheme. It extends battery life by using darker shades, which draw less power.
- On many laptops, noncolor LCD screens appear in an unsightly reverse video when you run Windows NT. Some laptops have a program or a switch that reverses this (the ideal solution). If yours doesn't, try one of the LCD color schemes to rectify the problem.

Choosing Your Own Colors

You can easily customize color schemes. To save time, start with one that's close to what you want. Then modify the scheme using the Palette and optionally save it under a new name. If you save it, you can easily switch to another scheme and then reload the custom color scheme later.

NOTE

There are two types of colors: solid and nonsolid (patterns). Solid colors must be used for some of the Windows elements: window frame, window text, window background, menu bars, menu text, active and inactive title bar text, button faces, button text, disabled text, highlights, and highlighted text. If you use nonsolid colors for these elements, they'll be changed to a solid color of a similar tint.

The following are the steps for customizing:

1. If you want, choose a color scheme close to what your desired outcome is.
2. Click on the Color Palette button. The dialog box expands to include the palette, as shown in Figure 9.3.
3. In the left side of the box, click on an area whose color you want to change. The listed Screen Element on the right side will reflect this. In some cases, repeated clicking cycles you through two or three elements. You also can choose from the drop-down list.
4. Choose a color or a pattern to assign to the chosen element.
5. When you're satisfied with the look, click on OK or save the color scheme by clicking on Save Scheme, typing a name for the color scheme, and clicking on OK. If you exit without saving, the colors will persist for future Windows NT sessions, but they will be lost if you select another scheme. However, you can create a scheme, save it, and then select or create another scheme without leaving the dialog box.

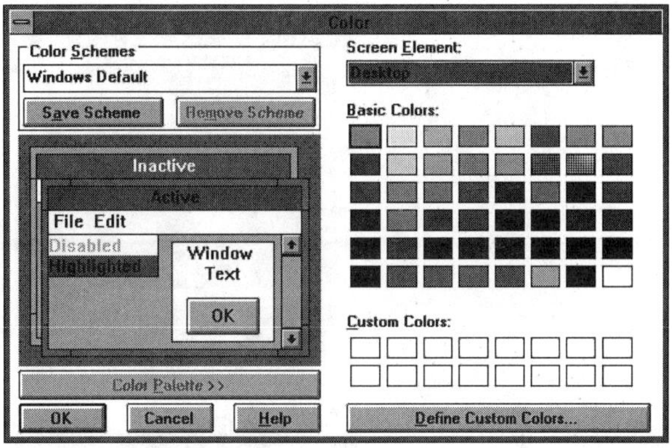

FIGURE 9.3.
The palette.

TIP

Some applications use particular settings in a color scheme, such as Button Face or Scroll Bar, for their own elements. If you're trying to change the color of a specific element in an application program, check whether it's the same color as one of the basic screen elements. Then try changing that element to see whether it's reflected in the application.

Color schemes are stored as a collection of numbers in the Registry and thus take up some disk space. It's not a significant amount of space, but you probably shouldn't create lots of color schemes that you won't use. To trash a scheme, select it from the drop-down list and click on the Remove Scheme button.

Creating Your Own Colors

Don't like the colors in the palette? Make up your own. The 16 slots at the bottom of the Color Palette let you store custom colors that you can assign to screen elements.

1. Expand the Color dialog box to show the palette. Click on Define Custom Colors. The Color Selector, shown in Figure 9.4, appears.
2. Use two cursors—the luminosity bar and the color refiner—by dragging them one at a time until the color in the box at the lower left shows the shade you want. As you do this, the numbers in the little boxes below the color refiner reflect the changes.

FIGURE 9.4.
The custom color selector.

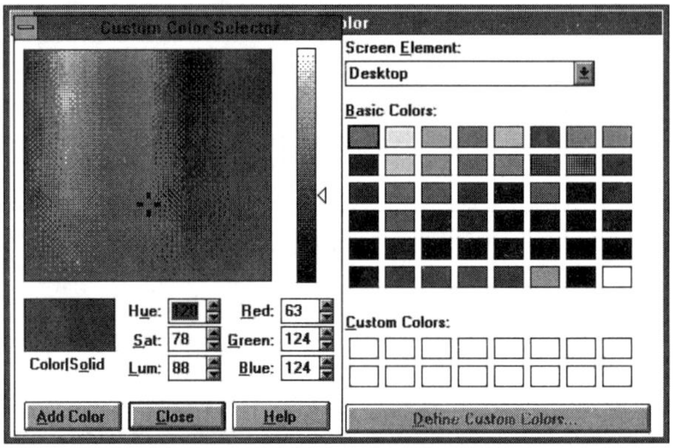

3. Click on Add Color. The new color is added to the palette. In case you're wondering what the terms in the box refer to, here's what they mean:

Term	*Description*
Luminosity	The amount of brightness in the color.
Hue	The actual shade or color. All colors are composed of red, green, and blue.
Saturation	The degree of purity of the color. Saturation is decreased when you add gray to the color and increased when you subtract it.

TIP

You can edit a custom color by clicking on it, moving the cursors around, and clicking on Add Color.

Fonts

As you probably know, the word *font* refers to type styles you set a document in. Fonts help get your message across through visual impact that spices up your document and increases readability. Fonts are specified by name, size, and style. Font styles include bold, italic, underline, double underline, subscript, and superscript. Others, such as small capitals, are available in some programs.

Windows NT comes with approximately the same set of fonts as Windows 3.1. The actual number and sizes of available fonts installed depends on the type of screen and printer you have. It also depends on whether you installed NT over an existing Windows 3.1. If you did, installed TrueType fonts will migrate into NT. Windows 3.1 TrueType fonts will work perfectly with Windows NT, so far as my experiments have shown.

After-market font packages often include installers, but those designed for Windows 3.1 might not work correctly with NT. If the font installer runs under Windows 3.1, you might be able to run it from NT without difficulty. However, because font installers for 3.1 want to modify the WIN.INI and not the Registry, changes might not take place appropriately unless the installer is designed for NT. The installer might copy the fonts into the appropriate directory, but it probably won't activate them.

This isn't a problem, however. Because installers usually decompress font files, go ahead and run the installer as a Windows 3.1 application under NT. Then use Control Panel's Font option to install the fonts. The Fonts option also lets you remove fonts from your Windows setup and lets you set various options for TrueType fonts.

TIP

Many font installers ask for a destination directory for the font files. I suggest keeping all your fonts (or at least ones not supplied with Windows) in a separate directory such as \WINDOWS\FONTS. This cuts down on clutter in your Windows directory. How to do this manually is explained in the section titled "Adding New Fonts to the System."

Classes of Fonts

Let's digress for a moment to discuss classes of fonts. You'll encounter several general classes of fonts in Windows.

- Screen fonts control how letters display on-screen. They come in predefined sizes such as 10-point, 12-point, and so on and match the printed fonts as closely as possible. However, the on-screen resolution usually is lower than the resolution of the final output because laser printers, bubble jets, and ink-jet printers have about 300 or higher dpi, as opposed to about 72 dpi on a typical screen.
- TrueType fonts debuted with Windows 3.1. They solve many of the earlier Windows fonts problems such as differences between how fonts appear on-screen and how they print. Depending on the printer and the font, TrueType fonts are either generated as bitmaps or downloaded as font files. TrueType fonts are stored in .TTF files. Matching screen fonts are stored as .FOT files. Both are necessary for printing and viewing a TrueType font on-screen.
- Non-TrueType fonts specific to your printer are called *printer fonts* by Windows NT. Typically they're stored in a printer as, for example, a PostScript outline font or an HP bitmapped font. The storage location can be a ROM or a plug-in cartridge in the printer. They also can be downloaded to your printer by Windows NT when you print. Downloaded fonts are called *soft fonts.*

- *System fonts* are fonts used internally by Windows NT to display dialog boxes, menus, and the like. These also are used for applications that don't support font choices, such as Cardfile and Notepad. System fonts are stored in .FON files such as MSSERIF.FON, which is the generic Microsoft serif font. Windows NT sometimes uses system fonts when it can't find an exact screen font to match a selected printer font. For example, if you have a PostScript printer installed and you set some selected text in Palatino, an appropriate system font will substitute for it on-screen, indicating as closely as possible the correct size, line breaks, and so on.
- *Vector fonts* are fonts that draw letters by using straight line segments and formulas. Vector fonts are used mostly on plotters.

TrueType has simplified font management and installation. Installing a TrueType font automatically takes care of both the screen and printer files. This wasn't always the case before Windows 3.1 and NT. A third-party font manager such as Adobe's ATM needed to be loaded as a separate program to coordinate screen and printer fonts and scale fonts on-the-fly for use by applications. Windows NT has an internal font scaler that, limited only by your printer's capabilities, provides applications with multiple font sizes from about 8 to 127 points. (A point is 1/72 of an inch.) Additionally, TrueType fonts will always look the same, regardless of the printer or screen (although they might have differences in smoothness). The TrueType font scaler engine performs these services for both 32-bit applications and those running in the 16-bit Windows 3.1 environment subsystem.

Adding New Fonts to the System

Here are the steps for installing new TrueType fonts into your system.

NOTE

Remember that fonts are not user-specific. Fonts that one user installs will be available to all other users on the same system.

1. Run the Fonts applet by double-clicking on its icon in the Control Panel window. Installed fonts are listed in the resulting dialog box, shown in Figure 9.5.
2. If you want to see what an installed font looks like, click on a font name. The name and a brief description of the font appear in the bottom of the dialog box. For bitmapped fonts, sizes are listed. For vector or TrueType fonts, no sizes are listed after the name because they can be printed or displayed in any size (typically up to a maximum of 127 points).

FIGURE 9.5.
The dialog box for viewing, installing, and removing fonts.

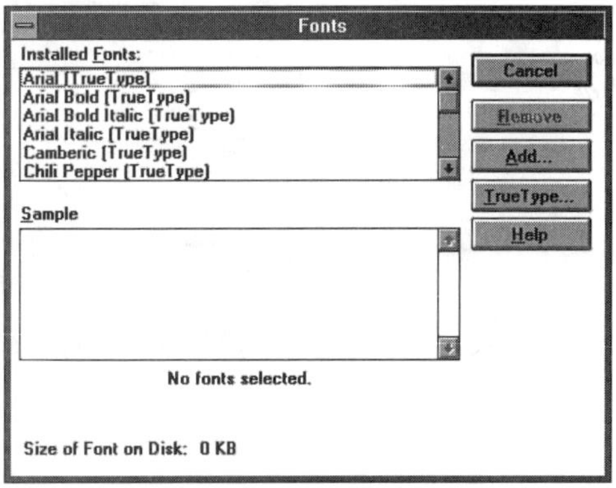

NOTE

A typical TrueType font file (.TTF) is approximately 30 to 50K in size. Its matching screen file (.FOT) will be about 1.3K.

NOTE

Unfortunately, you can't preview a font before you load it.

3. To add a new font, click on Add. The dialog box changes to include a file box, as shown in Figure 9.6. Choose the source drive and directory containing the fonts. Click on Network to choose a network drive that you're not currently connected to via File Manager. This brings up the Browser dialog box. You'll have to walk your way through the tree to find the fonts you want. However, this is a good way to snarf some TrueType fonts from other workstations. Typically you'll want to look in the \WINDOWS\SYSTEM or \WINNT\SYSTEM directory on another person's workstation to find fonts. You'll need to have read privileges on the directory, and it must be previously shared by its owner.

NOTE

Before you copy fonts from another person's computer, you might want to check on the legalities of such a move. Fonts typically have a single-CPU license associated with them. It's illegal to copy such a font to another machine.

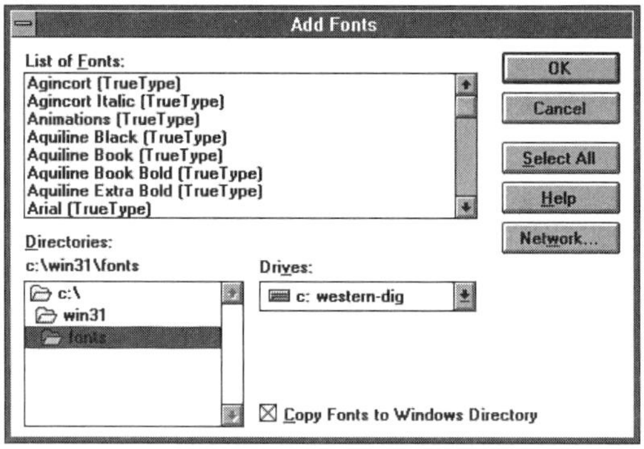

FIGURE 9.6.
Choosing the location of fonts to be added.

4. Select the fonts to add. Make multiple selections by Shift-clicking (to select a range) or Ctrl-clicking (to select individual noncontiguous fonts).
5. Note the check box at the bottom. Normally, fonts are copied from the source drive and directory to the Windows NT system directory. (Typically this is \WINNT\SYSTEM32, but if you installed over an existing Windows 3.1, fonts might be copied into the \WINDOWS\SYSTEM directory.) If you're adding the fonts from a floppy disk, this makes sense. But if the fonts are already on the hard disk, why make additional copies and take up more disk space? Turn off this check box if the fonts are already in a drive or directory that will be available when you start Windows.

TIP

As I mentioned earlier, you can make your \SYSTEM32 directory less cluttered and keep your fonts better organized by putting them in one place. Set up a directory for fonts, such as \WINNT\FONTS or \WINDOWS\FONTS, then move all your .TTF and .FOT files from the \SYSTEM or \SYSTEM32 directories to the new font directory. Run the Fonts applet and uninstall all your TrueType fonts, as explained in the section titled "Removing Fonts," making sure not to delete the files in the process (turn off the Delete check box). Then re-add each font. (Make sure that the Copy to Windows Directory check box is off.) Note that Windows NT *will* put a copy of each font's .FOT file in the \SYSTEM or \SYSTEM32 directory as you add the font. You can't control this, but because these screen font files are small, the impact on disk space isn't significant.

6. Click on OK. The fonts will be added to your font list.
7. Close the Fonts dialog box. The new fonts should be available for your Windows applications. You don't have to restart Windows NT.

TIP

The installer won't let you install a font that's already in your system, so don't worry about accidental redundancy.

TrueType Options

TrueType .TTF font files are not only large, but when installed in the system, they take up system RAM space and tend to slow down processes such as loading applications that might use them. This is because the whole font list is read each time such an application runs. Windows NT is memory-hungry as it is, so to help avoid memory shortages caused by RAM cram and exacerbated by TrueType fonts, try not to load more than you need.

If you, like many veteran Windows users, have become TrueType addicted, you can improve overall system performance by turning off non-TrueType fonts such as vector and printer fonts.

1. Click on the TrueType button in the Fonts dialog box.
2. The TrueType options box comes up with a single check box, Show Only TrueType Fonts In Applications. Turning this on disables other font types, freeing up some system memory. It also makes choosing fonts from a drop-down list easier.

NOTE

When you deactivate non-TrueType fonts, they aren't removed from your disk. You can still see them in the Fonts dialog box. You can reactivate them again from the same dialog box. The fonts just won't appear in applications. Some applications, incidentally, don't respond well to having TrueType fonts turned off. These applications won't list any fonts in their font choice lists if you use this option. If you have this problem, disable the Show only TrueType Fonts option.

TIP

There is a case to be made for using non-TrueType fonts. Using printer fonts built into your printer (not soft fonts) often increases print job throughput because the fonts are already in the printer and don't have to be downloaded at the start of each print job. Unless your printer setup specified (via Print Manager or an application's Printer Setup box) a substitution table that maps certain TrueType fonts to printer fonts, printing often will be faster using built-in printer fonts such as those in an HP cartridge or a PostScript font such as Helvetica. (Editing the substitution table is discussed in Chapter 4, "Print Manager.")

Removing Fonts

As I mentioned, removing fonts or font sets increases the available system memory. This means that you can run more applications simultaneously, or that processes will run more smoothly due to decreased paging. If you're having memory limitation problems, check your font list. If you have lots of TrueType fonts installed, try removing some you rarely use.

TIP

Normally, removing a font doesn't erase it from the disk. You can re-add it later.

CAUTION

Don't remove the MS Sans Serif font set. It's used in all the Windows dialog boxes.

Follow these steps to remove a font:

1. Open the Fonts window by clicking on its icon in Control Panel. The dialog box in Figure 9.5 appears, listing your installed fonts.
2. Select the font or fonts you want to remove.
3. Click on the Remove button.
4. A dialog box asks you to confirm the removal. If you want to remove the font from your disk as well as from your Windows setup, enable the Delete Font File From Disk check box.

TIP

Two tips pertain to this option. First, if you didn't copy the font into the Windows directory when you installed the font, you have only one copy of the font on your hard disk. If you delete the font file, you'll have to reload the file from a floppy, network, CD-ROM, or other source if you later want to use it again. Second, if you're not sure how often you use the font, you might try deleting it without removing the file, then do your work as usual. Do you or some applications miss the font? If so, reinstall it. If not, delete it from your disk later. You'll have to add it, then delete it again with the Delete Font File From Disk check box enabled.

5. Click on the Yes button. The fonts will be removed.

Ports

You can always use the DOS `MODE` command to initialize COM ports on a PC, but it's a hassle because you have to remember the command syntax. Windows 3.x and above has an applet in Control Panel to help you set up COM ports from a dialog box with desired baud, parity, flow control, IRQ, port ID, and so forth. Windows NT supports up to 256 serial asynchronous ports, from COM1 to COM256. Of course, you'll need some sophisticated I/O cards to supply you with 256 COM ports, but it's possible. More likely, you'll have a fax/modem board or data input devices using no more than the standard COM1 through COM4.

Actually, every communication, mouse, or fax program I've seen has built-in COM port initialization, rendering this Control Panel applet rather useless. Initialization from such programs will override settings you make in Control Panel. However, should you have to configure a port for a program that doesn't do its homework before trying to send and/or receive data across a serial port, you'll have to use this. An example might be when you're using a serial printer connected to a COM port, and the printer driver doesn't initialize the port.

NOTE

Parallel (LPT) ports can't be altered because they aren't serial ports and don't have settings.

Follow these steps to initialize a serial port:

1. Double-click on Control Panel's Ports icon. The dialog box shown in Figure 9.7 appears.

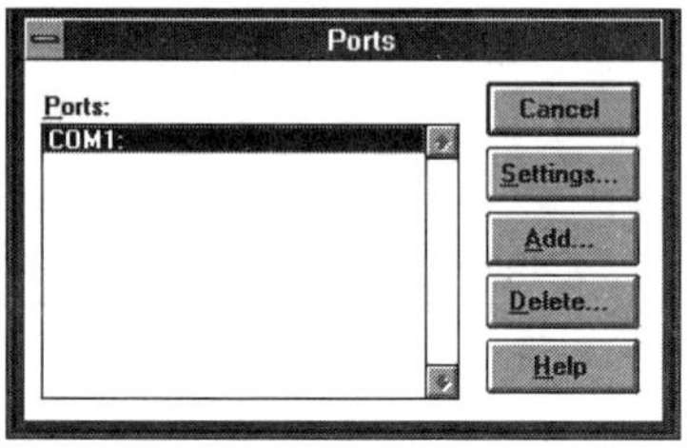

FIGURE 9.7.
Setting the COM ports.

2. You can set up the parameters of any of the four basic COM ports from here. Click on the port you want to alter. The dialog box shown in Figure 9.8 appears.

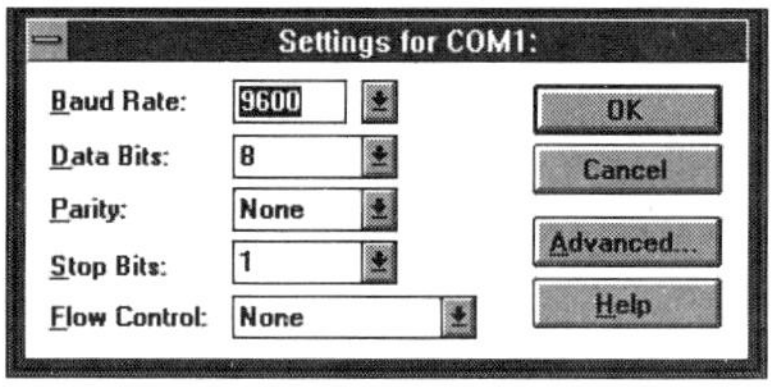

FIGURE 9.8.
Choosing the settings for a COM port.

3. Each section in the dialog box has a drop-down list. Your settings should match the settings of the equipment you're connecting to the port. If you're in doubt about requirements, consult the manual supplied with the external equipment. You might also want to refer to a book that covers the use of asynchronous serial communications interfaces.
4. Normally, you don't have to go any further. But if you're working with COM5 or higher, or if your physical serial ports are addressed oddly and you need to alter the port address or change the IRQ request line (hardware interrupt), click on Advanced. Make settings from the resulting dialog box. These settings require an understanding of the interrupt and port assignments of your hardware and possible conflicts with other ports or cards, such as network interface cards in the system, so make sure you do your homework first. Otherwise, leave them alone. Chapter 8, "Installing Windows NT," lists common IRQ and port addresses.
5. Click on OK. You'll be returned to the Ports dialog box. Change other ports if necessary, then click on Close when you're finished. The port is initialized immediately. The next time you boot NT, the ports will be initialized to the new settings.

Mouse

You can adjust three aspects of your mouse's operation:

- Tracking speed
- Double-click speed
- Left-right button reversal

NOTE

Mouse Trails was left out of NT because Microsoft assumed that you weren't going to be using NT on an LCD screen. This was a mistake on Microsoft's part, in my opinion. However, you could use an animated cursor (via the Cursors applet in Control Panel) to achieve a similar effect. Microsoft's version 9.x mouse driver for NT offers many of the features laptop users desire.

1. Double-click on the Mouse icon in Control Panel. The dialog box shown in Figure 9.9 appears.

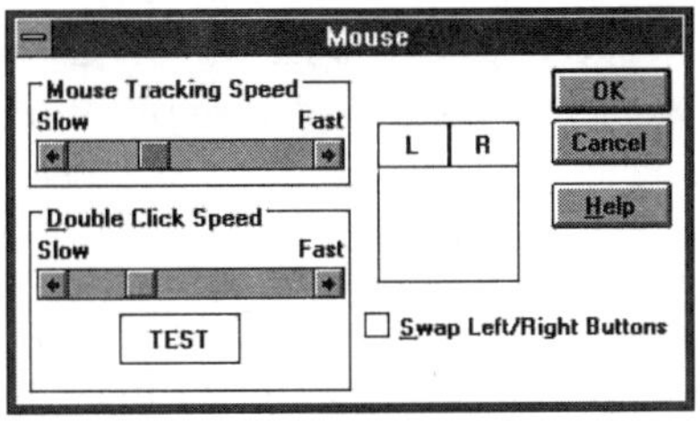

FIGURE 9.9.
Setting the mouse options.

2. Drag the sliders within the scrollbars to adjust the mouse speed parameters and set the check box to reverse mouse buttons.
3. Click on OK.

Now let's discuss the mouse options. *Tracking speed* is the speed at which the mouse pointer moves relative to the movement of the pointing device, whether track ball, pen, mouse, or what have you. Mouse motion is measured in "Mickeys," which equal 1/100 of an inch of mouse movement. The tracking-speed setting lets you adjust the relationship between Mickeys on the desktop and pixels (dots) on-screen. Decrease the tracking speed to increase your exactitude, requiring more hand motion for the same corresponding cursor motion. If you're especially coordinated or you have a large screen, you might want to increase the speed (fewer Mickeys per pixel). Notice that the tracking speed changes instantly as you move the slider in the dialog box. Move the cursor around to test the new speed. Double-click on the Test button to try out the new double-click speed. The color in the box changes if the double click registers.

TIP

If you use the mouse with non-Windows programs (such as Ventura Publisher or AutoCAD), you might want to match mouse speeds in the two environments. This way, you won't need to mentally adjust when you use non-Windows programs.

TIP

When you run a DOS window in NT, the mouse driver is supplied to the DOS environment automatically, unlike in Windows 3.1, which requires that it be loaded as a TSR or a device driver prior to loading Windows. Tracking speed in the DOS environment is controlled by the Control Panel setting—another nifty feature of NT.

Double-click speed determines how quick double clicks have to be to register with NT. If the double-click speed is set too fast, many users find it difficult to run programs from icons, select a word in a text file, and so on. If it's set too slow, you end up running programs or opening and closing windows unexpectedly. I find that the slowest speed works well for me. Double-click on the Test button to test a new speed. The button should change color each time you successfully double-click.

Left-right button reversal simply switches the function of your mouse's buttons. (If your mouse has three buttons, the middle one isn't affected.) If you're left-handed, being able to switch the mouse buttons might be a boon. If you use non-Windows programs outside of Windows or on other computers that don't support button-swapping, you might be adding some ergonomic confusion to your life. If you use the mouse only in Windows programs and you're left-handed, it's worth a try. Changes take effect immediately.

Desktop

You can make several alterations to the Windows Desktop. You can change the following:

- Background patterns
- Background wallpaper
- Sizing grid
- Border width of all windows

- Icon spacing
- Cursor blink rate
- Screen saver

The patterns and wallpaper settings let you decorate the desktop with something a little more festive. *Patterns* are repeated designs, such as the woven look of fabric. *Wallpaper* uses larger pictures that were created by artists with a drawing program. You can create your own patterns and wallpaper or use the ones supplied. Wallpapering can be done with a single copy of the picture placed in the center of the screen, or by tiling, which gives you multiple identical pictures that cover the whole screen.

The *sizing grid* is an invisible grid that causes the borders of windows to snap into place more easily. It makes aligning windows easier. It also affects the alignment of icons. The grid's setting is called *granularity*. The range is 0 to 49. If the setting is zero, the grid is turned off. Each increment of 1 corresponds to 8 pixels on the screen. I find a setting of 1 or 2 to be sufficient.

The *border* width settings let you make the borders of windows wider—for visibility purposes, I suppose. When windows are tiled, thicker borders help you distinguish between them more easily. When you resize windows, thicker borders are easier to grab. The range is 0 to 49.

The Applications section of the dialog box has two options: Fast Alt-Tab Switching and Full Drag. Normally, Fast Alt-Tab Switching is enabled. It causes Windows to display a thin dialog box in the middle of the screen when you press Alt-Tab to switch between applications, as shown in Figure 9.10.

FIGURE 9.10.
Pressing Alt-Tab.

Notice that the icon and the name of the application and document (if one is active) are displayed in the box. Each press of Alt-Tab cycles through the list of running applications in order. If you disable this feature, you won't see the dialog box in the middle of the screen. Instead, you'll see the application's window perimeter or icon with each press wherever it's currently located on-screen. But that means you have to look all over the screen to see which application will become active when you release the Tab key. I recommend leaving this option enabled.

If your video display adapter is fast enough, you might want to experiment with Full Drag. It causes Windows to display the complete window, instead of a window outline, when moving application windows or dialog boxes across the screen. If the window's painting is choppy, lower your video resolution or decrease the color palette.

Icon spacing determines the distance between icons, both on the desktop and in group windows. Increasing the spacing prevents icon names from overwriting each other, but it also can make icons harder to find because they get spaced out across more of the desktop and thus are more likely to be obscured by a window. I use a spacing of 106.

Cursor blink rate determines how fast the vertical bar (called the *insertion point* or *text cursor*) blinks. On some screens, it's easier to see if the speed is altered. The text cursor appears whenever you're editing text (in the text portion of a dialog box, in a Cardfile document, in a Notepad document, and so on).

Follow these general procedures to adjust any of the Desktop features. Some are covered in greater detail later in this chapter.

1. Double-click on the Desktop icon in Control Panel. The dialog box shown in Figure 9.11 appears.

FIGURE 9.11.
Setting the Desktop options.

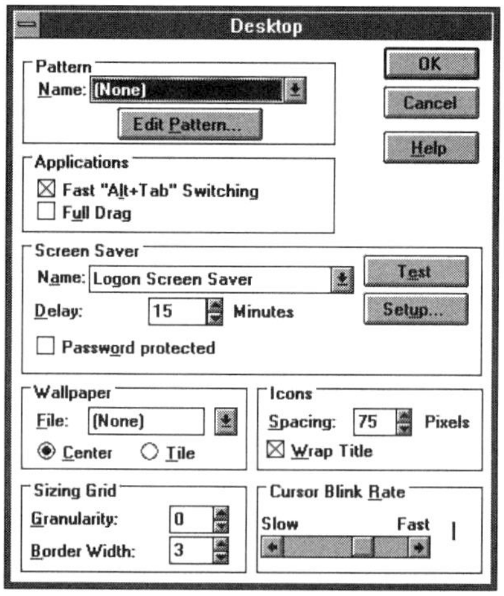

> **NOTE**
>
> As with color schemes, you can cycle through the choices in a drop-down list without opening the list. With the current selection highlighted, press the up and down arrow keys to see the other choices. You *won't* see the new selection here, however.

2. Open the drop-down lists for wallpaper or patterns and select the pattern or wallpaper you want. You have to try each one to see the effect because they don't go into effect until you leave the dialog box. You can have only wallpaper or a pattern showing at one time, not both. You can see a sample and a close-up of a

pattern (called a *cell*) by choosing Edit Pattern. From there you can edit the pattern by turning pixels on and off by clicking on them.

3. If you choose Wallpaper, click on Tile or Center.
4. Set the cursor blink rate by sliding the box in the scrollbar or by clicking on the arrows at either end of it. You can see the effect as soon as you move the mouse cursor off the slider button.
5. Adjust the border width and grid spacing (granularity) by clicking on the up and down arrows or by clicking on their assigned values and typing in the desired new value.
6. Select a screen saver if you want one and adjust the settings.
7. Click on OK.

Unfortunately, this is one of those dialog boxes that you'll have to open, reset, and OK a million times to see all the patterns and wallpaper choices and to see the effect of changing the border size and the granularity.

Changing a Pattern

If the supplied patterns don't thrill you, you can create your own with the built-in bitmap editor. You can either change an existing one or design your own. If you want to design your own, choose None from the Name drop-down list before you begin. Otherwise, choose a pattern you want to play with.

1. Click on Edit Pattern in the Desktop dialog box. A new dialog box appears, as shown in Figure 9.12.

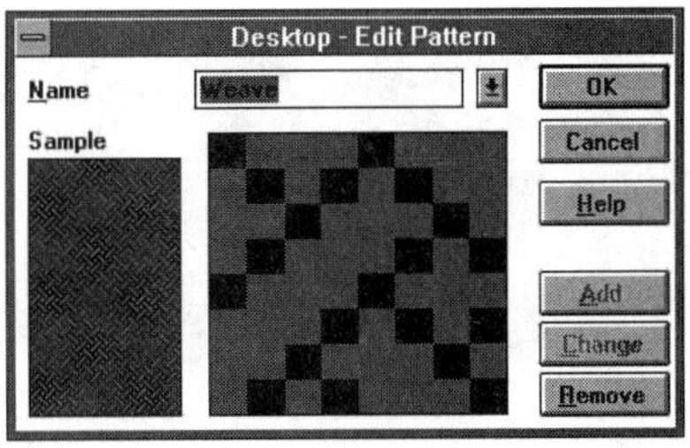

FIGURE 9.12.
You can edit a desktop background pattern with this box.

2. In the Name section of the box, type a name for the new pattern.
3. Create the pattern by clicking in the large box (this is the cell). What you're doing is defining the smallest element of the repeated pattern. It's enlarged to make editing easier. Each click reverses the color of one pixel. The effect when the pattern is applied across a larger area and in normal size is shown in the Sample section.

4. When you like the pattern, click on Add, and the pattern is added to the list. You can select it later from the Desktop dialog box.

If you later want to remove a pattern, select the pattern while in the editor and click on Remove.

Choosing a Specific .BMP File for Wallpaper

The images used in wallpaper are actually .BMP files—bitmapped files created by programs such as Paintbrush. Because many other applications create bitmapped .BMP files too, you can use things such as scanned images for wallpaper. Note, however, that wallpaper takes up more system memory than do patterns.

You also can edit the supplied .BMP files with Paintbrush if you want. Because Paintbrush will read .PCX files and convert them to .BMP files, you also can use virtually any .PCX file as wallpaper. Just load it into Paintbrush and save it as a .BMP file by choosing File | Save As | Options.

To change the wallpaper, follow these steps:

1. Create the image with whatever program you want, as long as it creates a .BMP bitmapped file.
2. Copy the file into the Windows NT directory (\WINNT, for example). Only then will it appear in the list of wallpaper options.
3. Choose the file from the Desktop dialog box. (If you leave Desktop open while creating your .BMP file in Paintbrush, the Wallpaper File list won't show the new file until you close Desktop and reopen it.)

TIP

You *can* choose a file in another directory if you enter its entire pathname in the Wallpaper File area. This way, you don't have to copy the file into the Windows directory.

Setting the Screen Saver

Screen savers reduce the wear on your monitor by preventing static images from "burning" the phosphors on the CRT's inside surface. The screen saver option lets you choose a blank screen or something more interesting when the system detects no activity from a human for a preset period of time. You set the pattern and the time interval before it kicks in.

1. In the Screen Saver section of the Desktop dialog box, choose a name from the drop-down list. (The default screen saver is basic black.)

NOTE

Before anyone actually logs on, the default screen saver is the Logon dialog box, which pops up in random locations on the screen. This screen saver is set to kick in after 15 minutes of waiting for a user to log on.

2. To see what the screen saver looks like, click on Test. The screen goes black and the screen saver starts. Move the mouse or press a key and the Desktop dialog box returns.
3. If you want to fine-tune your choice, choose Setup. Depending on which screen saver you choose, you'll have a few possible adjustments, such as text for a message, speed, placement, and details pertinent to the graphic.
4. If you enable the Password Protected check box, every time your screen saver is activated you have to type your password into a box before you can resume work. This option is handy if you don't want anyone tampering with your files or seeing what you're doing. It can be a pain if there's no particular need for privacy at your computer. Use your normal system password with the screen saver.
5. Set the number of minutes you want your computer to be idle before the screen saver springs into action. In the Delay space, either type a number or use the up and down arrows to incrementally increase the minutes.
6. When all the settings are correct, click on OK.

Keyboard

There's only one variable to adjust via the Keyboard applet—the key repeat rate. Most keys repeat when you hold them down. This setting lets you change the speed and how long a key has to be depressed before repeating begins.

1. Double-click on the Keyboard icon in Control Panel. The dialog box in Figure 9.13 appears.
2. Drag the sliders to change the key repeat speed and how long it takes before any key goes into repeat mode. You'll want to increase the delay if you find that keys are accidentally repeating when you or users don't really intend it.
3. Test the settings by clicking in the Test Typematic area and holding down a letter key. If it's too slow or starts repeating too soon, adjust and try again.

FIGURE 9.13.
Changing the key repeat rate.

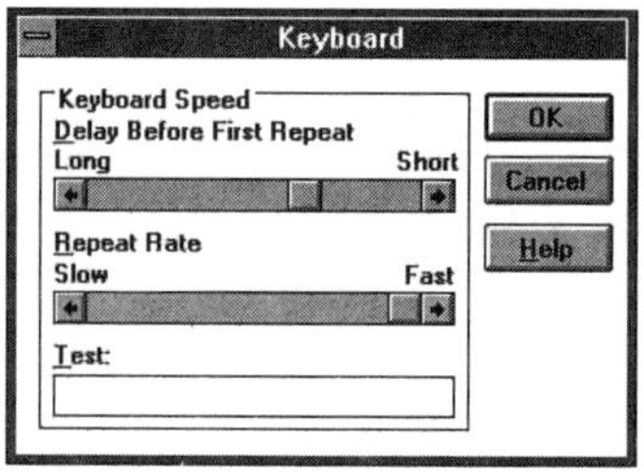

Printers

Running the Printers applet in Control Panel simply runs Print Manager. The Printer applet is in Control Panel as a convenience and to provide as much similarity with Windows 3.1 as possible. To alter printer setups, or to add and remove printer drivers, refer to Chapter 4, "Print Manager."

International

The international settings customize Windows NT for use in countries other than the one targeted by Microsoft when it sold you your copy of NT. It's likely that nothing needs to be changed. Note that the settings made from this box pertain exclusively to Windows NT and Windows applications. POSIX, MS-DOS, and OS/2 applications don't take advantage of them. Even some Windows applications don't. You should experiment with the settings to see whether they make any difference, or read the application's manual for information about how to set the formats.

Choosing International from Control Panel displays the dialog box shown in Figure 9.14. The international settings and their explanations are listed in Table 9.2.

FIGURE 9.14.
The International dialog box. Changes you make here affect only applications that use the internal Windows settings for such functions.

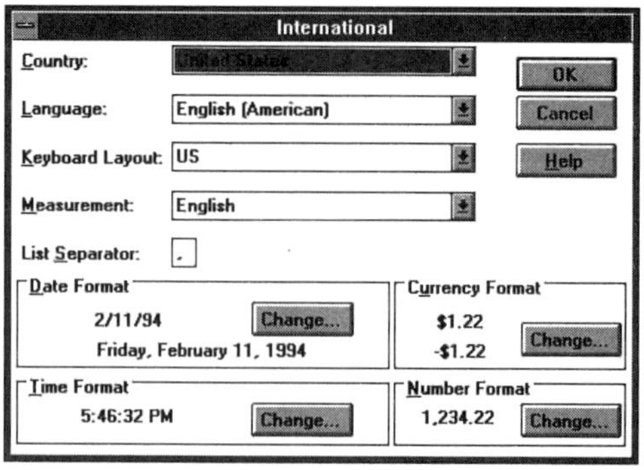

NOTE

You might be prompted to insert Windows NT floppy disks when you're making changes if driver files are needed.

Table 9.2. The international settings.

Setting	*Description*
Country	Selects which country you're in. All other settings change in accordance with the accepted practices in that country. You should change the other options only if necessary.
Language	Selects the language Windows uses as a default. Some applications use this information when processing your data or text—for example, when sorting data in a database—or when displaying foreign characters in a font.
Keyboard Layout	There are many types of keyboard layouts, with variations for each country and language. Choose the one that applies to yours.
Measurement	Metric or English.
List Separator	In the phrase "Matthew, Mark, Luke, and John," the list separator is a comma. In some other languages, items listed in a sentence are separated by different punctuation marks.
Date Format	You can choose from a myriad of date forms, such as 3/6/53, 03/06/53, 3/6/1953, 03-06-1953, March 6, 1953, and others. Useful for programs that pop a date into text at the touch of a key or that translate dates from one format to another.
Time Format	Similar to the date format options, this option allows 12- or 24-hour time indicators, a.m. or p.m. indicators, choice of separators, and leading zeros.
Currency Format	Chooses the currency indicator and the location and number of decimal digits.
Number Format	Numbers can be displayed with or without decimals, with or without commas, with or without leading zeroes, and with different decimal separators.

To change the settings, follow these steps:

1. Open the International dialog box.
2. Choose Country, Language, Keyboard Layout, and Measurement from the drop-down lists.
3. Set date, time, currency, and number formats via additional dialog boxes that appear when you click on the Change button in the respective sections. Examples of the current settings are shown in each section, so you don't need to change them unless they look wrong.

System

You use the System applet for five activities:

- To specify which operating system will boot if unattended when your computer has two operating systems
- To view or change the system environment variables and view or change the user environment variables
- To set the virtual memory (paging) file size
- To set the system recovery options for STOP (blue screen) errors
- To set the amount of CPU attention the foreground application gets relative to background applications

NOTE

Each user account on a system has its own settings, so if you want to change the settings for a given user, you must have that user log on or know his or her password.

Changing the Default Bootup Operating System

If you installed NT over an existing copy of DOS or OS/2, you had the option of wiping out the preexisting operating system or having NT live with it harmoniously. If you chose the latter, NT relocated the first 512 bytes of the existing boot track (the boot sector) to a new location on your hard disk as a file called BOOTSECT.DOS (regardless of whether the preexisting operating system was DOS or OS/2) and wrote the boot portion of the NT operating system into the normal boot sector.

When you turn on the machine, press Reset, do a three-key reset, or shut down and restart NT, the NT "boot loader" goes into action and presents a menu of the operating systems you can boot. By default, the NT operating system will start, but you can change this. For example, you or a user on the network might rather boot right into the MS-DOS or OS/2 environment rather than NT.

NOTE

Based on my experience installing NT on machines that previously contained another operating system, I suggest that the initial NT installation should always be a dual-boot setup, even if NT is eventually going to be the only operating system on the computer. It's better to keep the original operating system for a while. After a user-defined time limit is reached, the original operating system can be deleted and the disk converted to NTFS if you want. This way, users aren't locked into NT should they find an application that won't function under NT.

1. Double-click on the System applet icon in Control Panel. The dialog box shown in Figure 9.15 appears.

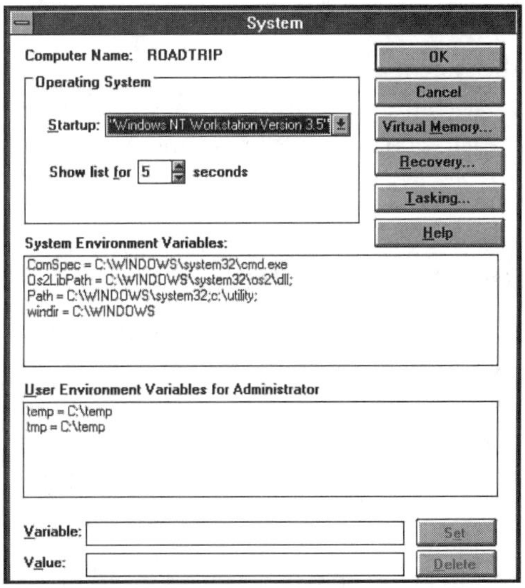

FIGURE 9.15.
Use this dialog box to set the startup operating system and system variables.

2. Open the drop-down Startup list and select the operating system that will boot by default unless you intervene by selecting the alternative operating system.
3. You can optionally set the time-out that determines how long the boot loader waits for you to choose the alternative operating system. By default, it's 30 seconds.

The next time you boot, the OS you chose will be highlighted in the boot loader menu and will load unless the keyboard is touched.

TIP

During the boot loader countdown, if any key on the keyboard is pressed, the countdown stops, essentially pausing the boot-up process.

Setting the Environment Variables

Just as DOS has provisions for setting system variables such as the \TEMP directory, prompt, and search path, NT provides a similar service that closely complies with the DOS variable definitions. The difference is that there are two sets of variables in NT: system and user. The System dialog box, shown in Figure 9.15, lists both sets.

The system variables apply to all users, whereas the user variables pertain to the logged-on user. They let each user set up a personalized environment that applications or command-prompt (DOS) sessions might benefit from.

Although the system and user variables are separate, the variables themselves are the same for both. That is, the list of variables you can specify is the same. When NT boots, the variables in each section, as well as in the AUTOEXEC.BAT file in the root directory of the boot disk, are examined.

NOTE

Contrary to what you might initially think, considering the existence of the Registry, the NT operating system looks at the AUTOEXEC.BAT file just as DOS does. This allows for greater software compatibility with Windows 3.1 and DOS applications, because some of these applications' setup routines modify the DOS startup files.

It's important to know how NT processes and prioritizes each of these groups of settings. First the system environment settings are loaded. Then the user settings are loaded. Finally, the AUTOEXEC.BAT settings are loaded. Whenever there's a conflict between the settings, the various settings take the following priority, from highest to lowest:

- System
- User
- AUTOEXEC.BAT

Because user settings take precedence over system settings, you can, in essence, edit the system settings by declaring a user setting for the same system variable, effectively overwriting it. For example, if the system variable for `temp` (the temporary directory) were set to \WINDOWS\TEMP and you wanted to change it to E:\TEMP, you would just enter this line in the User area of the dialog box. Note, however, that an exception to this rule applies to the `Path` statement, which isn't overwritten by the user or system commands. If you have different search paths declared in each section, NT adds them to one another, resulting in a cumulative path setting.

To change an existing system or user setting, follow these steps:

1. Select the variable line in the System or User Environment area.
2. Edit it in the Variable line at the bottom of the dialog box.
3. Click on Set. (If you want to delete the variable, click on Delete instead.)

Follow these steps to enter a new variable:

1. Select an item in the System or User Environment area.
2. Type the new variable in the Variable line and the value in the Value line.
3. Click on Set. The variable is added to the existing user variables list, but it won't go into effect until the user logs off then on again, or the computer is rebooted.

Setting the Virtual Memory File Size

If you're familiar with Windows 3.1, you probably know about the *swap file*. This is a file that temporarily stores data from the computer's RAM. It's treated by the operating system and applications as actual physical RAM. Swap files (sometimes called *paging files*) fool the operating system and applications into thinking that there is more physical RAM in the computer than actually exists, allowing more programs and operating system services to run than otherwise would be the case. Paging files have been around almost as long as digital computers. They were especially necessary back in the days when mainframes often ran with little more than 8K or 16K (not megabytes) of RAM. Whether the paging files were physically stored in the form of paper tape, punch cards, or magnetic tape didn't matter. The upshot was that only a very small amount of data was actually in RAM at any one time for processing, while the rest was "offloaded" momentarily until it was needed. From this technology grew the idea of swap files as we know them.

NT creates a swap file when it's set up. This file, which typically is stored on the NT boot partition, is called PAGEFILE.SYS. When NT runs out of RAM to dish out to applications or internal services, some of what's in memory gets paged out to this file for a moment. The result is that NT can continue to operate smoothly while all you know is that some hard-disk activity is occurring.

NOTE

If you try running NT with only 8M of RAM, you'll see some very heavy disk activity due to intense paging.

Setup calculates the optimum size of the file when NT is set up. (This figure usually is the amount of your physical RAM plus 12M.) You might want to experiment with this setting because your application mix might benefit from having a larger paging file (especially if your application is giving you "low memory" messages even when you don't have lots of other apps running).

Here's another reason for changing your paging file setup. NT is pretty smart about paging files and can use more than one. Each hard disk can have its own file. If you have a smart disk controller (or separate controllers for each drive), NT can actually use the paging drives simultaneously. For example, it could be reading from one and writing to the other, effectively speeding up paging operations. Even if you don't have such a setup, having paging files on multiple disks gives NT more breathing room and an option in case one drive suddenly fills up. (Paging files can dynamically expand—up to a limit declared by the user—unlike the permanent swap files in Windows 3.1 in Enhanced 386 mode.)

NOTE

You have to have administrator privileges to alter the paging file settings.

Here's how to modify the paging file sizes and locations:

1. In the System dialog box reached from the System applet in Control Panel, click on Virtual Memory. The dialog box shown in Figure 9.16 appears.

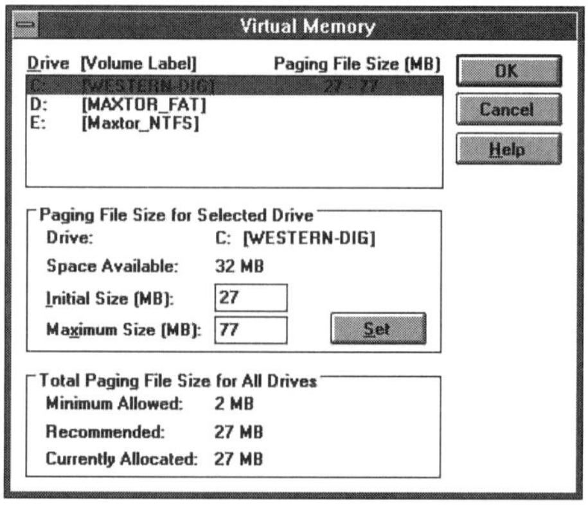

FIGURE 9.16.
Changing the paging file size.

2. In the Drive section, click on the drive whose file size you want to alter.
3. Enter the initial size and maximum size for the drive and click on Set. If the paging file size specified is less than the size of the physical RAM installed in the computer, and the recovery option to create a dump file is enabled, an error message will be displayed, as shown in Figure 9.17.

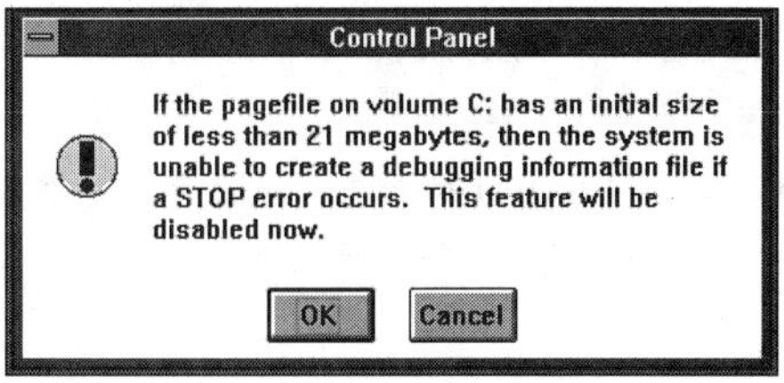

FIGURE 9.17.
Paging file size warning message.

TIP

Notice the information in the bottom part of the dialog box. It may prove helpful when you're making sizing decisions. You will want to allocate at least the minimum amount, and possibly more than the recommended amount if you're having low-memory trouble.

Setting the System Recovery Options

No matter how robust an operating system is, the potential to fail (encountering a marginal static RAM chip, for instance) does exist. If such a failure is detected with Windows NT, a blue screen with white text appears with a brief error message, a CPU register dump, and a stack dump. This type of error is known as a STOP error or the "Blue Screen of Death," as some of us frequently refer to it. There are four configurable recovery options.

1. In the System dialog box, click on the Recovery button. The dialog box in Figure 9.18 will appear.

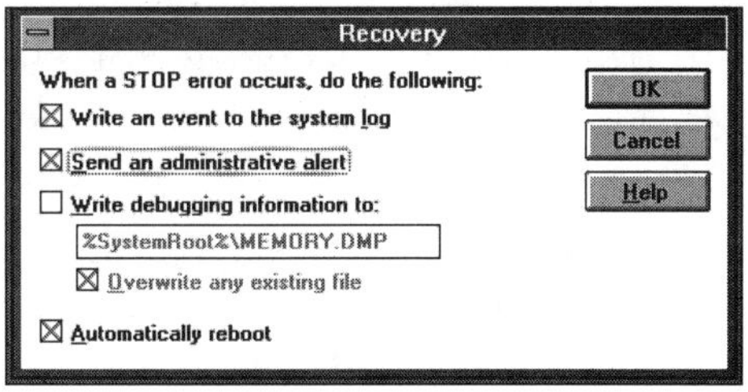

FIGURE 9.18.
Setting the system Recovery options.

2. Configure the settings for the desired action:

Setting	*Description*
Write an event message to the system event log	Creates an event message in the system event log, listing the error. Useful in isolating intermittent system failure.
Send an alert message to the system administrator	Informs the system administrator of the failure and cause.
Create a dump file with debugging information	Creates a dump of system memory. Can be used by technical support staff to determine the cause of the failure.
Automatically reboot the computer	Reboots the computer after a system failure.

Setting the Foreground Window Priority

Because Windows NT is a multitasking operating system, each running application receives CPU slices and is serviced in a round-robin fashion. However, the NT scheduler assigns a greater number of CPU cycles to the program that's running in the foreground window (the "active" window) than to background windows. This scheme is sensible, because normally you'll want the fastest reaction time in the window you're currently using. For example, you might be performing a spreadsheet recalculation, a database sort, or a word-processor spell check, and you don't care if NT is servicing a drawing program or a PIM's phone dialer in the background.

Normally, performance is tuned to result in best performance for the foreground window; therefore, it shouldn't need adjusting. In other words, you can't improve the active window's performance. (This can be particularly disappointing when you're running Windows 3.1 applications, because many will run more slowly under NT than under Windows 3.1. That's just the breaks until 32-bit versions are available.)

However, if the way you work involves lots of background processing that you'd like to speed up, the Tasking button in the System dialog box lets you alter (somewhat) the tasking priority level assigned to the foreground window relative to others. In other words, you can relinquish some CPU cycles from the foreground to speed up the background.

1. In the System dialog box, click on the Tasking button. The dialog box shown in Figure 9.19 appears.

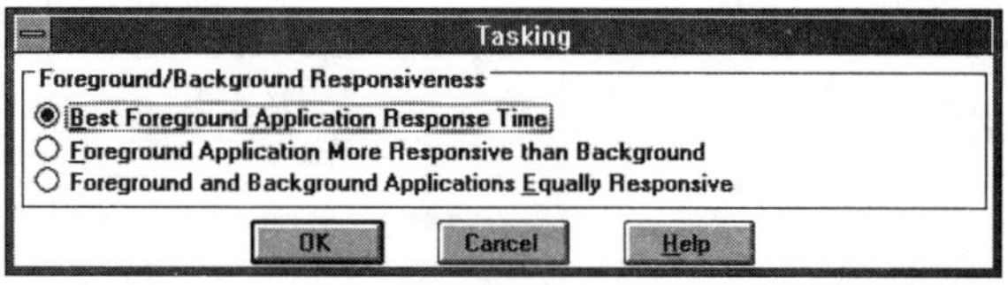

FIGURE 9.19.
Adjusting the foreground window's CPU priority.

2. Choose the option that best fits your needs:

Setting	*Description*
Best Foreground Application Response Time	This is the default setting. NT responds to background tasks as needed but does its best to steal as many CPU cycles as possible for the foreground application.
Foreground Application More Responsive	This setting slows down the foreground application somewhat while servicing background applications more rapidly, but still not equally.
Foreground and Background Applications Equally Responsive	This setting ensures equal treatment of all running applications. This might cause your foreground applications to respond a bit sluggishly (for example, when you're entering text from the keyboard).

Date/Time

The Date/Time icon lets you adjust the system's date and time. These settings are used for date- and time-stamping the files you create and modify, and for other time-related operations such as calendar alarms, automated backups, and so forth. This icon doesn't change the *format* of the date and time—just the actual date and time. To change the formatting, choose International from Control Panel.

Follow these steps to adjust the date and time:

1. Double-click on the Date/Time icon. The dialog box shown in Figure 9.20 appears.

FIGURE 9.20.
Changing the system date and time.

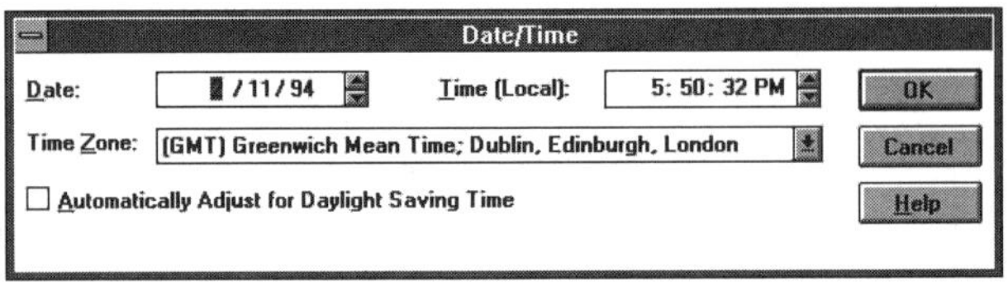

2. Adjust the time and date by typing the corrections or clicking on the arrows.

> **NOTE**
>
> You also can adjust the time and date using the `TIME` and `DATE` commands from a command-prompt session.

Network

Aside from connecting to and sharing printers and directories (tasks done from Print Manager and File Manager), all other essential network-related configuration is achieved via Control Panel. The Network applet is rich in features. If you're a system administrator, you should take time to become familiar with the many options. When you choose this applet, you see the dialog box shown in Figure 9.21.

FIGURE 9.21.
Configure the network from this box.

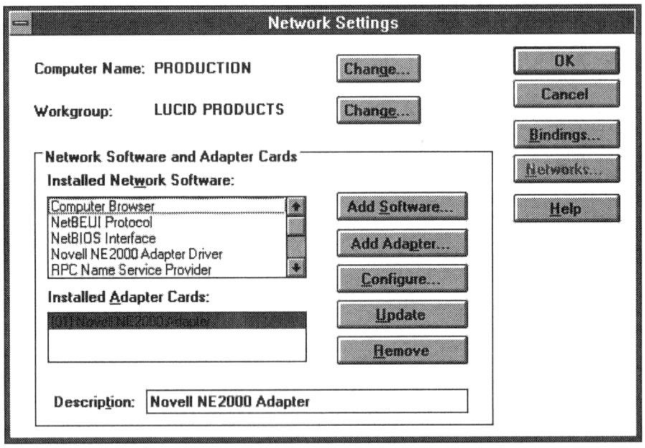

To some extent, what you see when you click on the various buttons will vary, depending on the kind of network you're running. However, Table 9.3 explains each option fairly accurately.

Table 9.3. Network configuration options.

Setting or Button	*Description*
Computer Name	Click on the Change button to change the name of the local computer.
Workgroup	Click on the Change button to connect to a different workgroup or domain.
Add Software	Lets you add network drivers and other supporting software (such as protocol modules) necessary for the local computer and network card to interact with the network.
Add Adapter	Tells NT you've added a particular type of network adapter card. A driver file will be requested.
Configure	Either configures a piece of network software or sets the particulars of an adapter card, such as IRQ, port address, and so on.
Update	Loads the latest version of some piece of network software.
Remove	Removes some network software or adapter card setup/driver.
Bindings	Adds or removes "bindings"—a type of network software used to sort of "glue" the main network components together.
Networks	Is an active button only if your computer is attached to a network containing multiple network types—for example, NetWare, Windows NT, and LAN Manager.

NOTE

Chapter 3, "Working with Windows NT," discusses connecting to and disconnecting from network drives.

Changing the Workstation's Computer Name

When you move a computer to another office, change administrators, or just decide that a computer's name is inappropriate for some reason, this is where you can change it. It's sort of like changing the volume label on a hard disk. There are three things to remember when you change a computer's name:

- When you change a workstation name, the official network path required to access the computer changes. This can throw off printer, disk, OLE, Clipbook, and any other connections other workstations might have made to that particular workstation.

- A computer name has to be unique on the network; no two computers can have that same name.
- If you're connected to a domain, you want to be extra careful before changing the name. Each workstation on a domain has an account based on the workstation name. If you change the name to something the domain server doesn't recognize, you won't be able to access the domain. Either have the domain administrator add an account under the new name and then change the workstation name, or vice versa.

To change the workstation name, follow these steps:

1. Click on the Change button just to the right of the Computer Name area. The dialog box shown in Figure 9.22 appears.

FIGURE 9.22.
Changing the computer's name.

2. Enter a unique name and click on OK.

Connecting to Another Workgroup or Domain

The significance of domains and workgroups is explained elsewhere in this book. When you set up NT on a workstation and a network card is detected, the networking interface software is set up and you're asked whether you want to join an existing workgroup or domain.

If you're joining a network after NT is installed, or you want to connect to a new domain or workgroup, use this option.

1. Click on the Change button to the right of the Workgroup/Domain name. The dialog box shown in Figure 9.23 appears.
2. Click on Domain or Workgroup. (If you're connected to an NT Server-based network, you'll want Domain.) Then enter the name of the workgroup.

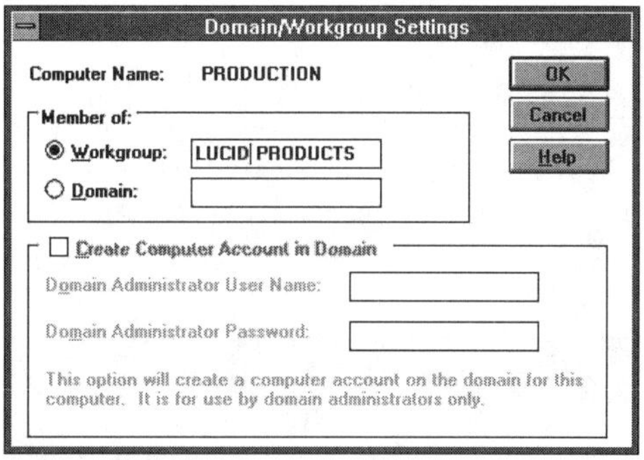

FIGURE 9.23.
The Domain/Workgroup Settings dialog box.

TIP

If you don't know the workgroup or domain name, you can browse the network using File Manager. Choose Disk/Connect Network Drive. The NT "browser" will scour the network and list workgroup and domain names.

NOTE

If you just changed your computer name and haven't rebooted NT so that it logs on with the new station name, you can't change the domain you're connected to. The Change button will be grayed. As a rule, you should change the domain name *before* the workstation name.

The lower half of the dialog box allows an administrator to create an account on the domain and join it simultaneously. Here's how:

1. Ensure that the computer's name is unique for the domain.
2. Choose the Domain radio button.
3. Enter the domain to connect to or create an account on.
4. Enable the Create Computer Account in Domain check box.
5. Enter the administrator account name and password, and OK the box.

TIP

The process is a little different if you don't directly have an account on the domain, but rather have an account on a "trusted" domain that's connected to the domain where you're attempting to set up a new account. In the User Name area, enter the trusted domain's name, a backslash, and your account name (for example, `marketing\johnd`). Note that Marketing must be a trusted domain and that the account `johnd` must have administrator status.

TIP

You also can connect to a domain if you're on the road or at home via the Remote Access Services (RAS). You have to log on to the network from your remote computer first. Also, you must have administrator privileges for your local computer and/or domain administrator privileges for the domain on which you're attempting to create an account. See Chapter 18 for more about RAS.

Adding a Network Adapter

If you want to add an additional network card or change the type of card you have, you use this option. The procedure is simple:

1. Click on the Add Adapter button. The dialog box shown in Figure 9.24 appears.

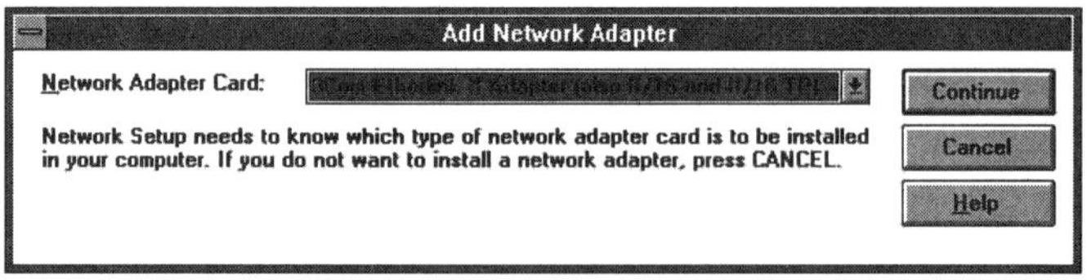

FIGURE 9.24.
Adding or changing a network adapter.

2. From the drop-down list, choose the type of adapter. If it's not listed, and you have a disk from the manufacturer, scroll to the bottom and choose Other.
3. Click on Continue.
4. If the driver files for the particular card aren't in the NT system directory, you're prompted to insert a disk or type in the path where they can be found, such as a CD-ROM drive.

NOTE

You might be prompted to specify other settings pertaining to the card, such as IRQ, base port address, DMA channel, and so on. If you're in doubt about settings, refer to Chapter 8's discussion of network card installation.

5. Close all dialog boxes. You might be prompted to restart the computer before the network card will become activated.

Configuring Network Software and Hardware

Sometimes you'll add a new card such as a fax/modem or a sound card to a workstation and find that it conflicts with an installed network card. The most common solution is to futz with the DIP switches, jumpers, and/or software configuration programs for the various cards to try to create a peaceful coexistence among them. You'll have to tell the NT network driver what you've done, however, when you change settings for a network card.

1. Choose the card from the Installed Adapter Card section.
2. Click on Configure. A dialog box relevant to the card appears. Make your changes to the settings and click on OK.

Some network software is configurable too. Notice that the upper part of the Network Settings dialog box lists all the installed network software. Configuration for software works the same way. Just click on the software you want to configure and then click on the Configure button. The most likely software items you might want to configure (although this is pretty technical stuff, and meant for administrators) are

- Server
- RPC Name Service Provider
- Remote Access Service
- NetBIOS Interface

A majority of the network software items can't be configured and will give you a message to that effect if you try to configure them.

Adding Network Software

Installing the network board and configuring it is only half of what a board needs to communicate with the network. It also needs a protocol driver. Protocol drivers fit in between the network card's driver and the higher-level network software, and they control how data is packaged and sent across the network. Setup installs the most popular small-network protocol, NetBEUI. For modest networks, this is all you'll need, so installing additional software isn't necessary. If you want to interact with UNIX or IBM mainframes, set up a wide area network (WAN), connect NetWare servers to your network, or connect printers directly to the network for sharing, you might need to load other network protocol software.

1. To add network software drivers, click on Add Software. The dialog box shown in Figure 9.25 appears.

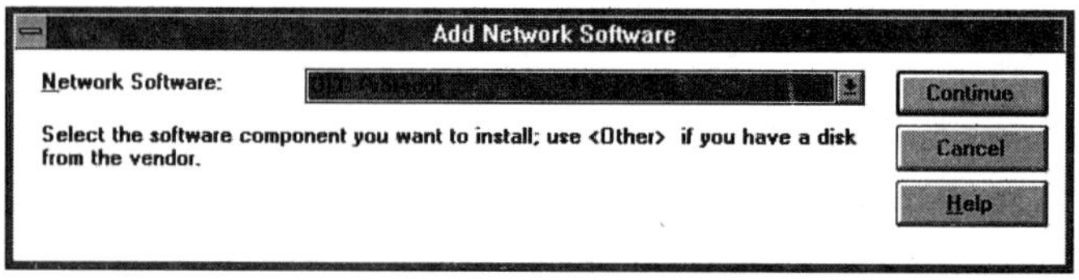

FIGURE 9.25.
Choosing network software to install.

As supplied in the first release of NT, the following software items are included:

Network Software	*Description*
Computer Browser	Lets you view and connect to other computers' shared resources and scan domains, workgroups, and workstations on the network.
Client Service for NetWare	Provides access to file and print services on NetWare servers.
DLC	Data Link Control is necessary for connecting to IBM mainframes or connecting printers directly to the network. This doesn't provide 3270-emulation capabilities, however. Additional software is required for that.
FTP Server	Provides TCP/IP clients access to your machine. Otherwise, TCP/IP clients couldn't utilize the File Transfer Protocol to download or upload files to the NT machine.
NetBEUI	Normally installed, this is an efficient and compact network protocol designed for PC networks.
NetBIOS	Network Basic Input/Output System. This is one level higher in the chain of software that connects a workstation to the network. It is the industry standard means of network communication for applications, much as the BIOS provides this means on a stand-alone computer.
Network Monitor Agent	Lets you monitor network activity using Performance Monitor. Also used for remote capturing of network packets with the System Management Server.

Network Software	*Description*
NWLink IPX/SPX Compatible Transport	This support is for Novell clients that utilize the IPX/SPX interface. It allows them to connect to the NT server for remote procedure calls (particularly for SQL Server).
Remote Access Service	Required to allow dial-in network service for a user. RAS must be installed on both the calling and the called workstations.
RPC Name Service	Remote Procedure Calling allows Provider applications to offload computing tasks to other machines on the network. This service allows the selection of either the MS Locator Service (for Microsoft clients) or the DCE-compliant interface (for VAX VMS services).
Server	This is the heart of networking features. It provides all of the support for clients to connect to the network. It then utilizes the other software components as needed. If the Server Software isn't running, there is no client networking support, no NetDDE, and no other basic networking operations.
Streams Environment	Needed for POSIX support, specifically for TCP/IP.
TCP/IP Protocol and Related Components	Supports UNIX connectivity and mainframe connectivity. Provides an interface that is routable for WANS. Its primary purpose is to provide more multiple operating system communications by utilizing an industry-standard mechanism. It's also utilized to provide socket support, and hence SQL Server support for UNIX clients. Includes such optional components as Connectivity Utilities, SMNP Service, TCP/IP Network Printing Support, FTP Server Service, and Simple TCP/IP Services. Also enables DHCP configuration. For further information, see the section titled "Windows NT and TCP/IP" in Chapter 17.

Network Software	*Description*
Workstation	This service provides the capability to support multiple users on the same machine when utilized in a stand-alone environment. When utilized in a networked environment, it plays additional roles.
Other	Use this option to install a protocol or other network-related software from a manufacturer that you have on disk (typically a floppy disk).

2. Choose the software you need from the drop-down list and click on Continue.

NOTE

If the software you need is from a manufacturer and on a floppy, choose Other.

Updating Network Software

If you get a new driver from Microsoft or a vendor, you'll want to update the software NT uses for your card or another network aspect. Follow these steps:

1. Open the Network Settings dialog box.
2. Select the software or adapter in question.
3. Click on Update. A Setup box appears, asking for the location of the update disk. Enter it and click on Continue.
4. Answer any additional questions.

You might have to reboot NT after the update.

Removing Cards or Software from NT

Suppose you decide to switch network cards from one brand to another or you decide you no longer need a particular piece of network software, such as Remote Access Services, on a workstation. It's a good practice to eliminate unused software or hardware drivers from an NT configuration. Additional services often consume CPU cycles and tie up system memory. Also, if you remove a piece of hardware and leave in the driver, you'll get an error message at boot time that says `At least one service couldn't be started.`

TIP

Whenever possible, you should install the new driver before you remove the old one. This can spare you the hassle of several reboots.

To remove a network card driver or a piece of network software, follow these steps:

1. Open the Network Settings dialog box.
2. Select the software or adapter card you want to remove.
3. Click on Remove. The message shown in Figure 9.26 appears. Click on Yes.

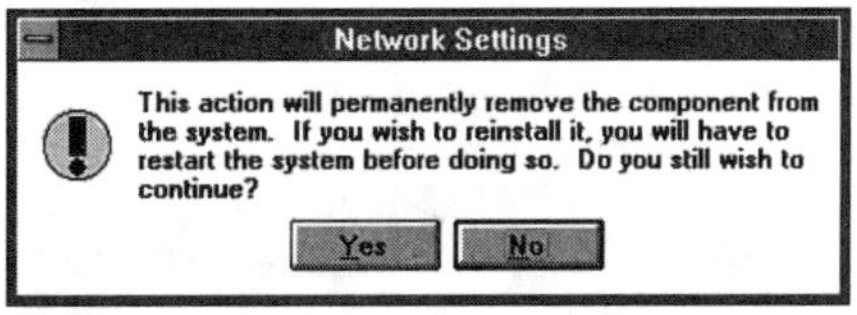

FIGURE 9.26.
Confirmation for removing a network component.

NOTE

If you remove an adapter card from the lower section of the dialog box, the associated software driver listed above will be removed automatically. You don't have to remove both.

Adding and Removing Bindings

Bindings are a class of software services that join various network software components. Bindings allow network components to work together and benefit from one another's built-in capabilities.

When you install a new adapter and driver, the bindings are configured automatically. However, you can tweak the bindings a bit if you like, or rearrange or disable some bindings to improve network performance.

1. In the Network Settings dialog box, click on Bindings. You'll see a dialog box like the one shown in Figure 9.27. Each line in the box shows the *binding path* for a specific network component, such as an adapter card. For example, in Figure 9.27, notice the first line. It shows the binding path for NetBIOS. Notice that the Novell NE2000 adapter card's name is in the far right. This represents the actual hardware. As you move left, higher-level software components are listed. Each component is separated by an arrow, which represents a binding.

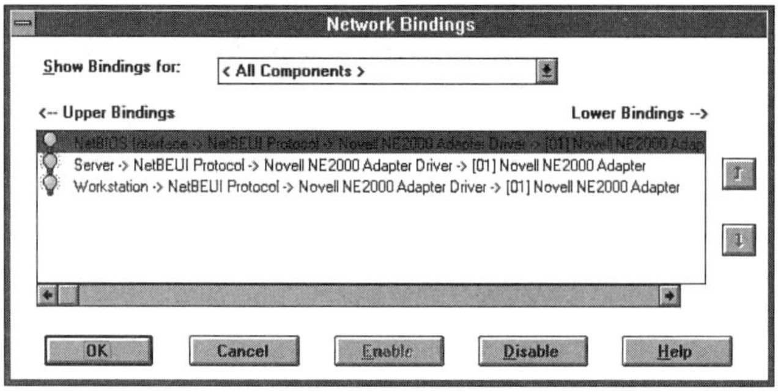

FIGURE 9.27.
Bindings.

Notice that although there is only one network card in this workstation, three components use the same card: the workstation, server, and NetBIOS. Each major component ultimately connects to the NE2000 network card.

TIP

You can choose which components to show bindings for from the drop-down list box.

2. You can disable or enable any binding path. For example, you might disconnect (unbind) a physical network card that you rarely use. Rather than removing it, you can just disable it and later re-enable it. Just select it and click on Disable or Enable. When something's enabled, the little light bulb looks lit up. When something's disabled, it's dim.

CAUTION

Disabling or changing binding settings can have unexpected ramifications if you don't understand the technicalities of NT network services. Use caution when disabling or rearranging bindings.

3. If you have multiple network protocols loaded (such as NetBEUI *and* TCP/IP), you can optimize the *binding path order*. Bindings normally are processed by NT from the top of the list to the bottom. If you use one protocol more often than any another, move it to the top of the list by highlighting it and clicking on the up arrow in the dialog box. This likely will speed up some network processing. Also, Microsoft suggests that some network protocols are speedier than others. If you put those protocols higher in the list and the slower ones lower, overall performance on the network can be improved.

NOTE

If the up and down arrows are grayed out, you don't have multiple protocols installed. Multiple binding path lines doesn't necessarily mean that you have multiple protocols installed. It just means that you have multiple network software components.

Specifying the Search Order for Other Networks

If your LAN topology has multiple network types connected, this can affect how quickly you'll be able to search for shared resources such as printers and files. If you usually look for resources on a particular type of network, you can move that type to the top of the search list. NT will terminate the search as soon as the resource is found, saving some time.

1. Click on the Networks button. (The button will be grayed if you don't have multiple networks installed at your site.)
2. A dialog box appears, listing the network types.
3. Highlight a network and click on the up or down arrow buttons to move it in the direction you want. Repeat the process until the networks appear in the desired order.

NOTE

This search order affects only the workstation you're using, not all workstations on the network. You might want to repeat this process for other workstations.

Cursors

Unlike Windows 3.x, Windows NT actually lets you choose the shape of cursors such as the I-beam, hourglass, and pointer. NT also supports animated cursors (such as a banana peeling itself or a barber pole rotating) and comes supplied with a number of replacement cursors, some animated and some static. To change a cursor, follow these steps:

1. Run the Cursors applet in Control Panel. The dialog box shown in Figure 9.28 appears.
2. There are several preset cursor configurations available. Then either select a prearranged configuration from the Cursor Schemes drop-down dialog box to configure all cursors at once or Select the individual cursor you want to change, and click on Browse.

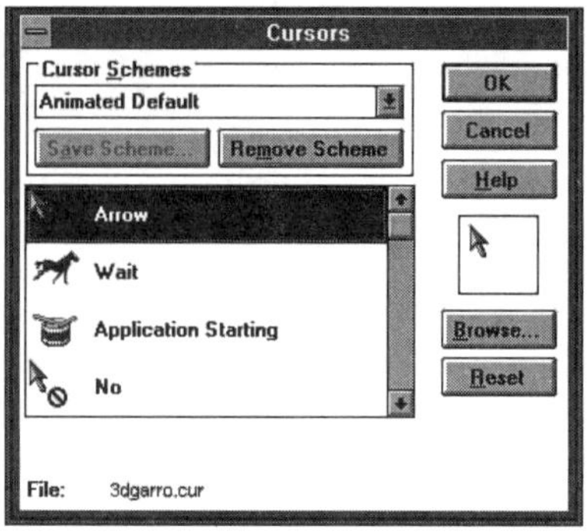

FIGURE 9.28.
Choosing cursors.

3. Find a directory containing cursor files and choose a file. Double-click on the filename. It will appear in a preview area in the Cursors dialog box.
4. If you want to save this configuration permanently, click on the Save Scheme button and name your configuration.

TIP

Check out some of the animated icons supplied with NT (they have the .ANI extension). I prefer the tapping fingers or the barber pole for "wait" or "application starting."

Sound

The Sound applet lets you turn on or off system sounds, such as the ubiquitous beep you hear when you've made an error or when NT or an application wants to get your attention. If you have a sound card installed, you can assign more interesting sounds to system events. In this case, system events are categorized such that distinct types of events (such as system startup, logoff, questions, information boxes, and so on) can each be assigned a separate sound. Something more than the simple beep is not only more entertaining, but it's also more informative.

You can record your own sounds for system events using the Sound Recorder program, or you can purchase sound files (which must be in the .WAV format) and use those instead of the somewhat meager offering of sounds supplied with Windows 3.1 and NT. If you have an audio-capable CD-ROM drive and the right software (such as the mixer supplied with the Pro-Audio Spectrum 16 board), you can record snippets from your favorite CDs, edit them, and use them for system sounds.

NOTE

To use .WAV files for system sounds, you must install and configure an NT-supported sound card and install a suitable device driver for it via the Device applet in Control Panel. Pay special attention to the sound card's IRQ, memory, and port addresses to ensure that they don't conflict with other devices and cards, particularly your network adapter. Refer to Chapter 8, "Installing Windows NT," for a discussion of such conflicts and typical device assignments.

1. Double-click on the Sound icon. The dialog box in Figure 9.29 appears.

FIGURE 9.29.

You can turn off the warning beep from this box if it bothers you.

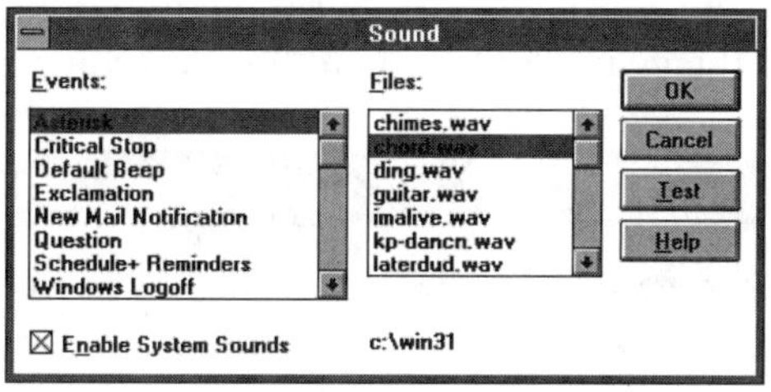

2. If you have no sound card, your only option is to turn the warning beep on or off by clicking on the check box at the bottom. This turns off all but the Windows NT startup and exit beeps. Choosing <none> has the expected effect of assigning silence to the selected event. If you're running NT on a well-endowed laptop, you might want to do this when you use the computer in a library, church, and so on.

   If your computer has a sound card, you can assign specific sounds by continuing with the following steps:

3. In the left box, choose an event category that you want to give a sound to.
4. In the right box, click on a sound file. Note that for any event, you can select a file from a different directory or drive. Before selecting a sound, double-click on its .WAV file (or highlight the file and click on Test), and the sound will play.

TIP

I suggest creating a \WINDOWS\WAV directory to store all your sound files. This makes it easy to find and reassign sounds. This is one more way to keep your Windows directory less cluttered.

5. Click on OK and the sound files go into effect.

Drivers

If you add a new piece of multimedia gear to your computer, such as a CD-ROM drive, sound card, video card, synthesizer card, or MIDI controller card, you'll have to install a driver file too. Just as with printers and network adapters, a driver file is necessary with these cards to act as a software bridge between the hardware and NT. Without the driver, NT doesn't know how to make the hardware work and can't communicate with it.

Some drivers provide nothing but control of an outside device such as a video player, external synthesizer, or audio CD player by providing on-screen controls similar to the front panel switches on a CD player or video disk machine. These drivers are called MCI drivers, which stands for Media Control Interface, not the telephone company. By contrast, other drivers are much more complex and support bidirectional data transfer and processing of such things as sampled sound files and compressed live-action video files.

NOTE

You must have system administrator status to add, remove, and configure device drivers.

In any case, you install, update, and remove drivers via the Drivers applet in Control Panel. In addition to installing and removing drivers, you also use Control Panel for fine-tuning certain drivers' settings, such as IRQ, port, and so on.

Windows NT comes supplied with a few drivers, at least the most popular ones. In time, more will become available. The bad news is that you can't borrow from the wealth of Windows 3.1 device drivers available these days. At least for the time being, you might have to suffer without a piece of gear until the NT driver becomes available. With rare exception, devices will work only with drivers specifically designed for NT.

TIP

Microsoft maintains a Windows NT Driver Library that contains new, tested drivers as they are developed for printers, networks, screens, audio cards, and so forth. You can access these drivers through CompuServe, GEnie, or the Microsoft Download Service (MSDL). You can reach MSDL at (206) 936-6735 between 6:00 a.m. and 6:00 p.m. Pacific Standard Time, Monday through Friday. As an alternative, you can order the library on disk from Microsoft at (800) 227-4679.

NOTE

If you're updating a driver, you have to remove the old one first. See the section titled "Removing a Driver."

Installing a New Driver

If you've purchased a board or other hardware add-in, read the supplied manual for details about installation procedures. If you're upgrading to NT and there are no instructions, take a look at the drivers that came with NT to see whether there's one for your device. Here's how:

1. Run the Drivers applet. You'll see the Drivers dialog box, shown in Figure 9.30. The drivers already installed in your system are listed.

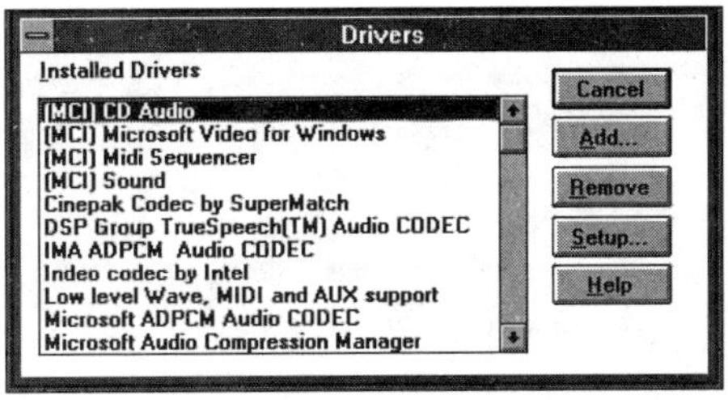

FIGURE 9.30.
Install, remove, and configure drivers from this box.

2. Note the drivers already installed. If the one you need isn't there, click on Add. The Add dialog box will appear, listing the drivers that came with Windows. Items preceded with "MCI" are Media Control Interface devices.
3. Check out the list to see whether the driver you need is there. If it's there, highlight it. If it isn't, and you have a disk with the driver or you suspect that it might be in a directory you know of, click on Unlisted or Updated driver.
4. Click on OK. If Setup finds the driver in your system directory, it asks whether you want to use the existing driver ("current" driver) or load a new one. Usually it's okay to use an existing driver unless you're updating.
5. You'll be instructed to specify a path where the driver can be found, just as when you install a printer or screen driver. Follow the normal procedure and on-screen prompts to add the new driver to your driver list. However, don't type the filename for the driver, just its path. Usually this will be just A:\ or B:\. If the driver is on a hard disk or CD-ROM and you don't know which letter drive or which directory, use the Browse button and subsequent dialog box to select the source drive and directory.

6. Some drivers need you to make additional settings. A typical example is the Sound Blaster card driver, which requires that you set the port address and interrupts for the board. If a setup dialog box appears for the driver, fill it in appropriately, using the board's supplied manual for guidance. Make sure that the settings don't conflict with a mouse, network, or other card. Pay special attention to interrupts (IRQ). IRQs must be unique for each device. If you make an error, NT is pretty good at alerting you to conflicts. The Event Viewer can be used to gain a little more information.

NOTE

You should also be aware of the program WINMSD that's supplied with NT. This program reports all I/O, IRQ, and DMA channels that have been allocated for use by the installed drivers. You'll find this program in the Program Manager Administrative Tools group.

TIP

If you're not sure which ports and interrupts your other boards are using, use the old trial-and-error method. For example, I installed a Sound Blaster card recently and used the default settings. But I kept getting dialog box error messages from Windows, indicating that there was a conflict. I repeatedly adjusted the IRQ and port settings until it worked. With two COM ports, a parallel port and a hard disk, a bus mouse on IRQ 5, and a Novell NE2000+ network board on IRQ 12 and port 300, I eventually found I could use port 220 and interrupt 7 with success. As described in Chapter 8, "Installing Windows NT," this switches the LPT1 printer output from interrupt-driven to polled I/O, with a consequential slowdown in NT's operations. Because my particular sound card doesn't allow for another acceptable IRQ setting, this was my only option. Ideally, a nonconflicting IRQ would have been a better choice.

7. When you're finished selecting any necessary settings, click on OK. Some drivers install several additional related drivers that might need you to make settings too, so more dialog boxes might pop up. Just fill them in as prompted.
8. New drivers won't work until you reboot Windows NT. Either wait until your next Windows session, or close any files you're working on and rerun Windows if you want to get the device working immediately.

Changing a Driver's Settings

Sometimes, when you're adding other pieces of hardware, for example, you have to alter some driver settings. One case in point is when you use the trial-and-error method of making the settings. Here are the steps to alter driver settings:

1. Choose the Drivers option from Control Panel.
2. Highlight the driver in question.
3. Click on Setup. The relevant dialog box from which you can make the settings appears. If Setup is dimmed, you've selected a device that doesn't have or require settings.
4. Reboot Windows NT for the driver changes to take effect.

Removing a Driver

When you remove a device such as a card or a CD-ROM from your system, you should remove the old driver from your Windows system. Drivers consume system memory, so leaving old ones installed affects your system's efficiency. You also should remove an old driver before installing an updated version of the same one.

Removing a driver from your system list doesn't erase the driver file. If you're certain you won't want to reinstall the driver and you're short on disk space, eliminate the driver and any associated files. (Figuring out the names of the files might require reading the device's manual.) If you think you'll want to use the driver later, don't erase it. When you're ready to reinstall it, use the Add button as explained earlier and enter the NT system directory (typically \WINDOWS\SYSTEM32 or \WINNT\SYSTEM32) as the path for the driver.

TIP

If you can't figure out the driver filename(s), take a look at the Registry instead. In all cases, you can trace through the various layers (if required) to find the actual name of the driver files.

CAUTION

Use forethought when removing driver files. Windows needs some drivers just to work. All the drivers that show up in the Drivers dialog box the first time you open it are the ones Windows must have. As a rule of thumb, don't remove a driver you didn't install, and make sure that any other files you erase from your disk aren't used by one of the supplied drivers.

Here are the steps for removing a driver.

1. From the list of installed drivers, select the driver you want to remove.
2. Click on Remove.
3. Confirm the removal in the resulting dialog box.
4. Restart Windows to have the removal take effect immediately.

Server

NOTE

The Server applet displays resource connections, the number of users connected to the workstation over the network, the names of files that are open, and who should be warned in case of administrative alerts. Because these items pertain to system administration more than to configuration, refer to Chapter 10, "Windows NT Administration," for details.

Services

As I discussed in detail in the first two chapters, Windows NT's design is very modular. This modularity has many advantages, not the least of which is that individual components can be added, removed, and updated with little upset to the remainder of NT. It also turns out that NT is designed to allow many individual internal components to be activated or deactivated without upsetting the rest of the apple cart—even in the middle of a workday while the workstation or server is attending to users' various tasks.

Many of NT's inner housekeeping chores are classified as "services." For example, the feature that allows you to create and share a Clipbook is a service, as is the *Event Log*—a feature that records every major activity on the workstation for administrators who want to monitor network use.

Eighteen services are included in Windows NT 3.5. In addition to being started and stopped through Control Panel, many of them can be configured to start at a specific time, such as at NT boot time, or to wait until an administrator starts them manually. Because services consume memory and CPU time, turning off a service might provide some additional computing power or memory room for particularly demanding applications. Or, if an administrator wants to deny a workstation or users on a workstation access to specific services, those services can be turned off pending manual intervention by the administrator.

To view and work with the various services' settings, follow these steps:

1. Double-click on the Services icon in Control Panel. The dialog box in Figure 8.31 appears.

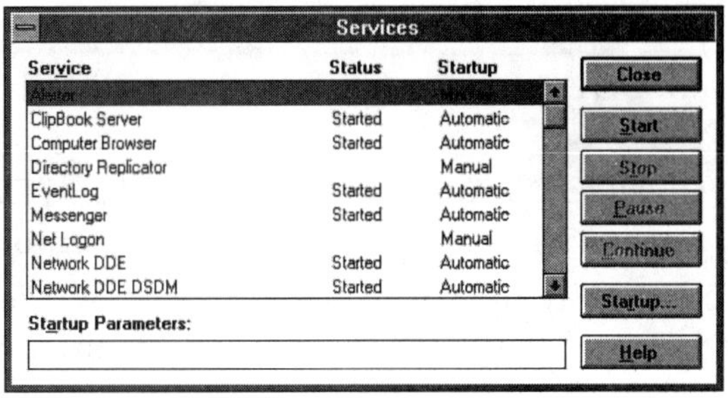

FIGURE 9.31.
The Services dialog box, listing services and each service's status, startup times, and optional parameters.

A list of services, along with their status and some buttons for working with them, appears. Table 9.4 describes the 18 services.

Table 9.4. The 18 services.

Service Name	*Description*
Alerter	Along with Messenger service, generates warning messages to administrators about problems on the local computer.
Clipbook Server	Allows sharing of Clipbook pages to network users.
Computer Browser	Allows browsing the network for resources shared by other workstations.
Directory Replicator	Performs directory replication service for administrators to easily copy complete directories to multiple workstations.
Event Log	Monitors the workstation's use by local and remote users, recording events of significance. Also reports internal error conditions such as malfunctioning hardware, drivers, and so on.
Messenger	Handles bidirectional communication between administrators. Also sends alerts generated by stations.

continues

Table 9.4. continued

Service Name	*Description*
Net Logon	Used to verify the authenticity of users logging on to a workstation, workgroup, or domain, depending on the system configuration.
Network DDE	Required for dynamic data exchange between workstations.
Network DDE DSDM	DDE Shared Database Manager. This service is used by Network DDE.
NT LM Security Support Provider	Supplies Windows NT security to RPC applications that do not use Lan Manager named pipes transports.
OLE	Provides OLE support to applications.
Remote Procedure Call Locator (RPCL)	Used by the RPC to locate available workstations to process remote procedure calls.
Remote Procedure Call (RPC)	Its primary use is to support client access to the NT machines. It's also a service that allows specialized NT applications to offload subroutines to network workstations to increase efficiency.
Schedule	Required for prescheduled commands, such as automated backup, to run at a specified time.
Server	Allows a workstation to share files, printers, named pipes, and RPCs.
Spooler	Allows a workstation to spool printer files.
UPS	Monitors the uninterruptible power supply and instructs the system to issue warnings, save files, and shut down prior to power outages.
Workstation	Gives a workstation the capability to connect and interact on a network and to allow multiple users to access a single stand-alone workstation.

2. In the Services dialog box, notice the Status column. Unless a service has been started, this column is blank. After a service is started, this changes to read `Started`. Now notice the buttons. You can start, stop, pause, continue, or configure the startup time for a service.

Starting, Stopping, Pausing, or Continuing a Service

Follow these steps to start, stop, pause, or continue a service:

1. Select the service in question. If you're starting it, it should be one that isn't already started.
2. Click on Start, Stop, Pause, or Continue.

NOTE

An optional Startup Parameter line allows you to enter a startup command that will be passed to the service as it's started. Startup parameter details vary based on the service. Most services utilize Registry settings for startup options, but startup parameters entered here will override those Registry settings.

CAUTION

Exercise caution when you stop the Server service. As explained in Table 9.4, this service is responsible for managing shared resources such as files and printers. If you shut it down, any users connected to your workstation will be disconnected from those resources. This could lead to data loss or a crashed application. The solution is to pause the Server service, then warn users that they should cease using resources on the particular workstation. Only then should you stop the service. Pausing the service keeps it running for users who are already connected but prevents new users from gaining access to the shared resources.

Specifying the Startup Time

As a final option, you can stipulate whether a service will start automatically when you start Windows NT on the workstation or whether it must be started manually. In general, this area of settings is better left alone unless you regularly need to stop a particular service. In that case, you can set the service to manual startup and then start it only when you need it.

The second column of the Services dialog box indicates the startup status of each service. Many of them are set to automatic, meaning that they start at boot time. To change a service's startup status, follow these steps:

1. Select the service.
2. Click on the Startup button. The Startup dialog box for the particular service appears. An example is shown in Figure 9.32.

FIGURE 9.32.
A typical Startup dialog box for a service.

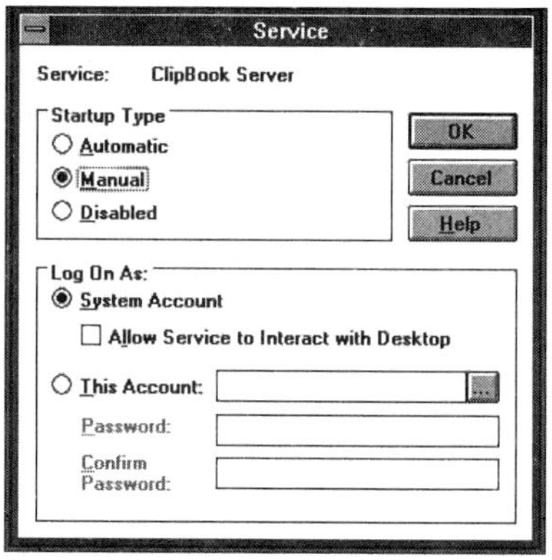

3. Choose a startup option:

Startup Option	*Effect*
Automatic	Starts at boot time.
Manual	Starts only when the Start button in the Services dialog box is clicked or an application or other service requests the service.
Disabled	Won't start when an application or service requests it. Won't start when the Start button is clicked. Must be reset to Manual or Automatic to be started.

NOTE

You must have at least 12M of memory in a computer or the Server service won't start automatically. It must be started manually.

Devices

As you know, the Windows NT operating system supports loadable device drivers just as DOS does. The advantage with NT is that many drivers can be loaded (started), stopped, and configured from within NT using dialog boxes. This is a far cry from having to exit Windows, carefully edit your CONFIG.SYS file, reboot DOS, and run Windows again.

NOTE

Unfortunately, not all devices and drivers can be loaded or unloaded without rebooting. Whether a particular one can be is determined by where it's layered in the startup chain (System, Automatic, Manual), as well as what other devices and drivers it depends on. For example, you can't change video modes or drivers without rebooting.

You use the Device applet in Control Panel to work with device drivers. The dialog box you see looks similar to others we've covered thus far, such as the Services box. However, remember the distinction between devices and services: Devices control physical hardware such as network cards, video cards, pointing devices, and CD-ROM drives. Services are higher-level software modules within NT that provide a complex capability such as sharing resources like directories or printers. When you run the Devices applet, you see the dialog box shown in Figure 9.33.

FIGURE 9.33.
Configure devices from this dialog box.

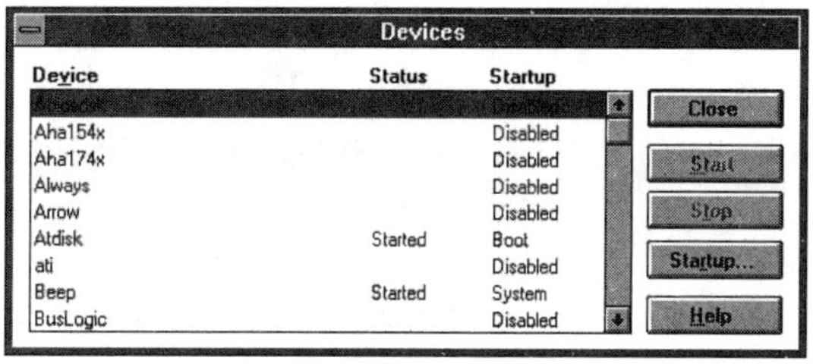

Just as with the Services dialog box, the listing has three columns. The first is the name of the device. Unfortunately, the name is rather cryptic. It takes some sleuthing to determine what a device name actually does. But with some guesswork, you often can figure it out. For example, the VGA item is the screen driver. The second column indicates whether a device driver has been started or not. If this column is empty, the device hasn't been started. The third column indicates when the device is set to start (there are four options, as explained later).

Starting or Stopping a Device Driver

To start or stop a device driver, follow these steps:

1. Select the device.
2. Click on Start or Stop. NT displays a dialog box telling you that it's trying to start or stop the device driver. A little clock in the dialog box has hands that turn as you wait.

NOTE

Sometimes the device can't be started or stopped. At least NT informs you that it can't do what you asked. In some cases you're told that the selected device is not something that supports being stopped or started. For example, if you try to stop something integral to system functioning, such as the screen or a mouse driver, you won't succeed. Some devices gray out the Stop button when selected for the same reason.

Configuring the Startup Time for a Device

You can set a device to start at several different times, as shown in Table 9.5.

Table 9.5. Startup time settings.

Setting	*Effect on Device Driver*
Boot	Starts the device as soon as NT begins to boot, just as with the old CONFIG.SYS. This is the first class of devices to be loaded. Used for starting drivers that are required for system startup—generally hard disk controllers, video, keyboard, and so on.
System	Starts the device after Boot devices are loaded. Use this setting for devices a notch less critical for early boot processes but still critical for bringing up the system. This setting generally is for software drivers that rely on a specific piece of hardware, such as the CD-ROM services.
Automatic	Starts the device after Boot and System devices are loaded. Use this setting for less-critical items not required for system bootstrapping or intermediate stages of operating. Also for basic services required for general operation, such as Server, Workstation, SQL Server, FTP, and so on.
Manual	Starts the device when the Start button in the Devices dialog box is clicked, or when a calling service or application specifically requests it.
Disabled	Won't start under any circumstance. Its startup status must be reset from this dialog box before it can be started.

A quick examination of the startup settings for your system's devices will show you which device drivers are critical for system bootup. Be careful not to change the startup settings for anything initially set to Boot or System. These devices are needed to bring up the system. If you set them to Automatic, for example, the system probably won't boot. Then you'll have to use the Last Known Good Boot technique, explained in Chapter 11.

Follow these steps to change the settings:

1. Click on a device driver.
2. Click on Startup. The Startup dialog box appears. Choose the desired radio button option for the startup type.
3. Click on OK.

Display

Windows NT 3.5 includes a nifty new Control Panel applet to configure your video display. It's a significant improvement over its predecessor, the Windows NT 3.1 Setup applet, which only let you specify the video resolution and refresh rate. With the new Display applet, shown in Figure 9.34, you can determine at a glance all the supported video resolutions and refresh rates your video driver supports, and select your color palette, font size, display area (or video resolution), and refresh rate. You can also change your video driver and even test a new video mode before final acceptance.

The most common use of the Display applet is to install and test a new video driver or display mode. To install a new video driver, follow these steps:

1. Click on the Change Display Type button. The Display Type dialog box, shown in Figure 9.35, will appear.

NOTE

The Display Type dialog contains several useful pieces of information. The Driver Information group lists the display driver's manufacturer, version numbers, and combined files. The Adapter Information group lists the video chip set, digital-to-analog (DAC) chip set, total adapter memory (which is useful knowledge to have when you're considering modifying a supported palette or resolution), and an identification string.

2. Click on the Change button to display the Select Device dialog box, shown in Figure 9.36. To display only compatible video device drivers, click on the Show Compatible Devices radio button. To display all available video device drivers, click on the Show All Devices radio button.

FIGURE 9.34.
The Display Settings dialog box.

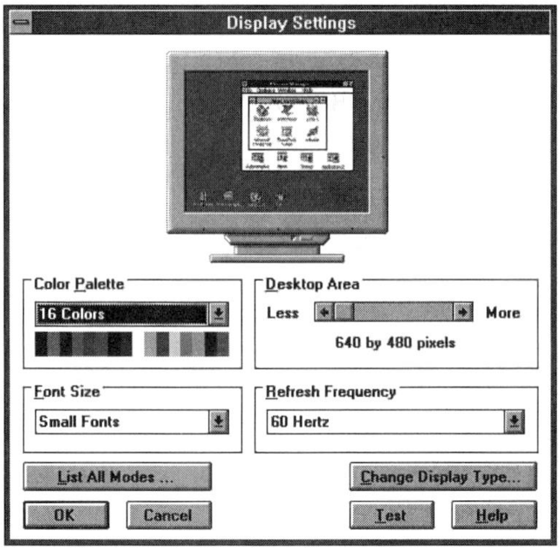

FIGURE 9.35.
The Display Type dialog box.

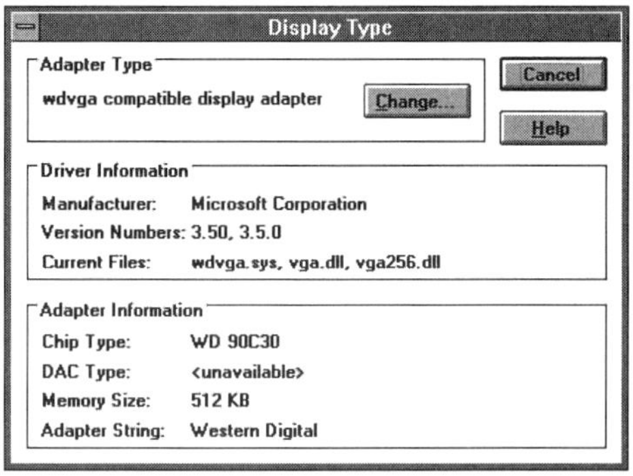

FIGURE 9.36.
Selecting a video driver from the Select Device dialog box.

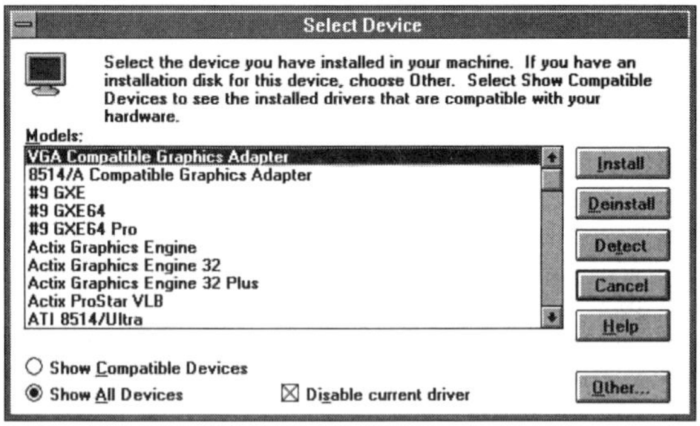

TIP

If you're not sure which video driver to install, click on the Detect button. This will copy all the available video drivers to your hard disk and attempt to install each driver in an effort to determine which drivers support your adapter. This process will require a system reboot of your machine in order to load and test each video driver.

CAUTION

Make sure the Disable current driver check box is enabled, or your current and new video driver will both be enabled on the next system startup, causing one of the installed video drivers to fail to start. Disable this option only if you have two video adapters supporting different video resolutions and designed to coexist with each other.

3. From the Models list, select the video driver to install and click on the Install button. If your video adapter isn't listed and no compatible driver exists (such as the Weitek P9000 Graphics Adapter, which also works for the Diamond Viper VLB), click on the Other button. To remove a video driver from your system, click on the Deinstall button.
4. After you've selected your video driver, click on OK. Then click on the close icon in the Display Type dialog box. If you haven't tested this driver before, you will be prompted to test the selected driver and resolution. A series of graphics will be displayed for approximately 5 seconds. If the graphics are visible, click on the OK button. If they aren't, select a different video driver, resolution, or refresh rate.

TIP

If for some reason the selected video driver doesn't work and you can't see the display, restart the computer and use either the Last Known Good option to restore your previous configuration or the `/basevideo` boot option at system startup. This will load NT with the default VGA video driver.

UPS

An uninterruptible power supply (UPS) is an AC-powered box containing a battery with enough power to keep a computer running for a short while after the AC input power has been lost. The UPS is plugged into the wall, and the computer is plugged into the box, as shown in Figure 9.37. A communications link using one of the computer's COM ports connects the UPS and the computer. When the UPS detects a power outage, it sends a message to the computer. Windows NT receives an interrupt on the COM port and responds to the alert by issuing messages to administrators (and optionally, users) that the computer is going to shut down within a certain number of minutes unless the power is revived. Then, after a preset period of time, NT begins an automated, safe shutdown. When power is restored, the NT machine resumes where it left off, with no loss of data.

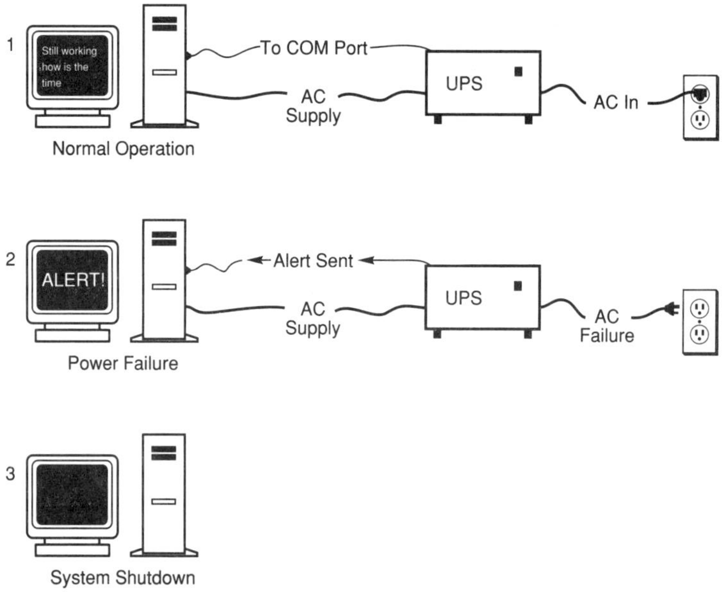

FIGURE 9.37.
A diagram of a UPS setup.

Typically, a UPS will be added to a server station (such as an NT Server station), but it could also be set up for any individual's workstation responsible for maintenance of crucial data, and where valuable work would be lost if the station were to go down unexpectedly.

If a UPS is installed on a workstation, the UPS settings from Control Panel are used to inform NT of the characteristics of the UPS. There are many brands and models of UPS devices, and each has its own power life capabilities, recharge times, and interface voltages. Also, you might want to specify the types of actions NT should take when a power outage does occur.

NOTE

Not all UPS devices interface with NT in such a way as to trigger an automated shutdown. Any UPS will keep the machine going after a power outage, at least for some period of time, so all PC-compatible UPSs will work with NT to some degree. But if you need unattended shutdown capability, you'll have to check with the manufacturer to ensure that the device and its cable are NT-compatible. The Hardware Compatibility List includes the appropriate settings for supported UPSs.

To configure your Windows NT-compatible UPS, follow these steps:

1. Read the manual supplied with the UPS and connect the AC lines and COM lines as instructed.
2. From Control Panel, double-click on the UPS icon. The dialog box shown in Figure 9.38 appears.

FIGURE 9.38.
The UPS configuration box.

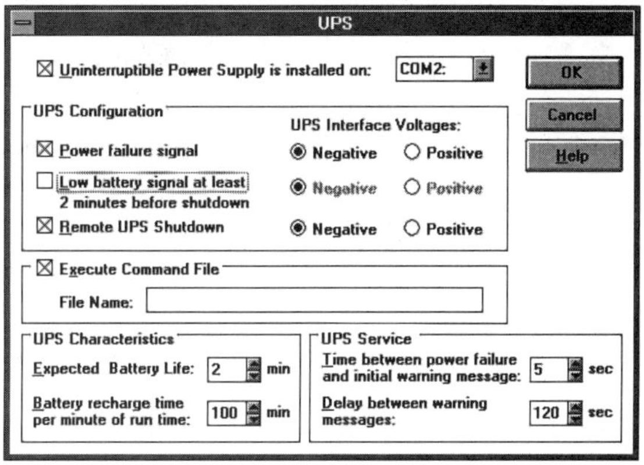

3. Fill in the settings in the box, using the following table for help with each setting:

Setting	*Notes*
UPS is installed on	Check this box if your UPS connects to a COM port. Then choose the COM port from the drop-down list.
Power failure signal	Can the UPS send a power failure signal on the CTS (clear-to-send) pin of the serial link? If so, check this box and indicate which voltage polarity (+ or -) signals the failure.

Setting	*Notes*
Low battery signal	Can the UPS send a low-battery signal on the DCD (data carrier detect) pin of the serial link? If so, check this box and indicate which voltage polarity (+ or -) signals the low-battery state. Note that the UPS must be able to maintain power to the computer for at least two minutes after the signal is sent, to allow NT a graceful shutdown.
Remote UPS Shutdown	Can the UPS receive a signal from the NT machine on the DTR (data terminal ready) pin of the serial link? (This signal is used to tell the UPS when the battery power is no longer needed either because the AC source was revived or because the computer shuts off.) If so, check the box and indicate which voltage polarity (+ or -) signals the cessation of battery power need.
Execute Command File	Do you want a command to execute just before the system shuts down? If so, check this box and enter the name of the .EXE, .CMD, or .COM file. The file must execute in no more than 30 seconds. It also must be stored in the \SYSTEM32 directory. A typical program would shut down a service (such as SQL Server) or broadcast user-specific messages. However, no such programs are supplied with Windows NT. (See the later discussion about alerting and disconnecting users prior to system shutdown.)
Expected Battery Life	Approximately how many minutes (2 to 270) can the battery keep the computer running after a shutdown? Err on the low side if you're not sure, or if the UPS is somewhat aged. Most batteries lose their staying power with age. You use this feature only if your UPS doesn't supply a low-battery signal.

Setting	*Notes*
Battery recharge time	For each minute of time the UPS is powering the computer (while the AC power source is on), how many minutes (1 to 150) are required for a full recharge of the UPS battery? Like the Expected Battery Life feature, use this feature only with a UPS that doesn't provide a low-battery signal. Its primary purpose is to make sure that NT doesn't restart without having enough battery power to support a safe shutdown (the minimum is approximately two minutes).
Time between power failure and initial warning	How much time goes by between the time the UPS detects a powerfailure and the power failure signal is sent to the computer? This figure is subtracted from the total expected battery life to determine when the system should begin shutdown. The range is 0 to 120 seconds.
Delay between warning messages	If the UPS can keep the system going for some time, how often (5 to 300 seconds) should the user be notified of impending doom? Too-frequent messages can be annoying. Messages sent too seldom can be overlooked.

4. After you've filled in the options, click on OK. NT will ask whether you want to start the UPS service. (Remember, as I mentioned earlier, that the UPS service is the internal software module that monitors the state of the UPS and performs the requisite messaging and automated shutdown when necessary.) Click on Yes, and the UPS service will be set to automatically start whenever NT starts.

NOTE

If you want to remove the UPS device and service from the machine, disable the first check box and click on OK. You'll be asked whether you want to stop the service. Click on Yes.

NOTE

Three other services must be running if you want the UPS and the NT UPS service to alert users of impending shutdowns and keep a log of what happened: the Messenger, the Alerter, and the Event Log. See the earlier discussion of the Services applet to review how to determine whether these services are on. Ideally, they should be set to start automatically upon NT bootup. You also might want to set who is to be notified in case of a shutdown. This is done with the Server applet, also discussed earlier.

NOTE

Of course, if your whole company's power goes out, everyone with a UPS should know better than to keep computing. They should choose Shutdown from Program Manager or Task List and get off their computers quickly. Users without a UPS will, of course, be dead in the water, and they will have to take their losses. Sometimes these losses will be minimized with help from the application software being run. For example, some better programs are fairly compassionate when it comes to power loss in that they keep track of temp files and recover them gracefully when you power back up.

Configuring with System Setup

Another means of configuration involves the use of the NT Setup program. Setup is used to change the screen, keyboard, and mouse types. It also can be used to add application programs to Program Manager groups, add and remove tape backup and SCSI drivers, delete user profiles, and add and remove significant portions of Windows NT components (such as help files, accessory programs, readme files, games, and so on) to free up disk space. The Setup program is described in Chapter 12.

Configuring Other Application Environments

As I discussed in Chapters 1 and 2, Windows NT runs non-NT applications that fall into four classes: MS-DOS, Windows 3.x, OS/2 1.x character-based applications, and POSIX character-based applications. NT achieves this by creating a simulated operating environment compatible with the application. The software modules responsible for providing the simulation are the environment subsystems. Some optimization and configuration of the various environments are possible, typically to allow for higher compatibility with non-NT programs. This section discusses options for configuring applications and subsystems. It also discusses some specific programs or classes of programs (such as DOS-based TSRs) and how best to run them under NT.

Recall from the discussion in Chapter 2 that NT provides a great deal of security for the core operating system. The security subsystem prevents an application that has run amok from wreaking havoc on other applications or the operating system. When an application is written in accordance with accepted I/O routines for the target environment, it's likely to run on NT. This is because NT's environment subsystems intercept standard I/O calls (to the screen, printer, and so on) and route them to the WIN32 subsystem's analogous calls. When a non-NT program doesn't play by the rules, it can fail when running under NT. When an illegal I/O attempt is made (such as an attempt to write directly to the hard disk), the NT security subsystem traps the call, reports it to the user (and the Event Log, if it's running), and terminates the application.

As a result of these rules, the following classes of applications either will need new drivers or might have to be updated altogether to run under NT:

- Disk compression software or other programs that attempt to write directly to the hard disk.
- Programs that expect to write directly to the printer and that come with their own printer drivers or print caching software.
- Some programs that write directly to the screen in order to speed up video performance, such as some graphics and MS-DOS high-speed game programs such as Flight Simulator. The success of these programs under NT may vary, depending on the version of the program, which video card you're using, and the display driver.
- Programs that need to write directly to other types of hardware, whether the hardware is an internal modem, video card, sound card, SCSI card, or another device.

TIP

If you're in doubt about a program, try it. NT will advise you if security has been breached. (NT won't allow any damage to your system.) Call the manufacturer of the board or device if the program doesn't work.

NOTE

Running programs in various environments is discussed in Chapter 3, "Working with Windows NT." Troubleshooting problems that arise when you run applications is covered in Chapter 10, "Windows NT Administration."

The remainder of this chapter discusses configuration for each environment.

Configuring the Windows 3.1 Environment

As I discussed in Chapter 8, "Installing Windows NT," installing NT over an existing Windows 3.1 can be a boon, because it uses configuration information from the Windows 3.1 setup for NT. This greatly simplifies things for the new NT user because it isn't necessary to create Program Manager groups and set other preferences such as Desktop settings. The WIN.INI and SYSTEM.INI settings are "migrated" into the NT Registry database, effectively giving users the look and feel of their familiar Windows 3.1 setup. The only groups that aren't migrated are the Main and Accessories groups. This is because NT wants the 32-bit versions of the programs in those groups (such as Control Panel), so it installs the new ones at setup time.

Many users will alternate between running Windows 3.1 and NT, particularly until 32-bit versions of their favorite applications become available. For this reason, NT continues to migrate key Windows 3.1 data at each NT bootup. When NT starts, it always reads the Windows 3.1 WIN.INI, SYSTEM.INI, and REG.DAT information from the Windows 3.1 directory (assuming that you installed NT over Windows 3.1).

Configuring the DOS Environment

There are a several ways to configure the MS-DOS environment:

- By configuring the user variables in the System dialog box, as discussed in the section titled "Control Panel"
- By making selections from the DOS window's Control menu
- By setting up PIF files for the DOS application

Making Command-Prompt Window Settings

Running DOS applications from the command-prompt window was covered briefly in Chapter 3, "Working with Windows NT." As you know, you can execute POSIX, OS/2, MS-DOS, and Windows applications from the command line.

When you run a character-based program, the window defaults to a standard size, background color, and font. Configuration options on the window's Control menu allow you to alter settings for the specific session. Options in the dialog boxes also let you save the settings to establish new defaults.

Windows 3.1 allows you to set the default font size (and thus the window size) for subsequent DOS sessions. Windows NT offers much more flexibility. You can

- change the font
- set the background and foreground colors for normal text
- set the background and foreground colors for popup boxes
- choose window or full-screen viewing
- set the default window position on the screen
- set the default cursor size
- use or turn off the QuickEdit mode
- use or hide the NT mouse pointer in the application

NOTE

In addition to these settings, you can set environment variables, specify memory requirements (for EMS and XMS), and set other nitty-gritty options using PIF files and the System option in Control Panel. Unless specified otherwise, NT uses the file _DEFAULT.PIF, stored in the \WINNT directory, as the basis for MS-DOS sessions and running applications that don't have a PIF. PIF files are explained in the section titled "Using PIF Files for DOS Programs." Command-prompt commands and syntax are covered in Appendix A, not in this chapter.

The great thing about NT's command-prompt sessions is that the Registry can store separate settings for each unique title bar text. This is not clearly explained in the manual, but what it means is this: When you run a command-prompt session, the title bar says Command Prompt until you run a program. When you run a program, the title bar changes. If the text that appears in the title bar is something you've saved the settings for before (as explained later), NT puts *those* settings into effect. For example, you can set up an icon in Program Manager for the MS-DOS editor Edit. Run the program, then alter the window characteristics and save them. The next time you run the icon, the settings go into effect.

TIP

Another way to do this is to run Edit from the command prompt. The title bar changes to say EDIT.EXE (or whatever the command is). Make the window changes and save them. The next time you enter EDIT at the command prompt, the settings go into effect.

1. Open a command-prompt window and click on the Control box (the button in the upper-left corner of the window). You'll see four relevant options: Settings, Fonts, Screen Size And Position, and Screen Colors, as shown in Figure 9.39.

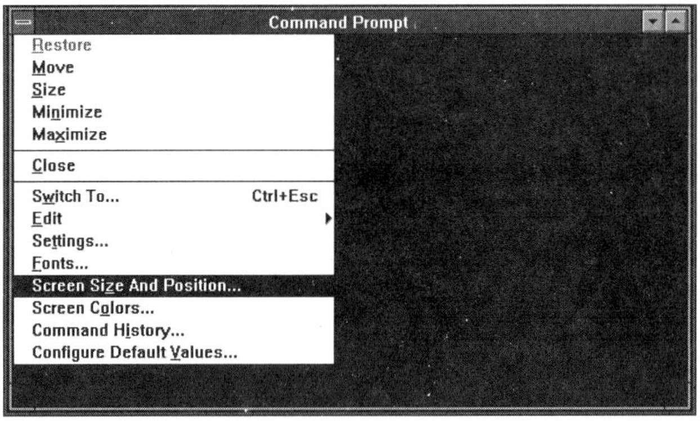

FIGURE 9.39.
Command-prompt settings that affect the operation of the session or setting defaults that affect all sessions.

NOTE

The Control menu's Edit command and its associated cascading menu options are covered in Chapter 5, which discusses the use of the Clipboard and OLE.

2. Choose Settings. You'll see the dialog box shown in Figure 9.40. From this box you can set whether the window is full-screen or windowed, and whether you want to use the Insert or QuickEdit mode. (QuickEdit lets you copy material to and from the Clipboard using the mouse cursor instead of having to use the Control menu's Edit commands and arrow keys.) Make your settings and click on the Save check box if you want the settings saved for the current title bar name.

   It's important to note that on RISC machines, all MS-DOS programs—character-based and graphics-based—can run only in a window. On x86 machines, character-based programs can run in a window, but graphics programs must run full-screen.

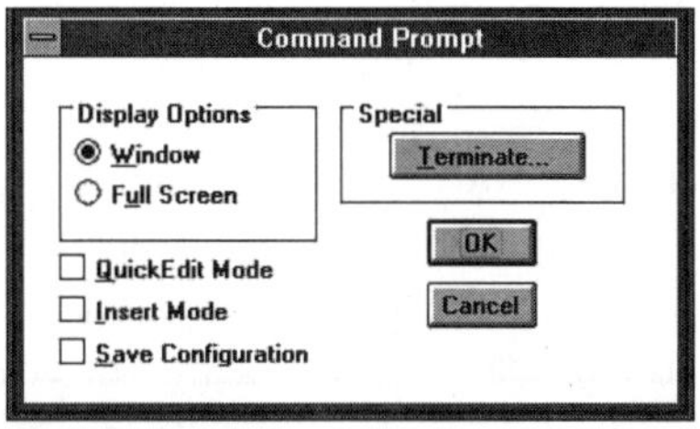

FIGURE 9.40.
Changing the window and QuickEdit settings.

NOTE

If the title bar reads Command Prompt and you make changes, these changes will become the default settings for future command-prompt sessions until you change them again. Also, if you don't save the settings, they'll still be in effect during the current session. This applies to all the settings discussed in the following steps.

3. Close the previous box, open the Control menu again, and choose Fonts. The Font Selection dialog box appears, as shown in Figure 9.41. From this box you can select the font type—TrueType or raster—as well as the font size, which in turn affects the size of the window. Click on each of the font sizes and notice the effect in the Window Preview and Selected Font boxes.

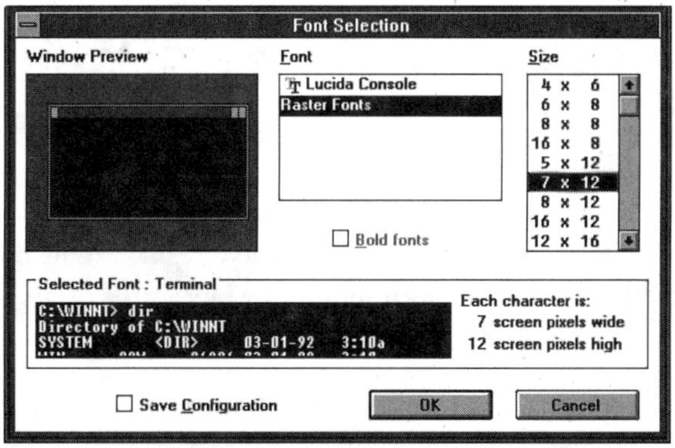

FIGURE 8.41.
Selecting a font (and window size) for a session.

TIP

In Windows 3.1, this is the extent of font control. In Windows 3.1, it's assumed that a character-mode screen is running in 80 characters by 24 lines. In NT you can increase this by upping the screen buffer size. Of course, a character-based application would have to be tweaked to deliver more than the standard 24 lines of text to take advantage of this. Setting the screen buffer size is discussed later.

4. Enable the Save Configuration box if you want to save the setting.
5. Check out the Size And Position command on the Control menu (see Figure 9.42). You've got three options here: size/position, buffer size, and cursor size. They don't really relate to one another, so don't worry about it. If you want to save the window's size and position, set the size and position on-screen before you choose this command. Then enable the check box for saving the position. If you want to alter the default buffer settings of 80 by 25 for the amount of memory that NT sets aside to remember what's on-screen (the number of characters by the number of rows) and initially how large to draw the window, do so. If you want to change the size of the cursor (small, medium, or large), make your choice and enable the Save cursor size check box.

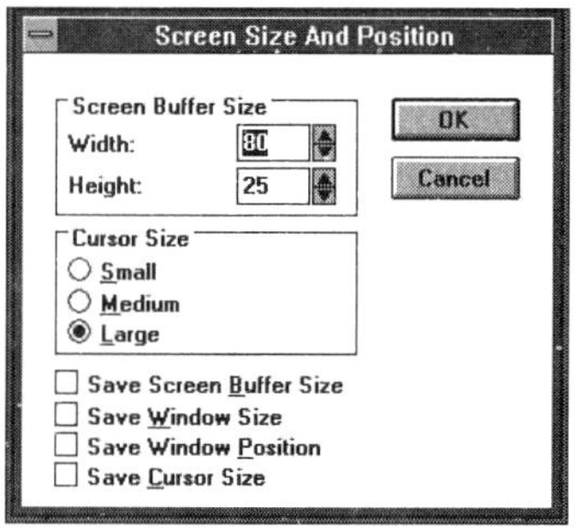

FIGURE 9.42.
Setting the window size and position.

TIP

If you're going to alter the buffer size, set it first, then click on OK. Adjust the position of the window, open the menu again, and save the position. Setting a large buffer size can be a real boon if you run batch files or other programs that normally cause text to scroll off the top of the screen. A large buffer enables you to scroll the screen back and check program flow and error messages.

6. To set the screen colors, open the Control menu and choose Screen Colors. The dialog box shown in Figure 9.43 appears.

NOTE

Color settings you make here are likely to be superseded by any color settings an application makes on its own. But if the application doesn't normally control colors (that is, when running in its native environment outside of NT), the color settings will apply.

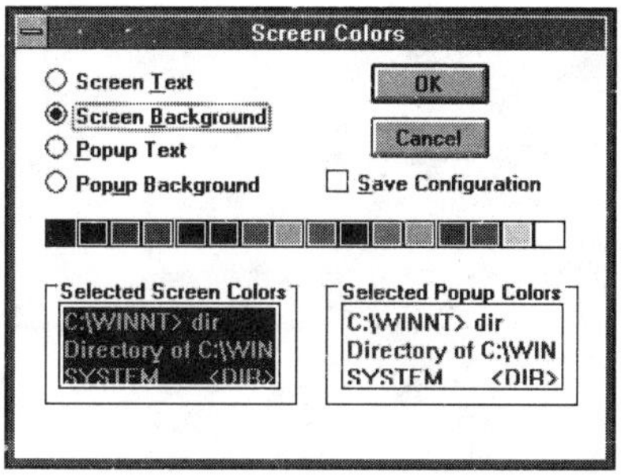

FIGURE 9.43.
Set the screen colors from here.

7. Click on the radio button that applies to the color you want to alter, then click on a color in the bar (or a shade if you're using a gray-scale screen). Most likely only the first two radio buttons will apply. Applications rarely use the preset colors for popup boxes. Enable the Save box if you want to have the same colors apply the next time you run the program or command prompt.

Using PIF Files for DOS Programs

Windows-based applications work well together and tend to peaceably coexist in the same workstation or on a network. However, DOS applications were never meant to run simultaneously—especially not with Windows programs or in the Windows or Windows NT environment.

NOTE

If you're having problems running non-Windows programs, you should read this and the next section as well as Chapter 12. You might also want to read the supplied documents README.WRI and NETWORKS.WRI for additional notes pertaining to specific programs and hardware.

MS-DOS applications were designed to run in solitude. They assume that they are the only application running and usually are memory hogs. Often they want at least 640K of RAM and perhaps even extended or expanded memory. Running several non-Windows programs simultaneously—especially DOS programs—is conceptually like trying to settle a boundary dispute at the U.N.

To accommodate the many DOS-based applications still in use, Windows NT has to be ingenious in managing computer resources such as RAM, printers, modems, mice, and display I/O. Significant sleight of hand is required to pull this off smoothly, but Microsoft has done this fairly well, partly due to the use of PIFs.

NOTE

In case you don't know, PIFs (program information files) are small files stored on disk, usually in the \WINNT directory or in the same directory as the application. They contain settings NT uses when it runs the related application. Correct PIF settings can spare you aggravation caused by program crashes, sluggish performance, memory shortages, and other annoying anomalies.

PIF settings can affect many aspects of an application's operation, such as (but not limited to)

- the directory that becomes active once an application starts
- full-screen or windowed operation upon launch
- conventional memory usage
- expanded or extended memory usage
- the application's multitasking priority level
- the application's shortcut keys
- foreground and background processing

PIFs have the same initial name as the application but use .PIF as the extension (123.PIF, for example). You create a PIF with the PIF editor. When you run an MS-DOS application from NT (using any technique), NT searches the application's directory and search path for a PIF with the same name as the application. If one is found, this file's settings are applied to the DOS environment by the DOS environment subsystem in order to run the application. If no PIF is found, Windows uses the default settings stored in a file named _DEFAULT.PIF, stored in the \WINNT directory. These settings work for most DOS applications, but not all.

NOTE

Both Setup and some installation programs create PIFs for you, so there might be some PIFs on your hard disk that you didn't create.

As you might expect, Windows 3.1 PIFs work fine in Windows NT, and, as in 3.1, you can use a PIF to launch a program. Just double-click on a PIF in File Manager, or click on a Program Manager icon that points to it. The PIF settings are loaded and the application is launched.

When the default settings don't cut the mustard, you'll have to fine-tune a PIF by making a few settings. The good news is that far fewer PIF options apply in NT than in Windows 3.1 because NT's DOS subsystem is more intelligent than its little brother. Only these PIF settings are of consequence to NT:

- Program filename
- Window title
- Optional parameters
- Startup directory
- EMS memory
- XMS memory
- Display usage
- Close window on exit
- Multitasking options
- Reserve shortcut keys
- Application shortcut keys
- Custom startup files

The PIF editor looks almost identical to that of Windows 3.1. It lets you set items that apply to Windows 3.1 so that the same PIFs may be used for each GUI. However, NT uses only the items just listed.

To bring up the PIF editor, double-click on its icon in the Main group. The complex dialog box shown in Figure 9.44 appears.

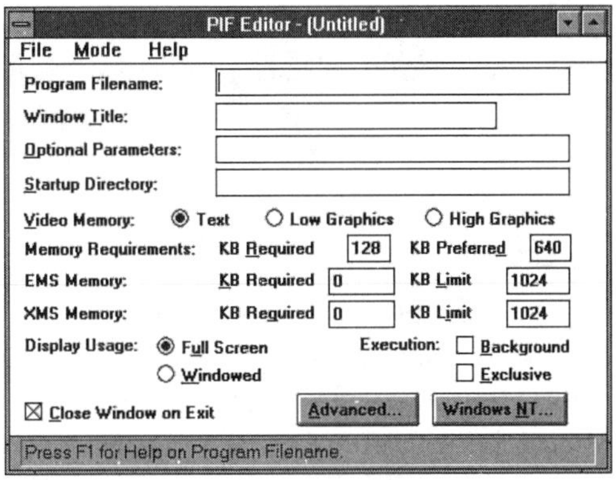

FIGURE 9.44.
The PIF Editor dialog box.

Make your changes, then save the PIF as you would any other file (using File | Save or File | Save As). It should have the same first name as the application it works with, and it should be stored in the \WINNT directory or in the application's directory.

The following sections discuss each of the options relevant to execution under Windows NT. Other options can be left alone, at least as far as NT is concerned. (For a discussion of other options, refer to a book or manual about Windows 3.1.)

Program Filename

Enter the program's executable name. It must be an .EXE, .COM, or .BAT file—for example, ED.EXE for PC-Write. You can use an environment variable if you want. For example, suppose you set a variable in AUTOEXEC.BAT with the line

```
set pcwrite=d:\ed\ed.exe
```

You could use the variable as the program name, entering `%pcwrite%` in this section.

Window Title

This is the name that displays in the title bar for the window and under the program's icon. You can make it descriptive if you like, such as Quicksoft PC-Write, Quicken for DOS, and so on. If you leave this entry blank, Windows NT uses the program's name instead. As with the program filename, you can use an environment variable with this option.

NOTE

If the program has an icon in Program Manager, the icon's Description line (as set from the Properties dialog box) takes precedence over the PIF window title setting. Therefore, if you run the PIF using the File | Run command, File Manager, or a command prompt, you could see a different title bar than if you ran it from Program Manager, assuming that there was a conflict between the two.

Optional Parameters

In this section, enter any parameters to be passed to the program when it launches. For example, you might want to instruct the application to load a particular file when it starts or instruct it to start in a specific mode. Commands entered here are added to the program's command line as if they were typed in manually at the command prompt. As an example, suppose you want the PIF to cause the application to load the file BUDGET.WK1. You would enter `budget.wk1` in the optional parameters area.

Several notes apply:

- Parameters can be up to 62 characters long.
- Some programs require a slash (/) before parameters entered from the command line. If your application does, be sure to enter it here.
- Putting just a question mark in the box results in a dialog box in which NT prompts you for parameters when you run the PIF. This is useful when you want to specify a file of your choice or a certain mode when you run the PIF.
- If you run the PIF using the File | Run command or the command prompt, parameters you enter there override those in the PIF.
- You can use environment variables to set this command as explained in the previous two items.

Startup Directory

This setting determines which drive and directory become the default directory once the application starts. If this is left blank, NT assumes the application's directory, which is fine because support files (for example, dictionaries or macros) often are stored in the same directory as the application. Again, you can use an environment variable to specify this setting.

CAUTION

Use care when changing this setting. Specifying a different directory can leave your application unable to find its support files, such as DLLs. Some applications use the DOS search path (as set by AUTOEXEC.BAT or AUTOEXEC.NT) to search for them, but not all do.

EMS Memory

Not to be confused with extended memory, EMS memory is another form of memory above the normal 640K DOS limit. Nowadays only a few programs use it. For example, Ventura Publisher for GEM (not Windows) greatly benefits from expanded memory, even though it will run without it. Check the software's manual to determine its needs.

Windows NT will supply simulated expanded memory on-the-fly for an application that requests it in a PIF. It does this by reallocating NT memory via its own expanded memory manager.

The KB Required setting tells Windows how much expanded memory must be available before it even tries to run the program. If that much is not available, a dialog box warns you to free up some system memory and run the PIF again. If you set the parameter to 0, this indicates that no EMS is needed for the application to run, even though it might benefit from having some. NT will try to provide EMS up to the limit.

The KB Limit sets to the top end the amount of EMS to supply the application. Having a limit prevents the application from taking all the available EMS. It also prevents NT from reassigning too much memory to the application, which can lead to lots of disk swapping and overall system slowdown. The default is 1024. A 0 entered here prevents Windows from assigning any EMS to the program. Entering –1 gives the application as much EMS as it wants, with a limit only being calculated by NT. (Use the –1 setting with caution, because the application might be greedy.)

XMS Memory

XMS is normal extended memory that complies with the Lotus-Intel-Microsoft-AST standard set several years ago. Although Windows and Windows NT love this kind of memory, few DOS applications can actually utilize it. A notable exception is Lotus 1-2-3 version 3.0.

Settings are similar to EMS Memory. In the KB Required area, set the amount of extended memory required for your program just to launch. As with EMS, if more XMS is available, NT will allocate it up to the limit. If not enough is available, a dialog box warns you. Leave the setting at 0 if your program doesn't require or use extended memory. Allocating extended memory is like taking RAM chips out of your computer—your system will slow down and disk swapping will occur more often.

In the KB Limit section, enter the ceiling you want your application to have. Try to minimize this amount, because Windows NT needs all it can get for its own use. Entering –1 in this box gives all available extended memory to the application, but it might affect overall system performance due to additional paging to disk that might otherwise be necessary.

Display Usage

This setting determines whether the application initially comes up windowed or full-screen. You still can toggle between views by pressing Alt-Enter. Of course, in full-screen display, the mouse is surrendered to the application. And, unless you stipulate otherwise via the application window's Control menu, when the application is running in a window, Windows takes over the mouse. Then it can be used only for Windows operations.

Remember that Intel-based machines can't run graphics-mode applications in a window. If a character-mode application running windowed switches to graphics mode (for example, the user changes Word for DOS to graphics mode), the DOS window will go full-screen.

NOTE

This option is meaningless on RISC-based machines, because all applications run in a window.

Close Window on Exit

If you want the program's window to disappear and dump you back into Windows when you exit the program, enable this box. Otherwise, the remains of the application stay on-screen when you quit, and nothing happens. You then have to press any key to return to Windows. In most cases, you'll want this box enabled. You'll want it disabled when you run an application such as Norton SI that measures the system speed or when you want to read the program's screen output after it completes execution.

Multitasking Options

This section determines the amount of CPU time given the application relative to other applications that are running. There are two settings: background and foreground. (The Background and Exclusive buttons are not functional in NT.)

To make settings, click on the Advanced button. You can enter a number for Background and a number for Foreground. Foreground defaults to 100 and Background defaults to 50. Numbers can range from 0 to 10,000. Numbers are relative, so they don't really mean anything in terms of a percentage. In general, if you want one program to have more CPU time when it's in the background, increase its background value. If a program is running too slowly in the foreground, increase its number.

NOTE

Unfortunately, you can't set up PIFs for Windows applications. Besides, it wouldn't help. The Windows environment divvies up CPU slices in a more egalitarian manner that doesn't allow fine-tuning.

You'll usually want to set the Foreground number higher than the Background number (as is the default) to ensure that the program runs faster when it's up front. Theoretically, at least, there are instances when you would want this number to be relatively low compared to other programs. Some programs don't do much but twiddle their thumbs, wasting CPU time. Character-based word processors, for example, need scant CPU time to stay alive and put characters on-screen as you type. If your background programs are suffering when this DOS program is in the foreground, try lowering its settings (both Foreground and Background).

The last tasking option is Detect Idle Time. If you enable this, NT keeps an eye on the application and can sense when it's twiddling its thumbs (waiting for you to press a key, typically). If the application is "idling," NT doesn't bother wasting CPU slices on it and works on other processes instead. Pressing a key gets NT's attention. This option is enabled by default and should be changed only if the application is dropping data or if it's malfunctioning in a way that indicates it's not being serviced often enough (for example, very sluggish performance).

Reserve Shortcut Keys

You access this option via the Advanced button. Its purpose is to reclaim key combinations normally reserved for Windows. If your application needs one of the Alt, Ctrl, Shift, or Esc key combinations that Windows usually interprets for jobs such as switching applications, opening Control menus, and so on, you should create a PIF for the application and reserve the necessary key combination. Specifying a combination prevents a conflict between your application and Windows when you press the keys. When a box is checked, Windows relinquishes use of the key (and its normal functioning with Windows) and allows your application to use it. Check one or more of these boxes only when your application needs the key combinations.

Application Shortcut Keys

You can set up application shortcut keys to quickly jump you to the running application. If Program Manager is the active window and you've set up a shortcut key for the icon, pressing the key combination launches the PIF. You also can set the shortcut key in the PIF editor using the Advanced Settings dialog box. Using a shortcut key lets you forego using the Task List or Alt-Tabbing your way to it.

As I suggested, you can create a shortcut key by modifying the PIF's icon in Program Manager via the File | Properties command. If you assign a combination here and another combination with the PIF editor, the icon's setting wins out.

To enter the shortcut key in the PIF editor, access the advanced settings and click on the Application Shortcut Key box. Press the key combination you want to assign to the application. The combination must include the Alt or Ctrl keys or both. Function keys can be used, and three-key codes are acceptable (such as Alt-Ctrl-Z).

CAUTION

Don't use a combination that other programs might use, such as Alt-F (which many Windows applications use to open the File menu), because this will cause a conflict. Also, remember that you can't use Esc, Enter, Tab, the Spacebar, Print Screen, or Backspace.

TIP

To delete a shortcut key, enter the combination Shift-Backspace. This works for Program Manager's Properties box and for the PIF editor.

Custom Startup Files

As I explain in the next section, Windows NT lets you further configure the MS-DOS environment with CONFIG.NT and AUTOEXEC.NT. These are the default files loaded into each DOS VDM (virtual DOS machine). If an application needs a particular environment that would normally be controlled by settings in CONFIG.SYS or AUTOEXEC.BAT, such as a memory-resident program, and you don't want *every* VDM to use these settings, you can control this. You simply create specialized files that the PIF loads instead of the defaults and declare the filenames in the PIF.

From the application's PIF, click on the Windows NT button. You'll see a dialog box that lets you name alternate files to be used. Enter the names of the files. You'll want to create your own modified files for this use.

TIP

Start by copying CONFIG.NT and AUTOEXEC.NT and then editing them with a plain text editor such as Notepad. You'll find the files in the \SYSTEM32 directory.

TIP

You can cause NT to execute a PIF from the command prompt. However, you have to use the Start command to do this. Otherwise the .EXE, .COM, .CMD, or .BAT file will run. Use syntax such as `start lotus`.

Using CONFIG.NT and AUTOEXEC.NT

Additional configuration of the DOS environment is possible by setting up two files that act much like CONFIG.SYS and AUTOEXEC.BAT do in normal DOS on a PC. These files are called CONFIG.NT and AUTOEXEC.NT. They're loaded when NT senses that you're running a DOS application.

When you run a DOS application, NT creates a DOS VDM by loading the DOS environment subsystem and sort of "booting up" DOS. In the process, it reads in settings from CONFIG.NT and AUTOEXEC.NT in just the same way real DOS does when it boots. The only difference is the filenames and the file locations. In this case, the files are in the \SYSTEM32 directory (usually \WINNT\SYSTEM32 or \WINDOWS\SYSTEM32) instead of the root directory.

By editing these two files, you can set up the DOS environment used by every DOS application (unless you declare different startup files using a PIF, as explained earlier). Recall that when you log onto NT, the AUTOEXEC.BAT file is read for path and environment information. These settings are added to the Windows NT environment and apply to any applications you run—Windows, DOS, POSIX, or whatever.

By contrast, *each time* you run a DOS application in a new window (each time a VDM is created), NT reads the CONFIG.NT and AUTOEXEC.NT files. The great thing about this is that you can change the settings and rerun a program and the new settings get read and go into effect. It's like rebooting DOS after fine-tuning CONFIG.SYS and AUTOEXEC.BAT, only faster.

NOTE

As I explained earlier, path statements found in AUTOEXEC.NT are appended to path statements already loaded from AUTOEXEC.BAT. Settings are cumulative.

The commands you can place in an AUTOEXEC.NT file are nearly identical to those in DOS. Refer to Appendix A for a listing of command-prompt commands pertinent to an MS-DOS window.

The commands available for CONFIG.NT are shown in Table 9.6.

Table 9.6. Commands available for CONFIG.NT.

Command	*Description*
`country=`	Sets the language conventions for the session.
`device=`	Used for installing loadable device drivers. Be careful with drivers that attempt to address hardware directly. They won't work. You *can* load display drivers such as ANSI.SYS and memory managers such as EMM.SYS and HIMEM.SYS. For a discussion of memory-resident programs, see Chapter 11.
`dos=`	Used for telling NT what to do with the upper memory area (where to load DOS, as in `dos=high`).

Command	*Description*
`dosonly`	Allows only DOS programs to be loaded from a COMMAND.COM prompt. POSIX, OS/2, and Windows programs won't run. Note that a COMMAND.COM prompt and an NT command-prompt window's prompt are not the same. If you run COMMAND.COM, you get a DOS box running the DOS command interpreter. Command-prompt windows run NT's command interpreter, whose command set differs and expands on MS-DOS.
`echoconfig`	Activates the display of CONFIG and AUTOEXEC commands as they are executed from the files.
`fcbs=`	Sets the maximum number of file control blocks (FCBs).
`files=`	Sets the maximum number of open files.
`install=`	Loads a memory-resident (TSR) program into memory before the window comes up or an application loads.
`loadhigh=`	Loads device drivers into the high-memory area (HMA).
`ntcmdprompt`	Replaces the COMMAND.COM interpreter with NT's interpreter, CMD.EXE. After you load a TSR or when you shell out of an application to DOS, you'll get CMD.EXE instead, from which you have the added benefits of the NT interpreter.
`rem`	Marks a line as a comment.
`stacks=`	The amount of RAM set aside for stacking up hardware interrupts as they come in.

Configuring the OS/2 Environment

Some configuration of the OS/2 environment is possible, though not as much as for the DOS environment. If you're running OS/2 as the other operating system on the workstation when NT is installed, NT will import the OS/2-related settings in CONFIG.SYS when it boots up the first time. These settings will be added to the Registry and will affect OS/2 sessions you run. For example, the `LIBPATH` information will be used to update NT's `Os2LibPath` environment variable. NT tacks the existing `LIBPATH` directory list onto the end of the following line:

```
%SystemRoot%\system32\os2\dll
```

If NT doesn't find a CONFIG.SYS file when it boots the first time, or if it finds a CONFIG.SYS file but it isn't an OS/2 CONFIG.SYS file (it's a DOS one instead), NT dumps default OS/2-related environment settings into its Registry:

```
PROTSHELL=c:\os2\pmshell.exe c:\os2\os2.ini c:\os2\os2sys.ini
%SystemRoot%\system32\cmd.exe
SET COMSPEC=%SystemRoot%\system32\cmd.exe
```

You can edit the OS/2 subsystem configuration information that NT uses when it runs OS/2 applications. You do this by running an OS/2 text editor in a window and opening the CONFIG.SYS file on the root directory of the startup disk. NT senses that you're doing this and loads the OS/2-related configuration information into a temporary file that you can edit. When you save the file, the changes are dumped into the Registry. When you restart the computer, the OS/2 subsystem settings go into effect.

NOTE

You must be an administrator to edit the OS/2 configuration information.

NT recognizes and uses seven OS/2 startup commands:

```
devinfo=KBD
country
protshell
codepage
set
libpath
devicename
```

NT ignores other OS/2 commands. You should consult an OS/2 manual to see how these commands are used. However, a few notes on how NT processes the last three commands just listed may be useful:

`libpath` is used to tell the OS/2 subsystem where 16-bit DLLs (dynamic link libraries) can be found. It's similar to the `PATH` statement in DOS. `set` is used to declare environment variables. `devicename` can be used to supply an NT device driver (that the user specifies) for use by the OS/2 subsystem. These three work as follows:

Command	*Notes*
`set`	These OS/2 `set` commands will be ignored: `vio_ibmvga`, `vio_vga`, `compspec`, `video_devices`, and `prompt`.
`libpath`	NT lets you change the OS/2 `libpath` from the command prompt. Enter `os2libpath` followed by the new path. If you have a `libpath` statement in CONFIG.SYS, NT appends it to the existing OS/2 library path with NT.
`devicename`	If you have an NT-compatible device driver that you want to use with your OS/2 application, use this command. The syntax is `devicename=os/2devicename [[`*`path`*`][`*`NTdevicename`*`]]` where `devicename` is the logical name for a device that OS/2 normally would supply an OS/2 application and where *`path`* and *`NTdevicename`* are the path and device driver name (filename) of the device driver to be assigned to OS/2. By default, it you don't specify the path and *`NTdevicename`*, Windows NT assumes it is `\DEVICE\`*`os2devicename`*.

Windows NT Administration

10

IN THIS CHAPTER

Administrative management of Windows NT is, in many ways, an IS manager's dream. Even in the best of circumstances, supporting PCs in a corporate setting is typically a nightmare. Novell has earned its market share in the PC networking niche due largely to its adept addressing of the manageability issue alone. Microsoft, based no doubt on its own experience in the corporate setting (which includes huge networks), has learned this lesson well. As a result, NT is quite rich in administrative tools and built-in security that often preclude the need for those tools.

For example, unless users have the proper authority, they can't alter files, directories, and NT settings of consequence. Internal Access Control lists and transaction logging make network and workstation management of critical data a reasonable (rather than an impossible) chore. Permissions can be modified over the network. That way, you don't have to visit the workstation in question. Even so, users still have the feeling that their PC is theirs because they still have control over desktop attributes such as color, fonts, Program Manager groups, and File Manager preferences.

When using NTFS partitions, managers can selectively lock out users from altering or even seeing specific files, directories, and even entire partitions. Also, lower-level users are not allowed access to administrative tools used for disk partitioning and formatting, or for setting up and altering user profiles, passwords, and permissions.

Many of the NT system administration techniques were discussed in earlier chapters. In particular, Chapter 9, "Configuring Windows NT," dealt with configuration issues that could be classified as system management. Topics such as font management, network software and hardware configuration, and system services and devices were discussed in that chapter. You might want to review Chapter 9 if you're managing a workstation or network. If you're running an MS-Mail post office or managing office time with Schedule+, refer to Chapter 6, "Network User Applications: MS-Mail, Schedule+, and Chat."

NOTE

Relatively effortless installation of NT onto new workstations over the network is covered in Chapter 8, "Installing Windows NT."

This chapter discusses system-related applications and techniques that are specifically administrative in nature, including

- the best methods for organizing Program Manager groups and icons
- replicating directories across the network
- managing shared workstation resources
- managing your users: permissions, passwords, access rights, and groups

- working from a distance: remote workstation administration
- managing the hard disk: partitioning and converting between file formats

Using these techniques in conjunction with Control Panel, File Manager, and Print Manager commands covered in previous chapters should give you a pretty good handle on the basics of local and network administration of NT. (Part III of this book covers network installation, usage, and optimization in more technical detail.)

NOTE

The Performance Monitor application (found in the Administration group), which helps locate network bottlenecks, is covered in Chapter 21.

NOTE

Windows NT 3.5 includes versions of User Manager, Server Manager, Print Manager, Event Viewer, and other tools that can be installed on any Windows NT or Windows 3.1 (or higher) workstation running in enhanced mode to aid in remotely administering the network. These tools are located in the CLIENTS \SRVTOOLS directory on the installation CD-ROM.

Organizing Program and Document Groups Effectively

I discussed the details of setting up application groups on the local machine in Chapter 3, "Working with Windows NT." There I reviewed the procedures for creating new Program Manager groups, adding applications to them, and setting the application icon properties. That and subsequent chapters covered additional techniques for running programs—from both the command prompt and (using associations) File Manager. If you're a veteran Windows user, you're sure to know the basics of running applications and organizing Program Manager and File Manager to work the way you like best. However, a few quirks that exist in NT and NT networking are worth keeping in mind. They could be seen as pertaining to system administration—especially when you're setting up working environments for others.

Organizing Local Workstation Applications

How you organize your groups depends on how many users are going to use the local workstation. Obviously, if you're the only person using the station, configuration is straightforward; simply set up your groups as you like them. If you imported your groups from a previous Windows 3.1 setup, they already are arranged according to your preferences (assuming you were using Program Manager as your shell in 3.1). If you were using Norton Desktop or one of the many other better alternatives to Program Manager, you have some work to do until you can buy your favorite shell for use under NT.

TIP

I use a program called Toolbox from PC-Kwik to organize my applications and documents because it supports group nesting. Although it's written for Windows 3.1, it seems to work fine under NT, and it doesn't replace Program Manager—rather, it works with it.

You want to keep Program Manager around because, at least at the time of this writing, it's the only shell that works with NT's Registry and that lets you create common as well as individual groups. Windows 3.1 shells write their changes into various .INI files, which the Registry wouldn't know about. So keep Program Manager as your system shell, at least for the time being.

If you've added an NTFS partition to your hard disk, this might cause trouble with the pointers in your Program Manager icons. For example, I've added an NTFS partition on my second physical drive, which comes up in NT as drive D, pushing my original drive D to logical drive E. Under DOS, the NTFS partition isn't seen, so the FAT partition on Drive 0 comes up as C, and the FAT partition on Drive 0 is D. The following table outlines the differences in logical drive assignments under DOS versus under NT.

DOS		*NT*		
Drive 0	Drive 1	Drive 0	Drive 1	Drive 1
FAT	FAT	FAT	NTFS	FAT
C:	D:	C:	D:	E:

This is OK, except that under NT I now have *three* partitions: C, D, and E. Therefore, Program Manager icons that were imported from Windows 3.1 might not point to the correct drive letter to find the application; thus, when you try to run some programs, you get an error message. Changing the property settings (from D:\123\123.EXE to E:\123\123.EXE, for example) fixes the problem in NT, but because the changes sometimes are reflected in Windows 3.1 settings, you get a similar message when you try to run the programs under Windows 3.1. The section in this chapter titled "Disk Administrator" offers partition management tips that can solve this problem.

In a nutshell, if you're running dual operating systems, you want to add any NTFS partitions in such a way that they're logically the highest-letter drive, even above the CD-ROM drive if possible. That way, all Program Manager icons pointing to your FAT, HPFS, or CD-ROM drives work fine in both operating systems. Then, when you boot NT, NTFS partitions are added to the end of the drive list rather than to the middle.

TIP

One work-around for erroneous pointers is to use environment variables in CONFIG.NT and AUTOEXEC.NT startup files, as explained in Chapter 9, "Configuring Windows NT." Use a declared variable as part of the application or document's pathname in the Program Manager icon's Path property field.

Administration-wise, if you're the only user on the workstation and your network administrator believes you're fit for the job, you want to set yourself up with full privileges. Create a new account for yourself (don't use the Administrator account—that should be reserved for emergencies) and give yourself Administrator status. Then set your Desktop colors, fonts, File Manager preferences, Program Manager groups, and so on.

Even if you're the only user on the workstation, you might want to create a few Common Program Manager groups anyway, rather than having them all be local to you. Why? Sometimes you might have a guest come over to use your computer, or you might want to log on using the real administrator's account (in case yours gets messed up, for example). If you have your most-used programs (such as a word processor, comm program, or whatever) in a Common group, it appears in Program Manager when you log in under these other accounts.

NOTE

Some application installation programs (for example, VCNT++) create Common groups, but still allow for the setting of user-specific details such as environmental settings. So, although the program group might appear for all users, other relevant settings created during installation might not appear for users other than the one who installed the program.

Multiuser Workstation Setup

If you're going to be sharing a workstation with other users, you'll have to coordinate who's going to be the big cheese on the workstation or if several of you are. In any case, you might want to share access to some programs and documents. So, from the Program Manager perspective, you should discuss this with your coworkers and decide which programs should go in Common groups. If you don't see the other workers, the discussion could transpire via e-mail. In any case, set up the applications in directories that are available to each person with access to the group. Take special note of whether the applications in question must have write access to their own directories, because this can affect the type of permission you assign the directory. You don't want people erasing the application's files, so if it can run with read-only privilege, all the better. However, many applications want to write to an .INI file when you change preferences or quit the program, so you might have to set the directory's permissions a notch higher.

NOTE

See the section titled "Security Options with File Manager" later in this chapter for details on setting permissions for directories and files.

Additionally, each user on the station will probably want to set up his or her own personal directories, permissions on those directories, and network connections (if networking). Don't forget that you can set up a home directory for each user via User Manager, as explained later in this chapter.

Organizing Network Applications

If the workstation is regularly running on a network, you have an additional headache when it comes to application organization. Again, two major issues—drive names and directory permissions—come up. But on top of this, you have share contingencies on the other workstations to contend with. Let's look at things one step at a time.

First, the problem of shifting drive letters gets even worse than it is on a single workstation with two operating systems and NTFS partitions. As you know, when you connect to a network drive, NT assigns it the next available drive letter unless you specify otherwise. If your Program Manager application or document icons point to Drive F, for example, and you or the user connected to a number of network drives in the wrong order, Drive F might be on Joe's computer instead of Jane's computer. The application you want to run might not be on Jane's computer, and the directory structure probably is different on Jane's computer anyway. The result is an error message.

Second, there's the issue of directory shares. If you set up Program Manager icons for yourself or a user, and those icons point to an application or working directory that is on another machine (or if the user is accustomed to saving files on a drive of a particular letter), you have to be careful. When setting up an icon for an application on removable media or on the network, Program Manager *does* warn you that you might not be able to access the application in the future, and the point is well taken. If the network workstation (in this case we could call it an *application server*) containing the application isn't up and running, or the directory holding the application(s) isn't shared, you also get an error message when you double-click on a Program Manager icon pointing to an application in that directory.

The moral of the story is twofold. First, consider whether using network workstations as application servers makes sense. Maybe it doesn't. Often, it's less of a headache for an administrator to copy entire application directories to each workstation (especially in a peer-to-peer network) than to deal with users who can't get their applications to run. Although this arrangement consumes more disk space, at least the user always has access to the application.

Second, if you *are* going to use remote workstations to hold applications, ensure that each user's File Manager is set to restore the necessary connections at boot time and that connections are assigned the correct drive letters. Also, explain to users that an error message probably means that the remote workstation isn't up or that the directory isn't shared, and tell them how to handle that. If you want to set up a dedicated application server (a computer just for dishing out applications and possibly data files), that's another solution. But just make sure that the server is always on and that permissions allow an adequate number of users access to the files and directories if there's going to be a heavy traffic load.

TIP

Set the user limit on a directory with File Manager's Disk | Share As command.

TIP

You can automate the process of restoring shares in the appropriate order by using a logon script. Logon scripts can be generic (for group-specific configurations) or user-specific.

Control Panel's Server Applet

The Control Panel's Server applet displays resource connections, the number of users connected to the workstation over the network, names of files that are open, and who should be alerted in case of administrative alerts.

This icon is mostly for use by system administrators or those administering their own standalone systems. It provides several important views of your network and lets you control aspects of network operations, called *server properties.* It lets you

- see who's connected to the local system's directories
- disconnect network users from the workstation
- see which local resources are shared
- see which local resources are open by others
- manage directory replication
- control who receives important system alert messages—for example, when a power outage occurs

Running the Server applet brings up the dialog box shown in Figure 10.1.

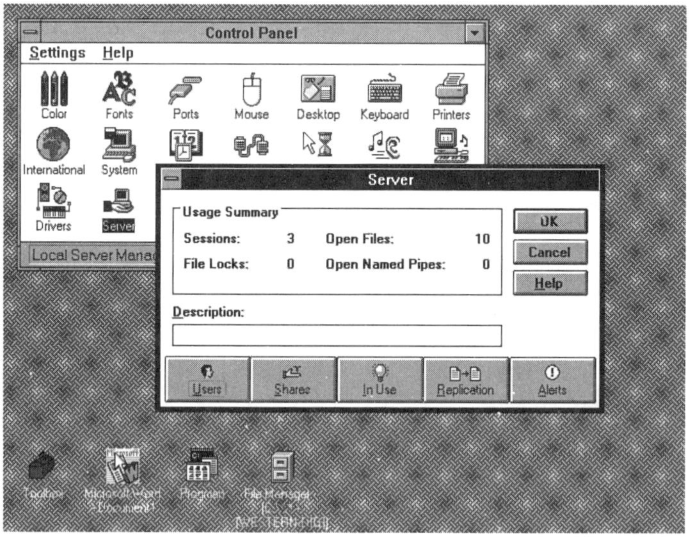

FIGURE 10.1.
The Server dialog box.

For starters, you see a report of several key factors of your server's usage:

Heading	*Description*
Sessions	The number of users connected
Open Files	The number of files users have open
File Locks	The number of files currently locked by users
Open Named Pipes	The number of named pipes currently open
Description	The description for your computer

What you can do on this particular screen is simply change the description of your computer. To reach the other functions, you have to click on one of the five buttons at the bottom. Here's what they do:

Button	*Description*
Users	Examines who's using your system resources, which resources are open by each user, and (if you wish) disconnects any user from such resources.
Shares	Basically the reverse of the preceding choice. Instead of showing a listing organized by user, this option lists your shared resources (printers or directories, for example) and shows who's using each one. Again, you can disconnect any or all users from the shared resource.
In Use	Displays which shared resources are open.
Replications	Manages the importing of a fixed set of directories and their files from an NT Server machine. NT Server machines can export as well as import.
Alerts	Chooses a list of computers to be notified when administrative problems crop up on your machine.

Managing the Users Currently Connected to Your Machine

An earlier section discussed the need for knowing who's connected to your computer, especially when it comes to shutting down the computer or unsharing a directory in which others might have files open. Also discussed were reasons for not unsharing a printer where a print queue exists and jobs are pending (doing so cancels those print jobs).

Administrators have a particular need to closely observe the number and nature of connections remote users have to a machine, especially before undertaking a system shudown.

Because not all users have the right to shut down the system, or share or unshare directories and printers, this type of activity is rarely of concern to them. But even from a security perspective, an administrator might want to know at any given time just how many users are connected, who they are, and the number of files they have open. If for some reason the user poses a threat or fails to terminate his or her connection when asked, the Server dialog box can be used to force such a disconnection.

In any case, here's how to check who's connected to the workstation:

1. Run the Server applet from Control Panel.
2. Click on Users. The dialog box shown in Figure 10.2 lists the currently connected users and the resource they're partaking of.

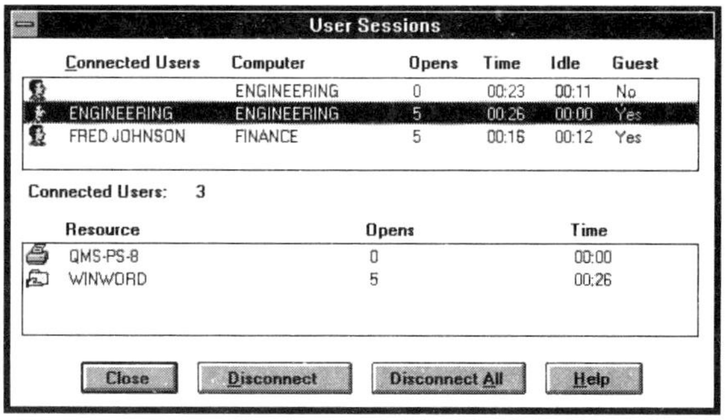

FIGURE 10.2.
Checking who's connected and which resources are being used.

3. When you click on a username in the upper portion, the resources that user is connected to are displayed below. Note in Figure 10.2 that some unnamed person on the ENGINEERING computer has five files open on the shared directory called WINWORD and is printing something to a shared printer called QMS-PS-8. Fred Johnson on the FINANCE computer also has five files open. Also listed are the elapsed time the user has been connected, how much time has elapsed since the user did something that affected this connection (such as save a file), and whether the user is logged on as a member of an account other than Guest.
4. You have only two real choices here if you're going to take action (besides closing the box, of course, if you're just observing):
   - You can select a user by clicking on that name and then clicking on Disconnect.
   - You can click on Disconnect All to get everyone off your system in one fell swoop.

   In either case, you're prompted to confirm your choice.

TIP

Want to know more about which files are open, and how to close only specific ones? Read the next section.

WARNING

You probably will cause a loss of data if you disconnect users with files open. Warn them first via a phone call, a visit to their office, or the Chat program, and give them time to close files and disconnect from your computer.

Seeing Which Specific Resources Are Being Used

Before you disconnect a user, you might want to know more than just that he or she has five or 10 files open. Getting a listing might be useful, even if just to examine network traffic flow and specific file demand.

1. In the Server dialog box, click on the In Use button. A dialog box listing all open resources (meaning those in use by another user) appears, as shown in Figure 10.3.

FIGURE 10.3.

Checking out the resources open by other users.

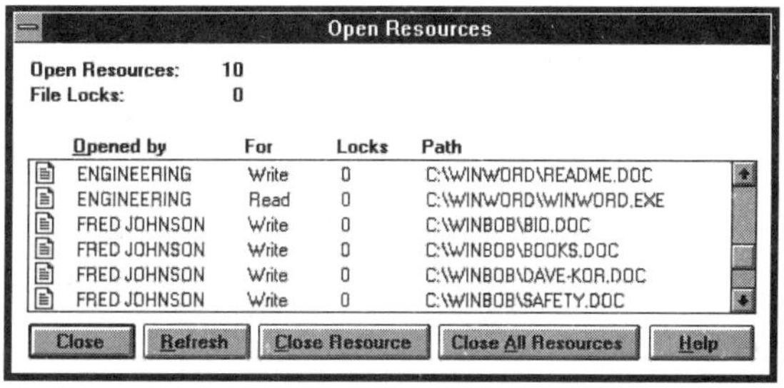

2. As with the previously described Users dialog box, you can pick a specific resource to close, or close them all. Clicking on Refresh updates the box to display the latest situation. (This is important, because people might have closed or opened files since you opened the box.)

Managing Shared Resources

Once you get in the sharing mood, it's sometimes hard to remember what you've offered to the world. How many directories have you shared? What are their sharenames? Which printers or other devices (such as fax modems) have you made available to other users? Which named pipes are available to others? The Shares button can tell you.

1. In the Server dialog box, click on Shares. A dialog box like the one shown in Figure 10.4 appears.

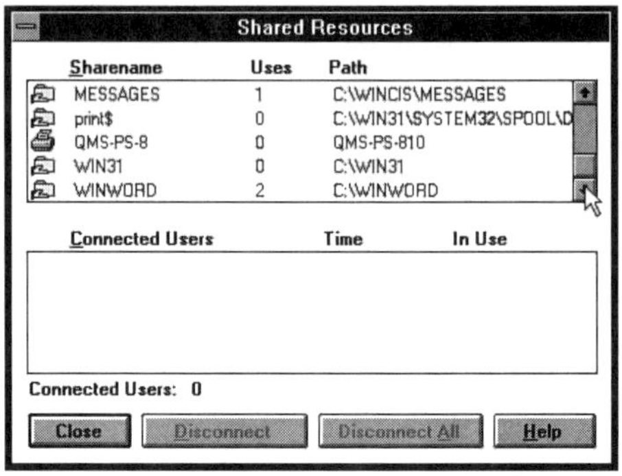

FIGURE 10.4.
Checking the list of your shared resources.

2. Scroll the list to see what's shared. In some cases, the items are things you didn't even know existed, much less that they were shared. Some of the items are so-called "special shares"—shares the computer arranged for all by itself. Don't worry about it. Each item has an icon suggesting, at least, the type of item it is:

What the Icon Looks Like	*What It Represents*
A hand holding a file	Shared directories
A plug	Shared named pipes
A printer	Shared printers
A question mark	Miscellaneous: other types of shares that NT can't classify for some reason

You also can see the following:

Item	*Meaning*
Sharename	Items available to others on the network. Remember that a share with a $ after its name is an administrative share. Only other NT administrators can access it.
Uses	The current number of connections to the resource.

Item	*Meaning*
Path	The pathname of the resource, typically a drive/directory path, although it could be a printer path—that is, the name the printer was given when it was created.
Connected Users	Who's connected to the selected resource. These people are listed in the bottom of the dialog box. When information about the user isn't available for some reason, the connecting computer's name appears.
Time	The length of time the user has been connected to the resource.
In Use	Does the user actually have a file open on the resource, or is he just connected to it? In other words, if you disconnected him, is he likely to lose data? If this column reads No, the answer is no.
Connected Users	This number near the bottom of the dialog box shows the total number of users connected to the highlighted resource.

NOTE

As I mentioned earlier, you might see special shares listed in the dialog box. These typically have the `$` after their names (for example, `C$` when drive C is shared).

Here's the scoop on common types of special shares:

Share Representation (Sharename)	*Description*
`driveletter$`	The default setting when sharing the root directory of a drive. It gives administrators and backup operators access to the drive (unless the machine is an NT Server, in which case server operators can access it as well).

Share Representation (Sharename)	*Description*
`ADMIN$`	A resource used by the internals of NT for its own purposes. The path of such a share always points to the directory where NT is stored. Only administrators, server operators, and backup operators are allowed access. Administrators use these heavily to access and troubleshoot user-related problems easily.
`IPC$`	An internal NT resource used for sharing named pipes. It concerns remote administration of a workstation.
`PRINT$`	An internal NT resource used for remote administration of printers.
`REPL$`	Only on NT Server. Pertains only to systems set up to act as "replication export servers."
`NETLOGON$`	Only on NT Server. Used by the system to manage a remote logon from another domain.

3. Click on the shared item you want to investigate. The names of the current users appear in the lower window of the dialog box, with an indication of how much time has passed since each user connected to the resource. Also, the total number of users is listed, along with a Yes or No in the In Use column indicating whether the user of the resource has files open at the current time.
4. To disconnect a user, select the user and click on Disconnect. To disconnect everyone, click on Disconnect All.

CAUTION

Note that this disconnects users from any and all resources they have open, which could cause loss of data, particularly if data files are open for the user's applications. You are alerted to that effect in a confirmation dialog box that you must okay before NT executes the disconnection.

Importing Replicated Directory Groupings

NOTE

Directory replication is an NT Server option that makes it easy to maintain (synchronize) identical directories of files on multiple computers, based on a single source computer called an *export server*. Because this topic pertains to NT Server–based networks and domains, it's covered in Chapter 16.

Managing Alerts

The final administrative option on the Server applet covered in this chapter is the Alerts button. This button enables you to view and manage who will be alerted to important system developments such as an impending power-down or other system alerts originating at the specific workstation. Typical messages pertain to the following:

- Access problems
- Printer problems
- Security violations
- User session problems
- UPS-controlled shutdown

Alerts won't happen unless two preconditions exist:

1. The source computer (the one you're configuring) must have the Alerter and Messenger services running.
2. The destination computer(s) must have the Messenger service running.

NOTE

To check whether these services are running, use Control Panel's Services applet. The Messenger service typically is started automatically at NT boot time. Alerter normally is started manually, which means either when an application or the operating system calls it or when you manually start it from the Services applet. If your alerts aren't being sent and received properly, check that the proper services are running. You might have to start Alerter manually with the Start button or change its setting to Automatic and reboot.

To manage system alerts, follow these steps:

1. Run the Server applet in Control Panel. The dialog box shown in Figure 10.5 appears.

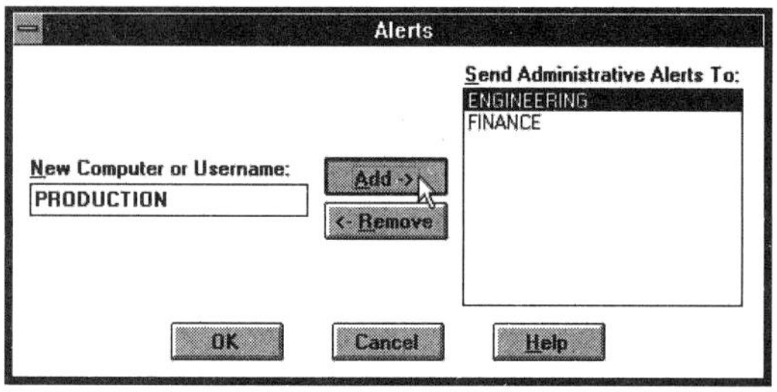

FIGURE 10.5.
Configuring recipients of alerts.

2. Type the name of the computer or user you want to be a recipient of alerts. If you enter a computer name, any user on the system receives the alerts. If you enter only names of specific users on a computer, only those users receive alerts. Other users on the computer at that time don't receive an alert.
3. Click on Add. (To remove a recipient or computer, highlight it on the right side and click on Remove.)
4. Click on OK in this box and in the Server dialog box.

NOTE

Although you can add Windows for Workgroups computers to the list of recipients, these computers won't receive alerter messages unless they're running Windows for Workgroups version 3.11 and are also running WINPOPUP, which can be enabled via their Control Panel's Network Logon button.

User Manager

User Manager is one of six applications found in the Administrator's group in Program Manager. As a system administrator, you'll rely on this program to

- add new user accounts to the workstation
- modify existing user account settings, such as name and password
- set a logon "script" or batch file that executes when the user logs on
- delete user accounts from the workstation

- assign a user to one of several permission sets, called "groups"
- assign or reassign the permissions given to each group
- set workstation policies such as minimum password length and account locking
- define which items you want in an optional audit trail of system activity

When you run User Manager, you see the window shown in Figure 10.6. The number of users varies, depending on your system.

FIGURE 10.6.
User Manager.

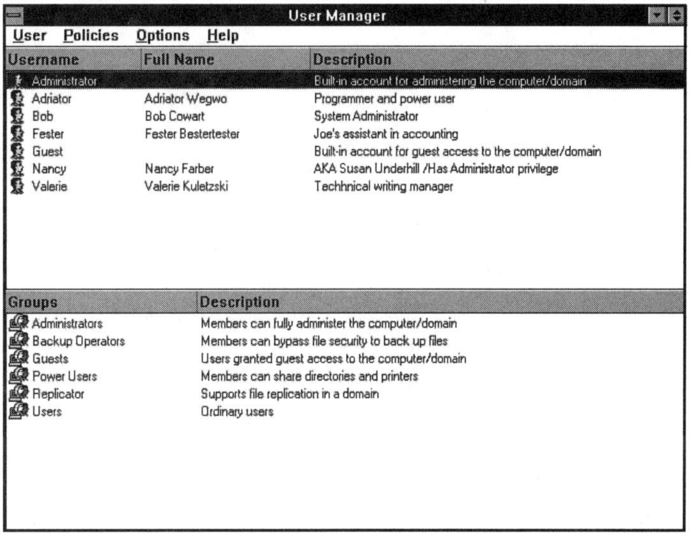

Note the upper and lower panes. The upper pane lists the accounts that already exist on the system. Each account has a name, a full name, and a short description line for identification purposes. The bottom pane lists the groups or categories of users that exist on the system. All accounts must fit into one of these groups. A group is defined by a set of rights and privileges. Assigning people to a group means that you don't have to construct their privileges from scratch. Because NT has so many security features, this would be a formidable job.

NOTE

However, if none of the existing groups meets your needs, you can fine-tune one of them or create your own group definition. You'll learn how to do this later.

Who Can Do What

Not all users can use User Manager equally. Because the program is primarily an administrative tool, it makes sense that its use is restricted to classes of users with higher privileges. Depending on your privilege level, you might or might not be able to execute all the menu commands. In other cases, it might look as though you're executing the command, but changes you make won't actually go into effect.

Here's the breakdown of who can do what:

Class of User	*Rights*
Users	Create groups, delete groups, and assign any account membership in the groups created by them. This doesn't mean that User group members can assign themselves membership in the Administrators or Power Users group in order to give themselves all rights on the computer. They can only create more User-level groups.
Power Users	Create, modify, and delete accounts and groups. This includes adding and removing accounts from the Power Users, Guest, and Users groups.
Administrators	Create, modify, and delete accounts and groups, assign passwords, set audit trails, set system-wide policies, and set user rights for each group.

Adding, Deleting, and Renaming User Accounts

The User Manager functions you're likely to use include adding or deleting user accounts. When NT is installed on a workstation, two accounts are automatically created—Administrator and Guest. At install time you're also given the option of configuring one user account (called the *initial user* account) by supplying a login name, full name, and password. Therefore, the typical newly installed system has two or three accounts. The Guest account is serviceable for occasional use by visitors to the system. However, you want to create separate accounts for any users who use the system regularly so that they can be given individual Program Manager groupings, File Manager connections, security privileges, and so on.

The initial Administrative account is created at setup, when you're prompted to enter a name and other information. By default, the name on this account is Administrator, and the password is *admin.* However, this can be changed via User Manager or by pressing Ctrl-Alt-Delete and entering a new password.

WARNING

If you forget this password, you're in trouble, because you won't be able to administer the system. There are a couple of fixes. First, the default User account that is added at installation time also has Administrative privileges, so logging in under that account allows password alteration. Second, you can use the Emergency Repair Disk. Finally, if you're on a network, another administrator can log onto the machine remotely and change the password. As a rule, however, it's a good idea to create an administrative account for each person who will have administrative privilege. Don't just let each administrative-level user use the built-in Administrator account. This way, if one account password is lost, another user will be able to access the administrative tools and commands reserved for administrators. Also, if each administrator has a unique account, auditing can be used to determine whose activities are adversely affecting system security.

TIP

If the Domain Admin group is removed from the local Administrator account, the computer can't be administered by any domain administrator except for those with local administrative accounts. If a new group is created and added to the local Administrator account, only members of this group will be able to administer the computer. This feature can be used to prevent access to sensitive computers or data on the network.

The guest account is a convenience that gives a casual user access to the computer but not the right to wreak havoc. The guest account is automatically created during setup and can't be removed, although it can be renamed to something like Visitor. Its rights can be altered by the administrator, however, so conceivably, a nefarious (or unwitting) administrator could give away precious rights to any passerby who logs on by typing `Guest` and entering no password. As a protection, an administrator might want to disable the guest account. On NT Server systems, this is the case by default.

Adding a New Account

To add a new account, follow these steps:

1. Choose User | New User. The dialog box shown in Figure 10.7 appears.
2. Fill in the Username, Full Name, Password, and Confirm Password areas. The Description is optional. The Username can be as long as 20 characters, but it must

be unique and can't be the same as a group name for the workstation (*administrators, users,* and so forth). Also, you can't use the following characters in the name: <, >, ?, *, +, ,, =, ¦, ;, :, [,], /, \, ", or a space.

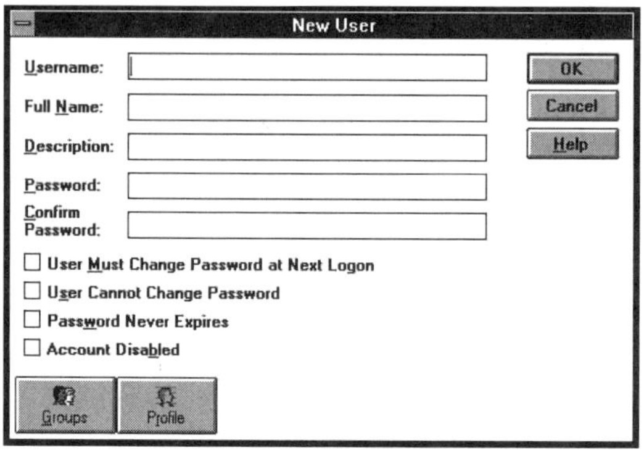

FIGURE 10.7.
Setting up a new user.

NOTE

Passwords can have up to 14 characters. Remember that uppercase and lowercase letters are treated differently. If you create a password of *ABRACADABRA,* entering `abracadabra` won't log you on.

TIP

Use a standard formula for usernames, because people will see them listed on the network or in various dialog boxes. The popular fashion is to use the first name followed by the first letter of the last name, such as *Johnd* for John Doe.

3. Fill in the appropriate check boxes, which are described in the following list:

Setting	*Effect*
User Must Change Password at Next Logon	Check this option if you're setting up an account for which you don't want to be the creator of the user's password. This typically is the case, because users should choose their own passwords.
User Cannot Change Password	Prevents the user from altering the password. Normally you want to do this

Setting	*Effect*
	only with accounts that aren't personal, such as Guest, for whom the password is, by default, blank (although this can be changed).
Password Never Expires	Prevents the password from expiring after the time set by the policies for the workstation. This time normally is set by the Maximum Password Age setting in the Account Policy dialog box (accessed by the Policy | Account command). You normally use this only with an account assigned to a service rather than to an individual. (The Scheduler and Directory Replicator services are typical services you might want to do this with. Custom services are another example. They can be assigned to an account via Control Panel's Services applet.)
Account Disabled	You can disable any account except the administrator's. Other accounts might call for disabling if a user is on vacation, for example. Or you might want to create and disable a standard user account template that you can easily copy for future new users using the User | Copy command. When you copy the template account, everything about the account is copied, but it's activated rather than disabled. You have to fill in the Username, Full Name, and Password for the new account.
Groups	Chooses which group(s) the user will be assigned to. This is explained in more detail later.
Profile	Sets the optional logon script (batch file) that will run when the user logs on, and the optional home directory (default directory) that the user's File Save and File Open dialog boxes default to for saving data files from applications. This is explained in more detail later.

4. After you click on OK in all necessary dialog boxes, the new user is added to the list of accounts.

Deleting an Account

Deleting an account is simple. You'll want to delete an account when a user moves to another department, quits the company, or no longer needs access to the computer.

WARNING

After a user is deleted, the account can't be restored, even if you create a new account with the same username and password. This is because NT assigns each new account a unique number (called a security identifier or SID) and uses that number internally—not the username and password. For this reason, it's safer to disable an account (from the Properties dialog box, as explained later in this chapter) for a while first, just to see whether the account is needed over time. If it isn't, delete it later.

Here are the steps for deleting an account on the workstation:

1. Bring up User Manager.
2. Select the account by clicking on it. You can select multiple accounts if you want, which lets you delete multiple users in a single blow.
3. Choose User | Delete. The warning box shown in Figure 10.8 appears. You might have to confirm your choice several times.

FIGURE 10.8.
Deleting a user's account.

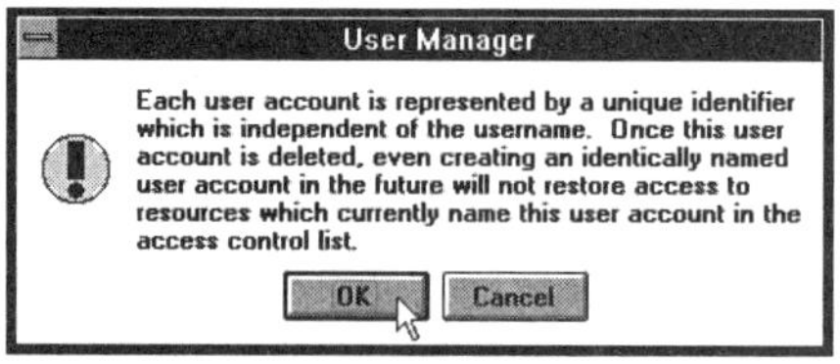

Renaming an Account

After an account is created, you might want to rename it. You can't do this from the Properties dialog box. Renaming is really nothing more than changing the username. For example, you might want to change Guest to Visitor, or Joe to Joseph.

1. Select the account.
2. Choose User | Rename. The dialog box shown in Figure 10.9 appears.

FIGURE 10.9.
Renaming an account.

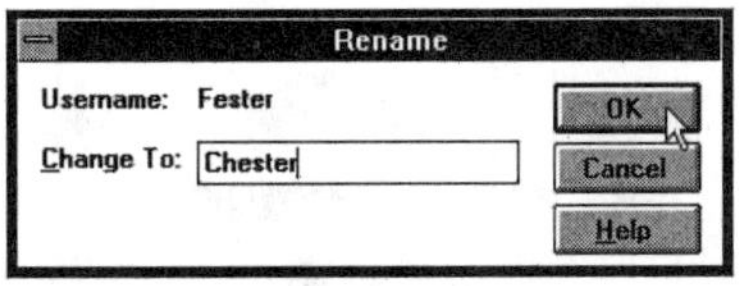

3. Enter a new name (up to 20 characters long) and click on OK.

Modifying Account Properties

Each account has a set of properties, just as files and Program Manager icons do. Modifying the properties for an account lets you redo everything you declared when setting it up (except the username, which is changed as explained in the preceding section).

1. Select the account. (You can select several accounts at once and change settings for all. Select multiple accounts just as you select multiple files in File Manager—by using Ctrl-click or Shift-click.)
2. Choose User | Properties. If you selected only a single account, the dialog box shown in Figure 10.10 appears. If you selected two or more accounts, the dialog box shown in Figure 10.11 appears.

FIGURE 10.10.
Properties dialog box for a single account.

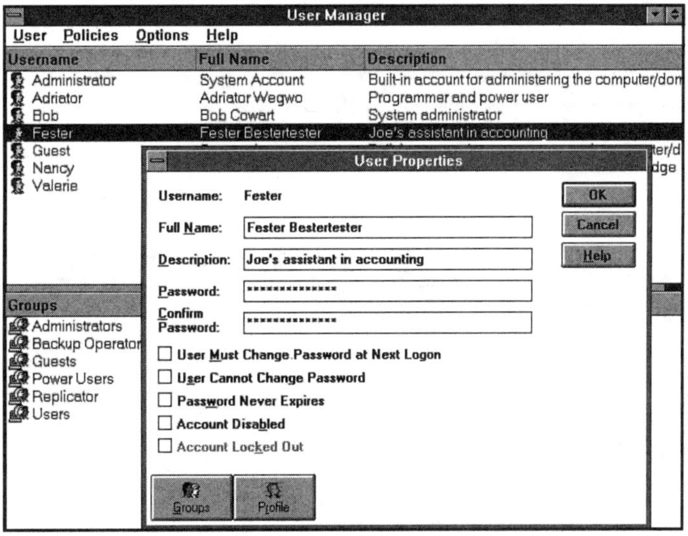

3. Change the properties as needed, including the Groups and Profile buttons. (Their use and meanings are described later.)

FIGURE 10.11.
Properties dialog box for multiple accounts.

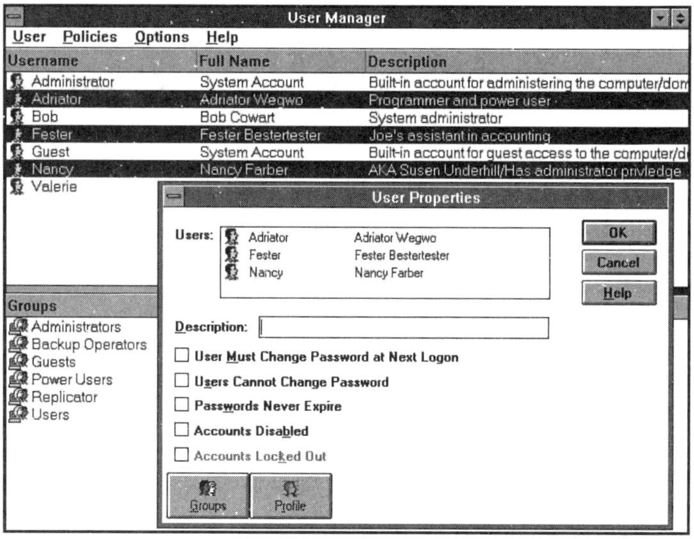

Note that if you're changing a group of users at once, the box has fewer settings. (This is useful when you want to change the description or the password requirements or disable a group of accounts quickly.) For example, you can't change the Username, Full Name, or Password because they're different for each user.

TIP

To change the properties for a single account, double-click on it.

NOTE

Property changes don't take effect until the next time the user logs on.

Managing Account Groups

Every account must be assigned to a group. The advantage of groups is that by defining a set of privileges for a group, you make it easy to add a user to the system and assign those privileges to the new user. Simply add the user to the group that has the desired rights.

As explained earlier in this chapter, NT sets up several groups at install time—Administrators, Power Users, Users, Guests, Backup Operators, and Replicators. However, you can create additional groups as you find the need. For example, you might like a group that has more rights than Users but fewer than Power Users. You also can redefine a group's rights and privileges so that all the members of that group have more or fewer powers when using the system. When you redefine a group's rights (properties), all accounts who are members of the group are quickly updated to reflect the changes.

In addition to all this, there's a little more confusion. There are two types of groups in NT—local and global. Mostly you deal with local groups when administering a workstation. Local groups are sets of privileges that can be used only on the local workstation. Global groups have a different icon and can be used anywhere in the domain or by trusted domains connected to your domain. (Refer to Part III of this book for more information.)

Assigning an Account to a Group

When you bring up User Manager, all existing groups are displayed in the lower pane. Based on this knowledge, you can then decide to which group you want to assign a new user.

Suppose you're creating a new user account. Here's how to assign its group membership:

1. After the upper section of the New User dialog box (Username and so forth) is filled in, click on the large Groups button at the bottom of the dialog box. The Group Memberships dialog box, shown in Figure 10.12, appears.

FIGURE 10.12.
Assigning a new account to a group.

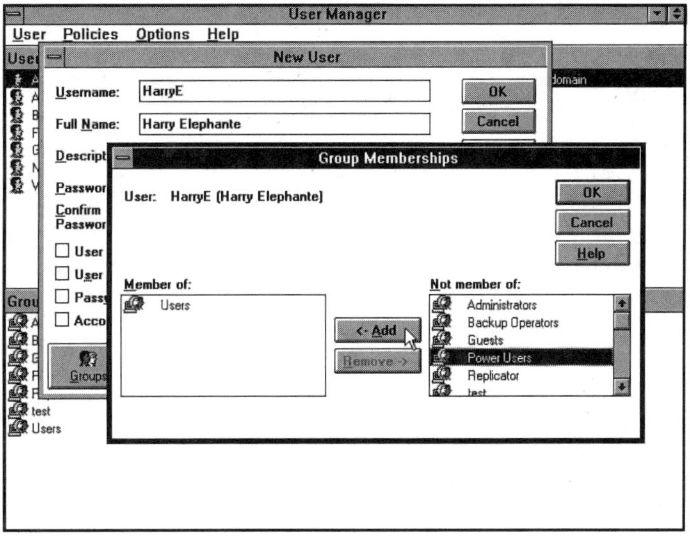

2. By default, new accounts are made members of the lowest-empowered group—Users. You can then add groups to or remove them from the list. In the list on the right are the existing groups from which you can choose. Click on any groups you want to give the new user admission to, then click on Add.

NOTE

An account can be a member of more than one group. You could be a member of, for example, Administrators *and* Users. However, because the rights of Users are a subset of Administrators, there's no need to be a member of both groups. For this reason, if you're upgrading a user's rights, you typically remove them from the previous assignment using the Remove button. However, some exceptions to this rule exist. Some groups have *capabilities* that others do not, and these capabilities can't be added to or removed from that group. Backup Operators, for example, have some capabilities that other groups don't. Thus, you might want to assign an account to the Users group and to the Backup Operators group. A table of the existing group rights and capabilities is included in the section titled "Managing Security Policies."

3. Click on any group in the left box from which you want to remove membership, then click on Remove.

TIP

You also can drag items between the boxes.

TIP

As explained in the section titled "Modifying Account Properties," you can alter the group assignment of an existing account or accounts via the Properties dialog box. Just select the account(s) in question and choose User | Properties. Then click on the Groups button and make the modifications, as explained earlier.

4. Click on OK.

Adding a New Group to the System

Normally, the canned groups are enough for typical networks and workstations. The rights and abilities of these groups were pretty well thought out by Microsoft, based on their in-house networks. Therefore, you're probably okay with just the Users, Power Users, Administrators, Backup Operators, and Replicators groups. Here's a brief breakdown of each of these groups:

Group	Description
Administrators	Can do anything on the workstation. The person who installed NT and the initial account are both assigned to this group. If the workstation is connected to an NT Server domain, all administrators on the domain are, by default, given this status on this workstation.
Power Users	Can add Program Manager groups, set the system clock, share directories, and install, share, and manage printers. Can create and manage User Manager groups, except the Administrator group.
Users	All new accounts are automatically given this level of permission. It supplies all the necessary rights to run programs. If the workstation is connected to an NT Server domain, all users on the domain are, by default, given this status on this workstation. Can't share or stop the sharing of directories and printers.
Backup Operators	Can use the Backup and Restore commands in the Backup utility provided with NT.
Replicators	Not intended for human users. This group is used with Control Panel's Services applet to set up the Replicator service. This option is covered later in this chapter.
Guests	Limited access only, such as logging on and using specific directories and files, but not changing any system settings, creating accounts, or managing and sharing resources.

If you're not happy with the supplied groups, create your own. Although the Microsoft manual suggests that copying an existing group saves you some legwork, it really only copies the account names, not the permissions and other settings, so you might as well start from scratch.

1. Choose User | New Local Group. You see the dialog box shown in Figure 10.13.
2. (Optional) Click on the Show Full Names button to see the full names of any users you add or who are by default already added (such as Administrator).
3. Fill in the Group Name and Description areas.
4. Click on the Add button to add members to the group. The Add Users and Groups dialog box, shown in Figure 10.14, appears.

FIGURE 10.13.
Creating a new account group.

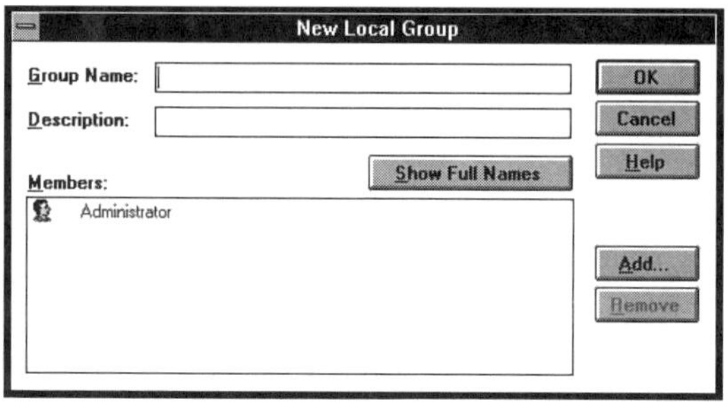

FIGURE 10.14.
Use this dialog box to add users to the new group.

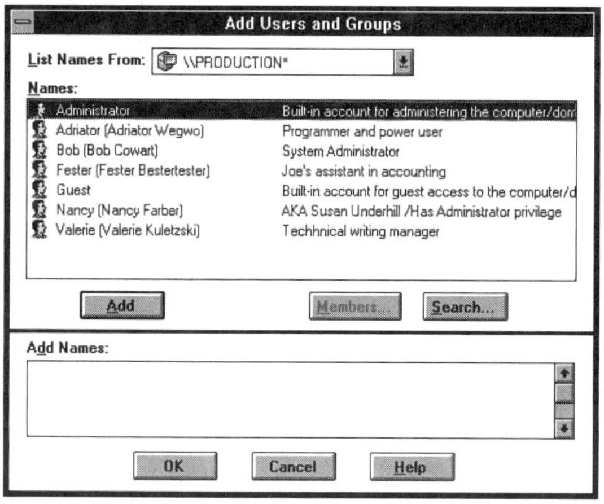

5. Click on a username, then click on Add. This adds the account to the list at the bottom of the dialog box.

NOTE

If you want to search the network for a particular user or group of users, click on Search. This brings up the Find Account dialog box, from which you can type in a user or group name and select which domain or workgroup to look in. This is how you add a remote user to a group on your workstation. Searching a large network can take some time, so use this command with care. For a large network, if you know the user's domain or workgroup name, select it first and click on the Search Only In radio button in the Find Account dialog box.

6. Repeat step 5 until all the desired names are added. When the list is complete, click on OK. The names are now added to the New Local Group dialog box.
7. Click on OK to create the new group, which appears in the User Manager window.

8. If you want, check the members by double-clicking on the new group name in the bottom half of the User Manager window. This brings up the Properties dialog box, which lists all members.

TIP

If you want to quickly assign a bunch of user accounts to the new group, select the user accounts *first*, before you choose User | New Local Group.

Changing a Group's Properties

The Properties dialog box lets you change the members in a preexisting group. It also lets you change the description of the group.

1. In User Manager, select the group whose properties you want to examine or alter.
2. Choose User | Properties. (Actually, the menu name "User" is a misnomer in this case; there should be a Group menu, but there isn't.) The Local Group Properties dialog box lists the current description and member roster, as shown in Figure 10.15.

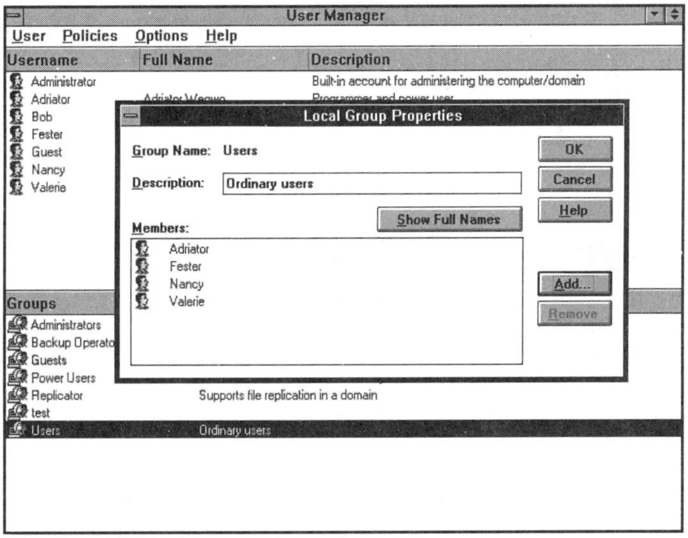

FIGURE 10.15.
A sample Properties dialog box, in this case for the Users group.

3. Type in a new description or edit the existing one if you want.

4. Edit the members list by clicking on Add, which brings up the Add Users and Groups dialog box (explained in the preceding section) or by clicking on an existing member and then clicking on Remove.
5. Click on OK, and the properties are altered.

NOTE

Rights and Permissions are different from one another, and each is different from Properties. Properties for groups, as you see here, include only the description of the group and who's in it. Rights apply to the system as a whole, enabling members of a group, for example, to share directories or printers. Rights are set using the Policies | User Rights command, as explained later in this chapter. Permissions apply to specific objects, such as a given file, directory, or printer. Permissions typically are set by the owner of the object using a dialog box's Share check box or by other means.

Deleting a Group

You can easily delete a group using the User | Delete command. However, just as when you delete a user, you can't reinstate a group. Even if the new group has the same name and members as the old one, it won't have the same properties and access rights. You have to re-create the group from scratch.

Follow these steps to delete a group:

1. Highlight the group name in the User Manager window.

CAUTION

Don't delete any of the NT-supplied groups—Administrator, Backup Operators, Guests, Power Users, Replicators, or Users.

2. Choose User | Delete. The box shown in Figure 10.16 warns against such an action.
3. If you're sure you want to delete the group, click on OK.

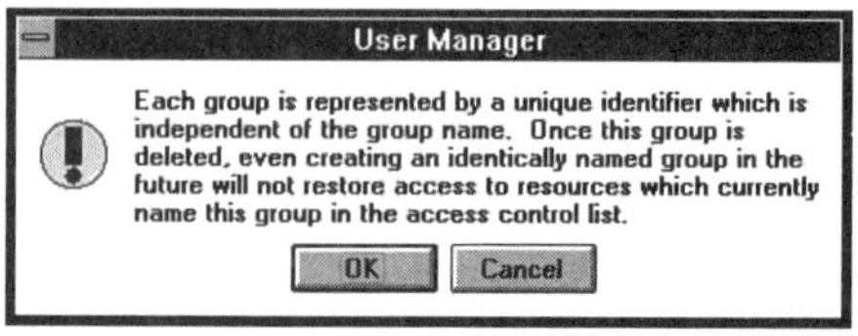

FIGURE 10.16.
Use care when deleting a group.

Managing Account Profiles

Each user account has special settings, called its *profile*. This profile contains some useful (though optional) settings:

- A *logon script*, which runs when the user logs on. This can be a .BAT file (DOS batch file), a .CMD file (NT batch file), or an .EXE file. This is not unlike putting such a program in the Startup group. The advantage is that the administrator can easily assign the startup script to a number of users.
- A *home directory*, which is the default directory that File | Save As and File | Open dialog boxes use when saving or loading files for use with applications. This makes easier work for administrators who want to back up or delete data files belonging to an individual user, because chances are good that the user's files will be in one directory. The home directory setting also determines the active directory when a command-prompt session is run. This directory can be a local or network directory.

To set up the profile, follow these steps:

1. Select the user's account in the upper half of the User Manager window. If you want to set the profile for a number of users, select them all. Shift-click for contiguous accounts, and Ctrl-click for noncontiguous accounts.
2. Press Enter or choose User | Properties. The Properties dialog box appears, listing the selected accounts.
3. Click on the Profile button at the bottom. The User Environment Profile dialog box, shown in Figure 10.17, appears.

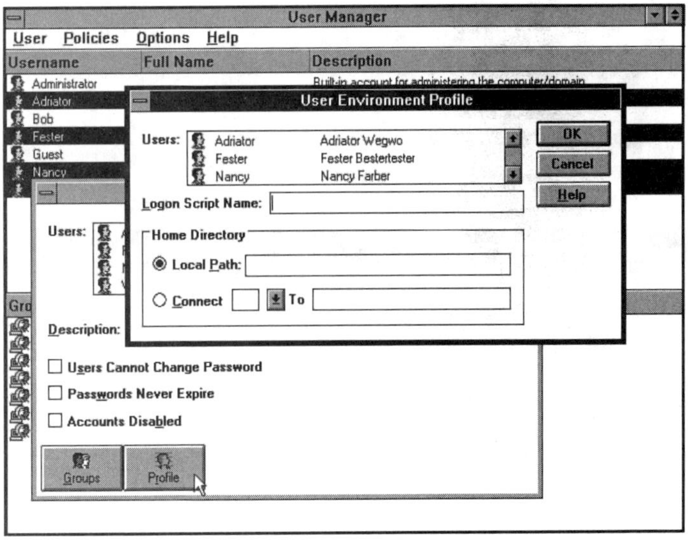

FIGURE 10.17.

Setting account profiles. In this case, several accounts are selected.

4. Enter the logon script name. By default, NT looks in the \SCRIPTS directory—\WINDOWS\SYSTEM32\REPL\IMPORT\SCRIPTS. You can use another directory if you specify it exactly as part of the file's pathname.
5. Next, you can optionally set the home directory. This can be on a local or network path. Choose the radio button that applies (Local Path or Connect). If you choose a local path, enter the directory name; for example, `c:\users\fredg` would store Fred G.'s files. NT creates the \FREDG directory under the existing \USERS directory for you. If you want to use a network directory, you must specify the logical drive letter the network directory will connect to, as well as the network path. This is similar to connecting to a remote directory in File Manager, but it happens before File Manager runs (right as the user logs on), so it won't interfere with File Manager. It just bumps up the drive letters a notch. Click on Connect, choose the drive letter from the drop-down list, and type in the network path (for example, `\\accounting\user\fredg`).

WARNING

If you're setting the profile for a number of accounts at once, you might not want to modify the Home Directory setting unless you want the whole group to have the same directory. It's better to modify the accounts separately for this.

TIP

You can have NT supply the directory name using one of its internal environment variables—*%username%*. Just enter this into the path (for example, `c:\users\%username%`). If the user's name is FREDG, the result is c:\USERS\FREDG. If the username is longer than eight characters, NT tells you it can't create the directory and that you must create it manually. Type in a shorter version of the username, such as `josephi` instead of `josephine`, and it will work.

NOTE

If you don't enter a home directory, NT uses the default home directory, which is \USERS\DEFAULT on the NT drive.

Managing Security Policies

Security policies are higher-level rights policies that are either system-wide in influence or, at the least, affect an entire group of users. Three security aspects can be set from User Manager (via the Policies menu): the Account Policy, the User Rights Policy, and the Audit Policy.

Policy	*Purpose*
Account	Sets details about passwords: how long before they have to be changed, minimum and maximum password length, number of bad logon attempts before locking the account, and how long old passwords are remembered.
User Rights	Sets the system rights (such as shutting down the system) assigned to a group of accounts. For example, you could use this command to keep all Power Users from changing the system time.
Audit	Sets what types of security-related events (such as system logon and logoff, changes of user rights, and system restart) are monitored and stored in an audit file, which can later be reviewed by an administrator to see what users have been up to. The audit file is read using the Event Viewer application.

Account Policy

Follow these steps to change the Account Policy:

1. Choose Policies | Account. The dialog box shown in Figure 10.18 appears.
2. Make settings as desired. Remember that these settings apply to all users on the workstation.

Setting	*Notes*
Maximum Password Age	How long can a user keep the same password? The range is between 1 and 999 days. If you never want to require a change of password, enable Password Never Expires.
Minimum Password Age	How long must a user use a new password before changing it? Range is 1 to 999 days. If Allow Changes Immediately is on, the user can change the password as often as desired.

Setting	*Notes*
Minimum Password Length	All passwords must be at least this long. Longer passwords provide greater security. Range is between 1 and 14. Enabling Permit Blank Password allows some accounts (such as Guest) to have a blank password.
Password Uniqueness	Can you reuse an old password immediately or not? If not, how many password changes must occur before you can use a previously used password again? If the Do Not Keep option is selected, a user being prompted for a new password can just enter the same old one. This doesn't do much for security. If the Remember option is selected, you have to choose a number between 1 and 8. This doesn't work unless Allow Changes Immediately in the Minimum Password Age section is disabled.
Account Lockout	How many times can an account be accessed with a bad password before the account is locked? Range is from 1 to 999. If account lockout is enabled, the lockout counter can be further limited to the number of attempts with a specified number of minutes. This ranges from 1 to 99,999 minutes. The locked account can be automatically enabled within the range of 1 to 99,999 minutes, or the account can be permanently disabled until an administrator manually enables the account via User Manager. This option can prevent local hackers from entering your system. I highly recommend it.

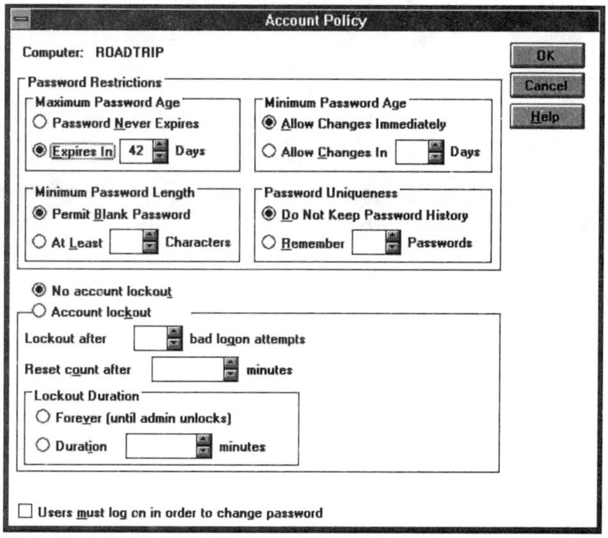

FIGURE 10.18.
Setting the account policy for the entire workstation.

User Rights Policy

To set the User Rights Policy, follow these steps:

1. Choose Policies | User Rights. The dialog box shown in Figure 10.19 appears. This box is a little confusing. What you set here is the rights that each *group,* not each *user account,* has on the system. Of course, all users in a given group are affected, but you aren't setting rights for individual users.

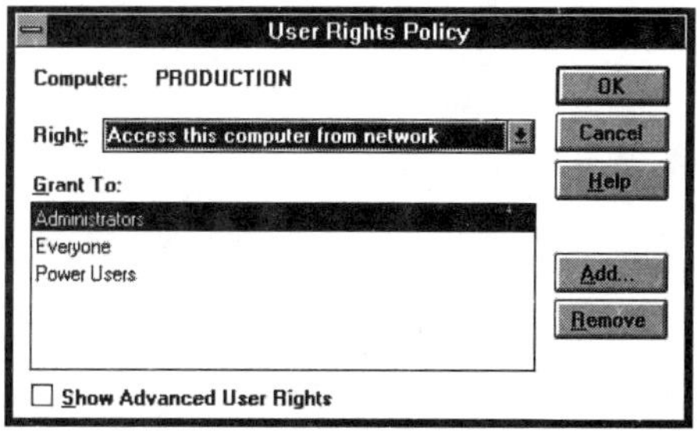

FIGURE 10.19.
Changing the rights for each account.

2. Select from the drop-down list the right you want to grant to a particular group. For example, say you want to grant the right to back up files and directories. Open the drop-down list and click on that right. In the bottom box are the names of groups that *already* have that right, so don't bother giving it to them again.

TIP

Some rights are pretty bizarre, and their meaning isn't immediately obvious. For example, "Create Permanent Shared Objects" is a pretty obscure right. Normally the rights displayed in the list make more sense, and complex rights aren't listed. You can show and grant the rights that are more advanced if you want, however. Just enable the Show Advanced User Rights box and reopen the drop-down list. The new items are added.

3. Now, suppose you want to give the selected right to a new group not listed. Click on the Add button. The familiar Add Users and Groups dialog box appears. Click on the group(s) you want to add to the list and click on Add, then click on OK. This adds the groups to the Policies box. If you click on the Show Users button, you can assign rights to individual user accounts.
4. Finally, click on OK to give the new right to the group(s).

Follow these steps to remove a right from an account group:

1. Select the undesired right from the drop-down list.
2. Click on the group from which you want to take the right.
3. Click on Remove.

Audit Policy

To set the Audit Policy, follow these steps:

1. Choose Policies | Audit. The Audit Policy dialog box, shown in Figure 10.20, appears.

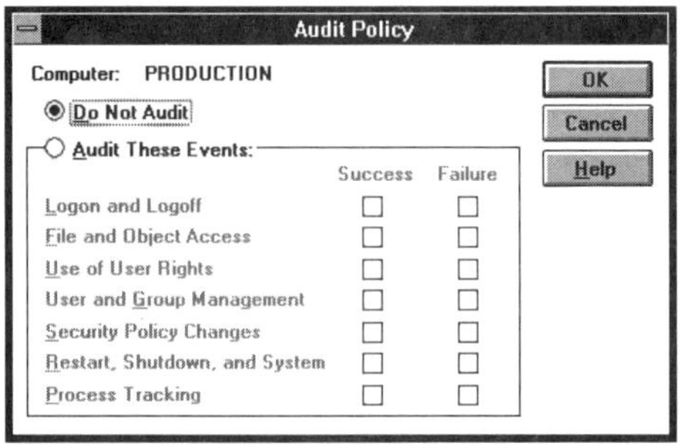

FIGURE 10.20.
Setting the system auditing policy.

2. By default, auditing is disabled. You might want to choose certain items to keep track of—for example, whether users are making security policy changes, or

whether a hacker has been trying to log onto the system. To activate auditing, enable Audit These Events.

3. Now the check boxes become available. Check one or both of the Success | Failure boxes for the event(s) you want to audit.

TIP

You should curtail your monitoring choices because the audit log's size is limited. Some events (such as File and Object Access) occur so often that they can fill up the log quickly. The size of the log is set via the Event Viewer's Log | Log Settings command. The Event Viewer is covered in Chapter 12, "Maintenance and Troubleshooting."

The following briefly describes your choices:

Event	*Notes*
Logon/Logoff	Makes entries when users log on or off the station. Also keeps track of remote users making a network connection to this station.
File and Object Access	Makes entries when users have accessed files, directories, or printers for which auditing has been set. Auditing of files and directories is set from File Manager's Security menu. Auditing of printer access is set from Printer Manager's Security menu.
Use of User Rights	Makes entries when any user takes advantage of an assigned user rights (as explained in the section titled "User Rights Policy").
User and Group Management	Makes an entry when a user changes a user account or group—for example, when an account is created, deleted, renamed, disabled, enabled, or has its password changed. Also when a group is altered by adding or deleting accounts or deleting the group totally.
Security Policy Changes	Makes a log entry when the Audit policy or User Rights policy is changed.
Restart, Shutdown, and System	Makes an entry when anyone restarts or shuts down the system. Does the same when any event happens that might jeopardize the system's security, including attempts to alter the Security (audit) Log.

Event	*Notes*
Process Tracking	Recall from Chapters 1 and 2 the discussion of processes. NT has many types of processes. Many simpler applications consist of only a single process; some contain multiple processes. The creation of file handles is considered a process, as are some accesses of objects (if done indirectly). In any case, entries are made indicating such processes. It might be of use to some managers to track the launch of and exit from applications. More obscure process tracking might be of lesser value.

Disk Administrator

Disk Administrator is the last of the major administration applications covered in this chapter. You'll find it in the Administrative Tools group (visible only to administrators).

With Disk Administrator, you can

- display various facts about your partition sizes and setup
- change drive letter assignments
- create and remove disk partitions of various types
- create, enlarge, and delete *volume sets*
- create and delete *stripe sets*

From the command prompt, you can

- change volume labels
- convert partitions from HPFS or FAT to NTFS format

None of these actions is likely to be necessary unless you find you need to rearrange your partitions, decide you want to convert FAT or HPFS partitions to NTFS, or have lots of extra room on your disks and want to improve performance or accommodate huge files with stripe and volume sets. Another possibility is that you've installed a RAID 5 disk controller and you want to set up stripe sets or volume sets on your machine (typically only on an NT Server machine).

When you install NT, Setup does disk formatting and system transferral automatically, essentially performing the same functions as the `FDISK`, `FORMAT`, and `SYS` commands in DOS. When you use Disk Administrator, the program partitions the disks for you. Then you can use the Tools | Format command to format the partitions.

CAUTION

Many of the changes you can make from Disk Administrator can erase entire volumes or hard disks. The good news is that the changes don't take effect until you exit Disk Administrator, at which time you're asked to confirm changes. Only if you say Yes are changes recorded. Make sure you want to save the changes you've made before you click on Yes.

Running Disk Administrator

NOTE

You must be logged on as an administrator to run the Disk Administrator program and make changes.

To run Disk Administrator, follow these steps:

1. Double-click on the Disk Administrator icon in the Administrative Tools group. If this is the first time you've run Disk Administrator, or if Disk Administrator determines that your physical hard-disk setup has been changed since the last time it was run, you see the message shown in Figure 10.21.

FIGURE 10.21.
Disk Administrator wanting to update its configuration record.

2. Click on OK if you get this message. Disk Administrator examines your disks and partitions, and then something like Figure 10.22 appears if you maximize the Disk Administrator window.

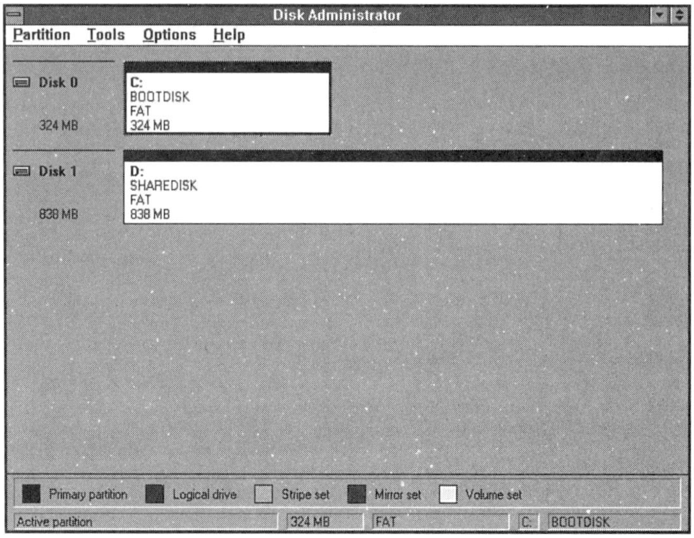

FIGURE 10.22.
The basic Disk Administrator screen with two disks.

3. Study the color key at the bottom of the screen. (This is a little more difficult on a gray-scale monitor, but it's possible.) Notice that divided disks have a primary partition and secondary partition(s). Also, it's likely that there's a little free space, especially if a disk is broken into several partitions. Disk Administrator displays unformatted free space as different from free space in an extended partition.

TIP

If you can't read the color key easily, you can assign different colors or patterns to partitions. Choose Options | Colors and Patterns. Choose a partition from the drop-down list, then a color or a pattern.

TIP

Note that early SCSI adapters maintained a test track (1M in size) when the drive was originally partitioned, but NT can format that 1 more megabyte if you want. Early Adaptec 1542b's and earlier have this feature. NT and newer SCSI controllers don't reserve this test track.

4. To work with a partition, simply click on it. A box appears around the partition, and the status line at the bottom reports a few facts about it—for example, whether the partition is the *active partition* (that is, the partition that contains the operating system and starts the boot-up process), the size of the partition, the type of file system, the letter assignment, and the volume name. This information also appears in the drive's representative box.

NOTE

If you have more disks than display at one time on the screen, scroll bars appear, letting you scroll down to the additional drives. Also, the program decides initially how to best display the sizes of drives and partitions relative to one another. You can change this for each separate drive with the Options | Region Display command. For example, you might want partitions displayed with bars representative of their relative sizes.

Working with Partitions

As you may know, hard disks often are divided into partitions. Until a hard drive is partitioned, the operating system can't use it. Partitions come in two types: *primary* and *extended.* Primary partitions can't be subdivided into logical drives; extended partitions can. (See Figure 10.23.) Extended partitions generally are more flexible in use than primary partitions. However, most operating systems require at least one primary partition.

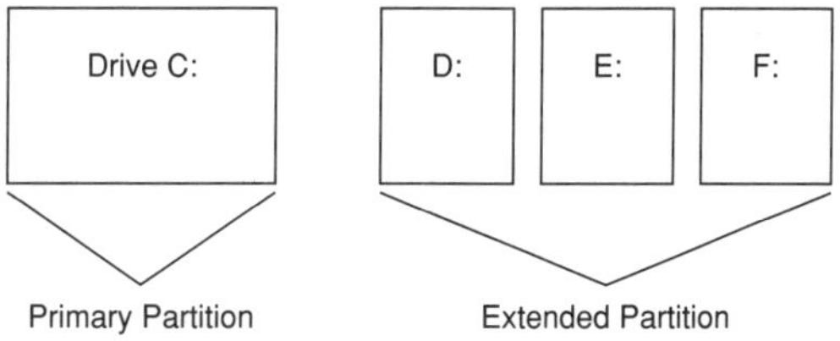

FIGURE 10.23.
The difference between primary and extended partitions is that extended partitions are more flexible.

Here are some rules about disk partitions under NT:

- Each drive can have up to four *primary* partitions or as few as zero.
- One partition per drive can be an *extended* partition. Each extended partition can be divided into many logical drives, each with its own letter, or none. Free space can be used for NT volume sets.
- If you're going to use DOS and NT on the same drive, the two operating systems can coexist only on a FAT partition, not NTFS.

- If you want operating systems other than DOS to coexist with NT, each needs its own partition. Check the manuals for the operating system to determine which type of partition is required.
- Intel-based systems always use Drive 0 to boot from, so the boot tracks have to be on that drive. RISC systems can have more than one system partition, letting you switch between them.

NOTE

Although on an Intel-based machine you have to put the boot files on Drive 0, NT lets you put the system support files and directories (\WINNT\...) on another drive or partition.

- Before a disk partition can be used, NT reboots and you have to format the partition from the command prompt.

Creating Primary Partitions

To create a new primary partition, do the following:

1. Click on any section of a drive's bar labeled as Free Space. Note that only two types of free space exist: *disk* free space and *extended partition* free space. You want disk free space.

TIP

Disk free space is represented by a bar with lines that slant to the right. Extended free space has lines that slant to the left. If you're in doubt about which kind you have, click on the bar and read the status line.

2. Choose Partition | Create. The Create Primary Partition dialog box, shown in Figure 10.24, appears.

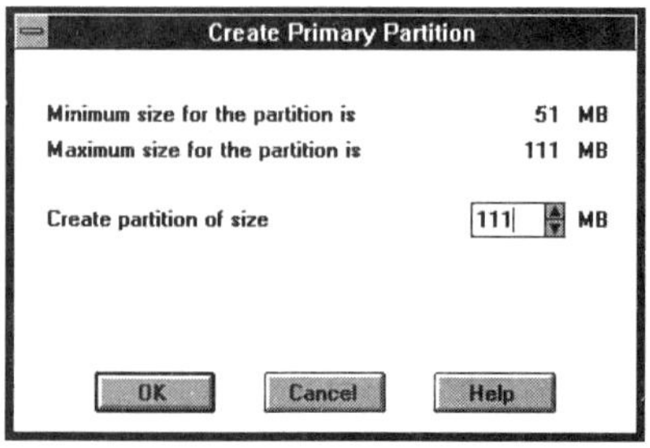

FIGURE 10.24.
Creating a new primary partition.

3. The program reports the minimum and maximum sizes that can be assigned to the partition. You don't have to use all the space. Remember that a disk can have up to four partitions, so you can leave one for use by another operating system, or you can assign some free space to an extended partition later. Adjust the size using the small arrows, or enter the desired size from the keyboard. Typically the size can't be less than 1M.
4. Click on OK.

You have to format the partition before it can be used, as described in the section titled "Preparing New Partitions for Use."

Creating Extended Partitions

If you have room on the disk, and if you don't already have an extended partition on the drive, you can create one.

1. Click on a free space bar. (This must be disk free space, not extended partition free space.)
2. As with creating a primary partition, a dialog box appears, asking for the size. Choose the size and click on OK.

If you want, you can create a logical drive in the new extended partition. This lets you use it to store directories and files. Otherwise, you must use the partition for fault-tolerance purposes within NT, such as volume sets and stripe sets. If you want to use some or all of the otherwise unused extended partition for setting up a logical drive, do the following:

1. Click on the extended partition space in the drive bar.
2. Choose Partition | Create. A dialog box asks the size of the logical drive. Choose the size and click on OK.
3. Move to the next section to format the partition for use.

Preparing New Partitions for Use

As I mentioned earlier, you must format a partition before the operating system can use it. This is done using either Disk Administrator's Tools | Format command or NT's `format` command, which is functionally identical to DOS's `FORMAT` command (with a few added capabilities):

1. Reboot the machine into Windows NT. This is imperative, because otherwise NT won't recognize any new partitions.
2. Log on using an administrator-level account.

3. Run a command-prompt session.
4. At the prompt, type `format x:` where *x* is the logical letter of the drive you just created. For more information about the syntax of the `format` command, type `format /?` or see Figure 10.25.

FIGURE 10.25.
The `format` command's syntax and arguments.

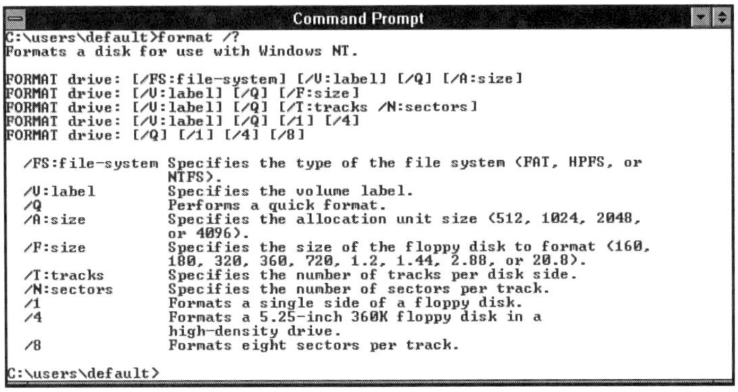
```
Command Prompt
C:\users\default>format /?
Formats a disk for use with Windows NT.

FORMAT drive: [/FS:file-system] [/V:label] [/Q] [/A:size]
FORMAT drive: [/V:label] [/Q] [/F:size]
FORMAT drive: [/V:label] [/Q] [/T:tracks /N:sectors]
FORMAT drive: [/V:label] [/Q] [/1] [/4]
FORMAT drive: [/Q] [/1] [/4] [/8]

  /FS:file-system Specifies the type of the file system (FAT, HPFS, or
                  NTFS).
  /V:label        Specifies the volume label.
  /Q              Performs a quick format.
  /A:size         Specifies the allocation unit size (512, 1024, 2048,
                  or 4096).
  /F:size         Specifies the size of the floppy disk to format (160,
                  180, 320, 360, 720, 1.2, 1.44, 2.88, or 20.8).
  /T:tracks       Specifies the number of tracks per disk side.
  /N:sectors      Specifies the number of sectors per track.
  /1              Formats a single side of a floppy disk.
  /4              Formats a 5.25-inch 360K floppy disk in a
                  high-density drive.
  /8              Formats eight sectors per track.

C:\users\default>
```

NOTE

If you created a partition but didn't give it a letter, go back to the preceding section and follow the instructions about assigning logical drives to a portion of an extended partition.

CAUTION

As usual, don't format a logical drive that already has data on it, unless you really want to trash the data. You'll be warned against this when you format.

5. You're prompted to enter a volume label.

TIP

To relabel the partition, use either Disk Administrator's Tools | Label command or the `label` command at the command prompt. Use the command syntax `label x:` where *x* is the drive letter. You are prompted to enter a volume label. If you change your mind about wanting to alter the label, press Ctrl-C. To display the current label from the command prompt, type `vol`.

Setting the Boot and System Partitions

So much for creating, formatting, and labeling partitions. Now for the story about which partitions boot the operating system.

As I mentioned in Chapter 8, "Installing Windows NT," and Chapter 9, "Configuring Windows NT," NT boots by first reading the boot track from what is known as the *boot partition.* This is the partition that the ROM BIOS points to for booting and is sometimes called the *active partition*—for example, by FDISK. The information in the boot partition is responsible for bootstrapping NT and getting it going. Assuming that happens successfully, numerous data files stored in the *load partition* are loaded. These are the files stored in the NT directory (for example, \WINNT and \WINNT\SYSTEM32).

> **NOTE**
>
> Both the boot and load partitions can be in the same partition or in separate partitions. They can be on separate disks, and even accessed by different controllers. They can be on partitions formatted as FAT, HPFS, or NTFS, and they can be on mirrored disks. However, they can't be located on a volume set, a stripe set, or a stripe set with parity.

Although the boot partition and the load partition don't have to be the same, they often are. If you installed NT on drive C of an Intel-based machine, the machine boots from drive C and gets all its system files from it as well. By contrast, if you installed NT on a drive other than C, the system and boot partitions won't be different. This is fine, and it offers you additional flexibility at install time—especially if you don't have 90M of free space on your boot drive.

What *is* imperative is that the boot partition be *active.* Being active means that the computer knows to use it to start up. Only one partition can be active at any one time, and the active partition must be a primary partition. In Disk Administrator, the active partition is the one with the asterisk (*) in its color-coded bar. On Intel machines, the active disk is always Drive 0. Only if you have multiple primary partitions on Drive 0 can you set another partition to be active.

The active partition on RISC machines is set using software that comes with the computer.

To set the active partition on an Intel-based machine, follow these steps:

1. Select the partition.
2. Choose Partition | Mark Active.
3. Click on OK.
4. Close NT and reboot. The operating system on the active partition will load.

NOTE

If there is only one partition on Drive 0 of an Intel-based machine, the Make Active command will be grayed out because no other possible active partitions exist.

NOTE

System partitions on RISC machines must be FAT partitions. Thus, you can't set security on just the NT system directories because FAT doesn't support this feature. If you want security on the system partition of a RISC machine, you must lock the whole partition for use only by administrators. Use the Partition | Secure System Partition command and then reboot to enable security. Issue the command again and reboot again to disable it.

Giving a Drive Letter to a Partition

Disk Administrator can pull an interesting and useful stunt. You can reassign logical drive letters in a permanent way. DOS lets you do this with the `ASSIGN` command, but it isn't permanent. When NT boots up normally, it checks out your hard disks and partitions and names them the same way DOS does. That is, the first primary partitions on each drive are named first, starting with Drive 0, moving to Drive 1, and so forth. These are named C, D, and so forth. Next, logical drives are named, continuing down the alphabet. Finally, additional primary partitions on each disk are named.

However, after you run Disk Administrator, things can change. Disk Administrator makes a record of the disk partition and logical drive assignments and stores them in a small database that doesn't change, even if you add a new hard disk or another piece of hardware—a CD-ROM drive, Bernoulli Box, or what have you—that might bump up the drive letters. This is called *static drive letter assignment.* (This is one solution to the troubles mentioned earlier in this chapter about Program Manager icons pointing to the wrong drives.)

You can alter the static drive letter assignments if necessary. Here's how:

1. Run Disk Administrator.
2. Click on the partition or logical drive you want to reassign.
3. Choose Tools | Drive Letter. The dialog box shown in Figure 10.26 appears. If you want to change the drive letter for a CD-ROM drive, choose Tools | CD-ROM Drive Letters. The dialog in Figure 10.27 appears.

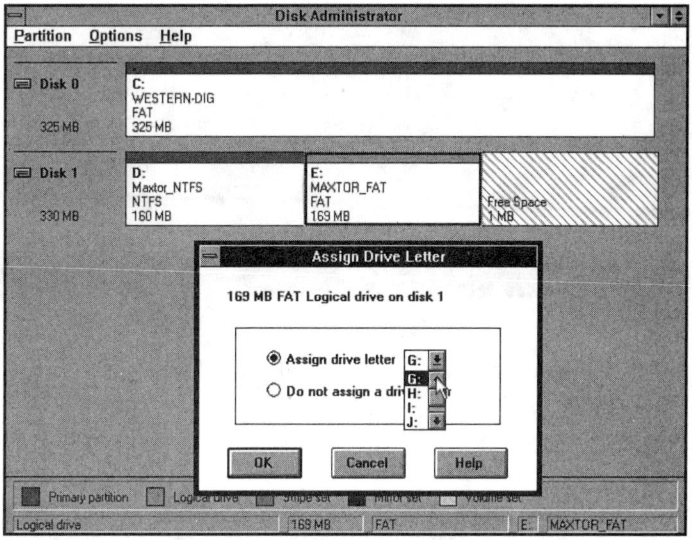

FIGURE 10.26.
Reassigning a logical drive to a new static letter.

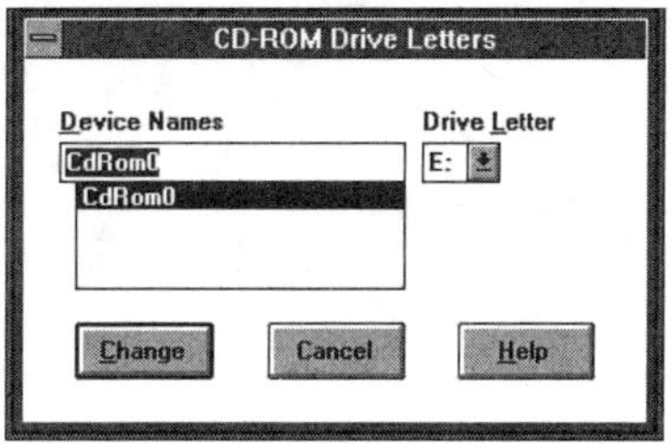

FIGURE 10.27.
Reassigning a CD-ROM drive to a new static letter.

4. Choose the letter from the drop-down list and click on OK. Alternatively, you can decide not to assign a letter at all by clicking on the Do not assign a drive letter option button. Then the partition isn't usable for storage of files and directories, but it still can be used by the operating system for stripe and volume sets.
5. Quit Disk Administrator. You're asked whether you want to save the changes you've made. Click on Yes, unless you've changed your mind. (Clicking on No abandons all the changes you've made this session.) You should see a dialog box informing you that `Disks were updated successfully` and that you should restart the computer. The dialog box implies that system shutdown occurs automatically, but I have had to do it manually. As reboot occurs, the NT Loader reports your partitions in the newly assigned order.

NOTE

You can't name more than 24 logical drives (C through Z). This is one of the reasons you can create volumes. You simply concatenate several physical drives into a single logical drive and give it one letter.

TIP

If you want to reverse the letters of two partitions, you must do a little shuffling. For example, to reverse D and E, rename E to F. Then rename D to E. Then rename F to D.

CAUTION

Be careful not to assign a new letter to the load partition (the one that holds the bulk of NT's files—for example, the \WINNT or \SYSTEM32 directory). If you do, NT has trouble locating the files. Also, be aware that reassignment of logical drive names might require adjustment of Program Manager icons, some Windows program .INI files, and some MS-DOS application pointer or initialization files.

Deleting Logical Drives, Partitions, and Volumes

You can delete drives, partitions, and volumes, with a few restrictions:

- On x86 machines you can't delete the partition containing NT's files.
- You can't delete just a portion of a volume or stripe set.
- Logical drives and volumes in an extended partition must be deleted before you can trash the partition.

1. Select the item you want to delete, be it a partition or a logical drive.
2. Choose Partition | Delete. A box warns of impending disaster, as shown in Figure 10.28.

CAUTION

Be sure you really want to erase the partition, volume, or drive. You can't restore it if you change your mind unless you first save the current configuration using Disk Administrator's Partition | Configuration | Save command.

FIGURE 10.28.
Make sure you want to delete the item before clicking on Yes!

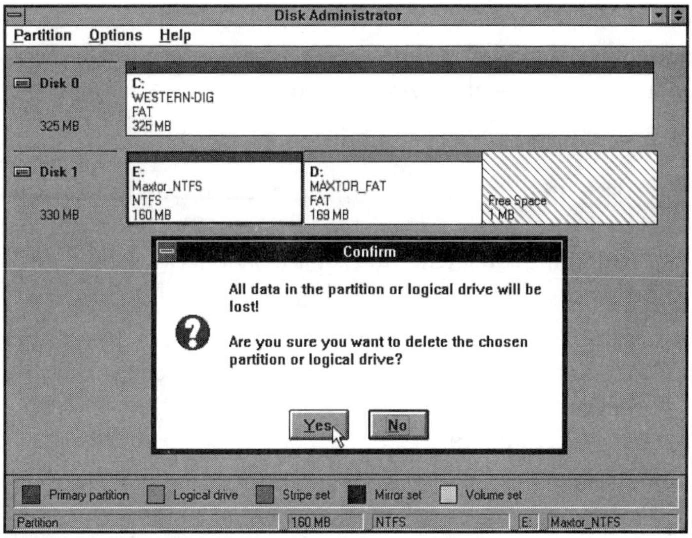

3. Click on Yes. The item is deleted, and free space becomes available on the disk.

Converting Partitions Between NTFS and DOS

In a typical Microsoft move to get you hooked, Windows NT makes it easy to convert existing FAT and HPFS partitions to NTFS format—much easier, in fact, than the reverse. You might want to do this as you become more comfortable with Windows NT and the available 32-bit Windows application mix grows richer. Eventually, I suspect most power users will bag their 16-bit applications and Windows 3.1 in favor of the more robust Windows NT. Obviously, this is what Microsoft is banking on too. The added security of file protection and convenience of long filenames offered by the NT file system are additional charms that might woo you away from the FAT system.

Whatever the reason, you can "upgrade" to NTFS using the `convert` command at the command prompt. The syntax is relatively simple:

```
convert drive: /fs:ntfs
```

`drive`	Specifies the drive to convert to NTFS.
`/fs:ntfs`	Specifies to convert the volume to NTFS.

NOTE

You can't convert the drive you're logged onto. Switch to another drive first.

Oddly enough, you have to specify the file system to convert to, even though the program only converts to NTFS. This suggests that later versions of `convert` will metamorphose a volume to additional file systems.

Want to convert an NTFS volume to FAT or HPFS? It's not so easy.

1. Back up the partition to whatever extent you feel is necessary. You can use the NT backup program (covered in Chapter 12) if you want, or any other means, such as bumming some temporary space on a network hard disk and copying all the files there.
2. Format the partition to the desired file system using the `format` command at the command prompt. Type `format /?` at the command prompt for the syntax, or refer to Figure 10.25.
3. Restore all the files and directories to the partition.

NOTE

There is one exception to the procedure just outlined. If the NTFS partition you want to reconvert has NT on it, neither the `format` command nor Disk Administrator lets you reformat it. However, you can get around this by running the Setup program (from the startup floppy disk, not the Program Manager icon in the Main group).

Setting Up Volume Sets

A volume *set* is a means of combining free space on a drive or a number of drives (up to 32) to form a single volume. In a sense, it fools the operating system into thinking that the volume is a single drive.

There are two primary advantages and one secondary advantage to using volume sets. The first primary advantage is that it provides a means of utilizing otherwise wasted disk space by combining small amounts of free space into a volume large enough to be useful. The other primary advantage is that it allows for the creation of huge volumes (in the gigabyte range, for example), combining several large partitions on separate disks. Such large volumes allow storage of huge files such as big databases. Finally, volume sets can improve disk I/O performance because data is more often read and written to several drives instead of just one. Because a disk controller can redirect data more quickly than a single disk can access the correct track and sector, using multiple disks effectively decreases the average access time of the volume.

NOTE

The down side to this scheme is that only NT can use the volume set. Other operating systems won't recognize it.

Windows NT fills up a volume set from the first drive in the set and moves along the chain. If a set consists of partitions A, B, and C, partition A is filled up first, then B, and then C.

Creating a Volume Set

Follow these steps to create a volume set:

1. Choose several areas of free space, either on one drive or across as many as 32 drives. Ctrl-click each area, just as you would to select multiple files in File Manager.
2. Choose Partition | Create Volume Set. You are advised of the size range possible. Choose the desired size for the total volume set.
3. Click on OK.

The volume set is created and assigned a drive letter. You must format the volume from either Disk Administrator or the command prompt, as explained earlier, before you can use it to store files and directories.

Enlarging a Volume or a Volume Set

You can enlarge a volume or a volume set to incorporate free space that might come available over time as your disk arrangement changes. Unfortunately, you can't *shrink* a volume. This would be a great feature, but Microsoft didn't build it in, at least not in version 3.5 of NT. To decrease a volume size, you must create a new volume and copy files into it, erase the original one, and rename the new volume.

NOTE

You can't extend a stripe set or mirror set.

To enlarge a volume or a volume set, do the following:

1. Select the volume or volume set.
2. Choose Partition | Extend Volume Set.
3. Enter a value within the range of acceptable values displayed in the dialog box.

4. Click on OK. The requisite free space is added to the volume and subtracted from the free space pool.

Deleting a Volume Set

You might want to delete a volume set to reclaim or reassign space or to remove a drive from the set. Unfortunately, you can't just remove one of the partitions from the set and keep on using the rest. Because data sectors are spread over the volume set as the set is used, this would be functionally akin to removing one of the platters of a hard disk and expecting it to continue being serviceable.

1. In Disk Administrator, select the volume set to delete.
2. Choose Partition | Delete.
3. Click on Yes in the Confirmation dialog box. All the data in the set will be lost, so you might want to back it up, copy it elsewhere, or check to make sure that nothing of value is stored in the volume.

Setting Up Stripe Sets

Stripe sets are similar in concept to volume sets. Free space on a number of disks (at least two and up to 32 physical disks) is combined to create a large volume. The advantage over volume sets is that overall throughput can be increased. Thus, a data stream destined for storage is broken up and *striped* across a number of drives, almost at once, rather than filling the volume from the "bottom up" (recall the discussion in the section titled "Setting Up Volume Sets"). The reverse happens when data is read from the disks.

In stripe sets, all the partitions must be the same size. For this reason, when you select a number of free areas across several disks, the smallest free space determines the common size for all the portions of the stripe set. Leftover space is returned to the system as free space that you can use in a volume set or a separate partition.

Stripe sets available in standard NT (not NT Server) are compatible with the industry standard known as RAID 0 (redundant array of inexpensive disks). RAID 0 is striping without parity, as opposed to RAID 5, which does record parity information and thus is less prone to catastrophic data loss in case of a single drive failure. RAID 0 has no fault tolerance, so if one drive fails, you lose all the data in the set. The improved throughput might be worth the gamble, though, and regular backups might be all the security you need.

NOTE

Stripe sets with parity (RAID 5), disk duplexing, and disk mirroring are limited to NT Server operation and are covered in Chapter 20.

Creating a Stripe Set

To create a stripe set, follow these steps:

1. Select multiple free space areas, starting with the first disk that has free space. Ctrl-click free space on subsequent disks (disks 2, 3, 4, 6, and so forth).
2. Choose Partition | Create Stripe Set. The maximum and minimum sizes are displayed in a dialog box. Set the desired size.
3. Click on OK.

Deleting a Stripe Set

Deleting a stripe set is like deleting a volume set:

1. Select the set in Disk Administrator by clicking on one of its portions.
2. Choose Partition | Delete.
3. Click on OK in the alert message box.

NOTE

Errors in volume and stripe sets are serious; when parity isn't used, the system can't recover from such a fault. If the error occurs while NT is booting, the set won't come online, and an error message is recorded in the Event Log. If the error occurs during the running of NT, you see a message of some sort reporting a severe disk error. Use the Event Viewer to examine the log for a description of the fault. You probably will have to delete and re-create the set.

Security Options with File Manager

Two last administrative measures need to be discussed before this chapter ends. Throughout this chapter, I've tried to emphasize the distinction between permissions and privileges. Again, permissions apply to specific objects, such as a file or a printer. Privileges are more global and apply to general actions a user might or might not have the right to perform, such as formatting a disk, changing passwords, or sharing a directory.

The two remaining topics pertain to permissions and a couple of other security measures (such as auditing) that you can set from File Manager and Print Manager. Most important, they determine which other users on the workstation have access to your resources. Less important, they let you see who's been using what.

Chapters 3 and 4 discussed sharing resources with others on the network and setting network access permissions. This section discusses the refinements you can make to access permissions. These options fall in the following three categories, which are listed on File Manager's Security menu:

Command	*Purpose*
Permissions	Lets you determine which group of users has access to files and directories and what they can do with them
Auditing	Lets you track who's using your directories and files
Owner	Lets you change who's in control of setting permissions

NOTE

These options are available only on the NTFS partitions. If the current window in File Manager is a FAT or HPFS drive, the Security menu options are dimmed. The only way you can control usage of FAT and HPFS partitions is when they're shared over the network; in that case, use the Share As dialog box to control access. NTFS partitions offer additional security over both the network and the local workstation.

File and directory security is managed by setting permissions. NT has a number of canned permission types that you can assign to individual users and to account groups. Choose file, group of files, or directory, then choose which permission(s) you want to assign to individuals or account group(s). The built-in permission sets for directories and files are different:

Security Option	*Directory Security*	*File Security*
No Access	■	■
List	■	
Read	■	■
Add	■	
Add & Read	■	
Change	■	■
Full Control	■	■

As you can see, there are a few more security features for directories—partly due to the nature of directories, such as the need to control the addition or modification of subdirectories.

The built-in permissions in the preceding list are called *standard permissions.* Standard permissions consist of various groupings of the more basic permissions, which are called *individual permissions.* When you assign a standard permission to a file or directory, the individual permissions implied by it are listed in an abbreviated form, as you'll see later. For reference, the following list gives the abbreviations you'll see:

Individual Permission Name	*Abbreviation*
Read	R
Delete	D
Write	W
Change permission	P
Execute	X
Take ownership	O

NOTE

You can mix and match individual permissions to create customized permission sets if you like, although this usually isn't necessary. These *custom access permissions* are covered later.

You should keep some things in mind when trying to administer file and directory access permissions. You can make this a big headache—or a cinch, if you plan carefully. First, figure out what really needs protecting and what doesn't. In general, data files need protecting, but applications don't. You usually can reinstall an application from another directory, network machine, or floppy without too much hassle. Second, try to work from the highest organizational level whenever possible. Following are three examples:

- Although you can create custom access permissions, try to use standard permission sets. It's easier.
- Although you can assign permissions to individual files, sometimes assigning permissions to whole directories is easier. That way, as the directory grows, you don't have to keep assigning permissions to each new file.
- Although you can assign permissions to individual accounts, try to work with groups instead. For example, create an account group and assign the whole group the permission of accessing a directory. When you want to remove a user's right to access the directory, simply remove him or her from the group. This beats the chore of having to individually exclude users from the permissions on every file in the directory.

TIP

If you're an administrator responsible for assigning permissions to a large number of users, you really should consider using group permissions if possible. It will save you a tremendous amount of work!

Keep these points in mind when setting up your permissions. Also, you might want to sketch some diagrams on paper to keep track of your overall game plan. After permissions are set up, it's a pain to go through all the directories or files and see who has permission to do what.

Also, keep a few other general operational rules in mind:

- Permissions are cumulative. If you give an individual's account one permission and give that account group another permission, the individual is granted both.
- The No Access permission is the exception to cumulative permissions. It overrides all others that might be set elsewhere. If Susie's individual account is given Change permission on a directory but her group is given No Access permission, she won't have access to the directory.

Setting Permissions on Directories

Assuming that you are the owner of a directory (or have permission), you can set the permissions on a directory. Setting permissions means declaring which people or account groups have the right to read, change, and delete the files in the directory. Note that any users or groups given Full Control can delete all files or even the directory itself.

Follow these steps to display a directory's permissions:

1. Click on the directory.

TIP

You can select multiple directories by Ctrl-clicking, but this can be done only from the file pane, not from the directory tree (left) pane. (If directories aren't listed in the file pane, choose View | By File Type and enable the Directories check box.)

2. Click on the Permissions button (the key) in the toolbar, or choose Security | Permissions. The Permissions dialog box, shown in Figure 10.29, appears.

   Until directory permissions are intentionally set, they inherit the permissions assigned to their parent directories.

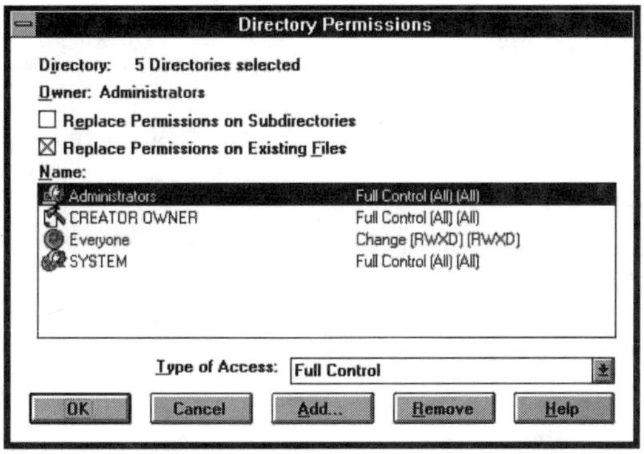

FIGURE 10.29.
Setting permissions for a number of directories.

NOTE

Newly created directories assume the permissions of the parent directory. However, changing the permissions on a directory doesn't, by default, affect the permissions on its subdirectories and files in those subdirectories.

Here's the breakdown of the Permissions dialog box:

Section	*Notes*
Directory	The name of the directory you are changing permissions on. If multiple directories are selected, the number appears here.
Owner Replace Permission on Subdirectories	Who owns the directory or directories? Should the changes you make here affect only the selected directory or all directories below it as well? Check the box if the answer is Yes.
Replace Permissions on Existing Files	Should the changes you make here be applied to the files in the directory, too? That is, if you give a group Change permission on the directory (such as the ability to change the directory's name).

Section	*Notes*
Name	Groups and user accounts for which permissions have already been set. When you choose multiple directories, only accounts or groups which have the same settings for all the directories are shown. Each named group or individual account's permissions is listed in the right side of the box. The first code in parentheses is the permission on the directory. The second code is the listing on the files in the directory.
Type of Access	Lets you change the permission(s) for the selected group or account. Click on a group or name in the Name section, open this drop-down list, and choose a standard permission. To set up a custom access permission, choose Special Directory Access or Special File Access and choose options from the resulting dialog box.
Add/Remove	These buttons let you add or remove users or groups from the Name list.

3. As a default, Replace Permissions on Existing Files is enabled. This makes sense, because the assumption is that you're setting a directory's permissions in order to affect the files in it. Enable or disable the check boxes as you see fit.
4. Look at the listing in the Names section and examine the rights assigned to each. Does the list include all the individuals or groups you want to give permissions to? Do you want to eliminate or limit some user permissions? If you do, click on a group or account in the list and choose the Type of Access from the drop-down list.

TIP

The codes (such as RWX) can be confusing. To see a longhand list of access types for an account or group, select the group, then open the Type of Access list and choose Special Directory Access. The check boxes in the resulting dialog box show an unabbreviated list of the current permissions.

5. To add or remove users or accounts, click on Add or Remove. If you choose Add, a large Add Users and Groups dialog box appears, from which you can choose, browse, and display the names of users from other domains or workgroups. See the section titled "Adding Users and Groups" for details about this box.

NOTE

The individual who creates a new file or directory automatically becomes its owner. He can give ownership away, or an administrator can claim it, but until either one of those events occurs, the creator owns the new file or directory.

Table 10.1 shows the breakdown of the actual rights each standard permission set grants to named users of directories.

Table 10.1. The rights each standard permission set grants to named users of directories.

Action Available to User or Group of Users	*Full Control*	*Change*	*Add and Read*	*Add*	*Read*	*List*
Show names of files in directory	■	■		■	■	
Show directory attributes	■	■	■	■	■	■
Switch to subdirectories	■	■	■	■	■	■
Alter directory attributes	■	■	■	■		
Add files (including subdirectories)	■	■	■	■		
Display owner and permissions	■	■	■	■	■	■
Delete directory	■	■				
Delete files (including empty subdirectory)	■					
Change directory permissions	■					
Assume ownership	■					

As a separate issue, consider the permissions granted to users of files in the directory you've changed the permissions on. The permitted actions are slightly different because the objects are files rather than directories (see Table 10.2).

Table 10.2. Permissions granted to users of files in the directory you've changed the permissions on.

Action Available to User or Group of Users	*Full Control*	*Change*	*Add and Read*	*Add*	*Read*	*List*
Read the file to display its contents	■	■	■		■	
Display owner and permissions	■	■	■		■	
Show file attributes	■	■	■		■	
Run an executable file	■	■	■		■	
Alter the file's directory attributes	■	■				
Alter the file	■	■				
Delete files (including empty subdirectory)	■	■				
Change the file's permissions	■					
Assume ownership	■					

Setting Permissions on Files

Read the preceding section about directories to understand the basic game plan. Selecting files, viewing current permissions, and assigning new permissions follow essentially the same rules.

As with directories, you can't change permissions on a file unless you're the file's owner or you've been given the Full Control permission to it. There are only four permission levels for files (as opposed to seven for directories): No Access, Read, Change, and Full Control. Table 10.3 gives the breakdown.

Table 10.3. The four permission levels for files.

Action Available to User or Group of Users	*Full Control*	*Change*	*Read*	*No Access*
Read the file to display its contents	■	■	■	
Display owner and permissions	■	■	■	
Show file attributes	■	■	■	
Run an executable file	■	■	■	
Alter the file's directory attributes	■	■		
Alter the file	■	■		
Delete files (including empty subdirectory)	■	■		
Change the file's permissions and ownership	■			

To change the permissions on a file or group of files, do the following:

1. In the file pane of File Manager, select one or more files on an NTFS partition.

TIP

Use the View | By File Type command to easily list and select just system files or program files, files with specific names or extensions, and so forth.

2. Choose Security | Permissions or click on the Permissions button (the key) in the toolbar. The File Permissions dialog box, shown in Figure 10.30, appears.

   The following are some things to note:

   - The files currently assigned permissions are listed to the right of the name to which they apply.
   - Permissions are shown only if they are identical for the groups or accounts listed.
   - The abbreviations described in the Directories section apply here as well.
   - To see exact permissions spelled out, click on the group or account, then open the Type of Access list and choose Special Access.

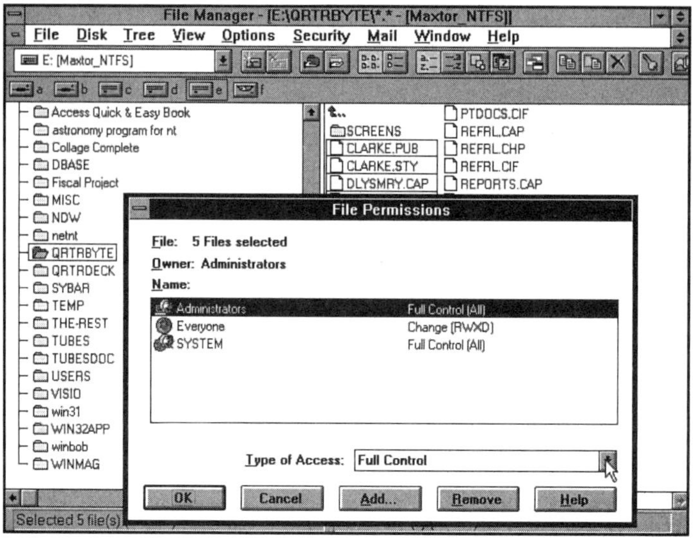

FIGURE 10.30.
Setting file permissions.

NOTE

Some directory permissions, when set, cause file permissions to be set to Not Specified. This means that unless you change the file permissions manually, the user or group is blocked from access to the files until permission is specifically granted when you set the file permissions.

3. Click on the group or individual whose permissions you want to set up or change.
4. Open the Type of Access drop-down list and choose the access you want to permit. Refer to Table 10.3 for help.
5. To add a group or account, click on Add and choose the group or account from the resulting dialog box. (See the section titled "Adding Users and Groups" for more about how to do this.) To remove an account or group, click on it in the Name area and then click on the Remove button.
6. Click on OK.

NOTE

Creating and maintaining account groups are covered in Chapter 9, "Configuring Windows NT."

Setting Up Customized Access Permissions

When the canned access permissions for files and directories don't cut the mustard for some reason, you can specify permissions to your own liking. This is called setting special access permissions. There's a great deal of flexibility here. You can set permissions for

- the directory itself, not including the files it contains
- the files only, not including the directory itself
- the directory and the files in it

> **NOTE**
>
> Setting permissions through shared directories (directories shared for network access) is covered in Chapter 3, "Working with Windows NT."

To set special access permissions, follow these steps:

1. Select the item whose permissions you want to set.

> **TIP**
>
> You can select multiple directories by Ctrl-clicking, but this can be done only from the file pane, not from the directory tree (left) pane. (If directories aren't listed in the file pane, choose View | By File Type and enable the Directories check box.)

2. Choose Security | Permissions.
3. Select the group or user whose permissions you want to modify. Note that, as explained earlier, only groups that have the same settings for the files or directories in question are listed. If no groups have the same permissions, nothing appears in the Name list. You have to add *someone* to the list before you can set special access permissions; otherwise, they won't apply to anyone, and you're wasting your time. Therefore, you should add a user or a group via the Add button.
4. Now you have to decide which type of permission you want to apply. Open the Type of Access drop-down list and choose. You have two options (you might see only one option—Special Access—if you've selected files, not directories):
   - Special Directory Access affects only the directory, not its files
   - Special File Access affects selected files, or a selected directory *and* all its files

A dialog box similar to the one shown in Figure 10.31 appears.

FIGURE 10.31.
Setting customized access with the Special File Access dialog box.

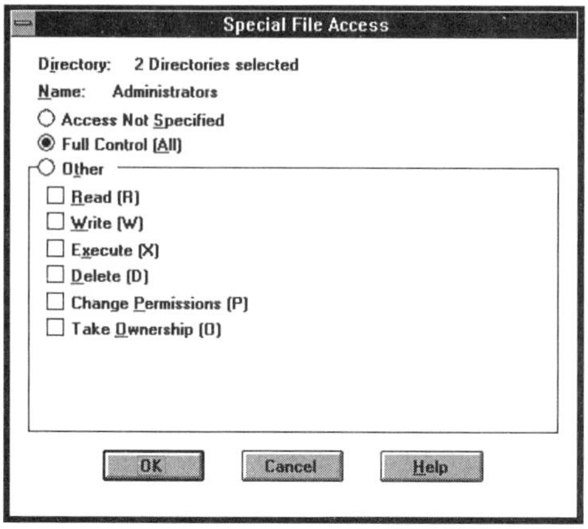

5. Fill in the appropriate boxes in the Special File Access dialog box, then click on OK for that box and for the Permissions box. Tables 10.4 and 10.5 might help you choose permissions. They list the special permissions granted for each setting. Table 10.4 applies to directories, and Table 10.5 applies to files.

Table 10.4. Actions available to a user or group of users when setting customized directory access permissions.

Action Available to User or Group	*Full Control*	*Take Ownership*	*Change Permissions*	*Delete*	*Execute*	*Write*	*Read*
Show names of files in directory	■						■
Show directory attributes	■						■
Allow new files and subdirectories	■					■	
Allow changes to directory attributes	■					■	
Allow access to subdirectories	■				■		

Action Available to User or Group	*Full Control*	*Take Ownership*	*Change Permissions*	*Delete*	*Execute*	*Write*	*Read*
Show directory owner and permissions	■				■	■	■
Delete directory	■			■			
Change directory's permissions	■		■				
Assume ownership of directory	■	■					

Table 10.5. Actions available to a user or group of users when setting customized file access permissions.

Action Available to User or Group	*Full Control*	*Take Ownership*	*Change Permissions*	*Delete*	*Execute*	*Write*	*Read*
Show file's contents	■						■
Show file's attributes	■				■		■
Allow changes to file contents	■					■	
Allow changes to file attributes	■					■	
Run an executable file	■				■		
Show file's owner and permissions	■				■	■	■
Delete file	■			■			
Change file's permissions	■		■				
Assume ownership of file	■	■					

NOTE

When you select all the files in a directory (by selecting the directory and then choosing Special File Access), a special feature lets you remove any permissions from the files in the directory and prevent new files from inheriting the permissions assigned to the directory (as is normally the case). In the Special Files Access dialog box, choose Access Not Specified.

Setting Up File Manager Auditing

You can set up an audit trail to keep track of who's been using specific files and directories and who's tried to use them but failed for some reason. A log listing events of your choice is created and stored on disk, and it can be read later using the Event Viewer application (covered in Chapter 12).

NOTE

You can request auditing only if you're an administrator.

For directories and files, six events can be audited:

- Read
- Write
- Execute
- Delete
- Change permissions
- Take ownership

Although the last three of these events are clear-cut and occur only when an object is deleted, has its permissions changed, or changes ownership, the first three events can be triggered by a number of activities. You might want to use Tables 10.6 and 10.7 to determine which events you want to monitor. In these tables, look for the events that trigger a particular category, then choose that category in the Auditing dialog box, explained later. Here's how to read the tables. Suppose you want an audit entry whenever someone views the attributes of a file. Choosing either Read or Execute in the Audit dialog box gives you that result.

Table 10.6. Directory-related auditing events.

Directory-Related Action You Want to Audit	*Read*	*Write*	*Execute*
List files in the directory	■		
View the directory's attributes	■		■
Change the directory's attributes	■		
Move to one of the directory's subdirectories			■
Create new subdirectories, directories, and files	■		
View the directory's permissions and owner	■	■	■

Table 10.7. File-related auditing events.

File-Related Action You Want to Audit	*Read*	*Write*	*Execute*
View the file's contents	■		
View the file's attributes	■		■
Change the file's attributes		■	
Execute the file if it's a program			■
Alter the contents of the file		■	
View permissions and owner	■	■	■

Okay, enough preliminaries. Here's how to establish auditing on directories and files:

1. Select the file or directory (in File Manager).
2. Choose Security | Auditing. The File Auditing or Directory Auditing dialog box appears, depending on whether you selected a file or a directory. See Figure 10.32.
3. At least one group or individual account must be listed before the audit actions become selectable; otherwise, they are grayed out. Use the Add button to add groups or individuals whose actions you want to audit. (See the section titled "Adding Users and Groups" for details on adding people to the audit lists.) Remove any entries whose activities you don't want to audit.
4. Click on an individual or group name in the Name list for whom you want to set auditing particulars.

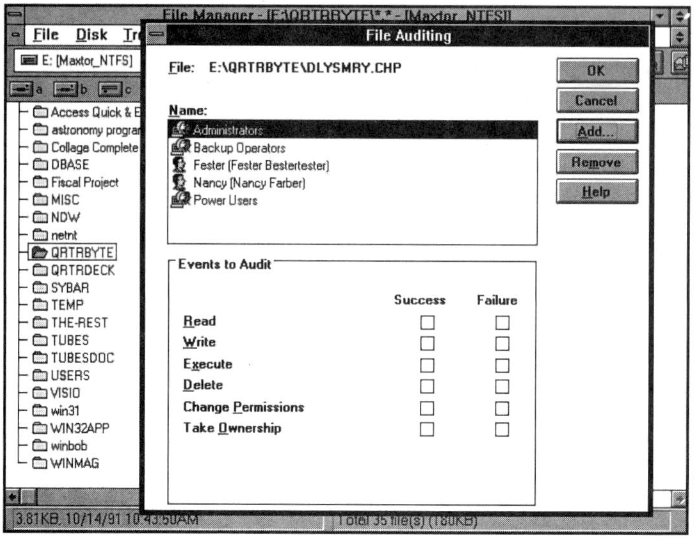

FIGURE 10.32.
Use this box to set up auditing specifications for a file. A similar box is used for auditing directories.

5. Set the check boxes in the dialog box to indicate all the events you want to audit. Note that you can choose to audit success and/or failure of each type of event. Failures typically occur when a user doesn't have the right to perform the activity he or she tries.

   If you're working with directories (rather than files), there will be two extra check boxes: Replace Auditing on Subdirectories and Replace Auditing on Existing Files:

Check Box	*Notes*
Replace Auditing on Subdirectories	Should the changes you make here affect only the selected directory and all directories below it as well? Enable this box if the answer is Yes. Enable this box if you want to affect only the directories and subdirectories, but not the files in them.
Replace Auditing on also Existing Files	Should the auditing changes you make here be applied to the files in the directory? If the preceding box is enabled, enabling this one also affects the files in any subdirectories. As a default, Replace Auditing on Existing Files is enabled. This makes sense, because the assumption is that you're setting a directory's auditing in order to audit the files in it in the same way.

6. Repeat steps 4 and 5 until all groups have their auditing set the way you want.
7. Click on OK.

If the Auditing Policy is not turned on in User Manager, you see an error message like the one shown in Figure 10.33. Run User Manager, choose Policies | Audit, and check the File and Object Access box. (User Manager's Audit dialog box is described earlier in this chapter.)

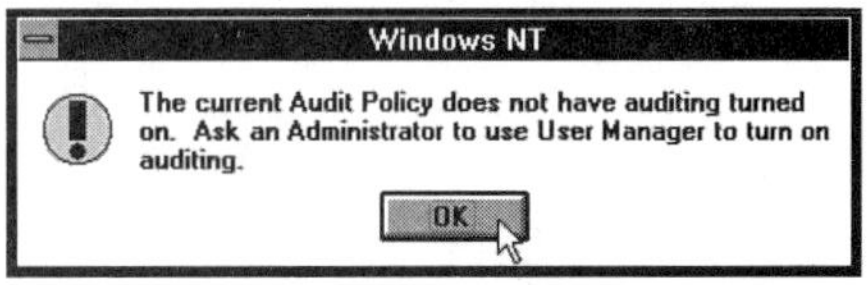

FIGURE 10.33.
If you see this message, auditing isn't activated.

Auditing now begins. Use the Event Viewer, covered in Chapter 12, to view details about the accesses.

Taking Ownership of Files and Directories

Every file and directory is owned by someone. If no specific ownership has been granted, the Administrators group owns the file or directory. However, when you create a new directory or file, it's all yours—you're the new owner. The advantage of being the owner is that you can grant permissions to other people to use the files or directories. Also, you can set permissions so that nobody can have access.

Well, almost nobody. An administrator can take ownership without asking—even if the permission is set to No Access. Otherwise, the creator of the file or directory remains its owner until someone else intentionally takes ownership.

NOTE

As you might recall from the discussion of permissions earlier in this chapter, you can grant the right to other users or groups to take ownership of selected files and directories. From the point of view of an administrator, you might want to take ownership of another's file or directory in order to change the permissions on it, copy files, or otherwise maintain the system.

1. Select the file or directory from File Manager. (You also can select multiple files and directories.)
2. Choose Security | Owner.

3. Click on Take Ownership. If several files or directories are selected, the box reflects that, as shown in Figure 10.34.

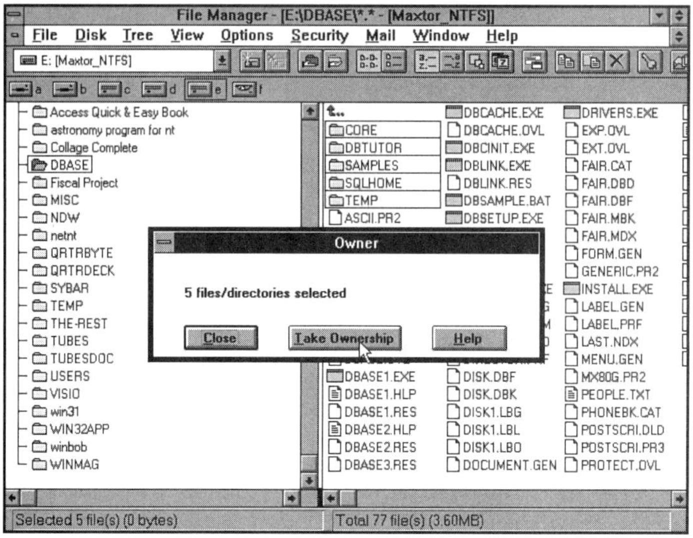

FIGURE 10.34.
Taking ownership of multiple files.

4. Click on OK.

NOTE

Even an administrator can't transfer ownership to another user. If you co-opt a user's file by taking ownership, you have to alert the user to have him or her reclaim it. Before doing so, you must set the permission on the file so that the desired user can claim it using the ownership command, described in step 3 of the preceding list.

Security and Administrative Options with Print Manager

Chapter 4 covered Print Manager in detail. However, a few topics weren't covered there because they pertained to printer administration. These topics are rather brief, compared to File Manager (luckily), and they address the following issues:

- Securing a printer to limit its use
- Auditing a printer so that you have a record of who's been using it

- Taking ownership of a printer so that you can alter its security and auditing

As an administrator of a printer, things might get to the point where, instead of just telling people not to use a printer, you might need to restrict who can use it. Also, you might want to grant a specific user control over the printer, as sort of a printer administrator. That person can then add users or groups, who can use the printer or administer it via the Print Manager window (pause the printer, delete files in the queue, rearrange the queue, and so forth).

Securing a Printer

Printers have permissions, just as files and directories do. In fact, the dialog boxes and commands you use to set permissions for a printer are very similar to those discussed in the File Manager sections of this chapter. For that reason, I won't go into great detail here. The main difference with Print Manager is that the permissions are different, because there are fewer variables when you give permission on a printer. For example, you don't have Read, Write, Execute, and other permissions to contend with. Only four permissions exist:

- No Access
- Print
- Manage Documents
- Full Control

Table 10.8 gives the breakdown of activities associated with each permission.

Table 10.8. Activities associated with each permission.

Permission	*Full Control*	*Manage Documents*	*Print*	*No Access*
Print documents	■		■	
Alter settings for documents	■	■		
Pause, resume, restart, delete documents	■	■		
Pause, resume, purge printer	■			
Change printer's properties	■			
Delete printer	■			
Change printer's permissions	■			
Assume ownership of printer	■			

As in File Manager, permissions are cumulative, so if a user belongs to several groups and permissions are set for each group (or even individually), permissions pile up for the user. There is one exception: If any group of which a user is a member is given No Access permission on a printer, that overrides other settings for the user, and he or she is blocked from using the printer.

When you print a document, you're given permission (by virtue of the Creator Owner group) to manage the document. Therefore, you can do anything with your own document that the Creator Owner group can do. (This group is assigned the Manage Documents permission; see Table 10.8.)

NOTE

You can change the permissions on a printer only if you are the owner of the printer (see the section titled "Taking Ownership of a Printer") or if you have been given the Full Control permission by the printer's owner.

Follow these steps to set a printer's permissions:

1. Run Print Manager.
2. Click on the printer's icon or window.
3. Choose Security | Permissions. The Printer Permissions dialog box, shown in Figure 10.35, appears.

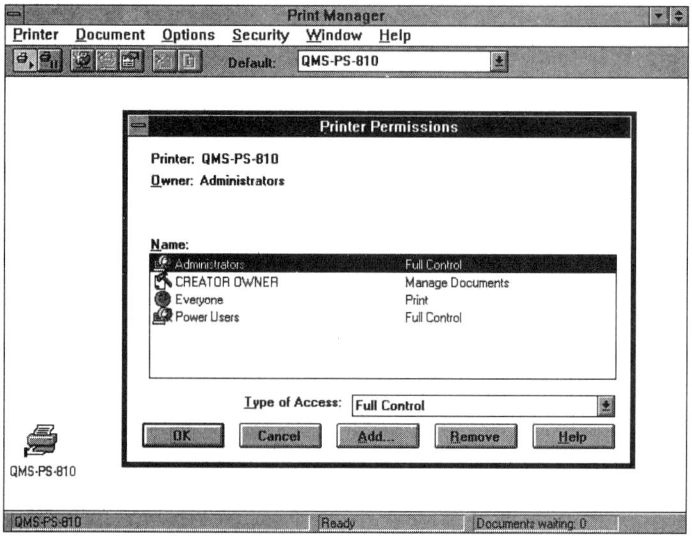

FIGURE 10.35.
Setting printer permissions.

4. Select an individual or group to whom you want to assign permissions. Note that existing permissions are displayed to the right. At this point, you might want to add or remove users or groups from the permission list for this printer. See the last section of this chapter if you don't know how to do this.
5. Open the drop-down list and choose the permission you want to assign.

Auditing Printer Usage

Auditing a printer helps you figure out who's been using it, how often it's been used, if and when its permissions have been changed, and other such events. This process is similar to auditing File Manager activities. Again, it requires that the audit policy for the machine (as set from User Manager) be set to Audit File and Object Access. The resulting log of printer use is stored on disk and can be viewed with the Event Viewer (covered in Chapter 12).

As with file and directory use auditing, you have two variables when setting up printer auditing—which users to monitor, and which activities of those users to monitor. You set these with the Auditing dialog box in Printer Manager. The dialog box lets you stipulate five event categories to audit. Table 10.9 gives the breakdown of how printer activities map to those events.

Table 10.9. Setting printer auditing options.

Activity	*Print*	*Full Control*	*Delete*	*Change Permissions*	*Take Ownership*
Print documents	■				
Alter job settings for documents		■			
Pause, resume, restart, move, delete documents		■			
Share printer		■			
Change printer's properties		■			
Delete printer			■		
Change printer's permissions				■	
Assume ownership of printer					■

To set auditing, follow these steps:

1. Click on the printer icon or window.
2. Choose Security | Auditing. The Printer Auditing dialog box, shown in Figure 10.36, appears.

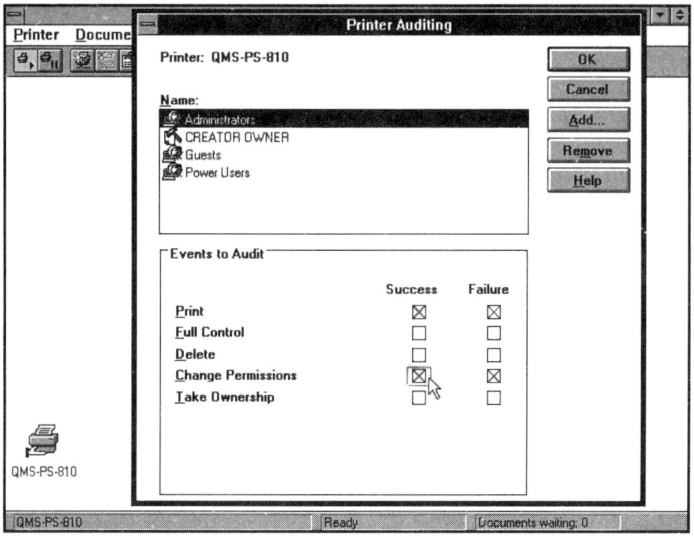

FIGURE 10.36.
Setting up auditing for a printer.

3. Add or remove users and/or groups from the list until the list represents everyone whose use of the printer you want to audit. (See the last section in this chapter to learn how to do this.) If anyone in the list should be removed, select them and click on the Remove button.
4. Click on a user or group, then set the permissions for that person. Repeat for each additional group or use.
5. Click on OK.
6. Repeat steps 1 through 4 for each printer you want to audit.

Taking Ownership of a Printer

If you have ownership of a printer, you can do anything with it you like—even delete it. Most important, you can change permissions for other users. There are three ways you might have ownership of a printer:

- If you create a printer
- If you're an administrator and you take ownership
- If you're given Full Control permission and you take ownership

The second two instances require that you *take* ownership when you don't already have it. Note, however, that either you have to be an administrator or you need to have been given Full Control permission by the current owner. In either case, to claim ownership, follow these steps:

1. Select the printer window or icon in Print Manager.
2. Choose Security | Owner.
3. In the resulting dialog box, click on Take Ownership.

Adding Users and Groups

A number of dialog boxes discussed in this chapter have an Add button. This button's purpose is to provide a way for you to add users and groups of users to the Name list in Auditing, Permissions, and other dialog boxes with NT. If you are administering an NT machine or network, you see this button and resulting dialog box often. It's just about as common as the old File | Save As or File | Open dialog boxes, at least when you're performing administrative chores. This section explains how that dialog box works, just in case you haven't figured it out with Help screens or by just playing around with the box (the way many of us learn to use most programs).

As the name implies, the Add Users and Groups button opens a dialog box whose purpose is to let you add users and groups to a list. The list is then assigned to some process, such as auditing. This dialog box, shown in Figure 10.37, lets you look around the workstation's registry, across the network (including across NT Server domains with trust). You can search for a specific user, or you can see who's in a group after you find a group.

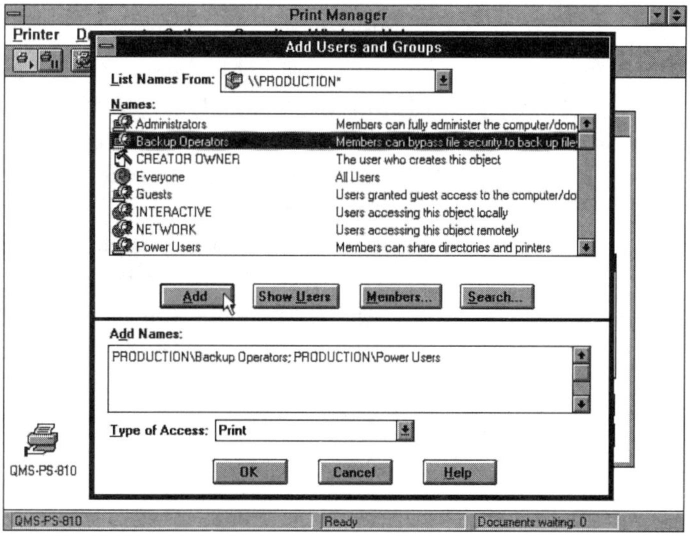

FIGURE 10.37.
The Add Users and Groups dialog box.

The following is the breakdown of the items in the box, with a few suggestions for their use:

Option, Button, or Area	*Description*
List Names From	Lists the name of the computer or domain in which the names and groups in the Name area reside. Open this list to choose other computers or domains. An asterisk after the name indicates that you'll see local groups for that computer or domain.
Names	Lists the names of groups or users who are members of the domain or computer shown in the List Names From box. To add a name to the Add Names area, double-click on it, or click on it once and then click on Add.
Add	Has the same effect as double-clicking on a name—adding the selected Name item to the Add Names list.
Show Users	Displays the names of users on the current domain or computer workstation. Normally, only the groups are shown. Click on this, then scroll to the bottom of the list (below the groups) to see the usernames.
Members	This displays the users within a given group. Click on the group in the Names section, then click on this button; the members of the group appear in a separate dialog box. You can then click on a member, then click on the Add button in *that* dialog box, to add the member to the Add Names list.
Search	You must know the domain for an account or a user before you can add it. This button helps you find individual users or account groups. Click on this button to bring up a new dialog box. Enter the user or group name at the top of the box and click on Search. You can narrow the search by clicking on Search Only In and choosing the domain, computer, or workgroup. You can find multiple names. Each found name appears in the Search Results area. Click on Add when the list is complete.

Option, Button, or Area	*Description*
Add Names	As you choose users and groups, they are strung together in this area in a list. Each user or group is separated by a semicolon. You can type in names, but be careful not to make typos. Use backslashes to separate the computer or domain name and the user or group name (for example, `finance\martha` or `finance\finance group`). When you finally click on OK, all the names in this box are added to whatever dialog box you were working with before, such as Printer Auditing.

Optimizing Windows NT: Performance Determinants

21

IN THIS CHAPTER

If you're reading this chapter, chances are good you're either the type of user who wants to squeeze every drop of performance from your machine, or you're suffering from some specific NT performance shortcoming you hope to resolve.

NOTE

Turn to Chapter 20 for a discussion of network optimization.

Let's consider what determines NT's performance—where the bottlenecks are and how your application mix and hardware affect system throughput.

If you're a veteran PC power user, you'll feel somewhat constricted when it comes to optimizing NT. As a writer who has pounded out hundreds of pages about supercharging Windows 3.1, I feel somewhat limited when writing about it.

Why the supercharging constraints? Partly because NT is new. As a result, there is still precious little in the area of add-ons, hardware and software optimizers, system-sleuthing software, shell replacements, and so on.

Second, because NT is a corporate animal, there's a disincentive against heavy "mods" to a workstation setup. I've already discussed this in earlier chapters, but it's worth repeating: Unless you're tweaking a single-user workstation (you're not going to share the machine), nonstandard shells, freaky hardware, and other novel arrangements can cause more headaches for your users than they're worth.

We've learned over time (it took a couple of years for those who got addicted to mods back in the do-it-yourself days of CP/M, early DOS, and UNIX) that the cost/benefit ratio of tweaking Windows might be more attractive in theory than in reality. Yes, you can pore over your Windows 3.1 .INI files till the wee hours or scan magazines weekly for the latest hot-rodding techniques, hoping to squeeze that additional ounce of performance from your speed-demon system. Overall, though, the time you spend usually isn't worth the reward.

Microsoft knows this too. The additional technical support headaches due to crashed Windows 3.x systems—resulting either from programs that toyed with the .INI files or from enthusiastic hobbyists—have been a royal pain for them. This is one reason why the analogs to the Windows 3.1 .INI files in NT are protected from accidental hacking. You have to dig into the Registry to get at them, and even then the Registry Editor helps prevent erroneous entries into the Registry.

NOTE

The other reason, admittedly, for protecting NT's internal settings is that Microsoft's design goal was to have NT meet government C2-level security—something that by definition must preclude easy tinkering with system settings.

Examining Your Needs

Of course, not everyone running NT needs to be concerned with optimization as it's discussed here. Other chapters of this book cover everyday NT operations, often with an eye toward efficient and effective organization of workstation and network operations. Efficiency tips pertinent to everything from application and user organization to workgroup appointment scheduling have already been discussed. That's not what this chapter is about. Even purely performance-oriented settings, such as tasking priority adjustments or the use of stripe sets, are discussed elsewhere. This chapter, by contrast, focuses on tricks for optimizing the hardware in your computer system.

Is optimizing of this sort something you need? Maybe not. If you've already bought a full-bore, state-of-the-art system such as a multiprocessor Compaq, a DEC Alpha, or a top-notch Pentium system and your system has a fast video accelerator, a SCSI drive, and lots of memory, there isn't much more to do. You might want to consider NT's peculiarities and throw as much RAM as possible at it, adjust the paging file sizes, or convert as many partitions to NTFS as you can. But that's all.

By the same token, if you're a single NT user doing common, everyday tasks such as word processing, and you're satisfied with the performance of your computer as a whole, you probably don't need to worry about performance boosters either.

However, if you're on a budget, working with 486s upgraded from DOS/Windows to NT, or a systems administrator who suddenly has the task of upgrading a slew of machines to NT for networking (and who has to concoct a machine to perform as a server), there might be a few tricks here worth considering.

Optimization Basics

With that in mind, let's take a look at your possible workstation optimization strategies.

NOTE

Network optimization, and therefore server performance tuning, is covered in Chapter 20, in which the Performance Monitor program is discussed.

The approach you take depends somewhat on your system type. Fine-tuning an x86 machine differs from fine-tuning a DEC Alpha or a MIPS machine. Even within a class of machine such as the x86, there are variations in hardware appointments such as RAM caching, disk caching controllers, video accelerators, CPU upgrades, and so forth.

NOTE

This chapter focuses only on the x86-based systems so common in the workplace nowadays. For fine-tuning other machine architectures, consult your manual or manufacturer.

This chapter organizes system optimization approaches from the bottom up—that is, from the cheapest to the most expensive. Thus, CMOS BIOS adjustments are discussed first because they're free. CPU, video system, and motherboard replacements are discussed last because they tend to cost big bucks.

TIP

By all means, you should study the manual supplied with the computer hardware. Often, significant proprietary performance-tuning features go unnoticed until they're discovered buried deep in the manual somewhere. A typical example is the hot key that turns on turbo mode, doubling the CPU performance.

BIOS Adjustments

A typical manual (as unreadable as they usually are due to their poor English translation) supplied with your common Intel 486 clone usually mentions the CMOS setup routine. Upon bootup, pressing Delete (or following some other on-screen instruction displayed at boot time) brings up a CMOS setup program that lets you view and change an extensive array of internal settings affecting memory usage, CPU speed, activation of the math coprocessor, video and BIOS shadowing, RAM wait states, hard-disk specifications, floppy drive capacities, and often much more.

These settings are called BIOS settings because they alter the basic input/output system. When the operating system needs to write to the hard disk, floppy disk, or screen, receive keyboard input, or perform other input and output tasks, it calls the BIOS—in other words, makes a "BIOS call." The BIOS, in turn, performs the requested action.

The BIOS is actually software stored in ROM plugged into the computer's motherboard. Although the BIOS's duties are standardized for each class of machine, particularly IBM

PC compatibles, the actual BIOS manufacturer varies. For example, two popular BIOS manufacturers for IBM clones are Phoenix and American Megatrends Inc. (AMI).

Because manufacturers of BIOS chips are legally prevented from copying each others' (and IBM's) software exactly, the user interface for setting BIOS parameters isn't identical for all PCs on which NT might be running. Usually, though, you'll see a menu listing a bunch of options, such as making "standard CMOS settings" and "advanced CMOS settings." Then you'll have a couple of options for saving the settings or quitting without saving. When you save the settings, they're stored in a CMOS chip (a chip whose contents can be modified and those settings maintained even when the power to the computer is turned off) that is powered by a small battery internal to the computer.

NOTE

With RISC-based machines, such setup screens are available via a supplied program, as was the case with the old IBM AT (80286-based) computers and most AT compatibles.

Depending on what's built into the motherboard (for example, what type of bus, CPU, video, and so on), the BIOS options will vary or be more extensive. Some fancy motherboards let you finely tweak the technique the system uses to refresh the RAM chips, let you specify blocks of memory that shouldn't be used by the operating system because a plug-in card needs that memory block, or let you set the internal clock source (tick rate) or CPU type and speed.

Be careful when futzing with the BIOS. If your machine is working okay, there probably won't be any problems that need addressing. If you're inexperienced in such matters, steer away from making changes to BIOS settings. You can view them, but leave the setup program without saving the changes. How you do this varies from machine to machine, but usually a series of Esc key presses gets you out safely.

The main BIOS optimizing options you should be concerned with are

- Setting the floppy drive sizes and types
- Ensuring that the hard-disk types are correct
- Setting the CPU to the highest possible startup speed
- Enabling or disabling the RAM checking
- Setting the RAM wait states as low as possible
- Enabling BIOS and video shadowing if possible

With some BIOSs, all these settings can be made from the "standard" settings screen rather than from the "advanced" one. Let's briefly look at these options one at a time.

Setting Floppies

First, you'll want to ensure that the floppies are set up correctly. This usually is done when the drives are installed, so unless the machine's battery has run down and the CMOS settings were erased as a result, the floppy drives will be set to the correct size and density. More important, some BIOSs let you declare the order of boot drives. Should the computer boot from drive C without looking for a floppy in drive A first? I like to set the boot order to C and then A so that I don't have the inconvenience of having to remove a disk I've accidentally left in drive A. It avoids the resulting error message, and it also means that booting NT will be faster because the floppy drive isn't scanned first.

Note that some computers, such as those from Gateway, offer a BIOS option to swap the A and B floppies. This swap option doesn't work with NT and should be disabled. Gateway sends out their machines with the A floppy set to the 5 1/4-inch as the default. Because this swapping option doesn't work with NT, you can't install NT from 3 1/2-inch disks.

Hard-Disk Type

Next, you need to make sure that the hard-disk type is correct. This is in the standard settings as well. A typical BIOS supports 47 different types of drives, each with its own specifications in terms of heads, tracks, sectors per track, landing zone, precompensation, and so forth.

CAUTION

Don't change this setting unless you know what you're doing.

If your system has been working fine, you don't need to futz with this setting. If you make the wrong modification, your system won't be able to boot until you reset it correctly. Some BIOSs have a feature, sometimes called "auto-detect hard disk," that sleuths out the hard disk's specifications by examining the disk. This can save you some hassles if you're adding a new hard disk and you don't know its specs, or if you accidentally change the hard-disk type on an existing drive. With most machines, you can't do anything to the BIOS to speed up hard-disk performance. You can, however, buy a faster drive and then use the BIOS to set the drive type. (Disk upgrading is discussed in the section titled "Upgrading Your Hard Disk.")

NOTE

One machine in particular *does* let you make hard-disk speed improvements from the BIOS. It's the Gateway 2000. This PC and others with the RIDE (rapid IDE) BIOS have three speed settings for hard-disk data transfers. The highest speed is 5M/second, which works fine with NT.

Turbo Mode

Most x86-based PCs, whether workstations or servers, have a speed switch, or a "turbo" switch. This switch is a throwback to the original IBM PCs and the 80286-based IBM AT, which had much slower processor speeds. On most PC clones, this switch gives you the option of slowing down the system to properly run older PC games. Some older games used the CPU clock signal (rather than the real-time clock) to determine how fast events occurred within the game. On super-fast systems, the games became unplayable, or they just bombed. In any case, there are few reasons these days to slow your system to a snail's pace by turning off the turbo switch, but you might want to ensure that the machine is actually running in turbo mode and that it *starts* in that mode. Some BIOSs let you set the motherboard to start in slow mode for the memory check or for another purpose (such as initializing cranky cards) and then go into high speed. Anyway, check this setting to make sure that the computer comes up full-speed ahead. Booting takes long enough without the processor running in slow motion!

Memory Amount and Memory Checking

Most systems ensure that the physical memory installed in the computer and the CMOS setting agree. If they don't, you usually get an error message indicating as much, and you're forced to enter the Setup program to make adjustments. After the comparison is made, a memory check ensues, which can be annoying if it runs too slowly or if you have tons of memory in the machine (for example, 16M or 32M). Some CMOS setups let you turn off the checking, enable or disable the "click" noise that emanates from the speaker as the check is executed, or opt to check only the "system" memory (the first 640K). If you want to speed up booting, turn as much off as possible. IBM PCs and clones use a parity checking scheme that reports memory errors if they crop up. I have yet to have one on a modern clone (although I have had them on old original IBM PCs). I've even turned off parity altogether, with no ill effects, when I was short on RAM SIMMs and had to use "4M by 8" rather than "4M by 9" SIMMs, which means SIMMs without parity checking.

NOTE

In support of RAM checking, let me say this: Although the RAM check at bootup isn't anywhere close to an exhaustive test that will turn up all manner of errors (you should buy a specialized program for RAM testing if that's what you want), at least it's something. If the computer in question is highly critical to your corporate or other needs, heck, a 15- to 30-second wait is no big deal. Leave it on.

Wait States

Most PCs have a CMOS setup option for setting the number of RAM "wait states," usually anywhere from zero to two. Wait states cause the system to insert the specified number of clock cycles (thumb twiddling) between processes involving the RAM chips (reading or writing). A wait state allows the data to settle reliably into the chip before another action is taken, such as writing another byte to a series of chips.

More expensive chips can read and write data as fast as the processor can dole it out, and therefore they need zero wait states, but cheaper ones can't. Typically, the slower chips were intended to perform up to snuff, but they didn't make the grade and were stamped as such and sold at a cheaper price. Slowness often is due to slight manufacturing imperfections.

Inserting wait states might be necessary if your RAM can't keep up with your CPU. Determining whether they're necessary isn't always easy. You might have to consult the manufacturer or systems integrator.

TIP

RAM chips are stamped with their reliable speed. Look for a number such as 70, 80, 90, or 100 on the chips.

Typically, you'll need no wait states for 70ns (70 nanosecond) RAM chips. Slower RAM chips (over 80 or 90ns) might need one or two wait states with fast processors such as 66 MHz 486s or Pentiums, but not always. I've used some 80ns chips at that speed with no adverse effects. If you're in doubt about whether your RAM can operate reliably with no wait states, try the wait state setting at zero. If you start getting lots of weird errors such as programs crashing, the system memory check reporting errors, or the operating system not loading, add a wait state and try again.

How much performance loss do wait states contribute? From my experience, not much. The major bottlenecks on most systems are threefold: processor, video, and hard disk. RAM speed comes in fourth. But if you're really trying to cut out the fat, it's something to consider. Benchmark programs that measure memory data transfers do show an improvement in system throughput when fewer wait states are used.

NOTE

See the discussion on memory caching in the section titled "About RAM Caches" for another approach to RAM optimizing that can be very effective.

BIOS and Video Shadowing

Most systems let you "shadow" the BIOS and video subsystem ROM software. Here's how it works. As I mentioned, the BIOS is a small amount of software stored in ROM (read-only memory) chips on the computer's motherboard. When the operating system needs to execute a low-level operation, such as writing to the hard disk, getting data from the keyboard, or sending data to a port, it makes a "call" to the software in the ROM (actually called *firmware*) to execute it. Having the BIOS in a chip means that the operating system itself (typically MS-DOS or NT) doesn't have to know about the physical structure of the machine. An application makes a call to the operating system, the operating system passes the call to the BIOS, and the requested service is performed.

NOTE

This modularization allows the BIOS to be upgraded without altering the operating system. In the early days of microcomputers, people had to write their own BIOS code to handle the keyboard, screen, printer, and I/O ports, assemble the code using a software assembler, carefully "patch" it into the operating system, reboot, and hope it worked.

This is all very convenient. BIOSs are now standardized enough that often you can even pull a BIOS chip out of one clone machine and drop it into another. (This works only if the chip sets—the CPU and support chips—of the two machines are identical, though.) It also allows for easy updating of BIOSs.

The bad news is that ROM chips are slow by design. They simply can't dish out the data very fast. This means that even with a screamer of a machine, when the operating system makes a call to the BIOS, the CPU will be cooling its heels, waiting for the BIOS code. The same is true of the firmware stored in ROM on your video card.

The solution is to copy the firmware code out of the ROM and into some of your much faster system RAM. Then fool the operating system into redirecting calls to the video card and BIOS to the new location of the code, from where it will execute much more quickly. This is what shadowing does.

Most CMOS BIOS setup routines let you turn BIOS and video shadowing on or off individually. You'll want to ensure that both are on, if possible. Sometimes you have the option of choosing the location of the RAM that will be used to hold the relocated code. This might be necessary only when you have an oddball card or another device that is mapped into a portion of system memory normally used for shadowing. I've never had to bother with this, and you probably won't either. Just check to see that the setup routine has video and BIOS shadowing enabled.

Optimizing Virtual Memory

Windows NT, like Windows 3.1, incorporates a virtual memory scheme. The virtual-memory manager provides the NT operating system with more apparent RAM for use by applications and the operating system than is physically present in the computer. This is done by using hard-disk space to simulate RAM, with the advantage that more applications and services can run simultaneously than would normally be the case. Data is temporarily shifted out of RAM and into one or more files called PAGEFILE.SYS.

When you install NT, settings controlling the virtual-memory manager are automatically adjusted to reflect your hard-disk space and drive designations. In NT, the virtual-memory files (called *paging files*) created on the hard disk are *dynamic,* unlike the *permanent* paging files that are possible under Windows 3.1. As available hard-disk space decreases, the paging files shrink in size, making room for your data files or applications. Also, under NT, each logical drive can support a single paging file (if you choose to set up this option), so if you have several disks, NT might decrease the size of a paging file on one drive and be intelligent enough to shift paging onto another drive.

NOTE

If the paging drives are physical (instead of logical), throughput can be increased for both paging and application services, because multiple requests can be processed simultaneously.

NOTE

Paging files can't be removed while NT is running, because important data could be lost if this were allowed. However, you can remove them under another operating system. Just look for the file PAGEFILE.SYS on each of your hard disks. Another way to remove them is from NT, if it's not in use. Just remove the paging file using Control Panel's System applet, reboot, then delete the inactive file.

Paging files are central to system optimization. NT is a huge operating system for a PC to run, and so tons of paging goes on. You've probably noticed that the hard disk, even of a simple workstation, can get very busy thrashing around with the simplest of operations. The moral is this: You'll want to ensure not only that your system has gobs of RAM, but also that you have ample paging file room for NT. See Chapter 9, "Configuring Windows NT," for details about setting paging file locations and sizes, which you do from Control Panel.

TIP

Also consider compacting your hard disk and upgrading your hard disk, hard-disk controller, and/or motherboard for faster disk performance. All these options are explained in the sections that follow.

Upgrading Your Hard Disk

There are a number of approaches for upgrading your hard-disk system:

- Delete unnecessary files
- Optimize the hard-disk interleave
- Repair fragmented files
- Defragment the hard disk
- Upgrade the disk controller
- Get a faster disk drive

Deleting and Managing Files

As you know, hard disks are never large enough. This is particularly true of NT. By the time you have NT (and possibly Windows 3.1 and DOS) on a disk, you're already pushing it. Add the almost infinite number of document files, electronic junk mail, applications, support files, help files, and temporary files, and pretty soon you're dreaming about gigabyte-sized drives. Because NT 3.5 doesn't work with disk compression programs, you can't just easily double your capacity with DoubleSpace, Stacker, or SuperStor, either.

What to do? Here are some ideas. Regularly sift through your files and delete old ones you don't use frequently. Back up important files to floppy disks. Erase programs you don't use, including accessory programs such as Paintbrush and Notepad and their associated help files (which have the same first name, but an .HLP extension instead of .EXE).

TIP

If you're sharing your workstation with other users, remember to clear the removal of an application with them.

Even though NT doesn't support on-the-fly disk compression programs, there's nothing to prevent you from running Windows 3.1, OS/2, or DOS applications that compress and decompress individual files. Use PKZIP or another compression application such as Kwik-Vault to crunch complete directories that you don't use regularly. When you need the files again, decompress them.

When you're searching for files to kill, remember that many applications (especially Windows applications) create and use temporary files while they're running. For example, when you edit a Word for Windows document, Word creates a file with a name such as ~doc1b2e.tmp to store the file as you edit. If such a program bombs, or if the computer loses power or is turned off before you properly exit the application, aside from probably losing your work, you'll also be left with a dead temp file. Such files can take up considerable room and will never be used again. Neither NT nor the application automatically deletes them.

The location of your temp files varies, depending on your system and the applications you use. Often they'll be in the \WINDOWS\TEMP directory. If they're not there, they might be in the same directory as the application or the document you're working on.

Temp files often use names that start with a tilde (~) and have the extension .TMP. Others start with the characters ~WOA and can have any extension. Thus, you can search for them using File Manager or the `DIR` command in a command-prompt window.

Another file of significant size you might want to look for is a Windows 3.1 temporary swap file. You won't have one of these if you're not running Windows 3.1 or if you're using a permanent swap file in Windows 3.1. Temporary swap files normally are deleted when you exit Windows 3.1, but if the system bombs or power is lost, the file might still be around. You'll want to delete the file \WINDOWS\WIN386.SWP.

NOTE

Some temp files might be hidden or system files and therefore won't appear in listings unless you opt to display such files (for example, by using File Manager's View | By File Type command).

To simplify cleanup, you might write a batch file that deletes temp files. If you run DOS regularly, you could add the following lines to your AUTOEXEC.BAT file or have your autoexec file call the batch file:

```
del c:\windows\temp\~*.tmp
del c:\windows\temp\~woa*.*
del c:\windows\win386.swp
```

CAUTION

Be careful when deleting temp files from within NT. Ideally, such files should be deleted only when you're not running Windows or Windows NT (that is, preferably from DOS), because this will ensure that the files aren't in use. But if you simply close all applications in NT except File Manager and Program Manager and delete the files, you should be okay. For most applications, NT alerts you if the file is still in use, because it will be locked by another process. But this might not always be the case.

TIP

You also can use the Windows NT Setup program to quickly and easily erase classes of programs, such as games, wallpaper, help files, and accessory programs.

Repairing Fragmented Files

Occasionally, an errant program or a system crash causes chunks of otherwise related data to lose their relationship to one another. When a disk is newly formatted, even large data files are written across the disk in their totality using consecutive sectors. As the disk fills up and files are erased, moved, copied, and so forth, this causes "holes" of erased data to open up, leaving sectors available for storing files. Any disk operating system (OS/2, DOS, NT, or UNIX) utilizes this space by breaking large files into pieces and fitting them in wherever possible. The disk directory (file allocation table, or FAT) remembers which pieces (or sectors) go with each other to constitute the letter to Uncle George, the business plan, and even the NT Registry file.

When a program freaks out or the system crashes, however, the directory might not be updated correctly, resulting in "lost" or orphaned sectors. The result is not only a corrupted file, but sectors that are marked as unavailable even though they're serving no purpose. In a word, you've lost some disk space. Such sectors are hidden, and they don't even display in a directory listing because they don't have names.

So much for the primer. As you may know, DOS's `CHKDSK` program is the cure for lost sectors (or, more typically, groups of sectors, called *clusters*). `CHKDSK` is a program in your DOS directory (assuming that you have an Intel-based machine with DOS on it) that, when used with the `/f` option (`chkdsk /f`, for example), scours your hard disk for lost clusters and reclaims them. If clusters are found, you're asked whether you want the data collected into files you can later edit. If you type `Y` (for yes), files with names such as FILE0000.CHK and FILE0001.CHK are created in the root of the checked drive. If you type `N` (for no), the clusters are immediately deleted and returned to the pool of available disk space.

NT does a cursory `CHKDSK` when it first boots up. It's not exhaustive, but it detects cross-linked files or confused directories and attempts to make repairs. This is a little daily housekeeping that NT does for you. For more exhaustive checking, NT includes a `CHKDSK` program that's much like the one that comes with DOS. In fact, it has the same name and can be executed from the command prompt from within NT. It can be used on any active drive (to fix problems) and causes a more thorough auto `CHKDSK` at boot time.

Also note that NT's `CHKDSK` will sometimes fail, particularly if there's an error in one of the system boot files. This book's technical editor, Art Knowles, commented that this has happened to him several times. He used `SCANDISK` (an MS-DOS 6.2 utility) to correct the errors that were found in the system Registry and Event Log files.

NOTE

See Chapter 12, "Maintenance and Troubleshooting," for details on maintaining and repairing damaged hard disks.

The moral of the story is this: One way or another, you should ensure that you don't have lots of lost clusters hanging around on your hard disk. If you run DOS regularly, or DOS and Windows 3.1, do a `CHKDSK` once in a while on your FAT partitions. OS/2 has a similar program. As NT matures, you'll see more disk maintenance programs such as the PC-Tools and Norton Utilities programs for Windows 3.1 that sleuth out all manner of errors, including lost clusters, cross-linked files, bad disk media, and so forth. You might want to choose one and use it. In the meantime, run NT's `CHKDSK` program on each drive from the command prompt once in a while.

Defragmenting the Hard Disk

As I mentioned, over time your files get broken into pieces so that they can most efficiently be shoehorned into available sectors on the hard disk's platters. However, your system pays a speed penalty for this ingenuity. When a file is read from or written to, the hard-disk heads must physically move around on the platters in order to reach sometimes far-flung tracks that otherwise might be consecutive. It's as if a song on an LP were broken up across the bands of the record, requiring the tone arm to jump to play one piece of music. Obviously, the song would be interrupted while the arm moved between portions. On a hard disk, such an interruption might be miniscule (on the order of 20 milliseconds), but it adds up—especially in NT, which does so much disk accessing.

The moral of *this* story is to *defragment* each hard disk on your system or on the network once in a while. Defragmenting rearranges all the data on a disk in such a way that files are written on consecutive sectors and tracks. This means that the heads have less moving to do in order to read from or write to a file. Thus, overall system throughput increases.

How do you defragment? Defragmenting programs for DOS, Windows 3.1, and OS/2 are widely available. For example, DOS 6 comes with a free `DEFRAG` program. When DOS 6 is installed, an icon for the program is added to Program Manager, allowing the program to be run from Windows 3.1. (Actually, it runs in DOS by temporarily closing Windows, because it's safer that way.) "Defragging" of NTFS partitions obviously can't be achieved from these programs. You have to rely on an NT-compatible defragging program for this purpose. Unfortunately, as of this writing none are available. The good news is that NT utilizes a 512 sector/cluster arrangement for NTFS partitions, and its indexes are very efficient. This means that there is less of a need to defragment NTFS partitions than FAT partitions. A good program can prevent disastrous data loss in case the power goes out during the process and can even be aborted in the middle of the process should you change your mind. Be aware that disk defragmenting (sometimes called *compacting*) can take quite a long time. It's the kind of thing you let the computer do overnight.

TIP

Actually, there's a way to defragment NTFS partitions, but it's roundabout. You have to back up and restore the partition.

Optimizing the Hard-Disk Interleave

Another approach to hard-disk optimizing is to ensure that the interleave is set to its optimum value. Some hard-disk controllers don't have electronics that are fast enough to read consecutive sectors as they pass by the heads on the hard disk. (Such a hard-disk controller isn't likely to be on an NT system, but it's possible if you're just now upgrading.) Instead, they read one sector of information, then need a bit of time to prepare for the next sector. Hard disks spin very fast, and as a result, magnetically recorded data flies by the head at an alarmingly rapid rate. To accommodate slower electronics, hard-disk controllers can be set to number the sectors nonconsecutively. Imagine numbering a pizza's sections with gaps between the numbers. Figure 11.1 illustrates this concept.

FIGURE 11.1.
A disk's interleave determines the order in which the sectors are numbered. This illustration compares an interleave of 1:1 to that of 2:1.

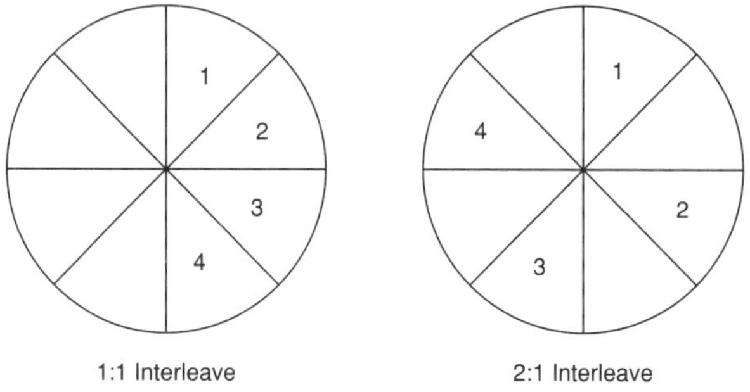

Spacing out the sectors gives the electronics more time to work between reading from or writing to each sector's data.

The fastest possible interleave is no interleave at all, meaning that sectors are adjacent. This is called 1:1 (one to one) interleave. On many computers, the interleave is set higher than it needs to be, such as 3:1, which would mean there are two added sectors between sectors 1 and 2. You might want to check your interleave setting using a good hard-disk utility program. Such a program will tell you the current setting, recommend a new optimum setting, and reorder the sectors for you. Some good DOS-based programs are Power Disk (Multisoft Corp.), SpinRite II (Gibson Research), and OPTune (Gazelle Systems).

NOTE

As with defragmenting, resetting interleave can take quite a long time, because major shuffling of data is required. Be prepared for a couple of hours of hard-disk activity. Also, you should make a backup of any important data before resetting the interleave. You might lose something important.

Upgrading the Disk Controller

The next stop is the disk controller. As you may know, the two elements of the disk subsystem are the disk itself and the controller that connects it to the computer. (There's also the bus that connects the controller to the computer, but we'll get to that in a bit.)

Several types of controllers have been available over the years, such as FM, MFM, RLL, ESDI, IDE, and SCSI. Each of these is an improvement over its predecessor, and each type of controller requires a matching drive of the same type. (An RLL controller requires an RLL drive, for example.) As of this writing, the bulk of current drives are either SCSI or IDE. Anyway, you can't just mix and match any drive and any controller.

Some disk controllers are smarter than others. The two prime considerations are the data path and the capability to cache data on the controller card itself rather than doing caching in system RAM with programs such as SmartDrive. Because there's always a delay (no matter what type of drive) when reading and writing, a caching disk controller speeds up processing by storing data in RAM on its card until the drive or the operating system can process it. An intelligent controller employs sophisticated algorithms to intuit which sectors or tracks are likely to be read by analyzing recent activity. It then reads in a mess of data (typically a whole track or two) and stores this data in the card's RAM, making it available for the operating system to grab.

Likewise, during a write, the operating system can quickly dump a large amount of data on the controller, believing that the data has been written to the disk when actually it's only been absorbed by the disk controller's RAM cache. The cache then hands it off to the disk while the operating system goes about its business. Good caching controllers have all the necessary hardware (including an on-board processor) to shuffle data to and from the hard disk without intervention by the main CPU or the operating system.

Aside from the inescapable mechanical slowness of hard drives (relative to the virtually speed-of-light performance from RAM), the other classic bottleneck for drives is the bus. The bus is the data path through which the CPU communicates with the drive. Typically, on an x86 machine, this is a 16-bit ISA (industry standard architecture) bus running at the standard 8 MHz data transfer rate popularized by the IBM AT-class machines. CPUs and plug-in cards such as disk controllers and video cards can now operate well in excess of this. Recognizing this fact, individual manufacturers such as IBM and vendor consortiums such as VESA have provided customers faster alternatives. As a result, we now have a mish-mash of acronyms. MCA, EISA, and VLB are new and competing bus standards, each of which at least doubles the old data transfer rate.

If your budget allows it and your system board supports it (changing the system board is discussed in the section titled "Upgrading Your CPU and Motherboard"), consider upgrading your disk controller to take advantage of a faster bus. In some cases this can be done for a very small outlay. For example, nowadays many system motherboards have at least one VLB connector—often two. This is a 32-bit high-speed data path designed principally for video and disk controllers. A clone IDE floppy/hard disk controller that will plug into a VLB slot costs only about $50, and it will work with your existing IDE drives (IDE controllers support up to two hard drives and two floppies). The cost/performance benefit of this upgrade is very high.

By and large, most pundits agree that for fastest throughput and greatest flexibility, SCSI is the way to go. SCSI is an industry-standard high-speed parallel interface designed for small computer peripherals. The Apple Macintosh has supported SCSI for years because it lets you daisy-chain a great number of dissimilar devices (printers, modems, scanners, hard disks, removable media drives, CD-ROM drives, and so on) on the same cable. Each device gets a device number, and each device driver is assigned to its respective number. Only one controller card is necessary, leaving more slots in your computer free for other uses. SCSI drives typically are faster (and more expensive) than their counterparts, such as IDE. Assuming that the SCSI spec doesn't change, buying SCSI devices also means that you don't have to keep buying controller cards. You buy one card and then just an extension data cable to add each new device to the chain.

In reality, though, SCSI has been an evolving standard, which is why some wary consumers (including me) have opted for IDE. Now in its second major iteration (SCSI II), the specification is settling down, and most devices seem to be working fairly reliably. Even though SCSI III is now being talked about, over the long haul, SCSI probably is the way to go.

CAUTION

Be aware that, as of version 3.1, NT doesn't have tremendous support for caching disk controllers. These controllers sometimes need NT-compatible device drivers. Check Chapter 8, "Installing Windows NT," and read the NT-compatible hardware listing supplied with NT before you drop big bucks for that fancy SCSI drive and/or intelligent controller. The same holds true for some SCSI controllers. I've heard of a few cases where even a very "industry standard" controller such as an Adaptec wasn't recognized by NT. You can rest assured that vanilla (and, incidentally, very affordable IDE drives using standard or VLB) controllers *do* work just fine.

Getting a Faster Disk Drive

Due to the expense of replacing drives, I discussed upgrading your system by changing controllers first. In reality, however, due to plummeting hard-drive prices, you can actually find controllers that outprice the drives. In any case, a general discussion of drive upgrades follows.

As you probably know, hard disks are rated primarily by type (SCSI, IDE, and so on), capacity (120M, 300M, 1G), and speed (12ms, 18ms, 20ms). Over the years, I've experimented with many speed upgrades to my systems, and I've concluded that one major Achilles' heel of a GUI system such as Windows is the hard disk itself. Regardless of changing the controller card, upgrading the CPU, or even upgrading the video controller card, getting a fast disk can appear to double your system's speed. I had read this in magazines, but I didn't believe it. It seemed intuitively wrong, and I thought it was just another industry ruse to sell expensive products. After all, a hard disk transfers data across its ribbon cable at about 5 megabits per second, and the platter is flying past the head at several hundred miles per hour. What could be slow?

Well, recall my earlier LP analogy. Even though the disk is spinning quickly and the data on it is always available, the heads that read and write the data have to be positioned on the track and then locate the right sector before any data is transferred. This is called *access time.* This is one major area where drives take a speed toll on your system. A drive's access time is averaged using a random pattern of track accesses. A drive with an average access time of 28ms will perform like a dog compared to one with 12ms, for example.

As with controllers, some drives have smart electronics. They might keep tabs on which tracks are being used the most, for example, and buffer (cache) data from those tracks into their on-board RAM. Typically, the cheaper drives don't have these features and are relatively dumb. However, drives with fast access times and relatively high storage capacity are so cheap that it doesn't matter.

For example, a typical x86-based NT workstation would perform admirably using a single 340M IDE hard disk. Such drives (for example, the Western-Digital Caviar) have a street price of about $300 or less as of this writing. Similar drives from makers such as Conner, Maxstor, and Seagate are readily available. Such drives have an average access time of under 20ms, and more often on the order of 12ms to 15ms. I have two such drives on my VLB-based IDE controller, which acts as a three-station server.

NOTE

As a rule of thumb, expect to pay about $1 or less per megabyte.

Drive technology changes quickly. We now have 3-inch and 1 1/2-inch drives, many removable-media drive technologies such as "floptical" drives, 8mm tape drives, and so forth. Hard-disk prices continue to drop, and capacities are hitting the multigigabyte range. (A gigabyte equals one billion bytes or a thousand megabytes.)

NOTE

See the previous discussion on disk economizing for alternatives to huge drives. Remember that having huge drives means losing huge amounts of data in case of a disk failure and that crashes are more prevalent with new technology.

Due to the rapidly changing nature of hardware, I can't offer too many specific recommendations. Suffice it to say that you should use time-tested, reliable media formats for mission-critical work, whether at home or in the office. If the choice is between buying new and flashy technology or a popular, boring drive, go for the latter. Remember that those babies will be spinning a zillion times a day. Also remember that new operating systems (NT is a good case in point) tend to ship only with drivers for popular, vanilla-flavored hardware.

If you must have a new whiz-bang toy, carefully compare specs on drives, including the MTBF (mean time between failure) ratings. Check the magazines for the latest scoop on drive recommendations, noting that long-term testing usually is beyond the reviewers' ken. If you're setting up stripe sets, consider upgrading from NT to NT Server and using stripe sets *with parity*. This way, if one drive of an array fails, you can still recover the data. This is not possible with standard stripe sets. Also remember to use backup disks with tape, as described in Chapter 12.

Upgrading Your Memory Subsystem

If only memory prices for RAM were as cheap as the cost per megabyte for hard disks! Then 16M of RAM would cost $16—a dream come true. Unfortunately, RAM prices have only gone up in the last year. Upgrades to NT in my business cost a pretty penny, with about $1,000 going into RAM alone, not to mention CPU and motherboard upgrades, new drives, and CD-ROM readers. Let's cover the worst of the news quickly and move on to more scintillating topics.

You'll want to take full advantage of your machine's physical endowments, not to mention NT's great capabilities. Like its little brothers, NT screams for extended memory (not expanded memory or anything else, incidentally). You'll want to give NT as much memory as possible. (You'd pay a dear price without it.) You might as well forget all the other fine optimizations mentioned earlier if you're short on RAM.

Vanilla NT (not NT Server) is remarkable in that it actually boots and appears to run with less memory than the "recommended" 12M. However, it will run at a snail's pace while sending your hard disk into conniptions and probably will wear out the stepper motor controlling the hard-disk heads way before its time. What's going on is almost continuous disk swapping, because the operating system components don't have room to load into RAM.

Microsoft says 12M will run NT on an x86-based client well enough. This is true. However, I suggest that this is marketing hype based on the negative press about NT's hardware requirements. I suggest splurging for the additional 4M and running with at least 16M. Certainly an NT server should have 16M or more. RISC clients need a minimum of

16M. For NT Server machines, I recommend a minimum of 20M and preferably 32M or more if SQL Server is running. The extra memory helps a lot!

How you install memory depends on your system. How much it costs depends on the position of the moon, the state of the economy, the current laws governing international import tariffs, and the whims of those in a position to concoct stories about the trickle-down effects of destroyed Japanese plastics plants. Check the manual that came with the computer or motherboard. Do you need proprietary cards and/or chips? If you do, expect to pay twice what a generic SIMM or SIP would cost. It's unfortunate, but true.

Next, what speed should the chips be? 70ns is considered the fastest. On an 80486 with a 66 MHz CPU, you'll probably want at least 80ns chips, and 70ns is better. (See the earlier discussion regarding wait states for slow memory.) A Pentium or fast RISC machine might have very stringent memory requirements. As a general rule, buy the fastest chips you can, because you might end up plugging them into a new, faster motherboard or machine later, particularly as system prices fall.

What will memory cost you? 1M of fast (70 or 80ns) memory costs about $40 to $50 as of this writing. Buying memory through the mail is easy, and shipping is negligible, so that's how I buy mine. Look through some magazines to find the cheapest prices, and buy that way. If your company policy mandates buying from a specific supplier, at least try bargaining based on competitive street prices. Remember, if you're upgrading a large number of machines, you're going to pay a mint for all that RAM.

TIP

Don't overlook the possibility of running Windows for Workgroups, DOS, Novell, Windows 95, or another alternative operating system on lower-priority workstations and just wait as system prices or RAM prices come down. Windows for Workgroups, despite some negative reviews, is now actually something to write home about. For starters, it's "plug and play" with NT. Second, because it's from Microsoft, it's been thoroughly tested with NT in-house. Finally, it's cheap.

Be careful when installing memory. RAM chips are static-sensitive. If you rub your feet across a carpet while carrying RAM chips, then discharge the buildup through the chips to something such as the computer's chassis, the chips can be blown. This has never happened to me, but I don't live in a dry climate. Stay in one place while doing your installation (don't walk around the room with the chips in your hand). Also, touch the computer chassis before picking up the chips, and try to touch only the fiberglass circuit board the chips are mounted on rather than the metallic circuit or chip legs themselves.

Most chips come three or nine to a card (called a SIMM—single inline memory module) that plugs into a holder on the motherboard. You must line up the chips in the right direction and line up little holes that engage with pins in the holder. Then the board snaps into place. The trick is to first insert the SIMM board at about a 45-degree angle and wiggle it to ensure that the contacts on the bottom of the board are fully inserted in the bottom of the connector cage. Then lift the SIMM, visually ensuring that it stays fully seated.

NOTE

When you power up again, be sure to set the CMOS settings to reflect the memory upgrade. Otherwise, NT probably won't take advantage of the new memory. See the section titled "BIOS Adjustments" for details.

NOTE

If an EISA system is used, it's also important to make sure that the EISA settings for memory amount and SIMM type are correct. Failure to do this can cause the ISA settings to be used, which might lead to NT not recognizing all of the installed memory.

CAUTION

Of course, memory should be inserted only when the power to the computer is off. Otherwise, you're likely to blow it out. This applies to all system upgrades. Unplugging hard disks with the power on, for example, isn't particularly dangerous, but it can trash the data on the drive. The voltages on a computer tend to be low (for example, +5, –5, +12, –12 volts), but the power supply box has high voltage. Even though the power supply is shielded from contact with users, to be extra safe you should unplug the computer before opening it and making modifications.

Upgrading Your Video Subsystem

The computer press has given Windows video a great deal of attention. Innumerable video system reviews, fancy benchmarking tests, and conflicting "editor's choices" appear monthly. It's impossible to keep up. One thing is for sure, however: Video system performance greatly affects most Windows (or other highly graphical) tasks. Even if the computer is already endowed with a fast processor and hard disk, sluggish video performance can make it seem to crawl when you move or resize a window, display a chart, or scroll a page of text.

Any version of Windows runs the video card in graphics mode, as opposed to the zippy character mode used by most DOS applications. Character mode is fast because it only requires pushing letters on the screen. A hardware-based character generator defines what an *A* looks like, and pushing it around only requires telling the generator where to put it. Pushing a line of text down the screen or scrolling only requires sending the video controller the appropriate command for line-down or line-up. Because the hardware knows that this means shifting everything up or down *x* number of pixels, it's fast. This is why DOS applications running in character mode (WordPerfect 5.1, PC-Write, WordStar, dBASE IV, and Lotus 1-2-3 version 2) run *fast,* even on an old clunker like a 286 or an old original IBM PC with a prehistoric 8086 processor. I still use some of these machines with DOS applications because, believe it or not, they're still darn fast at what they were designed for.

NOTE

The sad thing is that people throw out perfectly useful computer hardware instead of recycling it or giving it to schools or third-world countries, but that's another story.

Enter Windows. It became a hardware marketeer's heyday. Our machines suddenly came to a crawl, largely due to all the video overhead required to run in "graphics" mode on dumb VGA cards. Whenever you scroll a window, open a menu, or close a dialog box, Windows must redraw pixels on the screen. This process takes time, and the finer the screen's resolution, the more dots that have to be moved or redrawn. On a 1024x1280 monitor, we're talking 1,310,720 pixels! Each pixel on a monochrome monitor (purely black-and-white) equals one bit in the video board's memory. These bits typically are moved around and turned on and off (to create a black dot or a white dot) by the computer's CPU. On a color screen, the number increases dramatically.

Imagine being the CPU in a typical computer. The user has a document running full-screen and scrolls up a line. Suddenly, in addition to whatever else you're doing, you have to move a million bits of data around on the video board. This could get tedious and slow your system down a lot. The CPU in your computer has better things to do than redraw dots. And if the video card is drawing in color, there are many more bits per pixel, as many as 24 if you want "true color," which gives you 65 million colors. So, on a standard VGA screen at 480x640 resolution, in true color, we're talking 7,372,800 bits per screen. You get the idea.

There are four ways around the video bottleneck:

- Use fewer colors or lower resolution
- Get a faster CPU
- Use local bus video

- Get an accelerated video board

First, if you don't need true color, don't use the true-color driver. Move back to a 256-color driver, or even 16. At 16 colors, you can use a totally dumb video card available for about $50 (maybe even less) and run in 800x600 or 640x480 at zippy speeds. For many employees, such a system will be adequate. An entire color video subsystem can then be had for a song (maybe $200 to $300).

A similarly marked speedup results from decreasing the resolution. If you're running at 1280x1024, scale back to 1024x768 or 800x600. Sure, you see less on the screen, but the system response time speeds up considerably, and the text is larger, which is easier on the eyes.

NOTE

Video drivers are changed via the NT System Setup icon in the Main group. This is discussed in Chapter 9, "Configuring Windows NT."

If you've just got to have high resolution and/or lots of colors, then what? Using a faster main processor will help some, but the results are marginal, contrary to what you might hope. I recently moved up from a 25 MHz 486 to a 66 MHz one and didn't notice one bit of difference on my 1024x1280 gray-scale (16 levels of gray) 21-inch monitor's performance. The card for it does *not* have an accelerator chip, so the main CPU in my computer *is* doing all the work. Benchmark tests showed far less than the more than 100 percent improvement I had expected. The bottleneck obviously was elsewhere.

As with hard disks, the bottleneck is sometimes in the bus. The CPU just can't move data to and from the screen fast enough on the slow 8 MHz ISA bus. Proprietary systems such as the DEC Alpha shine in the video department because they're designed for high-speed video I/O. Ditto for EISA and VLB systems. If you're not fortunate enough to already be running with one of these faster buses, here are some tips:

- If you're using an ISA-based controller on an EISA/ISA motherboard, try dumping it for an EISA-based controller.
- If the motherboard has a VLB connector, dump the ISA video board for a VLB. Standard VLB Super VGA controllers that do 256 colors at 800x600 pixels are cheap. This is the affordable "middle path" between full-blown video systems and the vanilla job. If the computer has a pretty fast CPU, even graphics-intensive applications will perform admirably with this arrangement. (VLB motherboards are discussed later.)
- Some users report that a VLB/EISA combination makes a good server/workstation

platform. This arrangement gives you VLB for faster video, but an EISA 32-bit bus for faster disk I/O and network I/O (assuming that you get 32-bit EISA network adapters).

NOTE

VGA is the common name for 640x480 resolution. Super VGA is the common name for 800x600 resolution. The remaining two higher resolutions are referred to as 1024x768 and 1280x1024. The first number is the number of pixels from left to right. The second number is the number of pixels from top to bottom.

Coprocessor Boards

One sure way to spiff up performance is to switch to one of the coprocessor boards readily available these days. Coprocessor boards—sometimes called graphics accelerator boards—contain a dedicated graphics processor, a bunch of RAM, and some support chips. The RAM is used to store the screen's image. Often it's special RAM called VRAM (video RAM). This is particularly fast RAM fine-tuned for moving bits around at rapid rates. Special on-board programming in the graphics processor results in excellent performance when it comes to Windows-related tasks such as moving and resizing large areas of the screen. Moving chunks of images around is accelerated using what's called *bit blitting* or *bitblt* (which derives from the term *bit block transfer*). Simply stated, large blocks of bits (typically a window) constitute a block of pixels or bits. When you move a window by dragging it with the mouse pointer, Windows simply has to move a bunch of contiguous data bits from one place in memory to another. It's like moving a range of cells in a spreadsheet from one place to another. Windows graphics accelerator cards are designed around processors that excel at this task in particular.

The war is raging between card makers to get your vote (and dollar). Each claims theirs is the fastest, or the best bargain. Many use the same processor but add some bells and whistles such as "crystal fonts," zooming tools, virtual desktops, and so forth. Most at this point are designed for Windows 3.1, *not* for NT. Some cards excel at bit blitting, while others offer more colors. Some support more resolutions than others. Some offer higher refresh rates to prevent flicker—an ergonomic consideration. Some have VRAM, while others don't. You get the picture. There's lots of hype out there, and you'll have to pore over the magazines to keep up-to-date on the latest. We can't print this book every two months, so I won't bother to discuss the minutia. But some general rules might help:

- Consider your budget first. What can you afford? Prices range from about $350 to

$1,000 for accelerator boards. The more expensive ones have fully programmable coprocessors as opposed to less-intelligent graphics accelerator chips. This can theoretically make a difference because coprocessors can be programmed (by changing ROMs on the board or running a program in the computer that updates the card). In reality, I haven't seen much of this.

- Check to see whether the manufacturer or Microsoft makes a driver for the card. Just because it works under Windows 3.1 is no assurance that NT will support it.
- If possible, get a card that's popular or that uses the same accelerator chip as a popular card. At the time of this writing, the Weitek P9000 appears to be the item to buy, but NT has more thorough built-in support for cards using the S3 chip.
- How many colors do you need? If you're working on art projects, you might need 65 million (24-bit) colors. If you're doing text editing, stick with 4-bit, 16-color cards.
- Is flicker a problem for you? Even if you don't know it, your eyes might be taking a beating from flickering screens. (See the later discussion about the role of monitors with flicker.) Cards play their part in this. You'll want a card that can provide a 70 Hz (cycles per second) or faster (such as 72-90 Hz) refresh rate at the resolution you choose. As resolution increases, manufacturers tend to cut corners on refresh rate. You'll have to search to find a card that runs at the highest resolution (1280x1024) with a 72 Hz refresh.

NOTE

To take advantage of a card's high refresh rate, the monitor also has to support it at the chosen resolution.

Choosing a Monitor

Although this chapter concerns itself primarily with optimizing NT's performance in terms of speed, I'm going to digress a bit and discuss video displays—something a bit more aesthetic. Because video displays are the primary conduit through which we interact with computers and because they must dovetail with your video card choice, they merit attention.

As with video cards, numerous magazines have devoted a significant number of "special issues" to monitors. I suppose this is because monitors, especially with the advent of color graphical computing, are so nice to look at and can make boring old computing visually exciting. Or maybe it has something to do with our obsession with television. Anyway, color is here to stay, and with Windows, OS/2, and now NT, graphical interfaces are also here to stay. As a result, big, clear, easy-on-the-eyes monitors are on the rise. The problem is, how do you choose a monitor, especially a monitor for use with NT?

Let's discuss monitors in general and then go over some pointers pertinent to NT. As you know, monitors come in all shapes and sizes. Well, mostly square, but some are deeper than others, and certainly screen dimension varies. Most monitors these days are 14 or 15 inches and are used to display normal VGA resolution. However, the days are numbered for this size of monitor. Users are slowly becoming dissatisfied with the limitations imposed by a monitor this size. The scuttlebutt in the industry has it that 17-inch monitors might be taking the lead in sales soon.

NOTE

Recall that this measurement is taken diagonally across the screen's surface area. Often the image on the screen isn't even this large, so the figure can be misleading.

In any event, I concur that standard VGA doesn't really cut it if you want to see more than a third of a page of text (although I'm writing this on an LCD laptop with a standard VGA screen) or if you abhor the "jaggies" when you're writing a play, designing a house, or doing anything else that has you staring closely at screen details for any length of time. On the other hand, upping the resolution on a 14- or 15-inch monitor (for example, by using a Super VGA driver—800x600—if your video card supports it) will likely result in a blurry image and letters that are too small to read easily. Thus, the move to a larger monitor makes sense. Displaying 800x600 on a 17-inch monitor looks pretty good and increases your desktop by about 30 percent. A display of 1024x768 is also rendered nicely on a 17-incher. I wouldn't want to work in 1280x1024 on one, though. You'll probably want a 20- or 21-inch job for that.

If in doubt about the sagacity of purchasing a larger monitor, check one out in a store. Be sure to ask questions about how it works with your system, particularly with the video card you have now and ones you might upgrade to. Shopping for monitors is something I've made sort of a hobby of, and writing about the ergonomics of them is something I've made a profession of. I once wrote a long article for *PC Week* about the ergonomics of CRT (cathode ray tubes) and possible ill effects of long exposure to them at close range. Here's my personal list of points to consider when choosing a monitor:

1. Decide what screen size you want. As I mentioned, 17-inch is probably the best bet for serious day-in-day-out work by a power user. Obviously, for a server that doesn't get much direct attention, this is overkill and a waste of money. Use an old clunker monitor there. Ditto for workstations where simple tasks or character-based DOS, OS/2, or UNIX apps are being run.
2. Do you need color? Color is nice, but it blurs the image. Three dots (red, blue,

and green) make up each pixel instead of one dot on a gray-scale or black-and-white monitor. If color isn't really needed, great. You'll enjoy a lower price and a cleaner image on a gray-scale monitor. Most gray-scale monitors work with color cards. The monitor just turns colors to shades of gray. Check with the manufacturer on this. For typesetting and technical drawing particularly, gray-scale monitors are preferable. I have a 21-inch job I use for typesetting books.

3. Peruse the magazines and note whether they all agree on one model as the best in the size category you want. Typically, they won't. You'll find that maybe three models vie for the editor's choice among, for example, *Windows Magazine*, *PC World*, and *PC*. Typically the best models will be an NEC, a Nanao, and a Viewsonic (or a Mag). Note the names and *exact* model numbers (for instance, an NEC 5FG is *not* an NEC 5FGe).
4. Often the magazines have extensive tables listing features. Save the articles, copy them, throw the magazines in a corner, or something. You'll be glad later when you have to compare one little detail such as refresh rate or front panel adjustments.
5. Check the front panel adjustments for each. Are they easy to set? You should have

   Vertical height
   Horizontal width
   Horizontal and vertical position
   Brightness
   Contrast
   Pincushion
   Barrel
   Focus

   Optionally, you might want a color-matching control that lets you fine-tune color rendering to a standard color system such as Pantone. Some NEC monitors have this option. Also, settings for each video mode (character mode, graphics mode, and each resolution) should be savable, digitally stored in the monitor. The monitor should effortlessly sense the mode the card is in, switch to that resolution without blinking and making noise, and activate the appropriate presets. This prevents you from having to adjust the screen each time you run a full-screen DOS application, for example.
6. Compare the screen's specs with that of your video card. Specifically, decide which resolution you're going to be doing most of your work in. Then figure that you might want to move up a notch to a higher resolution at some time. Take that higher resolution and determine whether the card/monitor combination will work at a high enough refresh rate not to bother you with flicker. You should be able to run at 70 Hz or higher. 60 Hz is too slow for prolonged use. You can most easily

detect flicker out of the side of your eye because the retina has less persistence outside of its focal area. Try looking just past the monitor. When you find that it doesn't flicker much when looked at this way, when it's running in the desired resolution, you're doing well.

7. Check the monitor's *dot pitch*. This is a measurement of how focused the dots on the screen are. The smaller, the better. A dot pitch of .31 is too large. Look for .25 if possible. Monitors using Sony Trinitron tubes don't use dots. Instead, they use a grill whose aperture is about .26. A Trinitron tube doesn't always give a better picture than a conventional tube, but it's usually quite good. You often pay a premium for them. They aren't fully flat; they curve in the horizontal plane, like a vertical cylinder.
8. Observe the monitor, possibly even borrowing one to try in your office or at home for a day or two. Or, buy it with a no-questions-asked return privilege. Ask yourself these questions:

   Does it flicker?
   Is the image clear?
   Are the colors vibrant?
   Is it well focused in the corners and in the center?
   Can you adjust it easily to your liking?
   Does it make a high-pitched, bothersome noise?
   Would you prefer a fully flat screen?
   Does it look good at all resolutions you might use?
   Does it have a decent warranty?

NOTE

Speed of video performance has nothing to do with the monitor.

Finally, consider a couple more features:

- Most monitors have an antireflective etched tube. This prevents annoying, eye-straining glare, but it blurs the image just a bit. If you want the clearest image possible, buy a nonetched tube monitor such as the 5FG or 5FGe from NEC. You might have to adjust the room's lighting to prevent glare.
- Some studies suggest that long-term exposure to CRT-based monitors might be cause for health concerns. Specifically, even very low levels of electromagnetic radiation of various frequencies absorbed by the body over long periods of time may increase the risk of eye disease, and possibly birth defects and cancer. The jury is still out, even after years of research, but there is some evidence to suggest a possible problem. As a result, better monitors nowadays are designed to meet the

stricter standards being imposed in some European countries. If you're concerned about this, buy a monitor meeting the Swedac II low-emission standard. Magazine reviews in which monitors' radiation levels were tested seem to bear out manufacturers' claims of meeting this standard.

- Finally, consider buying "green." Some monitors power down to a fraction of their usual energy consumption level when they sit idle for a preset period of time. Instead of consuming a typical 200 watts, for example, a monitor might power down to 30 watts. When you move the mouse or press a key, it wakes up. Such "green" monitors are becoming more prevalent, but not all manufacturers make them yet. Also, be aware that they fall into two categories: those that don't power down unless used with a "green" video card that complies with the new standard, and those that power down by detecting a blank screen caused by a screen saver such as After Dark or Windows' own. You'll probably want the latter kind of monitor.

Before buying, shop around carefully. You can save several hundred dollars by checking the magazines for competitive pricing.

TIP

CompuServe's Ziffnet has a buyer's guide that lets you enter a model name and number and quickly see a listing of the cheapest mail order prices in the country. There's also lots of useful information about how to purchase equipment by mail order without losing your shirt. Log in and then type `Go Ziffnet` at the `!` prompt. Then follow the instructions for the Ziff Buyer's Market. Even if you don't buy from one of the vendors listed, it's a great way to get an idea of the latest street price of an item.

Upgrading Your CPU and Motherboard

Aside from buying a whole new computer system (which is often the easiest choice at upgrade time, considering the rock-bottom prices of many integrated systems these days), you might want to upgrade just the CPU or the motherboard. Whereas a new computer might cost you a couple thousand dollars, getting a new CPU or motherboard might cost only $500 to $1,000.

This past year I upgraded my system to speed up NT. The main upgrade consisted of pulling out the old motherboard and dropping in a fast 486 board. After a great deal of shopping and considering whether to drop a clock-doubled CPU into the old motherboard, I decided to bag the whole board and get a new one, complete with 66 MHz 486 CPU. The supplier was Hi-Tech in Milpitas, California, an outfit that often advertises in computer magazines. The price for the board was only about $750, complete with 128K memory cache and two VLB connectors. That was the best choice for me. But your system needs might be different. Let's consider the issues. Note that I discuss only Intel-based systems here. (I wish you could build a DEC Alpha or a MIPS R4000 system from inexpensive clone parts, but you can't. However, you *can* buy a bare-bones Alpha system with no monitor, keyboard, and so on.)

NOTE

In case you don't know, the *motherboard* is the main circuit board in the computer. It contains the edge connectors that the cards plug into, and it also contains the CPU, BIOS chip(s), and other support chips that make the computer work.

As I mentioned, you have to consider whether you want the hassle of installing a motherboard. It takes skill and know-how. I won't go into details here, but power connectors, screwdrivers, and removing all the boards and possibly the disk drives are involved. It can take a couple of hours or more.

You should decide what you're looking for:

- Faster CPU
- Local bus video
- Local bus hard disk
- EISA slots
- ISA slots

As a rule, you'll find that CPUs alone are expensive, almost as expensive as a complete new motherboard. What's more, a new motherboard often incorporates new technology that's worth investing in. You'll get a new BIOS, for example, with some fancy CMOS settings. You might also get some extra slots, a fast memory subsystem, or some RAM cache that your older board didn't have. (I'll get to those in a moment.)

If you're starting with a motherboard that has a zero-insertion-force Pentium upgrade slot, and the motherboard is pretty up-to-date, then purchasing a new processor alone might make sense. You just pop out the old one and pop in the new one. But remember that the old processor you'll be chucking might be worth more than you realize. Relatively fast processors alone (a notch down from top-of-the-line) tend to cost about $400, and you can almost always find a complete motherboard with CPU for this price. An added advantage is that you'll then have the old motherboard as the basis for another system.

Motherboards fall into two basic categories, just as complete systems do: clone and name brand. The name brands cost a bit more, but they tend to have slightly better performance. That is, for the same speed of CPU and RAM, you'll get faster performance. Often this is due to the design of the circuitry surrounding the CPU, particularly the memory subsystem. How fast the CPU can communicate with the RAM is a crucial determinant in system efficiency. If you already have a fast CPU, it's not even out of the question to buy a fast motherboard without CPU, plug your old CPU into it, and discard the old motherboard.

One trick I've used in choosing a motherboard is to check the magazines for reviews of clone computers. Some reviews have an accompanying chart listing performance and, if you're lucky, which brand of motherboard is used in each system. Look for fast performers and note who makes the motherboard. Often it will be a name brand such as Micronics, AIR, or Mylex. Then check your local systems integrator or supplier or scan the magazines for your board of choice.

Choosing a CPU

Choosing a new motherboard also can be confusing due to all the CPUs around, not to mention clock speeds. Ever since Intel was busted for monopolizing CPUs for PCs, we've been bombarded with confusing literature and ads. Everyone claims that their CPU is faster, smarter, and more compatible. Some are cheaper than others. Some use lower voltages so that they'll run longer in a laptop. Some are clock doubled, and others are not. Some have math coprocessors, and others don't. You'll have to do some research to determine what's best for your application mix. Because new processors seem to be born weekly, I'm not going to get into it here. But I have a few suggestions.

The first big decision is whether to go with a Pentium, an 80486, or an 80386 class of chip. This depends on your budget. If performance is no object, you'll want none of these, so you should get a 150 MHz DEC Alpha or one of the multi-CPU machines (for example, the AcerFrame 3000 MP50). Stepping down a notch, Pentium machines are now becoming affordable, and NT is no speed demon, especially when it runs Windows 3.1 applications. If you can afford a good Pentium motherboard, or if your current board allows a Pentium to be plugged in, consider it. In any case, a 386 is out of the question. It's too slow for NT.

SX chips (for example, the 486SX) don't have math coprocessors built in. This eliminates thousands of transistors from the chips, which means that they're significantly cheaper to manufacture. Of course, it also means that performance will slow down on tasks that benefit from having a high-speed floating-point calculator built into the chip, because the CPU has to do the math "longhand." If you do lots of work with applications that you *know* will utilize a math coprocessor, this will slow your work down. For a machine running NT, you're better off staying away from SX chips.

Then there are the non-Intel chips. IBM has a manufacturing agreement to make their own chips using the 486 name, and Cyrix makes the SLC (486) chips. There are others, such as AMD's. Look for performance specs that compare these with the Intel chips. Clone CPUs, which are a little cheaper, usually are fine. Many complete systems, including laptops, utilize these renegade CPUs, helping to keep the free-market system alive and kicking. Make sure you're not getting something without a math coprocessor, though.

Another big issue with CPUs is the data path—both internally and externally. The data path for your upgrade chip should be as wide as possible. For example, a Pentium is actually a 64-bit processor because it can push around 64 bits of information in a swipe. (Incidentally, it also can execute two instructions at once, a trick called *parallel processing*). A 486, by contrast, has a 32-bit internal bus. The width of the bus through which the CPU communicates with the outside world has an effect on its overall speed as well. The SX chips, in addition to not having internal math coprocessors, also communicate with the motherboard over a narrower bus (16-bit as opposed to 32-bit). DX chips use a 32-bit channel. Thus, data throughput between the CPU and the other elements of the computer (hard disk, video, adapter cards) is much faster with DX chips.

Yet another fertile field of battle in the war between the CPUs pertains to internal caches. Processors have varying amounts of internal speedy RAM that temporarily holds data that's being used repeatedly, just as a disk cache does. This caching can increase overall processing speed significantly. The larger the cache, the faster a certain processor can run. Caches typically range from 1K to 16K. A 486 CPU with only a 1K cache (such as a number of the Cyrix CPUs) might run almost as slowly as a fast 386. IBM's chips typically use 16K internal caches these days.

Next, consider processor speed. This is an important determinant of performance. The faster the better, obviously. Some CPUs, however, are *clock doubled* internally. This means that the CPU is working double-time on its own computations, and communicating with the board at *one half* the speed it's working inside. The clock-doubled chips are a cheap way of upgrading existing motherboards without having to install new timing crystals and high-speed support circuitry. It was a great idea on Intel's part to get PC makers to buy their new chips, because the computer makers didn't have to change the circuitry in the computers.

For example, consider a 50 MHz 486DX and a 66 MHz 486DX/2 (the 2 indicates that the chip is clock doubled internally). The 50 MHz 486DX actually sends and receives data faster than the 66 MHz 486DX/2. The DX/2 communicates at 33 MHz, while the DX chugs along at 50 MHz.

Which is faster in overall performance? It depends on your application mix. If the chip typically does heavy "thinking" (calculating internally), the DX/2 is faster. If the chip does lots of I/O, the DX is faster.

About RAM Caches

When you're shopping for motherboards, you'll see listings in magazines with descriptions such as

486/66DX2
128K
0K
no CPU

Here's the breakdown:

The first part means that the motherboard is set up for a 486DX/2 chip running at 66 MHz. The speed is determined by a crystal on the board. Often, such a board also will run a 33 MHz 486 as well, because the crystal speed is the same for each. Some boards list a number of CPU chips (for example, 386/386SX/486/486SX/Pentium) and a number of speeds. These boards have a couple of sockets for the different CPUs and jumpers for setting the clock speed.

The "128K" refers to RAM cache. RAM cache has been shown to be a very important asset when running Windows. The CPU must do a significant amount of memory accessing with Windows; thus, a fast memory system is crucial. Although dynamic RAM is fast as opposed to a hard disk, it isn't as fast as it could be. A 70ns wait for a chip to settle down after being written to, for example, can add up because the CPU executes millions of instructions every second. Just as hard disks use RAM caches to simulate hard-disk storage and allow the CPU to get back to work sooner, the memory system can have a cache of super-fast RAM, too. This is called *RAM cache*. It uses *static* memory chips that typically have a 20ns speed (normal memory chips are of the *dynamic* variety). Without going into the structural and operational differences between static and dynamic RAM, suffice it to say that static RAM is really fast and really expensive. You probably don't want to buy more than 256K, even though it would be nice if your whole 16M (or more) were of this variety. A good board will have at least 128K of cache that is set up for both "read" and "write-back" operations. Boards that don't have write-back cache should be avoided.

NOTE

If you buy a board or a machine with a write-back cache, make sure that you can turn it off if you need to. Some machines with write-back caches have been known to disagree with NT. Turning off the write-back caching action (but leaving the read cache on) is the only solution to the problem of random NT crashing.

The "0K" reference in the ad listing doesn't mean "OK" as in "OK Used Cars." It means that no RAM is installed in the board. You'll want to shop for RAM carefully (as discussed elsewhere in this chapter) and price-shop aggressively. You'll probably pay about $50 per megabyte of RAM. Make sure it's fast RAM.

Finally, if a board listed in a magazine or a flyer says "no CPU," this obviously means that you have to buy the CPU separately. "No CPU" boards usually are pretty inexpensive, and for good reason. Try to get one with a CPU if possible. Installing it isn't always easy, and you'll want to know that the board/CPU combination works before it leaves the factory or store anyway.

Slots

Even if you're not upgrading a machine yourself but are buying it new, you'll have to decide about slots—what kind and how many. As you probably know, the old standard is the ISA (industry standard architecture), a 16-bit slot. More cards are made for this format than for any other, and they're cheap. Clone ISA cards are plentiful, so if you're fabricating systems for the office and trying to keep costs down, this is the way to go. However, you'll want a couple of VLB (VESA local bus) slots in addition. Those will be for the hard disk or SCSI controller and/or video card.

Some power users like EISA (extended ISA) bus machines and will opt for that format. Some EISA motherboards have both ISA and EISA slots, so you can still plug your old I/O, sound, mouse, or other ISA cards into the EISA motherboard instead of chucking them. Others have VLB slots in addition to the EISA slots. The EISA bus is a wider bus (32-bit), just as VLB and IBM's MicroChannel are. But the EISA bus is not as fast as the VLB bus because it still runs at the standard 8 MHz, whereas the VLB runs at the clock speed for the CPU (for example, 33 MHz). The other down side is that far fewer EISA cards are available, and they are much more expensive. Some industry pundits feel that EISA is dead and that an ISA machine with a couple of VLB slots for I/O-intensive devices is the way to go. Other gurus say the EISA is terrific, and that an EISA/VLB makes the perfect high-performance workstation. A new 32-bit bus standard called PCI is emerging, and it might truly eclipse the EISA once it gets a strong foothold in the market. My advice is to wait and see how PCI pans out and hold on until the second iteration of PCI arrives before putting your eggs in that basket.

In any case, you'll need enough slots to accommodate your arsenal of cards, with a few left over for future expansions. Typically, you'll want about six to eight slots. Make sure that the slots are spaced properly for the computer chassis you have, and that the board actually fits in the chassis. Take some measurements. Although slot spacing is standardized for ATs and all machines after that, some older boxes (such as original PC boxes) don't accommodate today's motherboards.

General Buying Points

A number of benchmark tests are useful in determining how well a motherboard will perform when running Windows 3.1. As of yet, I know of none for Windows NT. However, the demands of both operating systems and GUIs are similar, so Windows 3.1 benchmarks most likely apply. Before settling on a particular motherboard, you might ask how it performs using popular benchmarks such as *PC Magazine*'s Winmark. Of course, video and hard-disk performance measures don't apply because those depend on the disk and video subsystem you plug into the board. You're interested only in the memory and CPU performance.

If you're going to upgrade the motherboard in your system, be ready to find someone who will put it in, or expect to spend the better part of the day doing it yourself. You will have few instructions (perhaps only a small block diagram and a cryptic translation), so you'll have to know something about how to disconnect and reconnect lots of wires, connectors, little LED lights, ribbon cables, speakers, and so forth.

You can figure most of this out by observing how the wires are connected to the existing motherboard. Although the layout of the new board will be different from the old one, most connectors (such as for the reset switch and LEDs) will be marked on the board to help you.

CAUTION

Pay extra attention to the power connectors, marked P8 and P9. They go back on with the black wires on each connector facing each other (all black wires grouped together). You don't want to blow out your new motherboard by doing this backwards.

Summary

This chapter discussed various approaches to upgrading your NT system in order to optimize its performance. We've covered the cost-free approaches of BIOS adjustments and hard-disk maintenance with interleave adjustment, defragmenting and using CHKDSK, and the more costly variations you can make such as upgrading your video and hard-disk subsystems or the motherboard and CPU. All of these were discussed with an eye toward the particular computational needs of Windows NT. Armed with this information, you should now be better equipped to make system purchases or optimization decisions. Keep in mind that system hardware is ever changing—and quite rapidly in the competitive PC hardware market. Frequent referral to the industry magazines is a must if you are to keep abreast. Here I have tried to present the most salient issues you will encounter while optimizing your system.

Maintenance and Troubleshooting

12

IN THIS CHAPTER

This chapter, the last chapter of Part II, comprises a miscellany of topics pertinent to Windows NT maintenance and troubleshooting. General system problems are covered first, and then more specific problems—those concerning video, networks, and hard disks—are discussed. Also covered are the following topics:

- Using the Event Viewer
- Using the Tape Backup program
- Specific MS-DOS and Windows 3.x applications notes
- How to recover from a crashed system
- How to attempt recovery of crashed hard disks
- Converting partitions between file formats
- How to reinstall NT from scratch
- The Registry Editor

General System Issues

This section addresses general system maintenance issues that might be useful if you're administering an NT machine or network.

How NT Boots

Understanding how NT boots might help you diagnose system startup problems. If you're having trouble booting, you should first make sure that the computer's system is set up correctly, using the CMOS setup utility or another program supplied with the computer. The computer needs to know which drive to boot from, and you must correctly enter the hard-disk type into the setup information. NT must be installed as explained in Chapter 8, "Installing Windows NT," and no IRQ, DMA, or other bus conflicts can exist. In particular, the video card must be set correctly; otherwise, NT might boot, but you might not know it because nothing recognizable appears on-screen.

Assuming that all is well with the physical system and that NT installed without incident, the boot-up drive's boot record was modified to cause the computer to load the NTLDR (NT Loader) program. When you boot, the following things happen:

1. NTLDR runs, then calls NTDETECT.COM. This program announces itself on-screen and checks out the computer's hardware attributes (the type of video card, hard disk, ports, memory, and so forth).
2. Based on the results of the search, NTDETECT compiles a list of hardware. This information is then placed in the Registry under the appropriate hardware keys.

3. NTLDR reads an ASCII text file called BOOT.INI to determine which other operating systems are on the hard disk. (This file, created during Setup, is found in the root directory of the boot partition.) Typically, the list is MS-DOS and NT, or OS/2 and NT.
4. After the countdown period ends, the default operating system (typically Windows NT) is loaded.

TIP

If you intervene by pressing the up or down arrow keys (not the Enter key because that will boot the highlighted item), the timeout clock stops and you can take as much time as you need to decide which operating system to boot.

5. NT starts the booting process by loading the low-level drivers and services. Which services start at boot time can be altered by settings made in the Services dialog box in Control Panel; these settings are stored in the Registry. A stock set of default services is started (unless you tinker with these settings, of course); they are the ones necessary for typical NT functionality.
6. The GUI and higher-level drivers load, and NT comes up on-screen, waiting for a user to log in.

The Structure of BOOT.INI

A typical BOOT.INI file looks like this:

```
 [boot loader]
timeout=30
default=multi(0)disk(0)rdisk(0)partition(1)\winnt
 [operating systems]
multi(0)disk(0)rdisk(0)partition(1)\winnt="Windows NT Workstation Version 3.5"
multi(0)disk(0)rdisk(0)partition(1)\winnt="Windows NT Workstation Version 3.5"
 /basevideo /SCSIORDINAL:0
C:\="MS-DOS"
```

The `[boot loader]` section indicates that the default operating system is WINNT, located on partition 1. It also states the time (in seconds) that the startup program waits before starting the default system automatically.

The `[operating systems]` section lists all the operating systems that are bootable and that will appear on the startup menu. All text between the quotes is what appears on the menu. You can edit this to read differently if you like, such as `MS-DOS version 6.2` or `Windows NT-Use this one, folks!`

NOTE

Currently, NT can boot multiple versions of NT, or NT Server and one prior operating system. This book's technical editor uses multiple versions of NT (a debugging version and a nondebugging version), as well as multiple versions of NT Server (debug, nodebug), and he expects to add the next NT release this way as well. Keeping the prior operating system is a convenient feature when it's time to upgrade, because it allows you to test the new release before committing to it.

NOTE

At first glance, it looks as if there are two duplicate entries for starting Windows NT. Although they're similar in appearance, they're not similar in functionality. The second instance, which includes the `/basevideo` switch, starts Windows NT with a default VGA driver. This entry can be used to start Windows NT if the user-installed video driver fails for some reason. For instance, selecting a video card refresh frequency that is higher than the monitor can handle results in an unreadable display.

TIP

You can change the default operating system, if you like, via the System applet in Control Panel. See Chapter 9, "Configuring Windows NT," for details. You also can do this by editing the BOOT.INI file found in the root directory of the boot drive once you've changed its attribute to read-write.

Back Up Your Configuration Information

As you add new users and make other changes to NT, you will want to update the repair information stored in the %SystemRoot%\System32\Repair directory and on the Emergency Repair disk. This is accomplished by running the Repair Disk Utility, RDISK.EXE, shown in Figure 12.1.

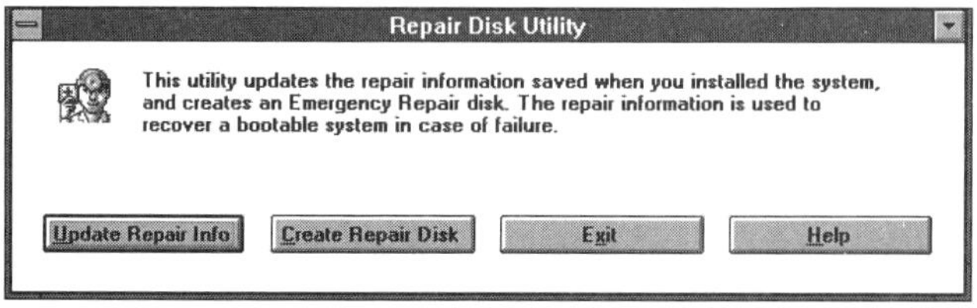

FIGURE 12.1.
Updating the system recovery data with the Repair Disk Utility.

NOTE

Some of these subsystem configuration settings are stored in the file \SYSTEM32 \CONFIG.NT. You'll want to back up this file (put it on a floppy) once in a while. You might have to use it if the system crashes and you use the Emergency Repair Disk to resuscitate it. You see, the Emergency Repair Disk has only the configuration information from when NT was installed or last updated with the Repair Disk Utility.

NOTE

Note that because the Registry files are always in use, you can't just copy them to or from a floppy disk unless they're stored on a FAT partition and the currently running operating system is MS-DOS. Otherwise, these files are locked.

The Repair Disk Utility can be used either to update the recovery information stored on the hard disk or to create a new repair disk. I recommend that after each major change (for instance, after you've installed and tested new software), you update the repair information stored locally on the hard disk. And after a hardware upgrade, or once a month, create a new repair disk. Don't just keep updating the existing repair disk; create new ones. This is so that you can have the option of restoring a configuration that you know is good. If you label your repair disks, you can keep a running history of your changes and have the option of restoring any of these configurations.

TIP

Use the RDISK utility to update the local copy of the repair information before you install new software on the system, just in case the software doesn't live up to the manufacturer's claims. If you have a tape drive attached, make a backup, too.

Trouble Booting Another Operating System

Although most users of NT version 3.5 will have had either MS-DOS or OS/2 on their machines previously, NT actually supports almost any prior operating system that was installed. If you decide to keep the prior operating system, the installation process simply grabs the boot record and relocates it in the file BOOTSECT.DOS. This file is then jumped to and used as the boot record when the optional secondary operating system is selected. Note, however, that you can have only one alternative operating system.

For a second operating system to boot (as an option from the menu displayed at boot time), a file called BOOTSECT.DOS must exist in the root directory of the boot partition. During NT installation, NT creates this file and copies into it whatever preexisting operating system boot record it found on the computer (such as DOS or OS/2).

When you choose to boot the alternative operating system, the NT boot loader must be able to locate this file, and it uses the statement in the BOOT.INI file to do so. If the pathname declared in BOOT.INI points to an incorrect or nonexistent directory, the alternative operating system won't boot. Typically, BOOTSECT.DOS is in the C:\ directory, so the line in the `[operating systems]` section of BOOT.INI should read

```
C:\="MS-DOS"
```

NOTE

For running MS-DOS, NT needs to find AUTOEXEC.BAT and CONFIG.SYS files. If you don't have these files in the root directory of the boot partition, add them using a plain text editor. Refer to a book about DOS for details on these files.

Trouble Logging Onto NT

Occasionally you or the user might have trouble logging on. Check the following items to determine the cause:

- Is the password being entered correctly? Remember that uppercase and lowercase letters are treated differently.
- Does the account require that the password be changed every so often? If so, perhaps the password needs updating. This option, as well as a new password, can be set via the User Manager program (see Chapter 10, "Windows NT Administration," for details). After the user can log on, he or she can change the password by pressing Ctrl-Alt-Delete.
- Is the workstation locked? A previous user might have locked the station in the middle of his or her session (to attend a meeting or go to the rest room, for example). Only that user (or anyone who knows the user's password) can unlock it. Station locking is achieved via the Ctrl-Alt-Delete dialog box.
- Is the user's account still active? Some accounts expire after a preset period of time. Again, the User Manager application must be employed.
- Is the user's account locked? If the account lockout policy has been set, you can't log onto the system until either the administrator resets your account or the lockout duration expires.

- Has the user (or have you) forgotten the password? This is a common problem, particularly when users are required to change their passwords frequently; it simply becomes difficult to remember them. Because there is no way to display the current password, the only solution is to assign a new one. Again, User Manager is the vehicle. See the next section for the exact steps.
- Recall from Chapter 10 that accounts can be assigned a property that limits login to times that fall between certain hours. Perhaps the user is trying to log in at a time that doesn't fall within the preassigned range.
- Consider that if the winlogin service fails to start, no authentication and therefore no logon will be permitted. Sometimes a reboot solves the problem. At the worst, you might have to invoke the Last Known Good option or reinstall NT to fix this. Administrators and users should be aware that this service should never be disabled via the Control Panel applets or Registry Editor. If this does happen for some reason, the Last Known Good option should be able to recover the previous configuration because no user can log on. (Hence, there will have been no Registry update of the Last Known Good configuration.)
- Finally, if the workstation with the logon problem is on a network, an administrator can remotely connect and possibly fix the problem.

If you're attempting to log in to a remote station over the network, other gremlins might be preventing login:

- Is the network up and running?
- Is your station communicating correctly with the workgroup(s) or domain(s) containing the station you're attempting to log to?
- Are you attempting to log into the correct domain? A domain that doesn't have a trust relationship won't allow you to log in.

How an Administrator Deals with a Lost User Password

So one of the users on a station you administer has forgotten his or her password. Here's exactly how to deal with the problem:

1. First, a little lecture is in order. Users should choose passwords that make sense to them but that aren't too obvious to anyone trying to break into the system. For example, `JOED` isn't a good password for Joe Derek. It's an acceptable username, but not a good password. Use something that's memorable, though, to prevent having to hassle the administrator. `DEOJ` (`JOED` backwards) is better. The name of the user's dog, wife, or something else memorable certainly beats `ERJ#(+p!`, which means nothing.

2. Log onto the system as someone with administrative powers.
3. Run User Manager.
4. Locate the user account for which the password has been lost, and highlight it.
5. Choose File | Properties.
6. Enter a new password and confirm it.
7. At this point you have a choice: You can opt for the new password to become official until it's changed at some future date, or you can require the user to *change* the password the very next time he logs on (thus making the password totally private). For the latter option, choose the User Must Change Password at Next Logon option in the dialog box.

NOTE

A third option, which gives the user an additional feeling of security, is to turn your back or leave the room while the user enters the new password at your computer. You might want to make sure that you don't leave the room long enough to allow the user to change privileges, though. Also, this works only for local workstations. Network workstations require that the administrator modify the domain account rather than the local account.

If this checklist doesn't solve the problem, administrators can use the Event Viewer to examine the Security log. If a user's account is set up (via User Manager) to record Failure for Login and Logoff, an entry appears in the Security log, listing the reason for the failure. By analyzing the log, an administrator can narrow down the cause. See the section titled "Using the Event Viewer" for a discussion of how to examine the Security log.

Video Problems

Some video adapters are not very graceful when it comes to switching video modes, particularly from character mode to graphics mode or vice versa. When you run an MS-DOS application, the application might run fine in a window, but when you switch back to full-screen, the display might become an indecipherable mess. The application might still be running, but you can't see anything recognizable. This is a known bug on a small number of video cards, such as ATI Graphics Ultra Plus. It's also been reported with the Diamond Viper card.

TIP

If you experience such a video problem, check the Hardware Compatibility List for notes on your video card. Also, see if your video manufacturer has an updated video ROM or an exchange policy. The Diamond Viper problem just mentioned can be fixed with a 3.08 or higher BIOS version.

If this happens, you have a couple of choices. The first is to switch back to windowed mode, save your work, and quit the application (or continue working if the application displays and responds correctly). If you can't get back into windowed mode, you have to terminate the application from the Task List or issue the necessary keyboard commands blindly (if you know them).

Another reported fix is to try other refresh modes. Some video adapter and monitor combinations just don't work as expected, particularly those that push the hardware past its rated capacity.

Network Problems

Chapter 8 and Part III discuss network installation and some troubleshooting issues. If you're having difficulty with your network, you might want to look in those parts of the book for specific discussions of network card and software installation and I/O port, DMA, and IRQ assignments. Some additional general troubleshooting hints are discussed in this section.

If your network isn't operating properly, there are several issues to consider: user settings, network card settings, conflicting computer names, conflicting protocols, and conflicting IRQs. Another possibility is physical cabling anomalies.

NOTE

Many of these typical problems—such as conflicting protocols, network card conflicts, and IRQ conflicts—will be reported in the Event Log. Check the Event Log using the Event Viewer (as described later in this chapter) for possible entries explaining the problem.

In terms of general system maintenance, remember that if you physically replace a workstation's network card, you might have to install an appropriate device driver. This is done through Control Panel (see Chapter 9). Make sure that the IRQ settings are set properly on the board and that the software driver in Control Panel is configured to that DMA (and/or other settings that the driver lets you change via its dialog boxes). Note that even if you're replacing a card with a so-called "compatible" card, such as a Novell NE2000-compatible card, the methods for setting up a card's IRQ, port, and so forth might differ. One might use hardware jumpers, while another might use a software setup program.

TIP

If you make hardware changes to a system, try to configure the software drivers before you switch the hardware. That way, the system stands a better chance of booting up properly the next time you reboot.

If you rearrange cabling, make sure you observe all rules pertaining to the network topography and the system employed. Did you use the proper repeaters, terminators, hubs, and cables? Did you exceed the maximum run length for your type of cable? You get the idea.

Finally, if you've upgraded to a network that utilizes a different protocol, you have to load the new protocol driver as well as the card driver. (Again, see Chapter 9 for how to do this from Control Panel.)

Finally, a problem can result from computers and domains not having unique names. Even with the most intelligent computer software, it's wise not to tempt fate by creating duplicate names. This applies to files and directories as well as workstations, workgroups, and domains. If, as NT is booting, it detects an existing domain, workgroup, or workstation with the same name as the workstation, the network connection will not commence. Check the workstation's name, or go to another workstation and browse the network for workstation, workgroup, and domain names to try to determine whether there is a name conflict. Note that some characters are illegal when naming computers, workgroups, and domains. These characters prevent the network from recognizing the name or can cause unexpected results:

Character	*Name*
•	Bullet
§	Section mark
¦	Pipe
¶	Paragraph sign
¤	Currency symbol

If network problems don't clear up and the station won't come online, check the Event Viewer for hints. Possible interrupt conflicts, and missing or inappropriate card drivers and software protocols, might be reported in the System log.

NOTE

Names must be unique only within a workgroup or domain. You can have a multiple-domain model in which each domain has a machine with the same name or user account.

Specific Computer Problems

A host of NT-related problems and fixes apply to specific computers. Of particular note for version 3.5 of Windows NT are the following:

ACER AcerFrame 3000 MP
Ambra Video Display
AST EISA Memory
AST Premmia
Dell
DFI 9800T
Digital Alpha AXP
Gateway 2000 and Micronics Gemini 486 Vesa local bus motherboards
Gateway Nomad and TI TravelMate Notebooks
IBM PS/2
IBM PS/2 models 53, 76, 76i, 77, and 77i
IBM ThinkPad models 700c and 720c
IBM ThinkPad portables
IBM ThinkPad Docking Station with built-in Future Domain SCSI
Olivetti LSX5030
Toshiba T4400SX Monochrome

Check the README.WRI file for details if you're having trouble with one of these machines. Be sure to search the file for all occurrences of your computer's brand name; often, discussions of the computer can be found in a number of places in the document.

TIP

If, when running any computer with NT, you get system error F002, this is most likely due to faulty hardware (typically video, network, or memory). Run a full diagnostic check on your computer, especially the RAM subsystem.

Using NT's Setup Program

The Windows NT Setup program performs a number of system maintenance functions. As with Windows 3.1, the primary function is for installing basic system drivers to control the screen, mouse, and keyboard. Typically, you need to modify only the mouse and screen drivers, because most keyboards have the same specifications.

Setup also can be used for installing and removing SCSI and tape backup devices; adding and removing large portions of related NT "components" such as Help files, accessories, and so forth (typically to free up disk space); deleting user profiles; and setting up applications.

Changing Screen, Keyboard, and Mouse Drivers

More often than not, you'll use Setup when you install a new mouse (or a keyboard designed for another language) or to delete user profiles that have accumulated from temporary users of the workstation.

Changing your keyboard or mouse doesn't necessarily require that you change the driver. If you change the keyboard or mouse, you'll have to change the driver only if the new device isn't compatible with the driver you had installed formerly. For example, many keyboards are "generic" keyboards that work with the standard NT keyboard driver even if they offer extended functionality (extra keys or a built-in calculator). Likewise, many mice are Microsoft Mouse-compatible.

NOTE

Remember that Windows 3.1 drivers can't be used with Windows NT. You must acquire a special NT-compatible driver for your multimedia hardware, fax modem, and so on, or it won't work from within NT.

NT comes with a good number of drivers, some of which are already installed in the \WINNT\SYSTEM32\DRIVERS directory. If you choose to install one that isn't, you're prompted to insert a source diskette containing the driver (and possibly other support files, such as screen fonts).

NOTE

Setup isn't used for printer, language, network, or multimedia driver alterations. You use Print Manager to install printer drivers, the International applet in Control Panel to change language settings, the Network applet in Control Panel to install network drivers, and the Devices applet in Control Panel to install multimedia drivers (for sound cards, for example).

To install a new driver, first run Setup; the icon is in the Main group. The dialog box shown in Figure 12.2 appears.

FIGURE 12.2.
Setup's main dialog box.

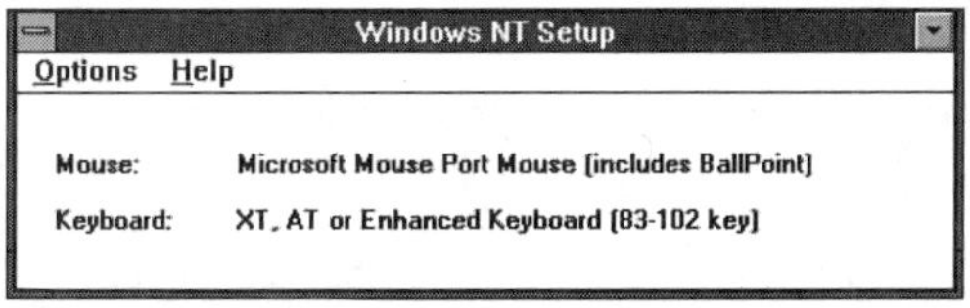

TIP

When NT Setup is running, no application installation programs, such as those shipped with Windows programs (either 16-bit or 32-bit), will work properly. You have to quit NT Setup first.

To change a driver, you have to be logged on with administrative privilege. Whether or not you install the new hardware first depends on the hardware. You'll want NT to be able to run while you make the alterations. If changing the hardware (for example, installing a completely different SCSI adapter that wouldn't run with the old setting) would prevent the system from running, installing the new hardware first won't cut it. You have to make the software changes first, then power down, install the hardware, and reboot.

Here's an example of changing a driver. Suppose you're installing a new mouse driver. First, make sure the new hardware (if any) is properly installed. Then do the following:

1. Choose Options | Change System Settings. The dialog box shown in Figure 12.3 appears.

FIGURE 12.3.
Change system settings from here.

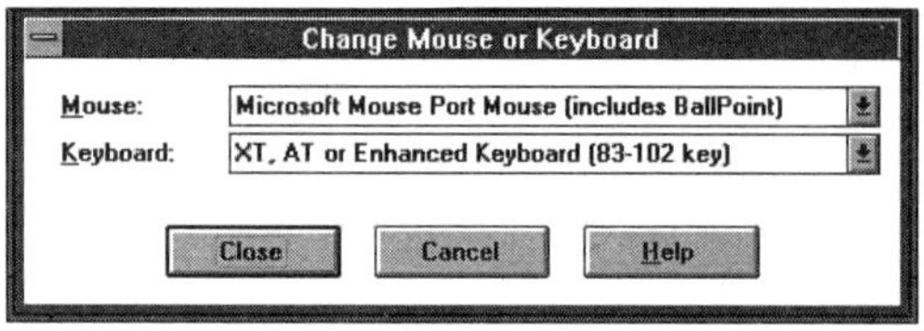

2. Open the appropriate drop-down list.
3. Choose the driver description that matches the new hardware or operational mode you want to use (for example, a Logitech Serial Mouse instead of a Microsoft Mouse Port). If the correct device isn't listed, you're out of luck unless you have a driver from another source, such as the hardware manufacturer. If you do, choose Other.

TIP

Microsoft maintains a regularly updated library of NT drivers. You can download drivers by calling (206) 936-MSDL between 6:00 a.m. and 6:00 p.m. Pacific time Monday through Friday. You also can access it on CompuServe and Genie, as well as the Internet at `ftp.microsoft.com`. Microsoft will mail you the library on disk if you call (800) 227-4679.

4. Click on OK. If you chose Other, or if the driver isn't already in the drivers directory, you're prompted to insert a disk or specify a drive and directory where the driver can be found. You can specify a location across the network, on a CD-ROM, or on a floppy drive. Grabbing a driver from another networked workstation is possible. If the needed driver is already on your system, you're advised of this in a dialog box and asked if you want to use the existing driver or load a new one. Choose to load a new one only if you're updating the driver. Otherwise, opt to use the existing one.
5. You must restart the computer via the File | Shutdown command in File Manager or the Ctrl-Alt-Delete dialog box before the changes will go into effect.

NOTE

You can't restart the system until you've properly exited Setup. Otherwise, you get a message telling you to exit the program properly.

TIP

If you think you'll want to be able to easily switch between different drivers (for example, so that you can switch between various keyboards to test your foreign-language skills), install them all by repeating steps 2 through 4 for each driver. (Do not reboot each time.) Then you'll have all the necessary support files on the system's hard disk. Next, choose the driver you want to work with now (Setup asks if you want to use the driver already found in the drivers directory, so say yes), then reboot. The next time you want to change drivers, just run Setup, choose the driver, and reboot.

Adding and Removing Tape and SCSI Drivers

You set up tape and SCSI drivers using Setup. It seems a little strange, because so many other device drivers are installed from Control Panel, but that's how it is. Think of Setup as the place from which you install the most basic and necessary hardware drivers—keyboard, disk, tape, and mouse.

When you install NT initially, the Setup program scans for SCSI devices and installs the correct one for the device it finds if an express installation was chosen. For a custom installation, Setup provides the ability to choose the drivers to test. Assuming that your SCSI device is one that Setup detects, you're in business—the driver is already installed. Only if you change your brand of SCSI controller, or if it wasn't detected to begin with, do you need to use Setup as described here.

NOTE

(This note pertains to users of the Media Vision Audio Spectrum 16 sound/SCSI card if used in conjunction with other SCSI controllers.) If NT detects a SCSI device upon booting, it installs the device's driver, even if the device isn't used. For example, I have a Media Vision Pro Audio Spectrum 16, but I don't use the SCSI on the card because I also have an Adaptec 1742a controller installed. The problem is that the Media Vision driver expects the SCSI device to be used for something, and their sound driver won't load (for wave, MIDI, and so on) unless the SCSI driver loads. But because I have no SCSI devices connected to the Media Vision SCSI port, the driver fails to load. The solution is to use Control Panel's Drivers applet to disable the TMV1 driver. Alternatively, you can remove the driver from the system using the Setup applet, as described a little later. Users of the Media Vision Basic cards without SCSI ports also require disabling this driver to be able to install the sound driver. Just select Polled I/O for the SCSI device in the dialog box for configuring the card.

The process of installing a SCSI or tape device works essentially the same way as that described for installing mouse and keyboard drivers.

1. Run Setup.
2. Open the Options menu and choose Add/Remove SCSI Adapters or Add/Remove Tape Devices.
3. In the resulting dialog box, click on Add to add a driver or click on Remove to get rid of one.
4. Another dialog box appears, from which you choose the adapter or unit driver to add or remove. Click on Install or Remove.
5. If you're adding the device, you're prompted to choose a directory or drive where the driver resides. There might be other on-screen directions.
6. After the driver is installed, click on Continue to get back to the NT Setup program.
7. Exit the program. You're reminded to restart the computer before the new driver will load.

TIP

Some devices—notably, SCSI ones such as CD-ROM readers, removable media units, or tape units—won't come online when NT boots unless they're powered up before booting. Check the power switch on external SCSI units before booting NT.

When You've Installed a Bogus Driver

With Windows 3.1, when you've accidentally installed the wrong driver for your hardware, you have to run the DOS version of Setup, choose the correct driver, and reboot Windows. However, you can't fix NT's setup from DOS, so don't try. NT uses another approach, one that's pretty intelligent.

Instead of remembering only one setup configuration of system drivers, NT remembers two—the last one that worked successfully (as far as NT knows, anyway), and the one you just created by adding, changing, or removing drivers. Therefore, when you reboot, NT knows if something didn't pan out. If the system doesn't boot properly (typically due to the wrong screen or mouse driver), the next time you reboot, NT reverts to the last known functional setup configuration.

The moral of the story is that if the system doesn't boot after you make driver changes from the Setup program, just reboot a second time. NT will try to fix itself. Then try making your driver changes again. Keep one thing in mind, though. Each time you log on, the Last Known Good configuration is updated. So don't log on if there is a serious problem and you want to use the Last Known Good option.

Removing User Profiles

User profiles are collections of settings that apply to certain users. For example, each profile stores Program Manager and File Manager settings, Desktop settings, mouse settings, and network and printer connections for a certain user. When the user no longer uses the system, you'll want to remove the user profile from the Registry.

To delete a profile, follow these steps:

1. Run NT Setup.
2. Choose Options | Delete User Profiles.
3. From the resulting dialog box, choose the name of the user account whose profile you want to delete.
4. Click on Delete.
5. Repeat the process for other profiles, if applicable.
6. Click on Close when you're finished deleting profiles.

NOTE

If the user is currently logged in, you can't delete that profile. Setup issues an error message if you try. Also, you must have administrative privilege to delete a profile.

Adding and Removing System Components

Setup lets you install or remove groups of NT-related files (called *components*). If you didn't choose a complete installation when you set up NT initially, you might want to use this option after the fact to load, for example, Help files, readme files, wallpaper files, games, or screen savers.

By the same token, if you did a complete install and are running tight on disk space, you might want to delete a class of files (or at least selected files in a class). For example, if you don't use the accessory Help files, deleting them frees up a fair amount of space.

Follow these steps to add or remove components:

1. Run NT Setup.
2. Open the Options menu and choose Add/Remove Windows Components. The dialog box shown in Figure 12.4 appears. Some components might have their option box checked, meaning that they're on the system already. If you want to remove a component, turn off its check box. If you want to add a component, turn on its check box.

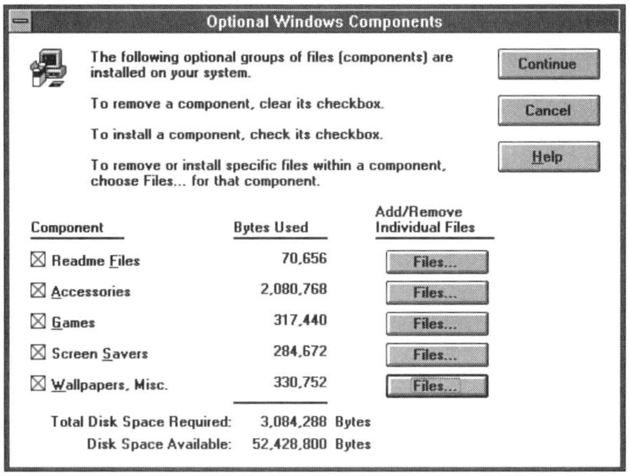

FIGURE 12.4.
Adding or deleting NT components.

3. (Optional) If you want to remove or add selected portions of a component, click on the Files button for that component. A Customize dialog box appears, listing the currently included files on the right side and files you can add to the list on the left side. Select files and click on Add or Remove as necessary. If you're adding files, keep an eye on the Total Disk Space Required number as you do so. Make sure that you have enough disk space to accommodate the new files. (The large components dialog box lists the available disk space.) Click on OK when the correct files are listed.
4. Click on Continue when all the options in the large dialog box are set. You're prompted either to insert disks with the source files (or to specify the location of the files, such as on a CD-ROM drive) or to confirm the deletion of files. Respond accordingly.

Setting Up Applications

NT Setup "sets up" applications by giving them icons in Program Manager. This is no big deal, because most installation programs supplied with applications do that for you. Also, if you migrated settings from a preexisting Windows 3.1 installation, your favorite programs are already set up in NT's Program Manager. As you probably know, you also can drag applications (any executable file) from File Manager into Program Manager, creating icons. However, if you want to do a clean sweep, searching for applications across one or more hard disks or through the system's search path, you may—if you're logged on as an administrator.

This method of installing applications has some drawbacks, however. For example, although the applications themselves might be installed, file associations, Registry information pertaining to DDE and OLE, and other such details won't necessarily be incorporated into the NT environment. Typically, if an application has a setup program, that's the better way to go.

1. From the Setup program, choose Options | Set Up Applications. The dialog box shown in Figure 12.5 appears, listing local and remote disks and the system path as options.

FIGURE 12.5.
Searching for applications to add to Program Manager.

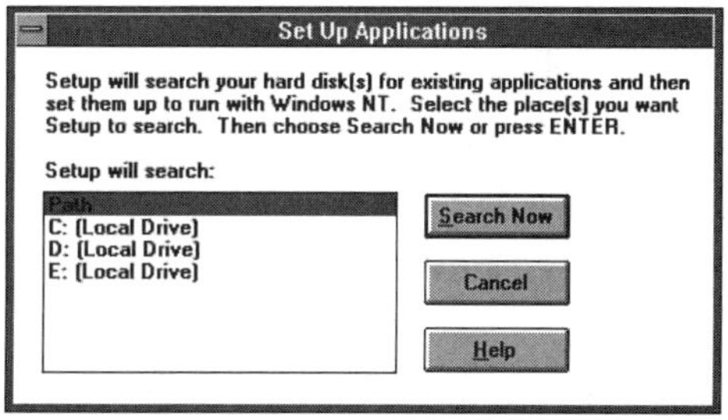

2. Choose the drives you want to search for applications and click on Search Now. The dialog box shown in Figure 12.6 appears, listing the names of applications that were found.
3. NT Setup uses an internal lookup table (database) of filenames to figure out which program an .EXE file is. You might be asked to confirm the names of applications if Setup is confused by the executable filename.

FIGURE 12.6.
Choosing which specific applications to add.

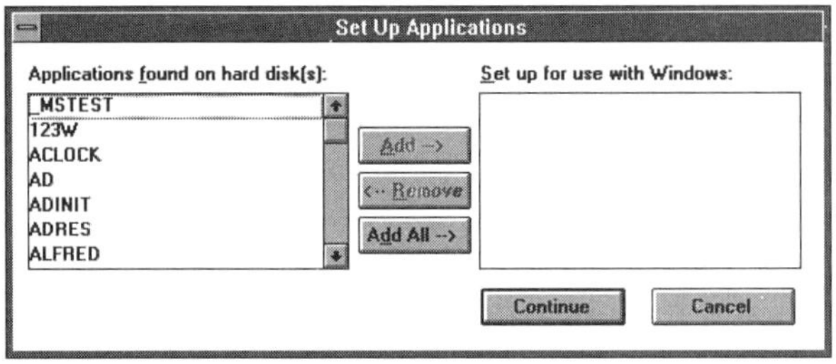

4. From the left side of the dialog box, choose the application you want to add to Program Manager, then click on Add. (Alternatively, you can click on Add All to choose them all at once.)
5. Click on Continue when you're satisfied with the list. Icons are added to the Applications group in Program Manager. These are available to all users, because Applications is a "common" group.

TIP

As soon as the applications have been found, it's a good idea to move them to a private group. You might not want all users to have access to them.

Hard-Disk System Maintenance

This section covers hard-disk maintenance and troubleshooting issues.

NOTE

Disk optimization and upgrading are discussed in Chapter 11, "Optimizing Windows NT: Performance Determinants."

Tips About SCSI Drives

In its current incarnation, Windows NT requires special attention to support more than two non-SCSI drives per machine. As I mentioned in Chapter 11, this is one of the primary limitations of IDE and other non-SCSI drive setups (such as ESDI). When you need more space than is available on two such drives (for example, when setting up stripe, volume, or mirrored sets), you have two choices.

If you have a machine that supports additional IDE cards or has additional controllers built in (such as some models from Compaq and Gateway), acquire and install the appropriate boards and drives, then reboot. NT recognizes up to six such drives. If you're in doubt about the compatibility of the hardware, ask the supplier or call Microsoft Product Support Services.

Another, perhaps easier, solution is to upgrade to SCSI drives. NT supports as many as seven SCSI drives while at the same time allowing two non-SCSI drives to coexist in the same computer. Therefore, you can keep your IDE or ESDI drives, for example, add a SCSI controller, and start buying SCSI drives.

NOTE

The SCSI spec allows multiple SCSI drives in each computer, with seven drives per card, and NT recognizes up to four SCSI controllers with seven drives per adapter at this point. If you're shopping for SCSI controllers and devices, the SCSI II spec is the preferred way to go.

SCSI drives have some peculiar requirements not characteristic of other types of drives. If you're having trouble installing or maintaining a SCSI drive, consider the following:

Windows NT supports many SCSI devices via SCSI controllers. The second released version of NT supported

94 SCSI adapters
72 SCSI CD-ROM drives
87 SCSI tape drives
24 SCSI removable media drives

The readme file supplied with NT contains information about particular brands and models of SCSI devices, such as those from NEC, Adaptec controllers, Compaq, Future Domain, and others. Special instructions for about 2,115 products are discussed there. I won't repeat them here, because you have the file already. Suffice it to say that if your SCSI adapter isn't working, you might have to change a switch, disable the adapter's BIOS, or alter the termination in some specific manner, as explained in that text file.

Two general rules pertain to SCSI cabling. First, SCSI cables (like some network cables) must be terminated properly at both ends in order to work. Second, either the SCSI device or the SCSI adapter has to supply termination power to the SCSI bus. You have to make sure that these two requirements are met.

TIP

SCSI termination comes in two flavors—passive and active. Active terminators are used to supply a more constant voltage to the SCSI bus and help in eliminating noise. Most SCSI I adapters use passive termination, and most SCSI II adapters use active termination. You can use active termination on either SCSI bus, however. If you suspect a problem, use active termination when possible.

Additionally, you'll want to make sure that SCSI devices are turned on before you boot NT, and that a CD-ROM drive is set to a SCSI ID number other than 0 or 1. Those are reserved for bootable media (typically hard disks, but this could include removable media). NT can get weird on you and think that the CD-ROM has multiple partitions if it's assigned to one of those ID numbers.

If a Hard Disk Isn't Recognized

Windows NT has stricter rules than MS-DOS for determining whether a hard disk has legitimate partitions. If sectors, boot tracks, or partition tables aren't encoded with absolute conformity to MS-DOS rules, NT might not recognize the disk even though DOS might. This can be unnerving, but the up side is that it offers more protection against viruses that alter the partition tables, FAT, or boot tracks. Such an altered drive simply won't come online.

To deal with such a drive, you have to reuse the MS-DOS `FDISK` and `FORMAT` commands on it. After making sure that the problem isn't due to another issue, such as SCSI settings, cabling, hard-disk termination, or hard-disk jumpers, follow these steps:

CAUTION

Some devices might not work after you perform an `FDISK` and `FORMAT` under DOS. Check the drive and/or controller's manual to determine if this is the case. If it is, attempt a reformat using Disk Administrator instead of following these next steps.

1. Back up all important data, including the DOS directory and related files (such as AUTOEXEC.BAT and CONFIG.SYS).
2. Boot DOS.
3. Use the `FDISK` command to prepare the disk for formatting.
4. Use the `FORMAT` command to format the drive.
5. Repartition as necessary, and restore the files to the drive.

Adding Hard Disks

When you add a new drive to an NT system, you can actually get away with not running Disk Administrator or declaring the addition of a new drive—just as it isn't necessary in DOS, OS/2, or Windows 3.1. Assuming that the controller and the system setup (CMOS or other BIOS-related settings) are correct and that the drive is formatted in a file system that NT can recognize, the drive simply comes online and is assigned the next available filename.

However, if you want to assign a static letter name to the drive that will not shift when new drives (such as CD-ROMs or additional hard disks) are dumped into the system, you should run Disk Administrator. When you do, the program detects that a new drive has been added since Disk Administrator was last run and prompts you to okay the process of updating the internal settings. Go ahead and do this. Then, if you want to assign a static letter name to the drive, use Disk Administrator commands to do so (as outlined in Chapter 10, "Windows NT Administration").

NOTE

As soon as a static label has been assigned in Disk Administrator, MS-DOS also recognizes the modified disk letter scheme. This can be a useful attribute, but it can cause havoc for the uninitiated when they boot DOS and wonder how their hard drive or CD-ROM letters got rearranged.

If a Hard Disk Is Removed from the System

If you remove a hard disk from the system, you might not get past the startup screen the next time you boot up. NTDETECT runs as expected (see the section titled "How NT Boots") but then can hang up. This is especially true if you remove the data cable from a drive but leave the power cable on and you don't change the CMOS BIOS settings to indicate that a drive is missing. Apparently, NT needs your BIOS settings to agree with your actual physical hardware.

NOTE

This problem of the system hanging when a drive is removed occurs only for Seagate ST-506/Western Digital 1003–compatible media. SCSI drives don't suffer from this problem (unless the removed drive is the boot drive). In many cases (IDE in particular), the master/slave arrangement is the cause of the problem.

In any case, the solution is to change the BIOS settings, then reboot. To be completely conscientious, you should inform NT that you have physically removed a hard disk from the system—particularly if you've assigned a static drive letter to that drive. To do this, run Disk Administrator, let it update itself, and make sure that drive letter assignments and partition information agree with your physical setup and that your disk letters are as desired.

TIP

Think ahead when removing or reassigning drive letters. If you have drives C, D, and E, for example, and you remove physical drive D, you might not want to have drive E fall back to the D drive's position. Pointers in Program Manager icons, and shared directories via File Manager, might both expect to find specific files on logical drive E. Just leave the hole where D was, and perhaps assign the CD-ROM drive to D (unless you want to adjust other settings, such as Program Manager icon properties, other workstation connections, and so forth).

Recovering Disk Configurations with Disk Administrator

NT is savvy in how it stores information about hard-disk volumes, stripe sets, volume sets, mirrored sets, and partitions. Much of this information is discussed in other chapters. Recall that a given machine's disk appointments are recorded in the NT Registry. A DISK section in the Registry contains the details of your disk partitions, their logical letter names, physical drive locations, and the role each partition plays in the NT system (for example, standard volume, volume set, and so forth).

What's intelligent about this system is that it stores most of this information (everything except static drive letters) in the Registry, instead of in each partition or the disk's boot sector. This way, if the boot sector becomes nonfunctional or is corrupted, you don't lose advanced partition information such as volume set and stripe set arrangements and each partition's role in running NT. Thus, you're more likely to be able to recover from disaster without losing data.

What's bad about this arrangement is that if the Registry becomes corrupted, thus trashing the partition map, you're out of luck. Unless you've backed up the repair information (as explained earlier) or the disk information via Disk Administrator (as explained in the following numbered list), you won't be able to recover such advanced disk utilization information.

Disk Administrator offers a security backup option that lets you make a copy of the disk partition arrangement on a floppy disk. Then, in case you have to reinstall NT, you can easily reset the partition map from the floppy disk and thus gain access to your files and mirrored, volume, and stripe sets. Here's how to use it:

1. If necessary, update the map using Disk Administrator. If you've added drives since running it last time, you're alerted to this fact, and you must allow the program to update the Registry.
2. Exit Disk Administrator and save any changes.
3. Restart the computer, NT, and Disk Administrator.
4. Choose Configuration | Save. Some information appears in a dialog box, and you're asked where you want to save the partition information. Indicate a floppy disk and insert either a blank disk, a disk you use for saving disk configurations, or even the Emergency Repair Disk you made when you installed NT.
5. Click on OK. The disk configuration information is stored on the backup disk. Mark the disk appropriately (including the date), and store it in a safe place.

NOTE

You should follow this procedure whenever you change partition arrangements with Disk Administrator so that you have a current copy on a floppy.

You can restore the partition information at any time. Simply do the following:

1. Run Disk Administrator again.
2. Choose Configuration | Restore.
3. Indicate the source of the partition information (for example, floppy drive A:) and insert the proper disk.
4. Click on OK.

If you have additional installations of NT on your hard disk(s), you can have Disk Administrator search for partition information in such setups. Just choose Configuration | Search. All preexisting configurations are listed, enabling you to choose.

CAUTION

This is dangerous stuff to play with. Obviously, you can render your system inoperable (and potentially lose data) if you activate a partition map that's out of date. Before restoring a configuration, save the current one in case you need to revert. Not only should you save the current configuration, but you also should back up the data when possible. After all, if the NT partition is destroyed, you can't boot NT to run Disk Administrator and fix the problem. In that case, you would have to reinstall NT and then restore all your data before NT would be returned to its prior state.

Repairing a Corrupted Volume

This section explains how to try to repair a FAT, NTFS, or HPFS volume that appears to be corrupted. Corruption often occurs because of broken chains or a disagreement between the file allocation table and the physical disk sectors. When you boot NT, the `AUTOCHK` program runs and tests the validity of your volumes. It also attempts to repair them. If the volume is NTFS, the repairs likely will cause less loss of data than on a FAT or HPFS volume. If problems continue, the solution is to run the `CHKDSK` program on the questionable volume using the following sequence, regardless of the partition's file system.

1. Boot NT.
2. Run a command-prompt session and issue the `CHKDSK` command on the volume in question.
3. If errors are reported, run `CHKDSK` again, this time with the `/f` option (for example, `chkdsk c: /f`), unless the volume in question contains the Windows NT files. If it does, jump to step 1 of the next procedure.

NOTE

The `/f` option causes `CHKDSK` to fix broken chains and dump lost clusters into files in the root directory. You can read these files with a text editor. These files are given names such as FILE0001.CHK.

4. If you're informed that `CHKDSK` can't correct the errors, look to see that no files are open on the volume. Close all applications except the command-prompt session and try running `chkdsk /f` again. If the errors still can't be fixed, restart the computer, reboot NT, log on, and try again.

If the volume in question contains NT and CHKDSK reports that errors exist, follow these steps:

1. Do a shutdown and then restart NT. AUTOCHK will run and possibly fix the problems. If it doesn't, go to the next step.
2. Run a command-prompt session and run `chkdsk /f` on the volume in question. CHKDSK knows that you're attempting to run it on the NT volume and gives you the option of scheduling an AUTOCHK at the next bootup. This should clear up the trouble.
3. If even this fails, consider this. NT won't fix all problems, particularly on files that NT accesses before the AUTOCHK program starts. The final solution is to boot another operating system (MS-DOS or OS/2) and run CHKDSK or SCANDISK on the NT partition to correct the problem.

Using the Tape Backup Application

NT comes with a tape backup system to help administrators manually or automatically back up important directories and files, then restore those items if and when needed. NT's backup program is surprisingly competent, considering Microsoft's history of backup programs supplied with DOS. Backups can be performed on local or remote FAT, HPFS, or NTFS partitions. The Backup program looks and works much like File Manager, so understanding the basics shouldn't be difficult.

NOTE

The Backup program was written by Arcadia Software—the hard-disk people. Like many programs derived from third parties, a more complete package is available from the manufacturer.

Other features include the following:

- Automates backups with batch files
- Examines a backed-up tape directory just as if it were a hard-disk directory
- Backs up huge directories or files across multiple tapes because file size is unlimited
- Organizes backups into *backup sets*—sets of files on a single tape
- Chooses for backup sets to be updated incrementally so that only modified files are backed up, or to have the entire set backed up again and appended to the tape as a new backup set

- Optionally verifies accuracy of all files copied to tape during a backup
- Optionally creates an audit log of backup operations for review by backup or system policy makers to ensure that data is regularly protected

As with any backup system, though, you'll want to put some forethought into developing a backup schedule and tape rotation scheme. You need to decide which directories or files are crucial and which can be skipped over because they could easily be replaced from other sources (application programs are a case in point). You should consider quite carefully the value of your data and the time required to re-create it if it should be lost. You also might want to consider making duplicate tapes from different locations on a network, and also how other data risk-reduction techniques (such as the use of fault-tolerant disk schemes) play into your overall information management policy.

TBU Hardware

To use the Backup program, you need an NT-supported tape backup unit (TBU). Check the NT Hardware Compatibility List or the docs supplied with the drive to determine this. Then, install the appropriate driver for the unit, using the NT System Setup program described earlier in this chapter. Initial support is included for inexpensive minicartridge QIC 40/80 tape drives as well as high-capacity SCSI 4mm, 8mm, and .25-inch drives. Other formats likely will follow in the future. You can install drivers for multiple devices, but only one will work at a time. Choose the target device from the Tape Backup program's Operations menu before doing the backup. This is akin to choosing a printer prior to printing a document.

NOTE

As of the release of NT version 3.5, QIC 40/80-compatible tape drives must be connected to the floppy-drive controller, not to a hardware data compression board or other proprietary board supplied with the tape unit.

TIP

You must have the TBU turned on before booting NT in order for the driver to load properly. If you've just added the driver with NT Setup, or if you forgot to power it up when you booted, you can load it manually with the Devices option in Control Panel instead of rebooting. After the system has been booted and the tape drive has been recognized, the tape drive may be powered down until it's needed.

Basic Operation

This section walks through the basics of tape backup. Note that the program has ample online Help, so you may want to refer to it for additional details.

Backing Up Files

Here are the steps for backing up specific files:

1. Run the program via its icon in the Administrators group or by typing `ntbackup` in a command-prompt session. The program comes up, as shown in Figure 12.7.

FIGURE 12.7.
Tape Backup's main screen.

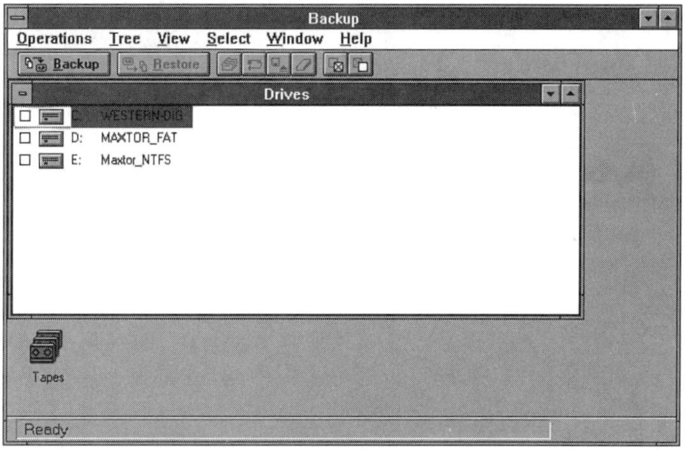

> **NOTE**
>
> To back up everyone's files, you must be logged on with Backup Operator or Administrative privileges. No special privilege is required to back up files, directories, or volumes that you normally have access to.

2. Choose which files you want to back up. Double-click to select a drive from the Drives window, then click on a directory in the resulting directory window to see its files. Note the check boxes beside each drive, directory, and filename. When the check box is selected, the item is set for backup. You select multiple items the same way you do in File Manager—by Shift-clicking and Ctrl-clicking.

TIP

Check out the Tree and View menus for viewing options that are identical to those in File Manager.

If you want to select all the files on a disk, simply check the drive's box. When you select a whole drive or directory, note again that only files accessible to the backup operator will be backed up. If a file is hidden, or if the user doesn't have read permission for a file in the selected drive or directory, such files are skipped during the backup.

NOTE

Minicartridge tape has to be formatted before it can be used. If your tape is new and unformatted, you must use the Operations | Format command to format it. Formatting some tapes takes much more time than formatting a disk, so be prepared to wait. 4mm DAT drives take a few seconds to format because only the initial label is replaced and the rest is performed on-the-fly. In striking contrast, QIC 40/80 tapes can take hours to format.

3. Choose Operations | Backup to begin the backup process. A large dialog box appears, asking for more information, as shown in Figure 12.8.

FIGURE 12.8.
The Tape Backup Information dialog box.

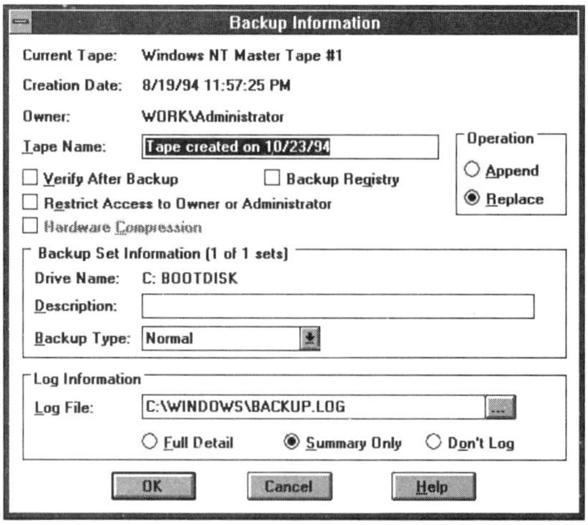

Fill in the box as required. Here's the breakdown of the options:

Setting	*Description*
Current Tape	Shows the name of the tape currently in the drive. If no name shows, check to see if a tape is in the drive. A blank tape will not have a name.
Creation Date	The date of the first backup made on this tape, or the date when the first set was replaced (overwritten) by a new set.
Owner	The person who created the first backup. That person's name is displayed here.
Tape Name	Use this section to change the name of the tape (see Current Tape). Not available if you're appending (see the following).
Append	Adds the backup data, beginning at the end of current data on the tape.
Replace	Starts backing up the data at the beginning of the tape and overwrites what's already there.
Verify After Backup	Determines whether or not files are verified for accuracy after they're copied to tape. Enabling this option slows down the backup process, *but it should be done.* After all, an unreliable backup is not really of any use. If a file fails the verification, it will be listed in the CORRUPT.LST file.
Restrict Access to Owner or Administrator	Not available if you're appending rather than replacing (see Append and Replace). If this option is enabled, it protects the tape's contents from usage by anyone other than the tape's creator, an administrator, or a backup operator. Also, if it's secured in this way, the tape must be used on the same computer with which it was created.
Hardware Compression	Enables hardware compression on supported SCSI tape drives.

continues

Setting	*Description*
Backup Registry	You can opt to include a copy of the Registry files for the machine as part of the backup. You might want to enable this option to ensure that you have a backup of Registry settings, especially if you do a daily backup. Note that the Registry can't be backed up unless at least one file is also selected to be backed up.
Description	Each backup set can have a 32-character description. A *set* is a set of files on a single drive that will be or has been backed up.
Backup Type	Each set you've chosen to back up can have a backup type set. There are five backup types. *Normal* backs up all the selected items and marks the archive bits accordingly. *Copy* has the same effect as Normal but doesn't mark the archive bit. *Incremental* backs up selected files that have been modified since the last backup and marks the archive bit. *Differential* is the same as Incremental, but it doesn't mark the archive bit. *Daily* backs up only selected files that are changed on the day the backup is run. The archive bit is not marked.
Log File	Enter the name of a text file log you want to have Backup create for you, in case you need to later audit backup activity on the system. Click on the ... button to browse for a filename of an existing log.
Full Detail	If selected, this option logs all backup events, including which drives, directories, and files were backed up.
Summary Only	If selected, this option logs basic Backup events: when the tape was loaded, when a backup was made, and if files fail to back up.
Don't Log	If selected, this option prevents a log file from being created.

4. After setting the options, click on OK. Another dialog box appears, reporting the status of the backup. See Figure 12.9.

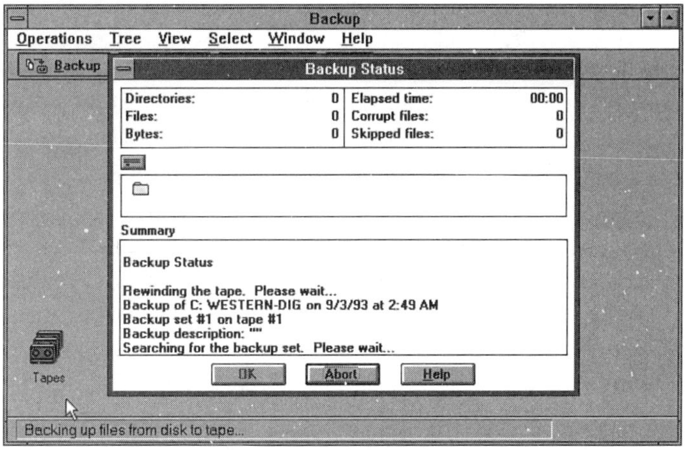

FIGURE 12.9.
The Backup Status dialog box.

5. Click on OK, and the backup process starts. If a tape runs out, you'll be prompted to insert another one.

Restoring Data from a Tape

When you realize that you need to restore some data from a tape, do the following:

1. Locate the tape that you think has the latest version of the volume, directory, or file contents, and place it in the tape drive. Note that when you restore data, you're restoring either a whole tape's contents, individual files you select, or a *backup set* (a set of directories or files that were backed up during the same session).
2. Run the Tape Backup program.

   Now things get a little tricky, because you might have to do a little work to locate the backup sets or files you're looking for. Normally, when you insert a tape, only the first backup set appears. If you want to look at other backup sets on the tape, you have to look at the tape's *catalog,* then get to the desired backup set, then view that set's catalog to select the desired files (or you can use the whole set). In other words, each tape has a catalog of sets and each set has a catalog of directories and files.
3. To see the catalog of backup sets on a tape, double-click on the tape's name in the tape window. After a while, the list of sets on the tape appears in the window. A question mark in the set's icon means that its catalog hasn't been loaded yet, so its contents aren't available for viewing.

To see the catalog of the set's contents, double-click on the set's icon. A list of all the directories and files in the set appears. A red X in a file or directory means that it's corrupted. A corrupted file or directory won't be restored.

4. Select the tape, backup set, or files to restore.
5. Click on Restore. The Restore dialog box that appears is similar to the Backup Status dialog box shown in Figure 11.9, with options similar to those described in the preceding numbered list. However, note the following:
   - If you're restoring items from an NTFS partition to an NTFS partition, you have the option of restoring file permissions. Do this only if you're restoring to the same computer from which the files were backed up; NTFS file permissions from one computer won't work on another computer. If this option is disabled, restored files adopt the permissions of the target directory.
   - If you want to restore to a driver or directory other than the original source of the files, enter the alternative target in the appropriate box(es).
6. Choose Log Options. See the preceding numbered list for descriptions.
7. Click on OK when the box is filled in correctly. A status box appears, keeping you apprised of the progress. You might be prompted to confirm the replacement of files in case conflicts arise.

NOTE

If the backup set you created uses two or more tapes, this is called a *family set.* Family sets have the set's catalog on the last tape, not the first tape. Sometimes when you use such a set you're prompted to insert the last tape of the series. If the last tape is lost, or if you ran out of tapes when you were doing a backup and then canceled the process, the first tapes won't have a concise catalog. You'll have to rebuild the catalog. The easiest way to do this is to run Backup from the command prompt with the command `ntbackup /missingtape`. A new backup set catalog will be created. However, be aware that this process can take quite a while because the tape must be scanned slowly.

TIP

If a disk drive crash causes you to have to reformat and reinstall NT, you will want to restore the NT system files from your backups (if you have any). Check the Readme file under "Restoring Data after Reformatting the System Volume" for details.

Using the Event Viewer

Many internal system occurrences trigger the display of error message dialog boxes while NT is running. For example, if a user attempts to access protected files or remove a printer over which he doesn't have control, a message usually appears. The same is true for an impending power-down, in the case of a UPS being triggered.

Due to NT's intelligent internal security design, many other subtler "events" internal to NT are equally well noted by the operating system, but they're not directly reported. Events such as applications being run, drivers being loaded, or files being copied between directories are common examples. Such events typically are not reported in dialog boxes. However, these events are stored in a log available for later examination by a system administrator. Many events are stored in the log by default. Others, as earlier chapters discussed, are optional. These optional events are set from File Manager, Print Manager, and User Manager.

NT generates three separate logs (files): the Security log, the Application log, and the System log. The Security log records events that might affect system security, such as logging on and off. The Application log is used only by applications that know about it and are coded to report to it. As an example, an application that can't find a support file or that runs out of disk space might report an error in the Application log. The System log contains numerous entries pertaining to system events such as bootup, shutdown, loading drivers, and errors with hardware conflicts such as conflicts between ports, CD-ROMs, SCSI cards, or sound cards.

Event Viewer is the application that displays each of the log files. Aside from simply displaying a log file, the Event Viewer also lets you

- apply sorting, searching, and filtering that makes it easier to look for specific events
- control settings that affect future log entries, such as maximum log size and when old entries should be deleted
- clear all log entries to start a log from scratch
- archive logs on disk for later examination and load those files when needed

NOTE

Only a user with Administrative privilege can work with the Security log. Other users can view the Application and System logs, however.

Working with Event Viewer Logs

The following steps explain how you can use the Event Viewer to open the three available logs and more easily view specific events.

1. You'll find the Event Viewer program in the Administrative Tools group. When you run it, the basic Event Viewer window comes up with the System log loaded by default. Figure 12.10 displays a typical example. (The meaning of each column is explained in the following section.)

FIGURE 12.10.

The Event Viewer displaying the System log of the local computer.

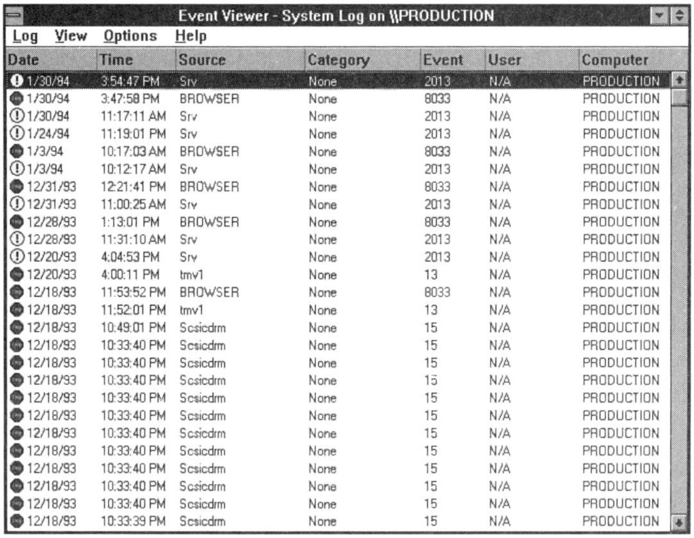

Date	Time	Source	Category	Event	User	Computer
1/30/94	3:54:47 PM	Srv	None	2013	N/A	PRODUCTION
1/30/94	3:47:58 PM	BROWSER	None	8033	N/A	PRODUCTION
1/30/94	11:17:11 AM	Srv	None	2013	N/A	PRODUCTION
1/24/94	11:19:01 PM	Srv	None	2013	N/A	PRODUCTION
1/3/94	10:17:03 AM	BROWSER	None	8033	N/A	PRODUCTION
1/3/94	10:12:17 AM	Srv	None	2013	N/A	PRODUCTION
12/31/93	12:21:41 PM	BROWSER	None	8033	N/A	PRODUCTION
12/31/93	11:00:25 AM	Srv	None	2013	N/A	PRODUCTION
12/28/93	1:13:01 PM	BROWSER	None	8033	N/A	PRODUCTION
12/28/93	11:31:10 AM	Srv	None	2013	N/A	PRODUCTION
12/20/93	4:04:53 PM	Srv	None	2013	N/A	PRODUCTION
12/20/93	4:00:11 PM	tmv1	None	13	N/A	PRODUCTION
12/18/93	11:53:52 PM	BROWSER	None	8033	N/A	PRODUCTION
12/18/93	11:52:01 PM	tmv1	None	13	N/A	PRODUCTION
12/18/93	10:49:01 PM	Scsicdrm	None	15	N/A	PRODUCTION
12/18/93	10:33:40 PM	Scsicdrm	None	15	N/A	PRODUCTION
12/18/93	10:33:40 PM	Scsicdrm	None	15	N/A	PRODUCTION
12/18/93	10:33:40 PM	Scsicdrm	None	15	N/A	PRODUCTION
12/18/93	10:33:40 PM	Scsicdrm	None	15	N/A	PRODUCTION
12/18/93	10:33:40 PM	Scsicdrm	None	15	N/A	PRODUCTION
12/18/93	10:33:40 PM	Scsicdrm	None	15	N/A	PRODUCTION
12/18/93	10:33:40 PM	Scsicdrm	None	15	N/A	PRODUCTION
12/18/93	10:33:40 PM	Scsicdrm	None	15	N/A	PRODUCTION
12/18/93	10:33:40 PM	Scsicdrm	None	15	N/A	PRODUCTION
12/18/93	10:33:40 PM	Scsicdrm	None	15	N/A	PRODUCTION
12/18/93	10:33:39 PM	Scsicdrm	None	15	N/A	PRODUCTION

NOTE

The first time you run Event Viewer, the System log is the default log. After that, the last log viewed is the default log.

2. Choose the log you want to view by opening the Log menu and choosing System, Security, or Application.
3. By default, the local computer's log is displayed. If you want to examine a networked computer's log, choose Log | Computer and use the Browse box to choose the desired workstation or server.
4. Just as with File Manager, changes to the log that occur while you're examining it won't always be immediately reflected. Press F5 to update the log if you suspect that some system activity has occurred while you've been running the program.

TIP

Use the low-speed connection check box in the case of slow or densely populated networks. This can save you time if you know the location or name of the computer you're looking for, because not all computers on the domain will be listed.

5. Normally the list is sorted with the most recent events at the top of the list. You can reverse this if you want by choosing View | Oldest First.
6. You can optionally filter out events that you don't want to wade through. For example, you can show events that occurred only during certain times of the day, events pertaining to a specific user or event ID, or event type (such as only errors or warnings). Choose View | Filter and fill in the dialog box. (The options are explained in the section titled "Filtering Events.")
7. You might want to search for a specific event. Use the View | Find command, and enter the relevant information in the dialog box.
8. If you want to see more information about an event, double-click on it. Another dialog box appears, listing details. An example is shown in Figure 12.11. Details of your Security log won't make much sense if you're not a programmer. Even then, the messages are cryptic. The System and Application logs offer more in the way of understandable English. Most useful is information about drivers failing to load (often leading you to IRQ and port conflict resolutions).

FIGURE 12.11.

You can display the details of an event by double-clicking on it.

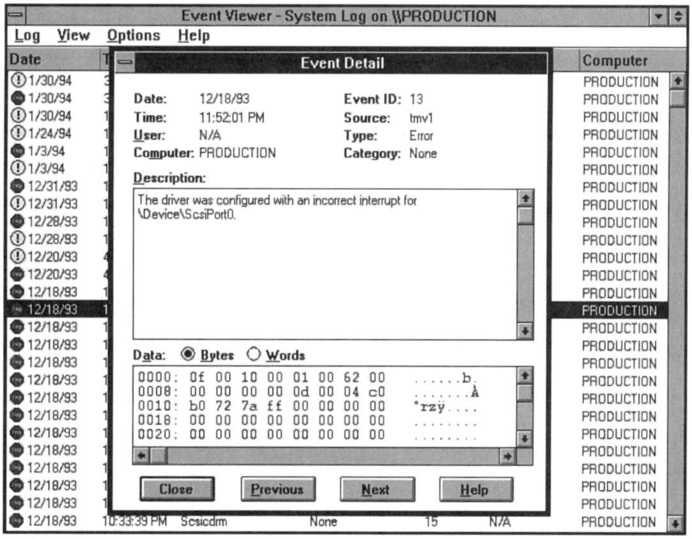

Log Breakdown

Essentially, each log file consists of a database with nine fields:

Type	Each type has an associated icon. There are five kinds of icons (see the following list), and they appear in the far-left margin of the listing.
Date	The date the event was logged (according to the system clock). This is another reason to ensure that the workstation or server internal clock is set correctly.
Time	The time the event occurred. Note that if it's necessary, all workstation clocks can be synchronized by using a command that pulls the time from the server machine for use in the log and other activities. Add the line `net time \\server /set` to the startup file for the machine, replacing the word *`server`* with the server's name. This line can even be included in the logon script for the user. (See the section in Chapter 10 titled "Adding a New Account.")
Source	The name of the application software or device driver that reported the problem to NT, which then logged it.
Category	Which general classification this event falls under. Each of the three logs has different categories of events.
Event	Event numbers are assigned to events based on a coding system Microsoft has designed. Event numbers help technical-support people figure out what's wrong with an errant system.
User	Many events are related to a specific user. For example, a user might be using the application that logs an error or other event to the Application log. That user's name then appears in this field. This is particularly useful for tracking down attempted security breaches.
Computer	The computer where the event happened. Of course, this will almost always be the same. The only time it will be different is if you export the log data into a comma-delimited format and merge it with exported data from other logs, then read it back into the Event Viewer. In this case, you might need to see which computer generated which entries. (You can export logs with the Log | Save As option.)

The icons in the left margin fall into the following categories:

Icon	*Description*	*Meaning*
Stop sign	Error	Serious trouble of some sort, such as the device driver not loading, IRQ or other hardware conflicts, missing network cards, and so forth.
! sign	Warning	Nonserious trouble, but worthy of attention soon, such as being low on hard-disk space (which could bring down the system).
i sign	Information	Nonserious. Typically, these notices concern successful operations achieved by applications.
Key	Success audit	A log entry indicating the success of a procedure. For example, if you opted to audit successful operations from Print Manager or File Manager's Security menu, a successful attachment to a shared printer or a successful drive connection by another workstation would be reported as a success audit.
Padlock	Failure audit	Similar to a success audit, but reversed—failed attempts are logged. Failures typically occur because the user making the attempt doesn't have the correct privileges.

Filtering Events

As mentioned in the preceding steps, you can cull all but the events you're interested in examining. When logs get quite large, or with a server that supports a high density of workstation activity, this might be the most effective technique for ferreting out what you need to examine. The Filter dialog box is shown in Figure 12.12. You reach it by selecting View | Filter Events.

See the previous lists for descriptions of the options in this box. It's worth noting that just as in File Manager, a filter remains in force until it's reset. Don't be alarmed if all your entries suddenly seem to have disappeared; they're probably just being filtered. Check the Event Viewer's title bar. It will read "Event Viewer—Filtered" if a filter is active. Also, if you choose Options | Save Settings on Exit, the filter will be activated the next time you run the program.

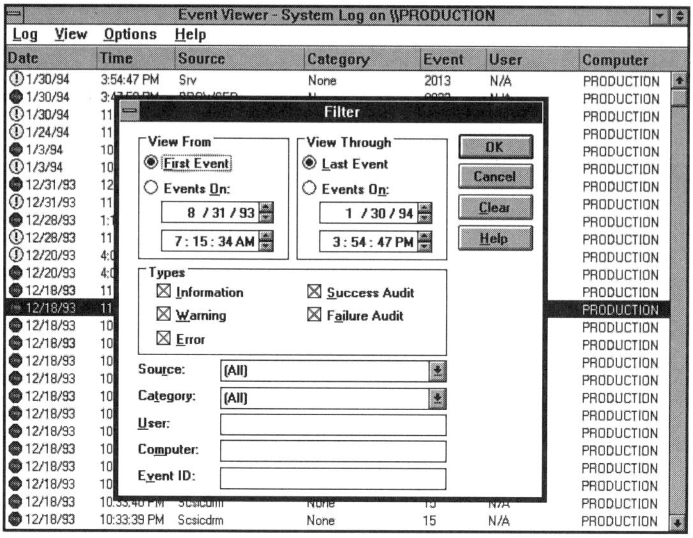

FIGURE 12.12.
The Filter dialog box.

Setting Logging Options

The Options menu lets you stipulate a few settings that affect how log entries are recorded. These settings are most useful in managing the size of your logs so that they don't eat up too much disk space. There are potentially so many loggable events that even a typical day on a busy network server could produce far larger log files than you would want to wade through, or that you'd want to devote disk space to.

To view or change options settings, choose Log | Log Settings. The dialog box shown in Figure 12.13 appears.

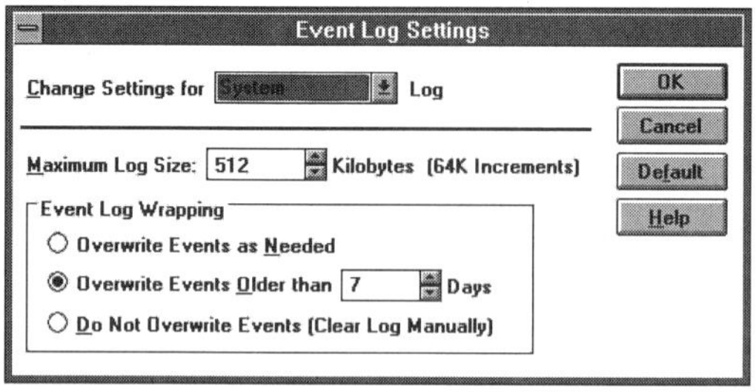

FIGURE 12.13.
Altering or viewing log settings.

The default log settings shown in Figure 12.13 suffice for most systems. Possible changes are explained in the following list.

Setting	*Description*
Change Settings for	Chooses one of the three logs you want to alter settings for.
Maximum Log Size	Declares the largest size of the log file (before old events are overwritten or entries cease to be written to the log).
Overwrite Events as Needed	When the log fills up, a new event takes the place of the oldest preexisting log entry.
Overwrite Events Older than	Only after the number of days you specify here will new entries replace old events.
Do Not Overwrite Events	Prevents events from being overwritten (and thus lost). The selected log might fill up if you enable this setting. If so, you'll have to use the Log | Clear All Events command to make room for new entries.

Using Archived Log Files

A final option in the Event Viewer lets you create archives of log files and to reload those files for later examination. As a rule, archiving log files isn't of much use unless you're running a very secure operation in which extensive background records of system or network usage are mandated by the government or the corporation where you work. Most likely, in such a secure operation, you'll be doing regular tape or other forms of backup, which might include backups of the log files anyway, and this regimen might meet your security requirements, depending on your tape rotation scheme. If it doesn't, you'll want to archive your event logs. It's a relatively simple process.

TIP

One case to be made for archiving is this: Logs can be useful in isolating network or machine failures. By keeping copies of past logs, you have something to compare with current versions that list new failures. By comparing logs, you can perhaps notice how and when the errors began to accumulate. Generally speaking, a network failure starts simple, then increases in frequency until a catastrophic failure occurs. Old logs can help here.

NOTE

The file created by the archiving process isn't affected by any filtering active at the time. All events in the log are written into the archive file.

1. View the log you want to archive. That is, run the Event Viewer and open the Security, Application, or System log. Only the log that's showing will be archived.
2. Choose Log | Save As.
3. You'll see a standard File box. Choose the drive and directory, and give the file a name.
4. The standard extension is .EVT. At the bottom of the box you have the option of choosing an alternative format for the file. You can save the file as an ASCII text file or as a *comma-delimited* text file for use by a database or spreadsheet program that can import that format. (Comma-delimited format separates columns with commas instead of tabs or spaces. Both text file formats, incidentally, omit nontextual, binary information from the event.) By default, both alternative formats are given the .TXT extension.
5. Click on OK.

NOTE

After you click on OK, the log is archived but the current log isn't cleared. Its contents are unaffected. If your log was full, you'll have to clear it manually.

To recall an archived log for later examination, do the following:

1. Run the Event Viewer.
2. Choose Log | Open.
3. Use the File dialog box to specify the file. Make sure to specify the type of file (in the File Type section at the bottom of the box) before actually opening it. This setting determines how the Event Viewer displays event detail data.

Repairing a Crashed System

There are several ways to repair a nonfunctional NT system. You should consider the following approaches in this order:

- Alter system settings from dialog boxes if NT can still be run.
- Revert to the Last Known Good configuration if NT won't start but was recently running before you made changes in the last session.
- Resort to the NT Emergency Repair Disk to attempt an NT recovery.
- Install another copy of NT on the system and boot it. Then do a restoration of the last system backup you made. Do this using the NT Backup program. This will let you restore all the security and administration settings from the previous installation rather than starting from scratch. Then delete the temporary NT installation.
- Reinstall NT from scratch.

NOTE

Dealing with crashed applications (rather than the operating system itself) is covered in the next section.

Windows NT is a complex animal. Aside from the stringent physical requirements NT places on your hardware (disk space, CPU speed, and RAM), NT's complexity can tax your system. NT's many features—security, network, multimedia, multiuser, environment subsystems, and internal services, just to name a few—offer the PC user a very rich mix. However, as with any software application, NT's complexity also can lead to problems.

Part of the original design plan for NT was for it to be less error-prone than DOS-based Windows, and in some important respects Microsoft has succeeded in its purpose. NT is certainly less prone to catastrophic crashing, for example. NT also is good at detecting system failings, logging errors in files for later examination, and, in many cases, recovering on-the-fly—for example, from a downed hard disk, a bad sector, or even a power outage (with the aid of an uninterruptible power supply, of course).

Still, serious problems might crop up from time to time. A system you work with might refuse to start, for example. Or it might become so bungled from mismanagement that reinstalling NT seems a less daunting task than sorting out all the user accounts and profiles. Or perhaps you've installed new hardware and made changes to the system as you thought appropriate but NT just won't start. In any case, the following are some troubleshooting points to consider in such circumstances. I suggest that you read them all before deciding which approach to take. Consider reinstalling NT as a last resort. Not only does a total reinstallation take time, but you'll lose lots of user account information and preference settings in the process.

- Try simply rebooting.
- Try logging on as a different user. The problem might lie in the user's profile or Registry settings. If you can log on as an administrator, try adjusting the defective user settings via User Manager or other accessories.
- Run Control Panel and make sure that the Workstation and Server services are running properly (refer to Chapter 9, "Configuring Windows NT"). These two services are required for all users and for basic NT functionality.
- If NT booted fine last time, but you have since made system changes (such as to the screen, mouse, keyboard, or another driver), try the "Last Known Good configuration" trick. Do a cold reboot. When you see the words "OS Loader" on-screen, press the Spacebar. You'll be given the option of choosing either of these two options:

  Current Startup Configuration

  Last Known Good Configuration

  Choose Last Known Good Configuration. NT always keeps two sets of configuration information on disk: the current one and the last one it perceived as being functional—at least functional enough to let you interact with the screen and with NT. Note that NT cans the Current setup when you revert to the Last Known Good setup. Also, of course, if you've changed your hardware (upgraded the video card, hard-disk controller type, and so forth) since NT stored the Last Known Good configuration, and then you revert to Last Known Good, the system still might not work because NT will try to use the old drivers with the new hardware! You might have to reinstall the old hardware, then invoke the Last Known Good. When you're up and running again, try reinstalling the new drivers (via NT Setup, Control Panel, an installation program, or whatever), power down, install the new hardware, and power up. Don't overlook the possibility that the software driver you're trying to install isn't correct for the new hardware.

Using the NT Emergency Repair Disk

If none of the options just listed solves the problem, the next approach is to use the Emergency Repair Disk you created at installation time.

1. Insert the same NT installation disk you used to set up the system in the first place. If you used WINNT.EXE for installation (in other words, if you installed over the network), you should have another set of disks that WINNT made at that time for just this purpose—unless a floppyless installation was performed. If it was, obtain the original setup disks from the system administrator. In any case, insert the proper disk and reboot.

NOTE

If you installed across the network with WINNT, this procedure will have limited usefulness. This is because, among other things, the Emergency Repair procedure compares the system files with the source files. Unless you have access to the installation floppies, or a portable CD-ROM drive, this part of the process won't work. This is the main reason why in Chapter 8, "Installing Windows NT," I advised you to set up network workstations with either a local CD-ROM or floppies.

2. A text screen appears, enabling you to do a complete installation or just attempt repairs. If you're having some trouble with NT options that might not require a complete reinstallation, you might consider the latter approach.

   If you choose to repair the current installation (by entering `r`), you have the option of using either your Emergency Repair Disk or the repair information stored on the local hard disk. Then the repair program offers you the following options, which might be effective in repairing the damage:

   - Check the boot disk for a corrupted boot track. If the boot track is corrupted, or if the boot partition has been accidentally reassigned via the Disk Administrator program, the program reassigns the partition using the configuration stored on the floppy disk. (Read the following Caution on this topic.)
   - Check the boot hard disk and the disk containing the system files for broken links (do a `CHKDSK`).
   - Check the system directory to make sure that all the necessary system files are present and okay. If a corrupted file is detected, it's replaced. (You'll be prompted to insert a disk containing the needed file.) If you've deleted some NT components since your last repair information update (wallpapers, fonts, games, or what have you), these unfortunately will be re-added to your system directory. You'll have to delete them manually.
   - Check the Configuration Registry for errors. If errors are detected, you have the option of replacing the Registry with the Registry file that was stored on the Emergency Repair Disk.

NOTE

Replacing the Configuration Registry effectively wipes out the security and user account settings, and probably some application initialization (.INI) settings for the workstation made since you installed NT. This is one important reason to be certain that the Repair Disk Utility (RDISK.EXE) is used regularly to update the repair information.

- As a final measure, the Repair program removes security blockages on the NT system files (only if they're stored on an NTFS directory) to ensure that NT can access its own system files. It's possible that you or someone could have accidentally restricted permissions on the files to prevent even NT from reading them. This would prevent NT from running.

3. If you go ahead with repairs, you see a screen with various options. Follow the on-screen prompts. You're prompted to insert the Emergency Repair Disk in drive A: and, if needed, NT disks along the way.

NOTE

If you don't have enough space on your hard disk, the repair program warns you after doing a media check. You'll have to eliminate some files and try again. If you can't even boot NT, you're stuck. You'll have to boot from a DOS disk in the floppy drive, or from another operating system on the hard disk (for example, DOS or OS/2) if you have two systems on the disk. You might be able to continue to the next screen anyway, but you'll probably get an error message later saying that the repair couldn't be completed.

NOTE

If the repair does bomb, you could end up with two or more Windows NT items in the boot loader menu. This also could happen after a reinstallation. One or more of them might not work. At the least, they're redundant. You can edit the boot loader startup choices by editing BOOT.INI with a text editor and eliminating the redundant line(s), as described in the section titled "Trouble Booting Another Operating System."

CAUTION

Often, a repair replaces the disk partition information as set in Disk Administrator and as detected by NT when you first installed. If you have changed your disk partition setup by adding or deleting partitions or hard disks or by converting partitions to another file format, you'll want to keep a copy of that information on a floppy disk for use after the repair or reinstallation. Make sure, however, that you haven't caused the problem in the first place by reassigning the boot partition to a partition that doesn't contain the NT boot tracks. Recovering such a setup only causes the NT bootup failure to recur. See Chapter 10 for more information about saving partition setups.

4. After performing the options you select, such as running a `CHKDSK` and checking the validity of the boot and system files (which can easily take about 10 minutes), the program then asks which major items you want restored from the Repair Disk's copy of the Configuration Registry:

```
[ ] SYSTEM
[ ] SECURITY
[ ] SAM
[ ] DEFAULT
[ ] SOFTWARE
```

CAUTION

As the on-screen message warns, restoring a configuration file is a last resort, because existing configuration information will be trashed.

Each item has a Help screen. Press F1 to read about each one before opting to replace any or all of them. If you don't check any item, you can still complete the repair and system validation by pressing Enter.

5. Reboot. NT should come up, at least in some form. If you replaced many files, you'll have to check the user profiles, accounts, disk partitions, security and auditing settings, Program Manager groups, and so forth. If you opted not to change too much but just to verify the disk media, system files, and boot track, NT should look pretty much the way it did before it bombed.

Reinstalling NT from Scratch

If you decide that you just can't cope with the old copy of NT, run Setup again and choose the directory. You'll be told there's an existing copy of NT around, especially if you're short on disk space. Running short of disk space is likely because NT installations are so large. It's not likely that you'll want to install two copies of NT on the same disk. Therefore,

Setup suggests "removing one of the NT installations" and indicates where they are—in C:\WINDOWS, for example.

NOTE

If the \WINNT\SETUP.LOG file has been deleted, NT won't be able to remove the prior version and/or files. SETUP.LOG contains the list of replaceable files.

You're reassured that removing the existing NT installation won't jeopardize your Windows 3.1 installation. This is because only the NT-related files will be wiped out (Setup has a large internal database listing its own files). Any files with the same names as Windows 3.1 files, such as WINFILE.EXE, live in the \SYSTEM32 directory to prevent collisions. You're asked to confirm that you want the files removed. Removal takes some time (about five minutes) because there are so many files. You're advised how much disk space was freed (typically about 45M).

If, after the files are deleted, there still isn't about 90M of free space, you can reboot and delete some files or choose a new path. If you choose a new path (for example, a different disk drive or partition), you're presented with a list of the detected partitions and the available space on each. You have a choice of reformatting the partition in a different file format (NTFS or FAT) or leaving it as is. Typically, you'll leave it as is.

Follow the installation instructions, and reboot the computer when prompted.

TIP

If you lose the boot loader menu and the computer boots right into NT instead of giving you the choice of NT or the preexisting operating system, you have to run Control Panel's System applet and make settings there. You also might have to examine or modify the BOOT.INI file stored in the root of the boot disk. The alternative operating system is stored in the file BOOTSEC.DOS (even if it's OS/2 and not DOS), typically in the root of the boot drive. NT itself always gets the real boot sector of your boot disk. The OS Loader and BOOT.INI enable you to branch to BOOTSEC.DOS to load the alternative operating system.

Dealing with Crashed Applications

If you're running a potpourri of Win16 applications, you'll encounter unexpected or erratic behavior from time to time. Contrary to bad press, it typically is not NT that is at fault, but rather the application developers. Many developers don't follow the Microsoft guidelines for developing applications. Instead, to maximize performance, they utilize undocumented APIs or nonstandard coding methodologies.

When your system dies due to such a runaway 16-bit application, you get a dialog box. Sometimes the whole WOW comes down; sometimes it just acts strangely. Sometimes Dr. Watson makes a log entry and offers a dialog box with several buttons on it. If you choose Ignore, the app might continue to run. Save your work if possible, then close. If the program doesn't let you run more than one copy of it, when you try to run the program again you get a message to that effect. Why? Because the internals of NT don't thoroughly close out the application. When you try to rerun the application, the application thinks that one instance of itself is still running, even though the Task List doesn't show it. What do you do now? Log off, then log on. This restarts WOW.

TIP

Another way to restart WOW is to use the program PVIEW.EXE, the *process viewer*. Run the program and kill the NTVDM session that contains WOW.

TIP

Note that interaction between 16-bit programs might be at issue in bringing down WOW. You might have to isolate the offender by loading one at a time or by a progressive process of elimination. I noticed, for example, that a mix of PC-Kwik Toolbox, After Dark, and WinCIS can spell disaster if you load the programs in the wrong order. Until more 32-bit versions of programs are available, or until manufacturers comply more strictly with Microsoft's guidelines for API calls, some ill-behaved programs are bound to pull down WOW. In general, the solution seems to be to load one 16-bit application at a time in order to experiment with the mix, then eliminate the troublemakers. In the worst case, you might have to find a replacement for a 16-bit application.

Sometimes when a WOW application crashes and you click on Ignore, the Task List doesn't indicate that it's running anymore, but the application thinks it is. You can't run it again. You'd think that shutting down all visible WOW apps would enable you to start from scratch by having NT reload the WOW subsystem, but this doesn't always work. You might have to actually restart NT. Oddly enough, you might be able to run other WOW apps just fine, even with the crashed or invisible one apparently still in memory.

TIP

If you have sufficient paging file space, you might want to consider running your 16-bit applications in separate memory spaces. This will prevent one 16-bit application from pulling down all 16-bit applications.

Running DOS and Windows 3.x Applications

As you know, in most cases Windows NT will run DOS and Windows applications with little configuration. Changes you make to .INI files associated with the programs when running them in other Windows products (such as 3.1 or Windows for Workgroups) will carry over and be used in NT. The only real adaptation you have to make with most Windows 3.x and DOS products is simply to expect them to run slower, and to realize that this is the price of security and robustness.

When running non–32-bit programs under NT, remember the cardinal rule: If the program accesses hardware directly, it probably won't run under NT. Windows NT will trap the hardware access, display a dialog box, and probably kill the program. The exception to this is when an NT device driver has been written to support such access. For instance, NT includes some video device drivers that support MS-DOS applications that directly access the video hardware. But even these don't work in all video modes or with all programs that directly access video, such as all DOS-based games. Certainly, any program that attempts to access the hard disk will fail.

Also, remember that all Windows 3.x programs run in one virtual DOS machine (VDM) (by default, this can be changed in the application's property-setting dialog), and if one program bombs, it can (but won't always) pull down other Windows 3.x programs that are running. DOS programs, on the other hand, each run in separate VDMs; one program crashing won't pull down others.

It wouldn't make much sense for this book to cover known bugs on existing programs, because vendors are constantly updating their software. Since the release of NT, many software developers have been busy updating their 3.1 applications to work with NT and, of course, Windows 95. Anything printed here likely would be out of date by the time you read this. Therefore, you should read the README.WRI file for details on specific applications.

Covered here are general notes about running non-NT applications—specifically DOS and Windows 3.1 applications, which are the bulk of applications that are run under NT.

NOTE

See Chapter 9, "Configuring Windows NT," for notes about creating PIFs for your DOS applications. See the following section for a discussion of tips and tricks that pertain to running memory-resident applications and specific DOS and Windows applications.

Tips About Windows 3.1 Program Errors

You might have already had a few cases of Windows 3.1 programs bombing under NT. In my many months of testing and using NT, I have too. In general, NT is very stable in and of itself. However, some Windows 3.1 programs aren't all that happy with it. As mentioned in Chapter 3, "Working with Windows NT," just as Windows 3.1 has some quirks (such as running out of resources), you might have to experiment with NT a bit to determine what it tends to gag on. Although Microsoft states that most Windows 3.1 apps that don't access hardware should run just fine, this isn't actually the case. I've had a number of programs, especially Windows 3.x communications programs, behave unacceptably one day, while on another day they seem to run just fine. Clearly, the program mix loaded at the time has something to do with this effect; in my case, loading WinCIM or WinCIS (communications packages used with CompuServe) *without* loading PC-Kwik's Toolbox program seemed to clear things up.

NOTE

You should use only communications programs that support dual-ended data flow control. Otherwise, data might be lost or the program might hang. Most protocols (such as Kermit, XModem, and CompuServe B+) use flow control. Flow control also is available for YModem-G and ZModem. Plain ASCII transferring routines often do not use flow control.

When NT traps a program error, a dialog box appears, reporting the offending error and offering several choices—none of which is very useful to the end-user. You can cancel the program, generate a Dr. Watson error log for dispatch to Microsoft or a programmer, or click on Ignore and continue with the program. The latter is supposed to allow you to save your work and exit the program gracefully; with some programs, none of the options actually allows you to do so. In reality, you can save your work *if* (and this is a big if) the application hasn't corrupted its internal memory management. If the program becomes very unstable and you continue to try to use it, you probably can kiss your work good-bye. But as in Windows 3.x, sometimes the application will restore to a known good state and allow you to save your work.

Not only that, but with some programs, some invisible internal stack continues to inform NT that the program is still alive. The application's name might or might not show up in the Task List, but even if it does, clicking on the End Task button in Task List doesn't always clear it from the Windows 3.1 subsystem. If you're trying to rerun a program that allows only one instance of itself in memory at one time, you might be stuck, because terminating the program isn't completely successful. When you try to run the program again, you might see a message from the application that says `You can only run one copy of _____ at a time.` Sometimes I've found that I have to log off (or possibly even shut down NT), reboot, and then try the application again. As I mentioned earlier, this is one way to clear the WOW subsystem. The other way is via the PVIEW.EXE program (mentioned earlier in this section) that kills the NTVDM session. Closing all Windows 3.1 applications, then running one in hopes of launching a new WOW subsystem, doesn't seem to help. Nor does any Control Panel applet allow termination and restarting of the WOW environment.

With a little experimentation, you will soon discover which Windows 3.1 programs are finicky under NT and which aren't. The real causes of these bugs will take a while to iron out, but you might as well relax and let the programmers do it. Improvements are continually being made in the compatibility arena. If you find major problems, you should ask the application's manufacturer for possible fixes, updates, or workarounds.

As a final note, installation routines for Windows 3.1 applications might occasionally bomb when run under NT. Microsoft claims that this is due to NT's "more stringent" floppy- and hard-disk formatting rules. The installation programs might work fine under DOS or Windows. One fix is to boot Windows 3.1 (or DOS, if that will work) and install under one of those environments. If you don't have DOS or Windows 3.1 on your machine, find a machine that does. Format some blank disks on your NT machine using File Manager or the command prompt. In the other machine, boot DOS and use `XCOPY` to copy your original application installation disks' files onto the new blank disks. Then rerun the installation on the NT machine.

Out-of-Memory or Out-of-Resources Messages

One of NT's great features is that system resources are no longer limited. Also, with the amount of memory that you'll likely be installing in NT systems and the dynamic use of hard-disk virtual space NT is capable of, memory shortages might be less common. So, when you get an "out of memory" or "out of resources" message from a Windows 3.1 application under NT, what's going on?

Chances are that the program is trying to use a Windows 3.1 printer driver, which is known to trigger such an error message. To fix the problem, run Print Manager and specifically set an existing printer (create one if necessary) as the "default" printer. Also, you might try choosing this new default printer from the application's Print Setup dialog box if it has one.

Tips About DOS Programs

The DOS emulator in Windows NT is pretty reliable. Again, don't forget that, unless they're supported by device drivers that allow such access, any programs that attempt to directly access hardware will bomb. Thus, DOS applications supplied with sound cards, communications programs, or anything else that circumvents standard DOS systems calls will display an NT-generated dialog box that announces an error.

Mouse Pointer Conflicts

One particular conflict pertains to the sharing of the mouse. The command-prompt window does supply mouse capability to DOS programs that request it. Although NT usually surrenders the mouse cursor to such applications gracefully, sometimes there is a conflict. To fix this, do the following:

1. Window the application.
2. Open the application's Control menu using the mouse or by pressing Ctrl-Spacebar.
3. Choose Hide Mouse Pointer. Now the pointer is exclusively under the control of the DOS application.
4. To return the mouse to use by NT, open the Control menu again and choose Display Mouse Pointer.

Tips About DOS Memory-Resident Programs

As you probably know, many DOS programs rely on or are themselves memory-resident, or TSR (terminate-and-stay-resident), programs. For example, most DOS-based remote-control programs (such as PC-Anywhere) load a memory-resident portion. SideKick is the perennial example of a TSR.

The NT User's Guide is pretty confusing on the issue of how to run TSRs. This is partly because there are so many different ways to do it and so many caveats. Here's the gist, in plain English.

The easiest way to run a TSR is to run it just as you would from DOS. First, run a command-prompt session. In the resulting command-prompt window, run the TSR as usual. It should pop up or otherwise work as expected. If you want to run another program in the same session (typically one that works with the TSR), run that one too by entering its name at the command prompt. Note that the TSR will be available only in the current window, not in every command-prompt window that you open from NT.

Want to easily load a TSR and a DOS application in the same window at once? No problem:

1. Create a batch file, and include the lines necessary to run both programs. For example, the following code loads a thesaurus program that I use, and then it loads PC-Write on top of it:

   ```
   thes
   ed
   ```

2. Save the batch file and create an icon for it in Program Manager.
3. Run the two programs by simply clicking on the icon.

So much for the simple approach. Want to get fancier? What if you want every command-prompt window to automatically have the same TSR loaded? This can be done, but be aware that each command-prompt window uses up that much more precious memory. To add the TSR to each command-prompt window you launch, follow these steps:

1. Edit either the CONFIG.NT or AUTOEXEC.NT file (depending on how the TSR is normally loaded—typically via AUTOEXEC.NT) to include a line such as

   ```
   SK2
   ```

   and save the file.
2. Check Control Panel's System applet to be sure that the startup files for command-prompt sessions actually match the names of the file(s) you edited.

TIP

If you need to set additional aspects of the DOS environment for a DOS application, such as reserving pop-up keys or requesting expanded memory, you have to create a PIF instead of just running the application with its usual name. You can use the same batch file or keyboard command techniques explained earlier, but use the file's PIF instead; just cite the PIF's name in the batch file (for example, ED.PIF). Additionally, you can set up the PIF to load a particular set of startup files (analogous to AUTOEXEC.BAT and CONFIG.SYS). Each PIF can stipulate its own set of startup files. Click on the Windows NT button in the PIF Editor to edit the name of the file. The AUTOEXEC startup file could include the name of the TSR you want to run prior to the main application running.

Finally, here's one caveat with respect to TSRs. Most pop-up TSRs (and even some standard programs) let you "shell out" to DOS to run DOS commands. For example, X-TREE has a command that brings up a DOS prompt. As another example, you might pop up SideKick, then close its window. In both cases, the idea is for the DOS prompt to appear. NT meets your expectations by running the MS-DOS command interpreter COMMAND.COM when you shell out from an MS-DOS program. This is in contrast to what NT normally supplies as a command-line interpreter, which is the 32-bit program CMD.EXE. Using COMMAND.COM speeds up a TSR's response time, which is good. However, the down side of this arrangement is that you might accidentally try to run an unsupported type of program (such as an NT, POSIX, or OS/2 application) and cause COMMAND.COM, the TSR, or your MS-DOS application to hang. You can prevent this possible problem by being careful about which commands you enter in such a window, of course. But to be extra cautious, you can alter the CONFIG.NT file (or another startup file if you've specified it in a PIF) by adding the line

```
dosonly
```

to the file. This allows only DOS programs to be run from the prompt.

Similarly, if you want the TSR or DOS application to shell out to NT's command interpreter so that you can use its extended commands, add the line

```
ntcmdprompt
```

to the CONFIG.NT file (or another startup file if you've specified it in a PIF). However, this might prevent a pop-up program from popping up when you press its hot keys.

Solving Printer Problems

One final area of troubleshooting to consider is printing. Almost by definition, printing is fraught with maladies and pitfalls. Murphy's law almost always kicks into high gear when you're about to print that last-minute report.

I said that *by definition,* printing is problematic because there are so many variables to contend with. Getting all those dialog boxes, printer drivers, and cables set up correctly with single-user Windows is bad enough. Now, with NT and multiple users attempting to share a printer, you'll have additional headaches. Where is the print queue? What are the priority settings? Who deleted my file from the queue or rearranged the queue to put my job at the end? Why are graphics printing as garbage characters? Compound the possible Windows errors with those of other application types (POSIX, OS/2, and DOS) and printer interfacing techniques (especially serial printer links), and you have all the ingredients for major frustration.

If you're lucky, after you install NT, your printer works right away. You share your printer, and others can easily print to it. If all your equipment is emblazoned with brand names, if NT comes with a printer driver for your exact printer model, if you happen to get all the DIP switch settings right, and if the printer is hooked up to an industry-standard parallel port, you might just be in business right away. Remarkably, this often is the case—but not always.

Unfortunately, there isn't room here or in any book for all the tips and tricks you would need to resolve every problem that can crop up in the software-computer-printer chain. Instead, I'll discuss only the most common problems that crop up in the data chain between Windows and your hard-copy printouts. Chances are good that you'll weed out the culprit and be printing correctly in short order.

General Printing Tips

Some of the solutions discussed here apply to problems other than those listed under the specific headings that follow. If you don't see your particular problem listed in one of those headings, check out the following points. These are the most common causes of printer problems:

- Make certain that you installed the correct printer driver, port, and printer name when you created the printer in Print Manager.
- Check the cable between your printer and your computer. Is it firmly seated? Are the little screws or clips that hold the connector secured?
- Check the switch settings and the power to your printer. Is it really on? If it's a laser printer, did it print a startup page successfully? Try powering it down and then up again.
- If you're using a docking station with a portable or other pass-through connection, check your parallel port settings. For instance, the Toshiba DeskStation IV requires the parallel port settings to be configured to output only rather than to the bidirectional default in order to print with an HP DeskJet 310.

Nothing Prints

If nothing at all prints, there might be a fast fix, because it means something's *really* wrong. Here are some possibilities:

- Check that the printer has paper.
- Some printers have an online switch. Check for it.
- Is there an error light or indicator to alert you to a problem with the printer? If so, check the manual to see what it means, and try to correct the problem. It could be

a paper jam, a dead ribbon, a toner cartridge that needs replacing, or a font cartridge that needs to be plugged in.

- Check the application you're trying to print from. Is the correct printer selected from the application's Printer Setup dialog box? If the application doesn't have a Setup dialog box, it assumes that you want to use the default printer. Check Print Manager to see that the default printer is the one you're trying to print to. (See Chapter 4, "Print Manager," for more information.)
- Is the printer driver set up to print to the correct port? Check the Configure dialog box. (Again, see Chapter 4 for details.)
- If the printer is connected to a serial port (COM1 through COM4), are the communications settings correct? They must be the same on both sides (printer/computer). For the computer, set them using the Ports icon in Control Panel. For the printer, check internal switch or software settings.
- Does the printer work with any application? Does it work outside of Windows? If it does, the problem is with your Windows setup.
- Are you trying to print to a networked printer? If so, check that the printer is really currently shared. Your workstation might have connected to the printer when you booted, but the printer's workstation might have powered down since then or unshared the printer. The printer might have limited permissions, preventing use by others or limiting it to certain hours of the day.
- Some Windows 3.1 applications don't want to print to network printers, and they assume that the printer is locally connected. You might have to connect a local printer to the machine, or at least print only when the network printer is immediately available; otherwise, the application might time out.

An Indecipherable Mess Prints

Another common printing problem is the appearance of *garbage.* This

```
!^&*(ghAU"YeW*%^#$!!
```

is an example of garbage.

- Severe garbage invariably results when a serial printer's communications settings are configured incorrectly (although other causes might be at work). Check the port settings from Control Panel and the switches on the printer. Baud rate, stop and start bits, and parity must all be set identically for the printer and computer. Try running at a slower baud rate. Note again that if a slower baud rate is used, both printer and COM port must be set identically.
- If, on a serial printer, output is correct for a few lines or pages, followed by lots of garbage, the *flow control* probably is incorrect. The printer is being overrun by

data faster than it can print it. The garbage starts because data is being lost. Check the flow control for the printer's COM port via Control Panel's Ports icon or Print Manager's File | Properties dialog box. The Xon/Xoff method is software flow control. The Hardware setting uses voltages on specific wires in your cable to control handshaking. Your printer and Windows NT must use the same flow-control method.

- It's possible that your serial printer cable is wired incorrectly and therefore isn't relaying the handshaking information to the correct pin on the computer's serial port. Check that the cable is intended for use with an IBM PC and that your serial interface card is configured with the correct port and handshaking.
- Try another cable. (A cable that's too long also could be the culprit.)
- Try another printer driver that's similar, or, for simple printing, try the Generic/ Text Only printer driver.
- Turn your printer off and on again. There might be leftover data in the buffer.

NOTE

A batch file or another command that ejects the current page often flushes the buffer.

- If the printer has an emulation mode, is it in the correct mode? It might be set to emulate another type of printer. For example, some laserwriters can emulate both PostScript and Hewlett-Packard printers.
- Try the printer's self test (if it has one). Maybe the printer is defective.

Incorrect Fonts Appear in the Printout

Sometimes downloaded fonts or font cartridge fonts won't print correctly. Other times, even TrueType fonts won't appear correctly.

- If you're using a cartridge, did you install the cartridge properly?
- If you bought TrueType fonts or another brand of fonts, did you carefully follow the instructions supplied with the fonts? Fonts often have to be installed in the correct directory, and you must tell Windows NT where the fonts are. Read the section titled "Fonts" in Chapter 9, "Configuring Windows NT."
- If the fonts are of the downloaded "soft font" variety, they're dumped from the computer into the printer. They'll be lost when the printer's power is turned off. You must download them again if the power was turned off at any time subsequent to the downloading.

- Is the printer's RAM already chock full of fonts? Perhaps you downloaded more fonts than it can handle, so the last few fonts weren't actually installed. Use a utility program to determine which fonts were successfully downloaded.
- Printed fonts might not reflect what you see on-screen if the screen fonts aren't installed properly. TrueType fonts consist of two files—one for the screen and one for the printer. If one of these gets lost, the two won't match. Use Control Panel to remove the problematic font, then reinstall it.

Only a Portion of a Graphics Page Prints

If only a portion of a page prints when you're printing graphics, consider the following:

- If your printer lets you add memory and it's likely that you've run into a memory limitation, you might have to install more memory. Typical laser printers have 3M or more of memory. This much can handle extra fonts and full pages of graphics easily. If you do a lot of complex printing, it's worth the price.
- Some laser or ink-jet printers have limited internal RAM that prevents them from printing a whole page of graphics in the highest resolution. Select a lower resolution and try printing again.
- Windows NT sometimes botches graphics pages when printing from Windows 3.1 or DOS applications on a "slower" computer, according to Microsoft. (What they mean by "slower" isn't clear, but knowing NT, it could mean a 33Mhz 486!) What happens is that a portion of a graphic prints on one page, and the rest of it appears on subsequent pages. This happens because the page of graphics isn't processed (rasterized) quickly enough, and NT starts sending the data anyway. Sounds like a bug to me. Anyway, the fix is to increase the amount of time NT waits before beginning actual printing. Increasing this time factor slows down all print jobs, so don't do it casually. You must make the change from the Registry Editor. (See the next section for details of Registry editing.)

  Perhaps an easier fix, at least for HP laser printers model III and above, is to enable *page protection.* Page protection ensures that there is always enough memory to print an entire graphics page. For some users, turning this option on solves the partial page-print problem without making them resort to Registry editing. Page protection must be activated in two places to be operative: first from the HP's front panel, and then in the printer driver's Options dialog box. In this dialog box, look for a check box next to the memory setting area.

Look for the value

```
LPT_timeout:REG_SZ:15
```

under the Registry key

```
HKEY_LOCAL_MACHINE\SYSTEM\CurrentControlSet\Control\WOW
```

The 15 stands for 15 seconds. Try a minute or so (60) for starters.

- Does the paper size selected in the printer's setup box match the paper you're using? Check and adjust it if necessary.

The NT Registry

The Registry is a database that contains information on system and application configuration. It replaces the multitude of .INI files utilized in previous versions of Windows. However, some 16-bit Windows applications directly access .INI files rather than relying on the services provided with Windows 3.x for this purpose. Therefore, Windows NT continues to support .INI file utilization for compatibility.

The Registry is divided into multiple sections, referred to as *hives*. To maintain hive integrity, modifications are first written to a backup of the current hive. Only after the system has confirmed that the changes have been successfully written to disk will the primary hive file be modified. Should a system crash occur before the primary hive has been modified, the system utilizes the alternative hive to update the primary hive. The files are stored in the SystemRoot\SYSTEM32\CONFIG directory, where SystemRoot is the directory where NT has been installed. Table 12.1 lists the normal hives in a Windows NT system.

Table 12.1. The normal hives in a Windows NT system.

Hive Name	*Files*
SAM, located in HKEY_LOCAL_MACHINE	SAM, SAM.LOG
SECURITY, located in HKEY_LOCAL_MACHINE	SECURITY, SECURITY.LOG
SOFTWARE, located in HKEY_LOCAL_MACHINE	SOFTWARE, SOFTWARE.LOG
SYSTEM, located in HKEY_LOCAL_MACHINE	SYSTEM, SYSTEM.ALT
DEFAULT, located in HKEY_USERS	DEFAULT and DEFAULT.LOG
HKEY_CURRENT_USER, located in HKEY_USERS	USER###, USER###.LOG or ADMIN###, ADMIN###.LOG

A hive consists of keys, subkeys, and value entries stored in a hierarchical manner similar to directories, subdirectories, and files. Although .INI files can't contain nested entries as a hive can, the same basic relationship for section, entry, and value still exists. For example, the WIN.INI file's `[windows]` section contains the `run` entry, which lists the applications to be executed at Windows startup. This same value appears in the Registry in the HKEY_CURRENT_USER hive under the Software\Microsoft\Windows NT\Windows subkey for the `run` value entry. Consider the Registry subkey the .INI section and the .INI value the Registry value entry.

A Registry value entry is composed of three parts separated by colons: the name, the data type, and the actual data value. For the preceding example, the name is *run,* the data type is *REG_SZ,* and the data value is a *null string.* Therefore, the subkey Software\Microsoft\Windows NT\Windows would appear as run:REG_SZ: . Table 12.2 lists the various data types for value entries.

Table 12.2. The various data types for value entries.

Data Type	*Description*
REG_BINARY	An uninterpreted binary data field.
REG_DWORD	A 32-bit numeric field.
REG_EXPAND_SZ	A text string that contains an insertion string. This insertion string is expanded to its actual data representation before the string is used. For example, ComSpec:REG_EXPAND_SZ: %SystemRoot%\system32\cmd.exe.
REG_MULTI_SZ	A multiple NULL-terminated text string field.
REG_SZ	A standard text string.

The Registry Editor

The Registry Editor can be utilized to directly edit the Registry hives on either a local or remote computer. I find the Registry Editor to be so useful for system administration that in every installation I automatically install the application in Program Manager's Administrative Tools group for the administrator account. The interface is very similar to that used in File Manager. Instead of directories, subdirectories, and files, the Registry Editor displays keys, subkeys, and value entries. This interface also includes the option to set permissions, audit, or take ownership of a Registry key.

WARNING

Editing the Registry manually with the Registry Editor can be a dangerous task, because a miskeyed value might prevent Windows NT from loading. Whenever possible, utilize Control Panel or other provided applications to modify the Registry.

Starting the Registry Editor

To start the Registry Editor, follow these steps:

1. From a console window, enter `start regedt32.exe` and press Enter.
2. From File Manager, double-click on regedt32.exe, located in the SystemRoot\SYSTEM32 directory, or choose File | Run and enter `regedt32.exe`.
3. From Program Manager, either create an application icon in your favorite group or choose File | Run and enter `regedt32.exe`.

NOTE

If you're only interested in browsing the Registry, be sure to select Option | Read Only Mode so that inadvertent modifications won't be recorded in the Registry.

Primary Registry Keys

When you launch the Registry Editor, four separate window panes, each containing a single root key, are displayed. These windows are labeled HKEY_LOCAL_MACHINE, HKEY_CLASSES_ROOT, HKEY_CURRENT_USER, and HKEY_USERS. These keys contain, respectively, state information for the local computer system, OLE, the current user profile, and all loaded user profiles.

Adding and Deleting Keys and Value Entries

To add a new Registry key, follow these steps:

1. Select the primary key in the left window pane where you want to add the new key as a subkey of the primary key.
2. Choose Edit | Add Key or press the Insert key.

3. When the Add Key dialog box appears, enter the name of the key in the Key Name field and leave the Class Name field blank. The Class Name box is reserved for future use by Microsoft.
4. Click on OK or press Enter. The new key will be displayed.

Follow these steps to remove a key:

1. Select the primary key in the left window pane where you want to add the new key as a subkey of the primary key.
2. Choose Edit | Delete or press the Delete key.
3. Click on OK in the warning dialog box or press Enter. The key will be removed from the Registry.

Do the following to add a value entry:

1. Select the key in the left window pane where you want to add the new value entry.
2. Choose Edit | Add Value.
3. When the Add Value dialog box appears, enter the value name in the Value Name box and scroll through the list box to select a data type (for example, REG_SZ, REG_MULTI_SZ, REG_EXPAND_SZ, REG_BINARY, or REG_DWORD).
4. Click on OK or press Enter.
5. The Resource dialog box appears so that you can enter the initial value of the entry. Enter the appropriate value and click on OK or press Enter. The new value will be displayed.

To edit a value entry, follow these steps:

1. Double-click on the value entry in the right window pane, or select the value entry and press Enter, or select the value entry and choose Edit | String, Edit | Multi String, Edit | Expand, Edit | Binary, or Edit | DWORD to display the Resource Edit dialog box.
2. Enter your changes in the dialog box and click on OK or press Enter. The new value will be displayed.

Saving and Restoring Registry Hives

Registry hives (a key, subkey, and value entries) may be saved and loaded to and from disk. I recommend that prior to making any changes to a hive, you save it first so that it can be restored if necessary.

To save a Registry hive, follow these steps:

1. Select the primary key in the left window pane.
2. Choose Registry | Save Key.
3. When the Save Key dialog box appears, select the drive and directory where the file is to be stored, and enter the name of the file in the File Name box.
4. Click on OK or press Enter. The Registry hive will then be saved for later use.

Do the following to restore a Registry hive:

1. Select the primary key in the left window pane.
2. Choose Registry | Restore or Registry | Restore Volatile.

NOTE

The Restore Volatile option works exactly like the Restore option, except that the modifications are in effect only until the computer is restarted.

3. When the Restore Key dialog box appears, select the drive, directory, and filename for the hive file to be restored.

NOTE

When you're restoring a key on a remote computer, the C: drive listed in the Drive box is the remote computer's C: drive, not the local computer's C: drive.

4. Click on OK or press Enter. The new entries will be displayed.

Remote Registry Access

Follow these steps to access a remote computer's Registry:

1. Choose Registry | Select Computer.
2. When the Select Computer dialog box appears, enter the computer name in the Computer box, or select a computer name displayed in the Select Computer box.
3. Click on OK or press Enter.

TIP

If the computer is on another domain, preface the computer name with the domain name—for example, WORK\SRV.

Registry Keys

Now that we've discussed the concepts of the Registry database and Registry Editor, it's time to consider putting this knowledge to use. From a user standpoint, the interface to the Registry is the Control Panel applets or another application. However, an administrator occasionally might need to delve deeper into the Registry to solve the occasional problem. This section discusses a few of the more useful Registry keys without a Control Panel interface and why an administrator might need to modify them.

Modifying the Windows NT Logon Process

Many corporations need to display a warning to unauthorized users to legally protect themselves from computer hackers. With a character-mode network client, the most commonly used method is to display a splash screen when the user signs on to the network. Windows NT and NT Server machines can accomplish the same task by displaying a dialog box with a custom caption and message with a single OK button to acknowledge their acceptance of the message. The Registry key HKEY_LOCAL_MACHINE\SOFTWARE\Microsoft \WindowsNT\CurrentVersion\Winlogon value entries include the following value entries:

`LegalNoticeCaption`: The caption to be displayed in the dialog box's title bar.

`LegalNotice`: The actual message to be displayed.

> **NOTE**
>
> In order to display a message, the `LegalNoticeCaption` value entry must be set to a non-NULL value.

If Windows NT or NT Server computer security is not an issue, the logon process can be automated. This will bypass the normally required logon dialog box at system startup. To accomplish this task, modify the following entries:

`DefaultPassword`: The user password to be used in the logon process.

> **NOTE**
>
> This value must be added manually by choosing Registry Editor's Edit | Add Value menu selection, and it must not be a NULL value.

`DefaultUserName`: The username to use in the logon process. By default, this is the current user.

`AutoAdminLogon`: To enable automatic logon, set this value to 1. To disable, set it to 0. The default is 0.

Normally, the logon dialog displays the Shutdown button on NT workstations but not on NT Servers. This can be modified by editing this Winlogon entry:

`ShutdownWithoutLogon`: To enable the Shutdown button, set this value to 1. To disable, set it to 0.

Locating .INI File Entries

If a Windows 3.x migration occurred during the Windows NT installation, or if an application is installed under Windows NT, the application's .INI file entries can be found in the Registry key HKEY_LOCAL_MACHINE\SOFTWARE\Microsoft\Windows NT\CurrentVersion\IniFileMapping. Generally these values are pointers to another key that contains the actual .INI entries. For instance, if you look for MSMAIL32.INI, you will find the value entry <noname>USR: Software\Microsoft\Mail and the actual .INI entries in HKEY_CURRENT_ USER\Software\Microsoft\Mail. Normally there is little reason to modify these settings directly. However, if the application fails to execute after a modification, the settings may be manually modified or deleted in their entirety to reestablish the default settings.

NOTE

Additional entries may contain the SYS: prefix, which directs the request to the HKEY_LOCAL_MACHINE\Software key.

NOTE

Only applications that utilize the Registry APIs will create an entry. Applications that directly access the .INI file will continue to do so and will not utilize any entries under this key.

Modifying Setup-Specific Information

When Windows NT is initially installed, certain information is stored in the Registry and is no longer available to the user for modification. Yet some of this information might need to be updated throughout the life cycle of the installation. This information is located in the HKEY_LOCAL_MACHINE\SOFTWARE\Microsoft\Windows NT\CurrentVersion Registry key. The following entries might be of interest:

`CSDVersion`: The service pack version if the installation has been upgraded by utilizing the Microsoft Service Pack.

`CurrentBuild`: The build number of the current installation.

`CurrentType`: The type of installation. Lists either the uniprocessor or multiprocessor and whether the build is a free (nondebug) or checked (debug) installation.

`CurrentVersion`: The version number of the installed product. Currently 3.5.

NOTE

The preceding data can be displayed by executing WINVER.EXE. However, this data shouldn't need to be modified. It's included for informational purposes only.

`RegisteredOwner`: This entry contains the registered owner of the software.

`RegisteredOrganization`: This entry contains the registered organization of the software.

`SourcePath`: The default source path used during setup.

`SystemRoot`: The root directory where NT was installed.

Configuring the WOW Subsystem

The HKEY_LOCAL_MACHINE\SYSTEM\CurrentControlSet\Control\WOW Registry key contains configuration information for the MS-DOS and Windows 3.x-compatible subsystem. Although you'll rarely have any need to modify these values, some unique software might benefit from a modification of the following value entries:

LPT_timeout: This value indicates the number of seconds that NT will wait before reusing the port. If your MS-DOS or 16-bit Windows applications have garbled print jobs, increasing the default value of 15 seconds might solve the problem.

Size: This entry lists the default amount of memory to be allocated in megabytes for an MS-DOS application. The default value of 0 lets NT determine how much memory to give an application based on the current memory configuration.

Wowsize: This entry isn't used on Intel platforms, but it's used on RISC systems to determine the amount of memory in megabytes to be allocated for use by the WOW subsystem. For each megabyte specified, NT actually uses 1.25M. The additional .25M is not available to applications.

NOTE

Setting this value to less than 3 generally causes the application to fail when launched.

Summary

This chapter discussed a great number of maintenance and troubleshooting issues. Topics ranged from the rather mundane (although never to be overlooked) chore of making backups to the elaborate—such as editing the Registry, troubleshooting networks, and dealing with crashed hard disks and applications. This chapter has a wealth of information—information compiled from a number of writers' and consultants' experience, information that is probably difficult to assimilate in a single reading. You might want to stick a bookmark at the beginning of this chapter and revisit it from time to time as maladies pop up in the NT systems under your purveyance.

PART III

Networking Windows NT

IN THIS PART

13

An Overview of Windows NT Networking

IN THIS CHAPTER

Networking is one of Windows NT's great strengths. Every PC running NT can, without shells or other add-ons, act as a LAN workstation accessing data on file servers, as a server offering its data to the network community to share, and as a Remote Access Service (RAS) access point allowing you to dial in from home and access the data on your machine at the office. Throw in a few machines running Windows NT Server, and you can easily build a secure network with sophisticated domain-based naming.

Installing a LAN card driver into Windows NT automatically loads a group of other programs and drivers that handle jobs such as carrying data across the network, making requests of file servers, and responding to the requests of other workstations. Each of these programs includes the instructions for Windows NT to use a specific protocol to handle each task.

A *protocol* is an agreed-upon way to do things. The protocol for a telephone call requires that you dial a 7- or 11-digit number, then wait for the person at the other end to answer and say hello. If you don't follow the protocol—by dialing only five digits, for example—you can't make a call. Computer protocols work the same way. For a workstation to open a file on the file server, it has to send the right kind of request.

In addition to the default protocols that are automatically loaded when you start, Windows NT also includes support for additional protocols that might have advantages over the default protocols for your network. So that you can understand the Windows NT protocols and choose the right combination for your network, this section takes a quick look at how LANs work.

Most books, including this one, use the ISO (International Standards Organization) open system interconnect (OSI) as a model to describe how communications networks work and for comparison with other specific networks. If you're familiar with other networking books, you'll recognize the following section as the requisite description of the OSI model. It turns out that the Computer Book Act of 1974 requires that any book discussing computer networking must include a description of the OSI model or bear a warning label on its front cover. I included the following section in order to avoid interfering with this book's fine cover art.

The OSI Model

The OSI model, or way of thinking, divides the processes of a computer network, which can be either local or wide area, into seven different layers. The bottom (or physical) layer defines the wire and other physical attributes of the network, and the top (or application) layer defines how the network interacts with the user. The model calls for each layer to talk only to the layers immediately above and below itself. This allows each layer to be well-defined without getting out of control with "featuritis." Each layer's protocol is responsible for shielding the higher layers from knowing how the layers farther down work.

Although the ISO has standardized protocols for each of the seven layers, most local area networks use older protocols that aren't OSI-compliant. The OSI model shown in Figure 13.1 is still useful for comparing these protocols.

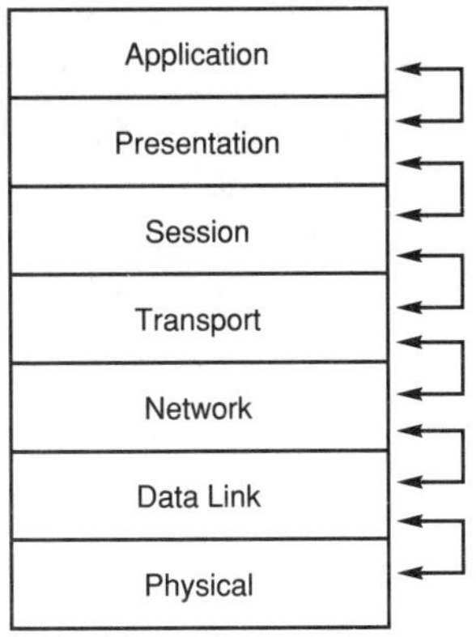

FIGURE 13.1.
The OSI model defines seven layers of network communications.

One good way to remember how the OSI model works is to think of a message, a request for data, a response, or an e-mail message as a letter. This letter needs to be delivered to Aunt Matilda, who is waiting for it with bated breath. The letter passes through several layers of handling, each of which puts the message inside a container—the envelope, the mail bag, the air freight container, and so forth. Similarly, each OSI layer adds a layer to the data it's sending and, as it receives a packet, removes a layer of wrapping and passes the data up.

The Physical Layer

The physical layer is responsible for sending bits from one end of the cable to the other. A physical layer specification such as 10Base-T defines the tangible aspects of the network, including the type of cable, the topology (how the cables are connected), how many pins are in the connector, and how they're used. Physical-layer protocols also define the voltages used on the cable, the bit rate, and the encoding method used.

The Data Link Layer

The data link layer packages the bits from the physical layer into *data frames*—a structured packet containing data. A frame is a group of data bits that also includes network control information such as addresses.

The details of the structure of a data frame change for different types of networks. As shown in Figure 13.2, each frame has several fields that carry important data about this packet for the network.

FIGURE 13.2.
An example of a Data Link Layer data frame.

The source address is the address of the workstation from which the frame was sent. The destination address is the address of the workstation to which the packet is being sent. The frame type is the type of data that is being carried in the frame, and the data is the data being transmitted over the physical connections of the network. The data link layer also adds error-correcting code information, typically a CRC (cyclical redundancy check) that allows the receiving station to make sure that the data was sent properly.

This layer provides error-free transfer of frames between computers over the physical layer. If a frame's CRC doesn't calculate to match the CRC in the packet, the packet is discarded so that the upper-layer protocols don't get data containing errors.

The media access and control (MAC) sublayer is the upper half of the data link layer that handles how workstation addresses are formatted and which station has access to the network at any given time. CSMA/CD is a MAC layer protocol. You might hear a product described as a MAC layer bridge, which is a device that links two networks at the MAC layer.

The network technologies discussed earlier define both the physical and data link layer protocols that will be used. So when you specify Ethernet, for example, you're calling for a particular set of data link and physical layer protocols.

The Network Layer

The network layer's primary job is to route data packets through the network, moving them from their source to their destination along the best route. To handle this task, the network layer adds an additional network address to the simple address used by the data link layer. Think of the network address as a street name and the MAC layer address as a house number. This layer also manages switching and packet congestion on the network.

The network layer bundles data frames into single packets that can be transmitted over the network, as shown in Figure 13.3. These packets, with their additional addressing and ECC information, are inserted into the data field of a data link layer frame. If packets are too large, the network layer protocol restructures them into smaller packets. On the destination computer, the network layer converts packets into their original structures.

FIGURE 13.3.
A network layer packet.

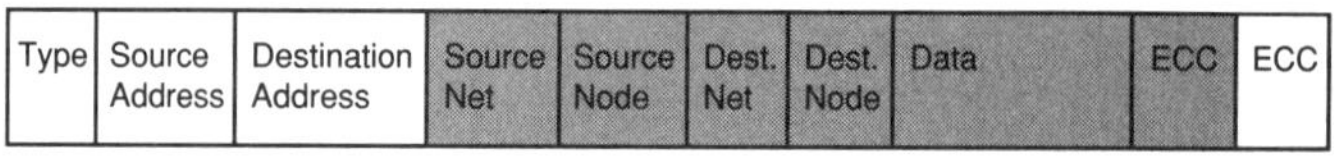

Windows NT supports IPX and IP as network layer protocols. The default NetBEUI (NetBIOS extended user interface) protocol has some of the features of a network layer protocol, but it doesn't actually support routing.

The Transport Layer

The transport layer manages error recognition and recovery. If the error-correcting code information in a packet indicates an error, or if a packet was not acknowledged, the transport layer tries several times to deliver its message before reporting a transmission error. This layer ensures the delivery of messages originating at the application layer. Like the network layer, the transport layer collects data frames and assembles them into packets. On the destination computer, the layer reassembles the packets into their frame structure.

Windows NT supports TCP, UDP, and SPX as transport layer protocols. Again, NetBEUI has some (but not all) transport layer protocol features.

The Session Layer

The session layer allows applications on different computers on a network to establish, use, and end a connection or session. This layer manages security measures and name recognition between computers.

The session layer synchronizes user tasks and manages the communication between processes. It regulates which computer transmits, when it transmits, and for how long. Functions such as remote file and print services generally are considered to be session layer services.

Windows NT uses the server message block (SMB) protocol as its primary session layer protocol. SMB provides message types for remote file and print services. With the addition of a NetWare requester, Windows NT also can use Novell's NetWare Core Protocol (NCP). Third parties such as NetManage and Sun also provide Network File System (NFS) support for Windows NT.

The Presentation Layer

The presentation layer determines how to exchange data between two computers. This layer translates the data sent from the application layer into an intermediary format. On the destination computer, this layer translates this intermediary format message into something the computer's application layer can use. The presentation layer also is responsible for data encryption.

The Application Layer

At the top of the OSI reference model is the application layer. It provides the means by which application processes can access network services. This layer directly supports user applications for e-mail, file transfers, and database access.

Now that you have a framework for talking about and describing the network connection in your computer, you might understand the Windows NT protocols as you install them. These protocols are the "languages" that allow Windows NT to communicate with other computers running the same protocols.

Windows NT provides Mail, Schedule+, File Manager, and many other application layer services.

Windows NT's Network Architecture

Windows NT's networking functionality was designed from the ground up, unlike earlier PC operating systems such as DOS and OS/2 1.*x*, which had networking strapped on as an afterthought. This early inclusion allowed Microsoft's programmers to make Windows NT's networking more efficient and elegant than any earlier PC operating system. They set out to make Windows NT the platform of choice for networked applications by building transparent file and print services into each Windows NT workstation. They also decided to provide a variety of powerful interprocess communications facilities to support client/server applications.

Microsoft also recognized, at least partially from their experience with OS/2, that we users weren't going to just toss out all of our existing networking applications and software. Therefore, they used several technologies to allow Windows NT to support standard network protocols so that Windows NT workstations could communicate with existing networks. The layered architecture that Windows NT uses (see Figure 13.4) mirrors the OSI reference model quite well. The presentation layer is thin to nonexistent, however, depending on the protocol and system used.

NDIS

The foundation of Windows NT's networking architecture is the NDIS (Network Device Interface Specification) 3.0 device driver. Early PC LANs used monolithic device drivers that not only interfaced with the LAN card but also implemented the network and/or transport layer protocols used by the LAN operating system. IBM's PC Network went so far as to implement NetBIOS in ROM.

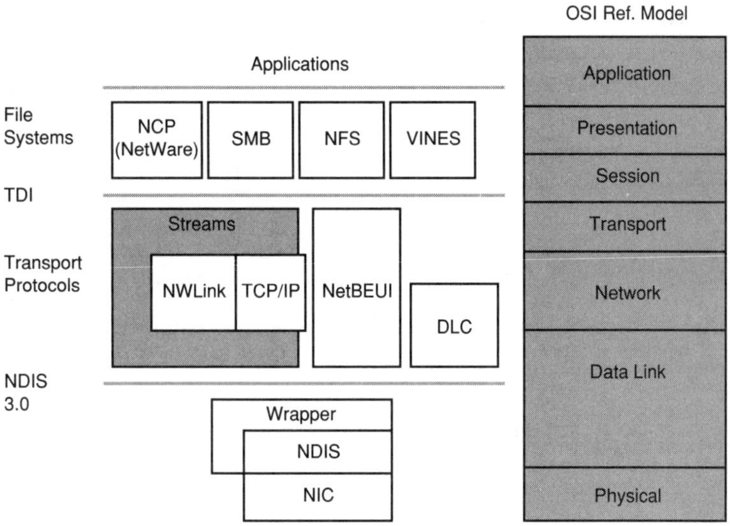

FIGURE 13.4.
Windows NT's networking architecture.

The problem with this monolithic approach is that it allows a LAN card to use only a single network layer protocol. If you use Novell's IPX.COM to talk to your Ethernet card, you can send only IPX data through that card. If you want to also send TCP/IP (Transmission Control Protocol/Internet Protocol) data to your UNIX machine, you're out of luck.

By 1989, the industry realized that the monolithic driver approach was a technological dead end. Microsoft, in cooperation with 3Com, developed NDIS as a solution to this problem. Rather than create a single piece of software that serves as both device driver for the LAN card and network layer protocol implementation, NDIS defines a data link layer interface so that multiple network layer protocols can access the same LAN card at the same time. See Figure 13.5.

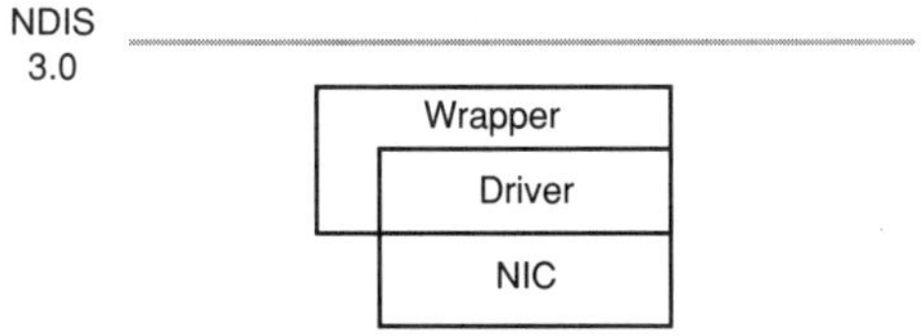

FIGURE 13.5.
NDIS.

NDIS 3.0 conforms to the device driver standards established for Windows NT. It calls for a C-call interface; NDIS drivers have access to the helper routines and are 32-bit, portable, and multiprocessor safe.

Unlike previous NDIS implementations used in OS/2 and Windows for Workgroups, Windows NT doesn't use a protocol manager or PROTMAN module to link the various components at each layer. Instead, the *bindings* (or relationships) between protocols are stored in the registry, and a small piece of code or wrapper around all of the NDIS device driver provides a uniform interface between protocol stack drivers and NDIS device drivers. The NDIS wrapper also contains supporting routines, which makes the development of an NDIS driver easier.

In addition to the usual LAN systems such as Ethernet and Token Ring, Windows NT also can use a serial port as a physical/data link layer protocol through the Remote Access Service. RAS allows a user to dial in to a Windows NT network and access data as if he or she were on a workstation connected to the network.

RAS is discussed in some detail in Chapter 18, "Internetworking: Remote Access Service and TCP/IP."

Multiple LAN Cards

One of the advantages of the NDIS approach is that it enables you to have multiple LAN cards in your system (see Figure 13.6). Adding a second, third, or sixteenth LAN card to your file server can let you extend your network beyond the distance limitations of your local area network technology by letting you run, for example, 100 meters of thin Ethernet cable from each of four LAN cards. Multiple LAN cards also enable you to support different LAN technologies for different users. Your CAD group, for example, can run FDDI or some other high-performance network, while the front office uses plain old Ethernet. Finally, you can provide greater bandwidth in and out of a system using conventional Ethernet or Token Ring cards by spreading the load over multiple cards. This can improve your network or server's performance.

FIGURE 13.6.
Windows NT supports multiple LAN cards.

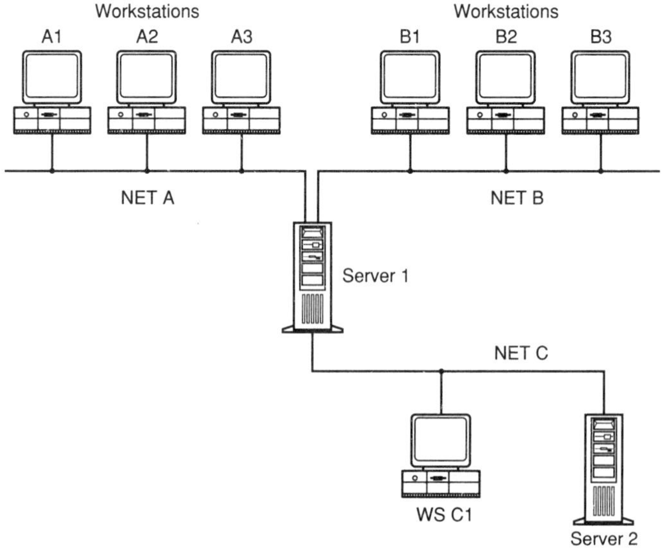

The one thing Windows NT doesn't do for multiple LAN cards is forward data from one network to another. NetWare users are familiar with the concept of internal routing, in which a NetWare file server forwards traffic from one network to another. As a result, the users on all the workstations in Figure 13.6 can access server 1, but users on the A1 through A3 and B1 through B3 workstations won't be able to access data on server 2 unless an additional bridge or router is added to the network.

Transport Protocols

Even though it's confusing, network people often use the term *transport protocols* to describe not only OSI transport layer protocols but also their associated network layer protocols. These combinations of protocols are collectively called transport protocols because their responsibility is to transport your data across the network. The higher layers relate more to specific applications than to simply carrying data hither and yon. In the Windows NT architecture, these protocols are just above the NDIS wrapper, and they use it for access to the LAN hardware. See Figure 13.7.

FIGURE 13.7.
Transport protocols.

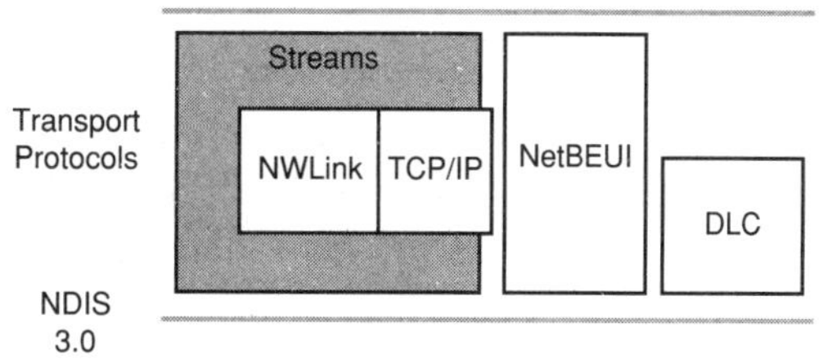

Windows NT ships with four sets of transport protocols. NBF, a simple protocol derived from NetBEUI, provides compatibility with existing LAN Manager, LAN Server, and MS-Net installations. TCP/IP provides a popular routable protocol for wide area networks and communications with UNIX machines. NWLINK is Microsoft's implementation of Novell's IPX/SPX protocols for communicating across NetWare networks and with NetWare file servers. Finally, DLC (data link control) provides an interface for access to mainframes and printers attached to networks. NT Server also provides Apple's AppleTalk protocol stack as part of its Services for Macintosh.

NetBEUI or NBF

The NetBEUI protocol is automatically loaded and bound to your adapter card when you install your LAN card into Windows NT. It's a self-tuning protocol that doesn't use very much memory, and it's fast because it has little overhead as compared to data.

NetBEUI is a good choice for regional sales offices or other small networks. NetBEUI also is used by Microsoft's LAN Manager and Windows for Workgroups. If you already run WFW or have LAN Manager, you can share those resources.

Although NetBEUI is fast for small networks, it's a bad choice for larger networks. Because NetBEUI uses your computer's name as its address, you won't be able to use NetBEUI effectively if you have multiple computers with the same name on your network. NetBEUI doesn't add a network address to your computer's name, so, unlike a true network layer protocol, it can't be routed. This means that as your network grows, so does the overhead of NetBEUI, because all messages that get broadcast by a station looking for the computer named, for example, Shlomo get forwarded across all your network links.

NetBEUI Isn't NetBIOS

When I talk about NetBEUI, it's important for you to understand that I'm talking about the transport layer protocol, not the programming interface NetBIOS. Most people think of NetBEUI and NetBIOS as being one and the same, because earlier implementations of NetBEUI on MS-DOS and OS/2 provided the NetBIOS programming interface as part of the NetBEUI device driver.

The important point to remember here is that the programming interface, NetBIOS, can be provided for use by higher-layer programs such as Windows NT's file and print services by protocols other than NetBEUI. This enables you to remove NetBEUI from your system and still take advantage of the higher-layer services.

Data Link Control

The data link control protocol is used primarily by IBM Token Ring networks. Strictly speaking, DLC isn't a transport protocol but a sophisticated data link layer protocol. Windows NT's file and print services don't use DLC, but NT provides DLC to enable connectivity to IBM mainframe computers. DLC also can be used to communicate with printers that are attached directly to the network, such as the HP LaserJet IIISi, instead of through the parallel or serial port of a print server.

NWLink

NWLink, or NetWare Link, is Microsoft's implementation of Novell's IPX (internetwork packet exchange) network layer and SPX (sequenced packet exchange) transport layer protocols. These protocols were originally developed by Xerox as part of their XNS protocol suite.

NWLink also includes a NetBIOS interface, which Microsoft calls NWBlink. It allows your Windows NT systems to communicate over networks that also use Novell NetWare and include routers.

Contrary to popular opinion, NWLink alone doesn't enable you to access data on a NetWare file server. For that you must have a NetWare-compatible transport protocol *and* a NetWare requester. Connecting Windows NT to NetWare networks is discussed in more detail in Chapter 19, "Integrating Windows NT with Other Networks."

TCP/IP

TCP/IP actually refers to a whole suite of protocols first developed for the U.S. Department of Defense in the 1970s as part of the ARPAnet (now Internet) development project. TCP/IP is the most widely supported protocol suite in the world, at least partially because the Department of Defense for years required all its computers to support TCP/IP. Because these are the people who think that $600 is a reasonable price for a hammer, no computer manufacturer wanted to write them off as a customer. TCP/IP also is the standard suite of protocols used by UNIX systems for their local area and wide area networking applications.

Windows NT's TCP/IP support has two advantages for you, the user. First, TCP/IP is the protocol suite of choice for large networks that are linked by routers. It's efficient on wide area and complex networks and well-supported by router manufacturers, wide area network providers, and, of course, the Internet. The other advantage of TCP/IP is its connectivity with UNIX and other non-PC systems.

Not only do users benefit from Windows NT's TCP/IP support, but system administrators and network architects will appreciate the Microsoft Dynamic Host Configuration Protocol (DHCP) and Windows Internet Name Service (WINS). These two services offer easier management of large networks and are discussed in further detail in Chapter 17.

Streams

Windows NT's TCP/IP and NWLink use another multiple protocol support facility called Streams, which was derived from AT&T's UNIX. Instead of being a single device driver bound directly to the NDIS device driver, these protocol drivers reside "inside a wrapper." Streams is a very popular method of implementing the TCP/IP protocol on UNIX-based systems. You can think of TCP/IP or NWLink as being surrounded by the Streams device driver. Calls to the TCP/IP or NWLink transport protocol driver must first go through the upper layer of the Streams device driver, then to the NDIS device driver via the lower end of the device driver.

Streams is a significant departure from the way protocol stacks were developed for MS-DOS and OS/2. Several reasons exist for the use of the Streams mechanism. Streams makes it easier to port existing protocol stacks to Windows NT. Streams also encourages protocol stacks to be organized in a modular, stackable style, thus moving closer to the original vision of the OSI model. Novell uses Streams in a similar fashion in NetWare 3.*x* and 4.*x* file servers.

Transport Data Interface

Above the transport protocols, Windows NT uses another boundary layer similar in function to NDIS called TDI (transport data interface), shown in Figure 13.8. This layer provides a common interface for file system and I/O manager processes to communicate with the various network transports. It's a "thin" layer, with very little code actually involved. TDI helps other vendors to develop their software, and it allows software developed above and below a level to be mixed and matched without reprogramming.

FIGURE 13.8.
Transport data interface.

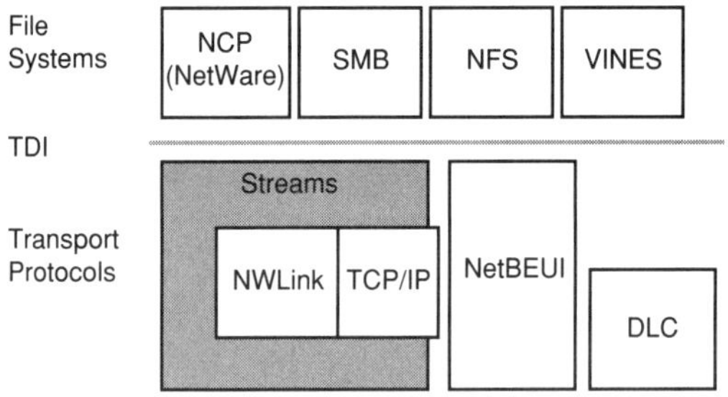

The TDI interface is based on 32-bit-wide handles. This increases the connection capacity between upper layers and protocols such as NetBEUI, which supports only an 8-bit Local Session Number—a real problem if you need to create a network with more than 256 stations.

The Session Layer and Above: File and Print Sharing on the Network

If all you wanted to do was pump data into a cable and receive it at the other end, transport protocols would be all you'd need. If you're not a programmer and you want to get work done using your computer rather than just sending packets back and forth, you need higher-layer protocols.

For most users, networking means file and printer sharing. These features also are important parts of Windows NT. The most significant components in providing these file and print services are the server and redirector, or workstation, service. These two components, with the help of several more to be identified later in this chapter, provide most of the functionality of the OS/2 version of LAN Manager available today. Both of these modules execute as 32-bit services.

The redirector service takes requests from applications, formats them into server message block (SMB) protocol messages, and sends them across the network to the server. The redirector service is a file system driver (FSD) that actually does the interaction with the lower layers of the protocol stack through the NetBIOS API. The server accepts the SMB messages, gets the requested data, and sends it back across the network to the requesting station.

When you access a resource on another system, you have to do it by referring to the resource's UNC (universal naming convention) name. First used by Microsoft in MS-Net and the PC Network Program, UNC is a naming convention for describing servers and sharepoints for those servers on a network. UNC names start with two backslashes (\\) followed by the server name. All other fields in the name are separated by a single backslash. A typical UNC name would appear as

```
\\server\share\subdirectory\filename
```

A *share* or *sharepoint* is the name assigned by the server's administrator to a disk drive or directory that he or she wants to make available to other users to share.

Multiple Protocols/Multiple Requesters

One of Windows NT's major advances over earlier PC operating systems such as DOS and OS/2 is its capability to support multiple requesters at once. This enables you to use the default Windows NT requester to access other Windows NT workstations and servers, Novell's NetWare Requester to access data on NetWare file servers, and a third-party NFS (Network File System) requester to access files on a UNIX server all at the same time.

The Multiple UNC Provider (MUP), shown in Figure 13.9, is responsible for managing these multiple requesters, or UNC providers. The most productive way to think of MUP is as a UNC name locator. The MUP can identify the right requester from a partial name; `\\server` is sufficient for the MUP to find a server and get a list of its sharepoints.

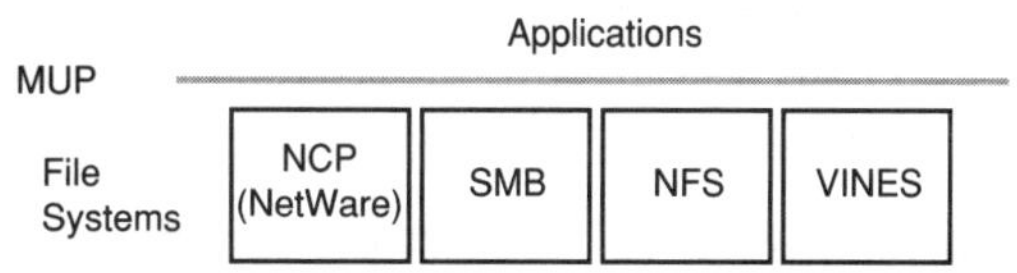

FIGURE 13.9.
The Multiple UNC Provider.

Unlike the NDIS and TDI boundary layers, which really just define how the protocols above and below them should communicate over specifically defined paths called *binds,*

MUP is actually a program. Like NDIS and TDI, MUP has defined paths to redirectors, but it also must know which requester to send any given request to.

When the MUP receives a command from an application, it checks the UNC name in that request against the table it keeps of UNC names and their associated requesters. If the MUP has seen this UNC name in a request during the past 15 minutes or so, the UNC name will be in the MUP's local name table, and the MUP will just pass it on to the right requester.

If this is a new UNC name, the MUP sends it to each requester, essentially going around the room asking, "Is this your mitten, Timmy? Is this your mitten, Joey?" until a requester fesses up. The redirector with the highest registered priority response that claims that it can establish a connection to the UNC is passed the command and the security context of the application generating the request.

For applications that don't make UNC requests but instead make Windows networking calls directly, Windows NT also provides a multiple provider router (MPR), which functions similarly to the MUP but for different function calls.

Additional Network Services

In addition to the workstation and server services, Microsoft ported a few other services from their older OS/2 LAN Manager. Alerter, Messenger, Browser, and Replicator all provide important services for network users.

The Alerter is used to forward alerts generated by events such as a full disk drive to remote computers or usernames. The Messenger receives messages and alerts and displays them on-screen in a dialog box. The Browser collects information about the machines in this domain or workgroup for use by other applications. File Manager uses the Browser's information to list the available sharepoints on another system, which enables you to connect to a new drive. The replicator service automatically copies the contents of a directory from an NT Server to another machine in order to create a real-time background backup.

Distributed Applications

It seems that all you need to do today to attract a big crowd at a seminar is to put "client/server" on the brochure's cover. Consultants also can make big bucks by using these magic words.

Don't get snowed by all the buzzwords. A distributed (or client/server) application is simply a program that has two parts. One typically interacts with the user and runs on one computer (called the client), and the other (called the server) typically provides some service, ranging from a database backend to a computing or communications service. These two parts of the program need to communicate with each other, and this is where Windows NT's interprocess communications facilities come in.

Just as with transport protocols, Windows NT provides a wide variety of interprocess communications (IPC) facilities, ranging from old and primarily historically interesting ones such as NetBIOS to the latest industry standard features such as remote procedure calls.

Windows NT actually provides six different IPC mechanisms: named pipes, mailslots, NetBIOS, Windows sockets, remote procedure calls (RPC), and NetDDE (network dynamic data exchange). Named pipes and mailslots were first introduced as part of LAN Manager. They're included in Windows NT to provide backward compatibility with existing LAN Manager installations and applications such as Microsoft's SQL Server. NetBIOS is the oldest of Windows NT's IPCs and is also provided for backward compatibility. Windows sockets is a Windows-based implementation of the Berkeley sockets APIs, which are popular in the UNIX world. Windows NT's RPC is compatible with the OSF/DCE (Open Software Foundation/Distributed Computing Environment) specification for remote procedure calls. NetDDE allows even the nonprogrammer to build distributed applications by extending standard DDE connections between Windows applications across the network.

Named pipes and mailslots, unlike the other IPC mechanisms, are written as file systems. As such, they share common functionality with the other file systems, including security access controls, which are part of NTFS and other file systems. In addition, processes can use named pipes and mailslots to communicate with other processes on the same machine, in addition to using them to communicate with processes on other machines on the network. As with other file systems, access to named pipes and mailslots is provided by the redirector.

The named pipes' APIs, while based on the OS/2 API set, have been ported to the Win32 base API set and extended, making support for client/server applications easier to implement. As a file system, named pipes can take advantage of the cache manager, improving the performance of some named pipe applications. This can improve performance by reducing the number of frames (and network overhead) generated.

Windows NT extends the named pipes support from OS/2 by adding an impersonation, which allows a server to change its security identity to that of the client on the other end. If, for example, you have a database server system that uses named pipes to receive read and write requests from clients when a request comes in, the database server program can impersonate the client before attempting to perform the request. Even if the server program does have authority to perform the function, the client doesn't, and the request would be denied. If not for this impersonation, a client could send a request to a server and have it fulfilled if the server had sufficient access rights, thus fooling the system. With impersonation, the server will pretend to be the client, but the client can't get a beer by asking the 21-year-old server to go to the liquor store for it.

The mailslot implementation in Windows NT is only a subset of full OS/2 LAN Manager implementation. LAN Manager provides both first- and second-class mailslots, but Windows NT provides only second-class mailslots. Mailslots provide so-called connectionless, basic broadcast messaging. Delivery of the message is not guaranteed.

Mailslots are most useful for discovering other machines or services on a network, or for advertising the availability of a service. Because of the broadcast nature of mailslots, they can easily clog your network with traffic, slowing down other important functions. Because most wide area networks don't forward broadcast messages across bridges or routers, mailslots are really useful only for local communications.

The use of NetBIOS as an IPC mechanism has existed since the introduction of the interface in the early 1980s. Even though higher-level interfaces such as named pipes and RPC are superior in their flexibility and portability, many applications use NetBIOS because of its wide acceptance in the PC network arena. The NetBIOS entry point in Windows NT's registry defines a common interface point from which multiple possible transport protocols can take the data across your network. Windows NT comes with NetBIOS interfaces to the NetBEUI transport protocol through the NBF driver; a device driver called Nbt provides NetBIOS support for the TCP/IP protocol stack and a NetBIOS interface to the NWLink IPX/SPX protocol stack.

Note that neither the NWLink nor the TCP/IP NetBIOS interface uses packet encapsulation or tunneling to put a NetBEUI packet inside an IP or IPX packet. Instead, they use the accepted methods defined by Novell in its NETBIOS.COM program for NWLink or RFC (request for comment) 1001/1002, which define how to use TCP/IP to carry NetBIOS traffic. This allows a workstation running Windows NT and, for example, NWLink NetBIOS to communicate with a workstation running DOS and Novell's IPX and NetBIOS.COM.

The sockets interface for TCP/IP was created at the University of California at Berkeley in the early 1980s. Since then, it has become a popular interface for developing distributed applications in the TCP/IP and UNIX environments. Microsoft, in cooperation with several other software vendors, developed the Windows Socket API set to migrate the sockets interface into the Windows and Windows NT environments and standardize the API set for all platforms. WinSockets is now used by almost all of the TCP/IP products for Windows 3.*x*, including Novell's LAN Workplace for DOS and NetManage's Chameleon. The Windows Socket interface for Windows NT runs as a layer above TCP/IP and uses TCP/IP as its transport. WinSockets is not available if you haven't installed TCP/IP support.

Remote Procedure Calls (RPCs) are one of Windows NT's most sophisticated interprocess communications facilities. First designed by Sun, RPCs are a transport protocol-independent medium. The basic concept is that a programmer can define a function that, rather than actually executing on the user's workstation, calls another program on a remote machine.

The RPC definition has been taken over by Open Software Foundation (OSF) as part of their Distributed Computing Environment (DCE) specification, which is supported by most of the major computer vendors. The Microsoft RPC implementation is compatible with the OSF/DCE standard RPC. Windows NT RPCs are completely interoperable with other DCE-based RPC systems, so a program running on a Windows NT workstation can call an RPC on an IBM RS/6000 or another DCE-compatible machine.

The RPC mechanism is unique in that it uses the other IPC mechanisms to establish communications between the client and the server. RPC can use named pipes, NetBIOS, or TCP/IP Sockets to communicate with remote systems. If the calling function (the client) and the actual program (the server) are on the same machine (as they may be for very small or test systems), the RPC mechanism can use the LPC (local procedure call) system to transfer information between processes and subsystems. This makes RPC the most flexible and portable of the IPC choices available.

A typical program has main (or backbone) logic, which defines what the program does, and a series of functions that actually do the grunt work of calculating pi or locating George Tirebighter's record in the "Shoes for Industry" database. In traditional programs, the functions and core logic are all statically linked into an executable program by the developer and then distributed.

In a multitasking environment such as Windows, these monolithic programs have a few disadvantages. First, because the functions and core logic are inexorably linked, a computer running five or six different programs has five or six different copies of the common functions such as "Display a File Open dialog box" in memory at the same time, which takes up valuable space. If you use DLLs (dynamic link libraries) instead, you can save memory and update the functions without updating the main logic of the program. With DLLs, the functions and main logic are stored in different modules.

RPC takes the concept one step further and places the main logic and the functions on different machines. A client application using RPCs is developed using a specially compiled "stub" library. The functions (or stubs) in this library actually transfer the data and the function to a module called the RPC Runtime. The RPC Runtime finds a server that can process the function and sends the function and data to the server, where they're picked up by the RPC Runtime module on the server. The server loads the DLL for the function, runs it, and sends it back to the client via the RPC Runtime module. When the function returns to the client application, it either has the appropriate returned data or indicates that the function failed in some way.

This is where distributed applications can make a big difference. If you build these apps with services in mind, you can do some really neat things with NT machines.

Summary

Like the OSI model, Windows NT uses a layered structure to give each workstation networking functions—from simple file and print sharing to sophisticated IPCs such as remote procedure calls. The layered structure—together with boundary layers and structures such as NDIS, TDI, and Streams—allows a single Windows NT workstation to run multiple transport protocols and requesters simultaneously in order to access servers and resources on the network.

The following chapters look at many of these networking features in more detail to help you design a Windows NT-based network and connect Windows NT to your existing computing infrastructure.

Designing and Installing Your Windows NT Network

14

IN THIS CHAPTER

This chapter discusses designing a local area network (LAN) with Windows NT, installing Windows NT's networking features, and configuring Windows NT to use your LAN card. If you're planning to use Windows NT as the basis of a new local area network, one of your first decisions will be what local area network technology to use.

If you've already started installing network hardware or if someone else in your company gets to worry about these things, you can skip ahead to the section on setting up your LAN card or configuring NT for your network card. If you're really lucky and someone else is responsible for installing and maintaining your network and you just want to know how to use it, you can skip to Chapter 15.

If you're planning a network with more than 30 or 40 workstations, you probably should divide your network into multiple segments connected by bridges or routers. This kind of design is beyond the scope of this book. Although there are several very good books on this kind of enterprise-wide networking, I, as a network consultant, firmly believe that a large network should be designed by a network professional who's made his or her mistakes on a previous client.

Network Cabling and Technologies

Over the past few years, two technologies—Ethernet and Token Ring—have emerged as the best choices for most users. Older technologies such as ARCnet and StarLAN have fallen by the wayside due to their limited data-carrying capacity.

NOTE

Some people use the term *topology* to describe LAN technologies such as Ethernet and Token Ring. Strictly speaking, a LAN's topology defines only how the stations are connected. Most networks use a bus or star topology.

Talking to LAN installers and managers might lead you to believe that Ethernet and Token Ring are completely different beasts and that choosing one or the other will be a fatal error. In reality, Ethernet and Token Ring have a lot in common. Both are widely supported by hardware and software vendors and have been immortalized as international standards by the 802 committee of the Institute of Electrical and Electronic Engineers. Either can be used to build a stable network for your NT users.

New multimedia applications such as desktop video conferencing and the overall growth of network use have started to push Ethernet's 10Mbps capacity and Token Ring's 16Mbps capacity past their limits, making the network cable the data bottleneck. Several new network technologies, including FDDI and the two so-called *Fast Ethernet* schemes, boost performance to 100Mbps. Alternatively, switching technology gives each user his or her own Ethernet to eliminate the bottleneck.

FDDI products are available (if quite expensive) now. Fast Ethernet products are available and reasonably priced now, and some of them can utilize your existing cabling.

Asynchronous transfer mode (ATM) is the LAN of tomorrow (if your idea of tomorrow is 1997 or 1998). It combines high speed (typically 155Mbps), cell switching to give each user his or her own data path, and wide area network capabilities to make a very attractive package.

NOTE

Wireless network adapters (utilizing either radio or infrared communications links) have been entering the market. They can be useful for small departments or low-traffic networks.

When you're choosing a LAN technology, as in any other endeavor you need to balance cost, reliability, and performance. Local area networks differ as to the type of cable they use, how fast they run, how easy it is to troubleshoot the system, and how easily they connect to larger computers.

People often make a big deal out of what I consider one of the least significant differences between networks: the *access method.* Most local area networks allow only one station on the network to send data at a time. The access method is the set of rules for how a station gets to be the one allowed to transmit.

CSMA/CD networks such as Ethernet control access to the network by making a station wait until the cable is quiet before sending. When the network gets busy, two stations may transmit their data at the same time. If this happens, the two stations figure it out and both stop transmitting. They each wait a random period of time and start listening for quiet again.

Token-passing networks use a special message called the *token* that is sent from station to station. When a station receives the token, it can either send a message to another station or pass the token, and therefore permission to send, to the next station.

Cable Type

Over the past 10 years, vendors have developed local area networks that can run on just about any type of cable. I wouldn't be surprised to find that some small Texas company has a LAN that runs on barbed wire for the computing cowboy market.

Luckily, the popular local area networks all use one of four types of cable:

- Unshielded twisted pair
- Shielded twisted pair
- Coaxial cable
- Optical fiber

Unshielded Twisted Pair

The unshielded twisted pair cable used by local area networks is very similar to the cable used by telephone companies, only better. An unshielded twisted pair cable is made up of pairs of wires that are twisted around each other. (See Figure 14.1.) This twisting causes the magnetic fields in the two wires to interact to improve the wire's capability to carry a signal. All other things being equal, cables with more twists, say 10 twists per foot, carry data better than cables with fewer twists.

FIGURE 14.1.
Unshielded twisted pair cable.

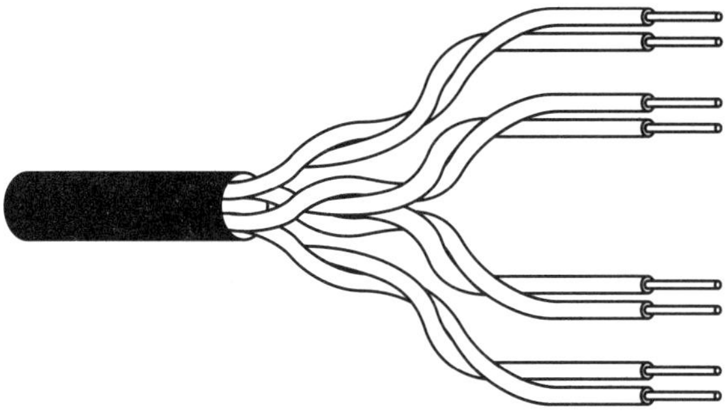

Unshielded twisted pair cable varies greatly in how it's made, and therefore how well it can carry high-speed data such as a local area network. Many early 10Base-T Ethernet and Token Ring network installations turned into disasters as users discovered that their telephone installers just didn't know what was needed to make a LAN work. Telephones can run on just about anything, but a high-speed LAN needs cable that won't scramble its data bits too much. Using just one 6-foot length of the flat wire you use between your home phone and the wall (which telephone installers call "silver satin") in a LAN cable system often prevents LAN data from passing through the entire cable segment.

Because computer networks are much less forgiving of poor-quality cable and poor installation practices than are voice applications, the EIA/TIA (Electronics Industries Association/Telecommunications Industry Association) recently came up with a grading system that ranks unshielded twisted pair cable in levels from 1 to 5. Higher-grade cables can carry progressively faster data traffic.

Levels 1 and 2 are of rather low quality and should be used only for telephone applications. Most commercial telephone systems installed before 1990 use these lower-quality cables that can't be used for LAN data.

Level 3 cable is good enough to use for 4Mbps Token Ring or 10Base-T Ethernet, but that's all. If you want to run 16Mbps Token Ring, you'll need to use at least level 4.

Level 5 is the good stuff. It can be used for 10Base-T, Token Ring, and all the new 100Mbps LANs. Well-installed level 5 cable can handle data at rates of up to 100Mbps and is the cable that new network technologies such as Fast Ethernet are designed for.

Because a cable plant should be designed to last 10 years or more, and because up to 80 percent of the cost of a cable plant is labor, I believe that any new UTP cable you install should be level 5. The small additional cost will save you big bucks when you can upgrade your network without pulling new cable.

NOTE

I occasionally hear that a LAN vendor has told a customer that level 5 cable can't be used for 10Base-T Ethernet, which requires level 3. This is not so. Each of the levels specifies only the minimum quality needed to make that level. All level 5 cable exceeds the level 3 specifications. The following lists the UTP levels:

Level	*Maximum Data Rate*
1	0Mbps
2	1Mbps
3	10Mbps
4	10Mbps
5	100Mbps

Shielded Twisted Pair

In order to reduce the cable's sensitivity to electrical noise, the shielded twisted pair adds a foil or copper braid shield around the wires just under the outer jacket. (See Figure 14.2.) The shield stops any noise that would cause a problem in unshielded pairs. Some cable also adds a shield around each pair in the cable to prevent signals on one pair from creating induced voltages in another pair.

The only shielded twisted pair cable in wide use today is the IBM Type 1 cable used with Token Ring. Some manufacturers of 10Base-T Ethernet cards also supply adapters that allow them to run on shielded cable.

FIGURE 14.2.
Shielded twisted pair cable.

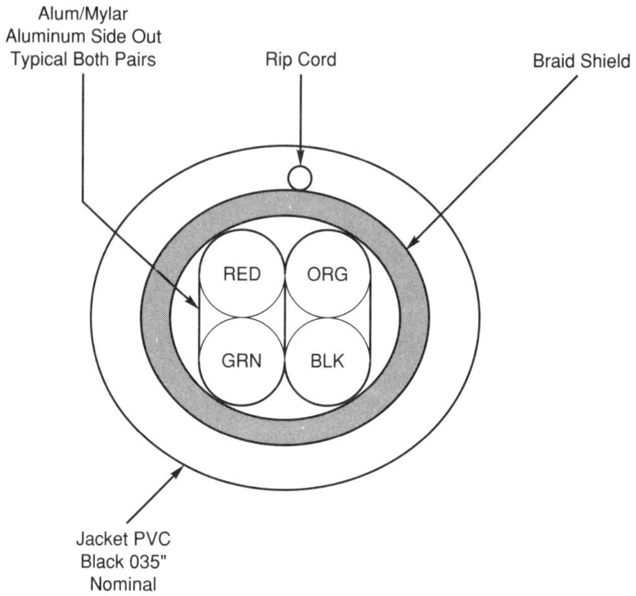

Shielded twisted pair cable is more expensive to buy and install than unshielded twisted pair. It's a good choice for Token Ring installations, especially those in electrically noisy environments such as factory floors. Shielded twisted pair usage has been declining since IBM endorsed the use of UTP for Token Ring.

Coaxial

Before 1990, almost all local area networks used coaxial cable that was similar to, but not the same as, the cable that brings Beavis and Butt-head into your home. Coaxial cable is made of a single conductor that is centered within a foil or copper braid shield.

Coaxial cable is simple to install and relatively inexpensive. Unfortunately, each local area network technology that uses coaxial cable uses a slightly different type. Coaxial cable is a LAN dead end because none of the new standard local area network technologies are designed to use coax. Figure 14.3 shows Thick Ethernet cable, the most sophisticated and most expensive coaxial cable in common use for LANS.

FIGURE 14.3.
Thick Ethernet coaxial cable.

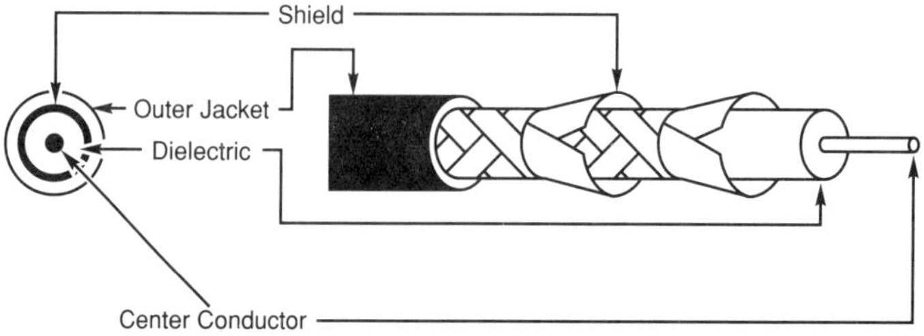

I currently recommend coax only for small networks, where it can be cost-effective. Large networks (and the future) belong to fiber optic and twisted pair networks.

Optical Fiber

Rather than sending your data down a wire as a series of electrical pulses, fiber optic networks use pulses of light running down a glass or plastic fiber. (See Figure 14.4.) Because fiber optic cables don't use electricity to send data, they are totally immune to electrical and magnetic noise. This makes them perfect for factory floor applications.

FIGURE 14.4.
Light follows a fiber optic cable.

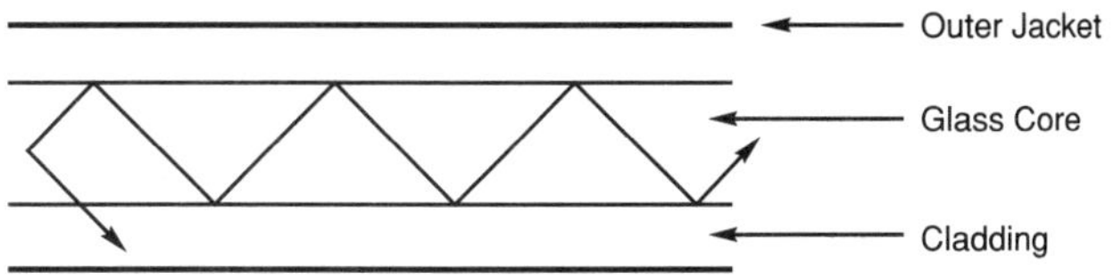

The real advantage of fiber optic networks is bandwidth. Using current technology, twisted pair and coaxial cables max out at about 100Mbps. Fiber optic long distance lines carry several Gbps. For this reason, fiber optic cable should be run where high traffic levels are expected in the future or where installation costs far outweigh materials costs like vertical risers.

Fiber optic LANs typically need a pair of fibers for each link, one for data to travel in each direction. (See Figure 14.5.)

FIGURE 14.5.
Typical fiber optic cable.

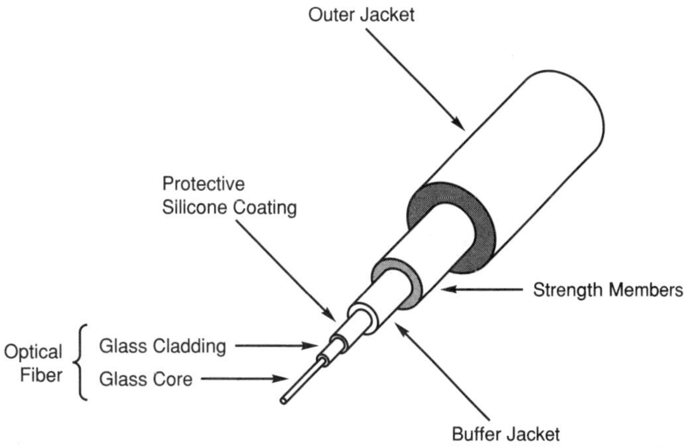

Fiber optic networks have developed a reputation as being hard to install, fragile, and very expensive. Over the past few years, fiber optic components have become less expensive. Several vendors, including 3M and AMP, have developed connector systems that are much easier and faster to apply.

Fiber optic networks also have a security advantage over copper networks. Some of the electrical signal we pump into a cable gets radiated out into the environment. It's possible that KAOS, or Dewey Cheetem and Howe (opposing council), could set up a van outside your building and decipher the data they pick up with the big dish antenna on top of their van. Because fiber optic cables don't radiate, that fancy spy van won't do Sigfried and the boys any good at all, even if they drive it to your building (see Figure 14.6).

FIGURE 14.6.
Security issues.

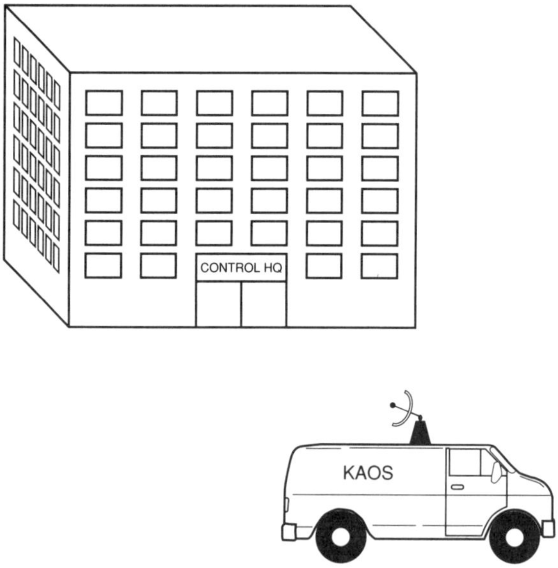

You should always use a fiber optic link when running your LAN from building to building. A school in Texas learned this lesson when they ran coaxial cable between two adjacent buildings. One day a thunderstorm came wandering over the school, looked down, and called out to its thunderstorm buddies, "Look boys, lunch!" After the lightning strike, more than 30 feet of cable apparently was completely vaporized. Also severely damaged were two active hubs, five PCs, a printer, and an electric typewriter that happened to be in the right place at the right time. Because fiber optic cables don't conduct electricity, the thunderstorm wouldn't have found them an attractive target.

A less dramatic, but more common, problem with copper cables between buildings is ground differentials. If copper cables are used to connect two buildings, a current (called a ground loop) may flow through the cable, interfering with the data.

Table 14.1 summarizes the differences between the types of cables used in most LANs.

Table 14.1. Cable types.

Type	*Advantages*	*Disadvantages*
UTP	Low cost Very flexible High performance Good management tool	Sensitive to RFI/EMI Cable lengths limited
STP	Flexible Less sensitive to electrical noise	Cable lengths limited Moderately high cost
Coaxial	Less sensitive to electrical noise Moderate cost	Different cable needed for each network Easily damaged
Optical Fiber	Completely immune to RFI/EMI Very high performance bandwidth Long distances supported No ground loops	Expensive to install Limited card choices Patch panels very expensive

Ethernet

Ethernet was developed in the mid-'70s by a team headed by Robert Metcalf at Xerox's legendary Palo Alto Research Center (Xerox PARC). Ethernet was just one of the computing breakthroughs developed at PARC, but it was never well exploited by Xerox. (We also can thank PARC for the laser printer and the concepts behind the Windows user interface, including icons and pull-down menus.)

That which we call Ethernet is usually a network that is compliant with the IEEE 802.3 standard. 802.3 was based on the Ethernet product Digital, which Intel and Xerox brought to market in the early '80s, but it's slightly different. Almost all current products sold as Ethernet are 802.3-compliant.

Over the years, vendors have developed, and the IEEE has standardized, a variety of cabling schemes for Ethernet. You can now run Ethernet on coaxial, twisted pair, or fiber optic cable. With Motorola's Altair, you can get rid of the cable altogether. Regardless of the cable used, Ethernet is always a 10Mbps network using CSMA/CD as its access method.

Ethernet's strengths are its low cost, good performance, and the fact that most DEC VAX and UNIX systems from Sun Workstations to huge servers have Ethernet ports available. Ethernet cards and other hardware are available from many vendors at commodity prices.

Thick Ethernet (10Base5)

The first Ethernet networks linked expensive minicomputers, workstations, and laser printers. Performance, reliability, and flexibility were stressed in the cable system design without great regard for cost.

This original cabling system has become known as Thick or "Yellow" Ethernet, after the special 50 ohm impedance coaxial cable it uses. The IEEE has given Thick Ethernet the designation of 10Base5.

Thick Ethernet cable, which is usually, but not always, yellow, is very thick compared to other LAN cables and quite expensive to install due to its .4-inch diameter size and 10-inch minimum bend radius. To protect the signal from electrical noise, the cable is extensively shielded with two copper braid shields and two foil, or metallized, mylar shields.

Computers are connected to the trunk through transceivers—little metal boxes with electronics—that are connected directly to the cable. Workstations are connected to transceivers through a DB-15 AUI (attachment unit interface) or a DIX (Digital, Intel, Xerox) connector and a length of AUI or transceiver cable. A transceiver cable can be up to 50 meters (164 feet) long.

A single Thick Ethernet trunk (see Figure 14.7) can be up to 500 meters (1,640 feet) long and have up to 100 transceivers. Each trunk must be terminated at each end with a 1W 50 ohm ±1 ohm resistor. Multiple Thick Ethernet segments can be connected, through repeaters, to create a single collision domain—that is, a single logical network up to 2,500 meters (8,200 feet or @1.5 miles) long with no more than four repeaters in the longest path between the two most distant nodes.

Thick Ethernet is expensive due to the cost of the special cable and transceivers. It's typically found in university environments.

Thin Ethernet (10Base2)

By 1982, Bob Metcalf had left Xerox and started his own company, 3Com. At 3Com, he and his team realized that $600 was a lot to ask someone to pay for the cable to connect two PCs in an office. They set out to make a variant of Ethernet that would be more cost-effective for smaller networks.

When they first unveiled their creation, they called it Cheapernet because it was cheaper than the traditional Ethernet. After they hired a few marketing people, they stopped calling it Cheapernet and started calling it Thin Ethernet because it uses a thinner cable than the traditional or Thick Ethernet.

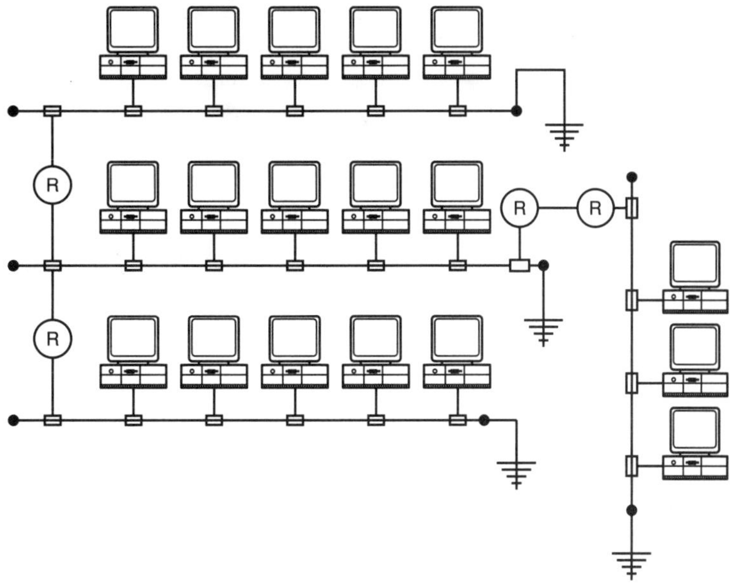

FIGURE 14.7.
Thick Ethernet.

In order to make Thin Ethernet less expensive, the engineers made two significant changes. Instead of using special cable that costs a dollar a foot, they used RG-58A/U, a stock item that costs about 12 to 30 cents a foot. They also decided to build the transceiver right into the network adapter, saving the AUI cable and the separate packaging of the transceiver.

Because the transceiver is part of the network interface card, you attach a PC to a Thin Ethernet segment by attaching a T-connector to the BNC (bayonet nut connector) on the back of the workstation's network interface on its base and attach the trunk cable to its arms.

Using drop cables between the BNC on the LAN card and the T-connector or main bus cable is a big mistake. Unpredictable problems will crop up. I've seen a case where adding a drop cable to one PC didn't affect that PC's access to the cable but did disable several other PCs on the network.

Thin Ethernet cable can be RG-58A/U, RG-58C/U, or cable specifically designed for use with Thin Ethernet. The specified cable has a nominal impedance of 50 ohms. A Thin Ethernet cable segment can be up to 185 meters (600 feet) long and can have up to 30 devices attached. Each segment trunk must be terminated at each end with a $^1/_2$W 50 ohm ±1 ohm resistor. A segment should be grounded at one, and only one, point to avoid ground loops. A typical Thin Ethernet is shown in Figure 14.8.

FIGURE 14.8.
A Thin Ethernet segment.

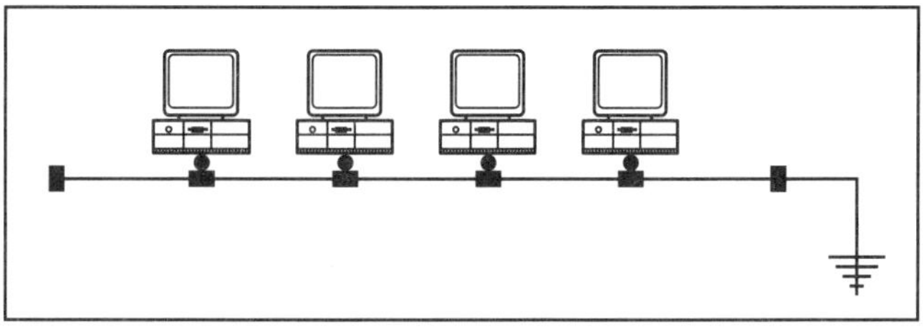

Thin Ethernet is one of the most popular LAN technologies in use today because of its simplicity, low cost, and relatively high performance. Unfortunately, Thin Ethernet has a few problems to go with these advantages. Thin Ethernet's biggest problem is that the main bus cable goes to each user's desk. If something goes wrong with the cable anywhere on the bus, the whole network goes down.

I currently recommend Thin Ethernet for small networks. Larger networks are better served by 10Base-T.

Twisted Pair Ethernet (10Base-T)

For many years, running Ethernet over twisted pair cable seemed like an unattainable technical achievement. In 1986, Synoptics, a Xerox PARC spin-off company, shipped its first Lattisnet products, which allowed Ethernet to run on the shielded twisted pair cable used in the IBM Cable System. By 1988, several companies, including Synoptics, were selling products that allowed users to run Ethernet on telephone-style unshielded twisted pair cable. These Ethernet products used a star wiring scheme with multiport repeaters (called hubs or concentrators by manufacturers) in the wiring closet on each floor.

The IEEE 802.3 committee decided that if there was this much demand for an Ethernet over a twisted pair system, they should add a chapter to the specification called 10Base-T. A 10Base-T workstation is connected to its hub by up to 100 meters (330 feet) of UTP cable that meets level 3 specifications.

The network uses two pairs of wires—one to send data from the workstation to the hub and the other for data going from the hub to the workstation. It's wired using the RJ-45 style 8 pin connector, so most people install a four-pair cable, which provides some room for broken wires and future growth. A typical 10Base-T network is shown in Figure 14.9.

10Base-T hubs with 8 to 128 ports are available. Several manufacturers, including Intel, have developed 12-port 10Base-T hubs on PC bus cards for use in a file server or router. Small unmanaged hubs are available for $50 to $100 per port. Typically, they include an AUI connector so that you can use fiber optic or Thick Ethernet backbones to connect your hubs. Hubs with expandable card cages and management features typically cost more.

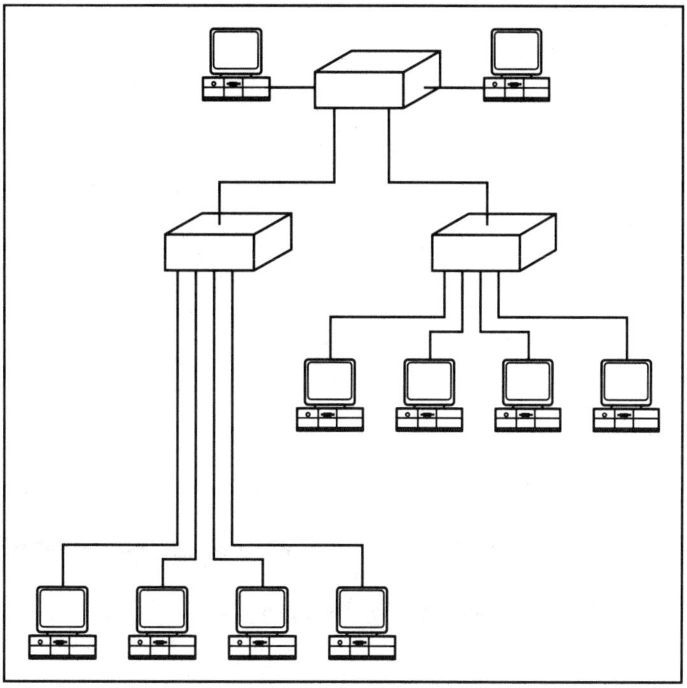

FIGURE 14.9.
A 10Base-T network.

All in all, 10Base-T has proven itself to be a reliable and cost-effective LAN technology. It's my recommendation for any Ethernet over about 10 workstations. Larger networks of over 50 stations should use hubs with management features that allow you to get status information and control the hub from your desk.

Token Ring

Token Ring was first developed by IBM and released in 1985 as a 4Mbps local area network running on shielded twisted pair cable. In 1988, IBM increased Token Ring's speed to 16Mbps and the IEEE issued a formal specification for Token Ring—number 802.5.

Each workstation is connected to a hub or MAU (multistation access unit), which connects that station to the next station on the ring. Token Ring usually is wired with twisted pair, but both fiber optic and coax Token Ring products exist.

Each hub or MAU (sometimes written MSAU) has a number of ports for lobe cables running to stations and a pair of connectors marked RI (for ring in) and RO (for ring out). MAUs are connected by running a cable called a main ring cable or a patch cable from RI on one MAU to RO on another MAU. Using shielded twisted pair, a single Token Ring can have up to 260 nodes. (See Figure 14.10.)

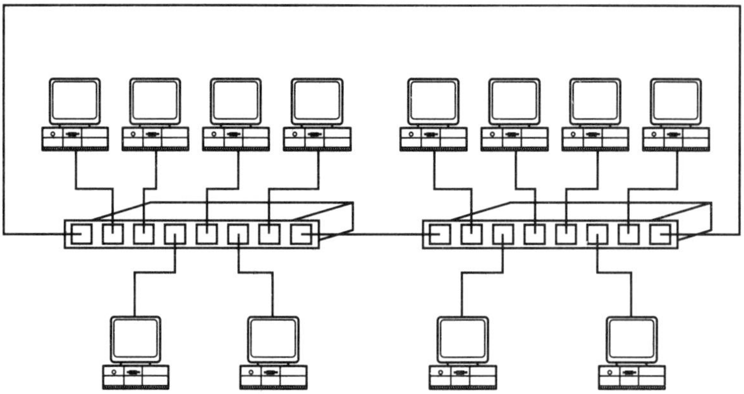

FIGURE 14.10.
A Token Ring network.

The rules for wiring Token Ring are rather complicated. If you have a small network, your cables can be up to 100 meters (330 feet) long between workstations and their MAUs.

The Token Ring architecture connects each station to the stations that are adjacent to it on the ring. A Token Ring card listens to the station on the network just before it and retransmits that data to the next station. (See Figure 14.11.) An IBM 8228 MAU, IBM's basic Token Ring hub, has a mechanical relay behind each port. When the MAU sees a DC phantom voltage of 3.5-7Vdc from the workstation, it opens the relay to connect the workstation to its neighbors. If the phantom voltage disappears, the MAU closes the relay connecting this station's neighbors.

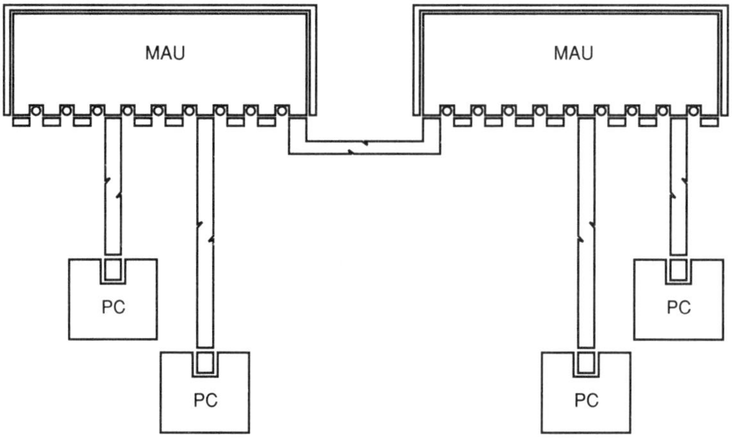

FIGURE 14.11.
The Token Ring data flow.

Token Ring's greatest strength is that it can be easily connected to IBM host computers such as 3090s and ES/9000s. The down side is that Token Ring is relatively expensive, at least twice the cost of an equivalent 10Base-T setup. It also has a well-deserved reputation as being difficult to troubleshoot.

The Short Story

If you need to make a quick decision about your network, try to remember the following rules:

- If you have to connect to an IBM mainframe, choose Token Ring.
- If you need to connect to Sun or other UNIX systems, use Ethernet.
- Thin Ethernet is good for networks of up to 10 stations.
- 10Base-T with four-pair level 5 cable is best for larger networks.
- Ethernet costs at least 50 percent less than Token Ring.
- Unless you have a lot of support staff and some Ethernet and Token Ring specialists, try to use just one technology.

Going Faster

If you have a very large network and an unlimited hardware budget, or if you're working on applications such as desktop video that need more than a shared 16Mbps data pipe, you have two ways to give your users the bandwidth they need.

The obvious approach is to simply use a faster network. If 10Mbps isn't enough, get 100Mbps. The Fiber Digital Device Interface (FDDI) was designed to solve your problems. Unfortunately, upgrading to FDDI means replacing all your LAN cards, cables, and hubs at a cost of at least $2,000 per station. Fast Ethernet promises 100Mbps at a lower cost, but it isn't available yet.

The alternative is to use 10Base-T Ethernet cards and replace some or all of your hubs with Ethernet switches such as the Kalpana Etherswitch or SMC ES/1. These switches, which are essentially high-speed bridges, effectively give each user his or her own 10Mbps data path by switching packets between multiple ports simultaneously. Using a 12-port data switch will allow you to provide 120Mbps total bandwidth to your users by giving each user or workgroup their own Ethernet segment.

FDDI

The Fiber Digital Device Interface at 100Mbps is the fastest standard local area network on the market and today's safe choice for the real power user. The ANSI (American National Standards Institute) standard for FDDI specifies a dual counter-rotating ring wired in a star using hubs such as 10Base-T or Token Ring.

Several vendors, led by Crescendo Communications with its CDDI product, have developed products that allow you to run FDDI on shielded or level 5 unshielded twisted pair cable. By the time you read this, an ANSI committee should have issued a standard for running FDDI over copper cable.

Due to its high cost (over $1,500 per station) and limited software support, FDDI is best suited to backbone networks that connect smaller workgroup networks.

Fast Ethernet

In early 1993, several vendors announced products that they claimed were the next logical step from Ethernet. In short order, these vendors divided into two camps. The 100Base-T group, led by Grand Junction Networks and 3Com, proposed a system that used two pairs of level 5 UTP cable to build a 100Mbps Ethernet. The 100Base-VG group, led by Hewlett Packard and AT&T, replaced the CSMA/CD access method with a demand protocol. It used a signaling system that could support send 100Mbps data across the level 3 cable most users had installed for 10Base-T by using all four pairs of wire in the RJ-45 jack.

When all these parties went to the IEEE 802.3 committee to get them to decide which product would become a standard, the IEEE, in an act of unique mediocrity, decided not to endorse one plan and reject the other but to standardize both approaches. 100Base-T is being specified by the 802.3 committee, and 100Base-VG, which now has Token Ring support added because IBM joined the group, will be defined by a new 802.12 committee.

We should now be seeing the first Fast Ethernet products with prices about half that of comparable FDDI products. Most vendors expect dual-speed 10/100Mbps to sell for about $400. They also will introduce mixed media hubs that have 10Base-T ports for workstations and fast Ethernet ports for file servers and backbones.

Choosing Your Cards

As soon as you've chosen Ethernet, Token Ring, or FDDI, you still need to choose LAN cards for all your workstations. Don't agonize too much over this decision. Unlike three or four years ago, when a slow Ethernet card could be two to three times slower than a fast one, the differences between competitive cards from different vendors are now pretty small.

The most important thing is to make sure that the card you pick has an NDIS 3.0 driver available for it. Microsoft ships Windows NT with drivers for some of the more popular Ethernet and Token Ring cards in the following list:

Ethernet

3Com Etherlink II, Etherlink III, Etherlink 16

AMD Am1500, Am2100, PCnet

Digital DECPA, LC, Turbo, Turbo/LC, Turbo Channel

Intel Ether Express 16

Novell/Eagle/Anthem/Microdyne NE1000, NE2000, NE1500, NE2100

Standard Microsystems (Western Digital) Elite 16

Token Ring

IBM Token Ring Adapter 16/4 and 16/4 A

Proteon Pronet 16/4 p1390

You can get drivers for other LAN cards from the manufacturer or from Microsoft's Windows NT Driver Library (WNTDL). You can download a list of all the hardware devices that have been tested by Microsoft in library 1 of the WINNT forum on CompuServe. This list is updated by Microsoft periodically as new drivers are added to the library. You can download the files from CompuServe, Microsoft Download Services, or GEnie. If you don't have a modem, you can obtain an individual driver from the WNTDL on a disk by calling Microsoft Product Support Services at (206) 637-7098.

NOTE

Windows NT 3.5 includes a list of additional drivers on the CD-ROM in the \DRVLIB directory. These include network drivers in the \NETCARD subdirectory.

You also need to make sure that you match your LAN card to your system's bus. Identifying your system's bus is pretty easy. Most PS/2 systems, including any machine that has a reference diskette, use IBM's 16- or 32-bit MicroChannel Architecture (MCA), which was designed as a faster successor to the 16-bit ISA (industry standard architecture), or AT bus slots used in most PCs. If you have a MicroChannel machine, you have to use MicroChannel cards. IBM's probably are the best choice.

EISA (extended industry standard architecture) systems, usually used for file servers and other I/O intensive tasks, have slots that can take a standard 16-bit ISA card or a 32-bit EISA card. If you have an EISA system, you should take advantage of it and use EISA Ethernet or Token Ring cards.

Newer systems might have ISA or even EISA bus slots and additional local bus slots that meet either the VESA VL-Bus or Intel PCI specification. VL-Bus cards interact very closely with the processor and require many processor resources to manage. If your system has VL-Bus slots, you still might get better overall system performance by using an ISA or EISA LAN card.

Pentium systems with PCI bus are just coming on the market as I write this. The 64-bit PCI bus shows great promise for disk controllers and LAN cards in addition to the video cards most often used with VL-Bus. PCI doesn't share VL-Bus's limitations when multiple cards are used. Therefore, if you have a PCI system and you find a PCI LAN card from a major vendor with NT drivers, buy it.

The vast majority of PCs connected to Ethernets use cards from 3Com, SMC, or Intel, or cards compatible with Novell's original NE-2000, such as those from National Semiconductor or Eagle. These cards have the widest variety of drivers available. You can't go wrong if you stick with one of these brands. It's not worth the $10 to $30 you might save to use a Taiwanese clone card.

When it comes to Token Ring, the vast majority of systems use IBM cards. Sticking with IBM Token Ring cards is safe, especially if you might need to use some IBM products such as AS/400 PC Support or PC3270 to access your host computer. SMC, Madge, Intel, and Olicom also make good Token Ring cards.

The other factor you might want to consider is the card's flexibility. The latest cards from SMC, Intel, and 3Com have both BNC and RJ-45 connectors. They can be used for both 10Base-T and Thin Ethernet and are software-configurable, so you don't need to fiddle with jumpers and switches to set the card up. Cards also differ in how many of your system's I/O ports and how much memory they take up, which can be important if you're also going to be running DOS on your system.

TIP

If at all possible, get a software-configured network card. It's much easier to set up and test because you don't have to remove the card to change the jumper or dip-switch settings.

Choosing a Network Card Configuration

NOTE

This chapter contains a very general discussion of setting up and configuring a network card. It covers procedures and general concerns, but it's not meant to be a substitute for your network card manual.

WARNING

Installing a network card is simple enough that just about any user can do it. However, electrostatic discharge, or static electricity, can destroy your motherboard, cards, and other components. Therefore, you should take some simple precautions if you're installing a network card. Touch a grounded metal surface—such as your computer's power supply—before you handle the card.

Most LAN cards use one interrupt line, between one and 16 I/O ports, and up to 64K of upper memory. Some older cards might also use a DMA channel. Before you install a LAN card on your system, you need to make sure that this new card won't have a resource conflict with a device that's already in your system. You need to check the resources that are already in use and then set your adapter to a set of unused resources.

If you have a PS/2, here's where you get off easy. You can just stick the reference disk in your machine and view what kind of card is in each slot and the resources it's using. When you configure your LAN card, the reference disk even tells you when you have a conflict with another card. If you have an EISA machine, the configuration utility can give you the same information for slots that have 32-bit EISA cards installed. Unfortunately, it can't tell you anything about any ISA bus cards your system might have.

The vast majority of people have ISA bus systems and will have to find some other way to figure out what resources are available. If you're setting up a new system or working on a system that has just the standard I/O devices such as COM: ports, you can use Tables 14.2, 13.3, and 13.4 to try to figure out what resources are available. If you can't remember whether you have fancy cards such as a SCSI host adapter or sound board, you can try using a diagnostic program such as CheckIt, Manifest, or the MSD that comes with Windows 3.1. These programs do a good job of identifying the I/O ports and memory addresses that cards in your system use. However, sometimes these programs tell you that an interrupt is free when it's actually used by a card in your system. This usually happens if you haven't loaded the device driver for the card before running the diagnostic.

Table 14.2. PC IRQ usage.

IRQ	Usual Use	Availability
0	System clock	Never available
1	Keyboard	Never available
3	COM2: and COM4:	Usually available; disable motherboard port if present
4	COM1: and COM3:	Sometimes available; disable motherboard if present
5	LPT2:	Usually available; disable motherboard port if present
6	Floppy disk controller	
7	LPT1:	Usually available via sharing
8	Real-time clock/calendar	Not available
9	Really IRQ 2 cascaded	Not available
10	No standard use	Usually available
11	Often used by SCSI adapters	Usually available
12	PS/2 mouse	Available if system doesn't have PS/2 mouse port
13	Math coprocessor	
14	Disk controller	
15	No standard use	Usually available

Table 14.3. PC I/O port usage.

I/O Ports	Common Usage
200-20F	Game port
230-23F	Microsoft bus or inport mouse
270-27F	LPT2:
2E8-2EF	COM4:
2F8-2FF	COM2:
280-29F	SMC/Western Digital Ethernet card default
300-31F	Novell and 3Com Ethernet card default
320-32F	XT hard-disk controller (including PS/2 model 30)

I/O Ports	*Common Usage*
330-33F	Commonly used by SCSI adapter and various sound cards
378-37F	LPT1:
380-38C	SDLC adapter
3B0-3BB	Monochrome adapter and LPT0:
3C0-3CF	EGA
3D0-3DF	CGA and EGA/VGA when in CGA mode
3E8-3EF	COM3:
3F0-3F7	Floppy-disk controller
3F8-3FF	COM1:
A20-A27	IBM Token Ring card default

Table 14.4. PC high memory usage.

Memory	*What It's Used By*
A000-C400	VGA
CC00-CDFF	Token Ring default
D000-DFFF	Default EMS page frame
D800-DBFF	Token Ring default
E000-FFFF	PS/2 extended BIOS or Plug-N-Play BIOS
F000-FFFF	AT and PS/2 ROM BIOS

TIP

If you're going to be running Windows 3.x or other DOS environments in addition to Windows NT on this system, it's a good idea to configure all your cards that use upper memory to keep all the used upper memory regions together. This makes it easier for memory managers such as EMM386 to load device drivers into upper memory.

If you can't use the default settings, the safest settings for an Ethernet card are IRQ 5, base I/O port 300, and base memory address CC00.

TIP

It's usually easiest to use the default settings recommended for your LAN card whenever possible. Change the settings only if they conflict with another device in your computer.

If you can't find the manual for your LAN card, you can find the default settings for some common network adapter cards in the Windows NT Installation Guide manual. See its section titled "Network Adapter Card Settings" on pages 50-56.

Connector Settings

When you're setting up your card, don't forget to set the card's option for which connector to use. Most Ethernet cards have at least two connectors for Thick Ethernet, Thin Ethernet, and/or 10Base-T. In addition to setting your card's IRQ, I/O ports, and memory address, you also have to tell it which of these connector options you're going to use. Some Token Ring cards have both STP and UTP connectors and need to be told which to use.

Speed Settings

Most Token Ring cards support both 4Mbps and 16Mbps operation. When you set up a Token Ring, all the stations on that ring must have their adapters set to the same speed because each station on a Token Ring repeats data to the next station on the ring. If you add a 4Mbps adapter to a 16Mbps ring, or vice versa, the whole ring will go down.

I expect that most Fast Ethernet cards will also have speed jumpers to adjust them from 10 to 100Mbps.

TIP

It's a good idea to make a list of the cards in your system, along with the resources they use, and tape it to the inside of your computer's case. That way, the next time you need to change anything, you'll have all the information handy.

Changing the Card Settings

If you're lucky, you can run configuration programs or reference disks to set your LAN card to the configuration you've selected. However, if you have older or more basic LAN cards, you must venture into the world of DIP switches and jumpers.

Jumpers are groups of little pins sticking out of the card and plastic covers that fit over a pair of pins, connecting them electrically. To change your card's configuration, you have to pull the cover off the pins it's currently connecting and move it to another position. Jumpers are harder to work with than software-configurable cards or even DIP switches, especially when there isn't enough finger room to get a good grip on the jumpers.

The other problem with jumpers is that they're easy to lose. Those little black pieces of plastic have a truly perverse nature. They jump out of your hand and into hyperspace at the worst possible times. In a true emergency, I've soldered the two pins together when I couldn't find a jumper.

Some cards, such as the Ansel Ethernet card, control all the settings using jumpers. These cards are tedious to set up and reconfigure when the need arises.

Your network card might also use DIP switches, which are simply banks of tiny little switches that fit into the same space as a small chip. As soon as you've found the DIP switches on your card, the first thing you need to do is find the mark on the switch bank that shows which way to flip the switch to close it. Most DIP switches say either *on* or *closed* at one edge. When each little switch is flipped toward the mark, it connects its two traces on the card. To change DIP switch settings, you move the small switch to the alternate position (either on/off or open/closed). Make sure that you move the switch all the way. Luckily, most click to tell you they've moved.

TIP

Don't use a pencil to change your DIP switches. Little pieces of pencil lead will fall into the switch and might cause short circuits. Use a paper clip instead. You can use a pen in a pinch, but it makes a mess.

Software-Configured Cards

If you're lucky (or smart), your cards don't have huge numbers of DIP switches or jumpers but instead are software-configurable. Some cards, such as the Intel Ether Express 16, which Microsoft uses in the Windows for Workgroups starter kit, have no jumpers at all. Others, such as SMC's Elite 16, have one or two jumper-selectable configurations and a jumper setting that lets you set their configuration via software.

Software-configurable cards come with a DOS-based application that enables you to tell the card how to behave. These programs range from well-written applications that scan your PC and recommend a configuration that doesn't conflict with any of the other devices in your system to crude command-driven setup programs.

As an example, you can configure an SMC Elite 16 card by installing it in a free slot in your system, setting its jumper for software configuration, and running SMC's EZSETUP.EXE. EZSETUP shows you the current adapter settings and enables you to change them as shown in Figure 14.12.

FIGURE 14.12.
The interactive screen in EZSETUP.EXE.

```
Board Type:    8013EWC
Node Address: 0000C02A5F70

                     Current Setup

I/O Base Address     320
IRQ                  5
RAM Size             16 K
RAM Base Address     0D0000
Add Wait States      Yes
Network Connection   BNC or 10BaseT

ROM Size             Disabled
ROM Base Address     Disabled

Do you want to change the setup ? (y) -> y

I/O base address ? (320) ->
IRQ ? (5) ->
RAM base address ? (0D0000) ->
Network Connection:
   1= BNC or 10BaseT
   2= AUI or 10BaseT
   3= Twisted Pair - No Link Integrity       ? (1) ->
```

After you change the card settings, typically you need to save your changes and reboot your computer. With some cards, you must turn your computer off for a few moments. After that, you're ready to test the card to see that it works. Remember to record your card's settings in your computer settings table.

TIP

Don't connect your card to a production network until after you've carefully configured it. A misconfigured card can take your network down, especially on a Token Ring.

After the Installation

As soon as you've installed your network card, you should test it to see that it's working properly.

Most LAN cards come with a disk that contains device drivers for popular network operating systems and a diagnostic program to test the card. Most LAN card diagnostics test the card's memory and configuration, verifying that the card is working and that it's configured the way you think it is. The better diagnostics also can send data between two machines that are running the diagnostic, which will also test the transceiver and cable system.

For example, SMC Ethernet cards come with the program DIAGNOSE.EXE. It enables you to test the RAM on the network card and test connections to a remote station.

When you run DIAGNOSE.EXE, you select your adapter card in a first menu, and then you select the tests you want to perform in a second menu. The Basic Adapter Test determines whether the adapter is properly installed and configured. This test will fail if there are hardware or software conflicts with the IRQ, I/O base address, or RAM base address, or if the network isn't properly terminated.

If you have another computer on the network with the adapter card correctly installed and configured, you can run DIAGNOSE.EXE and select the Respond to Test Messages option. On the computer where you are configuring the card, select the Initiate Test Messages option. When you run the test, the responding computer echoes the messages and the initiating computer checks to make sure it received the same message it transmitted.

If your adapter didn't come with diagnostic software, you'll just have to go ahead and install NT on your station, or add the LAN card to your existing NT, and hope it works. If it doesn't, see Chapter 15 for troubleshooting tips.

Installing Windows NT After the Card

If you've set up and installed your LAN card before installing Windows NT on your system, the Windows NT Setup program makes life pretty easy for you. Right after Setup asks you about your local printer, it scans the system for popular LAN cards. If you have a common card such as a Novell NE2000 or an SMC Elite 16, Setup will find it and ask you how it's configured.

If, for instance, you have an NE2000 card installed, Windows NT will find the card, check the card settings, and display them in an Adapter Card Setup dialog box (see Figure 14.13). If you have another LAN card or you want to use another set of settings, you can change the settings by clicking in the field and entering a new value or by selecting a value from the drop-down box.

NOTE

Because different LAN cards have different sets of configuration options, the dialog box for your card might look quite different from the one in Figure 14.13.

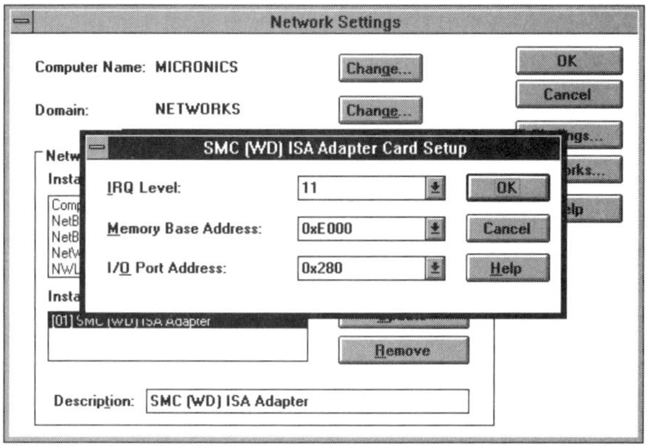

FIGURE 14.13.
The Adapter Card Setup dialog box for the SMC Ethernet network card.

If the information you enter here isn't actually how your LAN card is set up, you won't be able to finish configuring your network, communicate with other workstations, or join a Windows NT Server domain. After you complete the installation, you need to change the settings via Control Panel, as described in the next section.

Installing a Network Card After Installing Windows NT

If you're installing your network adapter card after you've installed Windows NT, you need to use the Network option in Control Panel to tell NT how to talk to your card. You also can use the following steps to add a second LAN card to your Windows NT system so that you can access more than one network.

TIP

Because most LAN card diagnostics run only under DOS, it's a good idea to configure your LAN card and test it under DOS.

1. Open Control Panel and double-click on the Network icon to open the Network Settings dialog box. Click on the Add Adapter button to add the driver for a new LAN card.
2. When the Add Network Adapter dialog box appears, from the Network Adapter Card drop-down box select the card you have installed. If your card is supported by a driver from the Windows NT Driver Library or a driver from the manufacturer, copy the driver to a floppy disk and select "<Other> Requires disk from manufacturer" from the drop-down menu. Windows NT prompts you to insert the disk. It copies the driver and displays the Add Network Adapter dialog box.

TIP

Be sure to check your CD-ROM's \DRVLIB\NETCARD directory for a driver for your network adapter before you spend money on connect time or long-distance fees.

3. Click on the Continue button. NT checks your card's settings and displays the Adapter Card Setup dialog box.
4. Check the settings to make sure that they reflect how your card is actually configured. If they don't match, you should change them so that they do. You can then click on the OK button for both the Adapter Card Setup dialog box and the Network Settings dialog box. Windows NT then installs the drivers and binds the default protocols to each card.

If you have trouble installing the software for your adapter, refer to Chapter 15.

Installing and Removing Network Software

Although Windows NT's Setup program or Control Panel will install a basic set of network protocols and services on your workstation automatically, you might need to add or remove a few pieces of network software when you install your LAN card. The protocols you choose to install largely depend on the size of your network and what you're planning to do with it. On small networks, the default set of software using Microsoft's NetBEUI protocol might be appropriate.

If your computer is part of a larger network, you might need to add TCP/IP or IPX/SPX support or install a requester to allow your workstation to access NetWare or UNIX NFS file servers. You might also want to remove the server service from your user's workstations if you're using a sophisticated server operating system such as NetWare or NT Server so that you'll have better control and security.

To add a network protocol or service, follow these steps:

1. Click on the Network icon in Control Panel.
2. Click on the Add Software button. The Add Network Software dialog box appears.
3. From the list, select the component you want to add and click on Continue. If you're adding a service other than those that come with Windows NT or NT Server, click on the <<<Other>>> button.
4. You see a dialog box that asks you for the path to the files needed to install the protocol or service. Enter the path and click on Continue. When Setup has finished copying the files, you return to the Network dialog box.

5. Click on OK. NT displays a progress dialog box as it binds the protocols to your adapter card.

Some network protocols, such as NWLINK and TCP/IP, prompt you for additional configuration information, typically network addresses. For details, see the discussions of these protocols in Chapter 15.

You'll have to restart your computer for changes to your network configuration to take effect. After you've made changes, Windows NT gives you an opportunity to restart the system.

If you installed Windows NT on this system from floppy disks, you'll be prompted to insert the appropriate disks. If you installed Windows NT from a CD-ROM drive or a network drive, you must enter the path to the CD-ROM or network directory that contains the Windows NT distribution files. If you no longer have access to the CD-ROM or network files because you installed from a CD-ROM drive that Windows NT doesn't support or from a file server that isn't currently available to your workstation, you have a problem.

The files that make up your new protocol or services will be copied to your \WINNT\SYSTEM32 directory.

To remove a network component, follow these steps:

1. Click on the Network icon in Control Panel.
2. In the Network Settings dialog box, select the protocol or service you want to remove in the Installed Network Software list.
3. Click on the Remove button and complete the dialog boxes that appear.
4. Restart your computer.

NOTE

If you remove NetBEUI, Windows NT won't be able to communicate with Windows for Workgroups computers or LAN Manager servers unless you reinstall it by clicking on the Add Software button.

Windows NT Networking Out of the Box: Peer-to-Peer Networking

15

IN THIS CHAPTER

If you're planning to build a small network—especially if the vast majority of the workstations are going to be running some version of Windows—you'll probably find all the networking software you need right in the Windows NT box. With just the standard Windows NT networking software, you can share data and printers across the network with other Windows NT and Windows for Workgroups workstations, as well as allow DOS machines access to shared resources.

Because all the Windows NT and Windows for Workgroups stations on the network can act as equals or peers, both offering their resources to be shared and accessing resources on other stations, this type of network generally is called *peer-to-peer networking*. In the DOS world, this kind of peer networking is provided by products such as Artisoft's LANtastic, Novell's NetWare Lite, and of course, Windows for Workgroups.

NOTE

The real-mode, or NDIS 2.0, network driver components of Windows for Workgroups are available from Microsoft and are known as the Microsoft Workgroup Connection. These drivers can be utilized on computers that are incapable of running Windows for Workgroups to provide network connectivity. With these drivers, you can access file and print shares on your workgroup or domain. If you have Windows NT Server, you can find an enhanced version of the network connectivity drivers for MS-DOS, known as the Microsoft Network Client version 3.0, in the \CLIENTS\MSCLIENTS directory. This version of the network software includes full support for DHCP and WINS services if you utilize TCP/IP as your primary transport protocol. Both of these client drivers support full access to file and print servers on the network.

This chapter takes a good look at how Windows NT's peer-networking features help you build workgroups that enable users to share resources with other systems. If you've used Windows for Workgroups, the concept of workgroups will be familiar to you because Windows NT workgroups and WFW workgroups work the same way, as do Windows 95 workgroups.

Why Workgroups?

A workgroup is a collection of two or more computers that share files or printers across a network. You might, for example, create workgroups on your network that correspond to your organization's structure. All that time the CEO spends making organizational charts could be put to good use as your Accounting department gets a workgroup, the Marketing department gets a workgroup, and so on.

Members of these departments could then exchange data among themselves and share printers. Whenever you needed to retrieve files from a computer that was in your workgroup, you could easily locate the shared directory and link a drive letter to it by using File Manager. If Windows NT didn't make you organize your computers into workgroups, or if you made the mistake of creating only one workgroup for a large organization, you'd have to scroll through a list of all the computers in your company to find your data. With workgroups, File Manager displays a tree—such as a directory tree—of the networks, workgroups, and servers available on the network, which makes finding your data much easier. Organizing computers into workgroups is a convenience; doing so makes it easier to browse network resources.

Your workgroups should have a lot more to do with the logical organization of computers than with the physical structure of a network. Creating workgroups for the second floor, third floor, and basement makes a lot less sense than setting up departmental workgroups.

If your company advocates the modern management practice of interdisciplinary teams in which designers, engineers, marketers, and musketeers all work together to bring a new musket to market, you can (and probably should) create a workgroup for each active team rather than each department.

Although workgroups help you organize network resources, they don't really simplify network administration. Each server, which can mean each PC on the system, is still administered individually. If the user WGATES is to access secure data on four, or 400, different machines, someone (and that means *you*) needs to create the user WGATES on each of those servers—one at a time. With a large number of computers, this can be an onerous task, about as much fun as having large, hairy men force burning bamboo under your fingernails, which we all know can be a bit annoying.

Users with large networks should use Windows NT Server, which goes beyond the workgroup concept to a domain-based naming and security scheme. Unlike servers in a workgroup, servers in a Windows NT Server domain are administered as a group. In fact, a *domain* is defined as a group of file servers that share a common user and group definition file. Because these servers all share the same user file, if you want WGATES to have access to data on 30 file servers that are all part of the same domain, you need to create an account for him only once.

Because all the servers in a domain must be running Windows NT Server, or some version of Microsoft's LAN Manager or LM/X (LAN Manager for UNIX), Chapters 16 and 17 discuss domains. Peer-to-peer networking workgroups, as opposed to domains, are the unit of organization.

Setting Up the Peer Network

Installing the LAN card driver into Windows NT automatically installs the server service (which enables you to give users at other computers access to your disk data and printers), the workstation service (which allows you to access other computer files and printers), and the computer browser service (which keeps a list of the other computers on the network). You then have to tell Windows NT your computer's name and the name of the domain or workgroup this computer will be a member of.

Although it's tempting to just rip off the shrink wrap and get that new software toy installed as quickly as possible, that's probably not a good idea. My experience has shown that organizations that spend a little bit of time and energy planning their installation spend much less time maintaining their system than organizations that allow their networks to grow piecemeal.

The first thing you need to do is come up with a convention for naming your computers, domains, and/or workgroups. A naming convention isn't just a way to keep people from using silly names, such as our NetWare file server Shlomo. It's also an important way to both prevent people from creating duplicate names, which can keep either of two objects with the same name from working, and add some valuable information about things such as the location of a computer or its most frequent user's name, which enables you to locate and fix problems that crop up.

What naming convention you use is less important than simply developing a convention. The most successful conventions are those that are simplest and most understandable when viewed. I had one client who successfully used the most common convention: the user's ID, made up of the user's first two initials and last name truncated to eight characters, plus `-COMP` for PCs and department names, plus `-DOM` for domains. Another client came up with a system that in eight characters included the company division, the user's initials and employment status, and a two-digit counter to ensure uniqueness. This code was so complicated that I was hired to create a client/server application to generate the codes and increment the counters as Jean-Paul Marat and John Patrick Murphy were assigned accounts.

NOTE

A computer's name can't be the same as any other computer on the network—even if they're in different workgroups—or the same as a Windows NT Server Domain. In addition, your workgroup name can't be the same as your computer name.

Joining a Workgroup

After you've got everything installed, you might find that you want to make your computer a member of a new workgroup. To change workgroups, follow these steps:

1. Open the Network applet in Control Panel.
2. In the Network Settings dialog box, shown in Figure 15.1, click on the button next to the workgroup's name.

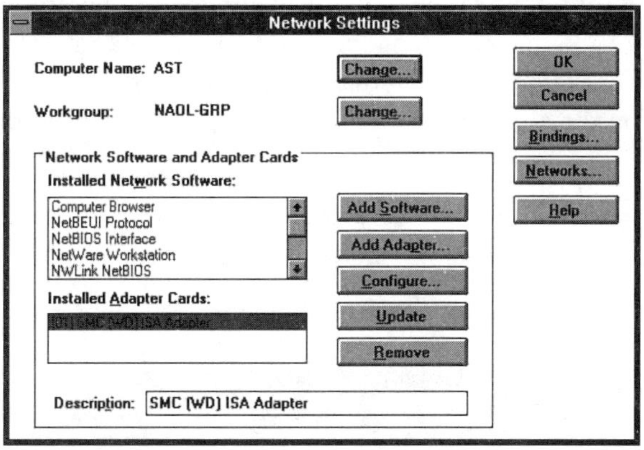

FIGURE 15.1.
The Network Settings dialog box.

3. When the Domain/Workgroup Settings dialog box opens (see Figure 15.2), enter the name of the workgroup that you want to join.

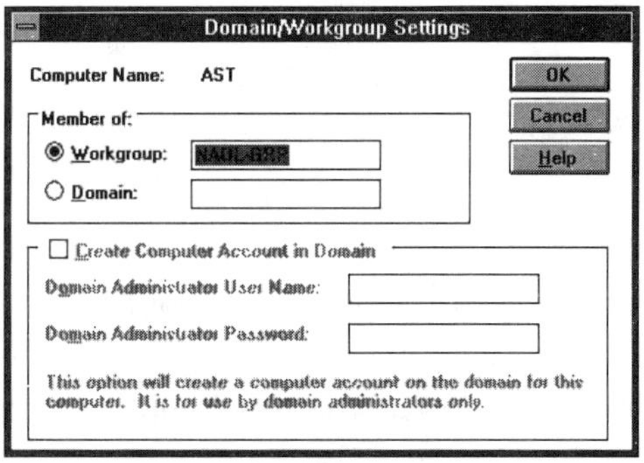

FIGURE 15.2.
The Domain/Workgroup Settings dialog box.

4. Click on OK to join the workgroup.

NOTE

A computer can be a member of only one workgroup at a time.

Joining an NT Server Domain

Joining a domain is similar to joining a workgroup. The difference is that anyone can join a workgroup at any time, but only computers and users who have accounts created by the network administrator can join a domain. As you can see from Figure 15.2, when you enter a domain name in the Domain/Workgroup Settings dialog box, you get the option of entering the domain's administrator account name and password.

If the computer's account already exists on the domain, or if you enter the correct administrator name and password so that the program can create one, your computer becomes a member of the domain. If not, you are rejected.

For more information on using domains, see Chapter 16.

NOTE

A computer can be a member of only one domain at a time.

WARNING

Your computer name can't be the same as any of the computers in the domain that you are about to join.

To join a domain, follow these steps:

1. Open the Network applet in Control Panel.
2. When the Domain/Workgroup Settings dialog box opens, click on the Change button next to the current workgroup or domain name.
3. Enter the name of the domain you want to join, as shown in Figure 15.3.
4. If the domain administrator has created an account for this computer, you can click on OK to join the domain.

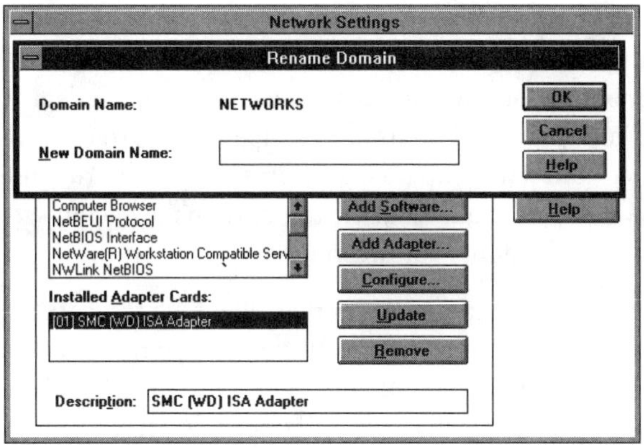

FIGURE 15.3.
Changing the domain name.

Creating a User Account in a Domain

If you're the domain administrator, you can save a step by having Control Panel create the computer's account as you install Windows NT on the system. All you have to do is enter your username and password.

1. In the Domain/Workgroup Settings dialog box, click on the Create Computer Account in Domain check box.
2. Enter the Domain Administrator User Name, and then enter the Domain Administrator Password.
3. Click on OK.

This creates an account for the user and logs this computer onto the domain as a workstation.

Setting Up a Workgroup

After you've configured a set of computers into a workgroup, your next step is to decide which computers are actually going to make their resources available for other users to share (called sharing in Redmondtonian)—that is, which ones will be servers and which will only be client workstations accessing the data on the servers. You don't have to make every Windows NT workstation a server just because you can.

It seems that there is a constant debate between network experts who feel that a small number of servers is better (the client/server camp) and those who advocate the freedom of a network in which each user's machine is a server (the peer-to-peer camp). On a bad day, you might hear them call each other "fascist" or "anarchist."

The client/server camp argues that fewer servers is better because you can back them up and make sure that they have better disk subsystems, UPSs, redundant disk drives, and plenty of memory so that the users accessing shared data get good performance easier. Even more importantly, they argue, a single administrator can manage a few file servers, creating users and setting up their security. They claim that users administering their own servers are slipshod about security, forget to make backups, and otherwise don't do the job as well as a professional administrator.

The peer-to-peer camp argues that they save the cost of additional dedicated server machines and a full-time administrator while empowering users, thereby building *esprit de corps* and boosting productivity. They also point to the advantage of not having a single point of failure at the file server. If one of 50 servers fails, you can get more work done than if the one and only server fails.

The truth is somewhere in between, and which approach you should take depends on your corporate culture, personal temperament, and users. If you're putting in a five-station network for a group of software developers, making all of them servers and letting those sophisticated users administer their own systems is a good idea. If, however, you're setting up a system to support a new airline's reservation system, you're probably better off with a single big server or multiple NT Servers in a domain.

Sharing Resources

After you've decided which machines are going to be servers, you have to set up their resources to be shared. Windows NT basically enables you to offer printers that are attached to your computer and directories on your local hard drives to be shared by other users. Whenever you want to offer a resource from your system, you need to give it a name—called a *share, sharename,* or *sharepoint*—that other users can then use to access the printer or directory.

NOTE

You can share a CD-ROM just as if it is a directory on your local computer. However, to prevent clients from receiving errors, always make the share read-only; otherwise, a network client might attempt to write to this share (on your CD-ROM). I have seen a few programs try this and fail, sometimes causing the Windows or MS-DOS client to freeze, requiring a reboot to restore. If this happens, you can be sure that there will be an accompanying data loss. One other point to consider when sharing a CD-ROM is that any client software that requires local access to the CD-ROM will fail as well. This type of software utilizes MSCDEX

(Microsoft CD-ROM Extensions) and will be unable to find its data files. In such a case, contact the manufacturer to see whether they have a network-aware version of the application.

When you first install Windows NT, it automatically creates sharenames for the root directory of each logical drive on your server and the directory you installed Windows NT into. The sharenames to the root directories are the drive letter with a dollar sign (`$`) added. The share to C:\ is therefore `C$`, you can access D:\ as `D$`, and so on. The Windows NT directory (typically C:\WINNT) is given the sharename `ADMIN$`. These shares are created to make administering the system easier. A network administrator can automatically update all of his or her servers by accessing just these administrative shares. Only members of the Administrators and Backup Operators groups can use, and only administrators can change, the properties of these sharenames.

Follow these steps to share a directory:

1. In File Manager, select the directory you want to share.
2. Either click on the Share Directory button on the toolbar—it's the one that has a hand passing you a file folder—or select Share As from the Disk menu.
3. When you see the New Share dialog box, shown in Figure 15.4, enter the name you want to use to share the directory in the Share Name box. The default sharename for a directory is the directory's own name. The sharename can be up to 12 characters long and should have some relation to the data that the directory holds, to make finding the right data easier.

FIGURE 15.4.
The New Share dialog box.

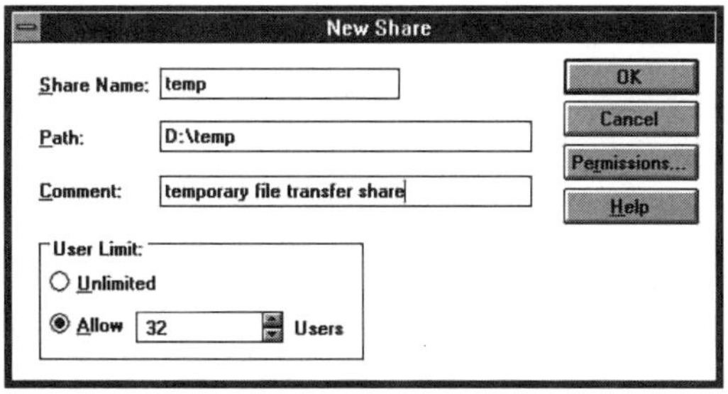

4. Enter a description of the data or the sharename's purpose in the Comment field. When users are browsing for data, they can view not only the directory's name but also this comment.

5. Now you can set a limit on the number of users that can access your data through this share at the same time and/or set the permissions for this share. The next section talks about what, if anything, you should do with these parameters in terms of security.
6. Click on OK to make the directory available for others to use.

NOTE

To share a directory, you must be logged in to the server machine as a member of the Administrators or Power Users group.

Securing Your Data: Setting Share Properties

As you saw when sharing a directory, each sharename has associated with it a user limit and a permissions filter. You can set the user limit either to limit the effect on your performance of other users accessing your hard disk, or as a primitive form of application metering. If, for example, you have five licensed copies of WinWord, you can set the WinWord sharename user limit to five. When the sixth user tries to link to that share—that is, assign a drive letter on his or her machine as an alias for the data in the directory on the server—this attempt will fail.

This user limit isn't really adequate as a software metering device, because most users try to share the directory as they log in as opposed to when they want to run the application; thus, 10 users need 10 shares, even if only two of them are running WinWord.

To limit user access to the data, you can set share permissions in addition to the user permissions that you might have already set up for this directory. A user is allowed to link to a directory only when that user, or a group that user is a member of, has permission to access the share or directory. When you link a drive to a directory on a Windows NT server, your station sends a series of messages to the server that essentially says, "Hi, this is IBM686. My local user WGATES really would like to use your SECRET_STUFF directory, okay?" If WGATES has permission to use the directory, the server acknowledges the request; if not, it sends a negative acknowledgment.

You can grant a user access to the data in a server's directory either by granting permissions to the directory, as described in Chapter 3, "Working with Windows NT," or by clicking on the Permissions button in the New Share dialog box to grant the user share permissions. Granting a user permissions through File Manager's Security menu gives the user access to the file or directory when the user is logged in at the machine that holds the data *and* if he or she is logging in from another workstation. Granting the user share permissions through the New Share dialog box gives the user access from another workstation but doesn't allow him or her to access the data from the local keyboard and screen.

You can give a user one level of access when he or she is sitting at the local keyboard, and a lower level of access when coming in over the network, by granting both directory and share permissions. The directory permissions act as the limit to rights, and the share permissions can then reduce access further. The user will have any given permission only if he or she has that permission through both the share and directory permissions.

NOTE

The group Everyone automatically has the Full Control permission to each sharepoint when the sharepoint is created. Unless you want everyone to have access to all your data, get in the habit of deleting this permission.

To create a set of share permissions, click on the Permissions button to open the Access Through Share Permissions dialog box, shown in Figure 15.5. Select the name of the user or group that you want to share the resource with, and then select a permission from the Type of Access box.

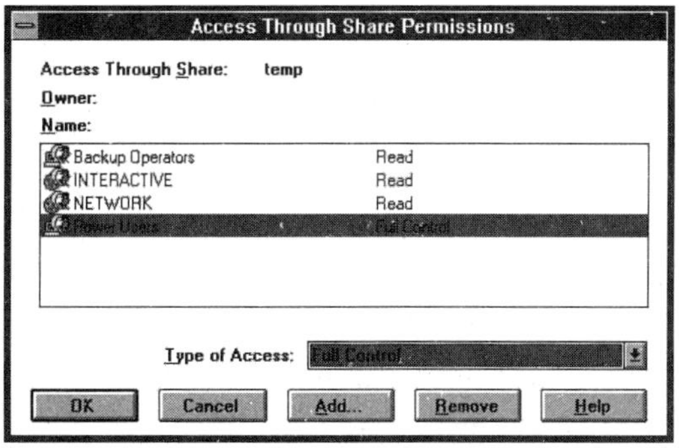

FIGURE 15.5.
The Access Through Share Permissions dialog box.

You'll notice that you have a lot less flexibility to set permissions for a sharename than for a directory. You can set a user's or a group's rights to only Read, Change, Full Control, or No Access. Table 15.1 shows the effect of each of these permissions.

Table 15.1. A list of directory permissions under Windows NT.

Permission	*Rights Granted*
No Access	None
Read	Read files, list subdirectories, and view file properties
Change	Write to file, create file/subdirectory, delete file/subdirectory, and change attributes
Full Control	Write to file, create file/subdirectory, delete file/subdirectory, change attributes, change permissions (NTFS), and take ownership (NTFS)

Because you have more detailed control over users through directory permissions, you should use directory permissions as your primary data protection screen. Share permissions should be used to protect very sensitive data that should be accessed or updated only from the local console. You can learn how to control directory permissions in Chapter 3.

WARNING

Giving your users full control over a directory can be a dangerous thing. Not only can they delete all your files, they also can lock you out. You would then have to use an Administrator-level account to take back ownership of the directory.

After you set the permissions for the directory, click on OK to close the dialog box and save your changes. At this point, your directory is available on the network for other users to connect to. You can tell in File Manager that a directory is being shared when a shared directory icon appears next to the directory's name.

Stopping Directory Sharing

If you decide that you no longer want to allow other users to share your computer's resources, you can stop sharing that resource. You should make sure that no users have any files open before you stop sharing (through the Server applet in Control Panel), or you'll start getting phone calls from annoyed users. If a user has a file open to read, he'll get errors when he next attempts to access the file, and he'll call you to yell. Even worse, if a user has the file open to write, he might not be able to save the data, and you might end up destroying the whole file. You can learn how to use the Server applet in Chapter 9, "Configuring Windows NT."

Just as you must be a member of the Administrators or Power Users group to share a directory, you must be a member of one of these groups to stop sharing.

To stop sharing a directory, follow these steps:

1. Open File Manager.
2. Click on the Stop Sharing button—the one with the picture of the hand snatching the disk drive back—or select Stop Sharing from the Disk menu.
3. When the Stop Sharing dialog box opens (see Figure 15.6), you see all the shared directories listed with their directory paths on your computer. If you select a directory before clicking on the Stop Sharing button, it will be the first share listed and will be selected.

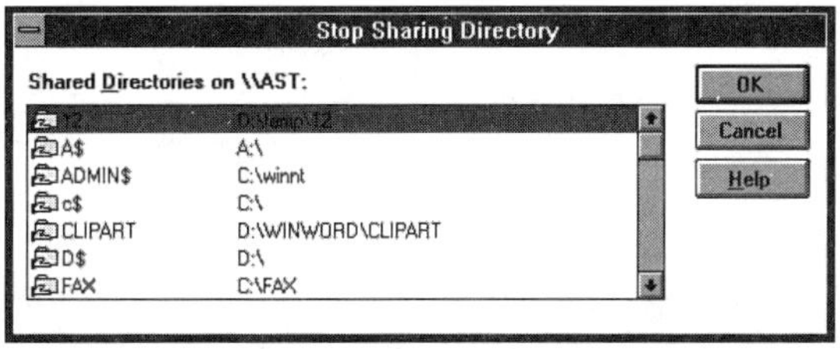

FIGURE 15.6.
The Stop Sharing dialog box.

Select the directories that you want to stop sharing, and then click on OK. If users are connected to the shared directory, File Manager asks you to confirm that you want to leave these poor slobs high and dry.

WARNING

Remember not to stop sharing if users have files open; it could lead to data loss or job loss.

Using Data from the Server

To access a directory that your network administrator has shared on a file server, you need to link that sharepoint to a logical drive letter on your workstation. You might hear old-timers call this process "mapping a drive" or "net using" because of the NetWare MAP, LAN Manager, and Windows NT commands used to perform this important function.

The easiest way to link a drive to a remote file share (see, I can use Microsoft-speak) is through File Manager.

1. Start File Manager, and either click on the Connect Drive button (the disk drive that sparkles as if someone cleaned one corner for a Formula 409 commercial) or select Connect Network Drive from the Disk Menu. The Connect Network Drive dialog box, shown in Figure 15.7, appears.

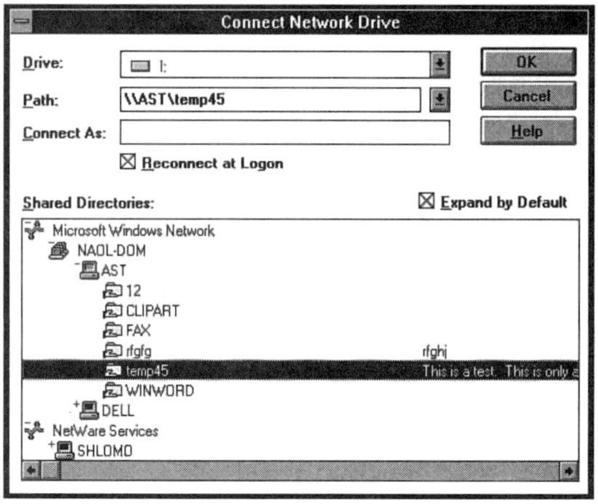

FIGURE 15.7.
The Connect Network Drive dialog box.

2. The Drive list box defaults to the first available drive letter on your system. If you want to use a different drive letter, such as W: for word processing or L: for lawsuits, select the letter you want to link.
3. The window at the bottom of the dialog box displays a tree of available shared directories. Double-click on the network where the data you're looking for is located (Microsoft Windows Network for Windows NT, Windows for Workgroups, Windows 95, and LAN Manager servers; or another network for directories available through an add-on requester such as the NetWare Services network).
4. The tree opens to show you the workgroups and domains on your network. Double-click on a workgroup or domain to see the file servers. If you enable the Expand by Default box, your workgroup or domain is automatically expanded to show its file servers the next time you open this dialog box.

NOTE

If you're on a slow or busy network, you might want to disable the automatic expansion feature because it creates quite a bit of traffic.

5. Double-click on a file server to make its available sharepoints appear.
6. Select a share and click on OK to link the drive. If you enable the Reconnect At Logon box, Windows NT reestablishes this link each time you log on.

If you're logged onto your system as a user who either doesn't exist on the server or doesn't have permission to use the directory you want to access, you can fill in the Connect As: field. This enables you to use different user IDs to access data on different computers. If the username you entered in this box has a password, you're prompted for it after you click on OK. If you want to use a name from another domain, you should type the domain name followed by the username (for example, `FBI\ENess` or `FBI\HHoover`).

If you aren't fond of all that clicking, you can type the sharename you want to link to, using the Universal Naming Convention (UNC) of `\\servername\sharename`. File Manager also remembers the last 10 directories you've linked to and puts them in a pull-down list for the Path field.

NOTE

If you're a member of the Administrators or Backup Users groups, you also can access the administrative shares (`C$`, `D$`, and so on) by entering them into the Path field. These shares don't appear in the display, which prevents nosy users from poking around where they shouldn't.

Breaking a Link to a Shared Directory

After you've established a connection to a shared directory, you might decide that you want to break the link. Again, the easy way is through File Manager.

1. Open File Manager and click on the Disconnect Drive button—the drive with an X through its sparkle—or select Disconnect Network Drive from the Disk menu. The Disconnect Network Drive dialog box, shown in Figure 15.8, appears.

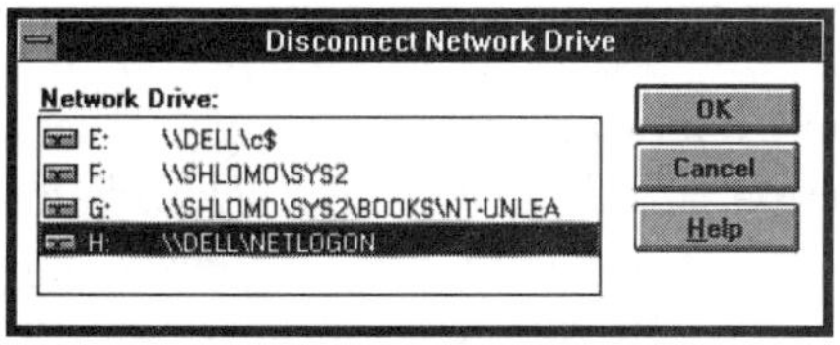

FIGURE 15.8.
The Disconnect Network Drive dialog box.

2. Select the drives you don't want to access anymore and click on OK. If you have files open on one or more of the drives you're trying to delete, you get a dialog box like the one shown in Figure 15.9. If you see this dialog box, you should click on the No button and go back and close the files—or better yet, exit the applications that had the files open and try again. If you click on the Yes button, you might lose any files you have open.

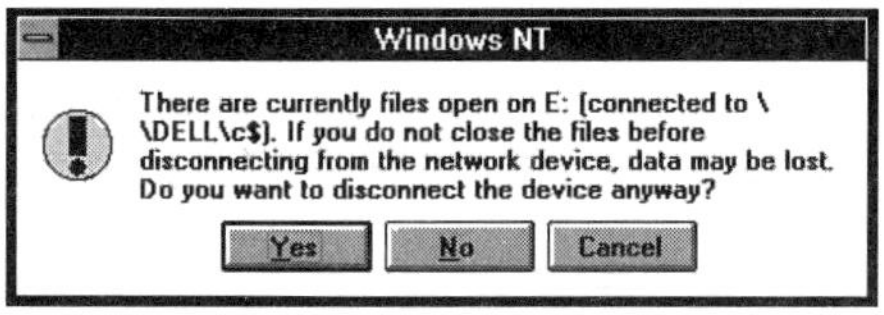

FIGURE 15.9.
Deleting a network drive with files open.

Sharing Printers

If you haven't already read Chapter 4, "Print Manager," now would be a good time to do so. This section discusses much of the same information, but it concentrates exclusively on the network-related aspects of working with Print Manager. If I've skipped something here, it most likely applies to both networked and stand-alone Windows NT systems and is discussed in Chapter 4. Some features that are available only on PCs connected to networks, such as usable print spooling, are integral to Windows NT—even for single-user systems.

In addition to sharing your data, you also can allow other users to send their print jobs to any printers you have on your system. Just as with directories, you can set permissions to control which users can access each printer or maintain the print queue for a printer.

As with any local area network, Windows NT provides shared printers by spooling data intended for the printer on the print server computer. At the risk of oversimplifying, when you tell an application to print on a remote printer, your application sends the data across the network to Print Manager on the print server, which then sends it to the printer.

Windows NT's printer sharing differs from what you might have become used to with networks such as NetWare or LANtastic, which primarily have DOS workstations. First of all, you can print directly from Windows 16- or 32-bit applications to network printers. With DOS and Windows 3.x networks, you must link a network printer to one of DOS's logical printer ports (LPT1: through LPT3:) before you can send the data to a network print queue. This makes it a lot easier to have multiple printer definitions for high- and low-priority print jobs, different output trays, or other printer configuration issues, because users have to select just the printer definition.

Secondly, because printer definitions include not only the printer's logical location on the network but also the printer's driver, users at Windows NT stations that have been properly set up can't send a print job to a printer using the new driver. No longer do users send their print jobs to bit heaven by selecting LaserJet III as the driver for your LaserJet III with the PostScript cartridge, nor do they print reams of PostScript code by selecting the reverse.

Windows NT goes even one step further, saving you from driver-mismatch migraines *and* from the print driver distribution blues. On most PC LANs, users must have the appropriate Windows 3.x print drivers for each printer on the network they might print to. When you get PageMaker 5.0 and discover that it works only with the newest version 99.99.99.22.9.9 of the driver for your Gutenberg WonderPress 10,000-page-per-minute printer, you might have a good day's work copying the Gutenberg WonderDriver to each machine on your network. With Windows NT on both the print server and the user's workstation, you need only to install the print driver on the print server; workstations simply use the server's driver.

If you've been working with NetWare and you're getting a bit confused by the new terminology, just bear in mind that what Windows NT calls a printer is actually more like a NetWare print queue (which can be serviced by one or more printers) than a NetWare printer (which is a specific port on the network, and therefore is really just one printer).

Sharing a Printer

You can share a printer that is attached to your computer for others to print to. Before you share a printer, it must be connected to one of your printer ports and have the printer drivers installed. Note that your workstation must be running the Server service to share a printer.

To share a printer, follow these steps:

1. Use Print Manager's Create Printer or Printer Properties menu choices to get to the Create Printer dialog box, shown in Figure 15.10.

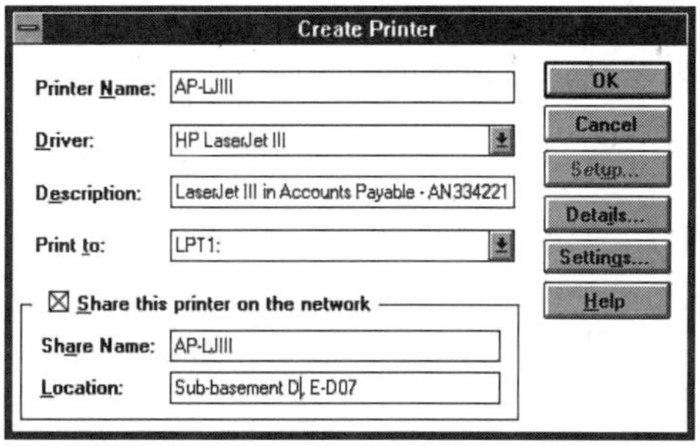

FIGURE 15.10.
The Create Printer dialog box.

2. Enable the Share this printer on the network box. Print Manager then creates a sharename for the printer in the Share Name box by truncating the printer's name and making it fit the DOS sharename conventions, removing spaces and other forbidden characters. If you don't like the name it comes up with, you can edit the sharename, but it can't be longer than 12 characters and it must follow MS-DOS naming conventions or those for MS-DOS and Windows for Workgroups.
3. If your printer-naming convention doesn't tell users where to go to pick up their print jobs, you should enter a description of the printer's location in the Location box. Because users see the location information in the Connect to Printer dialog

box, they can choose a printer convenient to them. If your travel department is a soft touch, some bright user might send his or her print job to the Paris office and then try to talk the travel people into a trip on the Concorde to pick it up.

4. Click on OK to share the printer.

Sharing a Networked Printer

Connecting printers directly to the local area network rather than to the serial or parallel port of a PC on the network has really taken off in the TCP/IP and NetWare worlds. Directly connected printers have a few significant advantages over PC-connected printers. Their biggest advantage is that the print stream is no longer at the mercy of the user whose printer is being shared. With a networked printer, you don't have to worry that Bill will try to run every TSR on his hard disk at the same time, or even that he'll just turn his PC off to go home in the middle of that 300-page report.

The other problem with PC-connected printers is the bottleneck at the parallel port. As 15 to 20 pages per minute laser printers have become common, the standard (or even enhanced) BiTronics parallel port can't keep up, especially on graphically complex documents. A 10Mbps EtherNet or 16Mbps Token Ring can deliver data to the printer a lot faster than a parallel port.

Windows NT includes support for the most common networked laser printers—HP LaserJets with HP Jet Direct cards. You can use a Jet Direct card with LaserJet IIs and LaserJet IIIs; more sophisticated printers such as the LaserJet IIISi and LaserJet IV come with JetDirect cards as standard equipment. HP's Jet Direct card is available in EtherNet and Token Ring versions. Both use the DLC (data link control) protocol to communicate with Windows NT print servers.

If you're planning to use JetDirect cards, you need to install the DLC protocol on the machines that will be acting as print servers for the networked printers. (See Chapter 13, "An Overview of Windows NT Networking," or Chapter 9, "Configuring Windows NT.") The print server is the machine that has on it the printer definition for the networked printer and shares that printer definition with other users. Users who connect to the printer definition don't need to load the DLC protocol, and probably shouldn't.

Follow these steps to set up a networked printer:

1. Install the Jet Direct card in your printer, connect it to the network, and turn it on.
2. Install the DLC protocol on the machine you'll be using as the print server.
3. Select Network Printer… from the Print To list box. The Print Destinations dialog box, shown in Figure 15.11, appears.

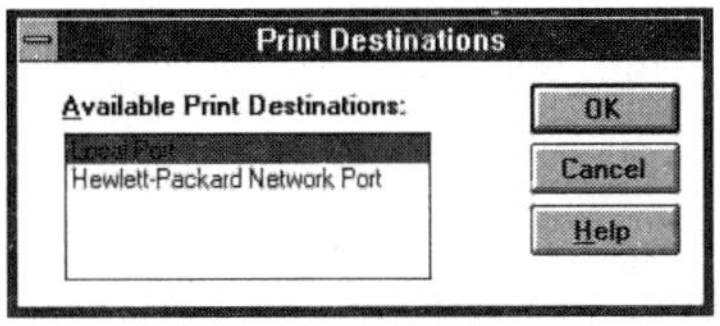

FIGURE 15.11.
The Print Destinations dialog box.

4. Select Hewlett-Packard Network Port. The Add Hewlett-Packard Network Peripheral Port dialog box, shown in Figure 15.12, appears.

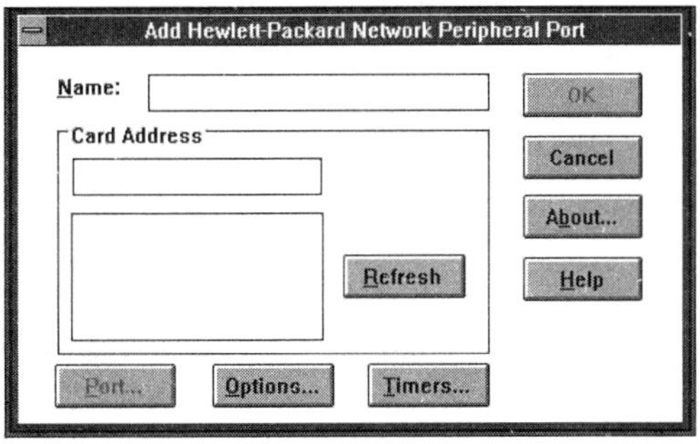

FIGURE 15.12.
The Add Hewlett-Packard Network Peripheral Port dialog box.

5. Enter a name for the port in the Name field. The name can be up to 255 characters long, but because DOS applications must send their data to this port and can accept only names similar to LPT*x*, they tend to be called LPT4 through LPT99.
6. Select the Card Address for the Jet Direct card you just installed. You did remember to run the test page and copy down the address that printed there, right? If you don't see the right address, something's wrong. Recheck all the cables, and if that doesn't work, see Chapter 21, "Troubleshooting Your Network."
7. If you have a LaserJet 4, 4Si, or later printer that supports bidirectional communications, or if you use locally administered addresses (LAA) on Token Ring, click on the Port button to access the Settings for Selected HP Network Port dialog box.

   If you have a LaserJet 4 or later, you should enable the Advanced Job Status box. This makes the print server pay attention to the data coming back from the printer. The most obvious advantage is that Print Manager won't delete the print job file for a print job until the printer tells it that the job has actually been printed and is in the output bin, not just in the printer's input buffer.

   Locally administered addresses are an option that enables a user to specify the node address of each workstation. LAAs are an advanced option and are best left alone by most users.

8. The Options button leads to other advanced options most users are better off leaving alone (see Figure 15.13). These options actually affect the DLC protocol, and changes affect all printers. Here you can change the DLC response timer, acknowledgment and inactivity timers, errors logged, primary or secondary adapter, and the number of link stations (printers) allowed. The number of link stations is the only parameter you're likely to change, and then only if you need more than 64 printers connected to a single print server.

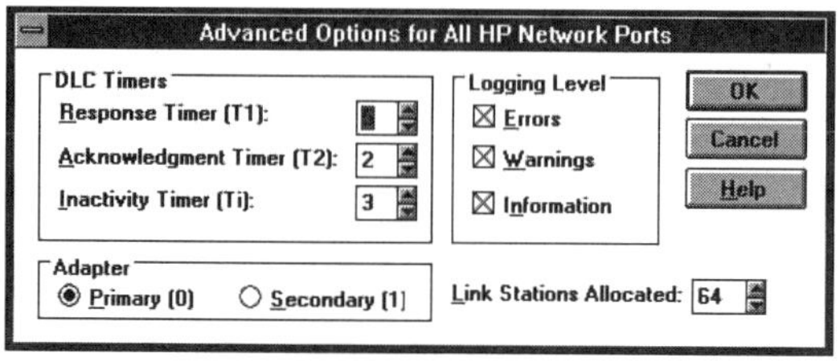

FIGURE 15.13.
Advanced options for all HP network ports.

9. The Timers button enables you to adjust how often the print server polls the printers to check on their status through the dialog box shown in Figure 15.14. A short time gives you a more accurate display of printer status in Print Manager and earlier alerts from printer errors so that you can get problems fixed before users start complaining—or, worse, try to fix it themselves. A longer time creates less network traffic. The default is 60 seconds.

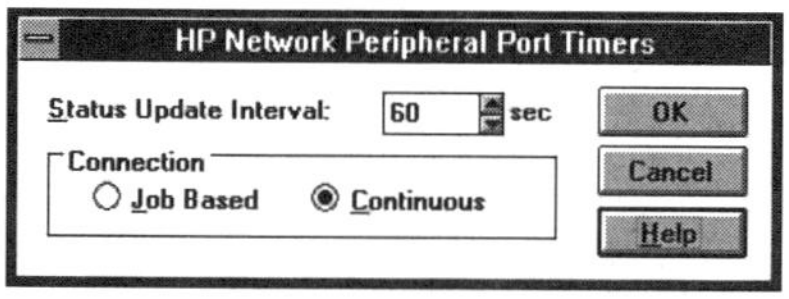

FIGURE 15.14.
The HP Network Peripherals Port Timers dialog box.

The Port Timers dialog box also enables you to set how the print server communicates with the printer. An HP printer running DLC can maintain a connection with only one print server at a time. If you set the connection type to Continuous, the print server connects to the printer and stays connected until it or the printer is turned off. If you select Job Based, the print server connects to the printer at the beginning of each print job and disconnects after each job, enabling another print server to then connect to the printer. If all the print servers are set to Job Based, you can have multiple print servers sharing a single printer.

If you're planning to have only one print server for the printer, a continuous connection generates less network traffic, establishing and tearing down the connections for each print job. If you have other print servers, especially if you have Windows for Workgroups print servers (which can run only in Job Based mode), you should run in Job Based mode.

Linking to Shared Printers

To use a printer on another user's computer, open Print Manager and do the following:

1. Click on the Connect Printer button (the one with a printer with a cable coming out of it and a bright spot) or select Printer | Connect to Printer to display the Connect to Printer dialog box, shown in Figure 15.15.

FIGURE 15.15.
The Connect to Printer dialog box.

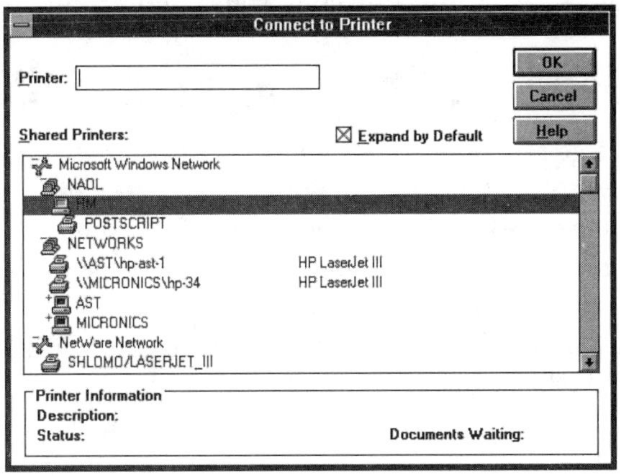

2. Expand the server tree, if needed, to find the printer share you want to link to, and then double-click on it. Click on OK to link to the printer.
3. If the server for that printer is a Windows for Workgroups system, a system with a different processor than your machine (RISC versus Intel), or a LAN Manager server, you won't be able to take advantage of a Windows NT 32-bit print driver at the server, and you see the warning box shown in Figure 15.16.

FIGURE 15.16.
What you see if your print server can't support your printer.

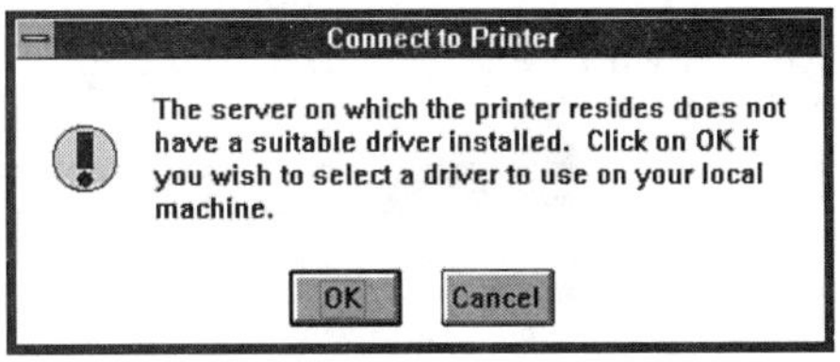

4. Click on OK and install the appropriate driver using the dialog box shown in Figure 15.17.

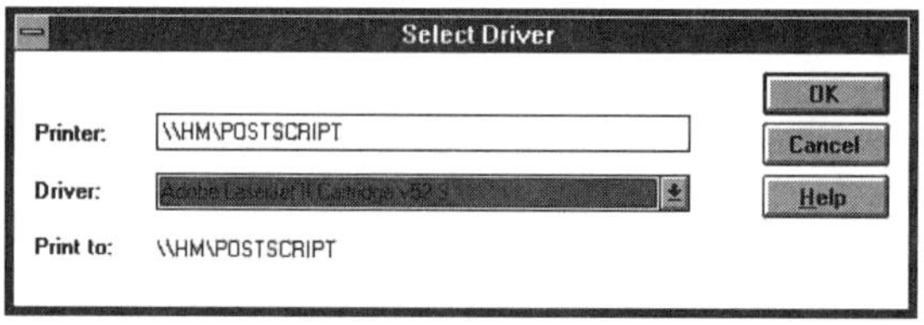

FIGURE 15.17.
Installing a print driver.

If you have sufficient permissions, you are now connected to the printer.

Connecting to Shared Printers on UNIX Servers

Many large networks include a mixture of print servers, including Windows NT Server, Windows NT, Windows for Workgroups, Windows 95, LAN Manager, Netware, and UNIX servers. All of these servers except UNIX support browsing with Print Manager. To connect to a UNIX printer, you need to know the printer name and IP address. Contact your system administrator if you don't have this information. After you've obtained the printer name and IP address, connecting to the UNIX printer is relatively trouble-free. Just do the following:

1. Open Print Manager and select Printer | Create Printer.
2. The Create Printer dialog box appears. At this point, you need to do the following:
   - Enter a name for the printer, something like `UNIX HP Laser Jet`.
   - Select a printer driver (HP LaserJet 4). If the printer driver is not already resident, you will be prompted for the source files.
   - In the Print To field, select Other. The Print Destinations dialog box, shown in Figure 15.11, will appear.
   - Select LPR Port in the dialog box. The Add LPR Compatible Printer dialog box, shown in Figure 15.18, will appear.

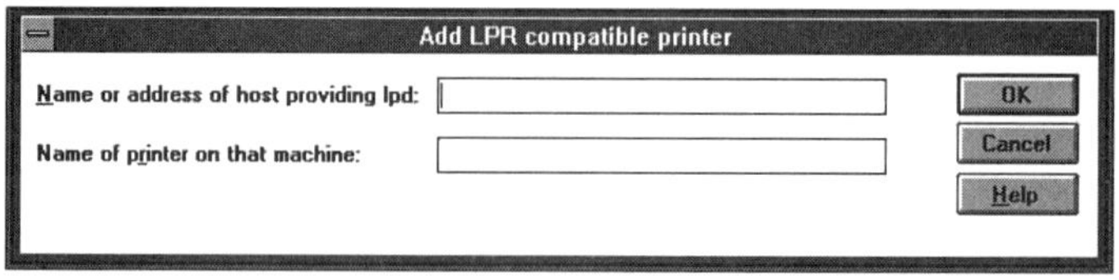

FIGURE 15.18.
Installing a shared printer on a UNIX server.

   - Enter either the DNS name (stored in the HOSTS file) or the IP address of the computer sharing the printer in the Name or address of host providing LPD field.
   - Enter the name that the printer was shared under in the Name of printer on that machine field.

3. Click on OK, and then finish filling out the optional fields in the Create Printer dialog box.

TIP

If you share the printer you have created, other computers will then be able to browse your computer and connect to it as well without having to know the printer name and IP address. From a system management viewpoint, it makes more sense to create and share these types of printers on a Windows NT print server.

4. Click on OK. If your privileges are accepted by the UNIX server, you will now be connected to the printer.

Controlling Access to Printers

This section discusses the *whats*, not the *hows*, of setting up printer security. The details of how to set up printer permissions can be found in Chapter 10, "Windows NT Administration."

The concept of securing a printer on a single user system seems strange to most people. If George can use the computer, he should be able to print. In the network environment, you can see good reasons to set printer permissions. Even if every user is going to be allowed to print to every printer, you might not want all 500 students in your university to have the power to move their print jobs to the top of the queue or to delete other users' print jobs.

A few good reasons can be found to prevent users from accessing a printer at all. Color, large format, and high-resolution printers have a high cost per page and a high "potential for abuse" for things such as birthday party invitations. Printers with specific forms such as invoices should be protected to prevent accidents, and the printer with check stock in it just begs for a little late-night PageMaking.

You also can restrict printer access to printers at remote locations to keep wide area network traffic down.

For most network printers, the default set of printer permissions (in which the administrators and power users have full control over the print queue, everyone gets to print, and users get to control their own print jobs) is just about the right combination. It wouldn't hurt to give a user whose desk is physically close to the printer the ability to manage the printer so that he or she can handle the occasional stopping and starting of the printer for a paper change or jam.

Network Printing Tips

If you follow these hints, your network printing will be relatively trouble-free:

- Make sure that print servers have enough disk space to hold all their print jobs.
- Use separator pages if print jobs are distributed to users. Skip them if users pick up their own jobs.
- Networked, high-capacity printers make life easier.
- Assign a *Key Operator* for each printer. This user is responsible for changing paper, clearing jams, and so forth. Give him or her full control over the printer definition.
- If you have both high- and low-priority users, create separate printers with different priorities rather than have users change their priority.

NT and Windows for Workgroups/ Windows 95

Even Bill Gates doesn't expect you to switch all your workstations to Windows NT right away. Most users' needs are met perfectly well by Windows 3.x or Windows 95, so they don't need Windows NT. Even more important, many users can't afford the 486 processor and 16MB of memory that NT needs to run well. Windows for Workgroups can run comfortably on a 386 with 8MB of memory. Windows 95 is happier with a 486, but 8MB is still OK.

Microsoft designed Windows for Workgroups 3.11 to be the best 16-bit client software for accessing Windows NT and Windows NT Server file servers. Even with Windows 95 available, this is still the case because, technically speaking, Windows 95 is a mixture of 16- and 32-bit code. At this point, Windows 95 is probably the best low-end client for NT. Graduation would be to NT Workstation, of course. But WFW itself graduated up to Windows 95, and when you can afford the upgrade to your workstations, it will make good sense to advance to Windows 95 on your various low-level workstations. Why? Windows 95 shakes hands with NT a little better, dishing up and understanding long file and folder names, for example; and using 32-bit drivers whenever possible—such as for printers, screen, and of course, network cards—speeds things up as well.

We're not going to delve into the differences between how the two operating systems interact with NT, because the distinctions between them on this level are minimal. If you know how to use WFW on the NT network, you'll pretty well understand Windows 95. Users on Windows for Workgroups or Windows 95 machines can link to resources on Windows NT machines as if they were other Windows for Workgroups or Windows 95 systems. Users on Windows NT stations also can access data on Windows for Workgroup and Windows 95 machines.

If you want Windows for Workgroups or Windows 95 stations to access your Windows NT machines, make sure that they all use the same protocol. If the WFW or Windows 95 systems will be accessing only Windows NT system resources that are on the same network, Microsoft's NetBEUI is the best choice. If they need to access servers across routers, you might have to configure Windows for Workgroups to use IPX/SPX-compatible transport with NetBIOS or an optional TCP/IP. As a default, Windows 95 stations are set up with both NetBEUI and IPX/SPX. From my experience it seems to be OK to leave the IPX/SPX drivers loaded even if they aren't being used, though it hasn't affected things when I've removed them, either.

NOTE

Although Windows for Workgroups/Windows 95 can support multiple transport protocols such as NetBEUI, IPX/SPX, or TCP/IP simultaneously, this is less efficient than utilizing a single transport protocol and can cause additional problems. Always try to use a single protocol for your network clients using MS-DOS or Windows for Workgroups.

Basically, Windows for Workgroups workstations look just like Windows NT workstations. To access resources on a Windows NT or NT Server from Windows for Workgroups, just use File Manager or Print Manger as you would to access another Windows for Workgroups machine. The same holds true of Windows 95. Just use the tools that are built into Windows 95 to access the NT or other WFW resources. Typically this will be done through the Network Neighborhood icon on the Windows 95 Desktop. It can also be done through the Windows Explorer, however.

Windows for Workgroups doesn't have a field in which you can enter a different username to access this resource. If you're supporting Windows for Workgroups users, you'll have to make sure that all users can get to all the resources they need from a single user ID.

When you go the other way and access a Windows for Workgroups or Windows 95 system's data, you might run into the dialog box shown in Figure 15.19.

Unlike Windows NT and NT Server, Windows for Workgroups and Windows 95 don't manage file access permissions by user *account.* Windows for Workgroups uses a less sophisticated system called share-based security. When you share a directory on a Windows for Workgroups or Windows 95 station, you get to assign a password that the user must enter to access the data. If a user at a Windows NT station tries to access the data in a directory that has been protected this way, he or she will see the dialog box shown in Figure 15.19 and will have to enter the resource's password.

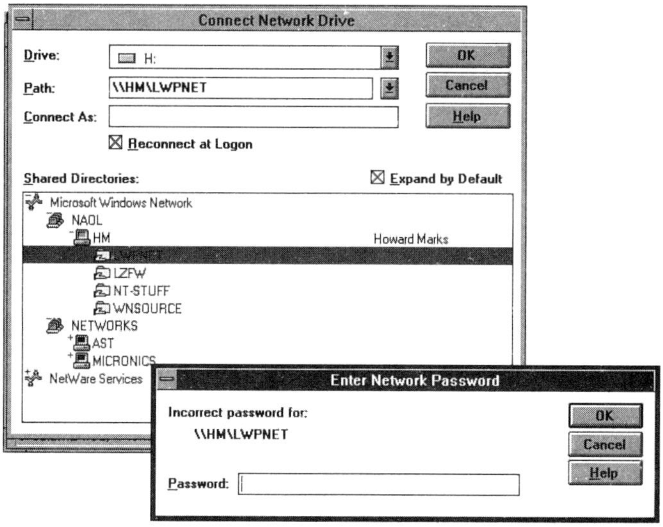

FIGURE 15.19.
What you see if there is a password-protected share on a WFW or Windows 95 station.

If you're running Windows NT Server, you need to tell Windows for Workgroups or Windows 95 machines to join a domain when the client machine is started; otherwise, they won't be able to access resources on the servers in a domain. To do this on a WFW station, follow these steps:

1. Open the Network applet in Windows for Workgroups' Control Panel and click on the Startup button. The dialog box shown in Figure 15.20 appears.

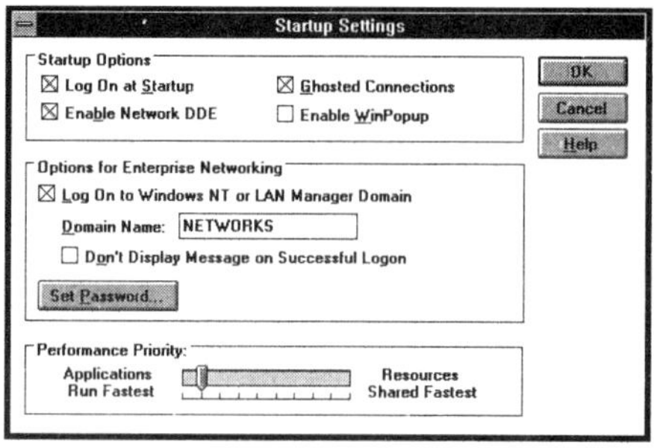

FIGURE 15.20.
Joining a domain from Windows for Workgroups.

2. Enable the Log On to Windows NT or LAN Manager Domain box.
3. Enter the name of the domain and set the password.

Procedures for adding a Windows 95 workstation to an NT network are detailed in the next section.

NOTE

Because of limited security and performance with Windows for Workgroups and Windows 95 machines and, even more importantly, because a remote user accessing your hard drive slows a Windows for Workgroups or Windows 95 station much more significantly than on a Windows NT station, you're better off keeping all your shared data on Windows NT systems. I would go so far as to recommend that you disable file sharing on Windows for Workgroups or Windows 95 machines.

Adding a Windows 95 Workstation to the NT Network

Due to slight differences between Windows 95 and WFW, I'll outline the exact means for getting a Windows 95 station on the NT network.

Firstly, make sure the Windows 95 machine is set up for one of the networking protocols installed on the NT server. Typically, this will be NetBEUI or IPS/SPX. On a huge network, this might be TCP/Internet provider. Again, recall that NetBEUI is the best choice for an Microsoft-only small network. It's lean and mean. The point to remember is that your client stations—Windows 95 or other—must be speaking the same language as the NT server machine. Use Control Panel in the Windows 95 end to check out the protocols installed.

After that is checked out, follow these steps to share resources on the network:

1. Right-click on any item you want to share on the network. This applies to printers, disks, and folders. Simply find the item with Explorer or via My Computer, right click, and choose Sharing. In the resulting box, activate the Shared As button and fill in the share name, comment, optional password, and possible security type and restrictions as desired.

   Note that you have to be part of an NT Domain to take advantage of user or group-level access rights.

2. On the NT machine, of course, you'll have to share any drives, directories, or printers you want to give the Windows 95 stations access to. Use File Manager and Print Manager on the NT machine to do this, using the Share As command. And remember that an NT machine can share not only local printers but also any printers on other NT stations to which it has access.

3. If the NT sever is a domain server, each Windows 95 client will need to have a user account set up for it on the NT server if it is to have access to resources on that server. Use the NT User Manager for Domains to set these up, and then use NT's File Manager and Print Manager to declare any specific sharing restrictions that might apply to those accounts.
4. Next, choose one of these options, as appropriate:
   - If you're using NT Workstation, make sure you have the same workgroup name specified on the NT workstation as you do for each Windows 95 station that will be part of this workgroup.
   - If you're using NT Server, set each Windows 95 station to log onto the NT domain and enter the correct domain in the domain field at each station. To do this, open Control Panel, choose networks, and double-click on Microsoft Client for Windows Networks. Click on the Domain check box and type in the name of your NT domain.

Now you should be able to open Network Neighborhood on any Windows 95 stations in the workgroup or domain and see an icon for the NT machine. Also, with the server browsers in NT's Print Manager or File Manager, the Windows 95 stations should show up as additional servers in the workgroup or domain.

TIP

If your office has one or more Novell print servers around, you can use NT's Server's Print Manager to share those printer servers. Using this technique, Windows 95, DOS, and WFW stations won't need Netware-specific network drivers loaded to print on the Novell print server. (You will need to install a printer driver for each printer, though.) This approach can only be done with Server, not NT Workstation. First, install and configure the Netware Gateway Services software that's supplied with NT Server. Then connect to the Netware print queue and share it.

Using Shared Printer Drivers

One important difference between WFW and Windows 95 connections with NT is this: Windows 95 (like NT) provides the capability to connect to a network printer without installing a printer driver. WFW doesn't support this feature. Here's how it works. You only need to install a printer driver on the computer that has the local printer attached to it. Then your NT and Windows 95 clients don't need to have a printer driver installed on their individual computers. When NT or Windows 95 access the remote printer, the driver on the computer that is sharing the printer is used. This eliminates unnecessary redundancy in drivers and allows for easier updating of drivers as new ones become available. Only when connecting to a WFW, UNIX, or Novell Netware printer server will you need to ensure that you've installed the requisite printer driver on Windows 95 or NT machines.

Mapping Drives in Windows 95

After you have your Windows 95 stations on-line, use of network resources is a snap. You might want to refer to a book specifically on Windows 95 for details (such as the author's *Mastering Windows 95*, from Sybex, 1995). But, suffice it to say that Windows 95 makes it easy for users to gain access to files and folders on remote machines, often without mapping them to logical drive letters. You just click on Network Neighborhood and work your way down the tree to the drive, folder, and files you want. Then, you can use them as though they are local. Alternatively, Windows Explorer can be used instead of Network Neighborhood, if you prefer that interface (I do).

There will be times when you'll need or want to map a network drive or shared folder (directory) to a logical drive letter, such as when a program you're using requires a conventional disk drive name for storing or opening data. Older 16-bit non-Windows 95 programs in particular will give you trouble because their File/Open dialogs and network browsers won't let you point to a remote folder as though it were local. In that case, you'll probably want to set up at least a temporary, and possibly a *persistent* logical drive allocation to a networked drive.

1. Find the drive or folder in question via Network Neighborhood, and right-click on it. (A folder/directory has to be formally shared from the server before it can be mapped to a drive letter, incidentally.)
2. From the right-click menu, choose Map Network Drive. The next available logical drive letter is automatically chosen and indicated in the box. Change it if you want to.
3. Click on Reconnect on Login if you want the remove drive/folder to be assigned this drive letter each time you bring up the workstation in question.
4. OK the box. You're mapped. Now you'll have a new drive show up in My Computer and Windows Explorer.
5. To disconnect from the network drive while at the Windows 95 workstation, right-click on the drive icon either via My Computer or Windows Explorer and choose Disconnect.

Managing Your Network from the Command Line

Although the fashion in operating system design nowadays is to create Mac-like graphical user interfaces, and although systems with graphical user interfaces such as Windows NT are easier to learn than cryptic, old-fashioned command-line systems such as DOS and UNIX, there are times when a command-driven system is better. Luckily, the designers of Windows NT have recognized this simple fact. So, unlike Apple's System 7, Windows NT does have a command-line interface that can be used to manage your network.

The most significant advantage that commands have over graphical applications such as File Manager and Print Manager is the capability to string a series of commands together in a batch file to automate some procedure that you perform on a regular basis (such as backing up your server). If you run a college computer lab or a similar network where you need to create user accounts in batches on a regular basis, you might find it easier to write a batch file that creates the users, their home directories, and sharepoints rather than to use User Manager.

Table 15.2 lists the commands (along with their syntax) that enable you to control your network. If you're moving up to Windows NT from a LAN Manager or MS-Net (PC LAN program) environment, many of these commands will look familiar. Each command is discussed in the sections that follow.

> **NOTE**
>
> Remember that you also can use these commands in user logon scripts.

Table 15.2. Commands for controlling your network.

Command	*Description*
`NET ACCOUNTS`	Displays and controls password and account restrictions on a server or domain
`NET COMPUTER`	Creates a computer account in a domain (NTAS only)
`NET CONFIG`	Displays workstation or server configuration information
`NET CONTINUE`	Reactivates suspended services
`NET FILE`	Displays information on file shares and locks; can be used to close shares and unlock files
`NET GROUP`	Maintains global groups

Command	*Description*
NET HELP	Offers help with these commands
NET HELPMSG	Gives a detailed description of an error message's meaning
NET LOCALGROUP	Maintains local groups
NET NAME	Maintains a workstation's messaging name list
NET PAUSE	Suspends a service or printer
NET PRINT	Displays and controls print queues
NET SEND	Sends a message
NET SESSION	Lists and disconnects user sessions
NET SHARE	Makes resource available to share
NET START	Starts a service
NET STOP	Stops a service
NET STATISTICS	Displays network statistics
NET TIME	Sets the workstation's clock to match the server and displays the time
NET USE	Creates a link to a shared resource
NET USER	Maintains user account information
NET VIEW	Displays a list of servers or shares

NET ACCOUNTS

NET ACCOUNTS is used to maintain the accounts database. You can use it to set password and logon requirements for all accounts. Changes you make with NET ACCOUNTS take effect only if user accounts have been set up (by using User Manager or the NET USER command) and if the Net Logon service is running on the server(s) you're trying to update. Net Logon is started automatically when Windows NT starts. NET ACCOUNTS changes affect all users on your server or domain.

If you type NET ACCOUNTS without any parameters, you'll see the current settings for password, logon limitations, and domain information.

Syntax:

```
NET ACCOUNTS [/FORCELOGOFF:{minutes ¦ NO}]
[/MINPWLEN:length][/MAXPWAGE:{days ¦ UNLIMITED}]
[/MINPWAGE:days][/UNIQUEPW:number] [/DOMAIN]
NET ACCOUNTS [/SYNC] [/DOMAIN]
```

Parameters:

`/SYNC`	Updates the user accounts database.
`/FORCELOGOFF:{minutes ¦ NO}`	Sets the amount of grace time a user can be logged on after his or her account expires or valid logon hours expire. Set this to `NO` if you don't want your users forced off.
`/MINPWLEN:length`	Sets the minimum password length from 0 to 14 characters. The default is 6 characters.
`/MAXPWAGE:{days ¦ UNLIMITED}`	Sets the maximum password age from 1 to 49710 days (136 years). Set to `UNLIMITED` to prevent passwords from expiring. `MAXPWAGE` can't be less than `MINPWAGE`. The default is 90 days.
`/MINPWAGE:days`	Sets the minimum password age from 0, for no minimum, to 49710 days. Must be less than `MAXPWAGE`.
`/UNIQUEPW:n`	Requires that a user's passwords be different than the last *n* passwords the user has used. The maximum value is 8.
`/DOMAIN`	Performs the operation on the domain controller of the current domain. Otherwise, the operation is performed on the local workstation if `NET ACCOUNTS` is run on a Windows NT machine that is part of a domain. By default, Windows NT Server computers perform operations on the domain controller.

NET COMPUTER

The `NET COMPUTER` command enables you to add or delete computers from a domain. It must be run from an NT Server machine that is a member of the domain.

Syntax:

```
NET COMPUTER \\computername {/ADD ¦ /DEL}
```

Parameters:

`\\computername`	Specifies the computer to add to or delete from the domain.
`/ADD`	Adds the specified computer to the domain.
`/DEL`	Removes the specified computer from the domain.

NET CONFIG

`NET CONFIG` displays the configuration of the workstation or server service. `NET CONFIG` with no parameters displays a list of configurable services.

Syntax:

```
NET CONFIG [SERVER | WORKSTATION]
```

Parameters:

`SERVER`	Displays information about the configuration of a server.
`WORKSTATION`	Displays information about the configuration of a workstation.

Examples:

```
C:\users\default>net config workstation
Computer name                         \\AST
User name                             Administrator
Workstation active on                 Nbf_SMCISA01 (0000C0295F70)
Streams\NWNBLINK (0000C0295F70)
Software version                      Windows NT 3.10
Workstation domain                    NAOL-DOM
Logon domain                          AST
COM Open Timeout (sec)                3600
COM Send Count (byte)                 16
COM Send Timeout (msec)               250
The command completed successfully.
C:\users\default>net config server
Server Name                            \\AST
Server Comment
Software version                       Windows NT 3.10
Server is active on                    Nbf_SMCISA01 (0000c0295f70)
Streams\NWNBLINK (0000c0295f70)
Server hidden                          No
Maximum Logged On Users                Unlimited
Maximum open files per session         2048
Idle session time (min)                15
The command completed successfully.
```

NET CONTINUE

`NET CONTINUE` restarts a service that's been suspended by `NET PAUSE`.

Syntax:

```
NET CONTINUE service
```

Parameter:	
service	The paused service, which can be one of the following: FTP Server Microsoft DHCP Server Net Logon Network DDE Network DDE DSDM Remote Access Schedule Server Simple TCP/IP Services Telnet Windows Internet Name Service Workstation

NET FILE

`NET FILE` displays, and optionally closes or removes, shared files and file locks. The listing includes the identification number assigned to an open file, the pathname of the file, the username, and the number of locks on the file. Type this command from the server where the file is shared.

> **WARNING**
>
> Closing a file that is actively in use might make the data in the file unrecoverable or corrupted. Use `NET FILE`'s capability to close files as a last resort.

Syntax:

```
NET FILE [id [/CLOSE]]
```

Parameters:

id	The identification number of the file.
/CLOSE	Closes an open file and removes file locks.

Example:

```
C:\users\default>net file
ID          Path                          User name          # Locks

-------------------------------------------------------------------
22          C:\FAX                        administrator      0
25          C:\FAX                        administrator      0
27          D:\WINWORD                    administrator      0
29          D:\WINWORD\CONVINFO.DOC       administrator      0
34          D:\WINWORD                    administrator      0
The command completed successfully.
```

NET GROUP

NET GROUP allows you to maintain global groups on servers. If you type just NET GROUP without any parameters, it displays the group names on the server.

Syntax:

```
NET GROUP [groupname [/COMMENT:"text"]] ¦ groupname {/ADD
[/COMMENT:"text"] ¦ /DELETE} ¦ groupname username
[...] {/ADD ¦ /DELETE}
```

Parameters:

groupname	The name of the group to add, expand, or delete. NET GROUP *groupname* displays a list of users in the group.
/COMMENT:"*text*"	Adds a comment up to 48 characters long for a new or existing group. You must enclose the text in quotation marks.
/DOMAIN	Performs the operation on the domain controller of the current domain. Otherwise, the operation is performed on the local workstation if NET ACCOUNTS is run on a Windows NT machine that is part of a domain. By default, Windows NT Server computers perform operations on the domain controller.
username [...]	A list of the users to add to or delete from a group, separated by spaces.
/ADD	Adds a group or adds a user to a group.
/DELETE	Removes a group or removes a user from a group.

Examples:

```
NET GROUP AR /add /Comment:"Accounts Receivable Group"
```

Creates a group called AR.

```
NET GROUP Beatles john paul george ringo/add
```

Adds John, Paul, George, and Ringo to the group Beatles.

```
NET GROUP BEATLES peteB /Delete
```

Kicks Pete Best out of the group.

NET HELP

`NET HELP` expands a network help message.

Syntax:

`NET HELP` *`command`*

or

`NET` *`command`* `/HELP`

Help is available for

NET ACCOUNTS	NET HELP	NET SHARE
NET COMPUTER	NET HELPMSG	NET START
NET CONFIG	NET LOCALGROUP	NET STATISTICS
NET CONFIG SERVER	NET NAME	NET STOP
NET CONFIG WORKSTATION	NET PAUSE	NET TIME
NET CONTINUE	NET PRINT	NET USE
NET FILE	NET SEND	NET USER
NET GROUP	NET SESSION	NET VIEW

`NET HELP SERVICES` lists network services you can get help on. `NET HELP SYNTAX` explains how to read `NET HELP` syntax lines. `NET HELP` *`command`* `¦ MORE` displays Help one screen at a time.

NET HELPMSG

`NET HELPMSG` displays extended information about Windows NT error network messages when you type `NET HELPMSG` and the error number (for example, `NET HELPMESSAGE NET2182`). Windows NT tells you about the message and suggests action you can take to solve the problem.

Syntax:

```
NET HELPMSG message#
```

Parameter:	
message#	The four-digit number of the Windows NT message you need help with. You don't need to type NET as part of the message number.

Example:

```
C:\users\default>net helpmsg 2182
The requested service has already been started.
EXPLANATION
You tried to start a service that is already running.
ACTION
To display a list of active services, type:
NET START
```

NET LOCALGROUP

NET LOCALGROUP is used to maintain local groups on servers. When used without options, it lists the local groups on the server.

Syntax:

```
NET LOCALGROUP [groupname]
groupname {/ADD ¦ /DELETE}
groupname name [...] {/ADD ¦ /DELETE}
```

Parameters:	
groupname	The name of the local group to add, expand, or delete. Typing just NET LOCALGROUP [*groupname*] results in a list of the users or global groups in a local group.
name [...]	A list of one or more users or groups, separated by spaces, to add to or delete from the local group being maintained. Names can be users or global groups, but not other local groups. If a user is from another domain, preface the username with the domain name (for example, SALES\RALPHR).
/ADD	Adds the users or global groups listed to the local group.
/DELETE	Removes users or global groups listed from the local group.

NET NAME

`NET NAME` adds or deletes a messaging name (alias) at a workstation. A messaging name is a name to which messages are sent. When used without options, `NET NAME` displays the names accepting messages at the computer.

A workstation can accept messages from three types of names:

- Message names, which are added with `NET NAME`.
- A computer name, which is added as a name when the Workstation service is started. This name can't be deleted.
- A username, which is added as a name when you log on (if it's not being used at another workstation). This name can be deleted.

Syntax:

```
NET NAME [name [/ADD | /DELETE]]
```

Parameters:	
name	The name, 1 to 15 characters long, to receive messages.
/ADD	Adds a name to the workstation. Typing `NET NAME` *name* works the same way as typing `NET NAME` *name* `/ADD`.
/DELETE	Removes a name from a computer.

NET PAUSE

`NET PAUSE` suspends a Windows NT service or resource. Pausing a service puts it on hold but doesn't remove it from memory. Typing `NET PAUSE NET LOGON` before you back up your system prevents a user from logging on and interfering with the backup.

Syntax:

```
NET PAUSE service
```

Parameter:	
service	The service to be paused. Can be one of the following: FTP Server Microsoft DHCP Server Net Logon Network DDE Network DDE DSDM

Remote Access
Schedule
Server
Simple TCP/IP Services
Telnet
Windows Internet Name Service
Workstation

NET PRINT

NET PRINT is used to manage print queues. It lists jobs for each queue, showing the size and status of each job and the status of the queue.

Syntax:

```
NET PRINT \\computername\sharename
[\\computername] job# [/HOLD ¦ /RELEASE ¦ /DELETE]
```

Parameters:

\\computername	The name of the server sharing the printer queue(s).
sharename	The name of the shared printer queue.
job#	The identification number assigned to a print job. A server with one or more printer queues assigns each print job a unique number.
/HOLD	Prevents a job in a queue from printing. The job stays in the printer queue, and other jobs bypass it until it's released.
/RELEASE	Reactivates a job being held.
/DELETE	Removes a job from a queue.

NET SEND

NET SEND sends a real-time message to other users, computers, or messaging names on the network. You can send a message only to a name that is active on the network. If the message is sent to a username, that user must be logged on and running the Messenger service to receive the message.

Syntax:

```
NET SEND {name ¦ * ¦ /DOMAIN[:name] ¦ /BROADCAST ¦ /USERS} message
```

Parameters:

name	The user, computer, or messaging name to send the message to. If the name is a computer name that contains blank characters, enclose the alias in quotation marks (" ").
*	Sends the message to all the names in your group.
/DOMAIN[:*name*]	Sends the message to all the names in your domain. If :*name* is replaced by a list of names separated by spaces, the message is sent to all the names in the specified domain or workgroup.
/BROADCAST	Sends the message to all the names on the network.
/USERS	Sends the message to all users connected to the server.
message	The text to be sent as a message.

NET SESSION

NET SESSION lists or disconnects sessions between the server and other computers on the network. When used without options, it displays information about all sessions with the server of current focus.

Syntax:

```
NET SESSION [\\computername] [/DELETE]
```

Parameters:

computername	Lists the session information for the named computer.
/DELETE	Ends the session between the server and *computername* and closes all open files on the server for the session. NET SESSION /DELETE with no *computername* closes all sessions.

Example:

```
C:\users\default>net session
Computer             User name         Client Type     Opens Idle time

----------------------------------
\\DELL               administrator     NT              5     01:34:02
The command completed successfully.
```

NET SHARE

NET SHARE makes a server's resources available to network users by creating a sharepoint for the resource. NET SHARE without parameters lists information about all resources being shared on the server. For each resource, Windows NT reports the device names or pathnames and the associated comment.

Syntax:

```
NET SHARE sharename
sharename=drive:path [/USERS:number ¦ /UNLIMITED] [/REMARK:"text"]
sharename [/USERS:number ¦ /UNLIMITED] [/REMARK:"text"]
{sharename ¦ devicename ¦ drive:path} /DELETE
```

Parameters:

sharename	The name that the resource will be shared by. Type `NET SHARE` *sharename* to display information only about that share.
drive:path	Specifies the absolute path of the directory to be shared.
/USERS:*number*	Sets the maximum number of users who can simultaneously access the shared resource.
/UNLIMITED	Specifies that an unlimited number of users can simultaneously access the shared resource.
/REMARK:"*text*"	Adds a comment to the sharename. Enclose the text in quotation marks.
devicename	One or more printers (LPT1: through LPT9:) shared by sharename.
/DELETE	Stops sharing the resource.

Examples:

```
C:\users\default>net share temp45=c:\temp45 /users:4 /remark:
"This is a test. This is only a tes..."
temp45 was shared successfully.
C:\users\default>net share temp45
Share name        temp45
Path              c:\TEMP45
Remark            This is a test.  This is only a tes...
Maximum users     4
Users
The command completed successfully.
```

NET START

`NET START` starts one of the Windows NT networking services or lists started services.

Syntax:

```
NET START [service]
```

NOTE

To get more help about a specific service, type `NET HELP START` *`service`*.

Parameter:	
`service`	One of the following services: Alerter Computer Browser Directory Replicator Event Log Locator Messenger Microsoft DHCP ServerNBT NBT Net Logon Network DDE Network DDE DSDM Remote Access RPCSS Schedule Server Simple TCP/IP SNMP TCPIP Telnet UPS Windows Internet Name Service Workstation

NOTE

`NET START` also can start network services provided by third parties, such as an NFS client or server.

NET STATISTICS

NET STATISTICS displays statistics for the server or workstation service.

Syntax:

```
NET STATISTICS [WORKSTATION | SERVER]
```

Parameters:

SERVER	Displays server statistics.
WORKSTATION	Displays workstation statistics.

Examples:

```
c>net statistics server
Server Statistics for \\AST
Statistics since 12/17/93 4:00PM
Sessions accepted                  1
Sessions timed-out                 1
Sessions errored-out               0
Kilobytes sent                     130
Kilobytes received                 30
Mean response time (msec)          142
System errors                      0
Permission violations              0
Password violations                0
Files accessed                     45
Communication devices accessed     0
Print jobs spooled                 0
Times buffers exhausted
Big buffers                      0
Request buffers                  0
The command completed successfully.
C:\users\default>
C:\users\default>net statistics workstation
Workstation Statistics for \\AST
Statistics since 12/17/93 4:00PM
Bytes received                               751060
Server Message Blocks (SMBs) received        1285
Bytes transmitted                            97926
Server Message Blocks (SMBs) transmitted     1196
Read operations                              7
Write operations                             1
Raw reads denied                             0
Raw writes denied                            0
Network errors                               0
Connections made                             2
Reconnections made                           2
Server disconnects                           0
Sessions started                             6
Hung sessions                                0
Failed sessions                              0
Failed operations                            0
Use count                                    54
Failed use count                             0
The command completed successfully.
```

NET STOP

`NET STOP` stops the selected service from running. Any users accessing the resource or open files will be denied access. Because some services (Nbt, for example) are dependent on others (such as TCP/IP), stopping one service might stop other services.

Syntax:

```
NET STOP service
```

Parameter:

service	One of the following services: Alerter Computer Browser Directory Replicator Event Log Locator Messenger Microsoft DHCP Server NBT Net Logon Network DDE Network DDE DSDM Remote Access RPCSS Schedule Server Simple TCP/IP SNMP TCPIP Telnet UPS Windows Internet Name Service Workstation

`NET STOP` also can stop network services provided by third parties for use with Windows NT.

NOTE

You must have administrative rights to stop the Server service.

NET TIME

NET TIME displays the time at a server or the time server for a domain, and it optionally synchronizes your system's clock with the time at the server or domain's time server.

Syntax:

```
NET TIME [\\computername ¦ /DOMAIN[:domainname]] [/SET]
```

Parameters:

computername	The name of the server you want to check or synchronize with.
/DOMAIN[:*domainname*]	Specifies the domain to synchronize time with.
/DOMAIN	Performs the operation on the domain controller of the current domain. Otherwise, the operation is performed on the local workstation (if NET ACCOUNTS is run on a Windows NT machine that is part of a domain). This parameter applies only to Windows NT computers that are members of a Windows NT Server domain but that don't have Windows NT Server software installed. By default, Windows NT Server computers perform operations on the domain controller.
/SET	Synchronizes the computer's time with the time on the specified computer or domain.

TIP

Although it's not documented in the online help, you can also specify the /YES switch. This will prevent the system confirmation prompt. This can be quite useful in logon scripts to synchronize all the computer clocks as users log onto the network.

NET USE

NET USE creates or deletes links between local aliases to shared resources. If you type NET USE with no parameters, you get a list of the resources you're currently linked to on other systems on the network.

Syntax:

```
NET USE [devicename] [\\computername\sharename [password ¦ *]]
[/USER:[domainname\]username]
[[/DELETE] ¦ [/PERSISTENT]:{YES ¦ NO}]]
NET USE [devicename] [/HOME [password ¦ *]] [/HOME[/DELETE]
NET USE [/PERSISTENT]:{YES ¦ NO}]
```

Parameters:

devicename	Assigns an alias to link to the resource, or specifies the device to be disconnected. There are two kinds of aliases: logical disk drives (D: through Z:) and printers (LPT1: through LPT3:).
computername	The name of the server containing the printer or directory you want to use. If the computer name contains a space, enclose *computername* in quotation marks (" "). The *computername* can be from the same (or different) workgroup as the machine where the command is run.
sharename	The network name of the shared resource.
password	The password needed to access the shared resource (if any).
*	Produces a prompt for the password. The password is not echoed as you type it at this prompt.
/USER	Specifies a different username with which the connection is made.
domainname	Specifies another domain. If *domainname* is omitted, the current domain is used.
username	Specifies the username to log on to.
/HOME	Connects a user to his or her home directory.
/DELETE	Cancels a network link connection and removes it from the list of persistent connections.
/PERSISTENT	Controls the use of persistent network connections. Persistent connections are reestablished automatically each time you log on.

YES	Saves connections as they are made and restores them at the next logon.
NO	Does not save the connection being made.

NET USER

NET USER is used to maintain the user accounts database on a server or domain. If you enter NET USER with no parameters, you see a list of the users on this server.

NOTE

This command works only on servers.

Syntax:

```
NET USER [username [password ¦ *] [options]] [/DOMAIN]
username {password ¦ *} /ADD [options] [/DOMAIN]
username [/DELETE] [/DOMAIN]
```

Parameters:

username	The name of the user account (up to 20 characters long) to add, delete, modify, or view.
password	Assigns or changes a password for the user's account. A password must be at least as long as the minimum length set by the system administrator and no more than 14 characters long. (See the NET ACCOUNTS command for more information on password restrictions.)
*	Produces a prompt for the password. The password isn't echoed when entered at the prompt.
/DOMAIN	Performs the operation on the domain controller of the current domain. Otherwise, the operation is performed on the local workstation (if NET ACCOUNTS is run on a Windows NT machine that is part of a domain). This parameter applies only to Windows NT workstations that are members of a Windows NT Server domain. By default, Windows NT Server computers perform operations on the domain controller.

continues

Parameters:

/ADD	Adds the user account to the database.
/DELETE	Removes the user account from the database.
/ACTIVE:{YES ¦ NO}	Activates or deactivates the account. A user can't log in with an inactive account. The default is YES.
/COMMENT:"*text*"	Enters a comment for this user (for example, Sammy "The Bull" Provano) up to 48 characters long. Remember to enclose the text in quotation marks.
/COUNTRYCODE:*n*	Uses the operating system country code to implement the specified language files for the user's help and error messages. A value of 0 signifies the default country code.
/EXPIRES:{*date* ¦ NEVER}	Causes the account to expire if *date* is set. NEVER sets no time limit on the account.
/FULLNAME:"*name*"	A user's full name (for example, John Fitzgerald Kennedy as opposed to ThePrez) in quotation marks.
/HOMEDIR:*pathname*	Sets the path for the user's home directory. The path must exist.
/HOMEDIRREQ:{YES ¦ NO}	Is a home directory required? If so, use the /HOMEDIR switch to specify the directory.
/PASSWORDCHG:{YES ¦ NO}	Can this user change his or her own password? The default is YES.
/PASSWORDREQ:{YES ¦ NO}	Must this account have a password at all times? The default is YES.
/PROFILEPATH[:*path*]	Sets a path for the user's logon profile.
/SCRIPTPATH:*pathname*	The location of the user's logon script.
/TIMES:{*times* ¦ ALL}	The logon hours. TIMES is expressed as *day*[-*day*][,*day*[-*day*]],*time*[-*time*][,*time* [-*time*]], limited to one-hour increments. Days can be spelled out or abbreviated. Hours can be 12- or 24-hour notation. For 12 hour notation, use am, pm, a.m., or p.m. ALL means a user can always log on, and a blank value means a user can never log on. Separate day and time entries with a comma, and separate multiple day and time entries with a semicolon.

`/USERCOMMENT:"text"`	Lets an administrator add or change the comment for the account.
`/WORKSTATIONS:{computername[,...] ¦ *}`	The list of up to eight workstations that the user is allowed to log on from. If you don't enter a list, or if the list is *, the user can log on from any workstation.

Examples:

```
C:\users\default>net users howard
User name                     howard
Full Name
Comment
User's comment
Parameters
Country code                  000 (System Default)
Account active                Yes
Account expires               Never
Password last set             12/3/93 8:57AM
Password expires              1/15/94 7:44AM
Password changeable           12/3/93 8:57AM
Password required             Yes
User may change password      Yes
Workstations allowed          All
Logon script
User profile
Home directory
Last logon                    12/16/93 11:01AM
Logon hours allowed           All
Local Group Memberships       *Administrators
Global Group memberships      *None
The command completed successfully.
```

NET VIEW

`NET VIEW` displays a list of resources being shared on a server. When used without options, it displays a list of servers in the current domain.

Syntax:

```
NET VIEW [\\computername ¦ /DOMAIN[:domainname]]
```

Parameters:

`\\computername`	The server whose shared resources you want to view.
`/DOMAIN:domainname`	Specifies the domain for which you want to view the available servers. If *domainname* is omitted, displays all domains in the local area network.

Examples:

```
C:\users\default>net view
Server Name            Remark

-----------------------------------------------------------
\\AST
\\DELL
The command completed successfully.
C:\users\default>net view \\dell
Shared resources at \\dell
Share name   Type         Used as  Comment

-----------------------------------------------------------
NETLOGON     Disk                  Logon server share
The command completed successfully.
```

NT Server

16

IN THIS CHAPTER

Windows NT is a good platform for a small workgroup network supporting word processing, e-mail, and other back office applications. Once you start talking about the so-called "mission critical" applications, from simple accounting to electronic data transfer and customer support, plain old NT just isn't a robust enough platform. For the real, industrial-strength file server, Microsoft has Windows NT Server. NT Server is a superset of Windows NT with several enhancements to make it a better file server.

What's Different About NT Server

NT Server's most important advanced feature is its domain-based naming and logon system. By combining your NT Servers into a domain, you can greatly enhance your control over access to your data and also simplify administering your file servers. All the servers in a domain share a single user database. You need to create a user (using the User Administrator or Net Accounts command) only once for all the servers in your domain, whether you have two or 200.

If you have a large network, you might want to divide it into multiple, separate domains. You might want to create multiple domains to allow departments, divisions, or subsidiaries to manage their own networks without granting too much administrative control to anyone outside the business unit. Multiple domains are also a good idea if you have a large, geographically distributed, wide area network. This will reduce the traffic over the slow WAN lines.

Once you create multiple domains, you'll discover that some of your users need access to data not only in their home domain but also in another. Rather than building walls between domains, or making you create a user ID for that user in each domain he needs data from and making him choose which domain's data he wants to access and log onto that domain, NT Server allows you to define trust relationships to allow users from one domain to access resources on another without logging out of one domain and into another.

If you've tried to manage a network of Windows 3.x workstations, you can attest to the difficulties of allowing users to log onto the network from any station and still get their familiar Windows Desktop and Program Manager groups. Windows NT Server gives you the ability to save users' desktops into User Profiles on a file server. Once you've set up a profile for a user, she will get the same desktop regardless of which Windows NT system she's using.

NT Server includes additional connectivity features including AppleTalk and therefore Macintosh client support. Users on Macintosh computers can access resources, including shared directories and printers on NT Servers, without any special software. Macintosh users will see NT Servers as AppleShare file servers and can access them using the same software and techniques.

Windows NT's Remote Access Service (RAS) is an invaluable tool for remote access to workstations and networks. Unfortunately, it's really useful only for remote network administration or users accessing their office machine from home, because a Windows NT system can support only one RAS session. NT Server adds support for intelligent serial cards such as Digiboards and IBM ARTIC cards to allow a single NT Server system to support multiple remote users.

Almost as significant as NT Server's domain management are its data integrity features. Windows NT supports disk mirroring and RAID level 5 disk arrays with error correction to protect file server data from loss in the event of a disk failure. In both schemes, redundant data is stored on additional disk drives so that a file server can have a drive failure but still continue to operate and serve its users.

The replication service lets you protect your data from server failures as well as drive failures. When you tell a Windows NT Server to replicate a directory, it will automatically copy any files that have changed in that directory and its descendants on the tree to another Windows NT system on the network as soon as the changes have been made. You can think of the replicator as either a file distribution system, sending the latest copies of some new driver to each Windows NT machine in the network, or as an automated backup system, all of which runs transparently to the user. Windows NT systems can receive replicated files, but only NT Servers can distribute files.

The network administration tools let you easily configure and maintain your TCP/IP network with the Dynamic Host Configuration Protocol (DHCP) Manager and Windows Internet Name Service (WINS) Manager. The DHCP Manager is used to dynamically issue client workstations IP addresses from a pool of IP addresses rather than statically assigning an IP address to a client workstation. The WINS Manager associates computer names to IP addresses. Also included is the Network Client Administrator, which is used to create installation diskettes to install network software, and the Remote Boot Manager, which is used to configure diskless workstation clients.

Of course, you also have to remember that NT Server is still Windows NT and has all the advantages of a true 32-bit, multithreaded, preemptive multitasking operating system with memory protection and a red racing stripe. But seriously, some of Windows NT's base features, such as support for RISC processors and especially symmetrical multiprocessing, are more likely to be used with machines running NT Server than users' workstations.

In fact, symmetrical multiprocessing and portability are NT Server's greatest strengths over competing LAN operating systems such as Novell's NetWare and IBM's LAN Server. With Windows NT, you can build a test server for a client/server database application on a simple PC and scale it up to a system with two 486s, four Pentiums, and more. Windows NT, and therefore NT Server, currently supports more than 30 multiprocessor computers from a dozen manufacturers ranging from ALR, AST, and Compaq to Siemens-Nixdorf and

NCR. Some of NCR's multiprocessor systems can have up to 64 486 processors. How's that for a database server?

NT Server Domains

Domains, and domain management, are the most important advance in NT Server. An NT Server domain is a group of NT Servers and LAN Manager 2.1 servers that all have the same user database along with the workstations they serve.

Sharing that common database means that, unlike operating systems such as NetWare 3.x, the user doesn't have to log onto each file server on the network individually. He or she just has to log onto the domain as a whole. As soon as the user is logged onto the domain, his or her access to all the file servers in the domain is established.

Even more important to you, the system administrator, you don't have to create an account on each server in the domain for each user. The user database for each domain is stored on every NT Server in the domain. When you set up your domain, the first file server in the domain becomes the Domain Controller, which stores the master copy of the user database.

NOTE

Although NT Server supports TCP/IP, NT Server domains and TCP/IP domains (that is, compuserve.com or whitehouse.gov) are completely unrelated. A Windows NT Server running TCP/IP will be a member of both an NT Server domain (Accounting, for example) and a TCP/IP DNS (domain naming service) domain. All the servers in an NT Server domain need not be members of the same DNS domain, and vice versa.

When you add or change a user account on an NT Server that is a member of a domain, it updates the master copy of the user database on the domain controller. All you have to do is select the name of the domain. Because the domain controller holds the master user database, User Manager for Domains won't let you edit the user database on NT Servers in a domain unless they are domain controllers.

The other NT Servers, and LAN Manager 2.x servers, that are members of the domain poll the domain controller, looking for changes to the user database about every five minutes. If the database on the domain controller has been changed, the domain controller sends the changes to the other server. In order to keep network traffic down to a reasonable level, NT Server doesn't send the entire database—just the changes since this server's last update.

User logon requests can be processed by any NT Server in the domain and normally are handled by the "nearest" file server to the user (the first to respond to a broadcast request). Because other servers will handle logon requests, if the domain controller should go down, it won't affect network availability except for the resources on the domain controller itself. Until you bring the domain controller back up or promote one of the other NT Servers in the domain to domain controller, you won't be able to add or edit user accounts.

NOTE

Although LAN Manager 2.1 file servers can be members of a domain and can validate logons for OS/2, DOS, and Windows for Workgroups stations, they can't validate Windows NT stations' logon attempts. I recommend upgrading your LAN Manager servers to NT Server as soon as possible.

NOTE

If you're going to mix LAN Manager and NT Servers in the same domain, you should have at least two NT Servers to prevent a failure at the domain controller from stopping your Windows NT users from logging on.

Large networks and networks that have departments that insist on managing their own servers (human resources, for example) can have more than one domain on the same network. You can create links, called trust relationships, between domains to allow users and Windows NT workstations from one domain to access servers in another domain.

This chapter concentrates on how to manage a domain. Chapter 17, "NT Server Gets Big," looks at multiple domain systems and how to plan your large network.

How Domains Are Different from Workgroups

As you saw in Chapter 15, which covered Windows NT's peer networking features, Windows NT servers and workstations can be members of workgroups, which, like domains, group servers together in users' dialog boxes to make it easier for users to find the resources they're looking for. Now we also have NT Server domains. I'm sure you're asking yourself, "Just how are domains and workgroups different, and why should I use either management approach?"

Workgroups are a casual affiliation of servers. Like a commune or co-op, they share their resources on an informal basis. In order to allow a user to access all the servers in a workgroup, you need to create the user's ID on each server individually. Workgroups can be made up of both Windows NT and Windows for Workgroups servers. Windows NT Servers can't be members of a workgroup; they must be members of a domain.

Domains are a more formal and somewhat more secure grouping of servers. Domain servers share a common user database that is replicated for fault tolerance and security. This makes domains easier to administer. Domains can have trust relationships, so a single user ID can be used throughout a large internetwork if you desire. Domains are made up of Windows NT Servers and Windows NT workstations and, to some extent, Windows for Workgroups 3.11 workstations. Chapter 17 talks more about domains.

Creating a Domain

A domain is created whenever you install Windows NT Server on a computer and configure that computer to be a domain controller. It's a good idea to finish planning before you excitedly rip the shrink wrap off the CD-ROM and type `setup`. You should have already come up with a naming convention for domains (or at least a name for the domain that the server you're installing right now is a member of), users, workstations, and servers. I can tell you from sad experience that just naming things willy-nilly leaves you with file servers named ObiWan and Kosher or Moe, Larry, and Curley. You then have to ask yourself, "Are the accounts receivable files on Sleepy or Grumpy?"

It's a good idea to have your names have some relationship in English to the function of the object you're naming. Domains named Accounting and Advertising with servers named AR, AP, and PAYROLL and Art, Media, and Research can help users find the data they're looking for quickly and with a minimum of your direct intervention. Because it's simplest to use user IDs as e-mail mailboxes, you also should somehow associate a user ID with the user (a real person). Wgates, WilliamG., and DaBoss are all user IDs that would pretty clearly identify Bill Gates better than AA001WG would if they were used on a Microsoft e-mail system.

To set up a new domain, follow these steps:

1. Start the Windows NT Setup program.
2. When the Domain Settings Dialog Box appears, click on the Controller in New Domain radio button.
3. Type the name of the new domain in the appropriate box. When you click on OK, your server will send a query over the cable to make sure that the domain you're creating doesn't already exist.

CAUTION

Be very careful when you type the Domain name. Although you can change the name of a domain, you can't move a server from one domain to another without installing all over again.

As soon as you've configured the domain controller and verified that it's working, you can install NT Server on the other servers in the domain. Because these systems have to communicate with the domain controller in order to install NT Server, I recommend that you bring up the domain controller and then try to access it from a Windows NT or Windows for Workgroups workstation to test the installation and LAN hardware. You don't want to find out that the cat ate the terminator after you blew a half hour or more trying to set up server number 2.

To configure a server as a member of a domain, select the Server in Domain option when Setup asks you to define this system as a server or domain controller. The domain controller must be available on the network to join a domain. In order to maintain the exclusive nature of the domain and to keep out the undesirable element, just as you can't join a country club without a recommendation from the membership committee, a server can't join a domain unless the domain administrator has created an account for the machine.

If, as is usually the case, you (the network administrator) are installing NT Server, you can just enter your user ID and password into the setup program's dialog box to have it create the account as you install the system, saving you the effort of entering the account names ahead of time. If you're letting mere users install NT Server and you don't want to trust them with the administrator's password (and who could blame you?), you should set up the server names ahead of time. As a side benefit, this prevents your users from being creative with their server names and makes them stick to the names you want.

As soon as you've given the setup program a name for this computer and a domain name, it asks you to enter the password for the administrator's account. Because the administrator's account has a great potential for abuse, you should definitely set a password. Make sure it's one that you can easily remember.

WARNING

If you forget the password for the administrator account, and you don't have another administrator-level account to use to change it, you'll have to reinstall Windows NT Server and create a new domain.

TIP

Write down the administrator's password and lock it away in a safe place after configuring your domain controller. You might want to keep the password in the same place you keep the Emergency Repair Disk.

TIP

Use User Manager for Domain to create one or two additional user IDs that are members of the Administrators group and record these account passwords right after you install NT Server on your domain controller.

Managing a Domain

If you go to an NT Server, log onto a domain with an administrative ID, and open the Administrative Tools group, shown in Figure 16.1, you'll find that it's just a little different from a standard Windows NT machine. Some of our old friends such as User Manager have changed—in this case into User Manager for Domains—and two new tools, Server Manager and User Profile Editor, give you better control of users, groups, and file servers than you had with workgroups.

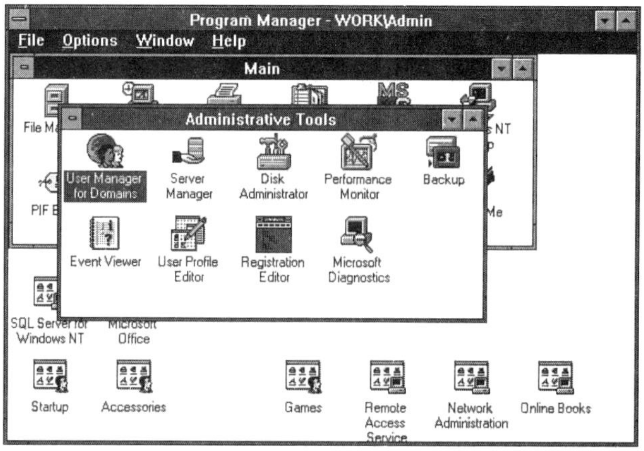

FIGURE 16.1.
NT Server's Administrative Tools group.

These tools let you control which users have access to your domain, when they have access, and what their computing environment and desktop will look like when they're logged in at a Windows NT workstation. With Server Manager, you also can control Windows NT Servers throughout your domain.

User Manager for Domains

You'll probably run User Manager for Domains, shown in Figure 16.2, more than any other NT Server administrative tool. As you saw in Chapter 10, "Windows NT Administration," User Manager is the primary tool system that administrators use for performing such day-to-day administrative tasks as creating users and user groups, maintaining group memberships, and, most important, changing users' passwords when they forget them. User Manager for Domains does all these things, just as Windows NT's User Manager adds several new features to improve system performance and security.

FIGURE 16.2.
User Manager for Domains.

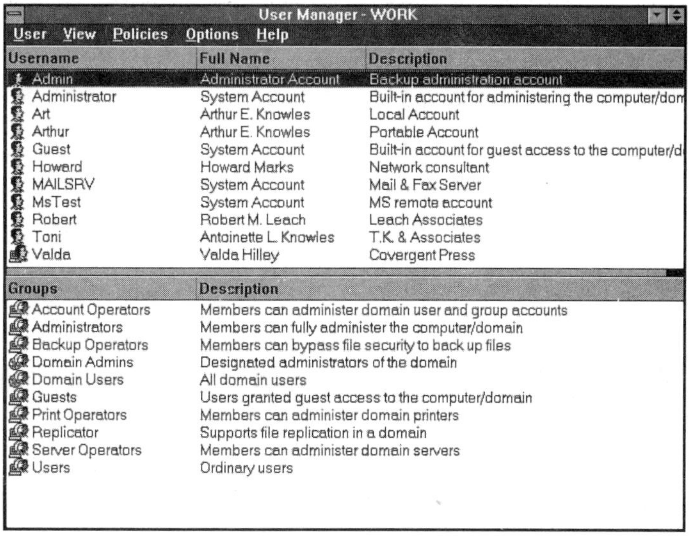

When you start User Manager for Domains, you'll notice two changes to the opening display. The first change is the addition of a View choice to the menu bar. The View menu enables you to sort the list of user accounts by the user account name or the user's full name.

> **NOTE**
>
> This chapter looks at only features of User Manager for Domains that are new or different from the standard Windows NT User Manager.

Because NT Server is designed to support large networks, Microsoft decided that multiple administrators should be able to maintain a single domain's user database at the same time through User Manager for Domains. If you're not the only administrator working on the domain at any given time, User Manager for Domains periodically refreshes your screen to let you see what the other administrators are doing. If you need to refresh your screen right now—to see whether someone else just created the Excel group, for example—you can select View | Refresh, as shown in Figure 16.3.

FIGURE 16.3.
User Manager's View menu.

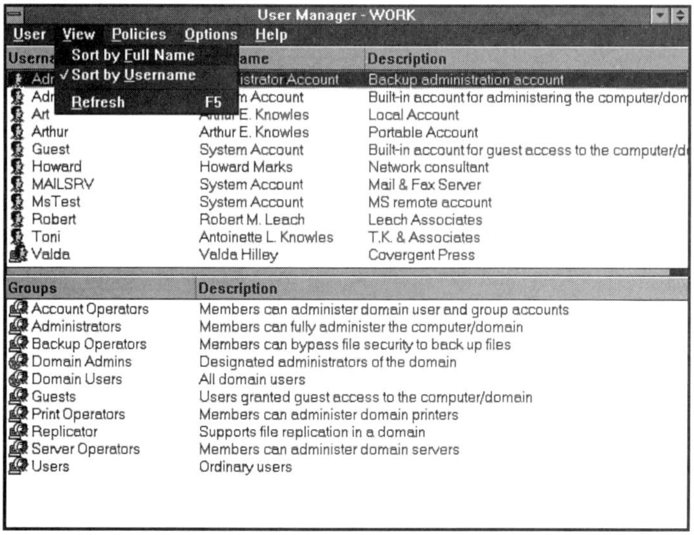

NOTE

If the Low Speed Connections option on the Options menu is selected, you won't be able to change your view or refresh it.

The other obvious change is that NT Server has several predefined groups that didn't exist in Windows NT. Even stranger, two of those groups, Domain Users and Domain Admins, have an icon different from the one you're used to.

Global and Local Groups

NT Server supports not only the user groups that were supported in Windows NT, now called local groups, but also global groups. The new world and users icon represents a global group, and the computer and users icon you know and love represents a local group.

Both global and local groups make administering your network easier by allowing you to grant rights and permissions to and perform actions and access resources for groups of users rather than giving them to each user individually. During my years of managing networks, I've found that the network administrators who have the most hair left on their heads do careful planning and use groups extensively.

After trying many theories and schemes for assigning users rights and permissions, I'm convinced that the easiest way to manage things is to create groups for logical workgroups—for example, users who need access to an application. This lets you set up a new user by simply making him or her a member of the groups that have access to the data this user needs access to. Because you can manage group memberships through User Manager for Domains but you need to set permissions for a single user through File Manager, groups generally are easier to deal with. You can make sure that the group has exactly the right set of permissions, which will, of course, be granted to the group's members. If you try to assign file permissions to each user, occasionally you'll miss a permission and will receive a support call.

I think all file permissions should be granted via groups, except when only two or three users will ever need access to the resource—such as when an assistant needs access to what is otherwise his or her boss's private data.

Global Groups

A domain's global group has as its members user accounts from within the domain. Global groups can't contain other groups, but they can, of course, have members in common and can contain only user accounts from within their home domain. They can't have users from other domains as members.

These groups are called global because they can be used—that is, granted permissions—not only within their own domain but also in any other domain in your network that trusts your domain. Basically, a domain that trusts another domain gives users from the other domain rights in the domain. If you need to know more about multiple domains, Chapter 17 discusses trust relationships in some detail.

Local Groups

Local groups enable you to include global groups, from the domain you're managing or from any domain that your domain trusts, as well as users from your domain and any domain that your domain trusts. Local groups can't contain other local groups. The net result of this is that you can nest groups only two levels deep. A local group can contain global groups, but a global group can contain only users. Because a local group can't contain other local groups, you get only two nested levels.

In addition to the fact that they can have global groups as members, local groups differ from global groups in two important ways. First, as their name implies, local groups are local to the servers that are members of a domain and are not available to other domains, regardless of any trust relationships with other domains. In fact, Windows NT workstations in a domain can even have their own local groups. A domain's local group can be granted permissions on the servers in that domain but not permissions to access resources on the Windows NT workstations. If you want to use a group to provide permission to both servers and workstation resources, you need to create a global group. Second, local groups can be assigned rights—to create new users, for example—as well as permissions to access server resources.

Comparing Global and Local Groups

The following list shows the contrasts between local and global groups:

Group Type	*Properties*
Global	Can contain only users from the same domain it exists in. Can be used to grant permissions. Can be used in its domain and domains that trust its domain.
Local	Can contain users and global groups from its domain and any domain its domain trusts. Can be used to grant permissions and rights. Can be used only on servers in its domain.

Just as user groups make managing a file server easier, global groups make managing a multiple domain system easier by allowing you to grant access rights and permissions to users from outside your domain in groups. You can allow senior executives from the home office to access your accounting data just by granting permissions to the group HQ\BigBrass in File Manager. Any members of the global group BigBrass in the HQ domain can then access the resources you've given them permissions to. This means that the administrator in the HQ domain is controlling which users have access to your data, because he or she has control over who's a member of the group.

Let's assume that you have a multidomain network and that each domain has a group called WINWORD that is the group of users allowed to run Word for Windows. If you make these groups global, it's a simple matter to grant permissions to the WinWord directory in your domain to the WINWORD group of one or two other domains. If they do the same for your domain, you can back each other up, providing all the users access to the Word for Windows program even if the server in their domain has crashed or is otherwise unavailable.

The ability of local groups to have global groups as members also makes managing the network easier. In the example just discussed, you could create a local group that contained your global WINWORD group as well as the WINWORD group for all the other domains you want to share data with. This way, only one group must have permissions, and adding new domains just means adding a member to my local group.

Built-In Groups

NT Server adds several new predefined groups to the set in Windows NT and changes how some others act. The Power Users group has been dropped. Let's take a quick look at each of the built-in groups and how they should be used.

Everyone

Everyone is not actually a group, because it doesn't show up in User Manager for Domains' list of groups. It's a placeholder for all users accessing the domain. If you grant permissions by using the Everyone entry on File Manager or grant rights through the Rights dialog box in User Manager for Domains, those abilities will be given to every user in the current domain, users in trusted domains, and guests who access the server.

Guests

The least-privileged group, Guests, is designed to be used to allow unknown users access to your domain. That might mean any user from a domain you trust or the Clanton gang. The only right the Guests group has by default is to log onto the domain across the wire.

Users

This local group contains every user in the domain. As new users are created, they're added to the Users local group. Being a member of the Users group gives accounts the capability to

- log on at a Windows NT workstation
- lock and shut down the workstation
- store a user profile on the workstation (user profiles are discussed later)
- create and delete local groups on the workstation
- maintain the membership list for groups the user has created

Note that members of the User group don't automatically get the right to log on at a machine running NT Server—just to log on across the network.

Domain Users

The Domain Users global group also includes all the members of the domain as they are created. The Domain Users global group also gives an administrator in one domain a convenient way to allow all the users in another domain to access his system just by making, for example, HQ\Domain Users a member of his Users local group.

When a Windows NT workstation is made a member of a domain, that domain's Domain Users group is automatically made a member of the local User group.

Backup Operators

The Backup Operators group has the capability to log onto a domain from a workstation or a server, back it up, and restore the data. Backup operators also can shut down servers or workstations.

Print Operators

The Print Operators group has the capability to log onto a domain from a workstation or a server and share, stop sharing, and manage printers on NT Servers. They also can shut down servers.

Because you want to have your file servers in centralized locations for security, power, communications, and environmental reasons, but you want your printers in the user environment to make life easier for the users, you'll probably want to connect your printers not to the printer ports on your file server but to selected workstations that will also act as print servers. If you do this, you'll probably want to give the Print Operators group the right to share printers on those workstations. Unfortunately, Print Operators is a local group, so you'll have to do a little extra work:

1. Create a global group in your domain that has as its members the users you want to give the ability to manage printers.
2. Make this global group a member of the Print Operators local group to give the users the rights they need in the local domain.
3. On each workstation whose printer you want to have these users manage, add the new global group to the workstation's Power Users group.

Account Operators

Account operators are sort of junior administrators. They have the ability to create and modify local and global groups, except the built-in Administrators, Server Operators, Account Operators, Print Operators, and Backup Operators groups and the user accounts for the members of the Administrators accounts.

Unlike administrators, account operators can't grant users rights.

If you're in the corporate MIS department, it might be a good idea to make a user in each department an account operator and delegate all the day-to-day password changes and new user account creations without giving them the power to lock you out.

Server Operators

If an account operator is a junior administrator who creates user IDs and changes passwords, a server operator is a technician maintaining the server itself. Server operators can share and stop sharing resources, make backups, format disks, and so on. Your departmental administrator probably should be a server operator too.

Administrators

Members of the Administrators group have all the rights and abilities of users in other groups, plus the ability to create and manage all the users and groups in the domain. Only members of the Administrators group can modify NT OS files, maintain the built-in groups, and grant additional rights to groups.

Unlike some other operating systems such as LAN Manager 2.x or Novell's NetWare, NT Server administrators don't have unlimited access to the data on the server. If an administrator is working at a file server, she can access data on NTFS partitions only if she has sufficient permissions. An administrator can access data she doesn't have permissions to only by taking ownership and granting herself permission, which can leave tracks a mile wide on the audit trail.

Domain Admins

The Domain Admins global group starts off with the administrators account as its only member. Because the Domain Admins global group is a member of the Administrators local group, any users you add to the Domain Admins group automatically get any rights and privileges you might grant to the administrators account.

When you create accounts that you want to be administrators on your domain, you should make those users members of the Domain Admins group rather than the Administrators group to allow them to also be administrators at each Windows NT workstation in the domain. When you make a Windows NT workstation a member of a domain, it automatically makes the domain's Domain Admins global group a member of its Administrators local group. Therefore, domain administrators are automatically administrators of not only the servers but also of the workstations in the domain. The Domain Admins group also allows the administrator of another domain to grant all your administrators access to their system by granting permissions to the Domain Admins group.

The User Menu

As soon as you start actually using User Manager for Domains, you'll see that the ability to sort your users and additional groups is just the tip of the iceberg. The User menu alone has several new choices, as you can see from Figure 16.4.

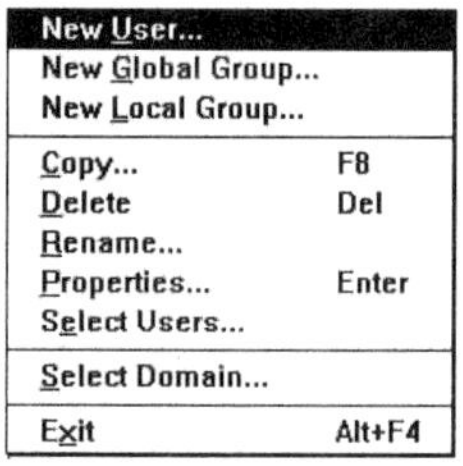

FIGURE 16.4.
User Manager for Domains' User menu.

New Global Group

The first new option enables you to create a new global group. As you can see from the dialog box shown in Figure 16.5, creating a global group is somewhat different from creating a local group. All you have to do is enter the new group's name and description and select the users you want to have as members of the group. You can select one or more users using the Windows Shift-click and Ctrl-click techniques. Click on the Add or Remove buttons as needed.

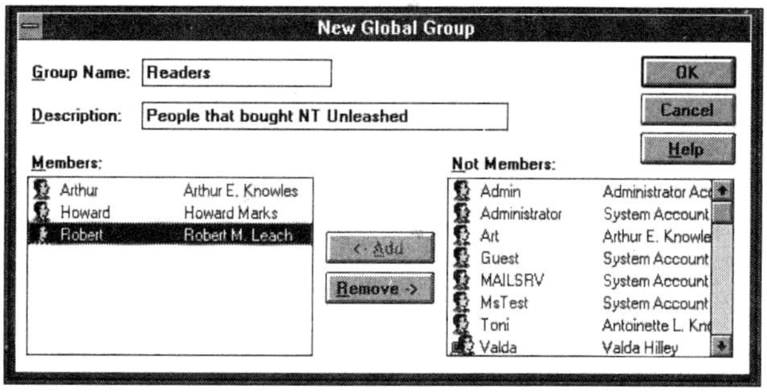

FIGURE 16.5.
Creating a global group.

User Properties

When you create a new user or try to change a user's properties, you see the dialog box shown in Figure 16.6. The Hours, Logon From, and Account buttons give you tighter control over users in NT Server domains that you have on Windows NT workstations.

Profiles

Because we usually think of a PC as having a single, primary user, most managers of standalone NT machines probably haven't spent much time working with user profiles. After all, if Steve is the only person who ever uses his computer, why should I spend a lot of time making sure that multiple users can log onto the system and each have a unique working environment down to Program Manager groups, color scheme, wallpaper, and finger-tapping mouse cursor? A user's profile is the user's Windows computing environment, including a home directory, logon script batch file that runs automatically every time the user logs onto the machine, and all the nuances of his or her Windows environment.

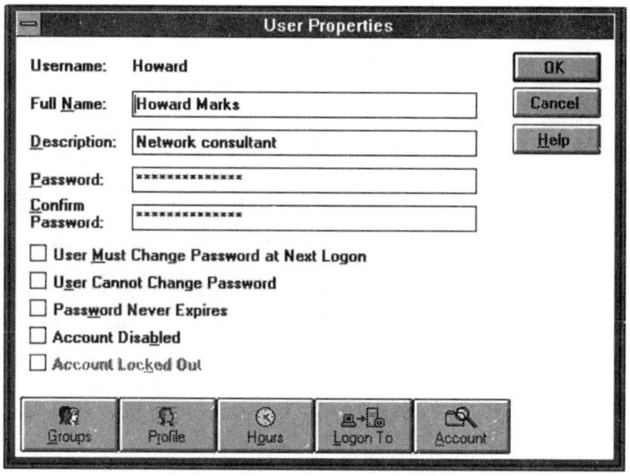

FIGURE 16.6.
The User Properties dialog box.

After you network your systems, you'll find that users actually try to log onto the network from workstations other than the one on their desks all the time. Bob might want to show Joe a report draft on the PC at Joe's desk, or you might log on from Susan's desk to troubleshoot her printing problems. Under Windows NT, the user's profile is stored on each machine that he logs on to, so the user will have a different computing environment on each machine on the network.

NT Server enables you to log in from any machine on the network and still get the same user profile. It also enables you as the system administrator to control users' profiles so you can keep FreeCell and Tetris off the desktops of your game addicts. User profiles are discussed later in this chapter in the section titled "User Profile Editor."

Click on the Profile button, and you'll see the dialog box shown in Figure 16.7. Here you can enter the filename for the logon script, the path or sharepoint, and the drive letter to use for the user's home directory, just like with Windows NT. You also can enter a path for the user profile file, which can be on an NT Server, which enables the user to have the same profile regardless of the machine he or she logs on from.

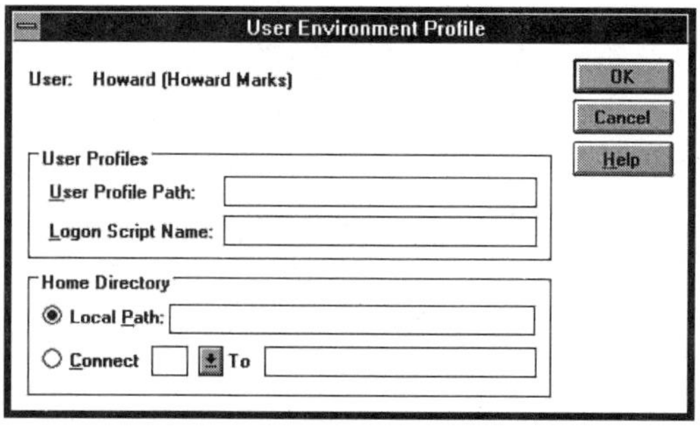

FIGURE 16.7.
The User Environment Profile dialog box.

Hours

By clicking on the Hours button, you can control when a user is allowed to log onto your network. (See Figure 16.8.) You might decide that you don't want students logging on between 4 and 6 a.m., when they tend to get messy. More likely, you don't want anyone logged on from 4 to 6 a.m. so that you can run backups or do other system maintenance.

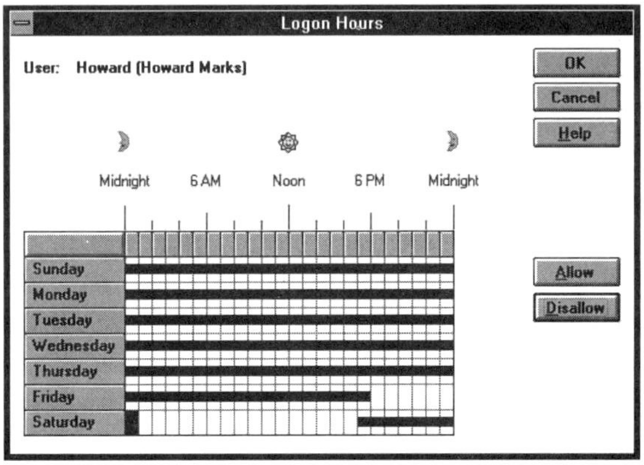

FIGURE 16.8.
Setting the user's allowed logon hours.

When you click on the Hours button and get the dialog box in Figure 15.8, you can control the user's allowed access times by selecting a block of time, in minimum half-hour intervals, during the week and then clicking on the Allow or Disallow buttons. Times users are allowed to log on are indicated by blue bars. Times they are forbidden access are empty squares. Click on the box above a time slice to select that time slice for all seven days a week. If you want to allow or disallow access for a whole day, click on that day to select all 48 half-hour slices.

Unlike most operating systems, NT Server lets you decide how to handle users who are logged in when their allotted time runs out. You can either allow them to continue working until they log off or have them forcibly bounced from the system at the end of their allotted time. Set this option through the account's policy function, discussed in the section titled "Setting Account Policies."

Logon From

You also can limit which machines on your network you want to allow any given user to log on from by clicking on the Logon From button. I've used this feature to limit administrator accounts to be valid only from stations in the MIS department or the administrator's own workstations.

I once got into trouble with this feature, though. The human resources department in a brokerage firm was very concerned about the fact that a network administrator under

NetWare automatically had access to every file on the file server (which isn't true of NT Server). They had us set up the system and show them how to change passwords and perform other basic administrative tasks. They got themselves in trouble by making the administrator account valid only from the human resources director's workstation. That system was sick in bed with a nasty virus from Duke Nuke 'em, which the director's son had downloaded from Larry's Pirate Paradise BBS. No one could administer the network.

You can limit the stations that a user or a group of users can log in at by clicking on the Logon From button to get the dialog box shown in Figure 16.9. Select User May Log On To These Workstations and enter the names of up to eight workstations the user can log on from into the boxes provided. The workstations need not be defined as having accounts in the domain or be turned in order for you to list them here. However, they will need accounts if a user is actually going to log on.

FIGURE 16.9.

Setting the allowed logon addresses for a user.

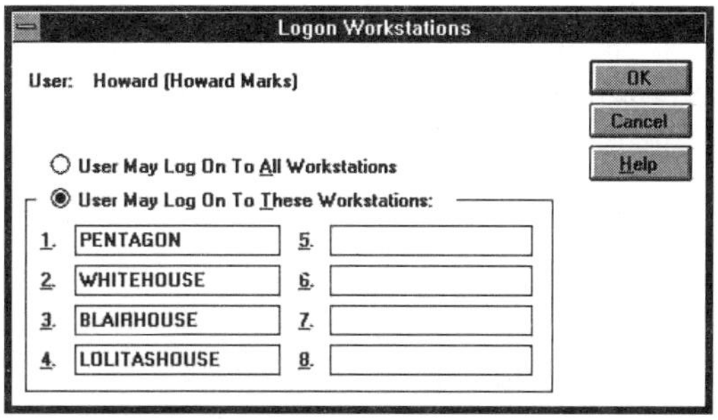

> **NOTE**
>
> Make sure that you have allowed for a failed workstation. You should be able to log on as an administrator from at least two workstations.

Account

If you click on the Account button, you can set a few more options for the user through the dialog box shown in Figure 16.10.

Here you can set an expiration date for the account, a useful feature for summer interns, students, and temporary workers. It prevents them from logging on if they can finagle their way to a workstation. You don't have to remember to delete or disable their account. If they should return to work, you can just change the date to re-enable the account.

You also can declare this account to be a local account. Most user accounts you create will be global accounts. A global account allows users to log on a server or a workstation, depending on their rights. Global accounts also are available in any domain that trusts your domain. You should use global accounts for your normal rank-and-file users.

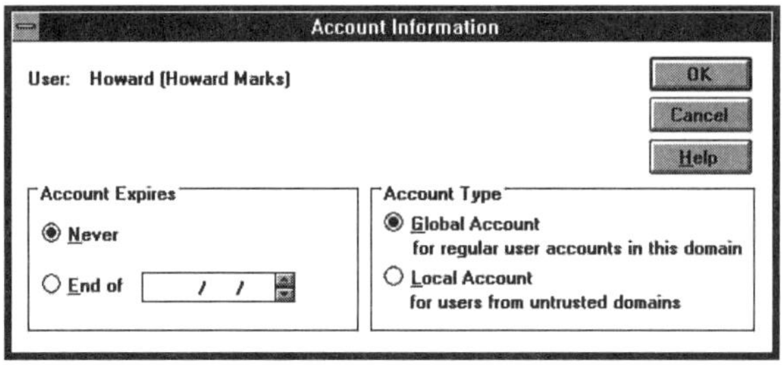

FIGURE 16.10.
The Account Information dialog box.

However, suppose, for example, that there is a user with an account in another domain that you don't trust, perhaps KGB\Sergi or Russia\BYeltsin. You can allow these users to access your domain across the network by either trusting their domain (but who really wants to trust the KGB even if the Cold War *is* over?) or by creating a local account for the user on your domain.

You can grant local users access rights and permissions just like you can with a global user, but your local accounts won't be available in domains that trust your domain. That's actually how you want it, because the administrator of the domain that trusts yours should be able to decide whether he trusts anyone at the KGB and not just take your word for it.

Select Users

The Select Users option enables you to highlight users who are members of a global or local group. Once these users are selected, you can change their properties or delete them. Of course, you also can use the normal Windows selection methods to select several users at a time.

When you choose Select Users, you see the dialog box shown in Figure 16.11. If you want to select all the members of the Domain Admins group, click on that group and then click on the Select button. If you want all the users that are members of the Domain Admins group or the Backup Operators group, select Backup Operators and click on the Select button again. If you want users who are members of Domain Admins but not members of Backup Operators, click on Backup Operators and then click on the Deselect button.

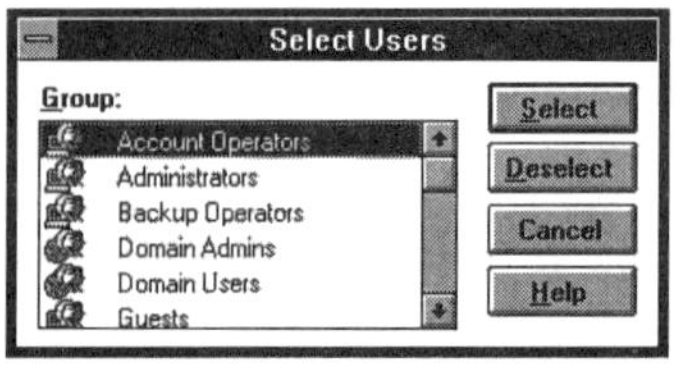

FIGURE 16.11.
The Select Users dialog box.

If you try to change users' properties after selecting more than one user, you'll get the dialog box shown in Figure 16.12 rather than the usual User Properties dialog box. Here you can change the properties for users en masse. Note that a few properties can't be changed for more than one user at a time, such as full names and passwords. Note that this is a good time to use the `username` environment variable to set paths, logon scripts, or home directories.

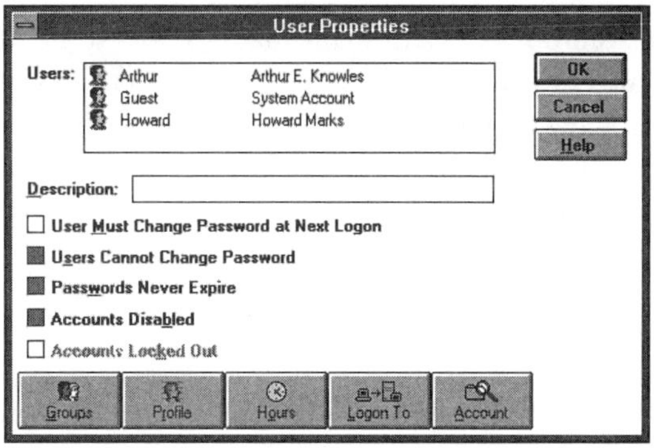

FIGURE 16.12.
The User Properties dialog box for multiple users.

If you decide that you don't want anyone from accounting logged in from 3 a.m. to 6 a.m., you can just click on the Hours button and change the allowed logon hours for all the users.

Select Domain

The Select Domain option enables you to manage other domains where your account is a valid administrator. When you click on Select Domain, you get a list box with the names of all the domains active on your network, as shown in Figure 16.13.

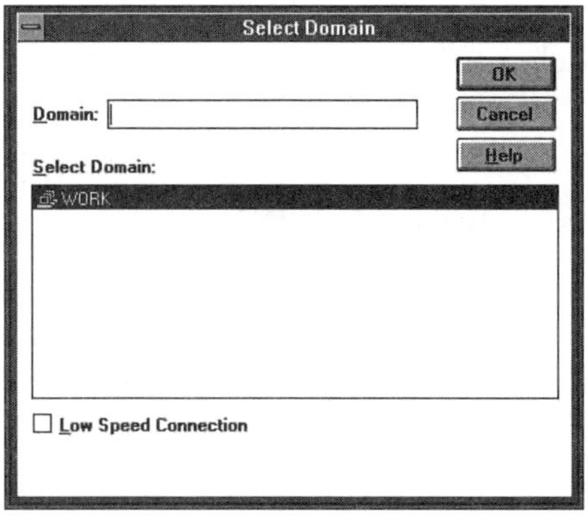

FIGURE 16.13.
Selecting a domain to manage.

If you select another domain and click on OK, you'll see the user database for that domain—assuming, of course, that you have the correct security clearance. You also can enter the name of a domain, or a computer that has its own user database, such as a Windows NT workstation, in the domain box. If you enter the name of a Windows NT workstation, you can edit the local users and groups on that station. Because NT Servers don't have their own user databases but copies of the domain database, entering an NT Server's name in the domain box is the same as selecting the domain name.

If you're administering a domain that is across some low-speed (or especially busy) connection such as a wide area link, you might find that User Manager for Domain's periodic user list updates and screen refreshes take a long time and/or clog the expensive low-speed link. If you enable the Low Speed Connection box, User Manager for Domains will take the following steps to minimize the required network traffic:

- The users in the domain won't be listed automatically. You'll have to enter a user's name in the appropriate dialog box to delete, rename, or otherwise modify that user's account.
- The groups in the domain won't be listed automatically. You'll have to enter the name of a local group in the appropriate dialog box to edit the group.
- You can't edit or create global groups. You *can* make users members of the group, or have them quit, by editing the user.
- Because there are no lists, the options on the View menu (Sort Order and Refresh) don't change how the list looks.

If you're not sure whether you should use the Low Speed option, you can either rely on User Manager for Domains to remember whether you selected it the last time (it keeps the last 20 domains you've managed and remembers whether they were managed over high- or low-speed connections) or let User Manager for Domains automatically test the connection and see whether it thinks the connection is fast enough to use a high-speed connection. If it's not, the system will automatically use its low-speed option.

If the system chooses low speed but you need to see the lists or modify a global group, you can change the connection speed through the Options menu.

Setting Account Policies

NT Server enables you to set the same password information as Windows NT. You can limit the minimum and maximum password age, minimum length, password uniqueness, and the maximum number of logon attempts to keep the hackers at bay through the Account Policy dialog box, shown in Figure 16.14.

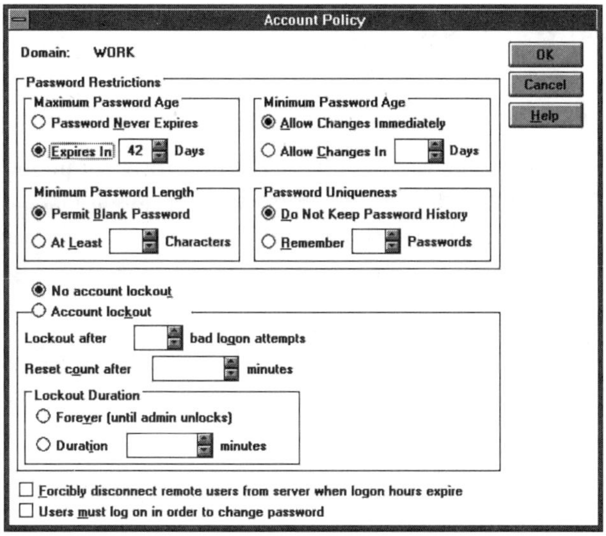

FIGURE 16.14.
The Account Policy dialog box.

You also can decide what to do when a user stays logged on past the end of his allotted time. If you enable the Forcibly disconnect remote users from server when logon hours expire option, users logged on to the server when their allowed time ends will be logged out. (You set the allowed time by clicking on the Hours button in the User Properties dialog box.) If you don't select this option, the user will be able to stay on the system indefinitely as long as he's logged in. He just won't be able to log back on if he logs off during one of his unauthorized periods.

Another option is to force users to log on before they can change their current password. This forces users with expired passwords to request a system administrator to change their password, rather than logging on with an expired password and then changing it. This is another tool that can help keep unauthorized people out of your system.

NOTE

If you're setting user time restrictions to allow housekeeping such as backups when no users are logged in and holding files open, select the Forcibly Disconnect option.

WARNING

With many DOS and Windows applications, forcibly logging a user out while he or she has a file open might corrupt the data in the file.

Trust Relationships

Chapter 17 is pretty much all about trust relationships, but because you set them through User Manager for Domains and that's part of *this* chapter, I have to say something, right?

A trust relationship is the ability of the administrator in one domain (the trusting domain) to use global users and groups from another domain (the trusted domain) to grant rights and permissions. By selecting Policies | Trust Relationships, you can have the domain you're managing trust other domains or have other domains trust yours.

NOTE

A trust relationship is a one-way path. If you want to have two domains fully share users and groups, you need to have the National Security Agency trust the CIA, as well as have the CIA trust the NSA.

NOTE

Trust relationships are nontransferable. If, for example, the CIA domain trusts the NSA domain, and the NSA domain trusts something so secret that you're not even allowed to know its name (let's call it Project X), that doesn't allow the CIA domain to trust Project X's domain.

When you select Trust Relationships from the dialog box shown in Figure 16.15, you see a list of the domains that this domain trusts and another list of the domains that trust this domain. To create a new trust relationship, first you have to add the trusting domain to the Permitted To Trust list on the trusted domain. When you do that, you have to enter the name of the domain and set a password that the trusting domain will use when it tries to trust this domain.

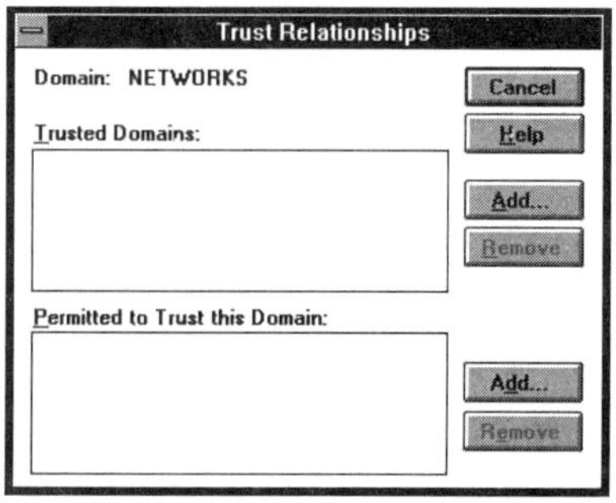

FIGURE 16.15.
Setting trust relationships.

Next, you have to manage the trusting domain and add the trusted domain to its trusted domains list, entering the password that was assigned by the administrator of the trusted domain.

NOTE

After the trusting domain logs onto the trusted domain the first time, the systems will agree on a new password, which will be unknown to both administrators. If you need to break a trust relationship and reestablish it, you need to remove both ends and start from scratch so that you can reset the password.

User Profiles

As you've seen, a user's profile defines how the user will interact with Windows NT. His or her Program Manager groups, network connections, and other information are all stored in the user's profile.

When a user logs into a Windows NT workstation for the first time, the system makes a copy of the default profile for that user. Any changes the user makes during a session, such as changing the wallpaper, are saved to the user's profile on the system drive. The next time the user logs in, she sees the changes she made in her previous session.

So what gets saved in a user profile?

- Program Manager groups, their arrangement on the Desktop, and all Program Manager settings
- File Manager settings, including network connections
- The configuration of the command prompt, including colors and fonts
- Network printer connections and other Print Manager settings
- Color scheme, mouse parameters, Desktop including wallpaper and screen saver, keyboard, international, and sound options as set in Control Panel
- Additional user data from applications such as Cardfile and Paintbrush

If you're still thinking in Windows 3.x terms, a user profile is made up of the .GRP files, most of WIN.INI, and most of the other .INI files, along with stuff Windows 3.x just doesn't do.

NT Server Enhancements

NT Server extends the user profile concept to enable users to store their profiles on the file server. That way, they can have the same desktop every time they log in at any workstation on the network. This lets Vice President Jane run her address book program from the Paris office or lets you log in at a user's workstation and use the diagnostic tools you've installed into your desktop.

You also get the ability to control users' profiles. You can have several users share a mandatory profile that they can't change. This makes managing groups of reservation clerks, bank tellers, or other users with a well-defined set of tasks to perform easier, because you can just set new users' profiles and know that all their options will be set properly. The fact that the various users can't change their profiles will save you hundreds of tech support calls as users try to figure out how to install their new games, not to mention the productivity boost provided by their not playing games.

Even if you decide to allow your users to change their environments, you can control how much they can change things. This can protect you from users who have a little less technical acumen than they think they do.

Mandatory and Personal User Profiles

A Windows NT profile is actually the registry hive of the user's information saved to a file on the local workstation, or, with NT Server, on a file server. When the user logs on, his or her profile is copied from the file into the registry to affect the current Windows NT session.

NT Server divides user profiles into two categories—mandatory profiles for users you want to use a working environment that you control, and personal user profiles for users you want to allow more control over their own environments. You can think of a mandatory profile as a read-only file. A user with a mandatory profile can rearrange icons or make other changes to his or her registry during a Windows NT session, but the user won't be able to save any of those changes to the profile file.

Personal user profiles, on the other hand, are read-write. Subject to the restrictions you set for him, each user who has a personal user profile can change his computing environment and save those changes for his next session.

Assigning multiple users the same user profile sounds like a good idea. You need to create only one profile rather than 10 or 15 profiles. If you later decide that you want to change the profile in some way, such as adding a new application or changing the user's wallpaper to the new corporate logo, you need to make the change in only one place.

If, however, you set up several users to use the same personal user profile, you'll find a little problem. Any change that any of the users makes to the profile will show up on all the other users' desktops the next time they log in. You're almost guaranteed to have one user who loves an orange-and-black color scheme, from her Princeton days, teamed with a die-hard Harvard fan who insists on crimson.

The solution is to share only mandatory profiles. Because the users can't save their changes anyway, they can share a profile without a problem.

Creating and Editing User Profiles

Your first step in setting up user profiles for your users is to run Program Manager and Control Panel to set the workstation's computing environment the way you want it. You can then use the NT Server User Profile Editor to save to a file the Registry hive with the configuration information you've set up. Because you've just finished spending the past three weeks getting your own account's configuration just the way you want it, you'll probably want to create a new administrator-level user ID to use while creating profiles.

As soon as you've saved the profile, you can use User Manager for Domains to tell the user's account to use the profile.

Remember that some of the information in a profile, including icons, window locations, and sizes, is dependent on the video display of the workstation. You should create user profiles on a system that has the same video subsystem as the users who will be using the profile. Multiple users with different video displays might not be able to share a mandatory profile. You'll have to set up a mandatory profile for each resolution.

If you really want your users to be able to log on from different workstations and be able to use the same profile, you have to make sure that all the application icons in the profile's Program Manager groups access programs and working directories that are accessible through the same paths from each workstation the user is likely to log on at. This could mean keeping all your applications on NT Servers with the network connections stored as part of the profile or keeping applications in exactly the same directory on each workstation so that the pointer to C:\WINAPPS\WINWORD is the Word for Windows directory for all the workstations your users are likely to log on from.

Default Profiles

If you log onto a Windows NT workstation using an account that doesn't have a user profile assigned to it, or if your profile is unavailable (for example, if the server you keep it on is down), Windows NT will load the local station's default user profile. Any changes you make to your configuration during that session will be saved as a local user profile for the account you used to log on.

Each Windows NT system also has a default system profile that's used to define how the system will behave when no users are logged in. If your boss thinks your company logo is the highest form of art and should be displayed on every workstation on your network, even when the users aren't logged in, you can edit the default system profile for each station (a thankless task not worth one percent of the energy it takes to perform).

User Profile Editor

In addition to simply letting you save your current configuration as a mandatory or user's personal profile, the User Profile Editor also lets you control how much a user will be allowed to change his or her configuration. Through the User Profile Editor, you get all the control that the Windows 3.x PROGMAN.INI restrictions section gave you and more.

1. Set Program Manager, Control Panel, and other options the way you want them.
2. Logged in as an administrator-level user, start up the User Profile Editor. You'll see the dialog box shown in Figure 16.16.

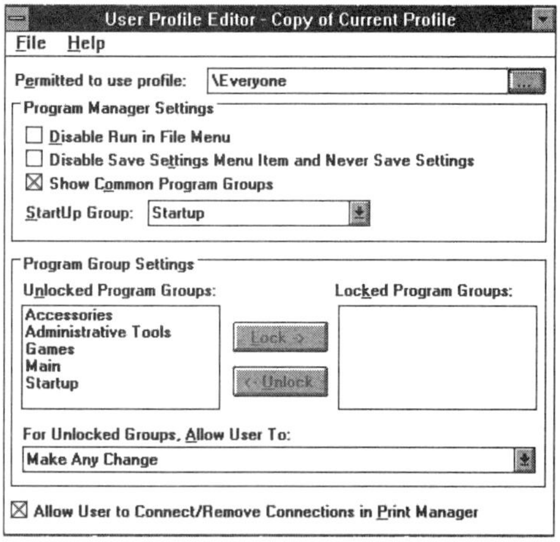

FIGURE 16.16.
The User Profile Editor.

3. Click on the Browse button (the one with the ... on it) to select the user or group that will be allowed to use this profile. Type the user or group name in the Permitted to use profile box. If you select a group, all the members of that group will be allowed to use this profile if you, or they, select it as their profile in User Manager for Domains.
4. Use the Program Manager Settings options to control how the user's Program Manager will act:

   Put an X in Disable Run in File Menu to gray out the Run command in Program Manager's File menu. This prevents a user from selecting Run from the File menu to run Duke Nuke 'em or some other forbidden application.

NOTE

Simply disabling the Run option won't prevent your users from running applications you don't want them to. At the very least, you'll also need to prevent them from opening a command-line window and running File Manager, where just double-clicking on an executable file will run it.

Put an X in Disable Save Settings Menu Item and Never Save Settings if you want the user to see the same Program Manager groups in the same places each time they log on, regardless of what they've done during their Windows NT session.

Put an X in Show Common Program Groups if you want this user to be able to access the common program groups. If you don't put an X here, the user will be able to see only his or her personal groups.

5. Select a group from the Startup Group pull-down menu to automatically start all the applications in that group when the user logs on.

NOTE

Editing an existing user profile requires that you log on as an administrative-level user who has the profile you want to edit as their logon profile. Because editing a profile with limited rights would be quite difficult, none of the check box limitations has any effect on administrator-level users. Administrators will be affected by the startup group you set.

6. The Program Group Settings area allows you to lock some or all of the Program Manager groups. Locking all the common groups that you give to most of your users makes it easier to provide tech support, because you can tell users to click on the file cabinet in the main group in order to open File Manager. If you've let the users change their groups, the file cabinet might have been moved to the furniture group. When you lock a group, you prevent users from changing the group or any of the icons in the group.
7. Even if you're leaving some of the users' groups unlocked, you might not want to give them complete control over the unlocked groups. You can limit users to one of four levels of control over their unlocked groups:

Level	*Description*
Make Any Changes	Allows the user to create and delete unlocked program groups and make any and all changes to unlocked groups.
Create/Delete/Change Program Items	Prevents the user from creating, deleting, or renaming groups. Allows the user to create, modify, and delete icons and their properties.
Change All Program Item Properties	Prevents the user from creating or deleting program items or groups. Allows the user to change properties of existing items.
Change Program Item Properties Except Command Line	Prevents the user from creating or deleting program items or groups. Allows the user to change the properties of existing items except the command line. This prevents a user from using an existing icon to run an unauthorized application.

8. You also can prevent users from changing their network printer connections. You'll find this especially handy when your users discover that the QMS color laser printer in the art department makes great birthday party invitations.
9. Finally, you need to save the profile. From the File menu, you can save the profile as a file on a file server to be used as a user or mandatory profile, or you can make this profile one of the default profiles for the system you're working on.

NOTE

NT Server uses a file's extension to determine whether a profile is mandatory or a personal user profile. Mandatory profiles must have a .MAN extension, and user profiles must have a .USR extension.

Server Manager

NT Server's Server Manager extends Control Panel's Server and Services applets to enable you to manage not only the server process on the computer you're now working at, but also other servers in your domain. Like Control Panel, Server Manager allows you to control user connections, shares, open files, and the replication service.

Server Manager is also the tool you use to manage the members of your domain, both servers and workstations, adding and deleting members and promoting or demoting Domain Managers and servers. You also can remotely manage file sharepoints on Windows NT workstations and NT Servers in your domain.

When you start Server Manager, you see the dialog box shown in Figure 16.17. It lists the computers that are members of the domain you're currently logged on to. One, and hopefully only one, of the NT Servers will be identified as a Windows NT 3.50 Controller; this is your domain controller. Other NT Servers will be identified as Windows NT 3.50 Servers. Windows NT systems in the domain will be identified as Windows NT 3.5 Workstations.

FIGURE 16.17.
The Server Manager screen.

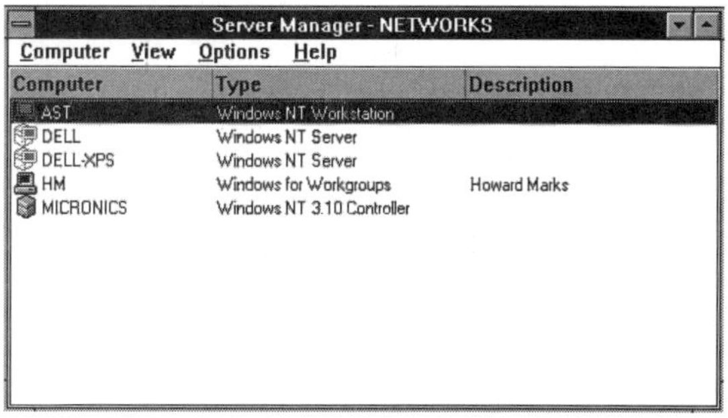

> **NOTE**
>
> In addition to Windows NT 3.5 Controllers, Servers, and Workstations, you might also see Windows NT 3.10 Controllers, Servers, and Workstations, as well as LAN Manager Servers and Windows clients.

> **NOTE**
>
> Only members of the Administrators, Domain Admins, and Server Operator groups can run Server Manager. Members of the Account Operators group can run Server Manager, but only to add computer accounts to the domain.

If you double-click on a computer's entry in the list, select it, and press the Enter key, or if you select Computer | Properties, you'll see the familiar dialog box shown in Figure 16.18. Through this dialog box you can view, and to some extent manage, user connections, shares, shared resources in use, the server's replicator, and how the selected server will respond to events that need attention.

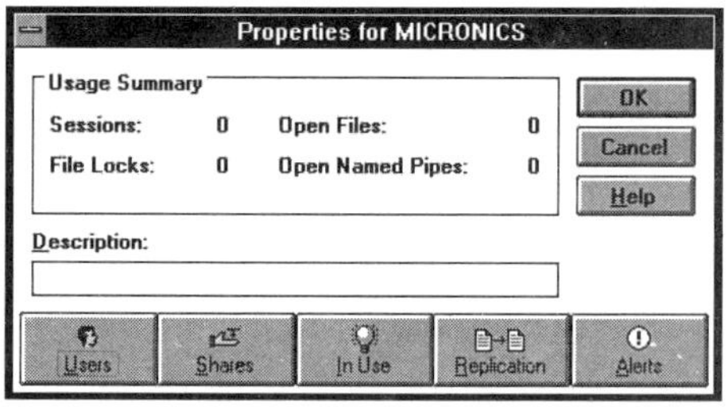

FIGURE 16.18.
The Server Properties dialog box.

Except for the ability to manage these resources on any computer in the domain being managed, this dialog box provides the same functions that Control Panel's Server applet does for the local system. See Chapter 10, "Windows NT Administration," for more information on the Server applet and this box.

Changing the View

When you first fire up Server Manager, you see a list of all the computers that have accounts in your domain. You can restrict the systems that are listed to just NT Servers or just Windows NT workstations. You can refresh the computer list using the View menu. Refreshing the view adds any computer accounts that have been added since you started Server Manager and removes any computers whose accounts have been deleted.

The computer list changes even more significantly if you disable Show Domain Members Only on the View menu. The list will change to show not only the members of your selected domain but also Windows for Workgroups and Windows NT systems on your network that might not be members of the domain. You'll also see each computer's status. If a computer isn't currently available on the network, its icon will be grayed out and a version number won't be displayed. Windows for Workgroups systems never display a version number.

Server Manager automatically updates the computer display after some actions, such as changing the domain controller. These refreshes can cause a significant amount of network traffic, because Server Manager polls all the computers in the list to check their status. If you're working on a domain across a low-speed or heavily loaded connection, such as a wide area link, you can reduce the traffic by selecting a low-speed connection from Server Manager's Options menu. As soon as you've selected the low-speed option, Server Manager stops updating the list automatically. Instead, it updates only when you select View | Refresh.

Managing a Domain or Peer Server

When you select Computer | Shared Directories, you see the dialog box shown in Figure 16.19. It enables you to control the shared directories for a selected server or Windows NT workstation. If you want to stop sharing a directory, select it and click on the Stop Sharing button. To change the number of users allowed to access the sharepoint or share level permissions on the directory, click on the Properties button. You'll see the same dialog boxes you see in File Manager for controlling these aspects of the sharepoint.

FIGURE 16.19.
The Shared Directories dialog box.

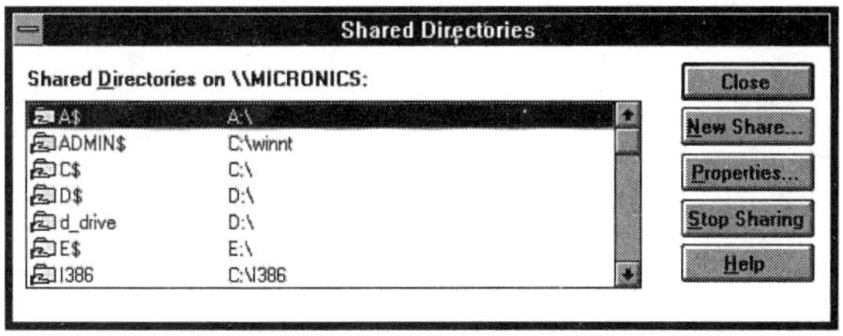

Click on the New Share button to have the computer you're managing share another directory. Again, it works just like File Manager, except that you can't browse for the directory on a tree display. You have to enter the directory you want to share in the Path box of the dialog box shown in Figure 16.20.

FIGURE 16.20.
The New Share dialog box.

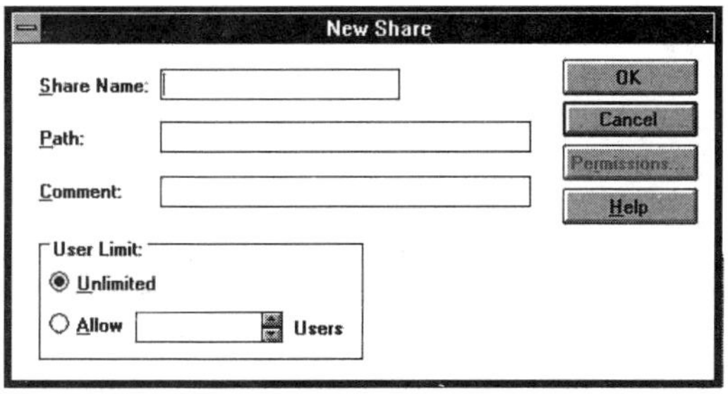

Choose Computer | Services to start and stop the Windows NT services running on the computer you're managing, such as the Clipbook server or replicator. This is just like going to that machine and running the Services applet from Control Panel. See Chapter 9, "Configuring Windows NT," for more information on managing services.

The Send Message option enables you to send a real-time message that pops up in a dialog box with an OK button to any user logged onto the selected computer. This comes in handy for sending `Server going down in 3 minutes` messages to your users. Note that WFWG 3.11 machines need to be running Winpopup to receive messages.

Managing Your Domain

Every computer in a domain needs to have an account in the domain database. Normally, you create that account when you install Windows NT by entering the computer's name and the name and password of the domain's administrator-level account. If your users are going to be installing Windows NT on their own systems and you don't want to trust them with an administrative account, you can create the computer accounts for their machines through the Add to Domain option on Server Manager's Computer menu. Doing so results in the dialog box shown in Figure 16.21. Just enter the new computer's name and whether it's running NT Server or plain old Windows NT.

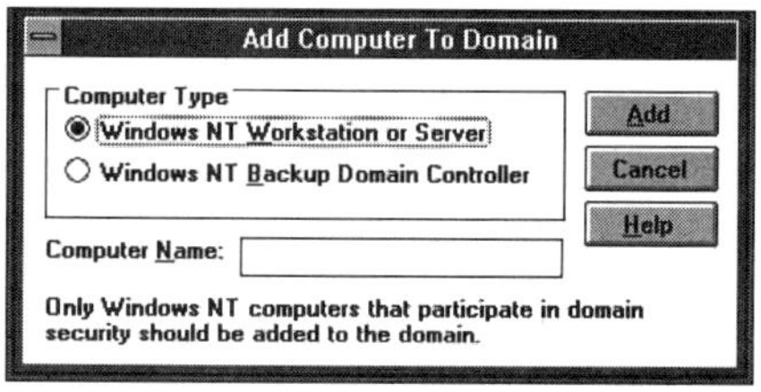

FIGURE 16.21.
The Add Computer to Domain dialog box.

As you've seen, any NT Server in your domain can validate user logons, but only one computer in each domain—the domain controller—has the master copy of the domain database. If the domain controller goes down, you won't be able to make changes to the domain database, such as adding users, until the domain controller is restored.

Because every Windows NT Server machine has a copy of the domain database, all you have to do to get your domain a working controller is promote that server to be the new domain controller. Just select the computer you want to promote and choose Computer | Promote to Domain Controller.

This causes the domain database on the computer you are promoting to be the master domain database for the domain. If you promote a computer in a domain that has a running domain controller, the controller will be demoted to a server automatically. It's a good idea to synchronize one of your servers with the domain controller and promote it before taking the domain controller down for preventative maintenance or upgrades so that your network will never be without a functioning domain controller.

If you promote a server to domain controller while the previous domain controller is down, you might have to manually demote the previous domain controller when it rejoins the network. If a domain controller tries to join a domain that already has a domain controller, it won't validate logon attempts until it's demoted.

Synchronizing Servers

Theoretically, the domain controller automatically updates each of the other servers in a domain after each change in the domain database. If a server has been off-line for a period of time, it might have missed these changes in the domain database. This can result in users occasionally not being able to log on. Even worse, a deleted user might still be able to log on if the out-of-date server validates his or her attempt.

To synchronize a single server with the domain controller, select that computer and then select Computer | Synchronize with Domain Controller. If your domain controller is off-line and a new controller got promoted, or if you're not sure which server needs synchronizing, select the domain controller. That menu choice will change automatically to Synchronize entire domain. Remember that synchronizing a domain, or even a single server, can generate a large amount of data traffic and either take a long time or slow everything else happening on your network or both.

Data Protection and Fault Tolerance

If you've ever had the misfortune of a hard-disk error, or even worse, a complete disk crash, you know how much time and money you can spend reconstructing the drive and lost data. Even if you make regular backups, you have to go through the time and aggravation of finding your last backup and restoring the data from tape. Of course, any work you've done since the last backup goes directly to data heaven, never to return.

On your personal workstation, even a disk crash is a controllable disaster. If you have a recent backup, you'll just have to reconstruct a few hours of work.

A disk error on a file server is another story. First of all, several different users will be saving their data to the disk, multiplying the amount of data you'll have to reconstruct (because it was created after the backup). Second, some users might not be technically astute (or just generally "with it") enough to know exactly what they've done on the system that day. You might end up sending out old versions of documents that haven't been spell-checked because Vice President Skippy found the file and forgot to redo the work he did on it that morning.

Even worse, you might have data that is simply irreplaceable. If you're developing an order entry system for L. L. Bean or J. Crew, in which a group of operators take orders over the phone and enter the data directly into their computers, a hard-disk error on the file server at 2 p.m. December 18th could mean that hundreds of orders totaling thousands of dollars would be lost forever. There would be no record of the orders, or even of the customers' telephone numbers and addresses, other than the data on that disk.

Of course, data loss can be the least of your problems. If you have a disk error on your file server, you'll have to take the server down, leaving your users sitting around twiddling their thumbs until you can repair the drive and restore your data. The cost of this down time can easily add up to many thousands of dollars as your company has to pay all those users and implement manual procedures to deal with customers and suppliers. Add in any loss of goodwill as customers don't get the level of service they're accustomed to and you might be looking for a new job and cursing your disk vendor.

After reading all this, you'll be glad to know that NT Server has several fault tolerance integrity features designed to allow your server to continue running right through a disk error, up to and including a drive crash. If you set up your servers right, your users will never know that your server just made one of its hard disks look like your college roommate's Bee Gees album you used when you couldn't find a Frisbee.

Mirrored Sets

Data mirroring is the simplest of NT Server's fault tolerant features designed to deal with a failed disk drive. Basically, if you configure two 500M disks to be a mirrored pair, they will from that point look to your users (both sitting at the server and at workstations on the network) like a single 500M drive. NT server will duplicate all disk writes so that it writes the same data to both drives.

When one of the drives has an error reading some data, NT Server will simply read the data from the other disk and place a message in the Event Log. Users at their own workstations won't even know anything went wrong. Even if one of the drives fails completely, the file server will take a lickin' and keep on tickin' using the other drive.

Unlike some other PC operating systems, including Novell's NetWare, NT Server's data mirroring doesn't require you to mirror whole disk drives. You can instead mirror disk partitions. This enables you to have different-sized drives in a mirrored pair without wasting the additional size on the larger drive. You can just create a mirrored pair of partitions the size of the smaller drive and an additional partition on the larger drive to use the extra space.

If you're short on disk space or money, you can carefully segregate your data between mirrored and unmirrored volumes. Put your most valuable or least replaceable data on your mirrored drive E: and less important data such as your collection of Leisure Suit Larry games or last year's accounting detail on the unmirrored drive F:.

If you can, you should put the two partitions of a mirrored pair on drives that are connected to different disk controllers or SCSI host adapters. Using multiple controllers protects your data from not only a drive failure but also a controller failure. Using multiple controllers also improves system performance by providing a higher bandwidth data pipe to the disk drives. Figure 16.22 shows examples of mirrored and duplex drives.

FIGURE 16.22.
Disk mirroring and duplexing.

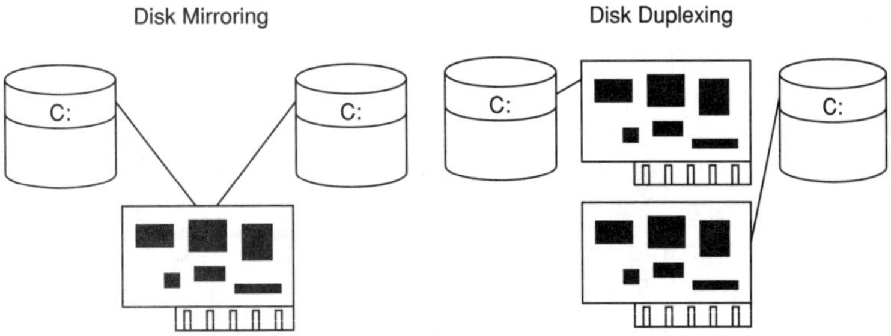

I've found that the protection against controller failure is less significant than it appears at first glance. This is because modern hard-disk controllers simply don't fail very often and because most of the controller failures I've seen have been so catastrophic that they take the server down by sending noise or excessive interrupt requests on the bus or by shorting out. The performance advantage alone is worth the extra cost of the second controller.

Creating a Mirrored Set

To create a mirrored set, you use Disk Administrator to create the first partition of the pair, select that partition, and Ctrl-click on an unused area of disk space on another disk drive so that both the unused disk area and the first partition are selected. Next, select Establish Mirror from Disk Administrator's Fault Tolerance menu. Disk Administrator will create a disk partition out of the selected free space. This new partition will be the same size as the original partition and will contain a copy of any data on the original partition.

Breaking a Mirrored Set

If one of the drives in your mirrored set fails, you might get desperate for disk space because your users insist on keeping every fax they've ever received on-line or you're adding additional drives to your server and you need to rearrange your partitions. You'll need to break one or more of your mirrored sets. Breaking a mirrored set doesn't destroy the data on either partition; it just stops the process of duplicating data between the two partitions.

To break a mirrored set, simply select it in Disk Administrator and choose Fault Tolerance | Break Mirror. Because breaking a mirrored set reduces the data integrity of your server, Disk Administrator makes you confirm your decision.

Beyond Data Mirroring: Disk Arrays

Disk mirroring first appeared in the computing world in the late '70s as part of special fault tolerant computers such as Tandem's NonStop. Disk arrays were first proposed in an article by three University of California, Berkeley professors as a solution to the problem of disk drive performance approaching theoretical limits and the growing cost of increasing drive speeds.

They proposed Redundant Arrays of Inexpensive Drives (RAID) as an alternative to a Single Large Expensive Drive (SLED). The article discussed five different methods by which an array of drives could emulate a single larger, more expensive drive, and it called these proposals levels 1-5. The concept has since been extended by others, including vendors, at both the high and low ends; therefore, RAID solutions of levels 0-7 are now available.

By using multiple disk drives and duplicating either data or error-correcting codes, RAID systems enable you to build very large (multiple gigabyte) volumes and improve your system's reliability.

RAID can be implemented in hardware, with special controllers such as those from Compaq, Dell, or Ciprico, or in software. Windows NT Server has built-in support for several RAID schemes, including level 5, without special hardware.

RAID Level 0 (Windows NT Stripe Sets)

Strictly speaking, level 0 isn't RAID because it doesn't improve system reliability by storing redundant data. A level 0 array simply distributes data across its drive. A typical level 0 array writes the first stripe of data to the first drive in the array, the second stripe to the second, and so on. Data stripes typically are a sector, track, or cylinder in size.

Level 0 arrays, which Microsoft calls stripe sets, have a performance advantage over single, larger drives because more data is under the disk heads at any given time. This reduces the number of seeks required for any given data transfer, and multiple data paths from the drives to the processor can eliminate the disk interface as a bottleneck.

Windows NT and NT Server both can build stripe sets out of standard drives. Because a failure of any drive in a level 0 array leads to the effective loss of all the data on the array, I don't recommend that you use stripe sets on your file servers.

RAID Level 1 (Windows NT Server Mirror Sets)

Level 1 is disk mirroring. In the original RAID paper, the authors assumed that mirroring would be on a disk drive basis as opposed to a partition or volume basis, but other than that, NT Server's mirror sets are a classic RAID 1 implementation.

For most systems, mirror sets give better performance than NT Server's other RAID options, especially when running with a failed drive. The down side to disk mirroring is that it requires you to buy twice the disk capacity you really need. This 50 percent capacity overhead can get expensive as you add additional gigabytes of disk to your servers.

RAID Level 2

Level 2 arrays stripe data across the drives of an array at the bit level. The first drive in the array contains the first bit, the second drive contains the second bit, and so on. Multiple additional drives contain error-correcting code (ECC) or parity information.

RAID 2 was designed for large computers with disk controllers that are as smart as or smarter than a typical PC rather than the microcomputers and technical workstations that run Windows NT. These controllers track drive errors through internal checksums on the disk and standard error flags performed by the drive and controller. As a result, RAID 2 systems are too complex and expensive for PC applications and generally aren't used on small systems.

RAID Level 3

Like RAID level 2, RAID level 3 systems stripe data across a series of drives. Level 3 differs from level 2 by using only one parity or ECC drive. Data can be interleaved at bit level, byte level (the most common), or any other logical size. Level 3 arrays typically have from 20 to 25 percent error correcting code overhead as opposed to the 50 percent overhead of a level 1 or data mirrored system.

Because data is interleaved across all data drives, a single read request is performed by multiple drives. Each drive reads a portion of the data, and all the drives transfer their portions to the controller in parallel. This yields high transfer rates, making RAID 3 ideal for applications that need high I/O bandwidth. But only one I/O transaction can be processed at a time, because every drive is involved in each read or write transaction.

RAID 3's parallel data transfers often work well for workstations that require fast sequential access to single large files, such as image processing systems. It's generally not recommended for transaction processing systems or environments in which most I/O transactions are for small amounts of data.

RAID Level 4

RAID 3's primary disadvantage is its inability to perform simultaneous I/O transactions because even small blocks of data are interleaved across all drives. Writing even the smallest file to a level 3 array requires that the system write to all the drives in the array.

A level 4 array, on the other hand, places the entire first transfer block, or cluster, on the first data drive, the second transfer block on the second drive, and so on. This process improves disk performance by enabling multiple reads.

Level 4 arrays still have a dedicated parity drive that contains error-correcting information for all the data drives. Therefore, it's involved in every write, forcing each write to be performed one at a time.

A multitasking operating system accessing a level 4 array can process independent read transactions for each data drive in the array. In an array with four data drives, for example, the array can perform three times as many reads as a single drive can in the same time period by accessing each of the data drives individually.

RAID Level 5 (Windows NT Server Stripe Sets with Parity)

The use of dedicated parity drives in RAID levels 1 through 4 limits each of these architectures to one write transaction at a time. Level 5, which Microsoft calls stripe sets with parity, spreads the ECC information across all the drives in the array. Therefore, each drive in a level 5 array contains both data and parity blocks. As in RAID 4, an entire transfer block is placed on a single drive, and the parity for that block of data is stored on another drive. When a drive fails, its data can be reconstructed from the remaining drives. Eliminating the dedicated parity drive removes the single-write bottleneck and lets RAID 5 perform multiple read and write transactions in parallel. See Figure 16.23.

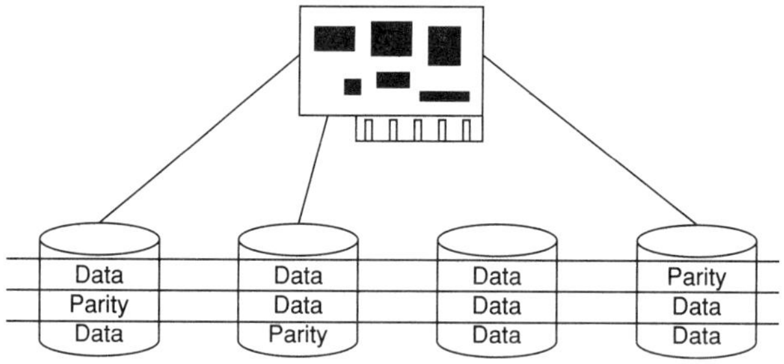

FIGURE 16.23.
A level 5 disk array.

Compared to a single drive, an array with four drives can perform four times as many reads and two times as many writes (because each write involves two drives) in a given time interval. In a combined read-write environment, the virtual transfer rates could be increased by a factor of one-half the number of drives in the array, compared to the single drive. As the ratio of reads to writes increases, the transfer rate increase factor approaches the number of drives installed. Theoretically, as you add drives to the array, performance increases, although not in linear proportion to the number of drives.

The elimination of the dedicated parity drive also reduces the performance effect of a drive failure. In any array that uses ECC instead of data mirroring to save disk space, the performance of the array is reduced when reading from an array with a failed drive, because calculating the original data from the ECC information takes time. In a level 4 array with a failed data drive, every read will require that the original data be reconstructed. In a 5-drive, level 5 array, 20 percent of the reads won't require the recalculation.

Hardware Arrays

In addition to the RAID features built in to Windows NT Server, you can add a drive array to your file server by buying a hardware-based array such as the Compaq Intelligent Drive Array or Micropolis Radiion. These hardware implementations have several advantages over software-based arrays. Because they have dedicated processors and possibly dedicated cache memory on their controllers, these hardware arrays can be faster than software-based arrays.

Hardware-based arrays also typically have cabinets that enable you to change drives in the array without turning the array off or bringing the server down. These systems can rebuild the array data onto a replacement drive in the background as users continue to access your array. These systems also can feature dual redundant power supplies to protect your data from a power supply failure.

Configuring Your Server's Disk Subsystem

Designing the disk subsystem for any given file server requires the careful balancing of cost, performance, and reliability. I firmly believe that any file server containing critical data, which includes the vast majority of file servers, should have some sort of data integrity feature enabled.

However, you shouldn't be lulled into a false sense of security because your data is protected from a disk or controller failure. Your data is more likely to be destroyed by user error, program bugs, or natural disaster than by a disk failure. In fact, the most important thing you can do to protect your valuable data is to have a regular schedule of backups.

The least-secure option is to use volume sets or stripe sets. Because a failure of a single drive that is part of a volume set or stripe set causes the system to lose all the data on that set, increasing the number of drives in the set also increases the odds of losing your data. In fact, the odds of losing data on a four-drive array are four times greater than those of losing data on a single drive.

If you can't afford to make your system truly fault tolerant, at least set up each volume to occupy only a single partition, limiting the amount of data you'll lose in the event of a drive failure.

Mirrored sets improve your data integrity at the cost of buying twice as many disk drives as you would otherwise need. Mirrored sets also typically have better performance than stripe sets with parity. If your drives are large enough to hold the largest volumes, mirrored sets probably are your best bet.

TIP

If possible, put the two drives in your mirrored set on separate controllers and connect them to different power supplies. This will protect your data against a controller or power supply failure, and multiple controllers will speed things up to boot.

Stripe sets with parity are a good solution if you need to create very large volumes or if you can't afford to buy enough disk drives to build mirrored sets. They provide a good level of data protection at a lower cost but are significantly slower than mirrored sets, especially for short writes. A small write to a stripe set requires that the system read all the stripes to calculate the ECC information and then write to both the changed stripe and the ECC stripe.

NOTE

Stripe sets with parity require more memory to manage, because the system needs to keep all the data described by a parity block in memory to calculate the error-correcting code. If you plan on implementing stripe sets with parity, figure on putting an additional 4M of memory in your server.

Hardware arrays can provide the best solution if your goal is to provide the most reliable system possible. Their hot swap capability and improved performance over stripe sets with parity are big advantages if you can afford them.

NOTE

Although disk arrays and mirrored sets protect you against a drive failure, they are no longer fault tolerant after such a failure. You should monitor your server's status regularly and swap a failed drive with a fresh one as soon as you notice that it has failed.

If you choose to use NT Server's data mirroring or stripe set features, you should use SCSI disk drives. If you use IDE or ESDI drives to build your mirrored or striped set, you might have a rude awakening in the event of a disk write error. Even though NTFS has a hot fix feature that automatically writes your data to an alternate sector if a write error occurs, this feature doesn't work properly for fault tolerant sets because it's part of the file system.

When using NTFS hot fix, a file is simply written to a different set of clusters on the disk if an error occurs and the bad cluster is marked as unusable. Because the error occurs on only one of the two drives in a mirrored set, and because a given cluster in the set contains the same data as its mirror, this technique breaks down.

If you're using SCSI drives in your fault tolerant set, NT Server will take advantage of SCSI's sector sparing to order the drive to assign the data to one of its spare sectors. From that point on, the drive will make it look to the system like nothing ever went wrong. If you're using IDE or ESDI drives, NT Server will disable the drive that has the error, breaking the set.

Setting Up a Stripe Set with Parity

To set up a stripe set with parity, install the needed drives and controllers, then follow these steps from Disk Administrator:

1. In Disk Administrator, select areas of free disk space on three to 32 drives by clicking on the first area and Ctrl-clicking on the others.
2. Select Fault Tolerance | Create Stripe Set With Parity.
3. In the resulting Create Stripe Set With Parity dialog box, enter the size of the stripe set you'd like to create and click on OK. The dialog box will show you the maximum- and minimum-size stripe sets you can create.

Disk Administrator then creates equal-size partitions on the selected drives. If the size you entered doesn't divide equally into the number of drives you selected, it will round off.

Deleting a Stripe Set with Parity

To delete a stripe set with parity, select the stripe set and choose Partition | Delete.

TIP

Make sure that you back up your data before you delete a stripe set. When you delete a stripe set, you lose all the data on it.

UPS Service

Windows NT's NTFS file system, which you should use on your file servers for security and performance reasons, holds some of your data in cache before writing it to the disk. Because writes to mirrored and striped sets take some time to complete, you should protect every file server with an uninterruptible file power supply and enable the UPS service, as described in Chapter 9, "Configuring Windows NT."

Remember that the UPS service requires a serial cable from the UPS to your computer so that the UPS can tell your computer when it's running on batteries. Just plugging your computer into a UPS will provide power monitoring. The UPS will beep when the power goes out, but it won't provide an automatic shutdown sequence. If the UPS and server are locked in a wiring closet and an electrician turns off the breaker for that closet, you won't hear the beeping before the battery runs out. If you haven't set up the serial cable and UPS server when the battery runs out, poof—there goes the server. It's a shame, but many people think that just adding a UPS solves all their problems.

There is a continuing debate on the best type of UPS. Online UPSs provide better power filtering because the computer runs from the batteries all the time. However, online UPSs are much bigger and more expensive and seem to break more often than standby UPSs. I've had good experience with UPSs from Sola, Best, and American Power Conversion.

NOTE

When you purchase a UPS, make sure it supports a true sine wave. Such UPSs include the SmartUPS and the Matrix UPS from American Power Conversion. APC also offers software that can provide additional electrical line statistics, which might prove useful for long-term monitoring.

Directory Replication

NT Server's directory replication service enables you to automatically maintain duplicate copies of one or more directories on your Windows NT Servers. When you change any files in the master copy of the directory, on the computer called the Export Server, the replication service will copy the files that have changed to one or more import computers. Export Servers must be running NT Server, while import computers can be running Windows NT or NT Server. See Figure 16.24.

FIGURE 16.24.
Directory replication.

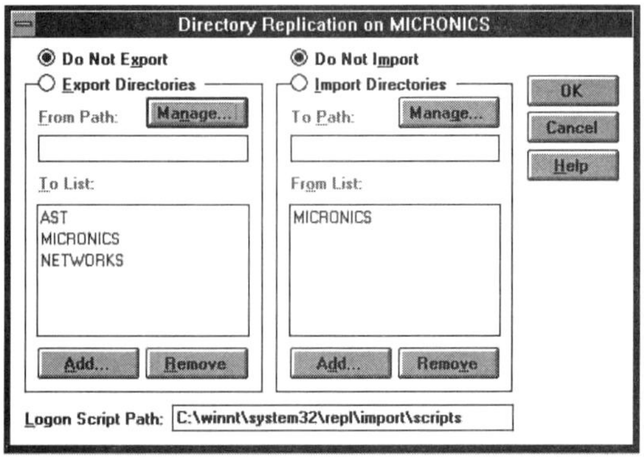

The replicator comes in handy for distributing files, such as from driver updates, to multiple destinations in order to keep all the copies up-to-date and in sync. If you set up WordPerfect directories on five of your file servers to balance the load, the replicator enables you to apply patches or copy new templates to only the master copy of the directory, vastly easing network administration.

If you have more than one Server in a domain, you'll find that you have to use the replicator to copy users' logon scripts to all the servers in the domain to enable users to get the same logon script regardless of the system they log on from.

Some users also will use the replicator to extend NT Server's fault tolerance. Setting up replication between multiple servers will, they say, protect their data against not only disk drive failures but also server failures. They'll tell you that even if a server fails, they'll have their system back up in seconds because users just have to access the backup data sets.

While this sounds good, in practice you might find yourself in the same situation as a new client who called me recently. Their network consultant, who had years of experience with networks but was new to NT, set up their system to replicate their data directories to an import machine and then back up that import machine to DAT tape nightly. Being the big mucky-muck network expert, he didn't actually test restoring a file from the tape but was confident that everything worked right because there were no errors.

What our friend forgot was that the replicator copies files only after they're both changed and closed. The replicator won't do you any good if what you want to do is protect your order entry database that is open by at least one user 24 hours a day. My new client had 24 tapes, each of which had none of their most valuable files.

Other users who have a large number of smaller files that get opened and closed as users work on them, such as law firms, can be well-protected by the replicator if they can live with the replication service's directory limitations.

How the Replicator Works

In order to copy files from the export server to the import computers, you need to run the replicator service on each system. When it's started, the replicator logs on to the systems using an account you've created just for that purpose. The service running on the export server then scans the subdirectories of the export directory (by default C:\WINNT\SYSTEM32\REPL\EXPORT) for new or modified files and subdirectories. When it finds changed files, it copies them to each of the specified import computers, where it copies the data to their import directory (by default C:\WINNT\SYSTEM32\REPL\IMPORT).

Although import computers have to run Windows NT or NT Server, they don't need to be members of the same domain as the export server. In fact, cross-domain replications are a good way to distribute templates and other corporate master files.

When configuring the replicator, you can tell it to copy specific subdirectories of the export directory, but you can't tell it to duplicate C:\WINWORD\DOCS, for example. If you have applications that update groups of files, such as a data file and its related index files, you should tell the replicator to wait for the directory to stabilize—that is, for all the files in the directory to remain unchanged—for two minutes or so to ensure that a synchronized set of files is duplicated.

You can even set up the replicator to copy from the export directory to the import directory on a single server to provide an instant backup copy.

Setting Up Replication

The first step in setting up the replication service, as it should be with anything, is to do a little planning. Figure out which of your NT Servers will be export servers, which data you want to replicate, and which machines will be import computers.

Remember that all this data being copied from one server to another adds to network and server traffic. If you put all your data directories under the export directory on all your servers, you'll flood your servers and Ethernet with data so badly that users trying to get work done will feel like they're swimming through molasses.

Next, you need to create a user account on each domain for the replicator server to use when copying your data.

Creating the Replication User

You create the replication user through User Manager for Domains, described earlier in this chapter. You must set several options, probably to allow the replication user access to the data being copied and the ability to copy files whenever they're changed. To create the replication user, follow these steps:

1. Launch User Manager for Domains and create a new user by selecting User | New User.
2. Enter a user ID, full name, password, and description into the User Properties dialog box, shown in Figure 16.25, as you would when creating any other user. Make sure that the Password Never Expires option is enabled so that the replication service won't be locked out.
3. Click on the Groups button. Make the user a member of the Backup Operators and Replicator groups using the Group Memberships dialog box, shown in Figure 16.26.
4. Click on the Hours button. Make sure that the user has access at all times by using the Logon Hours dialog box, shown in Figure 16.27.

FIGURE 16.25.
Replication service users need passwords that don't expire.

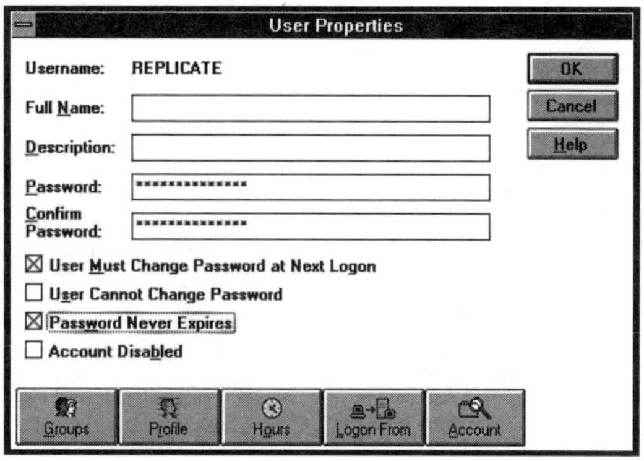

FIGURE 16.26.
The replication user's group memberships.

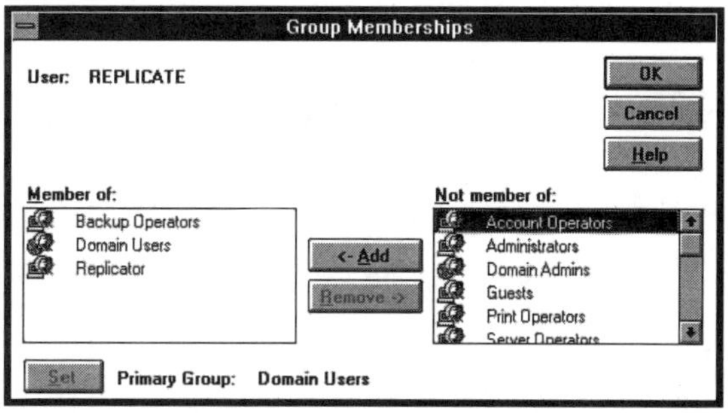

FIGURE 16.27.
Replication service accounts should have access at all times.

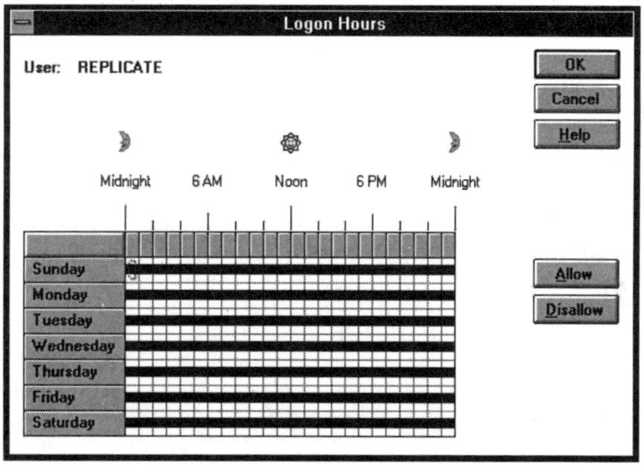

Setting Up an Export Server

Before you start configuring the replication service, you should create the appropriate user account and the directories you want to export. When planning your directory structure, keep in mind the following points:

- The Directory Replicator can copy only subdirectories of the export directory.
- An export server copies the same files and subdirectories to all its associated import computers.
- The total directory structure, from the export directory down, can be only 32 layers deep.

You don't have to copy the files into the subdirectories now. The replicator will copy them whenever you get around to it.

To turn your system into an export server, follow these steps:

1. Launch the Server manager, double-click on the server you want to configure, and click on the Replication button to get the Directory Replication dialog box, shown in Figure 16.28.

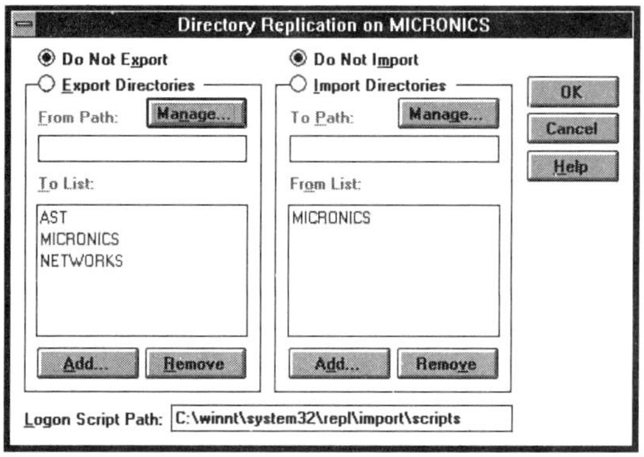

FIGURE 16.28.
The Directory Replication dialog box.

2. Click on the Export Directories radio button to enable your system's export function.
3. By default, the replicator will export the directory C:\WINNT\SYSTEM32 \REPL\EXPORT\SCRIPTS and its subdirectories. You can change this path by editing the From Path box.

NOTE

A Windows NT Server can export only a single directory and its subdirectories. Although you can choose to export only some directories of the export directory, you can't have two independent trees. Therefore, you can't export data from more than a single volume.

4. If you want to add additional directories to export, click on the Manage button to display the dialog box shown in Figure 16.29. Through this dialog box you can tell the system which directories you want to export. If you want to copy anything but the \SCRIPTS directory, click on the Add button to add another directory to the list.

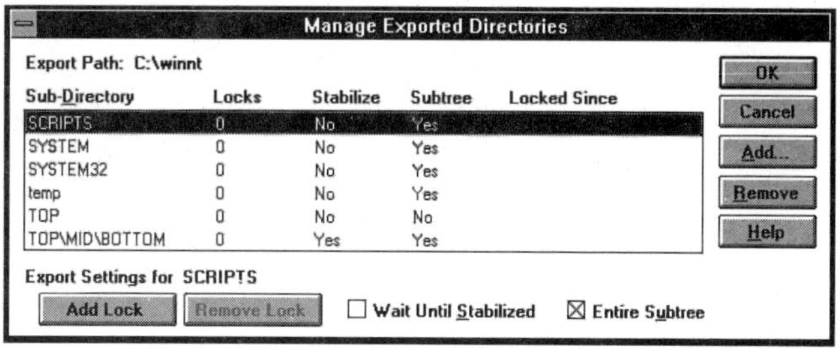

FIGURE 16.29.
The Manage Exported Directories dialog box.

5. When you see the Add Sub-Directory dialog box, shown in Figure 15.30, enter the path to the directory you want to replicate, starting from the export directory. Because you have to do things the old-fashioned way and type the directory name, you'll long for the missing Browse button.

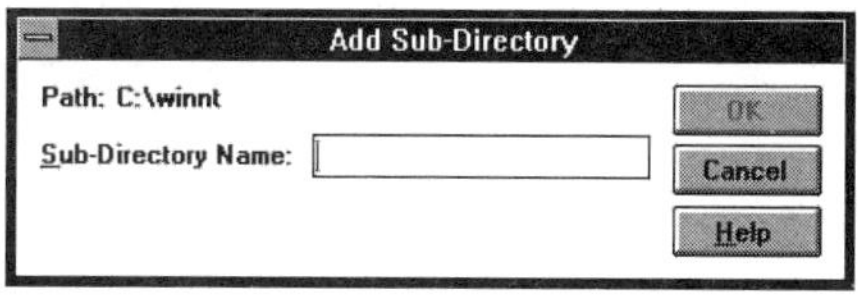

FIGURE 16.30.
The Add Sub-Directory dialog box.

6. After you add the directory, you can tell the replication service whether to copy its subdirectories and whether you want the directory to stabilize—that is, wait two minutes from the last file change to start the copy.

NOTE

Make sure that the directory replication user has full control permissions to the source directories of the replication. If it has less than full control, you won't get the file's permissions copied properly.

7. When you've listed all the directories you want to copy, click on the OK button to return to the Directory Replication dialog box.

NOTE

The Manage Exported Directories dialog box also enables you to apply a lock to a directory. To lock a directory, select it and click on the Add Lock button. You can apply as many locks as you want, but only the first one matters. If a directory has one or more locks, the replicator won't copy its files until the locks are removed. To remove a lock, click on the Remove Lock button.

NOTE

The Directory Replicator copies the same data to each import computer. There is no way to have the Replicator copy one set of data to one import computer and a different set to another import computer.

8. Now you have to tell the exporters where to send the data by maintaining the To list. In order to add a system to the list of systems that are to receive your data, click on the Add button to get the Select Domain dialog box, shown in Figure 16.31.

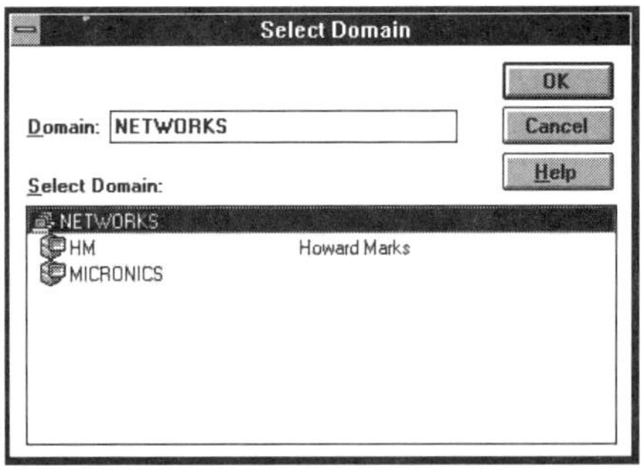

FIGURE 16.31.
Selecting import computers.

9. Now you can choose another NT Server, Windows NT workstation, or domain to receive the data. In order for the data to actually be transmitted, the import computer must also be running the replicator and must be configured to receive data from this server or domain. As a result, if you use a domain name in the To list, the server will export data to every machine in the domain configured to import its data.

NOTE

If the To list is empty, the replicator will export its data to its entire domain. As soon as you add the first server to the To list, this replication will end unless you put the local domain back in the list.

WARNING

You shouldn't specify a domain as the target for an export server if there might be a wide area network link. If there is a WAN link in your replication scheme, declare the server names explicitly in the export list.

You should avoid having a single import server receive the same data from more than one server. It wastes valuable network bandwidth and endangers data integrity, because a later version of a file can be replaced by an earlier version if the earlier version is replicated later. Loops, in which data gets back to its original server, are even worse, because they eat network bandwidth with great abandon.

Your export server is now configured. All you have to do now is configure the import servers and start the replicator.

Configuring the Import Computer

Configuring an import computer is almost exactly like configuring an export server. The right side of the Directory Replication dialog box works basically the same as the left side. Enter the directory you want your replicated data sent to into the To Path box, add servers to receive data into the From list, and so on. There are a few differences, though.

When you set up the import server, make sure that the replicator's user account has full access permissions to the data import directory so that it can write the data files and their properties.

Unlike with an export server, you don't have to tell the import computer which directories are going to be copied. When you click on the Manage button, you get the dialog box shown in Figure 16.32. It tells you the status of each directory that's been imported to this system.

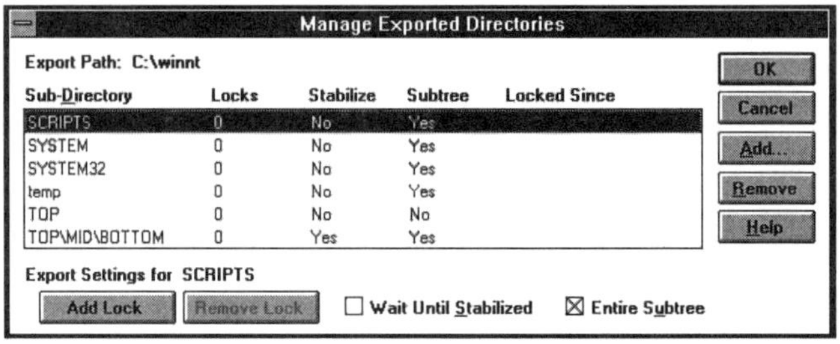

FIGURE 16.32.
The Manage Exported Directories dialog box.

This dialog box can be useful for making sure that all your replications are still running. Each directory is listed, along with the number of locks on the directory, the date and time of the last update received, and the directory's status. A status of OK indicates that the system is receiving updates from the export server and has a current set of its data. No Master indicates that the export server hasn't been heard from lately, and No Sync indicates that the two sets of data don't agree. (This can result from an open file at either end or a communications failure.)

Although this dialog box has Add and Remove buttons, there's really no reason to use them. Directories are added automatically when they're received, even if you've removed them. Therefore, there's no way an import computer can reject some data from an export server. If you're getting data from an export server, you're getting it all, so make sure that your import computers have plenty of free disk space.

The replication service import program treats an empty From list the same way the export program treats an empty To list. That means that an empty From list makes the import program accept data from any server exporting to its domain. As with the export server, if you want to include your local domain and other servers, you'll have to select your local domain manually.

Replicating Logon Scripts

When you log onto a Windows NT Server network, your computer might run a logon script created by the network administrator. As you saw earlier in this chapter, a user logging on to the network can be validated by any NT Server in the network, because each NT Server has a copy of the user database. As soon as a user logs on to the network, his or her workstation runs a logon script from the server where the user was validated.

A user's logon script is a batch file stored in the file specified in the User Environment Profile dialog box of User Manager for Domains in the path specified in the Server Manager Directory Replication dialog box in Server. Because this batch file is loaded from the validating server, you need to have the same logon script on each NT Server in your domain to allow a user to log on from any workstation and get the same logon script each time.

You should declare one server in each domain to be the master logon script server. This server, which can be, but doesn't have to be, the domain controller, has the master copies of each user's logon script and replicates this data to all the other NT Servers in the domain. This way, you have to update the logon scripts on only a single server.

On a small network, you probably should use the domain controller to store the master copy of the scripts. As the network grows and the domain controller gets busier, you can move this to another server to balance the load and therefore improve performance.

If you store your logon scripts in the default C:\WINNT\SYSTEM32\REPL \IMPORT\SCRIPTS directory, your logon script replication will be all set up as soon as you turn it on on each system and start the service. If you want to make a change to a logon script, edit the file in the \SCRIPTS subdirectory of the export directory. The changes will automatically be replicated to the \SCRIPTS subdirectory of the import directory on all the servers in the domain, including the master.

Starting and Controlling the Replicator Service

As soon as you have the import and export parts of the replication service configured, you need to tell the replicator what user ID to use to log into your system and start it. Because a service is just a special kind of program, starting a service is technically just launching another program. The replication service takes advantage of a service's capability to log on using a different ID than the user working on the station.

To configure the replication service, follow these steps:

1. Launch the Services applet in Control Panel. You see the Services dialog box, shown in Figure 16.33.

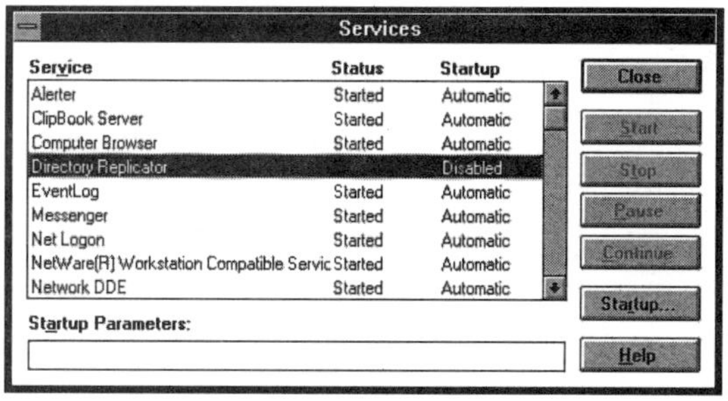

FIGURE 16.33.
The Services dialog box.

2. To configure the replicator, select Directory Replicator from the scroll list of services installed on this system. You'll see the dialog box shown in Figure 16.34.

FIGURE 16.34.
Replication user entry screen.

3. In order to have the replicator start every time Windows NT is loaded, select Automatic as the startup type. Doing so enables the automatic copying on this system. If you want to run the replication service only occasionally, select Manual.
4. Select This Account in the Log On As section to specify the user ID that the replication service should use. Although most Windows NT services use the System Account to log on, this account has no permissions to use data. Therefore, it's useless for the replicator.
5. To select the user you created earlier, click on the Browse button and select that account from the list of users in this domain (see Figure 16.35).

FIGURE 16.35.
The Add User dialog box.

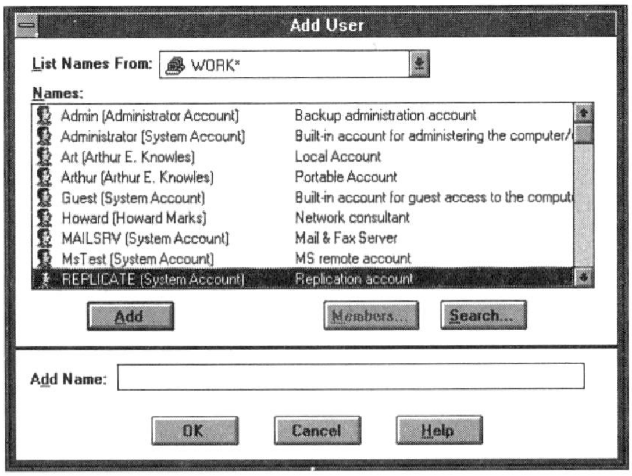

6. Select the user. Click on Add, then click on OK.
7. Make sure you enter the password correctly in the Directory Replicator dialog box. Click on OK.
8. Test everything by clicking on the Start button to start the service. If you've forgotten the password, a dialog box tells you.

Network Administration Tools

Windows NT Server's Network Administration group includes four very useful tools to help make an administrator's life less frustrating. These tools, shown in Figure 16.36, fall into two categories: TCP/IP network management and MS-DOS client management.

FIGURE 16.36.
The Network Administration group.

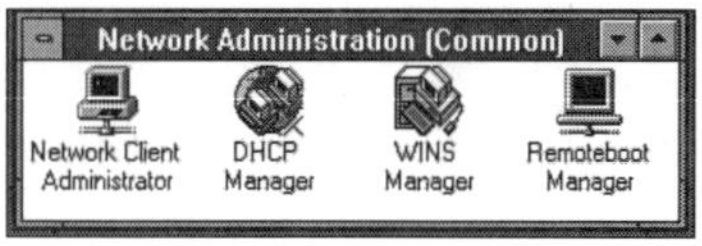

Normally, TCP/IP addresses are statically assigned by the system administrator and maintained by utilizing either an online database of assigned IP addresses and computer names or a scratch piece of paper that lists IP addresses in use. When a new user is added to the network, an IP address is assigned to that user based on a free pool of unassigned IP addresses. Sometimes the documentation is updated and sometimes it isn't, depending on the maintenance method in use. Sometimes a duplicate IP address is assigned because of the maintenance methodology. When this occurs, chaos follows.

In addition to statically assigning TCP/IP addresses, the administrator also has to update various files to associate a name with an IP address. After all, how many people can remember the 12-digit IP address for the resource they want to access? If these files get out of sync or become damaged, a call to the system administrator is in order. To address these issues, Windows NT Server includes the Dynamic Host Configuration Protocol (DHCP) and Windows Internet Name Service (WINS).

Continuing the theme of making network administration easier, Windows NT Server includes the Network Client Administrator and Remoteboot Manager. The Network Client Administrator is used to create a network startup disk or network client installation disk set. The Remoteboot Manager is used for diskless workstation management. You can also use the remote boot capability on computers with local hard disks to provide increased security, better system performance, and easier software upgrades while still providing custom configurations.

Managing Your TCP/IP Network

The DHCP Server service automates the assignment of IP addresses, and the DHCP Manager is an interface for service configuration. The WINS service provides name resolution services, and the WINS Manager provides configuration. Considering the complexity of these services, this section discusses only some of the more basic issues. For additional information, see Chapter 4, "Installing and Configuring DHCP Servers," and Chapter 5, "Installing and Configuring WINS Servers," of the TCP/IP online help files.

TIP

The online help files for Windows NT Server are located in the \SUPPORT\BOOKS directory on the installation CD-ROM. You can create a Program Manager Common Group (Online Books) and use File Manager to drag the help files into the group. An icon is supplied (BOOKS.ICO) if you want to use a different icon than the default HELP.EXE question mark. I find the built-in search capabilities of the online books help interface to be quite useful during system configuration, because the detail provided is far superior to the application's limited help facilities.

NOTE

DHCP Servers don't share a common database, so if you plan to use a single network segment, you should split the assignment of IP addresses between the DHCP Servers. For example, if you have two servers in a single segment, you can set the first server to use IP addresses from 128.0.0.1 to 128.0.0.127 and the second server to use IP addresses from 128.0.0.128 to 128.0.0.254.

Installing the DHCP Server Service

You install the DHCP Server service through Control Panel's Network applet. Follow these steps:

1. Start Control Panel and launch the Network applet.
2. Click on Add Software.
3. Select TCP/IP and related components and click on OK.
4. In the Windows NT TCP/IP Installation Options dialog, enable the DHCP Server Service check box and click on OK.
5. An icon for the DHCP Manager will be created in the Network Administration Group. Click on OK.
6. When prompted, restart the computer. If you intend to add more components, do so before restarting the computer.

Using the DHCP Manager

The first time you run the DHCP Manager, shown in Figure 16.37, it will display either the local machine if it's run on an NT Server with an active DHCP Server service, or a message box prompting you for a computer with a DHCP Service to manage. After you select one of these options, the scopes for the service will be displayed in the left window pane. The right window pane will display configuration options for the selected scope.

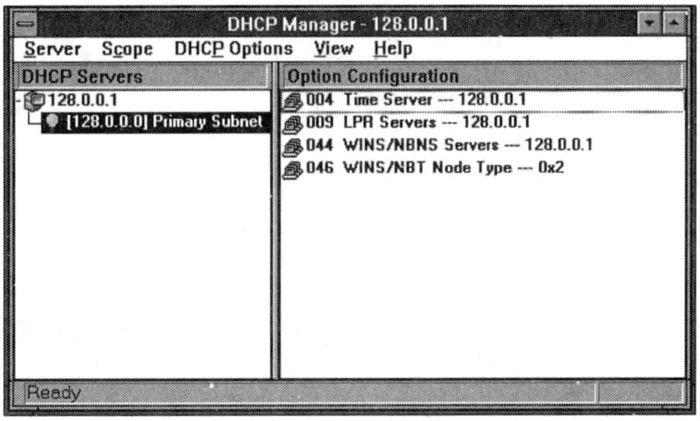

FIGURE 16.37.
The DHCP Manager.

To create a scope, follow these steps:

1. Select Server | Add. The dialog shown in Figure 16.38 will be displayed. Enter the IP address of the server and click on OK.

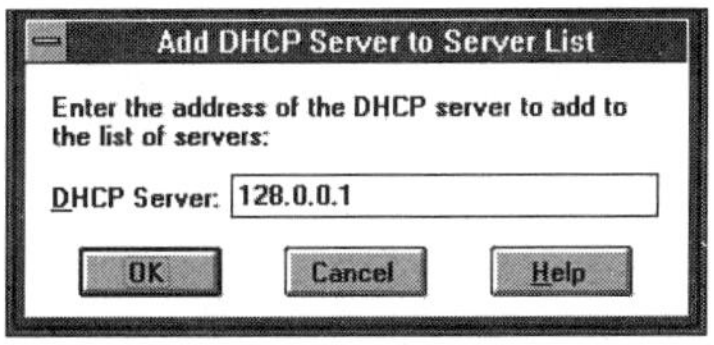

FIGURE 16.38.
Adding a DHCP Server to the server list.

2. Select the DHCP Server in the left window pane, then select Scope | Create. The dialog box shown in Figure 16.39 will appear.
3. Enter the start address and end address of the IP address pool. Then enter the subnet mask of the address pool. If you want to exclude a range of IP address from the pool, enter the start and end addresses in the appropriate Exclusion Range field, and then click on the Add button. Select your lease duration, enter a name and comment for your scope, and click on OK.
4. If you have additional scopes to create, repeat steps 1 through 3.

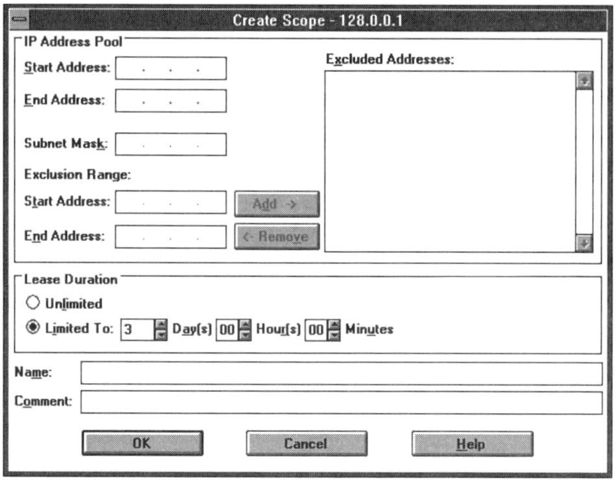

FIGURE 16.39.
Adding a scope to a DHCP Server.

NOTE

A *lease duration* is a maximum time limit that a workstation can use an IP address without renewing the lease from the DHCP Server. I recommend that you use a minimum lease time of twice your maximum DHCP Server off-line time. For instance, if you routinely perform system maintenance over the weekend, your lease time should be four days. This prevents your DHCP clients from releasing their lease on an IP address and then not being able to find a DHCP Server to give them a new lease or IP address. If you have multiple DHCP Servers, this is not an issue, as long as a DHCP Server is available.

To configure a scope, follow these steps:

1. Select the DHCP Server scope in the left window pane. Select DHCP Options | Scope. The dialog box shown in Figure 16.40 will appear.

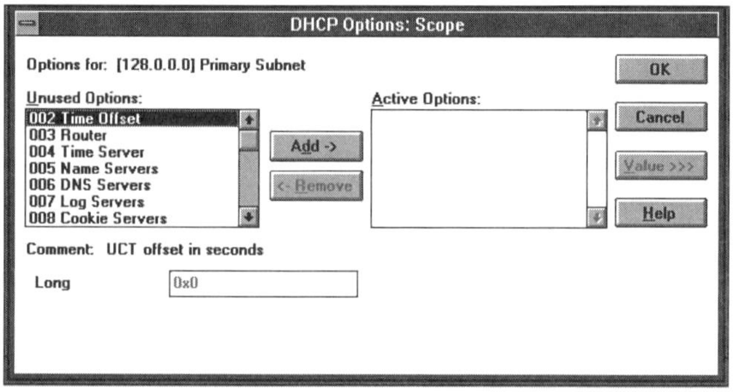

FIGURE 16.40.
Configuring a DHCP scope.

NOTE

You can make global changes to all scopes by selecting DHCP Options | Global. You can set default scope options by selecting DHCP Options | Defaults.

2. Select the desired option to configure from the Unused Options list box and click on the Add button. To change the default value, click on the Value button and change the entry in the bottom of the dialog box. Do this for each option you want to configure, then click on OK. Each option you select will then be displayed in the right window pane.

TIP

If you have an active network with many floating workstations, you can reserve IP addresses for them. Select Scope | Add Reservations. The dialog displayed in Figure 16.41 will appear. Enter the IP address to reserve, the adapter ID number, the client computer number, and a comment that describes the client workstation. Then click on OK.

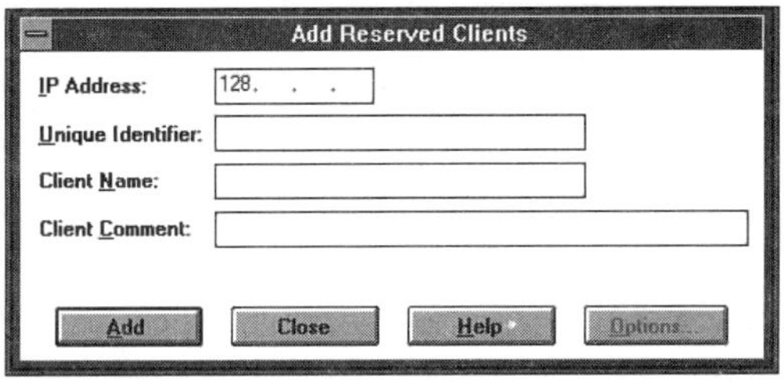

FIGURE 16.41.
Reserving an IP address for a workstation.

Select Scope | Active Leases to view active leases, including reservations. (See Figure 16.42.) To display only reservations, enable the Show Reservations Only check box.

Installing the WINS Service

You install the WINS service through Control Panel's Network applet. Follow these steps:

1. Start Control Panel and launch the Network applet.
2. Click on Add Software.
3. Select TCP/IP and related components and click on OK.
4. In the Windows NT TCP/IP Installation Options dialog, enable the WINS Server Service check box and click on OK.

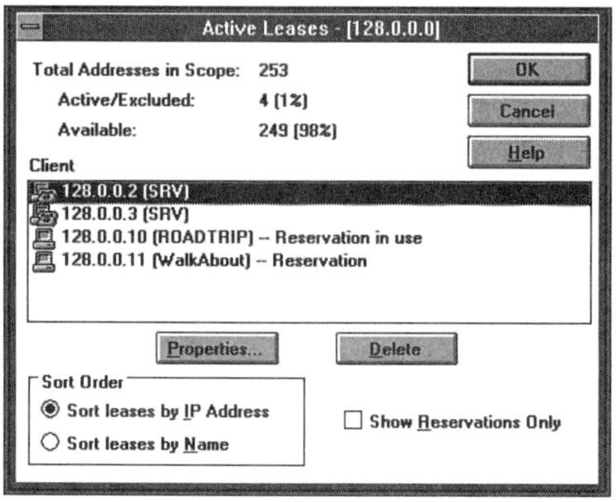

FIGURE 16.42.
Displaying the active leases.

5. An icon for the WINS Manager will be created in the Network Administration Group. Click on OK.
6. When prompted, restart the computer.

Using the WINS Manager

The WINS Manager has the look and feel of the DHCP Manager, and like the DHCP Service, the WINS service provides dynamic services. The primary purpose of the WINS service is to dynamically match NetBIOS computer names to IP addresses. Rather than requiring you to maintain a static list of computer names, the WINS service provides dynamic name resolution to WINS clients. As each client makes its initial access to the WINS service, it registers itself. It repeats this registration periodically.

The first time you execute the WINS Manager, there will be nothing to display until you add your first WINS server. After that, the application will display the WINS servers in the left window pane and the WINS statistics for the selected server in the right window pane (see Figure 16.43).

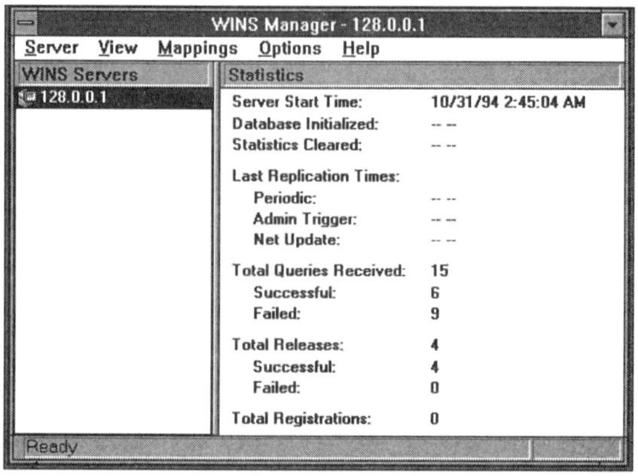

FIGURE 16.43.
The WINS Manager.

To add a WINS server, select Server | Add WINS Server. When prompted, enter the computer name of the server providing WINS services.

To display detailed information about the WINS server, select Server | Detailed Information. The dialog shown in Figure 16.44 will appear.

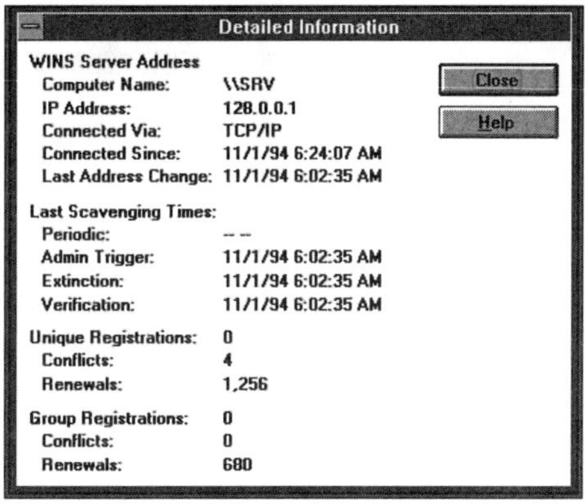

FIGURE 16.44.
Displaying detailed information about a WINS server.

To configure a WINS server, select Server | Configuration. To include advanced options, click on the Advanced button. The dialog box shown in Figure 16.45 will appear.

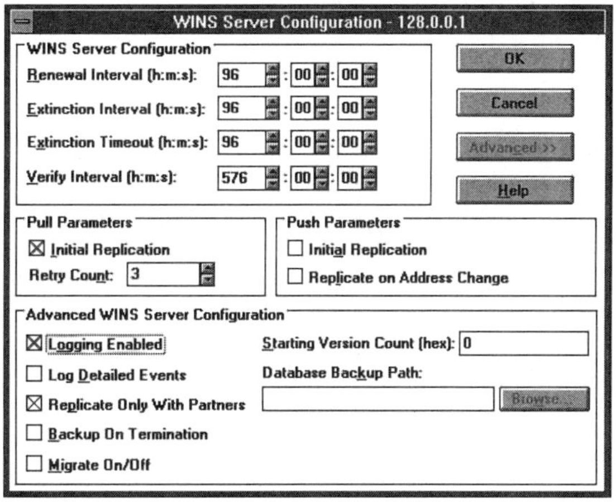

FIGURE 16.45.
The WINS Server Configuration dialog box.

One of the nicer features of the WINS service is that the database can be shared with other WINS servers. In fact, using multiple WINS servers can provide a performance increase. This sharing of the database is performed by creating replication partners. Each replication partner can send changes (push partner), request changes (pull partner), or make both requests.

To replicate the database, follow these steps:

1. Select Server | Replication Partners. The Replication Partners dialog, shown in Figure 16.46, will appear.

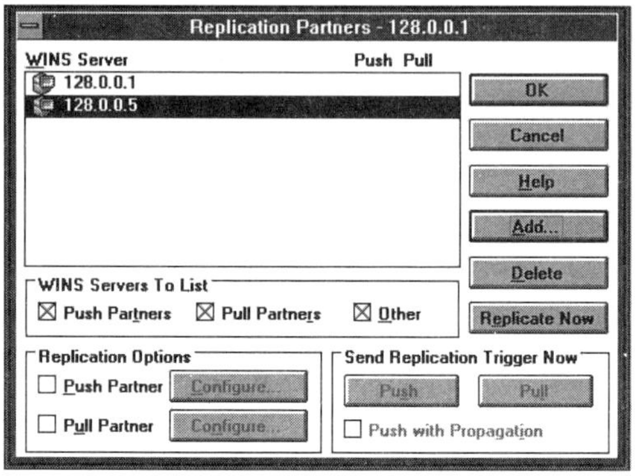

FIGURE 16.46.
Replicating the WINS database.

2. Before you can replicate a database, you need to add the WINS servers by clicking on the Add button.
3. When prompted, supply an IP address and computer name (if requested), and then select the WINS server you added. Next, specify whether this WINS server is to be a push partner, a pull partner, or both. If you want the replication to occur immediately, click on the Push or Pull buttons in the Send Replication Trigger Now group.

TIP

If you're migrating an existing TCP/IP installation, you can migrate your various host files by selecting Mappings | Static Mappings. This displays the Static Mappings dialog. Click on the Import Mappings button and load your host file.

Managing Client Workstations

A network administrator's life is tough enough without having to remember how to create installation diskettes for the various client operating systems and running around to each computer to install the software. Therefore, Windows NT Server includes the Network Client Administrator and Remoteboot Manager. The first can be used to create installation disks to install network client software for MS-DOS and OS/2, Remote Access for MS-DOS, TCP/IP-32 for Windows for Workgroups, and network administration tools for Windows NT Workstation and Windows for Workgroups. Remoteboot Manager can be used to provide remote boot capabilities to MS-DOS and Windows workstations equipped with a supported network card and remote boot ROM.

Creating Installation Disks

The Network Client Administrator, shown in Figure 16.47, has four options. Three of these options provide useful services to an administrator:

- Make Network Installation Startup Disk
- Make Installation Disk Set
- Copy Client-based Network Administration Tools

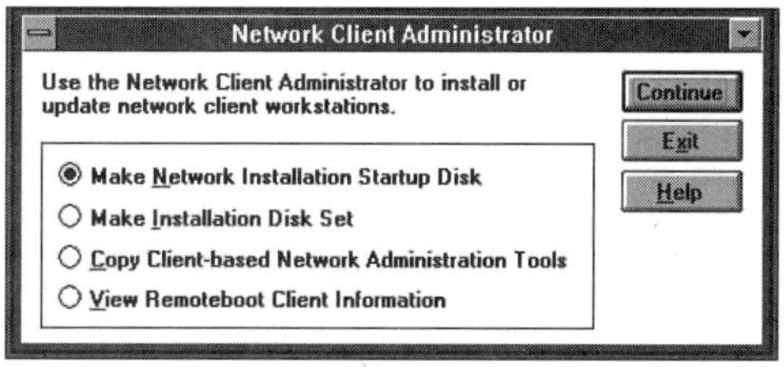

FIGURE 16.47.
The Network Client Administrator.

The fourth option, View Remoteboot Client Information, displays the dialog shown in Figure 16.48, but otherwise, it performs no useful function.

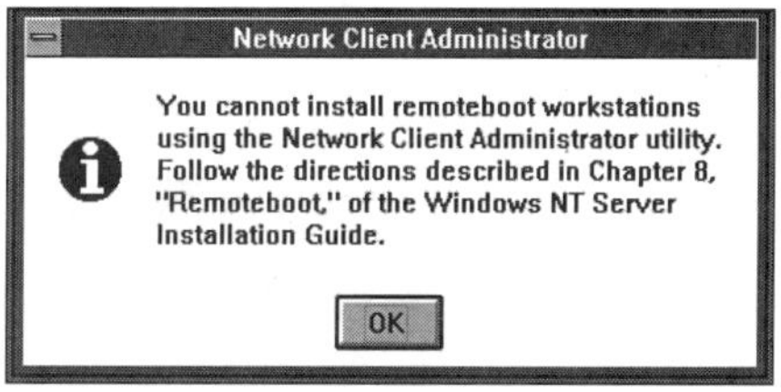

FIGURE 16.48.
The View Remoteboot Client Information dialog box.

Creating a Network Installation Startup Disk

The easiest way to install software on a client machine is to create a *startup disk*—a bootable MS-DOS system disk configured for a specific computer configuration. By specifying the computer configuration beforehand, you can use a network sharepoint to contain the client software installation files.

To create a network installation startup disk, follow these steps:

1. Start the Network Client Administrator. Click on the Make Network Installation Startup Disk radio button, and then click on Continue. The dialog shown in Figure 16.49 will be displayed.

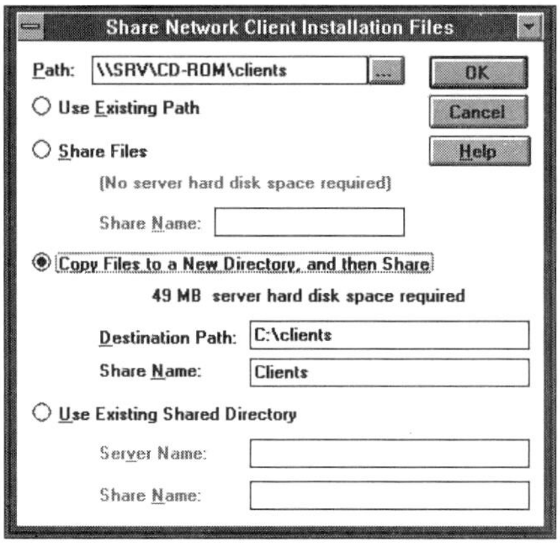

FIGURE 16.49.
The Share Network Client Installation Files dialog box.

2. If your network has limited disk space, you can use the CD-ROM as the source media by selecting either Use Existing Path or Share Files. If you use the Existing Path option, the CD-ROM containing the installation files must already have been shared, or your users won't be able to access the required files. If you have sufficient disk storage (at least 49M free), I recommend that you use the Copy Files to New Directory, and then Share option. Doing so will copy the required files to a directory you specify and then share that directory. If you have already copied the required files and shared the directory, you can use the Use Existing Shared Directory option. Once you've made your selection and copied the source files (if required) and clicked on OK, the dialog shown in Figure 16.50 will appear.

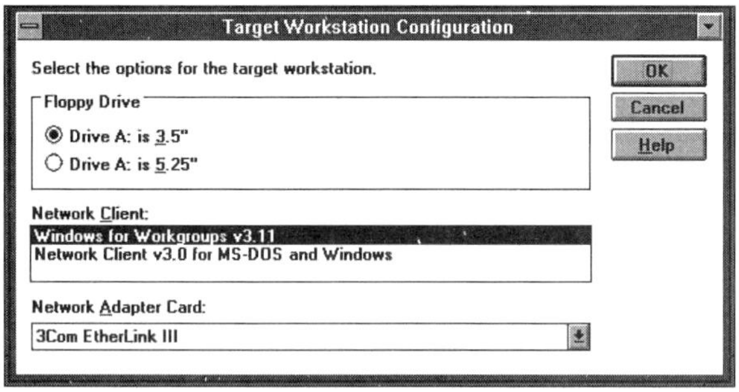

FIGURE 16.50.
The Target Workstation Configuration dialog box.

3. At this point, you must select the floppy drive type, network client software, and network adapter to be used on the client workstation. Once you've made your selections, click on the OK button.

NOTE

If you have multiple configurations (different floppy drives, client software, or network adapters), you will need to create a disk set for each of these configurations.

NOTE

The adapter configuration is based on the manufacturer's defaults. If your configuration is different, be sure to modify the PROTOCOL.INI file in the \NET subdirectory to match the target workstation's configuration.

4. If you decide to install Windows for Workgroups, a message box will inform you that you must have a legal license in order to use the supplied software. After you click on OK, the dialog shown in Figure 16.51 will appear.

FIGURE 16.51.
Configuring the default client installation.

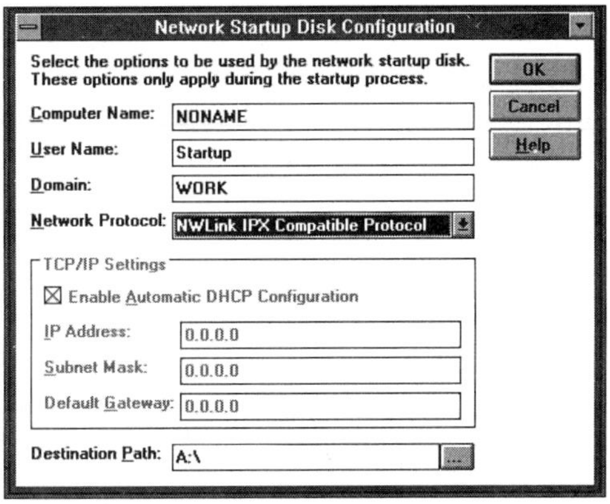

5. Enter the computer name, user name, domain name, and transport protocol to be used. If you select the TCP/IP protocol, you have the option of either assigning a static IP address or using DHCP to assign the IP address. You may also specify the default gateway IP address.

NOTE

If this installation startup disk is to be used for multiple installations, be sure to change the Computer Name on the client workstation after installation.

Otherwise, a duplicate computer name message will be displayed the next time the installation disk set is used, thus preventing a successful installation.

6. You will then be prompted for a formatted, bootable floppy of the selected type. Then you'll be asked to confirm your selections. Once you've accepted your configuration, the copy process will be initiated, and your installation disk will be created.
7. If you want to create another installation startup disk, repeat steps 1 through 6. Otherwise, click on Exit to terminate the application.

TIP

I recommend that you use DHCP to assign IP addresses if the installation startup disk is to be used for multiple installations. Otherwise, you'll need to change the IP address of the client workstation after installation to prevent duplicate IP addresses.

Creating an Installation Disk Set

Installation disk sets are used to create network client installation disks for MS-DOS and Windows, RAS for MS-DOS, TCP/IP-32 for Windows for Workgroups, LAN Manager for MS-DOS, and LAN Manager for OS/2. These generic installation disks may be reused without modification, unlike a startup disk.

To create a network installation disk set, follow these steps:

1. Start the Network Client Administrator, click on the Make Installation Disk Set radio button, and click on Continue. The Share Network Client Installation Files dialog, shown in Figure 16.49, will be displayed.
2. Select your source media options, as specified earlier. Once you've made your selections and clicked on Continue, the dialog shown in Figure 16.52 will appear.

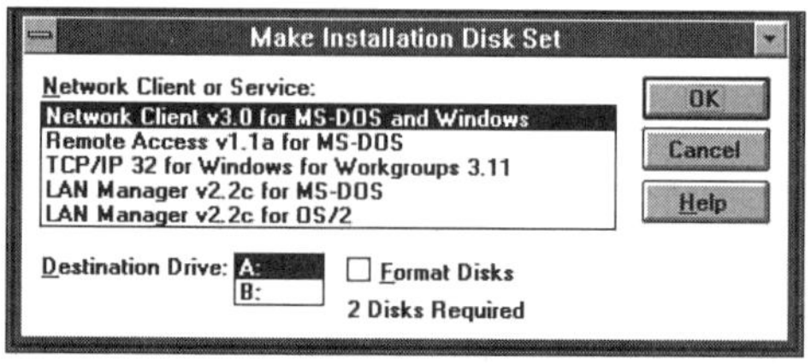

FIGURE 16.52.
The Make Installation Disk Set dialog box.

3. Select the network client or service and the destination floppy drive type. If you aren't using new floppies, enable the Format Disks check box. Once you've made your selections, click on the OK button.
4. As prompted, label each floppy before inserting it into the requested drive.
5. If you want to create another installation disk set, repeat steps 1 through 4. Otherwise, click on Exit to terminate the application.

Copying the Client-Based Network Administration Tools

The client-based network administration tools include versions of User Manager for Domains, Server Manager for Domains, DHCP Manager, WINS Manager, Remoteboot Manager, Remote Access Administration, and User Profile Editor for Windows NT and Windows 3.1.

To copy the client-based administration tools, follow these steps:

1. Start the Network Client Administrator, click on the Copy Client-based Network Administration Tools radio button, and click on Continue. The Share Network Client Installation Files dialog will be displayed.
2. Select your source media options, as specified earlier. Once you've made your selections and clicked on Continue, your users will be able to connect to the specified share and run the appropriate setup program to install the administration tools. Windows users will execute the SETUP.EXE program, located in the \SHARENAME\WINDOWS directory, and Windows NT clients will use the SETUP.BAT program, located in the \SHARENAME\WINNT directory.

NOTE

Unfortunately, the Windows NT setup doesn't create a Program Manager group or install any icons. Your users will have to do this for themselves.

Managing Your Remote Boot Clients

The remote boot service lets your client workstations boot MS-DOS and Windows 3.1 directly from the server. Instead of booting from a floppy or hard disk, a diskless workstation uses a *Remote Program Load* (*RPL*) ROM located on the network card. You can think of the RPL ROM as a replacement for your computer's disk controller ROM. Instead of initializing your disk controller ROM and reading the boot block from your hard disk, the RPL ROM is initialized and reads your boot block from a network server's hard disk.

Once the boot block has been executed by the client workstation, it will load either a common, or shared, configuration profile or a user-specific configuration profile. This configuration profile specifies the MS-DOS version to load and the CONFIG.SYS and AUTOEXEC.BAT to execute.

Installing the Remoteboot Service

You install the Remoteboot Service through Control Panel's Network applet. Follow these steps:

1. Start Control Panel and launch the Network applet.
2. Click on Add Software.
3. Select Remoteboot Service, and click on OK.
4. Once the Remoteboot Manager icon has been installed in the Network Administration Group, click on OK. Restart the computer as prompted.

Using the Remoteboot Manager

The Remoteboot Manager, shown in Figure 16.53, is used to create shared or personal profiles and workstation entries. A shared profile can be used by multiple workstations. A change to a shared profile affects all users of the profile. A personal profile, on the other hand, is user-specific and can be customized without affecting other profiles.

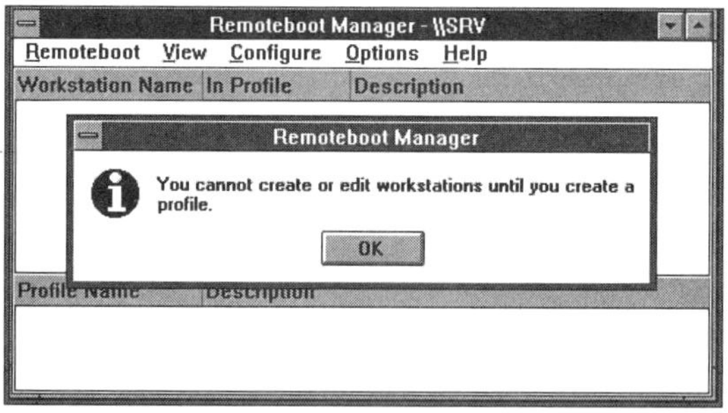

FIGURE 16.53.
Remoteboot Manager's initial display.

The first time you run Remoteboot, you will be informed that a profile must be created before you can create or edit workstation entries. A profile has a unique name, an operating system (which may be shared by multiple profiles), and a network adapter.

To create a profile, follow these steps:

1. Select Remoteboot | New Profile. The dialog box shown in Figure 16.54 will be displayed.

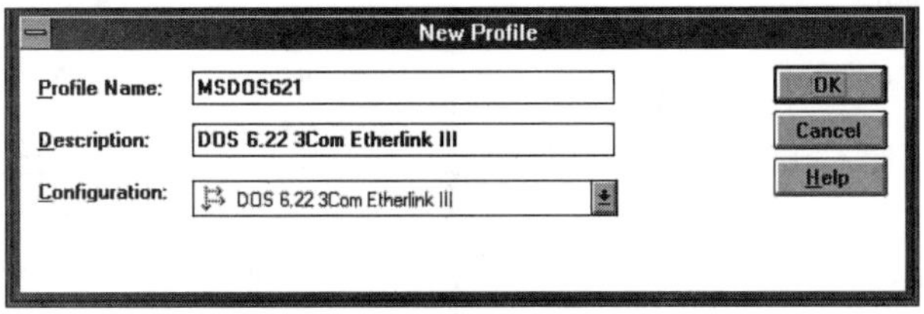

FIGURE 16.54.
Creating a new profile.

2. Enter a unique profile name—for example, `MSDOS621`—with no embedded spaces or backslashes (\) and a maximum length of 16 characters. Also enter a description, such as `MS-DOS 6.21 - Etherlink III`, and select a configuration, such as `DOS 6.22 Etherlink III`. Configurations depend on the operating system software you have installed on the server.

NOTE

After you've installed new operating system software on the server, select Configure | Fix Security to assign the correct file permissions. Then select Configure | Check Configurations to update the available configurations for use by the Remoteboot Manager.

Also note that until you install at least one MS-DOS operating system and execute the procedure just mentioned, you won't be able to create a profile, because no configurations will be listed in the Configuration drop-down list box.

NOTE

Any version of MS-DOS 6.2x will be displayed as MS-DOS 6.22 and must be installed in the \INSTALLROOT\RPL\RPLFILES\CONFIGS\DOS622 directory.

3. Click on OK to create the profile.
4. If you have multiple profiles to create, repeat steps 1 through 3.

Workstation entries, or records, require that the network adapter with the installed RPL ROM be active. This is because each workstation entry utilizes the unique adapter identification number assigned to the adapter by the manufacturer.

To create a workstation entry, follow these steps:

1. Select Remoteboot | New Workstation. The dialog box shown in Figure 16.55 will appear.

FIGURE 16.55.
Adding a workstation.

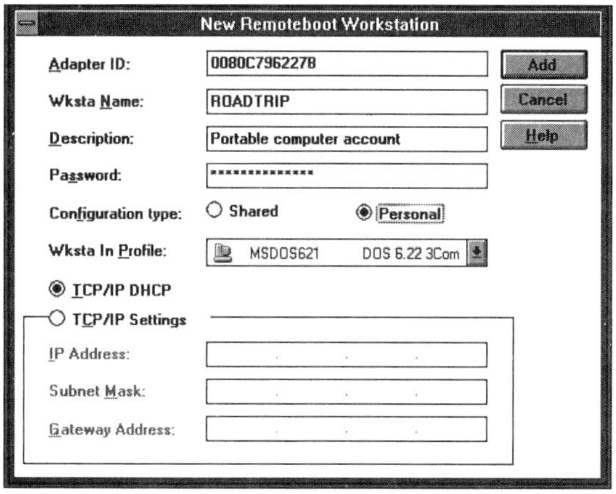

2. If you know the 12-digit hexadecimal adapter identification number of the workstation's network adapter, enter it in the Adapter ID field. If you don't know the adapter identification number, restart the workstation (to create a remote boot record), select View | Refresh (to update the display with the new workstation record), select the new record, and select Remoteboot | Convert Adapter.
3. Enter the workstation's name, a description of the workstation, a password for the workstation computer account, a configuration type (either shared or personal), and a profile for the workstation to use. If TCP/IP is used as a network transport, select the appropriate TCP/IP settings.
4. Repeat steps 1 and 2 for each workstation you configure.

NT Server Gets Big

17

IN THIS CHAPTER

Most small-to-medium-size organizations will find that including all their servers in a single NT Server domain is the best way to set up their networks. A single domain network is easier to design and administer than a multidomain network. Once your network starts to include wide area links, more than 300 users, more than 15 file servers, or independent divisions that don't want central MIS to control their systems, you will have to look seriously at dividing your network into multiple domains.

There are several advantages to dividing your network into multiple domains. For one thing, you eliminate a performance bottleneck at the primary domain controller. In a very large network, the domain controller could end up spending so much time distributing user database updates that it can't also provide regular file services with a reasonable response time. The network traffic created as the domain controller updates each file server in a network also can cause performance bottlenecks, especially on slow wide area network links.

Administratively, multiple domains let you group servers logically so that users browsing for data don't see lists of hundreds of servers. Multiple domains also enable you to easily assign the management of groups of users to different administrators.

Trust Relationships

Without trust relationships, dividing your network into multiple domains would limit a user's access to only the resources in his domain. If he weren't defined as a user in any of the other domains, he couldn't access data there without logging off from his current domain and logging onto the new domain with another account. Trust relationships enable users in one domain to access data in another without creating two accounts—one in each domain. (See Figure 17.1.) This enables the human resources department to manage their own network without allowing the MIS group any access, but it still allows them access to the corporate resources, such as e-mail.

When you establish a trust relationship between two domains, it enables the users and global groups in the "trusted" domain to be recognized, and therefore granted permissions to data and printer resources, in the "trusting" domain. If you want the network administrators from the MIS group, who have their own domain, to be able to manage your accounting domain, you can use User Manager for Domains to add the Domain Admins global group from MIS (domainadmins/mis) to your Domain Admins group, as shown in Figure 17.2.

Trust relationships don't carry forward and aren't transferable. If the Human Resources domain trusts the MIS domain and the MIS domain trusts the Audits domain, that doesn't mean that the Human Resources domain trusts the Audits domain. Each pair of domains that you want to have a trust relationship must have it explicitly. If you want the trust to go both ways, you have to establish a pair of trust relationships—one in each direction.

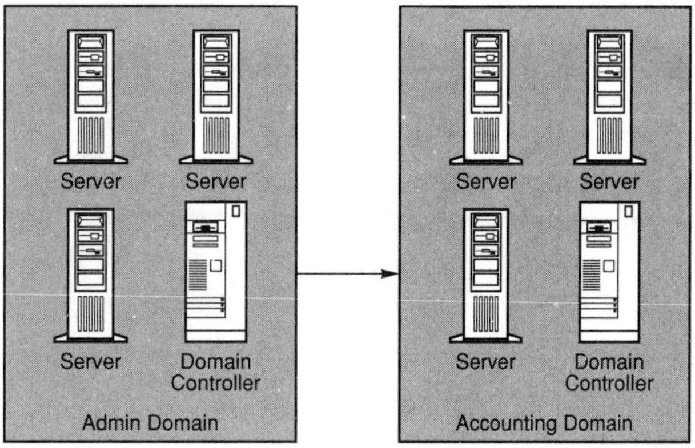

FIGURE 17.1.
The Accounting domain trusts the Admin domain.

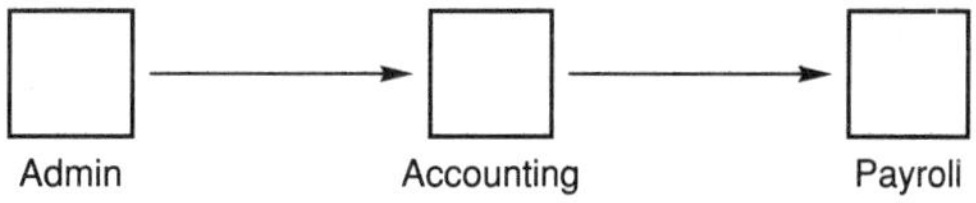

FIGURE 17.2.
The Accounting domain trusts the Admin domain, but the Payroll domain doesn't.

Microsoft suggests four different methods for organizing NT Servers. The single domain model, master domain model, multiple master model, and complete trust model should be treated as just that—models from which you can borrow ideas to come up with the most efficient configuration for your organization.

The Single Domain Model

The single domain model probably is best for you if

- you have a small network
- you have fewer than 15 or so servers
- you have the political power in your organization to be able to manage all the servers from a centralized MIS group
- your network doesn't have wide area or other low-speed links

By sticking to a single domain, you simplify things significantly.

In a single domain network, shown in Figure 17.3, any administrator can manage any of the servers in the domain. You need to worry only about creating one set of users and groups. You don't have to worry about which domains trust each other, and you don't have to create trust relationships.

FIGURE 17.3.
A single domain network.

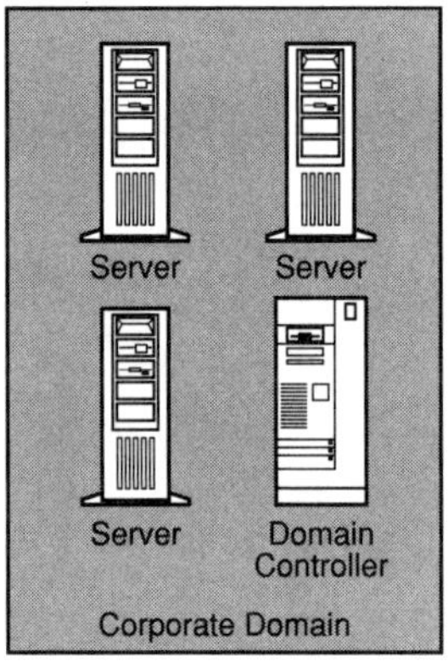

As your network grows, keeping everything in a single domain starts to cause problems. These problems can be broken into the following types:

- Convenience problems, which make using and/or administering the network more difficult
- Performance problems, in which simple domain access tasks create so much data traffic that the network gets clogged
- Security or political problems, in which quasi-independent departments or divisions want to join your network but don't want you, the MIS group, to manage their servers or have access to their data

The primary convenience problem is that, as the domain grows, all the lists in the network start getting uncomfortably large. Users browsing for data have to scroll through long lists of servers and resources, and administrators have to scroll through huge user and group lists. Dividing the network into multiple domains makes these lists easier to manage.

Performance problems rear their ugly heads on several occasions. Every time you create a new user or make some other change to the domain's user database, those changes have to be replicated to all the other servers in the domain. Therefore, the domain controller can become the network's bottleneck if it can't transport that data to a large number of file servers fast enough. Performance problems also can occur as users browse the domain and the servers send their information to the user's workstation.

Security problems are caused not by any technical factor in your network, but by the human factor in your organization. Someone in the executive suite might decide that it's not a great idea for you to have access to all the data on all the servers on your company's network. I've found that the most senior executives and human resources departments frequently want their own domain under their own management to secure their sensitive data. The following list describes the advantages and disadvantages of the single domain model:

Advantage	*Disadvantages*
Simple to administer	No groupings of users into departments No groupings of resources The domain controller can be a bottleneck Browsing resources can be slow and create large amounts of traffic

The Master Domain Model

If you're dividing your network into domains for convenience or to reduce the traffic on your backbone or a wide area link, you might want to set up your system with one master domain that all the other domains trust. (See Figure 17.4.)

FIGURE 17.4.
A master domain network.

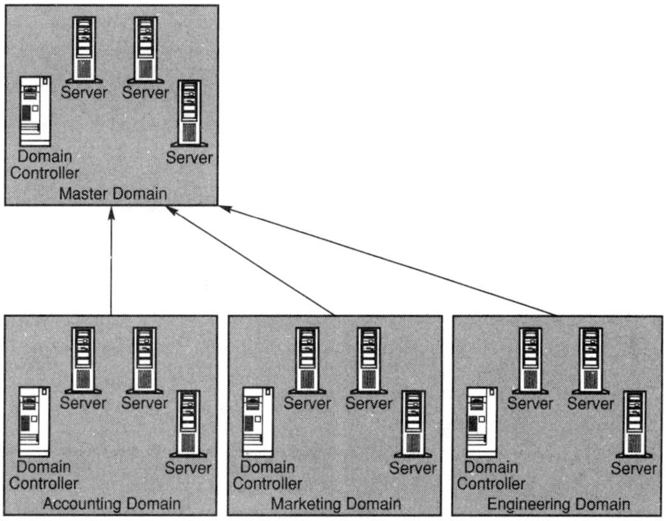

In the NT Server documentation, Microsoft talks about the master domain model, in which all users and groups are created only in the master domain. Trusting, or slave, domains don't have any users defined. This gives you centralized control and ease of administering the single domain model while shortening the browse lists and making the system easier to manage. If you have a central MIS department, it can run the master domain.

The servers in the slave domains refer all logon requests to the master domain, where all the users and groups are defined. If you have a large number of users, this model still gives you incredibly long user lists and might create a bottleneck at the domain controller.

Organizations that follow this model typically create a master domain that is used only to contain the user accounts and then subdomains that contain the actual resources to be shared. In fact, because only servers in the master domain contain the user database, if you don't put a second NT Server in the master domain, the domain controller becomes a single point of failure. If it goes down, no users can log on to the network at all.

The big advantage of the master domain model is that the user divisions can decide for themselves who has access to their resources. Although the central MIS department creates all the user accounts, it doesn't actually need to have administrator-level access to the resource domains. Therefore, the administrators there can keep the master domain administrators away from their data.

If you have a wide area network, all user logon requests from sites other than the one that has the master domain will have to travel across the wide area link. You can reduce the traffic slightly by distributing servers in the master domain throughout your network. The following list describes the advantages and disadvantages of the master domain model:

Advantages	*Disadvantages*
Central administration	Poor performance on wide area networks or with large numbers of users or groups
Resources can be logically grouped	Local groups must be defined on each domain
Departmental domains can have their own administrators for security	The master domain controller can be a single point of failure
Global groups need to be defined only once	

I think a better variant on the master domain model is to create user accounts not only in the master domain but also in the slave or resource domains. If you create the resource domains on a departmental basis, you can create the user accounts for users who will need access only to resources in their department on their departmental domain and users who will need access to data in multiple domains in the master domain. This will reduce network traffic because most logon requests won't need to be forwarded to the master domain.

The Multiple Master Model

As the number of users on your network grows, the single master model starts to break down. The domain database grows so large that resynchronizing file servers or adding a new server to the master domain takes a very long time, and managing a list of 1,000 or more users can be quite difficult.

In the multiple master model, shown in Figure 17.5, instead of declaring a single domain as the sole repository of user and global group accounts, you declare as masters a small number of domains, each with a domain controller and hopefully at least one other server to act as a backup. All the user accounts are created in one of the master domains, which the central MIS department can manage.

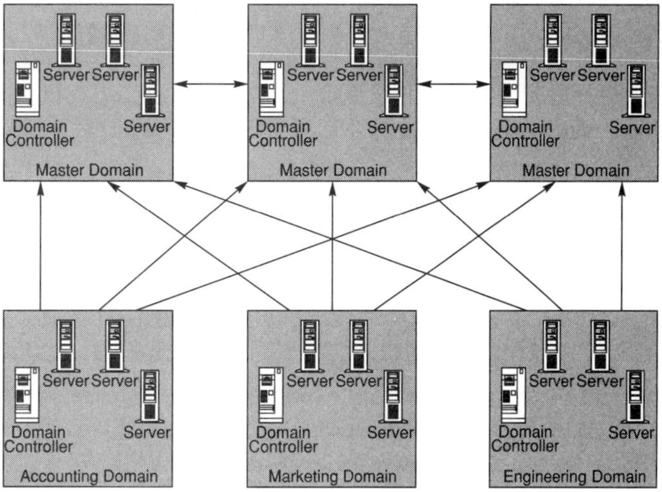

FIGURE 17.5.
A multiple master network.

As with the single domain model, shared resources such as directories and printers are located in a series of subdomains, which can be departmentally or geographically organized. The resource, or slave, domains can be managed by the central MIS department or by local administrators.

Each master domain both trusts and is trusted by each of the other master domains. The resource domains trust all the master domains. Therefore, any user, regardless of the master domain of his or her account, can be granted permission to access resources in any of the resource's domains.

If you start setting up your network following the multiple master model without properly planning the distribution of users among the master domains, you might have a bit of difficulty setting up global groups. Suppose that you wanted to group Excel users or marketing staffers by putting all the users with accounts starting with the letters A-G in one master domain, those starting with H-Q in a second, and the rest in a third. In order to create a global group that contains users from multiple master domains, you'd have to create a global group in each master domain for those users and then create a local group in the resource domains to contain all those global domains.

In order to simplify these groups, your best bet when running a multiple master network, you should spend some time planning how to divide your users among the multiple masters. The best approach usually is to match the master domains to your company's organization, creating a master domain for each division or subsidiary and slave domains for each department within the division. The following list describes the advantages and disadvantages of the multiple master model:

Advantages	*Disadvantages*
Can support large numbers of users with acceptable performance	Groups might need to be defined multiple times for different domains
Resources can be logically grouped	Many trust relationships to manage
Resource domains can be managed independently for security	Maintaining user accounts is more difficult, because they are in multiple domains

The Complete Trust Model

In the complete trust model, shown in Figure 17.6, all the domains in the network both trust and are trusted by all the other domains. Microsoft proposes this model for organizations that don't have a central MIS department to manage one or more master domains. Because there is no master/slave relationship between domains, each department can manage its own domains and be in total control of its own destiny.

FIGURE 17.6.
A complete trust network.

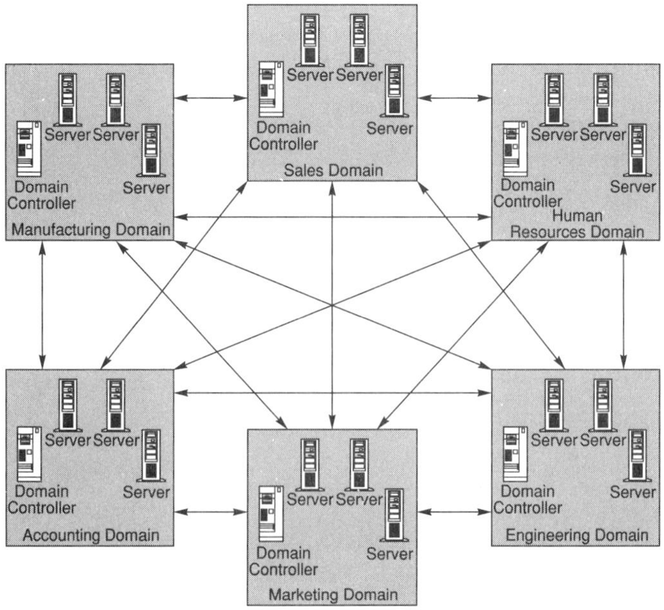

A fully implemented complete trust network requires that you set up a large number of trust relationships. This can make it unsuitable for large organizations with more than a few domains. In fact, the complete trust model requires that you create an $n(n-1)$ trust relationship, where n is the number of domains on your network. A network with five domains will require 20 trust relationships. By the time you're up to 15 domains, you'll need to establish 210 trust relationships. Just adding the 16th domain means adding 30 trust relationships to the other 15 domains on the net. The following list describes the advantages and disadvantages of the complete trust model:

Advantages	*Disadvantages*
Doesn't require central administration	A lack of central administration can lead to anarchy
Can support a large number of users	Requires creating very large numbers of trust relationships
Resources are grouped logically into domains	
Users are grouped logically into domains	
Each department can manage its own resources	

Designing Your Network

In my experience, real-world large networks aren't best designed by making them fit one of Microsoft's textbook models. True small networks are best set up as a single domain. Midsize networks might be best served by using a single master domain, but once the system grows beyond that manageable size, you're going to have to do some careful planning. I've found that, most of the time, a hierarchical structure fits the organizational structure of the company best and is therefore the most logical arrangement. However, you'll have to determine the best arrangement for your company yourself.

Remember that when you trust another domain and grant rights and/or permissions to global groups in that domain, you're really trusting the administrator of that domain, because that person controls which users are members of that group and therefore which users have access to your resources. If you're implementing a multiple domain network in order to have divisions or departments be in control of their data, the administrators in the domains that have your most sensitive data probably shouldn't use global groups from other domains.

If your network has any wide area links, you'll definitely want to use multiple domains. If you have multiple servers in your New York and Chicago offices, the domain controller in

New York will send each update to the domain database across the wide area link multiple times, once for each server on the Chicago side of the link. Because adding a user to a domain can send 1 to 2K to each server, a busy network administrator can really clog up a 9600bps or even a 56Kbps link, preventing real data such as e-mail messages and database requests from crossing the link.

You can cut down on this network overhead by creating a domain in each office and having them trust each other. If you create user accounts for the users in each office on the domain at that location, the only authorization traffic that needs to pass across the wide area link is access requests, when a user in one office wants to access data in the other, and logon requests, when Joe from New York tries to log on from Chicago during his monthly trip to the Windy City.

Internetworking: Remote Access Service and TCP/IP

18

IN THIS CHAPTER

There are basically two ways to allow users at remote sites to access data on your network. Remote control applications such as Carbon Copy and PC Anywhere actually run the remote user's applications on a computer at your site. They then send any data that the user's application sends to the screen across the phone line to the remote user's computer or terminal and send any keystrokes from the remote user's computer to the application. Remote node systems run the application on the remote user's computer and treat the phone line as an extension of the local area network, sending LAN-style traffic, including requests for file and print services, across the phone line. Each approach has its advantages and disadvantages, depending on the type of application you're trying to run across the phone line.

The main problem to be solved with any remote access system is that plain old telephone lines, even with the fastest modems, have a very limited capacity to carry data. The 9600bps modem that you thought was incredibly fast when you called CompuServe to download the latest games is more than 1,000 times slower than the Ethernet that connects your PC to your file server.

The answer is to keep the amount of data traveling across that link as small as possible. Back in the old days—1985—when everyone ran text-based DOS applications, remote-control packages performed much better than remote node systems because a DOS application just can't send too much data to the screen. After all, a full text-mode DOS screen is just 2K, but a graphics screen on a base VGA (640x480 in 16 colors) is well over 100K. If you use a high-resolution or high-color mode, a screen can be well over a megabyte.

When you start running a graphical user interface, everything changes. Updating an 800x600 screen can send 250K of data across the line. If you use a remote node system, such as Windows NT's Remote Access Service (RAS), only the remote user's file access needs to go across the line.

Although there are several remote-control programs for Windows 3.x on the market, I don't know of any for Windows NT. By the time you read this, however, Microsoft (hopefully) will have released the System Management Server (SMS), which will give you the ability to remotely control any MS-DOS, Windows 3.1, or Windows for Workgroups computer as part of its built-in administrative functions.

Remote Access Service (RAS) Features

RAS is a remote node system that allows Windows NT, Windows, Windows for Workgroups, and DOS workstations to access NT Servers across standard telephone lines or other asynchronous connections, X.25 packet switched networks, and/or ISDN lines. As soon as he's connected, the remote user can access resources on any Windows NT machine or NT Server that's connected to the RAS server he's dialed into, as long as they all use the same protocol to provide NetBIOS services.

A single RAS server running NT Server can support up to 256 remote users. Windows NT stations can act as RAS servers for a single dial-in line, so Windows NT users can, from home, dial in to their own workstations and access the rest of their network.

In order to maximize performance on limited-speed lines, RAS takes advantage of modem data compression features or compresses data in software when you use modems that don't do their own compression.

Because RAS treats the phone line as an extension of the LAN, it fully supports NT's security model, complete with trust relationships and centralized domain administration. You can further improve security by implementing callback security, where a user calls into the server, which identifies the user, disconnects the call, and calls the user back at the phone number the system administrator has stored as that user's valid location. RAS also supports additional security devices that can use cards, random-number generators, or other sophisticated techniques to validate users' identities.

Choosing Hardware for RAS

If you're like most PC system administrators, you've never given your system's communications ports much thought. You either ordered your systems with internal modems, which have their own COM ports built in, or worried more about the cables and connectors on your system's COM ports than how they worked. After all, you know that COM1: uses IRQ4 and that COM2: uses IRQ3, so all you have to do is plug in the modem and have a grand old time.

If all you want to do is run Crosstalk under DOS to download Duke Nuke 'em from your local bulletin board, that's all you really need to know about COM ports. If you want to use the latest modems at speeds about 9600bps, or if you want to be able to do something else while your computer downloads Duke Nuke 'em, you need to pay a little more attention.

Standard AT COM ports use 16450 UART (universal asynchronous receiver transmitter) chips to convert the parallel data on the PC's bus to serial data for the COM port. This particular chip has only a one-byte data buffer, so the COM port generates an interrupt every time a byte comes in. If the processor on your PC doesn't service that interrupt before a second byte comes in through the port, that first byte is lost. Supporting a single 9600bps modem for a file upload generates almost a thousand interrupts a second. A second true full duplex communication, with data going both ways on the line simultaneously, requires the processor to deal with almost 2,000 separate, single-byte data transfers every second.

Even a fast PC system such as a 486 DX/33 loses characters if you try to run a modem faster than 9600bps through a standard serial port. Because even a single lost byte in a RAS session forces a retransmission of the whole data packet, losing every 200th byte would result in a net data transmission rate of 0bps.

Most good 486 systems and most high-quality internal modems use the more advanced 16550 UART, which has a built-in 16-byte data buffer. Therefore, the processor can send data to the UART in blocks of 10 or more characters without having to pay attention to the port nearly as often. When receiving data, the processor similarly can empty the buffer 100 rather than 1,000 times a second. If you're investing good money in high-speed modems, you should make sure that all your remote systems are equipped with 16550s.

Using a 16550 UART can relieve the interrupt overhead of one or two serial ports, but even systems running 16550s start to lose data when they run multiple high-speed data streams. The other problem with standard, or nonintelligent, serial ports is that the overhead of actually touching every byte as it comes into or goes out of the system can really slow down the other processes on the system, because they get starved for processor time.

Conventional serial ports, even with 16550s, also limit the number of serial ports your system can support, because each port needs its own interrupt request line and, if you're using internal modems, its own slot.

If you want, or need, to support more than one dial-in line on your dial-in server, you'd better take a good hard look at an intelligent serial I/O card, such as a Digiboard or an IBM Artic card. Rather than connecting the UART to the computer's bus and generating an interrupt for each byte received, these cards have from two to 256 serial ports connected to a dedicated processor, typically a Z-80 or an 80188 with 64K or more memory, to buffer the incoming and outgoing data.

By using an intelligent serial card and external modems, a single RAS server can support eight or more simultaneous connections without losing data or significantly slowing down the other processes on the server. The RAS server can send data to and receive data from the intelligent serial card in 100-byte or larger blocks, just like a LAN card, greatly reducing the overhead on the server.

A Few Words on Modems

If you're like most PC experts (and you wouldn't be reading this book or be interested in Windows NT if you weren't already knowledgeable about PCs, would you?), you probably buy modems more out of habit and prejudice than out of any deep technical knowledge. Most PC managers buy the fastest modems they can afford from whichever vendor they've always bought them from. The biggest decision they're likely to make is whether to buy internal or external modems.

The internal modem supporters argue that internal modems are simpler to use, and that because they don't take up valuable desk space, the user is less likely to screw them up. External modem fans argue that the lights on their models make troubleshooting easier.

I tend to agree with the internal camp for remote sites and times when you have to install a modem in a user's PC and with the external camp for servers and other central site applications.

You do have to watch the design and quality of your internal modems. Many use nonstandard UARTs, which can cause compatibility problems with NT or even MS-DOS. For instance, this book's technical editor has a client with an off-brand internal modem that won't work with Remote Control (from Microcom). Yet the same software on an external modem works flawlessly. You also have to be careful about installation on internal modems. You wouldn't believe how many times I've had to fix problems with machines with two installed com ports, plus an internal modem. COM3 and COM4 aren't well-defined in the PC architecture, and even when you can set a modem to these addresses, they share interrupts with COM1 and COM2, which often causes more problems. If you need more than two serial devices in your system, you should look either at a bus mouse or at a better serial port card, such as a Digiboard 2 port card.

I prefer modular or rack-mount modems for central sites. Rather than making you stack 10 or 20 regular modems on a table and find a way to plug in 10 or 20 annoying little plug transformers, rack modems give you a rack, typically 17 inches wide and 6 to 8 inches high, which has a power supply and bus into which you plug up to 20 modem cards that have a serial port and lights like an external modem.

I developed this preference after working on a large bulletin board, where I discovered that Hayes used the aluminum case of their external modems as a heat sink. If you stacked them more than two high, the modems in the middle would fail due to the heat that developed in the stack. When I switched to rack modems, the internal fans kept everything humming right along.

Actually, more important than whether the modems you use are internal or external is how well they actually work. Whether a modem is the right choice for your application depends on how fast it is and whether it understands the commands RAS sends it and whether it sends back the status information in a way that RAS understands.

One of my first jobs as a writer was to evaluate high-speed modems for *PC Magazine* in 1987. Back then, most modems that sent data faster than 2400bps used proprietary technologies and could communicate only with another identical modem. In addition, there were big differences in how well the modems handled noisy phone lines. If you chose the wrong 9600bps modem for your application, it might not have performed as well as even a 2400bps modem would.

Luckily, the International Trade Union (ITU), formerly the Consultative Committee on International Telephony and Telegraphy (CCITT), has established standards for how modems take the digital data from your serial port and convert it into beeps and squawks that plain old telephone lines can handle. Any two modems that are compliant with, for example, the V.32bis standard will be able to communicate with each other at 14,400bps. The following table shows the modem standards commonly used with PCs and their transmission rates:

Modem Type	*Maximum Speed Before Compression*
V.22bis	2400
V.32	9600
V.32bis	14,400
V.32terbo (de facto standard)	19,200
V.FAST class	28,800
V.34 (not yet finalized)	28,800

Recently, AT&T proposed a new 19,200bps standard, which they called V.32terbo (a pun on V.32ter, which would be the next version of V.32 after V.32bis), and Rockwell, the leading manufacturer of modem chips, proposed a system, V.FAST, that would double V.32bis's 14.4Kbps speed. The ITU decided to reject V.32terbo because it wasn't a big enough advance to make a new standard worth it. They decided instead to make a few changes to V.FAST to turn it into V.34.

As of this writing, you can buy V.32bis modems for $150 to $200, V.32terbo modems—which also support V.32bis, of course—-for $350 or so, and V.FAST class modems for about $450. Because the V.34 standard is still being written, you can't buy V.34-compliant modems yet. However, Rockwell—and the manufacturers using Rockwell's modem chips, including Hayes—promise that they will allow you to upgrade their current 28.8Kbps V.FAST class modems to full V.34 compliance by just changing a ROM chip.

Because I've been burned in the past by both new modem technologies and vendor-promised simple upgrades that turned out to require sending the equipment back to the factory for a month or buying a $200 ROM chip, I remain leery of V.32terbo and V.FAST class modems. If you can live with 14.4Kbps for now, I recommend buying V.32bis modems and waiting until the dust settles on V.34. Six months to a year from now, V.34 modem prices will have come down to the point where you'll be able to buy V.34 modems and throw out the V.32bis modems you buy today without spending more in total than you'd spend for V.FAST class modems today. If you feel the need for speed now, skip V.32terbo and go all the way to V.FAST class.

In addition to just sending data across a phone line, most modems also perform error checking/correction and data compression. The ITU V.42 specification covers error checking and correction, while V.42bis defines a lossless data-compression algorithm that can compress some data up to 4:1. How much compression you'll actually see in the real world depends on the type of data you're trying to transmit. Bitmapped graphics files are the most compressible at about 4:1, and text files, including most word processing files, typically can be compressed at about 2:1. Some data, such as .ARC or .ZIP files that have already been compressed, can't be compressed at all. Sometimes you see a modem vendor claiming to send data across a phone line at speeds of 50 to 100Kbps. Those claims only really apply if you're trying to send 5,000 lowercase m's across the line. RAS users typically won't see more than a 2:1 compression ratio.

NOTE

When we talk about a 9600bps modem, the 9600bps refers to the speed at which data actually passes across the phone line. A modem with data compression, such as V.42bis, takes data in from your computer faster than its rated speed because it compresses the data after it gets it from your system. You should set your communications software, including RAS, to the highest speed your modem can accept data and turn on hardware (RTS/CTS) hand-shaking to get the best performance.

Regardless of the modem technology you choose, make sure that you deal with a reputable vendor such as Hayes, US Robotics, Multitech, or Intel. Off-brand modems generally aren't more than 10 to 15 percent cheaper than modems from the big boys, and they can mean significantly more trouble. As usual, buying a product that's on CompuServe's current supported hardware list—which, by the way, had more than 100 modems listed the last time I looked—probably will make your life easier and definitely will make it easier to get tech support from Microsoft.

MODEM.INF

Although the ITU clearly defines how modems should communicate with one another across the phone lines, no such standards-making body exists to define the commands that computers should use to tell a modem to dial or answer the phone line or to control various modem features such as error correction or data compression. Almost all the modems sold to the PC market claim to be "Hayes-compatible." Exactly what this means differs from vendor to vendor and even between different models of modems from Hayes itself. Just about any modem will dial when you send it an ATDT command, but at least half a dozen different sets of commands, used by different vendors, control the more advanced features.

If you're brave, if you think you know everything there is to know about modems, if you need to stick to the leading edge of technology, or if you're just an idiot, you'll decide to use a modem that's not on Microsoft's supported list. If you've chosen to accept this mission, you'll have to tell Windows NT how to communicate with your modem by modifying the MODEM.INF file.

MODEM.INF contains an entry for each model of modem that's supported by RAS. Each entry contains the modem's maximum data rate, the maximum port speed to use connected to the modem, and the character strings to send to the modem to make it dial, enable and disable data compression, and perform other tasks that RAS might want it to do.

If you're lucky, your modem vendor will be able to provide you with a MODEM.INF file, or at least the information you'll need to create one yourself. If not, see Appendix E of the Remote Access Service manual for more information.

When you get the latest model from Whizzo Datacomm, your regular modem supplier, you might try to take a shortcut and just tell RAS to use the same information for the new modem that it does for last year's Whizzo. To do this, just create an alias entry in MODEM.INF for the new Whizzo:

```
[Whizzo228]
ALIAS=Whizzo9600
```

If you create an alias that points to a modem definition that is an alias itself, your system won't work. If in the example you defined a Whizzo 3000 to use the Whizzo228 definition, it wouldn't work.

Beyond Modems: ISDN and X.25

Modems are a great way to let a few users dial in to your system at relatively low speeds. However, if you need to support a large number of users, or if you need to give your users a faster connection to your RAS server, you should look past modems and plain old telephone lines at X.25 or ISDN alternatives.

ISDN (integrated services digital network) has been billed by the telephone industry as the future of telecommunications. Like plain old telephone lines, ISDN provides a circuit-switched service so that your users with ISDN lines in their field offices or second bedrooms can dial into your RAS server just as they do with a modem. As with plain old telephone service (POTS), you pay the phone company a monthly charge plus a per-minute charge for the calls you make.

The big difference between ISDN and POTS lines is that ISDN lines are digital and can carry substantially more data. A primary-rate interface ISDN line provides two 64Kbps data channels and a 16Kbps control channel for call setup and other communications with the phone company. When a user dials into your RAS server using ISDN, he or she can use one or both of the B data channels to provide a 64 or 128Kbps connection. That's at least twice as fast as the fastest modems on the market.

RAS supports ISDN cards for your PCs from Digiboard.

The problem with ISDN is that, despite the fact that the phone companies have been pushing it as the next generation of telephone service, those B channels can be used for voice too. Since the 1970s, the phone company has been dragging its feet about actually making ISDN available. In the U.S., only about 40 percent of telephone customers can buy ISDN lines. In Europe, especially in the western zone of Germany, ISDN is more widely available.

X.25 is an older, better-established technology than ISDN. Unlike ISDN, it doesn't provide faster connections to your RAS server for your users. Instead, it gives you more flexible, and possibly less expensive, connections from your remote sites to your RAS server. If you've ever used CompuServe or a similar service, your data traveled from the local access node you dialed to CompuServe's data center in Columbus, Ohio across an X.25 network.

You can allow your field sales or service force to access your RAS server without paying the outrageous long-distance surcharges most hotels tack onto their bills by connecting your RAS server to a public X.25 network such as Sprintnet or the CompuServe network. Your users can then call the local node and, by sending a few commands to the X.25 PAD (packet assembler/disassembler), connect to your RAS server across the X.25 network.

X.25 connections are especially important if you're planning to build an international network. Just about every country in the world has at least one domestic X.25 network that is cross-connected to one of the domestic U.S. public data networks. In most countries, the telephone company is part of the government PTT (post/telephone/telegraph). The PTTs usually charge very high rates for long-distance and international calls. The PTT rates for X.25 connections can be as little as one-tenth the cost of a long-distance call.

X.25 is a packet-switched service, like a local area network, so multiple users' RAS sessions can share a single 56Kbps leased line connection from the Eicon X.25 card in your RAS server to your public data network's nearest node. They can connect to the public data network by calling the local node in their city with a standard 9600bps modem or with another 56Kbps leased line and an Eicon card.

Before you rush right out and set up an X.25 network, you should know that the packet-switching and error-correcting overhead of the X.25 protocol can substantially slow down communications with RAS.

Installing RAS

Installing RAS is a bit more complicated than installing a new network protocol. The basic steps are as follows:

1. Install and configure serial port hardware and modems.
2. Load the driver for the intelligent serial port card, if any.
3. Restart the system to start the intelligent card driver.
4. Add the Remote Access Service through Control Panel's Network applet.
5. Select and configure the transport protocols you want to support (NetBEUI, TCP/IP, or IPX/SPX) for your dial-up users.
6. Grant users permission to use RAS through the Remote Access Administrator utility.

If you're planning to use standard serial ports or an internal modem, as you would for a typical RAS client or a Windows NT machine that will be serving a single client, you don't have to worry about installing an intelligent serial card. If you're setting up an ISDN, X.25, or multiline server, you need to install the driver for your card through Control Panel's Network applet. Because Windows NT treats RAS as an alternative network protocol, you install intelligent serial cards, ISDN, and X.25 cards the same way you install an additional LAN card.

You install RAS itself through Control Panel's Network applet by clicking on the Add Software button. When you configure RAS, you have to specify a modem type for each port you want to support and whether each port is to be used for dial-in, dial-out, or both. See Figure 18.1.

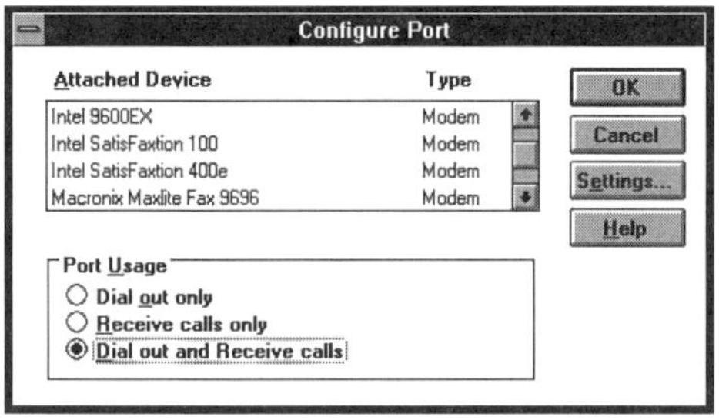

FIGURE 18.1.
The RAS port configuration dialog box.

When you click on the Network button, you can configure your transport protocols and select an encryption scheme, as shown in Figure 18.2. If you click on the Configure button, you can limit users' access to only resources on the RAS server, or you can let them access the whole network. See Figure 18.3.

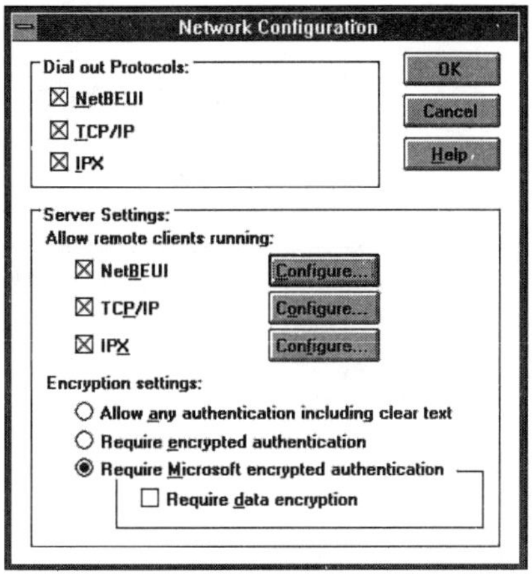

FIGURE 18.2.
The Network Configuration dialog box.

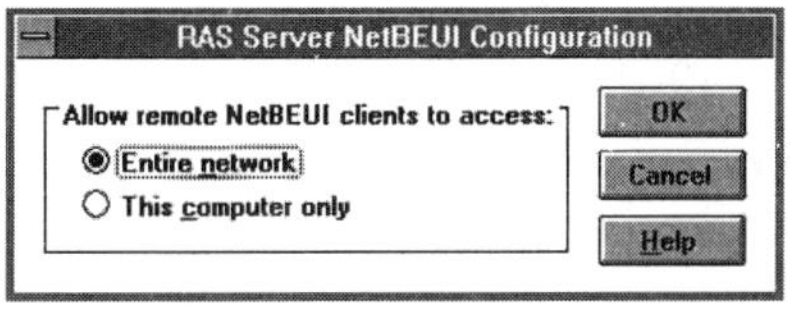

FIGURE 18.3.
The NetBEUI configuration dialog box.

For best performance, enable modem error control, disable modem data compression, and just use RAS's software compression. Testing indicates that RAS's compression is somewhat better than V.42.

Configuring RAS

After you've installed RAS and restarted your computer, you'll notice that you have a new program group for RAS with three programs in it:

- Remote Access: The program you use to call a RAS server
- Remote Access Monitor: Basically an external modem's lights, displayed as a window on-screen
- Remote Access Admin: The administrative tool

If the machine you're setting up will be a RAS server, start the Remote Access Admin application. Through this application's Server menu, you can start, stop, pause, and resume the Remote Access Service on any of the RAS servers on your network—assuming, of course, that you're a member of the Administrators group of the affected server.

Your first step in administering your RAS server is to grant some, or all, of the users defined in your domain permission to use RAS. When you select Users | Permissions, you see the dialog box shown in Figure 18.4.

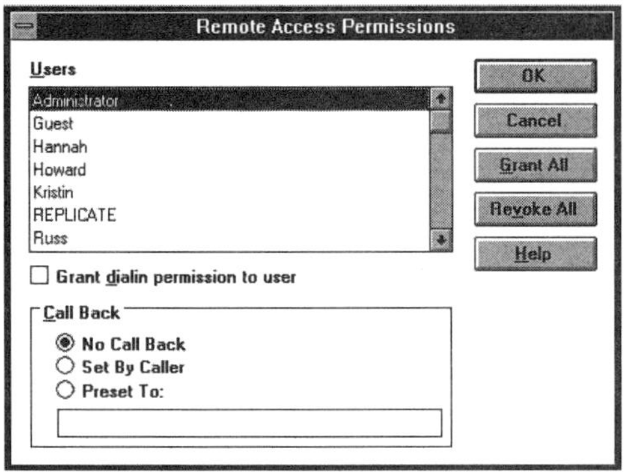

FIGURE 18.4.
User permissions.

Here you can select the users you want to have remote access to your network and grant them permission to use RAS. If you click on the Grant All button, all the users in your domain will be allowed to use RAS. If you click on the Revoke All button, the right to use RAS will be removed from all your users. Revoking all is a good idea if you're taking over a network that hasn't been managed well in the past. Start by revoking Remote Access permission from all your users, then give it back to those who need it.

RAS supports callbacks for security and convenience. When you enable call back, RAS will accept a call from a remote user, ask that user for his or her account and password, hang up the phone line, and call the user back.

If you want to limit your remote users to each being able to call in from a single remote site—for example, their office at home—to improve network security, select Preset To and enter the phone number RAS should call back for that user.

NOTE

Callback security is not absolute, especially if your RAS service is connected to your company's PBX. A skilled hacker can reprogram the PBX, or even the telephone company's central office switch, to redirect the callback number to another site.

If you want to support callback to prevent your field salesman from running up a big phone bill by having the server call back, and therefore pick up the cost of the call, you can select Set By Caller. When a user with this type of callback calls the system, RAS asks him where he should be called back.

At first glance, the Set By Caller option seems to be a great way to avoid hotel long-distance surcharges, customer site phone bills, and other similar problems. Remember, however, that the user's modem has to answer the phone automatically when the RAS server dials the number he enters. A hotel operator or other human intervention prevents you from using this callback option. An 800 number for your salespeople to call probably would work better.

To control how your users will access your system, and thus the network it's connected to, via RAS you should run the RAS administration program, shown in Figure 18.5.

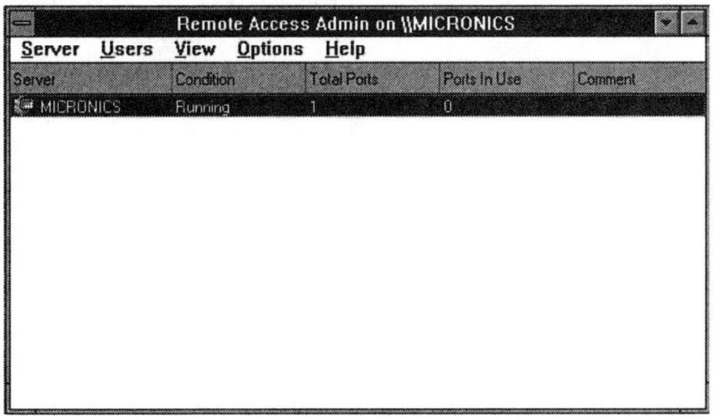

FIGURE 18.5.
The RAS administration program.

If you double-click on a server, or select a server and then select Server | Communication Ports, you get a list of the ports and modems on this RAS server. You can use this screen to reconfigure the server's communications ports if you upgrade your modems. More important, you can double-click on a port and get the status screen shown in Figure 18.6 to see how a session with a remote user is going.

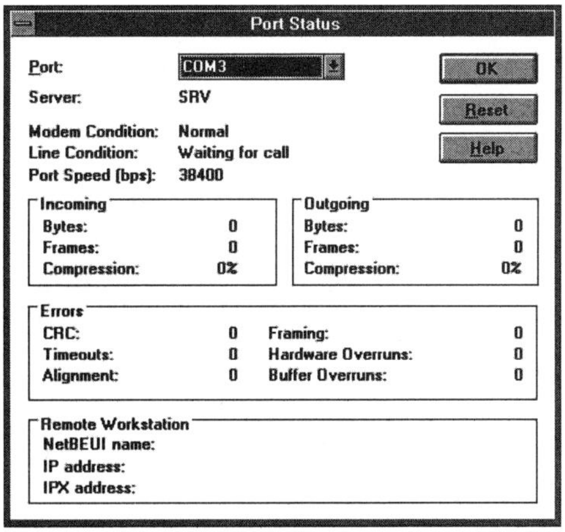

FIGURE 18.6.
The Port Status dialog box.

The Active Users option on the Users menu allows you to send messages to users and disconnect users from the RAS server.

Using RAS

When you want to call into a RAS server, open the Remote Access application. The first time you start Remote Access, you're prompted to create the first entry in your phone book through the dialog box shown in Figure 18.7. Here you can enter the number of the RAS server and once again set the modem or other hardware settings. As soon as you've got entries in the phone book, click on the Dial button and log on. When you're done, log off and hang up.

FIGURE 18.7.
Phone book entry.

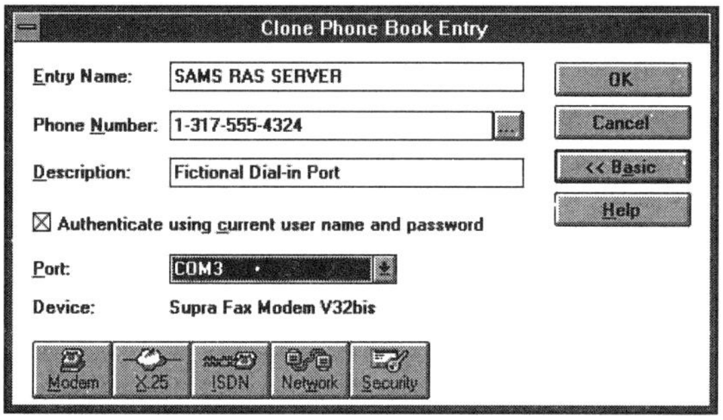

If you want to connect to the Internet or to any UNIX server, you can configure the RAS connection to use either the Point-to-Point Protocol (PPP) or the Serial Line Internet Protocol (SLIP) via the Network button. See Figure 18.8.

FIGURE 18.8.
The Network Protocol Settings dialog box.

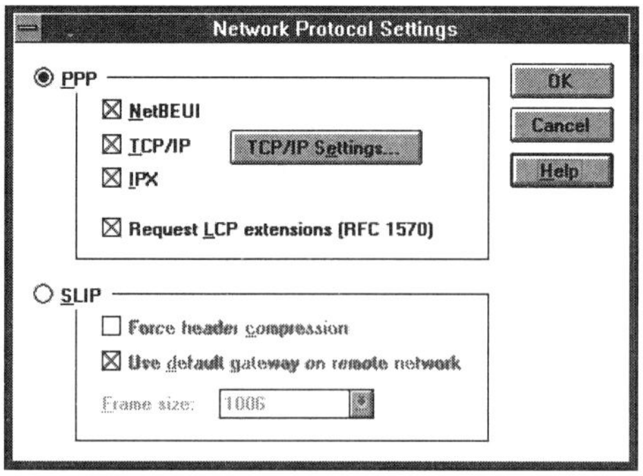

Connecting LANs

RAS is a good way to allow users to dial in to your network and access its resources from remote sites such as homes or hotels. If you have sites such as field offices that need continuous connections to your servers, or if you have more than one or two users who need simultaneous access, you'll probably be better off linking the LANs at these remote sites.

Bridges and Routers

To connect two networks, you'll need a bridge or a router at each site to connect the LANs to the wide area link. The bridge or router examines each data frame that comes across the LAN it's connected to and sends those frames that are intended for systems on the other side of the link across it.

Bridges and routers differ in how they determine which data should cross the link and which shouldn't. A bridge works at the MAC sublayer of the OSI data layer. It builds a table of all the node addresses that it's seen as source addresses on each of its Ethernet port and forwards those packets that are addressed to any port that hasn't been a source address on a frame so far.

Routers work at the network layer, examining the data packet's network address field and determining whether the packet is supposed to go to a different network. Routers, unlike bridges, rely on a particular network layer protocol. Routable protocols such as IPX or TCP/IP's IP (internetwork protocol) divide the address of a node on the network into a network (think of it as the street name) and a node (think of it as the house number).

Rather than keeping track of which nodes have sent packets to determine which packets should be forwarded, all the routers on the network communicate with each other, exchanging information about which networks they communicate with. Routers are responsible not only for forwarding packets but also for determining the best route any given data packet should take.

If you have a small network, bridges might be the right choice for you. As your network grows, bridges become a less attractive alternative. The problem with bridges is that they forward broadcasts and other data packets that routers would be smart enough to know didn't really need to be forwarded. In addition, if you build a network that has multiple paths that data can take—for example, your New York, Chicago, and St. Louis offices all connected in a triangle—your bridges will send any data packet from New York that is intended for either of the other offices to both, tying up your valuable wide area bandwidth.

Because routers know how to get from New York to Chicago, they would send only the data actually intended for machines in the Chicago office to the Chicago office. Routers, therefore, make more efficient use of the wide area network.

Routers do have two disadvantages. First, any given router can route only protocols that it's programmed to handle. If you buy a TCP/IP router and later decide that you also need to send IPX or Appletalk traffic across that link, you might need to update or replace your routers. Some routers, called bridging routers or brouters, bridge any data packets that aren't in one of the protocols that it knows how to route. The other problem with routers is that typically they're more expensive and more difficult to configure than simple bridges.

NOTE

If you have more than two locations, or more than five separate networks, even if they're all in one location, routers are a better idea than bridges.

Now that you've decided to use routers to link your networks, you have to actually find a real product to use. You can buy sophisticated routers from cisco, IBM, 3Com, or Wellfleet that can handle five or more local Ethernet or Token Ring connections and several high-speed WAN connections.

NOTE

If you're using DHCP or WINS, check with your router manufacturer for updates to support these services if necessary. Not all routers will support DHCP and WINS without software upgrades.

If your budget or your needs are more limited, you can build your routers from the PC platforms you know and love. Novell's MPR (multiprotocol router), Newport's LAN2LAN MPR, and several other products turn a PC with one or more Ethernet and/or wide area interface cards into a full-fledged router. PC-based routers, as you might guess, are slower than cisco or Wellfleet's RISC-based routers, but typically they can keep up with a single wide area network line at speeds up to T-1.

Phone Lines and Other Links

As you learned earlier in this chapter, plain old telephone lines, even with the fastest modems, are much slower than the LANs you're used to. If you really want the users in your Chicago office to be able to access the resources in New York without growing old and gray waiting for their applications to run, you'll have to set up a faster connection.

The traditional way to build a wide area network is to buy digital leased lines to connect your sites. Unlike dial-up or circuit-switched, leased lines provide a continuous connection between two locations at a fixed cost per month. If you're going to be using the connection between your offices more than about 60 hours a month, a leased line generally is cheaper than the equivalent dial-up service.

The basic building block of digital leased line services is a 64Kbps line called DS-0 (digital service-0). The telephone network was originally built to support voice communications. As AT&T started to change their system to use digital signals on the long-distance portion of a call, in order to allow them to give better signal quality and to send more voice calls across the same number of copper-wire pairs, they used a voice digitizing system that used 56Kbps of bandwidth to carry the voice signal and 8Kbps of call management overhead data. Therefore, here in the U.S. we can buy 56Kbps leased lines. In Europe, and in most of the world outside North America, the telephone companies give the user the full 64Kbps and use their own lines for the overhead.

Unless you've done a very good job of designing your applications and you compress your data within an inch of its life, your users probably aren't going to be very happy with a 56Kbps connection. The next step up, which generally is available, is called T-1 or DS-1 in North America and E-1 in the rest of the world. At 1.544Mbps (or 2.048Mbps in Europe), a T-1 line provides enough bandwidth for most applications, especially if you use bridges or routers with data compression.

Because T-1 lines can be quite expensive, up to several thousand dollars per month for a coast-to-coast line, customers started clamoring for something faster than a 56Kbps line that they could afford. Some innovative long-distance carriers developed a series of services they called fractional T-1. Fractional T-1 lines provide from 122Kbps to 768Kbps in multiples of 56 or 64Kbps.

If you're building a huge network, or if you just have incredibly data-hungry applications, such as CAD/CAM or multimedia applications, you might find that even T-1 lines don't give your users the kind of response times you'd like. If you want to go even faster, you can buy T-3 (45Mbps) or fractional T-3 services.

The following table shows a summary of the common line options you can use to build your wide area network:

Line Type	*North American Speed*	*European Speed*
DS-0	56Kbps	64Kbps
Fractional T-1	112Kbps to 768Kbps	128Kbps
T-1/E-1	1.544Mbps	2.048Mbps
T-3 and fractional T-3	3 to 45Mbps	4 to 45Mbps

If 45Mbps isn't enough for you, this book isn't adequate to get you set up. I strongly recommend that you hire an expert to design your network.

Packet Switched Services

Because you're paying the telephone carriers to give you a 56Kbps or faster data link 24 hours a day, seven days a week, leased lines are a relatively expensive way to build your wide area network. Packet switched services allow you to share communications facilities with other users while sharing the cost.

In a packet switched network, also called a public data network, if users from multiple companies are allowed to send their data across the network, each of your field offices is connected, via a leased line, to the data network's closest node or point of presence. There the data is multiplexed with the data from all the other users of the network at the network vendor's PAD (packet assembler/disassembler) or router and sent across the network to the point of presence where your other office is connected.

The first generation of packet switched networks used the CCITT X.25 protocol. I've already talked about these networks, because you can use them with RAS to allow your users to call into your RAS server from remote locations. X.25 networks were developed back when the long-distance locations were using analog technology and had relatively high data rates. In order to compensate, X.25 networks perform error checking as data crosses each router on the network. All of this error checking can slow your data (in technical terms, increase latency), making X.25 networks unsuitable for most LAN-to-LAN traffic.

Frame Relay networks, which are now available in most parts of the U.S., assume that the lines making up the network have low error rates and therefore perform error correction only at the final destination of the data packet. Because modern fiber optic lines have very low error rates, the fact that this end-to-end error checking is much slower if errors occur is more than made up by the fact that it is faster when there are no errors. If you have more than three or four sites in your network, you should take a good hard look at Frame Relay.

Asynchronous Transfer Mode is everyone's pick as the data communications medium of the 21st century. Like Frame Relay, it is a fast packet switching system. Unlike Frame Relay, it can be used for local area networks as well as wide area networks. ATM products are just now coming to market and are still very expensive.

The following table shows the commonly available packet switched services and their relative merits:

Network Type	*Suitability for LAN-to-LAN*	*Speed*	*Cost*
X.25	Low	9600 to 56Kbps	Moderate
Frame Relay	High	9600 to 1.544Kbps	Moderate
ATM	High	T-1 to 155Mbps	High

Hooking Windows NT to Your WAN

You could just set up a default Windows NT or NT Server network at each of your offices and use bridges and leased lines to connect them. This would be a big mistake. Although the NetBEUI protocol that NT uses by default to connect workstations to servers is very efficient on small networks, it's not really suitable for wide area nets. NetBEUI uses your computer's name as its address without any additional network address. This makes NetBEUI a nonroutable protocol.

NetBEUI uses broadcast messages to determine what computer names exist on the network. These broadcasts, combined with packets that get bridged in multiple directions, quickly bog down your network.

TCP/IP

Luckily, Windows NT also includes support for the TCP/IP protocol suite. TCP/IP was first developed under a U.S. Department of Defense contract for use on the ARPAnet, which has grown into the Internet, a very large wide area network, and it's well-suited to wide area network use. As a result, these protocols are frequently also called the Internet protocol suite.

TCP/IP's network layer protocol, IP, uses both network and node address fields, so it can be routed easily. In fact, almost all routers on the market support TCP/IP.

Unlike IPX or NetBEUI, the term TCP/IP doesn't refer to a single protocol, but to a set of protocols, also called a protocol stack, that performs the functions of all seven layers of the OSI model. In an effort to solve the problem of having at least one of every computer ever made and not being able to pass data between them, the DOD decreed that they would no longer buy computer systems that didn't support the TCP/IP protocol stack. Because these are the same people who think that $600 is a perfectly reasonable price for a hammer, no self-respecting computer manufacturer let this opportunity pass, and TCP/IP became the lingua franca of computing. The growth of TCP/IP was further accelerated by its inclusion in the 4.2bsd (Berkeley Software Distribution) version of UNIX.

The TCP/IP protocol stack is defined in a series of documents called RFCs (requests for comment), which are circulated on the Internet. There are RFCs to define the common TCP/IP protocols and applications listed in the next paragraph and for more obscure applications such as those in which you send voice or video data across a TCP/IP network.

The following are common TCP/IP protocols:

- IP: Internetwork protocol
- UDP: User datagram protocol

- TCP: Transmission control protocol
- SNMP: Simple network management protocol
- Telnet: A terminal emulation protocol
- FTP: File transfer protocol
- TFTP: Trivial file transfer protocol
- SMTP: Simple mail transfer protocol
- NFS: Network file system

The TCP/IP protocol suite isn't actually OSI-compliant, as you can see from Figure 18.9. The Internet protocol suite really defines three layers that sit on top of just about any data link and physical layer. TCP/IP is commonly implemented on Ethernet, Token Ring, FDDI, and serial telephone line networks (called SLIP for serial line IP).

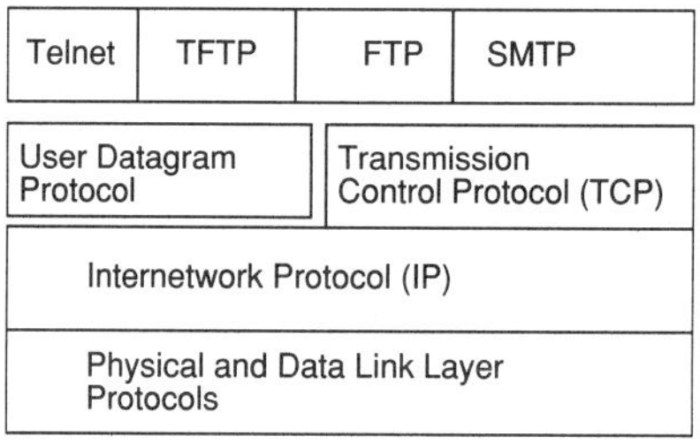

FIGURE 18.9.
The TCP/IP protocol stack.

Internet Protocol

The Internet Protocol (from this point on I'll call it IP) operates as a network layer protocol responsible for routing, addressing, and packet delivery. Like most network layer protocols, IP doesn't handle assured delivery, packet division and sequencing, or error correction. These functions should be handled in higher-layer protocols such as TCP.

IP Addressing

Every computer or other device on a TCP/IP network, called a host in TCP/IP-speak because all computers were host computers when the protocols were designed, must have a unique 32-bit address. IP addresses usually are written with the value of each byte of the address in decimal, separated by periods from the other bytes in the address—for example, 234.34.222.123.

A 32-bit IP address includes both the address of the network the host is connected to and the unique address on that network for this host. If you plan to connect your network to the Internet, you have to get a network address assigned to you by the Defense Data Network-Network Information Center (DDN-NIC). If you're using a commercial Internet access provider such as UUNET, Alternet, or PSI, they will take care of this for you.

In order to support both large and small networks, the Internet addressing scheme supports three different classes of networks. Class A network addresses have values from 1 to 126 for their first byte. The remaining three bytes are used for the host's address within the network. There are only 126 possible Class A network addresses on the Internet. A node with an Internet address of 46.23.42.243, therefore, is node 23.42.243 on network 46. Class A networks are designed for large networks, because each Class A network can have more than 16 million unique host addresses.

Class B networks use values of 128 to 191 in their first byte. The first two bytes of a Class B address identify the network, and the last two bytes identify the host address on that network. An IP address of 182.47.33.21, therefore, is host 33.21 on network 182.47. The 16,384 possible Class B networks can each have 65,534 hosts.

Class C networks have first-byte values of 192 to 223. The first three bytes of a Class C address represent the network number, and only the last byte is the host address. An IP address of 220.200.200.1, therefore, represents host 1 on network 220.200.200. Each of the more than 2 million possible Class C networks can each have up to 255 hosts.

As you can imagine, this addressing scheme can result in some very inefficient uses of the possible address space. Because your routers work better if each Ethernet segment in your company has a different network address, you're unlikely to have enough hosts on your network to use even a small fraction of the addresses available on your Class B network.

To solve this problem, or some users would say to make things more complicated, an IP network can be further divided into subnets. To do this, you create a subnet mask—a 32-bit data structure typically written in the dotted digital notation used for IP addresses. Your subnet mask should have a 1 in each bit of the IP address to represent the network and subnetwork and a 0 for each bit of the host address.

A Class A network's default subnet mask is 255.0.0.0, a Class B network's is 255.255.0.0, and a Class C network's is 255.255.255.0. If you want to divide your Class B network into 16 subnetworks, you would use a subnet mask of 255.255.240.0, which would reserve the first four bits of the third byte for the subnet number.

NOTE

All the computers on a single network segment—that is, connected to the same router port—must use the same network address and subnet mask.

Transmission Control Protocol

The Transmission Control Protocol, or TCP, is the most common higher-layer protocol in the TCP/IP stack. TCP is a connection-oriented, assured-delivery protocol with error checking and packet division and sequencing. A sophisticated protocol, TCP assures a transmitter that the data she's sending gets to its destination.

User Datagram

All of TCP's sophisticated features and error checking add some overhead and take time. If your higher-layer protocol is going to do its own error checking, it can use UDP, the user datagram protocol, instead of TCP. UDP is a simple protocol that doesn't do much error checking and is somewhat faster than TCP as a result.

Upper-Layer Protocol

FTP (file transfer protocol) and TFTP (trivial file transfer protocol) are used to exchange files between hosts. If you want to download a file from a site on the Internet, such as the latest patches to Windows NT from the Microsoft FTP server, you can use FTP or TFTP to make that transfer. TFTP uses UDP as its transport protocol and has less security checking than FTP, so it's frequently not supported on public access sites.

Telnet is a protocol designed to support terminal emulation programs, including the Windows NT Terminal. Because many TCP/IP hosts are UNIX systems, Telnet usually is used to allow a user at one host to emulate a terminal connected to another.

The network file system, or NFS, was first designed by Sun Microsystems. NFS, like Windows NT's SMB, is a file access protocol that allows users at one computer to access files on another.

SMTP, the simple mail transfer protocol, is used to send e-mail messages from host to host. Most UNIX e-mail systems use SMTP-based mail systems.

SNMP, the simple network management protocol, allows a user at an SNMP console to interrogate other nodes on the network—including hubs, routers, servers, and other network resources—and collect statistics from the device or control it. Typically, SNMP is used to collect error or traffic statistics and to control failed ports on hubs or routers. What information is available for controlling any particular device is defined by the MIB (management information base) for that device.

Domain Name Service

Although computers are perfectly comfortable thinking about other computers strictly by their IP addresses, most humans find it difficult to remember addresses such as 137.14.14.14. They would rather deal with names that seem more meaningful in human terms, such as `ftp.microsoft.com`.

Internet names typically consist of the host name, domain name, and type of domain, separated by periods. Several domain types have been defined, including `net` for network control and management hosts, `gov` for U.S. government hosts, `edu` for educational institutions, and `com` for commercial users. International hosts typically use their country code for the domain type.

Here are some typical host names:

`whitehouse.gov`	Bill Clinton and friends
`FTP.microsoft.com`	Microsoft FTP Server
`compuserve.com`	The CompuServe information service

In early (or simple) TCP/IP implementations, each host on the network has a table stored on it, which has a list of the other host names and IP addresses known to this host. Because these tables have to be maintained manually, it quickly gets to be a major administrative task to add the 100th host to your network.

The Domain Name Service allows a single or small group of name servers to store the host-to-address translation table. It allows other hosts to ask the domain name server how to find any given host.

Windows NT and TCP/IP

Windows NT can use TCP/IP as a transport protocol for its file and print services through the NetBIOS interface for TCP/IP, called NBT. This interface, defined in RFCs 1001 and 1002, doesn't encapsulate NetBEUI packets within IP but sends straight IP packets and communicates with other programs through the NetBIOS interface.

Windows NT users also can use TCP/IP to access other host computers across a TCP/IP network. Windows NT includes many of the usual TCP/IP applications:

Application	*Description*
Finger	Gets information about a host and its users
ARP	Converts IP addresses to Ethernet or Token Ring addresses
FTP	Transfers files
Ping	Confirms that a host can be communicated with
RCP	Remote file copy
Rexec	Runs program on remote host
Rsh	Runs shell script on remote host
Terminal and Telnet	Terminal emulation
Tftp	File transfers
Route	Builds routing tables

Windows NT also includes an FTP server program to allow other FTP hosts to exchange files with the Windows NT system.

Windows NT supports the Windows Sockets API to allow third-party products such as client/server database front-ends, terminal emulators, GUI file transfer utilities, and NFS clients or servers to take advantage of its TCP/IP protocol stack.

Installing TCP/IP

Like most other networking software for Windows NT, TCP/IP is installed through the Network applet in Control Panel. Before starting your installation, you should assemble a few pieces of information:

- Your domain name
- Your default gateway (nearest router)
- Your primary and secondary WINS server IP addresses (if any)
- The IP addresses of any DNS servers in your domain (if any)
- The LMHOST file for your network (if any)

If you aren't using DHCP configuration, you'll also need to know the following:

- Your network number
- Your subnet mask
- This station's IP address

To install TCP/IP and related services, follow these steps:

1. Open the Network applet in Control Panel, click on the Add Software button, and select TCP/IP protocol.
2. The dialog box shown in Figure 18.10 will appear. From it, you can select the TCP/IP services to be installed. After selecting the desired services, click on Continue. You will be prompted for the source media.
3. When exiting the Network applet, you'll see the SNMP Configuration dialog box, shown in Figure 18.11. From it, you can configure the SNMP service.

To configure the SNMP service, follow these steps:

1. Enter the names of the SNMP communities that you want the SNMP station to send messages to in the event of an error trap. On most networks, all the SNMP clients on the network are members of the public community. When an SNMP trap message is sent, the community name is part of the message.
2. For each community, enter the IP address or the host name of the SNMP console in that community that the SNMP trap messages should be sent to.

FIGURE 18.10.
The TCP/IP Installation Options dialog box.

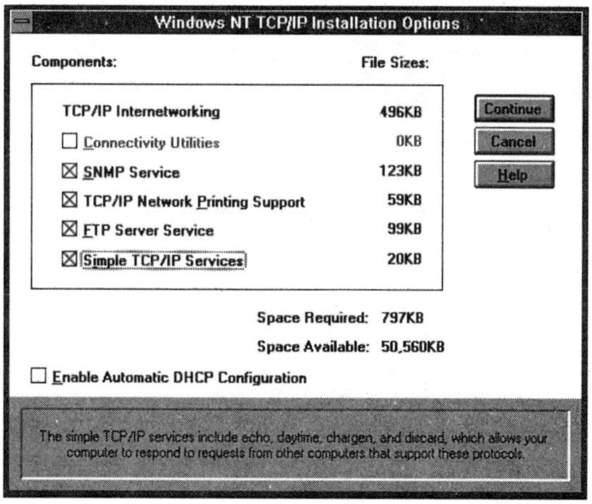

FIGURE 18.11.
The SNMP Service Configuration dialog box.

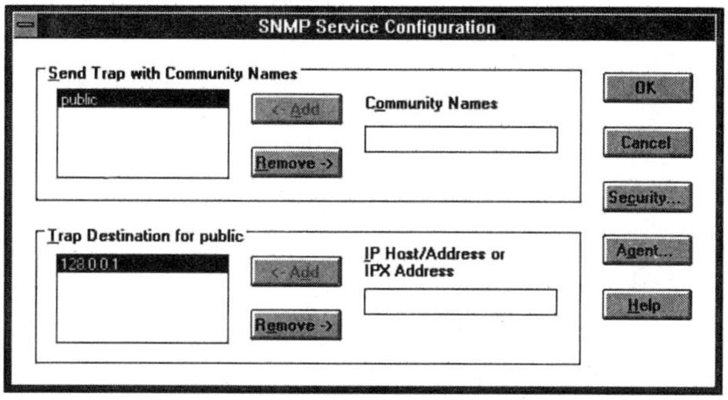

3. If you want to prevent unauthorized users from accessing the SNMP service and possibly resetting some valuable counters, click on the Security button. The dialog box shown in Figure 18.12 appears.

FIGURE 18.12.
The SNMP security configuration.

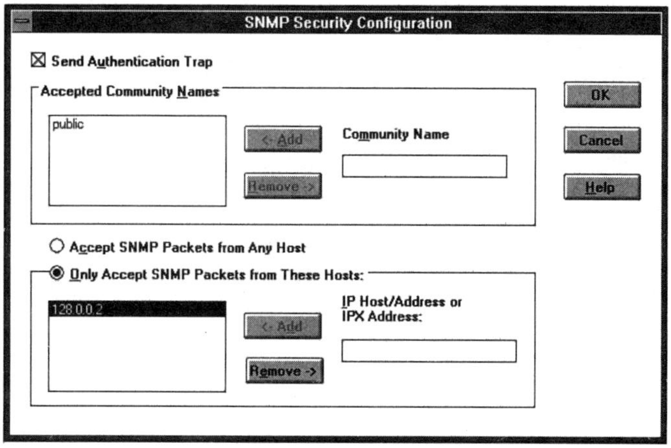

4. To limit access to the SNMP service to SNMP consoles in specific communities, enter the community names in the Accepted Community Names box. If security is really a concern, make sure that the public community isn't in the Accepted list.
5. Enable the Only Accept SNMP Packets from These Hosts radio button to further limit SNMP requests that will be honored by this station to the list of IP addresses you enter in the lower portion of the dialog box.
6. Put an X in the Send Authentication Trap box to have the system send out an error trap if an unauthorized host tries to access the SNMP service.
7. After configuring security, click on the Agent button (refer to Figure 18.11) to configure the SNMP agent through the dialog box shown in Figure 18.13.

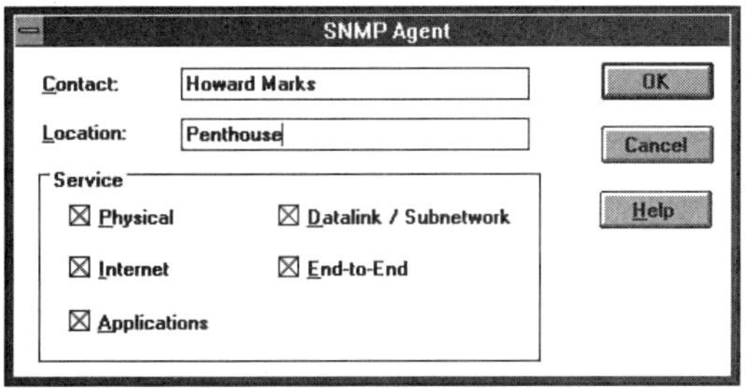

FIGURE 18.13.
The SNMP Agent dialog box.

8. Enter the contact name and the computer's location in the appropriate fields. This information will help the network manager at the SNMP console solve problems reported by the SNMP agent.
9. Put Xs in the Applications and End-to-End boxes to report data on those services.
10. If you chose to install the FTP Service, you'll see a warning box. It informs you that FTP logons send their passwords across the network in clear text, so anyone on your network with a protocol analyzer such as a sniffer can discover a user's password. Then the dialog shown in Figure 18.14 appears. From it, you can configure the FTP service.

To configure the FTP service, follow these steps:

1. Enter the maximum number of users who will be allowed to access the FTP server at the same time, up to a maximum of 50. Also enter the default or home directory for FTP access.
2. If you want to allow users to access your FTP server using the username of Anonymous and no password, enable the Allow Anonymous Connections check box.

   Anonymous FTP connections are commonly used for public file distribution servers on the Internet. When a user logs onto the server, he will be prompted for his e-mail address.

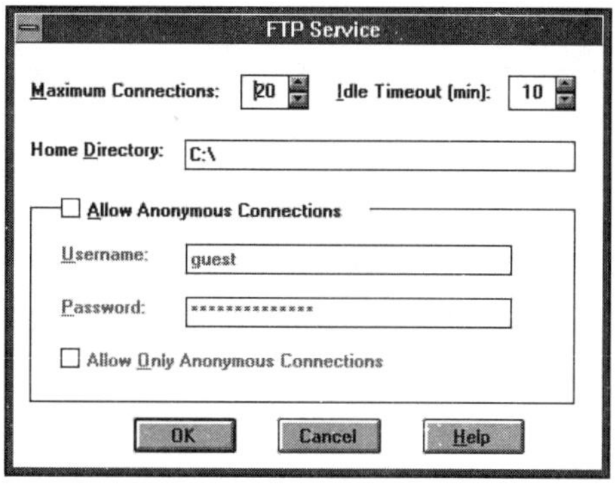

FIGURE 18.14.
The FTP Service dialog box.

3. Enter the user ID and password for the user, whose rights and permissions will be granted to users who log on as Anonymous.
4. If you enable the Allow Only Anonymous Connections check box, users won't be able to log onto the FTP service with their normal Windows NT account names. This prevents users from sending their passwords in clear text across the Net.
5. After you configure all the TCP/IP services, the dialog box shown in Figure 18.15 will be displayed. From it, you can configure the TCP/IP protocol.

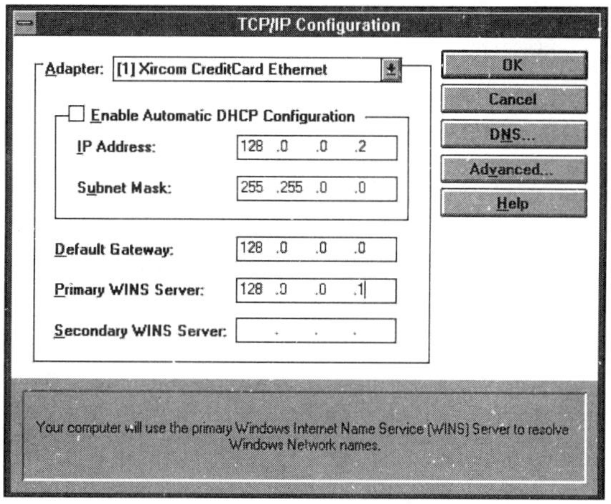

FIGURE 18.15.
The TCP/IP Configuration dialog box.

To configure the TCP/IP protocol, follow these steps:

1. If you're using DHCP to assign IP address, check the Enable Automatic DHCP Configuration check box. If you're not, enter the IP address for the network card shown in the IP Address field. Remember that every computer on the network must have a unique IP address, or it won't be able to communicate.

2. Enter your subnet mask into the appropriate field. Remember that all the hosts and routers on your network must be using the same subnet mask.
3. If this system is connected to an internetwork linked by routers, enter the IP address of the router port nearest to this station on the network into the Default Gateway field. A *gateway* is a TCP/IP term for what the rest of the world would call a router.
4. If you're using WINS to assign NetBIOS names, enter the IP address of your primary and secondary WINS servers into the Primary and Secondary WINS Server fields.
5. If you're going to be using TCP/IP for Windows NT file and print services, select one of the network adapters in your system to use for that purpose. Windows NT can support multiple network adapters in any given system for NetBIOS via TCP/IP, but each adapter must have its own IP address.

TIP

If you use multiple adapters with unique TCP/IP addresses, you can enable IP routing through the Enable IP Routing check box, accessed through the Advanced button.

6. If this computer is going to be a member of an NT Server domain on a different IP subnet, it must have an LMHOSTS file in its \WINNT\SYSTEM32 \DRIVERS\ETC directory. If you click on the Import LMHOSTS button, you'll be prompted for a path to an LMHOST file, which will be copied to the appropriate directory.

   If you're using NetBEUI as your transport protocol, your workstation will locate a domain server by sending out NetBIOS broadcast messages. Because IP broadcasts stay within the subnet they were sent in instead of crossing routers, a workstation won't be able to locate a server or domain controller on another subnet. The LMHOSTS file contains a list of IP addresses and NetBIOS names to allow the station to be able to locate the NetBIOS names listed. A typical LMHOSTS entry looks like this:

   ```
   122.22.22.3       AcctSrv
   ```

   Any other systems on other IP subnets that this computer's replication service is going to import data from or export data to must also be listed in the LMHOSTS file.
7. If you have a Domain Name Server on your network, click on the Connectivity button to configure your station to use DNS through the dialog box shown in Figure 18.16.

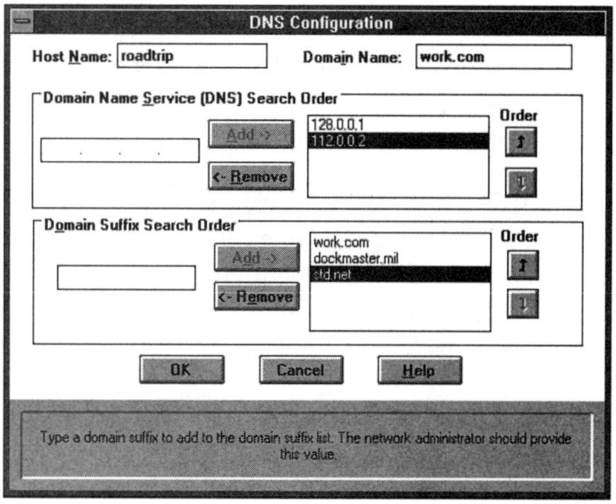

FIGURE 18.16.
The DNS Configuration dialog box.

8. First, you need to enter this system's DNS name. Put the host name, typically the same as the computer's NetBIOS name, in the Host Name field. Put the DNS domain name, which has no relation to any NT Server domain name, in the Domain Name field.
9. Next, you need to determine how you want your system to resolve host names into IP addresses. You can choose to use only the domain name service, to search the system's local hosts file and then the DNS servers, to search your DNS servers and then the local hosts file, or to use only the local hosts file.

   The local hosts file, which uses the standard bsd UNIX file format, is used to resolve host names to IP addresses. Here's a typical entry:

   ```
   133.33.4.21       powerpc.naol.com
   ```
10. In the Domain Name Service (DNS) Search Order box, enter the IP addresses of the domain name servers on your network. Place the DNS server closest to this station on the network at the top of the list to speed address resolution.
11. In the Domain Search Order box, list the domains to search for host addresses. DNS servers will give you the address of the domain, which must then be searched. You can list up to six domains.

Third-Party TCP/IP Products

Although Windows NT includes all the basics for using TCP/IP, if you're installing TCP/IP to provide better access to UNIX or other host computers, you'll find that the standard tools are a little weak. The command-line-driven FTP, Ping, and other utilities aren't exactly user-friendly, and although Windows NT's Terminal allows you to Telnet into your favorite host computer, it's pretty bare-bones.

Several third-party products, including Beame and Whiteside's NT/TCP, Net-Manage's Chameleon32, and the shareware QVT, include things such as improved terminal emulators with VT220 and 3270 emulations, GUI file transfer programs, and other improved user interfaces. Some also include Usenet news readers and other tools for Internet access.

The one thing missing from Windows NT's TCP/IP is any support for NFS—the network file system. Without NFS, you can only exchange, as opposed to share, files with UNIX systems such as SCO UNIX and Sun workstations. Both Beame and Whiteside and NetManage include NFS clients and servers as part of their packages, so UNIX machines can access files on your Windows NT server and you can access files on UNIX servers.

Integrating Windows NT with Other Networks

19

IN THIS CHAPTER

Earlier chapters discussed networks made up primarily of Windows NT workstations and/or Windows NT Servers. This chapter covers using DOS workstations to access Windows NT and NT Servers. It also looks at adding Windows NT systems (as both servers and workstations) into networks that aren't dominated by Windows NT but might be running some other network operating system or systems.

Because the majority of large corporate sites already had local area networks in place before Windows NT was widely available, you can assume that most corporate MIS managers are thinking about using Windows NT in one of four ways:

- As a new operating system to replace the existing operating systems
- As a new workstation operating system integrating with their current network
- As an application server platform for new applications
- As a file server/application server in conjunction with their existing network infrastructure

Contrary to what you might hear from your Microsoft rep (that nerdy guy who has a picture of Bill Gates with a little incense burner in his office down the hall), your favorite columnist in *PC World in Review,* or anyone else, corporate America is not going to abandon overnight all the systems they've spent millions of dollars on. Even if Windows NT Server made its competition look like Tinkertoys, inertia, budget cycles, depreciation schedules, and other business factors would slow its adoption; it would take from two to five years for NT to displace the previous generation of systems.

Given those truths and the fact that NT Server, as nice as it is, isn't a vast technical leap over competing network operating systems such as NetWare, IBM's LAN Server, or Banyan's VINES, you probably will have to deal with a mixed network at one time or another. Even if you've decided to replace your current network operating system with Windows NT and NT Server (which I strongly recommend if you're currently using Microsoft's LAN Manager), you might find that migrating to NT Server is much easier—and less stressful—than trying to make a massive conversion over a three-day weekend.

This chapter looks at the hows, whys, and especially the wherefores of integrating Windows NT—as a workstation, file server, and/or application server—into networks that predominantly run Novell's NetWare, Microsoft's LAN Manager, Banyan's VINES, or UNIX operating systems. We'll talk about the advantages, disadvantages, and pitfalls of some common techniques for allowing these varied systems to share not only the same cable but also data, printers, and other resources.

This chapter also looks at integrating Windows NT's servers with Macintosh computer workstations and workstations running DOS and/or Windows 3.x.

Using LAN Manager Server Resources

As you might expect, integrating Windows NT with Microsoft's own LAN Manager isn't really all that difficult. In fact, NT Server was often called "LAN Manager for NT" in the early Windows NT marketing materials.

Integrating LAN Manager and Windows NT is simple because they have a very similar architecture. Both LAN Manager and Windows NT use Microsoft's SMB (server message block) protocol with NetBEUI or TCP/IP transports, and LAN Manager 2.x has a domain-based administration system that is very similar to NT Server's. In fact, if all you want is to give users at DOS workstations access to both LAN Manager and Windows NT or NT Server, you don't have to do anything. As a later section in this chapter discusses, DOS workstations use the same requester to access Windows NT and LAN Manager servers.

I recommend that any organization currently running LAN Manager, except possibly for those using LM/X, should plan to upgrade to NT Server. Microsoft is clearly putting their new development efforts behind NT Server and future Cairo-based enhancements. Getting support for obsolete products such as LAN Manager gets harder and harder as time passes because even the tech support staff at Microsoft isn't being trained on old products. Once the old-timer tech support operators are promoted (or burn out), it becomes very hard to get support. In fact, at some point it becomes cheaper to upgrade than to stay put.

If your network is slow, if it's growing and needs more servers, or if you need some of NT Server's new features such as the Remote Access Service (RAS), a faster upgrade path is in your future.

LAN Manager Servers in NT Server Domains

Unless you choose to upgrade all your LAN Manager servers to NT Servers over a long weekend, you will, at least temporarily, be running a mixed network. When you're running LAN Manager and NT Servers on the same network, you can configure the network in one of two ways:

- You can build separate domains, so that some of your domains run Windows NT Server on all their file servers while other domains are made up of LAN Manager servers.
- You can include some LAN Manager servers in your NT Server domains.

LAN Manager 2.x servers (including LM/X LAN Manager for UNIX servers) can be servers or (in LAN Manager terms) backup domain controllers in NT Server domains. Because NT Server stores more information about users and other accounts in its domain database than does LAN Manager 2.x, the domain controller in a domain that has both NT Servers and LAN Manager 2.x servers must be running NT Server.

The LAN Manager servers in your domain store a copy of the domain database—at least for fields that LAN Manager supports. As backup domain controllers, they can validate logon requests for users at Windows for Workgroups, DOS, and OS/2 workstations. Because Windows NT workstations need some of the additional information found only in the NT Server domain database, a LAN Manager server can't validate user logon requests from Windows NT stations.

If you're going to be running a mixed LAN Manager/NT Server domain (whether permanently or as an interim step as part of your upgrade), you should have at least two NT Servers to act as the domain controller and a backup. That way, if the domain controller goes down or you take it down for preventative maintenance or an upgrade, you can promote the other NT Server to domain controller and keep on truckin'.

LAN Manager servers don't recognize a domain's local groups, because LAN Manager has no local group feature. Therefore, you can't assign access permissions to resources on a LAN Manager server to a domain's local groups. In addition, because LAN Manager domains are completely independent of each other without trust relationships, LAN Manager servers don't recognize trust relationships. This means that you can't assign access permissions to resources on a LAN Manager server to users from a domain other than the domain the server is a member of, even if the server's domain trusts the user's domain so much that it's signed an irrevocable power of attorney.

If a user wants to access data on a LAN Manager server in a LAN Manager domain, he or she must log on using an account in that domain, or the LAN Manager domain must enable guest logons to access the resource. If a user from a LAN Manager domain wants to access data on an NT Server domain, you'll have to create a local account for that user. Local accounts act just like regular user accounts, except that they don't let a user log on from a workstation in this domain and aren't available for use in domains that trust this domain.

When users with Windows NT workstations browse for resources, they see only LAN Manager 2.x domains—that is, domains in which the domain controller is running LAN Manager 2.x—if a Windows for Workgroups or Windows NT workstation is a member of the domain, or if the domain controller is explicitly told to look for it.

To add a LAN Manager domain to your NT Server domain's browser list, open the Network applet in the domain controller's Control Panel, select Computer Browser, and click on the Configure button. When you see the dialog box shown in Figure 19.1, you can add the names of LAN Manager domains to browse.

To make an NT Server domain available for users on DOS or OS/2 workstations using the LAN Manager 2.x client software, configure the server service and put an X in the Make Browser Broadcasts to LAN Manager 2.x Clients box.

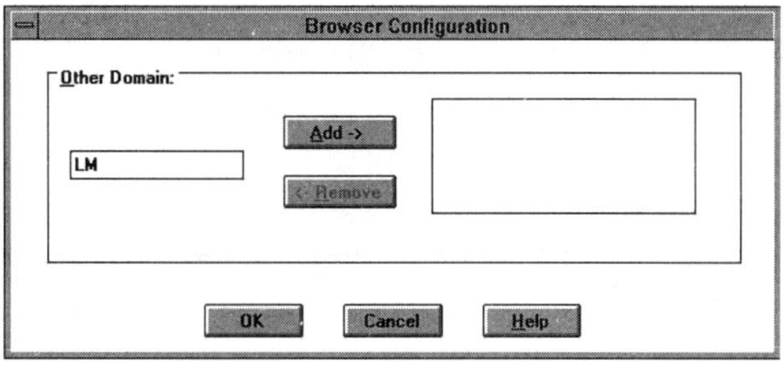

FIGURE 19.1.
Adding a LAN Manager domain to the browse list.

Managing LAN Manager Servers

With some limitations, you can manage LAN Manager servers through the NT Server management tools. Server Manager, User Manager for Domains, and other NT Server management tools enable you to administer features that exist on LAN Manager servers. The following are some of the more significant differences:

- LAN Manager user accounts can't be renamed.
- Users can't be forced to change their password at their next logon.
- Local groups don't exist.
- LAN Manager doesn't support user profiles but does support logon scripts.
- User rights, audit polices, and trust relationships don't exist on LAN Manager servers.
- Server Manager can't manage LAN Manager replication.

LAN Manager 1.x

If you're still running LAN Manager 1.x (including OEM versions such as 3Com's 3Plus Open), you have a harder row to hoe. At one time, Microsoft had a LAN Manager 1.1 to 2.x upgrade utility that copied your user accounts and other information from 3Plus Open or some other LAN Manager 1.x server to a LAN Manager 2.x server or domain. When I contacted the Microsoft sales department for information on this tool, they didn't have any record of it in their files. Your best bet is to find a reseller who worked with LAN Manager 1.x and therefore probably has the tools on the shelf somewhere.

Realistically, your LAN Manager 1.x network is now at least three or four years old, and in the intervening years you've found at least a few things you'd like to change. You can now take the opportunity to create new user accounts and groups while you install NT Server. You can still connect to both servers from a DOS or OS/2 workstation and copy your data files from the old LAN Manager server to your shiny new NT Server.

Supporting DOS Workstations

If your company is like most, you probably won't be installing Windows NT for all your users right away. In fact, even Bill Gates has been quoted as saying that 90 percent of the PC users in the field don't need the power of NT. Your comptroller and his divisions of bean counters probably aren't looking forward to upgrading all your users' machines to 16M 486s either.

Therefore, you're probably looking for a way to let your users with DOS workstations share the data and printers connected to your Windows NT workstations and NT Servers. Your best bet is to install Windows for Workgroups on those systems. Because Windows NT servers look just like Windows for Workgroups servers to Windows for Workgroups, you don't have to do anything special to enable your users with Windows for Workgroups to access your NT systems.

In fact, Windows for Workgroups goes with Windows NT so well that earlier chapters of this book discuss Windows for Workgroups right along with Windows NT. Windows for Workgroups has three big advantages over the kind of DOS requester often used with LAN Manager.

The first advantage is that Windows for Workgroups gives your users more available conventional memory than other requesters. Windows for Workgroups 3.11 implements its network features as 32-bit virtual device drivers. In addition to providing faster performance, this architecture uses very little conventional memory for device drivers, leaving it for your users' applications.

Second, Windows for Workgroups enables your users to access not only the NT servers on your network but also any NetWare or VINES servers. Doing this with conventional requesters leaves the user with very little conventional memory, because the requesters for both network operating systems the user is going to be accessing need to be loaded into memory simultaneously.

The third advantage is that Windows for Workgroups enables you to share printers connected to your users' workstations. This makes it much easier to place convenient printers where your users actually work, but it also adds some problems as users turn off their machines or make similar mistakes that screw up other users' print jobs.

There are times, however, when Windows for Workgroups just isn't the right answer. Users with old 1M ATs or even 4M 386 machines shouldn't use Windows for Workgroups. Other users might have applications, either commercial or developed in-house, that don't run with Windows for Workgroups or, like AutoCAD, that simply run better under plain old DOS because they can take full control of the machine. Interestingly, some of these programs themselves provide network services—forwarding e-mail messages between locations, sending faxes for users, and providing other communications services.

The LAN Manager Client

When Microsoft first released Windows NT and Advanced Server, they announced that you could buy client software for DOS PCs in multiuser packs. Shortly thereafter, as part of their campaign to make NT Advanced Server an attractive alternative to Novell's NetWare, Microsoft decided that they would stop charging for each user's client software and distribute it free of charge.

You can now download the LAN Manager requester from the MSCLIENT forum on CompuServe, the Microsoft download server (MSDL), or Microsoft's FTP server (`ftp.microsoft.com 131.107.1.11`) on the Internet. The package is made up of five files, which correspond to the five diskettes in the commercial distribution set. You download the files, decompress them to a set of five diskettes, and then install the requester as if you had bought the diskettes at your local Egghead Software. The files you need to download are self-extracting archives corresponding to the diskettes in the commercial distribution of the client software, as shown in the following list:

3 1/2-Inch Diskettes	*5 1/4-Inch Diskettes*	*Contents*
DSK3-1.EXE	DSK5-1.EXE	Setup
DSK3-2.EXE	DSK5-2.EXE	Drivers (disk 1 of 2)
DSK3-3.EXE	DSK5-3.EXE	Drivers (disk 2 of 2)
DSK3-4.EXE	DSK5-4.EXE	RAS
DSK3-5.EXE	DSK5-5.EXE	NetWare support files

After you download the files, you can install the LAN Manager basic or enhanced client for DOS. The basic client uses less memory and provides file and print services to LAN Manager, Windows for Workgroups, or Windows NT servers. It provides a command-driven user interface but doesn't support multiple protocol support or a menu-driven interface.

The enhanced client adds the menu-driven user interface, support for multiple protocols, and named pipe support. This is the client of choice if your users are going to be accessing client/server databases such as Microsoft's SQL Server. You'll also want the enhanced client if your computers have more than 2M of memory, because it loads most of itself into extended memory, giving you more net conventional memory than the basic client—even though overall it's larger.

If you don't have a modem, if your company has a policy against downloaded software, or if you'd just rather buy diskettes with those neat-looking Microsoft labels, you can order the requester package from the Microsoft inside-sales line at (800) 426-9400. Ask for part number 2723850V100.

The download package includes a detailed readme file on how to install, but it doesn't include the full documentation for the client software. If you've used LAN Manager 2.1, you can use the manuals from that product; if not, you can muddle your way through or order the manual set separately from the same 800 number (give part number 272-055-040). You might have to explain that you want the manuals for the network client software on CompuServe or the Internet; Microsoft usually doesn't sell manuals separately.

If you have Windows NT Server, the client software is included in the \CLIENTS directory on your CD-ROM. This is essentially the same software that I mentioned earlier, except that the Lan Manager client is version 2.2c and has been enhanced to use the DHCP and WINS services.

NetWare and Windows NT

Because Novell's NetWare operating system enjoys a 55 to 75 percent share of the PC LAN operating system market (depending on whose market research you read), you're probably reading this chapter to see how to get the Windows NT machine to print to a NetWare print queue or how to access a Windows NT application server from your DOS and Windows workstations that also access a NetWare file server.

When you buy Windows NT or NT Server, it comes with Microsoft's NWLink support for Novell's IPX (internetwork packet exchange) network layer and SPX (sequenced packet exchange) transport layer protocol. Because NWLink supports the NetBIOS API, you can use NWLink as transport protocol for Windows NT's SMB (server message block) protocol. This allows the usual Windows NT networking functions to run across a network carried by IPX rather than the usual NetBEUI protocol. This means that you can do peer-to-peer or NT Server networking across networks that can't—or, for management purposes, won't—carry NetBEUI traffic.

One of NetBEUI's limitations is that, because it uses a single-level naming system, it can't be sent from network to network through routers. If your company has a medium-to large-sized network running Novell's NetWare, Novell routers probably connect the network segments.

It's likely that you have Novell routers, because Novell includes a basic router program with NetWare (which you can use to make any AT class or better PC into a local router), and it builds even better routing software into NetWare file servers. If you have multiple LAN cards in a NetWare file server, it will automatically route IPX traffic between the segments. Because this routing function takes place at the network layer, you can even use a NetWare file server to link dissimilar networks by simply installing both Token Ring and Ethernet cards.

If you have a network in which a Token Ring network and an Ethernet network are linked by a NetWare file server, you could use NWLink on Windows NT workstations to enable stations on the Token Ring to share resources with servers on the Ethernet.

When you set up an IPX network, you need to assign each network segment—that is, each Ethernet or each Token Ring—a unique number. IPX then identifies each node on the network by the network number and the Ethernet or Token Ring card's MAC layer address. You can think of the network numbers as the name of the street and the node addresses as the house number.

NetWare routers exchange information about which networks they're connected to so that each NetWare router can build a table that shows how to get from its location to any other network number it's connected to.

NOTE

Every system connected to any given network segment must refer to that network by the same number. In addition, each network segment that is interconnected by routers must have a unique number that's different from those of all the other segments connected to it. Novell runs a network number registry, but most NetWare network administrators have come up with their own numbering systems.

Although you can use NWLink to connect Windows NT systems this way, it's really intended to let you access NetWare file servers or to allow NetWare workstations to access application servers such as Microsoft's own SQL Server for NT. If you load NWLink, you can use the IPX NetBIOS interface to send and receive messages from NetWare workstations running Novell's NetBIOS emulator for IPX.

Configuring NWLink

Because NWLink is part of the standard Windows NT distribution, you can install and configure it using standard Windows NT networking tools. To start using NWLink, follow these steps:

1. Fire up the Network applet in Control Panel and click on Add Software.
2. Select NWLink IPX/SPX Compatible Transport in the Network Software list box. The program prompts you for the path to the appropriate drivers and copies NWLink to your Windows NT system directories.

3. When you click on OK, the system configures and binds—that is, establishes the relationships between—the network protocols. When it gets to binding NWLink, it uses the dialog box shown in Figure 18.2 to enable you to choose the network number and frame type for each LAN card you're running NWLink on.

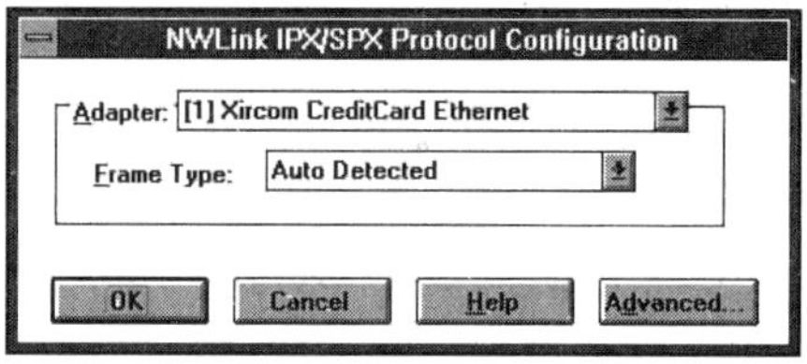

FIGURE 19.2.
The NWLink Configuration dialog box.

NOTE

The network number is configured from the Advanced Configuration dialog, accessed through the Advanced button.

The Frame Type field enables you to configure your Ethernet card to use one of a variety of slightly different MAC layer frame types. The Ethernet II frame is the oldest and is typically used for DEC and TCP/IP networks. Ethernet 802.3 is the IEEE 802.3 frame without an 802.2 header. Novell used 802.3 as their default frame type until NetWare 4.0. 802.2 is the full OSI-style frame and the default for NetWare 4.x and NetWare 3.12. SNAP is an extension of 802.2 used by Token Ring networks and networks with Macintosh computers.

4. Set the frame type and network number to match the other systems on your network and click on OK.

NOTE

You can find out what the current frame type and network address are for your network by typing `config` at the file server console.

5. NT prompts you to restart the system in order to start NWLink.

You can now install a network requester to access NetWare file servers or set up the application service, such as SQL Server, to use NWLink. An application service typically sends out Novell Service Advertising Protocol packets to let the client workstations on the network know that the server is available.

Sharing NetWare Resources

NWLink isn't, however, all you need to let your Windows NT workstations access data or print queues on your NetWare file server. To do that, you need software to support the upper layers of the NetWare protocols suite—the so-called NetWare Core Protocols. As of January 1994, you can equip your Windows NT workstations with the NetWare requester you need, *and* you have your choice of two different requesters, both of which are available free from CompuServe.

Due to a general deterioration of the relationship between Novell and Microsoft during the Windows NT development period (which felt like 10 years), Novell and Microsoft got into a name-calling contest around the time Windows NT was released. Microsoft had always assumed (possibly because Novell told all of their customers) that Novell would have a Windows NT NetWare requester available within 90 days of the official release of Windows NT. Novell did develop a requester for one early and widely available beta test version of Windows NT, but they didn't have one for the last beta and didn't have an available requester even after their self-imposed 90-day deadline came and went.

Novell, taking a little heat from users, issued a statement saying that prerelease Windows NT versions weren't stable enough to develop a real requester for and that the whole problem was in Redmond, Washington (home of Microsoft). Microsoft, meanwhile, seeing an opportunity to make Novell look bad and make their own customers happy, announced that they would just have to develop a requester themselves.

As of January 12, 1993, both companies started coming through on their promises. You can download a NetWare requester for Windows NT from both the Novell and Microsoft areas of CompuServe or from anonymous FTP sites on the Internet. Both Novell's NetWare Client for Windows NT and Microsoft's NetWare Workstation Compatible Service enable a user on a Windows NT workstation to access data and print queues on a NetWare file server.

As you might expect if you've spent any time working on Novell and Microsoft LANs, there are a few differences between the requesters. Each company decided that it could do the best job by taking as much control over the requester and its associated protocols as possible. Therefore, Novell's requester works best with Novell's IPX and LAN card drivers, and Microsoft's requester can be set up to work as a gateway to allow other Windows NT stations to access the NetWare file server without loading the NetWare requester themselves.

Unfortunately, early products were in a weird, not-ready-for-prime-time, free-for-the-download beta test period and could obviously have used more work. By the time you read this, both companies will have released new and improved versions of their requesters. I won't spend a lot of time talking about the bugs and work-arounds for the current versions. We'll just take a quick look at the features of each.

Novell's NetWare Client for Windows NT

Novell's NT requester seems to have been developed by a programming team that decided not to carefully study the Windows NT architecture and build a NetWare requester that would fit in comfortably, but instead to look over Windows NT and figure out how to take over as much of the networking as possible (because, presumably, they know networking better than anyone else).

In the first release, you had to replace the NDIS LAN driver from Windows NT with a Novell ODI driver (open data interface, a specification similar to NDIS but developed by Novell and Apple) that worked like Novell's NetWare and DOS LAN card drivers. If you wanted to use NetBEUI, TCP/IP, or some other NDIS protocol stack, you had to either have two LAN cards or use Novell's ODINSUP module, which lets NDIS drivers talk to ODI drivers.

Due to popular demand, the current release of the requester (November 3, 1993) can be used with either Novell ODI drivers and Novell's IPX/SPX II drivers or with Microsoft's NWLink. Using Novell's drivers allows the requester to automatically determine the right frame type. It can be somewhat faster for some applications, but using NWLink retains Microsoft's networking architecture and the NDIS driver you're already sure works.

After you download the requester (from the NOVFILES download section on CompuServe or from Novell's FTP server—`ftp.novell.com` on the Internet) and install it, you can access data and print queues on the NetWare file server, link to a NetWare directory, and so on. When you log onto your Windows NT workstation, it automatically attaches to your preferred server and to servers needed to reestablish any permanent connections you created in File Manager or Print Manager.

Because the requester tries to log onto your NetWare file server using the same username that you used to log onto the Windows NT workstation, it's a good idea to synchronize all your usernames. If you don't, you'll have to use the Connect As option in File Manager to connect to NetWare directories.

Because NetWare print servers don't run Windows NT print drivers, you have to load the printer drivers for any NetWare printers you want to access in all the Windows NT systems that will be printing to it.

The current requester isn't perfect. It has some bugs, particularly in the printing arena, and you can't run DOS or 16-bit Windows applications that take advantage of any NetWare-specific function calls or APIs. Therefore, you can't run SYSCON or any other NetWare management utilities under Windows NT. Windows NT workstations also ignore NetWare login scripts. A new version became available in the spring of 1994, but as of December 1994, it is still considered prerelease.

NOTE

You can't install both the Novell and Microsoft requesters, or even both NWLink and Novell's ODI IPX/SPX II protocol stacks, at the same time. In fact, if you decide to change from one to the other, be sure to delete all the files that were installed. Both use the same names for some of their DLLs—which, of course, include different code and entry points.

Microsoft's Client Services for Netware

Microsoft's Client Services for Netware differs from the NetWare requester in a few simple ways. The most significant is that the Microsoft requester is a better NT citizen, acting more like the Microsoft Workstation service. You can, for example, use Microsoft's UNC names to refer to NetWare resources in profiles, logon scripts, and dialog boxes. If I wanted to link my E: drive to the SYS:LOGIN directory on the NetWare file server named Porthos, I could use the following command line in a logon script or batch file:

```
NET USE e: \\porthos\sys\LOGIN
```

Microsoft's requester uses NWLink and normal Windows NT NDIS drivers. You install it through the normal Control Panel Network applet procedures you'd use to install any other network software into Windows NT.

NetWare's DOS APIs are supported better than in the current Novell requester. You can run some of the more sophisticated NetWare management utilities, but there is no guarantee that they will all run.

The other big difference is that you can use the Microsoft requester as a gateway. After connecting to a NetWare directory or print queue, you can then share that directory. This enables other users on Windows NT, Windows for Workgroups, or DOS workstations running the LAN Manager requester to access the NetWare server without having to load the NetWare requester themselves.

This pass-through feature really comes in handy, because you can install just one requester or shell on your DOS and Windows workstations, allowing them to access both Windows NT and NetWare resources. It's the only way that you can allow remote access users running Windows NT Remote Access Service (RAS) to dial into your network to have access to NetWare resources. The problem with this pass-through feature is that it creates a possible security problem. The user logged into the system running Windows NT and the NetWare requester can give another Windows for Workgroups or RAS system user access to NetWare file server data that the NetWare administrator didn't want that user to be able to see.

You can install the Client Services for Netware from Control Panel's Network applet.

All in all, I prefer working with the Microsoft requester rather than the Novell requester. This might change as both companies bring their products up to production levels.

Beame and Whiteside's MultiConnect Server

NWLink and a good NetWare requester for Windows NT (one might be available soon) still don't cover all the bases in Windows NT-NetWare interoperability. You can have Windows NT clients access NetWare file servers and set up your Windows NT application servers, but you still can't set up a Windows NT server that your workstations running the NetWare client-side software, NETX, or VLMS can access.

Beame and Whiteside's MultiConnect Server lets NetWare workstations access data and printer resources on Windows NT systems acting as servers. The program installs as a network service into Windows NT or NT Server and makes the system it's running on act like a NetWare 3.x file server on the network. The system running MultiConnect Server sends out Novell server advertising protocol messages, validates users against a bindery, and responds to NetWare Core Protocol requests like a NetWare file server.

Even if you plan on keeping NetWare as your primary file server operating system and are looking at Windows NT primarily as a power user's client and application server, MultiConnect Server might be worth a look. If your NetWare server goes down, you can run MultiConnect Server on a Windows NT workstation to act as a backup server. It even comes with Beame and Whiteside's own version of NetWare's Login, Logout, MAP, and other utilities, so you can use it even where no NetWare servers exist.

If you're planning a transition from NetWare to Windows NT, Advanced Server MultiConnect Server can relieve you of the pressure to change every user's client software overnight. Users can use their NetWare client software until you get around to updating them.

You can buy MultiConnect Server from

> Beame and Whiteside Software
> 706 Hillsborough St.
> Raleigh, NC 27603-1655
> (919) 831-8989
> Fax: (919) 831-8990

Prices range from $849 for one server supporting five users to $9,695 for one server supporting an unlimited number of users.

Banyan VINES and Windows NT

If you're currently using Banyan's VINES, which is probably the most sophisticated LAN operating system on the market for large networks, you'll be glad to hear that Banyan has made a requester for Windows NT available on their support bulletin board through their early availability program. Like both Novell's and Microsoft's NetWare requesters, the VINES requester is available to the general public; however, it's still classified as a beta test by Banyan, so it's not really a good idea to use it to run mission-critical applications.

As this was being written, the latest version of the requester ran on any Windows NT workstation with 16M of memory, an Ethernet or Token Ring card, and 3M of free disk space. It enabled you to access VINES servers running versions 4.11 (5) or later, including the current VINES 5.5.

The requester gives you full file and print services, including support for Banyan's VINES IP protocol (which is not quite the same as the TCP/IP IP protocol, even though they have the same name), VINES login, and support for StreetTalk and StreetTalk directory assistance. Currently missing is support for named pipes, OS/2 applications, NetBIOS applications on VINES IP, and support for Banyan's 3270 gateway.

You can download the requester package (currently NTEAP3.ZIP) from Banyan's support bulletin board at (508) 836-1834. You'll have to fill out a survey agreeing not to hold Banyan responsible if this beta test software makes your computer burst into flames.

After you have the package, run the enclosed setup program to install the VINES support, answer a few questions about your VINES setup, and restart your machine.

Unlike the NetWare requester, which automatically logs you in to your NetWare server when you log in to Windows NT, you won't be automatically logged in to your VINES network. To log in to the VINES network, run the login program from the VINES group on your desktop.

Macintosh Services

One of the Macintosh's advantages has long been the fact that every Macintosh includes a built-in network interface. Granted, LocalTalk interface runs at a snail's pace (just 230Kbps), but any network is better than no network. Just the fact that Apple included a network port on every Mac (and, therefore, networking software in every version of the Macintosh operating system) has resulted in Macs being networked to an even higher degree than Intel-based PCs.

If your organization is like most, a few Macintosh computers and their fanatical users are hidden away in the nooks and crannies of the advertising, art, and publications departments.

These users, totally convinced that their computers are the true personal computer and that all others are just the product of false prophets, will start wanting their own file server so that they can share their files and printers. Over time, they'll find that they don't only want to exchange files with their little clique of Mac users, but that they also need to see that Excel spreadsheet of the master budget and take advantage of corporate resources such as e-mail.

NT Server can support Macintosh workstations through its Macintosh services option. Macintosh services allow an NT Server to support Apple's AppleTalk protocol stack on Ethernet (which Apple and Mac users call EtherTalk), Token Ring (TokenTalk), and FDDI, as well as LocalTalk networks. Because the server will be "speaking" the AppleTalk protocol stack, Mac workstations don't need any special client software to access the NT Server. In fact, an NT Server looks just like an AppleShare file server to your Macintosh users.

A single NT Server can support up to 255 Mac workstations, providing file and print services, and serve as an AppleTalk Phase 2 router, passing AppleTalk messages between multiple network segments.

Requirements

In order to support Macintosh workstations, you need 2M of additional memory in your file server (more is better, of course). Because Macintosh files and filenames are more complex than DOS files, Mac users will be able to access directories only on NTFS disk volumes. Your Macs must be running System 6.0.7 or later; System 7 is fine. LocalTalk is fine for printer sharing and an occasional file transfer, but you'll need EtherTalk or TokenTalk cards in the Macs to get reasonable file-sharing performance.

How Macintosh Services Work

Providing file services for Macs and PCs on the same server presents a few challenges. Each Mac file is actually made up of two parts: the data fork contains the actual data for the file, and the resource fork contains descriptive information about the file (including which application created the file). In addition, Mac filenames can be up to 32 characters long. Some mechanism must be provided to shorten Mac filenames for users at DOS or Windows for Workgroups stations.

NT Server stores both the data and resource forks of Mac files in a single NTFS file through the use of multiple data streams. It also shortens Macintosh filenames that don't fit in the DOS "8.3" file convention to a six-character string followed by a tilde (~) and a number. Therefore, a filename such as JonesLetterhead would be seen as JONESL~1 by DOS users. If the Mac user then created a file called JonesLabels, DOS users would see it as JONESL~2.

Because NTFS filenames can be even longer than Mac filenames (up to 256 characters), a similar shortening function applies to NTFS files that are more than 32 characters long.

In order to make it easier for users on different platforms to share files, Mac services also does automatic translations between the DOS file extensions (used to identify which application created a file) and the Mac resource fork. Mac users automatically see .XLS files created by DOS users as Excel spreadsheets, .DOC files as Word documents, and so on.

TIP

You should recommend that your Mac users stick to valid DOS filenames and the extensions normally used by Windows applications for their file types when creating files that they expect to share with DOS or Windows users.

Macintosh users also can send data to printers connected to NT Servers, including printers such as HP LaserJets that don't include PostScript support (which is usually needed for a Macintosh to print). Macintosh print jobs are queued just like PC print jobs. Some Mac networks simply share printers, locking other users out when a user is printing. Spooling gives users the use of their workstations back faster.

Some Mac networks have a continuing problem, known as LaserPrep wars, which slows printing and forces the LaserWriter to print multiple startup pages. When a Macintosh tries to print to a LaserWriter or other PostScript printer, it asks the printer what version of the PostScript setup file (called a LaserPrep file) the printer is running. If the version doesn't match, it sends a new LaserPrep file and asks the printer to make it the resident file. The process of making a LaserPrep file resident takes some time for the printer to process and causes the printer to print a new startup page.

If users on the network have different versions of the Mac Chooser that use different LaserPrep files—a common occurrence—your printer will spend much of its time switching back and forth between LaserPrep files. NT Server solves this problem by sending a temporary LaserPrep file at the beginning of each print job. This slows things down a little if you have just one version of Chooser, but it speeds things up a lot if your users are running various versions.

Security

Like any other users, Macintosh users need to log onto the domain before they can access resources on the domain. Because they aren't actually part of the domain, Mac workstations don't need accounts the way Windows NT workstations do.

If you use the standard Mac networking software that is built into the Mac system, your users on Mac workstations will send their passwords across your network in clear text. If someone connected a network protocol analyzer such as a Network General Sniffer or a Novell LANalyzer to your network, they could capture the logon packets and discover the user's passwords. Microsoft has included a User Authentication Module for the Mac that, if installed on your Macs, encrypts passwords before they're sent over the wire.

Mac/AppleShare permissions are a little different from NT Server file permissions. On an AppleShare system, you can grant permissions to the owner of a folder, to a group that shares the folder, or to all the users on the network. Unlike with PC networks, you can't grant different permissions to different groups of users except for the owner, the group, and everyone. Mac administrators can grant the owner, the group, and everyone one of the four levels of access:

Level of Access	*Description*
See files	The user has read-only access to files and can't see folders in the current folder
See folders	The user has read-only access to files and folders in the current folder
Make changes	Full access
Cannot move, rename, or delete	Prohibits moving, renaming, or deleting folders or files in the folder

If you have applied more restrictive NT Server permissions, they will apply to the Mac users as well.

Setting Up Macintosh Services

This section discusses the process of installing and configuring NT Server Macintosh services. The process of designing an AppleTalk network, placing routers, choosing LocalTalk and/or EtherTalk, and configuring the AppleTalk network are beyond the scope of this book. If you don't already have a Mac network up and running and have no idea what a zone is or how to number your networks, you should read the *Services for Macintosh* manual that comes with NT Server, read a good AppleTalk networking book, or hire an experienced consultant. Note that an NT Server can act as a router, or seeding router, between two or more network segments, including acting as an Ethernet to LocalTalk router.

Macintosh Services installs on your NT Server just like any other network software. To install it, follow these steps:

1. Fire up the Network applet in Control Panel to get the Network Settings dialog box, shown in Figure 18.3.

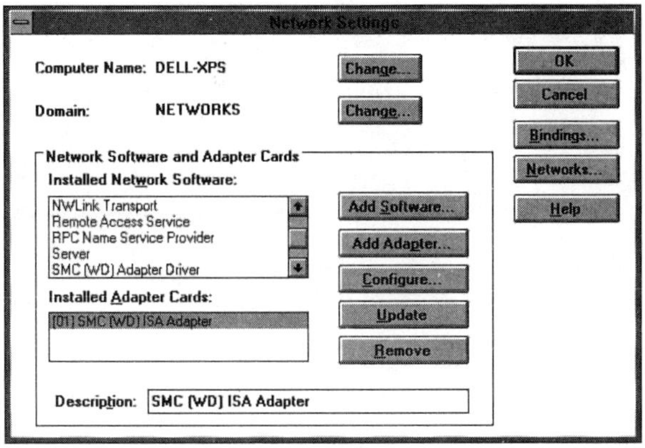

FIGURE 19.3.
The Network Settings dialog box.

2. Click on the Add Software button and select Services for Macintosh from the resulting dialog box. Windows NT prompts you for the path to the required files.
3. Click on OK and reboot your system to start the AppleShare servers for the first time.

As soon as you restart your system, you have to configure the AppleTalk protocol stack. Like any other protocol, it's configured through the Network applet in Control Panel. To configure AppleTalk, follow these steps:

1. Fire up the Network applet in Control Panel, select Services for Macintosh, and click on the Configure button. The dialog box shown in Figure 19.4 appears.

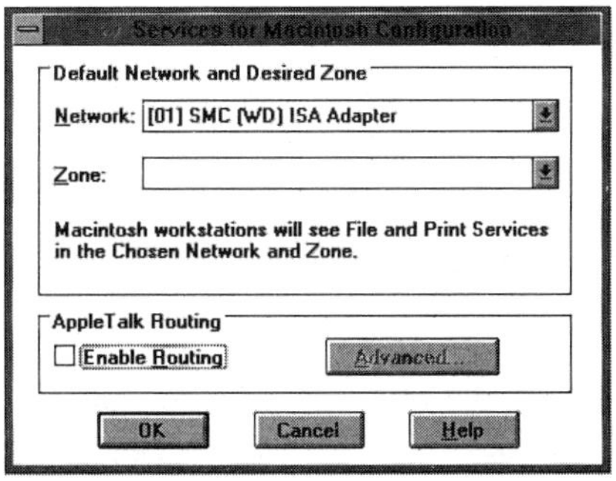

FIGURE 19.4.
The Services for Macintosh Configuration dialog box.

2. Select which of the network adapters in your system you want to use as the default network for AppleTalk from the Network list box.

NOTE

A LocalTalk adapter can't be the default AppleTalk adapter. If you want to serve Macs on a LocalTalk network, configure an Ethernet card in addition to the LocalTalk card.

3. Choose the zone you want this server's printers and volumes to appear in from the Zone list box.
4. If you want this server to also act as an AppleTalk router, put an X in the Enable Routing box and click on the Advanced button to configure the router. The dialog box shown in Figure 19.5 appears.

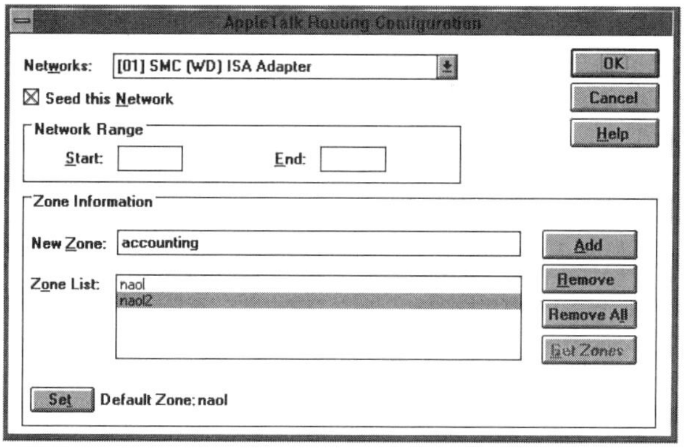

FIGURE 19.5.
The AppleTalk Routing Configuration dialog box.

5. From this dialog box you can select another network adapter, set the router to seed one or more network numbers, and configure AppleTalk zones.

TIP

If you want your users to send encrypted passwords from their Macs (PCs always send encrypted passwords), copy the Microsoft UAM from the AppleShare folder in the Microsoft UAM volume to the user's AppleShare folder in his or her System folder. Just in case the worst happens, copy the old UAM first.

Macintosh Printing

In addition to the print spooling that any Windows NT server provides to PC users, NT Servers providing Mac print services also allow PC users to print to network laser printers connected to an AppleTalk network (LocalTalk or EtherTalk) and convert PostScript print jobs to print on non-PostScript printers.

Because your NT Server can spool print jobs for your Mac users as well as your PC users, you probably want to capture—that is, lock—your printers to the NT Server, preventing other users from printing directly to the printer. Doing so maximizes printing performance and helps eliminate LaserPrep wars.

All the Mac users on your network will use a single user account to gain permission to the printers on your server. Create an account (I recommend that you name it MACPRINT or something similar) through User Manager for Domains and grant it permissions to some or all of your printers through Print Manager, just like you would for other users on Windows NT workstations. You'll then need to tell the Mac print server process on your server to use that username for Mac print jobs.

1. Fire up the Services applet in Control Panel and select Print Server for Macintosh.
2. Click on the Startup button to get the dialog box shown in Figure 19.6.

FIGURE 19.6.
The Print Server for Macintosh Service dialog box.

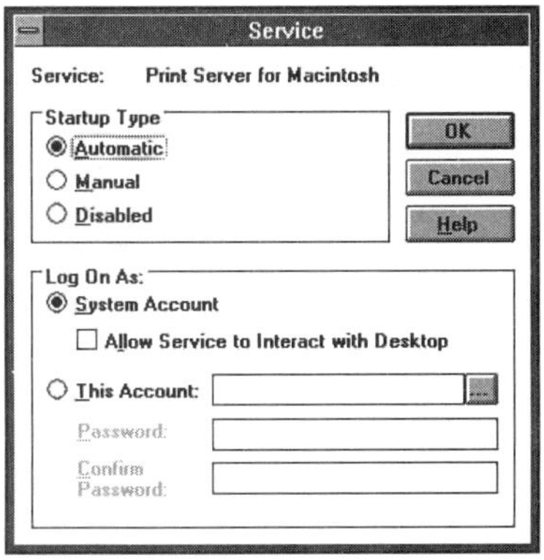

3. Click on the This Account button and enter the account that Mac print jobs should use.

Macintosh-Accessible Volumes

In order for Mac users to access data on your NT Server, you need to create one or more Macintosh-accessible volumes. Although you usually use the term *volume* as the equivalent of a logical disk drive, in this context a volume is roughly the equivalent of a Windows NT sharepoint. The rules for defining Macintosh-accessible volumes are somewhat different from those for setting up standard sharepoints:

- A volume name can be no more than 27 characters long.
- You can't define one volume to have its root under another volume. (This also means that you can't give one NTFS directory two different volume names like you can give it two different sharenames.)
- All the volume names on a server must fit within a single AppleTalk buffer of 4624 bytes. Note that two bytes are added to each name in the buffer.

To make a directory (and its descendants, of course) a Macintosh-accessible volume, follow these steps:

1. Start File Manager and select the directory you want your Macintosh users to be able to access.

NOTE

Remember that you can create Macintosh-accessible volumes only on NTFS or CDFS CD-ROM volumes. Mac users can't access data on FAT volumes.

2. Select MacFile | Create Volume (which exists only on servers with Mac support loaded) to get the dialog box shown in Figure 19.7.

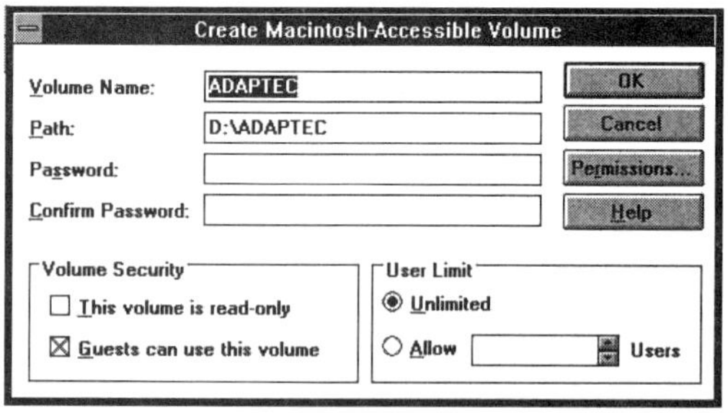

FIGURE 19.7.
The Create Macintosh-Accessible Volume dialog box.

3. The volume name defaults to the directory name. If you'd like to use a longer or clearer name, enter it in the Volume Name box. The path will default to the directory that was selected earlier.
4. You can assign a password to the volume by entering the same password into the Password and Confirm Password boxes. Users who want to access this data will have to enter the password you choose here before access will be granted. Note that assigning a password prevents users from connecting to the volume at startup.
5. You also can set the volume as read-only, prevent guest users from accessing the volume, and limit the number of users who can access this volume in this box.

If you decide to change any of the properties of the Mac volume, select MacFile | Properties.

You also can set Macintosh-style permissions for the volume through File Manager by selecting MacFile | Permissions. You see the dialog box shown in Figure 19.8, which allows you to set all the Mac-style permissions discussed earlier in this chapter. You can still set NT permissions in the usual way in addition to Mac-style permissions.

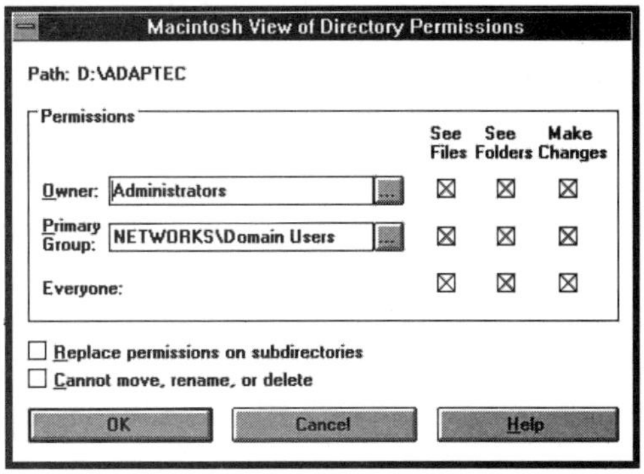

FIGURE 19.8.
The Macintosh View of Directory Permissions dialog box.

The MacFile menu, or at least some of its functions, is available through File Manager, Server Manager, and the MacFile applet in Control Panel. Select MacFile | View/Modify Volumes | Properties from Server Manager to access the dialog box shown in Figure 19.9.

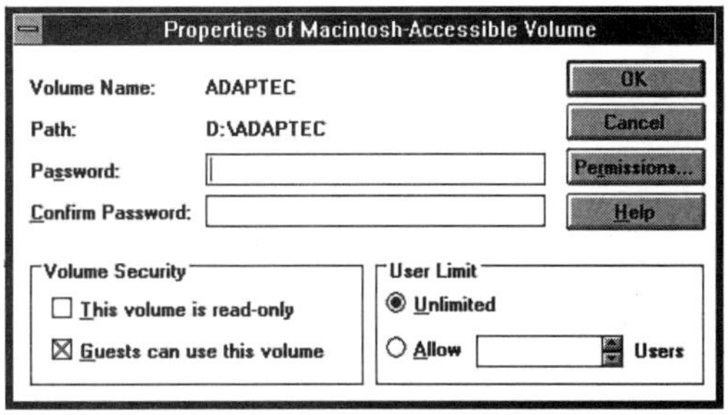

FIGURE 19.9.
The MacFiles Properties dialog box.

Click on the Permissions button to tighten your security. Here you can force users to use the Microsoft UAM (and therefore prevent them from sending clear text passwords across your net), prevent users who don't have a valid account from logging on as guest users, and prevent users from storing their passwords on their Macs.

NOTE

Allowing Mac users to store their passwords on their machines basically allows anyone who sits down at that Mac access to your server. If you want to run a secure system, you shouldn't allow workstations to store passwords.

This dialog box also allows you to set the logon message, displayed at logon time for users running Mac System 7.1, and limit the number of Mac users who will be allowed to access the server at the same time.

The User, Files, and Volumes buttons do basically the same things that the User, Shares, and Files buttons in Server Manager normally do: They allow you to manage logged-on users and open files.

As you've seen, NT Services for Macintosh uses DOS and NTFS file extensions to tell Mac users which application to run when a user double-clicks on a file that doesn't have a resource fork. You can maintain the table of associations to add new extensions or change the application to use for some file types through the Associate option on File Manager's MacFile menu. When you select Associate, you see the dialog box shown in Figure 19.10.

FIGURE 19.10.
The Associate dialog box.

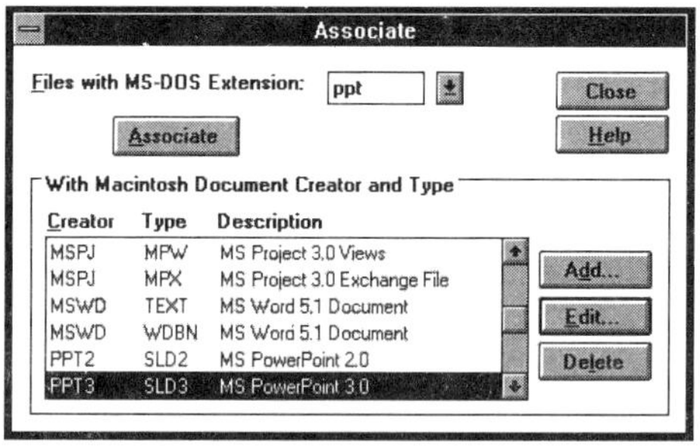

After you enter an extension or select an existing extension and click on Edit, enter a creator and file type for the extension to allow Mac users to access these files.

NOTE

If you have data that will be used only by Mac users, there is no need to share the directory that is the Mac volume.

Optimizing Your Network

20

IN THIS CHAPTER

Funny, isn't it, how the server that was plenty fast enough last year when you had 20 users on the network now feels like someone stole your 486 motherboard in the middle of the night and replaced it with the motherboard from someone's old XT?

Because there is no such thing as an infinitely fast processor, local area network, or disk drive, the art of network optimizing is a constant contest of locating the most significant bottleneck in your network and improving that component of your network. If 200 users are accessing one file server that has one disk drive to get their applications, it's pretty clear that adding another server, or maybe even another disk drive, to share the load will solve that bottleneck, thus improving performance. If, however, you have 20 file servers and 200 users on one Ethernet network, adding a 21st server isn't likely to improve things because the bottleneck is in the network cable, not the file server.

The sad truth is that as you upgrade your network and widen each bottleneck, you don't solve your performance problems. You simply shift the bottleneck to the next narrowest point. As your users' demands for network services increase, that bottleneck will become too narrow, and you'll need to figure out where the new bottleneck is.

Figuring out where your network's bottlenecks are, and which one has the most significant effect on your users' performance, is more of an art than a science. Several types of tools are available to help you determine whether some parts of your network are overloaded and therefore are holding things up. The Windows NT Performance Monitor, included with Windows NT Server and the Windows NT Resource Kit, helps you locate problems within NT file servers or workstations by letting you monitor how well Windows NT performs.

To find network bottlenecks, you can use

- the Performance Monitor with the Network Monitor Agent counters
- a network protocol analyzer such as a Network General Sniffer
- a software network monitor program such as Novell's LANalyzer for Windows or Triticom's Ethervision
- a hub management program such as Synoptics' Optivity
- the little tachometer display on your hub

What you're looking for is a display of what percentage of the available network bandwidth is in use.

NOTE

The Network Monitor Agent counters are an optional software component installed through Control Panel's Network applet. Click on the Add Software button, select the Network Monitor Agent, and install the counters. After the computer is rebooted, the Performance Monitor will include the Network Segment object that you can use to collect and monitor network statistics.

Luckily, NT is basically self-tuning. Unlike with other LAN operating systems, including LAN Manager, you don't have to manually set server parameters such as the maximum number of open files or the number of data packet receive buffers in order to get reasonable performance. NT can dynamically allocate processor resources and memory for different purposes, so you don't have to hand-tune it at installation time. That said, there are a few things you can do to speed your data on its way.

Using Performance Monitor to Locate Bottlenecks

Performance Monitor is a graphical application that allows you to graph, report, log, and set alerts based on the values of literally hundreds of counters that can track everything from the percentage of processor time used by any thread on your Windows NT machine to the amount of disk space that's free on a disk drive.

Performance Monitor can track these counters for the computer it's running on and for other Windows NT systems. It can even track counters on multiple systems at the same time, so it's easy to set up a Windows NT machine in your network control center that triggers an alert whenever any of the servers is running slowly, running out of disk space, or otherwise misbehaving. Performance Monitor can even run other applications in the event of an alert being triggered.

Performance Monitor can track counters related to several Windows NT objects. An object is a functional subsystem within Windows NT, such as TCP/IP or the processor. Each object type, such as the physical disk, can have multiple occurrences. For example, each drive on your server is an occurrence of the physical disk object type. The object types you can monitor with Performance Monitor are listed in Table 20.1.

Table 20.1. The object types you can monitor with Performance Monitor.

Object Type	*Description*	*Counters*
Browser	Computer announcements	Announcement totals, number of browse requests
Cache	The disk cache	Write hit ratio, read hit ratio
Logical disk	Disk volumes	Disk queue length, percentage of time disk is busy
Memory	Virtual memory management	Page faults per second, available cache, cache size
NetBEUI	The NetBEUI protocol	Bytes sent, number of timeouts

continues

Table 20.1. continued

Object Type	*Description*	*Counters*
NetBEUI resource	NetBEUI buffers	Number used
NWLink IPX	IPX protocol	Bytes transferred, window size
NWLink NetBIOS	IPX NetBIOS interface	Bytes transferred, window size
Objects	Windows NT multitasking	Events, threads
Paging file	Swap file	Percentage used
Physical disk	Physical disk drives	Time used, reads/writes per second
Process	Each process in system	Processor time, memory used
Processor	Each processor in system	Percentage time in user tasks, percentage time used
Redirector	File and print service I/O	Bytes sent/received
Server	Service process	Bytes sent/received, errors
System	All processors in system	Percentage time in user tasks, percentage time used
Thread	Each thread in system	Percentage processor time

NOTE

If you install additional optional components, such as RAS or an NFS server, you might find additional objects when you run Performance Monitor.

NOTE

In order to track physical or logical disk counters, you need to run the Diskperf program from the command line on each system where you want to track disk performance. Diskperf will enable collecting disk performance data, effective at the next reboot. Collecting disk performance data is disabled by default because it has a small effect on system performance (about 1.5 percent on 386 machines—less on faster systems, more if you have a large number of disk drives).

Within each of these object types, you'll find several different counters that you can track to keep an eye on your system's performance. Some object types, such as threads, allow you to track several counters for each occurrence, or each thread, in the system. Other data can be followed at different levels of detail. The System object type, for example, describes the aggregate data for all the processors in your system, while the Processor object type has independent counters for each processor.

If you're like most system administrators, you'll find the hundreds of possible counters to track intimidating. I've found that the counters listed in Table 20.2 provide the best information for server performance monitoring. You might find that others, such as percentage of disk in use, are useful for managing or monitoring your network, but the ones in Table 20.2 seem to be the simplest to manage.

Table 20.2. The counters that provide the best information for server performance monitoring.

Object Type	*Counter*	*Description*
System	% Total Processor Time	The aggregate time for all processors in the system that the processor is busy. Does not include time running the idle thread waiting for something to do.
Logical Disk	% Disk Time	Percentage of time the disk is busy.
Logical Disk	Avg sec/disk transfer	The average time it takes to process each disk transfer. Higher figures indicate that additional disk channels will help performance.
Logical Disk	Free Meg	Space remaining on the drive.
Logical Disk	Disk Queue Length	The number of requests waiting for the drive. A snapshot value, not the average over the time period. Higher figures indicate that additional disk channels will help performance.

continues

Table 20.2. continued

Object Type	*Counter*	*Description*
Server	Context Block Queue Time	The time, in milliseconds, that requests wait for file service processes.
Memory	Pages/sec	The number of page faults that require reading or writing to the paging file. A high figure indicates that more memory will speed server performance.
Network Segment	% Network Utilization	Percentage of network bandwidth in use. A high figure indicates that splitting the network segment will improve performance.
Paging File	% Usage Peak	The peak percentage of the swap file that is in use. Increase paging file size if over 75 percent.
Redirector	Current Commands	The number of requests pending service. If the number of pending requests exceeds the number of network cards in your server by more than two, your server is overloaded.
Redirector	Network Errors/sec	The number of serious network errors per second. Any value other than 0 needs attention.

When you start Performance Monitor, you'll see the screen shown in Figure 20.1. This graph screen is just one of four different views of your data that Performance Monitor can give you.

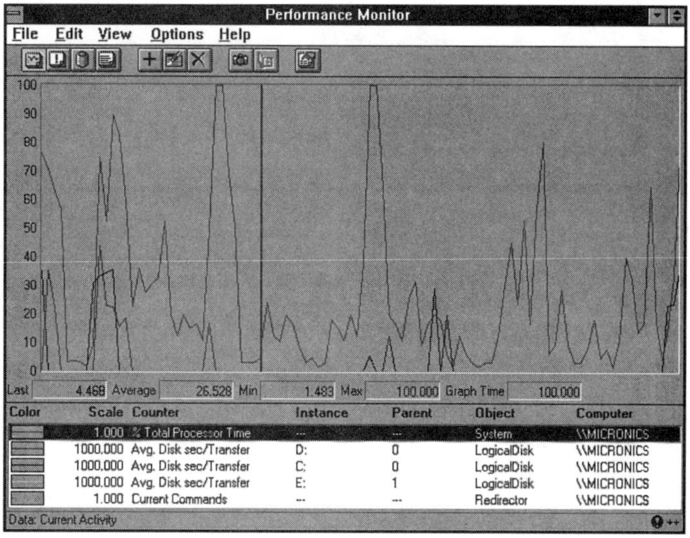

FIGURE 20.1.
Performance Monitor's graph screen.

Your first task is to select the counters that you want to graph. Click on the Add button, the one with the plus sign, to select the counters you want to track. When you do, you'll see the dialog box shown in Figure 20.2.

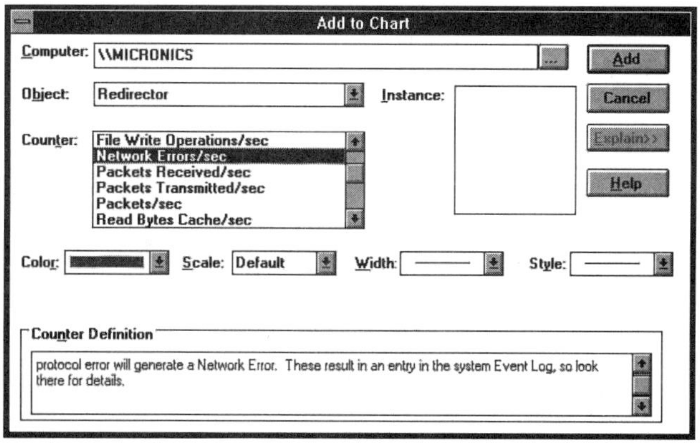

FIGURE 20.2.
Adding a counter to the graph.

Here you can select the computer, object type, counter, and occurrence that you want to track. You also can select the graph's scale, along with the color, width, and style for the line for this value. If you want a description of the counter like the one you see in Figure 20.2, click on the Explain button.

Select Options | Chart or click on the Chart Options button (the one on the far right) to adjust how the data will be graphed to your screen. In the resulting dialog box, you can set the update interval, whether you want a line graph or a bar histogram, and other options that affect how the graph looks.

After you've selected the counters you want to chart, you can display the average, current, minimum, and maximum values for that counter by selecting it at the bottom of the screen. You can edit the settings for any counter by double-clicking on it. You can remove a counter from the chart by selecting it and choosing Edit | Delete from Chart.

You can save the set of counters you're tracking in order to easily track those same counters at a later time by selecting File | Save Chart Settings.

If you want to set alerts, select View | Alerts or click on the alerts button (the one with the exclamation mark on it) on the button bar. Figure 20.3 shows alerts generated as the counters you're tracking accept the minimum or maximum limits you specify.

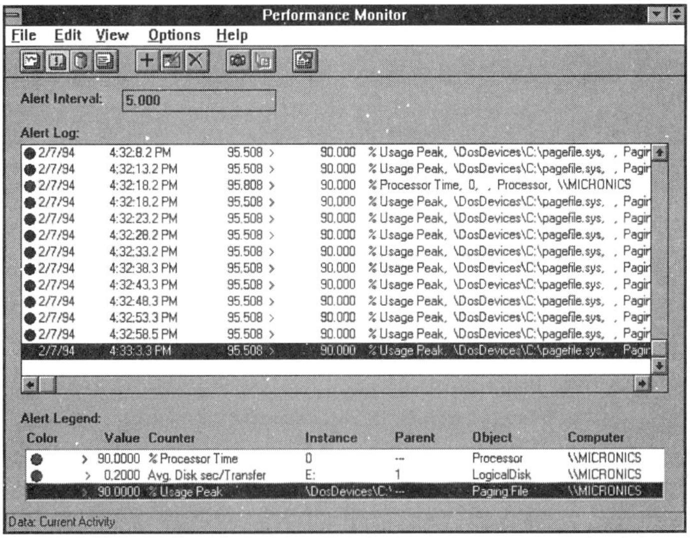

FIGURE 20.3.
The alerts screen.

Notice that the counters you selected in the chart view are not active in the alerts window. Each of the four kinds of Performance Monitor windows has an independent set of counters that it tracks. When you save your settings, if you choose Save Workspace rather than Save Chart, Alert, Log, or Report, you'll save the settings for all four windows.

To add counters, click on the Add button to get the dialog box shown in Figure 20.4. Here, as in the Add to Chart dialog box (see Figure 20.2), you can select the counter you want to monitor. You also can set the high or low limit for the counter and select an application to run when the limit is exceeded, such as WinBeep, which sends a message to your pager when a critical error occurs. You can choose to have the application run each time the limit is reached or just the first time.

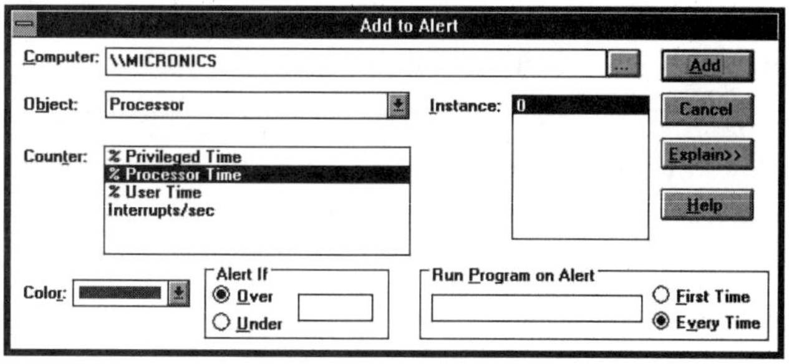

FIGURE 20.4.
The Add to Alert dialog box.

Choose Options | Alert to set options for how Performance Monitor should respond to any alert. Here you can tell it to switch to the alert window or send a message to another station on the network. You also can set the polling interval for how often the counters are checked or set it to check only when you tell it to manually.

If you want to collect data for later analysis, you can start a log file by clicking on the Log button (the one with a cylinder). When you create a log, you can select which object types you want to log information from. (See Figure 20.5.) Performance Monitor will then log data for all the counters in that object type to your file. Don't go overboard and log everything, or your log file will rapidly become the monster that ate Philadelphia and chew up all your disk space.

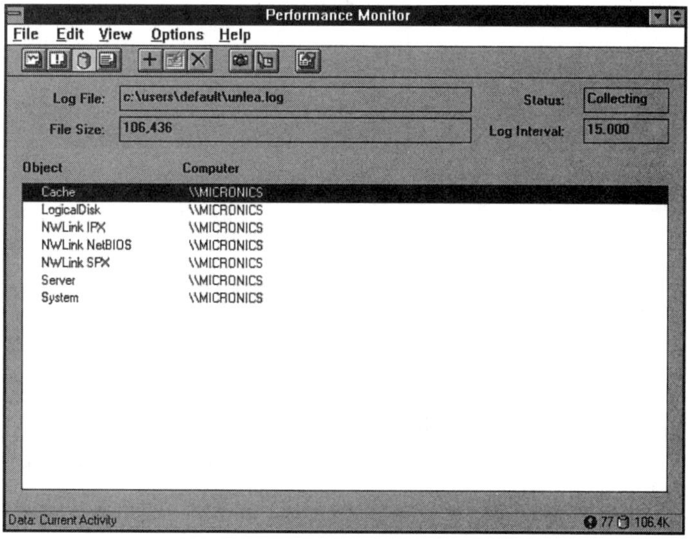

FIGURE 20.5.
The log file window.

To select which object types you want to log, click on the Add button in the Add to Chart dialog box. Because you can select only an object type, this is a very simple dialog box. You have to select Options | Log to set the name of the log file, set the polling interval, and start the log. If you select manual polling, the data will be entered into the log only when you click on the button with a camera to take a snapshot.

As soon as you've created a log file, you can use it as input for the chart, alert, or report windows by opening that window and selecting Options | Data From. You also can set bookmarks in the log file so that you can recognize what other actions were going on in the network at that point in time.

If you'd rather see your data in numerical form, select View | Report or click on the Report button (the one with a little report). You see a window like the one shown in Figure 20.6.

FIGURE 20.6.
The report window.

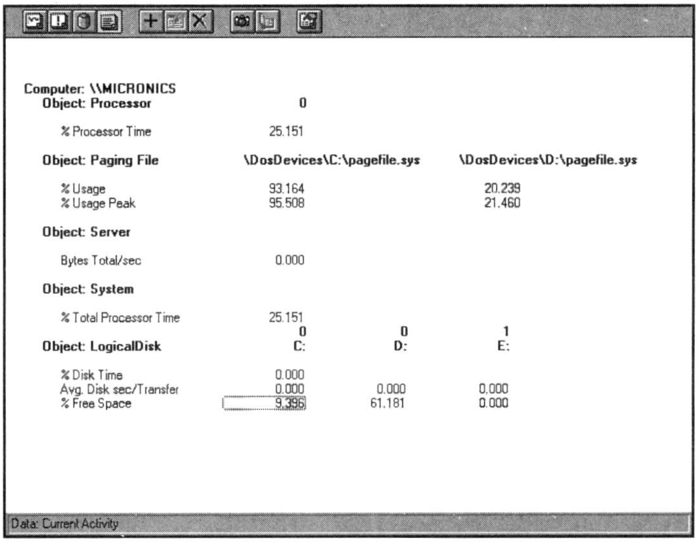

When you select Options | Report, you can set the polling interval.

Optimizing Your Server

The key to optimizing server performance is to keep clearly in mind what a file server's job is. A file server is responsible for responding to user requests for disk data by locating and retrieving data from its disks and sending it to the network or receiving data from the network and storing it on its disk drives. Your job is to balance the performance of the server's various subsystems.

Your first step is to buy a basic system for your server that's designed to provide high-speed I/O performance. I'd much rather see a server designed for I/O performance and reliability than a machine designed for flat-out computational performance that would make a great workstation.

There are basically five ways to improve your server's I/O performance. The first way, and the one that will give you the biggest payback at first, is to make your servers dedicated. You can dedicate your file servers by not using them to also run user applications and by setting the server's priority high. Even if you've decided to stick to Windows NT's workgroup approach and to not upgrade to NT Server, dedicating your file servers will speed up overall server performance and will eliminate the large performance variations created by users working on the server.

Next, increase the amount of memory in your server. At first, increasing the amount of real memory in the server will stop the server from using virtual memory, reducing the load on the disk subsystem and making all the processes needed in the server faster because they're memory-resident. If Performance Monitor's Pages/sec counter is high on your server, adding more memory will have a big impact on server performance.

Even if your server has enough memory to page only occasionally—to load a backup process from virtual memory, for example—adding more memory will have a positive impact on server performance. The additional memory will be used as additional disk cache, speeding up disk access and therefore file service.

The second most important thing you can do is optimize your disk subsystem. Just as with workstations, SCSI drives are better than IDE or ESDI drives, and 15ms drives are better than 20ms drives. When you're configuring the average workstation, you probably take a good guesstimate of how much disk space you'll need and then buy a single disk drive that size. Your server will need several times as much disk space as a typical workstation, probably more than a single disk drive can hold. Even if you can buy a single drive to hold all your server's data, you should consider breaking it up for performance.

Using multiple drives reduces the user's average access time to data by allowing the multiple drives to each service a different request simultaneously. The entire disk channel doesn't need to stop waiting for the drive to seek. If you add multiple disk controllers or SCSI host adapters, you also can improve the data transfer rate to the disk drives.

I recommend that you run your important server drives as mirrored pairs with each of the two drives on separate host adapters. In this duplexed configuration, the server can send write requests to both disk drives simultaneously. I also recommend that you have two drives per host adapter until you have four host adapters, or eight drives, total.

In general, the more drives and the more host adapters (up to four), the merrier. If you use striping, you can significantly increase throughput. If your budget can handle it, a hardware RAID solution is a good idea, too.

The next step is selecting the right bus architecture. Using an ISA bus system as a server will create a serious bottleneck at the bus. Modern SCSI II disks and multiple Ethernet or Token Ring adapters can transfer data faster than the poor old 8 MHz 16-bit ISA bus can. A fast server needs a faster channel between its processor and peripherals.

The traditional solution has been to use an EISA (extended industry standard architecture) bus system for your server. The 32-bit EISA bus supports bus master arbitration and burst transfers to transfer data many times faster than ISA. A wide variety of EISA disk controllers and network cards are available, making EISA a good platform to build a server around.

Over the past few years, systems have been coming out that use one form or another of a local bus to connect the processor to a few peripherals, usually including the video display card. The most common local bus, VESA's VL bus, basically connects the cards directly to a 486 processor's I/O bus. VL bus adapters can be very fast, even faster than EISA, but VL bus doesn't handle multiple adapters very well. I think VL bus systems are good choices for workstations, but the VL bus isn't well-suited to server applications.

NOTE

Remember that your servers aren't going to be running CAD or multimedia applications that require local bus video systems. In fact, a server with VL bus Ethernet and VL bus disk adapters will run faster with an ISA VGA than a fancy VL bus video accelerator.

Intel's PCI bus shows more promise as a server platform, even though there aren't many PCI adapters out yet. PCI bus, used primarily with Pentium systems, is 64 bits wide and has bus arbitration features that allow it to support multiple adapters without the processor overhead that VL bus imposes. Unfortunately, PCI bus is new and immature. Therefore, EISA is the safe bet. If you do decide to use PCI, don't buy it off the shelf and do it yourself. Purchase a complete system certified for Windows NT. This can help you avoid potential adapter conflicts and device driver problems and minimize the installation/configuration time. In addition, you should look for a PCI/EISA hybrid design. Doing so gives you the best option for configuring your server with high-performance 32-bit (or 64-bit if you can find them) peripherals. Don't even consider a PCI/VL bus/ISA combination, because these types of generalized motherboards perform poorly.

If you asked PC users how fast their computers were, most would answer as if you had actually asked them what processor was in their machines. In a workstation, the processor probably is the primary determinant of overall performance. In a server, the choice of processor plays a smaller, but still significant, part in determining file service speed.

NOTE

Your NetWare experience that the processor is of very little importance in server performance isn't really applicable to Windows NT or NT Server. Their performance is more sensitive to the server's processor than NetWare. In fact, NT Server requires more processor horsepower than NetWare to deliver similar performance.

If you're going to be using a processor-intensive application service such as SQL Server or SNA Server, or if you're supporting a large number of users, a RISC system or multiprocessor server such as a Compaq Systempro or Tricord "super server" is a good idea. I currently recommend 60 MHz Pentium servers over 66 MHz 486s, especially if they're PCI bus systems, due to the Pentium's 64-bit data transfer path. And if you can afford it, look at the new 90 MHz dual Pentium servers that have recently hit the market.

Now that you've built a system with multiple Pentium processors, 64M of memory, and a series of fast disk drives connected through the 128-bit miracle bus of tomorrow, you'll find that the bottleneck has moved to the network adapter. You just won't be able to move data in and out of the server fast enough through a single 10Mbps Ethernet or 16Mbps Token Ring card.

Reducing Network Bottlenecks

Network bottlenecks typically start to raise their ugly heads when you have 20 or more users and three or four file servers. A single file server is usually limited in how much data it can handle, so the disk channel or Ethernet card and bus is the bottleneck. As your network grows, the data capacity of the network cable itself becomes the limiting factor in your network's performance.

If you suspect that the network itself is becoming the most significant bottleneck on your network, your first step should be to find a way to measure just how busy your network actually is. There are several types of products that measure traffic on your Ethernet or Token Ring and report the percentage of the network's available bandwidth that's currently in use.

NOTE

I recommend that you think about upgrading or subdividing your Ethernet when it shows 20 percent or more bandwidth utilization on average and Token Rings when they hit 50 percent.

You can use a network protocol analyzer such as a Network General Sniffer or HP Network Advisor. A protocol analyzer typically is built from a portable or laptop computer and carries a price tag of $3,000 to $10,000 or more. Buying a protocol analyzer just to monitor network traffic is the computer equivalent of your average yuppie buying a Range Rover for his 10-mile freeway commute. It does the job, but it's overkill. Protocol analyzers can capture all the packets rushing by on your network and decode them to tell you onscreen what each packet is doing. They're great tools for an expert to use when debugging a troubled network but too much for just load balancing.

What you really need is a network monitor or probe that doesn't store every packet as it comes by for later decoding but just keeps statistics on how much data is going by. This is where the Network Monitor Agent counters and Performance Monitor can prove useful. If you need more information, you can buy stand-alone network probes, little boxes that you connect to your Ethernet or Token Ring and monitor from another computer, such as Novell's LANtern, for about $2,500. You also can find monitoring functions built into other network devices such as bridges, routers, and intelligent hubs from Cabletron, David Systems, and Synoptics. Some lower-end hubs include a simple tachometer display that gives you a quick view of your network traffic.

For a small network, less than 300 nodes or so, your best bet might be to buy a software traffic monitor such as Triticom's EtherVision or TokenVision. For just $4 to $500, they turn any computer on your network into a traffic monitor and can give you a "skyline" display showing network traffic levels over time.

For larger networks, you probably want to put a monitor on each network segment so that you can set SNMP alerts on the monitors. That way, when the traffic level on any of your networks exceeds the level you find acceptable, you'll get a message in your network command center.

The simplest way to speed up your network is to upgrade from Ethernet or Token Ring to a faster network such as FDDI. This is the simplest way to go if you're willing to replace all your current network hardware.

Another solution to network bottlenecks is subdividing your networks into smaller pieces. If you divide your 100-user network into three subnetworks—one each for users in the accounting, sales, and manufacturing departments—and give each network its own file servers, your users will see better performance because each of the three networks will need to carry only one-third as much data.

The problem with just subdividing is that you take a corporate-wide resource and turn it into three islands of technology. If someone in sales needs a special quote from someone in manufacturing or a credit check from accounting, he or she will need to resort to Sneakernet, carrying the appropriate data from one network to the other via floppy disk.

You can solve this problem by connecting each file server to all three networks through three different Ethernet or Token Ring cards. Each user can then access all the data on any of the file servers, but the traffic on each network is still limited to the traffic generated by the users in one of the three departments. See Figure 20.7.

FIGURE 20.7.
Using multiple LAN cards in your servers.

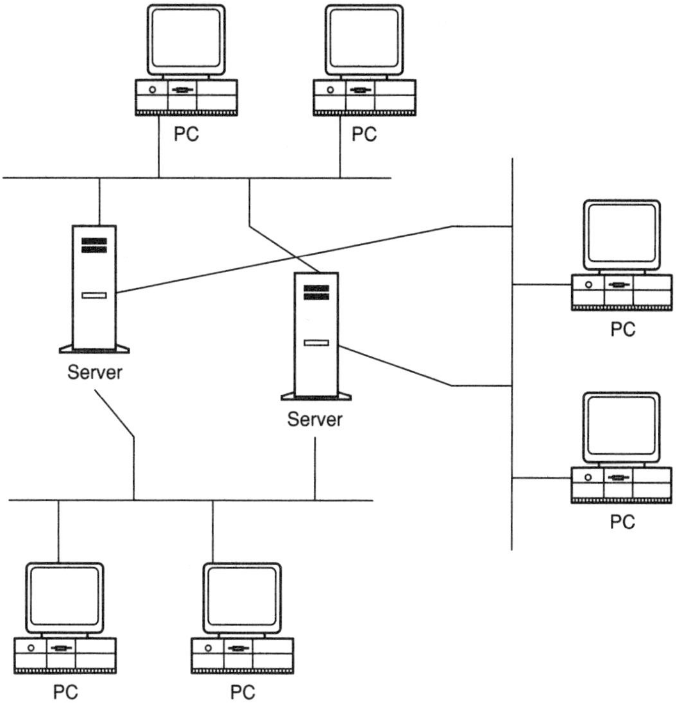

As soon as you get past two or three subnets, putting multiple LAN cards in each file server isn't really such a good idea. First, there are the physical connection problems. There is a relatively small limit on the maximum number of network cards in a server, so you can't have more than five or six networks before you run out of slots for LAN cards in a typical server. Even more important, you'll now be limited to keeping all your workstations within the maximum cable length of the network you choose.

If you have more than two or three subnets, you should use bridges, or routers, to connect your networks. (See Figure 20.8.) Just like in a wide area network, the bridges or routers will forward the data intended for other networks and keep communications between two stations on the same network on that network alone.

FIGURE 20.8.
Using bridges to build a large network.

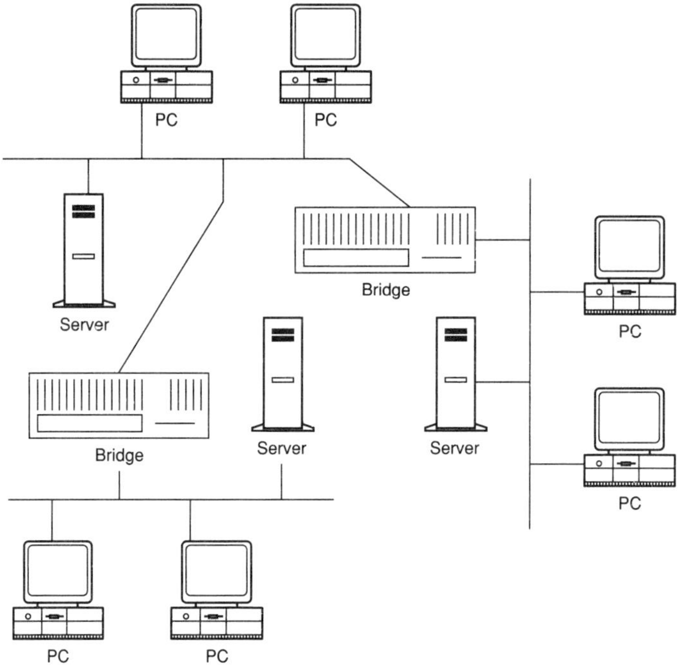

The disadvantage of bridges and routers is that it takes time for each packet to be received by the bridge, examined, and forwarded. Every bridge or router in the data path between a workstation and its file server reduces the performance of file service across that link by 10 to 40 percent. One common solution to this problem is to build a backbone network that connects all the user networks. (See Figure 20.9.) By using a backbone network, you keep each user network just two routers away from any other user network. Also, a failure of one user network doesn't prevent the users on the other user networks from communicating with each other.

As your network grows, you should look seriously at using TCP/IP rather than NetBEUI to carry your file and print service traffic. Although TCP/IP can be up to 15 percent slower on a single network than NetBEUI, it's more efficient when the delays of bridges or routers are added to the network.

NetBIOS can't be routed (you must use bridges to connect NetBEUI networks) and uses many broadcast packets to run. As a result, a NetBIOS network with bridges will have many overhead packets taking up valuable bandwidth. In a complex network, up to 40 percent of all the traffic can be overhead. TCP/IP, on the other hand, is routable and has much lower overhead on complex nets.

FIGURE 20.9.
A backbone network.

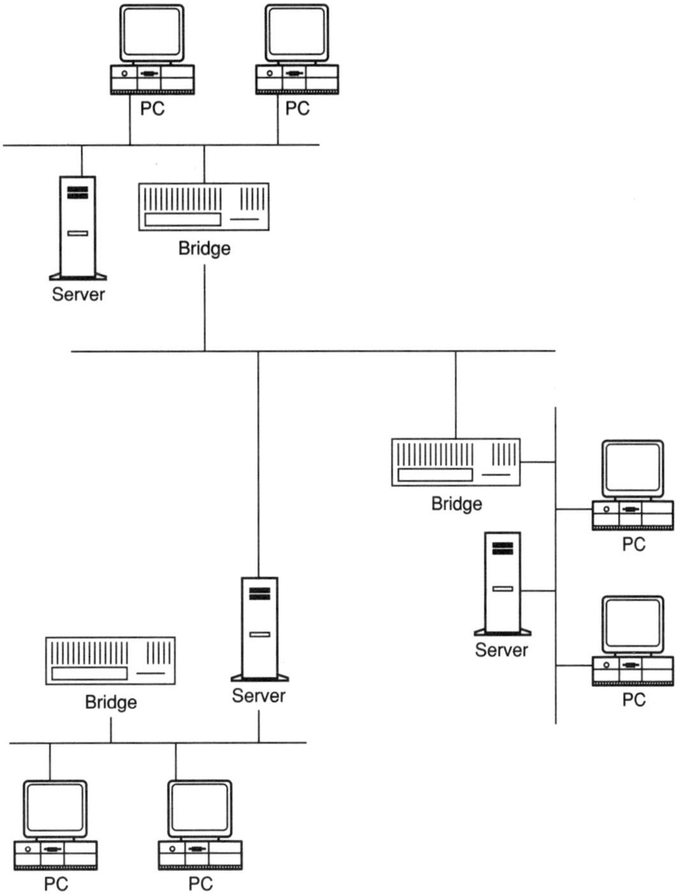

Troubleshooting Your Network

21

IN THIS CHAPTER

This chapter discusses ways to keep your network up and running. In addition to traditional, reactive troubleshooting, we'll discuss ways you can test and monitor your network and its components so you can prevent problems from occurring in the first place.

The first thing you need to realize about troubleshooting is that it's an art, not a science. The main thing you need to remember is to stay calm. As it says on the cover of *Hitchhiker's Guide to the Galaxy:* "Don't panic!" I've seen too many people make a bad situation worse by reformatting a hard disk or replacing all their network cables when a significantly less drastic solution would have worked better.

The key to successful troubleshooting is to take a careful look at the problem before doing anything. The first step is to determine how severe the problem is. If a single modem in a modem pool or one of your 20 laser printers fails, you have a much less significant problem than if all your file servers are destroyed in an earthquake. The first way to determine the severity of the problem is to classify the problem by the number of users affected and by how severely they're affected. There are several kinds of problems:

- Problems that prevent a mission-critical application from running or that prevent a large group of users from accessing their normal applications and data. Example: A file server or Ethernet hub failure.
- Problems that prevent a small group of users from accessing their normal applications and data. Examples: A user who forgets his password, or a failed LAN card.
- Problems that inconvenience the majority of users. Example: A failed drive in a stripe set with parity.
- Problems that inconvenience a small group of users. Example: A printer or communications server failure when others are available.

The second determination is the risk to your data. Just because the phone might start ringing sooner when your boss can't call Easy Saabre to make an airline reservation than when an overnight backup aborts, you shouldn't decide that it's more important. Your data probably is the most valuable asset your company has. A study several years ago sponsored by the Firemen's Fund insurance companies showed that more than half the companies that suffered a catastrophic data loss had gone out of business or merged with a competitor within two years.

Protecting Your Data

If you're following a good backup plan, your exposure to data loss should theoretically be limited to the single day's work since the last backup. If, however, you don't pay careful attention to your backup process, you might have a substantially larger exposure to data loss without even knowing it.

Network administrators make several common mistakes when it comes to backups. The most common is creating a batch file to back up the server and then just changing the tape in the tape drive every morning without looking at the backup program's output log or without ever trying to restore any files.

One of my clients made their backups this way for more than a year before they discovered, after a hard-disk crash, that one of their main database files hadn't been backed up in 17 days. Most backup systems, including this client's, can back up only files that aren't open or locked by another user or task. Because their new comptroller never exited the accounting applications and never logged out of the network, the files he used were always open and therefore not backed up.

If you're thinking that the best solution would be to design a backup system that backed up files even while they were in use, you'd be looking in the wrong place. If you tried to back up a database while it actually was in use, the backup program probably would back up the inventory table. Then, after a user entered a transaction that updated the inventory and sales order table, it would back up the sales order table. If you ever had to restore the data from that tape and use it to run your company, you'd find that the sales order table and the inventory table wouldn't be in sync.

The answer is either to make sure that you have database applications with well-designed backup functions that can log transactions and keep the database in sync or to make sure that your users aren't using valuable files during the backup process.

Another client checked his error logs, made sure he had all his files closed when his backup ran from 2 to 4 a.m., and securely transported copies of his tapes off-site every evening. However, he didn't know that his tape drive had a blown chip and that bit seven of every byte was always recorded on his tapes as a zero. If he had tried to restore any of his backup tapes, he would have found the problem before he needed one of the tapes. He actually found out when he was looking for an important file that a senior vice president had mistakenly deleted.

Even with a good backup plan, you might find yourself in a situation where you need to use all your skills—and the Norton Utilities for NTFS when they're released—to try to reconstruct some data on your server. Here your primary goal should be to follow the Hippocratic oath: "First, do no harm." Never delete a file or reformat a disk that has data you might need to recover. Specialized firms such as On-Track Data Recovery can do their magic only if you haven't wiped the slate clean.

Common Problems

The rest of this chapter is devoted to identifying and solving common networking problems. I'll start with the most common problem you're likely to find on any network—the well-known "My computer can't access network resources" phone call.

When a workstation can't communicate with the file servers on the network, one of many factors could be the cause:

- A bad network card
- A wrong protocol setup
- A bad cable
- Duplicate computer names
- A LAN card driver configuration that doesn't match the card setting

Determining exactly which problem or combination of problems is keeping your station from working is a process of elimination. Your detective work, like Sherlock Holmes's, consists of a series of deductions as you eliminate causes one by one.

Your first question should be, "When did this system last work properly?" If the answer is the day before yesterday, you should start by looking for things that have changed since the day before yesterday. If a major earthquake or hurricane tore through town yesterday, you'd probably be safe in assuming that your system problems were caused by yesterday's events.

It might be a bit more difficult to find more subtle events that could have caused the station to lose its connection to the server. If the user installed a new network protocol or service, such as TCP/IP, an NFS client or server, or especially Novell's workstation requester, it would be pretty safe to start by looking in Control Panel's Network applet to see if something there was inadvertently changed when it shouldn't have been.

A visit from the telephone installers is a giveaway that the problem is with a cable in the wiring closet.

After the user answers "Nothing" to the question "What happened yesterday?", walk to the back of his computer and make sure that his cables are actually connected to the right jacks in the back of his computer and in the wall socket.

More than once I've run to a user site to respond to a phone call that implied the user was going to jump out of his 45th-floor window if his computer wasn't working in 10 minutes, only to find that, while redecorating his office, the user plugged his computer into the jack for his phone and vice versa.

Once you're plugged in, you should fire up the Event Viewer to see whether there are any errors there that can help you find the source of the problem. Most problems related to LAN card configurations generate multiple entries in the system Event Log that you can use to diagnose the problem.

Using the Event Viewer

At system start time, any service that has difficulty starting places an entry in the system log. When any Administrator-class user tries to log into this computer, she gets a dialog box that informs her that something went wrong at system start time. You'll find that the Event Log is at least as good as, if not better than, your users at identifying where the problem is.

If you have a typical Windows NT workstation or NT Server, when you open the Event Viewer after seeing that dialog box, you'll discover that errors tend to domino or cascade. Therefore, you'll have six to 10 events in the Event Viewer from a single typical problem such as a bad or misconfigured adapter.

If your LAN card is configured to user I/O address 300 and IRQ3 but its driver is configured to use an I/O address of 200 and IRQ5, you'll start a chain reaction as the driver fails to load because it couldn't find the card. Then the LAN protocols, server service, and workstation service each can't start because they depend on the LAN card driver in order to run.

Bad LAN Card and Driver Configuration Problems

When your LAN card driver fails to load because of an error on the card or in its configuration, you can get a list in the Event Log with many resulting errors. When I changed the address of the Ethernet card in one of my test servers, all but one of the 26 entries in this Event Log were caused by the first error from the SMC8000 driver, which couldn't find the card.

The first step is to locate the first error in the log from the current session. The upper layer protocol errors are almost always there, because many other services and protocols rely on whatever service or driver failed first.

If that first error is from the LAN card driver, there could be a problem with either the driver's configuration or the LAN card itself. Your next step is probably to take the system down and run a diagnostic program for the LAN card. Most LAN card manufacturers provide DOS-based diagnostics that can test their cards and identify most problems.

NOTE

Remember that a LAN card with a bad transceiver can be identified only by diagnostics that use a loop-back adapter or another workstation. If you're running a thin Ethernet network, you can try using a T connector with two terminators attached as a loop-back. If that works, try a two-workstation test.

If your card passes its diagnostics, you need to go back to Control Panel's Network applet and check the driver's configuration. If the diagnostics fail, first check the card's configuration to make sure that a jumper or DIP switch isn't set wrong. If the card seems okay, try replacing it with a fresh one. It's usually better to just swap the card and figure out what was wrong with the old one back in the lab, because the user gets back to work faster.

Protocol Problems

If the errors in the log start with TCP/IP, NWLINK, or some other protocol, you'll need to configure the protocol through Control Panel's Network applet. Not having a valid IP address or using a IPX or IP network or subnet address different from the other devices on the network might start the error log cascade.

Setting two computers on your network to use the same NetBIOS machine name also is a protocol problem because it prevents the NetBIOS interface you're using—NetBEUI, IPX, or NBT for TCP/IP—from properly identifying a system on the network. Luckily, Windows NT scans the network to detect other computers on the network using this computer's name during the Setup process or when you change a computer's name. Unfortunately, unless you're using NT Server and making all your systems members of the same domain, there isn't a central database of names so that you can name a second computer MARY if the existing MARY is down or otherwise unavailable when you set up the new MARY.

Bad Cable Problems

A Novell study a few years ago indicated that as much as 75 percent of network downtime is caused by cable problems. Diagnosing cable problems can be relatively easy for star-wired architectures such as 10Base-T Ethernet.

If you have a star-wired network, and a single workstation can't locate the server at installation time or later, you can rule out cable problems by simply connecting a workstation that's working at another location on the network to the cable that's plugged into the failed workstation. If the new workstation works properly, you can be pretty sure that the problem isn't with the cables.

If that doesn't work, try replacing the patch cable that runs from the workstation to the wall jack in the user's office. These patch cords are the most likely part of your cable system to fail, because they're exposed to abuse from users. I've seen users roll over their patch cables with their chairs, rip the cable out of the connector and just jam it back in, and commit other innovative acts of patch-cable abuse.

While we're talking about patch cables, I want to throw in my two cents' worth about making your own. Don't. I've found that even skilled network administrators with the best tools don't always make great patch cables. It's hard to get all eight wires in the right positions and still get the strain relief bar on the RJ-45 to close on the jacket of the cable so that when the user pulls on the cable the actual electrical connections don't take the strain. Given that factory patch cables typically cost about $1 more than the cost of the components and that a good crimper costs more than $100, factory patch cables can be cheaper than the ones you make yourself, even before you figure in the cost of your own labor and the connectors you ruin getting it right.

If changing the patch cable doesn't solve the problem, you probably should check the wiring closet and make sure that no one accidentally disconnected this port from the hub or concentrator. After all, just plugging the cable back in might not show off your technical skills or your fancy tools and diagnostics, but it does get the problem solved, and that's what's important.

The next step is to check the cable end-to-end for conductivity. If you don't have a full toolbox, run down to Radio Shack and buy some alligator clip leads for connecting the two wires of a pair in your cable and a cheap volt-ohm meter. When you put the meter across the other ends of the wires, you should read well under 100 ohms.

Unfortunately, although this simple test can tell you that the problem is in the cables, it can't tell you that the problem *isn't* in the cables. High-speed digital signals such as Ethernet and Token Ring need more than just simple conductivity from a cable. They also need cables that meet certain specifications for signal loss, electrical noise, and length.

Remember that the quality of your installation is just as important as the quality of the parts you use. Running cables over fluorescent light fixtures, using telephone grade splices and punch-down blocks, and other installation errors can keep even the best cable from working properly.

Bus networks, on the other hand, can be quite difficult to figure out if you don't have the right tools and techniques. Because a problem in a bus network such as thin

Ethernet will cause the whole cable segment to go down, locating a cable break or other problem on a bus can be difficult.

Several manufacturers, including Microtest, Fluke, and DataComm Northwest, make hand-held cable testers designed specifically to test LAN cables to see whether they meet the appropriate specs. These testers typically have a signal injector that connects to one end of the cable and a main tester that connects to the other end of the cable and measures the noise and strength of the signal it receives.

These cable testers also take advantage of the fact that a break, a short, a bad connector, or another impedance mismatch in a cable causes any high-speed signal in the cable to be reflected, just like light is reflected by a mirror. By sending a high-speed pulse into the cable and measuring how long it takes for the reflection to come back, a cable tester or time domain reflectometer (TDR) can determine how far down the cable the problem is.

On a bus network, a TDR is the easiest way to find the problem. Without one, you have to split your network in half, putting terminators on both of the new ends at the break and checking whether the stations on each half can see each other. If there's just one problem, the stations on one half of your network will be able to see the others, and the stations on the other half won't. You just have to continue the process of dividing the network until you find the segment or connector with the problem.

If you have a cable tester, it's a good idea to check and document all your cable runs. That way, when you have a problem, you can throw the tester on the line and find out in seconds whether the problem is at one of the connectors or in the walls, where it's basically impossible to fix.

Replacing a Failed Drive in a Mirrored or Stripe Set with Parity

The first, and most important, step in replacing a failed drive in a mirrored or stripe set with parity is to recognize that it needs doing. I had one client, now out of business, who ran their computers in difficult conditions and therefore always built their servers with mirrored drives. What they forgot to do was check the status of their servers periodically. One day I got a panicked call after the second drive on one of their servers failed.

An examination of the error log from a backup tape showed that the server had run with a failed drive for three months. Had they swapped that drive, and had they not been indicted for mail fraud, they might still be in business today. If you want to avoid a similar fate, you should look at the error log for each of your NT Servers on a regular basis.

Once you know you have a drive you need to replace, the next step is to back up the volume in question. I know it sounds silly, but I always make a backup before doing anything to the disk subsystem on a server.

Fixing a Mirrored Set

When a drive in a mirrored set fails, the system automatically sends the data requests to the remaining drive, leaving the working drive as an orphan. You then need to go into Disk Administrator, select the mirrored set, and select Fault Tolerance | Break Mirror. This makes the mirrored set two separate partitions. The working drive gets the drive letter formerly used by the set, and the failed drive gets the next available letter on your system.

Next, you need to bring the server down, turn it off, and replace the disk drive. Your best bet is to look in the server documentation (you did document everything in this server, didn't you?) and configure another drive of the same make and model to replace the failed drive.

Once the new drive is in place, run Disk Administrator again and mirror the good drive by selecting the partition and the unused space on the new drive and selecting Fault Tolerance | Establish Mirror.

If you're using SCSI drives, and I hope you are, your best bet is to add the new drive to the same host adapter as the failed drive but to use a different SCSI address so that you can replace the drive and then run Disk Administrator once to break and make the mirrored set.

When you restart the computer, it will automatically copy the data from the good drive to the new secondary drive in the background and place an entry in the error log when the copy is complete.

Fixing Stripe Sets with Parity

When a drive in a stripe set with parity fails, it's automatically ejected from the set and orphaned. To fix the stripe set, you just need to add the new drive and run Disk Administrator to add it to the stripe set.

When the Domain Controller Is Down

One of NT Server's strengths is the fact that a user's logon request can be processed by any NT Server in a domain and not just at the domain controller. Because all servers in the domain have a copy of the domain database, they can continue to process logon requests for as long as the domain controller is down. In fact, the only thing you can't do when the domain controller is down is to update the domain database by adding users and changing group memberships and user rights.

The first decision you need to make when your domain controller is down is whether you're going to repair that server and bring it back up as the domain controller or if you're going to take one of the other servers in the domain and promote it to be the domain controller. If you're going to bring the domain controller down for an hour or so to add more memory or a new disk drive, promoting another server and then demoting it again when you bring the domain controller back up doesn't make a whole lot of sense. On the other hand, if a couple of wild-eyed terrorists machine-gun your domain controller into submission, you'll want to promote a server with less-severe wounds.

To promote a server to domain controller, you need to use Server Manager to select the server and then select Computer | Promote to Domain Controller. If the domain controller is running at the time, it will automatically be demoted.

You then have to decide whether you want to resynchronize the whole domain, which you should do if you have any reason to believe that the domain controller had changes that had not yet been duplicated on all the file servers in the domain. Resyncing a large domain can create a huge amount of network traffic, so you might decide to postpone it until off-hours, when it won't affect user performance significantly.

Restoring a Failed Server

If any of the other NT Servers in your domain fails or loses its connection with the domain controller, you should resync that server with the domain controller when you restore it to the network. Use the Server Manager, select the server, and choose Computer | Resynchronize Server.

Browser Errors

If, while scanning your system log, you run into an error that reads `The Browser has forced an election on network (`*`some network name`*`) because a Windows NT Server (or Domain Master) browser is started`, you have nothing to worry about. This message is simply telling you that your computer wanted to be the master browser—the computer that all the other computers ask for a list of computers in the domain—but that some other NT Server machine declared itself to be master browser first. Your network will continue to work without incident.

IN THIS PART

PART IV

Setting Up a World-Wide Web Site Using NT Workstation

22

Introduction to the Web, Web Sites, and Home Pages

IN THIS CHAPTER

This chapter will provide you with an introduction to the WWW, web sites, and home pages on the Internet. If you are already familiar with these topics, feel free to skip to the next chapter. The next chapter starts with an overview of various hardware platforms that can be utilized to host a Windows NT-based web site. By reading the next chapter, you will learn fundamental material about the WWW that's required to understand topics covered in later chapters.

Introduction to the WWW

Until the early 1980s, what is now called the Internet was a relatively small network called ARPAnet. This small network was mainly used as a research tool for about 15 years. After the Internet was created in the early 1980s, many universities and government organizations got connected to it to exchange and distribute information. Later, commercial organizations realized the potential of the Internet and started getting connected to the Internet as well. The recent increase in size of the WWW is a result of more and more commercial organizations establishing a presence on the web.

Until the creation of the World Wide Web (WWW), almost all information distribution was done via E-mail, FTP, Archie, and Gopher. E-mail became widely used for exchanging information between various groups of people as well as individuals. FTP was being used to transfer files from one host to another. Archie was used to locate various files on the Internet. Due to the very nature of the Internet, before long, information was scattered all over the Internet. Therefore, unless you knew where the information was, you had no way to search for the information you needed.

As a solution to this, "Gopher" was invented at the University of Michigan. Gopher is a database of information that's organized using a hierarchical menu interface. Gopher was designed to take someone looking for information from something general to something specific. This is done by offering the user selections of topics from various layers of menus. To extend the amount of information being provided, gophers were often connected to other gophers. Although this proved to be a more efficient way of locating and distributing information, its capabilities were limited. Mainly, the information being distributed was virtually limited to plain text, and access to information at various locations was not very well organized.

Due to this limitation of Gopher, a new platform-independent method had to be invented to distribute information on the Internet. This issue was addressed at CERN in Switzerland when Hypertext Markup Language (HTML) was created. HTML was derived from a document formatting language called Standard Generalized Markup Language (SGML).

HTML was designed to be a document markup language that's easy to learn, use, and transmit over the Internet. HTML is simpler to use and easier to learn than SGML. To transmit HTML documents, a TCP/IP (Transport Control Protocol/Internet Protocol) based protocol was invented. This protocol became known as Hypertext Transport Protocol (HTTP). Web servers speak HTTP to transmit HTML files, and web browsers use HTTP to retrieve HTML files. Web browsers display various objects, both static and interactive (such as text, images and Java applets), upon retrieving them from web servers.

With the unification of text and graphics, the WWW became an exciting medium of information interchange compared to Gopher. Someone looking for information finally could browse various information sources and easily travel from one source to another by following various *hyperlinks.* With the help of special applications and browsers, the WWW quickly became a vehicle of text and multimedia distribution. Also, locating information on the web has become a lot easier thanks to many search engines and web-site cataloging databases deployed on the web.

The World Wide Web is perhaps the most influential vehicle of information distribution since the invention of the television. The recent boom in the number of WWW sites on the Internet attests to this fact. As more and more people gain access to the WWW via online services or directly via a local Internet Service Provider (ISP), many organizations will focus more on using the WWW to keep their customers informed of new products, carry out business transactions, and provide customer service.

Compared to other information distribution vehicles, the WWW is a very attractive medium because the cost of publishing data and making it available to a global audience is relatively low. Furthermore, by registering a web site with various search engines and website cataloging databases, you can potentially get your customers to come to you for information when they need it. This is different from traditional ways of advertising, such as television advertising, in which advertisers take the information directly to their customers.

Clearly, by setting up a WWW site, you will be catering to a different kind of audience. Usually someone who is visiting your web site is there because she needs access to some information. Therefore, when designing your web site, you should keep in mind that your first priority is to make the information at your web site as accessible as possible.

Within the past few years, the Internet has grown by a scale of a few magnitudes. If you look at Figure 22.1, you will notice that the Internet has been almost doubling, annually, since 1991. The WWW is responsible for most of this growth.

FIGURE 22.1.
Growth of the Internet.

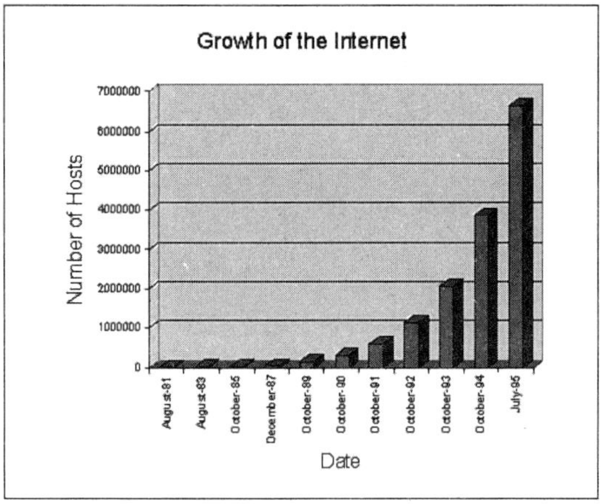

Introduction to WWW Sites

WWW sites can be thought of as TV broadcast stations. It's much less expensive, however, to set up and maintain a WWW site than to set up a TV broadcast station. You can generally have your own web site up and running in just a few weeks (in all likelihood, much sooner after reading this section!). Unlike TV broadcast stations, WWW sites broadcast information on a per-demand basis. When a client requests certain information from a web server, the web server delivers the information to the client and closes the connection. Refer to Figure 22.2 for a simple diagram of how web sites and web clients are connected to the WWW.

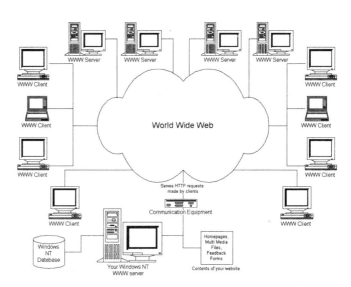

FIGURE 22.2.
Basic diagram of the WWW.

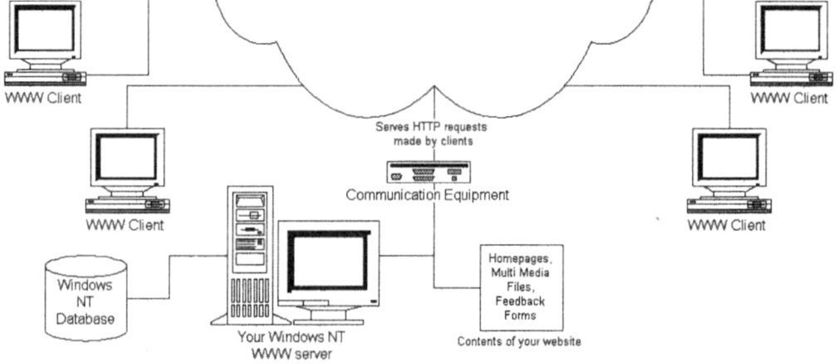

NOTE

This figure demonstrates how web servers and clients are linked to the Internet. As you can see, many web servers and clients are connected to the Internet. Because all these web servers and clients use HTTP to communicate with each other, various hardware platforms and operating systems can act as web servers and web clients.

The WWW is a collection of servers on the Internet that speak HTTP, which is a "connectionless protocol." Web servers listen for incoming HTTP requests, and when an HTTP request is received, the requested data is sent to the client. Refer to Figure 22.3 for a demonstration of this interaction.

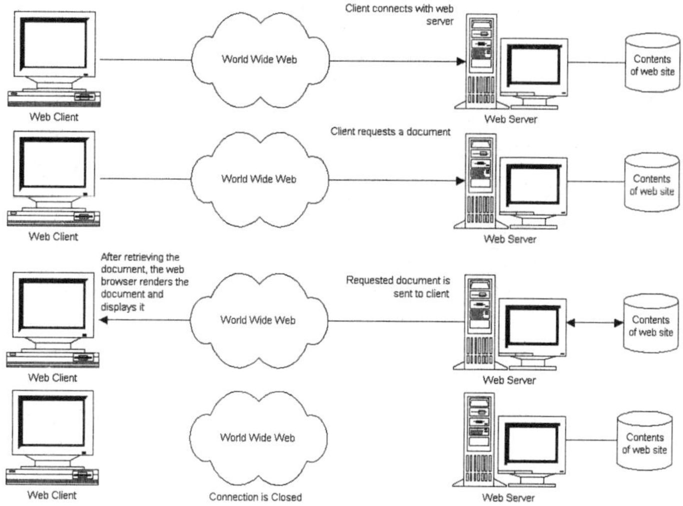

FIGURE 22.3.
How web servers serve HTTP requests by transmitting documents requested by web clients.

When someone accesses a page at your web site, usually more than one HTTP connection is made. Generally, one is made for each object, such as a graphics file or Java applet, that's embedded in the document being accessed. For example, if you type `netstat` at the command prompt when someone is accessing your web site, you will notice that usually more than one connection is made by the client accessing your web site. What you see in Figure 22.4 is the result of one page being accessed by a web browser. As you can see, several connections are made by the web browser accessing the page. This is because typically, a new connection must be made for each object (graphic, sound file, Java applet, and so on) on the page the client is accessing.

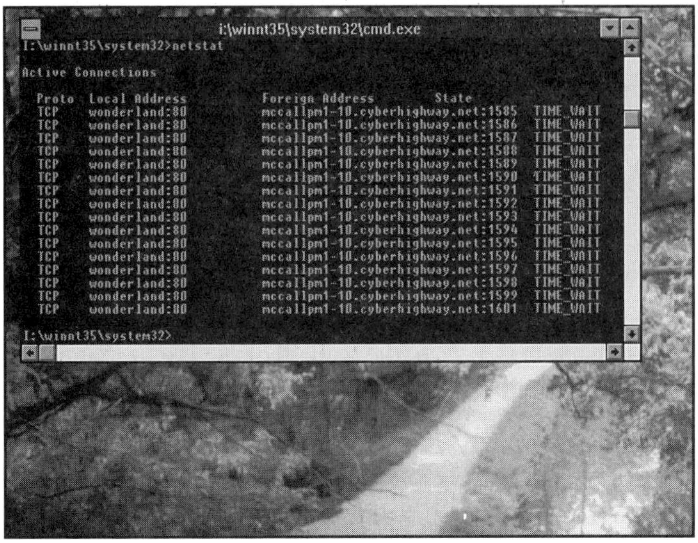

FIGURE 22.4.
Multiple HTTP connections for a web page access.

NOTE

A connectionless protocol is a protocol that does not need a persistent connection. When an HTTP request is received by a web server, the data is sent to the client. When the requested data has been transmitted, the connection is closed. Often a request for a page creates more than one connection. This happens if various inline graphics or other objects are on the page. Each connection is good only for retrieving one graphic or other object from the web server.

How Web Servers Work

If information requested by a client is simply a web page consisting of plain text, a few images, sound, or other objects, the web server simply transmits these objects at the request of the client. More work is involved, however, when dynamic content must be provided by the web server. Common Gateway Interface (CGI) is utilized by web servers to invoke various aplications on your server to provide dynamic content to users browsing a web site. Refer to Figure 22.5 for a graphical representation of how web servers invoke CGI scripts to provide dynamic content.

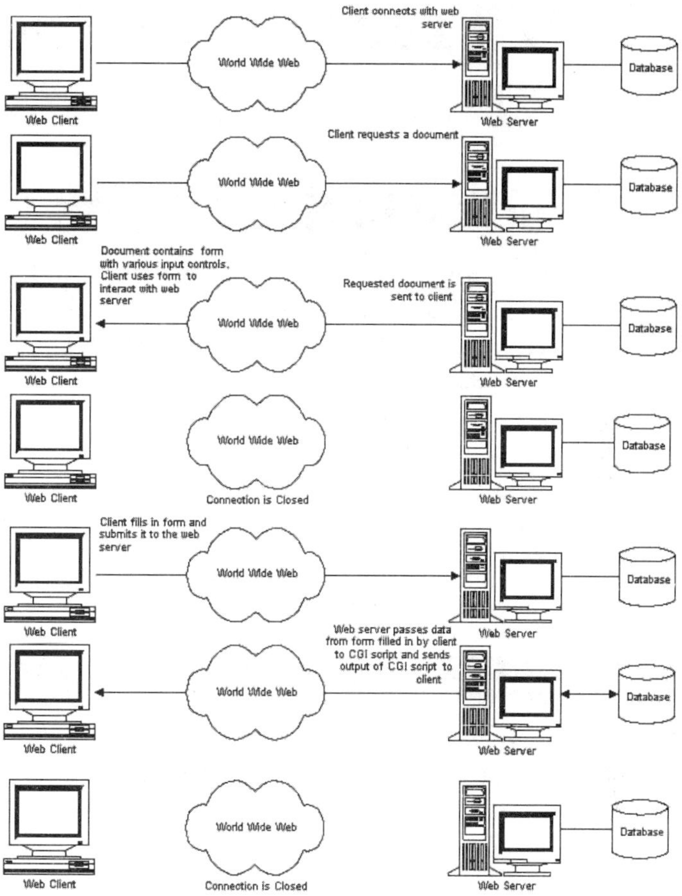

FIGURE 22.5.
How web servers use CGI to provide dynamic content to web browsers. The CGI script on the server typically processes input given by users browsing a web site, processes it (possibly by accessing a database), and sends a message to the user who invoked the CGI script.

Typically, CGI scripts receive input when a client fills in a form and submits it to the web server. The web server then invokes the CGI script after creating certain CGI environment variables. As shown in Figure 22.5, this process begins when a client first requests an HTML document containing a form from the web server. After the form is sent to the client, the connection is closed. When the user fills in the form and submits it to the server, the server executes the CGI script with the information that was put into the form. The CGI script then processes the data, possibly by accessing a database, and sends a message to the client who invoked the CGI script. This message typically contains the results of processing input provided by the client and provides a link to another page so that the user can continue to browse the web site.

NOTE

Web servers usually listen on port 80 for incoming HTTP requests.

Introduction to Home Pages

Home pages are documents formatted in HTML that might contain inline graphics or other objects. HTML documents are in plain text (usually ASCII) format and can be created with any text editor. In Chapter 24, "What Software Do You Need?" you will be shown various programs that can be used to create HTML files as well as various Windows NT web servers that can be used to host web sites. Just like the World Wide Web, HTML is evolving. More and more features are being added to HTML to accommodate various needs. HTML has been standardized by the WWW consortium. For more information about standard HTML and proposed HTML enhancements to standard HTML, you might want to visit

`http://www.w3.org/hypertext/WWW/MarkUp/`

NOTE

Just because a web browser such as Netscape or Microsoft's Internet Explorer supports a "neat" HTML tag does not mean that it is valid HTML. When using HTML enhancements that are beyond standard HTML, you should be aware that when someone looks at your web site with a browser that supports only standard HTML, your pages might not be rendered properly.

Home pages can contain inline graphics or other objects. Listed here are a few commonly used file formats found in web pages:

File Type	*Extension*
AIFF sound	.aiff
AU sound	.au
GIF image	.gif
HTML document	.html or .htm
JPEG image	.jpg or .jpeg
MPEG movie	.mpeg or .mpg
PostScript file	.ps
TIFF image	.tiff or .tif
Plain text	.txt

File Type	*Extension*
QuickTime movie	.mov
XBM bitmap image	.xbm

NOTE

When you embed various objects in file formats not commonly supported by web browsers, you should always include a link to software that can be used to view the files you make available.

Various graphics formats like the ones mentioned previously and new technologies such as Java and Virtual Reality Markup Language (VRML) home pages are capable of presenting information to a global audience in a way information has never been presented before.

Publishing on the Web with Windows NT

After you have your web site all set up, publishing on the web with Windows NT is very easy to learn. As mentioned earlier, content on the web is published through the use of a document markup language called HTML. To publish on the web, a basic understanding of HTML is required. This will change in the near future, however, when WYSIWYG HTML editors become common.

After consulting various reference materials on the web, you will be able to utilize HTML and publish information on the web. HTML is not a very powerful document markup language. Therefore, you might not be able to make everything look exactly the way you'd like it to look. By utilizing HTML, however, you will be able to present your content in an organized manner to web surfers browsing your web site. As you gain more experience in web publishing, you will be able to utilize various enhancements to standard HTML and create richly formatted web pages.

What's Needed to Publish on the Web

Many web authoring services will do all your web authoring for a price. If you are setting up your own web server, however, you might as well spend some more time familiarizing yourself with web publishing and do it yourself. The user-friendly environment of Windows NT can be exploited to publish on the web. Thanks to many web publishing applications available for Windows NT, even with no prior web publishing experience, it's easy to create an outstanding web site.

To learn how to publish on the web, the single most important thing you need is time. By spending some time on the project, you can familiarize yourself with HTML and how to publish on the web in just a few days. On the Internet, many resources are available that teach you how to publish on the web. For more information on publishing on the web by utilizing HTML, you might want to visit Yahoo's World Wide Web authoring resources page at

`http://www.yahoo.com/Computers_and_Internet/Internet/World_Wide_Web/Authoring/`

As more and more powerful web publishing tools are invented, however, HTML knowledge will not even be necessary. Very soon, what word processors such as Microsoft Word did for document publishing will be done to web publishing by web publishing suites. Before Word processors came into existence, a person who wanted to create a richly formatted document had to learn a rather complex document markup language and use that and a special compiler to design documents. Thanks to inexpensive microcomputers with feature-rich word processors, however, this drudgery is no longer necessary.

Web Publishing Tools

Various web publishing tools can be utilized to design web pages. Although most of these tools are simple HTML editors, a new breed of WYSIWYG web publishing tools is coming into existence. With these powerful tools, publishing on the web will become easier and less time-consuming.

Although initial versions of Microsoft Internet Assistant for Microsoft Word were limited in functionality, more recent versions have many added features to make web publishing tasks easier to handle. For example, the current version of Internet Assistant handles inline images, document backgrounds, various text colors, font attributes, tables, and many other document formatting attributes. Because all these attributes are accessible via an easy-to-use GUI, someone without any web publishing experience can publish content on the web by using Microsoft Internet Assistant. In addition to Microsoft Internet Assistant for Word, other WYSIWYG HTML editors will be available by the time you read this book. In the near future, thanks to these powerful tools, a knowledge of HTML will no longer be necessary to publish on the web.

In addition to Microsoft, several other companies, including Netscape and Vermeer Technologies, will be unveiling various web publishing suites that can be used to publish information on the web. These web publishing suites will make setting up and maintaining a web site easier by enabling you to concentrate on the contents of your web site instead of worrying about how it should be formatted with HTML.

Database Publishing Tools

Although providing plain text, images, and sound via the web has tremendous potential, the benefits are limited. Because the main goal of setting up a web site is to provide information, publishing databases on the web has a lot of benefits. Various database applications for Windows NT can be utilized to publish databases on the web. These database publishing applications are easy to install and offer a great deal of functionality. Through the utilization of such database interface applications, databases on an NT server can be made available to users browsing a web site. With CGI, such database interface applications can be set up to enable users browsing a web site to update and query a database.

Why Not UNIX?

Until recently, someone wanting to establish a presence on the web had very few available options apart from UNIX. For this reason, at the time of this writing, most web servers on the web are in fact UNIX web servers. These web servers are quite capable of hosting a web site and serving HTTP (Hypertext Transport Protocol) requests. However, the development environment UNIX offers for web site developers has much to be desired. Most often, web site developers on UNIX servers spend a fair amount of time worrying about operating system-imposed restrictions and inconveniences. These restrictions and inconveniences take time away from web site developers who can be better utilized working on the content of the web site. The often-cryptic user interfaces of various UNIX tools makes the task even harder for UNIX web site developers. On the other hand, Windows NT offers a user-friendly and robust environment in which to develop a web site. If you already have a UNIX web server acting as your primary web server, you will greatly benefit from making the switch to Windows NT.

Various Aspects of Publishing on the Web

You should be concerned about several issues when publishing on the web. Some of these issues are not too important and might not even be applicable to you. You should, however, pay particular attention to some issues, such as security.

Benefits of Publishing on the Web

Recently, many organizations have set up web sites on the Internet. If you know the name of a company, you can now almost get to its web site by guessing the company's web site address. Also, TV commercials and other product literature increasingly reference HTTP addresses. When the web becomes more widely used by the general public and becomes an even more popular medium of information distribution, customers will start visiting web sites of various companies for information. The cost savings of publishing on the web can be very large when it is no longer necessary to print color brochures and mail them to prospective customers. By utilizing the web, organizations can publish various pieces of product literature on the web and allow customers to access this information. All this can be done at a fraction of the cost involved in keeping customers informed through traditional methods.

Furthermore, when information is added to a web site, it is immediately available to millions of users. No other information distribution medium has the capability to distribute information to such a large audience at a relatively minor cost. In addition to your being able to provide information very quickly, by utilizing the web, you can also get customer feedback as soon as a customer transmits the feedback to your web server. The cost savings and time savings are two of the most significant advantages of using the web to distribute information. Also, by incorporating multimedia and new technologies such as Java to a web site, you can make the content of a web site richly interactive to make the information being presented more appealing to web surfers.

Drawbacks of Publishing on the Web

Using the WWW to distribute information has some drawbacks. One of the biggest drawbacks is the lack of security standards for transmitting sensitive data on the Internet. Because the WWW was born in an academic environment, initially, security was not a major concern. With the increasing commercial use of the web, however, security has become a major concern. Several companies such as Microsoft and Netscape have come up with various data encryption technologies that can be used to make the Internet a secure place to do business. These security mechanisms, however, are not widely implemented by all web browsers. Therefore, security concerns arise when sensitive data is transmitted on the Internet. In the near future, however, this will change when more and more web browsers (especially proprietary browsers of online services) support various data encryption mechanisms.

Another drawback of publishing on the web is the lack of content formatting control. Although standard HTML offers many document formatting attributes, its capabilities are somewhat limited. Use of Netscape or Microsoft Enhancements to HTML, however, enables content published on the web to be better formatted. Unfortunately, not all web browsers support these HTML "enhancements." This is a major drawback because with special HTML tags, the content might be made almost unintelligible for users who do not have browsers that support the HTML tags that were used. For example, users of various online services with *technologically challenged* web browsers will not be able to enjoy web sites as much as users who use Netscape Navigator and Microsoft Internet Explorer.

How to Use the Web to Your Advantage

Although there are certain disadvantages in publishing on the web, its advantages far outweigh the previously mentioned drawbacks. By utilizing the web judiciously, you will be able not only to provide content to your customers but also to do it in a timely and appealing manner to increase business and customer satisfaction. Also, the web can be utilized as an efficient medium to communicate with customers and get their feedback as well as other information. In chapter 28, you will be shown how to set up a feedback form that can be used to get feedback from users browsing your web site. Also, by using other Internet services such as FTP, you will be able to distribute software to those surfing your web site. By reading the next few chapters, you will be able to set up a web server and various CGI programs and unleash the potential of the web by using Windows NT.

Summary

This chapter covered various fundamental topics about the WWW that are required to understand topics covered in subsequent chapters. In this chapter, you were first introduced to the WWW, its architecture, and its evolution. Next, you were informed about web servers, how they work, and how home pages on web servers can be used to distribute information. The section on web publishing covered various web publishing tools that are available to publish on the web and how you can utilize these tools to make web publishing tasks easier to tackle. The web publishing section also covered various aspects of web publishing and how you can utilize the web to your advantage.

Before setting up a web site, you need to select proper hardware to host your web server. The following chapter discusses various hardware platforms that are available to host a Windows NT-based web server. By reading the following chapter, you'll know what hardware is needed to host your web site.

Choosing the Right Hardware for the Job

23

IN THIS CHAPTER

The hardware you need for your web site depends on the kinds of services you will be setting up on your web server. When you are hosting a web site, by far the most important factors as far as performance is concerned are input/output performance and the amount of memory available apart from the bandwidth of your Internet connection.

This priority changes somewhat dramatically when you start getting into 40 to 60 simultaneous users running various Common Gateway Interface (CGI) applications. If these CGI programs query and update a database on your server, raw input/output performance and RAM is not going to be enough. In such an event, although adding more memory will increase performance, you might need a powerful server to host your web server. Therefore, when choosing your hardware, you need to think about the magnitude of traffic you expect your web server to generate.

NOTE

Regardless of the hardware platform you go along with, be sure that your web server is on an NTFS partition. This will enhance the performance of your web server as well as provide better security. For security and performance reasons, you might want to set up your web server on another hard disk (not just another partition on the same hard disk, but a different physical hard disk).

Various Platforms Suitable to Run NT

Although Windows NT runs on several hardware platforms, Intel is the most widely used hardware platform. Lately, however, Power PC-based and Digital Alpha-based servers have been gaining popularity due to their high performance. Various tradeoffs are involved when you are choosing one platform over another. Depending on your current and anticipated needs, you need to choose the right server platform.

Going Along with an INTEL-Based WWW Platform

Hosting your web server on an Intel-based web server might be the most practical solution for you. INTEL-based servers are generally less expensive than Alpha-based or Power PC-based servers. If you do not need an extremely high-performance server, an Intel-based server will do fine. Often, your biggest bottleneck will be the bandwidth of the line connecting you to the Internet. Therefore, unless you are thinking about burdening your web server with various other tasks that require a fair amount of processing time, you will be fine by going along with an Intel-based server. Being able to utilize many applications written for Intel-based computers to develop your web site is another advantage in choosing an Intel-based web server. According to Robert Denny, developer of the popular Windows NT web server WebSite, an Intel-based web server running Windows NT is perfectly capable of saturating a T1 line.

TIP

If you'll be going along with an Intel-based web server, it might be a good idea to purchase a server that supports Symmetric Multiprocessing (SMP). By investing in a server that supports SMP under Windows NT, if you outgrow your server, you can simply add another processor.

NOTE

Be sure to talk about Windows NT compatibility issues with your vendor when going along with an SMP server.

Going Along with a Power PC-Based or DEC Alpha-Based WWW Platform

Power PC and Alpha servers are clearly high-performance servers that can be utilized for various other tasks in addition to hosting a web site. If you're employing your WWW server for internal use (it's an easy way of distributing information), you do want a fast system. If you're using it as a proxy server, you also want a fast system. A WWW server on a Power PC-based or Alpha-based server will do fine in the latter case.

On the downside, Power PC-based and Alpha-based servers generally require more RAM to run the same application programs that run on an INTEL-based computer. Lack of software or delayed release of software is another downside. Although this situation might change in the future, at the moment, most software vendors are focusing on Intel-based platforms.

NOTE

Although more and more applications are becoming available for non-Intel Windows NT platforms, support is still very limited. Make sure that you are comfortable with the available software for the Windows NT platform you'll be choosing.

Hardware Requirements for Each Platform

Listed next are the minimum hardware requirements for a basic Windows NT-based web server. Depending on whether you'll provide various additional services, such as hosting a database or providing mail services, you'll need more RAM and/or processing power.

Minimum Hardware Requirements for an Intel-Based Webserver

486 DX2/66 or better
16 MB of RAM
Around 100 MB of free disk space on an NTFS partition
At least a 28.8 PPP (Point-to-Point Protocol) link to the Internet
UPS that supports Windows NT
CD-ROM drive

NOTE

With 16 MB of RAM, you can basically get by for a web site. If, however, you are planning to run a few other applications or set up a database on your web server, a RAM upgrade to 24 or 32 MB will make a tremendous difference.

TIP

You can boost the performance of your webserver by using more than one hard disk and/or by using a dual-channel/wide SCSI card. By having Windows NT reside on one hard disk, your data files on another, and your application programs on another, you can increase the performance of your server. Also, when setting up swap file space, you can increase the performance of your server by splitting your swap files over two or more hard disks.

Minimum Hardware Requirements for an Alpha-Based or Power PC-Based Webserver

Any Alpha-based or Power PC-based server
32 MB of RAM
At least a 64/128 kbs ISDN link to the Internet

Around 100 MB of free disk space on an NTFS partition
CD-ROM drive
UPS that supports Windows NT

Price/Performance Issues

Although Power PC-based and Alpha-based web servers are inherently more powerful than existing Intel-based servers, they tend to be more expensive. Unfortunately, most software vendors don't seem to port their NT software to non-Intel platforms. Therefore, the number of application programs available for non-Intel platforms is limited. This might be an issue for you if you will be using the same machine to develop your web site because tools for non-Intel platforms are limited. With the recent Microsoft-Digital alliance, however, and the development of an Intel emulator for the Alpha, things might change in the near future. In most cases, the biggest bottleneck of your web server will be its link to the Internet. If you will be linking your web site to a large database or are planing to use one server for various other tasks such as Microsoft Mail Server, a DHCP server, or a RAS server in addition to hosting a web server, then going along with a Power PC or an Alpha server makes sense. If not, your best bet would be to go along with an Intel-based server. Also, with the introduction of new Pentium Pro-based servers that are optimized for 32-bit operating systems such as Windows NT, you will be able to enjoy a higher level of performance from Intel-based servers.

NOTE

Currently, an INTEL emulator for Alpha computers running Windows NT exists. This emulator, however, will run only those Windows applications that do not require Windows to be run in 386 enhanced mode. In other words, the new 32-bit applications will not work with this emulator. In the near future, however, you might expect to see an INTEL emulator that will run 32-bit Windows applications on an Alpha.

Importance of a UPS

The importance of having an Uninterruptible Power Supply (UPS) can't be stressed enough when you're dealing with an operating system like Windows NT that will be serving up documents on the web 24 hours a day. A sudden power failure in the middle of a disk read/write operation can be detrimental to the health of your server. What's really bad about such an incident is that a file might get corrupted and you might never know about it until you need the file. Although NTFS provides many safeguards to prevent such incidents from happening, you should never take a chance with your data. It's always wise to invest in a UPS that will shut down your server safely in the event of an extended power outage. Depending on your hardware, you need to choose a UPS that's at least capable of providing power until Windows NT has enough time to shut down various services and applications running on your server.

TIP

Be sure your UPS "supports" Windows NT. Although you can use the UPS applet that comes with Windows NT, many UPS vendors bundle software with added functionality that gives you more control and flexibility.

Summary

This chapter discussed various hardware platforms that are suitable for hosting a Windows-NT based web site. Although Alpha- and Power PC-based platforms are high-performance server platforms, software for them is limited. Therefore, you might be more productive by choosing an Intel-based server to host your web site.

The next chapter covers the software that you need to host your web site. The chapter also shows you how to use various tools to simplify web publishing.

What Software Do You Need?

24

IN THIS CHAPTER

After you have chosen your hardware, it's time to select your Web server software as well as other tools to develop your web site. Depending on the nature of the web site you will be setting up, you need to first determine the features you need your web server to support. Afterward, you will be able to select the web server that best satisfies your needs.

Choosing Your Web Server

About two dozen web servers are available for hosting a Windows NT-based web site. Various web servers support various features. Because capabilities of web servers change frequently, this chapter does not discuss features of various web servers. Instead, this chapter provides an overview of web server features and discusses features you should look for. This chapter will also list URLs of about two dozen Windows NT-based web servers. By visiting some of these URLs, you will be able to get the most up-to-date features of various web servers.

Things You Should Look For

When choosing your web server software, you should keep a few things in mind. One of the most important considerations is how easy the web server is to set up and administer. For example, the Netscape server uses forms to administer all aspects of the server. Therefore, by entering a user ID and a password, the web site administrator can administer all aspects of the server from a remote location. Such a feature might be very useful to you if you don't always have ready access to your web server.

Another feature you should look for is the degree of security each server provides. The level of security you need depends on what you will be using your server for. If your web site will be providing only unconfidential information to those browsing your web site, security will not be a major concern for you. When providing sensitive information over the web, however, you should ensure that such information is transmitted only via a secure medium in which the web server encrypts the data before it is transmitted. However, the server you choose should at least support restricting access to part of your server with user names and passwords. Some web servers allow the creation of user ID groups and assign various permissions to users on a per-group basis. If you will be dealing with a large user database, this feature will be very useful to you. There are also web servers that are capable of using the Windows NT user database to authenticate users who want to access various areas of your web site. Such a feature will be quite handy if you need to allow access to parts of your web site to users of your NT server. Having the capability to restrict access based on the client's IP address might be useful to you also. By utilizing this feature, you can deny access to visitors browsing your web site from various domains and countries.

CAUTION

You should never judge your web server's security based on the IP address of the web client. There are ways to trick your web server by misrepresenting the IP address from which the client is accessing your web server. Before transmitting secure data, you should authenticate the user with a user ID and password using a secure medium.

If you are using your web server to distribute security-sensitive data, you should make sure that your web server encrypts the data before transmitting it over the web. This is especially important if you will be transmitting or receiving valuable data such as customer credit-card numbers. Directory browsing is another feature your web server should give you control over. Directory browsing is the capability of a web server to list the contents of a directory when a URL is given without a filename but just a directory. If you want to make sure that web surfers can get to certain pages only if they know the complete URL name of a file, you should disable directory browsing. Otherwise, someone visiting your web site will be able to traverse your directory structure and obtain various files you did not intend anyone to have access to.

Support for CGI scripts is a definite must for a web server. CGI scripts enable you to interact with visitors browsing your web site by providing dynamic content and immediately responding to user input. You should make sure that your web server provides CGI scripts with access to CGI environment variables and supports server-side includes. Some web servers also enable you to interface with Visual Basic programs. This feature might be very useful to you if you are familiar with Visual Basic programming, because you can utilize the power and ease of Visual Basic to interact with those browsing your web site.

NOTE

By using server-side includes, you can make information in your static HTML pages change based on variables. Server-side includes should not, however, be used often because they tax your web server by making the processing of HTTP requests take longer.

In addition to the previously mentioned features, a few other features are standard for most web servers, but you should nevertheless ensure that your web server supports these features. As you host a web site for a while, you will realize that your web server's "log file" keeps getting bigger and bigger. This log file logs all your web server accesses; it is the key to determining who accessed what from your web server and when they accessed it. Many different log file analyzing programs are available. To use most of these programs, you should make sure that your web server generates logs in CERN/NCSA common log format. Having a mechanism to automatically archive log files is another plus. This feature renames the current log file, creates a new log file, and starts logging web server accesses to the new log file.

TIP

Depending on the number of hits your web site receives, you should typically recycle your log file about once a week. Old log files should be archived for future reference.

Last, but not least, is the price of the web server. Currently about two dozen web servers are available that will run on Windows NT. Some of these web servers are free and in most cases will meet your needs. If, however, you are very concerned about security and performance, you might want to go for a commercial web server that will suit your needs better.

To summarize the preceding discussion, listed here are the features you should look for when choosing a web server:

- The web server generates logs in CERN/NCSA common log format.
- The server includes performance measurement logs and tools.
- The server can be configured to prohibit access by domain name and IP address.
- Access can be controlled by requiring a password based on user IDs and user groups.
- Access to data hierarchies can be configured based on the IP address of the client accessing the web site.
- The server supports server-side includes.
- The server supports directory browsing.
- CGI scripts have access to all CGI environment variables.
- The server has a built-in search engine.
- Easy setup and administration are available via a GUI.
- The server can be administered while it is running.
- The server can be administered remotely.
- The server can serve different directory roots based on the IP address of the client.
- The server offers automatic archival of log files.

NOTE

Support provided by free web servers is limited if you run into a problem. If expeditious support is a must for you, consider using a commercial web server.

Following is a list of web servers for Windows NT. Because capabilities of different web servers change so rapidly, their features will not be covered in this chapter. Instead, by visiting the web sites listed here, you will be able to find the most up-to-date information.

WWW Server	For More Information
Alibaba	http://www.csm.co.at/csm/
Commerce Builder	http://www.aristosoft.com/ifact/inet.htm
Communications Builder	http://www.aristosoft.com/ifact/inet.htm
Folio Infobase	http://www.folio.com/
FolkWeb	http://www.ilar.com/folkweb.htm
FrontPage	http://www.vermeer.com/
HTTPS	http://emwac.ed.ac.uk/html/internet_toolchest/https/contents.htm
Internet Office Web Server	http://server.spry.com/
NaviServer	http://www.navisoft.com/products/server/server.htm
NetPublisher	http://netpub.notis.com/
Netscape Commerce	http://www.netscape.com/comprod/netscape_commerce.html
Netscape Communications	http://www.netscape.com/comprod/netscape_commun.html
PowerWeb	http://www.netclub.com/PowerWeb/pwrweb.htm
Purveyor	http://www.process.com/prod/purveyor.htp
SAIC	http://wwwserver.itl.saic.com/
SuperWeb Server	http://www.frontiertech.com/products/superweb.htm
Web Commander	http://www.flicks.com./
WebBase	http://www.webbase.com/
WebNotes	http://webnotes.ostech.com/
WebQuest	http://www.questar.com/webquest.htm
WebSite	http://website.ora.com/

TIP

If you find any mailing lists that have been set up to discuss issues about the web server you are using, you should join such mailing lists. By joining various mailing lists, you will be able to learn more about hosting a web site. Also, if you have a question, you can ask for help and get answers. Windows NT mailing lists are discussed in Chapter 30.

If you are looking for a free web server to get you started, you should consider the SAIC server as well as the EMWAC web server. These servers support many basic features that will enable you to get started very quickly. Both servers are administered by graphical user interfaces and are very easy to install and administer. For more information on installing and configuring these two servers, refer to their documentation found at the previously listed web sites.

Web Site Development Tools

Listed next are various tools you can use to simplify your web publishing tasks.

LView Pro

LView Pro is a very handy graphics manipulation program. You can use LView Pro to handle virtually all your basic graphics manipulation tasks. You can get LView Pro from

```
http://world.std.com/~mmedia/lviewp.html
```

Giftrans

Giftrans is a graphics file manipulation program that can be used to make backgrounds of .gif files transparent, and to save them as "interlaced" .gif files. You can get Giftrans from

```
http://melmac.harris-atd.com/files/giftrans.exe
```

Map Edit

Map Edit is very useful when you want to create an image map for one of your pages. An image map is a graphic with various "hot spots." Image maps enable you to send different pages to a web client depending on where on the image the user clicks the mouse. You can get Map Edit from

```
ftp://ftp.mcp.com/pub/software/Internet/mapedit.zip
```

Color Manipulation Device

Color Manipulation Device is a helpful utility for choosing background and text colors. By using this program, you can find out the HTML tag you should add to your pages to get a certain background and text color. If you are confused about various RGB color values, you can use this program to take the mystery out of things because you can just pick any color you want and assign it to a text element. You can get Color Manipulation Device from

```
http://www.meat.com/software/cmd.html
```

Programmer's File Editor

This is a very handy program that can be used for various tasks. You might find Programmer's File Editor to be very useful when you are editing large files, and it is a great substitute for Windows Notepad. Programmer's File Editor can be downloaded from

```
INTEL:       ftp://ftp.csusm.edu/pub/winworld/nt/pfe0602i.zip
Power PC:    ftp://ftp.csusm.edu/pub/winworld/nt/pfe0602p.zip
```

HTML Editors

Although it's possible to insert HTML tags manually, for large projects, this method is too time-consuming. Listed next are a few HTML editors that will make inserting HTML tags easy. You might want to try a few and pick the one you like the best.

```
Arachnid            http://bcpub.com/software/arachnid.zip
Hot Dog             ftp://ftp.sausage.com/pub/hotdog10.exe
HTML Easy           http://www.seed.net.tw/~milkylin/heasy13.zip
HTML Edit           http://www.ist.ca/~peterc/htmled12.zip
HTML Notepad        http://bcpub.com/software/htmln119.zip
Hypertext Master    ftp://ftp.tcp.co.uk/pub/ibmpc/windows/utils/htmled24.zip
Web Edit            http://wwwnt.thegroup.net/webedit/webedit.zip
```

Internet Assistant for Microsoft Word

Internet Assistant for Microsoft Word is a very useful application when it comes to adding a large number of Microsoft Word files to your web server. Although earlier versions of Internet Assistant for Word lacked many features, new versions have many added features to make web publishing easier. For example, the current version supports document backgrounds, tables, inline images, and various font attributes. Internet Assistant for Microsoft Word can be gotten free of charge from

```
http://www.microsoft.com/msoffice/freestuf/msword/download/ia/default.htm
```

NOTE

Internet Assistant for Microsoft Word is ideal for editing files saved in standard HTML. However, it might not handle various enhancements to HTML that well. Before loading one of your files containing HTML enhancements to Internet Assistant for Microsoft Word, and saving your changes, you might want to make a backup copy of your file. If your HTML files contain standard HTML, you need not do this.

HoTMetaL Pro

HoTMetaL Pro is a very feature-rich HTML editor that has a built-in thesaurus as well as a spell checker. When compared with other HTML editors, HoTMetaL Pro has one major difference. HoTMetaL Pro ensures that whatever you create with it conforms to standard HTML. Therefore, by using HoTMetaL Pro, you can make sure that your web pages are rendered properly by all web browsers. As you can see in Figure 24.1, HoTMetaL Pro also clearly marks HTML tags with special tags so that they are clearly visible when you edit HTML files. On the downside, HoTMetaL Pro makes it hard to create files with

HTML enhancements. A new version of HoTMetaL Pro will be released by the time you read this book. Therefore, you might want to visit the following URL for the most up-to-date information about HoTMetaL Pro:

```
http://www.sq.com/
```

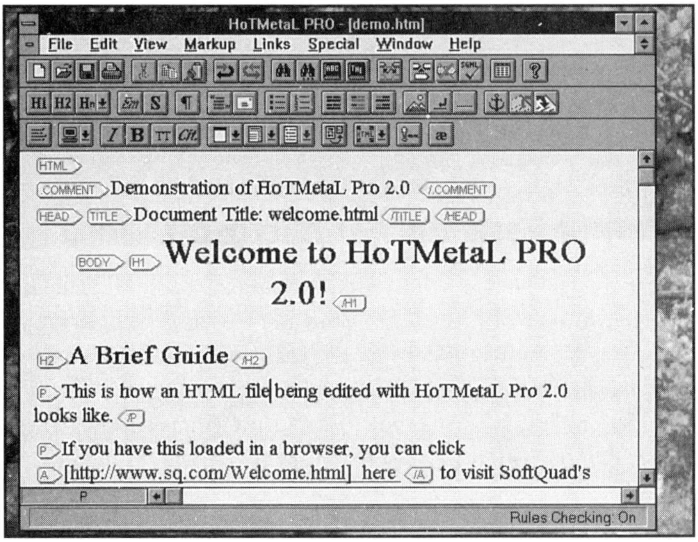

FIGURE 24.1.
HoTMetaL Pro marks HTML tags with special symbols when files are edited so that the HTML tags are clearly visible.

Log File Analyzing Tools

To determine various statistics about your web server, you need to analyze your web server's log file. Although some web servers come with utilities to analyze log files, by using different programs, you can obtain different information about various web server statistics. Listed next are two web server log analyzing tools you can use to analyze your log files. By using a spreadsheet application such as Excel, you can create a table like the one shown in Figure 24.2 by using the output of one of the web server log analyzing programs listed.

```
Analyze        http://www.net-shopper.co.uk/software/nt/analyse/index.htm
WebStat        http://www.huntana.com/webstat/index.html
```

FIGURE 24.2.
A table of web server statistics generated by Excel using the output of a web server log analyzing program.

For The Week Of	# New Hosts	# Repeat Visits	# Requests Served
07-Aug-95	8	12	445
14-Aug-95	189	248	5594
21-Aug-95	102	140	2995
28-Aug-95	109	152	3538
04-Sep-95	165	193	4534
11-Sep-95	301	356	8817
18-Sep-95	228	297	8196
25-Sep-95	276	321	7480
02-Oct-95	104	130	3670

WebTrends

Both log analyzing programs in the preceding list have command-line user interfaces and are not very easy to work with. If you'd rather use one program to analyze your web server's log file, create graphs, and provide other statistics for you, you should give WebTrends a try. WebTrends can be used to analyze your log file and provide useful statistics about your web site. If you have disabled DNS lookups on your server, WebTrends will also perform DNS lookups while analyzing the log file. You can get WebTrends from

```
http://www.egsoftware.com/webtrend.htm
```

As shown in Figure 24.3, WebTrends has a graphical user interface. Using this GUI, you can specify several options to customize the output of WebTrends as well as to define various log files to analyze.

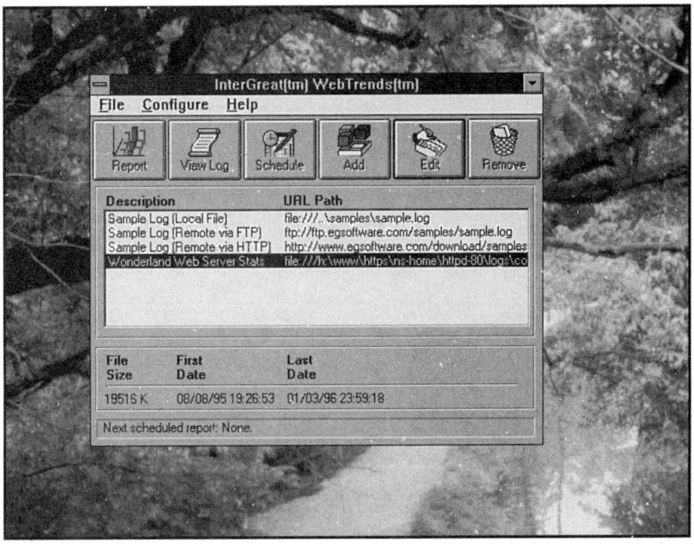

FIGURE 24.3.
WebTrends has a graphical user interface in which you can specify various log files you need to analyze.

If your web server is at a remote location and the log file is available via HTTP or FTP, WebTrends can be configured as shown in Figure 24.4 to retrieve the log file and analyze its content. WebTrends also has provisions for you to enter a user ID and password if the log file is to be obtained via FTP.

After analyzing the log file, WebTrends creates various comprehensive tables and graphics charts. By analyzing these charts and tables, you can determine various access statistics about your web site. A sample chart created by WebTrends is shown in Figure 24.5. About a dozen such graphs and tables are created after WebTrends analyzes your web server's log file.

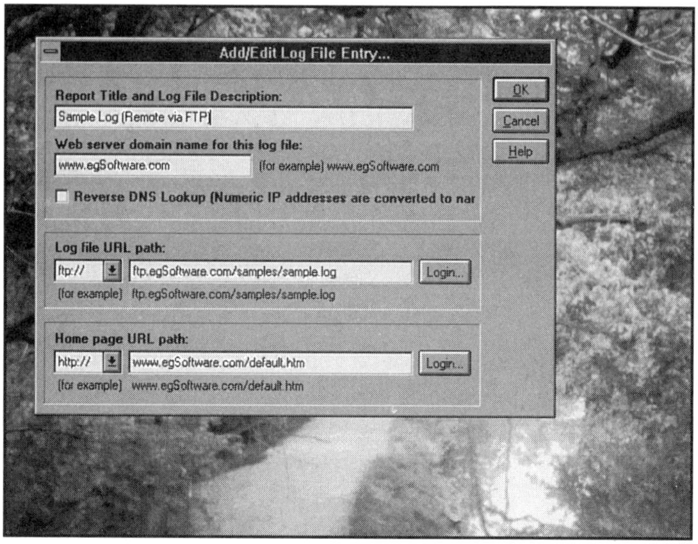

FIGURE 24.4.
WebTrends enables you to retrieve a log file via HTTP or FTP from a remote location before analyzing it.

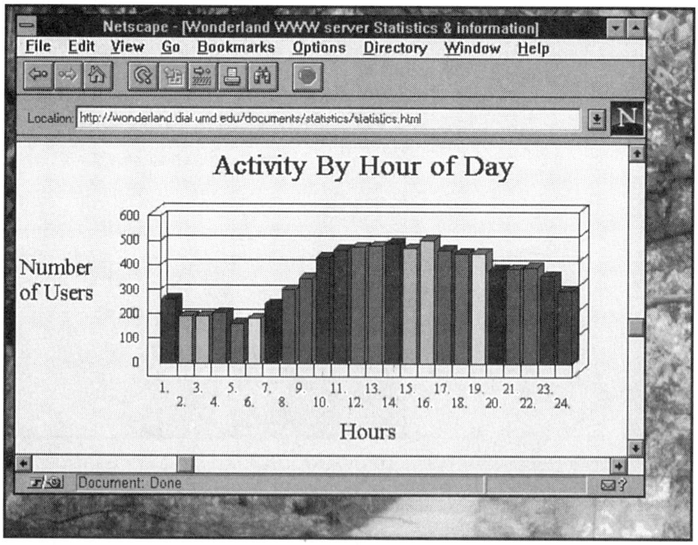

FIGURE 24.5.
An example of a chart created by WebTrends after analyzing a web server's log file.

Summary

This chapter discussed various web servers that are available to host Windows NT-based web sites. Various features you should look for, when selecting a web server, were also discussed in this chapter. After analyzing your needs, you will now be able to list all the features you need when you shop for a web server. This chapter also covered some Windows NT tools you can use to develop your web site. By utilizing these tools, you will be able to create an outstanding web site in the least amount of time possible. You were also shown how to analyze the access log file of your web server to create various tables and charts.

The next chapter discusses ways of connecting your web server to the Internet. The following chapter will help you analyze your needs and choose the right Internet connection for your web site. If you cannot afford a high-speed Internet link just yet, you will also be shown how to utilize the services of a web space provider and host your web site by using a regular 28.8 POTS (Plain Old Telephone Service) link to the Internet. By using a POTS line, you will be shown how to provide those accessing your web site near T1 or T3 access to most of your data in the next chapter.

Getting Your Lines Right: ISDN, POTS, and Service Providers

25

IN THIS CHAPTER

This chapter provides an overview of various Internet connection types and how to choose the best connection type based on your needs and other factors such as availability and affordability. By reading this chapter, following the discussions about Internet connection types and ways to get more from a POTS link, you will be able to make the best use of the Internet link you select.

Bandwidths of Various Connection Lines

Most likely, your web server's biggest bottleneck will be the limited bandwidth of your Internet connection. If possible, you should go with at least an ISDN (Integrated Services Digital Network) link to the Internet. As you can see from the chart below (Figure 25.1), even a basic, single B channel ISDN line is several times faster than a 28.8 POTS (Plain Old Telephone Service) link.

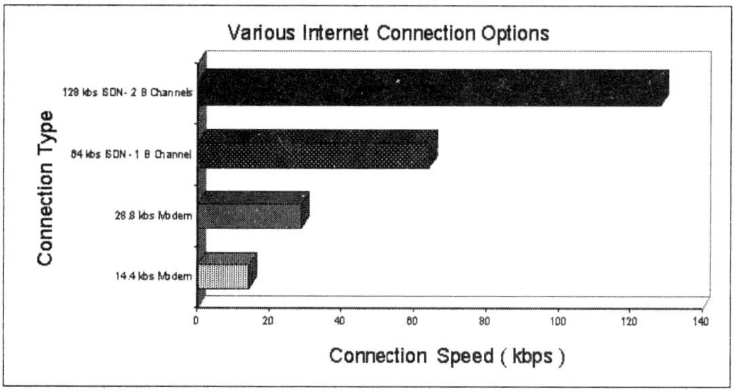

FIGURE 25.1.
ISDN Internet links have a higher bandwidth than POTS Internet links.

Another reason for using an ISDN link is that it does not need to be up all day for your Internet link; you will be using the line only when data is transferred, so you can disconnect when the line is not in use. This is practical with ISDN lines because of their fast call setup and teardown times—typically about one second. On the other hand, as you can see in Figure 25.2, a POTS link usually takes over 30 seconds to establish a call.

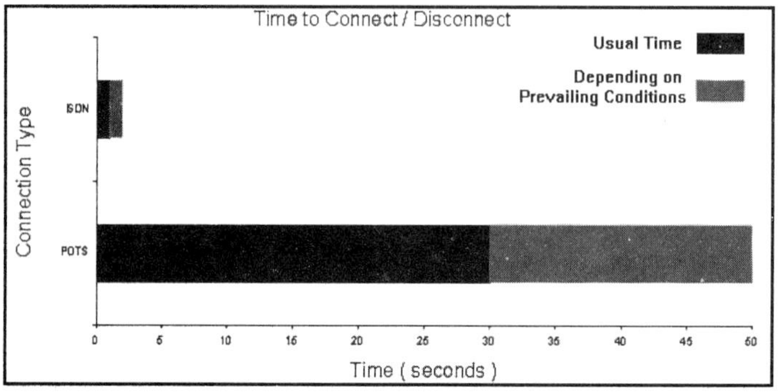

FIGURE 25.2.
ISDN connect/disconnect speeds are faster than POTS connect/disconnect speeds.

TIP

If you will be starting out with a 28.8 kbs (kilo bits per second) POTS link to the Internet, you should not get carried away with too many graphics. However, if you do have a few graphics and you start getting more and more hits, your web surfers might become frustrated with the slow data transfer rates of your web server. To avoid this, there is a very low-cost solution. You can simply find a *web space provider* with a fast link to the Internet (that is, T1 or T3) who rents out space on a web server. This service is inexpensive, usually less than $20 a month. Afterward, you can simply move all your graphics files to this web server. In your page, you can call the graphics files on the other web server rather than the graphics on your own server. This can make a significant difference since you will be providing only HTML (Hyper Text Markup Language) files to clients accessing your server; they will go to the other server for all your inline graphics and other objects. This frees up your relatively limited Internet bandwidth for transmitting plain-text HTML files and processing and responding to user input that interacts with a database on your server. If you are looking for such a location to store your graphics files, you might want to check out the following URL:

```
http://www.Four11.com/cgi-bin/SledPython?
Iside_UM_InfoWeb.html,200,2AC9CC,3775402,499E51B2
```

You might also be able to find similar web space providers locally in your area.

Using Another Server

As mentioned in the earlier tip, you can use another server to store all your graphics and other non-text objects if all you can afford right now is a POTS link to the Internet. Suppose you have a local inline image called "WindowsNT.gif" with the following HTML tag:

```
<img src="/graphics/icons/WindowsNT.gif">
```

You can free up your bandwidth for this graphic by moving "WindowsNT.gif" to another server (for example, www.server.com) and changing the above tag to the following:

```
<img src="http://www.server.com/graphics/icons/WindowsNT.gif">
```

NOTE

You can conserve your bandwidth by following the above tip because HTTP is a connectionless protocol. Therefore, once a connection is made for the web page, the page is transmitted, and the connection to your server is closed. Subsequently, for various inline images and objects of the page, the web browser will go to the other web server.

Suitability of Various Lines for Various Purposes

Obviously, a POTS link is suitable only for limited web traffic. By using another server to store your graphic files, you will be able to get the maximum from your POTS link by using it only for transmitting HTML text files. However, as you get more hits and the data on your pages increases, a POTS link may not be enough. In this case, you might need to consider an alternative, such as ISDN.

Although ISDN has been around for a while, it's still not as widely used as it should be. ISDN technology has a lot of potential. If you look at it from your telephone company's point of view, you'll see that providing ISDN is much simpler. Using new digital circuits means that virtually all your phone conversations are transmitted digitally within your phone company's circuits; only the line from your phone company to your site is analog. The phone company actually has to convert digital signals to analog before sending this signal to your site. By using ISDN, you make the job simpler for the phone company because the phone company doesn't need to worry about converting digital signals to analog. Unfortunately, current prices do not reflect this advantage. At the time of this writing, maintaining a 24-hour link to the Internet using a single-channel ISDN link (64 kbs) can cost as much as $650 for the ISDN line plus ISP (Internet Service Provider) charges. Ironically, a second phone line for a 28.8 kbs link to the Internet is about $17 plus ISP charges. This means that for about twice the bandwidth of a 28.8 kbs link to the Internet, one might have to pay more than 38 times! You might want to give your local phone company a call and consider what it wants to charge you and what you get in return before going with ISDN.

NOTE

The above cost of $ 650 a month was calculated for a 24-hour single channel ISDN line. Since you can bring down the line when it's not in use, the cost will be lower. However, it still costs several times more than a regular phone line.

If ISDN and POTS are not suitable for you, you have a third option for Internet access. You might be able to get a much better deal if your local cable company provides Internet services in your area. Due to the nature of the cable carrying your data, by choosing a cable-based Internet connection, you will typically get a bandwidth of over four mega bits per second! A cable connection to the Internet will give you a bandwidth up to 350 times faster than a 28.8 kbs dial-up modem connection. For more information about a cable-based Internet access provider, you might want to visit the following URL:

```
http://www.tci.east-lansing.mi.us/metshome.htm
```

Choosing the Right Connection

Choosing the right Internet connection is an equation that depends on several variables, such as your bandwidth requirements, expected web traffic, availability and cost of ISDN in your area, and, of course, your budget for the Internet link.

Recently, cable companies have been exploring the possibility of providing Internet service. If ISDN prices seem to be too high or unreasonable for you, you might want to check with your local cable company to see if they offer Internet service or if they plan to do so. The bandwidth your cable company can give you is much greater than what ISDN offers. If cable companies realize the potential of providing Internet services at a reasonable cost, everyone can afford high-speed Internet links, which will make the Internet a much nicer place to live in!

Summary

This chapter covered various issues related to choosing an Internet link for your web site. By reading this chapter, depending on your needs, budget, and the Internet links available in your area, you are now able to select the Internet link that best suits you. The chapter began with an introduction to various Internet connection types and outlined their capabilities and drawbacks. Because many companies can't afford a high-speed Internet link, you were also shown how to use a secondary web server to get the maximum out of a POTS link. Finally, an overview of various Internet connection types, their suitability, and choosing the right Internet connection to meet your needs was discussed.

The next chapter reviews several web publishing tools. You can use many Windows NT web publishing tools to make publishing on the web easier. By using various applications outlined in the following chapter, you'll be able to make your web site an outstanding Windows NT based web site.

Putting Your Pages Together: HTML Tools

26

IN THIS CHAPTER

This chapter will give you an overview of various tools that can be used to design your web site. You will be shown how to use these tools to add special effects to your graphics and convert them to different formats. Learning which graphics formats are suitable for various tasks will help you take advantage of the formats' features. If you use the tools and tips covered in this section, you will have an outstanding web site that's optimized for distributing information on the Internet.

HTML tags, their syntaxes, and how they are used are topics beyond the scope of this chapter. Instead of discussing such details, this chapter will cover web sites where you can find more information; you should also refer to Chapter 24, " What Software Do You Need?", to find out where you can locate the tools covered in this chapter.

HTML Resources On The Web

In case you are not very familiar with HTML, listed next are a few web sites that contain information about HTML. By visiting these web sites, you will be able to familiarize yourself with various HTML tags and find out how they can be utilized.

HTML Reference Manual

`http://www.sandia.gov/sci_compute/html_ref.html`

The Bare Bones Guide to HTML

`http://www.access.digex.net/~werbach/barebone.html`

A Beginner's Guide to URLs

`http://www.ncsa.uiuc.edu/demoweb/url-primer.html`

A Beginner's Guide to HTML

`http://www.ncsa.uiuc.edu/General/Internet/WWW/HTMLPrimer.html`

The Structure of HTML 3.0 Documents

`http://www.w3.org/pub/WWW/MarkUp/html3/overview.html`

HTML Writers Guild List of HTML Resources

`http://ugweb.cs.ualberta.ca/~gerald/guild/html.html#validation`

Web Publishing Issues

When publishing information on the web, keep in mind that your audience has a short attention span. For some people, browsing your web site is like "channel surfing" for a good TV program—the only difference is that the remote control is replaced by the mouse. Even though large graphics might look nice when you view them locally, remember that not everyone has access to high-speed connections to the Internet. You should use the content of your web site to captivate your audience; however, adding a few small graphics as "eye candy" won't hurt if they can be viewed easily by someone using a 14.4 modem. Users browsing the web via an online service, such as America Online, CompuServe, or Microsoft Exchange, are often limited to a 14.4 modem.

You should also make it easy for users to give you feedback or comments. People visiting your web site might get frustrated when they have a question or comments but have no way of e-mailing this feedback to you. It's a good idea to have a "button bar" or a standard set of selections at the bottom or top of each page; one of them should be a link to a feedback page. You will be shown how to set up an e-mail feedback form in Chapter 28, "Making Your Web Site Interactive." This form will allow users browsing your web site to answer questions on your feedback form and e-mail their comments to you.

Not Everyone Uses Netscape...

Although Netscapisms (or "Netscape enhancements to HTML") may look nice, not everyone uses Netscape, especially those accessing your web site with proprietary web browsers of online services like America Online, and Prodigy. These browsers may make your pages look entirely different from how they look with Netscape. By following proper HTML coding standards, you can be sure that no matter what browser is used, your page will look the way you intended it to be viewed.

If you use Netscape enhancements and discover that your pages look bad when viewed with another browser, but you really want to use Netscape enhancements, you can create two sets of pages—one for Netscape and one for other browsers. If you have just a few pages and are concerned about the appearance of your web site, this might be practical; however, it's not practical for a large web site. In the CGI programming chapter, you will be shown how to use a simple CGI program to offer a customized web page based on the browser used to access your web site. Because this example provides the program's source code, in Chapter 28, "Making Your Web Site Interactive", you will also learn the basics of writing CGI programs.

Optimizing Graphics by Reducing the Number of Colors

Graphics saved in .gif format can have up to 256 colors. However, unless you have a photograph saved in .gif format, you probably aren't using all 256 colors. Chances are you can use only a fraction of them and still have your graphic look remarkably similar to the original file. By reducing the number of colors used in a graphic, you can actually reduce the file size by as much as 40 percent, depending on the graphic. To reduce the number of colors, experiment with various amounts of colors until your graphic looks almost identical to the original graphic. Reducing the number of colors to 24 or 32 yields a workable combination of a smaller file size and good graphic quality. By using LView Pro, you can reduce the number of colors in your .gif files by choosing Retouch | Color depth, then clicking Palette Image, selecting Custom Number of Colors, and entering a value like 24, as shown in Figure 26.1.

FIGURE 26.1.
Reducing the number of colors to make .gif files smaller.

> **TIP**
>
> If the image does not look close to the original after you enter a number, you can choose Edit | Undo and try again with a few more colors.

You might wonder why you should go to all this trouble to reduce your graphics files by just a few kilobytes. Although the reduction of each file might not be that much, the kilobytes add up when you have more than one graphic on a page and more than one person accessing your web site at the same time. People with slow links to the Internet will appreciate the small graphics sizes.

Graphics File Size Issues

Make sure the images on your web site are as small as possible. If you have large graphics files at your website, users with slow modem links might get frustrated and leave your web site. After all the work you've put into setting up your web site, you don't want that to happen. If you need to have large graphics files, you should let the user decide if he or she wants to see them. This could be done by just showing a "thumbnail" representation of the graphic file that the user can click on to see the full picture.

Keeping your graphics small will make them load faster. In particular, try to limit the graphic's height. Vertical space is "golden" on a web page, quite apart from loading speed. When users look at your web pages, they generally expect to see some information. It might look rather unappealing if most of your user's screen is taken up by a large graphics file that takes several seconds to load.

TIP

After you have designed your web site, be sure to look at your pages on a monitor set to a resolution of 640 × 480 with 256 colors. If you designed your pages correctly, users should still be able to see all the information without using the horizontal scroll bar. Remember that not everyone has high-resolution super VGA monitors!

You can make your graphics files load faster by defining the graphic's dimensions in the HTML tag so that the browser can map around it and load the text before the image. For example, if you have an inline image called demo.gif, you should find the dimensions of the image and include this data in the HTML tag as follows:

```
<IMG SRC="/graphics/icons/ WonderlandNewIcon.gif"
     height=125 width=325 border=0 ALT= "Demonstration Graphic" >
```

TIP

You should always use the "ALT tag" and give a short description of your image so that if someone browsing your website has "tuned off" automatic display of images, they will see a description of the graphics file instead of just an icon with a graphic. Your LYNX users will also appreciate letting them know what they are missing! (Lynx is a nongraphical, text-based web browser.)

You can use almost any shareware or commercial graphics manipulation application to find out the dimensions of your graphics. A handy graphics manipulation utility called LView Pro is used for this demonstration. If you load a graphic in LView Pro as shown in Figure 26.2, you will see that the dimensions of the image are shown on the title bar of the application. You can get the latest version of LView Pro from `http://world.std.com/~mmedia/lviewp.html`.

TIP

Specifying the graphic's dimensions will give users the impression that pages at your web site load faster because they can start reading the text before all the graphics are displayed. Specifying the dimensions will also allow users to scroll a page before all images are loaded.

FIGURE 26.2.
The graphic's dimensions are shown on the title bar of LView Pro.

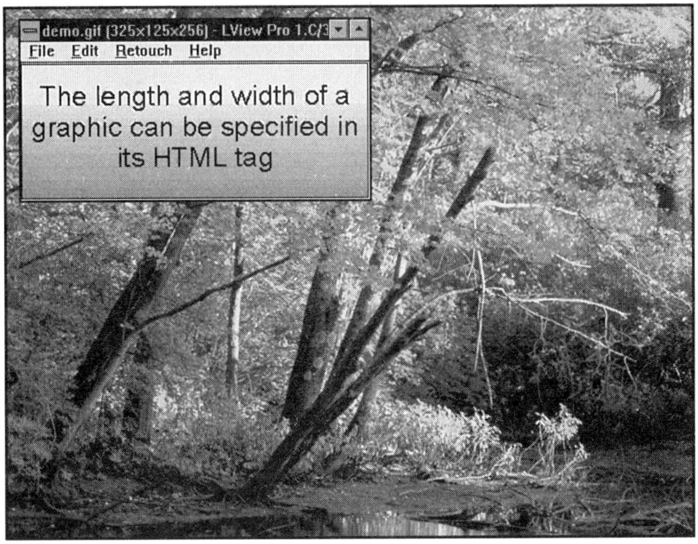

Using Graphics Formats

In addition to making graphics smaller, reducing the number of colors, and specifying dimensions of graphics in HTML tags, you can further optimize graphics at your web site by using different file formats. Two of the most commonly used formats are .gif and JPEG. Knowing their strengths and weaknesses will enable you to use these two formats judiciously and optimize graphics at your web site. The following sections will demonstrate how to enhance graphics at your web site and when to use what format.

Interlacing

If you have photographs at your website stored in the .gif format, it's a good idea to interlace them. What is *interlacing*? You might have noticed how some graphics on web sites appear in bands. First the graphic will look out of focus, then get clearer and more focused as more data about the graphic is sent to the web browser. Adding this effect to a .gif file is called "interlacing."

To save .gif files as interlaced files, first load the file into LView Pro, then choose File | Properties, select the ".gif" cross tab, and make sure that "save Interlaced" is checked. Next, when you save your file, be sure to save it as a "gif89a" file.

TIP

Interlacing photographs at your web site will allow someone who's not interested in the entire picture to go to another page rather than wait for the whole picture to load. You can use the interlace feature only on graphics stored in the .gif format.

NOTE

Be careful when using interlaced .gif files. Even though interlacing makes your graphics look "neat," interlaced .gif files are larger than non-interlaced .gif files and generally take longer to display, especially if the client's computer has a relatively slow processor. Therefore, don't get carried away with interlacing and interlace all the .gif files at your web site! Interlacing is a useful tool, but you should use it for the right job. Generally, interlacing should be used when displaying photographs because you can guess what the final photograph will look like from an early rendering of an interlaced .gif file. The same is not true for .gif files that contain text.

Creating Invisible Backgrounds

You can give your web site a professional look by making the backgrounds of .gif files transparent. When someone looks at your graphic with a browser, the graphic's background will become the background color of the browser. This gives the impression that the graphic is floating in the background, which adds a sophisticated touch to your graphic. You can make a particular background color of your .gif files transparent by using a utility program called `giftrans`, along with LView Pro.

Although you can create a similar effect by changing the background color of your graphic to the default background color of a browser like Netscape, as soon as someone changes the default color or looks at your web site using a browser with a different background color, your image will no longer appear to be floating in the background.

NOTE

.gif files of photographs are not suitable for making a certain background color invisible unless the background color does not appear anywhere in the photograph. Photographs are usually very rich in colors and a .gif file can have only 256 colors. Therefore, it is a good bet that the background color is used somewhere else in the photograph. Consequently, if you make that color "invisible," it's going to make the photograph look bad because parts of it will be invisible. If this happened in a photograph of a person, it could make him or her look like an alien! However, if a .gif file's background color is distinctly different from other colors in the graphic, you will have more luck making the photograph's background transparent.

It's very simple to make a background color of a .gif file invisible. As you can see in Figure 26.3, the graphic's background color is white, so it stands out against the background color of the web browser. If you make the white background of the image transparent, all you'll see will be the text "Having Fun With Windows NT!"

FIGURE 26.3.
Original graphic with white background when viewed with Netscape.

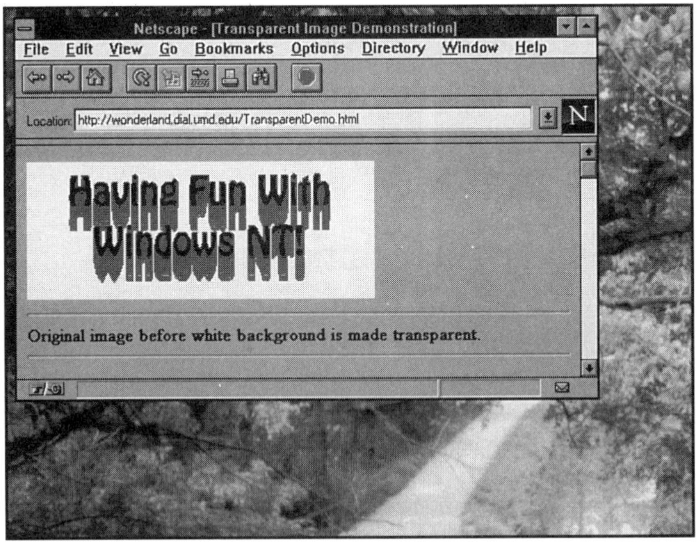

To make a color transparent, first load the .gif file into LView Pro. After loading the graphics file, you need to determine the "index color" that's been used for the image's background color. To do this, load the file into LView Pro and choose Options | Background Color. You will then see a color chart, shown in Figure 26.4. Since you need to find the "index color" of the background color, you have to mask out everything but the background color. Therefore, click the "Mask selection using" check box and select Black. Now when you click on a color in the color palette, every other color in the graphic will be shaded in black. For example, there's no red in the graphic (it's a grayscale graphic), so if you click on red, the whole image will be shaded in black. However, if you click on white in the color palette, everything but the background will be shaded in black. As you can see in Figure 26.4, this color has an index value of 215. You need to write down or remember this index value because you will be using it shortly.

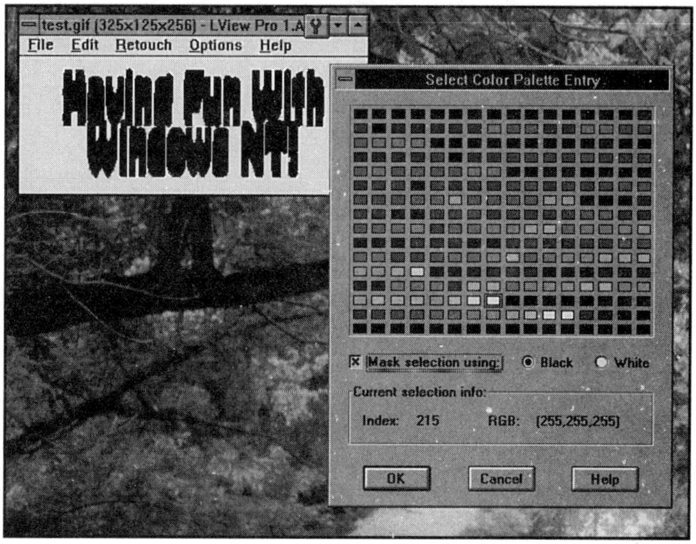

FIGURE 26.4.
Determining the index value of the background color.

After finding the index value of the background color, you can use giftrans to make the image's background color invisible. Although there are many command line switches for giftrans, this is the syntax to make a background color invisible:

```
giftrans -t <index value of background color> <original filename> > <new filename>
```

For example, since the background color's index value is 215 and the original file is called original.gif, use the following command:

```
giftrans -t 215 original.gif > new.gif
```

TIP

You can save time hunting for utility programs on your hard disk by creating a subdirectory called "utilities," adding this directory to your path, and storing all utility programs, like giftrans, in this directory. Then, whenever you need to access a utility program, you can just type its name without worrying about where you put the application.

As you can see in Figure 26.5, when you view the graphic with Netscape after making the background invisible, the graphic's background is the same color as the browser's background color.

FIGURE 26.5.
Original graphic with transparent background when viewed with Netscape.

Best Graphic Format For Photographs

When displaying photographs at your website, you should convert your pictures to JPEG (pronounced "jay-peg") format, which is a standardized image compression mechanism. *JPEG* stands for Joint Photographic Experts Group, the original name of the committee that wrote the standard. You can save a file in JPEG format by choosing File | Save As, then selecting .jpg as the file format in LView Pro.

> **TIP**
>
> Although most web browsers can display JPEG files, a few browsers do not have this capability. Therefore, you should make an identical file in the .gif format available for viewing in case a web browser does not support JPEG format graphics. However, almost all web browsers used today support the JPEG format.

JPEG can be used to compress color or grayscale images. JPEG compression works best when the image being converted to JPEG has "natural colors". JPEG works well on photographs, naturalistic artwork, and similar material. However, JPEG is a poor choice for any graphic containing letters, cartoons, sharp edges, or line drawings. Since you will typically gain a 4:1 compression ratio with JPEG, as opposed to .gif, your images will be much smaller. Having small images is a great advantage when pictures have to be transmitted over the Internet. Web surfers with slow Internet links will especially appreciate the small file sizes.

NOTE

You should never convert a cartoon or line art image to JPEG format. The resulting image will often be much bigger than the original! The same is true for images containing letters because JPEG has a hard time compressing graphics files that have sharp edges.

JPEG image compression is "lossy," which means that the resulting image is not exactly the same as the original image. The human eye has some limitations, and JPEG image compression is designed to take advantage of these limitations. Since the human eye perceives color differences less accurately than differences in brightness, JPEG images exploits a limitation in how we see things.

TIP

By using JPEG, your graphics can be in 24-bit color instead of the 8-bit color used in the .gif format, which supports only 256 colors. On the other hand, JPEG supports up to 16.7 million colors.

Choosing Colors with Color Manipulation Device

You can use Color Manipulation Device (CMD) to determine colors for the text elements of your web pages. By using CMD, you can pick the colors you want and assign them to text elements, as shown in Figure 26.6. After picking your colors, you can simply copy them to the Clipboard and paste the HTML tag to a web page.

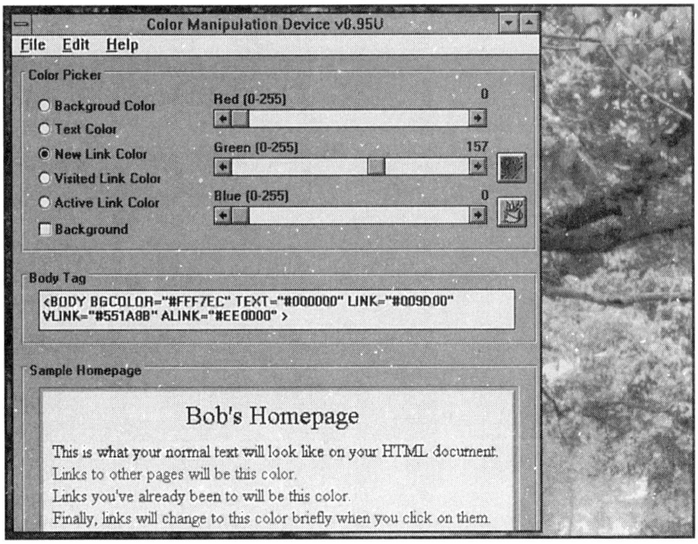

FIGURE 26.6.
Text element and background colors can be easily picked with the Color Manipulation Device.

Various HTML Formats

Due to the recent growth of the World Wide Web, many new web browsers have appeared in a short time. Although most of these browsers work fine for standard HTML, some of them do not handle enhancements to standard HTML (such as Netscape enhancements) that well. When you create your pages, you need to be aware of HTML standards so that a page created with a certain HTML standard will look the same no matter what browser is used to view the page. Please refer to the web sites listed earlier in this chapter for more information about HTML formats.

Web Page Publishing Tools on the Web

Listed below are a few web publishing tools found on the web that might be helpful when you're setting up web pages. You might want to add these tools to the bookmark file of your favorite web browser for future reference. The tools listed in the following sections are available free of charge on the WWW.

Online Spell Checker

If you make many typos or need help in spelling words, you might want to check out The WebSter's Dictionary at `http://www.eece.ksu.edu/~spectre/WebSter/spell.html`. This is a handy tool for spellchecking your web pages. The WebSter's Dictionary provides a forms-based gateway to a spellchecker for WWW documents. By simply typing the URL of your web page, the program will retrieve your web page, spellcheck it, and list all the words you misspelled so you can correct them. You can use this program to spellcheck your web pages without having to deal with a traditional spellchecker flagging every bit of HTML markup code.

Checking for Correct HTML

If you want to make sure your web pages conform to a certain HTML standard, such as HTML 2.0/3.0, use an HTML validating program to check your web site. Listed below are several HTML validating services that will check your web pages for correct HTML:

```
Weblint                               http://www.unipress.com/weblint/
A Kinder, Gentler HTML Validator      http://ugweb.cs.ualberta.ca/~gerald/validate.cgi
Doctor HTML                           http://imagiware.com/RxHTML.cgi
WebTechs HTML Validation Service      http://www.webtechs.com/html-val-svc/
```

TIP

Don't worry if you get a lot of error messages for one of your web pages. The HTML validator might be mistaking something you were doing correctly. Also, if you have used Netscape or Internet Explorer enhancements that are not part of standard HTML, they will be flagged by the HTML validator.

NOTE

By checking your web pages for correct HTML, you can increase the consistency and quality of the HTML documents at your site.

Online Web Page Color Selector

If you want to change your page's text or background colors, but are confused about what color is represented by a certain RGB (red, green, blue) value, you might find Color Selector Page at `http://catless.ncl.ac.uk/Lindsay/colours.html` to be a useful tool. By using a form to select colors for your text and background, you will be shown which HTML tag you should use and what your combination of colors will look like.

TIP

If you find yourself using this tool frequently to find RGB color values for your HTML tags, you might want to get a copy of Color Manipulation Device, described in Chapter 24.

Summary

This chapter discussed Windows NT utilities and tools that can be used when designing your web site. By using these tools, you can tackle virtually any web publishing task. You can also give your web site a professional touch by adding special effects to your graphics, such as interlacing them and making their backgrounds transparent. This chapter also covered various graphics file formats and how they are used.

What's Next

The next chapter will cover web site maintenance and legal issues you should be concerned about when providing information on the Internet.

Maintaining Your Web Site

27

IN THIS CHAPTER

After setting up a web site, you need to maintain it and keep it up-to-date. This chapter will cover maintenance and legal issues you should know about when providing information on the WWW. You will also be shown how to make your web site visible for users doing Internet searches by registering your web site with Internet search engines and web site databases.

Web Site Maintenance Issues

Once you have your web site up and running, you should take a few steps to ensure that people visiting your web site will return for more information. If you followed the guidelines and suggestions presented earlier, you should already have a user-friendly web site. However, there are other things you can do to make your web site outstanding.

Even though your web site's contents are the most important thing, you need to pay some attention to the appearance of the information you are presenting to the viewer. It's always a good idea to look at your web site with more than one browser to make sure your pages look the way you intended them to look. Sometimes a page that looks absolutely fabulous with the latest version of Netscape might look quite unattractive when viewed with another web browser.

Think of your web site as a channel in a large cable network. The cable network is, of course, the web, and the remote control is simply replaced by the mouse. When users can't find the information they're looking for or get frustrated with large graphics that take forever to load with a slow modem link, they will just change the channel (or visit another web site).

Keeping the Information Up-To-Date

By its very nature, information on the web is expected to be as current as possible. In the past, information needed to be prepared and sent to a publisher before it could be distributed; this was often a lengthy process. However, on the web, as soon as information is ready, it can be distributed to a large audience. You should take advantage of this by ensuring that the information at your web site is up-to-date.

TIP

It's a good idea to maintain a log of additions and changes that you make to your web site so that visitors can find out when information was added, modified, and so forth.

Registering with Internet Search Engines and Databases

One of the best ways to advertise your new web site on the WWW is to register it with Internet databases and online search engines. By registering your web site, those who are interested in its contents will be able to find it easily. WWW search database registering services are usually free.

> **TIP**
>
> When registering your web pages, be sure to register only pages or links that will not be changed in the future. If you have set up temporary links at your web site, do not register them. Also, be sure to keep any URLs (Uniform Resource Locator) you register the same. By keeping the URL names constant, those who are interested in the contents of your web site will be able to find it by doing a search.

To add your website to WWW search engines, you need to register your URLs with various databases; several are listed below. It's always best to register your site with as many search engines as you can so that your web site will be visible to as many web surfers as possible.

```
Yahoo                    http://www.yahoo.com/bin/add
WebCrawler               http://webcrawler.com/WebCrawler/SubmitURLS.html
Starting Point           http://www.stpt.com/util/submit.html
Lycos                    http://lycos.cs.cmu.edu/lycos-register.html
Infoseek                 http://www2.infoseek.com/doc/help/AddingSites.html
Galaxy                   http://galaxy.einet.net/cgi-bin/annotate?Other
Harvest                  http://harvest.cs.colorado.edu/Harvest/brokers/register-with-
CU-gatherers.html
Whole Internet Catalog   http://gnn.com/gnn/forms/comments.html
Apollo                   http://apollo.co.uk/
Pronet                   http://www.pronett.com/member/goldlink.htm
PowerLink                http://www.powerlink.com/powerlink/bin/doform?form=ecard
The Huge List            http://thehugelist.com/addurl.html
New Rider's WWW YP       http://www.mcp.com/newriders/wwwyp/submit.html
Nerd World Media         http://www.nerdworld.com/nwadd.html
```

If you wish to submit URLs of your website to more than one WWW search database at the same time, you might want to visit "Submit It!" at `http://www.submit-it.com/`. "Submit It!" allows you to fill in some information about the URL you are submitting (shown in Figure 27.1) and use the same information to submit your URL to more than one search database.

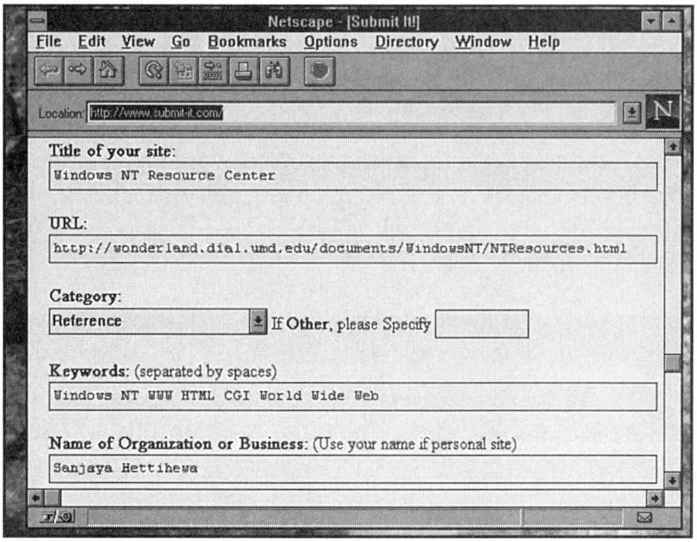

FIGURE 27.1.
"Submit It!" can be used to submit a URL to multiple WWW search databases.

Legalities: What You Should Know About Providing Information

When setting up a web site, you should be aware of certain legalities. By following a few guidelines, you can avoid unnecessary legal problems. The first thing to remember is that normal copyright laws do indeed apply to the web. Copyright laws do not change just because the medium of information distribution changes. If you own a copyright on something, you can "publish" it on the web; if others misuse your work, you can take legal action and they're as guilty as if they'd done the same thing in a non-electronic medium.

You should be concerned about copyright laws when designing your website and making information available to the public. The goal of the WWW and the Internet is to make information readily available to those who need it. On the other hand, copyright law is designed to restrict access and use of information to a certain degree. Therefore, there is a conflict between the intentions of copyright law and the spirit of the Internet. However, copyright law is part of the law and the spirit of the Internet isn't. Make sure your web site complies with copyright law.

It's also a good idea to have a link to a "disclaimer" page at your web site, which states that your company (or client) is not endorsing any product or other company; instead, the links are meant for informational purposes and to explore the web. Therefore, if someone doesn't like what you've linked to (even though you're not responsible for the content at the other end of the link), he or she can't complain to you about it or take legal action against you.

You should also be careful about using graphics that are trademarks of organizations mentioned in your web pages. If you want to use such a graphic, make sure you get permission first. You can get permission to use a graphic simply by asking permission from the webmaster of the web site containing the graphics you wish to use.

TIP

If you are concerned about your work, you can register it with the Copyright Office for a minimal price. Furthermore, you should also include a copyright sign [copy] on your work. You can insert the copyright symbol by using `©` in your web pages.

"Obtaining" graphics from other sites and adding them to your own pages can also get you into trouble. If you'd like to have something, you should first send some e-mail and ask for permission. If not, you can simply visit one of the public graphics icon archives and get all the graphics you need.

Here are some icon collections available on the Internet:

- http://www.infi.net/~rdralph/icons/
- http://www.meat.com/textures/
- http://www.cs.yale.edu/homes/sjl/clipart.html
- http://www.yahoo.com/Computers/World_Wide_Web/Programming/Icons
- http://www.sfsu.edu/~jtolson/textures/textures.htm
- http://www.stars.com/Vlib/Providers/Images_and_Icons.html

TIP

Ask nicely! If you need to use some information or a graphic on a web site, ask for permission to use the information or the graphic. As long as the information is not too proprietary, chances are that you will be given permission to use it.

Of course, you should also avoid issues that are illegal in the real world, such as slander, libel, or child pornography. Even though the electronic medium of the web might seem different from the real world, keep in mind that some things are illegal no matter what medium you're using. For more information about copyright law, please visit the following URL:

```
http://www.law.indiana.edu/law/lawindex.html
```

Summary

This chapter covered various issues that need to be addressed when providing information on the Internet. These issues include copyright laws and how they affect the information you provide on your web site. By following the advice in this chapter, you can make sure your web site is a legally safe web site. This chapter also covered maintenance issues for web sites and explained how to register your web site with search engines and cataloging databases on the web.

The next chapter will demonstrate how you can make your web site interactive by first introducing you to CGI and its capabilities. Afterwards, you will learn how CGI (Common Gateway Interface) can be used to provide dynamic content to users browsing your web site. You will also be shown how to setup PERL scripts as well as design and set up an e-mail feedback form.

Making Your Web Site Interactive

28

IN THIS CHAPTER

After you have set up your web site and have created some Web pages, it's time to think about making your web site dynamic. This can be accomplished by setting up a few CGI scripts on your server. By setting up customized feedback forms and database update/query forms, you can exploit the capabilities of your web site to its fullest potential. By reading this chapter, you'll learn about the basics of CGI and how you can utilize CGI to provide dynamic content to users browsing your web site. You'll also be shown a few CGI programming examples as well as how to install PERL on your web server. After installing PERL and writing a sample CGI script in PERL, you'll be shown how to execute PERL CGI scripts on your NT web server using a web browser. In addition to PERL, the chapter also shows how to use the C programming language to develop CGI scripts.

What Is CGI?

Common Gateway Interface (CGI) is a standard for linking various application programs to your web server so that clients accessing your web site can call these scripts to obtain and provide various information. Plain text HTML files retrieved by web clients are static. The information contained in these files never change unless you manually edit these files and make changes. On the other hand, by utilizing CGI scripts, you can have web pages that are dynamically created each time a client accesses your web site. To the client, it will look as if the page has been specially created for him or her based on the information being requested. Obviously, this is a very powerful tool for interacting with web surfers.

Suppose, for example, that you have a database that needs to be updated or queried. Depending on the information needed by browsers of your web site and the information you require from them, you need to set up a mechanism that allows updating and querying. Although you can use plain old e-mail to correspond with people, and to do the queries and updates manually, this option is not very practical once you start getting more and more visitors. Eventually you'll end up spending the whole day answering and responding to e-mail. (Maybe you do this already, but just imagine how much worse it will be!) By setting up a simple form, you can perform updates to your database utilizing a CGI script. You can also set up a CGI script to query your database so that your clients will get the most up-to-date information when they need it.

CGI programs can be written in almost any programming language that lets you either create an executable file or execute the program in real-time with an interpreter (as in the case of AWK and PERL). The following is a list of a few languages that can be used to create CGI scripts under Windows NT:

- AWK
- C/C++

- FORTRAN
- Pascal
- PERL
- Visual Basic

Depending on your expertise, what's available to you, and the type of CGI project, you'll have to choose the language that best suits your needs. Customarily, CGI scripts are stored in the CGI-BIN directory of your web server's document root directory.

Applications of CGI

Many organizations and individuals are using CGI for a variety of tasks. These tasks range from having a simple counter on a web page for counting the number of times a certain page is accessed to using a CGI script to manage an entire store front end. Such a CGI script can also allow users visiting a web site to look at the merchandise being sold and even to place orders for the merchandise. In addition to this, by using CGI, various web sites offer search capabilities of their web site to make finding information easier.

You can use CGI to interact with browsers of your web site, to get their feedback, and to provide them with dynamic content. Here's a list of a few applications of CGI that can be used to enhance the capabilities of a web site:

- Setting up a guest book
- Setting up a feedback form
- Adding a counter to a web page
- Designing a database front-end for the web
- Allowing web surfers to visit various web pages via a pull-down list
- Enabling users browsing your web site to e-mail you with their comments and feedback.
- Providing customized web pages based on web browsers used by clients
- Enabling your web site's browsers to search your web site

Before moving on to more advanced topics, an introduction to the fundamentals of CGI is in order.

Fundamentals of CGI

CGI scripts are typically used to provide dynamic content to the client who called the CGI script. CGI scripts communicate with web browsers, as illustrated in Figure 28.1. If the

CGI script is an interactive script, then typically a form with various input controls is sent to the web client. After filling the form, the client submits the form to the web server. The web server then uses CGI to call the CGI script with data from the web client. Afterwards, the CGI script processes the data, possibly accessing a database on the server, and sends a message to the client who made the request.

FIGURE 28.1.

A typical web server with CGI scripts.

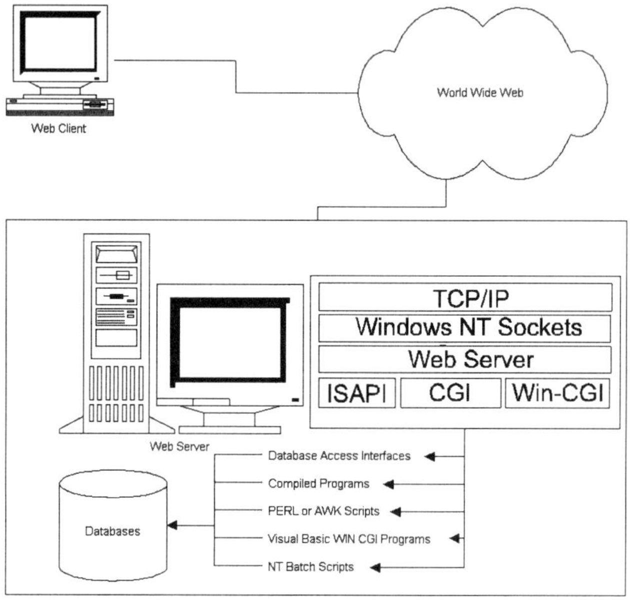

When a CGI script is called, the web server first examines the `REQUEST_METHOD` used to call the CGI script. This is done to determine how the web client is sending data to the CGI script. This process is shown in Figure 28.2. If the `REQUEST_METHOD` used to call the CGI script is **GET,** then any data supplied by the web client for the CGI script is found immediately following the URL name of the CGI script. In such a case, this information will be stored in the environment variable `QUERY_STRING`. On the other hand, if the `REQUEST_METHOD` used is **POST** or **PUT**, the size of input for the CGI script is stored in `CONTENT_LENGTH`, which contains the size of data supplied to the CGI script in bytes. The CGI script can then read from standard input the number of bytes returned by `CONTENT_LENGTH` to find the data given to the CGI script.

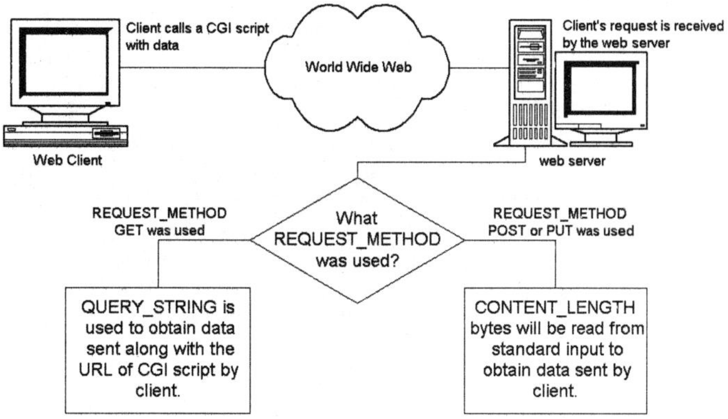

FIGURE 28.2.
Based on how a web browser invokes a CGI script, the web server executes the CGI script with the appropriate request method.

How CGI Works

CGI programs do not always need to be interactive. Non-interactive CGI scripts can be used to provide dynamic information that does not need user input. For example, in order to take advantage of various features offered by web browsers such as Netscape Navigator and Microsoft Internet Explorer, a CGI program can be written to determine the browser being used by a client and to send a page especially designed to take advantage of that browsers capabilities. Doing this is very easy. In fact, you'll be shown how to write an easy C CGI program for providing customized content based on the browser being used to access a page. In such an event, the CGI script will not need to interact with the person browsing the web site. Using a CGI program, dynamic content can be provided without any user intervention. For example, if the default web page of a web site is `welcome.html`, the main web page of the web site can be mapped to a CGI script. This can be done by creating a URL-CGI mapping, as shown in Figure 28.3. Such a script can determine the browser being used by the client as well as display a page with dynamic content optimized for the browser being used by the client. Refer to your web servers documentation for more information on creating URL-CGI mappings.

If a CGI script does not make use of user input, then what happens when a client accesses the page is very simple. First, the client connects to the web server and requests a web page. Because the document requested is linked to a CGI script, the web server executes the CGI program to which the page is linked. Output of the CGI program is then sent to the client who requested the page. Afterwards, the connection between the web server and the web client is closed. This interaction is shown in Figure 28.4.

FIGURE 28.3.

By mapping a web page to a CGI script, you can provide dynamic content based on various variables, such as the browser being used to invoke the CGI script.

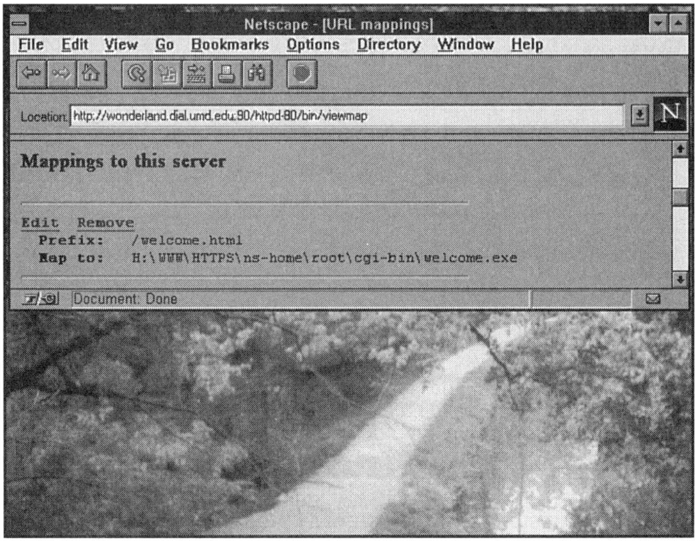

FIGURE 28.4.

How a non-interactive CGI script can be used to provide dynamic content.

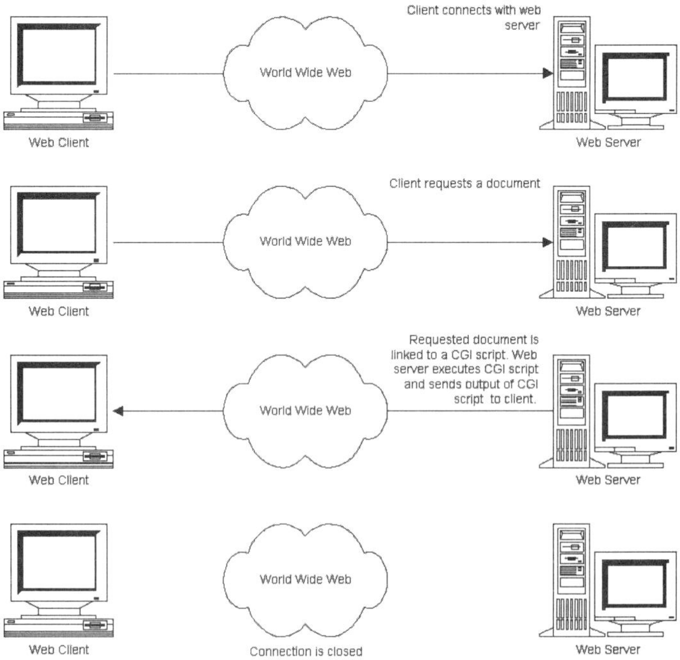

One of the greatest aspects of CGI is its capability to interact with your web site's browsers. This can be done by asking a user to fill in and submit a form. The CGI script can then validate the user's input, ask the user to fill in any missing information, and process the user's input. This process is carried out as shown in Figure 28.5.

FIGURE 28.5.

An interactive CGI script can be used to provide dynamic content.

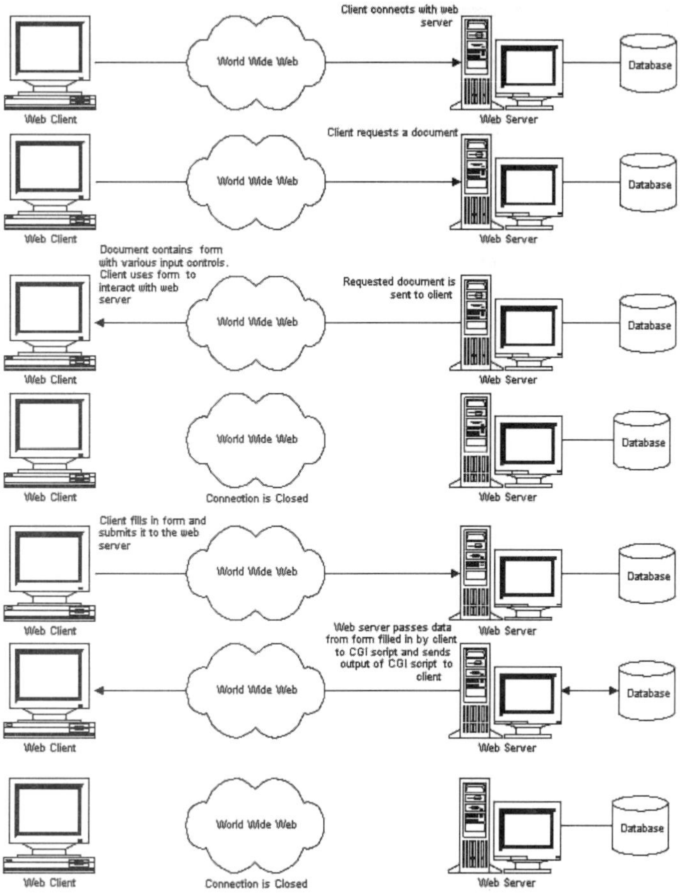

When a CGI script interacts with a web client to display customized output, a web page with various input controls is sent to the web browser. After the user fills in the form, it is submitted to the web server to be processed. Depending on the `REQUEST_METHOD` used to communicate with the CGI script, the CGI script obtains data sent from the client and then processes the data, displaying its output to *standard output*. Everything written to *standard output* by the CGI script will be visible to the client who called the CGI script.

CGI Issues

When setting up CGI scripts, there are a few things you should consider. Each time you allow a CGI script to be executed by someone surfing your web site, you are allowing someone to execute a program on your server. This can potentially lead to security breaches. Although this might sound a little perilous, it's actually not that bad, provided you follow a few guidelines. CGI is very safe as long as it is used properly.

Security

CGI is a very powerful tool for making information available to users browsing your web site. There are, however, certain issues you should be aware of. The first issue to be concerned about is *security*. By allowing CGI scripts to be executed, you are in fact allowing anyone browsing your web site to execute CGI applications on your server. Be particularly careful about CGI scripts that take input from a web client and use that same data without checking as a command line argument. Your CGI scripts should also always check for special control characters to avoid potential security breaches. If you have sensitive data in various sections of your web site, you might also want to disable directory browsing of your web server. This will ensure that unless the person browsing your web site knows the URL of a certain page or is transferred to a page from one of your own pages, he or she will not be able to "snoop around" your web site by browsing various directories and their contents.

Transmitting Sensitive Data

You should never set up CGI applications to distribute personal information that could be harmful in the wrong hands. If you are distributing valuable financial information such as credit card numbers, you should not use CGI unless you have configured your web server to encrypt data before it's transmitted over the Internet. If you need to transmit sensitive data and your web server does not encrypt data before transmitting, you should consider using a medium such as PGP (Pretty Good Privacy) protected e-mail to transmit such data. PGP is a very safe medium for distributing sensitive data.

Processing Time

Another issue to consider is the time it takes for a CGI script to fulfill a client's request. If you're providing data to users browsing your web site in real time, you should ensure that no one has to wait longer than five to ten seconds. If it's going to take longer to process a request, you should simply obtain the e-mail address of the person requesting the information and then e-mail the information as soon as the data is processed. If it takes longer than ten seconds to process a request, the user waiting at the other end will probably think that there's a problem and will simply stop waiting.

> **NOTE**
>
> If you really need to provide data in real time and the CGI scripts take longer than about ten seconds to execute, it's a very good indication that you are outgrowing your server and need more processing power and/or RAM.

Controlling Access to the CGI Directory

You should be cautious about who has access to your web server's CGI directory. It's very dangerous to allow users who upload files to your web site via FTP to have access to your CGI directory. It doesn't take too much programming knowledge for a user to write a malicious program, upload it to the CGI directory, and execute it with a web browser. Therefore, you should control who has access to your CGI directory via FTP or any other method.

Multiple Instances of the Same Script

Due to the nature of HTTP, it is possible that two or more clients will call the same CGI script at the same time. If the CGI script locks various files or databases when it is processing data, such an instance can potentially cause loss of data. CGI scripts should be able to handle such a situation without any problems.

CGI PERL Scripts

PERL (Practical Extraction and Report Language) is a very popular CGI programming language. By installing PERL on your web server, you'll be able to make use of many PERL CGI scripts to perform a variety of tasks. The purpose of this introduction to PERL is to let you know about PERL and how CGI PERL scripts can be set up on Windows NT web servers.

With the growth of the WWW, PERL is being used increasingly to write CGI programs. Most of the best features of C, sed, AWK, and sh, are incorporated in PERL. This allows PERL scripts to be developed in the least amount of time possible by not reinventing the wheel for fundamental tasks such as string manipulation. The expression syntax of PERL corresponds quite closely to the expression syntax of C programs. This makes PERL an easy language to learn for those who are already familiar with C.

PERL for Windows NT is provided free of charge on the Internet. PERL for Windows NT can be obtained from `http://info.hip.com/ntperl/`. After obtaining PERL for NT, create a directory for PERL and copy the PERL distribution file to this directory. Afterwards, decompress the distribution file. When decompressing the distribution file, be sure to use the option for using stored directory names in the archive. If this option is not used, all files will be extracted to the PERL directory you created and you'll find yourself in a mess! After the archive is uncompressed, run `install.bat` to install PERL on your server. Afterwards, `PERL.EXE` needs to be copied to the root CGI directory of your web server. This will enable your web server to execute PERL CGI scripts.

NOTE

When decompressing the .zip file, please be sure to use a 32-bit unzipping program that supports long filenames. Otherwise, the distribution files may not be properly installed. WinZip is a fine file uncompressing program that supports long filenames and a variety of file compression formats. Here's where you can obtain WinZip:

```
http://www.winzip.com/WinZip/download.html
```

NOTE

After installing PERL, you need to reboot your server in order for the installation directory paths to become effective. Failure to do this will cause PERL to greet you with an `Unable to locate DLL` message. (Yes, I was naive and tried it!) If you do not feel like rebooting your server, you can simply copy all files in the `PERL\bin` directory to the CGI directory of your web server.

For more information about PERL and sample CGI PERL scripts, you might want to give the following URLs a try:

Yahoo - Computers and Internet:
Internet:World Wide Web:Programming:Perl Scripts
http://www.yahoo.com/Computers_and_Internet/Internet/
World_Wide_Web/Programming/Perl_Scripts/

Yahoo - Computers and Internet:Languages:Perl
http://www.yahoo.com/Computers_and_Internet/Languages/Perl/

Your First PERL CGI Script: Hello World!

The purpose of this program is to provide you with an example of a simple PERL CGI script. You'll also learn how a PERL script is set up on a Windows NT web server and how a web client can invoke it. The script, which displays the text "Hello World," as well as some additional information about the web browser being used to invoke the CGI script, is very simple to write in PERL. Here's the code for this PERL script (the output is shown in Figure 28.6):

Listing 28.1. "HelloWorld.pl"

```
# Sanjaya Hettihewa, http://wonderland.dial.umd.edu/
# December 31, 1995
# "Hello World" CGI Script in PERL
# Display content type being outputted by CGI script
print "Content-type: text/html\n\n";

# Label title of contents being outputted
print "<TITLE>PERL CGI Script Demonstration</TITLE>\n";

# Display text
print "<H1>Hello World!</H1>\n";
print "<H3>Welcome to the fun filled world of<BR>\n";
print "Windows NT CGI programming with PERL!<BR><BR>\n";
print "The web browser you are using is:";

# Display value of the environmental variable HTTP_USER_AGENT
print $ENV{"HTTP_USER_AGENT"} , "<BR>\n" ;
print "Arguments passed in: ";

# Display value of the environmental variable QUERY_STRING
print $ENV{"QUERY_STRING"} , "<BR>\n" ;

# Obtain date and time from the system
($sec, $min, $hour, $mday, $mon, $year, $wday, $yday, $isdst) = localtime(time);

# display time
print "\nThe current time is: ";
print  $hour, ":", $min, ":", $sec , "<BR>\n";

# display date
print "\nThe current date is: ";
print $mon + 1 , "/", $mday , "/", $year, "<BR>\n";
```

Please pay particular attention to how the PERL CGI script is invoked by the web browser. In this example, the URL used to invoke the CGI script is

```
http://wonderland.dial.umd.edu/cgi-bin/
perl.exe?PERLScripts/HelloWorld/HelloWorld.pl+Argument
```

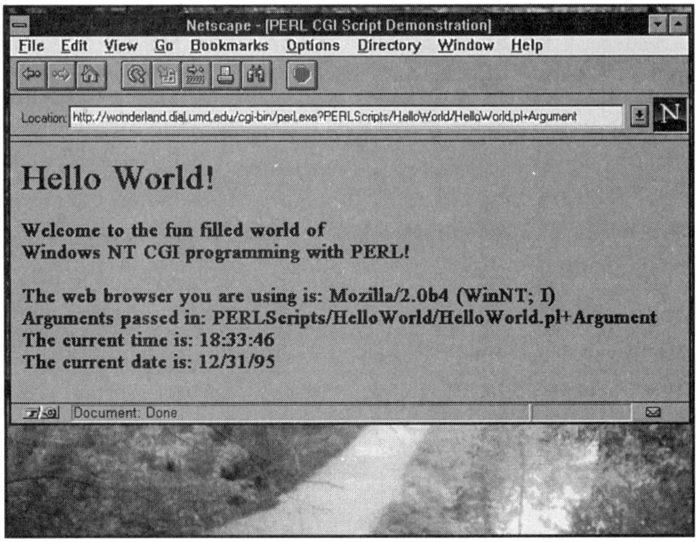

FIGURE 28.6.
Output of "Hello World" CGI PERL script.

When calling a PERL script on a Windows NT web server, the general syntax of the URL is

```
http://A/B?C+D
```

where `A` is the host name of the web server (`wonderland.dial.umd.edu`, in this example); `B` is the relative path to PERL.EXE (`cgi-bin/perl.exe`, in this example); and `C` is the location of the PERL script (the path is relative to the location of PERL.EXE). `D` contains any arguments passed into the PERL script. These arguments can be obtained by examining the contents of the CGI environment variable `QUERY_STRING`.

TIP

As you can see from this example, when PERL scripts are called with arguments, the length of URLs can become quite long. It is possible to avoid this situation by creating aliases for PERL scripts on your web server. For example, if an alias called "Hello" is created for

```
http://wonderland.dial.umd.edu/cgi-bin/
perl.exe?PERLScripts/HelloWorld/HelloWorld.pl
```

then the URL to call the PERL CGI script is reduced to

```
http://wonderland.dial.umd.edu/Hello+Argument
```

Please consult your web server's documentation for more information on creating aliases for URLs.

TIP

Whenever you have complex URLs for CGI scripts, you should create an alias for the CGI script. By hiding gory details such as long and complicated URL paths, your web site will actually look "friendlier" to someone browsing your web site. It will also save you time whenever you refer to such CGI scripts from one of your web pages, because you'll have to do less typing. If you are still not convinced, notice how much easier it is to remember this:

```
http://wonderland.dial.umd.edu/Hello+Argument
```

As opposed to this:

```
http://wonderland.dial.umd.edu/cgi-bin/
perl.exe?PERLScripts/HelloWorld/HelloWorld.pl+Argument
```

Providing Dynamic Content Based on Web Browser Used to Invoke CGI Script

Just like there are about two dozen web servers for Windows NT, there are many web browsers available for browsing the web. Unfortunately, apart from standard HTML, various browsers support various features. One of the most commonly used web browsers is Netscape Navigator. Because Netscape Navigator supports various additional HTML tags, information you provide can be richly formatted utilizing Netscape enhancements to HTML. If the appearance of your web site is very important to you, you might want to consider setting up a CGI script to provide a customized web page depending on the browser being used. Clearly this is not practical for a very large web site. However, by setting up a very simple CGI script, you can find out which web browser is being used by the user browsing your web site. If the browser being used is Netscape Navigator or Microsoft's Internet Explorer, you can provide a richly formatted web page with various HTML enhancements, or otherwise provide a basic page with the same content. The CGI script shown in Listing 28.2 works by utilizing the CGI variable `HTTP_USER_AGENT`, as shown in Figure 28.7.

The CGI script shown in Listing 28.2 provides customized content by examining the environment variable `HTTP_USER_AGENT`. Depending on the value of this variable, a page with Netscape enhancements to HTML can be displayed if the browser being used is Netscape. On the other hand, a page that only contains standard HTML 2.0 will be displayed if the browser being used to invoke the CGI script is not Netscape. By modifying the script, you can always add more customized pages for various other browsers. Such a script can be used for important pages such as the main homepage of your organization. By using CGI to provide dynamic content, you'll give a good impression to someone browsing the contents of your web site.

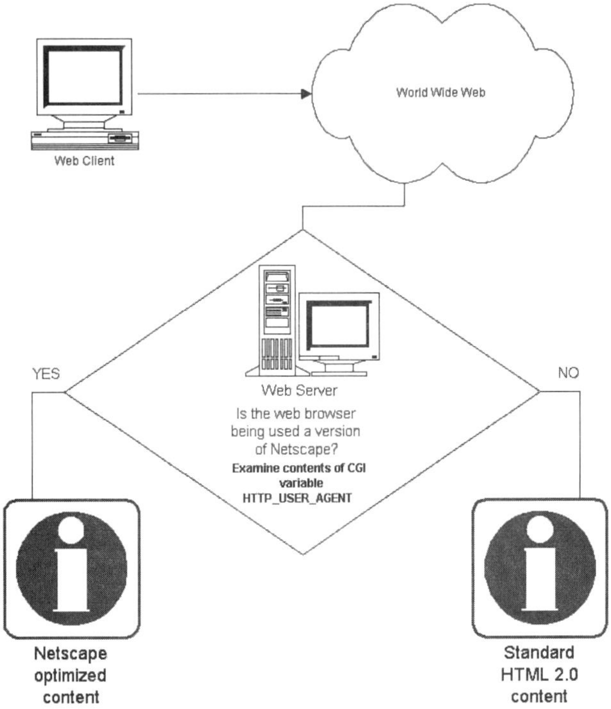

FIGURE 28.7.
How CGI variable HTTP_USER_AGENT can be used to display a customized web page.

TIP

The following program can be made more efficient by reading chunks of the file at a time rather than reading and outputting the file character-by-character.

Listing 28.2. CGI C program to provide customized content

```
/* (C) 1995 Sanjaya Hettihewa http://wonderland.dial.umd.edu/
 * January 1, 1996
 * Program to output a customized web page based on
   web browser being used.
 */

/* Special function libraries being used by this program */
#include <stdio.h>
#include <stdlib.h>
#include <string.h>
```

```
/* Please note the use of double quotes. This is because a single quote is
   used to quote the next charcter */

/* If you provide content specialy formatted for a different browser, please
   change the following */
#define  SPECIAL_BROWSER_SUB_STRING "Mozilla"

/* Please change the following to the full path name of the HTML file that's
    specially formatted. Please note that the following two lines should be a single
  line of code. (due to space limitations it's listed as two lines) */
#define  SPECIAL_BROWSER_PAGE "H:\\www\\https\\
         ns-home\\root\\documents\\WSDGNT\\special.htm"

/* Please change the following to the full path name of the HTML file that's
   formatted using standard HTML Please note that the following two lines
should be a single line of code. (due to space limitations it's listed as two lines) */
#define  OTHER_BROWSER_PAGE   "H:\\www\\https\\
         ns-home\\root\\documents\\WSDGNT\\regular.htm"

/* Please change the following to the e-mail address of your web site
   administrator */
#define  WEBMASTER            "mailto:webmaster@wonderland.dial.umd.edu"

static int DisplayPage ( char *pageName ) ;

main ( )
{

/* The "First Line" of all CGI scripts... */
  printf("Content-type: text/html%c%c",10,10) ;

/* Find out what web browser is being used */
  if ( getenv ( "HTTP_USER_AGENT" ) == NULL ) {
    printf("FATAL ERROR: HTTP_USER_AGENT CGI variable undefined!\n") ;
    return   ( 0 ) ;
  }

/* Display apropriate page based on browser being used by client */
  if (strstr (getenv ("HTTP_USER_AGENT" ), SPECIAL_BROWSER_SUB_STRING)!=NULL)
    DisplayPage ( SPECIAL_BROWSER_PAGE ) ;
  else
    DisplayPage ( OTHER_BROWSER_PAGE ) ;
  return   ( 0 ) ;

}

/* Contents of file passed into this function will be displayed to standard
   output. The web server will transmit what's displayed to standard output
   by this CGI script to the client that called the CGI script */
int DisplayPage ( char *pageName )
{

  FILE *inFile   ;
  char character ;

/* Check to ensure a valid file name is given */
  if ((inFile = fopen(pageName, "r")) == NULL) {
   printf ( "FATAL ERROR: Content file can't be opened! %s<BR>", pageName);
```

continues

Listing 28.2. continued

```
    printf ( "Please contact the  <A HREF=%s>Webmaster.</A><BR>",
             WEBMASTER );
    return ( 0 ) ;
  }

/* Displaying contents of file to standard output
   Please note that this can be done more efficiently by reading chunks of the
   file at a time */
  fscanf  ( inFile  , "%c" , &character ) ;
  while ( !feof(inFile) ) {
    printf ( "%c" , character ) ;
    fscanf  ( inFile  , "%c" , &character ) ;
  }
  fclose(inFile);
  return ( 1 ) ;

}
```

Listing 28.3 is the standard HTML web page designed for non-Netscape browsers. In case you are interested in knowing where this web page is referenced in the CGI program, for the purpose of this example, this file will be saved at

```
H:\\www\\https\\ns-home\\root\\documents\\WSDGNT\\regular.htm
```

Location of the above file is defined in the C program so that its contents can be displayed for non-Netscape browsers. In the C program, the location of the file is defined in `OTHER_BROWSER_PAGE`. Here's the listing:

Listing 28.3. Standard HTML page for non-Netscape browsers

```
<TITLE>Standard HTML page</TITLE>
<BODY>
Welcome to the standard HTML page for technically challenged web browsers.
<P>
Option One<BR>
Option Two<BR>
Option Three<BR>
</BODY>
```

Listing 28.4 is the Netscape-enhanced HTML web page that's specially designed for those browsing your web site with Netscape. This HTML code displays the same three options that are displayed by the standard HTML page. However, the options are displayed inside a table with some additional Netscape enhancements. Because the C program needs to know the location of this file, for the purpose of this example, the following page will be located at

```
H:\\www\\https\\ns-home\\root\\documents\\WSDGNT\\special.htm
```

In the C program, the full pathname of this file is stored in `SPECIAL_BROWSER_PAGE`. Contents of this file will be displayed by the CGI program whenever Netscape Navigator is used. You'll need to change this variable depending on where you store the Netscape-enhanced web page. Here's the listing:

Listing 28.4. Netscape-enhanced page for Netscape browsers

```
<TITLE>Netscape Enhanced page</TITLE>
<BODY>
<CENTER>
<TABLE BORDER=15 CELLPADDING=10 CELLSPACING=10 >
<TR>
<TD >
Welcome to the
<FONT SIZE=4>Ne</FONT><FONT SIZE=5>ts</FONT>
<FONT SIZE=6>ca</FONT><FONT SIZE=7>pe</FONT>
<FONT SIZE=6>En</FONT><FONT SIZE=5>ha</FONT>
<FONT SIZE=4>nc</FONT><FONT SIZE=3>ed </FONT>
 web page!
</TD>
<TD >Option One<BR></TD >
<TD >Option Two<BR></TD >
<TD >Option Three<BR></TD >
</TR>
</TABLE>
</CENTER>
</BODY>
```

After compiling this program and placing it in your web server's CGI directory, depending on the browser being used to call the CGI script, the appropriate page will be displayed. When compiling the C program, be sure to change `SPECIAL_BROWSER_PAGE`, `OTHER_BROWSER_PAGE`, and `WEBMASTER` to the appropriate values. The output of the CGI program for providing customized content is shown in Figures 28.8 and 28.9. For the purpose of this example, the web browsers Netscape and Mosaic were used. Notice how the enhanced HTML page is displayed when accessing the script with Netscape and how the standard HTML page is displayed when accessing the script with Mosaic.

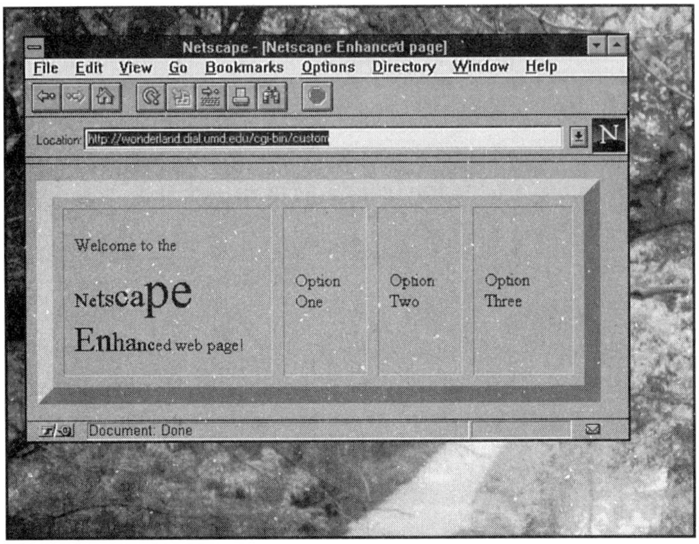

FIGURE 28.8.
Output of the CGI program when invoked by Netscape.

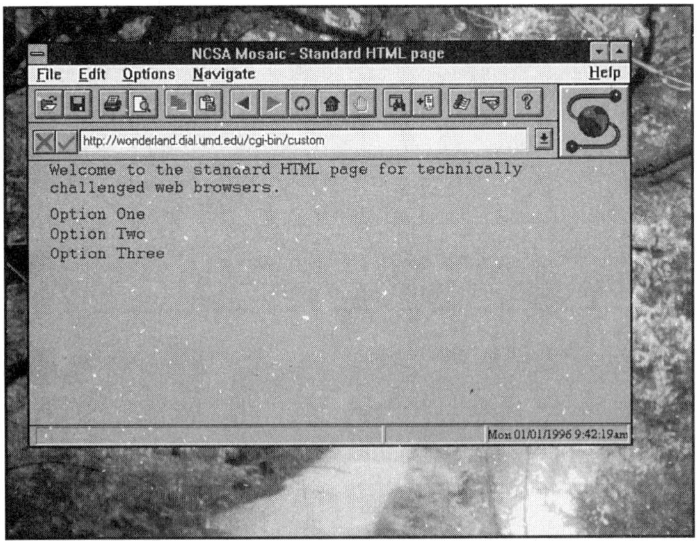

FIGURE 28.9.
Output of the CGI program when invoked by a non-Netscape browser (Mosaic, in this case).

Setting Up a Feedback Form

One of the best things about CGI is that it lets you interact with the people browsing your web site. What better way is there to interact with them than ask for their feedback? By using the Windows NT command line mail utility, called Blat, and another utility program that can be used to e-mail the contents of a form, you can set up a feedback form at your web site in just a few minutes.

The first thing you need to do is obtain a copy of Blat. Blat can be obtained from the following web site:

```
http://gepasi.dbs.aber.ac.uk/softw/blat.html
```

Blat is a public domain Windows NT console utility that sends the contents of a file as an e-mail message using the SMTP protocol. Blat is useful for creating scripts where mail has to be sent automatically (CGI scripts, results of backups, and so on.) In order to use Blat, you must already have an SMTP mail server installed and configured properly.

NOTE

If you have not set up a Windows NT SMTP mail server, you need to do so before installing Blat. You can download a free SMTP mail server for Windows NT from `http://www.emwac.ed.ac.uk/`. Please refer to the next chapter for installing the FREE EMWAC mail server for Windows NT.

After downloading Blat, you need to install it on your web server. Blat is distributed with the source code. The only two files you really need are blat.exe and gwinsock.dll. These two files should be located in the directory `%SystemRoot%\SYSTEM32`. After unzipping the Blat distribution file, you need to copy blat.exe and gwinsock.dll to `%SystemRoot%\SYSTEM32`. Afterwards, you need to install Blat by typing

```
Blat -install your_site_address your_userid@your_site_address
In my case,
your_site_address = wonderland.dial.umd.edu
your_userid@your_site_address = sanjaya@wonderland.dial.umd.edu
```

After this, as long as you have set up your SMTP server software properly, Blat will install and let you know that the SMTP server was set properly.

TIP

At this point, if you want to quickly e-mail a file, you can do so by typing

```
Blat <filename> -t <recipient>
```

After Blat is set up, you need to set up a form to e-mail your feedback. Before setting up the form, you need to download a program that will process the contents of the form once it's submitted. The program you need to download is wwwmail.exe; it can be downloaded from

```
http://www.esf.c-strasbourg.fr/misc/amsoft.exe?www
```

After downloading the program, you need to copy it to the CGI directory of your web server. Then, you need to set up a form that lets the user type in and submit feedback. You also need to create a page that is displayed after the user submits his or her feedback. This page should thank the user for the feedback and let the user choose another link to follow.

NOTE

In order for the program to work properly, you need to enable CGI on your web server. Please consult the manual for your web server to find out how this is done. Typically, the CGI directory is the `CGI-BIN` directory from the root directory of your web server. With some web servers, after creating this directory, you might need to define it as your CGI directory before you can execute CGI scripts.

Now all that's left to do is to create a feedback form and a response page that is displayed after the form is submitted. A sample feedback page is provided in Listing 28.5 for your reference. You can use a similar feedback page for your web site. All you have to do is change the following values:

```
name="mailto"
     value="user_ID@your.site"
name="WWWMail-Page"
     value="<Full Path of page to display after submitting the form">
action="<your CGI Directory>/wwwmail.exe/cgi-bin/feedback.hfo">
```

TIP

You can have a pull-down list using the SELECT/OPTION tag as shown in Listing 28.5.

After setting up a page similar to the one shown in Listing 28.5 as your feedback form, you'll have a feedback form that looks like the form in Figure 28.10.

Listing 28.5. Sample feedback form

```
<HTML>
<HEAD>
<title>Feedback Form Demonstration</title>
</HEAD>

<BODY>
<FORM  method=POST
       action="/cgi-bin/wwwmail.exe/cgi-bin/feedback.hfo">
<INPUT TYPE=hidden name="mailto"
       value="webmaster@wonderland.dial.umd.edu">
<INPUT TYPE=hidden name="WWWMail-Page" value="H:\www\netscape_commerce\ns-
home\root\documents\feedback\ThanksForFeedback.html">
```

```
<PRE>
<b>Subject:</b> <SELECT name="subject">
  <OPTION> I have some Feedback
  <OPTION> I have a comment...
  <OPTION> I have a suggestion...
  <OPTION> I need assistance with...
  <OPTION> Other
</SELECT>
<B>You E-mail address please:</B>    <INPUT name="sender" SIZE=30>
<b>Your name Please:</b>            <INPUT name="name" SIZE=30 >
<b>Your phone # (If you wish)</b>   <INPUT name="phoneno" SIZE=20 >
<b>Would you like a reply from me?</b> <SELECT name="Reply">
  <OPTION> If you wish
  <OPTION> Yes, please
  <OPTION> No thanks
</SELECT>
<b>Is this message urgent?</b>      <SELECT name="Urgency">
  <OPTION> Not particularly
  <OPTION> Yes, very urgent
  <OPTION> Not at all
</SELECT>
<b>And how are you doing today?</b> <SELECT name="Status">
  <OPTION> Oh, just fine, Thanks
  <OPTION> Doing great, Thanks!
  <OPTION> Don't even ask!
</SELECT>

<b>Please type your message and press the submit button:</b>
<TEXTAREA name="comments" cols=65 rows=3> </TEXTAREA>
<input type=submit value="Please click here to send message">
</FORM>
</PRE>
</BODY>
</HTML>
```

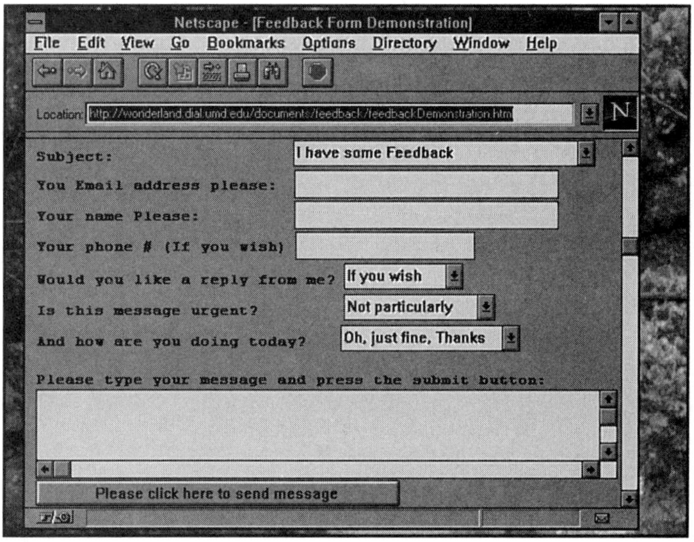

FIGURE 28.10.
A sample feedback form.

Benefits of CGI

The benefits of CGI are invaluable to any web site. These benefits range from having a customized input form for feedback to allowing someone browsing your web site to update and retrieve information from a database on your server. By using a customized e-mail feedback form, you can make sure you are provided with the information you need. By having a customized e-mail form, you can also ensure that your e-mail feedback form will always work—it does not depend on the setup of the client's web browser (in case it is not set up correctly for e-mail). Furthermore, if you need to set up a database that collects data from users browsing your web site, you can easily set up a CGI script to update information to a database on your server without any intervention on your behalf. ColdFusion (`http://www.allaire.com/cfusion/`) is a CGI application that can be utilized to allow users browsing your web site to update a database on your server. As you can see, the possibilities and applications of CGI are endless.

Summary

This chapter provided you with an introduction to CGI and demonstrated how CGI scripts can be set up on a Windows NT–based web server. You were also shown how to install PERL and run CGI PERL scripts on your web server. Various aspects of setting up CGI scripts, such as security, were also covered in this chapter so that the CGI scripts you develop and set up will not be a threat to the security of your web server. Various practical applications of CGI were also illustrated along with the source code so that you can modify these examples to enhance your web site and so that you can experiment with CGI.

The next chapter covers how you can extend the capabilities of your web site. You'll be shown how to extend the capabilities of your web server by setting up and configuring the Windows NT FTP server to distribute information on the Internet. You'll also be shown how to set up the FREE EMWAC mail server so that you can send and retrieve Internet e-mail.

Extending the Capabilities of Your Web Site

29

IN THIS CHAPTER

In this chapter you'll learn how you can extend the capabilities of your web site. The chapter begins showing you how to install the Windows NT FTP server. Afterwards, you'll be shown how it can be configured to meet your needs. By configuring your FTP server, you'll be able to make various files available to users. Also, by properly configuring your FTP server, web browsers will be able to access the contents of your FTP server as if it was a UNIX FTP server. After a demonstration on how to set up the Windows NT FTP server, you'll be shown how to set up the FREE EMWAC mail server. By using this mail server, you'll be able to send and receive Internet e-mail. The feedback form and CGI program described in the previous chapter, "Making Your Web Site Interactive," requires this mail server to be functional before the CGI script can be used to e-mail feedback to you.

Setting Up the Windows NT FTP Service

When hosting a web server, you should consider setting up an anonymous FTP site if you plan to distribute files. Setting up an FTP server will ensure that files are always available to users as long as they have access to the Internet (and not necessarily a web-browsing program). By having a separate service take care of file distribution, you can liberate your web server for processing regular HTTP requests.

Setting up the Windows NT FTP service is relatively simple. If you have not done so already, you need to install Windows NT's TCP/IP protocol by executing the Network applet from the Control Panel and choosing Add Software. Next, you need to install the FTP service by again going into Control Panel, executing the Network applet, choosing Add Software, and then selecting Simple TCP/IP Services.

Windows NT FTP Server Configuration Information

After you set up the Windows NT FTP service, you need to configure it by modifying a few Registry keys, depending on your preferences.

CAUTION

When making changes to the registry, be very careful and modify only specific registry keys listed below. Modifying other registry keys might adversely affect your server.

Although most Registry keys are optional, you must change one Registry key so that users can access your FTP site using a web browser. At this time, if you try to connect to your FTP server by using a version of Netscape prior to version 2.0, you'll not get a listing of files. This is because, by default, when a listing of files and directories is requested, the FTP server displays the data in the MS-DOS directory listing format. However, most web browsers, such as earlier versions of Netscape, expect the listing to be in the UNIX directory listing format. Therefore, in order for the directory listing to appear correctly, you need to add a certain Registry key. The utility to edit the Registry is located at

```
%SystemRoot%\SYSTEM32\REGEDT32.EXE
```

NOTE

After you make changes to the Registry, you need stop and restart the FTP service in order for the changes to take affect. You can stop and restart the FTP service by going into Control Panel, executing the Services applet, selecting the FTP service, and then stopping and restarting the FTP service.

NOTE

All the following Registry keys for the FTP service are relative to

```
HKEY_LOCAL_MACHINE\SYSTEM
        \CurrentControlSet
                \Services
                        \Ftpsvc
                                \Parameters
```

TIP

If you are making all the changes at the same time, you might want to edit the Registry and define all keys at the same time.

UNIX Style Directory Listing

In order to change the directory listing style to UNIX directory listing style, you need to add the following Registry key:

```
Registry key:      MsdosDirOutput
Data Type:      REG_DWORD, binary
Range:           0 or 1
Value:          1 for MS DOS style directory listing
          0 for UNIX style directory listing
```

When you add this Registry key with a value of 1, the output of the `LIST` command looks like the output of the UNIX `ls` command. This value also controls *slash flipping* in the path sent by the `PWD` command. When this value is 1 (true), the path contains backward slashes (\). If this value is 0 (false), the path contains forward slashes (/).

Displaying Messages to Users

When a user accesses a directory on your FTP server, you might want to display a message. This is done by changing the following registry key:

```
Registry key:      AnnotateDirectories
Data Type:        REG_DWORD
Range:             0 or 1
Value:            1 send directory annotations
0 do not send directory annotations
```

When `AnnotateDirectories` is set to 1, every time a user changes directories (that is, sends the server a `CWD` command), an attempt is made to open a file named ~FTPSVC~.CKM in the new directory. If this file is found, its contents are sent to the user as part of the successful reply to the `CWD` command. This may be used to attach annotations to specific directories.

TIP

The Directory annotation feature can be used to inform users where certain files are located and who to contact if they run into problems.

Setting Idle Time-Out Period

With the following Registry key, you can specify the idle time-out period for FTP sessions:

```
Registry key:      ConnectionTimeout
Data Type:        REG_DWORD
Range:             Value given in seconds
value            Can be set to the number of seconds the FTP service will allow
an FTP session to be idle
```

TIP

If you do not want your FTP service to disconnect people after a session has been idle, you can set the value of `ConnectionTimeout` to be 0. When `ConnectionTimeout` is set to 0, idle clients may remain connected indefinitely.

Displaying a Welcome Message

You can also have a welcome message displayed each time a client accesses your FTP server and is validated. In order to define a welcome message, you need to define the following Registry key with a greeting message:

```
Registry key:      GreetingMessage
Data Type:      REG_MULTI_SZ
Range:            Strings
value           Welcome message
```

NOTE

When a user logs on to your FTP server as an anonymous user and specifies an e-mail address that starts with a hyphen (-), your greeting message will not be sent.

Displaying a Goodbye Message

If you'd like to add a good-bye message to your FTP service that will be displayed when a user disconnects from your FTP server, you need to edit the following Registry key:

```
Registry key:      ExitMessage
Data Type:      REG_SZ
Range:            Text Message
value           Can be set to any text message you want to be displayed.
```

Limiting the Number of Connections

By defining the Registry key `MaxConnections`, you can limit the number of users who are able to connect to your FTP service at any given time:

```
Registry key:      MaxConnections
Data Type:      REG_DWORD
Range:            Number
value           Number of FTP users you allow.
```

NOTE

In order to allow an unlimited number of simultaneous users to access your FTP server, you can set the value of `MaxConnections` to be 0.

FTP Service Busy Message

You can also define the message that is sent out if a user tries to access your FTP server when it's already serving the maximum number of users allowed. In order to set the message, you need to define the following Registry key and specify the message that is sent to the FTP client requesting the connection:

```
Registry key:     MaxClientsMessage
Data Type:       REG_SZ
Range:            Message
value            Message to be displayed when the FTP server is servicing the
maximum number of FTP users allowed.
```

Defining Home Directories

There are two ways to define home directories for FTP users. One way is to go to Control Panel, execute the Network applet, and then configure the FTP service. The other way is to modify the following Registry key:

```
Registry key:     HomeDirectory
Data Type:       REG_EXPAND_SZ
Range:            Path name
value            Path to the users home directory
```

After defining this Registry key, if a user is validated, Windows NT attempts to change the user's directory to the directory defined in the Registry key. If the user does not have permission to access the directory specified, the user is refused FTP access. An event is written to the Windows NT event log if a user tries to connect to the FTP service and finds that his or her home directory is inaccessible.

NOTE

When allowing anonymous FTP, be sure to limit the permissions of the user account that runs as the FTP service. You should make sure this account only has permissions to access the directories you want to be made public.

NOTE

When setting up your server on the Internet, you should disable the Windows NT guest account. For anonymous FTP, you can create a new user and just give enough permissions for this user to access your public directories.

Setting Up the FREE EMWAC Internet Mail Server

In order to send and receive e-mail without using a remote e-mail server, you need to set up your own Windows NT mail server. Although there are several commercial e-mail servers for Windows NT, you can obtain a free e-mail server for Windows NT from

```
http://emwac.ed.ac.uk/html/internet_toolchest/ims/install.htm
```

NOTE

Although you can use the FREE EMWAC mail server for most of your e-mail needs, there are more advanced e-mail servers for Windows NT. These commercial e-mail programs provide additional functionality.

The following requirements have to be met in order to install the EMWAC mail service:

- Intel, Digital Alpha, or MIPS processor
- Windows NT 3.51 server or workstation with TCP/IP installed
- An NTFS partition
- At least 16MB of memory
- An Internet connection (of course)
- Access to a Domain Name server (this Domain Name server might be locally set up on your server or provided as a service by your Internet Access Provider)

NOTE

Please note that the following installation instructions apply to version 0.50 of the FREE EMWAC mail server. Installation instructions may vary for other versions.

How to Install the EMWAC Mail Server

Installing the EMWAC mail server is very easy. Before proceeding any further, you need to log in to your Windows NT system as a user with administrative privileges. Then, you need to obtain the EMWAC mail server software from the previously provided URL. The software comes in three flavors, depending on the platform you are using:

```
IMSi386.ZIP      Intel version
IMSAlpha.ZIP     Alpha version
IMSMips.ZIP      MIPS version
```

CAUTION

Please note that if you have a previous version of the EMWAC mail server, you need to remove it before installing the new version. You can uninstall the previous version by first stopping the mail services from the Control Panel's Service Manager applet and then running all three .EXE files with the argument `-REMOVE`.

After downloading the software, you need to install it by decompressing the distribution file. Additional installation instructions are available in the distribution file should you need them. After unzipping the distribution file, you should see the following files:

```
SMTPDS.EXE      The SMTP Delivery Agent.
SMTPRS.EXE      The SMTP Receiver.
POP3S.EXE       The POP3 Server.
IMS.CPL         The Control Panel Applet.
IMSCMN.DLL      A DLL containing common code used by mail server applications.
COPYRITE.TXT    The copyright statement for the software.
READ.ME         About the mail server and summary of new features, etc.
```

NOTE

Please note that you'll not be able to execute the .EXE files from the command prompt (without special arguments). The .EXE files are Windows NT services and need to be installed from the command prompt before they can be used.

Next, you need to copy the critical mail service files to a permanent directory. Because most other Windows NT services are located at `%SYSTEMROOT%\SYSTEM32`, you might want to copy the following files to the `%SYSTEMROOT%\SYSTEM32` directory. Here are the critical EMWAC mail server files:

- IMS.CPL (Must be located in %SYSTEMROOT%\SYSTEM32)
- SMTPDS.EXE
- SMTPRS.EXE
- POP3S.EXE
- IMSCMN.DLL

When you now invoke Control Panel from Program Manager, you should see the EMWAC mail services icon among the other Control Panel applets. You should install the three executable files by using the `-INSTALL` argument. This is done by going to the permanent directory where the executable files have been copied and then typing

```
SMTPRS -INSTALL
SMTPDS -INSTALL
POP3S -INSTALL
```

After you install these three programs, they'll register themselves with the Windows NT Service Manager. If you execute the Service Manager applet from the Control Panel, you should be able to see the following three mail services installed on your system:

- EMWAC POP3 Server
- EMWAC SMTP Delivery Agent
- EMWAC SMTP Receiver

Next, you need to configure the EMWAC mail service by running the Mail Server Configuration applet from the Control Panel. After the mail server is configured properly, you can start the three mail services by double-clicking the Services applet from the Control Panel and starting the three mail services.

Please note that before users can log in to the mail server from various mail clients to read e-mail, these users should be given the Windows NT right `Log on as a batch job.`

After following these steps, the EMWAC mail server should be operational under Windows NT. If you run into any problems during the installation process, please refer to the documentation that comes with the mail server for more information.

Summary

This chapter showed you how the capabilities of your web server can be extended by setting up and configuring a mail server and the Windows NT FTP server. The FTP server can be used to distribute various files on the Internet. By using the FTP server to distribute files on the Internet, anyone who has access to the Internet will be able to access the files you make available—even if the user does not have access to a web browser. On the other hand, to access information on a web server, one should have access to a web browser. Also, by using the EMWAC mail server you'll be able to send and receive Internet e-mail to and from your server. In addition to this, using this mail server, you can set up an e-mail feedback form, as described in the previous chapter.

The next chapter covers various Windows NT resources on the Internet. By learning more about Windows NT resources available on the Internet, you'll be able to use these resources whenever you have a question or problem with Windows NT. Also, by keeping up with the resources listed in the following chapter, you'll be able to keep up-to-date with new technologies and innovative ways of accomplishing various tasks.

Windows NT Resources on the Internet

30

IN THIS CHAPTER

One of the best things about the Internet is that generally people are willing to help you in whatever way they can. If you have a question about almost anything, for example, you can usually get an answer in about 24 hours if you know where to look for help. Numerous Windows NT resources are available on the Internet. Even though you can call Microsoft for questions related to Windows NT, you might first want to find out whether anyone else has come across the same problem and learn what was done to solve the problem; possibly saving you some time and money. Another advantage of posting questions on the Internet is that they are read by a diverse group of people. Therefore, responses you get will be greatly varied and will include a wide range of experiences. This will allow you to sift through and then select the best solution offered to suit your needs.

Where to Go When You Need Help

With a few exceptions, the Internet is generally a friendly place where people sometimes go a little out of their way to help you. If you are supporting Windows NT, consider joining one or more Windows NT Internet mailing lists. Later in this chapter, you will learn about various Windows NT mailing lists and directions for joining them. In addition to joining various mailing lists, you can visit Windows NT news groups and participate in various discussions; these Internet options enable you to keep up-to-date with new information.

Windows NT Mailing Lists

A great way to learn how to do various things with Windows NT is to join one or more Windows NT mailing lists. Most people who subscribe to these mailing lists are people who use Windows NT every day and are quite helpful when someone has a problem. Before you join a mailing list, be aware that some of them generate quite a few e-mail messages each day. If you don't want to receive multiple e-mails throughout the day, it's better to not subscribe to a mailing list. In my opinion, however, the knowledge that can be gained from being in one or more mailing lists is well worth the extra e-mail. By joining a mailing list, you not only get a chance to find solutions to your questions, but you are also able to discuss options with other NT users and learn innovative ways to accomplish your objectives. It's a safe bet that you will see me occasionally in some of the Windows NT mailing lists.

TIP

If your e-mail application supports "rules," use a rule to divert all e-mail from mailing lists to a folder. The dozens of messages you may get from various mailing lists then will not distract you from your personal and business e-mail. It's generally a good idea to use a different folder for each mailing list so that when you have some free time, you can open a folder and read all the messages.

To join any of the following Windows NT mailing lists, simply send an e-mail message to addresses listed. Be sure that your message body contains the appropriate text listed. Usually after a few hours, you will start receiving messages directed to the list.

TIP

When you are subscribed to a mail list, you will receive a "welcome message" that contains various information about the mailing list. Be sure to save this message; it also contains information regarding how to unsubscribe from the mail list in case you change your mind. Some list members are not very friendly when "unsubscribe messages" are sent to the main list!

A Few Windows NT Mailing Lists

For discussions related to Windows NT based WWW servers:

> Send e-mail to: `webserver-nt-request@DELTA.PROCESS.COM`
>
> Include this in body of message: `subscribe webserver-nt`
>
> Send e-mail to: `http_winnt@Emerald.NET`
>
> Include this in body of message: `subscribe` in the subject line; leave the body blank

For general discussions related to Windows NT:

> Send e-mail to: `list@bhs.com`
>
> Include this in body of message: `join iwntug`
>
> Send e-mail to: `mailbase@mailbase.ac.uk`

Include this in body of message: `join windows-nt`

Send e-mail to: `listserv@eva.dc.lsoft.com`

Include this in body of message: `subscribe winnt-l`

Windows NT Resources on the World Wide Web

There are many resourceful Windows NT web sites on the Internet. The following World Wide Web sites are devoted solely to Windows NT. You might want to add some of these sites to your favorite web browsers book mark list and visit them frequently to keep up-to-date with various Windows NT developments and find solutions to various problems.

Microsoft Windows NT Version 3.51 Hardware Compatibility List

`http://www.microsoft.com/NTServer/HCL/hclintro.htm`

Visit this URL to determine a peripheral in question is compatible with Windows NT.

Microsoft Windows NT from a UNIX Point of View

`http://www.microsoft.com/BackOffice/reading/nt4unix.htm`

This paper provides a technical overview of Windows NT for the information technology professional with a strong background in UNIX. It approaches the subject from the UNIX point of view and relates the concepts of Windows NT to corresponding ones found in UNIX. The paper begins with a technical comparison of the two operating systems and moves on to cover how the two can coexist in a heterogeneous environment. The paper finishes with a brief section describing some of the tools available to aid developers in creating applications for both platforms.

FAQ for Porting from UNIX to Windows NT

`http://www.shore.net/~wihl/unix2nt.html`

If you are interested in learning about NT versions of UNIX and TCP/IP utilities, visit this FAQ. You might find these utilities quite useful. This site also contains a list of frequently asked questions about how to port UNIX applications to Microsoft's Windows NT. It should be read by anyone who intends to port UNIX applications or who is actively porting UNIX applications. This FAQ is typically updated with new information about once a month.

Windows NT on the Internet

`http://www.neystadt.org/winnt`

This site contains many resources about using Windows NT to host a web site.

European Microsoft Windows NT Academic Center (EMWAC)

`http://www.emwac.ed.ac.uk/`

EMWAC acts as a focus for activities and events that support the use of Windows NT. This is a very informative web site to find various Internet tools and services for Windows NT. Be sure to browse the Internet Tool Chest for NT at this site for various Internet services such as Finger Server, Gopher Server, HTTP Server, Internet Mail, WAIS Server, and WAIS Tool-kit.

Digital's Windows NT Home Page

`http://www.windowsnt.digital.com/`

This URL leads you to the Windows NT resources page at Digital; this page contains many Windows NT information resources. If you are hosting your web server on an Alpha, you will find this web site particularly useful.

Beverly Hills Software Windows NT Resource Center

`http://www.bhs.com`

The Beverly Hills Software Windows NT Resource Center is a useful source of Windows NT resources and information. Beverly Hills Software is a complete Internet consulting and presence firm that specializes in the design, installation, and implementation of Microsoft Windows NT-based Internet Servers. Beverly Hills Software is also the home of The Windows NT Resource Center, a highly regarded web site for Windows NT information and resources.

Microsoft NT Server Web Site

`http://198.105.232.5:80/ntserver/`

This site contains many Windows NT server resources as well as information about creating web sites using Windows NT.

Self Reported Windows NT Links

`http://COBA.SHSU.edu/messages/nt-list.htm`

This site contains hundreds of Windows NT resources that are self reported. The goal of this page is to create a dynamic source of information on Windows NT, and to promulgate this information in as timely a manner as possible.

San Diego Windows NT User Group (SDWNTUG)

`http://www.fbsolutions.com/sdwntug`

The mission of SDWNTUG is to promote the use of Windows NT Server and Workstation and to act as a conduit for the free exchange of information and discussion of NT-related issues.

NT Web Server—Security Issues

`http://www.telemark.net/~randallg/ntsecure.htm`

Visit this site to find how you can make your NT web server more secure.

NT Web Server Resource Guide

`http://mfginfo.com/htm/website.htm`

A comprehensive list of Windows NT software and resources to host a Windows NT-based web site.

Rick's Windows NT Information Center

`http://infotech.kumc.edu/winnt/`

A large amount of Windows NT links about NT download sites, user groups and associations, news groups, mailing lists, and so on.

Information On NT

`http://infotech.kumc.edu/winnt/`

This site contains many Windows NT resources including resources for NT from Microsoft, Remote Access Server information, and Windows NT file archives, as well as other Windows NT resources on the Web.

Sanjaya's Windows NT Resource Center

`http://Wonderland.dial.umd.edu/~NT`

Contains various Windows NT information resources. This resource center is maintained by me and contains information about hosting a Windows NT-based web site as well as various issues that needs to be dealt with when using Windows NT. This resource center is updated frequently with new information.

Windows NT Software on the WWW

There are many web sites that distribute Windows NT software. You will be able to accomplish various tasks more efficiently by using the utilities and applications found in the following web sites. In addition, you will also find applications that will provide you with solutions to various limitations of Windows NT such as lack of a disk quota management and disk defragmenting.

Internet Shopper

`http://www.net-shopper.co.uk/`

Internet Shopper is a company dedicated to the promotion of Windows NT on all platforms. At the Internet shopper web site you will find a number of Internet services for Windows NT for mail, hosting a list server, NNTP news server, DNS service, and more.

California State University Windows NT Shareware Archive

`http://coyote.csusm.edu/cwis/winworld/nt.html`

This site contains a very extensive collection of Windows NT shareware applications as well as Windows NT drivers and Windows NT ports of useful UNIX utilities.

NT PERL Distribution Site

`ftp://ntperl.hip.com/ntperl/`

You can obtain the latest version of NT Perl free of charge from this FTP site. PERL is a very powerful programming language commonly used to develop web CGI programs.

NT DNS

`http://www.telemark.net/~randallg/ntdns.htm`

If you are setting up a Windows NT Internet server and need DNS (Domain Name Service), you will find the above link to be very useful. This link will provide you with a free Windows NT port of UNIX Bind.

Pragma Systems Telnet Server

`http://www.ccsi.com:80/pragma/`

Pragma Systems has a telnet server for Windows NT that can be used to connect to a Windows NT Internet server via telnet. An evaluation version of their telnet service can be downloaded from the above web page.

Sunbelt International

`http://www.ntsoftdist.com/ntsoftdist/`

At the Sunbelt International web site you will find numerous Windows NT disk management utilities—such as a utility to check your disk fragmentation.

Carmel Anti-Virus for Windows NT

`http://www.fbsolutions.com/ntav`

Carmel Anti-virus is a Windows NT virus detection and eradication utility.

Windows NT/Web Authoring Newsgroups

Listed below are a few Internet newsgroups that discuss various issues related to web site development. In order to keep up to date with new technologies and learn various procedures, it's a good idea to visit the following newsgroups every now and then:

```
comp.infosystems.www.servers.ms-windows
comp.infosystems.www.servers.misc
comp.infosystems.www.browsers.ms-windows
comp.infosystems.www.authoring.cgi
comp.infosystems.www.authoring.misc
```

A number of newsgroups have been set up on the Internet for discussions related to Windows NT. In order to take part in these discussions, you might want to check out some of the following newsgroups:

```
comp.os.ms-windows.nt.pre-release
comp.os.ms-windows.nt.misc
comp.os.ms-windows.nt.setup.misc
comp.os.ms-windows.nt.setup.hardware
comp.os.ms-windows.nt.admin.networking
comp.os.ms-windows.nt.admin.misc
comp.os.ms-windows.nt.software.backoffice
```

The Future of Windows NT and the WWW

As the World Wide Web evolves, many people will discover how the WWW can be used to effectively distribute information to a global audience and conduct business. Thanks to newly evolving technologies such as Java and VRML, the capabilities of the WWW will be further expanded. By using Windows NT, in very little time anyone can establish a web presence and take advantage of the various virtues of the web.

With the popularity of the WWW, higher bandwidths will soon be available to home users. Although Internet connections to homes are usually established using 14.4 or 28.8 modems, this trend will change soon, when ISDN becomes more widely available. When cable companies realize the potential of providing Internet access via cable lines, and start offering customers high-speed Internet access via cable, most home users will be able to connect to the Internet at higher speeds and use newly emerging Internet technologies such as MBone, which allows real-time video multicasting on the Internet.

As these new technologies become fused with the WWW, we might actually notice the television and the WWW merging into one device. Currently the only thing holding back video-on-demand on the Internet is low bandwidth communication lines. With the deployment of high-speed fiber-optic lines and multicast routers, more efficient ways of distributing information will evolve. The first Internet TV broadcast station might not be that far away after all.

All these technologies need robust operating systems that are easy to set up and manage. Windows NT is an ideal operating system for such a task. Although UNIX servers traditionally have been used to handle such tasks, they are often more expensive to set up and administer than Windows NT-based servers. By going with Windows NT, many organizations will be able to become part of the WWW and contribute something meaningful to the Internet community.

Summary

This chapter provided an overview of various Windows NT resources available on the Internet. These resources include Windows NT mailing lists, web sites, FTP sites, and newsgroups. By using these resources, not only will you be able to find help whenever you have a problem or a question, but you will also be able to keep up to date with new developments relating to Windows NT.

What This Section Covered

This section covered various aspects of setting up, managing, and administering a Windows NT-based web site. By reading this section and incorporating the tips and suggestions provided in earlier chapters, you will be able make your web site another outstanding Windows NT-based web site!

IN THIS PART

V

PART

Appendixes

An NT Command-Prompt Command Listing

A

IN THIS APPENDIX

As has been discussed throughout this book, the Windows NT command prompt is functionally a superset of the DOS prompt you're familiar with. In other words, it's a character-based interface in which you enter commands from the keyboard. However, this interface is significantly more capable than the DOS command-line interpreter.

The most striking difference is that NT doesn't issue an error message when you attempt to run Windows 3.1, Windows NT, POSIX, or OS/2 character-based applications from the prompt. Instead, NT detects the type of program you're running, spawns an instance of the appropriate environment subsystem, and launches the application in the environment.

In addition, the NT command prompt provides numerous commands not found in DOS, such as those for working with NTFS and HPFS partitions, for piping and redirection between subsystems, and for command-line editing. It also supports many LAN Manager commands for administering networks, and it even allows cutting and pasting of material between dissimilar subsystems.

NOTE

The basics of running the command prompt are covered in Chapter 3, "Working with Windows NT." Configuring the command-prompt window is covered in Chapter 9, "Configuring Windows NT."

This appendix lists the commands and functions available from the command prompt and offers some additional notes. Several categories of command-prompt commands are listed herein:

- Native commands
- Subsystem commands
- Configuration commands
- TCP/IP commands
- Network commands
- Utility commands

You can get detailed syntax about many day-to-day commands. At the command prompt, enter `help` followed by the command. For example, typing

```
C:> help attrib
```

displays all the switches, parameters, and values that can be applied to the command.

NOTE

Only *native* commands (discussed in the next section) supply help in this way. For nonnative commands, you must type the command name followed by a space, a slash, and a question mark. For example, typing

```
C:> append /?
```

displays help about the append command.

You can find help for all command-prompt commands, functions, and settings by running the Windows NT Help icon in the Main group. Choose Command Reference Help from the resulting screen.

Native Commands

Table A.1 is a list of *native* commands. These commands are built around the 32-bit NT Command Interpreter. Some of these commands run external programs, such as FORMAT.COM. Others are built into the Command Interpreter, so the Interpreter must be running in order for them to execute.

You can determine whether a command is internal or external using the `dir` command from the \SYSTEM32 directory. For example, typing `dir format.*` results in the on-screen listing of FORMAT.COM. Therefore, you know that this is an external command. External commands have the advantage of being callable directly from Program Manager or File Manager. For example, you could set up a Program Manager icon to run the Tree program to display the directory tree.

Table A.1. Native commands.

Command	*Description*
ACLCONV	Converts OS/2 Lanman Server access control lists.
AT	Schedules commands and programs to run on a computer. The Scheduler service has to be running for this command to function.
ATTRIB	Displays or changes file attributes, such as hidden, system, or read-only.
BREAK	Sets or clears extended Ctrl-C checking so that a user can't cancel an executing command.
CALL	Calls one batch program from another.

continues

Table A.1. continued

Command	Description
CD	Displays the name of the current directory or changes the current directory.
CHCP	Displays or sets the active code page number.
CHDIR	Displays the name of the current directory or changes the current directory. (Same as CD.)
CHKDSK	Checks a disk for directory and sector errors and broken chains and displays a status report.
CLS	Clears the screen.
CMD	Starts a new instance of the Windows NT Command Interpreter.
COMP	Compares the contents of two files or sets of files.
CONVERT	Converts FAT or HPFS volumes to NTFS. Note that you can't convert the current drive.
COPY	Copies specified files to another disk or directory, or to a new name in the current directory.
DATE	Displays or sets the date.
DEL	Deletes specified files.
DIR	Displays a list of files and subdirectories in a directory.
DISKCOMP	Compares the contents of two floppy disks.
DISKCOPY	Copies the contents of one floppy disk to another.
DOSKEY	Edits command lines, recalls Windows NT commands, and creates macros.
ECHO	Displays messages or turns command echoing on or off.
ENDLOCAL	Ends localization of environment changes in a batch file.
ERASE	Deletes one or more files.
EXIT	Quits the CMD.EXE program (Command Interpreter). Also quits a COMMAND.COM (MS-DOS Command Interpreter) session.
FC	Compares two files or sets of files and displays the differences between them.
FIND	Searches files for a text string.
FINDSTR	Searches files for a string.
FOR	Runs a specified command for each file in a set of files.
FORMAT	Formats a disk for use with Windows NT.
GOTO	Directs Windows NT to a labeled line in a batch program.

Command	Description
GRAFTABL	Enables Windows NT to display an extended character set in graphics mode.
HELP	Provides Help information, such as this listing, for Windows NT commands.
IF	Used in batch files for conditional processing (branching).
KEYB	Configures a keyboard for a specific language.
LABEL	Creates, changes, or deletes the volume label of a disk.
MD	Creates a directory.
MKDIR	Creates a directory. (Same as MD.)
MODE	Configures a system device, such as the screen or a COM port.
MORE	Displays output one screen at a time instead of scrolling off the top of the screen or window.
MOVE	Moves one or more files from one directory to another directory on the same drive.
PATH	Displays or sets a search path for executable files. This command typically is used from within the AUTOEXEC.NT file.
PAUSE	Suspends processing of a batch file and displays a message.
POPD	Restores the previous value of the current directory saved by PUSHD.
PRINT	Prints a text file.
PROMPT	Changes the Windows NT command prompt. The command prompt P_ is suggested.
PUSHD	Saves the name of the current directory for use by the POPD command, then changes the directory.
RD	Removes the directory you name. Only empty directories can be removed.
RECOVER	Recovers readable information from a bad or defective disk.
REM	Records comments (remarks) in batch files or CONFIG.SYS.
REN	Renames specified files.
RENAME	Renames specified files. (Same as REN.)
REPLACE	Replaces files.
RESTORE	Restores files that were backed up using the BACKUP command.
RMDIR	Removes a specified directory. (Same as RD.)
SET	Displays, sets, or removes Windows NT environment variables.

continues

Table A.1. continued

Command	*Description*
`SETLOCAL`	Begins localization of environment changes in a batch file.
`SHIFT`	Shifts the position of replaceable parameters in batch files.
`SORT`	Sorts input and writes the result to the screen, printer, or a file. Can be used to sort a file.
`START`	Starts a separate window to run a specified program or command.
`SUBST`	Associates a path with a drive letter.
`TIME`	Displays or sets the system time.
`TITLE`	Sets the window title for a CMD.EXE session.
`TREE`	Graphically displays the directory structure of a drive or path.
`TYPE`	Displays the contents of a text file.
`VER`	Displays the Windows NT version number.
`VERIFY`	Turns on and off the automatic verification that files are written to a disk correctly.
`VOL`	Displays a disk volume label and serial number.
`XCOPY`	Copies files as well as directory trees and files included in those directories. Has many options.

Configuration Commands

The commands listed in Table A.2 are used to customize the MS-DOS environment. As in 16-bit MS-DOS, these commands are used from within CONFIG.NT, the file that is analogous to the MS-DOS CONFIG.SYS file. CONFIG.NT goes into effect when NT runs the MS-DOS subsystem.

NOTE

Several of these commands are useful only for the OS/2 subsystem. See Chapter 9, "Configuring Windows NT," for details on modifying the OS/2 subsystem.

Table A.2. Configuration commands.

Command	Description
buffers	Determines how much memory space will be used for disk file buffering (caching). Windows NT and the MS-DOS subsystem don't actually use this command. It's included only for compatibility with files from MS-DOS that already include the statement.
codepage	For OS/2: Determines which code pages the system can use.
country	Determines which country's standards will be used for currency, time and date, decimal separators, and case conversion.
device	Used for loading a device driver into memory.
devicehigh	Loads device drivers into the upper memory area. Loading a device driver into the upper memory area frees more bytes of conventional memory for other programs.
devinfo	Prepares a device to use code pages. To use this command, place it in your OS/2 C:\CONFIG.SYS file.
dos	Specifies that the MS-DOS subsystem is to maintain a link to the upper memory area or is to load part of itself into the high memory area (HMA).
dosonly	Prevents starting applications other than MS-DOS-based applications from the COMMAND.COM prompt.
driveparm	Windows NT and the MS-DOS subsystem don't take action for this command. It is accepted only for compatibility with MS-DOS files.
echoconfig	Displays messages during the processing of the MS-DOS subsystem CONFIG.NT and AUTOEXEC.NT when the MS-DOS subsystem is invoked. If this command isn't present, messages won't be displayed. This command must be in the MS-DOS subsystem CONFIG.NT file.
fcbs	Specifies the number of file control blocks (FCBs) that the MS-DOS subsystem can have open at one time. A file control block is a data structure that stores information about a file.
files	Sets the number of files that the MS-DOS subsystem can access at one time.
install	Loads a memory-resident program into memory.
lastdrive	Windows NT and the MS-DOS subsystem don't take action for this command. It's accepted only for compatibility with MS-DOS.
libpath	Specifies the directories that the OS/2 subsystem is to search for dynamic link libraries. To use this command, use an OS/2 editor to edit the C:\CONFIG.SYS file.

continues

Table A.2. continued

Command	*Description*
`ntcmdprompt`	Runs the Windows NT Command Interpreter, CMD.EXE, rather than COMMAND.COM after you run a TSR or after you start the command prompt from within an MS-DOS application.
`protshell`	Windows NT and the OS/2 subsystem don't use this command. It's accepted only for compatibility with files from Microsoft OS/2 version 1.3 or earlier.
`shell`	Specifies the name and location of an alternative command interpreter you want Windows NT to use for the MS-DOS subsystem.
`stacks`	Supports the dynamic use of data stacks to handle hardware interrupts.
`switches`	Forces an enhanced keyboard to behave like a conventional keyboard. You use this command in your CONFIG.NT file.

Subsystem Commands

The commands listed in Table A.3 are, for the most part, throwbacks to the 16-bit MS-DOS world. They're not built in as NT native commands either because they're no longer useful or because their functionality has been incorporated into NT in another form.

Table A.3. Subsystem commands.

Command	*Description*
`append`	Enables programs to open data files in specified directories as if these files were in the current directory. The specified directories are called appended directories because, for the sake of opening data files, they can be found as if they were appended to the current directory.
`backup`	Backs up one or more files from one disk to another. You can back up files onto either a hard disk or a floppy disk. Files also can be backed up from one floppy disk to another, even if the disks have different numbers of sides or sectors. Windows NT displays the name of each file it backs up.
`debug`	Starts Debug, a program that enables you to test and debug MS-DOS executable files.

Command	*Description*
`edit`	Starts MS-DOS Editor, which creates and changes ASCII text files.
`edlin`	Starts Edlin, a line-oriented text editor you can use to create and change ASCII files. Edlin numbers each line of the text file that is located in memory. You can use Edlin to insert, modify, copy, move, and delete lines of the file. If you want to use a full-screen editor, use the `edit` command.
`exe2bin`	Converts .EXE (executable) files to binary format. `exe2bin` is included in Windows NT as a courtesy to software developers. It's not useful for general users.
`expand`	Expands one or more compressed files. This command is used to retrieve compressed files from distribution disks.
`fastopen`	Windows NT and the MS-DOS subsystem don't use this command. It's accepted only for compatibility with MS-DOS files.
`forcedos`	Forces Windows NT to load a program into the MS-DOS subsystem. To be used only if NT doesn't recognize the application as an MS-DOS application.
`graphics`	Loads a program into memory that allows Windows NT to print on a printer the displayed contents of the screen when you're using a color or graphics adapter.
`loadfix`	Ensures that a program is loaded above the first 64K of conventional memory, and runs the program.
`loadhigh`	Loads a program into the upper memory area. Doing so leaves more room in conventional memory for other programs.
`mem`	Displays information about allocated memory areas, free memory areas, and programs that are currently loaded into memory in the MS-DOS subsystem.
`nlsfunc`	Windows NT and the MS-DOS subsystem don't use this command. It's accepted only for compatibility with MS-DOS files.
`qbasic`	Starts Windows NT QBasic, a program that reads instructions written in the BASIC computer language and converts them into executable computer code.
`setver`	Sets the MS-DOS version number that the MS-DOS subsystem reports to a program.
`share`	Windows NT and the MS-DOS subsystem don't use this command. It's accepted only for compatibility with MS-DOS files.

TCP/IP Commands

These utility commands, listed in Table A.4, are useful when you connect to systems such as UNIX that utilize TCP/IP protocol. Note that many of these commands won't work unless you've installed the TCP/IP network protocol.

Table A.4. TCP/IP commands.

Command	*Description*
`arp`	Displays and modifies the IP-to-Ethernet or Token Ring address translation tables used by address resolution protocol (ARP). This command is available only if the TCP/IP protocol has been installed.
`finger`	Displays information about a user on a specified system running the Finger service. Output varies based on the remote system. This command is available only if the TCP/IP protocol has been installed.
`ftp`	Transfers files to and from a computer running an FTP server service (sometimes called a daemon). `ftp` can be used interactively. This command is available only if the TCP/IP protocol has been installed.
`hostname`	Prints the name of the current host. This command is available only if the TCP/IP protocol has been installed.
`ipconfig`	Displays the workstation's TCP/IP configuration values. This comand is available only if the TCP/IP protocol has been installed.
`lpq`	Displays print queue statistics. This command is available only if the TCP/IP protocol has been installed.
`lpr`	Prints a job to a remote printer. This command is available only if the TCP/IP protocol has been installed.
`nbstat`	Displays protocol statistics and current TCP/IP connections using NBT (NetBIOS over TCP/IP). This command is available only if the TCP/IP protocol has been installed.

Command	*Description*
`net start snmp`	Starts the SNMP service. The SNMP service allows a server to report its current status to an SNMP management system on a TCP/IP network.
`net start tcpip`	Starts the TCP/IP service.
`net start tcp/ip netbios`	Starts the NetBIOS over TCP service. Service names with two or more words, such as Directory Replicator or Computer Browser, must be enclosed in quotation marks (" ").
`net start telnet`	Starts the Telnet client service. The Telnet service in conjunction with the Windows Terminal program allows terminal emulation over TCP/IP.
`netstat`	Shows currently implemented TCP/IP connections and protocol statistics.
`ping`	Verifies connections to a remote host or hosts. This command is available only if the TCP/IP protocol has been installed.
`rcp`	Copies files to and from the computer running the RCP service. This command is available only if the TCP/IP protocol has been installed.
`rexec`	Runs commands on remote hosts running the Rexec service. Rexec authenticates the username on the remote host before executing the specified command. This command is available only if the TCP/IP protocol has been installed.
`route`	Manipulates network routing tables. This command is available only if the TCP/IP protocol has been installed.
`rsh`	Runs commands on remote hosts running the RSH service. This command is available only if the TCP/IP protocol has been installed.
`telnet`	Starts terminal emulation. The Windows Terminal program is started, the Telnet port is opened, and the Telnet prompt is displayed. This command is available only if the TCP/IP protocol has been installed.

continues

Table A.4. continued

Command	*Description*
`tftp`	Transfers files to and from a remote computer running the TFTP service. This command is available only if the TCP/IP protocol has been installed.
`tracert`	Displays the route for a destination, which includes the response time in milliseconds of each router and the router's IP address. This command is available only if the TCP/IP protocol has been installed.

Network-Related Commands and Utilities

The commands listed in Table A.5 are used from the command prompt to initiate network-related activities. Some of them are dependent upon specific network services or protocols.

Table A.5. Network-related commands and utilities.

Command	*Description*
`Nbtstat`	Displays protocol statistics and current TCP/IP connections using NBT (NetBIOS over TCP/IP). This command is available only if the TCP/IP protocol has been installed.
`Netstat`	Displays protocol statistics and current TCP/IP network connections. This command is available only if the TCP/IP protocol has been installed.
`Net Accounts`	Updates the user accounts database and modifies password and logon requirements for all accounts. The Net Logon service must be running on the computer for which you want to change account parameters.
`Net Computer`	Adds or deletes computers from a domain database. This command is available only on NT Servers.
`Net Config`	Displays the configurable services that are running, or displays and changes settings for a service.
`Net Config Server`	Displays or changes settings for the server service while the service is running.

Command	*Description*
`Net Config Workstation`	Displays or changes settings for the Workstation service while the service is running.
`Net Continue`	Reactivates suspended services.
`Net File`	Displays the names of all open shared files on a server and the number of file locks, if any, on each file. This command also closes individual shared files and removes file locks.
`Net Group`	Adds, displays, or modifies global groups on Windows NT Server domains. This command is available for use only on Windows NT Server domains.
`Net Help`	Provides a list of network commands and topics you can get help on, or provides help on a specific command or topic.
`Net Helpmsg`	Provides help for a Windows NT error message.
`Net Localgroup`	Adds, displays, or modifies local groups.
`Net Name`	Adds or deletes a messaging name (sometimes called an alias), or displays the list of names the computer will accept messages for. The Messenger service must be running in order for you to use this command.
`Net Pause`	Pauses running services.
`Net Print`	Displays or controls print jobs and printer queues.
`Net Send`	Sends messages to other users, computers, or messaging names on the network. The Messenger service must be running in order for you to receive messages.
`Net Session`	Lists or disconnects the sessions between a server and the workstations connected to it.
`Net Share`	Creates, deletes, or displays shared resources.
`Net Start`	Starts a service, or displays a list of started services. Service names of two or more words, such as Net Logon or Computer Browser, must be enclosed in quotation marks (`"  "`).
`Net Start Alerter`	Starts the Alerter service, which sends alert messages.
`Net Start ClipBook Server`	Starts the ClipBook server service. Service names with two words, such as ClipBook Server, must be enclosed in quotation marks (`"  "`).
`Net Start Computer Browser`	Starts the Computer Browser service.

Table A.5. continued

Command	*Description*
`Net Start Directory Replicator`	Starts the Directory Replicator service, which copies designated files to specified servers. Service names with two words, such as Directory Replicator, enclosed in quotation marks (" "). This service also can be started with the command `Net Start Replicator`.
`Net Start Eventlog`	Starts the event logging service, which logs events on the local computer. This service must be started before you use the Event Viewer to view the logged events.
`Net Start File Server for Macintosh`	Starts the File Server for Macintosh service, permitting the sharing of files with Macintosh computers. This command is available only on NT Servers.
`Net Start FTP Server`	Starts the FTP server service. This command is available only if the TCP/IP protocol and FTP Server have been installed.
`Net Start Messenger`	Starts the Messenger service, which enables a workstation to receive messages.
`Net Start Net Logon`	Starts the Net Logon service, which verifies logon requests and controls replication of the user accounts database domainwide. Service names with two words, such as Net Logon, must be enclosed in quotation marks (" "). This service also can be started with the command `Net Start Net Logon`.
`Net Start Network DDE`	Starts the Network DDE service.
`Net Start Network DDE DSDM`	Starts the Network DDE server service.
`Net Start NWLink`	Starts the NWLink service.
`Net Start NWNBLink`	Starts the NWNBLink service.
`Net Start Print Server for Macintosh`	Starts the Print Server for Macintosh service, permitting printing from Macintosh computers. This command is available only on NT Servers.
`Net Start Remoteaccess`	Starts the Remote Access service.
`Net Start Rpclocator`	Starts the RPC Locator service. The Locator service is the RPC name service for Microsoft Windows NT.

Command	*Description*
`Net Start Rpcss`	Starts the RPC Rpcss service, which is the RPC subsystem for Microsoft Windows NT. The RPC subsystem includes the endpoint mapper and other miscellaneous RPC services.
`Net Start Schedule`	Starts the Schedule service, which allows a computer to start programs at a specified time with the `AT` command.
`Net Start Server`	Starts the server service, which allows a computer to share resources on the network.
`Net Start SNMP`	Starts the SNMP service, which allows a server to report its current status to an SNMP management system on a TCP/IP network.
`Net Start TCP/IP NetBIOS`	Starts the NetBIOS over TCP service. Service names with two or more words, such as Directory Replicator or Computer Browser, must be enclosed in quotation marks (`" "`).
`Net Start TCP/IP NetBIOS Helper`	Enables the NetBIOS over TCP service.
`Net Start TCP/IP Protocol`	Starts the TCP/IP Protocol service.
`Net Start Telnet`	Starts the Telnet client service. The Telnet service in conjunction with the Windows Terminal program allows terminal emulation over TCP/IP.
`Net Start UPS`	Starts the Uninterruptible Power Supply service.
`Net Start Workstation`	Starts the Workstation service, which allows a computer to connect to and use network resources.
`Net Statistics`	Displays the statistics log for the local workstation or server.
`Net Stop`	Stops a Windows NT network service.
`Net Time`	Synchronizes the computer's clock with that of a server or domain. When used without the `/set` option, this command displays the time for a server or domain.
`Net Use`	Connects a workstation to or disconnects a workstation from a shared resource, or displays information about workstation connections. This command also controls persistent net connections.

continues

Table A.5. continued

Command	Description
`Net User`	Adds or modifies user accounts, or displays user-account information.
`Net View`	Displays a list of servers, or displays resources being shared by a server.

Other Utilities

Table A.6 lists several miscellaneous utilities that don't fall into the other command categories.

Table A.6. Other utilities.

Command	Description
`aclconv`	Converts OS/2 HPFS386 file and directory permissions to NTFS volumes.
`diskperf`	Starts and stops system disk performance counters.
`ipxroute`	Manages the source routing variables of the NWLink protocol on a Token Ring network. This command is available only if the NWLink protocol has been installed.
`portuas`	Merges a LAN Manager 2.x user accounts database into an existing Windows NT user accounts database.

Using the Messages Database

B

IN THIS APPENDIX

The Windows NT CD-ROM includes a little-documented program called the Messages database. It's essentially an online listing of many of the NT "information" and "error" messages that pop up in dialog boxes or that appear in command-prompt sessions. Some messages generated by Microsoft applications are also included. Purely informative messages that don't require any action on the part of the user are not included in this database, however.

The Messages database comes "wrapped" in a runtime version of Microsoft Access (the database program) with a specialized graphical interface, making it easier to display the messages and search through them. You can easily run the program from Program Manager and look up error messages as they occur in NT, scanning for the error and possibly dredging up some tasty, relevant information. Because you can search quickly through not only the messages themselves, but also through associated (albeit typically cryptic) explanatory material, you stand a pretty good change of discovering something applicable. The database also lets you look through all possible messages generated by a particular application or service (such as all File Manager messages) or discover the meaning of an error message that only reports an ID number when it occurs.

Installing the Database

You install the Messages database from the CD-ROM (it's not included on the floppies). To install the Messages database, follow these steps:

1. Start NT.
2. Insert the NT CD-ROM in an accessible CD-ROM drive.
3. Create a directory named \MESSAGES on a hard disk that has at least 3.3M of space on it. This directory will temporarily hold the files during setup.
4. Log onto the CD-ROM and copy all files in the \SUPPORT\WINNTMSG directory to the temporary directory you just created.
5. In File Manager, select the target directory and display its files. Notice that there is a SETUP.EXE program there. Double-click on it to run it.
6. Follow the on-screen instructions. Enter your name and company information. Next, choose a drive and directory for the database. Make sure you choose a partition with plenty of room. You'll need 4.58M of free space on the target disk.
7. What happens next is an installation of Microsoft Access. You'll be asked about joining an existing database workgroup so that you can share the database with others. If you don't have an existing workgroup, don't click on Yes.
8. Files are now copied from the temporary directory and expanded. A message reports that the setup is complete.
9. A common Program Manager group for the database is set up, as shown in Figure B.1.

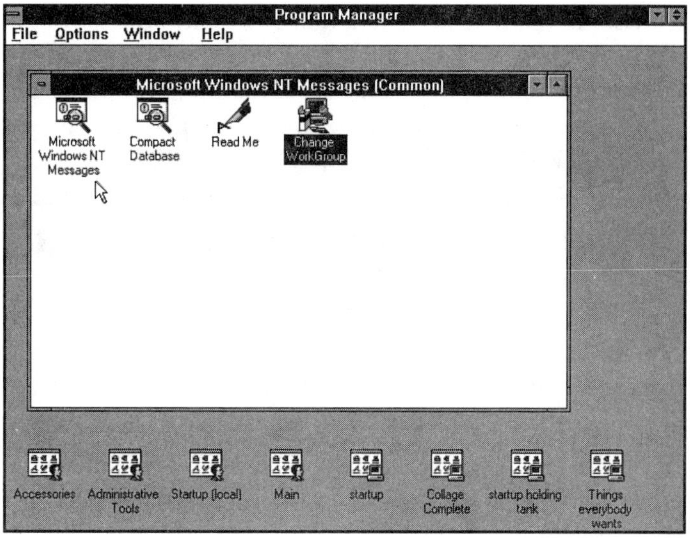

FIGURE B.1.
The NT Messages group that gets created when you run the setup program for the Messages database.

10. Delete the temporary files in the \MESSAGES directory. This will free up 3.3M of disk space.

Using the Database

To run the program, simply double-click on the Microsoft Windows NT Messages icon. Some disk churning will happen, and then you'll see the screen shown in Figure B.2.

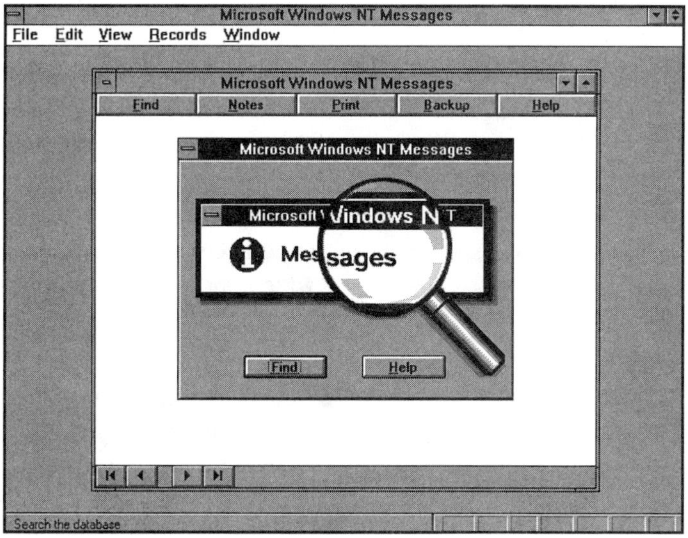

FIGURE B.2.
The startup screen for the Messages database.

It feels like you're looking in a mirror at first, because a number of screen elements are duplicated. There are two Find buttons, for example, and duplicate title bars. However, most of the menus don't work, and if they do, the options are grayed out, because this is only a runtime version of Access. So there isn't that much to figure out. The Help button does work, and some useful online help is available.

Finding a Message and Reading About It

Both Find buttons have the same effect. They're your entry into the world of error messages.

1. Click on Find. The dialog box shown in Figure B.3 appears.

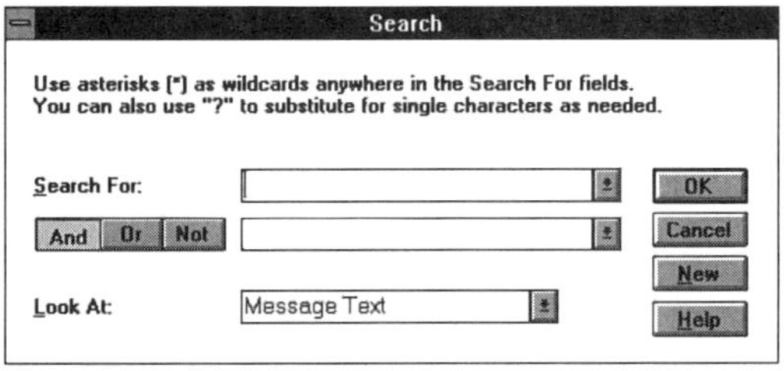

FIGURE B.3.
The Search dialog box that appears when you click on the Find button.

2. Fill in the boxes appropriately to help you find the message in question. Here's the breakdown:

Section	*Description*
Search For	Enter criteria for your search—for example, `incorrect password`. You also can click on the arrow at the end of each box to choose from a list of past searches you've conducted.
And, Or, Not	You can enter additional search criteria here if you want to do a more complex search. Use the And button to find instances in which both search criteria appear. Use the Or button to locate instances in which one *or* the other item appears. Use the Not button to exclude records containing such an item from the search (for example, `Program Manager`).
Look At	Lists the names of the fields in the Messages database. You can have the program look through all the fields in the database, but that takes additional time. To save time and possibly prevent errors, you can limit the search to specific fields:

Section	*Description*
	All Text searches the entire database.
	Message Text searches the text that actually appears in the error or system-information dialog boxes you see on-screen.
	Explanation and User Action searches through text in part of the database that explains what an error means and what to do about it.
	Net Message ID searches for the exact message number that some error dialog boxes report when the error occurs. Just enter the number in the Search For box and choose Net Message ID as the field to search.
	Notes is a field in which you can add your own notes about messages as you work with the database. This is like a Post-it that gets attached to an error message. (You add notes to a message by looking up the message and clicking on the Notes button.)
	Origin searches for messages based on the program or service that generates them. For example, to locate messages that are originated by Program Manager, select the Origin option and specify `Program Manager`.

NOTE

A type of message called a Windows NT Executive *stop* message can appear in a dialog box while you're using NT. To search for information about such a message, just type `stop:` in the Search For box, followed by the two significant digits following the block of 0s—for example, `stop:35`.

3. As soon as you've set up the criteria, click on OK, and the search begins. The program proceeds to locate all records that contain the search criteria you specified, then it reports the number of found records, as illustrated in Figure B.4. Here I searched all text for the words `software error`.
4. Click on OK. The first of the matching records is displayed in a box that lets you examine each possible error message and suggested remedies or interpretations. (See Figure B.5.) Notice that the actual error or information message appears in the top (gray) part of the box, and explanatory information is listed in the bottom portion.

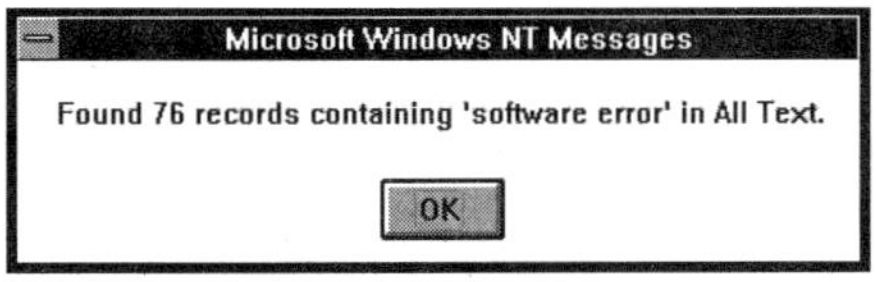

FIGURE B.4.
The Messages database reporting the number of found records.

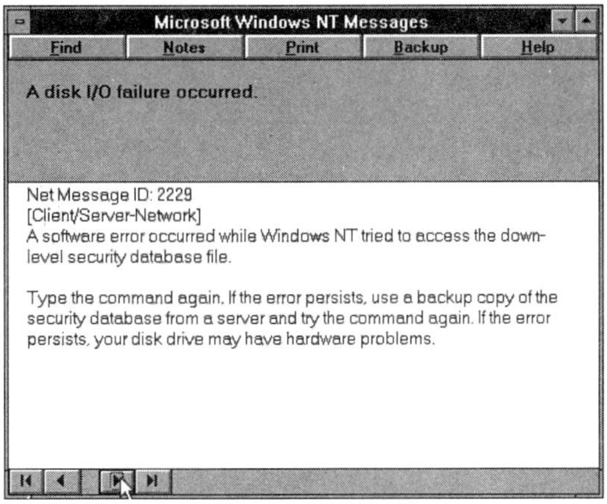

FIGURE B.5.
The first of the matching records.

5. You can move forward or backward through the matching database records by clicking on the little buttons at the bottom of the window, as shown by the pointer in Figure B.5. When you reach the end of the found messages, the status line at the bottom of the larger window reads `Last record`.

Options

You can attach your own notes to any displayed message by clicking on the Notes button and entering your notes. If you've already included notes about a particular message, clicking on this button brings up your old notes. You might want to use this feature to record a particular solution for future reference.

You also can print all the records that resulted from the current search so that you can examine them on paper. The messages will be queued up in Print Manager. Turn on your printer, load some paper, and click on the Print button. You can use the File | Print Preview command to see what the printout will look like prior to printing.

Finally, if you add lots of notes to a database file, you might want to back it up. Click on the Backup button and specify a path and filename for the backup file. Unless you add lots of notes to the database, though, backing it up doesn't make sense.

A Windows NT Glossary

C

account See *user account.*

account policy Determines how passwords are to be used by users on a workstation or on an entire domain.

active window The window that is "in front" of all others or whose title bar is in a different color or intensity from all others.

address The location in memory or on disk of a specified instruction or piece of data. Could also refer to the location of a workstation on the network.

administrative alerts Messages sent to specified groups of users, typically administrators, announcing system security problems, impending power loss, printer contention problems, and so forth.

Alerter service The internal NT service required for administrative alerts. The Messenger service must be running in order for the Alerter to work.

API Application Programming Interface. A collection of low-level software routines that programmers can use to send requests to the operating system.

application A computer program. Microsoft Word for Windows is an application.

application window The window an application is running in, as opposed to a document (or *child*) window, which runs inside an application window.

archive bit A single bit stored in a disk directory to indicate whether a file has been changed since it was last backed up. Backup programs clear a file's archive when they back up the program. Modifying the program sets the bit again so that a backup program knows to make a backup the next time you do a backup.

ASCII file American Standard for Information Interchange file. A simple text file with no formatting.

associate In File Manager, the process of informing Windows which program to run when a document file (not an executable file) is double-clicked on. For example, .WRI files will run Windows Write and open the document, because the two are associated.

asymmetric multiprocessing A multiprocessing scheme in which one CPU is dedicated to running the operating system and others are used for running applications, as opposed to symmetric multiprocessing.

attributes In FAT systems, settings for each file indicating whether the file is used by the operating system, has read-only status, has its archive bit set, or is a hidden file.

audit policy Determines whether and which types of events will be written to an audit log. Set via User Manager, Print Manager, or File Manager.

auditing A process whereby NT can keep track of certain security-related activities of users on the system, such as who logs on and who copies files. Audits are stored in audit logs, which can be examined through the Event Viewer application.

authentication The process by which NT determines whether a user is legitimate. This is done at logon time. If the user is interacting with computers on a trusted domain, authentication for the user is vouched for by one computer, and the others respect (trust) this authentication. Note that domain authentication is performed based on the domain controller rather than the local security database.

base-level synthesizer The lowest standard for the sound-effects section of Windows multimedia systems. A base-level synthesizer can play a minimum of six notes on three different instruments and three notes on three percussive instruments simultaneously.

batch program A text file that instructs NT to perform one or more tasks sequentially. Used for automating the loading or execution of programs. Batch files have a .BAT or .CMD extension.

binary A numbering system with only two values, 0 and 1.

binary-file transfer A data transfer process in which files aren't converted in any way. Typically used with a modem to send programs or complex documents from computer to computer.

bits per second (bps) A measurement of data transmission speed, usually over a serial data link. Roughly equivalent to baud rate. A single character requires approximately 10 bits, so a transfer rate of 9600 baud results in about 960 characters per second (cps) being transferred.

boot loader The most basic information NT needs to start loading when the computer is powered up or rebooted. The boot loader points to the system files so that NT can continue loading.

boot partition The hard-disk partition that contains the NT operating system. The boot partition is actually the active primary partition, and it doesn't have to include the NT OS files.

bps See *bits per second.*

browse To search through or examine a directory tree of files, directories, disks, workstations, workgroups, or domains. Often done via a Browse button in a dialog box.

buffer A temporary holding area for data, such as in a disk controller or printer.

C2-level security A computer security specification set by the U.S. Government's National Computer Security Council, a department of the U.S. National Security Agency.

Windows NT meets C2-level security because it requires password logon and authentication, and it supplies audit trails for operations affecting security.

check box A square option box in many dialog boxes. Clicking on it adds or removes an X from the box, indicating whether the setting is on (checked) or off (unchecked).

choose A term used in many instructions in this book and in Windows books and manuals. Usually means opening a menu and clicking on a command. Also can refer to dialog box items, such as in "Choose LPT1 from the drop-down list."

clear Typically refers to turning off the X in an option or check box.

click To click the left mouse button (unless a left-handed user has switched the functions of the left and right buttons).

client As opposed to a *server,* a client is a workstation that connects to another computer's resources. A client also can include RPC (that is, client/server) and doesn't necessarily have to be another workstation. Basically, a client is just another application, workstation, or whatever that utilizes resources from another process.

client application In OLE context, a program that uses an object (such as a graphic) supplied by another application (the *server* application). See *client.*

client/server networking As opposed to *peer-to-peer* networking, an arrangement in which central computers called *servers* supply data and peripherals for use by *client* computers (workstations). Typically, a server contains a large hard disk that supplies not only data but programs. It can even execute programs. A server might also supply printers and modems for use by clients on the network. In another sense of the term, client/server refers to an architecture for distributed processing wherein subtasks can be distributed between services, CPUs, or even networked computers for more efficient execution.

Clipboard An internal temporary storage area in all versions of Windows used for sharing data of various types (for example, text, graphics, sound, video) between applications. In NT, Clipboard works in conjunction with the ClipBook. The Clipboard is a local storage area only. It's not available to networked machines.

ClipBook An extension of the Clipboard that allows network users to share the contents of their Clipboard with other workstations.

ClipBook page As opposed to the Clipboard, a user's ClipBook can store any number of items, not just one. Each item, even of a dissimilar type, is stored on a ClipBook page. Pages are then individually "shared" for use by other network workstations. Like Windows for Workgroups, NT has a 127-page limit.

ClipBook service The internal NT service that allows you to share ClipBook pages over the network.

color scheme A selection of colors that Windows uses for screen display of applications, dialog boxes, and so forth, set from Control Panel.

command Usually an option from an application's menus. Also refers to commands typed in from a command-prompt session or from the Run dialog box from Program Manager or File Manager. In essence, a way of telling an application or NT to perform a major chore, such as running an application or utility program.

common groups As opposed to *local* groups, NT's Program Manager lets you set up groups of application and document icons that all users on the workstation will have access to in addition to their personal (local) groups.

compound device A multimedia device that plays files stored in the computer. For example, a synthesizer board is a compound device, as opposed to a *simple* device such as a CD-ROM drive that contains its own data (files on the CD-ROM disc).

Computer Browser service An internal NT service that keeps an up-to-date list of which computers are on the network. When an application supplies a dialog box that lets you choose a network computer, the information about workstations and servers in that box is supplied by the Browser service. If you terminate the service using Control Panel's Services applet, such an application will not be able to provide the list.

computer name Each computer on the network must have a unique name consisting of up to 15 uppercase characters. It can't be the name of another computer or domain. Names must be unique only within a workgroup or domain.

Configuration Registry A database of configuration information central to NT's operations. Similar to WIN.INI and SYSTEM.INI in Windows 3.1, it also contains settings similar to CONFIG.SYS and AUTOEXEC.BAT. Applications designed for Windows NT also store their own .INI settings in the Registry. The overall effect is to centralize all NT settings and provide security and control over system, security, and user account settings.

connect To tie into a shared resource on the network and give it a name, drive letter, or another assignment that allows your local computer to use the device.

Control menu A menu accessed by clicking on the control box in the upper-left corner of any window.

Control Panel Windows' primary configuration program for user-settable options such as screen colors, fonts, and printers.

controller Domain controller.

conventional memory System RAM from 0 to 640K.

current directory The directory that would be active if you logged onto the drive at the command prompt by typing the drive letter and pressing Enter. When you switch drives, the operating system remembers the directory that was current when you switched away. It will still be the active or current directory when you switch back, and it becomes the *default* directory where applications will store or look for files on that directory if they're not specifically told which directory to use.

DDE Dynamic Data Exchange. Implemented in Microsoft Windows products, a means by which running applications can exchange information, as opposed to OLE (Object Linking and Embedding), which has become more favored over time—especially OLE version 2. DDE is more often used by cooperating applications or tasks in the background, whereas OLE is used by people who want to link documents to create *compound documents.*

default button In almost every dialog box, one button has a darker line around it. Pressing Enter has the same effect as clicking on this button.

default printer The printer, as established in Print Manager, that documents will be sent to if the user doesn't specify another printer.

default profile When a new user is added to a workstation, the default profile sets up the user's account with a basic set of rights, privileges, and auditing setups. Can be altered via the User Manager.

dependent service Interlocking NT internal services. The Alerter service is dependent on the Messenger service, for example.

descendent key The Configuration Registry consists of a number of keys. Like subdirectories in File Manager, a descendent key is a subordinate key.

destination document The document *into* which a linked or embedded document is placed.

device contention A problem that occurs when two or more processes attempt to use the same physical hardware at the same time. For example, two communications programs could simultaneously try to use a modem hooked to a COM port.

device driver Software that allows NT to use a piece of hardware attached to the computer, such as a printer, modem, sound card, screen, or mouse.

DHCP See *Dynamic Host Configuration Protocol service.*

directory replication A process that easily copies and maintains a specific set of directories and files from a master computer to a number of remote computers. The Replicator service maintains (synchronizes) all the remote files so that they're updated whenever the master files or directories are modified.

Directory Replicator service An internal NT service responsible for performing and updating directory replication.

disabled user account A user account that has temporarily been disabled via User Manager. It can be enabled at any time, but for now, it prevents logging on.

disk configuration information Information stored in the Registry that tells NT how your hard disks are partitioned and what drive letters are assigned to the partitions. Also included is information about stripe, volume, and mirrored sets. The disk configuration information should be backed up onto floppies whenever you make changes to the disk settings via Disk Administrator.

disk duplexing Using a second hard drive as an exact replica of the first as a data security measure. The second drive has its own disk controller.

disk mirroring Using a second disk or partition to contain a complete copy of a disk or partition. This is a data redundancy technique that provides fault tolerance for disk systems.

disk striping Writing data across multiple disks to increase throughput.

document As opposed to an application, a document is a file such as a business letter that stores data created using an application.

domain In Windows NT Server, a group of computers that have the same domain database. The database maintains security on the system and allows workstations to interact with trust.

domain controller In each domain, one computer holds the domain database responsible for security and authentication of logons. This is called the *primary* domain controller. In addition, there can be normal domain controllers that have a copy of the domain database on them. These copies are kept synchronized by the primary domain controller. This is an NT Server function only.

domain database The security and logon authentication database stored in the domain controller.

domain name Each domain must have a name, much like a workgroup or username. This name appears in the Browser as users scan the network for workgroups, workstations, and domains.

domain synchronization The domain controller is responsible for keeping an updated copy of the domain database on all other domain controllers in a multiple-domain network. Synchronization is the process of ensuring that all databases are identical and up-to-date.

downloaded fonts Fonts sent to the printer from the computer prior to printing and stored in the printer's internal RAM. Downloaded fonts are lost when the printer's power is turned off.

DWORD A 4-byte hexadecimal data structure.

dynamic data exchange See *DDE.*

Dynamic Host Configuration Protocol service An optional TCP/IP services component to automate the assignment of client TCP/IP addresses.

embedded object Data stored in a document, but which was created by another application. As opposed to a linked object, this type of object doesn't have its own file on disk. However, it runs its source application for editing when you double-click on it. For example, a Paintbrush drawing embedded in a Write document.

EMS Expanded Memory Specification. An industry standard for allowing 8088/8086 and above Intel CPUs to access more than 640K of RAM, using a RAM banking method. Developed jointly by Intel, Lotus, and Microsoft, it was used by a number of programs such as Lotus 1-2-3 until it fell out of favor as Windows became popular and XMS came into widespread use.

encapsulated PostScript (EPS) file A file format for storing PostScript-style images that allows a PostScript printer or program capable of importing such files to print a file in the highest resolution your printer is capable of.

environment variable Settable from the System applet in Control Panel, the environment variables in NT are similar to those used in DOS to control operating system internals. For example, search path, aliases, system prompts, and so on.

Ethernet A LAN architecture devised by Xerox Corporation and later adopted by the IEEE. Also called the 802.3 standard.

event A significant NT happening worthy of user notification or a log entry.

Event Log service An internal NT service responsible for logging important events.

expanded memory Also called EMS. A memory specification developed by Intel, Lotus, and Microsoft. Allows for up to 32M of memory to be accessible even by computers based on 8088/8086 chips from Intel. Not widely used at this point. See *extended memory.*

export path Related to directory replication. A network path informing the replication server (export server) where to send files it's responsible for replicating. Typically, the path leads to another workstation (import computer). This is an NT Server-only feature.

export server See *export path.*

extended memory Memory above 1M in 80286 machines and above. See *XMS.*

extended partition One of four partitions on a physical disk can be made into an extended partition, which can be subdivided into zero or more logical drives.

extended-level synthesizer A multimedia definition as set by the multimedia PC council. More advanced than a basic-level synthesizer. Must be able to play 16 notes on nine instruments and 16 notes on eight percussion instruments at once.

extension The last three letters of a filename after the period.

external command As opposed to an internal command, a command that requires a separate file to run. The `format` command is a case in point, because it runs the executable file FORMAT.COM.

family set A collection of backup tapes made during the same backup session.

FAT See *file allocation table.*

file allocation table (FAT) The native DOS file system that uses a table called the file allocation table to store information about the sizes, locations, and properties of files stored on a disk.

file system The means an operating system uses to store files on a disk.

filename The name that a file system or operating system gives to a file when it's stored on disk. Filenames in NT's NT File System (NTFS) can be 256 characters long. NT differentiates between uppercase and lowercase letters in filenames when displaying them, such as in File Manager. However, it isn't case-sensitive when accessing such files.

full name When you establish an account in User Manager, the full name typically is a person's whole name—last name, first name, and middle initial. It's used for identification purposes in User Manager, but it doesn't show up on the network and it isn't required at logon.

General MIDI An industry specification governing the format of MIDI files. This is an evolving standard, but Windows adheres fairly well to it. Hardware and software you buy for a Windows system should be General MIDI-compatible.

global account A typical user account on an NTFS trusted domain is global in nature, as opposed to *local.* When an account is set to global status, the domain allows the user access to resources on the domain.

global group In an NT Server domain, a global group is a convenient means for setting up a number of users in a group, all of whom can be granted access to all the local domain resources as well as to resources in trusted domains. Can contain only accounts from its own domain.

group A collection of user accounts organized in User Manager to expedite the assignment of rights and privileges. Each person in the group is called a *group member.*

group icon In Program Manager, the icon that represents a minimized window containing program and document icons.

group name The name given to a group of users created in User Manager. See *group.*

HAL See *hardware abstraction layer.*

hardware abstraction layer (HAL) The most basic level of the NT operating system, which forms a bridge between the operating system and the computer's physical hardware.

header information Data sent to the printer to define aspects of the printout and prepare the printer prior to printing. PostScript documents include headers.

hexadecimal A base-16 numbering system with values ranging from 0 to 9, a to f, and A to F. Used in many programming languages. Not particularly relevant to users.

high memory area Also called the HMA, this is actually the first 64K (minus 16 bytes) above the 1M boundary. Therefore, actually it's the RAM address area 1024 to 1088 and is accessed by enabling the A20 line in real mode. Originally reserved for memory-mapped hardware such as video cards, it's often used by memory manager programs to relocate portions of DOS and used by device drivers in order to provide more conventional memory for applications.

high performance file system (HPFS) The file system used by OS/2.

hive A portion of the Registry that is recorded on disk as a separate file. Hives can be copied, but you need the Registry Editor to edit them.

home directory A default directory declared by an administrator (via User Manager) for a user that is the default directory for storing applications and documents. Use of a home directory makes backing up a user's files easier, because most document files for the user end up there.

HPFS See *high performance file system.*

I/O address Input/Output address. Many I/O devices, such as COM ports, network cards, printer ports, and modem cards, are mapped into an I/O address. This address allows the computer and operating system to locate the device, and thus send and receive data. Such I/O addresses don't tie up system memory RAM space, either. However, there are a limited number of them. You can access an I/O port in one of two ways: Either map it into the 64K I/O address space or map it as a memory-mapped device in the system's RAM space. Memory-mapped devices are easier to work with, because they can use any memory-related CPU command versus an in/out I/O port command.

import An OLE term. In Object Packager, you can import a file into a package for later embedding into a destination document.

import computer Relates to directory replication. The computer that receives replicated directories or files.

import path The path over which an import computer receives the copies of the master set of replicated directories from an export computer.

internal command A command embedded in CMD.EXE, the command interpreter for NT DOS, or in COMMAND.COM, the MS-DOS equivalent. Internal commands don't require additional support files. `DIR` is an example. See *external command.*

interrupt request line (IRQ) A line (conductor) on the internal bus of the computer (typically on the motherboard) over which a device such as a port, disk controller, or modem can get the attention of the CPU to process some data.

IPX/SPX Internetwork Packet Exchange/Sequenced Packet Exchange. The names Novell uses for its proprietary network layer and transport layer.

IRQ See *interrupt request line.*

Kermit A communications program popular on PCs. Kermit has a communications protocol to prevent data loss or corruption when files are transmitted between computers. Due to its popularity, many communications programs now support the Kermit protocol. It's not the fastest communications protocol around, but it's popular. See *Xmodem/CRC, Ymodem,* and *Zmodem.*

kernel The core of an operating system, usually responsible for basic I/O and process execution.

kernel driver A driver that has direct access to hardware. A hardware driver.

key In Registry Editor, analogous to a directory in File Manager. Keys are displayed in the left pane of the Editor window.

key map In MIDI terminology, a remapping of MIDI signals to appropriate key numbers (each key on a synthesizer has a number). Nonstandard keyboards might not comply with General MIDI specifications; thus, they will play the wrong sounds when sent a MIDI file for sound effects if a key map isn't set up to correct the mismapping.

keyboard buffer Memory set aside to store keystrokes as they're entered from the keyboard. Once it's stored, the keystroke data waits for the CPU to pick up the data and respond accordingly.

LAN Manager A network operating system product from Microsoft, developed for OS/2. LAN Manager can interface with NT Server without problems as a backup domain controller, but it can't be a primary domain controller. NT offers much of LAN Manager's functionality.

linked object In OLE terminology, an icon stored in the destination file, representative of the file that has been embedded.

local account An account type not necessary when trust exists between domains. If trust doesn't exist, a local account is set up for a user.

Local Area Network (LAN) A collection of computers connected to one another over high-speed cable for sharing data and resources. LANs tend not to utilize telephone or other leased lines from another source. Typically, computers on a LAN are located in the same building, as opposed to those on a WAN, or wide area network, which might be in different buildings, states, or countries.

local group A group of users that can be set up and given privileges and rights. These settings apply only to the single workstation on which the group was created. This is a way of easily giving a whole group of workers on the network access to your resources without risking giving those rights to everyone on the network or bothering with assigning rights individually.

local printer A printer connected directly to your computer.

local procedure call (LPC) Similar to RPC (remote procedure call) but used within a single system to pass data and commands between subsystems of NT.

logical drive A drive that isn't a physical drive, as in the floppy drive A or B. Instead, a logical drive is a drive created on a subpartition of an extended partition and given an arbitrary letter such as C, D, or E.

logon hours Hours during which a user is permitted to log onto the system.

logon script A batch file or other executable program that executes immediately when the user logs onto the system. The script is declared in User Manager.

logon script path The location of the logon script.

logon workstations In NT Server, the only stations on which the user is allowed to log on.

LPC See *local procedure call.*

Mach A kernel intended for use on PCs and relatively small computers, and based on the University of California's BSD 4.3 UNIX-derived operating system. Mach was developed at Carnegie-Mellon University and is the model after which NT was designed.

mandatory user profile In NT Server, a profile of rights and privileges assigned to a user that can't be altered by that user.

maximum password age The maximum time that a password can be in effect until the user must change it.

Media Control Interface (MCI) A standard interface for all multimedia devices, devised by the MPC council, that allows multimedia applications to control any number of MPC-compliant devices, from sound cards to MIDI-based lighting controllers.

Messages database A database supplied on the CD-ROM with NT that lists all the error and information messages that NT is likely to produce.

Messenger service Required to send and receive alert messages between computers when those messages originate from administrators or the Alerter service.

MCI See *Media Control Interface.*

microkernel The center of a kernel, containing the primitives of the operating system. Using a microkernel allows developers to easily extend the operating system's capabilities by adding alterable outer "layers" to it that perform additional functions, such as running programs of various types. See *kernel.*

MIDI Musical Instrument Digital Interface. Originally a means of connecting electronic instruments (synthesizers) and letting them communicate with one another. Computers then came into the MIDI landscape and were used to control the synthesizers. MIDI has been adapted for many purposes. Windows and Windows NT can play MIDI files.

MIDI setup To play MIDI files, NT needs to know the type of MIDI device you have and the port or other settings that pertain to it.

minimum password age The minimum amount of time that must pass before a user is allowed to change his or her password.

minimum password length The shortest possible password that the user is allowed.

mirrored disk set Several hard disks working together as a redundant fault-tolerant system preventing loss of data in case one of the drives fails.

mission-critical application An application program considered indispensable to the operation of a business, government, or other operation. Often these applications are transaction-based, such as for point-of-sale, reservations, or real-time stock, security, or money trading.

MS-DOS-based application An application that normally runs on a DOS machine and doesn't require NT.

multiprocessor system A computer containing more than a single CPU.

multitasking A process that allows a computer or operating system to concurrently run multiple applications or tasks by dividing the CPU's time between them so rapidly that it is not noticed or is not objectionable to the user.

multithreading A process that allows a multitasking operating system to, in essence, multitask subportions (threads) of an application smoothly. Applications must be written to take advantage of multithreading. Windows NT supports multithreading.

named pipe A vehicle that allows processes to communicate with one another without having to know where the sender and receiver processes are located. The name acts like an alias, connecting the two processes regardless of whether they're on the same computer or across connected domains.

Net Logon service In NT Server, an internal NT service that performs authentication of logons and synchronizes the user database among computers on the domain.

NetBEUI NetBIOS Extended User Interface. The network transport protocol used by all Microsoft's networking systems as well as IBM's LAN Server-based networks.

NetBIOS Network Basic Input/Output System. A network API (application programming interface), as opposed to the transport protocol, NetBEUI. NetBIOS allows networked computers to send, receive, and process input and output requests from each other over the network. NetBIOS is the standard API for all Microsoft's networking systems, as well as for IBM's LAN Server-based networks and most other PC-based networking systems.

Network DDE DSDM service The Network DDE share database manager. Required by the network DDE service to function.

Network DDE service Supporting DDE over the network.

network device driver A software driver required to interface the network interface card (NIC) with the computer and operating system.

network directory A shared directory.

network interface card (NIC) The network card that plugs into the computer and allows physical connection to the network.

NeXTSTEP A UNIX-based operating system from NeXT Computer, Inc. Recently ported from NeXT machines to run on x86-based PCs.

NIC See *network interface card.*

non-Windows NT application Any application other than one specifically written to run under NT's 32-bit operating system, including Windows 3.1 applications.

NT Executive The bulk of NT's operating system kernel. This portion is fully protected from user-mode applications and from the subsystems.

NTFS NT File System. The advanced file system supplied with NT that features numerous security features over competing FAT and HPFS file systems.

NT Server A robust, platform-independent, multiprocessing, fault-tolerant network file and print server sharing a common user database. Often utilized as an object or resource server in a client/server environment, such as an SQL Server database.

object Any item that is or can be linked into another Windows application, such as a sound, graphic, piece of text, or portion of a spreadsheet. Must be from an application that supports OLE.

object linking and embedding See *OLE.*

OLE A data-sharing scheme that allows dissimilar applications to create single complex documents through a cooperative scheme. The documents can consist of material that a single application couldn't have created on its own.

orphan One partition in a mirrored or stripe set that has crashed or failed beyond the point of return. With any luck, NT detects the problem and continues operating by redirecting reads and writes to another disk. In a mirrored set, continued operation is possible because the second partition will likely be able to pick up where the original left off. With a striped set, the set will fail unless striping with parity is used.

package In OLE, an icon that represents an embedded object that, when clicked on, opens, plays a sound, or becomes active in some other way.

paging file A virtual memory file stored on a physical hard disk. It's used to effectively extend the amount of physical RAM in the computer by shuffling data into and out of the RAM.

parity An additional portion of data added to each byte of stored or transmitted data. Used to ensure that the data isn't lost or corrupted. In NT Server, parity striping utilizes this principle to guard against loss of data in case one of the striped disks crashes. The parity information is created by "exclusive `OR`ing" the data being written to the stripe set before it's striped across the set. If one disk goes out, the Boolean reverse of this process can be used to figure out what was on the crashed disk and to reconstruct the stripe that was lost. Using this technique, any disk in the stripe set can fail. The parity information in conjunction with the other disks' data is adequate for restoration of the lost stripe. However, if two disks go down at once, there is no hope. Parity is also used on every RAM chip in IBM PCs and compatibles to determine if RAM errors have occurred. Parity also is used with communications programs to determine if data has been lost or corrupted in transmission.

partition A portion of a hard disk that behaves as a separate disk, even though it isn't.

patch map In MIDI setups, similar to key map but applicable to MIDI "patches," which are sound presets (marimba, piano, and so on). Nonstandard synthesizers might need patch maps to behave appropriately when playing MIDI files, multimedia CD-ROMs, or games in Windows.

path The location of a file or a computer in the directory tree or on the network.

peer-to-peer A type of networking in which no workstation has more control over the network than another. Each station may share its resources, but no station is the sole resource sharer or file server. Typically less expensive than *client/server* networks, peer-to-peer networks are also more difficult to administer and less secure because there is no central repository of data.

pel Picture element. The smallest controllable dot in a screen or printer image. Sometimes called a *pixel,* but actually not the same as a pixel. A pixel can be composed of several pels.

permission A property assigned to an object that controls who can have access to it. As opposed to a *right,* which is given to you or other users by an administrator.

personal groups As opposed to common groups in Program Manager, these groups contain icons only you can see.

personal user profile In NT Server, this profile allows the user to change some settings, as opposed to mandatory user profile. Applies to only a single user.

PIF See *program information file.*

port A connection or socket for connecting devices to a computer. See *I/O address.*

POSIX A UNIX implementation that ensures source-code compatibility of UNIX applications that comply with the standard. NT complies with character-based POSIX application requirements.

preemptive multitasking A multitasking scheme that empowers the operating system to override an application that is hogging the CPU, as opposed to *cooperative multitasking,* in which the applications are responsible for relinquishing the CPU on a regular basis.

primary partition A portion of hard disk that can be used by the operating system and that can't be subpartitioned like an extended partition can. Each disk can have up to four primary partitions, unless there is an extended partition on the disk, in which case only three primary partitions are allowed. Only primary partitions are bootable.

printer driver A software driver required to send documents to the printer. Translates the document into the codes necessary for actual printing.

printer fonts Fonts stored in the printer's ROM.

program file A program that runs an application directly (not via an association) when you click on it. In NT, such files have the extensions .BAT, .COM, .EXE, or .CMD.

program group A grouping of documents or applications in Program Manager.

program information file (PIF) A specialized file stored on disk. It contains settings that affect how the DOS environment in a VDM is constructed by NT prior to running a specified DOS application, such as to request expanded memory or to reserve shortcut keys for use by the application.

protected mode A memory addressing mode of Intel processors that allows direct "flat-memory" addressing (linear addressing) rather than using the awkward "segmented" scheme required by real mode, which was pioneered on the Intel 8088 and 8086 processors. Protected mode derives its name from the fact that sections of memory owned by a particular process can be physically protected from rogue programs that try to access those addresses. Windows NT utilizes protected mode at all times subsequent to bootup.

protected subsystem A major portion of the NT operating system that allows applications access to NT's core functions. For example, MS-DOS applications run in a protected subsystem that emulates the DOS environment and passes application calls (DOS API calls) to the NT operating system for handling.

queue Documents lined up and waiting to be printed, or commands lined up and waiting to be serviced. In printing, each printer on a local machine or shared on the network has a queue. Use Print Manager to view and manage the print queue.

quick format A quick way to format a floppy disk, quick format doesn't actually wipe the whole disk, nor does it test the media for bad sectors. It just erases the FAT.

RAM Random Access Memory. Physical memory chips located in the computer. Typical NT machines have 16 million bytes (16M) of RAM.

real mode As opposed to *protected mode,* real mode is a mode in which Intel x86 processors can run. Memory addressing in real mode is nonlinear, requiring a program to stipulate a segment and memory offset address in order to access a location in memory. Originally appeared on the Intel 8086 CPU and has been the bane of PC programmers ever since. Although subsequent CPU chips supported protected-mode linear addressing, backward compatibility with the thousands of real-mode applications has slowed the evolution of operating systems. Note that all Intel CPUs boot in real mode and require specific software support to switch into protected mode.

redirector A networking software module that traps requests for networked resources from the local computer and directs them to the correct supplier of that resource on the network. For example, a call for a printer, file, or named pipe on the network would be trapped by the redirector.

Registry See *Configuration Registry.*

remote administration Connecting to, altering settings on, making backups from, or otherwise managing a computer not at your desk, but from the computer at your desk.

remote procedure call (RPC) A programming term referring to a means that one program can use to ask another computer on the network to perform a task for it.

Remote Procedure Call service A service that must be running on both NT machines before an RPC can be initiated and properly responded to.

replication See *directory replication.*

resource A physical aspect of a computer that a process, application, or user might need access to, such as a disk, memory, a screen, or a sound card. In network terminology, *resource* typically refers to shared resources such as printers, directories, and modems.

right As opposed to a *permission,* a right is given to a user by an administrator, and, in general, it affects what the user can do on the network. For example, backing up files is a right. See *permissions.*

RIPL Remote Initial Program Load. This process utilizes a boot PROM on the network adapter to access a set of shared network files to boot the operating system instead of booting directly from a floppy or hard disk.

RISC Reduced Instruction Set Computer. A computer based on a CPU that has few instructions built into its internal microcode. Thus, more instructions are required to execute a particular task on a RISC chip than are required by a CISC (Complex Instruction Set Computer) for the same task. RISC theory postulates that simple instructions execute faster than more complex ones. Therefore, although more instructions are required per task, the actual computational throughput will be enhanced using such a chip. CISC chips, by comparison, perform many preprogrammed complex internal operations in response to a single request. Less programming code is required to achieve results from a CISC processor than from a RISC. The DEC Alpha, MIPS 4000, Hewlett-Packard HP-PA, and Sun SPARC processors are examples of modern RISC chips. Note that the 80486 and higher utilize a combination of RISC/CISC architecture, even though they're called CISC CPUs.

ROM Read-Only Memory. A type of chip capable of permanently storing data without the aid of an electric current source to maintain it, as in RAM. The data in ROM chips is sometimes called *firmware.* ROMs are found in many types of computer add-in boards, as well as on motherboards. CPUs often have an internal section of ROM as well.

RPC See *remote procedure call.*

RPC Locator service The service that keeps track of which networked machines are available to perform tasks for a distributed-server application (one that can spread its tasks across the network for faster processing).

SAM A protected subsystem that operates and maintains the Security Accounts Manager (SAM) database.

SAM database The database that contains the user account, password, and other settings for each user.

Schedule service An NT internal service required to allow a workstation to perform a service at a predetermined time via the AT command—for example, for scheduled automatic backups during off-hours.

screen buffer Some reserved memory space that stores the screen image when you switch between full-screen command-prompt sessions and back to the Windows screen display. The amount of memory required varies with the resolution and the number of colors in the display.

screen fonts Font files used to show type styles on the screen. Different files than those used by Windows to print the fonts. The two must match for accurate screen portrayal of final output.

Security Accounts Manager See *SAM.*

security database See *SAM database.*

security ID Each user or group of users is given a SID (security ID), which is used to identify the user or group when they log in. Even when a user account is deleted and re-created using the same information such as name and password, the SID will not be identical because each SID is unique and is never reused. Thus, after an account is deleted, it can't be resuscitated.

security identifier See *security ID.*

security log A log file that keeps track of events in NT that have affected security, such as password changes, alterations to user account management, and who has logged onto the system. The log can be viewed using the Event Viewer.

security policies Administrator-set rules that affect how security is maintained on an NT or NT Server network, or even on a given workstation. On an NT system, these consist of Accounts, User Rights, and Audit Policies. On an NT Server system, these include Trust Relationships. Use the User Manager or the User Manager for Domains to manage these settings.

server A machine on the network that has something to serve—that is, it contains a shared resource, such as a directory or a printer. In NT Server language, server refers to any machine that qualifies as a domain controller. See *domain controller.*

server application In OLE terminology, an application that supplies an object, such as a drawing, to a *client* application, such as a word processing program, for inclusion in a complex document.

Server Manager An NT Server application for managing domains, workgroups, and stations. Similar to User Manager in NT.

Server service The internal NT service required to share any local resource for network use.

service An internal software routine that can provide a particular function to an application. Similar to an API. All NT services are RPC- (remote procedure call) capable; thus, they can be used by other computers on the network if needed. However, the application on the remote computer must be designed around NT's RPC functionality.

shared pages ClipBook pages shared for network use.

shared resource See *resource.*

sharename When you share a resource, it must be given a name, such as `Joe's HP printer` or `Lotus directory`. The sharename appears in dialog boxes when network users are browsing the network.

shortcut key A key or key combination (such as F12 or Ctrl-F12) that performs a prescribed action, such as jumping to or launching an application. Program Manager allows the setting of shortcut keys to easily do just that. PIF files enable you to reserve shortcut keys for DOS applications rather than for Windows' use.

SID See *security ID.*

simple device In multimedia, a device that is self-contained and that can function without Windows sending it a file. A CD player and a video disc player are examples.

source document In OLE, the document that contains the information you want to link into (to appear in) another document (the *destination* document).

static object As opposed to OLE, where objects have a "hot" link to their original application, static objects are simply pasted into a destination document using the Clipboard. This is just the simple "pasting" that most Windows users use on a daily basis.

stripe set A data storage scheme using multiple hard disks. Data can be quickly written across several disks at a time rather than waiting for a sequential read from or write to a single disk. If *striping with parity* is used, data can be recovered even if a single drive in the set fails. This is not possible if parity is not used. Windows NT Server supports both forms of striping.

swap file See *paging file.*

synchronize To keep two or more copies of a file stored on different computers identical. The Replicator service, for example, keeps directories of files synchronized on a number of machines by updating files on all import machines when any of the marked files on the export machine are altered.

system default profile See *default profile.*

system disk The disk that contains the operating system, or at least enough of it to start the system and then look on another disk for the support files.

system partition A partition that contains hardware driver files that NT needs in order to interact with the computer—screen, mouse, printer, SCSI, and other drivers.

Task List Pressing Ctrl-Esc brings up the Task List, listing the running applications and allowing the user to easily switch between them.

TCP/IP Transport Control Protocol/Internet Protocol. UNIX systems' most popular transport protocol, used in both local and wide area networking. Although Windows NT's preferred transport protocol is NetBEUI, TCP/IP capability is supplied with the product and can be easily installed, allowing interoperability with UNIX-based systems.

time slice A small amount of CPU time given to each simultaneously running application, one after another. Sometimes multitasking is called *time slicing.*

timeout A period of time after which a device or driver might signal the operating system and cease trying to perform its duty. If a printer is turned off, for example, when you try to print, the driver waits for a predetermined period of time, then issues an error message. In computer terminology, the driver has *timed out.*

Token Ring A networking strategy relying on a single software *token* to determine which computer has the momentary right to use the network cabling for the transmission of data. The token is passed from computer to computer in rapid succession along with the data, much the way a multitasking operating system assigns CPU time to a task or thread. Nontoken schemes typically try to transmit on the network, and if a data collision is detected, they simply delay for a random amount of time and try again. This can result in additional noise and traffic on the system. On the other hand, Token Ring systems can come to a stop if the token is lost. IBM pioneered Token Ring networking.

TrueType fonts A font technology developed by Microsoft in response to Adobe's success in the scalable font business with its own Type 1 and Type 3 PostScript fonts and as a simple means for all Windows applications to have access to a wide selection of fonts for screen and printer output. TrueType fonts greatly simplify using fonts on a Windows computer. The same fonts can be used on Windows 3.1, Windows NT, and other Windows products, such as Windows 95 and Windows for Workgroups. Consisting of two files (one for screen and one for printer), hundreds of TrueType fonts are now available from a variety of manufacturers. Depending on your printer, the TrueType font manager internal to Windows, in conjunction with the printer driver, generates either bitmapped or downloadable soft fonts.

trust A relationship between domains that allows users or groups of users to cross domain boundaries without having to log on and be authenticated each time. The source domain machine sends a message to other domain servers on the network that have a trust relationship with it, indicating who might be coming online. It says, in essence, "These people are allowed into the party. Don't card them at the door."

Unicode A 16-bit computer encoding format that can represent all world languages that are currently involved in computing.

uninterruptible power supply (UPS) A device containing a large battery that can keep a computer going for at least a few minutes in case of a power outage. A well-equipped UPS can be hooked up to a COM port on a server to signal when a power outage is detected. NT can then begin a power-down, alerting connected users to save their work and log out before the server actually dies. Of course, if the power has already gone out for all other connected users, they're out of luck. They've probably already lost some work unless they, too, have UPSs. In either case, however, data loss on the server is minimized. If the server is set up as an application server, if each user stores his or her data on the server, and if automatic saving is set up (as can be done in Microsoft Word, for example), users' data loss can really be minimized using a UPS.

UNIX A multithreaded, multitasking operating system developed at Bell Labs and given to many institutions, particularly universities in the U.S. Many versions of UNIX now exist. However, it is large, complex, and, compared to Windows, relatively nonstandard. Applications written for one version of UNIX won't necessarily run on another version.

UPS See *uninterruptible power supply.*

UPS service An internal NT service that must be running in order for NT to respond to a message from a UPS that a power outage has occurred.

user account A listing of rights, privileges, passwords, group memberships, NT interface settings, and so forth that comprise a user's existence on an NT machine or NT Server system. Managed with User Manager or User Manager for Domains (in NT Server).

user account database The database that stores the information about all user accounts on the workstation. See *SAM.*

user default profile See *default profile.*

User Manager An application in the Administrators group (seen only if you log on as an administrator) for managing user accounts.

User Manager for Domains An application in the Administrators group (seen only if you log on as an administrator) for managing user accounts on a domain in NT Server.

user profile The personal settings that a user has made to his or her NT environment, such as screen colors, desktop settings, network connections, printer connections, Program Manager groups, File Manager settings, mouse settings, and more. Each user on an NT machine has a user profile that goes into effect when he or she logs on. See *default profile.*

User Profile Editor In NT Server, a program used to edit a user's profile.

value entry The string of characters on the right side of the Registry editor screen, showing the setting for the key that is selected in the left pane.

VDM Virtual DOS Machine. When you run a DOS or Windows 3.1 application in NT, a VDM is created to run it. The VDM fools the application into thinking that it's the only application running on an MS-DOS-based IBM PC.

virtual memory A scheme that allows hard-disk space to emulate physical RAM, allowing large applications to run in less physical RAM than they normally would require. When RAM runs low, the operating system uses a *virtual memory manager* program to temporarily store data on the hard disk (in a *paging* or *swap* file) as though it were in RAM, freeing up RAM for data manipulation. When needed, the data is read back from the disk and loaded into RAM again.

virtual printer memory In PostScript printers, this is the portion of memory reserved for downloaded fonts. It exists on a hard drive internal to the printer. The other portion of memory, called *banded* memory, is reserved for formatting the printed page and processing graphics.

volume Disk partition(s) formatted and available for use by the operating system.

wildcard A symbol that represents any character. Used in searching for or listing items, such as files. In Windows and many other operating systems and applications, * represents any number of characters, and ? represents any one character.

Windows Internet Name Service (WINS) An optional TCP/IP services component that automates the assignment of NetBIOS names to IP addresses.

WINS See *Windows Internet Name Service.*

workgroup A collection of networked PCs (optionally including Macintoshes) grouped to facilitate work that users of the computers tend to do together. The machines are not necessarily in the same room or office. Windows for Workgroups and Windows NT machines can both be part of a workgroup setup. Windows NT recognizes existing Windows for Workgroup groups. Domains are different from workgroups and are more sophisticated. See *domain.*

workstation A single computer on an NT network that is running NT, not NT Server. Machines running NT Server are called *servers* in Windows NT nomenclature.

Workstation service An internal NT service that must be running in order for network connections and sharing to work.

WOW Windows on Win32. The protected subsystem that allows any number of Windows 3.1 applications to run in NT. All Windows 3.1 applications run in a single VDM, unlike DOS applications, each of which gets its own VDM. Thus, if one Windows 3.1 application crashes, it's possible that they all will. However, NT contains the same robustness facility that Windows 3.1 incorporates. As such, if one application crashes, it won't necessarily crash the whole WOW. Often, you can kill just the offending program.

Xenix A version of UNIX developed by Microsoft. It was later marketed by the Santa Cruz Operation (SCO).

XModem/CRC An error-correction protocol used by the DOS application XMODEM and many other communications programs. CRC stands for Cyclical Redundancy Check, a means of detecting errors in transmission between modems or across wired serial links.

XMS Extended Memory Specification. An industry standard for allowing Intel 80286 and higher processors to access memory above 1M, as opposed to EMS (expanded memory specification). Not to be confused with actual extended memory, which is simply any physical memory mapped above 1M. Windows 3.1 and NT both require extended memory but don't require XMS memory.

YModem Another form of XModem that allows batch transfers of files.

ZModem Yet another version of XModem.

INDEX

SYMBOLS

A

J

K

L

O

P

Q

R

T

U

X-Y-Z

Book ISBN 0-672-30902-5